D1604176

OHIO

Source Records

From
The Ohio Genealogical Quarterly

*O*HIO

Source Records

From
The Ohio Genealogical Quarterly

GENEALOGICAL PUBLISHING CO., INC.
Baltimore 1986

Excerpted and reprinted from
The Ohio Genealogical Quarterly,
with added Publisher's Note, Contents,
Index, and textual notes, by
Genealogical Publishing Co., Inc.
Baltimore, 1986. Copyright © 1986 by
Genealogical Publishing Co., Inc.
Baltimore, Maryland. All Rights Reserved.
Library of Congress Catalogue Card Number 85-81230
International Standard Book Number 0-8063-1137-1
Made in the United States of America

Note

O HIO SOURCE RECORDS is composed of articles from *The Ohio Genealogical Quarterly,* a periodical so scarce that not even the Library of Congress has a complete set. Founded as a publication of the Columbus Genealogical Society in 1937, the *Quarterly* claimed all of Ohio, not just Columbus and surrounding Franklin County, as its domain. Despite this objective Franklin County records fairly dominated the *Quarterly,* though its coverage did eventually embrace many of the counties of central Ohio. By the time it wound up publication in April 1944 it had turned out a voluminous body of data, chiefly cemetery records, tax lists (the 1810 tax list, in particular), newspaper abstracts, and vital records.

Owing to the extreme scarcity of the *Quarterly,* this valuable data has been virtually inaccessible to the genealogist, and for that matter, few genealogists today are even aware that the *Quarterly* ever existed. It seemed a reasonable object therefore to gather all this material together and to bring it out in a reprint edition, which is now in hand, complete with index. Everything of a genealogical nature is included except news, notes, and queries, and the overwhelming majority of articles appear here in their entirety, reconstituted and rearranged as logic dictated.

Readers should note that the tax lists on pp. 101-159, already alphabetized, are *not* incorporated in the new index.

Genealogical Publishing Company

Contents

1810 Tax Lists*

Franklin County

Cemetery Records

---

*Not indexed in this work.

ix

Bible Records

Family History

Champaign County

Pickaway County

Greene County

Miscellany

OHIO
Source Records

From
The Ohio Genealogical Quarterly

EARLY SETTLEMENTS IN OHIO

Helen E. Swisher

A map is a visual instrument that enables men to understand positions of land-surfaces. Maps are used for different purposes. *Political maps* show countries; their boundaries, subdivisions, and cities. *Physical maps* show surface-features, such as creeks, rivers, hills, plains, and mountains; climatic conditions; vegetation; and soil conditions. *Relief maps* depict the elevations of the earth's surface, hills, and mountains. *Economic maps* are used to portray the economic problems of a country as population; products, such as corn and cotton; trade routes; water power; resources; standard time; and manufactures.

MAPS FOR THE STUDY OF GENEALOGY

Maps which contain many of the features described above, are useful in genealogical research. Political maps showing countries, states, provinces, counties and townships, as well as towns and villages obviously are necessary aids in genealogical work. Of interest to the genealogist also are the routes of travel taken by pioneer ancestors, and the physical and natural conditions of the country to which they came.

Maps also aid the genealogist in locating places where families lived. For example, certain lands in central Ohio were successively included in Franklin County, Delaware County, and then Morrow County, Ohio. In order to trace the movement of a family and its ownership of land, researches were necessary in the court houses of these three counties.

In this study maps will be presented showing the successive settlement and organization of Ohio's counties; the various land grants; and the subdivisions such as counties, townships, cities, and villages that may help in genealogical research. Maps pertaining to pioneer history of local communities in Ohio are solicited for possible publication in the QUARTERLY.

Map No. 1. Early Areas of Settlement

When the early settlers came to Ohio four-fifths of the land was covered with dense forests. Until roads could be cut through the wilderness, travel was chiefly along waterways as the Ohio River and its tributaries. There were five areas of settlement, each one with a town which became the center of the settlement. In the order of land grants they were: Virginia Military District, 1784; Connecticut Western Reserve, 1784; The Seven Ranges, 1786; The Ohio Company's first and second purchases, 1792; and the Symmes Purchase, 1794. In order of actual settlements upon the lands they were: The Ohio Company, Marietta; The Symmes Purchase, Cincinnati; The Seven Ranges, Steubenville; The Virginia Military District, Chillicothe; and the Western Reserve, Cleveland.

1

CLEVELAND

WESTERN RESERVE

CONGRESS LANDS

FORT RECOVERY

GREENEVILLE TREATY LINE

FORT LAURENS

GREENEVILLE

UNITED STATES MILITARY LANDS

STEUBENVILLE

CADIZ

SEVEN RANGES

VIRGINIA MILITARY LAND

SYMMES PURCHASE

CHILLICOTHE

CINCINNATI

OHIO COMPANY'S PURCHASE

MARIETTA

OHIO MAP NO. 1.

1. *The Ohio Land Company.*—Rufus Putnam, Manasseh Cutler, Robert Oliver, and Griffin Greene, obtained a patent from President Washington for 750,000 acres of land in southeastern Ohio, and made a second purchase of 214,285 acres adjoining the first tract on the west and north. Settlers were recruited from Massachusetts and other New England States. Their ancestors had come from England in search of religious freedom and in opposition to the Church of England. One hundred fifty years in New England had developed great differences between them and the Virginians.

2. *The Symmes Purchase* was acquired by Judge John Cleves Symmes of New Jersey, who had contributed liberally to the support of the Continental Army. Cincinnati became the center of the settlements upon the Symmes land which lay between the Great and Little Miami Rivers.

3. *The Seven Ranges* extended west of the Pennsylvania line and north of the Ohio Company's lands to the fortieth parallel of latitude. The early settlers came from Pennsylvania, some being of Quaker stock, and others of German origin. Other settlers came from western Virginia, especially Augusta County. Steubenville and Cadiz became the chief towns in these lands which was the first to be surveyed and offered for sale in the territory which is now Ohio.

4. *The Virginia Military District* lay east of the Symmes Purchase, between the Little Miami and Scioto Rivers. This land was reserved by Virginia for her troops that had served in the War of the Revolution. Chillicothe, early capital of the State of Ohio, became the principal town of this tract. Pioneers came to these lands through the passes in the Blue Ridge, often traveling through what is now Maysville, Kentucky, and up the Scioto River Valley to Chillicothe. The ancestors of many of them were English in nationality and Episcopalian in faith.

5. *The Western Reserve* (New Connecticut) extended one hundred twenty miles west from the Pennsylvania line and south from Lake Erie, a distance of about fifty miles. This land was owned and settled by inhabitants of Connecticut.

In addition to these five areas of settlement were the lands included in the United States Military Reservation. This reservation, which extended west of the Seven Ranges to the Scioto River and south of Wayne's Treaty Line, was settled by people from all the states and had no especial social peculiarities. New Jersey, New England, Virginia, and Pennsylvania contributed settlers to this area. Columbus and Zanesville became the chief towns.

THE ORGANIZATION OF THE COUNTIES OF OHIO
1788-1810

The year 1795 is very important in the history of the Ohio country for it marks the beginning of the great American migration to the West with Ohio as the gateway. Prior to this time no progress had been made due to Indian warfare; but with the settlement of these troubles by General Greene, and the signing of the Greenville Treaty, development was very rapid. Settlers came in such numbers by way of the few trails that led through wildernesses of Kentucky, Virginia, Pennsylvania, and from the Niagara district. Ohio, which in 1790, had but two counties, namely, Washington (1788) and Hamilton (1790), had by the year 1810 erected forty-one and organized thirty-four of the eighty-eight counties which comprise the state today.

COUNTY	ERECTED	ORGANIZED
Washington	1788	1788 (Marietta first land office.)
Hamilton	1790	1790 (Cincinnati 2nd land office.)
Adams	1797	1797
Jefferson	1797	1797 (Steubenville 3rd land office.)
Ross	1798	1798
Clermont	1800	1800
Trumbull	1800	1800
Fairfield	1800	1800
Belmont	1801	1801
Butler	1803	1803
Columbiana	1803	1803
Franklin	1803	1803
Gallia	1803	1803
Greene	1803	1803
Montgomery	1803	1803
Scioto	1803	1803
Warren	1803	1803
Muskingum	1804	1804
Athens	1805	1805
Highland	1805	1805
Geauga	1806	1806
Miami	1807	1807
Ashtabula	1808	1811 (Trumbull and Geauga 1808-11)
Cuyahoga	1808	1810 (Geauga 1808-10)

4

Delaware	1808	1808
Knox	1808	1808
Licking	1808	1808
Portage	1808	1808
Preble	1808	1808
Richland	1808	1813 (Knox County 1808-13)
Stark	1808	1809 (Columbiana County)
Tuscarawas	1808	1808
Wayne	1808	1812 (Col. 1808-09 Stark 1809-12.)
Darke	1809	1817 (Miami 1809-17)
Huron	1809	1817
Clinton	1810	1810
Coshocton	1810	1811 (Portage and Geauga, Muskingum and Tuscarawas)
Fayette	1810	1810
Guernsey	1810	1810
Madison	1810	1810
Pickaway	1810	1810
Champaign	1805	before 1810

THE QUAKER SETTLEMENT OF OHIO

By Harlow Lindley*

The period of a third of a century following 1680 marks the great migration of Quakers from England, Ireland and Wales to America, and most of these came to the region around Philadelphia. Previous to this date some Quakers had settled in New England, New Jersey, Virginia and the Carolinas. Most of the Quakers who early settled in Ohio came directly or indirectly from Pennsylvania. A majority came direct from Virginia and the Carolinas but most of them were direct descendants of Pennsylvania settlers. *The Encyclopedia of Quaker Genealogy* being prepared by William Wade Hinshaw is indispensible in following out these Quaker lines.

The membership of the Quakers in Ohio came very largely from Hopewell and Old South Monthly Meetings in Virginia; Cane Creek, New Garden, Deep River, Springfield, Center and Westfield monthly meetings in North Carolina; and Bush River in South Carolina. Friends from Pennsylvania and Virginia crossed the mountains and monthly meetings were established in Southwestern Pennsylvania near the present city of Brownsville and two monthly meetings were soon opened—one called Westland and the other Redstone. These served as the official base for the establishment of regular meetings in Ohio.

Groups of friends from Pennsylvania, Maryland, and Virginia, were augmented by a large movement from the Carolinas and Georgia. Probably the greatest contributing factor in this movement was the slavery issue, and after the passage of the famous Ordinance of 1787 Friends knew that the territory north and west of the Ohio would be forever free from slavery, although there were doubtless other contributing reasons.

In the year 1796, George Harlan and family, members of the Society of Friends moved to the Ohio region, stopping first at Columbia (Cincinnati) and the next year located on the little Miami River, within the present limits of Warren County, becoming the first sheriff of the county and later a member of the General Assembly of the State. So far as is known this was the first Quaker family to locate in Ohio.

*Mr. Lindley is the secretary, librarian, and editor of the Ohio State Archelogical and Historical Society.

In 1796, James Baldwin and Phineas Hunt, with their families, members of the Society of Friends, from Westfield, North Carolina, moved to the Virginia shore of the Ohio River. In February, 1797, Jesse Baldwin and Phineas Hunt crossed the Ohio River. Two families of Friends were now settled together in the Northwest Territory with one before mentioned (the Harlans) quite remote from them.

On May 8th of the same year, 1797, a group of Friends moved from Westland, Pennsylvania, and settled on the east side of the Scioto River below Chillicothe.

In the latter part of this same year, Jesse Baldwin moved from his first location opposite Green Bottom, some eighteen miles down the Ohio, and settled in what was called Quaker Bottom, in Lawrence County, opposite the mouth of the Guyandot River, and the present town of Guyandot. So far as can be ascertained, this was where Friends in the Northwest Territory first sat down to hold a meeting for divine worship.

John Warner, son of Isaac and Mary Warner, was born at High Bank, Ross County, Ohio, on July 12, 1798. So far as we know, he was the first child born as a birthright member of the Society of Friends northwest of the Ohio River, and, on November 11 of the same year, Rebecca Chandler, daughter of William and Hannah Chandler, was born near the same place.

In 1798, a group of Friends from Hopewell, Virginia settled at High Bank, and another group from North Carolina settled at Salt Creek in Ross County, Ohio. In 1799, Obediah Overman and his family from Grayson County, Virginia, arrived with Thomas Beals and his family. On their arrival, they opened a meeting for worship in the dwelling of Jesse Baldwin which was regularly held during their residence at that place. The nearest Meeting to them was Westland, Pennsylvania, about two hundred miles away.

Sometime during the year, 1799, Taylor Webster and family, from Redstone, Pennsylvania, settled at Grassy Prairies, five miles northeast of Chillicothe.

The intensified movement began around 1800. By 1800, settlements were being made west of the Ohio River, some miles out from Wheeling, Va. Just about the same time Friends from the South were migrating into southern and southwestern Ohio, and soon the Eastern and New England States were making their contributions. They constituted a meeting-going population. Those people, who, in the long march through the wilderness had rested on Sunday and at the accustomed hour, had gathered around their campfires for silent worship, or listened to vocal ministry from some of their own number, were not likely to neglect their religious duties when their travels were ended.

There is a tradition which probably is true, that at Con-

cord (Colerain) a group assembled first on the trunk of a
fallen tree, then were invited to the newly erected cabin of
Jonathan Taylor and later moved to the log meeting house,
which was one of the earliest structures.

The first Friends moved into eastern Ohio in September,
1800. In less than one year Friends so increased that two Pre-
parative Meetings were established, and, on December 19,
1801, Concord Monthly Meeting was established. The stream
of emigrants seemed unending and soon there were Friends
communities in Belmont, Jefferson, Harrison, Columbiana,
Morgan, and Washington Counties. Early in 1804 these meetings began to look to the establishment of a Quarterly Meeting.
Their request was granted by the Yearly Meeting in 1806 and
Short Creek Quarterly Meeting convened for the first time,
June 6, 1807.

We now go to another part of the State. In the latter part
of 1799 some families of Friends from Bush River Monthly
Meeting, South Carolina, settled near the present site of
Waynesville. Some months later a group of Friends arrived
from Hopewell Monthly Meeting, Virginia, and, during the
same year, a few from North Carolina. Other Friends continued to arrive and a volunteer meeting for worship was
established, April 26, 1801, at Waynesville. Twelve families
were represented in the meeting. All of these members were
certified to Westland Monthly Meeting, western Pennsylvania.
This Meeting was recognized by Westland Monthly Meeting,
December 26, 1801, and Miami Monthly Meeting was established October 13, 1803, and from this nucleus developed the
Meetings of Ohio west of the Hocking River, including what
later became West Branch Quarterly Meeting to the north,
and Whitewater Quarterly Meeting in eastern Indiana, as well
as all the Friends meetings in Indiana and farther west.

The rapid settlement of Friends in the valleys of the
Miamis is shown by the fact that in three years, from the
middle of 1804 to the middle of 1807, there were received at
Miami Monthly Meeting 367 removal certificates conveying to
that Meeting the membership of 1697 persons. These did not
all settle in the vicinity of Waynesville nor even in Warren
County, but were scattered through what are now Clinton,
Highland, Greene, Montgomery, Miami and Preble counties
in Ohio and Wayne County, Indiana.

In the planting of these Friends communities in Ohio a
number made contributions to the Nation far beyond the
ordinary. Chief among these in the earlier period were Mount
Pleasant, Salem, Damascus, Waynesville, Barnesville and New
Vienna. Mount Pleasant was founded about the year 1800.
Within a few years the thriving town became one of the leading business and industrial centers of eastern Ohio and com-
manded trade over territory of more than a hundred square
miles.

The proprietors of the first stores were Enoch Harris, Joseph Gill, and John Hogg. There soon developed a flouring mill, a woolen factory, a tannery, and one of the first and largest pork-packing establishments of the state. The most extensive meat market and one of the largest woolen markets of the state were here. John W. Gill built th first factory in the United States for the weaving of silk in 1840.

The chief glory of Mount Pleasant was not its material development but in the higher realm of mental and spiritual things. There were a number of college men among the early settlers and great interest was shown in the development of schools. In 1837 there was erected the Friends Boarding School. This school did valuable service. The main building was destroyed by fire in 1875 and the school was rebuilt near Barnesville, and has made a very creditable contribution to education for over a hundred years.

For many years, Mount Pleasant was considered the literary center of eastern Ohio. A large number of periodicals, magazines and books were published here. *The Philanthropist* published by Osborn, issued August 29, 1817, was the first American newspaper to advocate the abolition of slavery, and it was followed by Lundy's *Genius of Universal Emancipation.* The Ohio "Agents" were all men of prominence in their communities and two are worthy of special note—Benjamin Lundy, the pioneer leader in the anti-slavery movement in the United States, and Benjamin Hanna, the grandfather of Senator Marcus A. Hanna Abigail Flanner was an unusual woman for her day, and Mary Edmundson, the mother of Anna Dickinson, taught school in the Short Creek Meeting House.

Although the Quakers were small in number, relatively speaking, yet they made their impress upon the life of Ohio, particularly in the Counties of Jefferson, Columbiana, Belmont, Guernsey, Morgan, Washington, Ross, Highland, Clinton, Warren, Greene, Preble, Miami, Logan and Morrow·

BRIEF HISTORY OF REYNOLDSBURG, FRANKLIN COUNTY, OHIO.

By David Graham, May 9, 1885.

(1801-1886)

The following is an account of the village of Reynoldsburg and of the immediate neighborhood adjoining it; going back as far as the year 1805. About which time there were here and there a log cabin to be found along the streams of water, where the pioneers lived and began to clear off the forest, (which was very heavy) made up of the following kinds of trees: Beech, Sugar or hard maple, Oak of various kinds, Elm, Hickory, Soft maple, Sycamore, Ash, Sasafras, Willow, Cherry, Black and White Walnut or butter-nut, Swamp-beach, Spicebush, Crab-apple, Wild plum. Some of the last of the above trees are more properly called shrubs.

The settlement of the country progressed very slowly for several years on account of the presence of the Indians and the hardships to be endured. The want of a ready market and scarcity of grist mills and the great distance to be overcome in going to a mill, to the Post Office or to a store. When the first settlers came they hereabouts had to go to Chillicothe for their mail, their salt, their flour, etc. They had to get their hardware and glass from Pittsburgh, Penna.

The village of Reynoldsburg was laid out into lots by John French in, about the year 1830. The surveyor who was employed was Abiather Vinton Taylor of Truro township. It is situated on the Pike or National Road where it crosses Blacklick Creek, being about ten miles east of Columbus, the Capital of the State of Ohio. Soon after it's location there was a public offering its lots for sale. Several were purchased, James Taylor, William McIntire, and George J. Graham were among those who were successful bidders. The latter soon afterwards built a large frame house, in which he lived for over fifty years, until it was burned. Soon after the first sale a Mr. Sells of Columbus bought two corner lots and built on the two tavern stands that are known as the Upper and Lower Taverns. The latter was soon purchased by Mr. Samuel Gaver and a good hotel opened for the accommodation of all travellers, and they were not scarce, and for the residence of the town and vicinity, it was kept by him a goodly number of years.

The first dry-goods and grocery store in the village was kept by the Honorable James C. Reynolds in a hewed log cabin on

10

the lot where the United Presbyterian Meeting House now stands; owned then by Mr. Mathew Crawford, Esq. In this building he sold goods and groceries for several years, but after the road was finished he changed his location in town, and was appointed the first Post Master of the town. He was also elected to fill the office of Justice of the Peace. About the year 1840 he was elected by the county of Franklin a member of the Legislature of Ohio. His father had been a member of the Legislature several years previously, consequently his son was allowed to occupy the seat or desk which his father had graced years before in the old brick State-house. While he was in the Assembly he used his influence in getting the village incorporated, and in as much as he had been the means of advancing the interest of the town, the citizens of the town and vicinity held a public meeting and resolved that the town should be known by the name of Reynoldsburg in honor of J. C. Reynolds. He previously to 1840 built a large frame grist mill on the south-west corner lot, but its expense broke him up. He sold and moved to the town of Carroll on the Ohio Canal and built a water grist mill which he was only allowed to run for a few years when he was cut down by the malaria fever, which prevailed in that locality more or less every year.

The McEwen family have owned and occupied the Lower Tavern for about twenty years and have kept a saloon, besides some others which sold liquors contrary to the wishes of the majority of the inhabitants of the town and vicinity.

The pioneers of the village and the surrounding country have nearly all left this vale of tears. To record a few of their names may not be out of place here, Viz. Henry Johnson, John Coons, George Graham, James Graham, William (Little Billy) Graham, Joseph McIntire, Mathew Crawford, Esq., Robert, James and John McCrady, William and Thomas Ashton, Philip Rhoads, Archibald Cooper, J. B. West Esq., Robert Taft Esq., Nathaniel Mason Esq., Jeff, Learn, Moses Hunter, John and Alexander Frazier, William G., and John Graham, David Pugh, Moses Strang, John Livingston, Robert Forester, a minister of the United Presbyterian church, who was the Pastor of the Reynoldsburg U. P. Congregation for more than twenty years; Rev. John W. Thompson, Presbyterian, Thomas Longshore, Daniel and George Parkison.

The names of those who served as Justice of the Peace in the village were: Mathew Crawford, Jeremiah Nay, Robert Taft, John B. West, John Miller, George D. Graham, J. C. Reynolds, John Lynch, Charles Hutson, John Wright, and Nathaniel Mason Sr.

The first church organization was the Seceder (now the United Presbyterian congregation) church, which took place in 1819 by the election of two Elders and the acceptation of William Graham (for the other) of the congregation of Cambridge of the State of New York. The names of the other two were Mathew

11

Taylor and William Crawford. The election and ordination was conducted by the Rev. Robert Armstrong of Massies Creek, Greene County, Ohio, of Miami Presbyteria. The first Meeting House for public worship was built by said congregation about one half mile southeast of town on the Lancaster road where the Hebron road crosses it, on the southeast corner of the farm then owned by Mathew Crawford, but owned now by the widow and heirs of Josiah Medbury, deceased. There was regular preaching in this church for about forty years, until the new church was built in the village in the years 1860-1. The number of its members, on an average, have been about 100 or perhaps 110. The names of the pastors who have had charge of the said U. P. Congregation during its existence, are as follows: Rev. John Donalson, Stated Supply for two years, Rev. Samuel McLean two years, Rev. David Lyndsay seven years, Rev. Robert Forester twenty-one years, Rev. J. W. McNary eight years, Rev. J. C. McArthur three years and Rev. R. H. Park six years. The congregation has been blessed with the regular dispensation of divine ordinances nearly fifty years, which leaves seventeen years it has not enjoyed them.

But let us take up the account of the town again. The Meeting House was first built in the town for public worship was the Baptist brick church and which still stands, after an existence of over forty years. The little congregation has lately been divided on account of some practical questions.

The second church in the town was the Methodist Episcopal. It was a frame building located on the northwest corner of what is now the school house lot. It is taken down now and they have built a brick building situated on the south side of the national road. It has a steeple and bell.

The third was the Presbyterian church which was consumed by fire about 1860. Another one was built on the same lot immediately and is still used. This building also has a steeple and a bell.

The fourth church was built by the Universalists.

The fifth church built was the United Presbyterian, which was built about 1860, costing about two thousand dollars, It has a steeple and a bell.

The sixth church built was the brick Methodist Episcopal church with a steeple and a bell.

The seventh and last church built was the Campbellite church of brick construction, having a steeple but no bell yet.

The village has one of the largest school houses in the county and one of the best schools, which is kept up by Superintendant D. J. Snider. Mr. Snyder is a teacher of rare qualifications for the profession and is the only Superintendent the school has had. The school is divided into four departments, viz. Primary, Intermediate, Grammar and High School. The School District embraces territory besides the corporation of the village, which makes it necessary to have another small school house

12

for the accommodation of those who are located too far from the village, but they are governed by the same Directors and Superintendent. The Board consists of six members chosen out of the householders of the town and country. Two go out every year and two are elected at the Spring election to fill their places.

The town is bounded on the west by Blacklick, on the south by a line running east and west parallel with the new grave yard, on the east by a line taking in the grave yard on the hill, and on the north by a line running parallel with D. L. Graham's hedge fence and R. Spitler's north line until it reaches Blacklick creek, the place of beginning. Embracing about a half section of land.

The officers of the town are: a Mayor, a Marshall, a Treasurer, a Clerk and five Councilmen, who are chosen by the people of the village at the spring election on the same day that township officers are elected.

The Physicians who have practiced Medicine from time to time are Jacob Shaffer, Robertson, Lunn, Cowden, McCullough, Mathews, Goldrick, Carrol, Nourse, Fisher, France, Donnon, Brock, Alberry, Taylor, Dysart, Griffith.

The names of the most prominent merchants who have sold goods and groceries in said town, are as follows: Mr. Bronson, J. C. Reynolds, L. P. Rhoads, Wm. Goodwin, Abe Moore & Goodwin, Dickey & Ed. Moore, V. Hutson, Nat Mason Jr., Rhoads & Mason, John Rees, David Graham & Son, Thompson & Reid, Elias Weaver, Mason & Gayman, R. R. Johnson, Charles West.

The Post Masters have been J. C. Reynolds, Harvey Miller, D. Graham, Deputy John Miller, V. Hutson, John Lynch, Nathaniel Mason, Jr., William Rhoads, the present incumbent (1885).

The Wagon & Buggy Manufacturers, J. W. Thompson, Thomas Norris, Thomas Longshore, Abram Johnson, John Bryant, Mr. Abbot, Fred Norris, Harrison Long.

The names of the Blacksmiths, Joseph Reynolds, John Mitchell, Mr. Willis, George Shanks, Samuel Gillette, Saul Rush, Hays Brothers, William Hunt, James Banister, William & Josiah Rush, Mr. Hook, Mr. Feasel, and Mr. Rhodabaugh & Son.

The names of the Carpenters are, George J. Graham, Nathan Orcutt, Amariah Graham, Hack Long, Mr. Hathaway, Daniel Parkison, Samuel Parkison & Sons, James Hanna and Buel Gillett.

At the time the whites began to settle around where the village now stands the Indians had a sugar camp, and one of them took a little too much whiskey (of which they were all very fond) and loosing his balance fell into one of the kettles of boiling sugar water which caused his death. His comrades buried him near the said camp, and fenced in the grave with poles, which had not decayed and could be seen in the year 1817 when the writer with his father moved into the neighborhood. The first settler on the sight of the town was a Mr. Donahue; in the year 1816 he sold to Mr. John French.

13

Near the village there are several relics of the Mound Builders to be found. One is a mound near the southeast corner of the Corporation, situated on quite an eminence before the plow had disturbed it. It was about ten feet high and at the base about forty feet in circumference, but it has been nearly leveled down even with the surface on which it was erected. Another of these relics is situated near the northwest corner of the Corporation, on the farm owned by Ed. Parkison, lying across the road opposite his house and barn. It is a fort having a bank thrown up in a square, about twenty-eight or thirty rods on each side. The bank or wall was worn down by time so low that it was scarcely visible when the country was first settled. It can, however be traced out yet. Another fort, circular shaped, is to be found about a half mile south of said village, on the west side of the Lancaster road, the fence runs over the edge of it. It's circumference is about sixty or seventy feet. The wall was about three feet high when in a state of nature, but the husbandmen's implements have leveled it nearly even with the surrounding surface of the earth. This fort is on the land now owned by Mr. Joseph Ashton, and said fort is about forty rods south of the house which Mr. Nathan Orcutt occupies. About two and a half miles north-east of Reynoldsburg, near the south-east corner of Jefferson township, there is a fort similar in shape and size of the one just described, which has not been disturbed by the owner of the land (Dr. Lunn). The difference exists in the height of the wall and the depth of the ditch which was probably ten or twelve feet deep and the wall ten or fifteen feet high. The water stands in the ditch the most of the year. On the wall or embankment there was quite a large oak tree, showing that the wall is as ancient as the present timber around it and that they belong to some age of the world, when that was can only be decided by conjecture. One thing about the mounds we know from the fact that in many of them human skeletons are found, showing that they were used for burying the dead. It is held by some that the mounds were used as a tower where an enemies approach could be discovered, and that the forts were built for protection from animals and any other foe.

The village has a small hall where the Council holds their meetings, and attached to it is a Callaboose, in which to keep criminals, but to the credit of the citizens it is seldom needed, and it is likely, if the prohibition law was in force that it would not be brought into use often, perhaps not at all. A goodly number of the citizens are in favor of enacting some such prohibition law, as soon as possible.

There are very few villages more moral than the Burg, and where a larger proportion of the inhabitants are church going people, it is very seldom one will hear profane language in common conversation, and it is a very rare occurrence where quarreling and fighting takes place. The violation of the Holy Sabbath,

14

perhaps, is the sin which ranks next to the leading crime of drunkenness.

There has lately been organized a Company, which has purchased a lot on the south line of the Corporation, to be set apart for a graveyard. It has been run out into streets and family lots, and in it has been erected a nice vault for the accommodation of the village and the surrounding country.

In said town there is a large tile factory, where hundreds of dollars worth are sold every year. Also in connection with it a steam saw mill both run by the same steam engine which saws a very considerable amount of lumber. They sometimes fill a bill for a small number of brick to build houses and chimneys.

The town is blessed with plenty of water, both well and creek water, and the creeks are fed by durable springs which keeps them running the year round. In case of a fire there is an abundance of the element so essential to quench the flames.

One half mile north-east of the Corporation of said town is one of the largest freestone quarries in the state of Ohio. Some of the tiers are of the best quality and almost as durable as marble. It is owned and worked by Mr. William Forester, who keeps a double set of saws in operation night and day, furnishing step stones, caps and sills and range work for buildings in the city of Columbus and adjacent villages and in the country near the quarry. This work is done mostly during the summer season, but some is done during the fall and spring seasons if the weather permits.

Butchering is carried on quite extensively in the town and vicinity; there are five or six slaughter houses in operation, employing twenty-five or thirty hands, killing twenty-five or thirty head of cattle every week, besides a good many hogs and sheep.

The village has been more unfortunate than many others in respect to the number of fires it has had during its existence. The number of houses destroyed are not less than ten, and one of them was a meeting house worth about $2000.00. Another one, a large two story dwelling house worth twelve or fifteen hundred dollars. The others were smaller ones; one of them was owned by R. Spitler, but occupied by Mr. Jackson. It took fire in the night, and he and family were hard pressed to make their escape; his goods were mostly saved. Another fire consumed the building in which the Post Office was kept by V. Hutson. A stock of groceries in it, and two other houses, and the roof of the brick store on the north side of the National Road or Main Street; the goods were partly saved and partly insured. Again the large frame dwelling belonging to George Graham caught fire in the roof. It was in the day time but during a very high wind, which made it impossible for the citizens to stop it's progress until it was burned totally to ashes. Most of the furniture was saved. There was no insurance. Another fire consumed three buildings on the corner of the lot on which Nat. Mason's large brick store now stands. The grocery store owned by Mr. Craner was completely destroyed, but was insured, the other two buildings were totally destroyed.

The subject of temperance received the early attention of the citizens of the village and the surrounding territory. They strongly opposed the habit of using intoxicants as a common beverage, which they manifested by totally abstaining from frequenting the taverns and saloons for the purpose of treating and being treated, and refused to use it at rollings and raisings, or in harvesting or haying time. Also by joining the Washington Society and spending their money to get public lecturers to teach the people on the subject of tetotalism. The Women's Temperance Crusade was kept up for several months, but the earnest prayers sent up to the Throne of Grace by those Godly women prostrated on their knees on the hard pavement had no more effect on the hardened hearts of the retailers of liquid poison than their knees had on the cold brick pavement. The leading ladies who took an active part in the above movement should be remembered by recording their names in this historical sketch. Viz. Mrs. Rev. Ewen, the Widow Powers, Miss Hattie Turner, Mrs. William Howard, Mrs. William Baucher, and some others.

The Town Council have been doing all the law empowers them to do in order to prohibit the sale of liquor in the village. They have a lawyer hired to attend to the prosecution of the violators of the law. He has several cases pending in the court, taken there by appeal from the Mayor's docket, waiting their turn, or perhaps the pleasure of the court.

There have been several pretty serious accidents which took place in the village of Reynoldsburg during its existence that might be interesting to the citizens in time to come, and perhaps it might not be out of place to insert them here.

One of these accidents occurred in the blacksmith shop lately occupied as such by Mr. William Hunt, but now it is torn down and the lot is owned by Mr. William Johnson. One of the neighbors brought his rifle to the shop to have a bullet taken out of the barrel which had been put in before putting in any powder, he having failed to get it out in any way he could devise. The smith put the end of the barrel, where the bullet was, into the fire, intending to melt the bullet out. In the meantime the owner and others were standing near the forge watching the operation. As soon as the barrel got hot enought to set powder on fire, it went off, (it was supposed there was enough powder sticking to the inside of the barrel to cause the explosion,) and the bullet went through the thigh of its owner, causing him to fall which frightened the smith and bystanders seriously. A doctor was in town was called and the wound dressed. Finding no bones or large veins were touched by the ball the doctor pronounced it not necessarily fatal. The wounded man was about eighty years old, hence his relatives and friends were somewhat afraid that it might be fatal. However their fears were groundless for he survived for several years after the accident took place.

Another very serious accident took place while the workmen were engaged in raising the first Presbyterian Meeting House in the village. They had the body of the frame up and had the timber for the roof mostly up on the joists, about ready to raise the bents to support the rafters, (when the boss was warned by an old man who had had some experience in the business) that his prop was too light, and drove some boys from under the timbers. In the meantime the prop under the center beam broke and let the whole pile of timber, men and tools down on the sleepers with a crash, filling the bystanders with consternation and grief and rendering them more than ordinarily strong, they soon extricated their neighbors from their perilous situation. Which being done it was found out that four of them were dangerously if not fatally injured. Their names were, Joseph McCray, Mr. Sincebaugh, Mark Evans, Blythe Dixon and two or three others. Mr. McCray was hurt in the head, so that he did not know that he had been at the raising. Mr. Sincebaugh was jarred all over his body. Mr. Evans was hurt in his back and legs and Mr. Dixon was bruised on his head and face, leaving scars visible to this day, May 9th, 1885.

DAVID GRAHAM

HISTORICAL NOTES, MIFFLIN AND PLAIN TOWNSHIPS, FRANKLIN CO., OHIO

ROBERT WALDRON

MIFFLIN TOWNSHIP

The territory which now comprises Mifflin township was first settled about 1799 or 1800, by emigrants from Pennsylvania. William Read is believed to have been the first settler, but among other early pioneers were Frederick Agler, Daniel and John Turney, George Baughman, John Saul, Stephen Price, James Price, John Scott, Louis Patterson, John Dalzell, Zachariah Kramer, John Dill, James Park, George Harwood, Henry Carpenter, Matthias Ridenour, Ebenezer Butler, Libbeus E. Dean, Philander Patterson, Andrew W. Smiley, James Latta, John Starrett, William Smith, Nathanial Harris, D. Stygler, Geo. Bartlett, John Clark, Robert Paul, T. G. Schrock, Sarah Crouse Ramsey, Thomas Harward and others.

In the division of Franklin county into townships in 1803, this territory was included as a part of Liberty township. Then in September, 1811, Mifflin township was organized and established with its present boundaries, and named by the pioneers for their old Pennsylvania governor, Mifflin. It is designated as Twp. 1, in Range 17, of the U. S. Military Lands.

The first road in Mifflin township was the old Zanesville road, leading to Columbus and running through the southern part of the township. Some of the early settlers came in on this road, and then cut their way through the forest to their locations. It was afterward abandoned.

Several saw mills were established, including Dean's mill and Park's mill. The first grist mill in the township was built in 1859 by Joel and Jesse Baughman.

John Clark founded the town of Gahanna in 1849, at its present location, and Jesse Baughman followed in 1853 with the village of Bridgeport. There was considerable rivalry between the two towns, which were divided only by what is now Granville street.

A post office was established in Gahanna in 1849, and another at Park's Mill on Alum creek in 1851.

Two other communities, which have since been annexed to the City of Columbus, were originally in Mifflin township. East Columbus grew up along the Pennsylvania railroad, about the Ralston Steel Car Works. The modern residential section of Shepard was the site originally chosen by Dr. W. Shepherd for his private sanitarium and water cure. What is now Nel-

18

son road was then known as Alum creek road.

St. Mary's of the Springs, a Catholic seminary, was established in 1868. Several excellent springs were found on the property, including one or two with fine medical properties.

The first tavern in Mifflin township was kept by George Read, where the McMillen Sanitarium in Shepard now stands.

James Price, a Mifflin pioneer, earned quite a reputation as a deer hunter in those early days. He had a natural instinct for hunting, and his knowledge of woods and animals was very thorough.

The Lutherans and Presbyterians were the first to hold religious services in Mifflin township, with the Methodists and Evangelical following a few years later. The first Lutheran services are said to have been held in the homes of George Ridenour and Daniel Forney. The first church was built in 1838. The Presbyterians, led by Rev. Ebenezer Washburn, first held services in William Smith's barn, in 1819, but did not erect a church building until 1840.

Mifflin township's first school was erected on Big Walnut, where Gahanna is now located; the second, on top of the hill west of Alum creek; and the third, in the Park's neighborhood.

Mifflin Lodge of Odd Fellows, No. 518, was instituted June 27th, 1827.

PLAIN TOWNSHIP

The third time is the charm, it is said, and this axiom has proved true in the history of Plain township, where three separate attempts were made over a century ago to establish villages, before one finally succeeded.

In 1826, Lorin Hills and Lester Huphrey laid out a town which they called "Lafayetteville", on Granville road near where New Albany is now located. They had the plat recorded, but never made any improvements, and it was finally abandoned.

In 1835, Francis Clymer laid out a town on his farm, which he called "Mount Pleasant", but this also was a failure.

Then in May, 1837, Noble Landon and William Yantis laid out the town of New Albany. Each owned land on opposite sides of the street, and although they had the whole village platted together, each disposed of his own lots as he saw fit.

Early Settlers

There is some doubt among historians, as to who was the first settler in Plain township. The first authentic account of land transactions there, is the record of a patent issued to Dudley Woodbridge by President John Adams, in 1800, for 4,000 acres in the southwest corner of the township. In 1802, Woodbridge sold the land to John Huffman for 4,000 gallons of whiskey, delivered at Marietta.

Joseph Scott and a man named Morrison were perhaps the first settlers in Plain township, although some records claim that honor for Adam Baughman, whose daughter is said to have been the first white child born here. "Scott's Plains" and "Morrison's Prairie" are still familiar phrases.

Among other early settlers were: Samuel Baughman, Henry Huffman, Thomas B. Patterson, Lorin Hills, Jesse Byington, Gilbert Waters, William Yantes, Abraham Williams, Joseph Moore, Mathias, Daniel and George Dague, Mathew and George Campbell, John Robinson, William Goodhart, Roger Hill, David and Emil Cook, Jacob Wagner, John Clymer, John Alspach, Daniel Triplett, Christian Horlocker, Jacob Bevelhymer, Peter Quinn, Wayne Taylor, Ezekial Park, Samuel Riggle, David Morrison, Daniel Swickard and others.

The first saw mill was erected on Rocky Fork creek by Daniel Kramer, in 1827.

Early Churches Built

In 1837, the Methodists erected a brick meeting house which they called "Plain Chapel", in the northern part of the township. Later, in 1846, they built the frame church in New Albany. Circuit preachers at that time were G. G. West and Sheldon Parker.

The United Brethrens erected their church in 1836. The Albrites met about a mile west of Plain Chapel, and a small Presbyterian organization held meetings in New Albany.

Schools Of Township

Philip Walters and Jacob Smith were the first school teachers in the township. Smith taught a select school in the winter of 1820-21, before the days of public schools. The tuntion fee for one term was $1.50 per scholar.

Softhead school, a double log structure, was built in 1839. The Wagoner school building to the west was erected several years earlier.

School buildings served a double purpose, for education and religion, in those days.

Was Much Larger

When first organized, Plain township was much larger than at present. It then included all of what is now Blendon township, and about half of Jefferson.

The southeast quarter was laid out in 100-acre lots to satisfy claims of Revolutionary soldiers.

The first cemetery in Plain township was set apart on land donated in 1814 by John Smith, and he was the first to be buried there.

New Albany Incorporated

New Albany was incorporated in April, 1856. The first village officials were: S. Ogden, mayor; C. S. Ogden, recorder; R. Phelps, marshal; F. Johnson, J. McCurdy, C. Baughman, A. B. Beem and S. Stinson, councilmen.

"Hope" post office was established at New Albany in 1838.

Teetotalers Organized

An attempt to stop the dispensing of whiskey at public gatherings such as house raisings, corn huskings, and turkey shootings, was made as far back as 1820 when a group of "teetotalers" was organized.

Abraham Adams was the leader of this reform effort, but it met with so much opposition that it was finally dropped. Whiskey continued to be a prime attraction at gatherings where men predominated.

(Excerpts from Tri-Community News, Gahanna, Ohio, May 19, 1939)

ST. JOHN'S CHURCH, WORTHINGTON, OHIO

PHILLIP W. HULL, RECTOR

On February 6, 1804, there was founded in "Worthington and parts adjacent" in the new State of Ohio, St. John's Church, the oldest Episcopal Church west of the Allegheny Mountains. St. John's Church was incorporated by act of the legislature, in 1807 and became the second religious organization incorporated in Ohio.

Under these articles of incorporation St. John's remained an independent religious organization for more than a century. The parish was governed by three trustees who at times could be very autocratic. In 1919 these articles were changed by the state legislature so that St. John's could conform to the constitution and canons of the Episcopal Church and come into union with the Diocese of Southern Ohio.

In the fall of 1803, James Kilbourne, a friend of Alexander Viets Griswold—later to become bishop of the Eastern Diocese, led a band of one hundred settlers who were churchmen from Simsbury and Granby, Connecticut, to Ohio and founded the village of Worthington in Sharon Township, Franklin County, Ohio.

The village was named after Worthington, Connecticut, where James Kilbourne was confirmed, served as lay reader and later was ordained deacon.

Under the Articles of Agreement one town lot of one acre on the village green and one farm lot of one hundred acres were set apart for a Protestant Episcopal Church. Similar lots on the north side of the highway were allotted for a school. The first log cabin which was erected immediately after the arrival of the settlers in 1804, served as both church and school. The two farms lie immediately west of the village on either side of the road and extend to the Olentangy River.

The log cabin served for a church until 1808 when the Worthington Academy, a two story, red brick building, was built on the village green. Worship services were conducted in the academy for over twenty years. The present red brick church was started in the summer of 1827 and the first service was held in January, 1831. The building was erected by the church members themselves who were master workmen. But the financial limitations of the community prevented them from securing the materials which had to be bought and delayed its completion. The interior with its four columns supporting the roof (solid trees) and rear gallery is supposed to be copied from a London church, the rough design of which Philander Chase gave to John Snow, the architect and builder. The church has been in continuous use and is in a splendid state of preservation.

Behind the church is the old parish burial ground where lie the bodies of the pioneers with the grave of James Kilbourne in the center. Burials have not been made here since the Civil War. The angelus bell is rung every day at noon. In 1918, a beautiful marble altar and step with oak reredos were given by Florence R. Vance. The reredos consists of three panels which contain oil paintings. The central panel is a very fine portrayal of the reigning Christ. In 1926 a modern brick parish house was erected south of the church on the village green by Herman E. Vance, vestryman and senior warden for twenty-five years.

Among the members of the original colony were the following persons who settled in Worthington, many of whose gravestones are in the graveyard beside the church: James Kilbourne, Thomas T. Phelps, Abner Pinney, Russell Atwater, Jedediah Norton, Job Case, Levi Hays, Levi Buttles, Jeremiah Curtis, Zophar Topping, Ebenezer Street, Nathan Stewart, Roswell Wilcox, Lemuel Kilbourne, Jonas Stansberry, Abner P. Pinney, Josiah Topping, Azariah Pinney, Moses Andrews, Samuel Sloper, William Thompson, Alexander Morrison, Sr., Alexander Morrison, Jr., Samuel Beach, John Gould, Ezra Griswold, William Vining, John Topping, Israel P. Case, Israel Case, David Bristol, Glass Cochran, Lemuel G. Humphrey, Ambrose Case, Jacob Mills, James Allen, Nathaniel W. Little and Ichabod Plumb.

ST. JOHN'S EPISCOPAL CHURCH, WORTHINGTON, OHIO
"Oldest Church west of Alleghanies" Founded February 6, 1804.
Incorporated 1807. Church erected 1827-30. Parish House erected 1927.

James Kilbourne was the first minister of St. John's Parish and served for several years. He was a farmer, mechanic, mathematician, business man, soldier, and minister. He was the inn keeper and banker and his home still stands after 128 years. In later years James Kilbourne was a member of Congress and introduced the "Land Grant Bill" whereby public lands were appropriated to establish and support state universities.

Philander Chase, who resigned the rectorate of Christ Church, Hartford, Connecticut in 1817, came to Ohio, bought a farm south of Worthington (known today as Chaseland) and became the first rector of St. John's Parish. The next year a convention of the scattered churchmen in Ohio was held at Worthington and he was chosen the first bishop of the new Diocese of Ohio. He continued to serve as rector of St. John's until 1822. During this period he started a boys' school to educate men for the ministry of the Church in his farm home. This was the humble beginning of Kenyon College and Bexley Hall at Gambier, Ohio.

The late Dr. George F. Smythe in "A History of the Diocese of Ohio" writes of the beginning of St. John's: "For a quarter of a century thereafter, Worthington was the most important place in the history of the Episcopal Church in Ohio." And again: "To Ohio Churchmen, the public square at Worthington is, as it were, their Plymouth Rock."

The village of Worthington was laid out in May, 1804. Today Worthington is a village of fifteen hundred population within two miles of Columbus. In 1804 Columbus had not been settled, but in 1812 Worthington lost to Columbus in the choice of the state capitol.

BURIAL GROUND ST. JOHN'S EPISCOPAL CHURCH, WORTHINGTON, OHIO
Used from 1804 to Civil War. "Here lie the bodies of The Pioneers"

23

GLEANINGS FROM THE SUPPORTER
Printed by Nashee & Denny
CHILLICOTHE, OHIO
Blanche Collins

1809

For Sale—50,000 acres of land in the Virginia Military District. Terms: low for part cash, and annual installments. Thomas S. Hinde and Charles A. Stewart. November 3.

Notice—The estate of Jesse Phelps, Esq., late of Painesville, County of Geauga. Samuel W. Phelps, Adm. April 12.—To *Heirs*, executors, etc., of John Zane, deceased, that Horatio Clark Bowen, William Uruhart Bowen, and Christopher Bowen, heirs at law of John Bowen, deceased, have deposited with the treasurer of the State of Ohio, the full amount of the redemption money, interest etc., for part of a tract of land—889 acres, No. 3469, on Rokes Creek, entered in the name of John Bowen, of which 639 acres were sold to John Zane for the tax of 1800 and 1801. Now, therefore, the heirs will proceed in the next court of common pleas, Delaware county to exhibit proof of the right of redemption. June 8.

Notice—"That I have located 1000 acres of land on the waters of Paint and Indian Creeks, adjoining the lands of the two Mrs. Pattons, widows of Messrs. William and John Patton, deceased; of Peter Muhlenberg; James Crawford; Mr. Lumback; and others, on their west lines, and extending well purchasers under the sales made by my father . . . any persons trespassing or cutting timber from the premises will be made to account for so doing without descrimination. Those lands are for sale . . . just claims, or cash against my father, will be taken as payment", Angus L. Langham, September 22.

Notice—To debtors against the estate of William Murphy, deceased. Alexander Holmes, Adm., Licking county. October 10.

*Date following asterisk denotes date of publication.

24

MARRIED—On Sunday last, by Rev. John Collins, *Edward Tiffin,* Esq., to the amiable *Mifs Polly Porter,* Ross county. (*Apr. 20)—On Thursday the 19th ult. at Cincinnati, by Rev. William Lymes, *Thomas S. Hinde,* Esq., of this town, to the amiable *Mifs Belinda Bradford,* of Hamilton county, Ohio.—On Thursday the 19th ult., in Montgomery county, by Rev. Andrew Lemon, *Mr. Silas Atchison,* to the amiable *Mifs Polly Craig,* all of said county.—On the 2nd ult., at Urbana, Ohio, by Rev. Hiram M. Curry, *Mr. George Hunter,* to the amiable *Mifs Ruth* Fitch, all of Champaigne county. (*Nov. 3)—On Thursday last by John Ferguson, Esq., *Mr. James Bramble,* to the amiable *Mifs Eliza Poe,* of this town.—On the same evening, by the same, *Mr. George Scott,* to the amiable *Mifs Ann Thompson,* all of Chillicothe. (*Dec. 30)

DIED—At Belpre, in this county, on Monday last, Capt. William Dana, in the 65th year of his age.—*The Commentator*/Marietta, Nov. 4. (*Nov. 17)

1810

NOTICE—That Mary Parker, heiress of Alexander Parker, by her agent William Creighton, Jr., has placed the redemption money with the state for a tract of land entered in the name of Alexander Parker, No. 455, containing 1000 acres in Scioto county, on the Ohio river; 700 acres to Nathan Kennedy; 100 acres to John S. Wells; 199 acres to Hugh Bracken; and one acre to Moses Wright, Jan. 4, (*Jan. 27)

NOTICE—To debtors of the estate of Caleb Baldwin, Esq., late of Youngstown, Trumbull county. Henry Wick, Thomas Kirkpatrick, adms. March 21 (*Apr. 14)

DISSOLATION OF PARTNERSHIP—The firm of Thomas & David Gwynn is by mutual consent this day dissolved. Madison, August 5. (*Aug. 11)

MARRIED—At Lebanon, Ohio, on the 19th ult, by Enos Williams, Esq., *Mr. Nathaniel M'Clean,* one of the editors of the *Western Star,* to the amiable *Mifs Hetty Nut,* all of Warren county.—At Lebanon, on the 7th inst. by Enos Williams, Esq., *Mr. John Prill,* to the amiable *Mifs Sally Best,* late of the town of Cincinnati.—At Franklinton, on the 16th inst. Mr. Robert Russell, of Pickaway Plains, to the amiable *Mifs Polly Cain,* of Franklin county. (*Jan 27)—On Tuesday, the 27th ult, by the Rev. John Brice, *Col. John Ferguson* of this place to *Mifs Jane Denny,* of Wheeling, Va.—On the 18th ult, at Cincinnati, *Mr. Fair-*banks to *Mifs Polly Miles,* all of Hamilton county. (*)—At New Orleans, *General James Wilkinson,* to *Mlle. Trudeau,* handsome, ac-complished, and about 26 year of age. The general is about 55. (*Feb)—On the evening of the 22d inst. by Joseph Tiffin, Esq., *Mr. Jerome Smith,* to the amiable *Mifs Mary Keys,* of Union twp.—At Belpre, on Friday the 16th inst. by William Browning, Esq., *Mr. Nathan Bent,* to *Mifs Susan Dilley.*—At the same place by Daniel Goodus, Esq., *Capt. Cyrus Ames,* to *Mifs Polly Rice.*—On Feb. the 22d, at Georgetown, D. C., by the Rev. Dr. Gantt, the *Honorable William B. Giles,* Senator to the U. S. Congress, to *Mifs Frances Ann Gwynn,* eldest daughter of the late Thomas Peyton Gwynn of Virginia. (*Mar 31)—Near Franklinton, by Rev. Mr. Hoge, *Mr. William Long,* of this county, to the amiable *Mrs. Margaret Shaw* of Franklin county. (*May 6)—At Pittsburgh, on Thursday evening the 3d inst. by Rev. Mr. Taylor, *Thomas Enochs,* Esq., merchant, to *Mrs. Jane Porter,* all of that place. (*Sept 15)—At Washington, Pa., on the 18th inst. by

25

Rev. Mr. Brown, *Mr. John Shearer*, of this place, to *Mifs Rosanna* Wolff, of the former place. (*Sept 29)

DIED—At Marietta on the 20th ult. Mrs. Mary Gitteau, the amiable consort of Mr. Jonathan Gitteau, and the daughter of Col. Abner Lord of this place, aged 18 years. (*Mar 31)—Departed this life on the 28th ult. after a long and painful illness, Mrs. Ann Stockton, in the 56th year of her age.—At Portland (Vt.) on the 13th ult. Mrs. Ann Prentiss, consort of John Prentiss, Esq., of that place, in the 60th year of her age. (*April 7)—Obituary-same (*May 6).—Obit: Departed this life on the 13th of August Mrs. Mathilda Lawson, aged 37, consort of Jeremiah Lawson, Esq., late of Lebanon, Warren county, Ohio; now in Upper Louisiana, District of Cape Giradeau, Tawappity twp—35 miles above the mouth of the Ohio. She left a husband and four young children in a wild and almost uninhabited wilderness seated on the banks of the Mississippi. (*Sept 15)—In this town, on Monday evening last, after a short but severe illness, James Crockwell, in the 27th year of his age.—On Sunday last, Mrs. Trimble, consort of Mr. John Trimble, of Ross county. (*Sept 29)

1823

NOTICE—The estate of Alexander Collison late of Beaver twp, Pike county, deceased. Moses Collison, Admr. August 2.—The estate of Andrew Donally, deceased, late of Jackson county. Mary Donally, Exr. August 2.—The estate of Edward H. Edwards, late of Chillicothe, deceased. Samuel Edwards, Fred Edwards, Adms. October 13.—To debtors to the estate of Joseph Grayum, late of Gallipolis, Gallia county, Ohio. David Grayum, Luther Shepard, Adms. October 13.—The estate of Samuel Wettemore, late of Galliopolis, deceased. Wililam R. G. Udd, Thomas Rodgers, Adms. October 18.—The estate of Christian Leby, Jun., late of Green twp., Ross county. Mary Leby, David Leby, Adms. November 8.—The estate of Phillip Moore, Sen., late of Scioto county, deceased. Levi Moore, Adm. November 8.—The estate of Jehiel Gregory, deceased, Fayette county, Marion twp. Sally Gregory, Adm. November 1.—The estate of Alexander Walker, deceased, Twin twp, Ross county. Robert Dun, Exr. November 8.—The estate of Ebenezer Myers, late of Fayette county, deceased. Amos Hawkins, Adm. November 1.

MARRIED—On Thursday the 17th inst. by the Rev. R. G. Wilson, *Mr. Andrew McCollister*, to *Mifs Maria Kirkpatrick*, both of Huntington twp.—On the same evening, by the same, *Mr. Samuel Elliott*, Jr., to *Mrs. Margaret Walker*, both of this town.—At Jefferson, Pickaway county, on Monday last, *Mr. Abraham Thompson*, Jun., to *Mifs Sarah Hutsonpillar*, both of this town. (*July 26)

DIED—In Circleville, on the 28th ult. in the 22d year, Mrs. Nancy Thrall, consort of Mr. William B. Thrall, editor of *The Olive Branch.* (*Aug 2)—On Wednesday last after a long and painfull illness, Mrs. Margaret Elliott, consort of Mr. Samuel Eliott, in the 29th year of her age. (*Oct. 13)—At Troy, Miami county, on the 5th ult. Mr. Job Evans, formerly of this place, aged 28 years.—On the 29th ult. in the 55th year of his age, Major Isaac Brink, of this county.—On Monday evening last, Mr. John Shearer, of this place, aged about 35 years. (*Nov. 8)

26

NOTICE—The estate of Joseph M'Garrough, deceased, late of Union twp. Fayette county, James B. Webster, Adm. November 22, 1823.—The estate of David Knop, late of Cheshire, Gallia county, deceased. Joseph Mauk, Adm. February 19.—The estate of Hugh McKee, Jefferson twp, Ross county, William McKee, Adm. March 24.— The estate of Jeremiah Ulm, Ross county, deceased, March 20. Francis Nichol, Adm.—The estate of Mary Glover, late of Portsmouth, Scioto county. Elizabeth Glover, Exr. March 25.—The estate of Moses Kirkpatrick, Chillicothe, deceased. William Kirkpatrick, and Samuel Taggart, Adms. March 25.—The estate of Joseph Kirkpatrick, Sen., late of Chillicothe. William Kirkpatrick and Samuel Taggart, Adms. March 25.—The estate of Elijah Cockrell, late of Jefferson twp, Scioto county. Jesse and John Cockrell, Admrs. April 25.—The estate of Samuel Waddle, Washington, Fayette county, deceased. Robert Waddle, Norman F. Jones, Admrs. March 12.

MARRIED—On Tuesday morning last, at St. Paul's Church, by Rev. Intrepid Morse of Steubenville, the *Rev. Ezra B. Kellog*, rector of the P. E. Church of this place, to *Mifs Sobrina Bursh*, late of Duchess county, N. Y. (*Feb 7)—At Bainbridge, on Wednesday evening the 28th ult, by Elisha Kelly Esq., *Dr. William Blackston*, of Bloomingburgh, Fayette county, to *Mifs Julia Ann Doddridge*, daughter of Dr. Baron Doddridge of Bainbridge. (*May 6)—On Tuesday morning last, by Rev. Mr. Springer, *Mr. Joseph Wilson*, of Paris, Ky., to *Mifs Nancy McCoy*, of Union twp, Ross county.—On Tuesday last by James Miller, Esq., Mr. Nelson Shamblin, to Mifs Betsy Roby, all of this place. (*Aug 12)

DIED—On Friday the 26th ult. Mrs. Margaret Wolf, consort of Mr. J. Wolf of this place, in the 26th year of her age, leaving husband and three children. (*Jan 24)—On Wednesday last of pulmonary disease, Mr. Isaac Cook of this town, in the 53d year, leaving a widow and a large family. (*Feb 7)—On Thursday last, after a short illness, Mr. William Long, of this county, in the 80th year of his age. The deceased was one of the earliest settlers in this part of the country. On Saturday last, after an illness of two weeks, Mr. Matthew Long, son of the above, in the 34th year of his age. He usually resided in the neighborhood of Columbus, but was on a visit to Ross county when attacked. He leaves a widow and four small children.—On Sunday last, in the 44th year, Mrs. Mary Cook, of this place.—At Charleston, S. C. on the 1st of March Rev. Philander Chase, lately of Zanesville, and the son of Bishop Chase of St. Clairsville, Ohio. (*April 8)—Of pulmonary disease, at his residence in Huntington twp, on Thursday last, Mr. Martin Howard, in the 73d year of his age.—On Saturday last, at his residence in Concord twp, after a short but painfull illness, Mr. Hugh Stewart, in the 67th year of his age. His remains were interred on his farm on the day following. (*May 6)—On Tuesday morning last, after a short illness, Alison C. Looker, Esq., in the 33d year of his age. He was a native of New Jersey, and lately was a representative from Ross county to the General Assembly. (*July 26)

—In the city of Detroit, on Saturday the 17th ult, Major William Pultroff, formerly of this place, in the 44th year of his age.—In this town, on Tuesday last of pulmonary disease, Mrs. Martha McCoy, consort of Mr. Robert McCoy, of Columbus, in the 31st year of her age.—On Tuesday last, a dead body of a man was found in the west end of town which proved to be that of Henry Johnson, a stranger from Wilmington, Del. "His death was occasioned by some cause unknown". He was about 25 years old.—On Thursday last, at 12 o'clock, Owen Mason, son of Mr. Thomas Graves, of this township.—In Green twp, Mrs. Ostrander, consort of Dr. Edward Ostrander.—In Deerfield twp, on the 7th inst. Mr. John Hyde, aged 68 years.—In Twin twp. on the 5th inst. at an advanced age Mrs. Myers, consort of Mr. Joseph Myers.—At Galliopolis, on the 4th inst. James Hamlin, M. D., in the 20th year of his age. (*Aug 12)—In Twin twp. on the 21st inst. Mr. William Rogers, in the 75th year. He was an early settler in this country.—On the same day, James Gardiner, in the 13th year.—On Tuesday last, Mrs. Margaret Brown, in the 45th year. (*Aug 26)—On Thursday last, J. M. Shane, son of Joseph Shane, of this county.—On the 26th ult, after a short illness, Mr. James Taylor, in the 80th year. He lived in this vicinity for many years. (*Sept 9)—At Urbana on the morning of the 27th ult., aged 50 years, Mr. Marcus Heylin, merchant, formerly of this place. (*Sept 9)—On Friday 3d inst., Thomas Davidson, in the 60th year.—On Thursday, Thomas Fryer, lately from Cincinnati, aged 39 years.—On Thursday, Mrs. Sarah Thompson, consort of Abraham Thompson, aged 22 years.—On Friday evening, Mr. Robert N. A. Gregg, in the 22d year.—On Friday last, Mr. Joseph Keen, in the 24th year.—On Thursday last, Henry Peterson, late of New Jersey, aged 36 years (*Sept 16)

ADDITIONS

GLEANINGS FROM THE SUPPORTER, CHILLICOTHE, OHIO

1823—(Jan. 24)—Died—Dr. Jacob Jacobs, aged about 60.

(Jan. 7) Andrew Ensworth, aged about 50, on 6th.

(Nov. 22) Died Anthony Weaver, in Washington Twp., aged 50. In Amanda Twp. Phillip McDermeth, aged 36.

(Dec. 7) Married Dr. John E. Cooley to Mrs. Bethiah Harris, widow of late Rev. Timothy Harris on 26th. Died in Wayne Twp. on 23rd, Mrs. Mary King, wife of Caleb, aged 21 yrs.

(Dec. 13) Died—in Zanesville, Joseph Butler, aged 32, on 4th.

(Dec. 27) Estate of James Jackson, blacksmith, Mary Jackson, G. W. Dean, admrs.

ITEMS FROM THE OLIVE BRANCH,
CIRCLEVILLE, OHIO

These items are found in rare copies of this early Pickaway County newspaper preserved in the Circleville public library.

1821—(Feb. 27) Lost pocketbook, contents $1 note on Bank of Hamilton, due bill for $10, against John Craig, account against Jacob Larick, one in favor of John Creed against Elias Bixler. Copy of subscription list to collect for Rev. William Jones. Signed James M'Clelland, Tarlton, P. O. Estates—Mathias Fry's, (pro. Oct. 25, 1820), Elizabeth Fry admx.

(May 1) William Jones, James Bell, trustee; Jacob Howell, Madison twp. Pickaway Co., Benjamin Howell, admr; Jacob Haltzman, Saltcreek twp; Pickaway co., Phillip Shortle, admr; Isaac Cook, boarding and tavern (formerly occupied by John B. Bentley). Mentions—George Brown, John Ludwig, John Ely, James Renick, Daniel Hoffman, Charles Robertson, Thomas Robertson, Lucius Nebucker. Estrays—Charles W. Selby, Walnut twp.; James Wilson, John Wilson, John Shoup, J. P.; Alexander Gillispie, Abraham Van Meter, Benamin B. Beckett, Humphrey Beckett, J. P., Darby twp.; Isaac Miller, Andrew Reed, Theodore Mitchell, Nathan Perrill, J. P., Madison twp.; Christian Foust, Adam Zeahrung, Daniel Critz, Peter Parcels, J. P., Saltcreek twp.; Balzer Mantle, Obadiah Thomas, Samuel Silliband, David Henderson, J. P., Darby twp. Death infant of Capt. Thomas Haire.

(June 26) John Andrew Wiseman, boot and shoe apprentice runaway by Joseph Johnston. Robert Evans Tavern. Sheriff (Francis Kinnear)'s sale—Property of—John Hoffman suit of Peter Kinder, William B. Gould and John E. Morgan suit of Amasa Delano, Daniel Dresbach and John Ludwig suit of John Hoffman, Peter Apple suit of John Leavell, Jacob Zeager suit of Lewis Evans, Jacob Zeager suit of Stephen Short, Phillip Moots suit of John McCoy, Daniel Dresbach and John Ely suit of George Deffenbach, Thomas Haire suit of John Hoffman, John Keller suit of John L. Langhorn, Andrew Briner suit of John W. Leist. Thomas Bell, Storekeeper. Alexander Foresman, late treasurer of congregation of Circleville, for use of William Jones. Mentions, John B. Bentley, William Black, James Haswell, Charles Botkins, James Wilson, William Davis, James Jackson, James Crosby, George Wolfey, William Seymour, W. B. Thrall, James Renick, Robert Russell, George Brown, Robert Colwell, Job Radcliff, John Black, John Pancake, Henry Toland, William Hannaman.

(July 24) Estate of John Swisher, late of Pickaway Co. Abraham Swisher, adm'r. Estate of Ann Smith, Abraham Swisher, adm'r. Estate of Ann Smith, Abraham Swisher, admr. Brigade orders, 4th Brigade 2nd Division Ohio Militia, John T. Davenport, aide-de-camp. Estray—Christian Mickles, Wayne Twp. app. by Stephen Horsey, Isaac Bowen, Aaron Sullivan, J. P. Estray—Samuel Barnet, Walnut Twp. app. by John O'Harra, Jacob Keller, Daniel Swigart, J. P.

(July 31)   Estate of Stephen Short, Admrs. William Miller, William Renick.   Estate of Christopher East, Walnut Twp., admrs.   George East, Henry East.   John Hamill, bankruptcy. Married by Rev. Mr. Leist, William H. Norris to Catherine, daughter of John Weaver.   Mentions, William King, Thomas Evans, Charles Sody, George Lowther, William Montgomery, James Jobs, Alexander Frazier, James Cherry, John Harman, Jacob Greeno, John Cochran, J. P.   List of letters, unclaimed— William Dixon, Daniel Harmer, John Kemp, John Lape, Harman Moore, Jesse M. Farland, George W. Magee, Wesley Newman, George Pontiero, William Stump, Henry Speker, Elizabeth Start, Griffin Winstead, David Gilmore, Henry Kisner, Jacob H. Lutz, Valentine Lead, Alexander M'Bride, John Mitchel, John Morgan, James Owens, William Ramsey, Michael Saylor, Fanny Stall, Israel Todd.   Adam Nigh, P. M. Tarlton, O. (July 1, 1821) (August 7)   William H. Norris, tinware.   Estate of Catharine Chamerlin, Washington Twp. by Michael Harmon.   Married on the 31st, Robert K. Foresman to Jane, daughter of William Foresman.   Married at Athens, O. on the 5th by Rev. Jacob Lindley, the Rev. Solomon S. Miles to Eliza Ann Gilmore.

(August 14)   Caleb Atwater, books.

(JANUARY 1, 1822)   Daniel B. Hayes' estate, Thomas Evans, admr. Law office, James Pierce.   Died in Delaware, O.   Dr. Samuel Moulton, formerly of Castleton, Vermont.   Aaron Sullivan, tax collector and John Ludwig, asst.   Bankrupt, Eli Jester.   Estate of Giles S. Town, William Marquis, admr.   Estray Lawrence Shirley, Jackson Twp., John Williams, David Marsh, Jonathon Heath, J. P.   List of letters unclaimed in Circleville P. O., George Wolfley, P. M.   Caleb Atwater, George Alkire, Sam. Arnel, William Allison, George Aumiller, Jno. Barr, Joseph Brown, Humphrey Becket, Martha Baker, John Boggs, Horatio Bailey, William Black, A. F. Camp, Woolery Coonrad, Jr., Thomas Cunningham, William Crosley, Jacob Cramer, Mary Cook, Irila Decker, Marion H. Deval, Ebenezer Davis, Joseph Davis, Andrew Dukes, John Evans, Andrew Dukes, John Evans, Andrew Enswork, David Evans, Jacob Foster, William Foresman, John Galbreath, Caty Grove, Horsey H. Groves, Willis Gant, Benjamin Gibson, William Gouger, James Gardner, William Houghland, David Holdeman, Joseph M. Hayes, Abraham Haldeman, John Heath, Jabes Hedges, Thomas Haire, Paul Ike, William Irwin, Sarah Johnson, Peter Leist, John Lowry, Fergis Moore, Valentine Mutchler, Adam Meets, Douglas Moore, John E. Morgan, S. M. M'Cormick, Jr., George Morgan, Francis Neff, Archibald Owens, William Owens, John Nichols, Sarah Peters, John Pierce, Michael Pritchard, James Parcels, Barnet Preble, John Pancake, Thomas Robinson, Joseph Reed, John Ruggles, William Rout, Samuel Rout, Samuel Smith, William Rock, Aaron Sullivan, John Timmons, Sam'l Thomas, William Wiley, Benedict Wrench, Robert Wolverton, Elizabeth Webb, Sam'l Wilson.

(Jan. 8)   Dead Mrs. Elizabeth Justice, wife of Basil Justice, aged 20 yrs.   Married in Amanda Twp., Fairfield Co. on 27th, by Rev. Jones, Major John Shoup to Nancy Smurr.   John Chipman's estate, Wayne Twp., wife Susannah, Admx.   Dr. Gain Robinson's

estate, Aaron Sullivan, admr. Mentions—Charles Cook, James Simerman, Robert M'Affee, John M'Court, Joseph Olds, Courtney Tanner, Isaac Alkire, John Martin, Isaac Bradley, James Gunn. John Stonerock, John Rush, Henry M'Kinney of Monroe Twp.
(Jan. 15) Mentions—John T. Davenport, Phinehas Code, Hugh Miller, William G. Cantrall, Sam'l Watt, Charlie Cook, James Simmerman, James Moore, John Hamilton, John M. Hood.

(Jan. 22) Bankruptcy—James Wilson, Andrew Huston, clerk. Estray—Peter Miller, John Enochs, Samuel Harvey, John Cox, Pickaway Twp. Courtney Tanner, Isaac Alkire, John Martin, David Henderson, J. P., Deercreek-Darby Twp. Estate of Conrad Braucher, Isaac Braucher, Jacob D. Lutz, admrs. Estate of James Kinney, Jacob Kinney, Leah Kinney, admrs., Deercreek Twp. Married Scioto Twp. on 14th, Elias Pratt, Bloomfield, to Elizabeth Widner. Delinquent tax list—1822—Francis Ayrees, William Bell, Thomas M. Bailey, Isham Browder, Lawrence Butter, John Blackwell, Henry Brush, Isaac Beeson, Sam'l Bruckman, Nicholas Baldwin, George D. Blackie, John Beck, Cornelius Baldwin, Hance Baker, Sam'l Beaver, George Carrington, Joseph Conway, George Clark, Warren Cash, John Campbell, Thomas Carneal, Conrad Carr heirs, John Craiger, Amasa Delano, Ephriam Doolittle, James Denny, Dan'l Duwall, George Dawson, James Davis, John Dark, Francis Dade, George Emory, Jacob Eckehene, Joseph Evans, Patrick Finney, Henry Fox heirs, Nathaniel Fox Jr., Benamin Forsythe heirs, Samuel Findley, John Gibson, Alex. Gibson, R. Galbreath, James Galloway Jr., James Goldsby, Benson Goldsberry, George Greenway, Ashahel Heath, George Handy, Benjamin Harrison, reps., Christian Hoffman, George Hoffman, Jno. Hoffman, Daniel Hanson, David Henderson, Benjamin Hough, Thomas Hill, reps., Jno. Irwin, Jeremiah Joslin, Michael Kininel, Ephriam Knowls, Jno. Kerr, Joseph Kerr, Peter Kelly reps., Elias Langham, Joseph Ladd, David Larkin, John Larvin, Charles Leonard, Jno. Lacey, Angus L. Langham, Francis Muir, John McClain, David Mortimore, John McClean, Sam'l McFerron, James McDowell, James Muskemore, Stephen Mason, Ralph Morgan, Jesse McKay, William McCraw heirs, Henry Massie, William McMeechen, John Onlery, Jno. Oliver, William Ogburn, Jno. Overton, Ebenezer Petty, Edward Pritchard, Robert Pollard, Robert Porterfield, Alex Parker heirs, Sam'l Peebles.

(May 1) Daniel Swigart, J. P. Walnut Twp., Aaron Peters, William Stage. Orphans Court, Georgetown, Sussex Co., Delaware—case of Whettington Clifton's land. His sons, Whettington Jr. and James Clifton. Miss Howe opens school, terms $1.50 per quarter. Married George Boyer to Nancy Montgomery in Walnut Twp. on 24th. Jabez Hedges to Maria Williamson, daughter of William Bankrupt—Ebenezer Havers.

(May 7) Account of Ohio University signed by Ephriam Cutler, Stephen Lindsly, Edwin Putnam. "Hatting", Joseph Hossleton. Married by Rev. Jones, in Walnut Twp. Major John Leavell to Cynthia Hedges.

(June 7) Orphans Court, Georgetown, Sussex Co. Delaware—Estate of James King, sons, David and George. Estate of Charles Foster, John Foster, admr. Died James Hedges, son of Joseph, on the 9th, aged 8 yrs. Estate of Isaac Smith, Joshua Brownell admr. List of letters, unclaimed—(Additional names) Ann Corn, Michael Fink, John Fisher, Sam'l. Falmer, William Gauger, Catharine Grove, Benego Highwarden, Isaac Huffhines, Abraham Hight, Amos Hollenback, Peter Hott, William Irwin, Horatio R. Keys, Somerset Middleton, Sarah Marquis, Joseph Olds, John Osborn, C. J. Odell, Susannah Pontius, Moses Rawlins, Jacob Steely, Jno. Spangler, David Templeton, Aaron Teegarden, Jacob Teegarden, Henry Trace, Stephen Tiffin, Jacob Vandoven, Abraham Van Meter, Alex Vandgruff, Jno. Wolfley, James Wilson, Sarah Ward, Nancy Wood, James Wingate, Elijah Wright, John R. Yerkins.

(July 16) Estate of Phinehas Cade, Isaac Davis, Charles Cade, admrs. Married on 24th, William P. Benton to Anna Swope, both of Fairfield Co.

(August 6) Married Austin Jones to Nancy Moore, daughter of Joseph, of Ross Co. Died—John M'Cutchen, age 54 on 3rd ult. on return from New Orleans, at Pigeon Roost, Choctaw nation, Mississippi. Left widow and children.

(August 13) Died—John Wolfley, Esq. of Elizabethtown, Lancaster Co., Pa., aged 64 on visit to his children in Ohio on 5th. James Bell, native of Ireland, aged 50 yrs. on 10th. Married on 8th, William Fryatt to Miss Delilah Justice. Thomas Wright and Mary Clark.

(August 20) Died—George Fayette Mulliken, printer, aged 22 years, in Bloomfield, Pick. Co.

(Sept. 10) Died—Archibald M'Lean, at Chillicothe, born at York now Adams Co., Pa. aged 40 yrs.

(Nov. 5) Died George William Thrall, son of Col. Walter, aged 1 year.

(Nov. 12) Married Robert N. A. Gregg of Chillicothe to Martha, daughter of Thomas Evans.

(Dec. 31) Died—Samuel Hedges, of Berkley Co. Va. there. Father of Joseph Hedges of Circleville. William Myers, aged 50 on 27th.

NEWSPAPER NOTICES, COLUMBIANA CO., OHIO
BLANCHE COLLINS

DIED—On 29th of October, *Adam Finch* of Hanover twp., in the
70th year. (* 11/5/1852). On Monday, June 9, of typhoid fever, at
the residence of Dr. George L. McCook, his brother-in-law, Dr. *George
Fisher*, in the 24th year. He was among the first to volunteer for the
expedition sent from this city to relieve the sick and wounded soldiers
at Pittsburgh Landing. (*1/4/1860)

LEGAL NOTICES—Whereas my daughter, Hannah Crowl, has left
my house.—John Crowl. SLANDER—*Elizabeth Motlinger,* widow of
George, dec'd. vs. *Margaret Brinker,* (now Worman)—Adam Brinker
(*5/18/1816). ESTATE—*John Boyer,* late of Col. Co., dec'd.—Abraham
and Agnes Boyer, Adms. (*5/18/1816)—*Daniel Stewart,* late of Col.
Co. dec'd. Oct. 10, 1852. John Willyard (Williard) Adm. (*10/15/1852)
—*Christopher Williams,* late of Col. Co., dec'd, Henry Williams, James
B. Morrison, Exrs. (*11/12/1852)—*John Morrison,* dec'd. Harriet
Morrison, widow. Jacob Custard, Adm. (*8/27/1855)—*Thomas Holy,*
Wayne twp., SW Quar. Sec. 32. (*9/28/1855)—*Martha Abraham,* late
of Col. Co., dated Jan. 19, 1857, New Lisbon. Wm. C. Stewart, John
Foutts, Adms. *de bonis nom.* (*1/23/1857)—*Fred Wegerly,* dec'd,
Dungannon. Jacon Lindersmith, J. P. (*2/6/1857) Dower Rights—
Lydia Patterson vs John Patterson, SW Quar. Sec. 25.(*9/28/1855).
STATE OF OHIO 2, Apr. A. D. 1816: William Smith, George Atterholt,
and George Brown, Esquires, judges of said court, Petition of Joseph
Saint, to wit: *Thomas Saint,* late the father of the petitioner, died intestate seized of real property—SE Quar. Sec. 23, Twp. 7. R. 1-Steu-
benville. Deceased had six sons, John, Joseph, William, Thomas, Levi,
James, all under age except John and Joseph; that he left a grand
daughter——, of Beaver Co., Pa.; also Lucinda, heir of Joseph, dec'd,
who is also under age. Petition granted to effect a division of land.
Amos Stevens, John Underwood, Charles Hole, appointed to make
petition. (*5/18/1816)

MARRIED—On 29th, Sept. by Rev. Robert Hayes, Mr. *John Q.
Adams,* to Miss *Christiana Elliot.* On 4th of November, by same, Mr.
George Robinson, to Miss *Rebecca Travis.* On the same day, by same,
Mr. *John Y. Wan,* to Miss *Mary Shaiffer.* On the 11th of November, by
the same, Mr. *Thomas McCormick,* to Miss *Martha J. Chain.* (*11/19
1852. On Tuesday the 17th, by Rev. Wesley Lamphear, Mr. *Jacob
Hephner,* of Franklin twp. to Miss *Sarah Carlile,* of Centre twp. On
July 19th, by Rev. Walter Brown, Mr. *Levi Johns,* and Miss *Lucinda
McGlennon,* both of this county. (*9/28/1855). On Wednesday, Sept.
26, 1855, by Rev. Mr. Murrill, Mr. *Price Kuth* (Ruth) of Minerva, to
Miss *Elizabeth Colestock* of East Rochester. (*10/15/1855) On 2d
inst. by Rev. Walter Brown, Dr. *Lee Smith* of Bloomington, Ill., to Miss
Lizzie Rogers of N. Lisbon. On 29th ult. at Hamilton's Hotel, by John
Watts, Esq., *Henry Lambern,* to Miss *Sarah Ann Hartley,* of Knox
twp. (*2/6/1857) On 30th ult. by Rev. Robert Hays, Mr. *Daniel S.
Noble,* to Miss *Mary L. McCartney,* daughter of Rev. Wm. D. Mc-
Cartney, both of Madison twp. On 30th ult. by Rev. Samuel W. Clark,
Mr. *John Chaney,* to Miss *Mattie Asdel,* both of St. Clair twp.
(*11/17/1862)

Date following asterisk denotes date of publication. Ohio Patriot, New
Lisbon.

33

1830—August 26, Thursday. Married in this town on Thursday last by the Rev. H. Vandeman, Mr. *C. B. Campbell* to Mrs. *Adaline Linton*. Died—In this town on the 12th inst. Mr. Peter Bishop, saddler, aged about 26 years; On Sunday morning, 8th inst., near Washington City, George Graham, Esq., Commissioner of the General Office.

September 2, Thursday. Died—In Concord township on Wednesday last Mrs. Cummins, aged 54 years, wife of James Cummins one of the surviving soldiers of the Revolution.

September 30, Thursday. Died—In Berlin township, Mrs. Lucy, consort of Mr. Elisha Newel in the 42d year of her age; At Wakatomila, Ohio, Major Jonathan Cass, father of Governor Cass of Michigan.

October 7, Thurday. Married—On the 3d. inst. by John M'Leod, Esq., Mr. *Joseph M'Leod* to Miss *Velinda Williams*, all of Genoa township.

December 2, Thursday. Died—In this town on Tuesday last after a short illness, Dr. James H. Hills formerly of Farmington, Connecticut, aged 49 years. Dr. Hills has been long a citizen of Ohio and as a Physician has been extensively serviceable to suffering humanity;—In this township, a few days previously, Mr. John Lampson, aged probably 60 years (ab). He was an honest man and a good citizen.

December 30, Thursday. Married—In Kingston township on the 23d ult., by B. Carpenter, Esq., Mr. *William Vansickle* to Miss *Elcevann Lot*.

1831—January 27, Thursday. Married—In Marlborough township on the 9th inst., by Elder Martin, Major *Isaac Jones* to Miss *Harriet Drake*, daughter of the Hon. William S. Drake.

February 17, Thursday. Died—In Scioto township on the 5th inst., Mrs. Mary M'Keene in the 61st year of her age, consort of Mr. J. N. M'Keene. In Columbus on Sunday morning last after a few hours illness of the 'Cold Plague', General Jorn Warner, aged probably about 40 years.

March 3, Thursday. Married—In Marlborough township on the 24th ult., Mr. *Isaac Coldrain* to Miss *Mary Munson*.

March 17, Thursday. Died—In this town on Saturday last, Mrs. Barbra, consort of Mr. Gotlieb Albright, aged 50 years. Also, on yesterday Mrs. Abigail, consort of Mr. Edward Potter, aged 38 years. Each has left a husband and several young children.

April 21, Thursday. Married—In Frederick County, Maryland, on the 7th inst. Mr. *Robert Finley*, Merchant of this place to Miss *Elizabeth Lamar* of the former place.

April 28, Thursday. Died—In this town on Monday evening last, Miss Susan Kilbourn, aged 49 years. In Radnor township on Tuesday last, Colonel Joseph Dunlap aged 77 years, one of the earliest and most respectable citizens of the county.

May 5, Thursday. Married—In this town on Tuseday Evening last by the Rev. H. Van Deman, Mr. *N. B. Spurgeon* to Miss *Sarah A. Vining,* all of this place. Died—In Liberty township on Saturday last, Mr. Samuel Thompson, aged probably 55 years.

May 12, Thursday. Died—In this town on Saturday last, Mrs. Sally Alen, consort of Col. B. F. Allen, aged 39 years, one month and seven days, leaving a numerous train of 'connecions' and friends.—In the 32d year of her age in Troy township on the 5th inst., Mrs. Martha Cunningham, consort of Mr. Hugh Cunningham late of Belmont county, Ohio, leaving an affectionate husband and four children to lament her untimely end.

May 19, Thursday. Died—In Marlborough township on Friday last, Mr. John Welch in the 87th year of his age, the deceased has for many years been a resident of this town.

May 26, Thursday. Married—In Marlborough township on the 19th inst., by S. D. Wyatt, Mr. *Evan Norris* to Miss *Sarah Brundige.* Died—In this township on the 19th inst., Mr. Joseph Harter, aged probably 35 years.

June 2, Thursday. Married—In Radnor township on Thursday the 26th by John N. Cox, Esq., Mr. *John Jinkins* to Miss *Mary Jones.*—In Berkshire township on the 2d ult., by David Gregeory, Esq., Mr. *Reuben Hall* to Miss *Minerva Brown.*—By the same on the 19th ult., Mr. *Grandeson Benedict,* to Miss *Harriet Gregory,* all of Berkshire.—In the same township on the same day by the Rev. Jacob Drake, Mr. *Eleazer Dunham* of Berlin to Miss *Miriam Clark.*—In Berlin township on the 12th ult., by the Rev. Ahab Jinks, Mr. *Silas Dunham* of Berkshire to Miss *Arena Robeson.*

June 9, Thursday. Married—In this township on Thursday last, Mr. *Dexter Durphy* to Miss *Alma Pierce,* all of this township.—In Radnor on the same day Mr. *John Justus* to Miss *Jane Lloyd.*—Died—In Marlborough township on the 7th inst. of epeleptic fits, Mr. John Welchone, aged probably 40 years.

July 14, Thursday. Married—In Westfield township on Thursday last by the Rev. H. Van Deman, Mr. *Joseph W. Elliot* to Miss *Amanda Wade.*

September 15, Thursday. Died—In Sunbury on Friday 2d. inst., Col. Thomas J. Brown, aged 28 years, leaving a wife and one child.—In Worthington of consumption, on the 25th ult., Mrs. Janette Miller, consort of John G. Miller, Esq., she had been a member of the Presbyterian Church for several years.

September 22, Thursday. Married—In St. Peters Church on the evening of the 18th inst., by the Rev. Nathan Stem, Mr. *James T. Key* of Perryburgh, Wood county, to Miss *Susan C. Falley* of this place.

Died—In this vicinity on Tuesday morning last, Mr. Joseph Bierce, aged probably 28 years.—In Radnor township a few days since, Miss Jane Jones, aged probably 19 years.

September 29, Thursday. Married—In Union county on the 22d inst., by H. Van Deman, the Rev. *M. Dolbier* to Miss *Eliza Woods.*—On the same day, by the same, Mr. *Wolley* to Miss *Catharine Ann Cryder,* all of Delaware, Co.

October 6, Thursday. Married—In Marion county on the 29th ult., by Rev. H. Van Deman, *Rev. Eledad Barber,* to Miss *Mary Balantine.*

October 13, Thursday. Died—In this vicinity on Sunday morning last, Mr. Ebenezer Durphy, aged probably fifty years.

November 24, Thursday. Married—In this township on the 20th inst., by the Rev. R. Bigelow, Col. *Benjamin F. Allen* of this town to Mrs. *Elmyra Messenger.*

1832—June 28, Thursday. Married—On Tuesday the 12th ult., at St. Paul's Church, Rochester, N. Y., by the Rev. Mr. Johns, *Joseph R. Swan*, Esq., of this town to Miss *H. A. Andrews* or the former place.—On Thursday evening last by the Rev. J. Hoge, Col. *M. H. Kirby*, Secretary of State, to Miss *Emma Minor*, daughter of the late Isaac Minor, Esq., of this county (Ohio State Jour).

July 19, Thursday. Married—In Radnor on the 12th inst., by John N. Cox, Esq., Mr. *Robert M'Ilvain* to Mrs. *Mary Brockway.*

July 26, Thursday. Married—At Sunbury, On Tuesday last by the Rev. Mr. M'Ilroy, Dr. *Charles H. Picket* to Mrs. *Isabella Webb.*

August 9, Thursday. Married—In Hartoforf, Conn., on the 3 October ult., by the Rev. Dr. Hawes, Major *James Goodwin*, Jr., to Miss *Lucy Morgan*, dau. of Joseph Morgan, Esq.,

August 16, Thursday. Died—In this town on Friday last, Mrs. Sophronia, consort of Major Thomas Reynolds, aged about 25 years.

August 22, Thursday. Died—In Marion, on Saturday last after a short illness, Mr. David Campbell formerly of this place, aged about 35 years.

September 27, Thursday. Married—At Gambier, on Wednesday morning last by the Rev. William Sparrow, Mr. *Herman Dyer*, Principal of the Classified Department of the Grammar School, to Miss *Almira Douglass*, both of the above place. Died—Colonel John Brandt in Brantford, B. C.

October 4, Thursday. Married—Last evening in St. Peter's Church in this town by Rev. J. M'Ilroy, Mr. *James Westerfield* to Miss *Harriet Bills.* Died—In this township on the 28th of September last, Mrs. Betsey Thayer of inflamation of the bowels, aged about 35 years.

October 11, Thursday. Married—In Berlin township on the 30th of September, Mr. *Alfred Thompson* to Miss *Maria Janes.* Died—In the city of Baltimore on the 2d inst., Mr. Robert Finley, merchant of this place. The cause of his death is unknown. He was found in bed on the morning after he arrived in the act of expiring, it not having been known previously that he was ill.

November 15, Thursday. Married—In Troy township on the 1st of November by Ebenezer Wood, Esq., Mr. *Nicholas Jacoby* of Richland township, Marion county, to Miss *Elizabeth Worline* of the former place.

November 22, Thursday. Married—On the 8th day of November, by Levi Churchill, Jun. Esq., *Jeremiah Smith*, Esq., to Miss *Patty Marcy* both of Harmony township, Delaware county.

December 20, Thursday. Died—In Columbus on the 13th inst. Mrs. Mary Grover, consort of Mr. Ira Grover, aged 33 years. She was a most amiable and excellent lady.

1833, April 18, Thursday. Died (Communicated)—In Worthington, Franklin county on the 11th inst., Mrs. Nancy D. Holsclaw, eldest daughter of F. C. Johnes, late of Delaware county, deceased, aged 17 years, 7 months.

April 25, Thursday. Died—Saraj Jessup, Winfarthing, England, aged 102.

May 30, Thursday. Married—In Westfield township on Thursday 23d. Inst., by Sidney Moore, Esq., Mr. *James S. Elliot* to Miss *Sarah Wood* both of that place.—In Radnor on the 29th inst., by the

Rev. H. Van Deman, Mr. *Jeremiah Lee* to Miss *Maragaret Lawrence.*
Died—Suddenly, at the residence of her father, in the city of New
York on the 10th inst., Mrs. Sarah Ann Starret, wife of Dr. Starret
of this place, in the 21 st year of her age.

June 15, Thursday Died—Admiral Lord Gambier, and Rev.
Rowlad Hill in England.

June 30, Thursday. Married—In this town on the 13th inst. by
John N. Cox, Esq., Mr. *John B. Jones* to Miss *Gwen Jones.* Died—In
this town on Monday last of Pulmonary consumption, Mrs. Rebecca,
consort of James Ramsey, formerly of Springfield, Vermont, aged
43 years.

August 15, Thursday. Married—In this town on the 3d inst.,
by Sidney Moore, Esq., Mr. *James Durfy* to Miss *Jane Nafus,* all of
this town. Died—At Worthington, Franklin county, on the 3d inst.,
Worthington, the only son of Gen. G. H. Griswold, aged about 2
years and six months.

August 27, Thursday. Died—Of cholera at Bardstown, Ky., after a few hours indisposition, William Rowan and Mrs. Rowan his
wife——A. H. Rowan and Mary Jane Steele, son and daughter-in-
law, and granddaughter of Judge John Rowan. On Friday 26th inst.
all four of them were deposited in the same grave.

September 12, Thursday. Died—In Berlin township on the 4th
inst. Mrs. Barsheba, consort of Mr. William P. Smith, in the 24th
year of her age. —In Marlborough township in this county on the
4th inst., Rachel Ann daughter of William Millikan, Editor of the
Western Galaxy, aged 6 months.—At Columbus, of cholera, on the
9th of August, Ann Howard, youngest daughter of the late Horton
Howard, aged 22 years.

September 26, Thursday. Married—In this township on the
22d inst., by the Rev. L. B. Gurley, Mr. *Joseph C. Alexander* to Miss
Delight P. Sweetser. Died—In this town on Monday evening last, the
Hon. John W. Campbell, U. S. Judge for the District of Ohio, aged
probably 50 years.—In Radnor, on the 22d instant after seven days
illness, Mrs. Elizabeth Williams consort of David Williams, in the
25th year of her age. She was a native of Montgomeryshire, North
Wales. (Communicated).

October 3, Thursday. Married—On the 20th of September,
Nathaniel Handin of Scioto township, Dalaware county, aged 77
years to Miss *Hannah Wilcoc* of Franklin county, Ohio, aged 66
years.

November 14, Thursday. Married—In this town, on the 6th inst.,
by the Rev. James M'Ilroy, Mr. *Thomas Cox* to Miss *Ann Jones* all
of this town. —On Sunday the 10th inst., by the same, Major *Henry
Lamb* to Miss *Minerva Ann Stewart,* all of this place.

November 28, Thursday. Died—At Mobile, a short time since,
Mr. Erwin F. Finch, printer, aged 27 years, formerly of Delaware
county, Ohio.—Gal.

December 9, Thursday. Married—In this town on the 4th inst.,
by the Rev. H. Van Deman, Mr. *Charles C. Miller,* to Miss *Elizabeth
W. Vining.*—In Oxford township on Sunday the 28th ult., by Thomas
Reid, Esq., *Mr. Levi Varton* to Miss *Elizabeth Shoemaker.*

December 16, Thursday. Married—In Radnor on the 27th ult by
John N. Cox, Esq., Mr. *David Penry* to Miss *Joan Jones.*—In this
town on the 8th inst., by the Rev. H. Van Deman, Mr. *Robert Grant*
to Miss *Paulina Ann Ball.*

NEWSPAPER ITEMS
BLANCHE COLLINS
THE OHIO GAZETTE
DELAWARE, OHIO
Contributed by WILLARD E. WIGHT

December 23, Thursday. Married—In Sunbury, on the 15th inst., by Rev. J. C. Havens, Mr. *Benjamin Deuel* to Miss *Sarah Slocum.*— In this town on Wednesday evening by the Rev. J. M'Elroy, Dr. Ralph Hills to Miss Jane Evans.

1834—January 13, Thursday. Married—In Oxford township on the 9th inst., by Thomas Reid, Esq., Mr. *Ira M'Cloud* to Miss *Louisa Wood.* Died* Dr. Thomas F. Sargent, Minister of the Methodist Episcopal Church, died of apoplexy on Sunday evening the 29th inst., (*Cincinnati Gazette.*)

February 17, Thursday. Married—In Clinton township, Franklin county, on the evening of the 2th of January last by the Rev. William Jolly, Mr. *John Buck* to Miss *Fanny Anderson*, both of Clinton township.—In Westfield township on Sunday the 9th inst., by Thomas Reid, Esq., Mr. *David Smith* to Miss *Maria Monroe.*

February 24, Thursday. Married—In this town on Tuesday evening last, by the Rev. H. Van Deman, Mr. *Charles C. Chamberlain*, merchant, to Miss *Isabella Webb*, daughter of the late Joseph Webb.—In this town on the 13th inst. by Sidney Moore, Esq. Mr. George Slater to Miss Elizabeth Waggoner.

March 3, Thursday. Married—In Radnor township on Thursday last by the Rev. J. C. Havens, to Mr. *John Wolfley* to Miss *Julia Ann Adams.* Died—In Worthington on the 21st ult., Mrs. Eleanor N. Burr, consort of Mr. Ozias Burr, aged 57.—In this vicinity on Saturday last, Mr. Hiram Wilcox, son of Mr. Wilcox, aged 21 years.

March 10, Thursday. Married—In Oxford township on Thursday the 27th ult., by Thomas Reid, Esq., Mr. *Ralph Nicholas* to Miss *Rebecca Shearman.*—In Westfield township on the 6th inst. by the Rev. J. C. Havens, Mr. *Zibs Peake* to Miss *Amanda Torry.*—In this town on Thursday, by the Rev. H. Van Deman, Mr. *Ralph R. Ranney* to Miss *Harriet Storm.*—In this town on Tuesday evening last by Rev. H. Van Deman, Mr. *William F. Painter* to Miss *Sarah Ann Butler.* Died—In Radnor on the 19th ult., Mrs. Sarah, consort of Morgan Williams, Esq., aged 30 years.

April 5, Thursday. Died—In Scioto township on Sunday last, Mr. Richard Hoskins, aged 72 years.

April 19, Thursday. Married—In Berkshire township on Sunday last by the Rev. J. C. Havens, Mr. *Harlow Allen* to Miss *Evaline Carpenter.*

April 26, Thursday. Died—Drowned at Zoar on the 10th inst. William E. son of Mr. E. Gaylord Jr., aged 3 years and 3 months.

May 10, Thursday. Married—In this township on the 8th inst by Sidney Moore, Esq., Mr. *Harmon Howard* to Miss *Mary Ann Frederick.* Died—In Columbus a few days since, Richard M. only surviving child of the late Harvey D. Little, Esq., also, on Tuesday last Harvey D., posthumous son of said Little aged about 3 months. Both died of scarlet fever after a short illness.

May 31, Thursday. Married—In Berkshire on the 15th inst, by the Rev. J. C. Havens, Mr. *Benjamin Durling* to *Miss Matilda Leonard.*

July 5, Thursday. Married—In Delaware township on the 5th ult. by the Rev. J. Drake, Mr. *Spencer Dunham* to Miss *Eliza J. Alwood* all of this county.—In Orange township on the 26th by the same, Mr. *Elie Frey* to Miss *Alexia Nettleton.*

July 12, Thursday, Married—In Delaware township on the 30th ult, by Sidney Moore, Esq., Mr. *Henry Clark* to Miss *Julia Ann Cole,* both of Liberty township.

July 26, Thursday. Died—In this town on Thursday last, at halfpast 2 o'clock P.M. Mary Jane, daughter of Charles Sweetser, Esq., aged 6 months (Communicated).

August 23, Thursday. Died—On the 5th inst, at his home in Scioto township, Delaware county, the Rev. Christian Burge, Minister of the Gospel, in the 69th year of his age. The deceased was a soldier of the Revolution, and emigrated many years since from Greene county in Pennsylvania to Licking county, Ohio, where he resided until within two years past.

September 13, Thursday. Died—Departed this life on the 8th inst., at the residence of the Rev. A. Jinks of this place, Miss Lucy Washburn, aged 28 years. Miss Warshburn was a native of the state of Vermont and the only daughter of Dr. Daniel Wasburn who still resides in that part of the country. (Com).

1835—March 28, Saturday. Married—On Tuesday evening, the 17th inst., by the Rev. Mr. Snider, Mr. *Joshua Kline* to Miss *Mary Magdalene Harter,* all of this county.

April 4, Saturday. Married—In Berlin by the Rev. J. Drake, on the 25th inst. Mr. *Martin Benton* to Miss *Deborah Lewis,* all of this county.

May 9, Saturday. Married—In Oxford township on the 30th ult. by Ebenezer Wood, Esq., Mr. *John Hoffet* to Miss *Emily Faust.* Died—On Sunday morning last, of typhus fever, James Harvey Hills, aged 20 years and five months.

June 16, Saturday. Married—In Kingston, by the Rev. J. C.

Harris, cn Thursday the 11th inst., Rev. *Ira Chase* to Miss *Jane Wilcox.*

June 27, Saturday. Married—On Sunday the 14th inst, by the Rev. Andrew Kinnear, Mr. *Samuel Growel* to Miss *Barbara Stroub,* all of this place.—On Sunday the 14th inst., in Westfield township, by Thomas Reid, Esq., Mr. *Anson S. Wood* to Miss *Keziah Monroe.*—On the 21st inst. in Westfield by Anson Wood, Esq., Mr. Orrin Stantcn to Miss Sarah Poorman.

August 15, Saturday. Married—In Marlborcugh township on the 6th inst., Mr. *Walter Mitchell* to Miss *Nancy Phelps,* both of Marlbcrough township by Ebenezer H. Wood, Esq.,—On the 6th inst. in Westfield township by Anson Wood, Esq., Mr. *Aaron Shaw* to Miss *Betseyann Jenkins.*

August 22, Saturday. Died—In this town of bilious fever, on Tuesday the 18th inst., Mr. Reuben Stewart aged about fifty-five.

August 29, Saturday. Died—On Sunday evening last, John A., son cf A. H. Patterson of this place aged 14 months.

Octoter 3, Saturday. Married—In Radnor township on the 29th ult. by the Rev. James Davies, Mr. *John Davies* to Miss *Margaret Homcs,* bcth cf said township. Died—In Berkshire township on the 21st ult. John L. Crawford, in the 33 year of his age.

October 10, Saturday. Married—On the 5th inst., in Radnor township by Rev. James Davies, *Edward Jones* to *Edith Gallant,* both cf said tcwnship.—In Radnor township on the 4th inst., by the Rev. David Cadwalader, *Morgan Williams,* Esq., to Miss *Rachel Rogers* all of said township. Died—In Scioto township on Wednesday the 30th ult. Mr. David Shoup, Esq., aged 44 years.

October 17, Saturday. Married—By the Rev. Samuel S. Klein, on the 13th inst. Mr. *James M. Jamison* to Miss *Elizabeth Heigh* all of Delaware.

Octcber 31, Saturday. Married—In this town on Thursday the 29th inst. by the Rev. H. Van Deman, Mr. (——) *Nettleton* to Miss *Louisa Dobson.*

November 7, Saturday. Married—In Westfield township on the 22d ult, by the Rev. Levi Phillips, Mr. *Smith Aldrich* to Miss *Harriet Hamiston (Jamiston).*

November 14, Saturday. Married.—On Sunday last, by the Rev. Mr. Austin, *Mr. G. Durfee* of Marion to Miss *Mary Sweetser* of this place. Died—On Monday evening last, at his residence in Liberty township, Mr. Irwin Smith, formerly of this town.

December 5, Saturday. Married—In Zanesville on the 26th ult. by the Rev. James Culbertson, Mr. *H. G. Andrews* of this place to Miss *Emily Downer,* of the former place.—In Oxford township, on the 26th ult, by Thomas Reid, Esq., *Mr. Martin Jinkins* to Miss *Polly Erown,* both of Oxford.

1836, January 9, Saturday. Married—On Thursday the 7th inst., by the Rev. Henry Van Deman, Mr. *John Bean* to Miss *Sally Smart* all of this county. Died—In this village, on the 6th inst., after a lingering illness, Dr. Noah Spalding aged about 60.—On Thursday the 7th inst, in this place, Mrs. Smith widow of the late Irwin Smith.

January 23, Saturday. Married—On the 18th inst. by H. Moore, Esq., Mr. *John Gypson* to Miss *Rebecca Waggoner* all of this county.

February 6, Saturday. Married—On the 23d inst. by Anson Wood, Esq., Mr. *Madison Messenger* to Miss *Sally Oliver* all of this county.

March 5, Saturday, Married—On Sunday evening last by H. Moore, Esq., Mr. *Joseph Leiser* to Mrs. *Polina Grant* all of this

place. Died—On Sunday evening last, at his residence in this place, Mr. Samuel Bills.

March 12, Saturday. Died—In Peru township, Delaware county, on Sunday the 6th inst. Mr. John Gardner aged 77 years, an honest man and a good citizen.

March 19, Saturday. Married—On the 26th ult, by the Rev. H. Van Deman, Mr. *James Walling* to Miss *Mary M'Gee* all of this county,—On the 10th inst. by the same, Mr. *John Murphy* to Miss *Jane M'Clure*, all of this county.—On the 10th inst. by the same, Mr. *John Hults* of Ross county to Miss *Mathilda Beckley* of Delaware county.

March 26, Saturday. Married—On Thursday evening last, by the Rev. Mr. Austin, Mr. *Lemuel Herbert* to Miss *Mary Pew*, all of this place.—On the 13th inst. in Westfield, by T. Reid, Esq., Mr *Samuel E. Fout* to Miss *Cynthia Cutler.*

April 12, Saturday. Married—On the 31st ult. by the Rev. James B. Austin, Mr. *Robert Patton* to Miss *Martha Hull*, all of this county. —In Marlborough, on the 31st ult, by E. H. Wood, Esq., Mr. *James Brown, Esq.,* to Miss *Deleloh Griffith.*

April 16, Saturday. Married—In Scioto township on the 12th inst. by Sidney Moore, Esq., Mr. *Harvey Howard* to Miss *Ann Smith.*—In Berlin, on the 14th inst. by the Rev. J. Drake, Mr. *William C. Stone* to Miss *Harriet Andrus*, all of this county.

May 28, Saturday. Married—In Berlin on the 12th inst. by the Rev. Calvin N. Ransom, Mr. *Adam Fams* of Virginia to Miss *Sarah Irwin* of Martinsburg, Knox county.—On the 15th inst. by the Rev. James B. Austin, Mr. *Jonathan Baker* to Miss *Maria Wilcox*, all of Delaware county, Ohio.—On the 26th inst. by the same, Mr. *Stephen B. Allen* of Delaware to Miss *Margaret Jones* of Radnor, Delaware county.

June 4, Saturday. Died—On Saturday the 28th ult after a lingering illness, Mrs. Agard wife of Salmon Agard of this place.—Of consumption, in this village on the 3d inst. Mrs. Mellissa, wife of Caleb Howard, Esq., aged 38 years.

July 8, Saturday. Married—In Troy township, on the 4th inst. by Sidney Moore, Esq., Mr. *James Peters* to Miss *Sophia Starkweather.*

July 15, Saturday. Married—In this place, on the 12th inst. by Sidney Moore, Esq., Mr. *Charles Conklin* to Mrs. *Mary Rogers.*

August 12, Saturday. Died—At the residence of her father near this place, on Sunday the 6th inst., Miss Susan Weiser, aged 18 years.

September 9, Saturday. Married—On Sunday the 3d instant, by the Rev. S. S. Klein, Mr. *Jacob Jacoby* to Miss *Elizabeth Worline*, both of Marion county.—On Tuesday last, by the same, Mr. *John E. Kerbeckle* to Miss *Mary Heek* both of this county.—On Thursday last, by the same, Mr. *David W. Bradley* of Knox county, to Miss *Eunice Hawk* of this county.

October 21, Saturday. Married—At Columbis, Connecticut, on the 28th of September, by the Rev. Mr. Selden, Mr. *S. F. West* of Delaware, Ohio, to Miss *Charlotte Porter*, of the former place.— On Sunday, the 8th of October inst., by the Rev. Ashe A. Davis, Dr. *Charles S. Clark* of Sunbury, in this county, to Miss *Sarah Louise Wadsworth*, of Fredericktown, Knox county, Ohio. Died—On Sunday last, in Marlborough township, Mrs. Susannah Moses, aged 65 years.—On Tuesday last, in this place, Mrs. Chester, wife of Nathan Chester.

November 18, Saturday. Died—At his residence near this place, on Saturday last, Mr. Job Williams.

November 25, Saturday. Married—In Delaware, November 1837 by Sidney Moor, Esq., Mr. *Abraham Cole* to Miss *Harriet Lusk.*

December 2, Saturday. Married—In Berlin township, on the 16th November, by Henry Hodgins, Esq., Mr. *Nelson Brookhover* to Miss *Betsey S. Lewis,* all of Berlin township.—On the 23d ult, by O. D. Hough, Esq., Mr. *Ralph L. Slack,* of Oxford township, to Miss *Mary Ann Fleming,* of Peru township. Died—In Thompson township, October 2d, Capt. Benjamin S. Knight, in the 51st year of his age, late of Columbus, Ohio, and formerly a resident of Duanesburgh, of the county of Schenectady, N. Y. (Communicated).

December 30, Saturday. Married—In Berkshire township, on the 21st inst. by Henry Hodgden Esq., Mr. *Alfred Ruggles* to Miss *Eliza Barry,* all of said township.—In Delaware, on the 28th inst. by Sidney Moore, Esq., Mr. *Abraham Wolford* to Miss *Mary Carr,* both of Concord township.

1838—March 31, Saturday. Married—In Marlborough township, on Thursday the 29th inst. by the Rev. Nehemiah Martin, Mr. *Daniel S. Drake* to Miss *Clarissa Wilcox,* all of this county.

April 7, Saturday. Married—On the 29th ult. by Morgan Williams, Esq., Mr. *Elijah Adams,* Jr., to Miss *Elizabeth Landon.*—On April 21, Saturday. Married—In Radnor township, on the 11th inst. by Sidney Moore, Esq., Mr. *George Repert* of Delaware to Miss the 30th ult. by the same, Mr. *Thomas Humphreys* to Miss *Mary Phillios,* all of Radnor township.
Elizabeth Jones of the former place.

April 28, Saturday. Married—On the 21st inst. by Sidney Moore, Esq., Mr. *James Vining* to Miss *Philen Durfey,* all of Delaware township.

May 5, Saturday. Married—On the 30th ult. by S. Moore, Esq., Mr. *Jacob Richards* to Miss *Mary Metz,* all of Delaware township. Died—In Berlin on the 26th ult, Seth, infant son of Luther Closson.— On the 1st inst. Mrs. Mary, wife of Barney Cunningham. Mrs. C. has left a husband and a large family of children.(Communicated).

May 12, Saturday. Married—In Concord township, on the 9th inst. by Morgan Williams, Esq., Mr. *Edward Evans* to Miss *Malaban Jackson.* Died—In Westerlloo township, on the 5th inst. Mrs. Granger, wife of Daniel Granger, recently of this place.

June 2, Saturday. Married—On the 31st inst. In Concord township, by Morgan Williams, Esq., Mr. *Thomas C. Jones* to Miss *Catherine Owens.*

June 9, Saturday. Married—On the 7th by Rev. Mr. Webster, Col. *Nathan Chester* to Miss *Harriet Torrey,* all of Delaware township.—On the 26th ult. by Rev. Seldon Clark, Dr. *Samuel S. Page* of Bennington township, to Miss *Eliza Marvin* of Bloomfield township, Knox county.

June 25, Saturday. Died—Suddenly, on the night of the 19th inst. in Radnor, Joseph McGonigle, Esq., and aged and respectable citizen of Oxford township.

July 14, Saturday. Married—On the 8th inst. by the Rev. C. H. Allart, Mr. *John C. Wachter* to Miss *Frances Shoub,* both of this place.

September 29, Saturday. Married—In Liberty township, on the 26th inst. by the Rev. Mr. Labaree, Capt. *Samuel Wilson* of Worthington, to Miss *Elizabeth Edwards* of this place.

42

October 13, Saturday. Married—On the 4th inst. by the Rev. D. Cadwallader, Mr. *Samuel Nevours* to Miss *Sarah A. McGee*, both of Scioto twp. Died—On the 1st inst. after a lingering illness, John Montgomery Picket, the youngest child of Dr. C. H. Pickett, aged one year and two months..

October 20, Saturday. Married—On the 11th inst. by P. D. Hillyer, Esq., Mr. *Joseph F. Bivens* of Radnor, to Miss *Margaret Watkins* of Delaware.—On the 14th inst. by the Rev. A. Allardt, Mr. *John Heere* to Miss *Hannah Schmidt*, of Delaware township.—On the 15th inst, by the same, Mr. *Jacob Schmidt* to Miss *Christine Yeager*, both of Delaware township.

October 27, Saturday. Married—On the 18th inst. by O. D. Hough, Esq., Mr. *George Longwell* of Brown township, to Miss *Mary A. Sheets*, of Kingston.—On the 20th inst. by Sidney Moore, Esq., Mr. *John Mathias* to Miss *Ann Graham*, all of Delaware county (twp).—On the 23d. inst. by the Rev. W. S. Morrow, Mr. *David Stevens* of Troy township, to Miss *Rosanna Perry* of Delaware.

December 1, Saturday. Married—On the 29th ult. by the Rev. Henry Van Deman, Mr. *William Stienbeck* to Miss *Rhoda Foster*, all of Delaware.

December 22, Saturday. Married—On the 19th inst. by the Rev. W. S. Morrow, Mr. *William Smith* to Miss *Mary Thomas*, all of this place.

Contributed by WILLARD E. WIGHT

1839, January 5, Saturday. Died—On the 26th December, 1838, at her residence in Delaware county, Ohio, Mrs. Barsheba Eaton, widow of John Eaton, deceased, in the 73d year of her age. She was among the first settlers of the western wilderness, and endured the hardships and dangers of the frontier during the last war. She was a member of the Presbyterian Church until the year 1807, when she joined the Baptist Church of Delaware county.

February 2, Saturday. Married—On the 28th ult. by the Rev. J. W. White, Mr. *Samuel A. Griswold*, Editor of the Tiffin Gazette, to Miss *Etheline Kelley*, of this place.

February 9, Saturday. Married—On the 7th inst. by the Rev. H. Van Deman, Mr. *James M. M'Kibben* of Zanesville to Miss *Mary M, daughter of Thomas Butler*, of this place.

April 6, Saturday. Married—On the 2d inst. by P. D. Hillyer, Esq., Mr. *Adam Miller* to Miss *Lucy A. James*, all of this place.

April 13, Saturday. Married—On Thursday last, by the Rev. S. S. Klein, Mr. *David McElvain* to Miss *Harriet Trout*, all of this place.

April 20, Saturday. Married—In Berlin, on the 14th inst. by the Rev. Jacob Drake, Mr. *Charles G. Scott* to Miss *Zebiah Casell*, all of this county.

May 4, Saturday. Married—On the 23d ult. by Morgan Williams, Esq., Mr. *Barnabas Randall* to Miss *Roxanna Lusk*, all of Radnor.

May 18, Saturday. Married—On the 12th inst. in Berlin. By the Rev. J. Drake, Mr. *Gideon Richmond* to Miss *Lois Ames*, all of this county.—In Harlem, by Hurlburt Scovell, Esq., Mr. *Wheatey Closson* to Miss *Sally Fairchilds*, all of this county.—At Fayetteville, Washington county, Arkansas, in February last, *Royal T. Wheeler*, Esq., formerly of Delaware to Miss *Emily Walker*, of the former place.

May 25, Saturday. Married—On the 23d inst. by John Morrison Esq., Mr. *Levi Sonder* to Miss *Polly E. Carter.*—In this place, on the 23d inst. by the Rev. H. Van Deman, Mr. *Joel D. Butler* to Miss *Nancy Wells*, both of Marion.

June 1, Saturday. Married—on Saturday last, by the Rev. J. W. White, Mr. *William Dutcher* to Miss *Mariah Birch*, all of this county.—On the same day, by Rev. M. Allandt, Mr. *David High* to Miss *Angeline Seigfried*, all of Delaware township.

June 8, Saturday. Married—On the 26th ult. by O. Stark, Esq., Mr. *John Dumegan* to Miss *Polly Raymond*, all of Berkshire township.

June 29, Saturday. Married—On Tuesday last, by John Morrison, Esq., Mr. *Edward Erwin* of Scioto to Miss *Sally Ann Van Sickle* of Radnor.

July 6, Saturday. Married—On the 2d inst. by the Rev. Henry

Van Deman, Mr. *W. Woods* of Marysville to Miss *Martha Jane Thompson* of this vicinity.—On the 4th inst. by the Rev. S. S. Klein, Mr. *John Bloom* to Miss *Mary Smith*, all of this place.

August (?) Married—On the 25th inst. by Henry Patee, Esq. Mr. *Daniel D. Shaw* to Miss *Lodemia Dodge*, all of Westfield township. Died—At his residence in this place on the 26th inst. after a short illness, Mr. Thomas Wasson.—*Another Revolutionary Hero Gone*—Died—At the residence of his son in Harlem township, Delaware county, on the 20th inst. Jacob Rose, in the 79th year of his age. Mr. Rose entered the army of the revolution when he was quite young, and remained until it was disbanded. He was in several important engagements with the Indians in the State of New York. He was with General Sullivan in his expedition against the Six Nations in 1779, when they were completely subdued. He was at the capture of Cornwallis in 1718, which important event put an end to the British oppression. He also took part in the last war with Great Britain, which terminated so gloriously for American Liberty. Mr. Rose was distinguished through life for his exemplary and retiring habits, as well as his gentlemanly deportment. A great lover of his country and her republican institutions, and a devoted and ardent Christian, always ready to lend his aid to the afflicted. In a word he was a Christian in whom there was no guile; and he died as he lived, respected and esteemed by all who knew him. He has been gathered to his fathers after having lived long enough to see the fruits of his early toil in behalf of the liberties of his country crowned by the smiles of Heaven in its abundant posterity. . . STATESMAN.

September 7, Saturday. Married—On the 2d inst. by the Rev. H. Van Deman, Mr. *William A. Platt* of Columbus to Miss *Fanny A. Hays* of this place.—In Harlem by H.Scovell, Esq., Mr. *George Savage* to Miss *Remembrance Budd*, daughter of Dr. Budd of this place.—In Union county on the 22d ult. by the Rev. C. Rogers, Mr. *George McKittrick* of Delaware to Miss *Caroline M. Hill* of Union county.

September 14, Saturday. Married—On the 4th inst. by J. Morrison Esq., Mr. *John Burge* of Union county to Miss *Mary Meek* of Scioto township, Delaware county.—On the 12th inst. by the Rev. J. Drake, Col. *Samuel N. Adams* to Miss *Delia Lewis*, all of this county.—On the 12th inst. by Charles Steinbeck, Esq. Mr. *William Alldaffer* of Berlin, to Miss *Sarah Welch*, of Liberty (twp).

September 21, Saturday. Married—On the 16th inst. by the Rev. H. Van Deman, Mr. *Lewis C. Sturdevant* of Smithland, Ky., to Miss *Henrietta Smith*, of this vicinity.—On the 12th inst. in Berkshire township, by Elder H. D. Masin, Mr. *Peter V. Finch* of Trenton, to Miss *Marilla Wort*, of the former place.—On the 15th inst. in Lincoln township, by H. Patee, Esq., Mr. *Reuben Bunker*, of Marvin twp. Marion county, Ohio., to Miss *Lucretia White,*, of the former place.— On the 15th inst. in Oxford township, by J. W. Elliot, Esq., Mr. *David G. Coomer* of Marlborough township, to Miss *Phebe Clark*, of Oxford.—On the 19th inst. in Galena, by H. Scovell, Esq., *Robert Carpenter* Esq., to Miss *Philene Walker*, all of this county.

October 12, Saturday. Married—On the 6th inst. by the Rev. J. W. White, Mr. *Harrison Kanay* to Miss *Louisa Sweetser*, both of this place.—On the 10th inst. by the Rev. H. Van Deman, Mr. *D. N. Darlington* of Crawfordsville, Iowa, to Miss *Harriet Moody* of this place.

October 19, Saturday. Married—In Genoa, on the 17th inst. by the Rev. Ahab Jinks, Mr. *Warren H. Allen* of Delaware, to Miss *Sarah Keeler*, of the former place.

October 20, Saturday. Married—On the 22d inst. by the Rev. James McElroy, Mr. *Reuben A. Lamb* to Miss *Emily G. Howard*, all of this place.

November 9, Saturday. Married—On the 19th inst. by the Rev. H. Van Deman, Mr. *Leonard R. Tuttle* of Columbus, to Miss *Emily F. Howe* of this place.—On the 19th inst. by Elder B. Martin, Mr. *Frederick W. Koons* of Marion county, to Mrs. *Mary A. Brown* of Troy township, Delaware county.—On the 21st inst. by the same., Mr. *Daniel McDaniel* to Mrs. *Ann Tharp*, all of Delaware county.—In Radnor on the 14th by Morgan Williams, Esq., Mr. *Jacob Irwin*, of Marion county, to Miss *Elizabeth Fairchild*, of the former place.—In Delaware on the 19th inst. by the Rev. W. S. Morrow, Mr. *Levin L. Sands* to Miss *Sarah Ann Downer*, both of Tiffin.

November 30, Saturday. Died—At London, Madison county, on the 22d inst. Rev. Elias Van Deman (brother of Rev. H. Van Deman of this place) in the 34th year of his age.

December 7, Saturday. Married—On the 1st inst. by the Rev. W. A. Chapman, Mr. *Paul Randall* to Miss *Elizabeth Watkins*, all of this place—In Genoa on the 21st ult by E. Scovell, Esq., Mr. *William Starns* to Miss *Catharine Closson*, all of this county. Died—At the residence of her mother in this place, on the 30th ult, Miss Helen Wilson, aged about 16.

December 14, Saturday. Married—In South Bend, Iowa, on the 26th ult. by the Rev. J. S. Harrison, Mr. *John Millikan* (formerly of this place) Junior Editor of the *South Bend Free Press*, to Miss *Joannah R. Lewis*, of that vicinity.

December 21, Saturday. Married—On the 17th inst. by the Rev. H. Van Deman, *Abraham Thompson*, Editor of this paper, to Miss *Delia, youngest daughter of George Storm.*—On the 10th inst. by the Rev. S. S. Klein, Mr. *Charles Wotring* to Miss *Sarah Zeigler*, all of Delaware township.—On the 9th inst. in Galena by the Rev. Nathan Emery, Mr. *Charles Brown* to Miss *Sarah A. Dustin*, all of that place.—On the 12th inst. by Joel Mendenhall, Esq., Mr. *John Roloson* to Mrs. *Celinda Durfey*, all of this county.—In Troy township, on the 12th inst. by J. W. Elliott, Esq., Mr. *Phillip Wolf* to Miss *Elizabeth Queen.*—On the 19th inst. by the same, Mr. *William Worline* to Miss *Melinda, daughter of Jonas Main*, Esq., north of Troy township.

December 28, Saturday. Married—On the 25th inst. by John VanDyke, Esq., Mr. *Calvin Clark* of Peru, to Miss *Charlotte, daughter of Peter Coykendal* of Kingston.

1840—January 4, Saturday. Married—On the 26th ult. by S. T. Cunard, Esq., Mr. *Robert Blakely* to Miss *Hannah, eldest daughter of Joseph Kingman*, all of Lincoln.

January 18, Saturday. Marrried—On the 15th inst. by the Rev. James McElroy, Mr. *Haldemond Crary* of Columbus, to Miss *Mary E. Byxbe*, of this place.

January 25, Saturday. Married—In Westfield township on the 16th inst. by H. Patee, Esq., Dr. *George Granger* to Miss *Mary Bishop*, all of that place.

February 1, Saturday. Died—On the 17th ult. Mr. John Van Deman (father of the Rev. H. Van Deman of this place) in the 85 year of his age. "He fought for the liberties of his country in the Revolutionary war. He was a Christian man in his life, and in his death he left the precious (———) for his friends and relatives that he is now beyond the reach of sorrow and suffering."

February 8, Saturday. Died—On Wednesday morning last, William S. M., son of Joseph C. and Delight P. Alexander, aged 4 months and 3 days.

February 21, Saturday. Married—On the 6th inst. in Westfield, by H. Patee, Esq., Mr. *Benjamin C. Pickle* of Mt. Gilead, Marion county, to Miss *Olive S. Benson* of the former place.—On the 6th inst. by A. Patee, Esq., Mr. *Milton B. Smith* to Miss *Esther Riley*, all of Oxford township.

February 28, Friday. Married—At Galena, on the 5th ult. by Henry Hodgden, Esq., Mr. *Hiram P. Smith* of Delaware, to Miss *Sophia H.* daughter of *Ira Arnold, Esq.*, of the former place.—At the same place, on the 20th inst. by the same, Mr. *Carlton G. Scovelle* to Miss *Elizabeth Cook*, both of Galene—On the 25th inst. by the Rev. B. Adams, Mr. *William Cochran* to Miss *Therusha Adams*, all of this county.—On the 13th inst. by H. Patee, Esq., Mr. *James Aldrich* to Miss *Elizabeth Homiston*, all of Westfield. Married—On the 9th inst. by N. Jones, Esq., Mr. *Thomas B. Warner* to Miss *Hannah Tharp*, all of Troy township.—In Brown township on the 5th inst. by the Rev. B. Adams, Mr. *Marvin Adams* of Berlin, to Miss *Mary Ann McCombs* of the former place.

April 10, Friday. Married—In this place on the 8th inst. by J. Z. Mendenhall, Esq., Mr. *Joseph Saxton* to Miss *Dorcas Green*, all of this town.

April 24, Friday. Married—In this town on the 23d inst. by J. Z. Mendenhall, Esq., Mr. *Isaac Frost* of Bennington township, to Mrs. *Mina Strong*, of East Liberty.—In this town, on the 16th inst, by P. D. Hillyer, Esq., Mr. *Kilbourn Beach*, of Union county, to Miss *Margaret B. Evans* of Concord township, Delaware county.—In Orange township, on the 16th inst. by Rev. Philander Kelsey, Mr. *Blake W. Barrows* to Miss *Charlotte Janes.*—On the 5th inst. by Rev. D. Cadawallader, Mr. *R. Harris* to Miss *M. Bairns*, all of Radnor.—On the 30th ult. by the same, Mr. *D. Jackson* of Delaware to Miss *Nancy McCollister*, of Union county.

May 8, Friday. Married—On the 7th inst. by J. Z. Mendenhall, Esq., Mr. *David Rodgers* to Miss *Sylvia Phelps.*—On the 30th ult at Cardington, Marion county, by the Rev. J. G. Bruce, Dr. *Andrew McClure* to Miss *Eliza, eldest daughter of Robert Cochran*, of that place.

May 15, Friday. Married—On the 30th ult. by the Rev. Ahab Jinks, Mr. *Lewis Mulford* to Miss *Anna Miller.*

May 22, Friday. Married—On the 6th inst. at Cardington, Marion county, by Peter Doty Esq., Mr. *Obadiah Dunham* to Miss *Sarah Winship*, all of that place.—On the 17th inst. by Morgan Williams, Esq., Mr. *William Penry* to Miss *Mary Evans*, all of Radnor.

May 29, Friday. Died—In this village, on Friday the 22d, Henry Porter, infant son of S. F. and C. P. West, aged 20 months.

June 5, Friday Married—In Cardington, on the 21st ult. by Peter Doty Esq., Mr. *James L. Cumins* to Mis *Sarah Miller*, all of Canaan township.

June 12, Friday. Died—At Bellepoint, Delaware county, on the 3d ult. Capt. James Kooken in the 88th year of his age.

June 19, Friday. Married—On the 17th inst. by the Rev. William S. Morrow, Rev. *John White* of Cincinnati, to Miss *Anne C. eldest daughter of Hon. H. Williams* of this place.

July 3, Friday. Married—In Westfield on the 21st of June, by A. Patee, Esq., Mr. *George W. Switser* to Miss *Jane Travis*, all of Oxford.—On the 24th ult, by the Rev. J. Drake, Mr. *William Rose* to Mrs. *Ann Carpenter*, all of this county.—In Eden on the 29th ult. by O. D. Hough, Dr. *Isaac Leonard* to Miss *Nancy Thurston*, all of that place.—In this place on the 30th ult, by Joel Z. Mendenhall, Esq., Mr. *John Harris* to Mrs. *Altha Holmes.*—On the 25th ult. by O. D. Hough, Esq., Mr. *Jonas Waldren* of Kingston, to Miss *Eliza Gregg* of Brown.

July 10, Friday. Married—On the 30th ult. by the Rev. D. Cadwallader, Mr. *Samuel Wise* of Troy, to Miss *Susan Campbell* of Radnor.—On Thursday the 2d. inst. by Rev. Dr. Hoge, *John G. Miller*, Esq. Mayor of the City of Columbus, and Editor of the *Ohio Confederate*, to Mrs. *P. W. Crosby.*

August 7, Friday. Married—On the 5th inst. by the Rev. H. Van Deman, Mr. *Joseph Crawford* to Miss *Mary Lloyd*, all of this place.

August 14, Friday. Married—On the 6th inst. by Oliver Stark, Esq., Mr. *Chauncey Finch* to Miss *Mary Van Sickle*, all of Kingston township.

September 4, Friday. Married—On the 1st inst. by the Rev. William S. Morrow, *Andrew Patterson*, Esq., to Miss *Lucy Byxbe*, all of this place.

September 11, Friday. Married—On the 26th ult. by the Rev. Henry Van Deman, Mr. *William Chamdler* to Miss *Charlotte Leak.*— On the 27th ult, by the same, Mr. *Azra Thrall* to Miss *Mary G. Chandler.*—On the 6th inst. by the same, Mr. *William Null* to Miss *Susan Hedrick*, all of this county

September 18, Friday. Married—At Little Sandusky, on the 17th inst. by the Rev. M. Wheeler, Mr. *Victor M. Griswold* of Delaware, to Miss *Caroline, daughter of Col. P. McElvain*, of the former place.

October 2, Friday. Married—In this place, on the 1st inst. by Albert Pickett, Jr., Esq., Mr. *Elizur P. Mynier* to Miss *Millicent Lindenberger.*—In this town, on the 21st ult. by the Rev. W. S. Morrow, the Rev. *John Blanpied* to Miss *Sophia Dolbear.*—In this town on the 22d ult, by the same, Mr. *Egan Westervelt* of Galena, to Miss *Jane, daughter of John S. Brown.*

October 9, Friday. Married—In Berkshire on the 6th inst. by Henry Hodgden, Esq., Mr. *Harvey P. Lewis* to Miss *Jane Searles.* Died—On the 6th inst. at his residence in Troy township, after a short illness, Mr. John Alexander, in the 35 year of his age. The deceased has left a wife and four small children to mourn their irreparable loss.

October 16, Friday. Married—On Thursday the 8th inst. by the Rev. William S. Morrow, Mr. *Peres M. Dix* to Miss *Lovina Wise*, both of Troy township.

October 23, Friday. Married—On the 26th ult., by the Rev. H. Van Deman, Mr. *James Liggett* to Miss *Sarah Richardson.*—By the same, on the 14th inst. Mr. *George Miller* to Miss *Sarah A. Hedrick.* Died—At his residence, near this place, on the 12th inst, Robert Jamison, Senior, in the 73d year of his age. Mr. Jamison came early in the settlement of this county from the State of Pennsylvania, and though he had a numerous family, he was the instance of mortality in it since his residence in this state.

October 30, Friday. Married—On the 28th ult, by Charles Stienbeck, Esq., Mr. *Dalton W. Terril* to Miss *Catharine Roloson.*

November 20, Friday. Maried—In this place on yesterday evening, by the Rev. H. Van Deman, Mr. *Simeon C. Starr* of Marion, to Miss *Martha D. Sweetser,* of this place.—On the 4th inst by the same, Mr. *Jacob L. Felkner* to Miss *Elenor Carr,* all of Scioto township.—On the 17th ult. by the same, Mr. *Jonas Evans* to Miss *Rachel Smith.*

December 4, Friday. Married—On the 21st inst. by the Elder J. Drake, Mr. *William C. Haskins* to Miss *Martha W. Eaton,* all of Berlin township.

1841, January 8, Friday. Married on the 31ult. at Gambier, by the Rev. Joseph Muenscher, the Rev. S. G. Gassaway of Delaware, to Miss Isabelle Virginia, daughter of D. R. B. F. Bache, U. S. N., of the former place.—On the 24ult. in this place, by the Rev. A. Poe, Mr. James Carson to Miss Isabelle Johnson. On the 3 inst. by the same, Mr. Thomas Roberts of Columbus, Ohio to Miss Hannah Brentnall.

January 22, Friday. Married on the 31st. ult. by the Rev. H. Van Deman, Mr. John Cunningham to Miss Oliva Evans. On the 2 inst. by the same, Mr. Isaac Harrison to Mrs. Esther Fry.

January 29, Friday. Married—On the 28th. inst. by the Rev. H. Van Deman, Mr. Thomas Pettibone to Mrs. Sarah Downer, all of this place. On the 19th. inst., by the same, the Rev. Abner Dunham Chapman on Miss Alma E. Wigton, both of Kingston township. At Newark, Ohio on the 21inst. by the Rev. Mr. Duncan, Clark Dunham, Esq., Editor of the Newark Gazette, to Miss Lucretia A., daughter of Col. Hose Williams. In Berkshire township, on the 6th. inst. by Elder B. Adams, Mr. Nelson Collum to the accomplished Miss Jane Still, all of said township.

February 5, Friday. Married in Concord township, on the 28th. ult by Morgan Williams, Esq., Mr. Thomas J. Jones to Miss Sarah Freshwater. On the 7th. ult. by A. Patee, Esq., Mr. William Wood, of Oxford township to Miss Annis Turner of Westfield.

February 19, Friday. Married. In Cleveland township, Elkhart County, Indiana, on the 28th. ult. by Rev. Mr. Cooke, Mr. William Milikan, Senior Editor of the "South Bend Free Press" to Miss Emma, daughter of Mr. Hardin Cleveland of the former place.

February 26, Friday. Married—In Liberty township, on the 16th. ult. by the Rev. Joseph Labaree. Mr. Joseph Van Deman, of Ross County, to Miss Elizabeth Case, of the former place. On the 25th. inst. by O. Stark, Esq., Mr. Chauncey Sturdevant to Miss Lucinda Cahoun, all of this county.

March 12, Friday. Married. On the 4th. inst. by O. D. Hough, Esq., Mr. Joshua Berry to Miss Sarah Kensler, all of Brown township.

March 19, Friday. Married—In Columbus, on the 16th. inst. by Professor Shaver, Mr. F. C. Flieschmann of Delaware to Miss Charlotte Ketzel, of the former place.—Died. In this place on the 15th. Mrs. Powers aged 65 yrs.

March 23, Married—In Oxford township, on the 18th. by Henry Patee, Esq., Mr. Harman Birch, of Westfield, to Miss Alovia Benedict, of the former place. Died—In this village on the 19th. at the residence of her brother S. Finch, Esq., Miss Mary Finch, age 42 years. The deceased was a native of Fairfield County, Conn. and came to this place in August last. (Com.)

April 9, Friday. Died—In Brown township, on the 2nd. Mrs. Elizabeth L., wife of Horace J. Rice, of Ottawa county, and the daugther of C. M. and Sarah Thrall, aged 22 years and 7 mos.

April 23, Friday. Married: In Cardington, Marion County, on the 8th. by Peter Doty, Esq., Mr. Paul W. Purvis to Miss Lydia Bunker, all of that place. On the 18th. in Genoa township, by the Rev. James H. Frees, Mr. Milo Meacham to Miss Clarinda Learned.

May 7, Friday. Married. On the 22nd. by William M. Warren, Esq., Mr. John Thomas to Miss Drusilla Oller, both of Concord township.

May 14, Friday. Married. On the 11th. by the Rev. H. Van Deman, Mr. James Cellars of Liberty to Miss Elizabeth Ray, of this place. On the 13th. by the Rev. A. Poe, Mr. Isaac Beckover to Miss Mary Miller, all of this place. In Genoa township by H. Scovell, Esq., Mr. Isaac Jones to Miss Sally McWilliams, both of that place.

May 21, Friday. Married—On Sunday, the 12th. by the Rev. Samuel Sunton, Mr. Lloyd Freese, of Tiffin, Ohio, to Miss Lavinia Kelley, of this place. On the 6th. in Peru township, by Edmund Buck, Esq. Mr. David Baughman, of Zanesville, to Miss Lucy H. Buck.—At the same time and place, by the same, Mr. John S. Riley to Miss Nathilda Buck, all of Peru township. Died.—At the residence of her daughter, in Bellepoint, on the 3rd. Mrs. Mary Reynolds, after a short illness, of inflamation of the lungs.

May 28, Friday. Married—On the 27th. by the Rev. A. Poe, Mr. Alexander M. Rogers to Miss Martha Flanagan, both of Scioto township.

June 4, Friday. Married—On the 2nd. by A. Picket, jr., Esq., Mr. Hugh Lindsay to Miss Margaret Graham, both of this vicinity.— In Granville, Licking county on the 3rd. by the Rev. A. Jinks, Mr. William Jinks, of Delaware, to Miss Ann Farnham, of the former place.

June 11, Friday. Married—On the 20th. by O. D. Hough, Esq., Mr. Israel Potter, to Miss Phebe G. Whipple, both of Peru township. On the 3rd. by the same, Mr. George Taylor to Miss Mary C. Randolph, both of Peru township. On the 6th. by H. Hodgden Esq., Mr. Noble Landon of Berkshire, to Miss Hannah Plant, of Kingston.

June 18, Friday. Married—In Troy township, on the 13th. by J. W. Eliott, Esq., Mr. Robert G. McMaster to Miss Mary B. Worline.

July 2, Friday. Married—On the 30th. by the Rev. H. Van Deman, Mr. Rutherford Moody of New York, to Miss Eunice Kilbourne of this place.

July 23, Friday. Died. In Pittsburgh, Pa. on Friday, July 16th. Mrs. Maria Preston, consort of Rev. William Preston, late of this city.

August 6, Friday. Died in Troy township, on the 1st. Mr. Isiah Moses, aged 29 years and 10 months, leaving a wife and two children, together with a large circle of relatives, to mourn their early lose. (Communicated by one present).

50

August 13, Friday. Married. On the 5th. in Porter township, Mr. John W. Brown to Miss Mary Emeline Lindenberger, both of the former place. Died. On the 11th. after a short illness of five days, at the residence of his brother-in-law, Mr. Wm. McClure, of this vicinity, Col. James Crawford, aged 74 years.

September 3, Friday. Married—On the 29th. by H. Hodgden, Esq., Mr. Slome Ames to Miss Mabel W. Lewis, both of Berlin.

September 25, Saturday. Died—At his residence in Radnor, on the 23rd. Mr. Norman Harris, aged about 40 years. On the 24th. Mrs. Lucy Harris, his wife, aged about 34 years, leaving to the guardian protection of the 'Father of the Orphan' a large family of small children. Both bodies are to be interred today (25) inclosed in one coffin.

October 2, Saturday. Married—On the 19th. by Rev. Nathan Emery, Mr. Jeremiah Dunham of Berlin township, Delaware County, to Miss Amanda Blodget of Blendon, Franklin county.—In Radnor, on the 30th. of August by Rev. Reese Powell, Mr. Isaac Bowen of Columbus, to Miss Ann Jones, of the former place.—In the same place on the 16th. by the same Nathan Chaney to Miss Ann Williams.

October 9, Saturday. Married—In Brainbridge, N. Y. on the 23rd. by the Rev. Mr. Egenbrought, Dr. S. K. Bradley of Delaware, to Miss Eliza Craig of the former place.

October 16, Saturday. Married—In Harmon township, on the 17th by Edmund Buck, Esq, Mr. Adam Shoop, of Lincoln, to Miss Jane Kimball, of the former place

October 23, Saturday. Married.—In Columbus, on the 20th. by the Rev. S. G. Gassaway, Hon. Hosea Williams of this place to Mrs. Clarinda Starling, of the former place. In Berkshire, on the 15th. by H. Hodgden, Esq., Mr. Thomas J. Kerr to Miss Angelina Benton. On the 19th., by the same, Mr. Homer Carpenter to Miss Rebecca Pike. On the 26th. by the same, Mr. Isaac Wood to Miss Rebecca Jones. On the 17th., by the same, Mr. Joseph Hombeck to Miss Sarah Pike. Died. In this place, on Thursday morning on the 14th. William Harvey, son of T. W. & Alma Hitchcock, aged one year and two months.

October 30, Saturday. Married.—In St. Peter's Church, on Wednesday evening 28th. by the Rev. S. G. Gassaway, Mr. Pegleg Bunker to Miss Rachel Hills, all of this place.

November 6, Saturday. Married—On the 2nd. by the Rev. Ahab Jinks, Dr. Edward Rowland, of Sunbury to Miss Elizabeth, daughter of Col. F. Avery, of this vicinity. In Kingston, on the 3rd. by O. Stark, Esq., Mr. Calvin Vance, of Licking County, to Miss Jane Rosecrans, of the former place. In Berkshire township, on the 21st. by H. Hodgden, Esq., Mr. George Havens to Miss Mary M. Scott. Died. At his residence in Scioto township, on Sunday morning, the 31st. Mr. James Dean, aged about 70 years.

November 13, Saturday. Married—In Genoa township, on the 2nd.

51

by the Rev. W. Eastman, Mr. William H. Connell, of Melmore, Senneca county, to Miss Sarah C. Hough of the former place. On the 28th. by the Rev. P. Rosemiller, Mr. Noah Ewry, of this vicinity, to Miss Magdalene Tobias, of Green county.

November 20 Saturday. Married—In Kingston on the 17th. by O. Stark, Esq., Mr. Joel S. Stephens, of Porter township. to Miss Sophronia Rosecrans, of the former place.

December 4, Saturday. Married—In Delaware township, on the 24th. by Joel Z. Mendenhall, Esq., Mr. Benjamin D. Lyon to Miss Emeline Potter, both of Union county. In Genoa township, by Hurlburt Scovell, Esq., Mr. John Sebring to Miss Katy Ann Coe. Died.—At Columbis, Texas, in September last, Isaac Bunker, formerly a resident of this county. At the same place one week subsquent, Joseph Bunker, son of said deceased. In February last, near Houston, Isaac Bunker, jr., an elder brother of Joseph. On September 16th. last, near Caldwell, Miller county, Dr. George H. Dennison, a son-in-law of Isaac Bunker, Dr. D. was formerly a resident of Sunbury, in this county. he was drowned in attempting to cross the Brassos River.

December 18, Saturday. Died. In Berlin township, on the 9th. Mrs. Orrell Carpenter, aged 25 years, 2 months, 16 days.

NEWSPAPER ITEMS FROM THE OHIO GAZETTE

DELAWARE, OHIO

1842, January 1, Saturday. On the 28th, by Rev. S. G. Gassaway, Mr. Henry Z. Mills, of Columbus, to Miss Cynthia S., daughter of Dr. Reuben Lamb, of this place.

January 8, Saturday. Married. On the 28th. by S. Hubbell, Esq., Mr. Stephen F. Randolph, of Peru township, to Miss Charity Brown of Kingston.

January 15, Saturday. Married—On the 30th. by O. D. Hough, Esq., Mr. Andrew Heavlo, of Berlin, to Miss Elizabeth Pettijohn of Brown.

January 22, Saturday. Married. On the 20th. by the Rev. Mr. Pilcher, Mr. William E. Butler to Miss Sarah Ann Brees. Died. On the 20th. after a short illness, in the 75th. year of her age, Mrs. Anne, wife of Abraham Williams, of this place.

January 29, Saturday. Died. At St. Francisville, La., on the 9th. Stephen B. Aigin, aged 37.

February 19, Saturday. Married—On the 27th. by the Rev. H. E. Pilcher, Mr. John Boren, of Delaware to Miss Margaret Eatherton (Atherton) of this vicinity. Died. Departed this life, after an illness of about 8 hours, at her residence in Peru township, Delaware County, Ohio, on the morning of the 12th. Mrs. Mary Thatcher, consort of John Thatcher, Esq., aged 72 years. Mrs. Thatcher was, when quite young, taken prisoner by the Indians in the Revolutionary War, together with her mother, two brothers and a sister. They were taken into the interior of Pennsylvania; her mother, who had an infant which the Indians compelled her to carry "over the mountains and throughout the vallies" gave out after travelling about 12 miles, when she and the infant were tomahawked and scalped; the others were taken to Canada, and suffered much among the Canadians for seven years during which time her remaining brother died. Mrs. Thatcher and her sister were again permitted to see their father's face, who bought them back to Pennsylvania. She was in her youth, professed in Religion of Jesus Christ, was a member of the Baptist Church near a half century, sustained and umblemished Christian character. She was greatly beloved in life, and her death much lamented Feb. 14, 1842 (Com.)

February 26, Saturday. Married—On the 10. by O. D. Hough, Esq., Mr. James More, of Brown, to Miss Elizabeth Shadrick, of Kingston.

March 5, Saturday. Married—In Marlborough township, on Sunday evening last, by J. W. Elliott, Esq., Mr. Peter J. Brown to Miss Elizabeth Anderson, all of this place.

March 12, Saturday. Died—On Tuesday evening Martha Frances, youngest child of James & Martha Agin, aged 6 yrs. & 8 months.

March 19, Saturday. Married—On 3rd. by Rev. David Cadwalader, Mr. Japhet Hull to Miss Betsy Lush, all of Radnor. In Delaware, March 17, by Rev. Rees Powell, Mr. Rees Price to Miss Elizabeth Price, both of this place. Died—In Berkshire, Ohio, on Friday morning, 11th. Mr. Daniel Frost, late of Windham, Luzerne county, Pa. "Blessed are the dead who die in the Lord".

March 26, Saturday. Died—In this town, on the 19th. Mrs. Frances Holmes, wife of B. W. Holmes, and daughter of Thomas Butler, aged 26 years.

1843, December 16. Married—In Delaware on the 11th. by Rev. R. Powell, Mr. William Martin to Mrs. Elizabeth Thomas, both of Radnor. On 7th by Sidney Moore, Esq., Mr. George W. Crawford to Miss Mary Jones, both of the town of Delaware. On the 7th. by Rev. Jos. Labaree, Lieut. Cornelius Howe of the U. S. A. to Miss Ann Watson of Liberty. On Nov. 30th. in Cardington, Marion county by Rev. Mr. Allen, Mr. George P. Nichols to Miss Elizabeth St. John, all of the said place.

1844, January 27, Saturday. Married. On 18th. in Westfield by A. Wolf, Esq., Wm. B. Thornburgh to Miss Ann Hammond, both of Westfield. On 21st. by Rev. B. Pope, Mr. John Stimmel to Mrs. Mathilda Steckel, both of Delaware.

February 3, Saturday. Married. On the 25th. of December in Trenton, by Rev. Daniel Bennett, Mr. Ruliff Jacobus of N. Jersey, to Miss Laure Shellhouse of the former place. Died. On 24th. at the residence of her son in Delaware township Mrs. Susannah Worline, aged 83 yrs. 9 mos. and 8 days.

February 10, Saturday. Married. In Marlborough township on the 1st. by J. W. Elliott, Esq., Mr. Abraham Wolf to Miss Mary Simpkins. Died. On the 3rd. at his residence in this place, Mr. Hiram J. L. Brown.

February 24, Saturday. Married. In Delaware township on the 11th. by John Morrison, Esq., Mr. Jonathan Pike, to Miss Louisa Humble.

March 2, Saturday. Married. On the 16th. in Lincoln, by E. Buck, Esq. Mr Marion James of Peru to Miss Ann Barnard of the former place. Died. In Berlin township on the 9th. of lung fever, Helen M. eldest daughter of Thomas L. and Laura H. Hoadly, aged 13 yrs. In Fredericktown, Knox Co., on the 12th. while on a visit to her friend, widow Hannah Scott, of Berlin township, aged 64.

March 9, Saturday. Died. At the residence of his father, near Delaware, on the 3rd. Mr. John Brees, aged 26 years.

March 16th, Saturday. Married. On the 25th. by O. A. Hough, Esq., Mr. James M. Abrams to Miss Nancy Longwell, both of Brown. On 14th. by the same, Mr. Noe Brockover of Berlin to Miss Alma Lewis of Brown.

April 6, Saturday. Married. On the 3rd of March last by Rev.Gavit, Mr. Abraham Morehouse, School Director to Miss Amelia Baldwin, all of Peru. In Marion, on Thursday evening last, by Rev. H. E. Pilcher. Charles Smith to Miss Abigail, all of this place. Died. In this town on Monday last, Mrs. Lucinda G. Carpenter, wife of Ira F. Carpenter, aged 59 years.

April 20th., Saturday. Married. On the evening of the 10th. by Rev. Benjamin Pope, Mr. Abraham Sleeper to Miss Susannah Gordon, both of Galena in this county. On the 18th. by the same, Mr. Henry Ballyet of Richland to Miss Harriet Liehty of Delaware.

April 27, Saturday. Married. On the 20th. by Oliver Starl, Esq., Mr. Lewis Cutter to Mrs. Abigail Parker, all of this county.

May 14, Saturday. Married. On the 22nd. by the Rev. R. S. Elder, Mr. J. P. Maynard to Miss Fidelia Thrall. At the same time, by the same, Mr. Charles Sherman to Miss Roxanna L. Thrall, all of Berkshire township. At the M. E. Church of Delaware on 26th. by the Rev. Solomon Howard, Mr. Hector R. Pettibone to Miss Mary J. Hunte, both of this place. Died. In Scioto township April 26th. John Milton Dodds, son of William C. and Mary Dodds, in the 20th. year of his age. A professor of Religion and a consistant member of the Presbyterian Church.

June 8, Saturday. Married. On the 21st. by O. Stark, Esq. Caleb M. Quimby to Miss Lydia Marlwith, all of this county. On the 26th. by Edward Mason, Esq., Mr. Richard Keyes, of Sharon township. Franklin Co., O., to Miss Hanna Gould, daughter of William Gould of Kingston township. Died. In Berlin on the 2nd., Dr. Abram N. Wigton. aged 28. About a few months since he married a daughter of Mr. A. Smith, where he died.

June 15, Saturday. Married. In Westfield township, June 9th. by Adam Wolfe, Esq., Mr. Luke Irhie (Lake Erie) to Miss Philene Pattee.

June 29, Saturday. Died. At his residence in Delaware township on the 12th. James Osborne aged 69 years, 10 months, 21 days. In Norton on the 22nd. Lucy Ann, daughter of Wm. & Catherine Osborne, aged 5 months and 28 days.

54

July 6, Saturday. Died. In Troy township on the 26th. of June of the IRETHEMER, Lafayette, son of Sabeers and Sarah Main.

July 20th. Saturday. Married. On Wednesday morning last by the Rev. R. Putnam, Mr. Alexander C. Martin of Dresdin, Ohio to Miss Lucy M., daughter of Wm. Walker of this place.

July 27th. Saturday. Married. In St. John's Church, Worthington, on the 18th. by Rev. Elder, Mr. Charles J. Wetmore, merchant of this place, to Miss Phebe Ann Weaver, of Worthington. In Marion on the 22nd. by Rev. E. S. Shepherd, John E. Davids, Esq., to Miss Charlotte Bain, all of this place.

August 3, Saturday. Died. On the 29th. in Delaware, Mary Emily daughter of Jos. and Mary A. Harder, aged 5 mos., 9 days. On Thursday 25th. in Troy, Joseph Taylor, aged 18, son of Oliver Taylor, recently of this vicinity. Also on Friday following, Nancy Buck, sister of the above.

August 10. Saturday. Married. On the 1st. in Troy by N. Jones, Esq., Mr. George Helt, of Delaware to Miss Laura Wilcox, of the former place. Died. In this place on Tuesday morning last William L., son of Benjamin and Elizabeth Powers, aged 1 year and 8 months.

August 24, Saturday. Died. On the 17th. in Kingston, of the prevailing fever, James A. Wigton, aged about 20 years. On the 21st. in Berlin Mrs. Lois Richmond aged about 24 years.

September 14, Saturday. Married. On Thursday last in this place by the Rev. F. Putman, Mr. Moses Bangs of Worthington to Miss Alura Howard of Liberty. On the 1st. of August by the Rev. D. Cadwalader, Mr. Jacob Perry of Radnor to Miss Elizabeth J. Gastine of Concord. Died. In this place on Sabbeth evening the last of September of congestion of the brain, James Campbell, in the 38th. year of his age. He was a native of England and had resided in this country for about 3 years. He left a widow and 3 interesting children to mourn the loss of a father and husband.

September 21, Saturday. Married on the 19th. by Rev. J. Pitkin, Mr. James Torrence to Miss Abigail Dike, all of this township.

September 28, Saturday. Married on the 19th. by Oliver Stark, Esq., Mr. Charles R. Rosecrans to Miss Mary Eve Carney, all of this county.

ITEMS FROM OHIO GAZETTE

Contributed by Willard E. Wright

1845, February 14, Saturday—Died on the 9th. inst. at his residence in Troy township, after an illness of two days, Stephen Dix, aged 16 years, 6 months and 5 days.

February 28, Saturday—Married on the 17th. inst. by Elder Moon, Mr. Hire (m) Wilcox of Marlborough township, to Mrs. Mary Dutton of Marion.

Died—At the residence of Mrs. H. B. Janes in Norwalk, Feb. 2nd. Miss Jane Nettleton, aged 22 years. She was a native of Berlin, Delaware County, Ohio.

March 7, Saturday—Married on the 22nd. ult. by Oliver Stark, Esq., Mr. Lewis Roberts, to Mrs. Elizabeth Gillett, all of this county. On the 5th. inst. by Elder B. Martin, Mr. William H. Ferguson to Miss Sarah Main of Troy township.

March 14, Saturday—Married on the 22nd. ult. by the Rev. B. Pope, Mr. John Neufang to Miss Lorinda Watson, both of this county. On the 11th. inst. by the Rev. E. Washburn, Mr. Charles Dean of Blendon, Franklin county, to Miss Minerva Pelton of Genoa.

March 21, Saturday—Married on 13th. inst. by the Rev. D. Cadwalder. Mr. John Owens to Miss Mary Hugh, all of Radnor. On the 19th. inst., by the same, Mr. John Hugh of Cambria, Pa., to Miss Lucinda Pugh of Radnor.

July 4, Saturday—Married on the 26th. ult. by the Rev. D. Cadwallader, Mr. John Gillis to Miss Mary Pool, all of Troy.

1846, Feb. 4, Thursday—Married on the 15th. ult. in Bennington township by the Rev. Benjamin Martin, Mr. Thomas Gill to Miss Mathilda A. Burroughs. On the 4th. inst. by Oliver Stark, Esq., Mr. William Carpenter and Miss Mary Drake, both of this county. On the 1st. day of January last, by the Rev. Ira Chase, Mr. George W. Gould, Esq., of Wyandot county, to Miss Olive Cornish of this county.

Died—In the vicinity of this town on the 4th. inst. of consumption, George LePert aged 36 years. At his residence in Brown township on the 3rd. inst. William Bell aged about 62 years. At his residence in Bennington township on Sunday morning, February 1, William Voorhies, Esq., in the 48th. year of his age. Mr. Voorhies was a native of Woodbridge, N. J. and emigrated to this county in 1833.

February 13, Saturday—Married on Wednesday the 11th. inst. by the Rev. E. H. Canfield, Mr. Hartland D. Gowey of Logan county, to Miss Eliza A., eldest daughter of Mr. Benjamin F. Willey of this place.

February 20, Saturday—Married on the 6th. inst. by the Rev. H. E. Pilcher, Mr. James Kent, of Layfayetter (Ia) to Miss Emerelia Kent of Delaware co., Ohio. On the 12th. inst. by the same, Mr. Samuel Poland to Miss Adalinr Poland all of Delaware county. On the 12th. inst. by Israel Lucas, Esq., Dr. Guian Morrison of Bellepoint to Miss Margaret Beckley of Concord township. On the same day, by the same,

Mr. Walter Watson of Bellepoint to Miss Jane Beckley of Concord township.

February 27, Saturday—Married on the 26th. ult. by the Rev. H. E. Filcher, Mr. William LePert to Mrs. Delilas Stayner both of Waldo, Delaware county. On the 27th. ult. by Benj. Olds Esq., Mr. George Johnson to Miss Mary Sloan, both of Marion county. At the same time by the same, Mr. Amos Fulckey to Miss Lovina Sloan, both of Marion county.

March 15, Saturday—Married on the 11th. inst. by the Rev. E. H. Canfield, Gen. John T. Arthur of Zanesville, Ohio to Miss Martha H. Parish of this place.

March 20, Saturday—Married on the 3rd. inst. by the Rev. H. Vandeman, Mr. E. Stephens of Scioto to Miss Nancy Gaston of Kingston township. In Orange on the 15th. inst. by Elder Aaron C. Grover, Mr. James B. Osborn of Delaware county, to Miss Louisa Grover of the former place.

March 27, Saturday—In Mansfield, Richland county, on the 4th. of February, by the Rev. Mr. Magell, Mr. Otis Briggs of Ridgeville, Lorain county, to Mrs. May C. Storm of Delaware county. On the 19th. ult. by Benj. Olds Esq., Mr. John M. Smallwood, to Miss Margaret Smith.

April 10, Saturday—On the 7th. inst., by the Rev. Joseph Labaree, Dr. James M. Cherry of Middletown to Miss Mary Gooding of Orange.

April 17, Saturday—Married on the 11th. inst. by O. D. Hough, Esq., Mr. J. Randolph Hubbell to Miss Mary Longwell. On Wednesday, the 8th. inst. by the Rev. H. E. Pilcher, Mr. Abraham Styre to Miss Elizabeth R. Baldwin both of Delaware County.

Died at Eden, on the 9th. inst. Mrs. Louisa, wife of Seymour Scott, aged 39 years.

April 24, Saturday—Married on the 2nd. inst. by John Flemming, Esq., Mr. Wm. Osborn, to Mrs. Susannah Keen, all of this county. On Tuesday 14th. inst. in Kingston township by Rev. John Hunt, Mr. John Knox to Miss Esther Vansickle. On the 22nd. inst. by Rev. H. Vandeman, Mr. Wm. Arnold to Miss Ann P. Owens.

May 1, Saturday—Married on the 26th. ult. by the Rev. B. Pope, Mr. Forrest Meeker to Miss Mary a Seigfried, both of this county.

May 15, Saturday—Married on the 7th. inst. by the Rev. H. Van Deman Matthias Pound and Ruana Beckley, both of Scioto. By the same on the 7th. inst. Josiah M. Sanders and Mathilda L. Dodds, both of Scioto.

May 22, Saturday—Married on Thursday, 14th. inst. by the Rev. H. E. Pilcher, Mr. John H. Mendenhall to Miss Margaret E. Reynolds.

May 29, Saturday—Married on the 26th. by J. L. H. Esq., Mr. Elijah Shade of Logan county to Mrs. Emeline Lyons, daughter of E. Potter.

Died. After a short illness on the night of the 8th. of May, on board the steamboat "South America" on the Mississippi River, William W. Watts in the 47th. year of his age, late of Columbus, Mississippi, formerly of Bedford county, Virginia. The deceased was on his way to Ohio to rejoin his family after an absence of six months in Texas and Louisiana.

June 5, Saturday—Married in the city of Philadelphia, at the Church of the Epiphany, on the 19th. ult., by the Right Rev. Alonzo Potter D. D., the Rev. E. H. Canfield, Rector of St. Peter's Church, Delaware, Ohio, to Miss Martha C., daughter of the late John Hulme (Helm) of Brookfield, Lower Merrion, Pa. On the 4th. inst. by Leonard H. Cowles, Esq., Mr. Charles Sweetser to Mrs. Ann P. Pettibone, both of this place.

June 19, Saturday—Married on the 4th. of June, by the Rey. D. Cadwalder, Mr. Thomas C. Jones of Radnor to Miss Catherine M. Case of Oxford. Lied in Berlin, on Tuesday morning, the 9th. inst. Capt. John Lew's, in his 75th. year.

June 26, Saturday—Died in this place on the 21st. inst. after a protracted illness, Mr. George Storm, aged 66 years and 7 months. The deceased was a native of Virginia. He emigrated to Ohio in 1809 and settled in Delaware, since which time he has been a resident of our town.

July 10, Saturday—Married on the 30th. ult. by O. D. Hough, Esq., G. Hipple, Esq. to Mrs. Nancy Leonard, both of Brown.

July 31, Saturday—Married on the 38th. inst. by the Rev. H. E. Pilcher, Picton D. Hillyer, Esq. to Miss Mary Sweetser, all of this place. In Berkshire by the Rev. R. S. Elder of Worthington, Mr. John S. Fuller to Miss Margaret Veraman.

Died in this town on the 20th. inst. Sarah, second daughter of Hiram Covey, aged 15 years, 10 months and 24 days.

August 7, Saturday—Died in this place on Monday, August 2, of consumption, Miss Jane Day formerly of Woolavington, England. The deceased was the last of three daughters cut down by the fatal disease followed each other to the grave in the course of three years, leaving a widowed mother truely desolate. In this place on the 3rd. inst. Lovena, daughter of Hiram Covey, aged 18 years, 1 month and 9 days.

August 14, Saturday—Died on the 16th. ult. Rufus Whitney, youngest son of Charles and Philene Boyington, aged 3 months and 16 days. On the 7th. inst. Lucia Louisa, daughter of Charles and Philena Boyington, aged 8 years, 2 months and 24 days.

November 13, Saturday—Died in Cass, Miami county, on the 7th. inst. Titus K., son of Col. B. F. Allen of this place, aged about 19 years. On the 11th. inst. at the residence of his parents, after a short illness, Charles Henry, only son of Charles C. and Isabella B. Chamberlain, aged 3-10-0.

1847, April 2, Friday—Married on the 25th. ult. by Benjamin Olds, Esq., Amos Cook, to J. Devore. At Mr. Pope's Thursday Evening, April 1st. by the Rev. Prof. McCabe, O. W. U. Mr. Richard Rhodes of Reynoldsburgh to Miss Julia Kunkleman of Delaware.

Died in the village, of quick consumption on the 31st. ult. Maria, wife of John M. Bradley, late of Rochester, N. Y. aged 26 years.

April 9, Friday—Married on the 25th. ult. by the Rev. Joseph Labaree, Mr. Erastus Hardin to Miss Eliza Ann Seigfreid.

April 30, Friday. Married in Lincoln township on the 8th. inst. by E. Riley Esq., Mr. Collins Buck to Miss Nancy Stiner. By Rev. J. Drake on Sunday the 25th. inst. Henry C. Cowgill Esq., to Miss Sarah H. daughter of R. H. Thurston of Berlin.

Died at Greenham Farm, Somerset county, England, on February

1st. Mrs. Sarah Pratt, wife of Edward Pratt. Esq. In this place, on the 29th. inst. Mr. Samuel Bill in the 79th. year of his age.

May 7, Friday—Married in Delaware township on the 6th. inst. by Sidney Moore, Esq., Mr. Charles H. Ladd to Miss Elizabeth W., daughter of Edward Potter.

May 21, Friday—In Richwood on the 10st. inst. by the Rev. O. Burgess, Rev. John Burgess of the North Ohio Conference, to Miss Sarah Gray of Salt Rock township, Marion County. In Tiffin on the 10th. inst. by the Rev. Putnam, Robert McD. Gibson of Melmore, Seneca county to Miss Laura T. Hough, recently of Genoa, Delaware county.

May 28, Friday—Married on the 24th. inst. by the Rev. H. Van Deman, Mr. Charles Wilcox of Kingston to Miss Mary Van Sickle of Berkshire.

June 4, Friday—Died at Worthington, Ohio on Monday morning, 31st. of May ult. Ruth Griswold, relict of Ezra Griswold, formerly of Simsbury. Hartford county, Connecticut, in the 86th. year of her age. The family of the deceased emigrated to Ohio in the fall of 1803 arriving at Worthington, then a dense forest on the 29th. of October of that year and occupying the first cabin ever inhabited by a white family in that town. At the residence of his father in Blendon, Franklin county, on the 22nd. of April last, of pulmonary consumption, Moses Bradford Jameson, aged about 20 years.

NEWSPAPER NOTICES, JEFFERSON COUNTY, OHIO
BLANCHE COLLINS

NOTICE OF PUBLIC SALE—All personal property of John Iams, dec'd. John Iams, Adm. (*4-25-1817).

SALE OF LAND—Farm of Hugh Patton, dec'd; adjoining Michael Castners farm. Apply Wm. Patton, Andrew Anderson, Jas. McElroy, Admrs. (*5-2-1817).

ESTATE of Thomas McCausland, late of Island Creek, Jefferson county. William C. M'Causland, Adm. (*5-2-1817).

TRACT OF LAND—Late the property of Malichi Jolly, at Smithfield. John Burgess, Lewis Cary, Admrs. (*5-2-1817).

NOTICE—Estate of John Morton of Smithfield. Benj. Morton, John Morton, Admrs. (*5-30-1817).

REAL ESTATE—Of the late Col. Richard Brown on Ohio River, Hollidays Cove, Virginia. Bez. Wells, Adm. (*5-30-1817).

ESTATE of the late Hugh McConnely, late of Warren twp. Jefferson county. Henry West, James McCune, Admrs. (*7-4-1817).

NOTICE—To those indebted to estate of Anrew Duncan. late of Wayne twp., Jefferson county. Sam'l McElroy, Sam'l McNary, Admrs. (*8-1-1817).

NEW GOODS—200 Barrels of 1st quality Kenewha Salt, also a quantity of Yellow Creek Salt. Owner will take wheat at Myers mill, Hollow Rock fork of Yellow Creek; Richard's mill (formerly Gen'l Pattersons) and John Boyd's mil, Cross Creek. (*9-17-1817).

MARRIED—Tuesday evening by Rev. James B. Finley, Mr. George Burge to Miss Sarah Salmon, both of this town. (*5-30-1817).

STEUBENVILLE-CADIZ TURNPIKE COMPANY MEETING—At the house of Henry Rickey, Wayne twp., 29th April, 1817; at Steubenville, at the house of Wright Warner, under the direction of Bez. Wells, Benj. Tappan, and Alex. Sutherland; at Stoake's Tavern-Cadiz, under the direction of John Prichard, John Hannam Wm. Tingley; at Henry Rickey's, under the direction of Thos. Elliot, Jacob Shaplor, H. Rickey: at Smithfield, at the house of James Maholm, under the direction of Mordeccai Cole and Richard Price. (*5/2/1817)

SALE—Property in the town of Charlestown. Va., on premises, by James Stevenson, 11th September, 1817. (*6/4/1817)

ESTATE—Settlement of estate of Hugh McConehy, Sec. 29, tp. 4, R. 2, (Warren twp.) Warrenton road to Mt. Pleasant. Henry West, Jas McCune, Ams. (*9/12/1817)

A LOST BROTHER—Information wanted of John S. Klein, miller and mill-wright by profession, who formerly resided in Johnstown on the Mohawk river, N. Y. His brother will remain for 30 days at the house of Mordeccai Balderston, in Colerain twp., Belmont county, near Mt. Pleasant. Any information respecting him will be thankfully received. Frederick Klein, Rhinebeck, Duchess co., N. Y. (*7/11/1817)

TURNPIKE—(Reprint from Western Intelligencer—July 3 Columbus) Six or eight thousand dollars were on Monday last, subscibed to the stock for making a turnpike from this town to Granville and Newark. (*7/11/1817)

FOR SALE—Forty-eight valuable plantations or tracts of land (100 ac, 150 ac, 250 ac.) situated on Hugh's River, Wood county, Western Virginia. 10,000 acres of first quality bottom and upland. Hugh's River winds through this tract for 42 miles. Apply Jorh Nutter, or Major James Mealy, who live on the land, or to the subscriber in the borough of Milton, Pa. A. Addis. (*7/11/1817)

CAUTION—Wife, Mary Simos has eloped. Isaac Simos, Jeff Co. (*7/11/1817)

PUBLIC VENDUE—Estate of John Caufman, dec'd, farm one mile of New Richmond, Jefferson county. Adam Caufman, Mich. Castner, Adms. (*7/18/1817)

FARM FOR SALE—325 acres of land, the farm on which the late Hugh Patton dec'd, lived, situated in Island Creek twp., adjoining Michael Castners. Apply Andrew Anderson, Jas. McElroy, Adms. (*7/18/1817)

N. Y. JUNE 20—(Reprint)—Mr. Drenning had arrived in this city from Chillicothe, Ohio, with a dove of 600 fat cattle, having disposed of part of them at Baltimore and Philadelphia. Much credit is due Mr. Drenning for his care and attention in fattening and driving his cattle. They appear as fresh as if just taken off Long Island farms. This fact will be considered very remarkable when recollected that they have been driven 1000 miles. An offer of $12 per 100 for the beef of this drove was refused; but it is supposed $12½ will purchase them. (*7/18/1817)

NEWS—Proposals for publishing in Mt. Pleasant, Ohio, a weekly paper entitled *The Philanthropist*. Charles Osborn. (*7/18/1817)

NEW POST OFFICE—Richmond, Jefferson county. Mail starts every Wednesday morning at 5 o'clock and arriving at Richmond at 8. Alan Farquhar, P. M. (*8/1/1817)

*Western Herald—Steubenville, published by James Wilson. Date following asterisk denotes date of publication.

MARRIED—On Thursday, 17th ult., by Rev. Joseph Anderson, at the house of Joseph Morrison, Mr. Solomon Bently, of St. Clairsville, to Mrs. Jane Morrison formerly of Pennsylvania. (*8/1/1817)

NEW STORE—Steubenville, Third Street—by Thomas M. Coates. (*9/5/1817)

RAN AWAY—From subscriber, living in Pgh. on Aug. 28th, a black man, named, Peter. John Kerr. (*9/5/1817)

DANCING SCHOOL—Mrs. Marshel (late from N. Y.) will commence her dancing school in Market street, on the second Monday of September. N. B. Price will be $5 per quarter and the first quarter in advance. (*9/5/1817)

TAXES—Non-resident taxes. The subscriber has this day opened office for receiving taxes of non-resident land within the five non-resident districts. Composed of counties-Jefferson, Belmont, Columbiana, Stark, and Harrison. Non-residents who do not pay before the last day of December will be charged 100% on the amount due. Alex. Colleson, Ctr. (*9/12/1817)

PUPLIC SALE AT NEW SOMERSET—Dry Goods, Hwde—property of Baltzer Culp and Adam Hubler. (*9/12/1817)

NEW JERUSALEM CHURCH—Members for their mutual edification and improvement have agreed to hold a meeting at the home of Mr. Carlow, every Friday evening, to read and explain the scriptures, and the writings of Emanuel Swedenbourg, and other authors belonging to the N. C. (?) (*9/12/1817)

NEW SALEM—James Means has opened a new store, lately occupied by Mr. John Wilson, Market St., also has a store in Steubenville (*9/12/1817)

ATTENTION—Someone took away my great coat on Monday 11th instant from Mr. Houser's dwelling near where the regiment paraded on that day. Asabel Edgington, Island Creek twp., 2½ mi. of muster grounds. (*9/12/1817)

LOST BROTHE8—John Campbell, late from Chataguay county, N. Y. wants information about his brother, Robert, who left Trenton, two years ago and now resides in this state. John Campbell intends stopping at Steubenville 6 or 8 months. Information, letter, or otherwise to be sent there. J. Campbell. (*10/17/1817)

REWARD—$10—Ran Away on Sunday, 19th ult, an apprentice to the saddling business named *John Stuart*, between 18-19 years of age, dark complexion. Whoever returns said boy shall receive reward—James Hull. (*11/7/1817)—$10—Stolen from the bar on 25th day of Dec. A *Red Morocco Pocket Book* containing $40; also notes of hand in favor of subscriber against Jacob Huffman, John Huffman; and a certificate of an acquired section of land entered by Jacob Huffman. *Daniel Huffman*, Warren twp. (-2/10/1818)—$5—Ran Away on 21st. of Apr., an apprentice to the brick-laying business named *Stephen Tarlton*, 18 years-5' 9". Ambrose Shaw, Steubenville. (*5/2/1818)—Ran Away, 19th. of August last, *Samuel O'Donnell*, an indentured apprentice, about 19 years-5' 10", brown hair. Michael Smith, N. Phila.—$5—Eloped from my custody, Dorsey Viers, he lives on or near Lake Erie, John Moore, Constable, N. Salem. (*9/5/1820)—Ran Away, *James Bark*, a lad of 12 yrs, bound to subscriber by the overseers of the poor. Benj. Tappan. (*9/17/1820)—Ran Away on 12th. inst. *James Luckens*, an indentured apprentice, about 17 years-5' 6", red hair. Abel Wiley.—Ran Away, *Amos Hoglin*, an apprentice, 13 years-about 4½'. Pere Dempster, Smithfield. (*1/23/1819)—Ran Away, 13th. April, apprentice to stone-cutting, with tools, *Isaac Watkins*, about 20 years of age. John Hart. (*5/15/1819)

* Western Herald—Steubenville, Ohio.

NEWSPAPER NOTICES, JEFFERSON CO., OHIO
BLANCHE COLLINS

DIED—At Salem, very suddenly on board his favorite 'Cleopatra's Barge' Capt. *George Croninshield*, and *Samuel C. Ward*, Esq., who accompanied Capt. C. in his late voyage. (*12/19/1817)—On 23d. ult., Wm. White, of Island Creek twp. age 48 years, son of Mr. Isaac White of said township. (*8/8/1818)—Near Boon's Settlement on the Missouri, Col. *Daniel Boon*, the first settler of Kentucky, aged 84 years. He was found with his rifle in his hand, and cocked, and the muzzle resting on a log, and his finger to the trigger. In this position it appears he died without a struggle. (*9/12/1819)—On Saturday 19th inst., Dr. George Wilson of this town.—At Pittsburgh on the 17th. inst., Brevet-Major *John Pentland*, late of the 22d Reg't. U. S. Inf. He was at the taking of York and Fort George.—Drowned, on Thursday last, a Jerseyman, named *Fearis*. He was on board descending the river. (-9/26/1819)—At Dehassopolis, in this county, on Monday, the 14th. Mrs. Margaret Biles, dau. of the late Col. Wm. Wills of Northampton county, Pa., in the 47th year of her age. (*10/10/1819)—In Pittsburgh, on Tuesday 1st inst. Comm. *Joshua Barney*, lately of Baltimore. He distinguished himself during the Revolutionary War. He was on his way to Kentucky. (*12/12/1819)—In the vicinity of Bladensburg, on Saturday morning, General *Armistead T. Mason*, of Loudoun county, Va., aged about 33 years. He was killed in a duel with muskets. He is survived by his mother, wife, and child. (Reprint from Nat'l Intelligencer—Feb. 8) also In Wellsburgh, Brooke county, on 11th. ult., Miss *Eliza Maria Doddridge*, aged 15 years. The daughter of the Rev. J. Doddridge. (*2/20/1820)—On Tuesday 4th, Mrs. *Ealse Thompson*, consort of Samuel Thompson, jun., of 'Two Ridge' near Steubenville. (*5/15/1820)—At this place on Wednesday, Mr. *Garret F. Lynch*, printer, aged about 35 years. He was an inhabitant of the county of Philadelphia and was on a journey to New Orleans.—On the 5th of August last, on his passage from New Orleans to Philadelphia, *John Hales*, son of Mr. Robert Hales, merchant of this place. He had gone to New Orleans with a cargo of Flour. In the same vessel, on the 30th of July, also *George Riser, Elijah Wise*, and John Clare. The three latter persons being of this county.—Also, *John Fickes*, late of this town, at New Orleans, the 23d of July. He left a wife and several children.—On the 24th, at New Orleans, *James Henderson*, son of Thomas Henderson, late of this town. —In Columbus, on Thursday the 19th. ult., after twenty-one days of illness of fever, *Rhoda S. Smith*, consort of George Smith, editor of the Ohio Monitor, *(formerly extensively known as Rhoda S. Mitchell, of Boston)*, aged 33 years. (*9/11/1819)—At Chillicothe, on Saturday last, after a short illness, Mr. Benjamin Hough, former auditor of this state, leaving a widow and children. (*9/25/1819)—On Thursday last, in the 46th year, after an illness of several weeks, Mrs. *Elizabeth Means*, consort of James Means, merchant of this town. *(Washington and Pittsburgh papers please reprint.)* (*3/11/1820)—At his seat in Brooke county, Va., on Wednesday night last, after a short illness, Mr. John Edginton.—At St. Clairsville, on the 3d, after a painful and lingering illness, Mrs. *Jane Bentley*, consort of Solomon Bentley, aged 29 years. She is survived by her husband and two children. (*4/15/1820)—On Thursday last, Mrs. *Millar*, wide of James Millar, Esq. of this town. (*6/10/1820)—on Saturday 15th. inst. in Pittsburgh, Mr. *Daniel K. Page*, son of Mr. Samuel Page of this town. (*6/29/1820)

SETTLEMENT OF ESTATE—The estate of *Wm. Scott*, late of Croos Creek twp., Jefferson county, dec'd. Thos. & Wm. Scott, Adms. (*5/9/-1818)—Estate of *James Ross*, dec'd. D. Stanton, Adm. (*5/9/1818)—Estate of *Rob't Maxwell*, Sen, late of Wayne twp, dec'd. Emmy Maxwell, Ex'x. (*3/30/1818)—Estate of *Thos. Latta*, late of Wayne twp., dec'd. Martha Latta & Josiah Crawford, Adms. (*same)—Estate of the late *James Anderson*, Warren twp, dec'd. Fanny Anderson or Joel Staneart, Adms.—Estate of *David Moor*, late of Harrison county, Green twp. Nathan Nichols, Adm. (*9/5/1818)—Estate of *Wm. Bailey*, Island Creek twp., dec'd. John P. McMillan & George Watson, Exrs. (*3/27/1819)

HEIRS WANTED—About the year 1774 *George M'Candlish*, farmer, in Craig, near Whitehorn, in county of Wigtown, in North Britain, and *Agness Smith*, his wife, left Scotland and went to America. The advertisers understand they resided in Pennsylvania, and that they died about the year 1790 leaving children . . . Address Mr. John Bainbridge, 45 Bread St., London; Mr. James Smith, Wigtown, Scotland; Messers Joshua & Thos. Gilpin, Philadelphia. (*5/2/1818)—Information about William, James and John Abraham who emigrated to America about 1772. Apply to James Conningham, Baltimore. (*1/23/1819)

FOR SALE—100 acres lying on the road between Cadiz *(32 mi)* and Cambridge *(10 mi)*, for terms apply, George Wine, living in *New Winchester*, near the premises. Thomas Smith (*2/20/1919)—A lot opposite Todd's Tavern—*Sign of the Cross Keys*, Steubenville. Edw. Todd. (*5/9/1820)—Public Sale, All the real estate of the late *James Ayres*, dec'd Steubenville. N. Hutchinson, Adm.—In *Philipsburg*, a second sale of lots, Satur. 10th, Oct. P. Doddridge, prop. (*9/19/1818)—Public Auction, Wellsburgh, Va. (S. E. Quar. Sec. No. 20, twp. 11, Range 7,—160 ac.) Hugh Porter. (*7/17/1819)

FOR RENT—The tavern stand—*Sign of The Travellers Rest*, on Cadiz, Canton, and New Salem road near Steubenville, with 5½ acres of land. Apply Elizabeth Dundass on the premises.—For one or two years—'that 2-story house on 4th Street', next (2-doors south of Norton's Tavern, *The Sign of The Bear*) Apply Phillip Reilly. (*2/24/1818)

NEWS—FREE SCHOOL—In Smithfield at a meeting in the school house (5/5), it was agreed to open a free school under the direction of James

Carr, Benjamin W. Ladd, Abel Cary, Wm. Leslie, Robert Ritchie, jun, as Trustees. (*5/15/1818)—The annual meeting of the *Steubenville Library Company* was held at the home of Isaac Jenkinson. David Moodey, Sec'y. (*11/28/1818)—Caleb Atwater, Esq., Circleville, Ohio, has been elected an honorary member of the American Antiquarian Society of Massachusetts, and likewise a corresponding member of the Lyceum of Natural History of New York. (*8/8/1818)—Canton, Ohio: Col. Abraham Shane has been elected Brig. General, of the 3d Brigade, 6th Div. Ohio Militia. (*9/17/1818)

NOTICE—James Fowler wishes his friends to know his property is for sale by the sheriff not because of his own debt, but for Henry Fisher's for whom he became a surety through persuasion. (*11/28/1818)

CAUTION—My wife Nancy, has left me without just cause—*Moses Spicer* (*9/5/1818)—My wife Margaret, has left me without just cause. She has taken my children—if anyone will restore them to me they shall receive support, but none in their absence. David Kearns Island Creek twp. (*9/17/1818)—My wife Barbary, has eloped without just cause. Christian Henry Coler, Buffalo twp. (*2/20/1819)—My wife Rebecca Runyon and myself having separated, I will not be accountable for any debts. Joseph Runyon, Warren twp. (*2/27/1819)

MARRIED—In Steubenville, on Thursday 12th. ult., by the Rev. George Buchanan, Mr. *Thomas Lee* of Cadiz, to Miss *Nancy Wilson* of Steubenville, (*3/3/1818)—On Thursday 9th. unst., by the Rev. Archibald Hawkins, Mr. *Thomas E. Minor*, to Miss *Fanny Coil*, all of Jefferson count.—On Monday 20th. inst., by the Rev. John P. Finley, Mr. *James M'Kean* of Wheeling, aged 22 years, to Mrs. *Besser* of this place, aged 42 years. (*4/25/1818)—On Thursday the 21st. ult., by Moses Ross, Esq, Mr. *David Rogers*, to Miss *Jane Palmer*, both of Cross Creek twp. (*6/6/1818)—On Thursday, 2d. inst., by the Rev. Archibald Hawkins, Mr. *James Foy*, to the amiable Miss *Sarah Lendiff*, all of this county. (*7/4/1818)—On 4th. inst., by the Rev. George Buchanan, Mr. *John DeHuff*, to the amiable Miss *Amy Hines*, both of this town. (*8/8/1818)—On 27th. ult., by the Rev. John B. Finley, Mr. *Branson Gebbens*, to Miss *Jane Oddert*, both of this town. (*9/5/1818)—On Thursday eve last by the Rev. Obediah Jennings, Dr. *John McDowell*, jun. to Miss *Catharine W. Wells*, dau. of Beliziel Wells, Esq., all of this place. (*10/10/1818)—By the Rev. John B. Finley, on 18th. inst., Mr. *Samuel Monroe*, to Miss *Rachel Marple*; at the same time and place, Mr. *Josiah Harper*, to Miss *Elizabeth Marple*, sister of the former, all of this place. (*3/27/1819)—On Thursday eve last, by the Rev. George Buchanan, Mr. *John Kells*, to Miss *Sarah Parks*, both of this town. (*5/5/1819)—On Thursday evening last, by the Rev. Cornelius Springer, Dr. *P. S. Mason* to Miss *Rachel Wilson*, dau. of the late Dr. Wilson of this place. (*3/11/1820)—On Thursday last, by the Rev. Clement Vallandingham, Mr. *DeLorma Brooks*, to the amiable and accomplished Miss *Sila Harbaugh*, dau. of Wm. Harbaugh, Esq., all of this place. (*4/22/1820)—On Thursday eve last, by the Rev. Mr. Snodgrass, Mr. *James Hamilton*, merchant, to the amiable Miss *Esther Hunter*, dau. of Samuel Hunter, all of this town. (*5/10/1820)—At Chillicothe, on Thursday eve, 8th. inst., by the Rev. Mr. ———, the Rev. Cornelius Springer, late of Steubenville, to Miss McDowell of the former place. (-7/29/1820)—On Thursday eve, 24th. ult., by the Rev. Archibald Hawkins, Mr. *William Woods*, to Miss *Elizabeth Armstrong*, both of this town. (*9/2/1820)—At New Philadelphia on Thursday last 24th. inst., by A. Shane, Esq., Mr. *Dennis Sanders*, late of Cadiz, to Miss *Julianna Doddridge Murray*, day. of Capt. Nichlas Murray of Steubenville. (*7/8/1819)

* Western Herald-Steubenville, Ohio. Date following asterisk denotes date of publication

EXCERPTS FROM THE EAGLE

Established 1817, by John Herman, Printer and Publisher, Lancaster, Fairfield County, Ohio

Blanche Collins

DEATHS

1817—Departed this life Tuesday last, Miss *Alice Vanpelt*, dau. of Wm. Vanpelt of this town, aged 18 y. (*Feb. 6). Drowned on the Mississippi R., Major *Horace Stark*, U. S. A., and four others in crossing the river in a skiff near St. Louis. (*Apr. 10). *Henry Wilson*, son of Nathan Wilson, jr., died on Friday last from the falling of a tree. (*May 22). Suicide—*Jonathan Clark*, late proprietor, found in his cabin nine miles from here—Zanesville. (*Aug. 7).

1818—Mr. *Russel E. Post*, on 16th inst., a native of the state of Vermont, but for many years a resident of this state. (Jan. 29). On Sunday last. 10th inst. Mr. *Archibald Carnahan*, long a resident of Lancaster, drowned in attempting to cross the mill race of Mr. G. Ring adjoining this town. (*May 14). In Hocking township, Mr. *George Mauker*, in his 97th y. (*May 14). On Thursday last, 21st inst., after a short illness, Gen. *Jonathan Lynch*, long a resident of Lancaster, 46 yrs. of age. He leaves a widow and a large family. (*May 23). Mrs. *Jane Cox*, of near Lancaster, Friday, 29th ult., the widow of the late James Cox, deceased in the 53d yr. of her age. (*June 4). In the vicinity of Pilot Mountain, Surry co., Md., on the 30th ult., Mrs. *Priscilla Charmichael*, aged 113 yrs. She had nineteen children. Her eldest daughter has attained the great age of 93 yrs. One of her sons was in the French and Indian Wars, and was killed at the defeat of Braddock. (*June 4).

1819—Near Thornville, on the 27th ult., Mrs. *Mary Henthorn*, in the 76th year of her age. (*Sept. 23). Near Newark, on Sunday, after a few days illness, Miss *Leah Wells*, in the 21st year of her age. (*Sept. 23). On the 11th ult., at his residence near Somerset, *Peter Bugh*, Sr., Esq.; one of the commissioners of Perry co. (*Oct. 14).

1821—Mrs. *Margaret Cissna*, on Monday last, widow of the late Thomas C. Cissna of this city. (*Jan. 11). On Thursday last, 19th inst., *Abraham Miller*, of Rushcreek twp.; On Tuesday last, Miss *Lydia M'Ginnis*, aged 18 yrs., of Rushcreek twp. (*Apr. 26).

1822—At Somerset, on Thursday last, after a short illness, Mrs. *Anna Maria Stocker*, in the 73d yr. of her age; On Friday, 12th inst., at his residence in Hocking twp., Mr. *Samuel Thompson*, in the 67th yr. of his age. He left a widow and several children. (*July 18). In this township on Sunday, 21st ult., Mrs. *Hannah Stewart*, in the 69th yr. of her age, after an illness of 10 days. She left a consort and five children. (*Oct. 2). *Elizabeth Tallman*, dau. of Wm. Tallman of Pickaway county, died on Sept. 22; On Thursday last. Mrs. *Rachel Rush*, Hocking twp.; On Monday last, in Clearcreek twp., Mr. *Isaac Grover*, in the 59th yr.; On Wednesday last, Mr. *Ludwig Wolfley*.- One of the early settlers and an emigrant from Dauphin county, Pa. (*Oct. 3).

Caution—From trusting my wife Sallie Downey, *alias* Sally Lanfare, as she has absented herself from my bed and board without just cause.—*Henry Downey*. (*Mar. 5, 1817).

Divorce—Mary Springer *vs.* Joseph Springer, Absence 5 yrs. Thos. Ewing, Atty. (*Sept. 30, 1819).

*Date following asterisk denotes date of publication.

"The altar we with rapture greet; the chain is light, the bondage sweet."

MARRIED

1817—On Thursday last, in Richland twp. by David Swayzee, Esq., *David Swayzee*, jr. to Miss *Catharine Walters* of Rockingham co., Va.;—On Tuesday last, 28th ult., by Rev. John Wright, *Isaac Wilson* to *Jane Paden;*—On Tuesday, 14th ult., by Andrew Wickizer, Esq., the Rev. Mr. *Kemp* of Bloom twp., aged 70 y, to Mrs. *Barbara Wildermuth*, wid of the late Wm. Wildermuth of Greenfield twp., aged 76 y. (*Feb. 6). Last eve by Adam Weaver, Esq., *Jacob L. Eckert* of Bern twp. to Mrs. *Rebecca Johnston* of this town. (*Feb. 13). On Tuesday last, by Rev. Steck, *Frederick Shafer* of this town to Miss *Mary Boos* of Hocking twp.;—On Monday, 24th inst., by John Vanmetre, Esq., *Andrew Pierce*, son of Jas. Pierce, Esq., to Miss *Maria Carpenter*, dau. of David Carpenter, both of Bern twp.;—On Tuesday last, by Rev. Ellis, *Wm. Rigby* to Mrs. *Airy Williamson*, both of Hocking twp. (*Feb. 27). On Sunday, 2d inst., by Jacob Leef, Esq., *Samuel Coffman* to Miss *Sarah Bartmess*, both of Liberty twp.;—Same day, by Wm. Trimble, Esq., Major *John Whisler* of U. S. A., Commandant at Ft. Wayne, to Mrs. *Elizabeth James*, wid. of the late Wm. James, Esq., of Richland twp. (*Mar. 6). On Thursday, 10th inst., by Jas. Wimp, Esq., *Clement Green* to Miss *Maria Farmer*, both of Greenfield twp. (*July 17). At Newark on 25th inst., by Rev. Thos. B. Baird, *Edwin W. Coit* to Miss *Sally Woodruff*. (*Aug. 28). On Thursday, 28th Aug. by John Tallman, Esq., *Wm. Russel* to Miss *Elizabeth M'Arthur*, both of Violet twp.;—At Zanesville, on Sunday last, by Rev. David Young, *Daniel Limerick*, of this place, to Miss *Susanna Winters* of Zanesville;—At the same place, same day, by Rev. Charles Waddle, *Wm. Goff* to Miss *Ann Parker*, both of Zanesville. (*Sept. 11). On Thursday, 4th inst., by Jas. Wimp, *Nathan Plummer* to Miss *Elizabeth Crawford* of Greenfield twp.;—On Thursday, 11th inst., by the same, *Abraham Harris* to Miss *Sally Needles* of Bloom twp. (*Sept. 18).

1818—On Thursday last, by Michael Nigh, Esq., *Wm. Middlesworth* to Miss *Mary Leathers*, both of Fairfield co. (*Jan. 29). On Thursday, 9th inst., by Adam Weaver, Esq., *George Harrison* to Miss *Mary Hubble*, all of this town. (*Apr. 16). On Thursday, 23d inst., by Rev. John Wright, *Samuel Lefever*, to Miss *Rebecca R. Kelsey*, all of this county. (*Apr. 30). On Thursday, 30th April, by Michael Nigh, Esq., *Abraham Stall* to Miss *Agnis Young*, both of Fairfield co.;—On Thursday last, by Rev. John Wright, *John Burton* to Miss *Catharine Stewart*, both of Hocking twp.;—On the same day, by same, *Israel Carpenter* to Miss *Susan K. Hess*. (*May 7). On Sunday last, 10th inst., by Rev. G. Weise, *Wm. Shaug*, son of Dr. Shaug of this town, to Miss *Hannah Sherwood* of Perry co. (*May 4).

On Sunday eve last, by Jacob Ream, Esq., *Wm. Sturgeon* to Miss *Peggy Wolfley*, dau. of Lodowick Wolfley, all of this county. (*May 21). On Tuesday, 26th inst., by Rev. G. Weise, *George East* to Miss *Elizabeth Sackreiter*, both of Pickaway co. (*May 23). On Tuesday last, by Jacob D. Dieterick, Esq., *Samuel Bussard* to Miss *Margaret Smart*, both of this county;—At Carlisle, Pa., on Tuesday last, 19th ult., by Rev. Samuel Davis, the Rev. *John Swartzwalder* of that borough to Miss *Mary Marshall*, formerly of Maryland. (*June 13). On 16th ult., by John Hampson, Esq., *Jacob Giger* to Miss *Molly Howdeshall*, all of Fairfield co. (*June 20). On Thursday last, by Rev. Steck, *Andrew Alexander* to Miss *Polly Sterling*, all of Hocking twp.;—On 16th inst., by Wm. Irvin, Esq., *Robert Crawford* to Miss *Sarah Morehead*, both of Walnut twp. (*June 27).

1819—On Sunday, 4th inst., by Rev. Steck, *Charles Stevens* to Miss *Catharine Sterling*, all of Fairfield co.;—On Tuesday last, by same, *John Dunkel* to Miss *Catharine Morehart*, both of Bloom twp.;—On Tuesday, 24th ult., by Rev. A. Henkel, *David Martin*, Esq., to Miss *Catharine Bugh*, all of Perry co.;—On Sunday, 27th ult., by Roswell Mills, Esq., *John Warner* to Miss *Hetta Gordon*, all of Perry co.;—On Thursday, 1st inst., by same, *Zebulon Thennard* to Miss *Melinda Collier*, all of Perry co.;—On Monday, 5th inst., by Samuel Taylor, Esq., *Thomas Morton* to Miss *Elizabeth Pickering*, both of Jacksonville. (*July 8). On Sunday last, by Rev. Lewis Seitz, *John Bietz* to Miss *Lydia Seitz;*—On the same day, by same, *Noah Seitz* to Miss *Mary Stinekerner*, all of

66

Bern twp.;—On Thursday, 12*th* inst., by Roswell Mills, Esq., *Moses Riley* to Miss *Susannah Hall*, all of Perry co. (*Aug. 19). On 26*th* ult., Warton twp., Fayette co., Pa., by Rev. W. Brownfield, *Wm. Cox* of this place to Miss *Maria Briant*, dau. of Jas. Briant of the former place. (*Sept. 9). On 9*th* inst. by Rev. John M'Mahon, *Charles Brown* to Miss *Nancy Holmes* of Walnut twp. (*Sept. 16). On 24*th* Aug., by Rev. Gerhart, the Rev. *George Wise* of this place to Miss *Catharine Schuman* of Millerstown, Mifflin co., Pa.;—At Alexandria (D. C.) on Monday, 16*th* ult., by Rev. Joshua Wells, the Rev. *Christopher Frye*, Presiding Elder in the M. E. Ch., to Mrs. *Margaret Moss* of that place. (*Sept. 23).

1820—On Thursday eve last, by Rev. John Wright, *John Wright* of Green-castle, to Miss *Elizabeth Cox;*—At Zanesville, 13*th* inst., by Rev. Intripid Morse, Rev. *Lewis Shide* to Miss *Theresa Carhart*, all of this county. (*Dec. 21).

1822—On Tuesday last, by Rev. Horder, *Abraham Pitcher* of Hocking co., to Miss *Elizabeth Castle* of Perry co. (*July 18). On Sunday, 21*st* inst., by Wm. Ingman, Esq., *Henry Creaglow* to Mrs. *Rachel Merchant*, both of this county;—Last evening, by Rev. Carper, *Wm. Richards* to Miss *Lydia Arnold*, dau. of Daniel Arnold, all of this place. (*July 25). On Thursday, 7*th* inst., by Rev. Steck, *George Diffenbaugh* to Miss *Catharine Kern*, both of this county; On the same day, by Rev. J. Young, *John M'Elroy* to Miss *Axy Collins*, dau. of Jas. Collins, all of Bern twp.;—On Thursday last, by Rev. Jesse Spurgeon, *George Wilson* to Miss *Elizabeth Kemp*, all of this town;—Same day, by Rev. M. Steck, *Daniel Oburn* to Miss *Sarah Renshe*, both of this county;—Same day, by same, *Joshua Clark* to Miss *Mary Ann Baker* of this town;—Same day, by same, *Jesse Morrison* of this county, to Miss *Rebecca Combs* of Perry co.;—On Tuesday last, by Rev. G. Wise, *Jacob Bope* to Miss *Elizabeth Bury* of Pleasant twp. (*Nov. 21).

EXCERPTS FROM THE EAGLE

Established 1817, by John Herman, Printer and Publisher, Lancaster, Fairfield County, Ohio

Blanche Collins

DEATHS

1822—Died on Friday the 4th inst., of an illness of ten days, Mrs. *Ann Orr*, aged 78 yrs. She emigrated from Ireland to America in 1811, and resided in Frederick co., Md., (upwards of twenty years from that time, until about three months before her death when she removed to Ohio.) She was the mother of eleven children; three sons and one daughter still in Ireland; three sons and two daughters in America. On the following day interment took place at the family burying ground of Mr. Arnold, near this place, the Rev. Henry Matthews, of the M. E. Church officiating at the service. (*Oct. 17).

1823—Near Royalton on Thursday last, Mr. *Abraham Hagerman* in the 50th year of his age; At Lancaster, Pa., Mr. *Wm. Dickson*, editor of the Lancaster Intelligencer. (*Jan. 30). On Friday last, 31st ult. *Elijah Meason*, son of Isaac Meason, Esq., Greenfield twp.,' in the 19th year of his age. On Monday last, *Mary Cheney*, consort of John Cheney, Esq., of Bloom twp. (*Feb. 6). On the 4th inst., Mrs. *Torrence* of this town after a long illness. On Thursday last in Bern twp., after an illiess of eight years, Mrs. *Maria Carpenter*, widow of the late Emanuel Carpenter, Sr., in the 77th year of her age. (*Apr. 17).

1825—In this town on Saturday last, *Solomon Ruse*, in the 20th year of his age. On the 17th day of October last, at the residence of Mr. Samuel M. Hitt, Washington co., Md., the Rev. *Daniel Hitt*, in the 58th year of his age, and the 35th year of his (interent) ministery in the M. E. Church. (*Nov. 10).

1831—In Pleasant twp., on Saturday last the 22d ult., *Phillip Feeman, son* of Benjamin and Elizabeth Feeman, aged 3 yrs. In the same township same day, *Nicholas Rumser*, 82 yrs. On Sunday last in this town a son of Mr. *John Yeager*, aged 2 yrs. On the same day, *George*, son of George *Myers* of this town, aged 5 weeks. In Violet twp., near Waterloo, on Monday last, Mr. *Wm. Carty*, aged 60 yrs. (*Oct. 19). In Liberty twp., on Sunday 30th ult. Mr. *John Ulrich Bricker*, aged 56 yrs. (*Nov. 12). In Amanda twp., on Monday 14th inst. Mr. *John Hanaway*, aged 76 yrs. In Walnut twp., on Sunday last, Mr *McCanley*. In Pleasant twp... on Friday last, Mr. *Phillip Fetters*, a respected citizen, aged about 48 yrs. In this township on Tuesday last Mr. *John Green*, Sr., aged 66 yrs. and for the last 34 years a resident of this county. In this town on Tuesday last, at the residence of his uncle, the Hon. Thos. Ewing, after several weeks illness, Mr. *Charles Clarke*, in the 20th year of his age. In this township, Wednesday last, Mr. *John Strayer*, aged 68 yrs. (*Nov. 26). On Sunday last, in this town, *Martha Ann*, infant daughter of *Daniel D*. and Eliza Richman, aged 20 mo. (Dec. 3). On Thursday last, *Wm. Disney*, Esq., of the city of Cincinnati, arrived at the house of Mr.Nathaniel Wilson, near this place, on his way home, taking with him the remains of his wife, *Julia Disney*, who departed this life on 20th inst. at Middletown, Ohio. (*Dec. 24). In Madison twp., Monday 5th inst. Mr. *Wm. Dutton* aged 46 yrs. In Amanda twp., on Friday 8th inst. Mr. *Wm. Ashbrook*, aged about 44 yrs. In this town, on Monday last, 12th, inst| Mr. *Albert Stevens*, grocer, aged 62 yrs. In Bloom twp. Friday, Mrs. *Elizabeth Spurgeon*, wife of Rev. Elijah Spurgeon, after a few days illness, aged 51 yrs. In Violet twp., near Waterloo, on Friday last, after a few days illness, *Valentine Donaldon*, Esq., aged 45 yrs. In this town, on Friday last, fter a few hours illness, *James Weakley*, son of James and Eleanor Weakley. In Liberty twp. on Wednesday, Mr. *Casper Shaffner*, papermaker, aged 73 yrs. In Walnut twp., on Sunday last, Mr. *Henry Watson*, aged 50 yrs. In this town, on Saturday last, Mr. *John Wachter*, aged about 44 yrs. In Pickaway county, on Saturday 24th inst. Col. *Francis S. Muhlenberg*, aged 37 yrs., lately a member of U. S. Congress. Near this town, on Tuesday last, Miss *Catharine Vantrice*, aged 22 yrs. (*Dec. 31).

MARRIED

1823—On Thursday last, by Rev. Wm. Stevens, *James Walters* to Miss *Mary Sunderland*, both of this county. (*Jan. 30). On Sunday the 26th ult. by John A. Collins, Esq., *John Brannon* to Miss *Elizabeth Gordon*, all of Bern twp. On the 16th ult. in Montgomery co., by Rev. Peter Dechant, the Rev. *Henry Heinecke* to Miss *Catharine Hetzel*, of said county. On Thursday last, by Rev. John Wright, *Daniel Martin* to Miss *Anna Hood*, both of this county. Same day, by same, *Miles H. Gibbs*, of Meigs co., to Miss *Elvira Allen* of Royalton. (Feb. 6). On the 3d inst. by Rev. M. J. Steck, *Jacob Miller* of Perry co., to Miss *Sarah Miller*, of Pleasant twp. On Sunday 6th inst. by same, Capt. *James White*, of this town, to Miss *Rebecca M'Clelland*, of Perry co. On Tuesday 8th inst. by Rev. George Wise, *John Fertig* to Miss *Barbara Ream*, daughter of Sampson Ream, Bern twp. On Thursday last, by George Nigh, Esq., *Henry Dile* to Miss *Amelia Rumsey*, both of this county. On Sunday last, by same, the Rev. *David H. Young* to the amiable Miss *Elizabeth Myers*, both of Cleercreek twp. On Sunday last, by Rev. Wm. Stevens, *Jacob Binkley*, of this town, to Miss *Mahalah Booker*, late of Frederich co., Va. (*Apr. 17).

1825—In this town on Thursday last, by the Rev. M. J. Steck, *John Friend* to Miss *Mary Beard*, both of Columbus. On Thursday last, by Alex. Stirrat, Esq., *Joseph Johnson* to Miss *Mary Wilson*, both of this county. (*Nov. 10).

1828—On Wednesday eve the 13th inst. by Rev. Mr. Steck, *Richard Hooker*, jun., son of Capt. Hooker, late of this county, to Miss *Susan Graybill*, daughter of Samuel Graybill, of Greenfield twp. On Sunday 10th inst. by Rev. Mr. Wise, *Charles Wade*, of Pleasant twp., to Miss *Elizabeth Funk*, of Greenfield twp. On Tuesday last, by same, *John Conrad Miller* to Miss *Rebecca Rempour*, both of this county. On Thursday last, by same, *John Besore* to Miss *Elizabeth Strole*, both of Rushcreek twp. (*Feb. 23).

1829—On Thursday last by Rev. John Wright, *Thomas Watson* to Miss *Sarah McCollom*, both of this county. On Thursday 6th inst. by Isaac Schleich, Esq., *John Diver* (formerly of this place) to the amiable and accomplished Miss *Isabella Smith*, of Pickaway co. (*Aug. 22).

1831—On Thursday last, by Rev. J. Wagenhals, *David Good* to Miss *Susanna Beery*, all of Rushcreek twp. On 14th ult. by Samuel Wiser, Esq., *Emanuel Carpenter* to Miss *Mary Spears*, both of Greenfield twp. On Thursday last, by the Rev. Mr. Wright, *George M'Candless* to Miss *Margaret Ashbaugh*, both of Rushcreek twp. (*Oct. 19). At Somerset on Thursday the 3d inst. by the Rev. Charles Henkel, *Wm. Moeller*, one of the proprietors of the Western Post, to Miss *Eliza Ream*, both of that place. (*Nov. 12). On the 7th inst. by Rev. Mr. Weis, *Jonathan Fenstermacher* to Miss *Esther Evert*, all of this county. On the same day, by same, *Daniel Christ* to Miss *Catharine Smith*, all of this county. On Sunday last, by same, *Samuel Miller*, of Bern twp., to Miss *Margaret Lyons*, of Liberty twp. On Tuesday last, by same, *John Miller* to Miss *Barbara Poff*, all of Liberty twp. On Thursday last, by Rev. J. Wagenhals, *John Williams* to Miss *Isabella Williams*, all of Greenfield twp. In this town on Tuesday last, by Rev. Mr. Wright,

Adam Pyl, of Mt. Vernon, to Miss *Mary Keeler,* of this place. On Tuesday 8*th* inst. by Rev. C. McLean, the Rev. *Homer J. Clarke,* Professor of Languages in Madison College, Union Town, Pa., to Miss *Agnes Wilson* daughter of Thomas Wilson, dec'd., of Morgantown, Va. (*Nov. 26). At Philadelphia (Pa.) on Thursday 24*th* ult. by Rev. Mr. Barnes, *Andrew Jackson,* jun., son of the President of the U. S., to Miss *Sarah Yorke,* daughter of Peter Yorke, Esq., of that city. On Sunday last, in this town, by Rev. Henry Matthews, *Charles Bryant,* of Licking co., to Miss *Margaret Pugh,* daughter of Jesse Pugh, Esq., of this county. (*Dec. 3). On Monday last, by Rev. J. Wagenhals, *Jacob Fetther* to Miss *Mary Magdalena Walk,* of this place. On Tuesday last, by same, *Henry Marker* to Miss *Elenor Dener,* of this place. On Thursday last, at Col. Noble's, by Rev. Z. Connell, *John Wilson* to Miss *Harriet Ogdon.* On Tuesday last, by Rev. John Wright, *Christian Rudolph* to Miss *Clarinda See,* of Bern twp. (*Dec. 17). On Monday last, by Jacob Embich, Esq., *Jacob Goss* to Miss *Margaret Zopt,* all of this county. By the same on Thursday last, *Hugh Frill* to Miss *Sarah Trovinger,* both of Walnut twp. On Thursday the 15*th* inst. by Rev. J. Wagenhals, *Adam Crosby* to Miss *Lydia Coons,* all of Franklin co. (*Dec. 24). On 15*th* inst. by Rev. Geo. Wise, *George Westenberger* to Miss *Elizabeth Ream,* both of Bern twp. On 22*d* inst. by same, *Jacob Tarflinger,* of Seneca co., to Miss *Elizabeth Apt,* of Pleasant twp. On Thursday last, by Jacob Embich. Esq., *Joseph Westenberger,* of Pickaway co., to Mrs. *Susanna Brown,* of Hocking twp. Near Mansfield, on Thursday 22*d* inst. *George B. Arnold,* merchant, to Miss *Eliza Bartley,* daughter of Moredecai Bartley, Esq., late a Member of Congress. (*Dec.. 31).

CAUTION—To persons harbouring my wife, Betsey, as she has left without just cause or provocation . . . being exempt of her debts, unless compelled by law. *Elijah W. Lewis.* (*July 7, 1832).

The annual commencement of the Cincinnati College took place on 25th day of Septmber when seven young men received the degree of Bachelor of Arts. The Master of Arts degree was conferred on the Hon. John McLean, Rev. Nathan Bange, Rev. John P. Findley; and the degree of Doctor of Philosophy was conferred on Rev. Joshua L. Wilson of Cincinnati, Ohio. (from *The Ohio Eagle*—Lancaster, O. Oct. 17, 1822) *Date following asterisk donates date of publication.

FROM THE LANCASTER GAZETTE

LANCASTER, OHIO 1830-1833

August 10, 1830. Married—On Tuesday last, by the Rev. John Wagenhals, Mr. Daniel Holder to Miss Molly Wagner. All of Fairfield County.

May 17. 1831. On Sunday last, by the Rev. Geo. Wise, Mr David Wildermuth to Miss Anna Newkirk. All of this county.

May 31, 1831. For sale. 60 acres of land in Sept. 12, Township 12 and Range 20, of the County of Fairfield and possessed by Jacob Leathers deceased. Administrators: Andrew Pearse and Samuel Leathers.

November 8, 1831. Married—On Tuesday, the first inst. by Jason Frizzle Jr., Esq., Mr. John Wagner to Miss Sarah Hines, all of Richland Township. Died in Pleasant Township on Saturday the 22nd. ultimo, Philip, son of Benjamin and Elizabeth Freeman, age 3 years.

November 26, 1831. Married—Daniel Crist and Catharine Arine Smith, both of this county.

February 14, 1832. On Tuesday, married, by Rev. John Wagenhals, Jacob Slough of this county to Miss Mary Hall of Pickaway County.

June 30, 1831. Simon Crist and Joseph Crist, traders etc. under style of Simon Crist & Co. vs Elisha Barrett, atachment for the sum of $300.00.

May 10, 1832. Married—On Tuesday eve last by Rev. J. Wagenhals, Mr. John Bacher to Miss Magdalina Simpher of Franklin County.

October 25, 1832. Married—By Rev. J. Wagenhals Mr. John Shaeffer to Miss Mary Stukey of this county.

Novembeer 25, 1832. Married—On Sunday, Mr. Daniel Fisher to Miss Mary Wagner of Greenfield Township.

September 20, 1833. Married—By the Rev. J. Wagenhals on Sunday eve the first, Mr. Jesse Glick of Pickaway County to Miss Polly Glick of Bloom Township.

November 14, 1832. Married—On Thursday last by the Rev. J. Wagenhals, Mr. Jacob Weist to Miss Hannah Wildermuth, both of Greenfield Township.

December 13, 1832. Married—By the Rev. George Weis, Mr. Israel Rothon to Catherine Weist of Greenfield Township.

December 10, 1833. Married—At Lancaster, Pa. on the 8th. inst. by the Rev. S. Bowman, Mr. Carpenter McCleery, printer, formerly of this place, to Miss Catherine S. Danner of that city.

October 10, 1833. On Thursday last by the Rev. J. Wagenhals, Francis Sitterley to Miss Susanna Backer, of Franklin County.

October 17, 1833. On Thursday the 17th. by Rev. J. Wagenhals, Mr. William Creagmire to Catherine Neibling, both of this place.

On Sunday, January 26, 1834, by the Rev. Geo. Weis, Mr. Jacob Bolenbush to Miss Susanna Crist, both of Bloom Township.

January 28, 1834. By the Rev. Geo. Weis, Mr. John Danner to Miss Caroline Shaeffer, both of Lancaster, Ohio.

February 16, 1834. By Rev. J. Wagenhals, Mr. Stephen Cole to Miss Anna Glick, of Bloom Township.

February 9, 1834. By John Graybill, Esquire, Mr. Robert Smith to Miss Christina Bowman.

February 28, 1834. By Rev. Geo. Weis ,Mr. Henry Bradley to Miss Mary Glick of Amanda Township.

March 20, 1834. Married—By Geo. Weis, Mr. Jacob Wagner to Miss Susannah Swander, of Bloom Township.

March 27, 1834. Married—By Rev. J. Wagenhals, Mr. Jacob Wagner to Miss Susanna Macklin, of Pleasant Township.

March 31, 1834. Drounded in Madison Township, Mr Ezra Shaeffer, son of Abram Shaeffer.

October 23, 1834. Married—By Rev. J. Wagenhals, Mr. Daniel Wildermuth to Miss Lydia Weist, of Greenfield Township.

November 4, 1834. Married—By Rev. Mr. Snow, Mr. Lorenzo Dow Welsh to Miss Elizabeth Showman of Greenfield Township.

February 21, 1839. By Rev. Geo. Weis, Mr. Daniel Alspach to Miss Elizabeth Martin, both of Bloom Township.

October 16, 1834. Estate of George Neff. Abraham Neff, administrator.

July 7, 1836. Estate of Jacob Meeker, Aaron & Elisha Meeker, Administrators.

December 14, 1837. Great Bargins, Dry goods, Groceries, Hardware, Queensware, Drugs and Medicines. John Garaghty, assignee in trust for the creditors of J. & W. Wildermuth.

July 25, 1832. By Rev. J. Wagenhals, Mr. Benjamin Weist to Miss

Elizabeth Bowser of Pleasant Township.

November 25, 1879. Died—John Feemen.

October 11, 1832. Died in this town on Wednesday last George C., son of Jesse D. and Sarah E. Hunter, aged 6 months and 14 days.

February 26, 1832. Married by J. Crook, Esq., Major Othow Crawfis to Miss Sarah Wagner, both of Bern Township.

July 9, 1832. Died at his former residence in Earl Township, Lancaster County, Pa. John McCleary, in his 86th. year.

April 5, 1838. Married by the Rev. Lewis Madden, Mr. Wesley McArthur of Pickerington to Miss Susanna Westerberger of Violet Township.

October 23, 1826. Died—James McCleery, aged 69 years, at his residence in Greenfield Township, 3 miles north of Lancaster, Ohio, on the old Columbus road. He was a native of Lancaster Co., Pa.

March 26, 1826. Died, after a lingering illness, in her 17th. year, Esther Wagner, daughter of Adam Wagner of Greenfield Township.

May 8, 1827. Married on Sunday, May 6th, 1827 by the Rev. J. M. Steck Mr. Henry Alspach of Bloom Township to Miss Maria Wildermuth of Greenfield Township.

March 20, 1827. Married on Thursday last, by Rev. G. Weis, Mr. Valentine Hines to Miss Elizbaeth Wagner, both of Bern Township.

May 13, 1827. Married by Rev. J. M. Steck, Mr. John Neff to Miss Catherine Neff, both of Greenfield Township.

November 6, 1827. Married on Thursday last, by Rev. John Wright, Mr. Abram Hedges to Miss Alice McCleery, all of this county.

November 6, 1827. Married on Thursday last, by Rev. Geo. Weis, Mr. Isaac Wolf to Miss Rachel Shaeffer, both of Madison Township.

February 28, 1839. Married on Thursday last by Rev. J. Wagenhals, Mr. Jacob Shaeffer and Miss Deborah Welsheimer, of this city.

March 15, 1839. Please announce the name of Henry Rutter as a candidate for constable, at the ensuing spring election.

January 20, 1832. Died on Tuesday in Pleasant Township, Sarah Barbara, wife of Nicholas Radebaugh, Sr. at the advanced age of 82.

May 8, 1834. Wanted immediately—A teacher in School district No. 1 in the town of Lancaster, Ohio. One well versed in reading, writing, arithmetic, grammer and geography. None other need apply.

> Wm. Townsend,
> Jesse Waltz,
> Jacob Shaeffer, Directors.

NOTICES FROM THE WESTERN STAR

LEBANON, WARREN COUNTY, OHIO

BLANCHE COLLINS

MARRIED

1815—Yesterday evening by the Rev. William Gray, Mr. *David Skinner*, to Miss *Sarah Roe*. (*2/3)

1821—On Tuesday last, by the Rev. William Gray, Mr. *James L. Torbet* (late from Princeton, N. J.) to Miss *Hanah Winans*, daughter of Dr. John C. Winans, of this place. (*8/6) On Thursday, by the Rev. Eli Truitt, Mr. (frag.) *Jones*, to Miss *Nancy Marsh*, both of this county. (*8/13) On Sunday evening, the 19th inst., by the Rev. Eli Truitt, Mr. *John Prince*, to Miss *Johannah Gulick*, all of Lebanon.

*Date following asterisk denotes date of publication.
The Western Star was established, July, 1807, Nathaniel M'Clean, Editor. It is the oldest weekly newspaper published within the state and maintains a popular circulation.

(*8/20)· Dn Tuesday evening, Mr. *Joseph Henderson*, merchant of Lebanon, to Miss *Martha Knox*. —On Thursday evening, Mr. *Leyman Wakefield*, to Miss *Martha Strickler*. (*10/20) On Thursday evening last by the Rev. Eli Truitt, Mr. *Samuel Poland*, to Miss *Elizabeth Marsh*, all of Lebanon. (*11/24)

1822—On Wednesday last by the Rev. Wilson Thompson, *Thomas Corwin*, Esq., to Miss *Sarah Ross*, both of this town. (*11/16)

1823—On Wednesday last by the Rev. Wilson Thompson, Mr. *John Pauly*, to Miss *Sarah Smith*, daughter of Joseph Smith. —On Thursday last, Mr. *Lewis Griffith*, to Miss *Olive Sleasman*, all of Warren county. (*1/4) On Thursday last, by Rev. William Gray, Mr *Lew's Crane*, to Mrs. *Cathcrine James*. (*1/11) On Thursday the 6th inst. by the Rev. Elias Vickers, Mr. *William Russell*, to Miss *Ann Maria Morris*. (*3/15) On 1st April, by John M. Houston, Esq., Mr. *Henry Parrot*, to Miss *Mary Price*. —On the 2nd inst. by the Rev. Wilson Thompson, Mr. *George Parkinson*, to Miss *Lucretia Dawson*, all of this county. (*4/5) On Thursday eve. last by John M. Houston, Esq., Mr. *John F. Keys*, to Mrs. *Maria Phillips*. (*4/12) On Thursday the 15th inst. by the Rev. Matthew G. Wallace, Mr. *Abram Simpson*, to Miss *Fanny Longstreth*. On Thursday evening last, by the Rev. William Gray, Dr. *Caleb B. Clements*, to Miss *Susan Hurin*. (*5/24) On Thursday eve. last by the Rev. William Gray, Mr. *Frederick Bell*, to Miss *Eliza Cushen*, both of Deerfield, Union twp. (*5/31) On Thursday last by the Rev. William Gray, *Jacoby Hallack*, Esq., to Miss *Lucinda Dill*, all of this vicinity. (*6/7) On Thursday last by the Rev. William Gray, Mr. *David Silvers*, of Warren county, to Miss *Elizabeth Munger*, of Montgomery county. (*6/28) On Tuesday the 22d inst. by John M. Houston, Esq., Mr. *Tobias Burnet*, to Miss *Elizabeth Campbell*, both of this county. —On the 23d inst. by the Rev. Wilson Thompson, Mr. *William Willison*, to Miss *Polly Willson*, both of this county. (*7/26) On the 4th inst. by John M. Houston, Esq., Mr. *Joseph Evans*, Junior, to Miss *Amy Hormell*. —On the same day, by the same, Mr. *Leroy Pugh*, to Miss *Sarah Naylor*, all of this county. (*9/6) On Thursday the 27th ult. by the Rev. John P. Durbin, Mr. *Jacob Blinn*, to Miss —— *Thatcher*, both of this county. (*12/6)

1824—On Wednesday evening last by the Rev. John P. Durbin, Mr. *Richard Parcell*, junior, to Miss *Susan Earnfight*, all of this town. (*2/7) On Wednesday eve last by the Rev. John P. Durbin, Mr. *George Reeves*, to Miss *Elizabeth Brown*, all of this place. (*2/14) On Wednesday last by the Rev. John P. Durbin, Mr. *George King*, to Miss *Betsey Jeffrey*. —On Thursday last, by the same, Mr. *Harvey Gallaher*, to Miss *Ann Williams*, all of this vicinity. (*2/28) On Wednesday last by the Rev. John P. Durbin, Mr. *James Swaney*, to Miss *Clarissa Coffeen*, both of this vicinity. (*4/3) On Thursday last by the Rev. John P. Durbin, Mr. *Abram Fye*, to Miss *Nancy Shellar*, all of this vicinity. (*6/12) On the 6th inst., by James Benham, Esq., Mr. *P. P. Price* of Wilmington, to Mrs. *Mary R. Rook*, of this place. (*10/9)

1825—On the 23d ult, by the Rev. Richard Simonton, Mr. *Jeremiah Burns*, to Miss *Mary Harper*. —On the same day by the Rev. William Gray, Mr. *John Miranda*, to Miss *Bethany Campbell*. —On the 30th by John M. Houston, Esq., Mr. *John R. Russell*, to Miss *Charlotte Spinning*, —On the same day, by the same, Mr. *George Luther*, to Miss *Nancy Stephens*. (*1/1) On Tuesday last by the Rev. Richard Simonton, Mr. *Richard H. Smith*, to Miss *Hannah Jack*. (*1/29) On the 18th inst., by the Rev. Eli Truitt, Mr. *Isaac F. Posegate*, to Miss *Elizabeth Kean*, both of this place. —On the 25th inst., by the Rev. William Gray,

Dr. *Sylvan B. Morris*, to Miss *Catherine Knox*. —On the 29th inst., by the same, Mr. *William McKy*, to Miss *Polly Swinnard*, all of this vicinity. (*5/31)

DIED

1810—On Friday the 7th inst. Mrs. Patsy Low, consort of Jacob D. Low, Esq., Associate Judge of the Court of Common Pleas of this county.—On the 25th August in Chillicothe, Col. Moses M'Clean, aged 73. He was a patriot of the revolution, a gentleman of amiable manners, irreproachable character and a true christian. —Capt. Trippe of the U. S. Brig —— (Vixen) died on his passage from Havanna to New Orleans. —Also, Lieutenant Governor Broome of the State of New York. (July)

1815—On Saturday last after a short illness, Miss Lucy Hunt, daughter of Col. Ralph W. Hunt of this vicinity. (*2/3)

1821—On Saturday morning the 14th, Mary Carhart, aunt of the editor of this paper. (*4/5) On Thursday last, at Oxford, the Rev. James Hughs, a teacher of languages at Miami University. He has left a wife and a numerous family of children together with a large circle of relatives. —On the 4th April last Mrs. Sarah Yeman, of this county, consort of Mr. Moses Yaman, aged 71 years. —On the 30th April last, Mrs. Priscilla Yaman, consort of Mr. Samuel Ysman, of Warren county. (*5/7) On Tuesday last, Mary Ann, daughter of Absalom Runyan. —On Saturday Mr. Benjamin S. Rue. —On Sabbath morning, Caroline Mathilda, daughter of Matthias Corwin, Jun, Esq., (*7/16) On Saturday last, William M'Lean Bellar, infant son of Mr. Peter Bellar. —This morning, Mrs. Mary Fox, consort of Mr. Charles Fox, in the 66th year of her age. (*7/23) On Saturday last in this town, Phebe, daughter of Matthew and Ann Griggs. —On the same day, Mrs. Mary Drake, consort of Col. Lewis Drake, of this vicinity. (*7/30) On Thursday last, Mrs. Jemina Smith, in the 65th year of her age, widow of the late Abnor Smith of this town. (*8/6) On Thursday morning the 18th, Mrs. Elizabeth Crane, consort of Mr. Lewis Crane. (*10/20)

1822—On Sunday last, Mrs. Gibbs, consort of Mr. Thomas Gibbs. —On the same day,, Mr. Nicholas Rynearson. —On Thursday last, Wyllys Pearson, Junior. (*3/2) —On Tuesday last after a severe illness, Matthias Corwin, Junior, Clerk of the Court of this county. He has left a wife and two children to deplore their loss. (*10/12)

1823—On Wednesday the 26th ult. at his farm on Mill Creek, Hamilton county, Ohio, Mr. John Ludlow, Esq., in the 71st year of his age. He has left a wife and twelve children, fifty-four grandchildren, three great grandchildren. He has buried one wife, two children and twelve grandchildren. *Communicated* (*4/5) On Sunday the 18th inst. Capt. William Humphreys, an early settler of this county. —On the 28th inst. Ivory H. Chatburn, of this place. (*5/6) On Monday evening last, Miss Juliet Hunt, daughter of Col. Ralph W. Hunt. (*8/2) On Thursday last Capt. Benjamin Rue, in the 73rd year of his age. He served as a captain in the revolutionary war, and fought bravely in defending the liberties of his country. There has fallen another hero who acted a conspicuous part in that arduous struggle which terminated in American independence. On Thursday last his remains were interred with military honors. —On Sunday last, Mrs. Dyche, consort of Mr. Frederick Dyche of this county. —On Tuesday last, Mrs. Polly James, consort of Mr. Aaron James, of this county. —On Tuesday last, Mr. Samuel Gustin, an old and respected inhabitant of this vicinity.

after a short but severe illness, Mr. Joseph Eddye, an old and respected inhabitant of this vicinity. On the 11th, June, at Buenos Aires, the Hon. Caesar A. Rodney, Minister Plenipotentiary from U. S. (Interment Phila) (*8/28) On the 23d at his residence in this vicinity David Reeder, in the 76th year of his age. He was an old and respected citizen of this community. Fifteen minutes before his death, he was in full possession of health. —On Friday morning, Mrs. Mary Gill, of this place. (*9/25) On Monday last, Mr. John Martin, an old and respected citizen. —On last week in Hamilton township, Mr. Alexander Hamilton. (*10/16)

1825—On Sunday evening last, Mrs. Dorotha Mix, consort of Mr. George Mix of this town. (*1/1) On Tuesday last in this vicinity, John Hays, aged 70. His remains were interred in the Methodist burying ground with Masonic honors. (*2/5) On Thursday evening last, Daniel Hathway, of this town. (*4/23) On Saturday last after a short but severe illness, Mrs. Milka Adams, consort of Mr. Henry Adams, of this place. The deceased left four children. (*5/10) On Thursday last Eliza Ann Gordon, consort of Capt. John M. Daniel, her friends and society has sustained a very great loss. (*6/7) On last Thursday evening Jacob Ernfight, an old revolutionary soldier, in the 83rd year of his age. —On the same day, Mahlon Wells. —On Saturday last, John Tindall, of this vicinity. —On Monday last, Mrs. Benham, consort of James Benham, Esq., of this vicinity. —On Monday last after a lingering illness, James Armstrong, for many years a resident of this vicinity. —On Sunday last, Betsey, daughter of James Armstrong, dec'd. (*9/5) —On Wednesday last, Mr. James Parkinson, son of Mr. John Parkinson, of this vicinity. (*9/6) On Wednesday evening, 10th inst., at his residence near this place, Mr. Charles Fox, Junior, Esq., aged 34 years, leaving a wife and five children. (*9/13) On the 12th inst., after a short but severe illness, which he bore with Christian fortitude, Dr. M. D. Lathrop, of Waynesville. His remains were interred in the friends burying ground with Masonic honors. (*9/20) On Sunday last in this vicinity after a short illness, William Bogart. —On Monday last near this place, Robert Hays. —On last Tuesday evening in this place, after a short but severe illness, Christopher M. Jones. He was a member of the Baptist Church. His life was pious and exemplary. He has left a wife and seven children to lament their loss. —On Wednesday last, Robert Sale, in the vicinity of this place. —On —— day, Mrs. —— Perine, consort of Mr. James Perine. (*10/4) On Thursday last, Mrs. Sarah Morris, consort of Doct. David Morris. (*12/6)

1824—On Wednesday evening last, Mrs. Eliza Nixon, consort of Samuel Nixon, of this town, leaving a large family of children. —On Monday evening last, Mrs. Mary Ann Nixon, widow and mother of Mr. Samuel Nixon, in the 68th year of her age. (*2/7) On Sunday morning the 8th inst., James Decamp, for many years a resident of this town. (*2/14) On Wednesday last, Mrs. Cassandra Biggs, consort of Thomas Biggs, of this place. (*3/6) On the 20th ult. Mr. John Adams, for many years a respected citizen of this town. He has left a wife and five children to lament their loss. (*4/3) On the 24th last, at New Lisbon, after a severe illness of a few hours, John Laird, Esq., a senator of this state from Columbiana county. He was a young man justly entitled to the esteem of his friends and acquaintances. (*5/15) On Thursday last after a short illness Mrs. Nancy Crawford, of this vicinity. (*6/12) On Sunday last after a lingering illness, Mrs. Prudence Bone, consort of David Bone, of this town. (*7/17)

NOTICES FROM THE WESTERN STAR
LEBANON, WARREN COUNTY, OHIO
BLANCHE COLLINS

NOTICES

The partnership of Hollingsworth & Dill, this day dissolved by mutual consent. Signed Joshua Hollingsworth, Frances Dill. 1, March, 1821.

Of Harrison county in the State of Virginia, departed this life on the 19th, December, 1820, and left a large estate of both real and personal property in which his son Jacob Righter, who has lately resided in the lower part of the State of Ohio, but now unknown where to his friends, may be greatly interested by an immediate attention, which may be lost to him for want of it. The printers in the states of Ohio, Kentucky, will please give notice through public papers.—*From a disinterested person, a friend to justice.* 5, Mar. 1821.

Legal claims against the estate of Aaron Oxley, dec'd, late of Vernon twp, Clinton county. Josiah Biggs, Adm. 19, Feb. 1821.

The estate of John Stackhouse, dec'd, late of Vernon twp, Clinton county—Thomas Gaskill. 26, Jan. 1821.

Indebtedness to William Ferguson, or Ferguson & Voorhis, by note, or book accounts are placed in the hands of J. M. Houston, Esq., for collection. William Ferguson, Lebanon. 31, March, 1821.

Divorce: Eliza Newman vs. William Newman, willful absence of five years. Matthias Corwin, Junior Clerk, Lebanon. 29, January, 1821.

Public Sale: 5, May, 1821, at Lebanon, 60-70 acres, by heirs of Joseph James, dec'd. Matthias Corwin, Joshua Collet, Admrs. (*4/2/1821)

A certain Richard Ellis has established a glue factory and pretends to hold out an idea that he is well acquainted with the manufactury of glue, which is false and impositious . . . The subscribers have bought or used the glue, and they have no hesitation in stating that it is the worst glue that they have ever attempted to use. —Wm. M. Wiles, John W. Colbert, Daniel C. Penton, Samuel Ritchey, John Hathaway, George Miller, Abraham Delavere—Cabinet makers. The printers in Cincinnati are requested to give this to their papers, for we understand this fellow sends his loblolly there for sale. (*4/16/1821)

David Cutler, inventor of the new and useful improvement in distilling, has moved to the town of Lebanon, a few rods NE of the Presbyterian Meeting House. (*4/16/1821)

Whereas I am going eastward for some time, Dr. Daniel Egbert will attend to my practice . . . and collect all outstanding bills, John C. Winans, (do)

The tavern occupied by John Kephart, late of Clerkesville, Clinton county, dec'd will be rented on reasonable terms . . . Apply to Thomas Kephart Millgrove, Ruhannah Kephart . . Admrs. (*4/5/1821)

One Cent Reward—Ran Away 1, March last, John Martin, an indentured apprentice to the tailoring business . . Alanson Hill (do)

Public Vendue: 1, June next, at the late residence of Adam Sellers. William Sellars, Christian Sellers, Charles Null—Admrs. (do)

---

*Date following asterisk denotes date of publication.

The **Western Star** was established, July, 1807, Nathaniel M'Clean, Editor. It is the oldest weekly newspaper published within the state and maintains a popular circulation.

Lost—On Saturday last between Major Phillip's, Lebanon, and Esquire Williams, on the road leading to Deerfield, a ladies linsey dress, striped pale blue and deep blue, small stripes. A reasonable reward. Elen Goodpastor. (*5/7/1821)

The estate of Levi Smith late of Wayne twp., Warren county, Jane Smith, Admx. (do)

To lease the Mills on Todd Fork, formerly occupied by Jonas Whitacre, dec'd, for repairing the same. Apply to Samuel Nixon, Lebanon. Sarah Whitacre. 19. June. 1821.

To Joseph Cogley, son of John Cogley, dec'd, James Cogley, Polly Ruff, (who intermarried with John Ruff, since dec'd), Jane Fish, (who intermarried with James Fish), the children of James Cogley, dec'd, John Cogley, Joseph M. Cogley and Robert Cogley, the sons of Joseph Cogley, dec'd, Mary Henry, (who intermarried with William Henry), Sarah Cummins, (who intermarried with John Cummins), Robert Simmons, Elizabeth Simmons, George Simmons, Nancy Ebinger, (who intermarried with John Ebinger), and Joseph Simmons, the children of Nancy Simmons, dec'd (who intermarried with —— Simmons, since dec'd), the heirs and legal representatives of Robert Cogley, late of Armstrong county, Pa.,—Notice of inquest at the home of the said Robert Cogley, in the township of Buffalo, county of Armstrong, on Saturday, 15, next, for partition of real estate . . . according to law. Robert Robinson, Sheriff. Kittanning, 23, October, 1824. (*11/17/1821)

Executors Sale . . Dwelling house and 100 acres of John Egbert, dec'd. Apply to Stephen Bowers, or James Egbert, Exrs. (*12/29/1821)

A Card—The citizens of Lebanon are respectfully informed that Mrs. Catherine Forman will commence a school in this town about the 10th of April next for the purpose of teaching young Misses, reading, writing, sewing, and needlework. (*3/30/1822)

NOTES FROM THE FARMER
Published at Lebanon, Ohio, 1817
BLANCHE COLLINS

MARRIED
On the 24th ult, by T. Simonton, Esq., Mr. *Archibald Clinton,* to the amiable and accomplished Miss *Sarah Liggett,* all of Hamilton township, Warren county. This forenoon the Hon. *Jonathan Russell,* late minister to Sweden, will be married to Miss *Lydia Smith,* daughter of Barney Smith. The nuptials will be solemnized in Kings Chapel by the Rev. Dr. Freeman. (Copied from *The Boston Sentinel*) (*5/2) On yesterday, Mr. *Isaac Foster,* of Lebanon, and the amiable Miss *Hannah Aughee,* of Clear Creek. (*5/9) At Montgomery, the 21st inst, by the Rev. Mr. Hayton, Mr. *Jonathan Bailey,* to Miss *Ann V. Felter,* of said town. On the 17th inst. by the Rev. Mr. Stichts, Mr. *David Nichols,* to Miss *Hannah McCarty,* of this vicinity. On the 20th inst. by the Rev. William Gray, Mr. *John M. Christy,* to Miss *Sarah Clinton,* all of this vicinity. (*11/28)

* * * * *

DIED
Col. Appling, late of the U. S. Army, who distinguished himself in the late war, died at Fort Montgomery, in the Mississippi Territory. (*5/2) On the 5th inst, Mr. Martin Earhart, of this vicinity, at the advanced age of 96 years. On the 6th inst. Miss Harriet Halsey, daughter of T. B. Halsey of this vicinity. Her death was occasioned by a cut on the knee. (*5/9)

A hermit died at New Marlborough, Mass., on the 14th ult. Timothy Leonard, aged 70. He was born in Connecticut, brought up in Woodbury. After he was of age he went to Fredericksburgh, N. Y., where his father then resided. At 24 he came to this town. (*8/15)

* * * * *

NOTICES
NEWS—Both Houses of the Legislature of New York have agreed to a resolution of the members of the nest session—to appear in American manufacturers,—Franklin Square: the square in the city of New York, heretofore called St. George's Square, has by order of the corporation, been changed to Franklin Square. (*5/2)

LIME—The subscriber informs the public that he keeps on hand, at his kiln, 5 miles from Lebanon, on the Waynesville road, and near the Joseph Evans' sawmill, a quantity of lime . . . which he will sell at nine cents per bushel delivered. (*5/2)

Date following asterisk denotes date of publication. All items are from Volume 1.

PARTNERSHIP: William Wiles has taken John Wm. Colbert into partnership in cabinet making . . and will be hereafter transacted under the firm Wiles & Colbert. (*5/2)

BILLS— All my accounts up to a certain date have been placed in the hands of Benjamin Sayre, Esq., Lebanon, for collection. Jepthae F. Moore. (*5/2)

NEWS—The Little Miami Bridge Company will meet at the house of Cyrenus Jennings, on the first Monday of May at 2 o'clock, P. M. to elect officers of the said company, Warren county, Union twp. (*5/2)

PARTNERSHIP—The partnership heretofore existing in the shoe-making business is dissolved. Absolom Runion, Joseph Berry. (*5/2)

NOTICE: The subscriber wishes to inform the inhabitants of West-field and its vicinity that he continues to teach school at that place, at the usual price, but *not* on the same plan: to wit, The people may sub-scribe as entered for three months from and after that date. Anthony Geoghagan. (*5/2)

ESTATE of William Elstun, dec'd, late of Miami twp., Clermont county. Apply to Isaac Elstun, Adm. (*10/10)

PUBLIC VENDUE: On the 7th of November at the late dwelling of Martin Earhart, dec'd, personal property. Nicholas Earhart, George Earhart, Adms. On Thursday the 16th inst. 1½ miles east of Deerfield, and 1½ miles southeast of Lebanon on Dry Run, his property. Job Weeks. (*10/10)

TRACT OF LAND: For sale, lying six miles east of Lebanon where the state road from Cincinnati to Chillicothe crosses the Little Miami river. 60 acres cleared land, in high state of cultivation. Benjamin Rue. (*11/28)

SHERIFF SALE—At the court house in Lebanon, 16th day of August next, 60 acres part of Section No. 11, Twp. 4, Range 3, the property of Joseph James, at the suit of Walter Jenkins, and to be sold by me. Coonrad Snider, Sher. (*11/28)

ANNOUNCEMENT: The Rev. Abel M. Sargent will preach at the Court House in this town on Sunday next, at 3 o'clock. —On the 28th July, the 74th Annual Conference of the Methodists took place in Sheffield, England. About three hundred preachers were present (*10/10)

STRAY HORSES: Taken up by Thomas Roberts, dark bay filly, ap-praised by David Reed and David Evans, Samuel Reed, J. P. Clinton county, Richland twp. —Taken up by Elemuel G. Jackson of Richland twp., an iron gray filly . . appraised by Timothy Jones and John Ben-nett. Samuel Reed, J. P. —Taken up by John Reeder, of Salem twp., Warren county, a bay mare . . appraised by John Wilkerson and Daniel Thompson, James M. Manis, J. P. (*5/2) —Taken up by Joseph B. Staggs, a resident of Hamilton twp, Warren county, a yellow sorrel mare . . appraised by William Hopkins and Abraham Hany, John Hopkins, J. P. (*5/9) Five dollars reward . . ran away from Union Village on Saturday evening the 9th of this month, rig and bay mare . . John Wallace. (*5/9) —Taken up by Andrew Shiderly, Clermont county, a bay mare, appraised by John Erwin and Lewis Fryhagen. Silas Hutchinson, J. P. (*10/10)

ADVERTISEMENTS: Wrot and cut nails, George Rutter. —Sad-dling: Intends to carry on the saddling business at the shop where the firm of Hollingsworth & Adams subsisted. H. Adams, Jun. —New Store, William Heaton . . Mulberry Street, two doors east of *The Sign of General Jackson.* —New & Fresh Goods, Dry Goods and Gro-ceries . . the latest selection in Philadelphia . . will sell goods on as

81

good trems as can be had in the western country, for cash, whiskey, flour, sugar, linen, flax, hogs' lard, tallow, beeswax, butter, flaxseed, rags, and anything else the farmer has to exchange for this goods. Truitt & Wiles. —Merchandise consisting of Queensware, hardware, drygoods, groceries, foreign liquors, oil paints, and a variety of patent and other medicines. Robert Wood. —Plane Making Business: William Woodward.—One dollar per bushel given for clean merchantable wheat, delivered at this mill on the Little Miami, six miles east of Lebanon, T. & E. Graham.

Fifty-six and ¼ cents per bushel for any quantity of good clean Barley delivered at their store at Lebanon from this date, Jepthae F. Moore. —Constant supply of Embre's Beer, made in Cincinnati, to sell either by the barrel or gallon, Truit & Wiles.—Having commenced business in the log house adjoining Ichabod Corwin's new brick building on Broadway, will receive and execute orders for every description of stills, boilers', fullers', and hatters' kettles etc., Jacob Schwing. N. B. the highest price given for old copper, brass and pewter.—For sale, a few copies of *The Shorter Catechism*, with the Scripture proofs, in words at length. —Just received from Philadelphia, al large and general assortment of goods of the latest importations from England, and now opening at his Brick Store House, Mkt. St., & Broadway . . Alexander Crawford. (*5/2)

DISAPPOINTMENT . . The subscriber has for some time waited for those who stand indebted to him, hoping their generosity would prompt them to relieve his necessity . . he has, however, been disappointed: therefore those who wish future accommodations will do themselves a favor by calling and discharging their accounts . . He has a general assortment of wrought and cut nails . . George Rutter. (*5/9)

GROCERIES—Hardware, cutlery, china, and Queensware. G. Hansbarger. —Cash for hides, Broadway, Lebanon. Tobias Bretteny. (*5/9)

BOOTS & SHOES—Removal from the old stand on Mulberry to Mechanic Street, one door north of Richard Parcell's Tavern *The Sign of General Jackson*. Frederick Rook. (*5/9)

WANTED: Cabinet making. Howell & Baely. —Wheat at T & E Grahams Mills on the Little Miami River, William Lowery. (*5/9)

NEW STORE—Brown & Corwin's General Store, Hiram Brown and Matthias Corwin. —Wallace Bratton has just arrived from Philadelphia and is now opening his new frame store room one door south of J. Keenan's Tavern, *The Sign of The Cross Keys*, and adjoining N. Lane & Cos. store, Broadway. (*5/9)

FOR RENT—The tavern stand in Clinton county, on the state road leading from Lebanon to Chillicothe, heretofore known as Van Meter's Tavern. 100 acres cleared and 30 acres meadow and sugar camp. Immediate possession, Nathan Kelly. (*5/9)

BREWERY PURCHASED: Lately occupied by Daniel Symmes, Esq., dec'd, and will commence brewing as soon as the season will permit. 10,000 bushels of barley will be wanted yearly for a number of years. (62½c per bu.) Apply to P. Reily. Cincinnati, July 24. J. & S. Perry. (*5/9)

PLOWS—Made and sold at his farm ten miles north of Lebanon on the Dayton road. William Evans. (*5/9)

TOBACCO—In all its varieties, wholesale and retail, at Cincinnati. Christopher Erenfight. (*10/10)

TANYARD—For sale, subscriber desirous of declining business

cffers for sale his tanyard in Fairfield, Green county; this village 11 miles of Xenia, 12 miles east of Dayton and 13 miles east of Springfield. J. Smith. (*10/10)

REAL ESTATE—For rent, for one or more years an excellent farm lying on Turtle Creek, 3 miles below Lebanon, on the Cincinnati road. 80 acres improved land, orchard, meadow. J. F. Moore. —For Sale, House and lot on Mechanic Street, immediate possession. Coleman. Important—Two houses and lots for sale. John Wilson of Dayton or Mary Gilchrist of Lebanon. Exchange, Ground in Lebanon for carpentry work on a frame house, William Rockhill. (*10/10)

FULLING: Intends to continue in the business of Fulling & Coloring, David Tullis. (*10/10)

LOOK HERE! Subscriber has for sale in Clermont county; two valuable tracts of Land lying in said county, on the Ohio river, surrounded by the town of Neville. Tracts contain upwards of 300 acres. Gideon Minor. —EXTRA—I will sell the property with all the appurtenances thereunto belonging, where I now keep store, next to *The Cross Keys*, on Broadway, Wallace. —Sheriff Sale—At the Court House at Lebanon, Saturday, 20th December . . . the interest of Jonathan Smith, a certain tract of land lying between and being in the county of Warren, bounded on the Widow Mount's lower line, and thence down river 100 poles on the Little Miami. 5 acres . . . surveyed and taken in execution as the property of Jonathan Smith at the suit of John Campbell assignee of Amos Smith. Coonrad Snider, J. P. (*11/28)

1817—DIED—At Marietta, General Joseph Wilcox formerly of Killingworth, Conn., aged 68. (*2/13)   In this town Saturday last, Mrs. Harriet Jacobs, wife of Mr. Thomas Jacobs of Chillicothe. (*4/3) In Columbus, Miss Marie Hurlburt of Granville. (*4/3)   In Zanesville township on 15th inst. Mr. Valentine Best.   At Cincinnati, Hon. Daniel Symmes.   At the same place Dr. William Goforth.   At Saco (Me.) Mr. Cyrus King, aged 44, late a member from Mass.   At St. Clairsville, Mrs. Tirzah Ruggles, consort of Hon. Benjamin Ruggles. (*5/22)   In Jefferson twp, Guernsey county,   June 9,   Mrs. Eliza, wife of Dr. Job Walbridge, late of New Hampshire. (*6/19).   In Putnam, on the 4th inst.,   Mrs. Jane Thompson,   wife of Mr. John Thompson (*6/26)   At Painesville, on the 7th ult.   Hon. Samuel Huntington, aged 49, a native of Connecticut. (*7/8)   In Cincinnati. Miss Elvira Cooper. (*12/17)   In this town on Sunday last, Elijah B. Merwin, Atty-at-law. (*11/19)

MARRIED—On Thursday last by the Rev. Mr. Culbertson, *Mr. Benjamin Carter* to *Miss Jane Alison*, both of this county.   In Blue Rock twp. on Thursday last, by Christian Spangler, Esq., *Mr. Michael Waxler*, to Miss *Mercy Morris*. (*4/3)   On Thursday last by Rev. Mr. Culbertson, Mr. *Abraham Pollock*, to Miss *Jane Bigger*. (*4/17)   On Tuesday the 15th inst. by C. Spangler, Mr. *Johnson M'Ginnis* to Miss *Margaret Pennick*. (*4/24)   At Granville, Mass., July 20th, *Rev. Orlyn P. Hays* of Granville, Ohio, to Miss *Betsy P. Harvey*.   In Salt Creek twp. on Sunday last by C. Spangler Esq., Mr. *Eli Walls* to Miss *Judith Border*.   In Zanesville twp. on Thursday last, by the same, Mr. *James Basil* to Miss *Elizabeth Underwood*. (*8/27)   On Sunday the 30th ult. by Thomas Flood, Esq., Mr. *John Ryan* to Miss *Jane Wilcox*, both of Zanesville.   On the 9th inst. by the same, Mr. *Leonard Bowman* to Miss *Catherine Spilerfoch* of this city. (*12/17)   By Rev. Culbertson on the 16th inst.   Mr. *Jessie Lewis* to Miss *Mary Gabriel*, both of this county. (*12/24)

1818—DIED—In Maryland, Gen. Robert Bowie, formerly Governor of that state.   In Salem twp, Muskingum county, on the 27th ult., of smallpox, Mrs. Leanah Hardy, wife of Mr. Kinzie Hardy. (*1/28) In Stratford, Conn., on the 28th ult. Rev. . athan Birdseye, aged 108 years.   The whole number of his descendants was 258, with 206 of whom are living.   He had 12 children,   76 grandchildren,   163 great grandchildren, and 7 of the 5th generation.   He married but once and lived sixty-nine years with his wife who died at the age of 88. (*2/25)   In Wooster, Feb. 17th, William B. Raymond, Esq., Atty-at-law. (*3/4)   In this town on the 6th inst., the youngest child of Wyllys Silliman Esq., aged 9 months. (*3/11)   In Georgia, General John Millege, late governor of that state.   In New Haven, (Conn) Gen'l. David Humphreys, a patriot of 1776.   On the 20th inst. at Yorktown (N. Y.) John Paulding, one of the three incorruptible patriots who arrested Major Andre in the Revolutionary War. His funeral was conducted with military and masonic honors. (*3/18) Near Chillicothe, Mr. John M'Donald, in the 90th year. He was a native of Scotland, and was with Gen'l. Wolfe at the taking of Quebec in 1759. (*4/29)   At Wooster (O) on the 21st inst., Mrs. Barbara Smith, aged 100 years and some months. She was a native of Germany and emigrated to America at the age of 30. Her descendants are as follows: 14 children, 95 grandchildren, 176 great grandchildren, 285 descendants, most of whom are now living in Wayne county. (*6/3) In Cumberland county, Pa., Gen'l David Mitchell, aged 77. In New Orleans a few weeks since, Mr. Frederick K. Houck, of this town. In Cincinnati, Mrs. Hannah Piatt, wife of Jacob Piatt. (*6/24) In this town on the 22d inst. Jane, only child of Mr. Nathan C. Finlay, aged 12½ y. (*8/26) At Melton, N. Y. on June last, Alexander Ross, aged ab. 120. He was a native of Scotland and served in the army of the Pretender—1745. Afterwards he came to America, and was severely wounded at the Siege of Quebec. At the breaking out of the Revolutionary War he took up arms for his country and distinguished himself in action. At the age of 117 he joined a respectable church, and became a useful member. (*9/16) In this town on Thursday last, Mrs. Mary L. Stone, aged 36, wife of Capt. Noyce Stone. (*10/7) In Connecticut at an advanced age General Jedidiah Huntington. (*10/28)

MARRIED—In this town on Thursday last by Rev. J. Culbertson, Mr. *Alexander Wyley*, to Miss *Lydia Beaver*. By the same, Dr. *David Pardee*, to Miss *Mary Holmes*. (*2/11) In this town on Thursday last by the Rev. Mr. Culbertson, Mr. *Lyman Warner*, to Miss *Susannah Rees*, both of this county. (*2/25) In this town on Wednesday last, by the Rev. Mr. Culbertson, Mr. *David Kinkead*, of Chillicothe, to Miss *Narcissa Colhoun*. (*3/4) In this town on the 26th inst. by Chirstian Spangler, Esq., Mr. *Georges Parker*, to Miss *Ann Ashley* On Thursday the 3d inst. by the same, Mr. *William Lander* to Mrs. *Elizabeth Ashley*. (*3/11) In this town on the 2d inst. Mr. *Micajah T. Williams*, editor of the WESTERN SPY, of Cincinnati, to Miss Hannah Jones of the latter place. (*3/18) In this town on the 11th ult. by Thomas Flood, Esq., Mr. *A. Morrison* to Miss *Ann Smith*, both of this place. On the 18th ult, by the same, Mr. John W. Bradley to Miss Sarah Pierce. On the 18th ult, by Christian Spangler, Esq., Mr. *James Callihan* to Miss *Sarah Walters*. On Sunday last, by the same, Mr. *Jacob F. Herickle*, to Miss *Nancy Spangler*, both of this county. (*4/1) In this town by C. Spangler, Esq., Mr. *Cales Evans*, to Miss *Ann Lehew*. (*1/8) On the 23d inst. by J. W. Boyd, Esq., Mr. *Archelus Symonds* to Miss Eliza Willey, daughter of Mr. Waitman Willey of Delaware settlement. (*3/29) In this town on the 30th by C. Spangler, Esq., Mr. *John Walters* to Miss Alice Edwards. At China Grove (Md.) by Rev. Mr. Fiddler, Mr. *Wm. Campbell* to his former wife, Mrs. *Ann Campbell*. (*5/6) On Thursday last by C. Spangler, Esq., Mr. Stephen Emmons, to Miss Elizabeth Patterson. (6/24) In this town on the 28th ult. by Rev. Mr. Culbertson, Mr. *Peter Dugan*, to Miss *Maria Williams*. By the same, Mr. Jeremiah Dale, to Mrs. Maria Merwin. (*8/5) In this town on Thursday last, by V. Spangler, Esq., Mr. *John Bates*, to Miss Hannah Luck. On Friday evening by Rev. Mr. Culbertson, Mr. *Jacob R. Price*, to Miss Margaret Hart, both of this county. (*9/16) In this town on Sunday by C. Spangler, Esq., Mr. James Truesdell to Miss Laura Fuller. (*10/28).

*—The Muskingum Messenger, Published by Josiah Heard, Zanesville, Ohio

ITEMS FROM THE HISTORIAN & ADVERTISER, 1827
ST. CLAIRSVILLE, BELMONT COUNTY, OHIO
MAYBURT STEPHENSON RIEGEL

MARRIAGES—BARTON, Jesse son of Almer of Coleran Twp. to Catharine A. Mulvany, dau. of Mr. P. Mulvany of this place 2/15. CAVENDER, James to Jane C. Thornton 2/15. DILLON, Isaac P. son of Judge, to Mrs. Anne Smith 4/19. GANDY, John to Miss Elizabeth Gray 9/15. HOGE, Asa to Miss Asenith Mead, of Warren Twp 4/19. JOHNSON, Ashley, of Richmond, Indiana, at Friends Meeting House in Harrisville to Yydia Rhodes, dau. of Joseph 2/22. KUNTZ, Henry, to Mrs. Frances M'Caffrey 4/19. NEFF, Henry, Merchant of Jacobsburg, to Mary Bryson dau. of late Judge 12/5. O'HEARE, Thomas to Rebecca McCarroll 5/12. ORR, Thomas of Jefferson Co. to Lavina Thompson 7/4.

DEATHS—CASSADY, John 3/12. FAWCETT, Martha age 80 consort of Thomas dec'd. 2/4. KING, Hon. Rufus age 73, 4/29. PRIOR, Sarah consort of John, in Smith Twp. 2/15. SIDWELL, Benjamin age 30, formerly of Berkley Co., Va. 4/21. SPENCER, William son of Aaron, near Belmont 2/14. UPDEGROFF, Nathan—Early settler 3/3. WELLS, Abner near town 4/21. WILSON, Isaac in the city of Baltimore, formerly of this place, Member Society of Friends, age 70 5/15. WOODS, Ebenezer Zane age 23, 4/12.

NOTICE OF SETTLEMENT OF ESTATES—BRATTON, William by William & Joseph 9/29. CARTER, John by Elizabeth Carter & George W. Thompson 5/19. DICKSON, Rachel by Charles Eckles & James Hutchison 9/29. DOUGLAS, Joseph by Jane Douglas & Henry Long 11/3. DUNCAN, Robert by John & Jennet 6/2. FAWCETT, Martha by Stacy Bevan 3/31. GILLIS, Arthur by James Kelsey 6/23. GREEN, Alexander by Mary Green & Nehemiah Wright 9/22. HUGHES, Edward, of North Carolina, (Joice dau. of Judson Hughes) by Samuel Lef of Oley Twp. York Co., Pa., Exec. of Owen Hughes. 9/8. JALKES, Richard late of Jefferson Co. dec'd. by Thomas Merchant 7/7. KELLER, George—Rachel vs. Isaac & Absalom, adm. & heirs of George. (Thomas, Levi, Jonh, & Benjamin Keller and Louis Winzel & Anna his wife—also heirs) Rachel sues for alimony of her husband, Thomas at his father's death. 7/14. KNOUFF, Mary Ann by John 5/12. MERCER, John by Lydia, Richard & William DUNN. 12/22. MILHOUSE, William by Benjamin Wright 5/12. PLUMMER, Thomas by Mahlon Smith 3/31. PLUMMER, Robert by David Smith & Isaac Clendenon, Guardians of John, Abraham, Mary & Robert Plummer–heirs. 9/4. SHAEFER, John by Catharine Smith 3/17. SHARPE, Jeptha by John Vanlaw 12/22. SHAY, John—Robert Armstrong vs. heirs (Isaac, John, Abraham Shay—Elizabeth Cain & Iron—Ann McFarland & Robert—Sarah Morris & William—Polly Wilson & James —Catharine Daugherty & Henry—Rebecca Hare & Joseph.) 134 acres Range 6 Twp. 9 Section 34 S E ¼ in Belmont Co., O. 3/16. SKINNER, Nathaniel by Hannah 9/22. STUBBS, Joseph by Isaac Stubbs & David Smith 11/24. THOMAS, William by Camm 3/31. TOMPKINS, Mary—Late of Goshen Twp. Belmont Co. 4/7. WILSON, Daniel—Isaac Stevison & Anna his wife vs. John & Elizabeth Wilson, children and heirs of Daniel. 3/17.

MISCELLANY—Emmor Bailey offers farm—190 acres, 2 m. so. of Mount Pleasant and frame house in Smithfield, Jefferson Co. 2/15. Catharine Seamore vs. Randolph Seamore. Petition for divorce. 6/30. James Broonhall vs. Sarah Fields & John, Susan Moore & James, Martha Hoover & Abraham. Mentions John Lickey & Mary Dillon. 6/30. Margaret Rude vs. Caleb Rude. Petition for divorce. 7/7. John I. Reynolds assignee of William B. Reynolds vs. Moses Hill. Issue of November 24th contains list of St. Clairsville citizens meeting to promote re-election of John Quincy Adams. Robert Griffith, John Daugherty, Thomas Heanning & George Paull vs. Samuel Conway, David Jennings & William Kirkland. 11/24. John Townsend vs. Townsend Frazer. 11/24.

Contributed by BLANCHE COLLINS

DEATH NOTICES

BARCLAY, MR. HENRY, at the home of Isaac Case, Oct. 27th. One of the volunteers from Madison Co., Ky. He was on his way home from the battle of Trench. Methodist Church, Mr. Fisher. (*Nov. 3, 1813.)

BEACH, MILES, a. 20, d. last Thursday, Worthington. (*Nov. 27, 1811.)

BENEDICT, MRS. ANNA, consort of Hezekiah Benedict, d. Worthington, Aug. 27th, 1813. (*Sept. 1, 1813.)

BIGELOW, MISS DEMIS, a. 16 yrs., dau. of Russel Bigelow, Worthington, October 8th, their third child to die lately. (*Oct. 13, 1813.)

BROTHERTON, MRS. KEZIAH, consort of David Brotherton, in Franklinton, Aug. 11, 1811. (*Aug. 11, 1811.)

BROWNE, REV. JOHN W., editor of Liberty Hall, d. Cincinnati, Jan. 5, 1813. He fell from his horse into the river. Want of accommodations caused his death. (*Jan. 20, 1813.)

CASE, CAPT. SETH, a. 63 yrs. d. Middlebury, of apoplexy, June 4, 1813. Burial at Middlebury. (*June 9, 1813.)

CASTO, ASIAH, d. by suicide, Oct. 16, 1812, near Darby Creek. He was advanced in years, subject to fits of deliriousness. Baptist. He left a family. (*Oct. 21, 1812.)

DRAKE, PATIENCE, d. in Delaware (O.) 25th ult., dau. of Capt. Drake, Marlborough. (*Oct. 6, 1813.)

DRAKE, SYLVESTER, in Sunbury, Sept. 28, a. 26 yrs. Only brother of Rev. Jacob Drake, Delaware. (*Oct. 6, 1813.)

FLIPP, CAPT., who was wounded on his wagon on the Sandusky plains, died Aug. 25th, of his wounds. (*Sept. 1, 1813.)

GODARD, MOSES, d. in Delaware County, Mar. 28th, 1813, of typhus fever. A few weeks ago he buried his wife and his eldest daughter. Four infant children remain. (*Mar. 31, 1813.)

GREGORY, MUNSON, d. Worthington, Nov. 18th, son of James Gregory of Berkshire. (*Nov. 24, 1813..)

GRISWOLD, CAPT. SYLVANUS, a. 72 yrs. at Windsor, Co. (*Aug. 11, 1811.)

HARRINGTON, CAPT. STEPHEN, Delaware, (O.) d. July 9th, 1812, at the garrison at Lower Sandusky after a short but severe illness. (*July 17, 1812.)

HAWLEY, ELIZABETH, a. 40 yrs. consort of Amos Hawley, Worthington. (*Oct. 27, 1813.)

HAWLEY, SILENCE, a. 15 yrs. d. Oct. 27th, dau. of Amos Hawley. (*Nov. 3, 1813.)

---

*Notices from the Western Intelligencer. Est. Worthington. Ohio, 1811. Date following asterisk denotes date of publication.

OTHER OHIO RECORDS

Contributed by BLANCHE COLLINS

DEATH NOTICES

KILBOURN, CHARLOTTE, inf. dau. of Major James Kilbourn of Worthington, d. Nov. 10*th*. (*Nov. 17, 1813*.)

LITTLE, NATHANIEL, Esq. d. Delaware, Dec. 10*th*, 1812. He left a small family. (*Jan. 20, 1812*.)

MAYNARD, MRS. E., consort of Dr. Stephen Maynard, d. Feb. 12*th*, 1813. (Worthington). (*Feb. 17, 1813*.)

MORRISON, WIDOW MEHITABLE, Worthington, d. Feb. 21*st*, 1812. (*Feb. 14, 1812*.)

McGEE, COLONEL. Correspondence arrived from Texas confirming the death of Col McGee at Labatie, Feb. 6*th*, 1813. (*May 5, 1813*.)

McKNIGHT, JOHN, ESQ. Member of the House of Representatives of this state from Greene County, d. Monday morning last after three days illness. (*Feb. 14, 1812*, recopied from Zan(field) Messenger.)

NORTON, CAPT. JOAB, formerly of Worthington, d. Delaware (O.), July 17*th*, 1812, a. 33 yrs. He left a widow and four children. (*July 21, 1812*.)

PALMER, MISS PEGGY, dau. of Thomas Pamer, d. Oct. 14*th*, 1812, Worthington, a. 11 yrs. (*Oct. 14, 1812*.)

PRATT, LUCY, inf. dau. of Lemuel Pratt, d. Worthington last Sunday. (*Apr. 28, 1812*.)

POWER, AVERY, Esq. a. 76 yrs. d. at Liberty of quick consumption, May 3*d*, 1813. (*June 9, 1813*.)

RODGERS, MRS. ELISHA, D. Worthington yesterday. Funeral preached by Rev. Joseph Mitchell. (*June 18, 1812*.)

SMILIE, JOHN, at Worthington City, Dec. 31*st*, 1812, of typhus fever, a. 71 yrs. A member of the Congress. (*Jan. 20, 1813*.)

TAYLOR, NANCY, a. 17 yrs. d. Sept. 1, 1813, Worthington. (*Sept. 1, 1813*.)

TENNERY, GEORGE F., d. 21*st* ult. in Troy, Miami County. (*Aug. 11, 1811*.)

WEAVER, MRS. ELIZABETH, consort of Asa Weaver, Worthington, d. Apr. 19*th*, 1813. (*Apr. 21, 1813*.)

ZEIGLER, MAJ. DAVID, v. Cincinnati 26*th* ult. He was a native of Germany. He came to Penna. sometime during the Revolutionary War. During that war he was an officer. (*Oct. 16, 1811*.)

---

*Notices from the Western Intelligencer. Est. Worthington, Ohio, 1811. Date following asterisk denotes date of publication.

OTHER OHIO RECORDS

BLANCHE COLLINS

MARRIED—Sharon twp. last Tuesday by Ezra Griswold, Esq., Mr. Amos Hawley and Mrs. Sarah Buttles. (. *Dec. 3, 1814*); Mr. John Bailhache [edr. *Scioto Gazette*] to Miss Eliza Heath, both of this place, [reprint from *Supporter*, Dec. 24], (**June 2, 1817*); In Plumb twp. Fairfield co. Sunday 8th inst. by Rev. Camp, Mr. Christian Heyl of this town to Miss Esther Alspach. (. *May 14, 1814*.)

ELOPEMENT—Whereas, my wife Elizabeth, has eloped from my bed and board without just cause or provocation, therefore all persons are warned from harboring or trusting her on my account, as I am determined to pay no debts of her contracting after this date unless compelled by law. Daniel Murdick, Jr., Sept. 23. 1816. (**Oct. 24, 1816.*)

CAUTION—Whereas, on last Sept. two young men obtained a note of hand from my wife, Mary, payable to Elijah Warner, this is to caution all people from taking an assignment of said note, as I am determined never to pay it. Witness my hand 10*tk* day of Aug. 1816. Humphrey Beckett (*).

DIED—Franklinton, 7*th* inst. Mrs. Jane D. Lashmut, (. *March 26, 1814*); At Worthington in 19*th* Mr. David Dust. a drafted militia man from Gallipolis on his return home from a tour of duty. He left a wife and seven children, (. *March 26, 1814*): On Saturday last a lad, son of Mr. Stafford, instantly killed by a stroke of lightning, [M. Messenger copy], (. *June 1, 1814*); Mr. Joel Newton at Darby, 24*th* Nov. in 25*th* yr. Mild and intelligent he was particularly interesting to such of his acquaintances as were capable of enjoying the sympathies of a virtuous and polished mind. (**Dec. 19, 1816*); George Madison, Gov. of this state, d. Monday last at Paris, Ky., where he had been several weeks confined by illness. In consequence of this distressing event the government will be administered by Gabriel Slaughter [Lient. Gov. for 4 yrs.] The constitution does not provide for a new election. (**Oct. 31, 1816*); At Franklinton, Martha, w. of Stewart Baley. One week previous his inf. child; Columbus, child of the family of Mr. Vorhis, by name, Betsy Corbus, ag. 4 yrs. Died of a scald; Instances of drowning—one man at Kraymers Mills on Walnut Cr., one at Paint Cr., one at the mouth of the Scioto. (**Dec. 5, 1816*); Mr. James Wilson, ag. 60, Francestown, N. H., d. Troy twp. Delaware, on 10*th* inst. after a sickness of fever, leaving widow and many small children and grand-children; At Worthington, Monday 10*th* inst. of prevailing fever. Miss Amanda C. Little, 11 yr. dau. of Nathaniel Little Esq.; At Darby Cr. 5*th* inst. Mr. Elisha Knap, leaving a widow and children; In Franklinton, Monday last, Mr. John Thompson; Columbus, Monday last, Mr.

*Notices from the Western Intelligencer. Est. Worthington, Ohio, 1811. Date following asterisk denotes date of publication.

Joseph Miller, leaving numerous and very dependent family—and, on Thursday last, a young dau. of Mr. Jas. Culbertson; Clinton twp., Widow Delano, relict of Stephen Delano whose death was announced a few weeks ago. (*Sept. 15, 1821.) Mifflin twp. 28th inst. Miss Polly Read, ag. 21 yrs. after 5 days illness; In Franklinton 29th ult. Dr. John H. Lamber, phy. late from Illinois. Also on 30th ult. Mr. Matthias Swan. On 1st ult. Mr. John Coursen. In London—Mad. co., Dr. Elden Gage last from [we believe] Oneida co., N. Y., leaving a distressed wife. Columbus [Fri. 28th] after a painful illness of 24 da. Mr. Jas. Vickers, Deputy Marshall of this district, leaving a wife and six small children. (*Sept. 29, 1821.)

LEGAL NOTICES

BARBER, ISAAC, late of Marlborough Twp., Delaware Co. Adms. Ira Wilcox, John Millican. (*Feb. 21, 1812.)

CARPENTER, J., deceased. Sale of tract of land. Leonard Cowles. (Dec. 8, 1813.)

CARPENTER, JOHN, Delaware Co. Adm. Solomon Smith. (*Feb. 21, 1812.)

GODARD, MOSES, late of Liberty Twp. Adm. Lemuel G. Humphrey, June 1, 1813. (*June 2, 1813.)

HIGGINS, JOSHIAH, committed for counterfeiting, broke from Sheriff of Delaware County. $50 reward. Aaron Welch, Sher. D. C. (Oct. 20, 1813.)

LITTLE, NATHANIEL, dec. Adms. Wm. Little, Harriet Little, Delaware. Apr. 4, 1813. (*June 9, 1813.)

MESSENGER, ZEPHENIAH, late of Worthington, Claims. Adm. Adonijah Messenger. (*Nov. 24, 1813.)

NORTON, CAPT. JEREMIAH, late of Farmington, Hartford Co., Conn. Adm. Lawrence Lewis, Worthington, O. Feb. 25th, 1813. (*June 9, 1813.)

POWER, AVERY, late of Liberty Twp. Delaware Co. Adms. Leonard H. Cowls, Luther Power. (*Sept. 1, 1813.)

PRATT, LUTHER, late of Berkshire. Notice to Creditors. Adms. Worthy Pratt, James Gregory, Mar. 17th, 1813. (*June 2, 1813.)

WELCH, ISAAC. "Notice of Sale," Aug. 5th, property of the late Isaace Welch at home of Ezekiel Brown in Sunbury Twp., Delaware Co. Anna Fade. (*July 7, 1813.)

YOUNG, JOHN, late of Sunbury Twp., Delaware Co. Adms. John Leonard Jr., Andrew Young, May 20, 1813. (*June 2, 1813.)

*Western Intelligencer (Estab. 1811), Worthington, Ohio.

NEWSPAPER ITEMS FROM ZANESVILLE EXPRESS AND REPUBLICAN STANDARD

Zanesville, Ohio, Muskingum County

By Lorena B. Adamson

DEATHS

William Hamilton, d. 2-21-1813 "He was of advanced years". Publication date March 3, 1813.

Mrs. Margaret Culbertson, consort of William Culbertson, d. "near this town" Publication date Mar. 5, 1813.

David Campbell, d. 5-28-1813, age 16, in this county near Springfield, by a falling tree. Publication date June 2, 1813.

Alexander Carter, a private in Col. Dudles regiment of drafted militia from Ky., d. at Joseph Ogle's home at Wakatomaka on the Muskngum river. No date of death given.

Jesse Munson, d. at Granville 4-27-1813 age 72 years. "He was actively engaged at Bunker's Hill, being entrusted with a subordinate command". Publication date May 5, 1813

Miss Nancy Johnson, d. 1-10-1813 of "aconsumption".

Mrs. Lydia Carpenter, of Zanesville, d. 2-22-1813. Publication date February 24, 1813

Lt. Timothy E. Danielson, d. 1-21-1813 at Fort Winchester. Lt. Danielson "late of Marietta of Capt. Lingan's company, 19th Regt. United States Infantry, age 27 years. He was the son of the late Gen. Danielson of Massachusetts and step-son to Gen. W. Eaton, deceased". Publication date February 3, 1813

Miss Kiasiah Gallaher, d. 1-23-1813 in the 15th year of her age. Publication date January 27, 1813.

John Bailey, instantly killed by the fall of a tree 1-8-1813.

Robert Patterson, a schoolmaster, d. 12-2-1813 age 44 years.

Mrs. John Davis , wife John Davis, d. in Springfield, 12-7-1813 leaving a number of small children. Publication date December 8, 1813.

Miss Jane Ferguson, niece of Mr. Ferguson, d. in this town "of a Hectic". Publication date December 29, 1813.

Tmothy Rose, Esq. d. in Granville, 11-27-1813 aged 52. He enlisted as soldier in the Rev. War when 16 and "served until peace". He filled Civil War offices in his native state, Massachusetts and was a member of the company which settled Granville. Publication date December 8, 1813.

Miss Sally Irwin, of Zanesville, d. (no date) age 17 years. Publication date October 20, 1813.

James Kirker, of Westmoreland Co., Pa., d. in Zanesville 10-16-1813 aged about 52 years. Publication date October 20, 1813.

Capt. William Mason, d. in Washington Co., Ohio. (no date) Publication date October 6, 1813.

Miss Keziah Simonds, d. (no date) aged about 20. Publication date October 6, 1813.

Benjamin Sloan, Esq. one of the associate judges of the court of Common Pleas for Muskingum Co., d. at Springfield October 29, 1813 aged 36 years.

Mary Ann Craig, daughter of William Craig, Esq., d. (no date) aged 17 years. Publication date October 13, 1813

Stephen Buckingham, a merchant in Springfield, d. October 9, 1813 aged 38 years. Publication date October 13, 1813.

Snowden Stuart, d. 8-8-1813. Publication date August 11, 1813.

Oliver Wing, son of Enoch Wing, Esq., late of Washington Co., Ohio, d. August 18, 1813 aged 24 years. Publication date August 18, 1813.

Mrs. Houck, d. in this town. Publication date August 18, 1813

Son of A. M. Laughlin, d. age 21 months. Publication date August 18, 1813.

Rev. Joseph Spaw, of the M. E. Church, d. 8-28-1813 near Zanesville. Publication date September 1, 1813.

Albert Emmons, d. 7-24-1813. Publication date July, 28, 1813.

Capt. Benoni Peerce, Daniel Cunningham; killed and William Morrow, private, wounded in Battle of Massassinaway on the morning of the 18th, December and in the skirmish on the 17th. Publication date January 13, 1813.

MARRIAGES

Michael Hahn married Mary Allen 6-27-1813 by Christian Spangler. Publication date June 30, 1813.

Daniel Willer m. Kitty Miller, both of Jonathan's creek, Muskingum Co. 1-14-1813 by James Jeffrie. Publication date January 20, 1813

Bowes Boydston m. Polly Willey, dau. of Rev. John Willey of this county, on Sunday, 1-17-1813 by Christian Spangler. Publication date January 20, 1813.

Joseph Gale m. Mrs. Rebecca Moore (no date) both of this county by William Moore. Publication date December 22, 1813.

John Bowers m. Mary Vernon (no date) both of Muskingum Co., by Christian Spangler Publication date December 8, 1813.

Rev. James Culbertson of Zanesville, Ohio m. Sarah, dau. of late Joseph Milnor, merchant, of Trenton, N. J. in Trenton, N. J. 10-18-1813 by Rev. Armstrong. Publication date November 17, 1813

Jacob Messer, m. Polly Border 10-14-1813 by Christian Spangler. Publication date October 20, 1813.

William Lander m. Sarah Lawrence 10-14-1813 by Chris. Spangler. Publication date October 20, 1813.

Josiah Munro m. Rebecca Gold, both of Springfield, Muskingum Co., Ohio (no date)   Publication date August 11, 1813.

Major Horace Nye of Springfield m. Fanny Safford of Gallipolis, Ohio (no date). Publication date August 11, 1813.

Major Jeremiah Munson, of the U. S. Army m. Harriet, dau. of Daniel Warner 8-24-1813 by Rev. Culbertson. Publication date August 25, 1813.

William S. Richards, m. in Granville Miss Isabelle Mower, 9-9-1813 by Tmothy Harris. Publication date Sept. 29, 1813.

DIVORCE

Mary Ann Noland, "praying that her intermarriage with Barnabus Noland her husband might be dissolved for cause of voluntary absence of upwards of five years" Lancaster March 20, 1813. Publication date March 31, 1813.

Jacob Overmire of Fairfield County "praying that his intermarriage with Barbara his wife might be dissolved" Lancaster March 20, 1813. Publication date March 31, 1813.

Delilah Sprague, of Licking Co. prays that her marriage with John Sprague be dissolved. Newark 4-21-1813. Publication date

April 21, 1813.

James Stewart warns the public not to trust or harbor his wife, Jane, to whom he was married June 29, 1813, she having left his bed and board July 5, 1813. Publication date July 7, 1813.

James Stewart forewarns all persons from trusting or harboring his wife Hannah, she having left his bed and board July 5, 1813. Publication date July 14, 1813.

ALMINISTRATOR and TRUSTEE

Wm. Connell administrator for James Arnold estate 3-2-1813. Publication date March 3, 1813.

Edwin Putnam, trustee for said Col. Abner Lord, Springfield March 24, 1813. Publication date March 24, 1813.

Joseph Fickle, late of Hopewell Tp., Fairfield Co., Ohio notice by Edward Hamilton, Administrator December 12, 1813.

Amos Harris, late of Licking Co., Ohio notice by George and Jane Harris administrators Oct. 1813

Benjamin Sloan, deceased, notice of public sale by Nancy Sloan, administrator and I. V. Horne, administrator Springfield, Oct. 19, 1813.

Thomas Clayton, deceased, Joseph Clayton, Executor of estate advertises sale of furniture etc. in Clayton Twp., Muskingum Co., Aug. 20, 1813. Publication date August 25, 1813.

James Tanner, late of Tuscarawas Co., of Coshocton notice by James Robinson and Nancy Tanner, administrators 9-22-1813.

Nicholas Murphy, Thomas Speer, executor of last will and testament of said Murphy, Westland Twp., Guernsey Co., Ohio 3-29-1813. Pubication date March 31, 1813.

Benoni Peerce, notice of sale by Elizabeth Peerce, administrator and Wyllys Silliman, administrator of said Peerce estate, Zanesville 7-12-1813. Publication date July 7, 1813.

LETTERS IN POST OFFICE FOR

Adam Barr—Two letters in Post Office at Springfield, Muskingum Co., Ohio 1-1-1813. Publication date January 13, 1813.

Thomas Fouracres—One letter in Zanesville Post Office. Publication date October 6, 1813.

William Foreaker—Letter in P. O. at Springfield, Musk. Co., Ohio 7-21-1813.

Jacob Good—Letter in P. O. Springfield, Musk. Co., 7-21-1813.

MISCELLANY

L. Dent—wants 10 or 12 experienced boatmen "who will engage to go to New Orleans" Nov. 24, 1813. Publication date December 8, 1813.

Robert Fulton—Notice by Fulton to persons indebted to Kirker & Fulton, Zanesville Dec. 22, 1813. Publication date December 22, 1813.

Sally Holdsbury—offers a reward for the return of a bundle containing clothes and money. Bundle to be delivered to John Corbus at the sign of the Buck in West Zanesville." Publication date December 15, 1813.

James Murdock—of Cannonsburg, Washington Co., Pa. offers reward for information concerning Josephus Hunt, aged 19 or 20 years, a runaway apprectice to the millwright business. Nov. 24,

1813. Publication date Dec. 8, 1813.

James Reeves—Sign of the Western Star, Zanesville, furnishes accomodations for travelers. Nov. 10, 1813. Publication date Dec. 29, 1813.

James Taylor—I want to purchase a large quantity of Furs of all kinds, also a number of BEAR SKINS for which cash or goods will be given, Zanesville, Dec. 15, 1813. Publication date Dec. 15, 1813.

Mandly Taylor—of White Post, Frederick Co., Va. offers reward for the the return of his negro man, John, aged about 20 years. Oct. 6, 1813. Publication date December 8, 1813.

Luke Walpole—Merchandise for sale for cash or country produce. Springfield, Nov. 3, 1813. Publication date Dec. 8, 1813.

Mrs. Colerick—advertises the Zanesville Young Ladies Seminary, Zanesville, Dec. 29, 1813. Publication date Dec. 29, 1813.

William Burnham—For sale Salt & Cider by the barrel, Zanesville, Nov. 18, 1813. Publication date Dec. 15, 1813.

John Leavens—Hope V. Anchor Tavern offers to pay a good hostler $150.00 a year. Springfield Nov. 17, 1813.

Ichabod Nye—offers Whiskey for sale, Springfield 3-15-1813. Publication date March 31, 1813.

Elijah Ross—Gunsmith wants all old brass delivered at his shop in Zanesville. Feb. 10, 1813. Publication date March 31, 1813.

Jane Harris—advertises Blue Dying at the house formerly occupied by Jacob Ayes, Zanesville March 24, 1813. Publication date March 31, 1813.

REWARD

$20.00 reward offered for:

Deserted from the barracks at this place the following named Soldiers belonging to the 9th Regiment of the U. S. Infantry viz: JAMES KENT aged 23 years, born in Virginia. Also JOSEPH GRAHAM, born in old England, aged 40 years. He came from Mansfield to this place. Feb. 3, 1813.

LAND OFFICE AT ZANESVILLE, July 2, 1813, List of purchasers names and place of residence. Qr. Section, Tp. and Range of Tracts purchased and not completely paid for. Notice given of sale of tracts unless payment be made.

Jacob Reece, Muskingum Co. Sec. E TP. 26 Range 11

Jacob Bumgardner, Muskingum Co. Sec. N. W. TP. 15 Range 16 Publication date July 14, 1813.

List of 36 names

NEWSPAPER ITEMS FROM ZANESVILLE EXPRESS AND REPUBLICAN STANDARD

Zanesville, Ohio, Muskingum County

By Lorena B. Adamson

DEATHS

William Wells, Esq. d. in Springfield, Jan. 26, 1814 aged 60 years. Publication date February 2, 1814.

John Willy, a local preacher in the Methodist Episcopal Society, d. at his farm near Zanesville April 4, 1814. Publication date April 6, 1814.

Mrs. Daniel Warner, d. Oct. 11, 1814, consort of Daniel Warner. Publication date Oct. 12, 1814.

Col. Benjamin Tupper, d. in Springfield Feb. 4, 1814. He left a wife and five small children. Publication date Feb. 9, 1814.

Seamans, Drowned in the river at Springfield on the 6th. a child of the widow Seamans, about 3 years old. Publication date June 8, 1814.

Samuel Seamons, d. aged 62 years (no date). He came to this country from Novascotia about 24 years ago. Publication date Feb. 9, 1814.

Maj. William Reynolds, d. Nov. 13, 1814. Publication date Nov. 16, 1814.

Miss Kesiah Perry, dau. of Col. James Perry of this place d. Oct. 10, 1814. Publication date Oct. 12, 1814.

Martha Newell, consort of William Newell, d. at Springfield. Funeral sermon preached March 27, 1814. Publication date March 30, 1814.

William Newell, son of W. Newell, Esq. d. in Springfield age 17 years (no date) Publication date Mar. 9, 1814.

Marietta Frazey, dau. of Samuel & Esther Frazey of Zanesville died April 9, 1814 aged 2 months. Publication date April 13, 1814.

Mrs. Frisby, consort of James Frisby of Springfield. She has left a disconsolate husband and a number of small children to lament their irreparable loss. Publication date June 29, 1814.

Zeno Chandler, son of the late Dr. Chandler, d. Jan. 26, 1814 aged 16 years. Publication date Feb. 2, 1814.

Doct. Jesse Chandler, d. at his residence in Springfield Jan. 20, 1814 in the 50th year of his age. Publication date Jan. 26, 1814.

MARRIAGES

Alexander Tucker and Miss Hannah Bell married Oct. 16, 1814 by Christian Spangler. Publication date Oct. 19, 1814.

George Trusler m. Mary Dorothea Levingood Oct. 20, 1814 by Christopher Spangler

Capt. William Spry m. Sally Spry July 24, 1814 by Wm. Dixon. Publication date August 3, 1814.

Isaac Saucer m. Elizabeth Fletcher July 26, 1814 by Wm. Dixon. Publication date August 3, 1814.

Ensign Neil M'Fadden of U. S. Army m. Rebecca Bailey Aug. 18, 1814 by Christopher Spangler. Publication date August 24, 1814.

Col. George Jackson m. Mrs. Nancy Adams of Falls Tp. Muskingum Co. Nov. 6, 1814 by Rev. Joseph Thrap. Publication date Nov. 9, 1814.

Edward Harkness, of Springfield and Miss Elizabeth Usger of Zanesville were married on Sunday last by Christian Spangler, Esq. Publication date Nov. 16, 1814.

James Harper, late of Philadelphia m. Miss Juliet Wilcox of Lancaster by Adam Weaver on Nov. 6, 1814. Publication date Nov. 16, 1814.

David Cobb m. Peggy Whitacre, both of Zanesville, April 14, 1814 by Christopher Spangler. Publication date April 20, 1814.

William Eaker m. Miss Polly Ridgeway March 31, 1814. Publication date April 6, 1814.

Robert J. Bailey m. Miss Elizabeth Craft July 28, 1814 by Christian Spangler.

Alexander Britton m. Miss Charlotte Marsh in Clarksburg, Va. on Aug. 18, 1814 by Rev. Geo. Towers. Publication date August 24, 1814.

Mr. Arnold, of Virginia m. Prudence, dau. of Col. George Jackson of Muskingum Co., March 31, 1814. Publication date April 6, 1814.

ADMINISTRATOR & TRUSTEE

William Ward, late of Belmont Co., Ohio, dec'd. Notice by Edward Ward, Administrator, Guernsey Co., Ohio April 26, 1814. Publication date May 11, 1814.

James Thrall, late of Granville Tp., Licking County, Ohio. Notice by Charlotte Thrall, Extx., Silas Winchell, ad'tor June 18, 1814. Publication date June 22, 1814.

James Sinnati, dec'd. Notice of sale in Newark of 100 A. of land in 2nd. Quarter of U. S. Military Tract. Elias Gilman, Admr., Mary Sinnati, Admx. July 28, 1814. Publication date Aug. 10, 1814.

John Switzer, dec'd., late of Licking Co., Franklin Tp. Notice by Hugh Scott and Martin Grove, Administrators. Oct. 20, 1814. Publication date Oct. 26, 1814.

Elias Stanbury, late of Licking Co., O. Notice by William Stanbery and Ebenezer Granger, Executors, Newark, Ohio Jan. 27, 1814. Publication date Feb. 2, 1814.

Stephen Reed, late of Cambridge Tp., Guernsey Co., dec'd. Notice by John Taylor, admir. and Alice Reed, Admix. April 28, 1814. Publication date May 3, 1814.

Thomas Ramsy, dec'd. Notice by William Bogle and Peter Cochran, Executors, June 16, 1814. Publication date June 22, 1814.

Hananiah Pugh, late of Newark, Licking Co., Ohio. Notice by Sarah Pugh and Bradley Buckingham, Admrs., Newark, June 29, 1814. Publication date July 6, 1814.

Harp Peterson, dec'd. Notice by John G. Peterson, Admr. Jan. 14, 1813. Publication date Oct. 27, 1813.

Major Lewis Nye. Notice of sale by Margaretta Nye, Extrx. and Horace Nye, Executor. April 26, 1814. Publication date April 27, 1814.

Nicholas Murphy, dec'd. Advertisement of sale of land in Westland Tp. Guernsey Co., Ohio. Thomas Speer, executor. Sept. 7, 1814. Publication date Sept. 14, 1814.

Mary Murphy, estate, late of Guernsey Co., Ohio, dec'd. Thomas Speer, Administrator, June 17, 1814. Publication date June 22, 1814.

Clement Morgan, dec'd., late of Muskingum Co., Hopewell Tp. Notice by John Morgan and Joseph Thrapp, Executors and Mary Morgan, Executrix. Sept. 24, 1814. Publication date Oct. 5, 1814.

George M'Cullock, late of Coshocton Co., Ohio, dec'd. Notice by Catherine M'Cullock, Administratrix, May 10, 1814. Publication date May 11, 1814.

Thomas Means, late of Coshocton, Ohio. Notice by Charles Miller, Administrator, Jan. 24, 1814. Publication date Feb. 2, 1814.

James M'Calley, late of Licking Co., Ohio, dec'd. Notice by Henry Smith and William Gart, June 20, 1814. Publication date June 29, 1814.

Allen McKee, late of Ames Tp., Athens Co., Ohio by Notice by John McKee, Admir., Athens July 19, 1814. Publication date July 27, 1814.

Frederick Long, late of Guernsey Co., Cambridge Tp., dec'd. Thomas Witter, Admr. and Elizabeth Long, Admx., June 8, 1814. Publication date June 15, 1814.

Simeon Jennings, late of Oxford Tp., Tuscarawas Co., dec'd. Boaz Walton, Conard Westover, executors, April 28, 1814. Publication date May 25, 1814.

Philip Itzkin, deceased. Notice of sale of 700 acres of land about 15 miles from Coshocton. Abraham Kinsley and Jacob Kinsely, executors, May 20, 1814. Publication date June 1, 1814.

William Hull, dec'd. Robert Giffin, Admr. and Edy Hull, Admx. Coshocton Co., Newcastle T. p,, June 6, 1814. Publication date June 8, 1814.

Elizabeth Henderson, late of Pennsylvania. Petition by Daniel Flemming one of the heirs at law of the deceased E. Henderson, by his attorney, S. W. Culbertson, Zanesville, O., Nov. 7, 1814. Publication date Nov. 9, 1814.

Doct. Joseph Gray, late of Oxford Tp., Tuscarawas Co., dec'd. Notice by Boaz Walton & Jesse Walton, Admrs. April 28, 1814. Publication date May 25, 1814.

Aaron Gillet, late of Coshocton, dec'd. Notice by David Bookless, Admr., Oct. 24, 1814. Publication date Oct. 26, 1814.

Isaac Good, Jr. late of Oxford Tp., Tuscarawas Co., O., Dec'd. Notice by Nancy Good. Admrx. 4-28-1814. Publication date July 13, 1814.

Moses Hewitt, late of Athens Co., O. Notice by Henry Bartlett and Silas Bingham, Exrs., Athens, Ohio March 4, 1814. Publication date March 9, 1814.

Gilbert Devol, Jr., late of Marietta, deceased. Notice of sale by James Whitney, Admr. Marietta, Feb. 28, 1814. Publication date March 23, 1814.

Cornelius Donald, late of Salem Tp., dec'd. Notice by Boaz Walton, exr. and Rachel O. Donald, exx. April 28, 1814. Publication date May 25, 1814.

Daniel Cunningham, late of Salt Creek Tp., Musk. Co., O. Notice by Martin Chandler, Admr. Saltcreek Tp., April 22, 1814. Publication date April 27, 1814.

Doct. Jesse Chandler, dec'd. Notice by Abel Perrin, Admr. and Henrietta Chandler, Admx., Springfield Feb. 21, 1814. Publication date Feb. 23, 1814.

John Colver, late of New Philadelphia, Tuscarawas Co., O. Notice by Nathaniel Colver, Godfrey Westhaver, Executors. Gnadenhutten, Ohio, April 30, 1814. Publication date May 3, 1814.

Abraham Cherryholms, late of Oxford Tp., Tuscarawas Co., dec'd. Boaz Walton Admr. Elizabeth Cherryholms, Admx., April 28, 1814.

98

Publication date May 25, 1814.

Ethan Bancroft, late of Licking Co., Ohio, dec'd. Notice by Levi Rose, Admr. Lucy Bancroft, Admx. Publication date Aug. 3, 1814.

DIVORCES

Mary Richardson, late Mary Sellars, hath this day filed her petition praying to be divorced from her husband William Richardson, Muskingum Co. May 12, 1814. Publication date June 8, 1814.

Enoch Graves, whereas his wife Hannah refuses to live with him Graves forbids all persons from harboring or trusting his wife and his son Alonzo. Granville, Licking Co., Ohio April 18, 1814. Publication date April 20, 1814.

Adah Blanchard, late of Franklin Co., Vt. now a resident of Licking Co., O. has filed a petition for a divorce from her husband, Timothy Blanchard. Publication date April 27, 1814.

John Rankin. Notice of petition for benefit of the insolvent law. Feb. 15, 1814. Publication date Feb. 23, 1814.

Solomon Purdy. Wants Cooper stuff. Springfield. Publication date Feb. 23, 1814.

John H. Piatt, Flour & Whiskey wanted, Cincinnati. Publication date May 3, 1814.

Zerah Payne, advertises his shoe and Boot business, Zanesville Feb. 14, 1814. Publication date Feb. 16, 1814.

John Mathews. Liberal wages offered to a skillful Miller of Steady habits. Moxehale Mills. March 14, 1814. Publication date March 23, 1814.

George Hughes, advertises as Barber, Hair dresser etc. Publication date May 11, 1814.

Miss Guffin, advertises "Mantua & Bonnet Making" Aug. 22, 1814. Publication date Sept. 7, 1814.

Eb. Buckingham, Jr. and Increase Mathews, advertises for "A number of Stone Masons and Common Laborers" at the Springfield Bridge for the ensuing season", Springfield Feb. 23, 1814. Publication date March 2, 1814.

William Baker, advertises his Tayloring Business, Zanesville. Publication date March 9, 1814.

David Wirick, soldier in the 27th Infy. He was born in Washington Co., Pa. is 21 years old; a carpenter by profession; deserted from the Barracks of Zanesville March 6, $10.00 reward to any person taking up said deserter, etc. March 9, 1814. Publication date March 9, 1814.

Rachel Middleton, asked information about her husband, Thaddeus Andrews Middleton, who was to come from near Pittsburg, by land and to meet her in Springfield, Muskingum Co., Ohio. while she with baggage and two small children, came by water. After four weeks she had not seen or heard from him. Springfield. Publication date April 27, 1814.

James Crawford. Information wanted. He was a native of Pa., a distiller by trade, taken prisoner at Fort Michilimackinac and left Detroit in the brig Adams, landed at Buffalo at the time she was destroyed by the Americans. He has not been heard of since by his son-in-law, John Penny, who is married to his daughter, Hannah Crawford, who came to Pittsburg about the latter end of September 1812, with lieutenant

Darragh. Address Penny or Darragh, Pittsburgh, Pa. Aug. 3, 1814. Publication date Dec. 7, 1814.

Alfred Beard. Reward of six cents offered by Beard for information concerning Robert Olive aged about 16 years, a runaway apprentice to the hatting business. Madison Tp., Musk. Co., O. Publication date July 6, 1814.

John M'Donald, died near Chillicothe in the 90th year of his age. He was a native of Scotland and was with General Wolfe at the taking of Quebec in 1759. Publication date April 29, 1818.

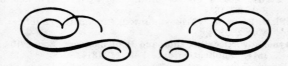

THE TAX LIST OF OHIO FOR 1810
Thelma (Blair) Lang

"An act levying a tax on land was passed at the first session of the eighth General Assembly of the State of Ohio, at Chillicothe, December 4, 1809, and was signed February 19, 1810 by Edward Tiffin, Speaker of the House of Representatives and Duncan McArthur, Speaker of the Senate.*

This Act provided:

1. "Taxes on all land owned by individuals, not exempted from taxation, yearly and every year hereafter*
2. The classification of all land into "first, second, and third grade land."
3. Rates of Taxation—"First class to be $1.25 per 100 acres, second class to be $1.00 per 100 acres, third class to be $.65 per 100 acres."
4. That a lister be appointed by the county commissioners to go to the dwelling of each and every resident owner of lands within the county and take a list of lands owned by the residents, with the name of original proprietors also;" Each lister to make two certified alphabetical abstracts of the names listed by him, one to be deposited with the commissioner of the proper county and the second, with the original list to be forwarded to the office of the state auditor before December 15, 1810.
5. Each County shall classify and assess as first class all lands on which the owner refuses to give the lister required information.
6. Collection of taxes of each County or Township by the Collector.
7. Taxes of proprietors not resident of State be collected by Special Collectors appointed by both houses of general assembly.
8. Distribution of tax monies.
9. Sale of land delinquent and on which no tax has been paid for three years.
10. Manner of enforcing the act.
11. Bonds.
12. Duties of Listers, Collectors, Commissioners, Auditors, etc. in relation to this act.
13. Failure to fulfill duties of those administering the Act.
14. Dates for taking tax lists and paying the taxes.
15. Disposition of lands on which taxes are delinquent.
16. Information to be secured by Listers.

Each lister to secure the following information:
- a. Name of proprietor in 1810.
- b. Name of original proprietor.
- c. Classification of land and number of acres to be taxed.

d. Original number of acres.
e. Fntry number, Survey nmber, Section number of Township number.
f. County in which land was situated.
g. Amount of taxes paid on land in 1810.

MAP OF OHIO—1810

INDEX TO TAX LIST OF 1810
ADAMS COUNTY

Thelma Blair Lang

John Adams, Henry Aldred, Andrew Alexander, John Alexander, James Allin, *Nath. Allin, James Anderson, Nathe. Anderson, Robert Anderson, William Anderson, Peter Andrew, David Armstrong, *John Armstrong, William Armstrong, *Jas. Arnell, *John Askhue, *Walter Ashmore, *Walter Askmore, Richard Askren, Amos Augustin, John Austin, Francis Ayres, Joel Bailey, *Walker Bailor, James Baird, Moses Baird, John Baker, William Baker, James Baldridge, James Baldridge, Sarah Baldridge, William Baldridge, John Baldwin, Stephen Baldwin, Samuel Baldridge, *Daniel Ball, Simon Ballard, *Daniel

102

Barbee, *Thomas Barbee, *William Barbee, *James Barkley, *The Heirs of John Barnards, John Barrett, John Barritt, John Bartlett, William Bartlett, Heirs of Elis Barton, George Bauman, *Henry Bayler, John Bayler, Stephen Bayler, Eldridge Bayler, Daniel Bayles, Daniel BaylesJr., Samuel Bayne, Joseph Beam, Thomas Bean, William Bear, George Beard, Benjamin Beasley, Jeptha Beasley, *John Beasley, Ellison A. Beasley, *Heirs of John Beasley, Nathaniel Beasley, Mathais Beavers, Michael Beavers, Alexander Beck, Andrew Bedinger, Stephen Beeck, *Clement Beedle, John Beekman, *William Berkley, Andrew Berry, Jonathan Bewle, Lewis Bible, John Bilbee, Peter Bilbee. Gabriel Black, Samuel Black, Thomas Black, William Black, *Tho. Blackwell, John Blair, Horatio Blanchard, John Boner, Jacob Boone, John Bovil, Thomas Bowen, Benjamin Bowman, Henry Bowman, James Boyd, Andrew Boyd, *Alex. Brackenridge, Robert Brackenridge, David Bradford, *Joseph Brady, Nan Brady, *Samuel Brady, Jacob Lratton, Charles Brewer, John Briggs, Joseph Britton, Demascus Brooks, *Humphrey Erooks, Greer Brown, Jane Brown, John Brown, James Brownfield, Joseph Brownfield, George Bryen, *James Bryen, John Bryen, Joseph Eryen, *Ambrose Buchannon, Thomas Burkett, David Burley, Charles Whilling Byrd, Cornelius Cain, James Cain, Jesse Cain, Alexander Campbell, Evan Campbell, Francis Campbell, George Campbell, James Campbell, John Campbell, Samuel Campbell, Curtiss Cannon, John Carbury, Devens Carey, *Thos. Carniel, Mark Carragan, Henry Carraway, *Mayo Carrington, James Carson, Joseph Carson, Peter Cartright, Michael Catt, *James Caward, John Cetty, John Chapman, James Charles, *Thomas Chilton, *John Chinnith, *Bawling Clark, James Clark, John Clark, Samuel Clark, Stephen Clark, *Benj. Cleft, Andrew Clemmer, *Mace Clemmons, *Benjamin Clift, George Coats, Joseph & John Cochran, Mary Coe, Ephraim Cole, James Cole, William Cole, Cornelius Colgin, Daniel Collier, Joseph Collier, Christian Collings, David Collings, Elijah Collings, Abraham Colven, William Colvin, Francis Combs, John Cone, John R. Connell, *Colin Cook, Catherine Cooke, John Coonrod, Daniel Copple, John Copple, Peter Conner, Lewis Coryell, Isaac Cox, Jacob Cox, ——— Crawford, George Crawford, Jonh Crawford, Thomas Crawford, William Crawford, Baurn Philip Creek, Jas. Criswell, John Cross, Samuel Cross, John Cruson, Benjamin Cultraugh, James Cummius, Samuel Cumpton, Thomas Cunningham, James Curry, Thomas Curry, Joseph Curtis, Elijah Cutchen, Joseph Daniel, Samuel Daniel, *William Dark, Joseph Darlington, Joe. Darlington, Lebediah David, Armstrong Davidson, John Davidson, William Davidson, Jeremits Davis, Richard Davis, Thomas Davis, William Davis, James Davis, Susannah Downing, *Philip Daws, *Joseph Deen, *T. Dempsey, *Aaron Denny, *James Deshman and others, David Devore, David Dillinger, George Dillinger, *Benja. Dillon, Job. Dinning, Elizabeth Donaldson, Israel Donaldson, William Donaldson, Joseph Douglass, Jacob Dowers, Andrew Dragoo, Bilterháser Dragoo, Daniel Dragoo, Davis Dryden, Samuel Dryden, Francis Duffy, Michael Duffy, Amos Duncan, David Duncan, Ennis Duncan, *Alexr. Dunlap, William Dunlap, John Dunlavy, Anthony Dunlavy, James Duren, John Eakins, David Earls, Isaac Earls, George Edginton, Sen., George Edginton, son of Joseph, George Edginton Jun., Isaac Edginton Jun., Jos. J. Edington, Joseph Edginton, Sen., Joshua Edginton, William Edginton, Isaac Edginton Sr., David Edie, *Thos. Edmonds, George

Edwards, Jess Edwards, *Richard Edwards, Jeremiah Ellis, Jeremiah Ellis Sen., Jesse Ellis, John Ellis, Nathan Ellis, Andrew Ellison, Arthur Ellison, James Ellison, John Ellison, John Ellison Jun., Robert Ellison, *John Elliott, Robert Elliot, Thomas Ellrod, Adam Erwin, *John Erwin, John Espy, Abraham Evans, Bej. Evans, *Edward Evans, John Evans, *Joseph Evans, *Susannah Evans, Thomas Evans, Abner Ewing, John Ewin, Robert Ewin, Samuel Ewin, Jeremiah Fenton, Jeremiah Fenton Jun., Samuel Fenton, Coonrod Fester, Charles Fields, Simon Fields, John Finley, John E. Finley, *Joseph S. Finley, Robert Finley, George Fisher, John Fisher, John Fisher Jun., *Bartholomew Fitzgerald, Adam Flaugher, Adam Falugher Jun., George Flaugher, *Osburn Flinn, Albright Florea, Andrew Foote, William Forbus, John Forsythe, William Forsythe, George Fortin, Nathaniel Foster, Robert Foster, Seth Foster, John Fowler, *Nathe. Fox, *James France, James Frame, Henry Franklin, Aaron Freeland, Aaron Freeman, Joseph Freeman, Michael Freeman, *John Fristo, Henry Fry, Nicholas Fry, William Gallagher, John Games, Benja. Gardner, Redman Gardner, Joseph Gaston, Robert Gaston, *Andrew Gatewood, *David Gilbans, Thos. Gibson, William Gilbert, George Gilgeer, James Gilleland, Robert Gilleland, Joseph Glasgow, Robert Glasgow, William Glasgow, Basil Glaze, Henry Glendening, John Glendening, John Glendening Jun., *Benja. Goodin, *Benja. Gooding, Basil Gordon, John Gordon, Lawrence Gordon, David Graham, *John Graham, *William Graham, *Francis Graves, *Richard Graves, *Robert Green, *John Green, *John Griffin, *John J. Griffin, Abraham Grooms, *Thomas Groves, James Gutridge, George Hains, Robert Haistings, John Hamilton, William Hamilton, William Hannah, John Hanover, Joseph Hanover, Henry Hardisty, Henry Hardman, Samuel Harlow, Nehmiah Harp, George Harper, Alexr. Harover, *John Harrice, *Charles Harris, *Jordin Harris, *Richard Harris, *Charles Harrison, George Harrison, *John Harrison, William Hatchison, Thomas Hatfield, John Hawk, * Hawkins, *John Hawkins, *Henry Heath, * Heddleston, Edward Hemphill, James Hemphill, Adam Hempleman, Robert Henderson, Byrd Hendrick, James Henry, *Henry Herdman, *James Herrin, Richard Hewitt, Aaron Hibbs, *William Hickman, *James Hines, *Isaac Hite, *William Holliday, *William Holliday and Hickman, *David Holmer, *David Holmes, James Holmes, * Hopkins, *John and Lyne Hopkins, *Samuel Hopkins, John Hood, James Horn, Joseph Horn, John House Jun., John House Sen., Milley Howard, Levi Howland, John Howland, *Robert Huggins, *Henry Hughes, Joseph Hughes, Benjamin Hunter, Abraham Hurst, William Hyett,

*John Inglish, James Inskip, *David Javkson, James Jacobs, William Jacobs, James January, Alexr. Jolley, Andrew Jones, Churchill Jones, Daniel Jones, David Jones, John Jones, John Johnson, Robert Johnson, Joseph Johnson, Samuel Jordan, *John Jouitt, *Robert Jouitt, David Keller for David Hensel, Hannah Keller, James Kendall, *Samuel Kendall, John Kendall, Abraham Kendrick, *Benja. Kendrick, *Curtis Kendrick, Samuel Kennett, Daniel Kerr, *Joseph Kerr, Paul Kerr, William Kerr, James Keskey, John Killin, Patrick Killin, Elijah Kimble, Voluntine Kinnett, John Kincaid, William Kinead, Thomas Kirker, *Thomas Kirkpatrick, Adam Kirkpatrick, Andrew Kirkpatrick, *Thomas Kirlin, John Knox, William Knox, Jacob Kratzer,

Cornelius Lafferty, *David Lahaw, *David Lambert, James Lang, Samuel Latters, John Laughlin, William Laughridge, Elias Law, James Lawson, John Leach, William Leedom, *Lewis Leinsford, Lewis Fanrin Co., *Charles Lewis, Philip Lewis, Thomas Lewis, William Liggett, John Linn, Andrew Livingston, Philip Locker, Philip Lockhart, Josiah Lockhart, Moses Lockhart, Thomas Lockhart, John Lodwick, Joseph Long, David Lovejoy, Joseph Lovejoy, *John Lovalace, James Lowrey, John Lucas, William Lucas, Robinson Lucas, *Lewis Leunsford, *Edmond Lyne, John Lyons, *William Lytle, John McBride, *Samuel McCall, Forgus McClain, James McClarin, William McClarin, *Thos. McClanahan, Francis McCleland, John McClenahan, *Thos. McCleland, Robert McClenehan, Mathew McClung, John McClure, Nathe. McClure, Ralph McClure, John McColm, Thos. McCollister, James McConnell, Robert McCoppen, William McCormick, Alexr. McCoy, Angus McCoy, David McCright, David McCright Sen., Nancy McCright, Alexr. McCullough, Thos. McCullough, Samuel McCullough, Alexr. McCutchen, John McCutchen, David McDemril, Michael McDonald, Sam McDonald, John McDowell, Moses McFadden, Arthur McFarland, Adam McFerson, David McFerson, Robert McFerson, William McGarrah, Alexr. McGehan, James McGoveney, John McHenry, Alexr. McIntire, Andrew McIntire, John McIntire, William McIntire, Joseph McKee, Samuel McKee, William McKinney, Duncan McKinzie, James McKittrick, James McNeil, Joseph McNeil, Gardner McNemar, William McNeshie, Alexander McNitt, Joseph McNitt, William McVay, *Robert Mack, George Mackey, John Mackey, William Maddox, Charles Magin, Andrew Mahaffy, John Mahaffey, William Mahaffy, Alexr. Mahany, Jesse Malany, John Mann, William Mannon, Jesse Markland, John Markland, William Markland, Ladock Markland, *John Marks, Daniel Marlott, Mary Marshall, *Richard Marshall, Elijah Martin, John Martin, *Henry Massie, *Massie & Kerr, *Nathe Massie, *Thos. Massie, Daniel Mathany, Michael Mattox, Thos. Maxwell, David Mears, William Meddleton, Thos. Melahan, Noble Melvin, John Merrill, Timothy Mershon, Elias Methany, Daniel Methany, John Middleton, Daniel Miller, David Miller, Henry Miller, James Miller, John Millegan, Samuel Millegan, *C. Minnis, Gavin Mitchell, David Montgomery, Jas. Montgomery Jun., Jas. Montgomery Sen., Patrick Montgomery, Samuel Montgomery, Aaron Moore, Andrew Moore, Daniel Moore, Elijah Moore, Henry Moore, Moses Moore, *Hosea Moore, James Moore, James Moore Sen., John Moore, Joseph Moore, Michael Moore, Nathe. Moore, Robert Moore, Samuel Moore, William Moore (E. F.), William Moore (W. F.), *Charles Morgan, *Daniel Morgan, *John Morgan, *Jonas Morgan, *Simon Morgan, Archibald Morrison, James Morrison, John Morrison, Robert Morrison, William Morrison, James Morrow, *Robert Morrow, *Henry Moss, James Mountain, *William Montjoy, Christian Mowrey, George Munroe, Samuel Murfin, Thomas Murfin, John Murphy, Recompence Murphy, Robert Murphy, William Murphy, Abraham Myers, John Myers, *William Nause, George Naylor, William Naylor, James Naylor, *William Nelson, *John Neauell, Joseph Nelson, *Presley Nevil, Thos. Newell, William Newell Jun., William Newell Sen., Jacob Newland, Christopher Newman, David Newman, Isaac Newman, John Newman, Joseph Newman,

The names preceded by an asterisk were original proprietors and not tax payers in 1810.

INDEX TO TAX LIST OF 1810
ADAMS COUNTY
THELMA BLAIR LANG

Richard Noleman, Philip Noland, *John R. Norton, William Nixon, Jane Nelson, Robert Newell, *John O'Banion, Charles O'Connor, Nathan Odell, Charles Osman, Thomas Ogle, Thomas Odell, William Ogle, David Oppy, John Orr, Archibald Oursler, *Joseph Oursler, Martha Ousler, Joseph Oyler, *John Pandall, Stephen Pangburn, Jonas Panther, Alexr. Parker, *Eliah Parker, *Iasiah Parker, James Parker, *John Parker, Elihu Parker, William Parris, Josiah Parker, Peter Parker Jun., Peter Parker Sen., Stephen Parker, Sylvanus Parker, William Parks, Ellis Parmer, Neeham Parry, Joseph Patton, Nathe. Patton, Thos. Patton, James Paul Sen., Jonathan Fawnell, William Pemberton, Isabella Pence, John Pence, Peter Pence, William Pence, John Pendall, Adam Penniwitt, John Penniwit, *Archillis Perkins, *Thos. Perkins, *Francis Peters, John Peterson, Ralph Peterson, William Peterson Jr., Amos Pattyjohn, John Pettyjohn, *Francis Peyton, *Heirs of Timothy Peyton, *Timothy Peyton, John Philips, Samuel Pilson, William Pittinger Jun., William Pittinger Sen., Jacob Platter, Peter Platter, James Poage, *Robert Pollard *William Pope, Rachel Portee, James Porter, John Porter, *Levin Powell, Hugh Powers, John Prather, Isaac Prickett, James Prickett, John Prickett, George Puntany, William Purdin, Benj. Pyealt, Henry Pyle, George Rader Jun., George Rader Sen., *John Rader, *Drurey Ragsdale, William Rains, Robert Ralston, Lawrence Ramey, Thos. Rand, Daniel Rankins, Peter Rankin, *Robert Rankin, *William Rankin, William Rawland, *Matthew Ray, Spencer Records, Daniel Redman, Elijah Redman, John Redman, Joseph Redman, Nevil Redman, Simon Reeder, Jonathan Rees, Barnett Reestine, Eli Reeves. *John Reid, Daniel Reynolds, Henry Reynolds, Joseph Reynolds, Joseph Reynolds Jun., Stephen Reynolds, William Reynolds, *Mathew Rhea, Anthony Rhoads, Israel Rhoads, John Rich, *Jas. Riley, Samuel Robarts, David Robe, Silas Robenson, Thomas Roberts, James Robins, Daniel Robbins, John Robinson, Thos. Robinson, William Robinson, *George Rogers, Henry Rogers, John Rogers, Thomas Rogers, William Rogers, Richard Roliston, James Rolston, Robert Polston, Richard Rounsavell, Michael Roush, Philip Roush, William Roys, John Russel, Patrick Russel, Robert Russel, William Russel, Jacob Sample, James Sanderson, Benja. Satterfield, David Satterfield, James Satterfield, *Charles Scott, Edward Scott, John Scott, Moses Scott, George Secrist, John Sellers, Samuel Sevin, Henry Sewell, Joseph Shaw, Peter Shaw, Russel Shaw, William Shelton, Abm. Shepherd, Jacob Shepherd, John Shepherd Jun., John Shepherd Sen., John Sherlock, Daniel Sherry, Daniel Sherwood, Jesse Shimer, Elizabeth Shoemaker, John Shoemaker, Simon Shoemaker, Solomon Shoemaker, Caleb Shreeves, Jonah Shreeves, John Shreeves, John Shroaf, Peter Shultz, Peter Simmons, Robert Simpson, Mary Simrall, *Philip Slaughter, Andr. Smalley, Jashua Smart, Philip Smeley, James Smiley, Ballard Smith, David Smith, Francis Smith, Jane Smith, *John Smith, Levi Smith, Mary Smith, *Obediah Smith, *Clewiah Smith, Robert Smith, Reuben Smith, William Smith, *Henry Sorber, Salathiel Sparks, *Andw. Specht, *Richard Speer, Uriah

Springer, John Spurgin, Samuel Starrett, Obadiah Staut, Thomas Staut, William Staurt, *John Steel, *John & Richard Steell, *John Stephens, William Stephen, Charles Stephenson, James Stephenson, John Stephenson, Mills Stephenson, James Stewart, James Stewart, Joseph Stewart, Robert Stewart, John Stickler, John Stivers, Jacob Storm, Aaron Stratton, *Beverly Stubblefield, Darby Sullivan, Jacob Sumalt, *Simon Summers, Ebenezer Sutherland, Jacob Swisher, Benjamin Sutton,   *Vincent Tapp, *Francis Taylor, *Richard Taylor, *Reuben Taylor, Newcomb Territ, Daniel Tharp, John Tharp, Richard Thatcher, Abrahm Thomas, David Thomas, Rees Thomas, Silas Thomas, William Tompkins, James Thompson, Jane Thompson, John Thompson, Mathew Thompson, Thomas Thompson, William Thompson, Samuel Thuraman, William Tomlin, Daniel Trackler, John Trebar, Robert Trevis, Christopher Trotter, Jeremiah Tryon, Osburn Tucker, Nathe. Tumbelson, Thos. Thoroman,   John Vance, Elizabeth Vanmeter, Benja. Vanpelt, Mary Vanpelt, Alexr. Varner, Edward Veach, Ralph Vores,   Josiah Wade, Lephemiah Wade, William Wade, James Wadman, Jonathan Waits, Elijah Walden, David Waldron, James Walker, Peter Walker, Samuel Walker, Delashhunt Walling, Jacob Walling, James Walsh Jun., *Lawrence Ward, *Thos. Warring, *William Washan, Ebenezer Washburn, Cornelius Washburn, Joseph Washburn, Nathe. Washburn, Nicholas Washburn, Thos. Wason, *Robert Watlins, Abraham Watson, John Wenston, Elinor West, John West, William West, Joseph Westbrook, Jesse Wetherenton, George Whaley, Levin Wheeler, James Wheery, Adam White, Uriah White, Charles Whitlatch, Elijah Whitlatch, Robert Whitlatch, Ezekiel Whitman, John Wickoff, Peter Wickoff, Peter Wickerman, Edmons Wildridge, Elizabeth Williams, *James Williams, John Williams, Joseph Williams, Morgan Williams, William Williams, Cornelius Williamson, Williamson, Means & Co., Samuel Williamson Jun., Samuel Williamson Sen., Thos. Williamson, William Williamson, John Wills, William Wills, Spencer Wilson, *Thos. Wilson, *Thos. Winslow, *John Winston, Jacob Wisner, Joseph Womack, Christopher Womsley, Isaac Womsley, Jonathan Womsley, William Wimsley, Abel Wood, Benjamin Wood, Jesse Wood, John Wood, Micah Wood, William Wood, Andrew Woodrow, Thos. Woods, *Robert Woodson, *Edmond Woolridge, David Worstell, James Works, John Wright, James Wright, *James Wright Sen., Robert Wright, Samuel Wright, William Wright,   William Yearley, John Yocum, David Young, Henry Young, James Young, Morgan Young, Thomas Young.

*—The names preceded by an asterisk were original proprietors and not tax payers in 1810.

INDEX TO TAX LIST OF 1810
ATHENS COUNTY

*Ainsworth, Jedh; *Alden, Jona; *Alden, Jne.; Alderman, Elijah; Alderman, Elisha; Alderman, Elisha Jun.; Ames, Silvanus; *Andrew, M Calla; *Angel, Joseph; *Angel, Israel; *Angel & Leavens; *Austin, Shadrach.

*Babcock, Abijah; "Babcock, Abijh; Bailey, John; Ballenger, Henry; *Barker, Isaac; Barrows, Ebenezer; Barrows, George; Barrows, Henry; Barrows, William; *Bartlett, William; Beaumont, Samuel; Beebe, Hopson; *Biggs, Zauheus; *Blanchard, A.; Boils, Jacob; Boils, Martin; Boils, Peter; *Bowers, Henry; *Bowers, Jhe.; Branch, Samuel; Brown, Benjamin; Brown, John; Brown, William; Buckingham, Ebenezer; *Buell, Jhe; *Buell, Jno. H.; Buffington, William; Burkingham, Stephen; *Burnham, Isaac; Burril, Solomon; Burroughs, Josiah.

Cartright, Caleb; Case, David; *Case, Eliphalet; Chadwicks, Levi; *Chevalee, Jno. A.; Clark, Obadiah; *Coleman, Samuel; Coleman, Thomas; Connett, Abner; *Converse, A.; *Converse, Alpheus; *Converse, B.; *Converse, Benja.; Cooley, Caleb; Cooley, Simeon; Cowdery, Jacob; *Cowdery, Joel; Crippen, Amos; Crippen, James; *Culver, Ebenezer; *Cummings, Jno. H.; *Cutler, Manh.

Dailey, David; Dailey, Silas; Dains, Jeptha; Danielson, Luther; Davis, Benjamin; Davis, Nehemiah 2nd.; *Davis, Push; Davis, Reuben; Dean, Silas; *Debbencourt, Francis; Dickey, Thomas; *Dodge, Jno.; Dorrough, Archibald; Doute, David; Doute, Thomas; Dutton, Kingsman; *Dyer, Eliphalet.

Eutsler, George; Ewing, George Jun.

*Fearing, Paul; *Fitch, Andw.; Free, Abraham; *Friend, Jno.; Frost, Abner; Frost, Abner, Jr.; Frost, Benjamin; Frost, Eland; Frost, Joseph; Fuller, Joseph; Fuller, Seth; Fulton, Robert.

*Gardner, David; Glazier, Abel; *Graves, Asa; Green, Ezra; *Greene, Catherine; *Greene, Charles; *Griffin & Phillip Greene; Griffin, Zebulum; *Grovenor, Nathan; Grow, Peter; Guile, Benjamin; Guthrie, Joseph;

Halsey, Edward; Halsey, Jacob; Halsey, Jesse; Hamilton, Thomas M.; Harrold, Christopher; Hatch, Elijah; Havener, John; Hecox, Truman; Hecox, William; Hewitt, Moses; *Hildreth, S.; *Hildreth, Saml.; Hoit, Ezra; Hoit, Abigail; Holbert, William; Hopson, Eizabeth; Humphrey, Jacob; Hurlbut, Reuben.

Johnson, Azel; Johnson, Henry; Johnson, John; Johnson, Joseph; *Judson, David.

Kimes, Jacob.

Latimore, Elisha; *Lawrence, Jno.; *Leavens & Angel; *Lee, Jona; Lewis, Daniel; Linscott, Amos; Linscott, Isaac; Linscott, Joseph; Linscott, Noah; *Lippet, Christr.; *Lord, Abner; *Lord, Elisha; *Lord, Thomas; *Lord, William; Lottridge, Bernadus B.; *Loving, Danl.

McGonagal, James; McCune, John; McCune, Samuel; McKee, Allen; *Manchester, M.; Mansfield, Martin; *Matthews, Jno.; *May, William R.; *Meigs, Jonathan; *Mercer; *Merrill, Capt.; *Miles, Benj.; Miller, Abel; Miller, John; *Morton & Tupper; Munroe, Solomon; *Munroe & White; Munsee, Danile.

*Nye.

Ogden, Alvan; Oliver, John; *Oliver, Robert;

Palmer, Robert; *Parsons, Saml. H.; Paulk, Cappas; Peirce, William; Perkins, Eliphas; *Peters, H.; *Petit, Jno. Gilbert; Phillips, Jole; Pilcher, Elijah; Pilcher, Stephen; *Poster Amos; Porter, Cummings; *Potts, Andw.; Pratt, John; Pratt, David; *Procter, Nathan; Pugsley, Abraham; Pugsley, Joseph.

*Ralstons, Ezehiel; *Reel, J.; *Revers, Abram.; Rice, Charles; Rice, Jason; Rice, Joshia; *Rice, Oliver; Rice, Reuben; Richardson, Abraham; Richardson, Susanna.

Sawyer, Artemus; Seamans, Joseph; *Seranton, Abram.; Shaw, Peter; Shipman, Daniel; Sloans, Joseph; Spencer, Joel; Starr, George; *Starr, Josiah; Stedman, Levi; Stephens, Isaac; Stewart, Andrew; Stewart, Archelaus; Stewart, Archibald; Stewart, Daniel; *Swart, Everett W.; *Swett, Jona; Swett, Jonathan, Jr.;

Thompson, William; *Thorndike, Israel; *Tichener, Elisha; Tippy, John; Tippy, Uriah; True, Josiah; *Trumbull, Jona; Tubbs, Daniel; *Turner, Peter; Tuttle, Solomon; Tuttle, Othniel; Tuttle, Elisha.

*Underwood, R.

Walker, George; Walker, John; Walker, Obadiah; *Walker, Robert & Jo.; Wariner, Philemon; Washburn, Eleazar; Washburn, Seth; Waters, Josiah; Wethes, Daniel; Wheeler, Cliphalet; *Whipple, Abram.; *White, Haffield; *White and Proctor; *Whitney, Elisha; *Wickham, Thomas; Wichingham, John; *Wilkins, Jno.; Wilkins, Timothy; Williams, John; Williams, Nathaniel; *Wilson, George; Wilson, John; *Winson, Christr.; Woodbury, Nathan; Wolf, Christopher; Wolf, George; Wyatt, Joshua;

Zin, Nicholas.

INDEX TO TAX LIST OF 1810 FOR BELMONT COUNTY, OHIO
RECEIVED JUNE 20, 1810 BY B. HOUGH, AUDITOR.
RECORDED JULY 16, 1810

Allen, John; Allen, Iseah; Allender, William; Alexander, James; Alexander, John; Alexander, James Sr.; Alexander, Peter; Alexander, Robert; Amerone, Abraham; Ami, Mussard; Anderson, Humprey; Anderson, Ira; Armstrong, George; Arnold, Joseph; Aull, Jacob; Aull, John; Aull, Peter; Aull, Phillip; Aull, Valentine.

Babb, Peter; Bailey, Benjamin; Bailey, David; Bailey, Michigan; Balderston, Mordecai; Ballenger, Daniel; Bane, Elijah; Barlow, Joseph; Barnes, John; Barton, David; Baswell, Demsey; Baswell, Zadack; Beam, Elizabeth; Beam, George; Belange, James; Bell, John; Bell, Joseph; Bell, Nathaniel; Bell, Robert; Bell, Robert Sr.; Bell, William; Biggs, Zacharias; Bivens, Samuel; Bivens, Steig; Bockhurd, Fanny; Boggs, Ezekiel; Boggs, William; Boman, John; Bond, Allen; Bondy, William; Bondy, William; Bones, Jacob; Bones, William; Boyd, Thomas; Boyles, James; Braderick, Isaac; Braderick, Absalom; Bradshow, John; Branson, Isaac; Branson, Jacob; Broomhall, Phebe; Brown, Abbie; Brown, John; Brown, Samuel; Brown, Simon; Bryson, Edward; Bunday, Josiah; Bunday, Thomas; Burns, Ignatious; Burres, Jeremiah; Buskin, Thomas; Byers, Andrew; Buchannon, George.

Carothers, Christie; Carpenter, George; Carr, George; Carroll, Michael; Carver, Henry; Casey, Samuel; Calderhead, Alexander; Caldwell, James; Calier, John; Camble, Thomas; Campbell, Andrew; Campbell, James; Campbell, John; Campbell, William; Caughey, John; Caven, Thomas; Cheldra, William; Clark, John; Clark, Samuel; Clavenger, Isaac; Close, Henry; Cocks, Joseph; Coffee, John; Cogle, Isaac; Cogle, Ralph; Cohran, Robert; Cohran, James; Coleman, John; Congleton, William; Connel, Samuel; Conner, Daniel; Conrow, Darling; Coon, George; Coon, Jacob; Coon, John; Cooper, David; Cooper, Francis; Corrather, James; Culberson, Joseph; Cunningham, John; Craig, William; Cramton, Henry; Crawford, Archibald; Crog, Mathias; Crosley, John; Croy, Richard.

Dallis, James; Danford, Ambrose; Danford, Peter; Davies, Jacob; Davis, Abraham; Davis, Harmon; Davis, Moses; Davis, Susan; Dawson, Jesse; Dean, Abraham; Deen, Thomas; Denham, William; Desellmes, Jesse; Devan, George; Deweese, Owen; Dille, Absolom; Dille, Dann; Dille, Joseph; Dille, John; Dille, Samuel; Dillo, Calleb; Dillon, Asa; Dillon, Ezra; Dillon, Job; Dillon, Joseph; Dillon, Josiah; Dixon, Rachel; Dixon, William; Dodd, Joseph; Doudney, John, Jun.; Doudney, Knows; Dougherty, John; Drum, Jacob; Duelen, William; Duff, James; Dunn, James; Dunn, Thomas; Dunn, William.

Eagleson, James; Ealon, Joseph; Eckles, Charles; Edgerton, James; Edgerton, Richard; Edgerton, Samuel; Edwards, Elizabeth; Edward, John, Jun.; Elles, Jonathan; Elliott, John; Engle, Joshua; Erwin, Arthur; Erwin, Joseph; Ewers, David; Ewers, William; Ewores, William.

Faris, John; Farmer, Isaac; Farquoir, William; Faucett, David; Faulk, Izaker; Fawset, John; Fawset, Joseph; Fawset, Mary; Fawset, Samuel; Feeley, Thomas; Finch, Jesse Sen.; Finney, Phebe; Finney, Robert; Flawerty, James; Flechasty, Amasa; Flora, Joseph; Ford, Hugh; Frazer, Daniel; French, Otho.

111

Gandy, Abraham; Garrison, John; Gasser, Jacob; Gaston, Alexander; Gatten, William; George, Travens; Gibben, Joseph; Gamble, Joseph; Giffin, George; Giffin, Robert; Giffin, William; Gillaspie, David; Gilkinson, Robert; Gilleland, Hugh; Given, George; Given, Moses; Goatz, George; Gorden, James; Graham, Arthur; Gorley, Samuel; Gray, Alexander; Gray, James; Gray John; Gray, Robert; Greenlee, Greer, Henry; Greer, John Jun.; Greer, John, Sen.; Gregg, Samuel; Griffeth, Joseph; Griffeth, Robert; Grigg, Abner; Grigg, Caleb; Grigg, Jacob; Grigg, Stephen; Grimes, Joseph; Grimes, William; Groves, Barnet; Groves, Joseph; Groves, William.

Hall, George; Hall, Isaac; Hall, Isaac, Jun.; Hall, Veachel; Hallaway, Asa; Hallaway, Joseph; Hambleton, William; Hamler, Jacob; Hammond, Charles, Esq.; Hanes, Abraham; Hanes, Jacob; Hanna, Henry; Hannah, James; Henry, John; Hardesly, Francis; Hardisty, Obediah; Hardisty, Richard; Harres, John; Hart, Leonard; Hatcher, John; Hatcher, Noah; Hatcher, Samuel; Havey, Charles; Hays, Motley; Hazlet, Margaret; Henderson, Robert; Harris, John; Henderson, John; Henson, Susan; Hines, John; Hinkle, Christian; Hoge, David; Hoge, Isaac; Hoge, Solomon; Hoge, William; Hodgen, Stephen; Hodgen, William; Hollingsworth, Levi; Holmes, George; Holmes, William; Hoover, Henry; Horn, Valentine; Hopper, Robert; Howard, Horton, Hulto or Hutto, William or Hutts; Hunnunt (?), Mirum Huntsman, James; Hutcheson, David; Hutcheson, William.

Ingle, Abraham; Ingle, Caleb; Ireland, George; Irwin, Charles; Irwin, Sarah; Israel, John.

Jones, Richard; Jenkins, Evans; Jenkins, Michael; Jenney, Emes, Johnston, Adam; Johnston, James; Johnston, Noah; Johnston, Sterling; Joston, Josiah.

Kelsey, James; Kenkard, David; Kenney, Richard; Kirkwood, Joseph; Kisor, Andrew; Kisor, William; Kitts, George; Kriller, George; Kring, James.

Lambert, Abner; Lappen, Mary; Larue, John; Lash, Jacob; Lattamore, Alexander; Lawson, Thomas; Lay, Jacob; Lee, Robert; Lefavour, Camptele, Lemley, George; Lewis, Samuel; Lift, John; Linder, Joseph; Lockwood, Benjamin; Lockwood, David; Londy, James; Loyd, John; Lyons, Hugh; Lyons, John; Lyons, Joseph; Lyons, Thomas; Lyons, William.

McBratney, Robert; McBride, John; McBride, Robert; McCalester, Wallace; McCalester, Isaac; McCall, Mathew; McCleland, David; McClure, James; McClure, John; McCoy, Hugh; McCoy, Jacob; McCoy, James; McConnel, Alexander; McConnel, James; McCribben, Mary; McFadden, James; McFadden, John; McFadden, Robert; McFarland, Robert; McFarland, William; McFerson, Samuel; McElroy, Archibald; McGee, Jesse; McIntire, David; McKemmons, Thomas; McKerk, James; McKune, Samuel; McMahan, Andrew; McMellon, William; McNabb, John; McNabb, George; McNichols, Nathan; McPeek, Daniel, Sen.; McPeek, John, Sen.; McPeak, Richard; MccWilliam, Abraham; McWilliam, Alexander; McWilliam, Alex., Sen.; McWilliam, David; McWilliams, George; McWilliams, William; McWilliam, Thomas; McWilliam, John; McWilliam, Samuel; Marcus, John; Marcus, William; Marcus, Thomas; Marret, Daniel; Marshall, Benjamin; Marshall, David; Maxwell, John; Medahmore, Samuel; Medley, Joseph, Jr.; Melhouse, William; Melton, Stafford; Menel, Joseph; Meredith, Benjamin; Merren, John; Middleton, Jehu; Milay, James; Milhouse, Robert; Milhouse, Wil-

112

liam; Millegan, Moses; Miller, Jonathan; Miller, Robert; Millner, Edward; Miller, Nathan; Mitchell, James; Mitchell, John; Mitchel, Thomas; Mitchell, Samuel; Mitchem, John; Moore, David; Moore, Isaac; Moore, John; Moore, Joseph; Moore, Robert; Moore, Thomas; Moorehea, Mses; Mrrison, Arthur; Moorison, Duncan; Morrison, Robert; Murphe, Abner; Murphey, Benjamin; Musk, William; Myers, Henry; Myers, Jacob.

Newell, James; Nichols, Eli; Nichols, George; Nichols, Hannah; Nichols, John; Nichols, Joseph; Neff, George; Nicholson, Joseph; Nixon, Andrew; Nixon, John; Norris, John; Norris, Mary; Nossinger, Nancy; Newport, Aaron; Nuswanger, David.

Ogan, Samuel; Outland, Margaret.

Pallon, Matthew; Panocoast, Joseph; Park, Hugh; Parker, Jacob; Parks, James; Parks, William; Parr, James; Patton, James; Patton, Samuel; Patton, William; Patterson, Andrew; Patterson, John; Patterson, Joseph; Patterson, Matthew; Parish, Joseph; Parish, James; Patterson, William; Paul, George, Esq.; Peason, Benjamin; Peckering, John; Peggot, Moses; Peggot, Nathan; Pegion, Charles; Perry, John; Perry, William; Phillips, Eavan; Picken, William; Pickering, Jacob; Pickering, Jones; Pickering, Levi; Pickering, Samuel; Pumphrey, Nicholas; Pirkins, David; Plummer, Eli; Plummer, Robert; Plummer, Robert; Plummer, Phebe; Plummer, John; Posery, Joseph; Potts, Samuel; Powell, Richard; Price, John; Purdy, John.

Reed, John; Rickey, David; Right, William; Riley, James; Roberts, Joseph; Reddle, William; Ralston, Joseph; Robinson, Sampson; Robinson, Samuel; Robinson, Thomas; Ruble, David; Rush, David; Rannel, Ananias; Russel, John; Russel, Samuel; Ramage, William.

Scott, Andrew; Scott, John; Scott, Matthew; Sebert, Adam; Sedwell, Nathan; Seills, Jonathan; Shannon, Jane; Sharp, George; Sharp, Joseph; Sharp, Samuel; Sharp, Thomas; Sharp, William; Sharplop, George; Sharplop, Preston; Sharplop, William; Shatwell, Titus; Sherer, Valentine; Shreck, Frederick; Simpson, John; Simson, John; Sinclair, George; Sinclair, James; Sinclair, William; Satterwaite, Thomas; Smith, George; Smith, John; Smith, Joseph; Smith, Mahlon; Smith, Samuel; Smith, Thomas; Smith, William; Snideker, John; Snideker, Jacob; Snideker, Nicholas; Snideker, Peter; Snider, David; Snyder, George; Spain, James; Spencer, John; Spencer, Nathainel; Spencer, William; Springer, William; Stanley, John; Stanton, Burdon; Starr, James; Steel, Benigah; Steers, Joseph; Stephenson, William; Steward, Allon; Stewart, John; Stookey, John; Stonebraker, Samuel; Stout, Jacob; Stubbs, Joseph; Sutton, John; Sutton, Jonathan.

Tagard, John; Taylor, Elizabeth; Taylor, Nable; Tepton, Solomon; Tepton, Thomas; Tepton, Absolom; Thavis, Richard; Thomas, Camm; Thomas, Daniel; Thompson, John; Thomas, Robert; Thompson, Samuel; Thompson, Thomas, Esq.; Thompson, William; Todd, Stephen; Trimble, Henry; Trimble, John; Truax, Richard.

Vail, Benjamin; Vail, Robert; Vail, Stephen; Vail, Robert, Jun.; Vance, David; Vance, William; Vanfasen, Benjamin; Vanmeter, Isaac; Vanlaw, Joseph; Vanpelt, John; Vanweys, John; Varner, James.

Waddle, George; Waddle, Robert; Walker, Andrew; Wallas, David; Walker, George; Ward, Seth; Warnack, John; Warner, Peter; Warnor, William; Watt, James; Weller, Peter; Wells, Levi; West, Enos; West, Henry; Whikear, Thomas; White, Isaac; White, Patrick; Wiley, Hance; Wiley, Samuel; Wiley, William; Wilkeson, John; Wilkins, James; Willace, Robert; Willes, George; Williams, Henry; Williams, Mary; Williams, Samuel; Williams, Thomas; Willis, Workman; Willson, John; Wilson, Aaron; Wilson, John; Wilson, Samuel; Wilson, Thomas; Wilson, William; Winman, Christian; Wiriack, John; Wiriack, Peter; Witchell, John; Wolman, Samuel; Wood, Aron; Woods, Elijah; Woods, James; Woods, William; Workman, Abraham; Workman, Benjamin; Workman, William; Worley, Samuel; Wright, Joseph; Wood, Robert; White, John.

Yost, Peter; Young, Alexander.

INDEX TO TAX LIST OF 1810
BUTLER COUNTY

Abbott, Benjamin; Abercromby, Hugh; Adams, James; Alexander, Samuel; Alger, Skilman; Alston, Thomas; Andrew, Malcomb; Armstrong, Archibald; Ashcraft, Nimrod; Ayres, Alexander; Ayres, James; Ayres, John; Ayres, Michael.

Beaty, David; Ball, Dennis; Ball, Isiah; Bigham, William; Brant, David; Bruce, Charles; Broadbury, Hezekiah, Blackburn, James; Baker, Daniel; Beach, Uzal; Butler, Joshua; Brown, Robert; Broadbury, David; Bailey, Nicholas; Bridge, Benjamin; Bryson, John; Ball, Ezekiel; Barnet, James; Beaty, John; Beaty, John R.; Baker, Ephriam; Baker, John; Baker, Mahlon; Barton, John; Blue, Frederick; Beckett, John; Brees, Moses; Bell, Jacob; Baldwin, William; Bowles, James; Ball, Davis, Bake, John; Bowman, Jonas; Blue, John; Barkalow, William P.; Barkalow, Derick; Barkalow, Tobias; Barkalow, Lebulon; Broadbury, James, Broadbury, Simeon; Bone, John; Blossom, Joseph; Beelor, Samuel Jun.; Beelor, James J.; Burk, Thomas; Blackburn, William; Blackburn, Bryson; Bolton, Joseph; Brown, John; Brosius, Daniel; Baldwin, William; Bebb, Edward; Beaty, Jeremy; Burns, Anthony; Baker, Thomas; Bell, Nathaniel; Bell, Benjamin; Buchanan, John; Baird, Joseph; Baldwin, Joseph.

Cassidy, John & Patrick; Cassidy, John; Cassidy, Patrick; Clark, Stephanus; Clark, James; Cummings, David; Clap, John; Colby, Joseph; Crane, Phebe; Crane, Moses; Clevenger, Samuel; Cullum, Edward; Carrick, Robert; Carsom; John; Craig, Robert; Coapstick, Samuel; Clark, Jacob; Conger, David; Carter, Reuben; Crane, Stephen; Conklin, Josiah; Cummins, James; Cristy, Andrew; Cox, Joseph; Cullum, Allen; Caldwell, Abram; Clark, Samuel; Calwell, Robert;

114

Caldwell, Daniel; Caldwell, John; Charles, Nehemiah; Clawson, Andrew; Campbell, Archibald; Catrow, Charles; Cox, Walter; Coon, John; Clark, Josannah; Clark, John; Clark, Jonathan; Compton, Joseph; Chamberlin, Nancy; Catrow, Peter; Cooley, William; Cooch, Thomas; Collins, Joel; Crooks, William; Coen, Edward; Charlton, James; Cowgnil, John; Campbell, Stephen; Careley, Justus; Clark, Samuel; Cornelison, Andrew; Crume, Moses; Cox, Gilbert; Case, Jacob; Clarke, John.

Dillon, Thomas; Doty, John; Doty, Daniel; Dixon, John; Davis. Margaret: Dick, George; Dewees, James; Davis, Vincent; Dickey. Samuel; Dickey, Adam; Dixon, Christopher; Dixon, Plat B.; Dungan. Josiah; David, William; Downing, John; Davis, John V. S.; Drollenger, Philip; Dubois, Daniel; Dubois, Benjamin; Dine, John; Denman. Moses; Driver, John; Dickey, Samuel; Drake, James; Deem. Adam: Dewit, Zachariah P.; Douglass, Joseph; Dewit, Jacob; Davis, John Jr.; Darr, Conrad; Deneen, James; Dunn, James; Dunn, John; Drybread. George; Daniel, John; Dearmond, King; Dick, Samuel; DeCamp, Joab: Delaplane, James; Duffield, David; Debolt, John; Drake, James; Drake, Moses; Davis, Samuel.

Enyard, John; Edward, Ural; Ewen, Margaret; Enoch, Abner; Enyard, Benjamin; Enyart, David; Evy, Daniel; Elliott, Arthur; Elliott, Arthur W.; Easton, Moses; Everinger, Nathaniel; Ely, Joseph: Emerson. James, Emerson, John; Elliott, James; Evans, Moses: Elliott, John.

Freeman, Ezra F.; Fleming, Thomas; Fleming, Robert; Fisher. John; Freeman, Abraham; Freeman, John; Freeman, Thomas; Ferris. Robert; Finney, John; Frazee, William; Flenner, David; Flowers. Aaron; Francis, John; Francis, Richard; Francis, William; Frazer. Samuel; Francis, David: Flenor, Rudolph; Ferguson, Samuel; Ferguson, Athel; Ferguson, Thomas.

Greer, Eleanor; Gibson, Isaac; Garrigus, David; Gregory, Margaret; Gobel, Daniel; Goudy, William; Griffin, Daniel; Gregory, Samuel; Griffis, David; Gard, Stephen; Gee, John; Gordon, Philip; Gard. Jeremiah; Gard, William; Gard, Aaron; Garrison, John; Garrison. Silas; Garrison, Samuel; Garrison, Aaron; Goble, Abner; Goble, Jonathan; Goble, Benoni; Guilkley, Robert; Graft, Abraham.

Heaton, James; Hough and Blair; Hawthorne, Hugh B.; Harlan. George; Hall, John; Hall, William; Hall, Cornelius W.; Hall, John Jun.; Hunter, Hannah; Hagerman, Margaret; Hueston, Matthew; Hahn, Joseph; Halloway, Joseph; Huff, Abraham; Hall, William; Heaton, David; Henry, Joseph; Harvey, William; Holmes, John; Henderson, Joseph; Hendsley, Gabril; Hyndman, Samuel; Hall, Sarah; Hildebrand, Michael; Hussam, Jacob; Hunt, Thomas; Harden, John; Holden, John; Harper, Samuel; Harrison, Andrew; Huff, Isaac; House. Henry; Hand, Enoch; Hannah, John; Hamilton, Andrew; Hinsey. Cornelius; Hinsey, William; Horner, Nathan; Hoag, Eleaser; Hancock, John; Harper, John; Hawk, Phillip; Holstead, John; Howard. James; Hamilton, John; Huffman, George; Houghman, Aaron; Heath, Abraham; Heaton, Daniel; Hatfield, George; Huffman, Jarvis; Huffman, John; Hittle, Solomon; Hartsell, Abraham; Hogue, James.

Iseminger, George; Irwin, John; Irwin, Thomas; Irwin, James; Irwin, Norton; Imley, John C.

Johnson, Thomas; Johnson, Thomas Jun.; John, Isaac; John, Elias; John, Thomas; John, Thomas Jun.; Jameson, John; Jones, Maurice; Johnston, John; Jones, William.

Kennedy, Samuel; Kerr, John; Kennedy, Joel; Kennedy, James; Kyle, Thomas; Kyle, Samuel; Kelley, Oliver; Kephart, John; Kemp, Jacob; Kemp, Philip; Kemp, John; Kemp, Daniel; Kearl, Thomas; Kelly, George; Kephart, John; Kemp, Philip; Kemp, Jacob; Kemp, John; Kemp, Daniel; Kearl, Thomas; Kelly, George; Kelly, Joseph; Knipe, John; Kerchiral, Reuben; Kinnen, Levi.

Lewis, Jacob; Line, Solomon; Line, Benjamin; Line, Henry; Logan, David, heirs of; Lowry, John, heirs of; Laramore, John; Larew, John; Loder, John; Line, John; Layman, David; Lee, George; Legg, William Jun.; Linn, John, Linn, Adam; Lowry, Samuel; Lucas, John; Lee, James; Long, David; Long David Jun.; Long, Gideon; Long, Noah; Lingle, John; Little, Squire; Lane, Hendrick; Loy, John; Loy, George; Lytle, Robert; Lewis, Andrew; Long, Benjamin; Logan, Patrick.

Millikin, Daniel; McCarren, Barney; McGonegal, Philip; McCullough, Thomas; Murray, William; McClelland, William; Moore, Patrick; McEowen John; McDonald, William; McCrea, Gilbert; McKean, Richard; Miller, Samuel; Maxwell, John; Marshall, James; McAdams, Thomas; McDonald, Daniel; Matson, Thomas; Murray, William; McClelland, James; McClelland, James Jun.; McClelland, Daniel; McIntire, James; McClure, Samuel; McClure, John; Mulford, David; Mulford, David; Mulford, Job; Merril, John; Murphy, James; Murphy, Cornelius; Moore, Levi; Markland, Matthew; McGarey, John; McCracken, John; Malally, Joseph; Montony, Abraham; Martin, Abraham; Morrow, John; McMahon, John; McMahon, Joseph; McMahon, Joseph Jun.; Machin, Patrick; Montford, Francis; Morningster, Michael; Martin, Anna; Martin, Isaac; Miller, Jacob; Miller, Abraham; McKeen, John; McCray, Phineas; McCray, Samuel; Marsh, Serring; Marsh, John; Martin, James; Martin, William; Marklin, George; McClary, Samuel; Miller, Jacob; Mitchel, William; Moorehead, Robert; Moorehead, Thomas; McClosky, John; Morris, William; Moore, James; McClain, William; McKinstry, William; McVicker, Duncan; Moore, Gersham; Moore Lewis; McKean, James; McDowell, Matthew; McClane, William; Mattox, John.

Nelson, Daniel; Nixon, Allen; Nickolas, Humphrey; Nicholas, James.

Osborne, Esther; Onspaugh, Michael; Ogle, Robert; Ogle, William; O'Neal, Patrick; Orlison, Matthew.

Powers, Jacob; Powers, David; Parson, Daniel; Potter, Joseph; Patton, William; Piatt, Abraham; Potter, Rhoda; Potter, Enos; Peek, Joseph; Paugh, Daniel; Perine, Daniel; Phelps, John; Patton, David; Powers, Thomas; Potter, Russell; Potter, Samuel M.; Pierce, Michael; Perry, Daniel; Parkison, Maxwell; Parkison, John; Parkison, James; Pierson, Bethea; Pierce, James; Paddox, William; Patton, Thomas; Pounds, Thomas; Prichard, John; Pottenger, Thomas; Pottenger, Samuel; Paine, Samuel; Page, John; Page, Daniel, Patterson, John; Paddox, Ebenezer; Patterson, Robert; Paddox, Ebenezer Jr.

Quick, John.

Randolph, Benjamin F.; Randolph, Joseph F.; Round, Jacob; Riddle, William; Reily, John; Robinson, John; Robinson, James; Rush, James; Russell, James; Russell, George; Rugless, James; Reed, William; Reed, David; Reed, Robert; Roby, George; Roby, Elias; Robison; William; Reeder, Reuben; Ross, William; Reed, Christopher;

Richardson, Matthew; Robinson, William; Reynearson, Reynard; Rood, Reuben; Richmond, John, Richardson, John; Ray, Jonathan; Richey, Adam.

Sutherland & Brown; Symmes, Celadan; Seward, Caleb; Stanley, Isaac; Spencer, Anderson, Snyder, George; Stevens, Oliver; Stuart, James; Stuart, Charles: Shields, Daniel; Sewell, Sarah; Sheafer, Peter: Sinkey, John; Spinning, William; Squier, Meeker; Squier, William Jun.; Squier, John; Skinner, Daniel; Smith, Jacamiah; Shaff, Frederick: Smalley, John; Stark, Archibald; Spinning, Jonathan; Schenck, Obadiah; Stacey, Warham; Seward, Samuel; Seward, Isaac; Swearingen, John V.; Segarson, Robert; Stuart, Samuel; Stuart, Joseph; Sharp, Horatia; Stephenson, Cornelius; Stephens, Joseph; Snyder, Jacob; Stump, George; Street, Abraham; Squier, William; Squier, Abraham; Squire, Caleb; Selvey, Zachariah; Simpson, Ephriam; Simpson, Abraham; Simpson, Jonathan; Simpson, Allen; Scott, James; Scott, Robert; Scott, David; Scott, John R.; Simpson, Jesse, Sutton. Jacob; Simmons, Thomas: Smith, Andrew; Stout, Able; Stuart, William; Schenck, John; Swift, Thomas; Sample, John; Slepher, Stephen; Saunders, Paul; Sutton, David; Sutton, George; Shaw, Knowles; Shaw, John; Shaw, Richard, Shaw, Sally; Stiles, Elizabeth; Simpson, Alexr.; Stonebreaker, Boston; Shuck, Michael; Shields, James; Smith, William; Smith, Robert; Swearinger, Charles; Stubbs, Nathan; Smith. Oliver; Smith, Christopher; Spencer, Joseph.

Talbot, Tobias; Torrence, John, heirs of; Taylor, Jacob; Tompson. James; Thompson, Wm. Jun.; Travis, Amos: Tietsort, Peter; Tietsort. Peter Jun.; Tietsort, Abraham; Tietsort, John; Thomas, Gabriel; Temple, Michael; Temple, Michael Jun.; Tapscott, James, Tapscott, Joseph; Tapscott, William; Taylor, Henry; Teagarden, Moses; Tolen, William; Tilson, Luther; Thomas, William; Talbot, Thomas.

Urmston, David.

Vinnedge, John; Vancleve, Benjm.; Vail, Henry; Vail, Shobal; Vail, Hugh; Vannest, Garret; Vannest, Isaac; Vannest, John; Vanduyne, Matthew; Vanduyne, Matthew Jr.; Vanduyne, Isaac; Vannest. George; Virgin, Brice; Vorhes, Peter; Vance, John; Vail, Randolph; Vansickle, John; Vaughn, John.

Walker, Joseph; Walker, Samuel; Walker, John; Walker, James; Wilkinson, Leah; Woodruff, Timothy; Woodruff, Elihu; Wagner, Godfrey; Wilcocks, Peter; Wilson, Hugh; Wiles, Isaac; Wingate, John; Wade, Thomas C.; Wilson, Samuel; Woolverton, David; Welch, John; Wilson, Ebenezer; Williamson, Joseph; Woods, Isaac; Woodruff, Daniel; Watts, Richard; Williamson, Peter; Williamson, David; Worth, Joseph; Woodmansee, Daniel; Woodruff, Timothy; Whittlessy, Duran; West, Eliazer; Waller, Ashbell; Waller, Levi; Waites, Andrew; Webster, William; Wier, Alexr.; Wagoner, Christopher; Wagoner, William; Woodward, Reuben; Woodward, William; Wilson, William; Weidner. Jacob; Webb, Obadiah; Weaver, Henry; Weaver, George; Williams. Marsh; White, Thomas; Warnock, Margaret; Wright, Jane; Whitinger, Deborah; White, William; Wilson, Josiah; Whitehead, Gerusha; Wason,, Henry; Winton, Matthew; Wilson, Alexander; Wilson, John; Withrow, John; Withrow, James; Whitson, John; Whitson, James; Weaner, Philip; Whitinger, Jacob; Whitinger, Nicholas; Wilson, James; Wilson, Thomas; Wilson, Ann.

Young, Sarah; Young, James; Young, John; Young, Alexander; Young, Robert.

INDEX TO TAX LIST FOR 1810
CHAMPAIGN COUNTY

Anderson, Thomas; Antrum, Thomas; Armstrong, Robert; Armstrong, Thomas; Arowsmith, Ezekiel.

Baker, Milini; Baldwin, James; Ballenger, Joshua; Baly, Henry; Barnes, William; Barret, Abner; Brown, John; Bay, David; Bery, Achory; Best, Francis; Bishop, John; Bracken, Jesse; Britton, John; Brown, Jonathan.

Caffy, Joseph; Calver, Samuel; Camron, Hugh; Cartmill, John; Cartmill, Nathaniel; Cary, Abraham; Cary, Samuel; Cary, Witsel; Chapman, William; Cheney, Benjamin; Cheney, Ebenezer; Cheney, William; Clark, Absalom; Clendenon, ———; Corbus, Richard; Cory, Elnathan; Coventon, Edward; Craig, Abraham; Crain, John; Crawford, Able; Crites, Conrad; Croft, George; Crowder, Herbert; Cummins, Joseph; Curry, Hivans.

Daniel, Hunt; Daniel, J.; Daugherty, Jervis; Davis, Jesse; Davis, Thomas; Davis, William; Dawson, John; Demint, James; Denny, James; Denunt, James; Dugan, ———; Donel, Jonathan; Dorme, Jonathan.

Easwood, John; Ewens, Moses.

Freakes, Robert; Freermood, Matthias; Foos, Griffith; Fithian, George.

Galloway, James; Garvey, Gray; Garwood, Daniel; Garwood, John Jr.; Garwood, Levi; Gibbs, Samuel; Gilleland, James; Gilleland, Samuel; Good, John; Good, Thomas; Grant, Robert; Gutridge, John Sr.; Gutridge, John Jr.; Garwood, Thomas.

Hacker, John; Hains, Caralisle; Hamilton, John; Harbour, Abner; Harbour, Elisha; Harbour, William; Harvey, John; Hazel, Henry; Hendrecks, William; Hendricks, William; Holycross, Howel; Homes, William; Howel, Aden; Huffman, Jacob; Hughs, Abraham; Humphreys, John; Hunter, Jonathan; Hurst, Daniel; Husted, John; Huston, Call.

Inskip, John; Inskip, Joshua; Irwin, John; Jackson, John; James, Thomas; Jarboe, Phillip; Johnston, Jacob; Johnston, Silas; Johnston, William; Jonathan, Daniel; Jones, Daniel; Jones, Justice.

Kain, John; Kenton, Simon; Kenton, Thomas; Kenton, William; Kenton, Mark; Kever, Abraham; Kirrel, Joseph; Kiser, Phillip; Kite, Adam.

Lafferty, John; Lamme, James; Land, Army; Langham, E.; Layton, Arthur; Layton, Joseph; Layton, William; Leiwes, Thomas; Lingle, John; Long, Jonathan; Lovet, Britton; Lowery, Archibald; Lowery, David.

McArthur, D.; McBeth, Alexander; McCoy, Daniel; McKinnon, Daniel; McKonkey, Archibald; McLain, Joseph; McLung, ———; McKinney, Samuel; McNutt, James; M'Colloch, Samuel; M'Colloch, Solomon; McPherson, Adam; McQuaid, Arthur; McPherson, John; Marmin, David; Marmin, Robert; Marmin, Samuel; Marriman, Martin; Marsh, Israel; Medzeker, David; Medzeker, George; Milice, Henry; Miller, Phillip; Millhollin, Jonnsthan; Minnick, Mikiel; Minor, Peter; Minturn, Jacob; Mitchel, Samuel; Moore, Thomas; Moots, Charles; Moots, Conrad; Morgan, Simon.

Need, Ever; Newel, Benjamin; Norman, John; Norman, Thomas. Offerrel, John; Outland, Josiah.

Paul, John; Paul, William; Pearce, John; Pearce, Jesse; Pearce, Thomas Jr.; Pearse, James; Pents, John; Penu, Henry; Penu, Jacob; Penu, John; Penu, John, Esq.; Penu, Joseph; Penu, Samuel; Perrin, John; Powel, William; Pickerel, Henry.

Ray, Robert; Reames, Jourdon; Rector, Charles; Reed, John; Renick, Robert; Renuk, R.; Reynolds, John; Reynolds, Joseph S.; Rhodes, Adam; Rhodes, William; Roberts, ———; Rock, Patrick; Runyon, John; Rusle, Robert; Rusle, Sydia.

Sample, William; Sanders, George; Sargent, Enoch; Sargent, George; Sayers, Thomas; Sentz, Nicholas; Sharp, Alen; Sharp, Job; Sharp, John; Sharp, Samuel; Shibby, John; Skiles, William; Sleeth, David; Smith, Abraham; Smith, Christopher; Smith, Joel; Smith, Peter; Smith, Peter Sr.; Smith, Samuel; Spain, Hezekiah; Spain, James; Spain, John Jr.; Spain, Joshua; Spain, Theodorick; Spain, Thomas; Stallard, Thomsa; Stanfield, Thomas; Steel, Archibald; Stevens, Christian; Stewart, Charles; Stoe, John; Stokes, Janamas; Stokes, Joseph; Stoneberger, John; Strickler, Martin; Stroder, S.; Swisher, George.

Talbert, Sampson; Taylor, John; Setsword, Isaac; Tharp, William; Thomas, John; Thomas, Richard S.; Tofflemire, David; Tompkins, William; Turman, Bn.; Turman, Isaac; Turnner, James; Tylor, ———.

Vanel, David; Vanmeter, Henry; Vous, Solomon; Vance, Joseph.

Walker, Joel; Wallace, Thomas; Ward, Abijah; Ward, William; Warner, John; Watters, William; Westfall, Able; Wilkeson, Thomas; Williams, Henry; Wilson, William; Winn, John; Win, Adam.

119

INDEX TAX LIST OF 1810 FOR OHIO
CLERMONT COUNTY
THELMA BLAIR LANG

Abbot, John; Abbot, Joseph; Abbot, Silas; Abanion, John; Abercrumbia, William; Abraham, James; Abraham, John; Aikens, Gabriel; Aldridge, John; Allen, Robert; Allison, Henry; Allison, Richard; Amacost, Christopher; Anderson, James; Anderson, John; Andrew, William; Apple, Andrew Jr.; Apple, Andrew Sr.; Apple, Christopher; Apple, Henry; Apple, John; Apple, William; Archer, Chapman; Archer, Richard; Armstrong, Jno.; Armstrong, John; Armstrong & Wells; Arnold, John; Arthur, Abner; Arthur, James; Ava, Joseph.

Babcock, David; Ball, James; Bailer, Robert; Baird, Alexander; Ball, Jas.; Bangheart, Michal; Barber, James; Barber, Nathaniel; Bartley, Isaac; Bartley, William; Barton, Edward; Baud, John; Baum, Charles; Baum, Charles Jr.; Baum, Michal; Baylor, Robert; Baylor, Walker; Beasley, William; Beck, Jeremiah Jr.; Beck, Samuel; Beck, Samuel; Beck, Stephen; Bedwell, James; Bennet, James; Bennet, John; Bennet, Patrick; Bennet, William; Bettle, Everad; Bhymer, John; Bhymer, Jonathan; Bhymer, Nathaniel; Bhymer, Samuel; Bitler, —; Blackmane, John; Blackwood, James; Blair, Robert; Blair, Alexander; Boggess, John; Bolander, Stephen; Boner, Mathew; Boocker, —; Booker, Lewis; Boothby, James; Boothby, Josiah; Boring, Ruben; Bornes, Jesse Rept.; Botts, George; Bowen, Thomas; Bowman, Joseph; Bowter, Peter; Bowyer, Henry; Boyed, Samuel; Boyd, Samuel; Boyer, H.; Boyers, T. Rep.; Boyers, Thomas; Brackenridge, —; Brackenridge, Alex.; Brackenridge, Jno.; Brackenridge, John; Brackenridge, R.; Bradbury, Benjamin; Bradbury, Gibbons; Bradbury, Moses; Bradford, Samuel; Bradford, D.; Bradford, William; Bradshaw, —; Bragdon, Latham; Bragg, Thomas; Brannon, Alex.; Brasher, Luben; Bredwell, Yelventon; Brice, Benjamin J.; Bridges, John; Broadwell, John; Broadwell, Moses; Brooks, Absalom; Brooks, John; Broughton, William; Brown, Cleaton; Brown, George; Brown, Henry; Brown, John; Brown, Joseph; Brown, Robert; Brown, Thomas; Brown, William; Brownlee, William; Bramager, William; Brunk, Joseph; Bryon, Daniel; Bryan, Morgan; Buchanan, Alex.; Buchanan, Andrew; Buchanan, James; Buchanan, Robert; Buckingham, Enoch; Buckner, P.; Buckner, Thomas; Buford, Abraham; Bunnel, Jonas; Burget, Jacob; Burget, Valentine; Burget, Valantine Jr.; Burk, Kelley; Burnet, Robert; Burns, James; Burton, John; Butler, —; Butler, Lawrence; Bhymer, Joseph.

Cade, Thomas; Calvin, James; Calvin, Joseph; Calvin, Stephen; Calvin, Vincent; Campbell, Charles; Campbell, John; Campbell, Joseph; Campbell, R.; Cambell, William; Candle, Lewis; Cantor, Thomas; Carmach, Jonathan; Carr, Robert; Carter, —; Carter, Henry; Carter, John; Carter, Nicholas; Corrothers, John; Corrothers, William; Cartwell, John; Casa, Peter; Chapman, Edward Jr.; Chapman, Henry; Chambers, James; Chambers, William; Charles, John; Church, Jonathan; Clark, Benjamin; Clark, Houton; Clark, John; Clark, Joseph; Clay, Matthew; Cleighton, Philip; Cleaton, Philip; Cliver, John; Collins, John; Coleman, Francis; Coleman, Samuel; Coleman, W. Rep.; Colther, John; Colther, John P.; Colther, Isaac; Colther, Matthew; Combs, Thomas, Comer, Daniel; Comer, Henry; Comer, John; Conover, Elias; Conrad, George; Conrey, John; Conrey, Jonathan; Cornick, Thomas; Cornwell, Daniel; Cornwell, William; Coshow, William; Cook, Thomas; Cotglazier, David; Cotteral, Thomas; Cowan, William; Cox,

John; Cox, Joshua; Crabb, Edward; Cradock. —; Cradock, Robert; Crane, David; Crane, Luther; Crane, Sears; Crawford. —; Crawford, John; Creamer, Adam; Creamer, John G.; Criss, Nicholas; Crist, John; Crist, William; Criswell, John; Cross, Benjamin; Crossley. Robert; Crossley, Ruben; Crossley, William; Crouch. William; Cuppy, Henry; Curry, Pheba; Curry, Robert; Custard, Christian; Curtis, Timothy.

Dannels, J.; Dandridge. John; Darby, Nathaniel; Darrell. William; Davidson, Mathew; Davidson; Robert; Davidson, William; Davis. Henry; Davis, Isechar; Davis. James; Davis, John; Davis, Joshua; Davis, Lewis; Davis, Thomas: Davis, William; Davison. George; Davison, James; Dawson. John; Day, Absalom; Day, John; Day, David; Day, John Jr.; Day, Lebus; Danley. James; Dangherty, Francis; Daugherty, James; Darby, Nathaniel; Daubyns, Robert B.; Debenevill, D.; Debeneville, Dr.; Deuth, William; Death. William; Denham, Obed; Denison, Rachel; Devore. Nicholas; Dewitt. Peter; Dial. John; Dial, Shadrick; Dichy, Robert; Dickey, Hugh; Dickson, William; Dimmet, Ezekiel; Dimmet, John; Dix, Thomas; Dobbs. N.; Dole. Joseph; Donham, Able; Donham. Gideon; Donham, Henry; Donham, Jonathan; Donham, John; Donham, John; Donham. John Jr.; Donham, Nathaniel; Donham, Robert; Donham, William; Donnals. William; Dougal. W.; Doughman, John; Doughty, Edward; Doughty, John; Doughty, Robert; Doughty, Samuel; Druley, John; Druley. Samuel; Drummond. John; Dudley, Ambrose; Dugan, Joseph; Duke. Ephriam; Durham. Benjamin; Dye, James; Dye, John.

Earhart, George; Earhart. John; Easton, Ph.; Eckord, Samuel; Eggleston, Richard; Eihony, J. W. & others; Ellis, Samuel; Ellis, William; Elsbury. Isaac; Elstun. Eli; Elston. George; Elstun, Isaac; Ely, George, Ely, Samuel; Emery, William; Emley, William; Empson. Thomas; English. Robert; Eppert, Frederick; Erwin, Andrew; Evans, George; Evans, Daniel; Evans, John; Eyestone, George.

Fagan, Abner; Fagan. John; Fagen, Joseph; Fairchild, Abigal; Franchard. Richard; Feagins, Daniel; Fee, Eligah; Fee, James; Fee. Sarah; Fee, Thomas; Fee. William; Feree, John; Ferguson, Hugh; Ferguson, Isaac; Ferguson. Isaiah; Ferren, Nathaniel; Fields, Lebner; Fields. Sarah; Finley. Samuel; Fiscus, John; Fisher, Adam; Fisher, Benjamin; Fisher, Jacob; Fishwater, Thomas; Fitzpatrick, James; Flack. John; Foot. Thomas S., Forsythe, John; Fountain, Samuel; Four. Joseph; Fox, Daniel; Fox, Jacob; Fox, Nathaniel; France, John; Frazee, Able; Frazzee, Benjamin; Frazee. Jacob; Frazee, John; Frazee, Moses; Frazee. Richard; Frazee, Stephen; Friberger, Andrew; Friberger, Jacob; Friberger, Lewis; Friberger. Peter; Free, Isaac.

Garland. James; Garret, James; Garret. John; Garver, Jacob; Gaskin, John; Gatch, Conduce; Gatch, Philip; George, William; Gest, Enoch; Gest, Johnas; Gest. Joseph; Gest, Nathaniel; Gibson, James; Gilbert, Micai; Gilleland, John; Gilman, Daniel; Gilman, J.; Glancy. Jesse; Glancy, John; Glancy. William; Glaze. Thomas; Glenn, Samuel; Godfre, James; Godfre, John; Goggan, Thomas; Gold, Jesse; Gold. Joseph; Golden, David; Golden. Jacob; Gorden, A.; Goudy, Thomas; Gould, Jesse; Gould, William; Graham, Francis; Graham. John; Grahm, ——; Gray. Andrew; Gray, Archibald; Gray, Benj.; Gray, James; Gray, Peter; Green. John; Gregg, Matthew; Gregory, Walter; Griffith. John T.; Grisham, Samuel.

Hackley. John; Haag, Davin; Hagg, Davin; Hains, Amos; Hair, Abraham; Hall, John; Hall, Patrick; Hall, Richard; Hamilton. James;

INDEX TAX LIST OF 1810 FOR OHIO
CLERMONT COUNTY
Thelma Blair Lang

Hamilton, John; Hand, David; Hanly, Thomas; Hannan, Catherine; Harden, Peter; Hare, Thomas; Harris, Abner; Harris, John; Harris, William; Harrison, Jno.; Harsh, Conrad; Hartman, Christopher; Harvey, John; Harvey, Jno. & others; Harwell, Lipscomb; Hastings, Peter; Hath, Henry; Hathaway, Daniel; Hawkins, John; Hawkins, Martin; Hays, John; Hedrich, John, Heightler, John; Henderson, James; Hendrix, Henry; Henry, James; Herren, ———; Herron, James; Hess, Samuel; Hewitt, Joseph; Hewitt, Robert; Heynes, Abraham; Heynes, Joshua; Hickey, Andrew; Hicks, Moses; Higbee, George; Highbee, Isaac; Hight, Isaac; Higgins, J.; Higgins, P.; Higgins, Robert; Higgins, William; Hill, Alexander; Hill, Jacob; Hill, Samuel; Hill, James K.; Hill, Thomas; Hillman, Joseph; Hiran, Arch'd M.; Hirons, Samuel; Hise, Frederick; Hodges, James; Hodkins, James; Hodkins, Samuel; Hoover, John; Hopkins, Archibald; Hoy, Adam; Huber, Jacob; Huber, John; Huggins, William; Hughs, James; Hughs, John; Hughes, William; Hughey, Alexander; Humphreys, Alex.; Hunt, James; Hunt, John; Hunt, Jonathan; Hunt, Levis; Hunt, Timothy; Hunt, Willson; Hunter, John; Hunter, William; Husong, Christian; Husong, Daniel; Huntington, Silas; Hutchinson, Aaron; Hutchinson, Ezekiel; Hutcheson, Joseph; Hutchinson, Silas.

Iler, Jacob; Ireland, James; Irwin, John; Irwin, Robert.

Jacobs, William; Jackson, Andrew; Jackson, David; Jackson, Joseph; Jeffreys, William; Jewel, Robert; Jinings, Israel; Jinkins, John; Johnston, ———; Johnston, James; Johnston, John; Johnston, John B.; Johnston, Jno. B.; Johnston, Thomas; Johnston, William; Jones, Cadwaleder; Jones, Churchill; Jones, David, Jones, Edward; Jones, Henry; Jones, James; Jones, Joseph; Jones, Thomas; Jones, William; Jones, Tame; John, Thomas; Jostlin, Israel; Jostlin, Jacob; Jostlin, Jeremiah; Jordan, Joshua; Jordan, Samuel; Juathard, J.; Judd, William; Jump, William; Justice, Jesse.

Kain, Daniel; Kain, James; Kain, John; Kain, Michael; Kanady, Alexander; Kanary, Charles; Kerns, Gabrail; Kibbs, John; Kindal, Curtis; Kinney, George; King, Elisha; Kilbreath, Samuel; Kinzar, Jacob; Kinzar, John; Kirgan, Daniel; Kirk, Capt.; Kirk Robert; Kirkpatrick, Andrew; Kirkpatrick, James; Kerr, James; Klinger, John; Knight, John; Knox, James.

Lacock, Nathan; Lacock, Ruben; Lahaw, Jeremiah; Laken, John; Laken, Joseph; Laken, Samuel; Lambert, Joshua; Lane, Archibald M.; Lane, Robert; Lane, Samuel; Lane, Shadrick; Lane, William; Latimoore, Samuel; Laughland, James; Lawson, George; Lawson, Robert; Lawson, R.; Lawson, William; Leads, James; Leeds, Absolom; Leeds, Aron; Leeds, Robert; Legate, John; Lemasters, Richard; Leming, Abraham; Leming, Ezekiel; Leming, Isaac; Leming, Jonathan; Leming, Samuel; Leming, Thomas; Lenord, Aaron; Lenord, Moses; Lewis, Charles; Lewis, Edward; Lewis, John; Lewis, Thomas; Light, Daniel; Light, Peter; Light, Jacob; Line, Isaac; Lindsey, Caleb; Lindsey, Edmond; Lindsey, Hezekiah; Lindsey, Stephen; Lindsey, William; Linton, John; Little, George; Liver, Adam; Liver, Catherine; Logan, John; Long, Christian; Long, Jacob; Long, John; Love, Alexander; Low, John; Lower, Matthew; Loyed, Catherine; Lucas, Nathaniel; Lynn.

Andrew; Lyons, William; Lytle, John; Lytle, William; Lytle, William & others.

McAdams, Ephraim; McBeth, Alexander; McCanchy, John; McClain, A.; McClane, Charles; McClelland, Daniel; McClure, Richard; McCollom, John; McConnell, Thomas; McConnell, John; McCulin, Cornelus; McDaniel, Valentine; McDenna, Rodmond; McDougal, John; McDowal, John; McFarland, Thomas; McGraw, John; McIntosh, James; McKee, John; McKibben, Hugh; McKibbin, Joseph; McKibbin, Richard; McKibbin, William; McKinnley, Richard; McKinney, Cain; McKinny, James; McLane, Archibald; McLane, Hugh; McLane, Peter; McMahan, William; McMains, John; Mabon, James; Machlin, Hugh; Madcalf, John; Madearas, Malaci; Magrue, Andrew; Magrue, Charles; Maglaughlin, Charles; Mahan, Samuel; Mains, John; Mallott, Daniel; Malott, John; Malott, Theodora; Malott, William; Manes, Philip; Manning, Elisha; Manning, John; Manning, Nathan; Manning, Richard; Manring, Joseph; Maranda, Thomas; Marsh, Richard; Marsh, Thomas L.; Martin, Alexander; Martin Benjamin; Martin, Fielden; Martin, Lewis; Massie, N.; Mattacks, Elijah; Mayham, Samuel; Mead, John; Meal, George; Medaras, Thomas; Meffard, John; Melott, Peter; Mesle, William; Metchar, Jacob; Metsgar; Conrad; Miller, Benjamin; Miller, David; Miller, George; Miller, Jacob; Miller, Javin, Miller, John; Miller, John Jr.; Miller, John Sr.; Miller, Lewis; Miller, Stephen; Miller, William; Millier, Abraham; Minnis, Francis; Minor, Gedeon; Mitchel, James; Mitchell, John; Mockins, Daniel; Molsbury, Samuel; Montjoy, John; Morgan Nathan; Moreland, Barton; Morning, Benjamin; Morning, Rodhan; Moore, Amos; Moore, John; Moore, Joseph; Moore, Mary; Moore, Samuel; Moore, William; Morecraft, William; Morris, Frazee; Morris, John; Morris, Levi; Morris, Thomas; Morrison, James; Morrison, R.; Morrison, Samuel; Morton, Samuel; Moseby, —; Mosley, Benjamin; Mosley, William; Moss, Moses; Mullin, Anthony; Mure, Francis; Musgrove, Moses; Myre, Abraham; Myers, Francis Sr., Myers, John; Myre, George; Myre, Jacob; Myre, Philip; Myers, Jacob; Myers, Thomas.

Nall, M.; Nancarow, John; Nancarrow, Jno.; Nash, John; Nelson, Samuel Nesbit, David; Newkirk, Henry; Newton, Ebenezer; Nichols, Philip; Nole, Andrew; Nole, M.; Nole, Martin; Noll, William; Norman, George; Norris, Abraham; Norris, Aquillah; Norris, Elisha; Norris, James; Norris, Nathan; Nott, Ignatious; Norwell, —; Norwell, Lipscomb; Norwell, L.

Obanion, John; Ogden, William; Oharo & Bousman; Oldridge, John; Ossinee, Donnals, Jr.; Overton, John; Overton, Thomas; Orr, Robert; Owen, Amasa; Owen, David; Owen, Thomas; Ozburn, Josiah.

Page, Thomas; Pague, James; Parker, Alex.; Parker, James; Parker, John; Parrish, Gerard; Paskey, Frederick; Paterson, Charles; Patterson, Charles; Patterson, James; Patterson, John; Patterson, Thomas; Patterson, William; Paxton, Thomas; Pay, Henry; Payne, John; Payton, Francis; Perrine, Joseph; Perns, Samuel; Perven, Enoch; Person, Thomas; Person, Thomas; Person, William; Phillips, Thomas; Picket, Younger; Pickle, John; Pickerel, Henry; Piginan, Joshua; Poage, James; Poague, James; Poe, Joseph; Pollock, John; Porter, Elias; Powell, Robert; Prather, Erasmus; Prather, John; Pricket, Isaiah; Pricket, John; Pricket, Joshua; Pricket, Nicholos; Purkiser, Michael ; Pursley, James; Pule, John.

Quarls, N.

Radford, William; Ragen, Thomas; Raglin, Jno. R.; Ralph, —; Ralston, Henry; Ralston, James; Ramsey, John;Raney, Francis; Ranson, Ambrose; Raper, Leonard;Raper Samuel; Rarden, Timothy; Rastler, George; Redibaugh, John; Reed. Clement; Reed, Isaac; Reed, John;Reed, Luther; Rees,Able; Reeves, John; Reeves. Stephen; Redinger, Henry; Rhea, Matthew; Ridlin. Abraham; Riggs, Amos; Riley, Gerard; Riley, John; Ritchey. William; Robb. Barbury; Robb, William W.; Roberts, John; Robinson, Samuel; Robinson. Thomas; Robinson, William; Rogers, Bernard; Rogers, Levi; Rogers. Thomas; Roney, James; Roney, Rosanah; Ross John; Ross. John Jr.; Ross, Lazerous;Roy, Bawler W.; Roy. Beverly; Roy, Bewler W.; Roy. Boler; Roy, Matthew; Rounds, James; Rounds Lemuel; Roudebush. David; Roudebush, Jacob; Roudebush. John; Roudebush, Christian; Rumery. Moses; Rust, Paul.

Salisbury, Samuel; Salisbury. Thomas; Sapp, Edward; Sapp. Frederick; Sapp, John; Sargent, James; Sargent, John; Sargent, Joshua; Sayers,R. & J. Taylor; Scott, Charles; Scott, Edward; Scott. George; Scott, Thomas; Sells, Benjamin; Seton, Alexander; Seton, Thomas; Sewell, William; Shalady. Andrew B.; Sharp, George; Shattorly. Andrew; Shaw, John; Shaw, Thomas; Shaylor, Joseph; Shearer. Andrew; Shelton, Cluff; Shepherd Solomon; Shick. John; Shick, Lewis; Shimmard, Samuel; Shingle, Christian; Shingle, John; Shingle, Julian; Shingle, Peter;Shinkle, John P.; Short, John; Shotwell, Jasper; Shultz, George;Simanton, Alley; Simanton; Theophilus; Simanton, William; Simon, Peter; Simons, William; Simmons. Adam; Simmons. James; Simkins, Ephraim; Simpson, Edward; Sims. John; Sinks. Nicholas; Siseglove, George; Slack, Jacob; Sly. William; Smiser. Philip; Smith, Adam; Smith, Amos; Smith. Christian; Smith. Dennis; Smith, Esther; Smith, John; Smith. Joseph; Smith. Michal; Smith, Obadiah; Smith, T.; Smith Stephen; Smith, Thomas; Smith. William; Smith. Wm. S.; Snell, Daniel; Snell, David; Snider. Benjamin; Snider, Christian; Snider, John; South, Daniel; South, James; South. William; Southall S. Southall Stehpen; Sparker. Josiah; Standard, G.; Stanley, Zecheriah; Stark, Lewis; Stark, Richard; Steapleton, Joseph;Stephens. Allen; Stephens, Archibald; Stephens, Edward; Stephens. J.; Stephens, Ruth; Stephenson, Lemuel; Stiers, Richard; Stoner, Philip; Stout. Abraham; Stouter, Joseph; Strecklin, Michal; Straws, George F.; Strigens, James; Stroup, Jacob; Stump, John; Stump. Lydda; Summers, Adam; Sutton, Nathan; Sweet, Henry; Swim, Jesse; Swing, George.

Talifaro, Richard; Talifaro, W.; Tate. Alex.; Taylor, Francis; Taylor, J. & R. Sayers; Taylor. James; Taylor, Jas. & others; Taylor. James; Taylor, Lewis; Taylor, Thos.; Taylor. Jas.; Taylor, J.; Taylor. Jonathan;Taylor, R.; Taylor. Reuben; Taylor, Richard; Taylor. Samuel;Taylor, Wm.; Teegarden, Daniel; Teal, Jacob; Temple, Benjamin; Tench. John; Test, Sarah; Thomas Lewis; Thomas, Phenehas; Thomas. P.; Thomas, William; Thompson Bernard; Thompson, Edward; Thompson, John; Thompson. James; Thompson, William; Tibbs, John; Tinkle. Charles; Tingley Levi; Tolls, Alberson; Tolliver, William; Tomlin, William; Townsley, James; Townsley, Robert; Trees, John Jr.; Trees. John Sr.; Trent, Lawrence; Tribble, Shadrick; Trout, John;Troy Benjamin; Troy Christopher; Troy, John; Troy, Simon; Trump, Sarah; Turner. Peter; Tweed, Archibald; Tweed, Coldwell; Tweed Samuel.

Ulery, Jacob; Utter, Joseph.

Vancaton. Isaac; Vancaton, John; Vanderman, Henry; Vanderman. Jacob; Vanosdol, Okey; Vaughn. William; Vaunce, John; Vaunce. Thomas; Vaus, William; Vodern, Henry; Vorhis, Jacob; Vowls, Henry.

Waights, Charles; Waights, James; Walker, D.; Walker, Davy; Walker, Joseph; Walker, Nicholas; Wall, Walter; Walldon. George; Wallravin, Samuel; W a r b e n t o n, Joseph; Ward, James; Wardlow, John; Wardlow; Robert; Wardlow, William; Waring. Roger W.; Waring, Thos.; Warren, John; Washburn, Cornelius; Washburn. George; Waters, Isaac; Waters, Richard C.; Watts, John; Watson, Zadock; Weaver, Frederick; Weaver, John; Wells, & Armstrong; Wells, Aaron; Wells. Joseph; Wells, Robert; West, Thomas; West, William; Whetsone, Jacob; Whilden, James; White, David; White. John; White. Levi; White, Tarpby; Whitecar, Margaret; Whitecar, William; Whitley, Robert; Whitemore, Benjamin; Whitmore, Conrad; Whorton. Francis; Whirton, John; Wickroy. George; Wiggins, Philip; Wiley, Elisha; Wiley, John; Williams, John; Williams, Wallen; Willis, Henry; Willis. Icabud; Willis, Stephen; Willson, John; Willson, Peter; Winlock, Joseph; Winston, John; Winters, James; Winters; William; Wise. Henry; Witham, Gedeon; Witham. Hannah; Witham, Nathaniel; Wood, David; Wood, Jane; Wood, Jeremiah; Wood, Joseph; Wood. Joseph Jr.; Wood, Margaret; Wood. Moses; Wood, Nicholas; Woods, Allen; Woods, Nathaniel; Woods, Samuel; Woolery, Henry; Wortman. John; Wright. Robert; Wright, Sarah.

Yates, Jonathan; Yates, Thomas; Young, Original.

Zimmerman, William; Zumalt, Henry.

INDEX TO TAX LIST OF OHIO FOR 1810
CLINTON COUNTY

Thelma Blair Lang

Adams, William; Allen, John; Anderson, Jas.; Armstrong, Walter; Arnold, George; Austin, Thomas;

Babb, Henry; Babb, Thomas; Baily, Daniel; Ballard, David; Ballard, Enoch; Ballard, John; Ballard, Simeon; Ballard, Spencer; Ballenger, John; Barkley, Edward; Barkley, John; Barnet, Arthur; Barney, Athanatius, Barnet, Thomas; Bartow, Wm.; Baxter, Joseph; Been, Thomas; Beggs, Josiah; Benet, Michael; Benet, Timothy; Biggs, William; Bardsale, James; Blackwell, Joseph; Bradford, Chas.; Bridges, Charles; Buck, Christian; Buckner, Thos.; Burr, Peter; Butler, William;

Calsea, Jesse; Camel, Archd.; Carter, David; Cast, Ezeliel; Casto, Jonathan; Casto, Thomas; Ceueu?, William; Clevenger, Aden; Clevenger, David; Cob, Semer; Cochran, William; Colter, John; Compton, Amoss; Compton, Stephen; Conklyn, Abegail; Cook, Isaac; Cook, Isaac, Jr.; Cook, John; Cook, Joseph; Cook, Wright; Copeland, William; Cox, Samuel;

Dakin, Preserved; Dakin, William; Dean, Joseph; Driks, Peter; Dillon, Daniel; Dillon, Jesse; Dillon, Jonathan; Dillon, Thomas; Draper, Thomas; Duval, Dan;

Eachus, Robert; Easterlan, Caleb; Edwards, Arch.; Edwards, William; Ellis, Abraham; Ellis, Henry; Ellis, Shobal;

Fairfield, David; Fannin, William; Farquhar, Benjamin; Farquhar, Mahlan; Faulkner, David; Ferriss, David; Flitcher, Henry; Fraziel, Alexander; Frazier, Ezekiel; Frazier, John; Furnace, John;

Garreston, Isaac; Garwood, Stacy; Gates, Horatio; Goggins, Elizabeth; Green, Jno.; Green, John; Grice, Joseph; Griffet, John H.; Griffin, James; Grines, Nancy;

Hawkins, Wm.; Hadley, John; Hadly, John; Hale, Jacob; Hale, Silas; Hale, Thomas; Hammer, David; Hanes, Charles; Hanes, John; Hardwick, Wm.; Harlan, Edith; Harlan, Nathan; Harlan, William; Harrel, John; Harris, James; Harvey, Isaac; Harvey, Joshua; Harvey, Samuel; Harvy, Caleb; Harvy, Eli; Harvy, William; Hawkins, Amos; Hawkins, Isaac; Hawkins, James; Haws, Abraham; Haws, Conradt, Jr.; Haws, Conradt, Sen.; Haws, David; Haws, Elizabeth; Haws, Jacob; Haws, Katharina; Haws, Mary; Haynes, Enoch; Haynes, Jacob; Haynes, Joseph; Haynes, William; Hayworth, Absalom; Hayworth, George; Hayworth, George, Jr.; Hayworth, John; Hayworth, Malon; Hayworth, William; Henderson, Arch'd.; Henderson, Rich; Hester, Francis; Hines, Nathan; Hoblett, David; Hobson, John; Hodgson, Amos; Hodgson, Daniel; Hodgson, Bur; Hodgson, Jonathan; Hodgson, Solomon; Hughes, Jesse; Hughs, Jesse; Hunt, William; Hyat, Ezekiel;

Ireland, William;

Jackson, Isaac; Jackson, James; Jackson, John; Jackson, William; Jeffus, Job; Jenkens, James; Jenkens, Charity; Johnson, Arch. & Co.;

Kelly, Robert; Kinnorthy, John;

Lawrence, Jonathan; Lee, Henry; Lee, Samuel Leonard, Ezekiel; Leonard, John; Lewis, John; Lewis, Thomas; Lewrus, Thomas; Lindley, James; Linton, Daniel; Linton, Nathan; Linton, Samuel; Luwus, Ebenezar; Lytle, John;

McDonald, William; McGrager, John; McManis, George; McManis, James; McMillan, David; McMillan, Jonathan; McMillan, Thomas; Madden, Eli; Magee, Elizabeth; Mangrum, John; Mann, Charles; Mann, David; Mann, Henry; Martin, John; Mason, Stephen; Mead, Edw.; Mendenhall, Nathan; Mendenhall, Step.; Millhouse, Henry; Miller, John, Jr.; Miller, Margaret; Miller, Samuel; Millhouse, Robert; Mills, Daniel; Mills, James; Moon, James;

Nelson, John; Nelson, Wm.; Newlin, John; Nickerson, Joshua; Nicklinson, Daniel;

Odle, Thomas; Owins, Samuel;

Palmer, James; Palmer, John; Pata, Charles; Patterson, Daniel; Patterson, Thomas; Phillips, George; Pirkins, Isaac; Porter, Wm.; Posey, Thos.; Ransdale, Thos.; Rees, Lewis; Rees, Robert; Rees, Thos.; Rhineart, Adam; Rhineart, Jeremiah; Rhonemus, Jacob; Ridley, Thos.; Right, David; Rightsmas, Peter; Roberts, Jno.; Roberts, John; Roucks, Joseph; Rowser, John;

Sanders, Joel; Sanders, John; Sanders, William; Sewel, Aron; Sewel, David; Sewel, John; Sheals, David; Sheals, William; Sherdon, John; Smally, Benj.; Smally, Benj. Jr.; Smally, William; Smally, Freeman; Smith, David; Smith, Joseph; Spay, Mordecai; Spotswood, Jno.; Spray, Samuel; Spurgin, Ezekiel; Stalker, Nathan; Stanbrough, Solomon; Stanton, Fred.; Stanton, Samuel; Steel, Jno.; Stephen, Christopher; Stoops, Robert; Stout, David; Stout, Isaac; Stout, John;

Tailer, Wm.; Tench, Jno.; Tench, John; Thatcher, Thomas; Throckmorton, Ed.; Titus, Phillip; Towler, James; Townsend, John; Townsend, William;

Vanhorn, Nathan; Venad, William; Vickers, Richard;

Walker, Azel; Walker, William; Wall, John; Way, Paul; Whinery, Thomas; Whitaker, Oliver; White, William; Whitson, David; Wickersham, Enoch; Wickersham, James; Wickersham, William; Wilson, Amos; Wilson, James; Wilson, John; Wilson, Joseph; Wilson, Isaac; Woodson, Woolman, John; Worker, David; Worton, Mahalan; Worton, Jonathan; Wright, Israel; Wright, James; Wright, John; Wright, Jonathan; Wrightsman, Abraham; Yeazle, Abraham;

INDEX TO TAX LIST OF OHIO FOR 1810
COLUMBIANA COUNTY
THELMA BLAIR LANG

Adams, Andrew; Adams, David; Adams, William; Adamson, James; Adgate, Elias; Aitenior, John; Alexander, James; Allen, Isaac; Allen, James; Allen, Jesse; Allen, John; Alltaffer, John; Alltaffer, George; Almon, John; Altman, Andrew; Altman, Peter; Altman, William; Altmore, Andrew; Anderson, Banjamin; Anderson, James; Antram, Levi; Antram, John; Armstrong, Andrew; Armstrong, James; Armstrong, John; Armstrong, Thomas; Armstrong, Robert; Arnold, William; Arter, Abraham; Arter, Catherine; Ashbaugh, Andrew; Ashbaugh, Thomas; Adamson, James; Altman, William; Anderson, Benjamin; Ashford, Aaron; Ashton, Thomas; Aten, Henry; Atterholt, George; Augustine, George; Augustine, Isaac; Augustine, John; Augustine, Philip;

Babb, John; Baightell, Samuel; Bailey, Joseph; Bair, Jacob; Bair, John; Bair, Rudolph; Baird, Paul; Baird, Henry; Baker, Gideon; Baker, Jeptha; Baker, Peter; Baker, Michael; Baley, John; Ball, Thomas; Ball, Nathan; Band, George; Barber, Isaac; Barns, John; Battin, John; Battin, Richard; Baughman, Henry; Baughman, Jesse; Baum, George; Beall, Reasin; Beans, William; Beats, Christian; Beats, Urban; Beaty, Samuel; Beck, Daniel; Back, Preston; Becht, Jacob; Becht, George; Beek, Preston; Beens, Levi; Beens, Moses; Beens, Moses; Beens, Timothy; Beens, William; Beeson, Henry; Beesson, Richard; Beevers, John; Beever, John; Bell, Smith; Bell, William; Bennet, John; Borners, Jacob; Bernes, Jacob; Bilger, Frederick; Bixby, Benjamin; Blackburn, Anthony; Blackburn, John; Blackburn, Moses; Blackledge, Abraham; Blackledge & Gloss; Blackledge, Joseph; Blackledge, Levi; Blackledge, Robert; Blackmore, Charles; Blackman, Charles; Blair, Robert; Blake, Edward; Blecker, Frederick; Boid, John; Boid, William; Bollman, Lewis; Booth, John; Bossart, Jacob; Bough, Henry; Bough, Henry Jr.; Boulton, James; Bowen, Owen; Bower, David; Bowers, Alexander; Bowman, Christian; Bowman, Isaac; Bossart, Jacob; Bowman, Jacob; Bowman, Michael; Bowman, Phillip; Boyce, Robert; Bradfield, Jonathan; Bradfield, John; Bradfield, Joseph; Bradfield, Thomas; Branaman, Richard; Brandberry, Conrad; Brandberry, Conrad Sr.; Brandberry, Jacob; Brandberry, Phillip; Brandberry, Rudolph; Brannon, James; Bricker, Henry; Bricker, Jacob; Bricker, John; Briggs, John; Brinker, Andrew, Brinker, John, Brittenstein, Martin; Brooks, Aaron; Brown, George; Brown, Herman; Brown, Nathan; Burger, Daniel; Burger, Nicholas; Burger, Peter; Burns, George; Burson, Edward; Burson, John; Burson, Silas; Burton, Robert; Bushong, Jacob; Bushong, William; Buson, John; Buson, Henry; Butz, George; Byers, Frederick; Byers, John; Byres, John; Beaty, Samuel;

Calder, Alexander; Calder, John; Caldwell, James; Callahan, James; Callahan, William; Calt, Catherine; Cannon, John; Cannon, Lindsey; Cannon, Matthew; Canole, John; Canole, Peter; Carle, Joseph;; Carle, Richard; Carman, James; Carrol, Edward; Carroll, Edward; Cattle, Jonas; Caulter, John; Cawgill, Henry; Cawgill, Thomas; Ceplee, Michael; Chain, Hugh; Chain, William; Chamberlain, Aaron; Chandler, Joshua; Chapman, Joseph; Clapper, George; Clapsadle,

Daniel; Clark, Ellin; Clarke, Eleanor; Clarke, Samuel; Clay, David; Clinker, Christian; Clippinger, Anthony; Coblentz, Jacob; Coblentz, John; Cochran, Samuel; Condon, James; Connel, John; Consor, John; Cook, J. Y.; Cook, Jacob; Cook, Job; Cook, John; Cook, Michael; Cook, Peter; Cook, Randolph; Cook, Thomas; Coon, Adam; Cope, Caleb; Cope, Jesse; Cope, John; Cope, Joseph; Cope, Nathan; Copperthwait, Thos.; Coulter, Beever & J. Bowman; Countryman, Chriestian; Courtney, Doziney; Cowgill, Caleb; Cowgill, James; Cowgill, Thomas; Coxton, M.; Coy, David; Coy, Henry; Craig,-----; Crane, William; Crawford, Daniel; Crawford, Edward Jr., Crawfoed, William; Crew, Littleberry; Crist, Abraham; Croombacker, Jacob; Croombecker, John; Cross, Thomas; Crosser, Adam; Crozer, John; Crumbacker, Jacob; Crumbacker, John; Crumbroke, John; Cullorn, William; Cunning, Dennis; Curle, Joseph.

Daniel, James; Daugherty, Thomas; Davis, Abraham; Diselham, John; Dixon, Emanuel; Dixon, Henry; Dixon, Joshua; Dolby, Abner; Donnaldson, James; Dorlen, Cornelius; Dorlen, C. & Moore, E.; Douglass, James; Douglass, William, Davis, Ellis; Davis, Isaac; Davis, Samuel; Dawson, Nicholas; Deal, Charles; Dildine, Richard; Devon, Edward; Dickenson, Jesse; Dickenson, & Aitenior; Dickinson, William R.; Dildine, John; Dildine, Richard; Dillon, Moses; Dillworth, Benj.; Duck, George; Dun, Michael; Dutterer, Conrad; Dutterer, Frederick; Dutterer, Michael;

Earl, Joseph; Easterly, Michael; Ebberhart, John; Ecces, John; Edgar, Robert; Edmondson, Thomas; Eighholtz, Phillip; Elkin, John Sr.; Ellis, Enos; Elsor; George; Elwood, Jermiah; Embrec, John; Embree, Moses; Emmonds, Cyrenias; Emmonds, Henry; Emrick, Peter; Engle, Josiah; Engledeer, William; Erwin, James; Erwin, Samuel; Estep, James; Evans, Jonathan; Eyster, John; Eyster, Peter; Eyster, Samuel;

Failer, George; Failer, Michael; Fariquhar, Thomas; Farmer, John; Farmer, Thomas; Forney, Henry; Faucett, Richard; Faucett, Thomas; Fauquhar, Thomas; Fauquher, Famuel; Fausneight, John Feets, John; Fegley, Abraham; Fernley, Thomas; Ferree, Jacob; Ferril, James; Ferril, William; Fast, Frances; Fetts, Henry; Fife, John; Filson, Davidson; Fink, George; Fink, George & Rual Henry; Firestone, John; Firiston, Nicholas; Forney, Adams; Forney, Andrew; Forney, Elizabeth; Forney, Henry; Forney, John; Forney, Nicholas; Forney, Peter; Foster, Thomas; Fought, Charles; Fox, Christopher; Fox, Henry; Franks, Henry; Frederick, G.; Frederick, George; Frederick, Thomas; Frederick, Henry; Frederick, Jacob; Frederick, John; Frederick, Joseph; Frederick, Conrad; Free, Jacob; Freed, Jacob; French, Brazilia; French, Elijah; French, Robert; French, Thomas; Friasier, William; Frifeogle, David; Fugate, John; Fugate, William; Fulks, Charles, Furgarson, Samuel;

Galbreath, James; Galbreath, Nathan; Galbreath, William; Gardner, John; Garwood, Isaiah; Garwood, John; Gaskall, Davis; Gaskall, Israel; Gattes, John; Gaunt, Jacob; Gause, Enoch; Gaver, Gideon; George, Thomas Gibson, Samuel; Gilbert, Jacob; Gilbert, John; Gillson, Richard; Gillingham, Thomas; Gillson, Samuel; Gisselman, Jacob; Glass, David; Glass, Jacob; Glass, James; Gloss, David; Gloss & Blackledge; Golden, John; Gonfallos, James; Gonway, Joseph; Goodwin, William; Goodyear, Samuel; Grace, William; Green, Joseph; Green, Lydia; Green, Thomas; Greenamire, Jacob; Gregg, Nathaniel; Gregg, Nathan; Griffith, Reuben; Grimm, D.; Grimm, Daniel; Grimm, Henry; Grissil, Thomas;

129

Hackins, Thomas; Hage, James; Hahn, James; Hahn, Adam; Hahn, Jacob; Hahn, John; Halley, Hannah; Hams, Hickman; Hana, William; Handman, David; Hanes, Ebenezer; Hanes, Hinchman; Hanes, John; Hanes, Jonathan; Hanes, Joseph; Hanes, Levi; Hanford, Abraham; Hanna, Benjamin; Hanna, Robert; Hanna, Thomas; Harbaugh, William; Harmon, Jacob; Harnish, John; Harnish, Samuel; Harris, Isaiah; Harris, Jonas; Harris, Thomas; Harrison, Benjamin; Harrison, William; Harson, Jonathan; Hart, Richard; Hartman, Adam; Hatcher, William; Hautz, Jacob; Haword, H.; Haword, Horton; Hay, Charles; Heald, James; Heald, John; Heald, John; Heald, Nathan Sr. Heald, William; Heald, William O.; Heck, Peter; Heckins,—; Hefflick, John; Hepbourne, Thomas; Herman, John; Herman, Frederick; Hester, John; Hibely, Michael; Hickenlibely, Jacob; Hickman, Adam; Hickman, William; Hinchman, Henry; Hindman, J.; Hindman, John; Hipfner, Jacob; Hively, Christopher; Hively, Michael; Hoah, George; Hoake, Martin; Hoge, James; Holderrieth, George; Hole, Nathan; Holland, Samuel; Holloway, Asa; Holloway, Ephraim; Holloway, Jesse; Homan, Ralph; Hoober, Jacob; Hooey, Thomas; Hoops, John; Hostetter, David; Hostetter, Jacob; Haword, H.; Howard, Horton; Howard, John; Huffman, Derrick; Huffman, John; Huffman, Michael; Hull, Reuben; Human, David; Humphreys, Joseph; Hunt, Caleb; Hunt, Elisha; Hunt, Nathan; Hunt, William; Hunter, Robert; Huston, Edward; Huston, Samuel; Hutton, Thomas;

Ilgenfritz, John; Isonhaur, John; Ivey, Phillip; Ivey, Samuel;

Jackman, Robert; Jackson, Isaac; Jackson, John; James, Isaac; James, J.; James, John; James, Thomas; Jennings, Obadiah; Jewel, John; Jinnings, Levi; Johns, Griffith; Johnson, Andrew; Johnson, G.; Johnson, James; Johnson, Jo.; Johnson, Robert; Jolly, Samuel; Jones, Catlett; Jones, Joseph; Jones, Lawrence; Jones, Samuel; Justice, David;

Kail, Jacob; Keatch, Thomas; Keek, Catherine; Kees, Henry; Keesly, Jacob; Kellar, Abraham; Kellar, Frederick; Kempf, Jonathan; Kempf, David; Keohl, George; Kerns, Abraham; Kerns, George; Kerns, Jacob; Kerns, John; Kerr, John; Kimberal, Samuel; Kimberling, Samuel; Kimpf, David; King, William; Kinnet, William; Kinney, Aaron; Kinney, Jacob; Kinney, Lewis; Kinney, Lewis, Jr.; Kinney, Peter; Kintner, Andrew; Knauf, Adam; Koffle, Peter; Koonts; Michael; Krauce, Jacob; Krebbs, Christian;

Langle, Casper; Lattimore,——; Laughlin, Robt; Laughlin, William; Lawer, Jacob; Lawer, Matthias; Lawrence, John; Lawry, James; Leeper, William; Lepley, John; Lepley, Michael; Leppenock, Frederick; Lewis, Enos; Lewis, Jesse; Lindersmith, Jacob; Lindersmith, John; Lindersmith, Joseph; Lipper, William D.; Lodge, Abel; Lodge, Jonathan; Long, Charles; Longnecker, Daniel; Longnecker, Joseph; Loop, Jacob; Lozer, Christopher; Lozer, Henry; Lozer, John; Lybert, Jacob; Lyder, Lewis; Lynn, Nicholas; Lyon, J.; Lyon, Jonathan;

McBane, Angus; McBane, Hugh; McBane, William; McBean, Angus; McBran, Ann; McClean, Allen; McCloskey, William; McConnel, James; McConnel, Joseph; McConnel, William; McCoomb, David; McCoombs, David; McCoombs, John; McConn, John; McCourtney, John; McCoy, Daniel; McCraken, James; McCredy, Joseph; McCredy, William; McDevolt, Charles; McDonald, Alexander; McDonald, John; McGilvory, Andrew; McGinnis, Hugh; Machelman, L. Lewis; Mc-

Herrin, Daniel; McIntosh, Alexander; McIntosh, John; McIntosh, Daniel; McIntosh, William; MacInterfer, George; McKaig, Patrick; McKeag, Patrick; McKegg, Patrick; Mackendurfer, George; Mackentusser, George; Mackenturfer, George; Mackling, George; Mackling, Jacob; McLean, Allen; McLaughlin, James; McLaughlin, John; McLerrin, Hugh; McLonery, William; McMillen, Catherine; McMilllen, John; McPhail, Cornelius; McPhail, John; McPherson, Andrew; McPherson, John; McPike, Hugh; Magriger, George; March, Elias Sr.; Marsh, Henry; Marsh, Jesse; Martin, Robert; Martin, Simeon; Mason, Charles; Mason, John; Mason, Martin; Mathews, John; Matinger, George; Matlock, Samuel; Malsberry, Benjamin; Matson, Isaac; Maunes, George; May, Jacob; Meaey, Micajah; Mease, John; Meeks, Samuel; Meese, Christian; Mellinger, Benedick; Mellinger, Joseph; Mendengall, Aaron; Mentser, Christopher; Mentson, Michael; Merrer, David; Merril, Abel; Metts, John; Miller, Abraham; Miller, Anthony; Miller, Miller, Christopher; Miller, Daniel; Miller, Henry; Miller, Jacob; Miller, Levi; Miller, Nicholas; Miller, Peter; Milner, Joseph; Millner, Milton; Mires, Henry; Mirl, William; Missia, Christopher; Mitts, Jacob; Moore, Thomas; Morcer, David; Morcer, Joshua; Moreland, Adam; Moreland, Jason; Moreland, Jason Jr.; Moreland, Jonah; Moreland, Stephen; Morgan, William; Morningstar, Adam; Moore, Mordaica; Moore, William; Moore, Thomas; Morran, Jane; Morrow, Joseph; Morris, J.; Morris, John; Morris, Lydia; Morris, Samuel; Morris, William; Morrison, William; Morton, Joseph; Montgomery, James; Mothersbough, Philip; Mauner, George; Mounes, George; Mounes, John; Mounse, George; Mowen, Baltzer; Mowen, John; Moreland, Joseph; Musser, Daniel; Musser, Jacob; Musser, John; Musser Michael; Musser, Peter; Musser, Samuel; Myres, Conrad; Myres, Daniel; Myres, Henry; Myres, John; Myres, Isaiah; Myres, Michael; Myres, William; Mason, John Sr.:

Neeley, Jacob; Neesly, Jacob; Neidig, John Sr.; Neie, James; Noble, Alexander; Neidig, John; Newhause, David; Nicholas, John; Nigh, John; Nudig, John; Nusley, Jacob; Nutton, Thomas; Nyswonder, John;

Ogden, Stephen; Ogle, William; Ogleby, George; Ohler, Phillip; Okelly, Patrick; Olliphant, Samuel; Oran, Thomas; Overholtzer, Jacob; Owen, Joshua;

Packson, Benjamin; Painter, Adam; Painter, Jacob; Pallate, Frances; Palmer, Christopher; Palmer, Joseph; Parker, John T.; Patton, William; Pearie, John; Pearpoint, Jonathan; Pease, James; Pence, Joseph; Pennock, Joseph; Pettit, William; Pidgeon, William; Piper, William; Pitts, Michael; Poe, Adam; Poe, Andrew; Poe, Thomas; Pollock, Samuel; Pontius, John; Pressell, Valentine; Preston, John; Pricket, Joab; Quail, John; Queen, Jonah; Quick, Susannah; Quigley, Samuel; Quinn, John;

Raab, Henry; Raab, John; Ramsey, Charles; Randolph, William B.; Rapp, John; Rassell, Caleb; Rawler, Baltser; Reamer, George; Redman, Jacob; Reeder, Thomas; Reeder, Samuel; Reeve, Joshua; Reeves, Benjamin; Reiley, John; Rich, Peter; Richardson, Fielden; Richards, Abijah; Richardson, John; Richardson, Samuel; Rhodes, Joseph; Rhodes, William; Richardson, Joseph; Rish, Jacob; Ritchie, David; Ritchie, Peter; Roberts, Samuel; Robins, John Sr.; Robison, John; Robison, Jonah; Robison, Wm.; Rock, George; Rogers, Alexander; Rogers; Evan; Rogers, George; Rogers, James; Rogers, Joel; Rogers, Robert; Rogers, Thomas; Rogers, Thomas Sr.;

131

Rogers, William; Rokenbrot, George; Roles, William; Roof, John; Rook, George; Roose, Andrew; Roose, Frederick; Roose, John; Rose, Charles; Rose, Hugh; Rosa, Hugh; Rossell, Job; Routzen, David; Rowler, Baltzer; Rowler, John; Rowler, Michael; Rudisyle, G. George; Rudisyle, Jacob; Rummel, Henry; Runkerberger, Frederick; Rupert, Adam; Rupert, John;

Saint, Thomas; Saitner, Christopher; Samms, John; Samsel, Nicholas; Saunders, Michael; Saunders, Mordaria; Scattergood, Benjamin; Schooby, Elisha; Scott, Benjamin; Seanor, Michael; Searninger, Bennoni; Seavingen, David; Seipe, Phillip; Semple, John; Scofield, David; Sharp, James; Shasley, Gutlip; Shaw, Samuel; Sheafer, Jacob; Shearer, William; Shearer, Joseph; Sheely, Nicholas; Sheets, Christian; Sheetz, Frederick; Shriver, Peter; Shelleberger, George; Shelleberger, Jacob; Shellenberger, Martin; Sheller, Henry; Shennefelt, John; Shinn, Mary; Shinn, Thomas; Shirts, Michael; Shisler, Jacob; Shively, Christian; Shively, Daniel; Shively, Frederick; Shriver, Jacob; Shriver, Lewis; Shriver, Peter; Shoemaker, Abraham; Shoemaker, David; Shoemaker, Phillip; Shook, Jacob; Shry, Henry; Shuby, Nicholas; Siddle, Isaac; Siddle, John; Silvers, Amos; Silworth, Benjamin; Simmison, Robert; Simonds, Andrew; Sinclare, David; Sinclare, George; Sitler, Martin; Skrinkle, George; Slagle, Daniel; Slater, William; Sloan, John; Smith, Daniel; Smith, David; Smith, Davis; Smith, Frederick; Smith, John; Smith, Jesse; Smith, Lenor; Smith, Peter; Smith, Phillip; Smith, S.; Smith, Samuel; Smith, William; Snider, Abraham; Snider, John; Snider, Michael; Snodgrass, Alexander; Snoke, John; Spencer, John; Sponceller, Frederick; Springer, Jacob; Spraughn, Daniel; Spraughn, John; Stalleup, William; Stanley, Jonathan; Stanley, Thomas; Stanley, Moses; Stuphn, Henry; Starkey, Levi; Staupher, Jacob; Steininger, George; Stephen, Michael; Stephens, John; Stephens, Peter; Stephenson, James; Stepper, David; Steward, John; Stewart, Archibald; Stewart, Hugh; Stewart, William; Stibbs, J.; Stibbs, Joseph; Stokesberry, J.; Stokesberry, John; Stough, John; Stoupher, Christian; Stoupher, Henry; Stout, Jehu; Stratton, Aaron; Stratton, Benjamin; Stratton, Daniel; Stratton, Jos.; Stratton, Joseph Jr.; Straughan, John; Street, Aaron; Street, Unice; Streeby, Michael; Stull, Adam; Summers, David; Summers, John; Swearinger, John; Switzer, Jacob;

Taggart, John; Taylor, James; Taylor, Joseph; Taylor, William; Teanor, Michael; Teegardin, William; Teeters, Elisha; Tset, Zacheau; Thomas, Dennis; Thomas, Enos; Thomas, Henry; Thomas, Jesse; Thomas, John; Thomas, John Jr.; Thomas, John Sen.; Thomas, Michael; Thomas, Nathaniel; Thomas, Peter; Thomas, Samuel; Thompson, Isaac; Thompson, John; Thompson, Joseph; Thompson, Thomas; Thoon, Isaac; Thorn, Isaac; Tullose, John; Tulloss, Richard; Unger, Jacob;

Vallandgham, Clement; Vanfusson, Jacob; Venneman, Benjamin; Votaw, Isaac; Votaw, Isaac Jr.; Votaw, John; Votaw, Joseph; Votaw, Moses;

Wallahon, Samuel; Walter, Peter; Walters, Henry; Walters, Peter; Walton, Benjamin; Walton, Gabriel, Watson, Joseph; Walton, Joseph; Wancy, Joseph; Warner, Israel; Warrington, Abraham; Warrington, Abraham Jr.; Warrington, Abraham Sr.; Watkins, James; Watt, Thomas; Webb, James; Webb, John; Welker, David; Welker, Jacob; Welker, John; Well, B.; Wells, Bazelell; Wills, Bazaleal; Wells, William; Welsh, Lauderick; West, George; Westright, Peter; Whann, John; Whinery, John; Whinery, Robert; Whinery, Thomas; Whinery,

William; Whitacre, Caleb; Whitacre, Edward; Whitacre, Jane; Whitacre, Joshua; White, Uriah; Whiteleather, Andrew; Whitmore, John; Whickersham, Job; Wickert, John; Wickert, Peter; Wilhelm, Frederick; Wilkes, Samuel; Wilkins, Joseph; Wilkins, John; Willits, John; Willits, Joseph; Willoby, John; Willyard, Phillip; Wilson, Israel; Wilson, James; Win, Tobias; Winterrode, Henry; Wirick; George; Wolg, John; Wolf, Henry; Woods, John; Woods, Joseph; Woods, Joshua; Woolman, Abner; Woolman, Asher; Woolman, Samuel Jr.; Wore, Asa; Worman, Conrad; Worman, Henry; Worman, Jacob; Worrel, George; Wright, Joseph; Wright, Thomas; Wright, John; Wright Joseph; Wright, Joseph Jr.;

Yates, Benjamin; Yates, James; Yates, Robert; Yerrian, Conrad; Yerrian, Matthias; Young, Baltzer; Young, Jacob;

Zacheus, Test; Zeppernack, Daniel; Zeppernack, Fredk.; Zimmerman, John; Zimmerman, Peter.

INDEX TO TAX LIST OF OHIO FOR 1810
CUYAHOGA COUNTY
THELMA BLAIR LANG

Abbot, David; Adams, Benoni; Austin, William; Baldwin, Samuel S.; Barnam, Eli; Barnam, Rachel; Bishop, Abraham; Blinn, Richard N.; Brooks, Benjamin; Brunson, Bela; Brunson, Daniel; Brunson, Harman; Brunson, Joseph; Brunson, Levi; Brunson, Seba; Bunel, David; Busk, Joseph; Burk, Silas; Burk, Sylvenus, Burres, David; Carr, Robert; Carter, Lorenzo; Chapman, Nathen; Clark, Marget; Cochran, Abner; Coleman, William; Comstock, Thomas; Cooper, Dennis; Cooper, Joseph; Cozard, Samuel;

Dodge, Samuel; Dille, Asa; Dille, David; Dille, Lewis; Dille, Luther; Dille, Neamiah; Dille, Samuel; Deane, Nathaniel; Deane, Seth; Deane, Timothy; Edwards, Henry; Edwards, Rodolfus; Edy, Caleb; Emy, Benjamin; Ensign, Ira; Ensign, Samuel; Fleming, John B.; Frost, Isaac; Frost, Elias; Gaylord, Alen; Grayham, Elisha; Gunn, Elijah; Hamilton, A. A.; Hamilton, James; Hoadley, Calven; Hoadley, Samuel; Holly, Ezekiel; Hook, John; Horace, Gunn; Jones, Benjamin; Jones, Samuel; Judson, Rufus; Kingsbury, James; Kyes, Frances;

McGrath, Elex; McGrath, Andrew; McGrath, Samuel; Miles, Charles; Miles, Erastus; Miles, Samuel; Miles, Theodor; Miller, Caty; Nobles, Elijah; Ofton, Thomas; Peek, Charles; Perry, Horatio; Perry, Nathan; Perry, Nathan Jr.; Prichard, Jared; Ruggles, Almon; Ruple, John; Rupie, Samuel; Seymore, Lothrip; Sharman, Dyer; Shartz, George; Shartz, John; Shaw, John; Sprague, Ezra; Strong, James; Tharp, Joel; Trillison, Isaac; Walworth, John; Walworth, John Jr.! Warner Noah; Warren, Daniel; Wert, Martin; White, Levi; Williams, Frederick; Williams, John; Williams, William; Wilson, Jeremiah; Woolcott, Benjamin.

INDEX TO TAX LIST OF OHIO FOR 1810
DELAWARE COUNTY

Abet, Charles; Adams, Samuel; Agard, Salmon; Alden, Daniel; Anderson, Bartholemoy; Armstrong, David; Aye, Jacob; Aye, John; Ayers, William; Barber, Isaac; Barber, Joseph; Barber, Orlando H.; Barns, Cumfort; Beard, John; Bennet, Elisha; Bennet, Henry; Bilings, Increase; Billington, Seth; Bon, Crastus; Boyd, William; Brown, Ezekiel; Brown, Thomas; Brundage, Nathanil; Buel, David; Buel, Peter; Buel, Thomas; Butler, David; Byxbe, Moses; Byxbe, Moses Jun.;

Carpenter, Benjamin; Carpenter, Gilbert; Carpenter, Ira; Carpenter, James; Carpenter, John; Carpenter Moses; Carpenter, Nathan; Case, Allen; Case, George; Case, John; Case, Silas; Case, Seth; Case Martin; Case, Truman; Catlin, Jonathan; Cellar, Thomas; Censler, William; Clark, Charles; Clark, Israel; Closson, Jacob; Cole, John; Cole, Joseph; Congale George; Cook, Benjamin; Cooper, James; Coper, Samuel; Cox, William; Curren, Joseph; Curtis, Jeremiah; Curtis, Warens; Davis, Thomas; Davis, Simon; Day, Charles; Dileeiver; Dix, David; Doake; Jacob; Driver, Samuel; Dumigan, Enoch; Dunham, Harlock; Dunham, Jonathan; Dunham, Silas; Eaton, Joseph; Ely, Michael; Evens, Edward;

Fairchild, Benjamin M.; Faneher, William; Filkey, Daniel; Filkey, Henry; Filkey, Jacob; Fisher, Jacob; Foard, Augustus; Foos, John; Foos, Valentine; Gah, J. Jun.; Gah, James; Gabriel, Richard;

134

Gabriel, William; Gallant, James; Gallant, John; Godard, Moses; Graham, Israel; Grigery, James; Grist, John;

Hall, Nathaniel; Harper, James; Harper, John; Harrop, Thomas; Haskins, J.; Haskins, Richard; Heath, Samuel; Helt, John; Hess, George; Hevelan, Andrew; Hevelan, Barnet; Higings, William; Hinton, Levi; Hoadley, Philo; Hoal, Obediah; Hull, Abraham; Humphreys, Samuel G.; Jinkins, Evans; Johnson, John; Johnson, Joseph; Jones, John; Jones, Leonard; Jones, Solomon; Kerr, Alex; Kile, Hugh; Keys, Robert; Kinton, Levi; Kipler, Morgan; Kirkpatrick, Samuel; Lamb, Reuben; Landon, Nathaniel; Latshaw, Joseph; Lawderwick, Elener; Lebar, Aaron; Leonard, John; Jeonard, John Jun.; Lewis, David Jun.; Lewis, John; Little, Nathaniel W.; Little, William; Longshore, David; Longshore, Euclydes; Loofborough, John; Loomis, Ruel; Loop, Christian; Luce, William;

McDonald, Thomas; McEwen, William; McHune, James; McWilliams, James; Main, Peres; Manvill, Eli; Manvill, Nicholas; Marks, David; Marvin, Matthew; Michener, Mordiea; Milikan, John; Minter, John; Moffit, James; Morgan, Samuel; Munro, Leonard; Murphy, Andrew; Nickins, Edward; Noble, Jonathan; North, Zachariah; Norton, Joah; Olney, Sally, widow; Owles, Comfort; Patterson, John; Patrick, Benjamin; Perfect, Thomas; Perfect, William; Perry, David; Perry, Henry; Phillips, John; Pinney, Menner T.; Plumb, Ichabod; Power, Avery; Power, Luther; Price, Joseph; Prince, David; Prince, Joseph; Pugh, David; Pugh, Thomas;

Rabaway, James; Reed, David Jr.; Reed, Elizabeth; Reed, George; Reed, Samuel; Reed, Samuel Jr.; Reed, William; Pieke, Noco; R. K. & L. S.; Roath, Nathaniel; Roberts, Ebenezer; Roberts, Amos; Roberts, Hezekiah; Robinson, Millen; Root, Azariah; Roush, John; Royce, Nijah; Ryley, John; Scott, Asa; Seribner, Hannah & Chas.; Shaw, John; Shaw, Jonathan; Sheals, David; Slack, Henry; Slack, Ralph; Smith, Ralph; Smith Samuel; Smith, Solomon; Smith, Stuart; Snodgrass, Robert; Stepjen Zachariah; Still, Oliver; Strong, Aaron; Strong, David; Staurt, Joseph; Sturdevant, Iar; Sturdevant, Noah; Sullivant, Lucas;

Thomas, David; Thomas Mordiae; Thompson, Jonathan; Thompson Richard; Tibit, Richard; Tuler, Roswell; Tyler, Samuel; Vanhorn, Ezekiel; Vanloon, Nicholas; Vining, Chas.; Waller, Thomas; Watkins, John; Watson, William; Webster, Charles; Weeks, Daniel; Welch, Ebenezer; Welch, John; Welch, Isaac; Wever, Samuel; Whiteas, Richard; Wilcox, Hira; Wilcox, Ira; Wilcox, Jaker; Williams, John; Wof, Jacob; Wood, Samuel; Wyatt, Nathaniel.

INDEX TO TAX LIST OF OHIO FOR 1810
FAIRFIELD COUNTY

Thelma Blair Lang

Abrams, Henry; Adams, John; Alen, Silas; Alexander, James; Allen, Jedediah; Allen ,Lemuel; Alspach, George; Alspach, Henry; Alspach, Jacob; Armstrong, Thomas; Arnold, Frederick; Arnold, George; Arnold, Henry; Ashbaugh, Adam; Augustus, John; Auspach, Jacob; Rabauch, Jacob; Bach, John; Baelor, Jacob; Bailey, Thomas; Bailor, Jacob Jr.,; Baker, Coonrad; Baldwin, John; Ballabach, Abrm; Ballabach, John; Banhore, John; Bare, John; Barnet, Absoleus; Barnhart, Henry; Barniger, Andrew; Barr, Adam; Barr, Andrew; Barr, David; Barr, John; Barr, Joseph Jr.; Barr, Samuel; Barr, Thomas; Barr, William; Barton, Jacob; Baugher, Henry; Bawyer, Jacob; Bawyer, Jacob Jr.; Beadle, Ben.; Beard, John; Beaty, Coonrod; Beaty, John; Beaver, William; Beecher, Hieleman; Beek, Andrew; Beekle, John; Beery, Henry; Beery, Jacob Jr.; Beery, John Sr.; Beery, Nicholas; Bell, Josiah; Benedam, Geo.; Berry, Abrm; Bibler, Barbara; Bibler, David; Bibler, Jacob Jr.; Bibler, John; Binkley, Henry; Binkley, Jacob; Bixler, Ellis; Black, John; Bly, Jacob; Bly, John; Bouder, Nicholas; Bough, Robt.; Boughard, Jacob; Bousey, Lewis; Bowman, George; Bowman, John; Bowman, Wendall; Boyd, Henry; Boyle, Hugh; Brand, Adam F.; Brats, Phillip; Braty, Valentine; Bratz, Jacob; Bressler, Peter Sr.; Brian, Coonrod; Bright, David; Bright, Major; Bright, Nemrod; Broadstone, Jacob; Brooks, James; Brown, James; Brown, William Sr.; Brumbach, Samuel; Bruner, Jacob; Buch, Peter; Buchannon, Andrew; Buckley, Adam; Burton, Jacob; Bush, Nicholas;

Cagy, Christian; Carpenter, David; Carpenter, Em'l Jr.; Carpenter, Em'l Sr.; Carpenter John; Carpenter, Samuel; Carpenter, William; Chaney, Samuel; Chrisley John; Christ, Simon; Clark, Heratia; Claud, Robert; Cleik, Geo.; Cleik,Henry; Cleik, Jacob; Cleik, Jonathan; Cleik, Peter; Cleik, Phillip; Cleymer, Charles; Cline, Geo.; Clymer, Massey; Cofman, David; Cofman, Frederick; Cole, Thos.; Cleburn, Robert; Coledran, Isaac; Collins, James; Collins, St. James; Compton, Conaway, Jereh.; Cook, John; Coomer, Philip; Coonrod, Daniel; Coonrod, John; Coonrod, Nicholas; Cooper, Joseph; Copman, Christian; Courtright, Abm.; Courtright, John; Cremer, Phillip; Crawford, William; Creed, John; Crocket, Andrew; Crowl, Geo.; Crowl, John; Cruchfield, Joshua; Crumb, Christian; Cup, Valentine; Curts, Lawrence; Dave, Henry; Davis, Anthony; Davis, Ben.; Davis, Jacob; Davis, John; Davis, Thomas; Decker, Cobstane; Decker, Jacob; Decker, John; Devebaugh, Geo.; Devebaugh, John; Dilshaner, Geo.; Dilshaner, Geo. Jr.; Dilshaner, John; Drake, Jephenah; Driver, Isaiah; Drum, John; Drum, Peter; Dudwiler, Jacob; Duman, James; Dumna, John; Dumma, Martin; Durst, Henry; Ebright, Adam; Emrick, Leonard; Erb, John; Evans, Thomas; Eversole, Peter; Ewing, David; Ewing, Mathew; Ewing, Thomas;

Fairchild, Abm.; Fairchild, Peter; Fasinger, Henry; Fasnaught, Adam; Faust, John; Fenstermaker, Geo. Feeman, Ben.; Feeman, John; Feltner, Marten; Fetters, Conrad Sr.; Firestone, Dan'l; Fisher, Jacob; Fisher, Henry; Fisher, John Sr.; Foglesong, Christian; Foust, Secastian; Fox, Jacob; Foy, Jacob; Fuman, Stason; Gairy, Geliad; Gardner, William; Gaup, Frederick; Gerey, John; Giger, Adam; Giger David; Giger, J.; Giger, Martin; Giles, Jacob; Goldthevaih, John;

Grafis, Jacob; Graybill, Samuel; Grayhart, Daniel; Green, Allen; Green, Eeginal; Green, John; Green, Thomas; Groves, John; Gundy, Christian; Hais, John; Hammond, Samuel; Hampson, John; Hamreckhouser, Geo.; Hamapacher, Conrad; Hanaway, John; Hand, James; Handwork, Frederick; Hannah, James; Harber, William; Harelaugher, Chrisitan; Harding, Iquetius; Harman, Frederick; Harman, Jacob; Harper, Samuel; Harrington, Nathaniel; Harrison, John; Harsbarger, Abm.; Harvey, Geo.; Hash, Jacob; Hastand, Joseph; Hay, Philip; Hay, Daniel; Hayman, Jacob; Hays, Mary; Hedges, Absolem; Hedges, Jesse; Hedges, Joseph; Heek, Frederick; Hsistand, Abm.; Henderson, Jams; Hensel, Michael; Hern, Christian; Herron, Phillip; Hiddle, Henry; Hinebaugh, Henry; Hite, Abm.; Hite, Andrew, Jr.; Hite, Andrew Sr.; Hite, Conrad; Hite, Isaac; Hite, John Sr.; Hite, John, Jr.; Hogman, Jacob; Holmes, Thomas; Holtz, Geo.; Hooker, Richard; Hooker, Samuel; Hooper, Jacob; Hopwood, William; Horn, Frederick; Hover, John; Huddle, Geo.; Huffer, Isaac; Hover, John Sr.; Huford, Gasper; Hufman, Henry, Humberger, Henry; Humberger, John; Humberger, Peter; Hunter, John; Hunter, Joseph; Husthaw, Geo.; Hyles, John;

Ijams, Isaac; Ijams, William; Jackson, John; Jasells, William; Johns, Reg.; Johnson, Benjamin; Jones, William; Jugmond, Conrad; Jugmond, Luke; Jugwood, Henry; Julien, John; Julien, John Jr.; Julien, Renne; Julien, Stephen Sr.; Kemp, Gabriel; Kemper, Daniel; Kemper, Isaac; Kemper, Jacob; Kester, Geo.; Kester, Jacob; Kester, John; Kester, Mathias; Ketner, Nicholas; Kiger, John; Kilis, Daniel; King, Christian; Kitswiller, Benjamin; Kittswiller, Elizabeth; Knoyer, Ulrich; Konig, John; Korfman, Jacob Jr.; Korfman, Martin; Kramer, Henry; Kromer, Michael; Krates, Jacob; Krienler, Henry; Kuntz, Isaac;

Lamb, Geo.; Lamb, Jacob; Lamb, John; Lamb, Peter; Lamb, Philip; Lame, Wilkinson; Lancaster, William; Landis, Martin; Lane, John; Lank, Adam; Lantz, Martin; Laremore, Isaac; Lashley, David; Leathers, Frederick; Leathers, Frederick Sr.; Leathers, Jacob, Lee, Zebulair; Leib, Joseph; Lephart, Henry; Lidey, Daniel; Lilenaker, Henry; Linebaugh, Geo.; List, John; Long, James; Long, William; Longbreak, Daniel; Lorish, Henry; Loughborough,————; Louis, Jacob; Loveland, Joseph; Lusk, Patrick; McArthur, Jun.; McCleland, James; McCleland, Robt.; McCoib, William; McCormack, Wm.; McFarland, Wm.; McFarland,————; McGinnis, Wm.; McInten, M. (?) McIntosh, John; McLin, ————; McLen, Robert; McLin, Peter; McLin, Phillip McLung, Charles; McMene, Job; McMullen, John; McMullen, Joseph; McNear, Joseph; McNottin, ? ; McNottin, John; McNottin, Thomas;

Magers, Abm.; Main, John; Mangol, Davy; Massee, ? ; Mask, Peter; Measey, James; Megey, Joseph; Miller, Catherine; Miller, Catherine; Miller, Daniel; Miller, Davy; Miller, Elizabeth; Miller, Jacob; Miller, John; Miller, Peter; Miller, Wm.; Misolle, John; Mix, Jacob; Moines, Frederick; Monly, John; Moore, George; Moore, Harmon; Moore, Henry; Moore, John; Moore, Wm. Jr.; Moorehead, John; Mooseheart, John; Morgan, John; Mortin, Wm.; Morton, Ulin (?) ; Morts, Jacob; Mounet (?), Isaac; Moyer, Abraham; Moyer, Daniel; Moyer, Jacob; Murphy, Edward; Musselman, Jacob; Musser, Theobold; Myers, Mo.;

Needless, George; Neely, Daniel; Neely, John; Neely, Mathew; Neely, Wm.; Neff, Abrm.; Nelson, Robert; Neoless (?), John; Newkirk, James; Newkirk, Newland; Nhome, (?), George; Noggle, Isaac;

Norris, George; Norris, W.; North, H, Polly; North, Wm.; Nye, George Sr.; Orving (?), Henry; Ottsbough, Jacob; Overmire, Peter; Owens, Nathan; Owens, Patrick; Owens, Thomas; Patten, John; Pauz (?), Jacob; Pearse, James; Pearse, John; Pennabaker, John; Peters, Abraham; Pew, Jesse; Pickle, Jacob; Pitcher, Frederick; Plimmer, Abrm.; Poorman, Barney; Poory, Wm.; Pope, Frederick; Powel, Moses; Power, David; Portts, John; Prough, Casper; Prough, Peter; Puhers (?), Wm.; Quin, Jonus;

Radabough, George; Raudabaugh, Nicholas; Read, James; Raed. Wm.; Ream, Abrm.; Rean, Jacob; Ream, Sampson; Ream, Wm.; Reber, Valentine; Reese, Jesse; Reese, Marvin; Reid, Francis; Reise, David; Revin, Christian; Reynold, John; Ricketts, Chas.; Rickets, China; Rickets, Reason; Rigby, Wm.; Rinehart, Peter; Ritten, Henry; Roberts, Henry; Roberts, John; Roberts, Moniel; Roland, James; Rolby, Jacob; Rolls, Jesse; Rouch, George; Rouch, Peter; Ruck, Peter; Rudolph; Peter; Ruffner, Benj.; Ruffner, Emanuel; Runcle, Daniel; Runfauf, Jonas;

Sanderson, Abm.; Sane, Philip; Sane, Peter; Saunders, Peter; Schistor (?), John; Scofield, Elnothon; Searls, John; Seitts (?), John; Selby, Thos.; Shaco, Wm.; Sharp, George; Shiptor, John; Shofer, Abraham; Shofer, George; Shofer, Isaac; Shofer, Samuel; Sholenberger, Henry;! Shoenberger, Samuel; Shoper, John; Shorick, Andrew; Shorlle (?), Philip; Shostle (?), Philip; Showley, Jacob; Shuer, Philip; Shull, Solamon; Sidenor, Nicholas; Sites, Peter; Skinner, Robt.; Slaughter, Robt. L.; Smart, John; Smith, Benj.; Smith, Christian; Smith, Martin; Smith, Nicholas; Snyder, Adam; Soladay (?), John Adams; Sorby, P.; Souft, Philip; Spereux, Wm.; Spitler, Jacob Sr.; Spitler, John; Spitler, Peter; Spitler, Wm.; Springer, Wm.; Spurgeon, Jesse; Spurgeon, Elijah; Spurgeon, Samuel; Staker, Michael; Stall, Wm.; Steerner, Henry; Sternus, Michael; Sterrit, Brice; Stevenson, Daniel; Stiers, Benjamin; Stinchacomb, George; Stites, Lewis; Stockborn, George; Stockborn, Peter; Stooky, John; Stooky, Peter; Stots, John; Strand, Edward; Strand, Jeremiah; Strouer, Jo.; Stroun (?), Thos.; Stuart, Joseph; Stuky, Christian; Sturgeon, Robert; Sucoveryen (?), Thos.; Swezey, David; Swope, David;

Teal Arthur; Teal, Edward; Teal, Nathaniel; Teal, Walter; Thompson, Samuel; Thompson, Wm.; Tifford, Catherine; Tomlinson, Henry; Tomlinson, Samuel; Tong, George; Trelor, Jacob; Trimble, Wm.; Turner, James; Turner, Daniel; Turner, Joseph; Turner, Wm.; Valentine, George; Vandamark, Daniel; Vanmeter, Daniel; Vanmeter, Jacob; Veary, Chrnistian;

Waggoner, Adam; Waggoner, Andrew; Waggoner, Daniel; Waggoner, Jacob; Waggoner, John; Waggoner, Ulrick; Walters, Casper; Walters, Henry Sr.; Ward, Wm. Sr.; Warner, Thos.; Watenhavez.—— Weadman, George Weaver, Jacob; Welty, John; Whiteman, Christian; Whitmore, Peter; Wickel, Jacob; Williams, Jeremiah; Williamson, David; Williamson, John; Williamson, Peter; Williamson, Peter Sr.; Willis, James; Willis, John; Wilson, John; Wilson, Joseph; Wilson, Nathaniel Jr.; Wilson, Robert; Wilson, Sarah; Wilson, Thos.; Wilson, Wm.; Winsiger, Adam; Wintermouth, Wm.; Winters, Jacob Sr.; Winterwith, David; Winterwith, Daniel; Winterwith, Wm.; Wiseby, Edward; Wiseler, Wm.; Wiseman, Jacob; Wiseman, Wm.; Wistenberger, John; Wolf, John; Wolfby, Lodwick; Work, Joseph; Wortsing, Peter Sr.; Wright, David; Wyman, David; Wilson, Nathaniel Sr.; Young, Adam; Young, Wm.; Zeigler, John; Zortman, Peter.

INDEX TO TAX LIST OF OHIO FOR 1810

FAYETTE COUNTY

By Thelma Blair Lang

Armstrong, Robert; Ayrs, Francis; Baldwin, David; Baldwin, Richard; Barger, Philip; Benegar, George; Buck, John; Bailey, Joshua; Bates, Daniel; Blair, William; Blue, John M.; Boner, Isaac; Brawley, William.

Carder, Sanford; Carrington, Clement; Carr, James; Clark, David; Cochran, Barnabas; Cochran, David; Coil, George; Coler, Abraham; Conn, Michal; Clark, Daniel; Coover, Samuel; Creamer, George; Devault, John; Devault, Nicholas; Devault, Thomas; Dickindon, Jacob Sr.; Dunlap, James; Dungan, Isaiah; Dyer, William; Davis, Benjamin; Doberty, James; Elis, Comton.

Fisher, Thomas; Flesher, Coonrod; Flesher, Henry; Funk, Adam; Good, John; Green, Thomas; Green, William; George, William; Hamilton, Alexander; Harper, William; Harvie, John; Heath, George; Heran, Patrick; Herod, John; Hill, Stephen; Hill, William; Hoil, Jacob; Hoppes, John; Horney, James; Hughes, John; Hamilton, William; Hampton, Jonathan; Hand, Jonathan; Hanes, Amos; Hanes, Enoch; Hankin, David; Huff, Thomas; Huff, Doctor; Haw, John; Haye, James; Hays, John; Hopkins, Joseph; Hurley, Leven; Jurey, Jesse; Jones, Thomas; Keller, Christopher; Koil, Oliver; Kiss, Adam; King, Elizabeth.

Lawyer, Jacob; Lock, Thomas; Laughan, Elias; Lucas, Nathaniel; McArthur, John; McDonald, Thomas; McElvane, David; Miller, John; McArthur, Duncan; McClean, John; McDonald, Thomas; Means, Robert; Massie, Nathaniel; Matthews, George; Monroe, George; Mooney, James, Judge; Mordeca, Ellis; Murphy, James.

Newman, George; Newman, William; Nisbett, David; Ogdon, Albert; Ohaver, Joseph; Patton, William; Pierson, William; Plymel, John; Pusley, Jacob; Painther, George; Parker, Aaron; Rankin, William; Richard, James; Robison, William; Robuck, George; Rogers, Benjamin; Rogers, Henry; Rowe, Isaiah; Rude, Jacob; Reed, William; Robinson, Nicholas; Robinson, Thomas; Rogers, Hamilton; Rogers, Thomas; Row, John.

Sellers, Samuel; Spotwood, John; Sowards, Solomon; Salmon, Benjamin; Salmon, Soloman; Sanders, James; Sawor, William; Shephard, Abraham; Steuben, Baron; Stogdon, David; Stout, Philip; Stroger, Adam; Suttle, Struther; Thomas, Ellis; Thompson, Isaac; Todhunter, Isaac; Todhunter, John; Todhunter, Richard; Tracy, Solomon; Tracy, Warner; Urestis, William; Walker, Horasha; Walker, William; Wood, William; Woodson, Worthington, Thos.; Webster, James B.; Workman, John; Zandole, John.

139

INDEX TO TAX LIST OF OHIO FOR 1810

FRANKLIN COUNTY

Thelma Blair Lang

Abey, George; Agler, Fredrick Anderson, I.: Andrew, Jesse: Andrews, Noah· Ashbaugh, John; Atwater, Russel; Austin, Elijah; Baldon, C.; Baldon, Cornl.; Ball, John; Baller, Percival; Bar, Andrew; Bard, Michael; Barker, Chancy; Barr, Mo.; Bartholomen, Martin; Bartlett, Isaac; Bassett, Alexander; Baughman, Geo.; Beach, Samuel Jr.; Beach, Samuel Sr.; Beaksly & Maryam; Bears, David; Bexla & Meryon; Blakely, Obed; Blew, James· Boyce, Robert: Brackenridge, Jas.; Breckinridge, Robt.; Bichle, John; Brisco, Reuben; Bristol, Adna; Bristol, David; Brown, Daniel; Brown, William; Butler, Avary; Butler, B.: Butler, J.; Butler, Joal; Butler, L.; Butler, Sarah W.

Campbell, Benj.; Campbell, William; Carder, Geo.; Carpenter, Rubin; Case, Isaac; Case, Israel; Case; Israel Jr.; Case, Joseph; Chapman, Ben:.; Cherry, Abraham; Chinoweth, Elijah; Chinoweth, Thos.; Cochran, Glass; Cochran, Simon; Cochran, Wm.; Coe, Ransom; Coldwell, Wm.; Coleman, Jas.· Colyeor, N.; Conine, John; Cooper, Robt.; Cooper, William; Cowgill, Joseph; Cramer, Christopher; Crawford, M.; Culbertson, Andrew; Culbert on, James; Culbertson, Robt.; Dark, Wm.: Davis, John; Daybon, Jas.: Decher, Elisha; Deerdurff, Abraham; Deerdurff, Paul; Dill, John; Dillino, Amassa; D'Lashmutt, Elea; D'Lashmutt, Eli; D'Lashmutt, M. K.; Donocan, John; Droddy, William· Dudly, Rich.; Duff, Edward; Dunn, Asa; Durkin, David; Dyer, John; Ebey, George.

Finch, David; Finley, S.; Fisher, Isaac; Fisher, Michael; Fleming, William; Follen, Thomas: Foster, Benjamin; Fulton, Elijah; Fulton, Hugh; Gail, Richard; Galaspa, Ennes; Galloway, Jas.; Gilpon, Geo.; Glen, S.; Goldsmith, Thos.; Good, Jos.; Goodle, L. Goodrich, Ebenezer; Goodridg, T.; Goodridg, M.; Graham, G.; Graham, M.; Grant, Kelly Widow; Grather, Joseph; Griswold, Ezra; Griswold, Isaac; Grubb, Jacob; Guilliford, John; Hamlen, Nathaniel; Hammond, Atthina; Hanna, Alland; Harmon, James; Harrison, Isaac; Harrup, Peter; Haughn, Nicholas; Henderson, Alexander; Henderson, Samuel; Henderson, Samuel Jr.; Henderson, William; Hess, Baltzer; Hess, Daniel; Hess, Margan; Hoffman, John; Hopper, Edward; Howe, Henry; Howser, John Jr.; Humphreys, Wm.; Hunter, Charles; Hunter, John; Hunter, Joseph; Ingram, Abraham.

Jackanias, Rose; Jamason, David; Johnson, Thomas; Jones, Abeole; Jones, David; Jones, Samuel; Justice, Robert; Keepsaw, Phillip; Kilbourne, James; Kilbourn, James; Kile, John; King, Jacob; Knight, M.; Lain; Daniel; Lambert, David; Landas, Samuel; Lemes, C.; Leonard, Abithan; Leonard, Preserved; Lerbeern, Andrew; Lewis, Sabia; Linch, M.; Lincoln, Goodle; Loundes, ?, Rep. D.; Lucas, Wm. Lyles, Robert; Lyles, Richard, Widow; McAfee, Joseph; McCloud, Charles; McCloud, Thomas; McCoy, James; McEleain, James; McEleain, William; McGill, Samuel: McGowen, John; McKingsbury; McMahon, Mageal; Mallon, M.; Mannon, Elisha; Mannon, Wm.; Mariam, William; Marshall, James; Mathews, Mathew; Maumon, M. B.; Maxfield, Amos; Mayborn, James; Maynard, Stephen; Medford, Wm.; Medlord, John; Mellington, Peter; Meryon & Bexla; Mickey, Thomas;

Millar, Jacin; Millar, Justice; Millingburgh, Peter; Mills, M. S. Moobury, William; Moor, Simeon; Moor, Thomas; Moor, Solomon; Moorhead, Thomas; Morgin, Dan'l.; Morris, Thomas; Morrison, Alex.; Morrison, Alex. J.; Morrison, Alex. Jr.; Morrison, William.

Nelson, David; Nelson, Robert; Norton, M.; O'Hana, Arthur; O'Hana, James; Orr, M.; Overden, Jacob; Overton, John; Overton, M.; Palmer, Ethan; Palmer, Thomas; Palmer, William; Park, Andrew; Park, Joseph; Parker, Thos.; Penn, Joseph; Penny, Abnor; Penny, Azariah; Penny, Levi.; Phelps, Edw.; Piper, Elazes; Pontious, Peter; Poppow, Jacob; Powel, Laton; Powel, Seymore; Powers, R.; Ramsey, James; Ramsey, Robert; Ramsey, Samuel; Ransom, Coe.; Reed, William; Rich, Ebenezer; Richeson, Saml.; Robe, William; Rochey, Christopher; Scott, Joseph; Scott, Saml.; Seeds, James; Selem?, Anthony; Sells, Benjamin; Sells, Ludwich; Sells, Mo.; Sells, Peter; Shannon, James; Shannon, Saml.; Sharp, No.; Shaw, William; Shedmore, Geo.; Shedmore, Josiah; Shedmore, M.; Shenn, Levy; Simmons, William; Simon, M.; Sirloff, George; Sloper, Samuel; Smart, Isaac; Smart, Joseph; Smith, Augustine J.; Smith, Rich; Spangler, David; Springer, Charles; Starling, Lynn; Steel, Wm.; Stephens, Rich.; Stewall, M.; Stewart, Jr., Heirs; Stewart, M.; Stokes, M.; Subblefield, Benj.; Sullivant, Lucas; Sullivant, Lucas, Jr.; Survey, Mathews; Swingston, Edward.

Tage, Mathias; Taylor, Robert; Terburn, Andrew; Thomas, L.; Thomas, Lewis; Thomas, Philip; Thomas, Thomas; Thomas, Stephen; Thompson, Charles; Thompson, William; Tool, Oliver; Toppong, Iasiah; Topping, Zoplus; Traube, M.; Tuller, Bela M.; Vance, Alexander; Vance, Joseph; Vance, Robert; Vanhorn, Isaac; Vineing, William; Vouis, Isaiah; Walker, Bay; Wallas, Rich. S.; Watts, Ino; Weatherington, Congration; Welscock, Roswell; White, John Jr.; White, Mo.; White, Saml.; White, William; Wiglon, Wm.; Wilcocks, Lymon; Williams, David; Wilson, John; Wilson, S.; Wilson, Samuel; Wood, Elizabeth; Writing, House M.; Yancy, Laton.

INDEX TO TAX LIST OF OHIO

FOR 1810, GALLIA COUNTY

THELMA BLAIR LANG

Alden, John; Aleshire, Abraham; Aleshire, Michael; Anderson, Andrew: Angel, Israel: Angel, Nathan; Ashley, Moses; Atkinson, John; Babcock, Abijah; Barford, John; Barker, Eleazer: Barker, Elaixer, Jr.; Barlow, Joel; Barlow, Sam. & Elnathan: Bauman, Sebastian: Bayers, Isaac: Beardsby,; Beardsby, John: Beers, Nathan; Benedict, Philip; Bing, John; Bing, John Jr.; Boarland, S. N.; Boggs, David; Boggs, Samuel; Boisvard, Joseph; Bowen, Joel; Bowers, Henry; Bowers, John, Bradford, James; Brice, John; Britt, Daniel: Brown, Nicholas; Bryan, Luke; Buck, Charles; Buck, Thomas: Buel, John; Buffington, Philip; Bullock, Squire; Burriss, William; Butler, Syms: Buveau, J. P. R.; Buveau & Safford;

Campbell, William; Carpenter, Amos; Carrington, Edw.; Case, John; Carrol, Rene; Collison, Wm.; Chandivert, P. M.; Chapman, Ezra; Chapman, Levi; Charrington, William; Cheetwood, Joshua; Christopher, Marshall; Clark, Elihu; Colt, Elisha; Colten, Abijah; Connup, David; Cook, Stephen; Cooper, Ezekiel; Cotton, Luther; Cunnington, Edward; Cuttler, Manassah; Dalliez, M. J.: Darst, Abraham; Darst, Abraham Jr.; Darst, John; Darst, Paul: Davidson, John Wm.; Davour, Francis; Dazet, Joseph; Dean, Nathaniel; Dexter, Timothy; Denham, Daniel; Derny, Samuel; Devacht, Joseph; Dhebecourt, F.; Dobois, F. A.; Dodge, John; Donnally, Andrew; Donnally, Dominic; Doughty, John; Downer, Elisha; Due, Andrew; Duport, Marion; Dust, David;

Elliot, Fuller; Entsminger, John; Eriswold, Sylvanus; Eteinne, Christopher; Evans, Israel; Evans, Jonathan; Everett, Moses; Ewing, John; Fee, John; Fee, William; Ferrard, John Babtist; Fitch, Andrew; Fleshman, Jesse; Fletcher, Joseph; Foster, Peregrine; Fox, Reuben; Fry, Frederick; Fuller, Oliver; Fuller, Sylvester; Gardner, Caleb; Gaston, Thomas; George, James; Gilman, Benj. J.; Gilston, Samuel; Glassburn, John; Greene, Catherine; Greene, Griffin; Green, John; Green, William; Griswold, Abial; Griswold, Sylvanus; Guilliland, James; Hall, Elias; Hall, John; Halves, E.; Hammon,; Hammon, Abijah; Hartshorn, Thomas; Heath, Peleg; Higley, Brewster; Higley, Joel Jr.; Hissel, Nimrod; Hitchburn, Samuel; Holton & Prince; Howel, Joseph; Hubbard, Namiah; Hubble, Abijah; Hubble, Abijah

Jr.; Hubble, Jesse; Hunt, Elijah; Humphreys, David; Hustaux, Nicholas; Huskins, Wm.; Ibert, Mathew; Irwin, David:

James, John; Jewett, Stephen; Jones, Benson; Jones, Phillip; Jones, Seth; Judd, Elizabeth; Judson, David; Kerns, Frederick; Kerr, Hamilton; Kerr, John; Koontz, John; Lalance, Peter; Larkins, Abel; Lastly, Abraham; Lastly, David; Lawrence, John; Lecterog?, Augustin; Lecterog?, Aug. Jr.; Lecterog?, Francis; Lellay, J. B. N.; Lischon, A. L.; Littleton, William; Livingston, B.; Lord, Thomas; Loucks, William; Lunt, Ezra; McCall, James; McCarty, John; McCarty, Jonas; McComb, Alexander; McComb, W.; McCombs, Elizabeth; McCormick, James, Maguet, Anthony; Maguet, Peter R.; Manring, Jordan; Marion, Francis; Marshel, Christopher; Masure, Michael; Mathew, Phinehas; Mathew, Witsele; Mavin, Picket; May, Fred; May, Henry K.; May, J.; May, Wm. R.; Menager, C. R.; Merril, James; Miles, John; Miles, Joshua; Miller, Abraham; Miller, Edward; Miller, Jacob; Miller, John; Mills, Charles; Moniss, James; Monroe, James; Montgomery & Wm. Lynn; Morrison, Wm.; Mounot, Stephen; Murrat, P.:

Nease, Henry; Newman, Walter; Nisewanger, John; Nisewanger, John Jr.; Nobel, Shubel; Northup, Daniel; Northup, Hampton; Northun, Thomas; Nourse, Joseph; Num?, Catherine & Griffon; Nye, Ichabod; Oliver, Alexander; Oliver, Robert; Olney, Cogshell; Parker, Wm. Jr.; Parker, William; Parmantier, John; Parsons, Harris; Parsons & Sproat; Parsons, Wm.; Patterson, James; Peter, John; Peters, Andres; Petit, Nicholas; Phelps, James E.; Phillips, Reter; Pierce, David; Pierpont, John; Piznoet, Ivachin; Prince & Holton; Putnam, Israel; Putnam, E.; Putnam, Jethro; Putnam, Rufus; Putnam, William; Questal, Nicholas; Raider, John; Rankins, James; Rathburn, Daniel; Reed, John; Rees, David; Rees, Samuel; Rhodes, Wm.; Rickabaugh, Adam; Robinson, Robert; Rodgers, George; Rodgers, John; Rodgers, Platt; Rose, John; Ross, Joseph W.; Richardson, Joseph; Rife, Joseph; Rhodarnr, Jacob; Robinson, James; Rodgers, Thomas; Rose, Jason; Rouch, Jacob; Rouch, Phillip; Rousch, George; Rousch, Henry; Roush, Henry Jr.; Roush, Michael; Runnels, John; Runner, Elijah; Rupe, Martin; Russel, John; Russel, Jonathan; Russel, Moses; Sacour, L. A.; Safford, Robert; Saldere, L.; Sampson, Crook; Sargeant, W.; Sarguithan, F. A.; Saucent, James; Savary, John; Sayre, David; Sayre, David Jr.; Sayre, Ephriam; Sayre, John; Sayre, John Jr.; Sayre, Thomas; Schuyler, Derick; Scott, Sabre; Shearwood, Solomon; Sheffield, Hannah; Shepard, Enoch; Shepard, Thomas; Sloan, John; Smith, Benjamin; Smith, Calvin; Smith, James; Smith, James Jr.; Smith, Joel; Smith, Melanton; Smith, Pascal M.; Smith, Therasa; Smith, Timothy; Smoke, Garret; Somner, Job; Somner, Jesse; Spincer, Wm.; Sproat, Ebenezer; Sproat & Parsons; Stacy, Wm.; Stanton, John; Sterns, Asa; Sterry, Cyprean; Stevens, Geo.; Stilwell, Elias; Story, D.; Stouts, Elijah; Stow, Erastus; Strong, Daniel; Strong, Oraska; Strong, Stephen; Sweat, Sam.; Swift, Stephen; Switzer, John; Switzer, Phillip; Syan, John; Symer, Abraham B.

Terry, Paul; Thayer, Simon; Thevenin, Nicholas; Thomas, David; Thomas, Jacob; Tupper, Anselm; Tupper, Benjamin; Tupper, Edw. W.; Underwood, Robert; Vail, Thomas; Varian, David D.; Vibert, A.; Vining, Josiah; Waddle, Wm.; Wadsworth, Elijah; Waldo, John; Walrous, John; Watrous, John B.; Waugh, Andrew; Waugh, George; Waugh, John; Webster, S.; Wells, Rufus; Whiteman, Edw.; Whitsel, Mathew; Wilkes, Charles; William, Jeremiah; Williams, Benjamin; Williams, Robert; Willis, Samuel; Willys, Samuel; Wilson, Wm. Wilson, Stephen; Wolf, Elizabeth; Wolf, Peter; Womelsdorff, Daniel; Worth, Alexander; Yeager, Nicholas.

143

INDEX TO TAX LIST OF OHIO
FOR 1810, GEAUGA COUNTY

Allen, David; Allison, David; Allison, David Jr.; Anderson, Noah; Andrews, Amos; Andrews, Jaivus S.; Archer, William; Atkins, Joseph; Atkins, Josiah; Atkins, Qintius; Atkins, Thomas; Austin, Elephat; Austin, Joab;

Bacam, Ralph; Badger, Joseph; Baldwin, Daniel; Barlett, Joseph; Barnum, Enoch; Bartholomew, Abigail; Bartholomew, Abraham; Bartholomew, Benjamin; Bartholomew, Daniel; Bartholomew, Isaac; Bartholomew, Jacob; Bartholomew, John; Bartholomew, John B.; Bartholomew, Joseph; Bartholomew, Samuel; Bartholomew, Thedal?; Bartholomew, Uriah; Bates, Benjamin; Bates, Caleb; Beach, Luman; Beard, Amariah; Beard, Jedediah; Beckwith, Geo.; Beckwith, Samuel; Bemas, Samuel; Benton, Lyman; Biglow, John; Blackman, Elijah; Blackman, Hiram; Blisard, John; Blish, Benjamin; Blish, Benjamin J.; Bond, Stephen; Bond, Elijah; Bradley, James; Bradley, Thadeus; Breakman, Chirst; Breakman, John; Brooks, Hannaniah; Brooks, John; Brooks, Jon; Brown, Alexander; Brown, John; Brown, Josiah; Brown, Stephen; Burnet, David; Burton, Samuel; Burnet, Syrenus; Button, Elijah;

Caldwell, Timlj?; Canfield, & Bond; Carlton, Adolphus; Carlton, Darius; Carlton, John; Carrel, Hercules; Carrel, John; Case, Asakel; Case, Cephas; Case, Joseph Mills; Case, Sidia Wm.; Castle, Daniel & Amasa; Chandler, David; Chapin, Amariah; Chapman, Caleb; Chappel, Nathaniel; Clapp, Paul, Jr.; Clark, Joseph; Clark, Lemuel; Cleveland, Orson; Conrod, Stuntz; Cook, Isaac; Cook, John; Cook, Merriman; Cowce, Andrew; Cowles, Edna; Cowles, Joseph B.; Cowles, Levi; Cowles, Noah; Creighton, Tobt.; Crosby, Elijah; Crowel, William; Cunning, Robt.; Davis, Abednego; Davis, Eleazer; Dayton, Daniel; Drennen, John; Durland, Andrew; Edward, Obed; Ellis, Rowland; Elliot, John; Ferguson, William; Ferris, Gilbert J.; Finch, Gideon; Fish, Amos; Fleming, James; Flowers, Erastus; Fober, Lemuel; Fobes, Walter; Ford, John; Fowler, Eli; Fowler, Isaac; French, John; French, Peter;

Gillet, Nathan; Gordon, Thomas; Gray, Samuel; Gregory, Eli; Gregory, Ezra; Gregory, Jonathan; Griffith, William; Hall, Daniel; Henderson, John; Hardy, Samuel; Hardy, William; Harper, Alexander; Harper, James; Harper, James A.; Harper, John A.; Harper, John C.; Harper, John J.; Harper, Joseph D.; Harper, Wm. A.; Hawley, Chauncey; Hawler, Geo. W.; Hawley, Jeff D.; Hawley, Orestes K.; Hawley, Timejk?; Hayes, Daniel; Hayes, Ebenezer; Hayes, Eli; Hayes, Joseph; Hayes, Seth; Heathman, Bennet; Heathman, Jona; Heathman, Thomas; Helvins, Ebenezer; Hendry, David; Herriman, Stephen; Herrington, Jona; Herrington, Seth; Hewet, John; Hewins, William; Hibbard, Daniel; Hickcox, Eleazer; Hickcox, Uri; Hill, David; Hill, Hesekiah; Hill, Simeon; Hitchcock, Peter; Hix, David; Holcomb, Timothy; Hopkins, Benjamin; Hopson, Samuel; Hotchkiss, Ebn.; Hotchkiss, Joseph; Hubbard, Manoah; Hubbard, Mathew; Hulbert, Seth; Humphrey, Ambrose; Huntington, Samuel; Hyde, Freeman; Jack, Man Wm.; Jackson, Dunham; Johnson, Benjamin; Johnson, Joseph; Jones, Benerah; Jones, John; Jones, William; Jordan, Thomas;

Kellog, Jacob; Kellogg, Daniel; Kennedy, James; Kennedy, John; Kerr, Joseph; King, Elisha; King, Hezekiah; King, Nathan; King, Nehenia; King, Peter; King, Peter Jr.; Kinzerty, Thos.; Kneippe, Charles; Kneippe, Christian; Knoulton, Calvin; Knoulton, Stephen; Lement, Robert; Lect, Gideon; Lyman, Epaphras?; Lyon, Aaron; Lyon, Christopher; McDaniel, James; McDaniel, William; McFarland, William; McNough, Samuel; McNought, John; Martin, Robert; Martin, Thomas; Merry, E.; Mills, Starling; Mines, John; Mendel, Reuben; Merry, Ebenezer; Merry, Hosmer; Miller, James; Miner, Justus; Miner, Philo; Minees, John; Mixer, Phinias; Morse, Benj.; Moss, Simeon; Mt. Gomery, Eli; Mt. Gomery, John; Mt. Gomery, Levi; Murry, John N.; Niles, David; Niles, Leonard; Nittleton, Roger; Northrap, Daniel; Norton, Elisha; Noyes, Daniel; Noyes, Jordon; Noyes. Joseph; Nye, Benjamin; Nye, Ebenezer; O'Daniel, Joshua; Oilverthron, Thos.; Olds, Ezekial; Olds, Thomas; Olmstead, Zachariah; Opp, Conard; Owen, Joel;

Padan, Jacob; Page, Noah; Paine, Edward; Paine, Edward Jr.; Paine, Hendreck; Paine, Joel; Palmer, Isaac; Parker, C.; Parks, Nathan; Parker, Charles; Parker, Clark; Patchen, Eleazer; Pepoon, Joseph; Perrin, William; Phelps, Clark; Phelps, Isaac H.; Phelps, Jesse; Pittney, Lewis; Pomeroy, Daniel; Pomeroy, Ichabod; Pomeroy, Stephen; Pool, Elijah; Potter, Samuel; Punderson, Lemuel; Quiggle, John; Rawlings, James; Reed, John R.; Rin, Paul; Robinson, Israel; Rockwell, Caleb; Rockwall, Joshua; Root, Jona; Rose, Simeon; Royes, Thedore; Ruack, John C.; Rusark, Shadrick; Rudd, John Jr.; Russel, Jona; Russel, Luther; Russel, Nathan; Russel, R.

Sawin, Purchase; Sawtell, Daniel; Sessions, Anson; Sheffield, Harvey; Sheffield, John; Shephard, Pelatiah; Skinner, Abraham; Skinner, Hannah; Smith, Hall; Smith, John; Smith, Noah N.; Spaldings, Solomon; Starr, Beverly; Starr, William; Steel, Zadock; Stevens, Rosswell; Stewart, Amasa; Stockwel, Abner; Stone, David; Stone, James; Stone, Calvin; Stone, Vene; Strong, Nathan; Sweet, Benjamin; Sweet, Peleg; Swift, Philip; Tappen, Abraham; Thayer, Seth; Thompson, Caleb; Thompson, Isaac; Thompson, Zadock; Thurston, Jason; Townsley, Daniel; Tiffany, Jacob; Townsley, John; Tubbs, Joseph; Turney, Asa; Umbufield, Theo.

Vidito, Jasper; Vidito, John; Vosbury, Martin; Wackley, Jona & David; Wallace, John; Warner, Jona; Waterous, John B.; Waterous, William; Webster, Daniel; Webster, George; Webster, Luman; Webster, Michael; Weiss, John; Wheeler, Aaron; White, Samuel; Whitmore, Collins; Waid, Elisha; Widener, Michael; Wilcox, Hosea; Wilcox, Elnathan; Willey, Clerment; William, Calvin; William, Davidson; Williams, Joseph; Williams, William; Wilmot, Asa; Wood, John; Wood, Palmer; Wood, ?; Woodworth, Ezekiel; Woolcott, John H.; Wright, Aaron; Wright, David; Wright, Ewins; Wright, James; Wright, James Jr.; Wright, Jhol.?; Wright, Moses; Wright, Timothy; Young, Dalas.

INDEX TAX LIST OHIO 1810

By THELMA LANG

GREEN COUNTY

Agun, William; Aldridge, Littleberry; Alexander, Matthew; Alexander, Nathaniel; Alcxander, Samuel; Allen, Benjamin; Allen, Jackson; Anderson, James; Anderson, John; Anderson, John H.; Anderson, Richard C.; Anderson, Seth; Anderson, William; Andrew, Hugh; Andrew, Read; Ankey, Henry; Apperman, Richard; Armstrong, Alexander;

Armstrong, Robert.

Bagwell, Thos.; Baileff, Thomas; Bailes, Elsha; Bain, James; Bain, John; Baird, John; Baisseau, Benjamin; Baker, Francis; Baldwin, Reese; Barnes, James; Barns, John; Barrett, James; Barrett, John; Bayley, Thos. M.; Beal, Robert; Beatty, William A.; Beck, John; Beddle, Cement; Beeson, Amazeah; Beeson, Margaret; Bell, Henry; Bell, Joshua; Benson, James; Biddle, —; Bird, Andrew; Birt, William; Blessing, John; Blue, John, Sr.; Bodkin, George; Boggess, Robert; Bole, Margaret; Bone, Martha; Bone, Samuel; Bone, Volentine; Bonner, David S; Bonner, Frederick; Booker, Lewis; Bowen, Ephriam; Boyd, Nancey; Bozworth, John; Bradfort, Margaret; Bradford, Charles; Bradford, David; Brady, Joseph; Brasilton, Samuel; Brill, Henry; Britton, Mary; Bromagem, Elias; Browder, Harmon; Browder, Thomas; Browder, William; Brown, Jacob; Brown, Samuel; Bruner, Elias; Bruster, Samuel; Buckles, Robert; Buckles, William; Bull, James; Bull, William; Bunting, James; Burris, Joseph; Butler, James.

Caine, John; Campbell, Henry; Campbell, John; Campbell, Jonathan; Campbell, Smaule; Campbell, William; Camron, Hugh; Canker, Andrew; Carman, Joseph; Carneal, Thomas; Casbole, Robert; Cason, William; Chambers, Adam; Chambers, John; Clancey, James; Clark, Jonathan; Clarke, John; Clayborne, Butler; Cole, John; Collett, Moses; Collier, James; Collier, Moses; Compton, Amos; Compton, Joseph; Compton, Samuel; Compton, Stephen; Conwell, Elizabeth, W.; Cosslee, Lewis; Cox, John; Coy, Jacob; Cozad, Aaron; Cozad, Jacob, Sr.; Cozad, Jacob, Jr.; Cramer, John; Crawford, Robert; Crichfield, John; Crittenton, John; Croghan, William; Cronk, Andrew; Crow, Mathias; Crusen, Cornelius; Culberson, James; Culley, Thomas; Cunningham, James; Currie, David; Currie, James; Currie, John; Cutler, Jacob; Cutter, Benjamin.

Dark, William; Darst, Jacob; Davis, David; Davis, Owen; Davis, Phillip; Davis, Robert; Deed, Francis; Denney, James; Dolby, Joel; Dorsey, Luke; Downey, John; Downey, William; Dunwoddly, John; Durnbough, Jacob; Dynes, Chambers.

Ealey, Isaac; Eaton, Henry; Edge, George; Edge, William D.; Edwards, Mills; Elam, Josiah; Ellis, John; Ennis, John; Ennis, Jeremiah; Ennis, Samuel; Ennis, Thompson; Esnbree, Thomas.

Faliferer, William; Farmer, Upton; Farmer, William; Faulkner, David; Faulkner, Jesse; Faulkner, Robert; Faulkner, Thomas; Ferguson, Zachariah; Fiers, John; Findley, Samuel; Flood, Jonathan; Folk, George Sr.; Forgey, James; Forgey, Stewart; Forquhar, Jonah; Fowler, John; Frakes, Robert; Frazier William; Freeman, William; Friskett, George; Funor, James.

Gallowoy, George; Galloway, George, Jr.; Galloway, James B.; Galloway, James; Galloway, James, Jr.; Galloway, James, Sr.; Galloway, John; Galloway, Samuel; Galloway, William; Gamble, Samuel; Garlough, Adam; Garrard, Isaac; Garrison, David; Gates, H.; Gates, Horatio; George, William; Gibbons, Robert, heirs; Gibson, J.; Godfrey, Thomas; Goldsby, John; Goode, John; Gough; Gowdy, Andrew; Gowdy, James; Gowdy, John, Sr.; Gowdy, Samuel; Gray, George; Greene, Timothy; Gregg, John; Grimes, Benjamin; Grimes, Mary; Grimes, Nancy; Grover, Josiah.

Haines, Amos; Haines, David; Haines, Henry; Haines, Jacob; Haines, John; Haines, Noah; Hale, John; Hall, Richard; Hamill, Robert; Hamilton, William; Hanna, Robert; Hardman, Peter & Henry; Harner, George Sen.; Harrow, John; Harshman, John; Harshman, Philip; Hatfield, Levin; Hayes, James; Heath, Tinsley; Heaton, John; Hefley, Charles; Henderson, Alexander; Herbert, William; Herring, Jacob; Hill, Baylor; Hite, Isaac; Hittle, George; Hivling, John; Hoblett, Boston; Holland, George; Hoop, John; Hoover, Felix; Hopping, Ezekiel; Hopping, Jeremiah; Hopping, Moses; Horner, Benjamin; Horner, Jacob; Horney, William; Hoscher, Frederick; Hosier, Jacob; Hosier, Joseph; Howell, Ezekiel; Hubble, Jacob; Hufford, Jacob; Hulick, Samuel; Hunt, Josiah; Hunter, Thomas; Hurley, Zadock; Hussey, Christopher; Husted, Joseph M.; Huston, David.

Inlows, Abraham; Irwin, John; Irwin, William; Isham. George; Isham, George, Sen.

Jackson, Philip; Jamison, John; John, Jno.; John, Samuel; Johnson, Aaron; Johnson, Arthur; Johnson, Reuben; Johnson, William; Johnston, Christopher; Johnston, James; Johnston, Rodd; Johnston. Simeon; Jones, Churchill; Jones, Peter; Jones, Richard; Jones, Robert; Judy, Jacob; Jusy, John; Junkin, James; Junkin, Lancelot; Junkin. William.

Kendall, Robert; Kendall, William; Kent, John; Kerr, Alexander; Kerr, Joseph; Kersner, Soloman; Kirkpatrick, John; Kirkpatrick, Samuel; Kiser, John, Jr.; Kiser, John Sr.; Knox, John; Koogler, Adam; Kyle, Joseph; Kyle, Samuel.

Lambert, Aaron; Lambert, Joseph; Lambert, William; Lamme, Nathan; Larne, Abraham; Lessley, John; Laum, Jacob; Lee, Samuel; Leonard, Nave; Lewis, A.; Lewis, Addison; Lewis, John; Lewis, W.; Lewis, Warner; Lindsley, Jeremiah; Lingo, A.; Lingo, Agnes; Linn, Samuel; Loose, Justus; Loughhead, David; Low, William; Lowrey, Ann; Loyd, James; Lucas, Claeb; Lucas, John; Lucas, Joseph.

McCabe, Armstrong; McCalley, John; McClane, John; McClellan, John; McClelland, William; McClelland, Robert; McClure, William; McConnel, Adam; McCormick, James; McCoy, Alexander, Jr.; McCoy, Alexander, Sr.; McCoy, David; McCoy, James; McCoy, John; McCully, Soloman; McCune, Joseph; McDaniel, Dempsey; McDaniel. Isaiah; McDaniel, Reuben; McDermed, Edward; McFarland, William; McKaig, John; McKay, Moses; McKnight, John; McKnight, William; McMichael, William; Maltbee, Ammi; Marshall, John; Marshall, Robert; Martin, John; Martin, Samuel; Mason, David; Mason, Owens; Mason, Stephen; Massenburg, John; Massie, Nathaniel; Mastin, Ezekiel; Matthews, A.; Maxey, Bennett; Maxey, Horatis; Maxwell, William; Maxwell's heirs; Mayson. David; Mead, A.; Means Robert; Mendenhall, Aaron; Mendenhall, John; Mendenhall, Martin; Mendenhall, Richard; Menick, John; Mercer, Aaron; Mercer, Edward; Mercer heirs; Mill, Jacob; Miller, Christlery; Miller, Isaac; Miller, Jacob; Miller, James; Miller, Moses; Miller, William; Mitchell, James; Mock, John; Mock, Phebe; Moody, Robert; Moore, William; Mooreman, Thomas; Morgan. Isaac; Morgan, Sarah; Moseby, Benjamin; Mure, Francis; Murphy, John.

Nane, Leonard; Nelson, William; Newman, Joseph; Nicholson, Simon; Niswonger, Jacob; Nott, William.

Painter, David; Paris, Thomas; Parker, A.; Parker, Alexander; Parker, James; Parker, Thomas; Paul, John; Paul, Jonathan; Paulin, Uuriah; Pearce, William; Pelham, Peter; Pelham, Samuel; Perkins, Thomas; Perry, Samuel; Petro, Nicholas; Peterson, Michael; Phillips, Charles; Popence, James; Porter, William; Posey, Thomas; Poter, James M.; Powers, Daniel; Prince, David; Pride, John, heirs & Co.; Price, Frederick; Price, Peter; Price, Susannah; Pults, John; Puterbough, Magdelena.

Quinn, Matthew.

Ralls, Nathaniel; Ralston, Joseph; Rawlins, John R.; Read, Andrew; Reed, James; Repp, Henry; Ritch, Jacob; Rittenhouse, Garrett; Ritter, Tobias; Robinson, Edward; Robinson, Joseph; Rodgers, William; Rose, Jesse; Ross, Robert; Rowen, Edward; Rowen, McCalley; Rush, Jesse; Russell, A.; Russell, Albert; Russell, Alfred; Russell, James; Ryalls, James.

Sackett, Cyrus; Sale, John; Sanders, John; Sanders, Forrest; Sanders, William; Sandley, William; Schooley, Samuel; Scott, George; Scott, Moses; Sergant, W. H.; Shall, John; Shannon, George; Shaw, William; Sheley, Davis; Sheley, John, Jr.; Sheley, John, Sen.; Sheley, Samuel; Shillinger, Adam; Shingledecker, Jacob S.; Shoup, George; Shoup, Samuel; Shover, Simon; Simerman, George; Simmerson, Robert; Simpson, Thomas; Sipe, Francis; Small, James; Smalley, William; Smelser, Andrew; Smith, Jacob; Smith, Joseph; Smith, Mathais; Smith, Minor; Smith, Thomas; Smith, William; Snodgrass, James, Sr.; Snodgrass, John; Snodgrass, Robert; Snowden, James; Sparks, Ann; Spencer, Charles; Spencer, Michael; Srofe?, Sebastian; Staley, Daniel; Stanfield, William; Stanton, Frederick; Stanton, William; Steele, Samuel; Steele, William; Stephens, Evan; Sterret, Mary; Sterrett, John; Stewart, Andrew; Stevens, James; Stevens, John; Stevenson, James; Stevenson, John; Stevenson, Thomas; Stevenson, William; Stites, Samuel; Stokes, John; Stone, Thomas; Stowe, Alexander; Stratton, Joseph; Strong, Noah; Strong, Reuben; Stubblefield, B.; Stubblefield, Beverly; Stump, Leonard; Summers, Simon; Sutton, Amariah; Sutton, Cornelius; Sutton, Isiah; Sutton, Jeniah?; Sutton, John; Sutton, William G.; Synip, Rinehart.

Taliafur, Wm.; Tanner, Robert; Tanner, William; Tatman, James; Tatman, Joseph; Taylor; Francis; Taylor, William; Thatcher, Ruth; Thomas, Absalon; Thomas, Daniel; Thompkins, William; Thorm, William; Tibbs, William; Tiffin, Edward; Tingley, John; Tingley, William, Jr.; Todd, James; Todd, John; Torrence, John; Towler, James; Townsend, Abraham; Townsend, Levi; Townsley, John; Townsley, Thomas; Townsley, William, Sr.; Trader, Moses; Trubee, Christopher; Turner, Hercules; Turner, Joseph.

Umphreville, David.

Vance, Joseph; Vandolah, Joseph; Veneaton, Abraham.

Wallace, John; Walton, Edward; Ward, George; Ward, William; Warfield, Richard; Warren, Edward; Washington, William; Watson, Jesse, Jr.; Watson, John; Watson, John Sr.; Watters, James; Watts, J.; Webb, Lucey; Wheeler, Ebenezer; Whichar, Matthew; White, William; Whiteman, Benjamin; Whiting, Francis; Wiland, Christian; Williams, John; Williams, Remembrance; Wilson, Daniel; Wilson, Jacob; Wilson, James; Wilson, John, Jr.; Wilson, John, Sr.; Wilson, Joseph; Wilson, Thomas; Winget, Reuben; Winlock, Joseph; Wolf, George; Wolf, John; Wolf, John, Sr.; Woodcock, Robert; Woodfords, Heirs of John; Worman, Henry; York, Jeremiah.

INDEX TAX LIST OHIO 1810

GUERNSEY COUNTY, OHIO

By THELMA LANG

Adair, John; Allen, William.

Basil, Israil; Beatty, Zaccheus; Beham, James; Beham, John; Biggs, Zaccheus; Borton, Benjamin; Bratton, James; Bryant, John; Burt, David; Burt, Luther; Burns, Samuel; Buymer, George.

Callis, William O.; Cannon, John; Carey, Rufus; Carter, William; Caruthers, John, heirs; Casey, Ezra; Chambers, Robert; Chapman, John; Clark, Joseph; Cochran, Alexander; Cook, Thomas; Corbett, John; Cowan, Edward; Cunningham, Wm.

Daugherty, Daniel; Dawson, William; Dickerson, Richard; Dickerson, John; Dillon, James; Downey, Williams.

Edwards, James; Emely, John; Enslow, David.

Frame, John; Frame, James; Frame, David.

Goldsmith, Charles; Gomber, Jacob.

Hall, John; Hauna, Andrew; Helger, Henry; Henderson, Thomas; Henderson, Thomas, Esq.; Henderson, John; Hillioner, William; Hite, Andrew; Huffman, Michael; Hughs, Levy.

Isaac, Perkins; Israel, Basil.

Jacoby, Nicholas.

Kiggins, John; Knapp, Azael; Kinowley, Thomas; Kolenger, George; Kirkpatrick, Thomas.

Lantz, William; Leath, Samuel; Leru, James; Long, Frederick.

McCluney, William; McConnell, William; McGiffen, Archibald; McKinney, John; McMurdy, Adam; Martin, John; Martin, Nancy; Masters, Benjamin; Meek, John; Miller, George; Miller, Isaac; Moffit, John; Morehead, William; Murphy, Nicholas.

Obresson, Patrick; O'Farrises, Joseph, heirs; Ogier, William.

Poalk, Samuel.

Reasoner, William; Reasoner, John; Reeves, Stephen; Reeves, Joseph; Rice, George; Roberts, Patrick; Roseman, Philip; Russells, John Assigns.

Sarchett, Peter; Shiman, Morey; Sickman, Priestly; Sickman, John Smith, Elisha; Smith, Joseph; Smith, Samuel; Smith, Thomas; Speer, Robert; Speer, Thomas; Stiers, Samuel.

Talbut, William; Thompson, Thos., heirs; Tuigh, George R.

Vernon, Frederick; Verry, Jona; Vouis, John.

Wheery, David; Wheery, D.; Williams, Joseph; Wilson, Joseph; Wilson, Samuel; Wine, Christian; Wine, George; Wyrich, Peter.

149

INDEX TO TAX LIST OF OHIO FOR 1810

HAMILTON COUNTY

By Thelma Blair Lang

Abbot, Dominicus; Abbot, Elisha; Abbot, Nathaniel; Able, James; Agnew, Samuel; Ailes, William; Allen, Jacob; Allen, Joseph; Allen, Samuel; Alston, Alexander; Alter, Frederick; Anderson, Benjamin; Anderson, Eizabeth; Anderson, Isaac; Andrew, John; Andrews, James; Andrews, John; Armstrong, James; Armstrong, John; Armstrong, W. & John; Armstrong, N. Shepherd; Armstrong, T. & S.; Arnold, Richard; Ashburn, Cyrus; Askreen, Thomas; Atherton, Aaron; Atherton, Peter; Atherton, Aaron, Jr.; Atherton, Benjamin; Atherton, David; Auter, Ralph; Ayres, Richard; Ayres, Samuel; Ayres, Bennagh; Ayres, Ebenezer;

Backburn; Hannah; Badgely, William; Baegdley, Robert; Baits, David; Baits, Seth; Baker, David; Baldwin, Abraham; Baldwin, John; Balser, George Balser, Henry; Balser, Henry, Jr.; Balser, Henry A.; Balser, John; Balser, Joseph; Balser, Peter; Barkdoll, Stephen; Barnes, John; Bates, Clark; Bates, Isaac; Bates, Othniel?; Bates, Usal; Baum, Martin; Baum, Martin; Baxter, James; Beazly, John; Beeke, Hannah; Beel, Samuel; Beler, Henry; Bell, John; Bell, Peter; Bellis, Wiliam; Bennet, Samuel J.; Bennet, Samuel, Sr.; Bennau, Richard; Bennefield, John; Berry, Samuel; Bett, William; Betts, John; Batsion, John; Bickle, Christian; Blau, ?; Blach, David; Blau, John; Blue, John; Blue, David; Bodian, Richard; Boman, John; Boneham, John; Boon, William; Boother, Abraham; Boram, Aaron; Bowers, Phineas; Bradley, Robert; Bram, Jeremiah; Bran, David; Bran, John; Bray, Peter; Brand or Braud, William; Brecount, David;

Bridges, John; Brinton, Samuel; Broadwell, Jacob; Broadwell, Jonah; Brocan, Isaac; Brocan, Michael; Brown, Ehpraim; Brown, F. & A.; Brown, Grace; Brown, John; Brown, Joshua; Brown, Mathew; Brown, Ruth; Brown, William; Brown, John W.; Bruen, Faber; Bryant, Nathaniel; Buckingham, Enos; Buckingham, Levi; Bunnell, Benjamin; Bunnel, Lewis; Bunnel, Samuel; Burge, Jonathan; Burnes, James; Burnet, J. J. Findlay; Burnet, Jacob; Burnet, J. J.; Butler, Stephen; Butler, William; Butterfield, Jeremiah; Buxton, Lydia;

Caldwell, Robert; Canahan, Robert; Cannahan, Robert; Canaham, James; Campbell, Albert; Campbell, John; Campbell, Robert, Sr.; Camron, Daniel; Camron, Duncan; Canington, George; Cannady, David; Cannady, Francis; Card'e, James; Carey, William; Carpenter, John, Sr.; Carpenter, Joseph; Carson, Agnes; Carson, Enoch; Carson, Juliet; Carson, Robert; Carson, W. G.; Carver, Abraham; Carver, John; Case, Henry, Sr.; Case, Henry, Jr.; Casto, John; Chalmers, Andrew; Cahrters, James; Chase, Abraham; Cilley, Joseph; Clark, Ichabod; Clark, James; Clark, John; Clark, Jonathan; Clark, Joseph; Clarke, John; Clevenger, Ann; Creary, John; Coots, John; Cochran, William; Cockner, William; Cockner, John; Codderman, Wido; Coil, John; Collins, Robert; Colwell, James; Compton, Nathan; Compton, Jacob R.; Compstock, Joab; Concklin, Joseph; Cone, Charles; Conger, Moses; Connor, D.; Conover, John; Conover, Joseph; Coons, Frederick; Coons, Frederick, Jr.; Coons, Henry; Cooper, William; Cooper, Leonard; Corbly, John; Concklin, Stephen; Couston, David; Couston, Michael; Covalt, Cheniah; Covalt, Jonathan; Covalt, Bethuel; Cox, Andrew; Cox, John; Cox, Jacob; Cox, William; Crain, Jonas; Crain, Lyhu; Crain, Sayers; Cram, Abraham; Cram, William; Crane, Ichabod; Crane, Noah; Crane, Polly; Crane, Samuel; Cregar, Peter; Crish, Moses; Crisman, Felix; Crist, George; Crist, Joseph; Crist, Peter; Crossley, Josiah; Crosley, Ross; Crossley, Henry; Crowell, Peter; Cullom, George, Sr.; Cullom, George, Jr.; Cullom, William; Cumming, John; Cunningham, James; Curpler, Mathias;

Darham, Daniel; Davies, Charity; Davies, Peter; Davies, Stephen; Davies, William; Davis, James; Day, Daniel; Day, John; Day, Timothy; Dayton, Aaron; Dayton, J.; Dayton, Jonathan; DeBalt, Michael; Deguller, Anthony; Delaney, Jacob; Demerit, Nicholas; Denman, Abrion; Denman, Joseph; Denman, Nathaniel; Demford, William; Dennison, Mary; Denniso, Mary; Devie, Isaac; Dickey, Patrick; Dill, Richard; Dodson, Edward; Dodson, John, Sr.; Donaldson, William; Downey, James; Drake, William; Dunn, Micajah; Dun, Samuel; Dunseth, James; Durham, Aquilla; Durkham, Joshua; Duskey, Dennis; Duskey, Eli; Durkey, Lemon; Dye, Jno.; Dye, Nancy;

Earhart, George; Eason, Alexander; Eas, Henry; Ecclebarger, Joseph; Edward, Isaac; Edwards, Joseph; Edwards, Thomas; Elloot, John; English, William; Enyard, Benjamin; Enyard, Sylas; Evans, Walter; Evans, William; Evingham, Jacob; Eversal, Christian; Eversal, John; Everson, Rich; Ewing, James; Ewing, John;

Fagan, Aaron; Fagan, George; Farmer, George; Farran, Charles; Fawble, Jacob; Feght, Christopher; Felter, Cronymus; Felter, David; Felter, Jacob; Felter, William; Finney, E. W.; Fenton, R.; Fenton,

Jacob; Ferguson, James; Ferguson, Hutson; Ferris, Henry; Ferris, Isaac; Ferris, Jash.; Ferris, Eliphabit & Brothers; Ferris, John; Feinsler, Paul; Findlay, James; Finney, John; Fleak, Peter; Flemming, Daniel; Flin, Stephen; Flinn, Agnes; Flinn, David; Flint, Hazekeah; Fordyce, James; Fordee, Thomas; Forll, Thomas; Foster, Gabriel; Foster, Luke; Fox, Stephen; Frazee, Isaac; Frazee, Jonah; Frazee, Jacob; Frazee, Levi; Frazer, Thomas; Fraser, Jonas; French, Geremiah; French, Sop; Fulton, David;

Gamble, Robert; Gano, J. L.; Gano, John S.; Gano, Seth; Gardner, Esther; Garrard, Jonathan; Garrison, Elyah; Garrison. Levi, Sr.; Gaston, Hugh; Gaston, R. John; Gaston, Robert; Gates, Uriah; Gay, Joseph; German, Caleb; Gest, Enoch; Gibson, Alexander; Gibbs, Justus; Gifason, David; Giffin, Margaret; Gile, Andrew; Glisson, Thomas; Goble, Isaac; Goff, William; Goforth, Aaron; Golden, John; Goldtrap, John; Gonston, Michael; Gonston, David; Goudy, Robert; Gordon, George; Gow, Samuel; Gray, David; Gray, Lewis; Gray, Samuel; Gray, William; Greenham, David; Grier, James; Grinnel, Barney; Grooms, John; Gwaltney, Josiah; Goulding, Bernard; Goulding, James; Gwinup ?, George;

Haden, Christopher; Haden, Daniel; Hageman, Adrian, Sr.; Hageman, Christopher; Hageman, Adrian, Jr.; Hageman, Simon; Hainback, Isaac: Hale, Stephen; Hall, John; Halley, Samuel; Hamil, John; Hamil. Andrew; Hamilton, Alexander D.; Hammit, William; Hand, John; Handford, Thadens; Handford, Henry; Hankins, William; Hansbrook, Daniel; Harden, James; Harmer, Josiah; Harness, Michael; Harper, Robert; Harper, Thomas; Harrider, Rosannah; Harris, Aaron; Harris, Joseph; Harrison, Terazie; Hasbrook, Archibald: Hawkins, Carvil; Hawkins, Joseph; Hawkins, Blairs; Hawkins, Richard; Hank, John; Hankins, Richard; Hay, Jacob; Hedger, Elias; Heifleigh, Jacob; Helmick, Jacob; Helmick, Peter; Henry, Arthur; Hervy, Christopher; Hetchler, Jacob; Higgins, Thomas; Highfill, Phillip; Highlands, Anthony; Hilditch, Samuel; Hill, Andrew; Hill, John; Hinkle, Asa; Hinton, William; Hoffman, Jacob; Hoffman, Robert; Hole, Bamobar; Hole, John; Hole, Walter; Holland, Thomas; Holoway, Joseph; Hopple, Andrew; How, Ezenezer; House, Jacob; Hubbard, John; Hubble, Thomas; Hugher, Esekiel; Hughes, Thomas; Humes, John; Hunt, Edward; Hunt, Isaac; Hunt, Jesse; Hunter, Daniel; Hunter, John; Hunter, William; Hurin, Enos; Huston, Paul; Huston, Samuel; Hutchinson, Ezikiel; Hutchinson, Isaiah; Hutchinson: Jacob; Hutchinson, John; Hutchinson, Jonathan;

Ingersol, Abel: Ingersol, Daniel; Ingersol, Joseph; Ingersol, James; Irwin, Samuel, Irwin, William; Isgrig, Daniel; Isgrig, Joshua; Isgrig, Michael;

Jackman, Atuell; Jackman, Edward; Jackson, William; Jacobs, John: James, Joseph: James, Scot. Sr.; Jenkinson, John; Jennings, Jacob: Jessup, John: Jessup, Judith; Jessup, Stephen: Jesup, Daniel; Jesup, Nancy; Johnston, Samuel, Johnston, Walter; Johnson, Samuel J. McKnight; Johnson Abner; Johnson, Andrew; Johnson, Carey; Johnson, Edward; Johnson, Samuel; Johnson, Samuel, Jr.; Johnson,

Thomas; Jones, James; Jones, John; Jones, Jonathan; Jones, Phillip; Jones. Thomas; Jones, William; Jones, Isaac; Jones, Isiah; Joyce, Elizabeth; Julay, Peter;

Kantz, Jacob; Keen, Peter; Kelly, John; Kelley, David; Kemper,

Peter; Kneiper, Caleb; Kempton, Robert; Kerns, Jacob; Kerns, Peter; Kerr, Thomas; Ker, Hugh; Kindle, Thomas; King, Thomas; Kitchel ?, Benjamin; Kitchel, Samuel; Kitchell, John; Kitchell, Joseph; Kitchell, Mary; Kitchell, Moses; Kitchell, Wichleff; Kizer, Jacob; Knapper, Jacob; Knapper, Margaret;

Laboteux, John; Laboteux, Peter; Lachey, Andrew; Lacing, Jacob; Lamburt, M.; Lamburn, Samuel; Landon, William; Lane, Aaron; Largdon, Oliver; Langoon, John W.; Larnard, Desire for Heirs of E. Larnard; Larrison, Jonathan; Lee, Adam; Lee, David; Lee, Henry; Lee, Levu; Lee, Peter; Lee, Samuel; Leeper, Allen; Leming, Samuel; Lemon, William; Leonard, David; Leonard, Luther; Lincicub ?, Jacobus; Lieby, George; Lindley, Abraham; Little, Cornelius; Little, Samuel; Little, William; Logan, William; Long, Michael; Longworth, Nicholas; Looker, Othniel; Lovain, John; Love, Henry; Lowes, James Ludlow, Henry; Ludlow, Isaac, (heirs of); Ludlow, John; Ludlow, William; Lyans, Samuel; Lyon, John; Lyons, James; Lyons, Samuel; Lyst, John; Lytle, Taylor & Armstrong;

McAdams, James; McAdams, John; McAdams, Thomas; Mc-Adams, William; McCash, James; McCash, William; McAuley, Ezekee; McCausland, Henry; McChesney, Ann; McCleleane, James; McClelland, James; McCormick, Francis; McCormick, James; McCormick, John, Sr.; McCormick, Thomas; McCown, Benj.; McCullough, Eleanor; McCullom, Patrick; McCullough, Sampson; McGaughy, David; McGee, Joseph; McGlaughlin, Tebrey; McHenry, Dan; McHenry, Hannah; McHenry, Samuel; McIntire, William; Mack, Pritchard; McKee, James; McKee, John; McKee, Samuel; McKinney, David; McKnight, Joseph; MaMahon, Francis; McMillan, Constance; McMillan, Samuel; McMillan, Arch.; McNutt, James; McNutt, Alexander; McNutt, John; Malston, Thomas; Mantrees, Conrad; Markland, Thomas; Marm, Mehetarnel; Marsh, Lemon; Marsh, Jacob; Marsh, Robert; Marshall, George; Marshall, Henry; Martin, Abner; Martin, John; Martin, Samuel;; Marvin, Robert; Marsh, Samuel; Massie, Nathaniel; Mathews, James; Mathers, James; Mathers, John; Matson, James; Matson, John; May, Andrew; Mean, John; Meek, Hugh; Meek, John; Meeker, John; Meeker, Nathaniel; Meeks, Edward; Mennepier, Francis; Mercer, Susanna; Merrit, Jesse (heirs of); Miles, Abezer; Miles, John R.; Millar, Abraham; Millar, John; Miller, Burgan; Miller, Ezra; Miller, Henry; Miller, J. B.; Miller, John; Miller, William W.; Mills, Abner; Mills, E. Philenion; Mills, Isaac; Mitchell, William; Monison, Moses; Moor, Robert; Moore, Robert; Moore, Adam; Moore, Bustard; Moore, Charles; Moore, Jacob; Moore, John; Moore, Samuel, Sr.; Mordock, James; Morely, William; Morgan, Matheas; Morgan, Richard; Morris, Aquila; Morris, John; Morris, Robert; Morrison, Isaac; Morrison, W. C.; Morrows, ————; Morse, Joseph; Morton, Henry; Muchmore,

Samuel; Muchmore, Benjamin; Mulford, Joseph; Mundle. Jonathan; Myars, John;

Newcomer, Peter; Nicely, Peter H.; Nickels, Jonathan; Orr, Robert; Owens, Peter;

Parks, Culbertson; Patten, Robert; Patterson, Charles; Patterson, James; Patterson, John; Patterson, William; Pattmore, Abraham; Payton, Elizabeth; Pearson, Harmon; Pecker, John; Pecker, Lewis; Pennghough. Frederick; Penory, Alexander; Penory, Ralph; Perice, Benjamin; Perry, William; Peters, Andrew; Phillips, James W.; Phlilips, Richard; Phillips, Thomas; Piatt, Jacob; Piatt, John H.; Pierson, Anraham; Pierson, Daniel; Pierson, Mathias; Pierson, Samuel; Pittman, Jonathan; Pollock, James; Porter, William; Powell, Robert; Preston, Joseph; Price, Clarkson; Price, Daniel; Price, Hezekiah; Prottsman, John; Pryer, Andrew; Pryer, John; Puterson, Hays;

Ralston, Susannah; Ramsey, John, Jr.; Ramsey, William; Rankuss, Samuel; Ray, William; Raymond, Samuel; Reddick, Joseph; Redenbaugh, Henry; Redenbaugh, John; Redenbaugh, Phillip; Reed, John; Reed, William; Reeder, David; Reeder, Morrison; Reeder, James; Reeder, ex. as of P.l. Hanes; Reeder, George; Reeder, Jonathan; Reeder, Joseph; Rees, Henry; Repsher, John; Rich. Thomas; Rickey, Robert; Richardson, Robert; Rickey, Tho.; Riddle, John; Ridenour, Joseph; Riggle, George; Risk, David; Roase, Jacob; Robenson, Cuthbert; Robertson, Ephraim; Robertson, Samuel; Robson, Alexander; Rockenfield, Anraham; Ross, Ogden; Rogers, Andrew; Rogers, Simeon; Role, Edward; Role. John; Roler, George; Roll, Abraham; Rood, James; Rood, Felix; Rood, Rachall; Rop. Ignatius; Rop, John; Rop, Thomas; Roseberry. Thomas; Ross, Daniel; Rowan, Robert; Rve, Thomas; Rue, Benjr.; Ruffin, William; Runyan, Benjamin, Sr.; Runyan, Benjamin, Jr.; Runyan, Henry; Runyan. John V.; Runyan, Noah; Rute, Samuel; Ryan, William; Rybalt, Jacob;

Sampthan, Joseph; Sandusky, & Patteyon; Sayre, Sevi; Sayre, Levi; Schooley, John; Schoggin, Aaron; Scot, James, Sr.; Scott, Andrew; Scroyer, John; Scudder, Henry; Seaman, John; Sears, Benjamin; Sears, John; Sears, Gideon, Sedam, Cornelius; Settle, Francis; Seuteny, Wm.; Seward, James; Seward, Samuel; Sexton, Joseph; Shannah, Daniel; Shaw, Albin; Shearer, Lodowick; Shearer, Michael; Shears, Benjamin; Sheats, Thos.; Sheward, Richard; Shewart, Cornelius; Shuff, John; Shul, Vincent; Shule, Burk; Shuman, Jacob; Silber, John; Simon, Joseph; Skillman, Jacob, Sr.;. Smith, Abraham; Smith, Charles; Smith, Constantine; Smith, Edward; Smith, Isaac; Smith, Jeremiah; Smith, John; Smith, Jonathan; Smith, Peter; Smith, Samuel; Snodgnaf, William; Snyder, Cornelius; Spear, John; Spaiks, Isaac; Spencer, O. M.; Spencer, Oliver; Spring, David; Stacy, Thomas; Stanley, William; Stansbury, Thomas; Stebeck, William; Steel, Robert; Steel William; Stephenson, Thomas; Stephenson, Ladock; Stepp, Henry; Sterret, Isaac; Stewart, John; Stewart. John, Jr.; Stebbans. Liba: Steward, Jacob; Stite, Samuel; Stite, W. S.; Stites. Hezekiah: Stites, John; Stormes, Jacob; Stout, Benjamin; Stout, Charles; Stout, James; Stout, Jesse; Stout, Ruben;

Strong, Chloe; Stuart, William; Studderd, George; Sturger, Isaac; Sutton, Stephen; Swallow, Isaac; Swan, Caleb; Symmes, Daniel; Symmes, J. C.; Shining, Ichabod; Symes, J. Jm. Cleve; Symmes, John C.;

Taulman, Harmonius; Taulman, John; Taulman, Joseph; Terry, William; Terwillegar, Catherine; Terwillegar, Daniel; Terwillegar, John; Terwillegar, Mathias; Thomas, John; Thompson, Enoch; Thompson, James; Thompson, John; Thompson, Price; Thompson, Thomas; Thrailkell, Moses; Throckmorton, Richard; Tibbin, David; Tiffin, Joseph; Tise, Henry; Todd, John; Tompkins, Bennet; Torrence, William; Townley, Martha; Trim, John; Trinkle, John; Tucker, Benjamin; Tucker, Ephriam; Tucker, Henry; Tucker, John; Turpin, Phillip;

Ulery, Henry;

Vail, George; Vance, James; Vancoler, Jesse; Vancyke, Dominicus; Vancyke, Henry; Vancyke, Peter; Vanjilder, David; Vanhorne, Joseph; Vaurankin, John; Vantrees, Hartman; Vanzant, Isaac; Vanzant, Massey; Viley, Cornelius; Voorheese, Abraham, Sr.;

Wade, David E.; Waggoner, Aaron; Wakefield, Andrew; Walden, Benj.; Waldsmith, Christian; Walker, Christopher; Walker, David; Wallace, Mathew; Wallace, John S.; Walton, David R.; Ward, Cyrus; Ward, Joseph; Ward, Stephen; Ward, Uzal; Waring, Jonathan; Warwick, Robert; Washington, G.; Watson, James; Watson, John; Watson, William; Webb, Clayton; Webb, John; Webb, William; Weller, Andrew; Wells & Armstrong; Wells, Samuel; Whaleon, James; Wheatley, Robert; Wheeler, Jacob; Wheeler, Rhode; Whetstone, John; Whetstone, Ruben; Whitaker, Jonathan; Wightsite, James; Wilkens, Daniel; Wilkens, Michael; Wilkens, Peter; Willey, Noah; William, Joel; William, John; Williams, George; Williams, Joel; Williamh, Jonathan; Williams, Joshua; Williams, Samuel; Williams, Thomas; Williamson, George; Williamson, Joseph; Williamson, William; Willis, Benjamin; Willis, Nathaniel; Willis, Henry; Wilmoth, Thomas; Wilson, John; Wilson, Joshua L.; Winans, Phillip; Wingate, Benjamin; Wimmen, Jacob; Winnings, John; Witham, Morris; Wolverton, Mary; Wood, James; Wood, Stephen; Woodruff, Denias; Woodruff, Nathaniel; Woodruff, Stephen; Woodruffe, Lewis; Woods, Stephen; Woodward, William; Woodworth, Daniel; Wooley, Anthony; Wooley, John;

Yeatman, Griffin; Young, Peter; Youngblood, Thomas; Youst, Anraham;

Zeigler, David.

INDEX TAX LIST OHIO 1810

HIGHLAND COUNTY

By THELMA LANG

Amos, Martin; Anderson, R. C.; Antrim, Thomas; Arthur, Charles; Arthur, Duncan M.; Arthur, Pleasant; Ashinfetter, Jacob; Ault, Henry; Anthony, Garrett.

Badge, Andrew; Bailet, Thomas; Bails, Bowater, John; Bails, Curtis; Bails, Jacob; Baldwin, Jesse, Sr.; Ballard, Robert; Ballard, William; Ballow, Robt.; Barlow, William; Barnard, Frederick; Barns, Jacob; Earns, John; Barr, John; Barrere, George W.; Barrett, Jonathan; Barrett, Richard; Baytop, James; Beeson, Banjamin; Bell, John; Bell, Samuel; Bell, Richard; Bells, Mains; Bennett, Joshua; Bernard, John; Bernard, Richard; Berreman, Jonathan; Berriman, Eli; Bigger, Head; Bingerman, Adam; Bloomer, Benjamin; Blunt, Elizabeth; Boatman, William; Bond, Henry; Boyd, John; Boyd, James; Boyd, William; Bowers, Dorothy; Bowers, Jacob; Bradford, David; Bradley, John; Branson, David; Branson, Jacob; Brian, Jesse; Brodus, Richard; Brouse, Adam; Bronson, Robert; Brooks, Benjamin; Brooks, James; Brooks, Nancy; Brougher, Frederick; Brown, David; Brown, Edward; Brown, Joel; Brown, John; Bruse, James; Bucknor, Phillip; Buford, Abraham; Burson, Aaron; Butcher, Jacob.

Caily, Frederick; Caily, George; Callins, Isaac; Calmes, Marquis; Campbell, Nathaniel; Campbell, William; Canady, Walter; Connel, James; Caplinger, John; Caplinger, William; Caps, Dempsey; Carlisle, James; Carter, William; Carter, Wm.; Casey, Peter; Cass, Elizabeth; Champ, Evans; Chany, Benjamin; Chany, Edward; Chany, Edward, Jr.; Chany, Gabriel; Chapman, David; Chapman, Isaac; Charles, Andrew; Christy, Thomas; Chriswell, George; Clark, Daniel; Clevinger, Abram; Clifton, Charles; Coffin, Samuel; Coffman, Jacob; Colain, Thomas; Colames, Marquis; Cole, John; Combs; Cook, John; Cooker, Jacob; Coplinger, John; Coryell, Joseph; Couger, Michael; Cox, John; Cox, Thomas; Craig, James; Crane, Samuel; Creed, Mathew, Sr.; Creed, Robert; Creek, Jacob; Creek, Joseph; Creens, John; Crieger, John; Criger, John; Crockett, Pressley; Cummings, James; Cuntryman, Henry; Cuntryman, John; Cuntryman, Martin; Curp, Frederick; Curry, James; Curry, William.

Daily, William; Davidson, John; Davidson, John Esq.; Davidson, Robert; Dick, Thomas; Dicky, Arthur; Dodson, Joshua; Donohoo, John; Dougherty, William; Douglis, A.; Drake, Joel; Drake, Joshua; Drake, Jourden; Drake, Richard; Duckwall, Lewis; Dugas, Robert; Duncan, McArthur; Duncan, Robert; Dunham, Samuel; Dutton, David.

Eakins, John; Eakins, Joseph; Earl, Edward; Earls, Robert; Easter, Adam, Jr.; Easter, Adams, Sr.; Easter Jacob; Easter, John; Edgar, Nancy; Eggleston, Joseph; Elliott, Temple; Ellis, Jehu; Emastace, John; Ensly, Job.; Eubanks, William; Evans, A.; Evans, Amos; Evans, D.; Evans, David; Evans, Dan.; Evans, Evan; Evans, George; Evans, Richard; Evans, S.; Evans, Samuel; Evans, Samuel Jr.; Ewell, Samuel.

Fanning, James; Feely, Michal; Fender, George; Fenner, James; Fenwick, James; Ferguson, Nimrod; Finley, Robert N.; Fisher, Cephas; Fisher, Jacob; Fisher, James, Sr.; Fitzhugh, Peregrine; Fitzpatrick, James; Fitzpatrick, Robert; Fitzpatrick, Thomas; Folk, John; Fraley, Daniel; Franklin, Anthony; Franklin, Thomas; Fullerton, Alexander.

Garrett, John; Gasman, Peter; George, Mercy; George, William; Gibbs, Richard; Gibler, Frederick; Giblar, John; Giblar, Lewis; Gibson, S.; Gibson, Samuel; Gice, Erasmus; Gillispie, Hugh; Gillon, John; Gossett, John, Sr.; Grady, John; Graham, John; Grant, Jeremiah; Gray, William; Green, John; Griffen, James; Grigg, Moses H.; Grove, Benjamin.

Hadley, James; Hair, John, Sr.; Hamie, Ebenezer; Harden & Gray; Hare, Jacob; Harris, Charles; Harvey, Richard; Harvey, Samuel; Hatter, John; Hatter, Peter; Hayes, John; Hays, John; Hayse, John; Hayworth, James; Hughs, John; Head, William; Hearst, Andrew; Heyson, Anthony; Hiestand, Jacob; Hiett, John; Hill Corneleus; Hill, Walter; Hill, William; Hindman, Samuel; Hinton, Thomas; Hodgeson, Solomon; Hodgeson, George; Hodgeson, John; Hoggett, Stepehen; Holliday, Samuel; Holmes, David; Holton, Samuel; Hoop, John; Hoop, Peter; Horsefan, Joseph; Hough, Joseph; Houser, Jacob; Huffman, Isaac; Huffum, Runyon; Huffman, Felix; Hugh & A. Evans; Hughey, Charles; Hulett, Richard; Hume, Wm.; Hunt, Asa; Hunt, John; Hunt, Jonathan; Hunt, Phineas; Hunter, John; Hunter, Robert; Hunter, Thomas; Hupp, Dan; Hupp, Phillip; Hussey, Christopher; Hussey, Joshua; Hussey, Stephen; Huston, Robert.

Inskeep, Daniel.

Jackson, Gideon; Jackson, Jacob; Jameson, John; Jennings, Lewis; Jessup, John; John Ebenezer; John, Thomas; Johnson, Asshley; Johnson, Ashley; Johnson, Benjamin H.; Johnson, Charles; Johnson, Elisha; Johnson, James; Johnson, Thomas; Johnson, William; Jolly, David; Jolly, James; Jonaean?, Drury; Jonaean, Isaac; Jones, Richard.

Kays, G. Allison; Kays, John; Kelley, Ezekiel; Ken, Joseph; Kerr & Massie; Kessinger, Andrew; Keys, Samuel; Kibbon, John M.; Kibbon, John, Jr.; Kibbon, Joseph; Kiff, William; Killburn, John; Killgore, Mathew; Kingery, John; Kinsey, Alex. M.; Kinworthy David; Kinworthy, David, Sr.; Kinworthy, Elisha; Kinworthy, Isaac; Kinworthy, Joshua; Kinworthy, William; Knighten, Jesse; Knowlton, Daniel.

Lame, A. George; Layman, Isaac; Ledgs, Jozabas; Lemmings, Daniel; Leonard, James; Leverton, Foster; Lewis, Charles; Lewis, Nathaniel; Liggett, John; Little, Samuel; Lucas, James; Lucas, Jesse; Lucas, Joshua; Lucas, Richard; Lucas, William, Jr.; Lucas, William, Sr.

McCarr, F. G.; McMillen, George; McMillen, Thomas; McMillen, William; McPherson, Isaac; McQuttie, Samuel; Machie, John; Malcom, John Sr.; Marsh, James; Martin, Elizabeth; Massie, Henry; Massie & Kerr; Massie, Nathaniel; Matthew, Joel; Mathews, George; Matthews, John, Jr.; Means, Robert; Menfin, William; Metzger, Jacob; Metzger, Michal; Miller, Frederick; Miller, Isaac; Miller, Jacob; Miller, John, Sr.; Milligan, James; Millner, Beverly; Milner, Dudley; Minnis, Cal.; Minnis

Callohill; Minn's, Callowhill; Mitchel, David; Mobberly, Rezin; Moore, John; Moore, Peter; Moore, Bob.; Moore, William; Morrow, Alexander; Morrow, James; Morrow, Robert; Morrow, William; Morton, Hezikiah; Mougher, Peter; Mulenbrugh, Peter; Murphy, Hector; Murray, James; Myers, Joseph.

Nelson, John; Nevill, D. & Co.; Nichols, George; Noble, William; Nixon, Robert; Nordyke, Abram; Nordyke, Israel; Nordyke, Micaijah; Norse, Robert; Nowel, Bukard.

Odell, James; Overman, Dempsey; Overman, Obadiah; Overman, Zebulon.

Packer, Jacob; Palmer, John; Patterson, Moses; Pavy, Isaac; Pettjohn, Thomas; Pence, Henry; Phillips, Edmund; Pool, Joshua; Pool, Thomas; Pope, Nathaniel; Pope, William; Porter, John; Porter, Joshua; Puckett, Benjamin; Pulse, John; Pusey, Mary; Pye, Thomas.

Rapp, David; Rasdall, Thomas; Ratecap, George; Reece, James; Reede, Leonard; Reede, James, Sr.; Reede, Samuel; Reely, Michal; Rees, Samuel; Richards, George; Richards, John; Richardson, J. C.; Richardson, John E.; Ricky, William; Roads, Abram; Roads, George; Roads, Jacob; Roads, Jacob. Sr.; Roads, John; Roads, John Esq.; Roads, Phillip; Roberts, Isaiah; Robinson, Thomas; Rogers, James; Rogers, Thomas; Rollins, Sealy; Roose, Aaron; Rose, Robert; Ross, David; Ross, Isaiah; Ross, Oliver; Ross, St. Clair; Rotrough, Jonas; Roush, Henry; Roush, John.

Sahm, Frederick; Sahm, Jacob; Sanders, John; Sanders, Jonathan; Sanders, Samuel; Sanders, Thomas; Sanderson, Margaret; Satterthate, John; Savet, Peter; Scott, James D.; Sears, John; Seatch, James T.; Sharp, Isaac; Sharp, William; Shaver, Andrew, Sr.; Shields, John; Shin, Joel; Shockly, Benjamin; Shockly, John, Jr.; Shoemaker, Martin; Shoemaker, Samuel; Shoemaker, Simon; Skilman, William; Sloane, John; Small, Joseph; Small, Knight; Smalley, Daniel; Smally, David; Smith, Archibald; Smith, David; Smith, Enoch; Smith, Jeremiah; Smith, N.; Smith, Nathan; Smith, Seth; Smith, William; Snoggs, Ebenezer; Sparger, Joseph; Speers, Jacob; Spottwood, Jacob; Spottswood, John; Springer, Jacob; Stafford, Fanny; Stafford, James; Stafford, Jarvis; Stafford, John; Stafford, Jonas; Stafford, Mary; Stafford, Robert; Stafford, Shadrack; Stanley, Strongerman; Starr, Alexander; Stephen, Hoggett; Stevens, John; Stewart, Isaac; Stewart, Wilson; Stitt, Samuel; Stockwell, Isaac; Strain, David; Strain, Samuel; Streskley, Thomas; Stroup, Anthony; Stroup, Michael; Stutts, John; Stutts, Michael; Stutts, Peter, Jr.; Summer, Absolom; Summer, Bowater; Summer, Joseph; Summers, Lewis; Summer, Thomas; Sultors, George; Sullevant, David; Supton, William; Swearingen, Joseph.

Tallifero, Wm.; Tallefero, William; Taylor, R.; Taylor, Richard; Taylor, William; Temp in. Salmon; Templin, Tesah; Teowler, William; Terrel, David; Tarry, David; Thompson, William; Thornburgh, Edward; Thornburgh, John; Timberlake, John; Timberlake, Richard; Tomlinson, Josiah; Trimble, Ailen; Tucker, Thomas.

Underwood, Alexander.

VanMatre, Abram; Vanmatre, Absolom; Vanmatre, Isaac; Vamatre, Joseph; Vanmatre, Morgan; Vanmatre, Peter.

Walder, Elizabeth; Walker, Archibald; Walker, Charles; Walker, Elijah; Walter, James; Walter, John; Warring, Thomas; West, Charles; West, James; West, John; West, Joseph; Weyer, Daniel; Weyer, Jacob; Wheatley, Samuel; Wilkins, John; Wilkins, John, Jr.; Wilkin, Phillip; Wilkin, Rachel; Wilkin, John; Willbum, Richard; Williams, Elias; Williams, Elisha; Williams, Enion; Williams, Isaac; Williams, James; Williams, John; Williams, Jonathan; Williams, William; Willis, William; Willson, James; Wilson, George; Wilson, James; Wilson, John; Wisby, Thomas; Woodrow, Joshua; Woolpack, Richard; Worley, Jacob; Worsham, Wm.; Wright, Alexander; Wright, Hanna; Wright, James; Wright, Jerima.; Wright, Solomon; Wright, William; Wright, William, Jr.; Wright, William, Sr.

Yarger, Joseph.

159

SETTLEMENTS OF ESTATES
ABSTRACTS OF FRANKLIN COUNTY, OHIO RECORDS

MRS. JOHN M. TITUS

The settlements of estates of Franklin County, Ohio, are found in the Probate Court, Court House, Columbus, Ohio. The numbers preceding each settlement appear as they are filed in their envelopes and as given in the Index Book of "Settlements of Estates." These abstracts state the number of the case; the name of the deceased person; the date of administration; the administrators; the appraisers; and the place of residence of the deceased, whenever given.

ABSTRACTS OF SETTLEMENTS OF ESTATES

01. Fleming, William dec'd. Sept. 6, 1803. Exrs.—Joseph Fleming, Robert Fleming, & William Bennett. The widow· was Elizabeth Fleming by afft. of Valentine Foos on Oct. 6, 1804. Bill for coffin for widow on Aug. 17, 1803. Appr'd by Ezekiel Bogart, & John Robinson, Oct. 12, 1803. Mentions that the widow had given a horse to Mitchell McDowell (McDole).

02. Foos, John dec'd. May 3, 1803. Adm.—Jane Foos, Joseph Foos and Lucas Sullivant. Appr. not found.

03. Williams, David dec'd. Apr. 10, 1806. Appr.—Zachariah Stephens, William Domigan, & Jacob Grubb at Franklinton. Adm.—Richard Hoskins, Abraham Dearduff & Benj. Sells, appointed Feb. term of court, 1810. Mentions money collected in Penn. by David James. Also says that Robert Williams swore to the correctness of a bill at Marietta.

04. Kepler, Benjamin dec'd. Franklin Twp., Nov. 29, 1805. Appr.—Nathaniel Hamblin (Hamilton), Samuel McElvaine & Thomas McCollum (McColm). Widow was Marian Kepler. Adm.—Marian Kepler & John Overdear. Widow was appointed guardian to Samuel, Sally, Rachel & Mary Ann Kepler, infant heirs of dec'd under age of 14 yrs. Adm.—On Nov. 26, 1805, was Balser Hess, Joseph Hunter & Marian Kepler.

05. McIlvaine, Samuel, dec'd. Apr. 16, 1806. Adm.—Elizabeth McIlvaine, John Dill, Wm. McIlvaine, Thomas Moore and Samuel King. Appr.—John Lisle, Baltzer Hess and Arthur O'Harra.

06. Pinney, Capt. Abner, late of Worthington, May 6, 1805. Appr.—James Kilbourne, Reuben Lamb & Wm. Little. Adm.—Azariah Pinney, widow Ruth Pinney. Mentions Dr. Reuben Lamb.

07. Buttles, Levy, Liberty Twp., Sept. 30, 1805. **Appr.**—Ezekiel Brown & Wm. Thompson. **Adm.**—The widow, Sarah Buttles, Joel Buttles & Levi Hays. Recorded, Apr. 13, 1808. Sarah Buttles was appointed guardian to Julia, Polly & Levi Buttles, infant heirs of Levi Buttles. Wm. Thompson was appointed guardian of Rora Buttles, infant son of dec'd. On July 26, 1805. **Adm.**—Sarah Buttles, Joel Buttles, Levi Hayes, Nathan Stewart & Ichabod Plumb.

08. Pinney, Betsy, & Harvey, guardianship. Infant son and daughter of Abner Pinney, dec'd. (See 06.) July 23, 1806. Appointed—Azariah Pinney and Roswell Tuller, guardians for Betsy Pinney, under age of 12, and chosen by Harvey Pinney, over age of 12.

09. Pinney, Betsy, guardianship, Jan. 12, 1810. Chose William Vining as guardian with Bela M. Tuller and Samuel Sloper as securities. (See 08.)

010. Hess, Balser—Will—Clinton Twp. Proven December 27, 1806. Exrx. wife, Mary Eva Hess, son Daniel Hess and Robert Culbertson. Appr.—none found.

011. Hedges, Joshua, dec'd, Harrison Twp., Apr. 16, 1805. Adm.—Mary Hedges, Joseph Vance, and Benj. Sells. Appr.—James Short, William Williamson & Joseph Buck, April 22, 1805.

012. Grant, Hugh, dec'd, Harrison Twp., Apr. 6, 1807. Adm.—Joseph Dickson, Wm. Brown, Jr., David Jamison, & Lucas Sullivant. Appr.—John Dill, Asa Dunn & James Blue.

013. Young, Robert, dec'd., Franklin Twp., Jan. 3, 1807. Adm.—Wife, Jane Young, Thomas Morehead, and Lucas Sullivant. Appr.—Jacob Grubb & Charles Hunter.

014. Breckenridge, Samuel, dec'd., Dec. 10, 1805. Adm.—Robert Culbertson, David Jameson, Zachariah Stephens and Arthur Parks. Appr.—John Pursell, Asa Dunn and Andrew Park.

015. Breckenridge heirs, Dec., 1806. John Dill appointed guardian for Alexander Breckenridge, Andrew Parks for Agnes Breckenridge, and Robert Culbertson, for Margaret Breckenridge, infants of Samuel, dec'd. Robert Culbertson & David Jameson appointed guardians of Polly, Samuel, and John Breckenridge, infants of Samuel. dec'd.

016. Smith, Polly (Envelope empty). Order Book A-214. Infant heir of Thompson Smith, dec'd, over the age of 12 yrs., chose Thomas Hart as guardian. Securities—Lucas Sullivant & Lewis Williams. Apr. 10, 1807—the date.

017. Missing.

018. White, Benjamin, deceased. Date—Apr. 9, 1807. Adm.—Frances White, widow, with Joseph Dickson, Benj. Sells, & James Marshall, Appr.—not found.

019. Bogart, Ezekiel, dec'd.—Will, proven—May 20, 1807. Adm.—Joshua Bogart & Michael Fisher, May 6, 1807. Appr.—James Short, Edw. Williams & John Robinson, May 6, 1807.

SETTLEMENTS OF ESTATES

ABSTRACTS OF FRANKLIN COUNTY, OHIO. RECORDS

MRS. JOHN M. TITUS

020. Bogart, George—Guardianship. Minor of Ezekiel, dec'd. Date—Feb. 17, 1808. Guardians, Edward Williams, with Joseph Bogart & John Barr, as securities.

021. Buck, Joseph, dec'd., Walnut Twp. Date—Aug. 17, 1807. Adm.—Elizabeth Buck, Jacob Grubb & Moses Donaldson, with Wm. Bennett & David Denny. Appr.—Wm. Ward, Wm. Williamson & James Short. Adm.—June term, 1813, Elizabeth Buck, Jacob Grubb, & Moses Donaldson.

022. Brannon, Wm., Date—Oct. 21, 1807. Adm.—Rudolph Landes, Phillip Cherry & Barnabas Lambert. Appr.—Wm. Rankin & Samuel Landes, Nov. 14, 1807—Hamilton Twp.

023. Lewis, Jedidiah H., dec'd. Late of Worthington. Will, Oct. 21, 1807. Adm.—Sabra Lewis, Stephen Maynard, Thomas Palmer, & Ezra Griswold. Appr.—Alexander Morrison, Jr., & Bela M. Tuller. (See 056 & 057.)

024. Scrivener, Samuel, dec'd. Liberty Twp. Will.—Date, Oct. term, 1807. Adm.—Hannah Scrivener (Scribner), wife. Appr.—not found.

025. Grant, Hugh, dec'd., Heirs of. Catherine, widow of Hugh Grant, dec'd, relinquishes her right of administration, and Wm.

Brown & Joseph Dickson were appointed. Guardians, appointed Feb. 20, 1808—Joseph Dickson & Samuel White.—Grdn. app. June 14, 1813, was James Seeds.

026. Johnston, Michael, dec'd. Date—June 14, 1808. Adm.—Mary Johnston, Alexander Blair & John Graham. Appr.—Thomas Foster, Jonas Bradley, and John Downing, June 23, 1808.

027. Ingram, Rotha, dec'd. Date—Oct. 13, 1808. Adm.—Luther Winget, Alexander Blair & Michael Dickey. Appr.—Michael Dickey, Wm. Lapping & John Johnston. Nov. 5, 1808, mentions Katherine Ingram. June 13, 1813, John Moore was appointed to complete the settlement of the estate as Luther Winget died, and the estate not settled.

028. Mickey, Daniel, dec'd. Date—Oct. 14, 1808. Adm.—Elizabeth Mickey, Thomas Mickey, & Jacob Grubb. Appr.—Benj. Grace, George Eby & Paul Deardoff. Filed Feb. term, 1809.

029. Noble, Seth, dec'd. Date—Mch. 24, 1808. Adm.—Martin Bartholomew, Wm. Domigan & Josiah Vorice (Voris). Appr.—Nathaniel Hamlin, John Hunter, & Edward Livingston. Filed, Jan. 1811. Adm. filed claim for $20. for keeping two children.

030. Myers, Joseph, dec'd. Date—Feb. 17, 1809. Adm.—John Dyer (dec'd 1812) & John Sandusky. Appr.—Lewis Foster, Calvin Carey, & John Turner.

031. Myers, Joseph, dec'd. Date—June term, 1814. Adm.—Wm. Dyer, adm. of the estate of John Dyer who had been adm. of estate of Joseph Myers, dec'd, with Robert Dyer, & E. N. DeLashmutt.

032. Lyle, John, dec'd. Will—Exr. Wife, Rachel & oldest son Robert Lyle (Lisle). Appr.—Joseph Hunter, Elijah Fulton & John Wilson—Mch. 1, 1809. Settled 1824. In will mentions wife Rachel Lisle, youngest son John, oldest son Robert, second son James, oldest daughter Margaret, & each of his daughters not mentioned should receive $400, in money. In settlement of estate mentions wife, Rachel, sons, John, Robert & James; Margaret McElvaine, and other daughters, Jane Maynard & Rachel Sackett.

033. Topping, John, dec'd. Late of Worthington. June 17, 1809. Adm.—Zopher Topping, Azariah Pinney & Stephen Maynard. Appr.—Moses Maynard and Israel Case.

034. Price, William—(missing).

035. Creighton, Robert, dec'd. June 14, 1809. Adm.—Hugh Creighton, George Lowther, & Michael Rawlings. Appr.—July 14, 1809. David & John Denny.

036. Greer, Robert, dec'd. Oct. 9, 1809. Adm.—Polly Greer, Jonathan Holmes, John Martin, & Edward Williams. Appr.—Oct. 26, 1809. Abram Inskeep, Jr., John Barr & Ishmael Davis.

037. Hoover, Sebastian, dec'd. Oct. 9, 1809. Adm.—Elizabeth Hoover, Isaac Huffhines, & John Woodruff. Appr.—Oct. 17, 1809, George Hayes, Jeremiah White, & Matthew Michell.

038. Foos, Guardianship of Nicholas, Margaret, & Polly Foos, infants of John Foos, dec'd (see 02). Oct. 11, 1809. Guardians, Jacob DeLong, John F. Craun & Frederick Peterson.

039. Hammond, Jonas, dec'd. July 23, 1811. Adm.—Althina Hammond, Alexander Morrison, Jr., Zophar Topping, & Azariah Pinney, Worthington. Appr.—Oct. 26, 1809, Ezra Griswold, Moses Maynard, & John Goodrich.

040. Cowen, Moses, dec'd. Oct. 14, 1809. Adm.—Zabud Randell, Wm. Foley, & Jenks Wait. Appr.—Oct. 4, 1809, Robert Culbertson, Joseph Hickman, & John Foley.

041. Ingram, Rotha (See 027). Feb. 1810. Adm.—John Moore, Michael Dickey & Peter Paugh. Appr.—Nov. 5, 1808, Michael Dickey, Wm. Lapping, & John Johnston.

042. McElvaine, Joseph & Purdy, Guardianship. Feb. 15, 1810. Thomas Moore, John Dill, & Solomon Moore, guardians of Joseph and Purdy, infant heirs of Sam'l. McElvaine. Dec. 15, 1826, Andrew McElvaine was appointed guardian of Joseph V., aged 11 yrs. and Samuel McElvaine, aged 9 yrs., with Joseph Hunter & Robert Brotherton.
   Order Book X-52 says: Samuel McElvaine, Franklin Tp. Appr.—John Lisle, Baltzer Hess & Arthur O'Harra. Adm.— Elizabeth McElvaine, widow, Wm. McElvaine and John Dill.

043. McElvaine, Andrew, Guardianship. Feb. 17, 1810. Grdn.— Samuel King chosen by Andrew McElvaine, infant heir of Sam'l. McElvaine, over 14 yrs.

044. Irwin, Wm., dec'd. Oct. 26, 1809. Adm.—Zabid Randell, Jenks Wait & Wm. Foley. Appr.—Robert Culbertson, Joseph Hickman & John Foley. Mentions—Wm. Irwin & wife, Harriet, late Whiteman.
   Order Book X-152 says Dr. Wm. Irwin, Aug. 15, 1810, Hamilton Twp. Appr.—Samuel Landes and Wm. Caldwell.

045. Overdear, John, dec'd. May 26, 1810. Adm.—Martha Overdear, Wm. Brown, Jacob Grubb, Elias DeLashmutt & Wm. Domigan. Appr. June 1, 1810. Arthur O'Harra, James Marshall and Jacob Overdear.

046. McNutt, James, dec'd. Nov. 30, 1809. Adm.—Samuel McNutt, John McNutt, Samuel Blair, Robert McNutt, & Thomas Gwynne. Appr.—Thomas Gwynne, John Arbuckle & John Graham.

047. Robinson, Henry, dec'd. Will (missing). Sept. 28, 1810.

048. Knode, Elizabeth, Guardianship. Jan. 23, 1811. Elizabeth Knode, above the age of 12 yrs. chose John B. Johnston with James Blue & David Lambert as guardians. (No others of the name Knode in books. Does not give parents names.)

049. Noble, John, Guardianship. Jan. 25, 1811. Martin Bartholomew appointed guardian of infant heir of Seth Noble, dec'd. (See 029.) Adm.—Martin Bartholomew, Wm. Domigan, & Wm. Merrian.

050. Hornbaker, John, dec'd. Will. Oct. 2, 1811. Adm.—Widow Elizabeth and Isaac Weatherington. Appr.—John Barr, Emmor Cox, Samuel Landes. Heirs mentioned—E. Hamblin, Mary Witmer, nee Hornbecker, Catherine Seeds, and John Hornbecker.

051. Peney (Pinney), Azariah. Nov. 3, 1811. Appr.—Alexander Morrison, Samuel Beach, Isaac Case. Adm. Nov. 11, 1811, Wm. Robe, Alexander Morrison, Jr., Bela M. Tuller.

052. Stewart, Lydia—Guardianship. Minor of John Stewart, dec'd., aged about 16 years, chose John Dill as guardian with Michael Fisher as security. Nov. 12, 1811.

053. Stewart, Adam—Guardianship. Nov. 12, 1811. Adam Stewart, aged about 15 years, chose Wm. Reid as his guardian with Robert Culbertson.

054. Grace, Benjamin, dec'd. Will. Dec. 2, 1811. Adm.—Nov. 30, 1811—Jacob Grubb, Arthur O'Harra, Jacob Overdear. Appr.— Daniel Brunk, Benj. Britton, Dec. 26, 1811. Washington Twp.

055. Lambert, David. Will. Appr.—Apr. 20, 1812—David Spangler, John Barr, Thomas Gray. Adm.—June 16, 1813—Polly Lambert, Thomas Morris.

056. Lewis—Guardianship. (See 023.) March 9, 1812. Sabra Lewis appointed guardian to Lucy Lewis, aged 10, Eliza Lewis, aged 8, Jedidiah H. Lewis, aged 6, heirs of Jedidiah H. Lewis, dec'd, with John Goodrich and Recompense Stansberry.

057. Lewis—Guardianship. (See 023 & 056.) June 24, 1812. Elias Lewis, aged 16, Prudence Lewis, aged 14, Martin Lewis, aged 12, heirs of Jedidiah H. Lewis, dec'd., chose their mother Sabra Lewis as guardian.

058. Morrison, Alexander, dec'd. Will. May 23, 1811. Exr.— Wm. Morrison, James Kilbourne, June term, 1811. Appr.— May 23, 1811, Daniel M. Brown, Stephen Maynard, Simeon Wilcox.

059. Hamilton, Joseph—Guardianship. March 10, 1812—minor orphan of Wm. Hamilton, dec'd. Stewart White appointed guardian with John M. Goetchius and James Marshall.

060. Dyer, John. Will. March 22, 1812. Adm.—Jane Dyer, Samuel Dyer, Charles Hunter. Appr.—Oct. 11, 1814, Alexander Blair, Thomas Roberts.

061. Taylor—Guardianship. June 22, 1812. Zilpha Taylor appointed guardian of Nodiah, Isaiah, George, Washington Taylor, infant heirs of Isaiah Taylor, dec'd, with John Goodrich, Samuel Beach.

062. Taylor, Nancy—Guardianship. June 22, 1812. Samuel Beach appointed guardian of Nancy Taylor, minor heir of Isaiah Taylor, dec'd. Adm.—June 20, 1812—Zilpha Taylor with Alexander Morrison, Worthington. Appr.—Feb. 11, 1811— Samuel Beach, Wm. Morrison.

SETTLEMENTS OF ESTATES

Abstracts of Franklin County, Ohio Records

Mrs. John M. Titus

063. Ramsey, Robert L., dec'd. June 22, 1812. Adm.—Samuel Ramsey, Mary Ramsey, John Stombaugh & Wm. Domigan. Appr.—Aug. 22, 1812, John Wilson, John Parsel, & Emmor Cox. Appr.—Jan. 12, 1813—Emmor Cox & John Wilson.

064. Topping, Miranda—Guardianship. June 23, 1812. Grdn.—Lewis Gay appointed guardian of Miranda Topping, infant heir of John Topping, dec'd. aged three yrs., with Recompense Stansberry. Miranda died Jan. 1827, heir—Dayton Topping.

065. Topping, Miianda, Order Book 5–83—Sept. 1827, died Intestate. Adm.—Arora Buttles, Recompense Stansberry & Robert Brotherton. Appr.—James Russell, John W. Ladd and R. W. Cowles.

066. Bacchus, Harriet Maria. June 25, 1812. Guardians appointed for Harriet Maria Bachus, infant heir of Elijah Bachus—Thomas Bachus, Elias N. DeLashmutt and Henry Brown.

067. Same as 066.

068. Bachus, Elijah, dec'd. June 25, 1812. Adm.—Appointed by the court—Thomas Bachus, E. N. DeLashmutt & Henry Brown. The widow Hannah released her right of administration as she lived too far away. She was living in Kaskaskia, Ill. Appr.—June 25, 1812—Gustavus Swan, Sam'l. Parsons and David Scott.

069. Cramer, Christopher, dec'd. Oct. 26, 1812. Adm.—Catherine Cramer, John Cramer, Lucas Sullivant and Lynn Starling. App.—Nov. 3, 1812, by Billingslea Bull, Frederick Peterson, and George Kalb.

070. Hoover, Phoebe. Oct. 27, 1812. Elizabeth Hoover was appointed guardian of Phoebe, aged 4 yrs., minor daughter of Sebastian Hoover, dec'd., with Charles Rarey.

071. Morrison, Henry—Guardianship. Oct. 27, 1812, Henry Morrison, aged 18 yrs., chose Isaac Case, Preserved Leonard & Richard Gale as guardians.

072. Lewis, Thomas, dec'd. Adm —Oct. 28, 1812, Benjamin Foster, John Harvey, and Reuben Golliday. App.—Nov. 17, 1812, Elijah & Thos. Chenoweth.

073. Simmons, William, dec'd. Adm.—Oct. 29, 1812, Jacob Grubb, Jacob Overdear, and Titus Dort. App.—Oct. 6, 1812, Joseph Smart and Daniel Hess.

074. Walling, Elisha, dec'd. Oct. 19, 1812. Adm.—Wm. Center, Asa Walling, Moses Pursell, and Percival Adams. Appr.—not found.

075. Powers, Avery, dec'd. Exers.—Oct. 29, 1812, Prudence Powers by will with Jacob Grubb and Jacob Overdear. Perry twp.

075a. Power, Avery, Jr., dec'd. Appr.—Dec. 10, 1812. Adam Hosack, Jacob Grubb, John O'Harra.

076. Powers, guardianship for Benjamin, Mary and Hiram Powers. Oct. 29, 1812, Prudence Powers appointed guardian to said infant heirs of Avery Powers, dec'd, with Jacob Grubb and Jacob Overdear.

077. Goldsmith, Thomas, dec'd. Franklin twp. Mch. 30, 1813. Adm.— John Goldsmith, John O'Harra, and Wm. Brown. Appr.—Samuel White, Michael Fisher and John Dill.

078. Norton, Jedediah, dec'd, late of Farmington, Conn. June 1821, Adm.— Phineas B. Willcox, Orris Parish, Recompense Stansbury. and Stephen Frothingham. Appr.—May 8, 1814, Gustavus Swan and Joseph Vance.

079. Grant, Hugh heirs (see 012.), May 20, 1811. Adm.—Joseph Dixon and William Brown. No appraisers.

080. Henderson, Samuel, dec'd. Will. Excr. June 14, 1813. Alexander Henderson and Elijah Fulton.

081. Winget (or Wingate), Luther, dec'd. June 15, 1813. Adm.—John Moore.

082. Johnson, Wm., dec'd. Franklin twp. June 28, 1813. Adm.—Sally Woolcott, John Shields, and Townsend Nichols. Appr.—John Shields, Daniel Howser, and Townsend Nichols.

083. McGown, Robert, dec'd. Adm.—Aug. 17, 1813, John McGown. Appr.— July 19, 1813, John Shields, Joseph Hunter, and John Donovan.

084. Lambert, Rebecca, Isaac, and David, guardianship. June 12, 1813, Polly Lambert and Jacob Grubb appointed guardians of the children of David Lambert, dec'd. Adm.—Thomas Morris and Polly Lambert. Appr.—Apr. 20, 1813, David Spangler and John Barr.

085. Grace, heirs of Benjamin, dec'd. Sept. 28, 1812, Catherine Grace was appointed guardian of Josiah aged 18 yrs. Lair aged 16 yrs. Stephen aged 13 yrs. 8 mo. Benjamin aged 12 yrs. Jesse aged 10 yrs. and William aged 7 yrs. infant heirs Benjamin Grace, dec'd, with Jacob Grubb and Benjamin Sells.

086. McGown, Mary, infant heir of Robert McGown, dec'd. Sept. 28, 1813, Joseph Hunter, John Shields and Nathaniel Hamlin were appointed guardians.

087. McGown, Matilda. Sept. 28, 1813. Appointed guardians were, Wm. Merrion, John Moler and Samuel G. Flenniken.

088. Anderson, Ezekiel, dec'd. Sept. 28, 1813. Adm.—Margaret Anderson, John Edgar, John Inks and James Scott. Appr.—Wm. Reed, Frederick Fagler, and Mathias Ridenour. Order book 3-133, Mary and Jane Anderson, over age of 12 yrs. chose their mother Margaret Anderson as guardian and the court appointed their mother as guardian of John, aged 9 yrs., Esther, aged 4 yrs. and Margaret, aged 2 yrs.

089. Messenger, Zephaniah, dec'd. Adm.—Sept. 28, 1813, Adonijah Messenger, Israel Case, and Ezekiel Tuller. Appr.—Wm. Robe, Abiel Case and Buckley Comstock.

090. Simmons, William, dec'd. Admr.—Oct. 29, 1812, widow, Anna Simmons, relinquished her right of administration, the court appointed Jacob Grubb, Jacob Overdear, Titus Port. Appr.—Joseph Smart, Daniel Hess, Elijah Fulton. Dier age 16 yrs., Hanson age 15 yrs., chose as guardian their mother. She was appointed guardian of Judson, age 13 yrs., Nancy age 11 yrs. and Samuel age 7 yrs. with Joseph Stewart, and David Jones.

091. Marks, John, dec'd, Mch. 1, 1814. Admr.—James Marks. Wm. Marks, John McGown. Appr.—Nathaniel Hamlin, Joseph Hunter, John Collett.

092. Sordon, Jonathan, died intestate. Admr.—Quinton Sorden, William Mooberry, Samuel Ramsey, Mch. 1, 1812. Appr.—Mch. 1, 1814, James Kile, Thomas Gray.

093. Williams, Mathew, Estate of. Mch. 2, 1814. Admr.—Fergey Moorhead, Edward Livingston, Thomas McCollum. Mch. 22, 1814. Appr.—Asa Dunn, William White, James Blue.

094. Lee, Jonathan, dec'd. Will. Exrx.—wife, Sarah Lee and John Craum, Oct. 1814.

095. Hughes, William, dec'd, of Franklinton. Will.

096. Reed, Charles, dec'd. Admr.—June 21, 1814, Thomas McFeeley, William Moore, Solomon Moore. Appr.—Wm. Domigan, Joseph Cowgill, Joseph Gorton.

097. Hadley, Jacob, Estate of. Admr.—June 21, 1814, Andrew Scott, John Edgar, John Wagner (Waggoner). Appr.—Jacob Sharp. John Strate, Moses Ogden.

098. Monroe, John, Estate of. Admr.—June 20, 1814, Percival Adams, James Lindsey, James Taylor. Appr.—James Culbertson, Thomas Johnston, James Brown.

099. Davis, John, estate of. Widow relinquishes her right of administration and requests that her father, Robert Parish, be appointed. Admr.—Robert Parish, Meredith Parish, John Turner, June term, 1814. Appr.—June, 1814, Robert Parish, Thomas Roberts, Abram Domigan.

0100. Morehead, Thomas, Estate of. Admr.—Rachel Morehead, Stephen Thomas, Wm. Brown, Jr., John Huffman. Appr.—May 8, 1813, Wm. Badger, John Ramburg, George Skidmore.

0101. Norton, Joab, dec'd. June 2, 1814. Admr.—Lucy Morton, Cruger Wright.

0102. Guardian of Nancy and Clorinda Vance, heirs of Alexander Vance. June 22, 1814, Jos. Vance, Samuel Shannon, Gustavus Swan were appointed Appr. Joseph Vance, Admr. Joseph Vance was appointed guardian June 3, 1814, of Nancy and Clorinda Vance, infants under age of 12 yrs. until they reach the age of 12.

0103. May 3, 1817, Joseph Vance was chosen guardian of Nancy, heir of Alexander Vance.

0104. Palmer, Luther, Worthington. Will. Exr.—Ethan Palmer. Appr.—Isaac Griswold, Isaac Harrison, Cruger Wright.

0105. Dukes, John, Will of June 22, 1814. Admr.—Mary Dukes, Asa Dunn, Henry Brown. Appr.—David Spangler, Asa Dunn, Thomas Cunningham.

0106. Nickerson, Aaron, dec'd. June 22, 1814. Adm.—Uriah Nickerson, John Brickle and Thomas McFeeley. Appr.—None given.

0107. Cady, Wm., dec'd. Adm.—June 22, 1814, Esther Cady, Uri Nickerson, and John Brickle. Appr.—Richard Stevenson, Thomas Wood, and Benjamin Clevenger.

0108. Overdear, John, Jr., minor of John Overdear, Sr., June 3. 1814, Jacob Overdear was appointed guardian of John Overdear, Jr. until he arrives at the age of 14 yrs. with Jacob Grubb and Wm. Brown. Jacob Overdear was appointed guardian of John Overdear, Jr., Aged 10 yrs. with Jacob Grubb at Dec. term, 1816. Apr. 2, 1822, John Overdear chose Jacob Overdear, Jacob Grubb, and John Laughrey as guardians.

0109. Lane, Peter, dec'd. Will. Aug. 20, 1814. Adm.—David Broderick,
0110. Henry Brown, and Lincoln Kilbourne. Appr.—George Skidmore, Orris Parish, and Frederick Stimmel.

0111. Hobbs, George, dec'd. Aug. 20, 1814. Adm.—Catherine Huff and Cutleb Lighnecker.

0112. Cornet, Thomas. Will. Madison twp. Feb. 2, 1814. Appr. of the estate were, Wm. D. Henderson, John Coons, and Benjamin Clevenger.

0113. Chenowith, Thomas, of Pleasant twp. Oct. 10, 1814. Adm.—John Chenowith, John Harvey and Jacob Grubb. Appr.—Reuben Golladay, William McKibben and Abraham Romines.

0114. Fleming, Joseph. Oct. 10, 1814. Adm.—Sarah Fleming, Wm. D. Henderson, Nelson Punteney.

0115. Guardian, of Margaret, Jean, and Willy Fleming, heirs of William Fleming. July 26, 1805, Joseph Fleming and John Dill were appointed. Oct. 10, 1814, Benjamin Clevenger was appointed guardian for Margaret, Jane, and William Fleming.

0116. Taylor, Matthew, Estate of, Madison twp. Oct. 10, 1814. Adm.—David Taylor, Richard Suddick, Abiathar Taylor. Appr.—David Nelson, Daniel Ross and Benjamin Clevenger.

0117. Taylor, James, Estate of. Truro twp. Oct. 12, 1814. Adm.—Francis Taylor, Edw. Long, John Long and David Long. Appr.—Mathew Taylor, Thomas Wood and David Taylor.

0118. Guardians of Samuel Taylor and Jenny Taylor. infant heirs of Matthew Taylor. Oct. 12, 1814, David Taylor, A. V. Taylor and Edw. Long were appointed.

0119. Guardian of Rebecca Taylor. Oct. 12, 1814. Matthew Taylor, Edw. Long, A. V. Taylor were appointed.

0120. Guardian for John, Mary, Jane, Esther and Margaret Anderson, heirs of Ezekiel Anderson, dec'd. Oct. 13, 1814. Margaret Anderson and John Edgar were appointed.

0121. Gillispy, Enos, dec'd. Estate of. Oct. 13. 1814. Adm.—Obediah Benedict, Glass Cochran and Joseph Pool.

0122. Guardian for Shelburn Gillispy, infant heir of Enos Gillispy. Oct. 13, 1814, Glass Cochran, Obediah Benedict, Joseph Pool were appointed.

0123. Guardian for Thomas Jeff Pinney, Azariah, Dorcas, James, Alexander, and Charles Pinney, heirs of Azariah Pinney. Oct. 13, 1814. Dorcas Pinney, William Robe, Levi Pinney were appointed.

0124. Will of Hugh Watt. Exr.—William Read.

0124. A. Watt, Hugh, Estate of. Exr.—Adam and Alexander Read.

0125. Radcliff, Benj., Estate of. Adm.—Thomas Renick, Christian Radcliff. Appr.—Feb. 10, 1810, William Seymour, Thomas Chenowith, Elijah Chenowith.

0126. Wilson, Samuel, Estate of. Dec. 12, 1814. Adm.—Dr. John Smith, Dolly Wilson, John Wilson, Jason Bull. Appr.—Bulkley Comstock, Glass Cochran, John Wilson.

0127. Taylor, Samuel, Estate of. Jan. 8, 1814. Adm.—Matthew Taylor, Edw. Long, John Faulkner, Matthew Taylor. Jr. Appr.—John Long, Zachariah Stevenson, James Taylor.

0128. Wilson, Daniel, Estate of. Feb. 20, 1815. Adm.—John Wilson, Robert Wilson, Samuel Henderson. Appr.—John Stipp, Emmor Cox, William Caldwell, George Sharp.

0129. Guardian for Isaac Thomas, minor heir of Stephen Thomas. March 23, 1825. William Brown, Robert Brotherton, William Miller. Dec. 1814, Guard.—John Kile.

0130. Guardian for Isaac Thomas, aged 18, heir of Stephen Thomas. Oct. 9, 1830, William Miller, Ralph Osborn, Christopher Heyl.

0131. Thomas, Stephen, Estate of. Nov. 27, 1813. Adm.—Hannah Thomas, John Ransburg, Wm. Benedict, John Kile. Appr.—John Huffman, William Badger, William Brown.

0132. Vandyke, John, Estate of. Empty.

0133. Blue, James, Estate of. Adm.—Daniel West. Elizabeth Blue. Appr.—Levi Shin, Fergus Moorhead, David Spangler.

0134. Linn, Abigail, Estate of. Apr. 22, 1815. Adm.—Samuel Ramsey, Robert Williams.

0135. Furbee, Mathias, Estate of. May 27, 1815. Adm.—Caleb Ferby, James R. Tucker, Samuel McElvain.

0136. Graham, Nathan, Estate of. June 12, 1815. Adm.—Stephen Maynard, Hanne Graham, Recompense Stansbury, John Goodrich, Jr. Appr.—Jesse Andrews, Richard Andrews, Harvey Stivens.

0137. Johnson, Wm., Estate of. Empty.

0138. Plum, John, Estate of. June 12, 1815. Adm.—Rachel Plum, Jacob Plum, Percival Adams, Michael Stimmel. Appr.—James Culbertson, James Lindsay, Michael Fisher.

0139. Wrightman, James, Estate of. June 12, 1815. Adm.—Geo. Wrightman, James Kilbourne, Michael Stimmel. Appr.—Asa Dunn, James Lindsay.

0140. Beach, Samuel, Will of. Ex.—Levi Pinney, Samuel Beach, Alex. Morrison, Samuel Shannon.

SETTLEMENTS OF ESTATES

ABSTRACTS OF FRANKLIN COUNTY, OHIO RECORDS

MRS. JOHN M. TITUS

0140a. Beach, Samuel, Estate of, missing.

0141. Guardian for Jesse Tomlinson, orphan of Hugh Tomlinson. June 14, 1815, Thomas Tipton, and Samuel Starks were appointed by the Common Pleas Court of Franklin Co.

0142. Guardian of Sally Moorhead, child of Thomas Moorhead. June 14, 1815, Arthur O'Harra and John M. White were appointed.

0143. Guardian of Jane and Lincoln G. Moorhead, children of Thomas Moorhead. June 14, 1815, Lincoln Goodale and Sam'l G. Flennikin were appointed.

0144. Vance, Alexander, Estate of. Apr. 1, 1814. Adm.—Joseph Vance, Elias DeLashmut, Henry Brown.

0145. Baucher, Jacob, Estate of.

0146. Gray, John, Estate of. May 14, 1815, Thomas Anderson appointed adm. Joseph Barker, Thomas Anderson, Wm. Bowman, as sureties. June 15, Mary Gray requested her brother, Thomas Anderson, be made administrator of John Gray's estate with Thomas Cochran and Wm. Chipps as appraisers.

0147. Guardian of John Grate, son of Joseph Grate, appointed June 15, 1815, signed by Joseph Grate and Jeremiah Hews.

0148. Barker, Eliphalet, Estate of. July 22, 1815, James H. Hills and Cynthia Barker appointed adm., signed by James H. Hills, Cynthia Barker, Ezra Griswold and Peter Barker. Receipts to adm. of estate from Chandler Barker, Simeon Barker, Orange Johnson, Samuel Baldwin, Frances Stewart, Burkley Comstock, Jacob Fairfield, Jesse Andros, James Allen, Israel P. Case, Jacob Keller, Lemuel Humphrey, Betsy Wallace, Griswold & Kilbourne, Orton Goodrich, James Norris, Hezekiah Benedick, Moses Maynard, Samuel Sloper, Joel Buttles, Abial Case, Geo. Case, Ebenezer Goodrich, Calvin Case, Isaiah Wallace, Josiah Topping, Ralph Case, Warren Wever, Warren Andros, John Goodrich.

0149. July 22, 1815, John Dill appointed adm. of Armstrong (Armstead) Dill Abbott, dec'd., signed John Dill, Lincoln Goodale and Samuel Shannon.

0150. Thompson, Benj., Estate of. Fanny Thompson appointed adm. of estate. Signed, Fanny Thompson, Coonrod Christman, Samuel Keys. Appr.—John Collett, Robert McCoy, John Kerr. Amounts paid to the following: James English, John and Robert McCoy, James A. Seraton, Francis Baldwin, Geo. Scott, Sam'l Barr, Henry Haynes, Stewart Baily, Clayton Harper, Jacob Armitage, Wm. Sterrett, Wm. Waggoner, John W. Edminston, Edw. Long, Christian Hoyle, John Greenwood, Amasa Delano, John Carlisle, Benj. Drummond, John Lacy.

0151. Dearduff, Paul. Will. Estate of.

0152. Wright, John, Estate of. Oct. 9, 1815, Geo. Long appointed adm., signed, George H. Long, David Wright, John Todd, Catherine Wright, widow. Sales to Andrew Dildine, Philemon Needles, John Chaney, Frederick Fruchey, Wm. Cornal, Walter Huse, Henry Schoonover, Andrew Cramer, Jacob Algier, Owen Roberts, Andrew Needles, Richard Stevenson, John Welton, Richard Derrick, Nicholas Winterstein, Edw. Hathaway, John Fraily, Phillip Swisher, Jacob Luf, John Kalb.

0153. Kalb, John, Estate of. Oct. 9, 1815. Adm.—George Kalb, John Coons, Walter Hughes. Appr.—John Stevenson, Zachariah Stevenson, John Todd.

0154. Hughes, James, Estate of. Madison twp. Oct. 9, 1815. Exr.—Mary Hughes, Joseph Wright appointed. Signed, Mary Hews, Joseph Wright, Geo. Rall, Moses Starr.

1054a. Appr. Graun, Richard Courtright, William Smith.

0155. Noble, Mary, Estate of. Oct. 9, 1815, Samuel McGill appointed Adm. Signed, Samuel McGill, Samuel Henderson, Arthur O'Harra.

0156. Weaver, David, Estate of. Oct. 9, 1815, Elizabeth Weaver asks that Wm. H. Richardson be appointed Adm. of her dec'd husband's estate. Appr. appointed, Wm. Henderson, Emmor Cox, George Sharp. J. P. was Frederick Peterson.

0157. Oct. 9, 1815, Mary Watt appointed guardian of children of Hugh Watt,
viz: (1) Sam Watt, 14 yrs., Sept. 20, 1815. (2) John Watt, 13 yrs., Sept. 20, 1815. (3) Sarah Watt, 10 yrs., May 2, 1815. (4) Elizabeth Watt, 6 yrs., Dec. 23, 1815. (5) Adam Watt, 4 yrs., Dec. 14, 1815. (6) Mary Watt, 1 yr., Dec. 14, 1815. Signed, Mary Watt, Robert Shannon, Joseph Vance.

0158. Kuts, George, Estate of. Oct. 12, 1815, James Kirk appointed Adm. Signed, James Kirk, John Shields, William Caldwell. Wife was Patience, oldest son George, also a son James.

0159. Oct. 12, 1815, George Bogart appointed guardian of Wm. Blue, son of James Blue. Signed, George Bogart, Joseph Gorton, Benj. Sells.

0160. Feb. 12, 1810, David West appointed guardian of George Blue and Polly Blue, children of James Blue. Signed, David Spangler, Daniel and George West.

0161. Feb. 12, 1816, John Thompson appointed guardian of Anne Blue, child of James Blue. Signed, John Thompson, James Lindsay, Andrew Barr.

0162. Topping, Zopher, Estate of. Oct. 10, 1815, Ezra Griswold and Hector Kilbourne appointed Adm. by request of wife, Lois Topping.

0163. Oct. 13, 1815, Daniel Krouse appointed guardian children viz: Michel. age 15 yrs., Mary, age 13 yrs., Nancy, age 11 yrs., Lydia, age 9 yrs., Hannah, age 7 yrs., children of Daniel Krouse.

0164. Hugh Fulton appointed guardian of Mary Fulton, child of Elijah Fulton. Signed by Hugh Fulton, Samuel Henderson.

0165. Hugh Fulton and Samuel Henderson appointed Adm. of the estate of Elijah Fulton.

0166. Smith, George, Madison twp., Estate of. Nov. 1, 1815, Mary Smith and Daniel Ranier appointed Adm. Signed by Mary Smith, Dr. Daniel Ranier, Phillip Pontius, James McLeish. Inv. by Ezekiel Groom. Charles Rarey, Elisha Decker.

0167. Corbus, Andrew, Estate of. Mch. 1816, David Broderick, Adm. accts. against estate, by Nicholas Gutches, John Ransburg, John Cutler. Alexander Morrison, John Wolcott, Wm. Newbrough, Christopher Beard, Henry Brown, Samuel Parsons, David Broderick.

0168. Justice, David, Estate of. Dec. 15, 1815, Nancy Justice, Adm. Signed by Nancy Justice, David Scott, Francis Stewart.

0169. Chambers, Robert, Estate of. Feb. 12, 1816. Adm.—Wm. Badger and Elizabeth Chambers. Signed by Elizabeth Chambers, William Badger. Jos. Badger, Percival Adams.

0170. Brown, Samuel, Estate of. Feb. 12, 1816, William Reed, Margaret Brown appointed Adm.

0171. Feb. 12, 1816, John Thompson, David Spangler appointed guardians of Richard, Nancy, Susannah, Lewis, Dellia, Nicholas, children of John Dukes, dec'd.

0172. Wellmouth, Joseph, Hamilton twp., Estate of. Benson Goldberry Adm. Appr.—Joseph Gifford, Cornelius Marmon, James Blue, Apr. 1. 1812.

0173. Perrin, John, Estate of. Feb. 13, 1816, Mary Perrin Adm. Signed. Mary Perrin, John Rogers, John Postle.

0174. Breckenridge, James, Estate of. July 22, 1816. Robert Brotherton. Adm. Signed by Robert Brotherton, Thomas Moore and John A. McDowell.

1075. Will of Mathias Ridenhauer.

0175a. Empty.

1076. Feb. 15, 1816, Daniel Dearduff appointed guardian of Samuel, son of Abraham Dearduff.

0177. Feb. 15, 1816, John Dearduff appointed guardian of Joseph, son of Abraham Dearduff.

171

0178. Dearduff, Abraham, Estate of. May 9, 1812, David and Daniel Dearduff, adm., signed, Chas. Hunter, Isaiah Vorhees, E. L. DeLashmutt.
0179. Will of John Dill made June 5, 1802.
1079a. Filed Mch. 31, 1817. Adm.—Samuel G. Flenniken, Robert Dill, Michael Fisher.
0180. Apr. 29, 1816, Elizabeth Fulton appointed guardian of Margaret and James, children of Elijah Fulton, signed by Elizabeth Fulton and Sam'l Henderson.
0181. Dec. 30, 1816, Joseph Smart appointed guardian of William, son of Elijah Fulton, signed, Joseph Smart, Joseph Hunter.
0182. Apr. 29, 1816, Philomen Needles appointed guardian of Archibald, Nancy, Elizabeth, Elijah, Polly and Sarah, children of John Needles, signed, Philomon Needles, John Cole, and Richard Courtright.
0183. Apr. 29, 1816, Margaret Brown appointed guardian of Martha, Alexander, and Elizabeth, children of Samuel Brown.
0184. Apr. 29, 1816, James Lindsay appointed guardian of John, son of Samuel Breckenridge, signed, James Lindsay, Wm. Badger.
0185. Apr. 29, 1816, Wm. Badger appointed guardian of William, son of Samuel Breckenridge.
0186. Apr. 30, 1816, William Badger appointed guardian of Robert, Martha, and William, children of Robert Badger, legal rep. of Robert Chambers.
0187. May 1, 1816, Cotton M. Thrall appointed guardian of Timothy S., son of Samuel Thrall, signed, Cotton Thrall, Levi Pinney.
0188. Jesse Pancake—empty.
0189. May 2, 1816, Wm. Harrupp and Francis Smith appointed guardians of Catherine and Polly, heirs of Isaac Hess.
0190. Hickman, Townsend, Estate of. June 29, 1813, Wm. Stierwalt, Jane Hickman, Joseph Grate, John Skidmore, Adm. Appr. were Henry Skinner and John Skidmore.
0191. Brisbine, James, Estate of. June 8, 1816. Adms.—James Brisbine, Wm. Moore, Nelson Punteny & Joseph Moore, of Plain twp. Apprs.— Thomas B. Patterson, Jacob Clouse, Phillip Roose. He left wife and children not named.
0192. Swope, John, Estate of. Aug. 26, 1816. Adms.—Betsy Shofe, Jacob Plum, Samuel Andrews, James Lindsey. Apprs.—Thomas Morris, Andrew Barr and George Jarmor (?); wife, Elizabeth Shoaf.
0193. Gibson, William, Estate of. Aug. 27, 1816. Adms.—wife, Margaret Gibson, John Shields, Samuel Gillet. Apprs.—John Shields, Wm. McElvain and John Stranahan.
0194. Aug. 27, 1816, Adms. was Mary Smith, James McClish, Phillip Pontius. Mary, guardian of Sarah, daughter of George Smith.

SETTLEMENTS OF ESTATES

ABSTRACTS OF FRANKLIN COUNTY, OHIO RECORDS

MRS. JOHN M. TITUS

0195. May 5, 1817, Adms.—Mary Smith and Daniel Ranier. Mary Smith appointed guardian of Samuel Smith.

0196. Inks, John, Truro twp. Aug. 27, 1816. Adms.—Sarah Inks, William Cornell, John Edgar. Apprs.—John Hanson, George Young and Richard Rhoads.

0197. Hughes, Elizabeth, Estate of. Adms.—Elijah Thomas, Wm. Ballenger. Signed, Elijah Thomas, William Ballenger, Wesley Thomas, and Richard Hughes, Aug. 27, 1818.

0198. Hosack, Adam, Estate of. Nov. 13, 1813. Eunice•Hosack, Samuel G. Flenniken, Elias DeLashmutt. Apprs.—Jacob Grubb, David Scott, Elias DeLashmutt.

0199. Aug. 28, 1816, Woolry Coonrod was appointed guardian for Hugh, Nancy and Mary, children of Hugh Grant, dec'd. Sureties were Woolry Coonrod, Lucas Sullivant, Nicholas Haughn.

0200. Massie, Thomas, Estate of. Sept. 13, 1816. Adms.—Robert Massie, John McDowell, and A. McDowell.

0201. Grace, Catherine, Estate of. Nov. 7, 1816. Adms.—Daniel Brunk, Thomas Backus, Robert Elliott. Apprs.—Alexander Bassett, John Thomas, Benj. Britton, Norwich twp.

0202. Bartlett, Isaac, of Harrison twp., Estate of. Nov. 1816. Adms.—Recompense Stansbery, Jacob Fairfield, Obadiah Benedict.

0203. Dec. 30, 1816, John Cutler appointed guardian of John Willbourn, heir of Thomas Willbourn.

0204. Purcill, John, Estate of. Jan. 30, 1816. Adms.—Sarah Purcill, Morris Purcill, Emmor Cox, Wm. Caldwell. Apprs.—Isaac Worthington, Robert Wilson, Andrew Barr. Heirs were Moses, Samuel, and John Purcill.

0205. Dec. 31, 1816, Mathew Matthews appointed guardian of Harriet, Anna, and John, children of Ashael Hart.

0206. DeLong, Jacob, Estate of. Adms.—John Crone, Jane DeLong, Peter Lewis.

0207. Burnett, Henry, Estate of. Jan. 3, 1817. Adms.—Anthony Burnell and James Lindsey.

0208. Perrin, Jeffrey, Estate of. Pleasant twp. Jan. 3, 1817. Adms.—Thomas Roberts, Samuel Dyer. Apprs.—Charles Hunter, James Gardner.

0209. Miller, Justice, Estate of. Jan. 15, 1814. Adms.—Alex Bassett, Jacob Grub, Elias DeLashmutt, Jacob Overdear.

0210. Faulkner, John, Estate of. Adms.—John C. Broderick, Wm. Martin, Edward Livingston, Mch. 21, 1837.

0211. Hopper, Alexander, Franklin twp., Estate of. Mch. 31, 1817. Adms.—Agnes Hopper, Wm. Hopper, George Skidmore, Wm. Domigan.

0212. Barringer, Em., Estate of. Apr. 28, 1817. Adms.—Sarah Barringer, widow, Robert Campbell, Dr. John M. Edmiston. Apprs.—John Ridenour, Hugh Jeams, Robert Campbell.

0213. Apr. 28, 1817, Sarah Barringer, Robert Campbell, John M. Edmiston appointed guardian of James Mathew and Celesta, children of Wm. Barringer.

0214. Apr. 28, 1817, Henry Glick appointed guardian of John, David and Sarah, children of John Wright. Signed, Henry Glick, Arthur V. Taylor, Andrew Dildine.

0215. Sylvester, Obadiah, Estate of. Feb. 20, 1832. Adms.—Robert Kelso, Abraham Stagg, Thomas Stagg. Apprs.—John H. Smith,

William Carr, Michael Stagg, Mary Sylvester, administratrix.
0216. O'Harra, Charles. Rebecca O'Harra appointed administratrix.
0217. Havens, Robert, Estate of. May 5, 1817. Admrs.—John McIlvaine. Robert Brotherton. Appr.—Robert Armstrong, Jeremiah Armstrong, H. Brown.
0218. May 6, 1817, Arthur O'Harra and David Jameson appointed guardian of Stephen, Benjamin, Jesse, and William Grace.
0219. Oct. 30, 1823, Stephen Grace appointed guardian of Jesse Grace. Signed, Amazian Hutchinson, Jacob Ebey.
0220. Hopper, Robert, Estate of. Mch. 2, 1814, Admrs.—Alexander Hopper, John Skidmore, David Dearduff.
0221. Brandon, James, Estate of. June 3, 1817. Adm.—Jacob Roberts; surety, Jacob Plum, Henry Brown. James Brandon (Bratten) died May 12, 1817.
0222. Thompson, William, Estate of. Aug. 19, 1817. Admr.—Chas. Thompson; surety, Israel Baldwin, Ezra Griswold, Jr. Apprs.—Recompense Stansbury, Reuben Carpenter, Mathew Matthews.
0223. Aug. 29, 1817, Wm. D. Henderson, Benj. Clevenger, appointed guardian of Mary Booker, heir of John Booker.
0224. Aug. 29, 1817, Wm. Reed appointed guardian of Daniel Redenhauer, heir of Mathew Redenhauer.
0225. Henderson, Adam, Estate of. Oct. 15, 1817. Admr.—Samuel Henderson, Alex Henderson, and John Wilson.
0226. Will, Daniel Case.
0227. Nov. 26, 1817, Calvin H. Case chosen guardian by Wm. Case, minor of Daniel Case.
0228. Gilmore, Jane, Estate of. Nov. 28, 1817. Admrs.—John A. McDowell, Lucas Sullivant, Samuel McDowell. Heirs—James Gilmore, Jr., appointed guardian for Samuel, Adison, Sally and atty for Nash (Noah) Pitzer and James Davidson, heirs of Robt. Gilmore.
0229. Nov. 29, 1817, Anthony Burnett and James Lindsey appointed guardian of Belinda, heir of Hiram Burnett.
0230. Hunter, Robert, de'cd. Admr.—Deborah Hunter, Joseph Hunter, and Thomas Moore, Dec. 3, 1817.
0231a. Will of John Decker.
0231. Decker, John. Will filed Feb. 21, 1818. Admr.—David Williams and David Spangler.
0232. Dec. 6, 1817, Michael Fisher, Samuel Flenniken appointed guardian of John Sites, minor.
0233. Dec. 10, 1817, Hannah L. Orr appointed guardian of Wm. Orr. Admr.—John Shields and Isaiah Vorhes.
0234. Dec. 24, 1817, Estate of Samuel McGill.
0235. Mch. 13, 1818, Daniel Dearduff, Wm. Fleming appointed guardian of William, Minor of John Stierwell.
0236. Mch. 14, 1818, Horace Wolcott and Henry Brown appointed guardian of Hannah Stark, minor of Samuel Stark, dec'd.
0237. Mch. 20, 1818, Benjamin Sells appointed guardian of Sophia and William King, heirs of Jacob King.
0238. Mch. 1818, Benj. Sells, John Gorton, and Wm. Sells appointed guardians of Peggy and John King, heirs of Jacob King, dec'd.
0239. Sept. 13, 1827, John Brickle, John McElvain and David Dearduff were chosen guardians by John, age 14 yrs., heir of Jacob King, dec'd.
0240. John Ball, property sold June 22, 1818, will filed Mch. 3, 1819. Admr.—May 18, 1818. Polly Ball, Francis Stewart, Wm. Domigan, Edward Pennix.
0241. Aug. 11, 1818, Amasa Jones, Increase Mather appointed guardian of Bathsheba Matthews.

0242. Aug. 10, 1818, John A. McDowell, Wm. Gillmore appointed guardian of Sally Irwin.
0242. Will of Israel Case, missing.
0243. Sloper, Samuel, Estate of, Sharon twp. Oct. 30, 1818. Admrs.—Lydia Sloper, Stephen Maynard, Jr., Tracy Willcox, Oliver Lockwood. Apprs.—Moses Maynard, John Goodrich and Stephen Maynard.
0244. Aug. 15, 1818, John Long and Wm. Richardson appointed guardian of Polly Alkeltree.
0245. Aug. 18, 1818, Wm. H. Richardson, John A. McDowell, T. C. Flournay appointed guardians of Jacob, David and Catherine Weaver, heirs of Jacob Weaver.
0246. Aug. 19, 1818, Robert Brotherton, Eli C. King chosen guardian by Marlin Baldwin.
0247. Guardians for Chas. Ball, age 11, Lucius Ball, age 9, John Ball, age 7, Maryann, age 5, and David, age 3, minors of John Ball, dec'd.
0248. Aug. 20, 1818, Wm. B. Henderson appointed guardian of William, Eliza, age 13, Margaret, age 11, Sarah, age 7, heirs of Joseph Fleming, dec'd.
0249. Apr. 18, 1826, Jacob Gander appointed guardian of Sally, age 13, heir of Joseph Fleming.
0250. Wm. Gander, guardian of Peggy, age 18, heir of Joseph Fleming.
0251a. Estate of Ethan Palmer, will.
0252. Aug. 21, 1818, John Hunter, Joseph Hunter, T. C. Flournay appointed guardian of John McGown.
0253. Aug. 21, 1818, Chloe S. Palmer, Francis Olmstead appointed guardian of Meriam, infant heir of Ethan Palmer, dec'd.
0254. Dec. 17, 1825, Farrin Olmstead, Cruger Wright, Francis Olmstead, guardians of Meriam Palmer, age 11 ys. 9 mo.
0255. Sept. 16, 1816, will of Charles Bennett, Muskingum Co., O.; wife, Mary, sons Stephen and Nathan.
0256. Aug. 22, 1818, E. C. King, P. H. Olmstead and Wm. Platt appointed guardian of William Frazer.
0257. Guardianship of Abraham Kepler, missing.
0258. Oct. 19, 1818, eter Clover, Joshua Clover appointed guardians of Daniel and Polly, heirs of Daniel Teter.
0259. Estate of John Barly.—Book.
0260. Oct. 21, 1818, Julia Mead and Joel Buttles guardians of George, Nash, Elizabeth, and Julia, age 11 yrs., heirs of Hezekiah Mead.
0261. Oct. 21, 1818, Lucas Sullivant and John A. McDowell guardians of Henry Howe, heir of Stanislus Howe.
0262. Lucas Sullivant and John A. McDowell guardians of Richard Howe, heir of Stanislaus Howe.
0263. Will of Joseph Park.
0263a. Park, Joseph, Estate of. Admrs.—James Hoge, Jos. Miller, John A. McDowell, Wm. Stewart and John McElvain, Oct. 31, 1818. Dec. 18, 1824. Admrs.—Francis Stewart, John Barr, and Robert Brotherton.
0264. Dec. 10, 1818, Wm. John and John Armstrong appointed guardians of John, minor of Daniel Dale.
0265. Estate of Peter Harruff.—Book.
0266. Will of Michael Rohr.
0266a. Rohr, Michael, Estate of. Dec. 12, 1818. Admrs.—John Rohr, Geo. Rohr, Samuel Bishop, Henry Bunn. Apprs.—John Sharp, Thos. Rathmell, Jacob Leningood.
0267. Mch. 13, 1819, Orris Parish. Gustavus Swan, and John Parrish guardian of Thomas Purdy, age 14, on July 4, next.
0268. Mch. 3, 1818, Robert Brotherton, John A. McDowell, Gustavus Swan chosen guardians by Arthur, minor of Andrew Park.

SETTLEMENTS OF ESTATES
ABSTRACTS OF FRANKLIN COUNTY, OHIO RECORDS
MRS. JOHN M. TITUS

0269. March 5, 1818, Elizabeth, minor daughter of David Weaver chose Wm. Richardson, Robert Brotherton, and Thomas G. Flourney as her guardians.

0270. Will of John Delong, missing.

0271. Will of Elias Turner.

0271a. Turner, Elias, Estate of. Admrs.—Mary Turner, Michael Patton, and Wm. Sells. Apprs.—Eli C. King, Michael Patton, and Caleb Houston.

0272. Guardianship of James and Elizabeth Falkner, missing.

0273. Apr. 12, 1824, Robert Taylor, David Pugh, and John Lang, appointed guardians of Elizabeth Falkner, age 7 yrs., minor of John Falkner. June 14, 1823, James Hoge and John A. McDowell, appointed guardian of Elizabeth Falkner.
Marshall, John Starr, Jr. and James Marshall. Apprs.—Thomas Mrashall, John Starr, Jr. and James Marshall. Apprs.—Thomas Moore and Joseph Hunter.

0275. Springer, Elizabeth, Will of, Mch. 27, 1819.

0275a. Admrs.—David Dearduff, Jacob Grubb, Jos. Foos, and Adam Brotherton.

0276. Scott, David, Estate of. Admrs.—Thomas Barker, Gustavus Swan, and Orris Parish. Apr. 26, 1819.

0277. Webb, Thomas Smith, Estate of. Aug. 2, 1819. Admrs.—John Snow, Benjamin Gardiner, and Amasa Delano.

0278. Aug. 3, 1919, Thomas Moore and James Culbertson, chosen guardians by Mary Harruff, age 14 yrs. minor of —— Harruff, dec'd.

0279. May 5, 1819, Jacob Strader, and Arthur O'Harra, chosen guardians of Isaac Borror, age 18 yrs., Minomi Borror, age 16 yrs., and Absalom Borror, age 15 yrs., heirs of Jacob Borror.

0280. Aug. 7, 1819, Lucas Sullivant and John A. McDowell, chosen guardians by Henry Howe, age 17 yrs., heir of Henry Howe.

0282a. Read, William, Estate of. Aug. 9, 1819. Admrs.—Adam Reed, and Alex Reed. Exec.

0283. Aug. 10, 1819, Hannah Haddock and John A. McDowell appointed guardians of Enoch Haddock.

0284. Ritter, Frederick, Will of.

0284a. Missing.

0285. Missing.

0286. Pike, Isaac, Estate of. Aug. 14, 1819. Admrs.—James Pike, Benjamin Pike and Ralph White.

0287. Vandenburg, Jasper M., Estate of. Oct. 2, 1819. Admrs.—Jennett Vandenburg, John Jeffords, James Kooken, and Robet Armstrong.

0288. Andrus, Richard, Will of. Nov. 1, 1819. Admrs.—Stephen Maynard, Ezra Griswold, and William Derrikson.

0289. Andrews, Richard, Estate of. Oct. 28, 1822. Apprs.—Samuel Baldwin, Billias Skeel, and Aristarchus Walker.

0290a. Smith, William, Estate of. Nov. 1819. Admrs.—Stephen R. Price, Jos. Miller, John Cunning, James Smith, J. A. McDowell, and Alex Read. Apprs.—Samuel Gillet, Adam Read, and And. Smiley.

0291. Chester P. Cole, Joseph Miller, appointed guardians of Bateman Cole.

0292. Myers, John, Estate of, Book.

0293. Smith, John, Estate of. Nov. 2, 1819. Admrs.—John Sharp, George

W. Williams, and Adam Rarey with widow. Elizabeth Smith. Apprs.—John Gander, Jacob Decker, and Matthias Wolf.

0294. Michael Patton, Thomas Moore, Feb. 3, 1819, appointed guardians of Cynthia Cady, age 17 yrs., Kessiah Cady, age 15 yrs., and Almira Cady, age 12 yrs., heirs of Arthur Cady.

0295. William Godman, Nicholas Clabaugh, and William Crosley, Nov. 4, 1819, appointed guardians of Lydia, daughter of Joseph Myers.

0296. Martin Ballou, Jacob Tinker (Tinkham), and John Fall, Nov. 5, 1819, appointed guardians of James McLaughlin.

0297. Malbone, Solomon. Estate of. Nov. 5, 1819, Clinton twp. Admrs. —Aristarchus Walker, Austin Goodrich, and Abiel Case. Apprs.— Billias Skeele, Rodney Cooke, and David Colvin.

0298. Denney, James, Estate. Missing.

0299. Hubble, Burr, Estate of. Nov. 9, 1819. Admrs.—Arora Buttles, Orris Parish, Recompense Stansbury. Apprs.—Amos Hawley, Daniel Upson, Potter Wright.

0300. John A. McDowell, and George Anthony, Nov. 1819, appointed guardians of William Bailey.

0301. Robert Armstrong and Orris Parish, Nov. 12, 1819, appointed guardians of James Scott.

0302. Reuben Skeels, John Saul, and Roswell Wilcox, Nov. 10, 1819, appointed guardians of Hiram, age 19 yrs., Betsy, age 16 yrs., Amelia, Mary Ann, and Samuel, minors of Richard Andrews.

0303. Alice Case, and William Case, Nov. 13, 1819, appointed guardians of Rodney Case, minor of Daniel Case, dec'd.

0304. Park, Jonathan, Estate of. Sharon twp., Nov. 13, 1819. Admrs.— Jonathan Park, Levi Pinney, and Peter Barker. Apprs.—Amos Hawley, Samuel Abbott and Charles Thomson.
In the same envelope—Estate of John R. Stokes, Aug. 29, 1816. Admrs.—John Collett, Joseph Vance, and Robert Armstrong.

0305. Jacob Hoyt (Hoit), Peter Barker, Nov. 13, 1819, appointed guardians of Worthington Taylor, age 13 yrs.

0306. Levi Pinney, Peter Barker chosen guardians of George Taylor, age 17, Nov. 13, 1819.

0307a. Bristol, David, Estate of. Mch. 13, 1820. Admrs.—Adna Bristol and Stephen Frothingham. Apprs.—Preserved Leonard, Levi Pinney, and Asa Weaver.

0308. Thomas Johnston, and Orris Parish, Mch. 15, 1820, chosen guardians of Joseph Hunter, age 11 yrs. next Aug.

0309. Anson Smith and Benjamin Pike, Mch. 16, 1820, chosen guardians of Daniel Bradford Smith, age 17 yrs. on Dec. 17, 1819.

0310. Thomas Johnson and Jacob Grubb, Mch. 17, 1820, chosen guardians by Luther Smith.

0311. Stokes, John R., Estate of. Admr.—John Collett. Filed Mch. 18, 1820.

0312. Duke, William. Estate of. Mch. 21, 1820. Admrs.—Ishmael Davis, Emmor Cox, and William Caldwell.

0313. Delano, Oliver, of Clinton twp. Will.

0313a. Apprs.—John Smith, Elam Jewett, and Levi Pinney. Admrs.— Thomas Bull, Stephen Hoit, Hiram Bull, and Alanson Bull.

0314. Wherry, James, Estate of. Mch. 24, 1820. Admrs.—Margaret Wherry, John R. Parrish. Alexander Crone, and John M. Strain. Apprs.—J. B. Gardiner, William Stoll, and Eli King. "Had widow and six small helpless children."

0315. Case, Rachel. Estate of.

0315a. June 10, 1820. Admrs.—John Smith and William Case.

0316. Daniel Upson, Arora Buttles, and Orange Johnson, June 16, 1820 appinted guardians of Nobles, Eleazer B., and Mary Hubble.

0317. Lewis, Joseph, Estate of. Aug. 22, 1820. Admrs.—Obadiah Benedict, Stephen Maynard, and Joab Hoit. Apprs.—Amos Hawley, William Vining, and Chandler Rogers.

0318. Gorton, Joseph, Estate of. Oct. 10, 1820. Admrs.—Horace Wolcott, Lewis Risley, and John Watts. Apprs.—Edward Pennix, and Lewis Risley.

0319. Poole, Joseph, Estate of. Oct. 11, 1820. Admrs.—Samuel R. Norse, Daniel Upson, Recompense Stansbury, and Bulkley Comestock. Oct. 19, 1820, Daniel Upson was chosen guardian of Simeon and Joshua Poole. Also of Abijah, Thomas, and Phebe, heirs of Joseph Poole.

0320. Oct. 13, 1820, Isaac Case, Asa Weaver, and Josiah Fisher, chosen guardians of Polly and Martha White.

0321. Oct. 14, 1820, John R. Parish, and Jacob Overdear guardians of James Perrin.

0322. Oct. 16, 1820, George Goading, and Thomas Hart, guardians of Cloe and Selam Case.

0323. Oct. 18, 1820, Ozias Burr, and Stephen Maynard, appointed guardians of Hannah Lewis (widow and relict of Joseph Lewis) a "lunatick," of Sharon twp. (not to be committed).

0324. Guardians of Simeon, Joshua, Abijah, Thomas, and Phoebe Pool, missing.

0325. Oct. 19, 1820, Chloe Pool and Preserved Leonard, guardians of Annie, heir of Joseph Pool, dec'd.

0326. Heath, Joseph, Estate of. Nov. 4, 1820. Admrs.—Amos Heath, Joseph Gundy, John Harvey. Apprs.—Jacob Gundy, Benjamin Foster, Elijah Chenowith.

0327. Hopper, Edward, Estate of. Nov. 18, 1820, Prairie Township. Admrs.—John Hunter, Samuel Hunter, David McMillen. Apprs. —William Stierwalt, Israel P. Brown, William Willcox.

0328. Ferguson, John, Estate of. Dec. 8, 1820. Admrs.—Thomas Ferguson, Sarah Ferguson, Samuel Dyer, John Chenowith.

0329. Higgins, Richard, Estate of. Feb. 23, 1821. Admrs.—Mary D. Higgins, Samuel Higgins, John Hunter.

0330. Higgins, Richard, Prairie Twp. Admr.—Samuel Higgins. Apprs. —Henry Clover, William Willcox, George Skidmore.

0331. Ogden, Moses, Will of.

0331a. Ogden, Moses, Estate of. March 17, 1821. Admrs.—Lidia Ogden, Elias Ogden, Joseph Edgar.

0332. Culbertson, Robert, Will of, d. Apr. 14, 1821. Book.

0332a. Admrs.—James Hoge, Ralph Osborn, Samuel Culbertson, Robert Russell. Apprs.—Jacob Grubb, Robert Armstrong, Joseph Miller.

0333. March 16, 1821, Abram J. McDowell, Lucas Sullivant, guardians of Peter, age 10, James, age 8, minors of Peter Hoover, dec'd.

0334. Dec. 17, 1825, Reuben Golliday, Jacob Ebey, John Robinson, guardians of Peter, age 14, heir of Peter Hoover, dec'd.

0335. Sept. 13, 1827, Reuben Golliday, Adam Brotherton, David Deardurf, guardians of James Hoover, age 14, 1st of last March.

0336. March 16, 1821, George McCormick, Joseph Miller, guardians of James, son of Elias Turner, dec'd.

0337. Abner Pinney, Samuel Beach, Mch. 20, 1821, appointed guardians of Azariah Pinney.

0338. Lane, Lemuel, Estate of. Feb. 23, 1831. Admrs.—Benjamin Sells, Orris Parish, and Christopher W. Kent.—Mch. 20, 1821, Elizabeth Lane, Orris Parish, and Benjamin Sells were admrs. Apprs.—R. Osburn, J. Robinson, and J. Lane.

0339. Tuller, Bela M., Will of, Mch. 22, 1821.

0339a. Tuller, B. M., Estate of. Lydia Tuller, wife. Admrs.—Horace Tuller, Ezra Griswold, Chandler R——, and Roswell Wilcox.

0340. Lord, Abner, Estate of. Jan. 14, 1821. Admrs.—A. McDowell, Jacob Grubb, John McElvaine. Apprs.—L. Goodale, John Starr, Jr., John Hunter.

0341. Yantis, John, Will of.
0341a. Yantis, John, Estate of. Empty.
0342. John Cutler, George McCormack, and Henry Brown, chosen guardians of Matilda, heir of Robert McGowan, June 13, 1821.
0343. Guardianship of Elizabeth, Daniel, and Magdaline Kendall, missing.
0344. Guardianship of Jonah Carson, missing.
0345. Swain, Matthias, Estate of. Oct. 12, 1821. Admrs.—William Stierwalt, Jacob Grubb, William Fleming. Apprs.—Horace Wolcott, Edw. Pennix, Adam Brotherton.
0346. Guardian of Catherine Burr. Oct. 23, 1821. Chandler Rogers and Ozias Burr, chosen.
0347. Davis, Ishmael, Estate of. Oct. 13, 1821. Admrs.—John Swisher, Emmor Cox, William Caldwell. Apprs.—David Spangier, wm. Hendren, and Thomas Rathmell.
0348. Harvey, John, Estate of. Oct. 16, 1821. Admrs.—John Chenowith, Sarah Harvey, Benj. Foster, and Benj. Chenowith. Apprs.— George Goodson, Elijah Chenowith, and Samuel Dyer.
0349. Miller, Joseph, Estate of. Oct. 17, 1821. Admrs.—William Doherty, Ralph Osburn, James Harris.
0350. Lambert, John H., Estate of. Oct. 17, 1821. Admrs.—Jacob Grubb, Joseph Hunter, Abram J. McDowell, Ann Lambert widow of John H.
0351. Case, Abiel, Estate of. Oct. 19. 1821. Admrs.—Chandler Rogers, Samuel Beach, and Alpheus Bigelow.
0352. Evans, David, Estate of. Jan. 9, 1822. Apprs.—Jacob Grubb, Robert Armstrong, and William Domigan.
0353. Jeffords, John, Estate of. Dec. 24, 1821. Adm.—Sally Jeffords. Apprs.—William McElvain, Andrew Backus, James Kooken.
0354. Lucas Sullivant, and William Domigan, Dec. 8, 1821, appointed guardians of Samuel Richard, George W., Maria A., Wealtha, Clark, and Thomas, children of Richard Higgins, dec'd.
0355. Kooser, Daniel, Estate of. Dec. 24, 1821. Admrs.—Elizabeth Kooser, Peter Putman, and John Putman.
0356. McDavitt, Patrick, Estate of. June 10, 1822. Admrs.—Nathaniel McDavitt, Andrew Dill, and William Fleming. Apprs.—Thomas Johnson, Israel Plum, John Cochran.
0357. Lane, William, Estate of. Jan. 10, 1822. Admrs.—Andrew Dill, William Domigan, and Jacob Grubb. Apprs.—George Williams, Elijah Merion, William Stewart.
0358. Curry, Moses, Estate of. Hamilton twp., Jan. 17, 1822. Admrs.— Mary Curry, Elijah Merion, Thomas Reynolds. Apprs.—Samuel Henderson, Moses Morrill, and Wm. Stewart.
0359. Apr. 2, 1822, John Overdear, Joseph Overdear, Jacob Grubb, and John Laughry, appointed guardians of John Overdear, minor son of John Overdear.
0360. Apr. 2, 1822, John Crone, William Godman, and George Sharp, were chosen guardians of James Lee, age 19, minor of Jonathan Lee.
0361. Apr. 2, 1822, Bela Lathem, Orris Parish, and P. B. Wilcox, were chosen guardians of Joseph Lee.
0362. Apr. 2, 1822, John Crone, William Godman, and George Sharp, chosen guardians of Elijah Jacobs, age 18, heir of Benjamin Jacobs.
0363. Apr. 2, 1822, William Godman, John Gander, and George Sharp, chosen guardians of Sally Myers, age 12 yrs. and George Myers, age 14 yrs., heirs of John Myers.
0364. Apr. 4, 1822, Francis Steven (?), Samuel Shannon, Gustavus Swan, appointed guardians of James jr., minor of Robert Shannon.
0365. Apr. 4, 1822, Andrew Dill, Lucas Sullivant, and John R. Parish,

appointed guardians of James and George, minors of William Lane.

0366. The same guardians were appointed for John, minor of William Lane.

0367. Apr. 6, 1822, Amos Hawley, George H. Griswold, and Adna Bristol were chosen guardians by Lucius Strong.

0368. Apr. 6, 1822, Thomas Jones, and Arthur O'Harra were chosen guardians by David Pancake.

0369. Apr. 6, 1822, James Peters, Marly and Joseph Billingsley were chosen guardians of Eliza Barkley.

0370. Apr. 8, 1822, John Ball, Andrew Dill, and John R. Parish, chosen guardians by John Ball, age 16 yrs., minor of William Ball, dec'd.

0371. Will of Stephen Smith.

0371a. Smith, Stephen, Estate of. Nov. 2, 1822. Admrs.—Robert Williams, John W. Smith, and Adam Earhart. July 12, 1822, Mary Smith, Robert Williams, and George Williams.

0372. July 8, 1822, James Vanderhugh, David W. Deshler, and James Kooken, appointed guardians of James, minor of Joseph Vanderburgh, dec'd.

0373. July 8, 1822, Samuel Barr, and Jacob Grubb, chosen as guardians by Daniel Rumsey.

0374. July 8, 1822, Lucas Sullivant, and Jacob Grubb, appointed guardians of Lucas, age 15 yrs., minor of William Marshall.

0375. July 8, 1822, Lucas Sullivant, and Jacob Grubb, appointed guardians of Mary Marshall, minor of William Marshall.

0376. July 8, 1822, Isaac W. Flenniken, and Thomas Martin, chosen as guardians by Thomas McLaughlin.

0377. July 8, 1822, Amos Hawley, Arora Buttles, and Levi Pinney, appointed guardians of Milton, Darwin, Sophrona, and Alex. Morrison.

0378. Will of William Badger, sr.

0378a. Badger, William, Estate of. Jackson twp. Aug. 15, 1822. Admrs. —William Badger, Archibald J. Badger, and Arthur O'Harra. Apprs.—William Brown, Woolrey Coonrod, and Nicholas Haughn.

0379. Beers, George, Estate of. Oct. 19, 1822. Admrs.—John Beers, Adam Sarber, and Christian Sarber. Apprs.—N. Goetchius, Daniel Brown (?), and Abraham Shoemaker.

0380. Griswold, Ezra, Estate of. July 3, 1822. Sharon twp. Admrs.— Ezra Griswold, and Geo. Harlow Griswold. Apprs.—A. Hawley, C. Pinney, and J. Sherman.

0381. Maynard, Stephen, Estate of. Sharon twp., Oct. 28, 1822. Admrs. —Abner Pinney, Stephen Maynard, jr., Samuel Abbot, Selah Wilcox. Apprs.—Obadiah Benedick, Abraham Ingham, and Archibald Douglass.

0382. Oct. 28, 1822, John W. Ladd, and Orange Johnston, appointed guardians of Marcus Strong, minor of David Strong.

0383. Britton, Hosea, Estate of. Oct 30, 1822. Admrs.—Benj. Britton, Robert Elliot, and Samuel Brunk. Apprs.—Daniel Brunk, Moses Hart, sr., and Ephraim Fisher.

0384. Wilber, Elijah, Estate of. Oct. 31, 1822. Admrs.—Nathan Cole, Horace Wolcott, and Lewis Risly. Apprs.—Ezekiel Curtis, Edward Pinnix, and Adam Brotherton.

0385. Little, Nathaniel, Estate of. Nov. 1, 1822. Admrs.—Stephen N. Frothingham, Adney Bristol, and Joseph Greer. Apprs.—John W. Ladd, James Pierce, and Ira M——.

0386. Nov. 2, 1822, Joel Buttles, and Orris Parish, appointed guardians of Justin, minor son of Alex Morrison.

0387. Sparks, Elijah, Estate of. Perry twp., Nov. 2, 1822. Admrs.— Elizabeth Sparks, Benjamin Porter, and Jacob Eby, Jacob Kunkle, and Jacob Keller. Apprs.—John Crider, Alanson Perry, and Amaziah Hutchinson.

SETTLEMENTS OF ESTATES

0338.* Landes, Samuel, Estate of. Jan. 1, 1823. Admrs.—Alex Crone, Peter Stimmell, Isaac Plum, and Michael Stimmell. Apprs.— Thomas Johnston, David Spangler, and Andrew Barr.

0389. Robe, William, Estate of. Jan. 25, 1823. Admrs.—Daniel Upson, Arora Buttles, Joel Buttles, and Charles Whitmore. Apprs.— Recompense Stansbery, Charles Whitmore, and Jonathan Sherman.

0390. Taylor, James, Estate of. Jan. 14, 1823. Admrs.—Abiathar Taylor, Matthew Taylor, Billingsley Bull, and Orris Parish. Apprs.— William Patterson, Daniel Ross, and Richard Courtright.

0391. Mch. 3, 1823, John McElwain, Gustavus Swan, and A. J. Mc-Dowell, were appointed guardians of Wm. Doherty, minor of John Doherty.

0392. John A. McDowell, and Abram McDowell, appointed guardians of Keziah Doherty, minor of John Doherty, same date (Mch. 3, 1823).

0393. Mch. 6, 1823, the same guardians appointed for John Daugherty.

0394. Mch. 6; 1823, Henry Brown and A. J. McDowell, appointed guar-

*this should be 0388

dians of David, minor of John Doherty.

0395. Mch. 7, 1823, Emanuel Doherty, Wm. Doherty, and Abram Mc-Dowell, appointed guardians of the minors of John Doherty.

0396. Thos. Johnston, Jacob Grubb, and Philo Olmstead, were appointed guardians of Benj. Hunter, minor of Robert Hunter, Mch. 7, 1823.

0397. Mch. 7, 1823, John A. McDowell, and John T. Martin, were appointed guardians of James Gibson, age 16 yrs. in May.

0398. Dean, Libbeus, Estate of. Mch. 10, 1823. Admrs.—Ebenezer Dean, Samuel Gillett, Jeremiah McLene, and James Smith. Apprs.—William Dalzell, Luther Patterson, and John Agler.

0399. Mch. 15, 1823, John M. Edmiston, and Joseph Hunter, appointed guardians of Madison and John Hunter.

0400. Smith, Jones, Will of.

0400a. Smith, Jonas, Estate of. Apr. 12, 1823. Admrs.—Silas C. Smith, Nicholas Demorest, Dan'l Demorest, Gillian Demorest, and John Lane. Apprs.—John Watts, John M. Goetchius, and Stewart White.

0401. Decker, Jacob, Will of.

0401a. Empty.

0402. Mitchell, Charles, Will of.

0402a. Mitchell, Charles, Estate of. June 13, 1823. Admrs.—James Howey, Jane Mitchell, Brice Hayes, and Peter Sells.

0403. June 11, 1823, Jacob Neff, and Jacob Grubb, were appointed guardians of John Hopper, age 15 yrs. and of Margaret Hopper.

0404. June 11, 1823, James Gardner, and John G. Neff, were appointed guardians of Solomon, Edward, and Alex Hopper. On Apr. 12, 1826, James Gardner was appointed guardian of Alex Hopper, age 15 yrs., minor of Edward Hopper.

0405. Schoonover, John, Estate of. June 11, 1823. Admrs.—John Schoonover, Joseph Schoonover, Billingsley Bull, and Phillip Cramer.

0406. Turney, John, Estate of. June 11, 1823. Admrs.—Daniel and Joseph Turney. Apprs.—Ebenezer Butler, Frederic Agler, and John Agler.

0407. Shlusher, Tobias, Estate of. June 12, 1823. Admrs.—Dannie Shlusher (in German), George Lang, Nathan Bennett, Conrad Ware (in German). Apprs.—Daniel Krouse, Geo. Bishop, and Cotton Tabor.

0408. Strain, John M., Estate of. June 1823. Admrs.—Elizabeth Strain, Wm. McElvain, Moses Jewett, and John McElvain. Apprs.—W. T. Martin, C. Heyl, and C. Huston.

0409. Chapman, Benjamin, Will of.

0409a. Chapman, Benjamin, Estate of. Empty.

0410. June 14, 1823, John R. Parish, Gustavus Swan, and Abram McDowell, were appointed guardians of William Steele.

0411. Ross, Daniel, Estate of. June 14, 1823. Admrs.—Jane Ross, John F. Ross, Caleb Huston, and Alex. Ross. Nov. 13, 1830, Hugh Ross, Elias Chester, and Thaddeus Smith.

0412. Frazer, John, Estate of. June 16, 1823. Admrs.—John French, Isaac Crawford, and Matthew Crawford. Apprs.—John B. French, Jos. McIntire, and James McCray.

0413. Adams, Eli, Estate of. Nov. 6, 1823. Admrs.—John Cary, George B. Harvey, John Wilson, and Joseph Booth. Apprs.—Henry Brown, Daniel Deshler, and Jeremiah McLene.

0414. McKee, Samuel, Estate of. Aug. 30, 1823. Admrs.—George Anthony, George B. Harvey, and Orrin Parish.

0415. Buttles, Levi, Estate of. Aug. 30, 1823. Admrs.—Joel Buttles, Henry Brown, D. W. Deshler, and John Greenwood. Apprs.—John M. Walcutt, and John Cary.

0416. Truman, Charles, Estate of. Aug. 30, 1823. Admrs.—David Deshler, John Greenwood, Henry Brown, and James Cherry. Apprs.—John Wilson, Joseph Booth, and George B. Harvey.

0417. Jameson, David, Will of. Missing.
0417a. Jameson, David, Estate of. Aug. 30, 1823. Adam Brotherton, Arthur O'Harra, Excr.
0418. Huff, John, Estate of. Sept. 27, 1823. Admrs.—Emmor Cox, John Thompson, and Robert Brotherton.
0419. Parks, Jane, Will of.
0419a. Parks, Jane, Estate of. Sept. 27, 1823. Admrs.—Arthur O'Harra, Adam Brotherton, and James O'Harra.
0420. Sullivant, Lucas, Estate of. Oct. 7, 1823. Admr.—Lynn Starling— Securities, Francis Stewart, and Abram McDowell.
0421. McDowell, John A. Oct. 7, 1823. Lynne Starling, Excr. (brother-in-law).
0422. Kerr, Samuel, Estate of. Oct. 8, 1823. Admrs.—Reuben Golliday, Lawrence Foster, and William Beatty. Apprs.—Samuel Flenniken, Edward Livingston, and Thomas Johnston.
0423. Gillett, Samuel, dec'd of Mifflin twp. Oct. 22, 1823. Admrs.— Benjamin Platt, and David W. Deshler. Securities, Jeremiah McLene, and Samuel Shannon.
0424. Slosher, Daniel. Oct. 30, 1823. Admr.—George Bishop. Securities, Nicholas Goetchius, and William Elder.
0425. George William, appointed guardian of Lewis Davis, infant heir of —— Davis.
0426. Vandemark, Jeremiah, Estate of. Oct. 30, 1823. Admrs.—Nicholas Goetchius, and Daniel Vandemark, with Adam Pontius, and George Bishop as securities. June 23, 1825, William Godman was appointed Admr. with George Bishop, and Daniel Crouse as security.
0427. William Miller, appointed guardian of William, son of Andrew Seeds. Oct. 30, 1823, Matthew Miller, and William C. Duff securities. Sept. 1, 1834, Matthew Miller, Absolem Barker, appointed guardians of William Seeds, jr.
0428. Seeds, Aaron, Estate of. Oct. 30, 1823. Admrs.—William Seeds, Woolrey Coonrod, and William Miller.
0429. Ross, Jane, Estate of. Oct. 31, 1823. Admrs.—Abithar Taylor, David and Matthew Taylor.
0430. Crossett, Samuel, Estate of. Oct. 31, 1823. Admrs.—Matthew Taylor jr. 3rd., William Crosset, Abithar Taylor, and Hugh W. Ross. Apr. 14, 1824, Admrs.—William Crossett, Ebenezer Smith and Elias Chester.
0431. William McElvain, and Orris Parish, appointed guardians of James McGill, Oct. 31, 1823.
0432. Baker, Henry, Estate of. Oct. 31, 1823. Admrs.—Andrew Dill, and Sarah Baker, with Jeremiah McLene, and George Williams as securities.
0433. Edward Livingston, William Doherty, and Robert Brotherton, appointed guardians of Mary, Edward M., and Ann Ross, heirs of Daniel Ross, dec'd, Nov. 1, 1823.
0434. Taylor, John D., Estate of. Nov. 1, 1823. Admrs.—Joseph Wright, Nicholas Hopkins, and Billingsly Bull.
0435. Seeds, Aaron, Estate of, Nov. 1, 1823, admr. William Seeds with Woolry Coonrod and William Miller as securities.
0436. Clark, John C., Estate of, Admr. William T. Martin appointed Nov. 1, 1823, with William Sells and William Long as securities.
0437. Nov. 1, 1823, Abram J. McDowell appointed guardian of Samuel C., minor heir of Richard Higgins, with Jacob Grubb as security.
0438. Nov. 4, 1823 Abram J. McDowell appointed guardian of Joshua aged about 10, Ann Maria aged 15 yrs. George Washington, Willy Ann minor heirs of Richard Higgins. Security, Jacob Grubb.
Mch. 16, 1825, Abram McDowell chosen guardian of Richard aged 15 yrs. heir of Richard Higgins. Securities, James A. Paxton and Samuel Higgins.

May 20, 1831, Clark Higgins appointed guardian of Ann Maria, and Joshua heirs of Richard Higgins dec'd. Securities, Lyne Starling and Francis Stewart.

0439. Fulton, Hugh, Estate of, Nov. 3, 1823, admr. John Smith, with Alexander Henderson and Samuel Henderson as securities.
Nov. 3, 1823, Samuel Henderson appointed guardian of Alexander aged 18, Samuel aged 17, David aged 15, and James aged 9 yrs. minor heirs of James Fulton dec'd.

0440. Nov. 3, 1823, Samuel Henderson appointed guardian of Elizabeth C. Curry, (late Elizabeth Campbell Henderson (Elizabeth Curry in 1829), and John Curry. heir of Adam Henderson. Securities, John Smith and Alexander Henderson.

0441. Bull, Thomas, Estate of, Nov. 3, 1823, admrs. Alanson and Jason Bull with John Smith and Samuel Henderson as securities. (Thomas Bull was a Revolutionary Soldier).

0442. Sells, Ludwick, Estate of, Nov. 3, 1823, admrs, William and Peter Sells, with Jacob Grubb and John McElvain as securities. (Ludwick Sells was a Revolutionary Soldier.)

0443. Ferguson, Thomas, Estate of, Nov. 3, 1823, admr. Thomas Ferguson with Wm. Ferguson and James Gardener as securities.

0444. Bidwell, Joshua, Estate of, Nov. 3, 1823, admrs. Isaac Bidwell and Rodney Comstock. Securities, Ozias Burr and William McCloud.

0445. Wright, Brazilla, Estate of, Nov. 3, 1823, admrs. Susan and M. B. Wright with Cyrus Fay and George McCormick as securities.

0446. Broderick, David, Estate of, Nov. 3, 1823, admr. George Broderick with Henry Brown and John M. Wolcott as securities.

0447. Todd, John, Estate of, admr. Benjamin Todd, Nov. 3, 1823, with George Stephenson and George Cork as securities. Dec. 10, 1824, Joseph Wright was appointed appr. instead of Billingsley Bull, dec'd.

0448. Craun, John, Estate of, Nov. 3, 1823, exers. John Craun, Jacob Craun, Abraham Craun, and Isaac Craun. Securities, Nicholas Goetchus and James Purcy.

0449. Hutchinson, Amaziah, Estate of, Nov. 3, 1823, admr. Amaziah Hutchinson jr. Securities, William Sells and Ebenezer Richards. (Amaziah Hutchinson was a Revolutionary Soldier.)

0450. White, James H., Estate of, Nov. 11, 1823, Nathaniel Benton appointed admr. with John Britton and Thomas Ingals as securities.

0451. Kerr, John, Estate of, Nov. 8, 1823, James Robinson and John Cutter appointed admrs., with Ralph Osburn, John Greenwood and Charles Lofland as securities.

0452. Kilbourne, William, Estate of, Nov. 8, 1823, Arius Kilbourne appointed admr. with John Sells and Aurora Buttles as securities.

0453. McElhaney, Robert, Estate of, Nov. 11, 1823, Hugh McElhaney and George W. Williams appointed admrs., with Jacob Grubb and Samuel Shannon as securities.

0454. Pursel, John, Estate of, Jan. 3, 1824, Susan Pursel and Isaiah Pursel appointed admrs., with Robert Lisle and William Caldwell as securities.

0455. Rohr, Michael, Estate of, Jan. 3, 1824, George Rohr appointed admr. with Thomas Rathmell and Robert C. Messmore as securities.

0456. Gilmore, Robert, Estate of, Feb. 3, 1824, William Bennett appointed admr. with Francis Stewart and George W. Williams as securities.

0457. Dunn, Asa, Estate of, Feb. 3, 1824, Percival Adams appointed admr. with Francis Stewart and James Lindsay as securities.

0458. Fisher, Michael, Estate of, Feb. 19, 1824, Michael Fisher jr. appointed admr. with William Stewart and Ferbus Moorhead as securities.

SETTLEMENTS OF ESTATES

ABSTRACTS OF FRANKLIN COUNTY, OHIO RECORDS

MRS. JOHN M. TITUS

0459. Coleman, Abraham, Estate of, Mch. 11, 1824, Abraham and James Coleman appointed admrs. with Andrew Dill and Robert Breckenridge as securities.

0460. Mar. 11, 1824, Benjamin Foster, appointed guardian by choice of Orson aged 18 yrs., Joseph aged 16 yrs., Nancy aged 14 yrs. and of Robert aged 8 yrs. Jackson aged 4 yrs., Clarissa, and Samuel and Elijah minor heirs of Samuel C. Kerr, with Elijah Chenowith and Samuel Dyer as securities.

0461. Mch. 11, 1824, Andrew Dill appointed guardian of Sally Hays minor heir of ——— Hays, with William Domigan, security.

0462. Apr. 12, 1824, William Stewart and Elias Chester appointed guardians of William Crossett under 14 yrs. of age, minor heir of Samuel Crossett. Securities, Ebenezer Smith and William Crossett.

0463. Apr. 12, 1824, William Stewart and Elias Chester appointed guardians of Elizabeth Crossett minor heir of Samuel Crossett. Securities Ebenezer Smith and William Crossett.

0464. Feb. 16, 1835, William Long appointed by choice, guardian of Elizabeth Aged 13, yrs. minor heir of Samuel Crossett. Securities, Charles Wood and David Taylor.

0465. Apr. 14, 1824, Recompense Stansbury appointed guardian of Mary aged 12, Olive aged 10, and Harriet aged 6 yrs. infant heirs of Joshua Bidwell. Security, William McCloud.

0466. Long, Matthew, estate of, Apr. 14, 1824, admr. John Long, with Thomas Gray and William Cornell as securities. Appraisers appointed, June 27, 1825.

0467. Apr. 14, 1824, John Cochrane appointed guardian by choice of David aged 16 yrs, minor heir of John Lightner, with John Hutson as security.

0468. Sowers, Christopher, Estate of, Apr. 14, 1824, admr. John Cutler, with John Greenwood and Henry Brown as securities.

0469. McCloud, Thomas, Estate of, Apr. 14, 1824, Exec. William McCloud, with Recompense Stansbury and Noah Andrews as Securities.

0470. Apr. 14, 1824, Richard Courtright appointed guardian of Samuel aged 17, heir of John Black dec'd. with Thomas Gray and Joseph Schoonover as securities.

0471. Apr. 14, 1824, Henry Brown appointed guardian of Thomas Wiseman age 16 yrs. heir of ——— Wiseman dec'd., with William Doherty and John Cutler as securities.

0472. Apr. 15, 1824, Matthew Taylor appointed guardian by choice of Thomas aged 16 yrs. heir of Thomas Skeed dec'd with John Long and William Crossett as securities.

0473. Apr. 16, 1824, Thomas Johnston appointed guardian by choice of Michael Fisher aged 20 yrs. minor heir of Michael Fisher dec'd. with George W. Williams as security.

0474. Apr. 16, 1824, Thomas Johnston appointed guardian of Milton aged 10 yrs. infant heir of Michael Fisher dec'd with George W. Williams as security.

0475. Apr. 16, 1824 George W. Williams appointed guardian by choice of George aged 18 yrs. and Jacob aged 15 yrs. minor heirs of Michael Fisher with Thomas Johnston as security.

0476. Jan. 14, 1830, George W. Williams appointed guardian by choice of Milton aged 15 yrs. minor heir of Michael Fisher dec'd. with Michael and Sarah Fisher as securities.

0477. Apr. 16, 1824, David Spangler appointed by choice guardian of Matthew aged 17 yrs. and Asa aged 19 yrs. minor heirs of Asa Dunn dec'd. with George W. Williams as security.

0478. Apr. 16, 1824, Mary Dunn appointed guardian of Mahala aged 11 yrs., minor heir of Asa Dunn, with David Spangler as security.

0479. Martin, John, Estate of Apr. 16, 1824, David Deshler admr. with Levi Adkinson and Jacob Hare as securities.

0480. Peterson, Frederick, Estate of, Apr. 17, 1824, Frederick Peterson Jr. appointed exec. with Billingsly Bull and Joseph Wright as securities. June 24, 1825, John Swisher was appointed admr. after the death of the exec., with William Godman and Jacob Gander as securities.

0481. Apr. 17, 1824, James Condren appointed guardian of David Herdman aged 4 yrs on Feb. 7, last, minor heir of Elias Herdman with John R. Parish and James Condren jr. as securities.

0482. Apr. 20, 1824, Richard Howe appointed guardian by choice of George aged 16, yrs., minor heir of Stansilaw Howe, with William S. Sullivant as security.

0483. Apr. 20, 1824, John Greenwood appointed guardian of Maria Ritter aged 8 yrs., heir of Frederick Ritter. Security, David Deshler.

0484. Apr. 20, 1824, William S. Sullivant appointed by choice guardian of Joseph aged 14 yrs. minor heir of Lucas Sullivant dec'd. Securities, Jeremiah McLene, William Doherty and Lyne Starling.

0485. Dec. 18, 1824, Henry Brown appointed guardian of Michael L. Sullivant aged 17, and upwards, minor heir of Lucas Sullivant dec'd. Securities, Lyne Starling, and Abram McDowell. Aug. 26, 1826 court ordered that Henry Brown be removed.

0486. Davis, Joshua, Estate of, Apr. 20, 1824, admr. Samuel Davis, with John and William Davis as securities.

0487. Fulton, John, Estate of, Apr. 20, 1824, exec., Cristena Fulton with Richard and James Suddick as securities.

0488. Shields John, Estate of, May 1, 1824, Edward T. Shields, admr. with Benjamin Sells and Abram Stotts as securities.

0489. Sibliss, Thomas, Estate of, May 1, 1824, admr. John R. Parish, with David Dearduff and James Suddick as securities.

0490. Blakesley, Thomas, Estate of, May 29, 1824, admr. George Bishop, with Henry Dildine and Daniel Crouse as securities.

0491. Rathbone, Amos, Estate of, May 29, 1824, admrs. Thomas Rathbone and Amos Jenkins, with James Harris and William Sells as securities.

0492. Nelson, Robert, Estate of, Sept. 7, 1824, admrs. Martha Nelson and John Barr. with Robert Brotherton and Jeremiah McLene as securities.

0493. Coldshine, John, Estate of, Sept. 27, 1824, admr. Moses Morrill, with Elijah Marion and Elijah Glover as securities.

0494. Wait, Jencks, Estate of, admr., Sept. 27, 1824, admr. William Wait, with John Loughery and Jacob Overdear as securities. (Jencks Wait was a Revolutionary soldier).

0495. Chaney, John, Estate of, Sept. 29, 1824, admrs. Charles Chaney and John Hanson, with Richard Courtright and Robert Taylor as securities. June 16, 1834 Mease Smith was appointed to examine the accounts.

0496. Besser, John, Estate of, Nov. 6, 1824, admr. Robert Brotherton, with Adam Brotherton and Francis Stewart as securities.

0497. Nichols, Townsend, Estate of, Nov. 13, 1824, admrs. Mary Nichols and Jarvis Pike, with John McCoy and John Cutler as securities.

0498. Jackson, William, Estate of, Nov. 13, 1824, admr. Catherine Jackson, with Andrew L. Burke and William T. Martin as securities.

0499. Ringrose, John, Estate of, Nov. 13, 1824, admr. Robert Brotherton, with Thomas Moore and John White as securities.

0500. Wilcox, Selah, Estate of, Nov. 16, 1824, admrs. Recompense Stansbury and Tracy Wilcox, with Daniel Upson and Darius P. Wilcox.

0501. Starr, James, Estate of, Nov. 23, 1824, John Starr appointed admr. with will annexed, with Samuel Abbott and Francis Stewart as securities.

0502. Crosby, Harry, Estate of, Nov. 23, 1824, non-cupative will proven and Augustine W. Sweetland with Demas Adams and Samuel Abbott as securities.

0503. Bull, Billingsley, Estate of, Dec. 9, 1824, Caty Bull appointed admix. with Thomas Ashton and Joseph Wright as securities.

0504. Agler, Frederick, Estate of, Dec. 9, 1824, admrs. Margaret Agler and John Agler, with Peter Putman and Samuel Baughman as securities.

0505. Hopkins, Nicholas, Estate of, Dec. 10, 1824, Ann Hopkins appointed admix. with William Stevenson and George Stevenson as securities.

0506. Culbertson, James, Estate of, Dec. 11, 1824, Emily Culbertson appointed admix. with Francis Stewart and Samuel Barr as securities.

0507. Vance, Joseph, Estate of, Dec. 15, 1824, Cinthea Vance appointed admix. with Jeremiah McLene and David Deshler as securities.

0508. Jewett, Elam, Estate of, Dec. 15, 1824, will proven and Benjamin F. Jewett and Alexander Shattuck appointed executors, with Jason Bull and Bellias H. Skeeles as securities.

0509 Dec. 18, 1824, Mathew Matthews appointed guardian of Cyrus aged 11 yrs. and Nancy aged 9 yrs. infant heirs of Eliphat Barker dec'd, with Aurora Buttles and Noah Andrews as securities.

0510. Patterson, Luther, Estate of, Dec. 18, 1824, admrs. Sarah Patterson and Joseph Booth, with George B. Harvey and Thomas Johnston as securities.

0511. Downs, James, Estate of, Dec. 18, 1824, admr. Robert W. Riley, with George Williams and John McElvain as securities. Nov. 21, 1828, admr. cited to appear and show cause why he should not be removed, Apr. 14, 1829 was removed and George Reardon was appointed with John C. Broderick and Robert Brotherton as securities.

0512. Dec. 18, 1824, Andrew Dill appointed guardian of Phoebe, infant heir Mathew Swain dec'd, with William Domigan and Robert Riley as securities. Apr. 12, 1828, court order removed Andrew Dill, appointing Betsy Swain as guardian of Phoebe aged 8 yrs. minor heir of Mathew Swain, with John Young and Andrew Jameson as securities.

0513. Dec. 18, 1824, Charles Loffland appointed guardian of Sally aged 11 and John aged 13 yrs. minor heirs of John Loffland dec'd., with Ralph Osburn and Bela Lathem as securities.

0514. Dec. 18, 1824, David Nelson appointed guardian of David H., under 14 yrs., Martha, Margaret, Caroline M., and Mary Ann all under 12 yrs. of age, minor heirs of Robert Nelson dec'd with William McElvain and Edward Livingston as securities.

0515. Starr, John, Estate of, Dec. 20, 1824, admr. John Starr jr., with Benjamin Platt and John Greenwood as securities. (John Starr was a Revolutionary soldier.)

0516. Colshine, Henry, Estate of, Dec. 20, 1824 admr. Moses Morrill with Frederick Stambaugh and Elijah Marion as securities.

0517. Jerman, William, Estate of, Dec. 21, 1824, admrs. Sally Jerman and Robert Lisle, with Samuel Keys and Riley Jerman as securities.

0518. McCafferty, Thomas, Estate of, admix. Rachel McCafferty, with John Cochran and John Palmer as securities.

0519. Lofland, John, Estate of, Dec. 21, 1824, admr. Charles Lofland with Ralph Osburn and James Robinson as securities.

0520. Mch. 14, 1825, Ruah Dean appointed guardian of Albert aged 20, Joseph aged 18, Mariah aged 16, Alfred aged 18, Charles aged 13, Betsy Ann aged 10, John aged 8, and Catherine Esther aged 5 yrs. minor heirs of Libeas Dean dec'd. with Ebenezer, Samuel and George Dean as securities.

0521. Apr. 3, 1830, Dennis Faris appointed guardian of Charles aged 18, and Betsy Ann aged 15 yrs. heirs of Libeas Dean dec'd. Securities, James Bryden and P. H. Olmstead.

0522. June 20, 1825, David Pugh and Jonathan Whitehead appointed guardian of Joel Sylvester minor heir of Obediah Sylvester (Record from N. J. of suit brought against the estate cost $20.)

0523. Mch. 14, 1825, James Pierce appointed guardian of Samuel Comer aged 18 yrs. minor heir of Samuel Comer dec'r., with Daniel Upson and Demas Adams as securities.

0524. Littlejohn, Jos., Estate of, Sept. 6, 1828, admr. Samuel Dyer, with Jeremiah McLene and David Brooks as securities.

0525. Mch. 14, 1825, John W. Smith appointed guardian of Charles C. Hand with John Greenwood and William Merrion as securities.

0526. Mch. 16, 1825, John Long, Charles Chaney and William Long appointed guardians of Charles aged 12, Phillip H. C. aged 4, John C. aged 8, and Robert aged 6 yrs. minor heirs of John Chaney dec'd.

0527. Mch. 16, 1825, John Young, Charles Chaney and William Long appointed guardians of Anson aged 14 yrs and Candace, minor heirs of John Chaney dec'd.

0528. Galbraith, Mary, Estate of, Dec. 17, 1825, exec. John Galbraith with Robert Lisle and Fergus Morehead as securities.

0529. Mch. 21, 1825, Thomas Ingals appointed guardian of James aged 5 yrs and Irvin aged 3 yrs. minor heirs of James White dec'd. with John Cornell and Nathaniel Penton as securities.

0530. Saul, George, Will of, Mch. 21, 1825, admr. Leonard Saul, with Adam Read and Goetleib Leightenecher as securities.

0531. Frothingham, Deborah, Will of, Mch. 22, 1825, exec. Stephen Frothingham with Recompense Stansbury, Jacob Fairfield and Henry Ogden.

0532. Sharp, Andrew, Estate of, Mch. 22, 1825, admr. John Cornell, with Benjamin Sells and Thomas Johnson as securities.

0533. Smith, David, Estate of, Mch. 22, 1825, admrs. William Thomas and Andrew Dill, with John McElvain and John Kile as securities.

0534. Bennett, John, Estate of, admr. William Godman Mch. 22, 1825, with Nathan Bennett and George Sharp as securities.

0535. Clendening, John, Estate of, Mch. 23, 1825, admr. Jonathan Clendening with John Hanson and David Pugh as securities.

0536. Crumb, Anthony, Estate of, Mch. 23, 1825, admr. George Smith, with Abraham Crumb and Jacob Crumb.

0537. Hays, George, Estate of. Mch. 23, 1825, admix. Mary Hays with John Greer and John Champe as securities.

0538. Mch. 23, 1825, David Nelson appointed guardian of Nancy Nelson aged 16 yrs. minor heir of Robert Nelson dec'd, with William McElvain and Edward Livingston as securities.

0539. Lawrence, Isaac, Estate of, Apr. 14, 1825, admr. George W. Williams, with Christian Heyle and Robert Brotherton as securities.

0540. Menely, Jesse, Estate of, June 20, 1825, admrs. Hannah Menely and Joseph S. B. Menely. Security, Reuben Golliday. (Jesse Menely was a Revolutionary soldier).

0541. June 20, 1825, George Bishop appointed guardian of Jeremiah Vandemark aged 10 yrs. minor heir of Jeremiah Vandemark dec'd. with John Sharp and Andrew Cramer as securities.

0542. Aug. 24, 1829, Daniel Vandemark chosen guardian by Jeremiah aged 14 yrs. minor of Jeremiah Vandemark dec'd. Securities, Jacob Gander and Isaiah Jacob Chandler.

SETTLEMENTS OF ESTATES

ABSTRACTS OF FRANKLIN COUNTY, OHIO RECORDS

MRS. JOHN M. TITUS

0543. Ogden, Elias, Estate of, June, 20, 1825, admix. Hulda Ogden, with David Pugh and Jonathan Whitehead as securities.

0544. June 20, 1825, Jacob Gundy appointed guardian of Polly aged 15 yrs. minor heir of John Campbell dec'd. Securities, Daniel Links and Jonathan Couch.

0545. Shofe, Elizabeth, Estate of, June 23, 1825, exr. appointed, Daniel Stimmell; securities, Jacob Plum and Abraham Shofe. Apprs. George Gearman, Andrew Barr and Thomas Moore.

0546. Shofe, Guardianship, June 23, 1825, Michael Stimmell appointed guardian of Polly aged 12 yrs., and chosen as guardian by Betsy aged 14, Joseph aged 16, Henry aged 18, and John aged 19 yrs. minor heirs of John Shofe dec'd. Securities, Jacob Plum and Samuel Riley.

0547. Haven, William, Estate of, June 29, 1825, Admr., appointed, William Headley. Court ruled to Elizabeth Waggoner (late Elizabeth Havens) and husband Martin Waggoner to show why they should not administer on said estate. Securities, Jonathan Whitehead and Michael Stagg jr. Apprs. Lewis Martins, Abraham Hamaker and Thomas Havens.

0548. Littlejohn, Guardianship, June 27, 1825, James Gardiner chosen as guardian by James aged 14 yrs. and appointed guardian of Abraham aged 12, Isabella aged 9, William aged 7, and Alice aged 3 yrs. minor heirs of Joseph Littlejohn. Securities, Benjamin Foster and Isaac Griffith.

0549. Coleshine, Guardianship of, June 28, 1825, Adam Reed, appointed guardian of Margaret aged 7 yrs. 3 mos. and Jackson aged 4 yrs. infant heirs of John Coleshine, dec'd. Securities, Francis Stewart and Abraham J. McDowell.

0550. Coleshine, Guardianship of, May 11, 1835, Thomas McCauley guardian by choice of Jackson aged 14 yrs. minor heir of John Coleshine, dec'd. Securities, Augustus Platt and Moyler Northup. Accounts and vouchers referred to Thomas Sparrow, Master Commissioner.

0551. McCormick, Guardianship of, June 25, 1825, James Stagg appointed guardian of Caty aged 14 yrs. minor heir of William McCormick, dec'd. Securities, William Carr and Jonathan Whitehead.

0553. McCormick, Guardianship of, Dec. 7, 1830, Moses R. Spurgeon appointed guardian of John, minor, heir of William McCormick, dec'd. Securities, George McCormick and William Armstrong.

0553. Wilcox, Simeon, Estate of, June 29, 1825, admr. appointed, John B. Beard. Securities, Tracy Wilcox and Elam Barker. Apprs., Homer Tuller, Joshua Gale and Belial Skeele.

0554. Kammel, John, Estate of June 30, 1825, Admr. appointed, Abram J. McDowell. Securities, Orris Parish and James C. Cory. New apprs., appointed Aug. 6, 1825, Apprs., Jacob Grubb, Adam Brotherlin and Thomas Reynolds.

0555. Evans, Guardianship of, July 1, 1825, Ralph Osborn chosen as guardian by Richard aged 15 yrs. on Apr. 25 next, minor heir of Richard Evans, dec'd. Securities, Orris Parish and John Cummings.

0556. Smith, Guardianship of, July 1, 1825, Sarah Smith appointed guardian of Josiah aged 10 yrs. infant heir of William Smith, dec'd. Securities, John Cummings and Ralph Osborn.

0557. Smith, Guardianship of, Sept. 30, 1831, Mease Smith chosen as guardian by Josiah aged 16 yrs. minor heir of William Smith, dec'd. Securities, James Hoge and Phineas B. Wilcox.

0558. Smith, Guardianship of, Sept. 20, 1831, Phineas B. Wilcox appointed guardian of Angeline aged 9 yrs. infant heir of William Smith, dec'd. Securities Nathan B. Kelley and Joseph Hunter.

0558½. Ross, Christena, Estate of, July 2, 1825, Admr. appointed, Samuel C. Andrews. Securities, Orris Parish and Phineas B. Wilcox. Apprs. Christian Heyl, Robert Brotherton and Francis Stewart.

0559. Evans, Harvey D., Estate of, July 16, 1925, Admrs. appointed, William Doherty and William Neil. Securities, Ralph Osborn and Lyne Starling. Sept. 1829, Mease Smith was appointed Admr. with Joseph Ridgeway, Ralph Osborn and Jeremiah MeLene as securities. Apprs. Francis Stewart, W. S. Martin and D. W. Deshler.

0560. Bigelow, Daniel, Estate of, July 23, 1825, Admr. appointed, Thomas Johnston. Securities, John Greenwood and George Anthony. Apprs. William Long, David Smith and Thomas Johnston.

0561. Seeds, James, Estate of, Jackson twp. July 16, 1825, Admrs. appointed, Robert and William Seeds. Rule to Sarah Seeds to show cause why she should not be appointed Admix. Security, Philo H. Olmstead. Apprs. John Fisher, John Kious and Woodbury Coonrod.

0562. Johnson, John, Estate of, Aug. 6, 1825, Admr. appointed, Arthur O'Harra. Securities, Francis Stewart and Robert Brotherton. Apprs. Joseph Hunter, Andrew McElvain and Joseph M. Hunter, Jr. Mentions Margaret, wife of the dec'd.

0563. Marshall, James, Estate of, Franklin twp., Aug. 16, 1825, Admr. appointed, John Starr. Securities, James O'Harra and John Hunter. Apprs. Joseph Hunter, Sr., Joseph Hunter, Jr., and Andrew McElvain. Mentions wife Charity Marshall.

0564. Perrin, Mary Ann, Estate of, Truro twp., Sept. 16, 1825, Admrs. appointed, John Long and Jonathan Perrin. Securities, Jonathan McComb and Samuel Davidson. Apprs. Zachariah Paul, William Patterson and George Powell.

0565. Stagg, Michael, Estate of, Jefferson twp. Oct. 8, 1825, Admix. appointed, Lydia Stagg. Securities, David Smith and Joseph Edgar. Apprs. J. H. Smith, Andrew Allison and Jonathan Whitehead.

0566. Cochran, John, Estate of, Truro twp. Oct. 8, 1825, Admix. appointed, Elizabeth Cochran. Securities, Solomon Barrack and John Hutson. Apprs. John French, George Graham and John Coons.

SETTLEMENTS OF ESTATES
ABSTRACTS OF FRANKLIN COUNTY, OHIO RECORDS
MRS. JOHN M. TITUS

0567. Barr, Peter, Estate of, Oct. 8, 1825, Admr. appointed, Adam Brotherton. Securities, Jacob Ebey and Jacob Grubb. Apprs. Reuben Golliday, John P. Robinson and Lewis Risley.

0568. Lake, Guardianship of, Dec. 12, 1825, Thomas Vause chosen as guardian by William aged 14 yrs. on Sept. 26 last, minor heir Thomas Lake dec'd. Securities, Joseph Ridgeway and Hugh H. Giles.

0569. Moore, Benjamin, Estate of, Blendon twp., Dec. 12, 1825, Admr. appointed, Abram Phelps. Securities, Edward Phelps and Chandler Rogers. Apprs. Francis C. Olmstead, George Osborn and Isaac Greenwood. (Benjamin Moore was a Revolutionary soldier).

0570. Heindle, Guardianship of, Dec. 12, 1825, George Wightman chosen as guardian by Magdalena aged 19 yrs. on June 1, 1825, minor heir of Adam Heindle dec'd. Securities, Jacob Heindle, Daniel Helsell and Nicholas Helsell.

0571. Howey, James, Estate of, Dec. 12, 1825, Admrs. appointed, Sarah Howey and James Mitchell. Securities, William Mitchell, Joseph Hunter and Charles Mitchell. Apprs. Elisha Hays, Joseph Hunter and Brice Hays.

0572. Cochran, Guardianship of, Dec. 13, 1825, Henry Johnson chosen as guardian by Ezra aged 15 yrs. on Aug. 13, 1825 minor heir of John Cochran dec'd. Securities, Williams, Henry Johnson and Matthew Crawford.

0573. Long, Guardianship of, Dec. 14, 1825, Percival Adams appointed guardian of Hopkins aged 4 yrs. infant heir of Henry Long dec'd. Securities, John Ransburgh and Andrew Dill.

0574. Davidson, Guardianship of, Dec. 14, 1825, Joseph Davidson appointed guardian of Mary aged 9 yrs. infant heir of Joseph Davidson dec'd. Securities, Reuben Golliday and Jacob Ebey.

0575. Evans, Guardianship of, Dec. 19, 1825, Jacob Waggoner chosen as guardian by John aged 17 yrs. on Sept. 8, 1825, minor heir of Mark Evans dec'd. Securities, Peter Sells and John H. Smith.

0576. Clark, Samuel, Estate of, Jan. 14, 1826, Admrs. appointed, John Clark and Samuel M. White. Apprs. William Brown, Woolery Coonrod and William Miller. Securities, John M. White, Stewart Bailey, William C. Duff.

0577. Christy, Henry, Estate of, Dublin, Dec. 19, 1825, Admr. appointed Edward R. Christy. Securities, Chandler Rogers and Jesse F. Dixon. Apprs. Charles Rogers and Jesse Dixon.

0578. Boothe, Joseph, Estate of, Dec. 19, 1825, Admr. appointed, William T. Martin. Securities, George B. Harvey and Thomas Johnston. Apprs. John Cutler, John Greenwood and Michael Dulty.

0579. Moore, Simeon, Estate of, Blendon twp. Dec. 19, 1825, Admr. appointed, Simeon Moore jr. Securities, Nelson Putenney and and Samuel McDonald. Apprs. Gideon W. Hart, Isaac Harrison and Charles P. Hempstead. (Simeon Moore was a Revolutionary soldier).

0580. Rarey, Charles, Estate of, Madison twp. Jan. 14, 1826, Exrs. appointed, Adam and Charles Rarey. Securities, Samuel D. Havely and William Rarey. Apprs. John Huston, Amaziah Hutchinson and Andrew Little.

0581. Dearduff, Isaac, Estate of, Perry twp. Jan. 16, 1826, Exr. appointed, Daniel Beard. Securities, David Smith, John Friend and Peter Bower. Apprs. William Davis, G. Thomas and Noah Clark.

0582. Zinn, Phillip, Estate of, Mch. 23, 1826, Admrs. appointed, David W. Deshler and Henry Zinn. Securities, Gottileb Leightnecker and Jeremiah McLene. Apprs. John Wilson, Robert Armstrong and George B. Howey.

0583. Hendren, William D. Estate of, Madison twp. Apr. 10, 1826. Admr. appointed, William H. Richardson. Securities, William Doherty and Adam Rarey. Apprs. John Guffy and Jesse Blair.

0584. Johnston, Isaac, Estate of, Apr. 10, 1826, Exrx, Sarah Johnston. Securities Hugh Iams and Henry Johnston. Apprs. Andrew Smiley and James Price.

0585. Slusher, Guardianship of, Apr. 10, 1826, John Nothstine appointed guardian of Catherine aged 4 yrs. 6 mo. and Susan aged 3 yrs. 3 mo. infant heirs of Daniel Slusher dec'd. Securities, Christian Sarber and Henry Hill.

0586. Rager, George, Estate of, Apr. 12, 1826, Admr. appointed, Anthony Bole. Securities, Joseph Bell and James Cutler. Apprs. Lynd L. Latmore, Ephraim Fisher and David Thomas.

0587. Agler, Guardianship of, Apr. 15, 1826, William Shaw chosen as guardian by William aged 20 years., Margaret aged 18 yrs. minor heirs and Lewis aged 15 yrs. Elizabeth aged 12 yrs. and Frederick aged 8 yrs. infant heirs of Frederick Agler dec'd. Securities Arthur O'Harra and Francis Olmstead.

0588. Fulton, Guardianship of, Apr. 18, 1826, John Smith chosen as guardian by Alexander aged 18 yrs., Samuel aged 17 yrs. and David aged 15 yrs. minor heirs, James aged 9 yrs. infant heir of Hugh Fulton dec'd. Sceurities, Alexander and Samuel Henderson.

0589. Greer, Guardianship of, Apr. 19, 1826 Aurora Buttles chosen as guardian by Urial O. aged 17 yrs. minor heir of Joseph Greer dec'd. Securities, Daniel Upson and Bulkley Comstock.

0590. Clark, Guardianship of, Apr. 18, 1826, Gilliam Demorst appointed guardian of Ann Maria aged 5 yrs. and Lucinda aged 3 yrs. infant heirs of Charles Clark dec'd. Securities, Silas Smith, Nicholas Demorst, John Goetchius and William Patrick.

0591. Lord, Thomas, Estate of, Apr. 20, 1826, Admr. appointed, John McElvain. Securities, James K. Corey and Abram McDowell. Apprs. D. W. Deshler, Peleg Sisson and Robert Brotherton.

0592. Johnston, Guardianship of, Apr. 26, 1826, Margaret Johnston appointed guardian of Richard aged 7 yrs., Ann, 5 yrs. Jane, 3 yrs. and John W. aged 1 yr. infant heirs of John Johnston dec'd. Securities, James and Thomas Woods.

0593. Long, Guardianship of, Apr. 27, 1826, Robert Taylor appointed guaridan of Robert, Henry B. Edward and George, infant heirs of Matthew Long dec'd. Securities A. V. Taylor and Zachariah Paul.

SETTLEMENTS OF ESTATES
ABSTRACTS OF FRANKLIN COUNTY, OHIO RECORDS
MRS. JOHN M. TITUS

0594. Culbertson, Andrew, Estate of, Apr. 28, 1826, Admix. Esther Culbertson, with Andrew Dill, William W. Shannon, Nathaniel Smith and John Emerick as Securities. Apr. 15, 1828, order removing Admix. and David W. Deshler was appointed instead. Apprs. George W. Williams, William Stewart and Moses Morrill.

0595. Postle, Gabriel, Estate of, May 29, 1826, Admr. appointed, John Postle. Securities, Israel P. Brown and John Hunter. Apprs. Reuben Golliday, William Wilcox and Samuel Hunter.

0596. Watts, John, Estate of, June 24, 1826, Admr. appointed, Gilliam Demorst. Securities Stewart Bailey and John Goetchius. Apprs. Richard House, Samuel M. White, John Goldsmith and Samuel Hunter.

0597. Shepherd, John, Estate of, June 24, 1826, Admr. appointed, Robert Armstrong. Securities, John Armstrong, and Robert Brotherton. Apprs. Amaziah Hutchinson, Robert H. Clay and Robert Elliot.

0598. Kimmons, Robert, Estate of, June 24, 1826, Admr. appointed, James Kimmons. Securities. Henry Brown, and Abraham Romaine. Apprs. Robert Cade, William Beatty and Josiah Brown.

0599. Backus, Thomas, Estate of, June 24, 1826, Admr. appointed, Abram J. McDowell. Securities, Henry Brown and Robert Brotherton. Apprs. Francis Stewart, Eli W. Gwynne and Lincoln Goodale.

0600. McAfferty, Guardianship of, Aug. 15, 1826, John French chosen as guardian by Thomas aged 18 yrs. minor heir and Nancy aged 12 yrs., James, 10 yrs., Hiram 8 yrs. and Almire 8 yrs. infant heirs of Thomas McAfferty dec'd. Securities, Abithar Taylor and John Iams.

0601. Turney, Guardianship of, Aug. 18, 1826, Jesse Baughman chosen as guardian by Daniel aged 18 yrs. and George 15 yrs. minor heirs and John infant heir of John Turney dec'd. Securities, George Baughman and Andrew Dill.

0602. Garnett, Ann, Estate of, Queens Co. Md., Aug. 18, 1826, will and accompanying certificate recorded. (Will printed in Vol. I, No. 3, O. G. Quarterly).

0603. Davidson, guardianship of, Aug. 18, 1826, Jacob Gander chosen as guardian by Abednigo aged 17 yrs. minor heir of Adonijah Davidson dec'd. Securities, Samuel Barr and Andrew Dill.

0604. Hendron, Guardianship of, Aug. 21, 1826, Nancy Hendron chosen as guardian by Thomas aged 20 yrs. and Daniel, 16 yrs. minor heirs, and Samuel, 14 yrs., William, 12 yrs., Sarah Ann, 7 yrs. in Dec., Robert 4 yrs., and Rebecca, 6 mos. infant heirs of William D. Hendron dec'd. Securities, Emmor Case and John Swisher.

0605. Hendron, Guardianship of, Aug. 25, 1826, Nancy Hendron chosen as guardian by Louisa aged 18 yrs. minor heir of William D. Hendron dec'd. Securities, Emmor Case and John Swisher.

0606   Anderson, John, Estate of, Aug. 22, 1826, Admr. appointed, Thomas Anderson. Securities, Westley Cochran and Joseph Barker. Apprs., Simeon Cochran, James Gardiner and Baltzer Mantle.

06 7.   Greer, Guardianship of, Aug. 22, 1826, Percival Adams chosen as guardian by Thomas aged 19 yrs. minor heir of Nancy Greer, widow, dec'd. Securities, Michael Fisher and John Colcman.

0608.   Ferguson, Guardianship of, Aug. 23, 1826, Samuel Dyer appointed guardian of James aged 12 yrs. infant heir of James Ferguson dec'd. Securities, Benjamin Foster and David Dearduff.

0609.   Sharp, Guardianship of, Aug. 25, 1826, Clarissa Sharp chosen as guardian by Sally aged 17 yrs., Andrew, 14 yrs. and Parthena, 10 yrs. minor heirs of Andrew Sharp dec'd. Securities, Abraham Jaycocks and Matthew Westervelt.

0610.   Fishel, Guardianship of, Aug. 23, 1826, John Fishel chosen as guardian by Mary aged 16 yrs and Michael, 14 yrs. minor heirs. Rachel, Margaret, Daniel and Caty, all under 12 yrs of age, infant heirs of John Fishel dec'd. Securities, Woolery Coonrod and Peleg Sisson.

0611.   Watts, Guardianship of, Aug. 26, 1826, Stewart Bailey and William Lusk appointed guardian of William aged 10 yrs., Catherine, 8 yrs., John, 6 yrs., Hiram, 5 yrs. and Sarah, 1 yr. infant heirs of John Watts dec'd. Securities, Nicholas Dem orest and Samuel Hunter.

0612.   Watts, Guardianship of, Dec. 21, 1826, John Goetchius chosen as guardian by Nicholas aged 20 yrs., Joseph, 18 yrs. and Maria, 15 yrs. minor heirs of John Watts dce'd. Securities. Charles Harrison and John Briggs.

0613.   Postle, Guardianship of, Aug. 26, 1826, Stephen Postle appointed guardian of Lewis aged 4 yrs. infant heir of Gabriel Postle dec'd. Securities, John Postle and Reuben Golliday.

0614.   Postle, Guardianship of, Aug. 26, 1826, Joseph Cade Young appointed guardian of Franklin aged 2 yrs. infant heir of Gabriel Postle dec'd. Securities, Reuben Golliday and John Postle.

0615.   Postle, Guardianship of, Dec. 19, 1826, Mary Postle appointed guardian of Jane aged 1 yr. infant heir of Gabriel Postle dec'd. Securities, Woolery Coonrod and David Dearduff.

0616.   Case, Alice, Estate of, Clinton twp. Nov. 30, 1826, exr. appointed, Aurora Buttles. Securities, Matthew Matthews and William Case. Apprs. Aristarchus Walker and David Dearduff.

0617.   Hunter, John, Estate of, Clinton twp. Nov. 30, 1826, Admr. appointed, Charles Hunter. Securities, Joseph Hunter and Robinson P. Hunter. Apprs. Thomas Moore, Peter Carson and Samuel Henderson.

0618.   Smith Sarah, Estate of, Plain twp. Nov. 30, 1826, Admr. appointed, Daniel Smith. Securities, Joseph Edgar and Abraham Stagg. Apprs. Abraham Williams, John Daniel and Andrew Allison.

0619.   White, Guardianship of, Dec. 11, 1826, Abraham Stagg chosen as guardian by Catherine Adaline aged 17 yrs. minor heir of John White dec'd. Securities, Aurora Buttles and David Smith.

0620. Hunter, Guardianship of, Dec. 15, 1826, Andrew McElvain appointed guardian of Joseph V. aged 11 yrs. and Samuel, 9 yrs. infant heirs of John Hunter dec'd. Securities, Joseph Hunter and Robert Brotherton.

0621. Hunter, Guardianship of, Dec. 18, 1826, Charles Hunter appointed guardian of William infant heir of John Hunter dec'd. Securities, William Hunter and Andrew McElvain.

0622. Taylor. Matthew, Estate of. Marion twp. Dec. 20, 1826, Exrs. were Ann Taylor and William Sheilds. Securities, John Cunning and John Armstrong. Apprs. William Peterson, John Long and Zachariah Paul.

0623. Moore, Guardianship of, Dec. 20, 1826, Samuel Andrews chosen as guardian by Washington aged 17 yrs. and Jane, 15 yrs. minor heirs of Thomas Moore dec'd. Securities, Thomas Moore and Orris Parish.

0624. Truman, Guardianship of, Dec. 20, 1826, John Greenwood chosen as guardian by Maria aged 16 yrs. minor heir of Charles Truman dec'd. Securities, John Jones and Joshua Folsom.

0625. Truman, Guardianship of, Dec. 20, 1826, John Jones appointed guardian of Esther aged 14 yrs. infant heir of Charles Truman dec'd. Securities, John Greenwood and Bela Lathem.

0626. Truman, Guardianship of, Dec. 20, 1826, Robert Armstrong appointed guardian of Hannah aged 12 yrs. infant heir of Charles Truman dec'd. Securities, not given.

0627. Truman, Guardianship of, Dec. 20, 1826, Orris Parish appointed guardian of Sally Ann aged 8 yrs. infant heir of Charles Truman. Securities, Thomas C. Flannery and Samuel Andrews.

0628. Gilbert, Guardianship of, Dec. 20, 1826, Thomas Moore appointed guardian of John aged 14 yrs. infant heir of John Gilbert dec'd. Securities, Joseph Moore and Lewis Ringle.

0629. Moore, Guardianship of, Dec. 20, 1826, Samuel C. Andrews chosen as guardian by Mary minor heir of Thomas Moore dec'd. Securities, Thomas Moore and Orris Parish.

0630. Sullivant, Guardianship of, Dec. 20, 1826, Isaac Minor chosen as guardian by Michael aged 19 yrs. minor heir of Lucas Sullivant dec'd. Securities, Thomas Moore and Gustavus Swan.

0631. Stotts, Uriah, Estate of, Dec. 21, 1826, Admr. appointed. Abram Stotts. Securities, Jacob Goodhue and Robert Pollock. Apprs. Moses Morrill, William Merion and George W. Williams.

0632. McGown, Olive, Estate of, Dec. 21, 1826, Admr. appointed, Hugh McMasters. Securities, Jacob Goodhue and John Cutler. Apprs. Abram Stotts, James Cherry and Andrew Backus.

0633. Case, Guardianship of, Dec. 21, 1826, Matthew Mathews appointed guardian of Douglas aged 8 yrs. infant heir of Calvin Case dec'd. Securities, Aurora Buttles and Phineas B. Wilcox.

0634. Cashman, Christian, Estate of, Hamilton twp. Dec. 21, 1826, Admr. appointed Thomas Johnston. Securities, Archibald Benfield and George Cashman. Apprs. Percival Adams, James Lindsay and Michael Stimmell.

0635. Campbell, John, Estate of, June 30, 1825, Admr. appointed, Abram J. McDowell. Securities, James K. Corey and Orris Farish. Apprs. Jacob Grubb, Thomas Reynolds and Adam Brotherton. Mentions wife, Eleanor Campbell.

195

0636. Kerr, Guardianship of, Dec. 22, 1826, Charles Hinkle appointed guardian of John about 6 yrs. infant heir of John Kerr dec'd. Securities, William Doherty and James Robinson. Apr. 10, 1827, guardian removed, and Joseph Ridgeway appointed with John Cutler and Otis Parish as securities.

0637. Kerr,, Guardianship of, Dec. 22, 1826, Mary Kerr appointed guardian of Mary aged 15 yrs. infant heir of John Kerr dec'd. Securities, James Roninson and William Doherty.

0638. Kerr, Guardianship of, June 29, 1830, Joseph Ridgeway appointed guardian of John aged 10 yrs. infant heir of John Kerr dec'd. Securities, James Robinson and William Doherty.

0639. Huffman, James, Estate of, Dec. 25, 1826, Admr. appointed, Peter Rodes (Roth). Securities, Jacob Huffman and Jacob Chandler. Apprs. William Miller, William Smith and Richard Howe.

0640. Dunn, Caleb, Estate of, Dec. 25, 1826, Admr. appointed, Percival Adams. Securities, Arthur O'Harra and Archibald Benfield. Apprs. David Spangler, Fergus Whitehead and James Lindsay. (Hamilton twp.)

0641. Corey, James K. Estate of, Jan. 10, 1827, Admix. appointed, Maria Corey. Securities Phineas B. Wilcox and Abram J. McDowell. Apprs., William Neil, Orris Parish and William Doherty.

0642. Turney, Daniel, Estate of, Jan. 10, 1827, Admix. appointed, Samuel Denny. Securities, Jeremiah Minor and Ralph Osborn. Apprs. James Robinson, Robert Brotherton and John Cunning.

0643. Thrall, Joel, Estate of, Feb. 12, 1827, Admix. appointed, Rebecca Thrall. Securities, Matthew Crawford and Lyman Thrall. Apprs. William Graham, James McCray and Horace L. Thrall.

SETTLEMENTS OF ESTATES
ABSTRACTS OF FRANKLIN COUNTY, OHIO RECORDS
MRS. JOHN M. TITUS

0644. Gillett, Asa, Estate of, Worthington, Feb. 27, 1827, Admrs. appointed, Aurora Buttles and Rensellar J. Cowles. Securities, Demas Adams and Peleg Sisson. Apprs. Rodney Comstock, Clark Thompson and Isaac Hamlin.

0645. Baker, John, Estate of, Feb. 27, 1827, Exrx., Ann Baker. Securities, William Merion and Thomas Templeton. Apprs. George W. Williams, Hugh McElhaney and John Shannon.

0646. Vandenberg, Guardianship of, Apr. 9, 1827, Matthew Matthews appointed guardian of Elliot aged 11 yrs. and Louisa aged 4 yrs. infant heirs of Jasper Vandenberg dec'd. Securities, Phineas B. Wilcox and Benjamin Sells.

0647. Jeffords, Guardianship of, Apr. 9, 1827, Matthew Matthews appointed guardian of Caroline aged 11 yrs. and Mary aged 9 yrs. infant heirs of John Jeffords dec'd. Securities, Benjamin Sells and Phineas B. Wilcox.

0648. Davis, Guardianship of, Apr. 10, 1827, David Williams chosen as guardian by John aged 17 yrs. and William, 15 yrs. minor heirs and James, 14 yrs., Alfred 11 yrs. and Isaac Newton, 9 yrs. infant heirs of Ishmael Davis dec'd. Securities, Jacob Plumb and Lyne Starling.

0649. Hays, Guardianship of, Apr. 12, 1827, Horace Wolcott chosen as guardian by Samuel aged 17 yrs. minor heir of George Hays dec'd. Securities, Charles Lofland and John B. Broderick.

0650. Hayden, John Estate of, Apr. 13, 1827, Admr. appointed, David Hayden. Securities, James Moore and Robert Ross. Apprs. Adam Blount and James Boyd. (Wife Sarah).

0651. Forrer, John, Estate of, Apr. 16, 1827, Admr. appointed, Joseph Ridgeway. Securities, William Doherty and David W. Deshler. Apprs. Orris Parish, Otis Crosby and William Neil.

0652. Delashmutt, Guardianship of, George W. Williams, appointed guardian of William aged 13 yrs., Harriet, 11 yrs., Porter, 9 yrs. and Van, 7 yrs. infant heirs of John K. Delashmutt dec'd. Securities, Jeremiah McLene and Lyne Starling.

0653. Badger, Robert, Estate of, Jackson twp. June 18, 1827, Admr. appointed, Archilbald J. Badger. Securities, William and James Badger. Apprs. William Miller. John Goldsmith and

0654. Nashee, George, Estate of, July 18, 1827, Admr. appointed, John Bailhace and David W. Deshler. Securities, William Doherty and Moylan Northup. Apprs. Nathaniel McLean, Jeremiah McLene and Zachariah Mills. (Jane K. Nashee, wife).

0655. Sherman, Jonathan, Estate of, Sept. 3, 1827, Admr. appointed, Aurora Buttles. Securities, Phineas B. Wilcox and Orris Parish. Apprs. C. H. Wetmore, Samuel Abbott and E. Washburn.

0656. Putman, Guardianship of, Sept. 3, 1827, Demming L. Rathbone appointed guardian of Julia Putman Rathbone aged 3 yrs. infant heir of Aaron W. Putman dec'd. Securities, Philo H. Olmstead and William H. Doherty.

0657. Long, Thomas, Estate of, Madison twp. Sept. 6, 1827, Admr. appointed, William Patterson. Securities, John Swisher and John Wright. Apprs. John Lang, George Kalb and Joseph Wright.

0658. Badger, Guardianship of, Sept. 10, 1827, Arthur Park appointed guardian of May aged 2 yrs. infant heir of Robert Badger dec'd. Securities, Arthur O'Harra and Robert Breckenridge.

0659. Badger, Guardianship of, Sept. 11, 1827, Robert Breckenridge appointed aged 6 yrs. Aug. 3, 1827, and Sarah Ann, 4 yrs. oin Sept. 15, 1827, infant heirs of Robert Badger dec'd. Securities, Samuel Shannon and Benjamin Sells.

0660. Lawson, John P., Estate of, Sept. 10, 1827, Exrs. appointed, Samuel Cope and Peter Lawson. Securities, John Bishop and Ebenezer Goodrich. Sept. 4, 1829, Orris Parrish appointed Admr., with Elson Wilson and Thompson Bull as securities. Apprs. Lyman Andrews, Nathan Carpenter and Benjamin Bartholomew.

0661. Saul, Leonard, Estate of, Sept. 10, 1827, Admrs. appointed, Samuel Saul and Andrew Read. Securities, Isaac Taylor and David Nelson. Apprs. William Dalzell, John and William Barr.

0662. Harvey, Sarah, Estate of, Pleasant twp. Sept. 10, 1827, Admr. appointed, Joseph Chenowith. Securities, Samuel Dyer and John Lewis. Apprs., Josiah Browning and Elijah Chenowith.

0663. Nashee, Guardianship of, Sept. 11, 1827, James Hoge chosen as guardian by Sarah W. aged 16 yrs. on Mch. 2, 1827, and Esther A., 14 yrs. on Dec. 15, 1826, minor heirs of George Nashee dec'd. Securities, William Doherty and David W. Deshler.

0664. Crosby, William, Estate of, Sept. 11, 1827, Admr. appointed, William Godman. Securities, Benjamin Sells and David Smith. Apprs., David W. Deshler, William McElvain and Robert Brotherton.

0665. Smith, Joseph, Estate of, Sept. 11, 1827, Exr. appointed, Abraham Smith. Securities, David and John Smith. Apprs., Uriah Clark, Joseph H. Marsh and Daniel Beard. (Perry twp).

0666. Mahan, Neil, Estate of, Hamilton twp. Sept. 11, 1827, Admr. appointed, James Mahan. Securities, John Stambaugh and George Clickenger. Apprs., George W. Williams, Thomas Johnston and Samuel M. Kilgore. (Neil Mahan was a Revolutionary soldier).

0667. Dill, Guardianship of, Sept. 13, 1827, Andrew Dill chosen as guardian by John A. aged 20 yrs., Andrew C., 17 yrs. and Esther, 15 yrs; appointed guardian of Isabella, 12 yrs. and Thomas 8 yrs. minor heirs of Andrew Dill dec'd. Securities, Jeremiah McLene and Frederick Stombaugh.

0668. Dill, Guardianship of, May 19, 1832, Thomas Moore appointed guardian of Thomas aged 14 yrs. next Jan. infant heir of Andrew Dill dec'd. Securities, Mease Smith and Robert Brotherton.

0669. Duff, William, Estate of, Jackson twp. Admr. appointed, Stewart Bailey. Securities, William Brown and John Kile. Apprs., Nicholas Clabaugh, William Miller and John Streacher.

0670. Topping, Miranda, Estate of, Sept. 13, 1827, Admr. appointed. Aurora Buttles. Securities, Recompense Stansberry and Robert Brotherton. Apprs., R. W. Cowles, John W. Ladd and James Russell.

SETTLEMENTS OF ESTATES
ABSTRACTS OF FRANKLIN COUNTY, OHIO RECORDS
MRS. JOHN M. TITUS

0671. Turner, John W., Estate of, Truro twp. Oct. 27, 1827, Admrs. appointed, Jonathan McComb and Adam Turner. Securities, Samuel McComb and Elijah Glover. Apprs., John Barr, Zachariah Paul and Daniel Whitsel.

0672. Ferguson, Thomas, Estate of, Pleasant twp. Nov. 22, 1827, Admr. appointed, William Bigger. Securities, John Bigger and Thomas Roberts. Apprs., Charles Hunter, James Walker and Jacob Gundy.

0673. Athey, Elijah, Estate of, Pleasant twp. Dec. 11, 1827, Admr. appointed, John Buck. Securities, John Tomlinson and John Ross. Apprs., Jacob Gundy, Thomas Roberts and James Gardiner.

0674. Zinn, Guardianship of, Dec. 11, 1827, Elizabeth Zinn appointed guardian of Adam aged 15 yrs. and 43 das., Nancy, 11 yrs., Peter, about 7 yrs. and Catherine about 3 yrs. infant heirs of Phillip Zinn dec'd. Securities, D. W. Deshler and Gottileb Leightnecker.

0675. Lampson, William K., Estate of, Mch. 23, 1827, Admr. appointed, Nathan Lampson. Securities, Evan Gwynne and Joshua Baldwin. Sept. 1832, Mease Smith appointed Admr. with P. B. Wilcox and J. R. Swan as securities. Apprs., Matthew Matthews, John Greenwood and Thomas Wood. (Mentions wife, Sarah).

0676. Cunning, Samuel, Estate of, Dec. 18, 1827, Admix, Mary Ann Cunning. Securities, James Hoge and Ralph Osborn. Apprs. Robert Brotherton, John Wilson and Samuel Shannon.

0677. Saul, Guardianship of, Apr. 8, 1827, Mary Saul appointed guardian of Aaron aged 11 mos. infant heir of Leonard Saul dec'd. Securities, G. Leightnecker and William Allman.

0678. Saul, Guardianship of, June 30, 1830, George Saul appointed guardian of Aaron aged 3 yrs. infant heir of Leonard Saul dec'd. Securities, Christopher S. White and William Allman.

0679. Olmstead, Francis, Estate of, Blendon twp. Jan. 1828, Admr. appointed, Aurora J. Olmstead. Securities, Simeon Moore and Gideon W. Hart. Apprs., Abram Phelps, John Bellington and Isaac Griswold. (Francis Olmstead was a Revolutionary soldier.)

0680. Ferguson, John, Estate of, Pleasant twp., Apr. 11, 1828, Admr. appointed, James Walker. Securities, David Smith and John Foster. Apprs., Charles Hunter, James Walker and Jacob Gundy.

0681. Ferguson, Thomas, Estate of, Apr. 14, 1829, Admr. appointed, James Gardiner. Securities, William Ferguson and John Calumber. Apprs., Jacob Gundy, James Walker and Charles Hunter.

0682. Kooser, Guardianship of, Apr. 11, 1828, Elizabeth Kooser appointed guardian of Sarah aged 14 yrs., Margaret, 7 yrs., and Daniel 6 yrs. infant heirs of Daniel Kooser dec'd. Securities, Peter Putman and Gottileb Leighnecker.

0683. Kooser, Guardianship of, Apr. 11, 1828, Gottileb Leightnecker appointed as guardian of Frederick L. and Gottileb both aged 11 yrs. infant heirs of Daniel Kooser dec'd. Securities, Henry Brown and Orris Parish.

0684. Kooser, Guardianship of, Apr. 12, 1828, Gottileb Leightnecker chosen as guardian by John aged 18 yrs. minor heir of Daniel Kooser dec'd. Securities, Henry Brown and Orris Parish.

0685. Powell, William, Estate of, Apr. 11, 1828, Admrs. appointed, John Dukes and Mary Powell. Securities, David Spangler and Francis Stewart. Apprs., Henry Bartel and David Williams.

0686. Smart, Isaac, Estate of, Hamilton twp. Apr. 13, 1828, Admr. appointed, Joseph Fisher. Securities, Moses Morrill and Samuel Shannon. Apprs., George Clickenger, James F. Forney and Friedrich Nambath. Mentions wife, Hannah.

0687. Brickle, Guardianship of, Apr. 12, 1828, Davidi Smith appointed guardian of Theodore aged 15 yrs. infant heir of John Brickle dec'd. Securities, Jacob Overdear and Robert Brotherton.

0688. Nichols, Guardianship of, Apr. 14, 1828, Mary and John Gilmore appointed guardian of Townsend Z. aged 4 yrs. on Sept. 13, 1827, and Elizabeth Missuri Ann, aged 5 yrs. on the 14th, next, infant heirs of Townsend Nichols, dec'd. Securities, Jacob Overdear and Robert Brotherton.

0689. Culbertson, Guardianship of, Apr. 14, 1828, James Hoge chosen as guardian by James aged 17 yrs. minor heir of James Culbertson dec'd. Securities, Benjamin Sells and Jeremiah McLene.

0690. Culbertson, Guardianship of, Nov. 21, 1828, Henry Brown chosen as guardian by Elizabeth about 16 yrs. minor heir of James Culbertson dec'd. Securities, Ralph Osborn and Robert Brotherton.

0691. Culbertson, Guardianship of, Jan. 15, 1830, Phineas Wilcox appointed guardian of Andrew aged 12 yrs. and Samuel, 8 yrs. infant heirs of James Culbertson dec'd. Securities, Mease Smith and Joseph R. Swan.

0692. Smith, Guardianship of, Apr. 15, 1828, Nathaniel W. Smith appointed guardian of Mary Jane aged 8 yrs., Esther, 5 yrs., Martha, 4 yrs. and Culbertson, 2 yrs. infant heirs of Joseph Smith dec'd. Securities, Andrew Dill and John Emmick.

0693. Davis, John, Estate of, Perry twp. May 28, 1828, Admr. appointed, Christopher Davis. Securities, Job Postle and Samuel Hunter. Apprs., Jacob Gundy, Josiah Bivans and James Gardiner.

0694. Cunning, John, Estate of, May 31, 1828, Admrs. appointed, James Hoge and Ralph Osborn. Securities, John McElvain and Joseph Ridgeway. Apprs., A. Benfield, Henry Brown and John Wilson.

0695. Ogden, Guardianship of, Sept. 4, 1828, Daniel Smith chosen as guardian by Charles aged 16 yrs. minor heir and appointed guardian of George, 13 yrs infant heir of Moses Ogden dec'd. Securities, William Shields and Joseph Edgar.

0696. Kious, Solomon, Estate of, Jackson twp. Sept. 4, 1828, Admr. appointed, Woolery Coonrod. Securities, John and William Seeds. Apprs., Moses Pursel, William Miller and James L. Holton.

0697. Stagg, Lydia, Estate of, Sept. 5, 1828, Admr. appointed. Jacob Smith. Securities, Jeremith McLene and Bela Lathem. Apprs. John H. Smith, William Sisco and John Kelso.

0698. Fruchey, Guardianship of, Sept. 6, 1828, Jacob Gander chosen as guardian by John aged 18 yrs. minor heir of John Fruchey dec'd. Securities, Frederick Fruchey and Christopher Heyl.

0699. Lorin Guardianship of, Sept. 6, 1828, Peter Lawson chosen as guardian by Ezekiel C. aged 16 yrs. minor heir of ———— Lorin, dec'd.

0700. Bartlitt, Guardianship of, Sept. 6, 1828, Oliver Clark chosen as guardian of Sumner aged 16 yrs. minor heir of ———— Bartlitt, dec'd.

0701. Nash, Guardianship of, Sept. 6, 1828, Peter Lawson chosen as guardian by George W. aged 15 yrs. minor heir of James Nash dec'd. Securities, Benjamin Smeltzer and Stephen Brinkerhoof.

0702. Taylor, Robert, Estate of, Mch. 6, 1827, Execs., his sons, David and James W. Will proven and ordered to be filed. (A-191).

0703. Shepherd, Guardianship of, Sept. 8, 1828, Robert Armstrong appointed guardian of Alexander aged 12 yrs., Ruhama, 10 yrs. James, 8 yrs. and Sally, 3 yrs. infant heirs of John Shepherd dec'd. Securities, Bela Lathem and G. Leightnecker.

0704. Shepherd, Guardianship of, Sept. 13, 1828, John Swisher chosen as guardian by Jane aged 16 yrs and Sarah, 14 yrs. minor heirs of John Shepherd dec'd. Securities, James Cherry and Teunis Peters.

0705. Keller, Guardianship of, Sept. 13, 1828, Abraham Keller appointed guardian of John, Harrison, Lewis, Margaret aged about 15 yrs., and Susannah L. minor heirs of John Keller dec'd. Securities, Robert Russell and William Godman. (Dec'd. wife was Eve)

0706. Cunning, Guardianship of, Sept. 20, 1828, Ashael Renick appointed guardian of Margaret aged 7 yrs. infant heir of John Cunning dec'd. Securities, Ralph Osborn and William Baldwin.

0707. Cunning, Guardianship of, Nov. 24, 1828, Samuel Crosby appointed guardian of Samuel aged 9 mos. and 14 days, infant heir of Sam'l Cunning dec'd. Securities, Joseph Ridgeway and Thomas Johnston.

0708. Edwards, George, Estate of, Madison twp. Nov. 24, 1828, Admr. appointed Samuel M. Kilgore. Securities, John Kile and Robert Lisle. Apprs., George W. Williams, David Taylor and John Hetsel.

0709. Woods, Thomas, Estate of, Madison twp. Nov. 24, 1828, Admr. appointed, Samuel M. Kilgore. Securities, John Kile and Robert Lisle. Apprs., David Taylor, John Hetsel and George W. Williams.

0710. Woods, Guardianship of, Nov. 28, 1828, Elizabeth Woods appointed guardian of Susan Jane aged 8 yrs. on Aug. 12, '28, Mary, 6 yrs on Jan. 6, '28, George, 4 yrs. on Dec. 14, '28, Lewis, 3 yrs and Marcus Richeson, 1 yr. on Jan. 13, '28. infant heirs of Thomas Woods dec'd. Securities, Samuel and David Ramsey.

0711. Woods, Guardianship of, Feb. 14, 1834, David Ramsey appointed guardian of Susan aged 14 yrs., George, 10 yrs., Lewis, 9 yrs. Mary, 12 yrs. and Marcus, 5 yrs. infant heirs of Thomas Woods dec'd. Securities, Alexander Mooberry and Samuel Ramsey.

0712. Ramsey, Guardianship of, Nov. 24, Samuel Ramsey appointed guardian of Sally Ann aged 10 yrs. and Elizabeth, 8 yrs. infant heirs of William Ramsey dec'd. Securities, Robert Brotherton and J. C. Broderick.

0713. Edwards, guardianship of, Nov. 24, 1828, Rebecca Edwards appointed guardian of Francis aged 15 yrs., John Gill, 13 yrs., Lucius H., 11 yrs., Stephen S., 9 yrs. and Charles, 6 yrs. infant heirs of George Edwards dec'd. Securities, John Kile and Samuel M. Kilgore.

0714. Neiswander, Frederick, Estate of, Aug. 14, 1829, Admrs. appointed, George Redenhauer and Mary Neiswander. Securities, David Redenhauer and Francis Stewart. Apprs., Stephen R. Price, A. Allison and Hugh Iams.

0715. Munger, Timothy, Estate of, Apr. 6, 1829, Admix. appointed, Elizabeth Munger. Securities, Walter Field and Matthew Matthews. Apprs., John Wilson, Henry Innis and Jason Bull.

0716. Dunn, Guardianship of, Apr. 6, 1829, Nancy Dunn appointed guardian of Susan aged 4 yrs. in June next, and Mary, 2 yrs. infant heirs of Caleb Dunn dec'd. Securities, Asa Dunn, Joseph Davidson and Peter Potter.

0717. Chenowith, Elijah, Estate of, Apr. 7, 1829, Admr. appointed, Elijah Chenowith. Securities Thomas Reynolds and Benjamin Foster. Apprs., not given.   Mentions children, viz., Joseph, Cassander Morgan, Elizabeth Carr, Rachael Wood, Ruth Davidson, Sarah Haines, John L. and Thomas, to be given $100. each.

0718. Fetters, Peter, Estate of, Plain twp. Apr. 7, 1829, non-cupative will proved and ordered to be recorded. No securities or appraisers given.

0719. Gay, Guardianship of, Apr. 9, 1829, Benjamin E. Gray chosen as guardian of Allen H. aged 17 yrs. minor heir of John Gray dec'd. Securities, Thomas Shreaves and John Tipton.

0720. Gray, Guardianship of, Apr. 9, 1829, Benjamin E. Gray chosen as guardian by William aged 19 yrs. minor heir of John Gray dec'd. Securities, John Tipton and Thomas Shreaves.

0721. Landes, Guardianship of, Apr. 10, 1829, Peter Stimmell appointed guardian of Elizabeth aged 11 yrs. infant heir of Samuel Landes dec'd. Securities, Joseph Fisher and William St. Clair.

0722. Falkner, Guardianship of, Apr. 13, 1829, David Taylor appointed guardian of Elizabeth aged 11 yrs. infant heir of John Falkner dec'd. Security, Jeremiah May. Feb. 23, 1832, William and Elizabeth Henry appointed guardian of Elizabeth aged 15 yrs. heir of John Falkner dec'd. Securities, Benjamin S. Wilson and William Hunter.

0723. Lolliker (Lolliger), Guardianship of, Apr. 14, 1829, Phineas Wilcox appointed guardian of May aged 13 yrs infant heir of ———— Lolliker dec'd. Securities, Joseph R. Swan and Orris Parish. (There was a Rudolph Lolliger, tavern-keeper, licensed June 21, 1829 and Oct. 21, 1822).

0724. Lolliker, Guardianship of, Apr. 14, 1829, John McElvain appointed guardian of John aged 10 yrs. infant heir of ———— Lolliker dec'd. Security, Wm. Doherty.

0725. Lolliker, Guardianship of, Apr. 14, 1829, Benjamin Sells appointed guardian of Hester Ann aged 8 yrs. infant heir of ———— Lolliker dec'd. Security, John Young.

0726. Bolton, Guardianship of, June 16, 1829, Matthew Matthews appointed guardian of Martha Jane aged 4 yrs. infant heir of Thomas Bolton dec'd. Securities, Phineas B. Wilcox and John McMullin.

0727. Parish, John R., Estate of, June 18, 1829, Admr. appointed, Philo H. Olmstead. Securities, Charles Loffland and Thomas Johnston. Apprs., Phineas B. Wilcox, Joseph R. Swan and David W. Deshler.

0728. Ramsey, James, Estate of, Madison twp. July 14, 1829, Admr. appointed Emmor Cox. Securities, Joel Buttles and Francis Stewart. Apprs., Robert Lisle, Thomas Rathmell and John Sharp. (Ruth Ramsey, widow).

C729. Keys, Sarah, Estate of, Madison twp. July 21, 1829, Admr. appointed, Thomas Cavender. Securities, Phillip Hooper and John Kalb. Apprs., William Patterson, George Powell and Richard Courtright.

0730. Ramsey, Guardianship of, Aug. 24, 1829, Ruth Ramsey chosen as guardian of Rebecca aged 16 yrs. minor heir of James Ramsey dec'd. Securities, Jacob Chandler and David Ramsey.

0731. Grove, Jacob, Estate of, Plain twp. Aug. 24, 1829, Admr. appointed, Daniel Swickard. Securities, Anthony Taylor and Daniel Smith. Apprs., Anthony W. Taylor, William Campbell and Jonathan Swickard.

0732. Lanning, Guardianship of, Aug. 25, 1829, Henry Bunn chosen as guardian of John aged 16 yrs. minor heir of Joseph Lanning dec'd. Securities, Parker Rarey and Alexander Cameron.

0733. Stewart, Guardianship of, Aug. 25, 1829, Thompson Bull chosen as guardian of Spencer aged 16 yrs. in Apr. 1829, minor heir of ———— Stewart dec'd.

0734. Hart, Valentine, Estate of, Aug. 25, 1829, Admr. appointed John Hart. Securities, Joseph and Moses Hart. Apprs., Robert Elliot, Daniel Brunk and George Beach. Norwich twp. Widow, Gracy Hart.

0735. Conner, Charles, Estate of, Aug. 25, 1829, Admr. appointed, John Swisher. Securities, Jacob Gander and Phillip Hooper. Apprs., Richard Courtright, Ebenezer Smith and Phillip Hetsel.

0736. Wilcox, Guardianship of, Aug. 28, 1829, Recompense Stansberry appointed guardian of Anna Eliza aged 10 yrs., John O., 12 yrs., Mary, 8 yrs., Albert, 6 yrs. and Celia, 4 yrs. infant heirs of Roswell R. Wilcox dec'd. Securities, Chandler Rogers and Daniel Upson.

0737. Neiswander, Guardianship of, Aug. 29, 1829, Michael Neiswander appointed guardian of Reuben aged 4 yrs. infant heir of Frederick Neiswander dec'd. Securities, Christian Heyl and Jesse Baughman.

0738. Hopper, Guardianship of, Aug. 31, 1829, William Doherty chosen as guardian by Solomon aged 16 yrs. minor heir of Edward Hopper dec'd. Securities, John McElvain and John L. Starling.

SETTLEMENTS OF ESTATES
ABSTRACTS OF FRANKLIN COUNTY, OHIO RECORDS
MRS. JOHN M. TITUS

0739. Downing, Guardianship of, Aug. 31, 1829, Francis Downing appointed guardian of Dorcas aged 12 yrs., Simeon, 11 yrs. and Elizabeth, 5 yrs. infant heirs of Mary Downing dec'd. Securities, John and Joshua Foster.

0740. Backus, Guardianship of, Sept. 1, 1829, Temperance Backus appointed guardian of Alexander aged 13 yrs. in Sept. 1829, and Abner S., 11 on June 27, last, minor heirs of Thomas Backus dec'd. Securities, Mathew Matheny and Joseph Ridgeway.

0741. Greer, Joseph, Estate of, Sharon twp. Sept. 1, 1829, Admr. appointed John McMullin. Securities, Demas Adams and

Mathew Matheny. Apprs., Potter Wright and John W. Ladd. Names wife. Nancy and children. Isabella, George, Laura, Johanna, Elizabeth, Henry and Richard.

0742. Higgins, Guardianship of, Sept. 2, 1829, Samuel C. Higgins chosen as guardian by George aged 15 yrs. minor heir of Richard Higgins dec'd. Securities, James Greer and John L. Greer.

0743. Cook, Justin H., Estate of, Dec. 24, 1829, Admr. appointed, James McDowell. Securities, Ralph Osborn and James Johnson. Apprs., Phineas B. Wilcox, Mease Smith and James Robinson.

0744. Wood Guardianship of, Dec. 25, 1829, John Swisher appointed guardian of George aged 12 yrs. infant heir of Charles Wood dec'd. Securities, Jacob Gander and Adam Sarbor.

0745. Wood Guardianship of, Jan. 14, 1830, Thaddeus Smith appointed guardian of George aged about 14 yrs. minor heir of Charles Wood dec'd. Securities, James Wiley and David Miller.

0746. Johnston, Thomas, Estate of, Dec. 24, 1829, Admrs. appointed, William Stewart and William Johnston. Securities, Francis Stewart and Archibald Benfield. Apprs., George W. Williams, Percival Adams and Michael Stimmell.

0747. Keys, Guardianship of, Jan. 12, 1830, Phillip Hooper appointed guardian of Rachel aged 14 yrs., Sally Ann, 12 yrs. and Rebecca, 8 yrs. infant heirs of James Keys dec'd. Securities, Thomas Cavender and Zachariah Stevenson.

0748. Higgins, Guardianship of, Jan. 15, 1830, Samuel Clark Higgins, appointed guardian of Willey Ann aged 13 yrs. infant heir of Clark Higgins dec'd. Securities, Samuel Reynolds, William Baldwin and James Gardner.

0749. Riley, William, Estate of, Will proven and ordered to be recorded. Exr. William Brown; witnesses, William C. Duff and Andrew Armstrong.

0750. Cummings, Guardianship of, Jan. 16, 1830, George McCormick chosen as guardian by Samuel Parker Cummings aged 14 yrs. minor heir of Alexander Cummings dec'd. Securities, William Armstrong and Benjamin Sells.

0751. Cummins, Guardianship of, Feb. 14, 1834, Jacob Hockman chosen as guardian by Daniel aged 17 yrs on Apr. 1st. last, minor heir of Alexander Cummins dec'd. Securities, John C. Broderick and Robert Brotherton.

0752. Gibson, Guardianship of, Jan. 16, 1830, James, aged 3 yrs. Feb. 26 next, infant heir of ———— Gibson dec'd. Securities, Henry Butler and Orris Parish.

0753. Leightnecker, Gottileb, Estate of, Jan. 16, 1829, Admrs. appointed, David W. Deshler and Lincoln Goodale. Apprs., Francis Stewart, John L. Starling and John M. Wolcott.

0754. Nelson, David, Estate of, Jan. 26, 1829, Exrs., John Barr, Edward Livingston and David Taylor. Securities, John and James Wilson. Apprs., John Woods and John Wilson. (David Nelson was a Revolutionary soldier.)

0755. Hubbard, Guardianship of, Feb. 16, 1830, Hiland Hubbard appointed guardian of Mary E. aged about 7 yrs. daughter of Hiland Hubbard dec'd. Securities, James Hoge, Daniel Upson and Recompense Stansberry.

0756. Harrison, William, Estate of, Feb. 27, 1830, Admr. appointed, Charles Harrison. Securities, James Bailey and John Stranahan. Apprs., not given.

0757. Ramsey, Guardianship of, Mch. 29, 1830, Ruth Ramsey chosen as guardian by Nancy minor heir and Susannah infant heir of Ruth Ramsey. Securities, James Porter and John Stombaugh.

0758. Davis, Francis, Estate of, Mch. 29, 1830, Admr. appointed, James Harris. Securities, James Johnston and John G. Broderick. Apprs., William C. Long, Benjamin Sells and Amon Jenkins.

0759. Bumgardener, Henry, Estate of, Mch. 30, 1830, Admr. appointed, John L. Starling. Securities, Jacob Grubb and George Reardon. Wife, Nancy. Apprs., not given. (He was a Revolutionary soldier). Wife was Nancy Bumgardner.

0760. Groves, Guardianship of, Mch 30, 1830, Daniel Swickard chosen as guardian by Peter aged 16 yrs. and Jonas, 14 yrs. minor heirs of Jacob Groves dec'd. Securities, Jacob Smith and John Alspaugh.

0761. Williams, George W., Estate of, Mch. 31, 1839, Admr. appointed, John L. Starling. Securities, Jacob Grubb and Francis Stewart. Apprs. William Stewart, Robert Breckenridge and Samuel M. Kilgore.

0762. Williams, Guardianship of, Mch. 31, 1830, Hugh McElhaney appointed guardian of Oliver P. aged 17 yrs., Mary about 11 yrs. and David, 7 yrs. heirs of George W. Williams dec'd. Securities, Samuel Shannon and Joseph Leiby.

0763. Williams, Guardianship of, Mch. 30, 1830, Alexander Mooberry chosen as guardian by Eli about 15 yrs and Jane about 13 yrs. of age, minor heirs of George W. Williams dec'd. Securities, Thomas Rathmell and John Thompson.

0764. Springer, Benjamin, Estate of, Apr. 2, 1830, Admr. appointed, Neal Osborn. Securities, Thomas Clark and James Cutler. Apprs., Peter Putman and John L. Starling.

0765. Johnston, Guardianship of, Apr. 2, 1830, Elizabeth Johnston appointed guardian Samuel aged 11 yrs. last Sept., infant heir of Thomas Johnston dec'd. Securities, William Stewart and Archibald Benfield.

0766. Johnston, Guardianship of, Apr. 2, 1830, Francis Stewart chosen as guardian by Thomas Johnston aged 18 yrs. last Dec. and Edmond, 14 yrs. last Jan. minor heirs of Thomas Johnston dec'd. Securities, William Stewart and Arthur O'Harra.

0767. Johnston, Guardianship of, Sept. 25, 1832, Francis Johnston appointed guardian of Samuel aged about 14 yrs. minor heirs of Thomas Johnston dec'd. Securities, William Stewart and James Lindsay.

0768. Turner, Guardianship of, Apr. 3, 1830, John McComb appointed guardian of Samuel aged about 7 yrs., James, about 5 yrs. and John, about 3 yrs. infant heirs of John L. Turner dec'd. Securities, Jonathan McComb and Robert C. Henderson.

0769. Young, Guardianship of, Apr. 3, 1830, Edward Livingston appointed guardian of George W. aged 11 yrs. infant heir of James Young dec'd. Securities, Isaac Taylor and Ralph Osborn.

0770. Berringer, Martin, Estate of, Montgomery twp., June 24, 1830, Admr. appointed, Robert Howell. Securities, Daniel Smith and John Young. Apprs., Peter Putman, Christian Heyl and John Wilson.

0771. Childs, John, Estate of, Madison twp., June 25, 1830, Admrs. appointed, Lydia and Isaac Childs. Securities, Thomas Grooms and Samuel Bishop. Apprs., Jacob Gander, Adam Havely and Alexander Cameron.

0772. Smith, Guardianship of, June 26, 1830, John H. Smith appointed guardian of Russell aged about 7 yrs., Nelson, 4 yrs. and Juliana aged about 3 yrs. infant heirs of Josiah Smith dec'd. Securities, Jacob Smith and Michael Stagg.

0773. Thompson, William, Estate of, Sharon twp., June 26, 1830, Admr. appointed, Charles Thompson and Moses S. Wilkinson. Securities, George H. Griswold and Demas Adams. Apprs., Ozias Burr, William McCloud and Rodney Comstock.

0774. Springer, Benjamin, Estate of, Madison twp. Oct. 15, 1823, Exer. John More and Adam Shepherd. Will given in Vol. 1, No. 4, O. G. Quarterly.

SETTLEMENTS OF ESTATES
ABSTRACTS OF FRANKLIN COUNTY, OHIO RECORDS
MRS. JOHN M. TITUS

0775. Domigan, William, Estate of, June 30, 1830, Exr. appointed, Francis Stewart. Securities, Joseph R. Swan and John McElvain. Apprs., Lewis Risley, Jacob Grubb and A. Brotherton.

0776. Jones, Thomas, Estate of, Sept. 8, 1830, Admr. appointed, John C. Broderick. Securities, R. Brotherton and John Thompson. Apprs., Lincoln Goodale, Robert Brotherton and Gardner Woods.

0777. Brown, William, Estate of, Oct. 9, 1830, Admr. appointed, Francis Stewart. Securities, Ralph Osborn and Christian Heyl. Apprs., William Miller, James Walcott and Adam Brotherlin.

0778. Decker, Guardianship of, Nov. 29, 1830, Daniel P. Miller, appointed guardian of Joseph aged yrs., John, yrs. and Elisha 11 yrs. minor heirs of Conrad Decker dec'd. Securities, Jacob Weaver and Jacob Gander.

0779. Decker, Guardianship of, May 4, 1835, John Decker was chosen as guardian by Elisha aged 16 yrs. minor heir of Conrad Decker dec'd. Securities, Samuel Watt and Andrew Dildine.

0780. Ross, John F., Estate of, Nov. 30, 1830, Admr. appointed, Hugh M. Ross. Securities, Elias Chester and Thaddeus Smith. Apprs., Alexander Mooberry, Richard Courtright and John Swisher.

0781. Bailey, David, Estate of, Nov. 30, 1830, Admr. appointed David Smiley. Securities, Peter Latmore and Zephaniah Rodgers. Apprs., H. Coffman, Jesse and Jacob Miller.

0782. Mickey, Thomas, Estate of, Perry twp., Dec. 1, 1830, Admix. appointed, Jane Mickey. Securities, Samuel Davis and Jesse Miller. Apprs., Amos Brelsford, Joseph Davis and Uriah Clark.

0783. Shields, William, Estate of, Dec. 2, 1830, Exrx., Margaret Shields. Securities, and appraisers not given. Will given in Vol. 1, No. 4, O. G. Quarterly.*

0784. Albright, Elijah, Estate of, Dec. 2, 1830, Admr. appointed, Joseph S. Brooks. Securities Elijah Ellis and Andrew McElvain. Apprs., Robert Brotherton, Peter Sell and Christian Heyl.

0785. Grove, Guardianship of, Dec. 2, 1830, Jonathan Swickard appointed guardian of Martin aged 13 yrs. in Nov. last, Jacob, 11 yrs. on July 28, last, Elizabeth, 9 yrs. on Apr. 8, last, William and Michael (twins), 7 yrs. on Mch. 23, last, Lavina 15 yrs. on Oct. 15, last and John, 3 yrs. Dec. 26, this mo., infant heirs of Jacob Grove dec'd. Securities, Daniel and Andrew Swickard.

0796. Widener, Henry, Estate of, Dec. 20, 1830, Knowlton Bailey appointed Admr., securities, Solomon Clover and Joseph A. Wood. Estate found insolvent; dividend declared, 77½ cents on the dollar. Apprs., Peter Clover, William Steirwalt and William Willcox.

0797. Godman, Julius, Estate of, Jan. 18, 1859, Admr. appointed, William T. Martin. Securities, James Cherry and David W. Deshler. Apprs., Peter Putman, Perry McElvain and Jesse F. Wixom.

0798. Warner, John, Estate of, Feb. 15, 1831, Admr. appointed, Christian Heyl. Securities, John Young and Joseph Leiby. Apprs., Hiram Platt, M. Matthews and P. H. Olmstead.

0799. Akins, Guardianship of, Feb. 21, 1831, James Akins chosen as guardian by Samuel aged 17 yrs., Martha 12 yrs., Margaret M. 14 yrs. and Elizabeth A. Akins minor heirs of John Mathers dec'd. Securities, Charles B. and Richard Akins.

0800. Blakely, Guardianship of, Feb. 21, 1831, William Smith appointed guardian of Robert aged 12 yrs., Rossman, 11 yrs., Sally, 7 yrs. infant heirs and Matilda aged 16 yrs. minor heir of Thomas Blakely dec'd. Securities, Henry Dildine and John Fairchild.

0801. Boyd, Guardianship of, Feb. 21, 1831, Abram Kellar appointed guardian of Lucius infant heir of Benj. Boyd dec'd. Securities, Thomas O'Harra and William Hunter.

0802. Parish, Guardianship of, Feb. 21, 1831, Thomas Shreves appointed guardian of Polly Parish an insane woman. Securities, John Moler and Abram Romine.

0803. Thompson, John, Estate of, Hamilton twp. and Circleville. Feb. 24, 1831, Alfred Thompson appointed Admr. Securities, James Lindsay and Robert Lisle. Apprs., Jacob Plumb and Michael Stimmel. (John Thompson was a Revolutionary Soldier).

0804. Holton, James T., Estate of, Feb. 25, 1831, William H. Jolley appointed Admr. Securities, Darius P. Wilcox and William Nolan. Apprs., John Dunn, Henry Baumgartner and Moses Pursell.

0805. Clark, Guardianship of, Feb. 25, 1831, William Clark chosen as guardian by Isaac Ambrose Clark aged 18 yrs. minor heir of John Clark dec'd. Securities, Thomas Johnston and John Watson.

0806. White, Guardianship of, Feb. 25, 1831, Henry Enoch chosen as guardian by Henry aged 14 yrs. and George aged 16 minor heirs of Samuel White dec'd. Securities, David Royce and James Bigwood.

*p. 282, this volume

0807. Piper, Thomas, Estate of, Feb. 28, 1831, Hannah Piper appointed Admix. Securities, Peter Sells and William McElvain. Apprs., Moses Jewell, Peter Putman and W. T. Martin.

0808. Jameson, Sarah, Estate of, Feb. 28, 1831, A. Jameson appointed Admr. Was removed May 14, 1831 and William Scott was appointed. Securities, Robert Brotherton and Francis Stewart. Apprs., Joseph Breckenridge, W. M. Badger and David Dearduff.

0809. Warner, Guardianship of, Feb. 28, 1831, Mary A. Warner appointed guardian of Mary Ann and Chauncy infant heirs of John Warner, dec'd. Securities, Conrad Heyl and Robert Brotherton. June 11, 1834, Conrad Heyl appointed guardian. Securities, Phillip Read and John Marcy.

0810. Smith, Sarah, Estate of, May 13, 1831, Admr. appointed, Robert Smith and George Ridenhour. Securities, Robert Brotherton and Daniel Swickard. Apprs., David Ridenhour, Andrew L. Smiley and Adam Read.

0811. McGown, John, Estate of, May 13, 1831, Jared Shead appointed Admr. Securities, Hugh McMasters and Thomas Carpenter. Apprs., not given.

0812. Kilbourne, John, Estate of, May 14, 1831, William Long appointed Admr. Securities P. B. Wilcox and Cyrus Parker. Apprs., L. Goodale, J. M. Whiting and P. H. Olmstead.

0813. Green, Caleb, Estate of, Perry twp. May 14, 1831, Catherine Green appointed Admix. Securities, William Hays and Hugh McMasters. Apprs., Abner Brelsford and Thomas Watson.

0814. Piper, Eleazer, Estate of, Perry twp. May 14, 1831, Admr. appointed, William Hays. Securities, Amaziah Hutchinson and Amos Brelsford. Apprs., G. Thomas and Amos Brelsford.

0815. Ramey, Guardianship of, May 14, 1831, Asa Dunn appointed guardian of Elizabeth aged 10 yrs. infant heir of William Ramey dec'd. Securities, Percival Adams and John Dunn.

0816. Ramey, Guardianship of, May 14, 1831, Asa Dunn chosen as guardian by Sarah Ann aged 12 yrs. minor heir of William Ramey dec'd. Securities, Percivlal Adams and John Dunn. June 9, 1934, John Greenwood chosen as guardian by Sarah Ann Ramey. Securities, P. B. Wilcox and N. H. Swayne.

0817. Ramey, Guardianship of, July 5, 1833, Asa Dunn chosen as guardian by Elizabeth aged 12 yrs. minor heir of William Ramey dec'd. Security, Otis Crosby.

0818. Jameson, Guardianship of, May 14, 1831, Francis Stewart chosen as guardian by David aged 14 yrs. minor heir. Thomas aged 10 yrs. and Mary infant heirs of Joseph Jameson dec'd. Securities, William Stewart and John M. Wolcott.

0819. Jameson, Guardianship of, Feb. 27, 1835, Francis Stewart chosen as guardian by James aged 15 yrs. minor heir of Joseph Jameson dec'd. Securities, Philo H. Olmstead and Michael Sulivant. Accounts settled June 15, 1840; due each heir $599.62.

0820. Giberson, Guardianship of, May 16, 1831, Zebulon Giberson chosen as guardian by Charles aged 15 yrs. minor heir of Harmon Giberson dec'd. Securities, Parker and William Rarey.

0821. Hoover, Guardianship of May 17, 1831, John Hoover chosen as guardian by Peter, John, Polly, and Anna, minor heirs of John Hoover dec'd. Securities, Joseph Moore and Daniel Swickard.

209

0822. Weatherington, John, Estate of, May 17, 1831, exrs. appointed, Isaac and John Weatherington; securities, Andrew Dill and George Clickenger. Apprs., Robert Lisle, Emanuel Weaver and Robert Breckenridge.

0823. Rohr, John, Estate of, May 20, 1831, Margaret Rohr appointed admix. Securities, Owen Roberts and Henry Dillinger. Apprs., Peter Line, William Smith and Thomas Rathmell.

0824. Howell, Robert, Estate of, Sept. 26, 1831, Thomas Wood appointed admr. Securities, Philo H. Olmstead and Robert Brotherton. Apprs., Francis Stewart, John M. Wolcott, and Mathew Matthews.

0825. Reader, Guardianship of, Sept. 26, 1831, Michael Neiswander appointed guardian of John aged 9 yrs. and Elizabeth 6 yrs. infant heirs of———Reader dec'd. Securities, William Doherty and Abraham Stagg.

0826. Stevenson, Mary, Estate of, Sept. 26, 1831, George H. Stevenson appointed admr. Securities, Phillip Hooper and Richard Stevenson. Apprs., not given.

0827. Stevenson, John, Estate of, Madison twp. Sept. 26, 1831, Joshua Stevenson appointed admr. Securities, Thomas Cavender and Zachariah Stevenson. Apprs., Samuel Barr, Philemon Needles and John Kile. (John Stevenson was a Revolutionary Soldier).

0828. Starling, John L., Estate of, Sept. 26, 1831, William Armstrong appointed admr. Securities, John C. Broderick and Mathew Matthews. Apprs., John Bailhache, M. Matthews and C. Heyl.

0829. Brown, Guardianship of, Sept. 27, 1831, William Stranahan chosen as guardian by William Mary Ann minor heir and appointed guardian of John, Patsy, and Samuel infant heirs of William Brown dec'd. Securities, James Conger and Abraham Vanmeter.

0830. Brown, Guardianship of, May 23, 1836, William Miller chosen as guardian by William minor heir of William Brown dec'd. Securities, Francis Stewart and Christian Heyl.

0831. Brown, Guardianship of, Mch. 22, 1837, Griffin R. Minor chosen as guardian by John minor heir of William Brown dec'd. Securities, Robert Neil and Joseph Sulivant.

0832. Ferguson, Guardianship of, Sept. 29, 1831, Charles Hunter chosen as guardian by James minor heir of Thomas Ferguson dec'd. Securities, Lyne Starling and John Marcy.

0833. Hews, James D., Estate of, Oct. 1, 1831, Joseph Wright appointed admr. Securities, John C. Broderick and Robert Brotherton. Estate settled by Mease Smith. Master Commissioner.

0834. Taylor, Nancy P., Estate of, Oct. 1, 1831, David Taylor appointed admr. Securities, Purdy McElvain and James Taylor. Apprs., not given.

0835. Downs, Guardianship of, Oct. 1, 1831, Joseph Ridgeway chosen as guardian by James minor heir of James Downs dec'd. Securities, Isaac Taylor and Joseph R. Swan.

0836. Downs, Guardianship of, July 3, 1833, Moses R. Spurgeon chosen as guardian of Wilber minor heir of James Downs dec'd. Security, Philo H. Olmstead.

0837. Alspaugh, David, Estate of, Madison twp. Oct. 29, 1831, Joseph Wright appointed admr. Securities, Mathew Matthews and Cyrus Fay. Apprs., Abraham Shoemaker, George Kalb and William Patterson.

0838. Courtright, Richard, Estate of. Dec. 13, 1831, Sarah and John Courtright appointed admrs. Securities, Philemon Needles and John S. Miller. Apprs., John Swisher, John Long and Abraham Shoemaker.

0839. Ramey, William, Estate of, Jan. 5, 1832, Elizabeth Ramey appointed admix. Securities, Robert Brotherton and John C. Broderick. Apprs., Fergus Morehead, David Slaughter, and Alfred Thompson.

0840. Spangler, Eli, Estate of. Jan. 8, 1832, May Spangler appointed admix. Securities, Robert Brotherton and John C. Broderick. Apprs., James Lindsay, William Johnston and Robert Breckenridge.

0841. Elder. William, Estate of, Jan. 24, 1832, Thomas and William Elder appointed admrs. Securities, John Welton and Alexander Cameron. Apprs., Henry Dildine. George Bishop and Jesse Seymore.

SETTLEMENTS OF ESTATES
ABSTRACTS OF FRANKLIN COUNTY, OHIO RECORDS
MRS. JOHN M. TITUS

0842. Backus, Guardianship of, Feb. 4, 1832, Temperance Backus chosen as guardian by Elijah Lucretia, William, and Alexander, minor heirs of Thomas Backus dec'd. Securities, Phineas B. Wilcox and Mathew Matthews.

0843. Benfield, Archibald, Estate of, Feb. 4, 1832, Francis Stewart appointed admr. Securities, William Stewart and Gustavus Swan. Apprs., Adam Brotherton, John W. Wolcott and Phillip Read.

0844. Wilcox, Roswell. Estate of, Feb. 4, 1832, Dorcas and Daniel P. Wilcox appointed admrs. Securities, Jason Bull and John Fips. Apprs. Aristarchus Walker, Belias M. Skeele and Hiram Andrews.

0845. Cook, Rodney, Estate of, Feb. 20, 1832, Laura Cook and John Buck appointed admrs. Securities, Elihu Webster and George H. Andrews Apprs., Aristarchus Walker, Hiram Andrews and Belias H. Skeele.

0846. Morrison, Guardianship of, Feb. 20, 1832, Aurora Buttles chosen as guardian by Alonzo minor heir of ———— Morrison. Security, A. H. Pinney.

0847. Swashgood, John, Estate of, Feb. 20, 1832, Stewart White appointed exr. Securities, Samuel M. White and Thomas Shreves. Apprs., Jacob Grub, Reuben Golliday and John Robinson.

0848. Hartman, Henry, Estate of, Feb. 21, 1832, Jacob Hartman appointed admr. Securities, Arthur O'Harra and William Champe. Apprs., Andrew Dill, Robert Breckenridge and Thomas Wright.

0849. Davis, John, Estate of, Feb. 25, 1832, Samuel S. and Joseph Davis appointed exrs. Securities, Griffin Thomas and Abner Brelsford. Apprs., Adam Brelsford, Robert Boyd and William Sells.

0850. Decker, Andrew, Estate of, Feb. 25, 1832, George Bishop appointed admr. Securities, Amos Crum and Isaac Decker. Apprs., Daniel Kious, Henry Dillenger and Alexander Cameron.

0851. Hedges, Guardianship of, Mch. 13, 1832, John Hedges appointed guardian of Nancy D. R. aged about 3 yrs. and Ann R. aged about one month infant heirs of Daniel Hedges dec'd. Securities, John Ross, William Baldwin and Samuel Reynolds.

0852. Burnet, Hiram, Estate of, May 14, 1832, Margaret Burnet appointed admix. Securities, William T. Martin and Joseph Hunter jr. Apprs. none given.

0853. Watt, Guardianship of, May 14, 1832, Elisha Chambers chosen as guardian by William aged 16 yrs. and Catherine, about 15 yrs. minor heirs of John Watt dec'd. Securities, James Conger and William Armistead.

0854. Fox, Guardianship of, May 14, 1832, Michael Thomas appointed guardian of Elinda and Mary minor heirs of ———— Fox dec'd. Securities, David Wright and William Johnson.

0855. Robbins, Guardianship of, May 14, 1832, Eliza Robbins appointed guardian of Minerva, David and Westley minor heirs of Samuel Robbins dec'd. Securities, William Johnston and David Wright.

0855. Robbins, Samuel, Estate of, May 14, 1832, Admr. appointed David Wright; Securities, William Johnston and Michael Thomas, Apprs., not given.

0856. Goetchius, Henry, Estate of, May 17, 1832, Elizabeth Goetchius appointed admix. Securities, Stewart Goldsmith and Thomas Goldsmith, Apprs.

0857. Dill, Andrew, Estate of, Hamilton twp., May 18, 1832, admr. appointed, William Champe; securities, John Emmick and George Reed. Apprs., William T. Martin, Robert Armstrong and George Riordan.

0858. Jameson, Joseph, Estate of, Sept. 4, 1829, admr., appointed, Francis Stewart; securities, William Stewart and William Doherty. Apprs., Adam Brotherlin, John Stambaugh and Robert Brotherton.

0859. Lilly, Guardianship of, May 19, 1832, John W. Campbell, appointed guardian of Mitchell D. aged 12 yrs. in Oct. next, minor heir of John D. Lilly dec'd. Securities, Gustavus Swan and William T. Martin.

0860. Whitsell, David, Estate of, May 19, 1832, Polly Whitsell, appointed admix. securities, John Gallion and Aaron Meeker. Attest., Mease Smith and Lynne Starling.

0861. Price, Stephen, Estate of, Mifflin twp. Mch. 4, 1832, admrs. appointed, John Clark and James Price. Securities, not given. Apprs., George Wittenmeyer and John Scott.

0862. Noble, Jonathan, Estate of Sept. 15, 1832, Hannah Noble and John Billington appointed admrs. Securities, Abram Phelps and John Wait. Apprs., Grove Pinney, Isaac Griswold and Arora J. Olmstead. Blendon twp.

0863. Postle, Shadrack, Estate of, Sept. 16, 1832, Stephen Postle appointed admr. Securities, William Stierwalt and Washington Hickman.

0864. Embry, Joseph, Estate of, Aug. 21, 1832, ?Michael Sullivant appointed admr. Securities, William T. Martin and Thomas Embry.

0865. Keller, John, Estate of, Montgomery twp., Dec. 29, 1832. Abram Keller appointed admr. securities, Mayborn Northorp and Robert Russell. Eve Keller, widow. Margaret, daughter was aged 14 yrs. and 10 mo. at time of father's death. Apprs., Joseph Ridgeway, James Johnston and Isaac Taylor.

0866. Gray, Guardianship of, Sept. 14, 1832, Thomas Gray jr. appointed guardian of Richard E. aged about 6 yrs., Sarah Jane about 4 yrs. and Eliza Ann about 1 yr. minor heirs of Thomas Gray dec'd Securities, Thomas Gray sr. and Matthew Brown.

0867. Courtright, Guardianship of, Sept. 24, 1832, Edward Courtright was chosen as guardian of Hiram aged 17 yrs., Jesse aged 15 yrs. and Lucinda aged 11 yrs. minor heirs of Richard Courtright dec'd. Securities, John Courtright and Archibald Powell.

0868. Betts, Guardianship of, Sept. 25, 1832, Isaac Betts appointed guardian of Francis aged about 11 yrs. minor heir of Jacob Betts dec'd Security, John Wilson.

0869. Saul, Guardianship of, Sept. 25, 1832, George Saul chosen as guardian by John aged 19 yrs. minor heir of Leonard Saul dec'd. Securities, William Caldwell and Frederick Launsby.

0870. Bailor, John, Estate of, Montgomery twp. Sept. 25, 1832, admr. appointed, William Stewart; securities, James Lindsay and Francis Stewart. Apprs., Moses Morrill, William W. Shannon and William H. Richardson.

0891. Elder, Guardianship of, Sept. 25, 1832, Alexander Cameron chosen as guardian by Jesse Elder aged 16 yrs. minor heir of William Elder dec'd. Securities, Abraham Shoemaker and William H. Richardson.

0872. Brickle, George, Estate of, Sept. 25, 1832, admr. appointed John Brickle; securities, Benjamin Sells and Edward Davis. Apprs., Thomas Moore, Joseph Hunter and Peter Lawson. Montgomery twp.

0873. Weistell, Guardianship of, Sept. 25, 1832, Charles Knoderer jr. appointed guardian of John, Samuel, Mary and Susannah infant heirs of David Weitsell dec'd. Securities, Charles Knoderer and Edward Davis.

0874. Sanford, Guardianship of, Sept. 26, 1832, Robert Brotherton chosen as guardian by William Sanford aged 16 yrs. minor son of William Sanford dec'd. Securities, Henry Vanhorn and A. V. Taylor.

0875. Black, Guardianship of, Sept. 26, 1832, H. Wolcott was appointed guardian of Hays Black minor heir of John Black dec'd. Securities, Mathew Matthews and Robert Brotherton.

0876. Shultz, Bolzer, Estate of, Truro twp. formerly of Berwick twp. Adams Co. Penn. Jacob Shultz appointed admr. securities, Robert Brotherton and George W. Williams, Apprs., Alexander Mooberry, John Courtright and John Switser. Heir, Samuel Shultz of Breckneck twp. Lancaster Co. Penn.

213

0877. Case, Israel, Estate of, Sept. 29, 1832, Lucinda Case and Alexander Shattuck appointed admrs. Securities, Ezekiel Brown and Alvin Tuller. Apprs., Hiram Andrews, Stephen Maynard and R. Stansberry.

0878. Hays, Guardianship of, Feb. 28, 1832, P. B. Wilcox appointed guardian of Julia M. aged 10 yrs. and Caroline 8 yrs. infant heirs of Michael L. Hays dec'd. Security, Joseph R. Swan.

0879. Hays, Guardianship of, Feb. 28, 1833, William Preston chosen guardian by Jane aged 16 yrs. minor heir of Michael L. Hays dec'd. Security, P. B. Wilcox.

0880. Denune, John, Estate of, Apr. 15, 1833, Robert Henderson appointed admr. Securities, Robert Breckenridge, Michael Stimmel and Michael Fisher, Apprs., not given.

0881. Hews, Mary, Estate of, Madison twp., April 15, 1833, John Courtney appointed exr. Securities, John Hanson and John Cramer.

0882. Dyer, Jane, Estate of, Apr. 16, 1833, John Dyer appointed admr., securities, Jeremiah McLene and John Hunter. Apprs., not given.

0883. Weeks, Guardianship of, Apr. 16, 1833, Jonathan Whitehead chosen as guardian by Abi aged 14 yrs. of age minor heir of ————— Weeks, dec'd.

0884. Weeks, Guardianship of, Dorman aged 12 yrs., Jane aged 8 yrs. and Miranda aged 6 yrs. minor heirs of ————— Weeks dec'd. Securities, Levi Pinney.

0885. Brown, Putman, Estate of, Apr. 16, 1833, Chandler Rogers appointed Admr. Securities, H. D. Little, and John Weaver. Apprs. Obadiah Benedict Jacob J. Lewis and Daniel Field.

0866. Spangler, Guardianship of, Apr. 16, 1833, Mary Spangler appointed guardian of Susannah aged 10 yrs., February last. Margaret aged 8 yrs. in March last, John aged 3 yrs. March 15, last, Ann aged 3 yrs. March 15, last and Eli aged 1 yr. Apr. 1 last minor heirs of Eli Spangler dec'd. Securities, John Kious, and David Barber.

0887. Spangler, guardianship, June 11, 1836, David Spangler appointed guardian of Susan aged 13 yrs., Margaret 11 yrs., Mary Ann 8 yrs., John and Eli minor heirs of Eli Spangler dec'd. Securities, Robert Brotherton and Moylan Northrop.

0888. Crawford Guardianship of, Apr. 17, 1833, George Jeffries chosen as guardian by John aged 17 yrs. minor heir of John Crawford dec'd. Securities, Benjamin Sells and Moses Spurgeon.

0889. Lawyer, John, Estate of, Apr. 17, 1833, Hugh Huston appointed Admr. Securities, William Mitchell and Jesse Miller. Apprs., William Sells, Charles Michel and Thomas Michel.

0890. West, Guardianship of, May 16, 1833, Israel Cowden chosen as guardian by Benjamin West aged 16 yrs. on May 1, 1833, minor heir of ————— West dec'd. Security, Thomas Stagg. On Apr. 17, 1833, Benjamin West was chosen as guardian by Benjamin West minor heir of ————— West dec'd.

0891. Talman, Guardianship of, Apr. 18, 1833, James Tallman appointed guardian of the minor heirs of Samuel Tallman dec'd.

0892. Sells, Peter Estate of, Apr. 18, 1833 Sarah Sells appointed Admix. Securities, Benjamin Sells and Jeremiah McLene. Apprs., William McElvain, John Brickel and James Bryden.

214

SETTLEMENTS OF ESTATES
ABSTRACTS OF FRANKLIN COUNTY, OHIO RECORDS
ROSALIE HADDOX

0893. Spangler, John, Estate of, Apr. 21, 1833, Joseph Spangler and Joseph Murray appointed Admrs. Securities, David Spangler and William Doherty.

C894. Wilson, Guardianship of, Apr. 22, 1833, John McCarty appointed guardian of Margaret aged 10 yrs. minor heir of James Wilson dec'd. Securities, John Wilson and A. J. McSowell.

0895. Work, Guardianship of, Apr. 23, 1833, John Work chosen as guardian of Franklin aged 14 yrs. and Elizabeth aged 15 yrs. minor heirs of ———— Work. Security, R. W. McCoy.

C896. Shirey, Guardianship of, Apr. 25, 1833, Samuel Dearduff chosen as guardian of Michael Shirey aged 16 yrs. minor of Michael Shirey dec'd. Security, James Graham.

C897. Jones, Guardianship of, Apr. 25, 1833, Elias Gaver chosen as guardian by Jesse Jones minor heir of Thomas Jones dec'd. Security, Phillip Reed.

C898. Walcott, William, Estate of, July 1, 1833, Robert Walcott appointed exec. Securities, Joshua Baldwin and George Jeffries, Apprs. Thomas Legg, John Brickell and John Kenny.

C899. Swashgood, Guardianship of, July 1, 1833, Reuben Golliday appointed guardian of Samuel and Mary aged 7 yrs, May last, (twins) infant heirs of John Swashgood dec'd. Securities, Charles Hunter and Robert Brotherton.

C900. Swashgood, Guardianship of, July 1, 1833, Reuben Golliday chosen as guardian by Sarah aged 16 yrs., William aged 15 yrs. and Elizabeth aged 12 yrs. minor heirs John Swashgood dec'd. Securities, Charles Hunter and Robert Brotherton.

C901. Waddle, John, Estate of, July 2, 1833, William and Alexander Waddle apointed Admrs. No security or appraisers given.

C902. Ball, Charles Estate of, July 2, 1833, Washington Risley appointed Admr. Securities, Lucien Ball and Orville Risley. Apprs., Thomas Killpatrick, William Caldwell and Reuben Golliday.

C903. Boyd, Benjamin, Estate of, July 16, 1833, Joseph Wright appointed Admr. Securities, John Cramer and Samuel D. Havely. Apprs. James Peircy, Joseph Williams and William Smith. (Madison Twp.).

C904. McCormack, Evans, Estate of, July 16, 1833, Samuel D. Havely appointed Admr. Securities, James Kooken and Joseph Wright. Apprs., Joseph Williams, James T. Peircy, Alex. Cameron and William Smith.

0905. Schoonover, Henry, Estate of, July 18, 1833, Sarah Schoonover and Charles Rarig appointed Admrs. Securities, Samuel D. Havely and John B. West. Apprs. Joseph Wright and William Smith.

0906. Hews, Walter, Estate of, July 18, 1833, Samuel D. Havely appointed Admr. Securities, Robert Brotherton and Charles Rarey, Apprs., James Wiley, Daniel Miller and James Peircy.

C907. Schoonover, John, Estate of, July 27, Isaac Painter appointed Admr. Securities, Isaac Baldwin and Peter Mills. Apprs., J. Gander, Isaac Decker and George Berman.

215

0908. Stagg, Josiah, Estate of, July 27, 1833, Maria Stagg and Peter Mills appointed Admrs. Securities, Isaac Baldwin and Isaac Baldwin and Isaac Painter, Apprs., John H. Smith, Philemon Parcel and Joseph Edgar.

0909. Woods, James, Estate of, July 31, 1833, Robert Neil and Lyne Starling appointed Admrs. Securities, Demas Adams and William Miner. Apprs., Ralph Osborn, Isaac Taylor and Robert Riordan.

0910. Jewett, Henry, Estate of, July 31, 1833. Admr. appointed Benjamin F. Jewett. Securities, Otis Crosby and Samuel Crosby. Apprs. J. Ridgeway, Ira Grover and J. Ridgeway jr.

0911. Whyte, James, Estate of, Sept. 3, 1833, Admrs. appointed Joseph Ridgeway and Robert Brotherton. Securities, Ralph Osborn and John Young. Apprs. Robert Cutler, Joseph Leidy and Frederick Iseler (Eisler).

0912. Collins, William, Estate of, Sept. 12, 1833. Admr. appointed Samuel C. Flenniken. Securities, John C. Broderick and John Wilson. Sept. term 1848, Robert Neil appointed Admr. Securities, John Baldwin and W. Dennison. Apprs., R. W. McCoy, James Kooken and Eli W. Gwynne.

0913. Jones, Lydia, Estate of, Admr. appointed, George Jeffries, Esq. Sept. 19, 1833. Securities, Moses R. Spurgeon and Andrew McElvain May 23, 1846. Exec. removed and Tunis Peters appointed. Securities George W. Peters and L. Peters.

0914. Platt, Benjamin, Estate of, Admrs. Augustus Platt and Luther Hillery appointed Sept. 19, 1833. Securities, Jeremiah McLene and Robert Rierdan. Apprs; Ralph Osborn, Joseph Ridgeway and Lewis Mill.

0915. West guardianship of, Sept. 19, 1833. John Coons, appointed guardian of Buley West, aged 11 yrs., Marian West, aged 9 yrs. and Guy West, aged 5 yrs., infant heirs of George West. Securities James C. Reynolds and Samuel Shannon.

0916. Howard, Horton, Estate of, Sept. 20, 1833. Executor appointed, Joseph and John Howard and Samuel Torrer. Securities, Lyne Starling and Joseph Ridgeway.

0917. Ramelsberry, Guardian appointed Sept. 19, 1833, John Patterson of Ernest aged 7 yrs. and William, aged 5 yrs. and Augustus, aged 9 yrs. minor heirs of —— Ramelsberry dec'd. Securities. C. Heyl and P. B. Wilcox.

0918. Parks, Samuel, Estate of, Sept. 20, 1833, Admr. Ezekiel Park. Securities, Wyllys Spencer and Abraham Crist. Apprs., Jacob Wagner, Daniel Swishard and Peter Quinn.

0919. Mattison, guardianship, Sept. 21, 1833. John Hanson was appointed guardian of William Mattsion, aged 7 yrs., and Mary Mattison, ager 55 yrs., minor heirs of William Mattsion, dec'd. Security, John Greenwodd.

0920. Schoonover, guardianship, Sept. 21, 1833, George Beals appointed guardian of Abraham, aged 13 yrs., Charles W. aged 8 yrs., Margaret, aged 7 yrs., William, aged 5 yrs., and Angeline, aged 2 yrs., minor heirs of John Schoonover, dec'd. Securities, Isaac Painter and Edward Hedden.

0921. Schoonover, guardianship, Feb. 11, 1834, Alva Schoonover chosen by John, aged 17 yrs., minor heir of John Schoonover, dec'd.

0922. Wright, guardianship, Sept. 21, 1833, ——————Buttles chosen as guardian by Samuel, aged 12 yrs., minor heir of Moses Wright, dec'd. Securities, A. H. Pinney.

0923. Lee, Asa, Estate of, Sept. 21, 1833, Admr. appointed, Timothy Lee. Securities, Samuel McDonald, William Jameson. Apprs. Ebenezer Washburn and Samuel McDonald.

0924. Lee, guardianship, Sept. 21, 1833, Sally Lee was chosen guardian of Newton D. Lee, George A. Lee, Charles B. Lee, Oren A. Lee and an infant not named——infant heirs of Asa Lee. Security, Samuel McDonald.

0925. Dildine, (Elisha) Estate of, Sept. 23, 1833, Charles Rarey appointed admr. Security, Joseph Schoonover and Benjamin Britton. Apprs., William Smith, Alex Cameron and Thomas Patrick.

0926. Lindsay, James, Estate of, Sept. 23, 1833, John Barr and William Lindsay appointed Execs. Security, Frances Stewart and John Stambaugh.

0927. McAffee, guardianship, Sept. 23, 1833, Daniel Decker chosen guardian by Thomas B. McAffee and Dinah McAffee, minor heirs of Joseph McAffee, dec'd. Security, Anthony Barrett and William McAffee.

0928. Mann, Johnston, Estate of, Sept. 24, 1833, Admr. appointed Samuel G. Flenniker Security, George Rierdan and John Emick.

0929. Morrill, Merit, Estate of, Sept. 23, 1833, Moses Morill appointed Admr. Security, John Wilson and E. Glover. Apprs., William Bennett, James Fleming and Philip Winkleblack.

0930. McBratney, Robert, Estate of, Sept 25, 1833, Admr. appointed Jeremiaj McLene Security, Orris Parish and John Marcy.

0931. Campbell, John W., Estate of, Sept. 26, 1833, Exrx. appointed Eleanor Campbell and John Patterson, William Miner and N. H. Swayne appointed executors. Security, Samuel Parson and Bela Latham. Apprs., Ralph Osborn, D. W. Deshler and J. Ridgeway.

0932. Winkleblack, Michael, Estate of, Oct. 1, 1833, Admr. appointed John Ziegler. Security, Jacob Overdier and John C. Work.

0933. Dedrick, James B., Estate of, Oct. 12, 1833, Admr. appointed George L. Salsberry. Security, George H. Andrews and Isaac N. Case. Apprs., Isaac Case, Elias Vinning and Joseph Hyde.

0934. Andrews, Titus D., Estate of, Oct. 12, 1833, Admr. appointed George Josiah H Fisher. Security, Isaac H. Case and George H. Andrews. Apprs., Isaac Case, Orlando Case and Elisha Hard.

0935. Little, Harvey D., Estate of, Oct. 14, 1833, Mary Little Executrix and Samuel Forrer and Joseph Howard, Executors. Security, Lyne Starling and Joseph Ridgeway.

0936. Thomas, Ebenezer, Estate of, Oct. 14, 1833, Admr. appointed Ebenezer Thomas Jr Security, Joseph Ridgeway, and Charles Scott. Apprs., David Smiley, Jacob S. Rogers and John Weedon. Elizabeth H. Thomas mentioned.

0937. Howard, Hannah, Estate of, Oct. 14, 1833. Admr. appointed, Joseph Howard and Samuel Torrer. Security, Lyne Starling and Joseph Ridgeway.

0938. Leonard, Isaac, Estate of, Oct. 17, 1833, Abner Leonard appointed Executor Security, Joseph McComb and William Patterson. Apprs., Jonathan McComb, John Lang and Zachariah Paul.

0939. Beard, Charles C., Estate of, Oct. 17, 1833, Jarvis Pike appointed admr. Security, Ralph Osburn and John McElvain. Nov. 11, 1833 Mease Smith appointed admr. Sec. Ralph Osburn and Jarvis Pike.

SETTLEMENTS OF ESTATES
ABSTRACTS OF FRANKLIN COUNTY, OHIO RECORDS
ROSALIE HADDOX

0940. Lindsey, guardianship, Oct. 28, 1833, John Barr was appointed guardian of Wilson Lindsey, Fulton, James, Susan A., Jane C., and Martha A. Lindsey, infant heirs of James Lindsey, dec'd. Security, Francis Stewart and John Stambaugh.

0941. Knoderer, Frederick C., Estate of, Nov. 11, 1833, admr. appointed Frederick C. and Frederick W. Knoderer. Security, Frederick Bentz and Christian Karst. Apprs. John Brickell, Michael Stimmell.

0942. White, John M., Estate of, Nov. 29, 1833, Admr. appointed Rachel D. White Security, Jacob Stimmell and Frances Stewart. Apprs., J. Lerby, T. Eister, and Robert Cutter.

0943. Taylor, Samuel, Estate of, Dec. 5, 1833, Exec. appointed John Long, Security, Littleton R. Gray and Thomas Gray.

0944. Sells, Ephraim, Estate of, Jan. 6, 1834. Admr. appointed, Benjamin Sells. Security, Andrew McElvain and Edward Davis. Sept. 19, 1837 James Cherry was appointed Admr. instead of Benjamin Sells, dec'd. Security, James Harris and James Bailey. Record mentions Martha Sells. Apprs., William McElvain, Christian Heyl, James Bryden.

0945. McCoy, John, Estate of, Jan. 6, 1834, Admr. appointed Benjamin Sells. Security, Andrew McElvain and Edward Davis. Apprs., W. McElvain, C. Heyl, and James Bryden.

0946. Clymer, John, Estate of, Jan. 6, 1834, admr. appointed, Mary Clymer. Security, Frederick Henry and Francis Clymer and

218

Louisa Clymer. Apprs., Joseph More, Frederick Henry and Cubbage Needles.

0947. Guy, Ann, Estate of, Jan. 8, 1834, Admr. appointed, Hiram Guy. Security, Nathaniel Medbury and Charles Love. Apprs., Andrew J. McDowell and J. Northrup.

0948. Osborn, John, Estate of, Jan. 24, 1834, Admr. appointed, Mease Smith. Security, Orris Parish and James McDowell.

0949. Osborn, guardianship, Jan. 24, 1834, P. B. Wilcox appointed guardian cf William, aged 15, Michael 11, Eliza E. 7, and Penelope, 5, infant heirs of John Osborn, dec'd. Security, Mease Smith.

0950. Meyers, John, Estate of, Feb. 11, 1834, Admr. appointed, Christian Myers. Security, Jacob Turney and John Whitsell.

0951. McCan, John, Estate of, Feb. 11, 1834, admr. appointed, Benjamin Carter. Security, Henry Miller and Robert Thompson. Apprs. David Smiley, Jacob S. Rogers and John Weedon.

0952. Morris guardianship of, Feb. 11, 1834, Clark Higgins appointed guardian of Jacob, Louisa, Albert and May Morris, infant heirs of Jacob Morris, dec'd. Security, Robert Brotherton and Christopher Davis.

0953. Swisher, Michael, Estate of, Feb. 11, 1834, admr. appointed, William Stewart. Security, Frances Stewart and Jacob Fisher. Apprs., William W. Shannon, Robert C. Henderson, and Michael Fisher.

0954. Scott, guardianship, Feb. 11, 1834, Orris Parish appointed guardian of George Scott, infant heir of ————Scott, dec'd.

0955. Warner, guardianship, Feb. 12, 1834, John Starr was appointed guardian of Henry Warner, 19, minor heir of Osborn Warner, dec'd. Security, William T. Martin and Isaac Case.

0956. Lunn, Benjamin E. Estate of, Feb. 13, 1834, Admr. appointed, Thomas Lunn. Security, Daniel Whitsell and Adin G. Hibbs. Apprs., James Edgar, John Martin, John Painter.

0957. Jackson, Benjamin, Estate of, Feb. 14, 1834, admr. appointed, John Courtright. Security, Joseph Wright and John D Cress Apprs., James Carson, John Young, and Elias Chester.

0958. Cochran, guardianship, Feb. 18, 1834(P. B. Wilcox chosen as guardian of John Cochran, aged 14 yrs., minor heir of John Cochran, Dec'd. Security, Mease Smith.

0959. Weaver, guardianship, Feb. 19, 1834, Bela Latham appointed guardian of Michael, aged 5 yrs., and John aged 7 yrs., infant heirs of Michael Weaver dec'd. Security, Samuel C. Andrews.

0960. Hutchinson, guardianship, Feb. 20, 1834, P. B. Wilcox appointed guardian of Lewis 4 yrs. and Samuel 2 yrs. Hutchinson, infant heirs of John Hutchinson, dec'd. Security, N. H. Swayne.

0961. Dyerd, John, Estate of, Feb. 20, 1834, Mary Dyer and John Reid appointed as admrs. Securities, Joseph Foster and Reuben P. Mann, Apprs., Charles Hunter, William Walker and Thomas Tipton.

0962. Kious, John, Estate of, Feb. 21, 1834, John H. Kious appointed admr. Securities, George Hoover and William Miller. Apprs., William Miller, Moses Persol and Jacob Stimmell.

0963. Kious guardianship, Feb. 21, 1834, George Hoover was chosen as guardian by Zeniah minor heir of John Kious dec'd. Securities, John H. Kious and Jacob B. Diemer.

0964. Kious guardianship, Feb. 24, 1834, Jacob Borrer appointed as guardian of Maria aged 10 yrs. and John aged 8 yrs. infant heirs of Solomon Kious dec'd. Securities Woolery Coonrod and Chandler Rodgers. Receipt for $93., dated Sept. 13, 1841, signed by Maria White and Isaac White, "for my share of my father's estate".

0965. Wallace, William, Estate of, Feb. 22, 1834. Elizabeth Wallace appointed as admix. Securities, David W. Deshler and Joseph Ridgeway. Aug. 10, 1835, R. G. Walling was appointed admr. instead of Elizabeth Wallace dec'd. Securities, Otis Crosby and Robert Cutler, Feb. 22, 1836 Samuel Crosby was appointed admr. of this estate and also of the estate of Elizabeth Wallace dec'd. Apprs., S. Crosby, Robert Cutler and R. G. Walling.

0966. Ogden, Elas, Estate of, Feb. 26, 1834, John Kelso appointed as admr. Speaks of Hulda C. Ogden and also of Lewis Ogden.

0967. Vorys, Isaiah, Estate of, Apr. 3, 1834, Charlotte Vorys was appointed exrx. Securities, George McCormick and John M. Walcott. On the settlement of the estate John Greenwood was allowed $43.37, for services rendered.

0968. Bishop, John, Estate of, late of Madison twp. Apr. 5, 1834, John Young was appointed admr. Securities, Samuel Bishop and Elias Chester jr. Apprs., William Kile, John Wilson and Abraham Shoemaker.

0969. Baughman, George, Estate of, May 7, 1834, James Price and Jesse Baughman appointed as exrc. Securities, John Saul and Daniel Swickard.

0970. Darby, John, Estate of, June 2, 1834, Moses M. Hunter appointpointed admr. Securities, Luther Pratt and Nicholas Demorest. Apprs. John McCafferty and David Westenberger.

0971. Ogden guardianship, June 2, 1834, Charles H. Ogden chosen as guardian by George H. Ogden minor heir of Elias Ogden dec'd. Securities, Samuel Reynolds and William Armstrong.

0972. Kilbourn, James, Estate of (Madison twp.), June 2, 1834, Samuel D. Haverly appointed admr. Securities, John Swisher and Samuel Watt, Apprs., Jacob Gander and Jesse Welton, and Jacob Hockman. Mentions wife, Martha Kilbourn. Jan. 13, 1836 she signs her name as Martha Haverly.

0973. Sager, John, Estate of, Blendon twp. June 2, 1834, Christiana Sager appointed admix. Securities, Daniel Swickard and Jonas Sowder. Nov. 5, 1834, Daniel Swickard appointed admr. Securities, John Havens and Shuah Mann. Apprs., Jacob Smith, John H. Smith and George Beals.

0974. Sells guardianship, June 3, 1834, John McElvain chosen as guardian by Benjamin Sells jr. aged 20 yrs. minor heir of Peter Sells dec'd. Securities, William Sulivant and Moylen Northrop.

0975. Sells, guardianship, June 3, 1834, Benjamin Sells chosen as guardian by Cyrus Sells aged 18 yrs. minor heir of Peter Sells dec'd. Securities, John Brickle and James Harris.

0976. Sells guardianship, June 3, 1834, Benjamin Sells appointed guardian of Miles Sells aged 12 yrs. minor heir of Peter Sells dec'd. Securities not given.

0977. Sells guardianship, June 3, 1834, Benjamin Sells appointed guardian of Sarah Sells aged 8 yrs. infant heir of Peter Sells dec'd Securities, John Brickle and James Harris.

0978. Sells guardianship, June 3, 1834, Benjamin Sells appointed guardian of Luke Sells aged 6 yrs. infant heir, of Peter Sells dec'd. Securities John Brickle and James Harris.

0979. Wilcox, Israel, Estate of, June 3, 1834, Will proven and R. W. Cowles appointed excr. Securities, Matthew Matthews and Moses Maynard jr. Apprs., John W. Milligan, Joseph Roberts and Thomas Vause.

0980. Fisher guardianship, June 10, 1834, Lyne Starling appointed as guardian of Jane Fisher aged 2½ yrs. infant heir of Michael Fisher dec'd. Securities, Francis Stewart and Henry Brown.

0981. Purdy guardianship, June 11, 1834, George W. Purdy appointed as guardian of Catherine aged 8 yrs. and Emeline aged 6 yrs. infant heirs of George Purdy. Securities, John Young and John Courtright.

0982. Flagg, Edmund, Estate of, June 12, 1834, John Hunter appointed admr. Securities, Robert Brotherton and Amaziah Hutchinson.

0983. Hunter, Joseph, Estate of, June 14, 1834, will and codicil probated and referred to the Supreme Court. June 6, 1834, Joseph and William Hunter appointed execs. Securities, Francis Stewart and John McElvain.

0984. Lamson, guardianship. June 14, 1834, William Preston appointed guardian of James Lamson aged 15 yrs. minor heir of William K. Lamson dec'd. Security, P. B. Wilcox.

0985. Coruse, Daniel, Estate of, Aug. 9, 1834, Isaac Decker appointed admr. Securities, George Bishop and Elias Decker. Apprs., Henry Dildine Henry Dellinger and Alex. Cameron.

0986. Robinson, James, Estate of, Montgomery twp. Aug. 18, 1834, Godfrey Robinson appointed admr. Securities, Gustavus Swan and Samuel Reynolds. Apprs. A. Chittenden, M. Northrop and John M. Walcott. Mentions widow, Mary Robinson. Also Miss Ann Robinson.

0987. Smith guardianship, Sept. 15, 1834, Hiram Richards appointed guardian of Lois Smith aged 10 yrs. infant heir of C. Smith dec'd. Securities, Ebenezer Richards and Amaziah Hutchinson.

0988. Maynard, Eber P., Estate of, Sept. 15, 1834, Robert McMains appointed admr. Securities, George Richey and Clark Bowers.

0989. Maynard, Moses, Estate of, Sept. 15' 1834, Moses Maynard jr. appointed exec. Securities, Recompense Stansberry and Ozem Gardner. Apprs., Aseph Allen, John W. Ladd and John McMahan.

0990. Miller, William, Estate of, Jackson twp., will proven and Matthew Miller and Jacob Strader appointed execs., Sept. 15, 1834. Securities, John Mitchell and Absolom Borror. Apprs., Woolery Coonrod, William Miller and David Spangler.

0991. Phelps, Abram, Estate of, will proven and Mrs. Lucy Phelps appointed exrx. Sept. 15, 1834. Securities, Homer M. Phelps and P. H. Olmstead. May 28, 1839 accounts filed and referred to John G. Miller, Special Commissioner. Wife, Lucy Phelps sole heir married Jeremiah Armstrong before May 27, 1840.

0922. Edgar, Harriet, Estate of. Will proven and ordered to be recorded.

0993. Miller guardianship, Sept. 15, 1834, Absolom Borrer appointed guardian of William Miller aged 20 yrs. minor heir of William Miller dec'd. Securities, Matthew Miller and Jacob Strader.

0994. Wilson Guardianship, Sept. 15, 1834, John McCarthy appointed guardian of Margaret Wilson minor heir of James Wilson dec'd. Securities, Andrew McElvain and John Wilson.

0995. Edmiston, Dr. John M., Estate of, Sept. 15, 1834, Eli W. Gwynne and Thomas M. Gwynne appointed admrs. Securities, Joshua Baldwin and Gustavus Swan. Apprs., Samuel Barr, John Wilson and Andrew Backus. Mentions widow and five children.

0996. Chandler, Jacob, Estate of, Sept. 19, 1834, Elizabeth Chandler appointed admix. Securities, Abner Leonard and John Champe. Apprs., Abraham Shoemaker, John Wilson and Jacob Weaver.

0997. Shepherd guardianship. Sept. 20, 1834, Joel Buttles appointed guardian of Mary Shepherd aged 16 yrs. a colored girl. Security. Aurora Buttles.

0998. Kooser guardianship, Sept. 30, 1834, Elizabeth Kooser chosen as guardian by Frederick Kooser aged about 17 yrs. minor heir of Conrad Kooser dec'd. Securities, William T. Martin and Jacob Hare.

0999. Kooser, guardianship, Sept. 30, 1834, Elizabeth Kooser chosen as guardian by Gottilieb Kooser aged about 17 yrs. Securities, William T. Martin and Jacob Hare.

01000. Warner guardianship, Sept. 22, 1834, Charles Scott appointed guardian of Horatio Warner aged 12 yrs. infant heir of Alva S. Warner dec'd. Security, Matthew Matthews.

01001. Switzer, John, Estate of, Sept. 22, 1834, Betsy Switzer appointed admix. Securities Thomas Johnson and John Courtright. Apprs., Edward Livingston, Alexander Mooberry and Edward Courtright.

01002. Switzer, Benjamin, Estate of, Sept. 23, 1834, Elizabeth Switzer appointed admix. Securities, William Doherty and Jonas Pike.

01003. Layton, David, Estate of, Sept. 24, 1834, Josiah Bevan appointed admr. Securities, John Neff and Abram Romine. Apprs. John Hunter, Christopher Davis and James Gardener.

01004. Robinson guardianship, Sept. 27, 1834, Mary Robinson chosen as guardian by Ann Robinson aged 14 yrs. minor heir of James Robinson dec'd. Securities, Matthew Matthews and David W. Deshler.

01005. Mead, Linus, Estate of, Sept. 27, 1834, Louisa Mead appointed admix. Securities, Lynne Starling and Matthew W. Gilbert.

01006. Seely guardianship, Sept. 27, 1834, Moses Jewell chosen as guardian by Phoebe Seely aged 15 yrs. minor heir of——— Seely dec'd. Securities ,Andrew McElvain and O. Parish.

01007. Young, John, Estate of, Oct. 27, 1834, John Long appointed admr. Securities, William T. Martin and James Young. Apprs., Jonathan McComb, Matthew Taylor and William Thompson.

01008. Eberlee, Peter, Estate of, Nov. 4, 1834, Jacob Eberlee and Christian Heyl appointed admrs. Securities, Francis Stewart and Andrew Sights. Apprs., M. Matthews, William Awl and Otis Crosby.

01009. Lawson, Peter, Estate of, Nov. 11, 1834, Losana and David Lawson appointed admrs. Securities, Robert Brotherton and John Marcy.

01010. Bates, Aquilla, Estate of, Nov. 24, 1834, George White appointed admr. Securities, Philip Read and John Lakin.

01011. Williams, David, Estate of, Dec. 30, 1834, Margaret Williams and Abraham J. Williams appointed admrs. Securities, Jeremiah Minor and Kernes. Apprs. G. R. Minor, Jacob Stimmel and Peter Stimmel.

01012. Connelly, Edward, Estate of Blendon twp. Feb. 16, 1835, William H. Connely appointed admr. Securities, Simeon Moore and John Heer. Apprs. Timothy Lee and Robert Paul.

01013. Reece, Thomas, Estate of, Feb. 16, 1835, Nancy Reece appointed admix. Securities, John Coons and Jacob Reese. Apprs. Daniel Whitsell, George Parkinson and John D. French.

01014. Roney guardianship, Feb. 16, 1835, James Roney was chosen as guardian by Margaretta Roney aged 15 yrs. minor heir of Mary Woodside dec'd. Securities, Jacob Falkner and M. J. Gilbert.

01015. Roney guardianship, Feb. 16, 1835. James Roney appointed guardian of Mary Jane Roney aged 7 yrs. and Isaac L. Roney aged 10 yrs. and Eliza Ann Roney aged 11 yrs. infant heirs of Mary Woodside dec'd.

01016. Thompson, John, Estate of, Feb. 16, 1835, Samuel Thompson, appointed admr. Securities, Adam Read and P. H. Olmstead. Apprs. A. J. McDowell, William Long and John Emmick.

010017. Hunter, Joseph, Estate of; Will proven and William and Joseph Hunter appointed execs. Securities, Francis Stewart and John McElvain. Apprs. Thomas Moore, Jacob Slyh and James O'Harra.

01018. Kells, John, Estate of, Feb. 18, 1835, Jane Flagg apointed admix. Securities, A. J. McDowell and George Richey.

01019. Baldwin, Archibald K. Estate of, Feb. 18, 1835, Sylvanus Baldwin appointed admr. Securities, Otis Crosby and Samuel Crosby.

01020. Clymer guardianship, Feb. 19, 1835, Matthew Westervelt appointed guardian of Louisa Clymer aged 7 yrs. infant heir of John Clymer dec'd. Securities, Stephen Brinkerhoof and John Watt.

SETTLEMENTS OF ESTATES

Abstracts of Franklin County, Ohio Records.

Rosalie R. Haddox

01021. Shannon, guardianship, Feb. 19, 1835, William W. Shannon appointed guardian of Amanda, aged 16, Samuel, aged 14 and Hadessa I., aged 12. Security, Samuel Shannon and Fergus Moorehead.

01022. Shannon, guardianship, Feb. 23, 1835, William Shannon appointed guardian of Nathaniel W. S.

01023. Blount, Adam, Estate of, May 12, 1835, Admr. appointed, James M. Paxton. Security, Miner Pickle and Owen T. Barbee.

01024. Modlee, George, Estate of, Feb. 20, 1835, Admr. appointed, George Parkinson, Security, Jeremiah Hay.

01025. De Noon, guardianship, Feb. 21, 1835, John Kissinger appointed guardian of Edmund, aged 8 years, heir of John DeNoon. Security, David Beers and Lewis Agler.

01026. DeNoon, guardianship, Feb. 21, 1835, John Kissinger appointed guardian of John DeNoon, aged 11 years, heir of John DeNoon. Security, David Beers and Lewis Agler.

01027. Patterson, guardianship, Feb. 21, 1835, David Beers appointed guardian of Charles, aged 20, Angeline, aged 16 and Maria P., aged 14 years. Security, John Kissinger and Peter Agler.

01028. Groomis, Mary, Estate of, Feb. 21, 1835, Admnr. appointed, Benjamin Britton. David Groomis mentioned. Security, David Smiley, Miskell Saunders.

01029. Maynard, guardianship, Feb. 25, 1835, Hiram Andrews appointed guardian of William W., aged 20, Jefferson T., aged 16, and Horace, aged 15 years, heirs of Stephen Maynard, deceased. Security, Elnathan Maynard and Amaziah Hutchinson.

01030. Lehmann, guardianship, Feb. 26, 1835, Nicholas Barth appointed guardian of Herrman, aged 18 and Gabriel, aged 15 years. Security, P. B. Wilcox and Christian Rader.

01031. White, guardianship, Feb. 26, 1835, Clark Higgins appointed guardian of Marcella, aged 11 years, heir of John White, deceased. Security, John Greenwood and Frances Stewart.

01032. White, guardianship, Feb. 26, 1835, Clark Higgins appointed guardian of John McDowell White, aged 18, and Samuel C. White, aged 20 years, heirs of John White, deceased. Security, John Greenwood and Frances Stewart. On Oct. 26, 1841 a note was signed by John McD. White, Samuel C. White, Marcella. White Cherry and John Cherry.

01033. Cochran, guardianship, Feb. 27, 1835, P. B. Wilcox appointed guardian of Michael, aged 19 years. Security, Mease Smith.

01035. Thomas, Cornelius, Estate of, Feb. 28, 1935, Admnr. appointed Mease Smith. Security, Lynn Starling and P. B. Wilcox.

01036. Price, William, Estate of, Feb. 28, 1935, Admr. appointed, Mease Smith. Security, P. B. Wilcox and George B. Harvey.

01037. Johnson, Henry, Estate of, March 9, 1835, Admnr. appointed, William Perrin. Security, R. Brotherton and William Garvin.

01038. Spangler, Joseph, Estate of, March 11, 1835, Admnrs. appointed, John Landis and William Spangler. Mary Spangler, widow of Joseph Spangler mentioned. Security, William Spangler, David Spangler and Benjamin Landis.

01039. Connell, William, Estate of, March 20, 1835, Admnrs. appointed Daniel Whitsell and William Connell. Widow mentioned but no name. Security, John Long, David Pugh.

01040. Whims, Charles, Estate of, May 4, 1835, Admnr. appointed, William Whims. Those mentioned in the papers are Sarah, widow of Charles; Martha, Andrew, children; and the Admnr. William was the eldest son. Security. Zachariah Stevenson and John Wright.

01041. Parks, guardianship, May 4, 1835, Elizabeth Parks appointed guardian of Silas, aged 10, Elizabeth C., aged 8, Eliza, aged 6, and Sarah Jane, aged one year, all heirs of Samuel Parks, deceased. Security, Asahee Carter and George Parks.

01042. Van dorn, Ralph, Estate of, May 8, 1835, Admnrx. appointed, Mary Ann Van dorn; Admnr. appointed, William Thompson. Security, Dr. Ezekiel Whitehead and George Parkinson. Appraisers: Daniel Taft, John Hanson and Benjamin Bronson.

01043. Whims, guardianship, May 5, 1835, Sarah Whims appointed guardian of Martha Whims, aged 14, Andrew Whims, aged 17, heirs of Charles Whims. Security, William Whims and John Swisher.

01044. Hunter, guardianship, May 7, 1835, Joseph Hunter appointed guardian of Mandelburt, aged 18, Return I., aged 16, Orville S., aged 15, Andrew and Eunice aged 4 years and Livonia P., aged 12 years, all heirs of Eunice Hunter, deceased. Security, Joseph McElvain and Robt. Brotherton.

01045. Bishop, guardianship, May 7, 1835, Sarah Bishop and Daniel Whitsell appointed guardians of Adam, aged 6 years, Samuel aged 3 years, and John, aged 1 year, heirs of John Bishop. Security, Matthias Wolf and Frances Stewart.

01046. Cramer, Andrew, Estate of, Feb. 24, 1835, Executor, John Swisher. Ludwig and Anthony Cramer (Kramer) mentioned in papers. Security, Samuel Hamilton and John Helsel.

01047. Burgett, George, Estate of,

01048. Bayley, Thomas M., Estate of,

01049. Cown, guardianship, May 12, 1835, Moses H. Kirby appointed guardian of John Cown, aged 13 years. Security, R. Brotherton and George Riordan.

01050. Kensel, guardianship, May 12, 1835, Henry Brown appointed guardian of Mary Kensel, heir of William Kensel, deceased. Security, Robert Neil and Moses H. Kirby.

MARRIAGE RECORDS, FRANKLIN COUNTY, OHIO

Blanche Tipton Rings

All records are taken from Record Book—Volumes 1 to 8, inclusive. The volume and page follows the name of by whom married. Many times there is no indication of whether it is minister or Justice of Peace.

—A—

†Aaron (I.) & Anson (Rec.), Ann—Knobs, William—Sept. 2, 1839. (Aug. 31)† by W. T. Martin, J. P.   3–222.
(†William Knobs—Ann Anson—Aug. 31, 1839.)

Abea, Miss Catherine—Arnest, Jacob—Feb. 5, 1856.   John Charles Hennaman, M. G.   6–260.

Abbe, Catherine—Langmeister, Henry—Feb. 21, 1839.   Wilhelm Schmidt, M. G.   3–220.

Abby, George F.—(Abbe)†—Schultz, Margaret (Schutz)†—March 30, 1843.   C. F. Schaeffer, M. G.   4–4.

†Abby, John—Rew (I) and (Kerr),† Betsy—July 28, 1843.   Charles Rarey.   4–4.

†Abel, Catherine—Guldner, John—May 12, 1855.   C. H. Borgess, C. P.   6–209.

†Abell (Abel),† John—Benedict, Rachael—April 16, 1833.   G. W. Hart, J. P.   3–54.

†Abell, John—Enos (Rec) & Ems (I), Catherine—Apr. 25, 1857. K. Mees, M. G.   6–358.

Abner, Margaret—Bolsley, Michael—May 9, 1842.   Joshua Young, J. P.   4–25.

†Abner, Simon (signed in German)—Junker, Caroline—Nov. 16, 1858.   William F. Lehman, M. G.   7–181.

†Abbott, Catherine—Everest, George S.—Feb. 12, 1838.   Hiland Hulburd, M. G.   3–238.

†Abbott, Hattie—Neil, James H.—Oct. 19, 1858.   James Hoge, M. G.   7–168.

The marriage records of Franklin County have been copied as given in the Marriage Record Books. Marks and abbreviations used in this chapter are as follows:
I.—Marriage Record Index.
Rec.—Marriage Record as given in the Record Books.
M. G.—Minister of the Gospel.
C. P.—Catholic Priest.
J. P.—Justice of Peace.
†—Original Records. These original records are fragments of paper stored in the Probate Court Rooms.
O. S. J.—Ohio State Journal.
W. I.—Western Intelligencer, predecessor of the Ohio State Journal.
Consents—Consents to marriages are given where found. They have been obtained from original documents and from record books.
Returns—Records have been copied even when "no return" is marked after them. In a great many instances the minister or Justice of Peace failed to return the official papers. The Probate Court cannot give certified copies of marriage records unless a "return" has been made.
Many original records, affidavits, and consents have been found which are not included in the record books at the court house. These will be printed later in a supplement to the regular records. The word "Colored" is used whenever it is given in the records. The term "contraband" also refers to negroes.
All dates are given in the return of the minister as when married, not the date of license. When there is no return given, the date of issuance of license is stated.

ABBOTT, Henry J.—Stanley, Mary E.—April 20, 1859. C. E.
Lewis, Rector of St. John's Church, Worthington. 7–263.

†ABBOTT, Hester Ann—Mackey, Joseph J.—Oct. 23, 1847. A.
Patton, J. P. 5–79.

ABBOTT, James S.—Neley, Martha—July 1, 1832. William T.
Snow, J. P. 3–43.

　†(Consent of his father, Samuel Abbott) O. S. J. (At Worthington—James S. Abbott and Miss Martha Neeley, of Somerset,
Perry County, Ohio—rest same.)

†ABBOTT, Joel—McDowell, Melinda and Melina—Nov. 4, 1813.
John B. Johnston. 1–126.

†ABBOTT, Lena (Rec) and Sena (I)—Myers, Jacob—Mch. 19, 1854.
John Charles Hennamon, M. G. 6–108.

　†(Jacob Myers and Helene Abbert, both of Rome, Franklin
County, rest same.)

†ABBOTT, Loice (Rec) and Lois (I)—Purse, Zedina—Nov. 16, 1822.
Eli C. King, J. P. 2–116.

ABBOTT, Mary Ann—Burr, Philo—Sept. 21, 1825. Ebenezer
Washburn, V. D. M. 2–177.

†ABBOTT, Mary—Webb, Henry—May 1, 1856. J. D. Smith,
M. G. 6–281.

　O. S. J. (Henry Webb, of Dixon, Illinois, and Miss Mary
Abbott, eldest daughter of J. S. Abbott, rest same.)

†ABBOTT, Philan S.—Fisher, Molly L.—Aug. 1, 1858. Mary B.
Bruny, Elder in Christian Church. · 7–136.

†ABNETT, William (of Pickaway County)†—Miller, Mariah S. (Miss
of Hamilton Township)†—March 5, 1840 (Feb. 5, 1840).† Lewis
Madden, M. G. 3–235.

†ABRAMS, Catherine—Kingery, Jacob—Jan. 14, 1863. J. G. Miller,
J. P. 8–118.

ACHERSON, Sarah Elizabeth (Ackerson)†—Johnson, Francis—Mch.
4, 1852 Joseph S. Brown, Minister.

†ACHESON, James C.—Northrup, Lavinia—Oct. 15, 1838. James
Hoge, M. G. 4–1.

　O. S. J. (James C. Acheson & Lavinia, youngest daughter of
M. Northrup.)

†ACHESON, Thomas—Hooker, Catherine—Sept. 21, 1840. James
Hoge, M. G. 4–1.

　O. S. J. (Thomas Acheson, son of the late T. Acheson, of
Washington, Pa. & Catherine L. Hooker, daughter of Thomas H.
Hooker, late of Hartford, Conn.)

†ACHEY, Almina—Staley, James—Sept. 8, 1864. John C. Tidball,
M. G. 8–404.

†ACHEY, Benjamin—Shaffer and Schaeffer, Almira—March 25, 1850.
N. Doolittle, M. G. 5–224.

†ACHEY, George—Sourden, Catherine—May 25, 1843. David Lewis,
M. G. 4–3.

†ACHEY, Henry—Saul, Susanna—Dec. 13, 1843. Philip Gast,
M. G. 4–4.

†ACKAMON, Nancy A.—Rendalan, Joseph—Dec. 9, 1837. Thomas Wood, J. P. 3–186.
 †(Knadalon, Joseph & Ackerman, Nancy, Dec. 9, 1837.)
 O. S. J. (Joseph Knodoean & Miss Nancy Ackerman, all of here, Dec. 9, 1837.)

ACKERMAN, Sarbara—Igel, Peter—1845. William Schonatt, Catholic M. G. 4–149.

†ACKERMAN, Caroline C.—Cain, Samuel—June 26, 1860. William L. Heyl, J. P. 7–449.

†ACKERMAN, John—Coe, Lovella—Feb. 14, 1848. D. S. Cherry, M. G.

†ACKERMANN, Levi—Philbrick, Permelia—Nov. 25, 1850. R. K. Nash, M. G. 5–265.

†ACKERMANN, Magdalina — Pusecker, Charles — Jan. 22, 1857. William F. Lehmann, M. G. 6–332.

†ACKERMAN, Peter—Keys, Cariline—Dec. 22, 1844. H. L. Richards, M. G. 4–5.

†ACKERMAN, Philip—Koch, Magdalina—Mch. 16, 1851. Konrad Mees, M. G. 5–317.

†ACKERMAN, Valentine—Schoedinger, Mary—Apr. 26, 1853. William F. Lehmann, M. G. 6–30.

†ACKERS, Robert—Murphy, Bridget—July 8, 1864. William L. Heyl, J. P. 8–380.

ACKERSON, Joseph W.—Mossman, Huldah—Oct. 13, 1861—vouched by William Brown. George Wagner, J. P. 7–638.

†ACKLES, Rebecca—Kreamer, Joseph—Aug. 20, 1853. Robert King, J. P. 6–54.

†ACRES, Jane—Beeson, and (Beason)† Peter—Sept. 24, 1857. James Poindexter, M. G. 7–6.

ACTON, Caleb H.—Crawford, Sidney—Apr. 5, 1854 (Apr. 15).† Elisha C. Wright, M. G. 6–104.

ACTON, Elizabeth — Petticord, Caleb — Nov. 10, 1842. David Howard. 4–212.

†ACTON, John—Bigelow, Susannah—Apr. 15, 1847. J. S. Rogers, J. P. 5–55.

†ACTON, N.—Wilson, (Wilcox),† Almira—Sept. 9, 1839. Samuel Dearduff, J. P. 3–222. †(William N. Acton and Almyra Wilcox.)

†ACTON, Rachel—Fickle, Nelson, age 18 years—Apr. 7, 1859. T. W. Dobyns, J. P. 7–255
 †(Rhoda Fickle is willing for "my son" Nelson Fickle to marry Rachel Aston. Wit.—Joseph Fickle, Banjamin Hiser.)

ACTON, Richard—Biggert, Margaret—Aug. 27, 1846. No return. 5–22.

ACTON, Sarah Ann—Armentrout, Gideon—July 26, 1842. J. S. Rogers, J. P. 4–2.

ACTUN, William—Pinckney, Elizabeth Ann—Aug. 10, 1851 (Aug. 19).† John B. West, J. P. 5–324. (Pickering).†

†AKER (I) & Acher (Rec.), Mary—Kuehlwein, George L.—July 4, 1854. K. Mees, M. G. 6–123.

MARRIAGE RECORDS, FRANKLIN COUNTY, OHIO

BLANCHE TIPTON RINGS

All records are taken from Record Book—Volumes 1 to 8, inclusive. The volume and page follows the name of by whom married. Many times there is no indication of whether it is minister or Justice of Peace.

—A—

†ADAIR, Joseph H.—Trumbo, Mary Alma—July 4, 1860. Daniel D. Mather, M. G. 7–450.

†ADAMS, Addison—Ortman, Ann W.—Nov. 24, 1859. Rev. Henry Williard. 7–349.
> O. S. J. (At Union Church, Perry Township, both of the county.)

†ADAMS, A. H.—Konitzer, C. F.—†May 27, 1851. John W. Weakley, M. G. 5–309. O. S. J. (Both of City. Mr. A. W. Adams.)

†ADAMS, Amanda—Phipps, James—Nov. 2, 1848. B. Boyd, J. P. 5–135.

†ADAMS, Andrew—Bergnitz, Dorothy—Dec. 28, 1854. W. Slaughter, M. G. 6–174.

†ADAM, Anthony—Magley, Anna M.—Apr. 21, 1853. K. Mees, M. G. 6–29.

†ADAMS, Bailey—Timmons, Sealy—Feb. 28, 1847. Robert Seeds, J. P. 5–47.

†ADAMS, Barbara—Jackson, John—Dec. 12, 1847. George J. Archer. 5–84.

†Adam or EDEM, Catherine—Nochbar, George. Nov. 18, 1854. K. Mees, M. G. 6–164.

†ADAMS, Charles B.—McClellan, Mary A.—March 24, 1864. J. S. Cantwell, M. G. 8–330.
> O. S. J.—Miss Mary A. McClellan, all of Columbus, rest same.

The marriage records of Franklin County have been copied as given in the Marriage Record Books. Marks and abbreviations used in this chapter are as follows:

I.—Marriage Record Index.
Rec.—Marriage Record as given in the Record Books.
M. G.—Minister of the Gospel.
C. P.—Catholic Priest.
J. P.—Justice of Peace.
†—Original Records. These original records are fragments of paper stored in the Probate Court Rooms.
O. S. J.—Ohio State Journal.
W. I.—Western Intelligencer, predecessor of the Ohio State Journal.
Consents—Consents to marriages are given where found. They have been obtained from original documents and from record books.
Returns—Records have been copied even when "no return" is marked after them. In a great many instances the minister or Justice of Peace failed to return the official papers. The Probate Court cannot give certified copies of marriage records unless a "return" has been made.
Many original records, affidavits, and consents have been found which are not included in the record books at the court house. These will be printed later in a supplement to the regular records. The word "Colored" is used whenever it is given in the records. The term "contraband" also refers to negroes.
All dates are given in the return of the minister as when married, not the date of license. When there is no return given, the date of issuance of license is stated.

†ADAMS, Chloe—Havens, George—Aug. 29, 1864. J. Kronenbitter, J. P. 8–400.

ADDAMS, Delia—Chew, Anthony S.—March 7, 1837. L. L. Sader, M. G. 3–158. O. S. J.—Anthony S. Chew and Miss Delia, daughter of Demas Adams, Esq.

ADAMS, Demas—Barns, Susan—Sept. 27, 1818. Rev. Philander Chase.

†ADAMS, Edward—Miller, Martha—Nov. 13, 1851. Edward Davis. 5–358.

ADAMS, Elisa—Mas, Conrad—Sept. 20, 1844. Rev. Martin Schaad. 4–194.

†ADAMS, Elizabeth—Inman, Esack (Rec.) or Esau (I)—April 1, 1818. Joseph Gorton, J. P. 2–47.

†ADAMS, Elizabeth—Ferguson, John M.—Nov. 13, 1856. David Shrom, V. D. M. 6–315.

†ADAMS, Elizabeth B.—Gutches, Paul M.—Sept. 8, 1860. B. N. Spahr, M. G. Vouched by John Warren. 7–480.

†ADAMS, Eri—Cross, Mary Ann—Oct. 16, 1864. George Wagner, J. P. 8–429.

ADAMS, Fredona—Spring, Homer—Jan. 6, 1861. J. F. Snoddy, J. P. 7–533.

ADAMS, George W.—Grate, Mary—Dec. 22, 1856. No return. 6–326.

†ADAMS, Harriet G.—Gill, Stephen A.—March 8, 1848. James B. Finley, M. G. 5–95.

†ADAMS, Harriet J.—Strohm, Henry C.—June 26, 1855. J. D. Smith, M. G. 6 210.

†ADAM, Helena—Wellman, Hubert—Oct. 30, 1858. K. Mees, M. G. 7–175.

†ADAMS, Henry—Postles, Emanda Jane—April 7, 1839. Samuel Dearduff, J. P. 3–213.

(Consent of her father Stephen Postle, April 6, 1839.†)

†ADAMS, H. L.—Hildreth, Emma A.—Oct. 10, 1854. H. L. Hitchcock, M. G. 6–154.

O. S. J.—H. S. Adams of Sandusky, and Mrs. Emma A. Hildreth of Circleville. Rest same.

ADAMS, Isaac J.—Dennis, Sarah—July 29, 1861. No return. 7–611.

†ADAMS, James—Jameson, Jane C.—Sept. 17. 1835. Nathan Emery, M. G. 3–124.

†ADAMS, James W.—Bowman, Leah A.—Sept. 20, 1859. William Hanby, M. G. 7–322.

(She is three days under age of 18 years.)

†ADAMS, Jane—Frank, Samuel—Jan. 12, 1842. James Hoge, M. G. 4–98.

†ADAMS, John—Smothers, Hannah—April 29, 1821. Russell Bigelow, M. G. 2–89.

(John Smothers says his sister, Hannah Smothers, is of lawful age to marry John Adams and that the parties is not nearer related than first cousins.†)

†ADAMS, John—Linton, Philipena—April 4, 1841. John Starrett, J. P. 4–1.

Adams, John N.—Clemings (or Clemmins†), Jane—Oct. 15, 1832. Jacob Grubb, J. P. 3–47.

†ADAMS, John N.—Lee, Margaret (Rec.) or Nancy (I)—Aug. 26, 1847. W. T. Martin, J. P. 5–69.

†ADAMS, John Quincy—Dickerson, Susannah—Dec. 18, 1863 (Dec. 20, 1863†). Daniel Bonebarke, M. G. 8–276.

ADAMS, Joseph—Reed, Emeline—July 16, 1842. William T. Martin, J. P. 4–3. July 16, 1841. 4–2.

†ADAMS, Joseph—Huffman, Barbara—May 16, 1844. Jesse Bright, M. G. 4–4.

ADAMS, Joseph—Luster, Catherine—Oct. 31, 1854. No return. 6–160.

†ADAMS, Lucinda—Ross, Robert L.—Sept. 26, 1850. J. L. Chadbourne, M. E. M. G. 5–259.

†ADAMS, Margaret—Avery, Daniel—Jan. 4, 1821. A. Allen, J. P. 2–86.

†ADAMS, Margaret—Barbee, Franklin—Oct. 21, 1828. James Hoge, M. G. 3–61.

O. S. J.—William Barbee and Miss Margaret Adams, daughter of Percival Adams, Esq., Oct. 23, 1828, Hamilton Township.

†Adams, Margaret—Lewis, Wesley—Dec. 29, 1850. Rev. Lewis A. Burt. 5–279.

†ADAMS, Margaret A.—Brackenridge, John S.—Sept. 8, 1863. H. L. Whitehead, M. G. 8–222.

†ADAMS, Martha—Ranney, David—Sept. 25, 1855. J. C. Bright, M. G. 6–233.

ADAMS, Mary—Horlocker, William—Sept. 4, 1842. Daniel Hamaker J. P. 4–134.

†ADAMS, Mary Ann—Shadle, Solomon D.—Nov. 9, 1843. Josiah D. Smith, M. G. 4–251.

†ADAMS, Mary E.—Beatty, Robert W.—Aug. 6, 1848. Jesse Bright, M. G. 5–117.

†ADAMS, Mary E.—Swan, Lewis—Sept. 24, 1848. G. C. Crum, M. G. 5–125.

†ADAMS, Mary—Fristo, G. G.—March 31, 1853. John M. Leavett, M. G. 6–22.

†ADAMS, Mary—Newberry, Lewis M.—Jan. 24, 1858. Lovett Taft, M. G. 7–57.

O. S. J.—Miss Mary Adams and Lewis I. Newberry, all of county. Rest same.

†ADAMS, Minerva Ann—Elliott, David—Sept. 27, 1860. G. M. Clover, J. P. 7–490.

(Mary A. Bryant gives consent for the marriage of David Elliott to Minerva Ann Adams, my daughter, Sept. 20, 1860. Daniel Brunk and Mary A. Brunk, Norwich Township. Witness—George McCombs and David Elliott.†)

†ADAMS, Nancy—Stumbaugh, John—Jan. 30, 1833. James Hoge, M. G. 3–67.

MARRIAGE RECORDS, FRANKLIN COUNTY, OHIO

Blanche Tipton Rings

Adams, Nelson—Coleman, Abigail—Oct. 16, 1832. John F. Solomon, M. G.
3–49.

†Adams, Percival—Brown, Elizabeth—Nov. 4, 1847. James Hoge, M. G.
5–80.
    O. S. J.—Percival Adams, of Hamilton township and Miss Elizabeth
Brown, of this city, rest same.

†Adams, Percival—England, Mary C.—Feb. 25, 1863. G. M. Scott, V. D. M.
8–129.

The marriage records of Franklin County have been copied as given in the Marriage Record Book
Marks and abbreviations used in this chapter are as follows:
I.—Marriage Record Index.
Rec.—Marriage Record as given in the Record Books.
M. G.—Minister of the Gospel.
C. P.—Catholic Priest.
J. P.—Justice of Peace.
†—Original Records. These original records are fragments of paper stored in the Probate Court Rooms.
O. S. J.—Ohio State Journal.

†ADAMS, SARAH B.—(Miss)*—Riordan, Robert—Nov. 29, 1831. Robert Spencer, M. G.—3–27.

†ADAMS, Sarah—Morrison, Robert (Aged 17 years, consent of David Morrison)—Dec. 25, 1864. Rev. G. M. Peters. 8–475.

†ADAMS, Susan—Stewart, William—June 12, 1856. W. C. Brooks. 6–288.

ADAMS, Susan C.—Gorman, Thomas—Sept. 16, 1861. Julius C. Grammar, M. G. 7–631.

†ADAMS, Thomas—Barber, Elizabeth—July 18, 1829. James Hoge, M. G. 3–63.

†ADAMS, Thomas—Breckenridge, Margaret—Feb. 25, 1819. Percival Adams, J. P. 2–60.

†ADAMS, Thomas J.—Miller, Mary Frances—March 3, 1864. L. Davis, M. G. 8–311.

†ADAMS, William—Rudisill, Jane—Sept. 26, 1837. William Preston, M. G. 3–240.

O. S. J.—William Adams and Miss Jane C. Rudilson, of this city, rest same.

†ADAMS, William A. (Rec.) and Edmond C.*—Palsgrove, Kate—Jan. 7, 1862. M. K. Earhart, J. P. 7–691. Vouched for by E. C. Stevenson.

†ADAMS, William J.—Eastwood, Jane—Oct. 30, 1834. Thomas Wood, J. P. 3–110.

ADAMS, William L.—Simmons (I. & Rec.) & Timmons, Nancy—May 3, 1843. (March 9, 1843).* William Walker, J. P. 4–3.

ADE, Josephine—Moretz, Joseph—May 24, 1853. No return. 6–37.

†ADEY, Anne—Brennan, Michael—Jan. 12, 1853. James Meagher, Catholic M. G. 6–3.

ADLER, Eliza—Seiter, Henry—Sept. 18, 1860. No return. 7–486.

†ADLER, Samuel—Fleischhauer, Cecilly—June 12, 1859. J. Goodman, Priest. 7–289.

*AGATHA, Anna—Stutz, Charles—Nov. 3, 1863. J. Kronenbitter, J. P. 8–256.

AGNEW, Thomas—Golding, Mary—April 30, 1852. Jonathan Furlong, J. P. 5–376.

†AGILO (Rec.) & Agile,† Messlus—Blakely, Nancy—Nov. 10, 1831 (Rec.) and Dec. 10, 1831.† Abraham Shoemaker, J. P. 3–33.

†AGIN, David—McCoy, Hannah (aged 17 years, consent of her father, Jacob McCoy)—Dec. 23, 1858. John Kilgore, J. P. 7–190.

†AGIN (Rec.) & Egan,† Peter—Sullivan, Julia—March 8, 1859. Edward M. Fitzgerald, C. P. 7–239.

†AGLER, ANDREW J.—Goodwin, Laney—Jan. 1, 1850. Dudley A. Tyng, M. G. 5–206.

AGLER, Clinton W.—Goodwin, Mary Jane—Dec. 26, 1857. No return. 7–48.

†AGLER, Elizabeth—Horlocker, Peter—June 3, 1834 (Rec.) and April 3, 1834.† David Beers, J. P. 3–86.

AGLER, Elizabeth—Carr, Daniel—Nov. 17, 1840. Thomas Wood, J. P. 4–49.

†AGLER, Emma—Dill, James A.—July 21, 1863. J. C. Tidball. M. G. 8–202.

*AGLER, FRANKLIN—Brake, Christian—Dec. 5, 1858. Moses Beers, J. P. 7–189.

†AGLER, Frederick—Denoon, Barbara—June 22, 1840 (Rec.) June 11, 1840.† David Beers, J. P. 3–250.

†AGLER, Flora—Kissinger, Andrew (aged 20 years, consent of his guardian, Lewis Agler)—Jan. 13, 1860. David Beers, J. P. 7–373.

AGLER, George W.—Drake, Hannah—April 7, 1842. T. R. Cressy, M. G. 4–3.

†AGLER, George—Drake, Lucinda—Sept. 18, 1849. J. P. Bruck, J. P. 5–170.
†(The mother of Lucinda Drake gives consent for her to marry George Agler, June 27, 1849.)

†AGLER, John—Otto, Rebecca A.—March 4, 1847. Granville Moody, M. G. 5–48.

O. S. J.—Miss Rebecca A. Otto, both of city, rest same.

AGLER, John A.—Coe, Eliza Ann—June 24, 1855. Samuel Kinnear, J. P. 6–216.

†AGLER, Lewis—Denune, Lucinda—Oct. 24, 1833. David Beers, J. P. 3–75.

†AGLER, Lovina—Cornwell, John W. (aged 20 years, personal consent of his father, Daniel Cornwell)—Aug. 28, 1862. David Beers. J. P. 8–42.

†AGLER, Lucinda—Lamon and Leamon, Isaac—April 3, 1856. J. W. White, M. G. 6–273.

†AGLER, Luther—Goodwin, Elizabeth—March 22, 1855. George W. Williard, M. G. 6–195.

AGLER, Margaret—Park, James—May 27, 1831. David Beers, J. P. 3–14.

†AGLER, Mary Ann—Denune, Alexander—Dec. 1, 1831. David Beers, J. P. 3–28.

†AGLER, Mary A.—Brady, Francis Schuyler—Dec. 26, 1828. David Beers, J. P. 7–199.

†AGLER, Mary Adaline—Shull, Adam—April 24, 1862. J. C. Tidball, M. G. 8–1.

†AGLER, Matilda Ida—Kiner, Jacob—March 24, 1864. Samuel Kinnear, J. P. 8–327.
Record says, "Father's consent in writing." Does not give ages of either. Consent not found in originals.

AGLER, Peter—Patterson, Louisa—Jan. 7, 1830. David Beers, J. P. 2–237.

†AGLER, Peter—Atwell, Eliza C.—April 15, 1858. J. D. Smith, M. G. 7–99.

†AGLER, Sally—Betell, Benjamin—March 18, 1834. David Beers, J. P. 3–82.

AGLER, Sarah—Zinn, Henry—July 19, 1825. C. Henkle, Lutheran M. G. 2–170.

† (Peter Agler says his sister Sarah Agler is over 18 years.)

†AGLER, Sophia D.—Steward, John N.—Dec. 31, 1854. J. C. Bright, M. G. 6–171.

†AGLER, Susan Ann—Eaton, William, Jr.—Dec. 5, 1850. John Starrett, J. P. 5–273.

†AGLER, William—Chambers, Mary—Nov. 15, 1830. James Hoge, M. G. 3–64.

†AHLEFELD, Nathan—Wiley, Celia E.—May 22, 1856. William T. Snow, M. G. 6–284.

†AHLER, Wilhelmenia—Walters or Wahlter, Lorenz—Sept. 15, 1864. C. H. Borgess, Catholic M. G. 6–139.

†AINSWORTH, Juliett M.—Ellis, Francis M.—Sept. 7, 1853. J. D. Smith, M. G. 6–58.
O. S. J.—Francis M. Ellis, of Lancaster, and Miss Juliett M. Ainsworth, of this city, at the residence of D. G. Deshler. Rest same.

†AKENBRECK or Eggenbrecht, Elizabeth—Krug, George—March 22, 1857. K. Mees, M. G. 6–349.

AKIN, Charles B.—Brentlinger, Phebe—July 14, 1832. John F. Solomon, M. G. 3–49.

†AKINS, James—Ballinger, Catherine—Feb. 18, 1816. Joseph Gorton, J. P. 2–18.

ALBANY or (Alberry),* Rhoda—Havens, William—June 6, 1841. Jacob Smith, Jr., J. P. 4–130.

†ALBEN, Elijah—Romine, Miranda—Sept. 13, 1846. D. P. Cole, M. G. 5–23.

†ALBERRY, Delila—Burton, Isaac Jefferson—May 28, 1847 (May 24, 1847).† Shuah Mann, J. P.
(Consent of his father, John Burton, May 28, 1847.)

†ALBERRY, Eliza Jane—Needles, James A.—Dec. 7, 1845. Danial Hamaker, J. P. 4–202.

†ALBERRY, Emily—Beaver, John—July 11, 1847. Shuah Mann, J. P. 5–63.
(Consent of James M. and Anna Alberry for their daughter Emily to marry John Beaver, July 9, 1847.)†

†ALBERRY, Hannah—Rhodes or Roads, Joseph G.—Feb. 14, 1856. Shuah Mann, J. P. 6–262.

†ALBERRY, Harvey—Harden, Lavina H.—March 13, 1851. S. Mann, J. P. 5–294.

*ALBERRY, Henry M.—Hills, Emma or (Elmira)†—Feb. 9, 1838. Jacob Smith, J. P. 3–188.

†ALBERRY, Henry M.—McOwen, Rachel—Nov. 31, 1850. Joseph S. Brown, M. G. 5–345.

†ALBERRY, Herman B.—Smith, Julia—Oct. 14, 1847. George G. West, M. E. M. G. 5–76.

†ALBERY, Jerusha B.—Whitehead, Edward B.—March 5, 1863. Daniel U. Mather, M. G. 8–142.

†ALBERRY, John—Baldwin, Sarah—Dec. 30, 1832. George Beals, J. P. 3–71.

†ALBERRY, John—Hills, Maria—May 21, 1838 (March 19, 1838*). Daniel Swickard, J. P. 3–192.

234

*ALBERY, Jonathon—Hardin, Sophia—Nov. 13, 1853. Daniel Hamaker, J. P. 6–76.

†ALBERRY, Mary—Baughman, Jesse—May 3, 1840. Uriah Heath, M. G. 3–251. (Consent of her father, Pater Alberry.)†

†ALBERRY, Mary Ellen—Vickery, Pater—Aug. 4, 1850. Shuah Mann, J. P. 5–251.

†ALBERRY, Matilda Ann (Albenny)†—Baldwin, Thomas R. (K.)†—Aug. 15, 1844. Shuah Mann, J. P. 4–33.

ALBERY, Philip—Beaty, Elizabeth—Aug. 8, 1843. Daniel Hamaker, J. P. 4–4.

†ALBERY, Philip G.—Beatty, Mary M.—Feb. 8, 1852. Shuah Mann, J. P. 5–356.
(Consent of her parents, she will be 17 years old next June.)†

†ALBERRY, Thomas J.—Evans, Caroline J.—March 8, 1860. George Wagner, J. P. 7–395.
O. S. J.—He of Licking County, she of Franklin County.

†ALBERRY, William—Stagg, Maria—March 27, 1836. Jacob Smith, J. P. 3–149.

†ALBERS, John H.—Brown, Sophia M.—April 10, 1849. Benjamin Overmire, J. P. 5–159.

†ALBERT, Ann—Lewis, Daniel—Aug. 8, 1855. M. M. Clark. 6–222.

†ALBERT, Anton or Anthony—Scheiff, Louisa—Oct. 12, 1854. K. Mees, M. G. 6–153.

†ALBERT, Barbara—Frison, Joseph—May 10, 1859. J. B. Hemsteger, Catholic M. G. 7–271.

ALBERT, Elizabeth—Lensh, Henry—June 15, 1855. Gotlieb Nachtrieb, M. G. 6–215.

†ALBERT, George—Henbeck, Catherine—Dec. 1, 1855. K. Mees, M. G. 6–248.

†ALBERT, Heman—Hold, Eliza N.—July 31, 1862. Rev. H. Willard. 7–33.

ALBERT, John—Knedel, Mary A.—Jan. 2, 1853. Rev. J. B. Hemsteger, Pastor Holy Cross Church. 5–431.

†ALBERT, Levi—Salor, Melicia V.—July 4, 1839. William Walker, J. P. 3–222.

ALBERT, Regina—Marywort, Peter—March 25, 1853. No return. 6–21.

ALBERT, Susan—Pickard, John—Sept. 20, 1862. J. Kronenbitter, J. P. 8–56.

†ALBERTSON, Dorothy—Stevenson, Alfred—March 7, 1833. George Jefferies, M. G. 3–57.

†ALBIN (Alberm),† Susan Ann—Dikes (Dykes),† James—June 20, 1847. John Dunn, J. P. 5–60.

ALBRECHT, Andrew—Schwarz, Catherine—Oct. 30, 1842. Charles F. Schaeffer, M. G. 4–3.

†ALBRECHT, Catherine—Axel, Phillip—March 10, 1863. William F. Lehmann, M. G. 8–143.

†ALBRIGHT (Albrecht),† Andrew—Babbitt (Babbett),† Anna—Feb. 8, 1864. J. B. Hemsteger, Catholic M. G. 8–301.

†ALBRIGHT, Thomas—Dunham, (Miss)† Fanny—Sept. 1, 1864. Samuel Tippett, M. G. 8–403.

†ALCHEINS, Elizabeth—Loelckes (Loelkes),† John—March 3, 1853. C. Speilman, M. G. 6–15.

†ALCORN, Hiram—Olbert (I.) or Albert (Rec.), Susan—Aug. 11, 1863. K. Mees, M. G. 8–210.

†ALDER, Angelina—Betz, John—Sept. 5, 1850. Henry Francis, J. P. 5–256.

†ALDER, David—Pierce, Ruth—Nov. 11, 1850. G. W. Evans, J. P. 5–269.

†ALDER, Margaret—Frazell, Jason—Aug. 22, 1839 (Aug. 8, 1839).† J. S. Roger, J. P. 3–224.
(Consent of her father, Jonathan Alder, as they are of full age Aug. 7, 1839. Witness—Lewis Alder.)†

†ALDER, Paul—Francis, Mary—May 17, 1838. Paul Alder, J. P. 3–197.

†ALDEN, Mary—Warner, John H.—Aug. 12, 1849. Henry Francis, J. P. 5–175.

†ALDERFER, Polly (widow of George Alderfer)—Sohl, Leonard—March 30, 1824. C. Henkel, M. G. 2–119.
O. S. J.—Leonard Saul and Mrs. Mary Alderfer, in this town. Rest same.

†ALEBRION (Abbison),† Sarah—Peterbrook, John—Jan. 10, 1824. Robert W. Riley, J. P. 2–117.

†ALEXANDER, Ephriam K.—Kellar, Miss Chloe H.—May 14, 1864. William C. Roberts. 8–355.

235

†ALEXANDER, George—Benshuter, Elizabeth—May 6, 1830. Daniel Swickard, J. P. 3–5.

ALEXANDER, James—Watson, June—May 21, 1864. J. Kronenbitter, J. P. 8–342.

†ALEXANDER, Mary Jane—Wiswell, Theodore—May 14, 1846. Granville Moody, M. G. 5–8.
(James Alexander, father and guardian of Mary Jane Alexander, gives consent for her to marry, she being a minor. Witness—Elisha Wilson. Rebecca Wiswell gives consent for her son Theodore Wiswell to marry, he being a minor. Witness—Joseph A. Wiswell.)†

†ALEXANDER, Rachel—Cooper, William—June 24, 1851. J. P. Bruck, J. P. 5–323.

†ÁLEXANDER, Sarah F.—Sheehy, William—Sept. 13, 1863. Edwin Fitzgerald. 8–216.

†ALEXANDER, Thom. J.—Park, Charlotte—Sept. 26, 1845. Uriah Heath, M. G. 4–6.

†ALEXANDER, William G.—Flenniken, Martha—Nov. 2, 1839. T. R. Cressy, M. G. 3–229.
(Consent of her mother, Ann Flenniken.)†

†ALDRICH, Edson—Elliott, Margaret—April 1, 1847. Granville Moody, M. G. 5–53.

ALFORD or Erfurd, Frederick—July 12, 1852. K. Mees, M. G. 5–389.

†ALGER or (Algire),† George—Stephenson or (Stevenson),† Susan—Aug. 7, 1834. Peter Stephens, M. G. 3–91.

†ALGER or (Algire),† Jacob—McClara, Sarah—Feb. 13, 1833. Peter Stephens, M. G. 3–71.

†ALGIRE, Alphous—Hershey, Elizabeth C.—Oct. 16, 1856. Charles Jucksch, J. P. 6–309.

†ALGIRE, Nicholas—McClary, Pheby—Oct. 4, 1837. Thomas Wood, J. P. 3–177.

ALGIRE or Allgire),† Ruth—Wildermuth, William—Aug. 30, 1840. Philip Pence, M. G. 3–254.
(John W. Kile, as guardian of Ruth Algire, says to let William Wildermuth have license, Aug. 28, 1840.†)

ALGIRE or (Allger),† Sarah—Davis, Amoss or (Amasa)†—Feb. 8, 1844. Abraham Shoemaker, J. P. 4–72.

†ALGIRE, Sarah Jane—Kile, William—March 28, 1850. Moses Seymour, J. P. 5–244.

†ALGIRE, William K.—Stevenson, Mary Jane—Aug. 7, 1845. James Laws, M. G. 4–6.

ALGIRE, Zacherah—McClary, Sarah J.—Aug. 10, 1842. Thomas Wood, J. P. 4–2.

†ALKIRE, Elizabeth—Powell, Samuel (recorded) Jan. 15, 1810. John Smith, J. P. 1–67.
(John Alkire, her father, gives consent. Witness—Joseph Powell. Signed, Sept. 25, 1809.†)

†ALKIRE, Elizer—White, Jacob—Jan. 16, 1831. Benjamin Lawrence, M. G. 3–10.

†ALKIRE, George (W.)†—Baltimore, Matilda—June 8, 1839. Jacob Fisher, J. P. 3–217.

†ALKIRE, George W.—Brant, Rebecca—Nov. 28, 1850. John Gantz, J. P. 5–272.

†ALKIRE, James—Goetchius, Sarah—Jan. 12, 1845. S. F. Conrey, M. G. 4–5.

†ALKIRE, Jesse—Coartney, Margaret—April 10, 1832. James Rose, Preacher. 3–42.

†ALKIRE, Joseph—Courtney, Almira—April 19, 1846. James T. Donahoo, M. G. 5–6.

ALKIRE, Margaret—Dennis, Isaac—Feb. 9, 1832. Matthew Peters, M. G. 3–33.

MARRIAGE RECORDS, FRANKLIN COUNTY, OHIO

Blanche Tipton Rings

†Alkire, Martha J.,—Elmore, William, Oct. 9, 1851. Daniel Evans, J. P. (She a non-resident.†) 5–336.

†Alkire, Matilda—Henderson, William—July 9, 1848. James Harrison, M. G. 5–115.

†Alkire, Nancy—Gardiner, William—Jan. 11, 1848—W. T. Martin, J. P. 5–89.

Alkire, Nancy—Peat, John R.—March 7, 1854. W. H. Marble, M. G. 6–105.

Alkire, Richard C.—Watts, Amanda—June 30, 1861. T. H. Phillips, M. G. 7–601.

†ALKIRE, Robert—Like (I) or (Inglis*), Elizabeth—June 20, 1809. John Smith, J. P., of Pleasant Township. 1-61.

(Page 4—Sir: I want you to grant license for to marry Robert Alkire given under our hands and seal this 4th day of April, 1809. James and Hannah Douglas. Witness—Thomas Denison.)

†ALKIRE, Robert—Hoffman, Margaret—March 22, 1858. William Fields, J. P. 7-85.

†ALKIRE, Sarah—Nicholas, William—April 22, 1855. Thomas H. Hall, M. G. 6-203.

†ALKIRE, Weeden H.—Walrath, Catherine—Oct. 23, 1858. No return. 7-172. March 16, 1859, by Edward Lilley, J. P. 7-248.

†ALLAMON, Samuel—Nichols, Elizabeth M. A.—Nov. 5, 1839. W. Herr, M. G. 3-227.

(Mary Gilmer says she is willing for my daughter, Elizabeth Missouria Ann Nichols to marry Samuel Allamon. Witness—Rachel Needles and J. F. Kelly, Columbus, Monday, Nov. 4, 1839.†)

†ALLBERRY, Esther—Smith, Josiah—Aug. 9, 1846. Shuah Mann, J. P. 5-17. (Consent of his father, Kelley Smith, he being a minor.†)

ALLBERRY, or (Albery†), Francis—Kinner, Hanner—March 13, 1828. A. Allison, J. P. 2-196.

†ALLBERRY, Hester—Woodruff, Aaron E.—May 29, 1845. Nathan Emery, M. G. 4-302.
Vouched by James M. Woodruff.

†ALLBERRY, Noah—Smith, Almira—March 22, 1846. Shuah Mann, J. P. 4-6. Vouched by Samuel Roberts.

†ALLEN ADELAIDE—Booth, Henry F.—March 17, 1846. Granville Moody, M. G. 4-38.
O. S. J.—All of city, rest same.

†ALLEN, Andrew—Matters, Joanna—Nov. 26, 1857. J. M. Jamison, M. G. 7-35.

†ALLEN, Any Matilda—Bender, William—April 13, 1856. Rev. S. K. Reed. 6-275.

†ALLEN, Archibald—Brown, Adelia. Colored. May 28, 1864. William L. Heyl, J. P. 8-364.

†ALLEN, Charles H.—Park, Amanda S.—April 15, 1852. D. B. Cheney, M. G. 5-373.
O. S. J.—All of city, rest same.

†ALLEN, Cyrus—Coe, Mina—May 1, 1821. James Hoge, M. G. 2-106.

†ALLEN, Elizabeth—Bell, William—Jan. 29, 1851. Elder Ezekiel Fields. 5-284.

†ALLEN, Esther—Thacher, Stephen P.—Feb. 21, 1859. G. W. Gowdy, M. G. 7-229.

ALLEN, Francis E.—Benadum, William S.—March 19, 1863. D. A. Randall, M. G. 8-148.
O. S. J.—He of Lancaster, she of Winchester, rest same.

†ALLEN, George H.—Miller, Sarah Jane—March 24, 1853. H. Lomis, M. G. 6-21.
O. S. J.—George H. Allen and Miss Sarah Jane Miller, all of county, Rev. H. Lomis, rest same.

†ALLEN, Georgianna—Williams, Luther—July 2, 1863. O. Allen, M. G. 8-195.

†ALLEN, Harvey O.—Burr, Agnes C.—July 18, 1855. Rev. O. Allen. 6-221.
O. S. J.—All of city, rest same.

†ALLEN or Ellen, Jerusha. (I) or Margaretha J. (Rec.)—Freeman, Nimrod—April 7, 1860. Rev. C. Vogel. 7-412.

ALLEN, Jesse—Latimer, Mary A. (Mercy†)—March 22, 1829. John Weeden, J. P. 2-228.

†ALLEN, John R.—Werth, Anna E.—Contraband—Dec. 10, 1863. D. A. Randall, M. G. 8-270.

†ALLEN, Livinia—Chambers, William—April 16, 1851. R. K. Nash, M. G. 5-311.

†ALLEN, Lucinda—Rivers, Frank (Colored)—Sept. 30, 1864. J. Kronenbitter, J. P. 8-421.

†ALLEN, Lucinda Jane—Wheeler, George T. or S.—Feb. 20, 1862. John E. Woods. 7-713.

†ALLEN, Lucy Frances—Carlisle, Abram—March 17 (March 16†), 1843.   Joseph M. Trimble, M. G.   4–57.

ALLEN, MARY—Davis, John W.—June 7, 1855.   T. N. Stewart, M. G.   6–213.

ALLEN, Minnie A.—Awl, Woodward—May 16, 1861.   O. Allen, M. G.   7–586.   O. S. J.—Both of Columbus, rest same.

†ALLEN, Minus—Classpill, G. W.—July 16, 1826.   Henry Mathews, M. G.   2–174.

†ALLEN, Mitchell—Heser, Elizabeth—June 11, 1850.   J. S. Weisz, M. G.   5–239.

ALLEN, Oril—Rinehart, Samuel—Oct. 15, 1848.   H. M. Phelps, J. P.   5–130.

ALLEN, Owen W.—Scott, Miss Flora M.—Oct. 17, 1862.   Joseph M. Trimble, M. G.   8–71.

ALLEN, Rosella—Andrews, George C. (T.†)—Aug. 11, 1831.   Zachariah Cornell, J. P.   3–32.
(William C. Ray says that Rosella Allen, daughter of Asa Allen, is over 18 years of age and wants to marry George T. Andrews, Aug. 10, 1831.†)

†ALLEN, Sarah—McKillip, Patrick—Dec. 7, 1848.   Dudley A. Tyng, M. G.   5–141.

†ALLEN, Miss Sarah—Coleman, John L.—Aug. 25, 1864.   James Heffley, V. D. M.   8–399.

†ALLEN, Stephen—Mann, Nancy Jane—May 24, 1849.   J. C. Havens, M. G.   5–166.

ALLEN, William—Faram (Farmer), Mary—Oct. 6, 1842.   Abraham Shoemaker, J. P.   4–3.

†ALLEN, Wilson D.—Beecher, Almina—July 28, 1853.   J. A. Bruner, M. G.   6–49.   O. S. J.—Wilson D. Allen and Miss Almenia Beecher, all of city, rest same.

†ALLENSWORTH, William—Dawson, Mary—May 29, 1864.   D. D. Mather, M. G.   8–363.

†ALLER, Catherine—Schaub, Frederick—May 18, 1854.   William F. Lehmann, M. G.   6–121.

†ALLER (Oller†), John—Hess, Catherine—Nov. 10, 1808.   James Hoge, M. G.   1–54.

†ALLER, Phebe—Fischer, Henry—April 2, 1863.   J. Kronenbitter, J. P.   8–159.

ALLER, William—Johnson, Marilla—Aug. 6, 1857.   Jesse Alkire, J. P.   6–375.

ALLEY, Eleanor—Shambo, Alexander—Aug. 29, 1862.   J. G. Miller, J. P.   8–46.

†ALLGIRE or Allgier (I), Adaline—Hersley (Hersey†), Henry—Aug. 23, 1855.   Richard Pitzer, M. G.   6–224.

†ALLGIRE, Henry—Holbert, Eleanor—Feb. 4, 1855.   Peter Appleman, Elder U. B. Church.   6–182.

†ALLGIRE, Joshua—Eyer, Lavina M.—Feb. 22, 1849.   W. W. Kile, M. G.   5–152.
(T. C. Hendren, guardian of Joshua Alkire, gives consent for Joshua to marry Lavina M. Eyer, Feb. 17, 1849.†)

ALLGIER, Eliza—Cowgill, Daniel M.—May 29, 1851.   James T. Bail, M. G.   5–310.

†ALLIN, Asaph—Williard, Cora—Aug. 3, 1826.   Samuel Abbott, J. P.   2–174.

†ALLIS, Edwin J.—McDonald, Julia H.—Dec. 9, 1858.   Edward Lilley, J. P.   7–192.

ALLIS, Phebe Ann—Otstott, John H.—May 28, 1856.   No return.   6–285.

†ALLIGER, Angeline—Kern, William J., age 20 years—March 13, 1859.   James T. Finch, M. G.   7–244.
(Consent of her mother for Angeline Allager, age 16 years.†)   (I, Virginia A. Dunn, mother of William J. Kern, whose father is dead, do hereby consent to his marriage with Angeline Alegre, March 11, 1859.   Witness—Jabob Dunn and F. M. Allegre.†)

ALLISON, Nancy—Scott, Charles—July 12, 1827.   H. Matthews, M. E. M. G.   2–186.

†ALLMAN (I) or Alltman,† Eve—Taylor, Moses—Feb. 2, 1831.   Thomas A. Morris, M. G.   3–13.

†ALLSPATCH, Charles—Kissell (Russell†), Elizabeth—Sept. 2, 1852.   J. S. Weisz, M. G.   5–396.

ALLSPAUGH, Jacob—McCracken, Ruth (aged 16 years, consent of her father)—March 6, 1862.   J. Kronenbitter, J. P.   7–719.
(Elihu McCracken gives consent for my daughter Ruth E. McCracken

to marry Jacob Alspaugh, March 5, 1862. Wit.—William McCracken and Jane McCracken.†)

†ALLWOOD, Samuel—Wright (Knight†), Jemima—March 2, 1845. Shuah Mann, J. P. 4-5.

ALLWOOD, Maria—Looker, William—Jan. 8, 1852. Shuah Mann, J. P. 5-352.
(James A. Looker says Maria Allwood is 16 years old and both parents give consent for her to marry William Looker.†)

†ALLWOOD (Altwood†), Eliza Jane—Readinghouse, William—Oct. 30, 1851. J. P. Bruck, J. P. 5-340.
(Columbus McArthur says that William Readinghouse has full consent of his father to marry Miss Eliza Jane Allwood. She is 18 years old.†)

†ALLWOOD, Cynthia—Norton, William—Feb. 1, 1855. D. K. Wood, J. P. 6-181.

†ALSPACH, Catherine—Hatch,† Fairchild—Sept. 6, 1853. Daniel Hamaker, J. P. 6-57.

ALSPACH, Christena—Brown, John—Jan. 12, 1843. Abraham Shoemaker, J. P. 4-28.

†ALSPACH, Christena—Needles, Samuel—Sept. 19, 1845. J. Williams, J. P. 4-202.

ALSPACH, Elizabeth—Ruse, Solomon—Sept. 24, 1854. Jeremiah White, J. P. 6-148.

†ALSPACH, Jacob—Henry, Elizabeth—Oct. 21, 1851. J. C. Winter, M. G. 5-337.

†ALSPACH, Jonas, Jr.—Henry, Sarah—Sept. 20, 1846. William W. Davis, M. G. 5-25.

†ALSPACH, Judy—Hevy, Samuel—March 10, 1839. Morris Roe, M. G. 3-213.

†ALSPACH, Levi—Artle, Mary Ann—Jan. 17, 1847. Joshua Glanville, J. P. 5-40.

†ALSPACH, Rebecca—Onet, John—July 9, 1846. Conrad King, M. G. 5-15.

†ALSPACH, Rebecca—Shook, Elias—Nov. 14, 1858. William F. Lehmann, M. G. 7-180.

†ALSPACH, Sarah—Click, Andrew—March 5, 1837. John Starrett, J. P. 3-153.

†ALSPACH, Susannah—Clouse, David—Dec. 17, 1846. Daniel Hamaker, J. P. 5-36.

†ALSPACH, William—Kramer, Mary Ann—April 13, 1848. M. Livingston, M. G. 5-101.

ALSPAUGH, Hannah—Rohr, John—April 28, 1840. P. Pence, M. G. 3-243.

ALSPAUGH (Alspau†), Jonathan—Parrorf (I and Rec.) (Pattors†), Polly—Dec. 22, 1832. Daniel Swickard, J. P. 3-50.

†ALSPAUGH (I) Alspach (Rec.), Susan—Lehman, John K.—Aug. 28, 1864. James Heffly, V. D. M. 8-393.

†ALSPAW & Alspaugh (I), Susan—Kissel, Martin—Jan. 10, 1856. Andrew Barr, M. G. 6-256.

ALSTON, Anthony—Carter, Miller. (Colored.) Feb. 7, 1860. No return. 7-389.

†ALSTON, Peter—Revels, Mary—May 26, 1859. William Hanby, M. G. 7-281.

†ALT, Adam—Dreshmann, Mary—March 24, 1857. William F. Lehmann, M. G. 6-350.

†ALT, Adam—Lewer (Loeber†), Mary—Jan. 24, 1864. William F. Lehmann, M. G. 8-296.

†ALTES (Althes†), Charles—Ritzmann, Fredericka—July 5, 1860. William F. Lehmann, M. G. 7-450.

†ALTHALN (Althan†), Elizabeth—Brandt & Brunt (I), Henry—Aug. 23, 1853. K. Mees, M. G. 6-55.

†ALTHEN, Ann Maria—Trot, Benedict—Dec. 6, 1849. C. H. Borgess, Catholic M. G. 5-198.
(The original has Olding and Althen is crossed out.†)

†ALTHEN, Henry L.—Rehr, Mary—Sept. 8, 1862. William F. Lehmann, M. G. 8-51.

†ALTHEN, John—Henkel, Anna Eliza—Nov. 1, 1835. Wilhelm Schmidt, M. G. 3-130.

†ALTHOLHN (I) (Althohn†), George—Walter (Walther†), Barbara—Oct. 28, 1863. K. Mees, M. G. 8-252.

MARRIAGE RECORDS, FRANKLIN COUNTY, OHIO

BLANCHE TIPTON RINGS

†ALTHOUSE, Christian—Schott, Sophia—Oct. 15, 1844. C. Spielman, M. G. 6-238.

†ALTHOUSE, Isaac–Webb, Levina–May 1, 1845. H. L. Hitchcock, M. G. 4-6.

†ALTIN, (Althohn†), Katherine—Dabus (I) (Debus†), Adam—May 3, 1863. K. Mees, M. G. 8-173.

†ALTMAN, Caroline M.—Pike, Nathaniel—April 16, 1857. J. M. Jameson, M. G. 6-357.

ALTMAN (Allman†), Elizabeth—Johnston, Chester—Aug. 26, 1832. Robert O. Spencer, M. G. 3-47.

†ALTMAN, Elizabeth—Jenkins, George—Oct. 20, 1849. William Walker, J. P. 5-190.

†ALTMAN, Frederick—Crumley & Gramlich, Catherine—April 21, 1863. K. Mees, M. G. 8-167.

†ALTMAN, John G.–Denig, Maria–Feb. 1, 1844. H. L. Hitchcock, M. G. 4-4.
*–John G. Altman and Miss Maria, dau. of Dr. G. Denig, all of city.

†ALTMAN, Lavina A.–Fitz, John–March 18, 1841. Thomas Wood, J. P. 4-94.

†ALTMAN, Margaret—Canady, James—June 2, 1850. John Dunn, J. P. 5-247.

†ALTMAN, Maria—Edwards, Joseph R.—Oct. 14, 1849. William Davis, M. G. 5-189.

ALTMAN, Mary M.–Wolf, J. H.–April 2, 1844. W. T. Martin, J. P. 4-295.

†ALTMAN, Salome—Berryhill, Stephen—April 5, 1825. C. Henkel, M. G. 2-138.

†ALTMAN, Silome (Miss Seloma†)–Parks, James–Feb. 23, 1840. Henry Willard, M. G. 3-244.
*–James Parks and Miss Salome Altman both of this city, rest same.

ALTMAN, Sophia—Hare (Hane†), Benjamin F.—Nov. 21, 1852. H. L. Hitchcock, M. G. 5-420.

†ALTMAN, William H.—Spangler, Henrietta—May 13, 1858. William F. Lehmann, M. G. 7-112.

†ALTMON, Catherine–McDonald, William–Sept. 4, 1831. Truman Strong, M. G. 3-21.

†ALTUN, & Altman,† David—Olstot, Elizabeth—Oct. 3, 1828 (Oct. 8†). James Hoge, M. G. 3-61.
*–David Altman and Miss Elizabeth Utstol, in Hamilton Township, Oct. 19, 1828.

†ALTMEYER, Martin—Dorsam (Rec.) & Lieson (I), Catherine—Aug. 14, 1855. C. H. Borgess, Catholic, M. G. 6-221.

†ALVORD, George–Baty, Suvina–June 4, 1848. William Walker, J. P. 5-109.

†ALVORD, Elijah S.–Atcheson (I) (Acheson†), Julia–Aug. 22, 1864. J. E. Grammer, M. G. 8-397.
*–He of Indianapolis, Indiana, and Miss Julia Acheson, rest same.

†ALWARD, Elizabeth–Pee, Samuel–June 7, 1853. Nathan Brooks, J.P. 6–40.

ALWOOD, Miss Susan–Johnson, Washington–Dec. 14, 1857. Hugh Calvin McBride, Pres. M. G. 7–41.
No ages given. (Consent of her parents, A. A. Allwood and Susan Allwood. Wit.—Washington Johnson and Henry Johnson.†)

†ALWOOD, Mary Jane–Davenport, David–Jan. 5, 1860. John G. Miller, J. P. 7–369.

†AMANN, Johanna–Schoffhauser, John G.–Oct. 26, 1858. C. H. Borgess, Catholic, M. G. 7–173.

†AMAS & AMOS, Geòrge–Dex & Dix, Rachel–June 17, 1818. Eli C. King,
J. P. 2–62, 2–64.

†AMBOS, Caroline–Glock, Frederick–Aug. 26, 1855. Charles Jucksch, J. P.
6–299.

AMBOS, Caroline–Uhlmann, Frederick–Sept. 6, 1860. No return. 7–479.

†AMBOS, Peter–Jager & Jaeger, Doroty & Dorothy–Aug. 1, 1841. Charles
F. Shaffer, M. G. 4–1.
*–Miss Dorothy Yager, all of city, rest same.

AMBROSE, D.–Loy, Rachel–April 16, 1842. Samuel Kinnear, J. P. 4–2.

AMBROSE, Margaret J.–Bailey, Samuel–March 17, 1842. M. Ambrose,
J. P. 4–24

†AMBROSE, Margaret Jane–Kramer, Henry–June 16, 1853. W. W. Davis,
M. G. 6–41.

†AMBROSE, Silas J.–Zinn, Mary Jane–Aug. 27. 1850. David Warnock,
M. G. 5–255.

†AMBROSHER & Ambroshier, John–Koons (Kearns†), Matilda–June 11,
1836. Isaac Painter, J. P. 3–145.

†AMBURGE, Theresa–Rosenberg, L.–Sept. 29, 1864. J. Kronenbitter, J. P.
8–418.

AMES, Catherine–Shlitt, Henry S.–July 1, 1852. No return. 5–388.

†AMOLD, George J.–McComb, Sarah L.–March 25, 1847. Josiah D. Smith,
M. G. 5–51.

AMOLD (Arnold†), Lavina–Blodget, Harry & Harvey–June 3, 1829.
Abram Philips, J. P. 2–232.

AMOLD, Sarah L.–Rimer, Daniel–Jan. 22, 1852. J. D. Smith, M. G. 5–355.
(Sarah L. Amold†).

†AMLIN, Eliza J.–Sharp, William W.–Sept. 1, 1864. D. D. Mather, M. G.
8–404.
Vouched by Zeloria Amlin.

†ALMY, A. O. (Amy, Francis A. C.†)–Crew, Samuel Jackson. Recorded
June 22, 1843. By Lester James, M. G. 4–58.

†AMOS, John–Smith, Miss Ruth–May 8, 1855. Rev. G. L. Archer. 6–208.

†AMOS, Mary–Lane, John–Nov. 3, 1853. Z. G. Waddle, J. P. 6–73.

†AMOS, Walter–Simmons, Mary E.–Oct. 20, 1862. E. P. Goodwin, M. G.
8–72.

†AMSPHER, Amos–Sewell, Sarah–Feb. 4, 1845. Henry Shenefelt, J. P. 4–5.
(I agree that the Clerk may issue license to my son Amos Amspher
to be joined in marriage to Sarah Sewell. Jan., 1845. Wit.–Elizabeth
Deyo, Aaron Deyo, David Deyo, Thomas E. Hudson and George M.
Smith.†)
Thomas E. Hudson, says he saw Elizabeth Deyo sign her name to
this instrument, Feb. 1, 1845.

ANDER, Mary–O'Brien, John–Feb. 4, 1865. No return. 6-260.

†ANDERICK (I and †) & Andrick, John W.–Geyer, Annie–Nov. 20, 1860.
William F. Lehmann, M. G. 7-513.

†ANDERS, Abram Y.–Wickson, Elizabeth–May 30, 1840. William Walker,
J. P. 3–247.

†ANDERS, Lucinda (Andus, Lorinda†)–Cook, John P.–Dec. 12, 1839. John
Chandler Rogers, J. P. 3-231.
*–In Sharon township, Dec. 12, 1839, Miss Lavina Andrews of
Sharon township and John P. Cooke of Clinton township, by
Chandler Rogers, Esq.

†ANDERS, Timothy–Fisher, Ruth B., of Sharon Tp.–Dec. 16, 1819. Isaac
Fisher, M. G. 2–68.
(Isaac Fisher gives consent for his dau., Ruth B. Fisher, to marry
Timothy Andrews of Delaware County. Wit.–Daniel Week.†)

†ANDERSON, Andreas–Uriens, Catherine–Dec. 16, 1864. K. Mees, M. G.
8–468.

†ANDERSON, Andrianas M.–Middleton, John–Jan. 31, 1860. George W.
Brush, M. E. M. G. 7–383.

†ANDERSON, Daniel–Ortman, Manziliah–Oct. 16, 1862. Rev. J. H. Groff, 8–67.

ANDERSON, Edmund–Fisher, Mary–Nov. 1, 1848. George C. Crum, M. G. 5–139.

†ANDERSON, Eliza J.–Cromwell, John S.–Dec. 27, 1849. Solomon Dunton, M. G. 5-204.

†ANDERSON, Elizabeth J.–Coleman, John C.–Oct. 2, 1862. G. G. West, M. G. 8–63.

†ANDERSON (Anders†), Elmira–Impson, Benjamin–July 29, 1852. G. W. Evans, J. P. 5–391.

†ANDERSON, Fanna & Fanny–Buck, John–Jan. 12 (Jan. 10†), 1834. William H. Long. 3–80.

†ANDERSON & Andres, George H.–Wiles & Wites, Mariah–Sept. 5, 1824. Isaac Fisher, J. P. of Sharon Tp. 2–130.

†ANDERSON, Georgianna–Cassels, Hiram–Jan. 29, 1863. James Poindexter, M. G. 8–124.

†ANDERSON, Hannah–Rusk, Robert–March 2, 1837. T. R. Cressy, M. G. 3–158.

†ANDERSON, James—Hamilton, Mary Ann—April 4, 1858. William Porter, M. G. 7-95.

†ANDERSON, James–Spade, Rebecca–Sept. 8, 1859. K.Meese, M. G. 7-317. Vouched by Samuel Spade.

†ANDERSON, Jane–Feasle & Feasel, George–Oct. 27, 1823. Isaac Painter, J. P. 2-116.
    (Jacob Feasel, Jr., made oath that George Feasel, son of Jacob Jacob Feasel, Sr., is over 21 years of age and wants to marry Jane Anderson, dau. of ———— Andreson, deceased, and she is over 18 years of age, Oct. 24, 1823.†)

†ANDERSON, Jane—Butler, Amos (Amon)—Oct. 8, 1835. Thomas Wood, J. P. 3-126.
    *—Amon Butler and Jane Anderson, rest same.

†ANDERSON, John—Leps, Mary Ann—March 31, 1839. Thomas Wood, J. P. 3-212.
    *—John Anderson and Miss Mary Ann Leps, all of this county, April 31, 1839.

†ANDERSON, John—Murray, Caroline—March 12, 1858. Edgar Woods, M. G. 7-78.

ANDERSON, John M.—Hayes, Elizabeth—June 8, 1830. Isaac N. Walters, Elder in Christian Church. 2-251.

ANDERSON, John T.—Welch, Elizabeth—March 3, 1842. Benjamin Britton. 4-2.

†ANDERSON. Joseph R.–Flenniker (Rec.) (Flenniken†), Eliza S.–Dec. 24, 1857. James Hoge. M. G. 7-45.

†ANDERSON. Levi—Jones, Magdaline—April 4, 1847. H. L. Hitchcock, M. G. 5-54.

†ANDERSON, Louisa–Threet, Edward H.–June 26, 1851. Daniel Evans, J. P. 5-318.

†ANDERSON, Lucinda–Baily, John–Aug. 14, 1844. T. N. Stewart, M. G. 6-227.

†ANDERSON. Mary—Jefferson, Thomas—Jan. 25, 1838. T. R. Cressy, M. G. 3-187.

ANDERSON. Mary—Headden, James—Dec. 29, 1844. Daniel Eldridge, M. G. 4-141.

†ANDERSON, Mary—Cassel, Edward—March 24, 1864. James Poindexter, M. G. 8-331.

†ANDERSON. Mary E.—Perril, Hugh—May 31, 1848. H. L. Hitchcock, M. G. 5-109.
    (May 31, 1848. Mary E. Anderson's late husband having been absent over six years, is believed to have died soon after leaving her and she wants to marry Hugh Perril.†)

†ANDERSON, Mary E.–Hall. James–Feb. 1, 1853. Uriah Heath, M. G. 6-7.

243

BLANCHE TIPTON RINGS

†ANDERSON, Nancy—Webster, Elihu—Oct. 15, 1817. Eli C. King, Acting J. P. 2-43.

†ANDERSON, Polly–Painter, Nathaniel–Nov. 16, 1823. Jacob Smith, J. P. 2-116.

†ANDERSON, Rebecca A.—Waterman, Augustus F. —April 5, 1855. J. D. Smith, M. G. 6-199.

†ANDERSON, Rebecca Jane—Mouser, David—Jan. 24, 1858. Jacob Hathaway, M. G. 7-60.
Vouched by H. Anderson.

†ANDERSON, Robert D.—Goldsmith, Mary J.—Aug. 24, 1854. Archibald Fleming, M. G. 6-142.

†ANDERSON, Rose A.—Brodrick, William H.—Dec. 17, 1845. Granville Moody, M. G. 4-37.
*—W. H. Brodrick and Miss Rose M. Anderson, dau. of John Anderson of Winchester, Va., Dec. 17, 1845.

†ANDERSON, Sarah—Lee, John. Colored persons. Oct. 18, 1832. Abram S. Phelps, J. P. 3-51.

ANDERSON, Sarah–Ring, Robert–April 27, 1834. James Hoge, M. G. 3-108.

†ANDERSON, Sarah D.—Miller, James B.—Sept. 27, 1855. J. W. White, M. G. 6-235.

†ANDERSON, William F.—Moler, Hannah—March 4, 1856. J. A. Bruner, M. G. 6-266.
*—William T. Anderson of Ann Arundel County, Md., and Miss Hannah Moler of this vicinity.

†ANDERSON, William H. (M.†)—Georgianna, Ann—Dec. 29, 1836. George Jefferies, M. G. 3-161.
NOTE: In the Index books the name is given under G, but in the original record as "Georgianna Ann *Watson*."

ANDERSON, W. J.—Flowers, Mary E.—Feb. 7, 1842. H. L. Hitchcock, M. G. 4-2.

†ANDERSON, Wilson–Jones, Betsy–Feb. 13, 1845. W. T. Martin, J. P. 4-5.

†ANT DESS, Thomas, (Francis†)—Fischer, Jacobine—May 14, 1839. H. D. Juncker, Catholic Clergyman. 3-224.

ANDLITZ, Anna—Hilendale, Adam—June 2, 1857. No return. 6-365.

†ANDOVER, Maria—Sanders, Robert—Aug. 12, 1853. J. A. Bruner, M. G. 6-53.
*—Robert Sanders, formerly of Scotland, and Miss Maria Andrews of this city, rest same.

†ANDREA, Joanna Maria Sophia—Frey, Joseph Carl—Jan. 8, 1851. K. Mees, M. G. 5-281.

†ANDREGG (Anderegt†), Conrad–Stelzer (Heltzer†), Elizabeth–May 15, 1856. Charles Jucksch, J. P. 6-282.

†ANDRES, Charles—Reamy, Jenny—Sept. 7, 1864. J. Kronenbitter, J. P. 8-407.

ANDRES, John—Basing, Josephine—May 18, 1842. H. D. Juncker, Catholic M. G. 4-2.

ANDRES (Andress†), Mahala—Strong, L. C. (Lucius†)—Dec. 23, 1827. H. Hullburd, M. G. at Worthington. 2-193.

†ANDREWS (Andrus†). Abner—Westervelt, Mary—Jan. 15, 1852. John C. Bright, J. P. 5-354.

†ANDREWS, Abner L.—Buttles, Emma—Dec. 26, 1859. William Dent Hanson. 7-366.

†ANDREWS, Adam—Sharp, Nancy—Dec. 5, 1822. William C. Duff, J. P. 2-111.

†ANDREWS, Amanda—Weaver, David—July 17, 1825. Aristarchus Walker, J. P. 2-154.
(David Weaver said, "from the family records of Richard Andrews, deceased, father of Amanda Andrews, she is over the age of 18 years.†)"

†ANDREWS, Anne—Dodge, Luther—March 17, 1840. William T. Martin, J. P. 3-239.

ANDREWS, Annjennett—Rogers, Thomas B.—June 17, 1861. David Rogers, J. P. 7-597.

†ANDREWS, Betsy of Worthington—Wallace, John of Franklin County—April 17, 1817. Ezra Griswold, J. P. 2-38.

†ANDREWS, Betsy—Skeels, Harvey—Oct. 24, 1821. Nathaniel Little. 2-95.

†ANDREWS & Andrus, Bradford L.—Hymrod, Jennie Z.—Oct. 17, 1860. Thomas H. Phillips, M. G. 7-494.
*—He of Rochester, N. Y.

†ANDREWS, Clara Ann—Davis, Beriah—June 13, 1850. William Graham, J. P. 5-240.

†ANDREWS, Clarinda—Stith, James—April 30, 1847. Granville Moody, M. G. 5-57.

†ANDREWS, Clarissa of Delaware County—Goodrich, John—Nov. 29, 1818. Stephen Maynard, J. P. 2-54.

ANDREWS, Clarissa—Davis, Brice—Sept. 29, 1849. No return. 5-187.

†ANDREWS, Cynthia—Barker, Eliphalet—April 15, 1813. Ezra Griswold, J. P. 1-116.

†ANDREWS, Edward—Waters, Magdaline—Jan. 13, 1852. William Parry, German M. G. 5-354.

†ANDREWS, Edwin—Lamson (Lampson†), Harriet—Dec. 11, 1839. Truman Skells, J. P. 3-232.
*—Edwin Andrews and Miss Harriet Thompson in Clinton Township, Dec. 11, 1839.

†ANDREWS, Eliza—Smith, Elias C.—June 17, 1856. Robert Forrester, M. G. 6-288.

†ANDREWS, Elizabeth—Williams, Aron—July 30, 1857. John Helpman, J. P. 6-374.

†ANDREWS, George B.—Farrell, Marsilla (Marcella†)—July 14, 1861. Joseph M. Trimble, M. G. 7-606.

ANDREWS, George C.—Allen, Rosella—Aug. 11, 1831. Zachariah Cornell, J. P. 3-32.

†ANDREWS, James—Collins, Mary E.—March 14, 1860. John E. Woods, Lithopolis. 7-401.

†ANDREWS, James—Kirby, (Miss†) Anna—July 19, 1864. Joseph M. Trimble, M. G. 8-382.

†ANDREWS, James L.—Thompson, Catherine—March 8, 1857. H. W. Parsons. 6-345.

ANDREWS, John (of Steubenville, O.†)—Lord, Phoebe (I. and Rec.)—Dec. 18, 1827. Philander Chase, Bishop of the Protestant Episcopal Church in the Diocese of Ohio. (Phoebe D. Lord of Columbus.†) (At Franklinton.†) 2-193.

ANDREWS, John—Gwynne, Lavinia—Oct. 8, 1835. William Preston, M. G. 3-163.

†ANDREWS, John C.—Tone, (Miss†) Mary A.—Sept. 26, 1858. William Toser, M. G. 7-157.

†ANDREWS, John W.—Tharp or Thorp, Permelia—Nov. 17, 1846. Joshua Glanville, J. P. 5-33.

†ANDREWS, Juliet—Kellog, Burr—July 27, 1834. Erastus Burr, M. G. 3-94.

†ANDREWS, Laura–Bull, Horace J.–March 12, 1825. Joseph Carper. 2-133. Horace J. Bull says Laura Andrews, daughter of Jesse Andrews, is over 18 years of age.

†ANDREWS, Lydia–Pinney, Miles–May 1, 1831. John W. Ladd, J. P. 3-19. (Consent of his father, Levi Pinney. Wit.–William C. Andrews and G. H. Griswold.†)

†ANDREWS, Lyman—Vining, Persy M.—Dec. 6, 1818. Vinal Stewart, Preacher. 2-54.

ANDREWS, Mahala—Strong, Lucius C.—Dec. 23, 1827. H. Hulburd, M. G. 2-230.

†ANDREWS, Maila R.–Douglass, A. J.–Sept. 20, 1849. R. K. Nash. 5-185.

ANDREWS, Margaret–Yarger, Adam–Feb. 10, 1861. Patterson Harrison, J. P. 7-548.

†ANDREWS, Martha—Pierce, William—Oct. 13, 1847. David Rogers, J. P. 5-76.

ANDREWS, Mary—(Makintosh†) McIntosh & Makendish, Clark—Nov. 5, 1840. Chandlers Rodgers, M. G. 4-181. (Both of Sharon township.†)

ANDREWS, (Andrus†), Mary Ann—Hunt, Asher—March 5, 1829. Adam Miller, M. G. 2-222.

†ANDREWS, Mary Lucinda—Wilcox, John—April 18, 1850. George Taylor, J. P. 5-229.

†ANDREWS, Mary L.–Rogers, William K.–July 1, 1862. Julius E. Grammar, M. G. 7-23.

†ANDREWS, Myra—Case, Orier (Orren†)—March 29, 1812. Ezra Griswold, J. P. 1-96. Both of Worthington.

†ANDREWS, Noah–Griswold, Miss Ruth–Feb. 22, 1807. James Kilbourn, J. P. 1-25. Both of Worthington.

†ANDREWS, Peggy–Lewis, James–Oct. 3, 1833. W. T. Martin, J. P. 3-56. Darkies (Blackies†).

ANDREWS, Qualzy—Connard, John—Jan. 18, 1852. Nathan Brooks, J. P. 5-354.

†ANDREWS, Ray W.–Wisewell, Mary–Oct. 18, 1849. William Davis. 5-189.

†ANDREWS, Samuel–Clark, Mary–June 27, 1825. Henry Matthews, M. E. M. G. 2-146.

†ANDREWS, Samuel C.–Hutchinson, Emorilla–March 12, 1835. Thomas Wood, J. P. 3-106.

ANDREWS, Simon P.–Conroy, Margaret–Aug. 28, 1851. K. Mees, M. G. 5-327.

†ANDREWS, Sylvester W.–Lazell, Jeanette–Feb. 15, 1853. William Preston, M. G. 6-12.
*—Gen. S. W. Andrews and Miss Jeanette Lazell, dau. of Judge John A. Lazell, all of city.

†ANDREWS, Thomas–Rose, Ruth–Nov. 29, 1812. Jacob Tharp, J. P. of Plain Tp. 1-109.

ANDREWS, Thomas of Steubenville–Dlowd, Miss Phoebe D. (I. and Rec.) of Columbus–Dec. 10, 1827. Philander Chase. 2-252.

ANDREWS, Titus A.–White, Marthy–Jan. 15, 1830. Josiah Fisher. 2-252.

†ANDREWS, William–Dellinger, Amanda–Dec. 3, 1857. J. S. Weisz, M. G. 7-38.

†ANDREWS, Zelda–Andrus, Richard–Nov. 27, 1855. Thomas Woodrow, M. G. 6-247.
*–Richard Andrus and Miss Zelda, youngest dau. of Capt. George H. Andrews of Sharon Tp.

ANDRICKS, Ann–Harris, Morrison H.–Feb. 2, 1854. Nathan Brooks, J. P. 6-99.

†ANDRICK, Christian, aged 20 years–Walters, Malissa–March 25, 1858. William B. Preston, M. G. 7-87. (Consent of John Andrick, parent.†)

†ANDRICK, Elizabeth–Walter, Peter–Oct. 17, 1861. D. D. Mather, M. G. 7-652.

†ANDRICK, Lydia–Sarber, George–Aug. 5, 1834. Alexander Cameron, J. P. 3-101.

†ANDRICK, Mary M.–Harris, Harvey D.–March 7, 1854. William Haddock, J. P. 6-105.

†ANDRICK, Rufus Edward–Siance, Eizabeth–Dec. 24, 1857. John G. Miller, J. P. 7-46.
Vouched for by John Andrick.

†ANDRICK, Sarah E.–Temple, Caldwell–Aug. 27, 1861. Daniel Hamaker, J. P. 7-617.
Vouched by John M. Andrick.

ANDRICKS, Daniel–Clevenger, Polly–March 16 (Feb. 27†), 1830 Abram Shoemaker, J. P. 2-244.
Abraham Smith says he heard the guardian of Daniel Andricks give his consent for his ward to marry Polly Clevenger, Feb. 24, 1830.

ANDRIX, Mary A.–Weaver, Daniel C.–Dec. 23, 1852. William Haddock, J. P. 5-428.

†ANDROS (I.) (Andrews†), William C.–Toppin, Eunice G.–Aug. 12, 1840. Albert Helfenstein, Rector at Worthington. 4-1.

†ANDRUS, Catherine–Carpenter, James H.–June 22, 1854. Thomas Woodrow M. G. 6-127.

†ANDRUS, Harvey–Davis, Ellen Jane–Dec. 27, 1853. A. R. See, M. G. 6-89.

†ANDRUS, Polly–Carpenter, Nathan–Jan. 6, 1848. Louis A. Bruner, M. G. 5-86.
*–Nathan Carpenter and Miss Polly Andrews, eldest dau. of Maj. Hiram Andrews of Sharon Tp.

†ANDRUS, Richard–Andrews, Zelda–Nov. 27, 1855. Thomas Woodrow, M. G. 6-247.

ANDRUS, Samuel–Case, Diana–May 21, 1842. George Taylor, J. P. 4-2.

†ANDRUS, Sarah L.–Pritchard (I.) Prichard (Rec.), George W., aged 19 years, consent on file (not found)–Feb. 14, 1861. William Graham, J. P. 7-549.

†ANGEL, Michael–Lindamon, Magdalina–March 16, 1848. Konrad Mees, M. G. 5–97.

†ANGLE, A. R.–Douty, Cora L.–March 31, 1864. C. Moore, M. G. of Cincinnati. 8-333.
*–He a conductor on C. O. R. R. and Miss Cora L. Douty, dau. of G. Douty, Esq., of city.

†ANGLE, Jacob B.–Lamb, Emily R.–Dec. 31, 1862. Daniel D. Mather, M. G. 8-78.

†ANLINE, (Rec.) Anlon (I), Jacob–Corder, Hannah–Nov. 11, 1838. Benjamin Britton, J. P. 3-205.

*ANNMEILLER, Frederick–May or Mai, Katherine–April 14, 1856. K. Mees, M. G. 6-276.

†ANNOLD (Rec.) Arnold (I.) (Armold†), Cathron–Diens (Dicus†), Aaron–Dec. 21, 1843. Daniel Hamaker, J. P. 4-72.

†ANNOLD (Armold†), George W.–Park, Charlotte E.–Aug. 28, 1853. Daniel Hamaker, J. P. 6-55.

†ANNOLD (Armold†), Martha–Carpenter, Newton–June 1 (June 9†), 1849. Daniel Hamaker, J. P. 4-50.

†ANNON, (Miss†) Margaret–Washington, Daniel (of Columbus†)–June 27, 1845. Elder Ezekiel Fields. 4-300.

†ANTHONY, Anna Eva–Lang & Long, John M.–July 11, 1863. J. Kronenbitter, J. P. 8-200.

†ANTHONY, Annie J.–McFarland, N. C.–May 25, 1864. Henry McCracken, M. G. 8-362.

247

†ANTHONY, Caroline S. (aged 17 years, personal consent of her mother, Anna Anthony)–Melhorn, Daniel–Nov. 28, 1863. J. Kronenbitter, J. P. 8-266.

ANTHONY, Frederick–Anthony, Rosina–Nov. 1, 1832. Thomas Wood, J. P. 3-48.
*–Both of this town.

†ANTHONY, George–Bailey, Margaret–Sept. 26, 1816 (Recorded). James Hoge, M G. 2-30.

†ANTHONY, George–Baily, Margaret–March 27, 1817 (Recorded). James Hoge, M. G. 2-34.

†ANTHONY, George–Parish & Parrish, Clarissa–Oct. 21, 1823. Charles Waddell, L. M. G. 2-115.
*–George Anthony and Miss Clarissa Parish, all of here. Oct. 16, 1823.

†ANTHONY, Jacob–Smith (I.) (Schmidt†), Caroline–Feb. 23, 1837. Wilhelm Schmidt, M. G. 3-167.

†ANTHONY, Lewis–Ruster, Rebecca–Oct. 21, 1834. George Jefferies, M. G. 3-127.

†ANTHONY, Lewis–Bever, Anna Eve–Dec. 30, 1849. Solomon Shultz (K. Mees, M. G.†) 5-205.

†ANTHONY, Nicholas–Cebearger & Cebarger, Alice–Aug. 18, 1864, William F. Lehmann, M. G. 8-396.

ANTHONY, Rosina–Anthony, Frederick–Nov. 1, 1832. Thomas Wood, J. P. 3-48.

†ANTHONY, Rosina–Schille, Frederick–Dec. 18, 1850. K. Mees, M. G. 5-276.

ANTHONY, Susannah–Plettner, Augustus–May 22, 1862. Wm. F. Lehman M. G. 8-10.

†ANTONI, Sophia–Donaworth, George–March 31, 1834. Wilhelm Schmidt, M. G. 3-97.

†ANTONY, Nicholas–Lichti, Rosina–April 13, 1841. Charles F. Schaeffer, M. G. 4-1.

†APPLE, Jane–Becker, Frederick–Dec. 1, 1836 Wilhelm Schmidt, M. G. 3-166.

†APPLE, Thomas–Barr, Susan–Nov. 27, 1859. J. D. Smith, M. G. 7-355.

†APPLEGATE & APPLEGAIT, Anna–Engeroff, Frederick–Feb. 15, 1855. William F. Lehmann, M. G. 6-188.

†APPLEGUTS (I.) and (Rec.), William–Thompson, Mary–May 26 (May 17†), 1837. William Walker, J. P. 3-169.

†APPLEMAN, Lucinda–Stouffer, Amos–Feb. 17, 1864, Abner F. Jones, V. D. M. 8-303.

†APOLS. DOROTHEA–Long, Prarrrd (Konrad†)–Jan. 28, 1845. K. Mees, M. G. 4-175.

†ARCHER, Robert H.–Soovers, Susann–May 29, 1851. Abraham Wright, M. G. 5-307.

†ARCHER, Sarah, alias Sarah Smith–Triplet, Daniel–June 3, 1821. John Davis, J. P. 2-92.

†ARCHER, William–Flood, Elizabeth–July 30, 1846. W. T. Martin, J. P. 5-19.

†ARDLE & Ordel (I.) John D.–Hannah Ann–Aug. 4, 1857. John Helpman, J. P. 6-375.

†ARRINGTON, John A.–White, Anny–Dec. 28, 1854. Patterson Harrison, J. P. 6-173.

†ARRISON, (no name given)–Dean, Rachael–Oct. 8, 1835. Ebenezer Washburn, M. G. 3-180.
*–Alexander Arrison of here to Mrs. Rachael Dean of Blendon Tp. Rest same.

ARMENTROUT, Jemima–Lotridge, Dyer–Jan. 2, 1848. J. S. Rogers, J. P. 5-88.

†ARMENTROUGHT (Armentrout), Martha–Francis, Joseph–Nov. 29, 1835. John D. Acton, J. P. 3-132.

†ARMENTROUT, Elias–Bigelow, Nancy–Feb. 29, 1848. William Walker, J. P. 5-94.

(Consent of her parents, (Sttei?) and Mary Bigelow, Feb. 18, 1848.†)

ARMENTROUT, Gideon–Acton, Sarah Ann–July 26, 1842. J. S. Rogers, J. P. 4-2.

ARMENTROUT, Ishmael–Warner, Lysetna–June 3, 1846. No return. 5-10.

†ARMENTROUT, Lydia–Jones, Edmund–April 5, 1847. John Rathburn, M. G. 5-52.

ARMENTROUT, Marion–McCann, Ann E.–Feb. 5, 1861. John Kilgore, J. P. 7-543.

(Lide Jones gives consent for my son Marion Armentrout to get license. Wit.–James Duffy, Edmund Jones and Jacob Fist. Marion Armentrout says his mother is late Armentrout. Jan. 31, 1861.†)

†ARMENTROUT, Ruhama–Hays, Martin–July 31, 1864. Chauncey Beach, J. P. 8-387.

ARMINTROUT, Clarissa–Walker, Nathan–Jan. 11, 1849. Henry Francis, J. P. 5-145.

AMINTROUT, Fannie–Latham, David–Nov. 13, 1859. J. T. Britton, J. P. 7-356.

†ARMINTROUT, Jacob–Crawford, Rose M. (age 17 years, written consent file)–March 30, 1864. T. W. Dobyns, J. P. 8-335.

(Mrs. Meribah Crawford has given up her dau., Rose Manta Crawford, to marry Jacob Armentrout. Wit.–Merion Armentrout and A. Grace.†)

†ARMISTEAD, Sarah–Brackenridge, Joseph C.–April 6, 1837. Warren Frazzell, M. E. M. G. 3-170.

†ARMISTEAD (Armstead†), William–Wait, Lucy–Aug. 11, 1810. Benjamin Lakin, G. M. G. 1-77.

†ARMITAGE, Eliza–Golliday, Reuben–Nov. 8, 1838. Samuel Dearduff, J. P. 3-204.

†ARMITAGE, Elizabeth–Wyne, Isaac–Oct. 18,1835. Thomas Wood, J. P. 3-127.

*–Isaac Wynn.

ARMINTAGE (Rec.) (Armitage†) James–Jameson, Eliza–July 24, 1828. Jacob Grubb, J. P. 2-201.

†ARMITAGE, Mary–Truzill, Jacob–June 23, 1833. William Lusk, J. P. 3-80.

†ARMITAGE, Rebecah–Bogart, Jorge–Sept. 8, 1820. Robert Elliott, J. P. of Norwich Tp. 2-76.

†ARMITAGE, Sarah–Clover, William A.–Sept. 5, 1850. Rec. D. P. Cole. 5-256.

†ARMOLD, Lucinda–Kidner, William–Nov. 27, 1856. Daniel Hamaker, J. P. 6-320.

†ARMSTEAD (Armstid†), Lafayette–Jones, Joanna–Sept. 7, 1860. B. Tresenrider, J. P. 7-477.

†ARMSTEAD, Mariah (Miss Maria†)–Walton, Michael–Feb. 24, 1853. Uriah Heath, M. G. 6-14.

†ARMSTEAD, Mary Ann–Moler, John–Nov. 4, 1847. Cyrus Brooks, M. G. 5-80.

*–John Moler and Miss Mary Armistead, both of vicinity.

†ARMSTEAD, Phebe Ann–Gaines, John M.–Nov. 25, 1860. A. J. Martin, J. P. of Jefferson Tp. 7-515.

†ARMSTEAD, William–Gorton, Mary (Rec.) (Nancy†)–June 2, 1825. Rev. Joseph Carper. 2-143.

(William Armistead says Rachel Gorton is widow of Colo Gorton, deceased, of Franklinton, May 30, 1825.†)

†ARMSTEAD, William M.–Walton, Elizabeth M.–July 31, 1855. Uriah Heath, M. G. 6-224.

*–At residence of William Crum, William M. Armstead and Miss Elizabeth M. Walton, all of county.

MARRIAGE RECORDS, FRANKLIN COUNTY, OHIO
BLANCHE TIPTON RINGS

†ARMSTED, Mahetabel–Stone, Enos–July 6, 1848. John Miller, J. P. 5-114.
  ARMBRUSTER, Matthias–Baehr, Sarah–Dec. 3, 1861. William F. Lehmann, M. G. 7-677.
†ARMBRUSTER, Mathias–Hagele, Catherine–Aug. 28, 1864. William F. Lehmann, M. G. 8-400.
  ARMOLD, Elizabeth–Patterson, Benjamin–July 15, 1846. No return. 5-16. Signed by David Patterson.
†ARMOLD (I.) (Arnold†), Emoretta–Hardin, Nathan–Aug. 22, 1854. William Slaughter, M. G. 6-139.

†ARMONTROUT, George–Bigelow, Rachel–Oct. 22, 1853. Chauncey Beach, J. P. 6-67.

†ARMSTRONG, Abram S.–Craig, Eliza Ann–April 10, 1862. John G. Miller, J. P. 7-737.

ARMSTRONG, Alcinda–Goetchius, George–Nov. 30, 1843. James Armstrong, M. G. 4-113.

†ARMSTRONG, Ann–Jones, William–Sept. 20, 1853. Joseph M. Trimble, M. G. 6-62.

†ARMSTRONG, Ann C.–Smith, Philip–Nov. 23, 1845. James Laws, M. G. 4-261.

†ARMSTRONG, Amy S.–Bratton (Britton†), Edward D.–Feb. 2, 1852. Chauncey Beach, J. P. 5-363.

†ARMSTRONG, Aquilla–Lishalier, Sarah–June 17, 1847. No return. 5-61.

ARMSTRONG, Bella A.–Murch, Robert L.–July 11, 1861. Robert Forrester, M. G. 7-604.

ARMSTRONG, Charles H. Snouffer, Ellen L. (aged 19 years, consent on file†)–May 19, 1861. David Rogers, J. P. 7-587.
    (Dr. D. S. Armstrong gives consent for my son, Charles H. Armstrong, to mary Miss Ellen L. Snouffer, May 14, 1861. Wit.–Charles H. Armstrong and William S. Eyman.†)

†ARMSTRONG, Deby A.–Light, Charles H.–April 13, 1854. J. A. Bruner, M. G. 6-113.
    *–Charles H. Light of Indiana and Miss Delia A. Armstrong of the county.

ARMSTRONG, Ellen–Barker, William–June 2, 1842. Rev. Chandler Rogers 4-25.
    June 3, 1842. Charles F. Schaeffer, M. G. 4-28.

†ARMSTRONG, Ellen M.–Johnson, Orville, M. D.–June 17, 1856. Henry Floy Roberts, M. G. 6-288.

†ARMSTRONG, Elizabeth–Smith, Louis P.–Jan. 24, 1857. Daniel Hamaker, J. P. 5-41.

†ARMSTRONG, Elizabeth–Henderson, William M.–March 29, 1860. Henry Whorton, M. G. 7-409.

†ARMSTRONG, Fanny (Tacy†)–Caldwell, William–Jan. 21, 1836. Jacob Grubb, J. P. 3-134.

†ARMSTRONG, Flourannah–Green, Rufus W.–March 30, 1847. J. S. Rogers, J. P. 5-51.

†ARMSTRONG, Henry A.–Tone, Sarah A.–Jan. 5, 1848. E. H. Field, M. G. 5-87.

†ARMSTRONG, James–Nelson, Mary Ann–May 23, 1842, James Hoge, M. G. 4-4.
    *–James Armstrong, Esq., of New Lisbon, O., and Miss Mary A. Nelson of Columbus.

†ARMSTRONG, James R.–Scott, Maria L.–July 3, 1845, H. L. Richards, M. G. 4-6.
    *–James R. Armstrong, printer, and Miss Maria Louisa Scott, both of city.

†ARMSTRONG, Jane–Shepard, Henry C.–Dec. 11, 1862. Joseph M. Trimble, M. G. 8-100.

†ARMSTRONG, Jeremiah–Minter, Polly–April 12, 1807, James Marshall, J. P. 1-27.

†ARMSTRONG, Jeremiah–Phelps, Lucy–Nov. 6, 1838. Albert Helphenstine, M. G. at St. John's Church, Worthington. 3-233.

†ARMSTRONG, John–Thompson, Ruhama–June 15, 1819. James Hoge, M. G. 2-104.

†ARMSTRONG, John–Morrison, Catherine–Nov. 7, 1850. N. Doolittle, M. G. 5-268.

†ARMSTRONG, John–Spellman, Florena–April 1, 1856. J. H. Ralston. J. P. 6-269.

* Varified by news items in the Ohio State Journal of the same period.

†Armstrong, Joseph–Herd, Louisa M.–June 20, 1855. Elder Hiram Hendren. 6-215.

†Armstrong, Joshua–Trish, Victoria E.–March 26, 1863. J. G. Miller, J. P. 8-153.

†Armstrong, Julia–Schrock, William–April 17, 1862. William T. Snow, M. G. 7-736.

†Armstrong, M. Lacey–Wasson, G. W.–April 6, 1847. James Hoge, M. G. 5-54.
   *–G. W. Wasson of Wooster, O., and Miss M. Lacey Armstrong, dau. of Robert Armstrong of this city.

†Armstrong, Laughlin–Hall Mille–Jan. 31, 1854. John Eberly, J. P. 6-94.

Armstrong, Lucinda J.–Davis, Charles E.–Oct. 15, 1857. No return. 7-15.

†Armstrong, Lucy Ann–Myers, Henry M.–June 31 (Jan. 31†), 1838. James, Hoge, M. G. 4-183.
   *–Henry Miser, of Putnam Co., and Lucy Ann Armstrong, of this county, Feb. 1, 1839.

†Armstrong, Maggie–Gay, Oliver–Dec. 26, 1859. Rev. H. Williard. 7-361.

†Armstrong, Margaret J.–Starrett, Robert M.–April 3, 1862. Rev. H. Williard. 7-732.

†Armstrong, Mariah D.–Trimble, Robert–April 27, 1852. Archibald Fleming, M. G. 5-374.
   *–Robert Trimble of Fairfield Co., and Miss Maria D. Armstrong of Hibernia, Franklin County.

†Armstrong, Mattie L.–McMillen, J. F.–June 9, 1864. Isaac N. Langhear. 8-365.

Armstrong, Nancy J.–Green, Rufus–Nov. 18, 1852. J. T. Britton, J. P. 5-419.

Armstrong, Nancy R.–Bowers, Newman H.–Nov. 27, 1862. James H. Gill. 8-91.

†Armstrong, Robert–Thompson, Sarah–Dec. 21, 1818. James Hoge, M. G. 2-104.

†Armstrong, Robert, Jr–Nichols, Margaret-Nov. 7, 1850. N. Doolittle, M. G. 5-268.

†Armstrong, Robert L.–Kennedy, Mary E.–May 8, 1862. J. D. Smith. M. G. 8-6.

†Armstrong, R. C. (Ruhama†)–Heffnar, David S.–Dec. 14, 1841. Charles Fox, Rector of Trinity. 4-131

†Armstrong, Rose A.–Martin, W. D.–March 10, 1859. Silas Johnson, M. G. 7-229.

Armstrong, Rosetta–Williams, James–May 28, 1863. No Return. 8-183.

Armstrong, Sample R.–Kidd, Alice–Dec. 25, 1861. E. Washburn, V. D. M. 7-686.

Armstrong, Sarah–Domigon & Domigan, William–Feb. 8, 1830. Davies Francis, J. P. 2-245.

†Armstrong, Sarah A. D.–Wills, David–Dec. 30, 1849. S. Mann, J. P. 5-204.

Armstrong, Sullivant L.–Noe, Emma–May 19, 1861. Joseph M. Trimble, M. G. 7-583.

†Armstrong, Sullivan L.–Grovenbery, Salinda E.–Sept. 3, 1863. James T. Finch, M. G. 8-217.

Armstrong, Susan–Borland, John–Oct. 11, 1842. Stephen Maynard, J. P. 4-26.

†Armstrong, Susan–McClane, John–Oct. 10, 1844. James Price, J. P. 4-192.

†Armstrong, Thomas–Dulin, Francis C.–June 19, 1856. William Field, J. P. 6-289.

†Armstrong, Thomas–Lee, Sarah Jane–Jan. 8, 1863. J. Kronenbitter, J. P. 8-115.

†Armstrong, Virginia Trafzer (Traftzer†), Frederick–Dec. 13, 1863. James M. Paxton, J. P. 8-271.

†ARMSTRONG, William–Delano, Jane–Nov. 7, 1822. Rev. James Hoge, 2-133.

†ARMSTRONG, William–Morrison, Elizabeth–Nov. 7, 1850. N. Doolittle, M. G. 5-268.

ARNDT, Samantha S.–McNeal, William H. H. –Sept. 19, 1861. Joseph S. Cromwell, J. P. 7-634.

ARNEST, Jakob–Abea, Miss Catherine–Feb. 5, 1856. John Charles Hennaman, M. G. 6-260.

†ARNET, John–Boyd, Elizabeth–Feb. 16, 1853. William Haddock, J. P. 6-11.

†ARNET, Vynal–Hall, Mary Jane–Nov. 14, 1844. D. P. Cole, M. G. 4-5.

†ARNETT, Ephraim–Harper, Martha Jane, age 15 years, personal consent of her mother, Frances Harper. Dec. 4, 1862. Elder Allen Brown. 8-93.

†ARNOLD, Ann Maria–Ward, William S.–Dec. 21, 1848. W. T. Martin, J. P. 5-143.

†ARNOLD, Barbara–Borshert, George–Sept. 7, 1857. H. Bauer, Pastor. 6-381.

ARNOLD, Christian J. D.—Wild, Sarah–Dec. 29, 1842. Charles F. Schaeffer, M. G. 4-3.

†ARNOLD, Emily–Burwell, William–Jan. 23, 1850. William Davis, M. G. 5-210.

†ARNOLD, Francis–Boden, Ernestine–July 14, 1856. William F. Lehmann, M. G. 6-293.

†ARNOLD, (Armold†), Ira–Ingram, Lena–Dec. 14, 1814. Recompense Stansbery, J. P. at Worthington. 2-1.

†ARNOLD, Jacob–Park, Eliza A.–Sept. 18, 1851. J. C. Winter, M. G. 5-331. (Jacob Ulry says Jacob Arnold and Eliza A. Parke are of age.†)

†ARNOLD, Magdalena–Porchet, Johann George–Nov. 27, 1859. H. Bauer, Evan. Luth. M. G. 7-353.

†ARNOLD, Mary Ann–Barnhands, ePter (I. and Rec.)–Feb. 3, 1839. Morris Roe, M. G. 3-213. (Adam Hamaker says he heard Mrs. Arnold give consent for her dau. Mary Ann Arnold to marry Peter Barnhard, Jan. 28, 1839†)

†ARNOLD, Nathan–Cutler, Betsey–Jan. 1, 1818. Venal Stewart, Preacher. 2-45.

ARNOLD, Randall R.–Baldwin, Mary–Sept. 15, 1827. Gideon W. Hart, J. P. 2-189. Both of Blendon Tp.

†ARNOLD, Samuel J.–Manly, Georgiana–April 1, 1855. Elder S. Jones. 6-198.

†ARNOLD, Thomas–Gabriel, Angeline E.–Oct. 28, 1847. Uriah Heath, M. G. 5-79. *–Thomas Arnold and Miss Angeline Gabriel, both of city.

†ARNOLD, Whitmore–Helser, Harriet L.–May 2, 1861. John W. Miller, J. P. 7-576.

ARNOLT, Peter–Kesler. Barbara–Aug. 3, 1853. No return. 6-51.

†ARROWS, Christianam–Snider, Jacob–May 30, 1833. Jacob Grubb, M. G. 3-55.

†ARTHUR, Ann–Owen, George–March 23, 1859. John H. Jones, M. G. 7-251.

†ARTHUR, John–Humphries, Ann–April 26, 1853. William Perry, G. M. G. 6-30.

†ARTHER, John–McComb Rebecca J.–June 7, 1853. J. D. Smith, M. G. 6-37.

†ARTHUR. Mary–Hughes, John E.–March 6, 1860. Edward T. Evans, M. G. 7-400.

†ARTHUR, Thomas–Blindon, Jane–July 22, 1863. John H. Jones, Pastor. 8-203.

†ARTHUR, Watkin–Jones, Mary–Oct. 4, 1861. R. H. Evans. 7-638.

ARTHUR, William–Gravner, Elizabeth–Jan. 13, 1857. No return. 6-330.
†ARTHUR, William–Davis, Rebecca Jane–Sept. 17, 1857. John W. Miller, J. P. 6-383.
†ARTIS, Adeline–Jones, Jabez–Jan. 7, 1858. James Poindexter, M. G. 7-53.
†ARTLE, Mary Ann–Alspach, Levi.–Jan. 17, 1847. Joshua Glanville, J. P. 5-40.
†ATHEY, NANCY–Hand, Isaac–Jan. 27, 1849. D. P. Cole, M. G. 5-148.
†ATHEY & Athe (*), POLLY–Lain, William–Dec. 23, 1829. John Tipton, J. P. 2-237.
†ATHEY, SARAH–Gardner, George–Apr. 30, 1857. William Walker, J. P. 6-358.
†ATHEY, SUSAN–Age 17 years, consent on file–Leiter, Daniel J. vouched by James J. Sheaders–Jan. 24, 1860. Rev. Levi. Johnson 7-378. (Dec. 18, 1860. I am willing for you the probate court to issue licenses to Daniel Liter to marry Susan Athey for I am the parent and Guardian, Malindy Athey. John M. Athey. Malindy Athey is the two witness. James Sheaders, Elijah Atehy, James J. Sheaders says John M. Athey & Malinda Athey are parents of Susan Athey.)
†ATKINSON, MARY–Green, Benjamin S.–June 9, 1853. Edward Davis, M. G. 6-40.
†ATKINSON, JAMES–Darby, Ruth–June 5, 1856. Thomas S. Lloyd, Preacher. 6-287.
†ATWOOD, (I) & Attwood (Rec), JOHN H.–Bushang, Sarah–June 25, 1864. Geo. W. Meeker, J. P. 8-373.
†ATWOOD, PATRICK–Gould, Mary–May 6, 1859. William L. Heyl, J. P. 7-268. (Both of Jefferson Tp.)
†AUBERT, CHARLES–Reisel, Elizabeth–Nov. 4, 1863. William L. Heyl, J. P. 8-256.
†AUBORN, MARTHA M. H.–Field, Frederick B.–Mch. 6, 1864. Julius E. Grammar, M. G. 8-314.
†AUBURN (I & Rec). (Dulen in*), JULIA–Britton, John T.–May 24, 1830. Benjamin Britton, J. P. 2-254.
†AUEY, POLLY–Hutchinson, Amaziah, Jr.–Apr. 2, 1818. See Hutchinson, this should be EBY. Robert Elliott, J. P. 2-45.
†AUGMAN & Ohnsmann (*), CATHERINE–Conrade, Frederick–Sept. 10, 1863. K. Mees, M. H. G. 8-124.
†AUGUSTUS, SALEM W.–Cook, Amelia G.–Mch. 31, 1852. H. L. Hitchcock, M. G. 5-370.
*—(Miss Amelia G. Cook, teacher at the Deaf and Dumb School. The brides mother and grandmother were both present, rest same.)
†AULD, JAMES C.–Sheesley, Rovenia–Oct. 1, 1863. Edward D. Morris, M. G. 8-235.
†AULT, MELINDA–aged 16 years, consent of her parents on file Kitsmiller, Thomas–Dec. 15, 1864. J. A. Schulze, M. G. 8-467. (Gahanna, O.— Dec. 7, 1864–Valintine & Mary Ault give consent for daughter Molinda to marry Thomas Kitsmiller. John Kitsmiller gives consent for my son Thomas to marry Miss Malind Ault, Gahanna, Dec. 7, 1864)
†AULTMAN, CATHERINE–Ritchie, James–Mch. 7, 1864. Joseph M. Trimble, M. G. 4-231.
†AUMILLER, CHRISTINA N.–Koch, George–Nov. 12, 1849. K. Mees, M. G. 5-195.
†AUMILLER, H. FREDERICK–Smith, (Schmitt)*, Elizabeth–Mch. 7, 1856. K. Mees, 6-267.
†AUSTIN, EMILY–Blade, Richard–Oct. 18, 1849. Thomas Hughs, M. G. 5-190.
†AUMILLER (Aumuller), LAWRENCE–Frank, Barnary–May 4, 1852. K. Mees, M. G. 5-376.
†AUSTIN, JOHN A.–Bacon, Harriet–Aug. 9, 1855. Henry Floy Roberts, M. G. 6-225.

†Austin, Margaret A. (Miss)*–Hart, Moses W.–Mch. 27, 1864. E. H. Heagler, V. D. M. 8-329.

†Austin, Mary–Gains, Atkin–Sept. 25, 1861–colored. Silas Johnson, M. G. 7-635.

†Austin, Sarah E.–Billingsley, John B.–Mch. 7, 1855. William Graham, J. P. 6-192.

†Austin, Thomas W.–Lattimer, Lucy J.–Oct. 28, 1863. D. D. Mather, M. G. 8-251.

†Auten, John F.–Tevenderf, Jane–July 21, 1821. Robert Reiley, J. P. 2-91.

†Auten, Lucinda–Crosby, William–Aug. 6, 1841. Charles Fox, M. G. at Trinity. 4-53.

†Auter, Harriet (Auten)–Osgood, James W.–Sept. 14, 1841. Joseph M. Trimble, M. G. 4-205.

*–(J. Wentworth Osgood, printer of Boston, Mass. & Miss Harriet Auter of this city,

†Avery, Betsey–Butterfield, Free–(Green)* of Sharon Tp.—Sept. 19, 1826. Amaziah Hutchinson, J. P. 2-179.

†Avery, Christopher–Hays, Axah S. or L. (Asah)*–May 1, 1845. Charles C. Lybrand, M. G. 4-6.

†Avery, Daniel–Adams, Margaret–Jan. 4, 1821. 2-86. A. Allen, J. P. 2-86.

†Avery, Horace B.–Miller, Roxie–Apr. 22, 1859. D. A. Randall, M. G. 7-264.

†Avery, Sylvester–Kidwell, Martha E.–Oct. 24, 1858. B. Britton, Elder. 7-167.

†Avery, William–Pickle, Margaret–Feb. 25, 1828. Lyndes L. Latimer, J. P. 2-196.

(Consent of her father, Minard Pickle. Wit., David Avery, Jr.)

†Avry, Anne–West, Benjamin–both of Perry Tp.–Apr. 15, 1824. Uriah Clark, J. P. 2-118.

*(Daniel and Sally Avery, parents of Aney Avery give their consent, Apr. 16, 1824.)

Awl, Woodward–Allen, Minnie A.–May 16, 1861. O. Allen, M. G. 7-586.

†Awlston, Agnes–Dickson, Moses–Dec. 31, 1860. William T. Snow, M. G. 7-531.

†Axel, Phillip–Albrecht, Catherine–Mch. 10, 1863. William F. Lehmann, M. G. 8-143.

†Axell, Ami & (Amzi)*–Thrall, Cassander & Cass Andra–Dec. 2, 1837. J. A. Watterman, M. G. 3-184.

†Axt, George–Brunn, Eliza–Dec. 21. 1854. K. Mees, M. G. 6-172.

†Ayle, John, Widower–Kenady, Elizabeth, Widow–June 30, 1825. Jacob Gundy, J. P. 2-143.

†Ayers, (Myers)*, Lavinia–Searls, (Serls), Selvester–Oct. 19, 1820. T. Lee, J. P. 2-77.

*(Thomas Myers gives consent for his daughter Levinia to marry Selvester Soils,–Jefferson Tp.–Oct. 7, 1820.).

†Ayers, Samuel–Canfield, Eliza–Mch. 21, 1825 (Mch. 31)* Jacob Smith, J. P. 2-143.

†Ayers, Abigail–Smith, Stephen–June 15, 1856. M. K. Earhart, J. P. 6-288.

†Ayers, Charles–Rochel, Dency–Sept. 4, 1851. S. Mann, J. P. -328.

(Charles J. Ayers (by him) says her parents John and Lucinda Rochell give consent, she being under age.)

†Ayers, Elizabeth N.–Gates, John B.–Jan. 23, 1849. Milton B. Starr, M. G. 5-147.

†Ayers, James J.–Alberry, Amanda A.–Feb. 1, 1862. No return. 7-704.

†Ayers, Mary J.–Deviney, Jacob C.–Aug. 16, 1853. John Painter, J. P. 6-53.

†AYRES, Mary J.-Deviney, Jacob C.—Aug. 16, 1853. John Painter, J. P.
—6-53.

†AYRES, Susan-Perry, John—June 19, 1845. Charles M. Putnam, M. G.
—4-218.

†AYRES, Temperance-Carpenter, Royal—Jan. 3, 1833. Samuel P. Shaw,
M. G.—3-59.

†BABB & Bebb, Samuel-Brown, Elizabeth—Aug. 6, 1843. R. S. Kimber,
M. G.—4-29.

†BABBERT, Frederick-Fischer, Mary—Nov. 8, 1862. J. B. Hemsteger,
C. P.

†BABBETT, Sanford, Widower-Norris, Widow Phebe Q.—Mch. 30, 1824.
Aristarchus Walker, J. P.—2-119.

†BABBETT, Sanford-Cory, Lydia–Sept. 8, 1842. J. Pegg, J. P.–4-26.

†BABBITT & Babbett, Anna–Albright & Albrecht, Andrew–Feb. 8, 1864.
J. B. Hemsteger, Catholic M. G. 8-301.

†BABBITT, Catherine–Campbell, James–June 21, 1863. C. Spencer,
V. D. M.–8-192.

†BABBITT. Cyyrus B.-Johnson & Johnston, Sarah J.–Feb. 2, 1864. Joseph
M. Adair, M. G.–8-295.

†BABCOCK, Benjamin–Hunter, Margaret–Dec. 3, 1854. William Graham,
J. P.–6-167.

†BABCOCK, Ellen Jane (Ellener Jane†)–Morrison, George–Aug. 28, 1852.
G. W. Evans, J. P.–5-396.

†BABCOCK, Jacob–Wilcox, Nancy–Jan. 7, 1841. J. S. Rogers, J. P.–4-19.

†BABCOCK, Olive–Wilcox, Francis–Oct. 19, 1848. J. S. Rogers, J. P.–
5-131.

†BABCOCK, Rosemanly–Smith, Nathan–May 6, 1838. Jacob S. Rogers,
J. P.–3-195.
(Jacob S. Rogers says he believes Nathaniel Smith and Rosemanly
Babcock are of age, Apr. 21, 1838.)

BABCOCK, Roswell–Hainly & Hainley, Jane–July 1, 1830. David Bailey,
J. P.–2-252.

BABCOCK, Wealthy–Watts, John–Jan. 31, 1832. William Seeds, J. P.–
3-32.

BABST (1) & Papst (Rec.); Regina–Fahrenkapp (Rec) & Farrankopp
(1) Valentine–May 9, 1858. C. H. Borgess, C. P.–7-111.

†BACCHUS, Emily–McElvain, J. W.–May 26, 1840. James Hoge, M. G.–
3-183.

†BACCHUS, Hannah–George, William–Jan. 24, 1818. James Hoge, M. G.–
2-103.

†BACCHUS, Thomas–Williams, Temperance–Nov. 25, 1811. James
Marshall, J. P.–1-147.

†BACH, Edward, aged 20 years, consent of his mother–Kemmerer, Emma
May 14, 1859–Edward Lilley, J. P.–7-275.
† I give consent for my son, Edward Bach to get married with
Emma Kemmerer, Katherine Bach. May 14, 1859–Wit; Katherine
Allen & William Bach.

†BACH, William–Krayer, Sophia–Nov. 28, 1856. K. Mees, M. G.–6-320.

†BACHELDER, James L.–Cloud, Margaret P.–Apr. 21, 1851.
N. B. (This follows Apr. 25, 1850 not 1851)
D. B. Cheny, M. G.–5-230.
*Apr. 22, 1850–James L. Bachelder of Cincinnati & Miss Margaret
P. Cloud.

---

*—Asterisk denotes verification in newspaper items.   †—Original record.

†Original Record.
*Verified by news items in the Ohio State Journal of the same period.

†BACHELOR, Alonzo–Cole, Barbara A.–Mch. 17, 1859. E. C. Green, J. P.–7-247.

BACHELOR, Lucy–Chrysler, Elias–Oct. 13, 1852. Nathan Brooks, J. P.–r-409.

BACHER, John–Coontz, Susanna–May 29, 1846. No. return–5-10.

BACHER, John–Salidee & Salida, Juliann–Mch. 12, 1856. J. W. White, M. G.–6-267.

†BACHER, Julia A.–Click, Josiah–May 1, 1860. P. Eirick–7-422.

†BACHER, Mary Ann–Recher, Peter–Oct. 18, 1848. C. Weinle, M. G.–5-131.

BACHMAN, Christian–Schneider, Catherine–Jan. 12, 1860. Edward Lilley, J. P.–7-373.

†BACHMAN, Jacob–Kulp, Margaret–Apr. 1, 1855. William F. Lehmann, M. G.–6-196.

†BACHMANN, Joseph–Hesler, Elizabeth–Jan. 18, 1855. K. Mees, M. G.–6-178.

†BACHMANN, Louisa, Miss–Schnitzer, Frederick F.–Jan. 11, 1863. J. S. Cantwell, M. G.–8-109.

†BACHMAN, Magdalene–Louis, Jacob–Apr. 30, 1858. Konrad Mees, M. G.–7-106.
   † (Maria Layman or Loerfmoun gives consent for her daughter Magdalena Bachman (under 18 years) to marry Jacob Louis, her father is dead. Witness–Valentine Schneider and Griffin Loerfman? (On outside of paper it says "Consent of Mrs. Bachman."

†BACHMANN, Mary–Schneider, Balentine–Jan. 18, 1855. K. Mees, M. G.–6-179.

†BACKAR, Henry–Lee, Margret–Sept. 30, 1819. Richard Courtright, J. P.–2-69.

†BACHNER & Bachner, Michael–John, Mar. Ann–1845. William Schonatt, Catholic M. G.–4-36.

†BACKUS, Alexander–Keys, Sarah–Sept. 29, 1845. A. Patton, J. P.–4-37.

†BACKUS, Elijah–Wheeler, Caroline–Nov. 7, 1843. Alexander F. Dobb, M. G.–4-30.
   *(Elijah Backus, attorney & Miss Caroline Wheeler, all of city, Nov. 6, 1843.

†BACKUS, Elizabeth–Niswander, Jesse–Aug. 30, 1830. Jacob Gander, J. P.–3-4.

†BACKUS, Lafayette, M. D.–Dering & Denig, Harriet L.–May 5, 1846. James Hoge, M. G.–5-7.
   † (Consent of her father George Denig, Wit.–O. Backus & A. L. Denig.
   *(Youngest daughter of Dr. Denig of this city.

BACKUS, Lucretia–Guitteau, Abner L.–Mch. 13, 1832. William Preston, M. G.–3-40.

†BACKUS, Mary (Ann)†–King, Lyman–Dec. 25, 1846. A. P. Freeze (Freese), M. G.–5-37.

†BACKUS, Mary Ann–Shott, Charles–May 31, 1849. Conrad Gahn, M. G.–5-167.

†BACKUS, Shannon–Moore, Elizabeth E.–Aug. 8, 1844. Shuah Mann, J. P.–4-32.

BACKUS, W. H.–Woolf, Mary A.–Jan. 15, 1842. William Caldwell, J. P.–4-27.

BACON, Anna–Tripp, Stephen–Mch. 27, 1828. Jason Bull, J. P.–2-200.

BACON Arlow G.–Kilbourne, Cunthia M.–Nov. 6, 1847. No return–5-81.

BACON, Bulsona L.–Otstotts, John S.–Nov. 21, 1841. R. J. Elder, M. G.–4-206.

†BACON, Danie L.–Beal, Maple (Mable)†–Feb. 22, 1841. W. T. Martin, J. P.–4-20.

†BACON, Daniel–Bull, Lucy C.–Nov. 27, 1844. James Armstrong, M. G.–4-34.

257

*(Daniel Bacon & Miss Lucy, daughter of Rèv. Jason Bull, all of county.

†BACON, Harriet–Austin, John A.–Aug. 9, 1855. Henry Floy Roberts, M. G.–6-225.

BACON, James–Topping, Mary S.–Oct. 10, 1854. No return–6-153.

†BACON, John–Galbraith, Anne (Jane)†–Mch. 3, 1843. Jason Bull, M. G. –4-28.

†BACON, John G.–Groom, Elizabeth–Aug. 27, 1848. John Gantz, J. P. –5-120.

BACON, Lucy–Weaver, Hiram–Mch. 30, 1854. J. L. Grover, M. G.–6-110.

†BACON, Narcissus W.–Timmons, Solomon–Sept. 15, 1864. John C. Tidball, M. G.–8-407.

†BACON, S. A. (Selah) †–Fisk, Emma–May 31, 1840. William Preston, M. G.–4-20.

†BACON, Sarah E.–Davis, Henry F.–Dec. 25, 1859. David Rogers, J. P. –7-361.

†BACON & BADOR, Abigail–Reed, Danforth B.–July 2, 1841. William Caldwell, J. P.–4-229.

BADER, Andrew–Zeiser, Antoie–Aug. 10, 1854. No return–6-138.

†BADER, Frederick–Frey, Mary S.–Mch. 11, 1860. K. Mees, M. G.–7-402.

†BADER, Hyacinth & Hiazinth–Fischer, Sophia–Oct. 11, 1854. C. H. Borgess, C. P.–6-150.

†BADER, John–Walzer & Waltzer (1), Josephine–Oct. 26, 1858. C. H. Borgess, C. P.–7-167.

BADERFIELD, Lewis–Briber, Christian–Mch. 6, 1842. Charles F. Schaeffer, M. G.–4-24.

†BADGE (1) & BERTCH (Rec), Catherine–Hite, James–Apr. 10, 1860. William F. Lehman M. G.–7-416.

†BADGE, Archibald–Seeds, Mary–May 21, 1818. William Brown J. P.–2-49.

†BADGER, Archabald–Park, Kesia–Nov. 18, 1824–both of Franklinton Tp. Joseph Badger, J. P.–2-127.

†BADGER, Archibald–Gray, Rebecca–Apr. 9, 1857. William Field, J. P. –6-354.

†BADGER, Elizabeth–Gentry, Benjamin–July 30, 1840. Robert Seeds, J. P. –3-252.

†BADGER, James–Rizer & Riser, Elizabeth–Apr. 24, 1831. Stewart White, J. P.–3-16.

†BADGER, John–Pick (I & Rec) & Perk, Milesse–Oct. 24, 1839. Nathan Emery, M. G.–3-228.

†BADGER, Margaret–Conrad, Jesse–Sept. 12, 1834. Jacob B. Diemer, J. P. –3-101.

†BADGER, Margaret–Borar & Borror, Absolom–Feb. 28, 1839. John Gantz, J. P.–3-209

†BADGER, Martha–Foley, Moses–Apr. 15, 1819. Joseph Gorton, J. P.–2-57.

†BADGER, Mary B.–Smith, Joseph H.–July 16, 1857. G. W. Gowdy, V. D. M.–6-373.

†BADGER, Robert–Park, Nancy–Mch. 22, 1820. James Hoge, M. G.–2-105.

†BADGER, William–Breckenbridge, Margaret–July 31, 1814. James Hoge, M. G.–1-137.

†BADO, Elizabeth–Goetchius, John–Oct. 19, 1840. William Sutton, M. E. M. G.–4-110.

†BADO, Sarah E.–Watkins, Elijah–Jan. 19, 1857. No return (William Field, J. P.)–6-333.

†BADOW, William–Hooker, Eliza–Jan. 13, 1859. Lovett Taft, M. G.–7-212.
*(All of vicinity)

†BAECHER or BALCHER, Conrad–Kline & Klein, Catherine–June 18, 1863. K. Mees, M. G.–8-191.

†BAEDER, Frederick–Kellar, Margarethe–Mch. 19, 1844. Conrad Mees, M. G.–4-233.

†BAEHR, Andrew (in German) ††Fuchs Magdalena–Jan. 28, 1862. William F. Lehmann, M. G.–7-703.

BAEHR, Charles (in German)–Odel, Catherine–Aug. 25, 1862. K. Mees, M. G.–8-43.

BAEHR, Sarah–Armbruster, Mathias–Dec. 3, 1861. William F. Lehmann, M. G.–7-677.

BAEHR, Susan–Dice, Charles–May 8, 1851. Rev. B. Braumiller–5-311.

†**BAER**, Magdalen–John, Peter–May 16, 1855. C. H. Borgess, C. P.–6-210.

†**BAERLIE**, Cather ne–Nagle, John Martin–Apr. 26, 1864. Charles Helwig, M. B.–8-349.

†**BAERERLING**, Maria–Luntz, Conrad–September 12, 1851. K. Mees, M. G. –5-331.

†**BAESLER & BESLER** Louisa–Lachenmeur & Laghenmur, Gottlieb–Sept. 23, 1858. Konrad Mees, M. G.–7-159.

†**BAETY**, Susanna–Grifee, William–Nov. 2, 1824. Jacob Gundy, J. P. –2-126.

†(Consent of her father, William Baety for his daughter Susan to marry William Griffe–Oct. 17. 1824. Wit.–William S. Baety)

†**BAEUERLE**, Louisa–Beck, Joshua–Mch. 28, 1864. Wm. F. Lehmann, M. G.–8-333

BAGG, James–Smith, Caroline–Oct. 3, 1861. Edward Fitzgerald, C.* P. –7-642.

†**BAGGART**, Dandelion–(Rec) & Daniel (1)–Schorempf, Sellina–Nov. 8, 1837. H. D. Juncker, M. G.–3-179.

†**BAGLEY**, Darcus–Athey, Elijah–Nov. 23, 1820. Reuben Golliday, J. P. –2-78.

†**BAHR**, Simon–Magley, & Magli, Melissa–Oct. 7, 1855. K. Mees, M. G. –6-236.

†**BAHTEL**, Selena Jane–Martin, Charles–Mch. 28, 1863. Benjamin D. Evans, M. G.–8-152.

†**BAIER**, Frederick–Murray, Eliza–Aug. 21, 1851. J. P. Bruck, J. P.–5-325. (Fredrick Baier says Eliza Murray is 17 years old).

†**BAILE**, Elias–Strain, Jane–Sept. 17, 1864. Wm. L. Heyl, J. P.–8-414.

†**BAILEY**, Asenath–Reason, John–Sept. 21, 1854. D. P. Cole, M. G.–6-148.

†**BAILEY**, Catherine–Reel, Henry, Jr.–Mch. 6, 1851. Wm. F. Lehmann, M. G.–5-294.

BAILEY, Eli–Clark, Sarah M.–Colored–July 14, 1859. No return–7-299.

BAILEY, Eliza–Murphy, John–Apr. 27, 1852. C. H. Borgess, Catholic M. G.–5-375.

†**BAILEY**, Eliza–Deltz, Amos K.–May 12, 1853. D. P. Cole, M. G.–6-33.

BAILEY, Elizabeth—Tully, W. A. (Tulley, Wm. A.)—Apr. 3, 1827. Samual Hamilton, Elder in M. E. Church—2-184.

BAILEY, Emily—Rowley, James M.—Dec. 16, 1846. G. W. Evans, J. P. —5-35.

BAILEY, Frances—Dearth, Aaron—Dec. 19, 1856. John G. Miller, J. P. —6-324.

BAILEY, George W.—Crosby, Libbie—Dec. 22, 1864. Edward D. Morris, M. G.—8-471.

BAILEY, Isaac, aged 19 years, consent of his father, Thomas Bailey. Ward, Martha L.—July 5, 1862. John Kilgore, J. P.—8-24.

BAILEY, J.—(Male)—******Sells, E.—(female)—Apr. 27, 1836. E. W. Sehon, M. G.—3-138.

BAILEY, James M.—Ebberton, Lucinda—Oct. 3, 1844. Albert Bowers, J. P. of Perry Tp.—4-33 (should be Allen Bowers)*

*—Ohio State Journal.

*–Both of city.

BAILEY & Baily*, Jane—Frey & Fry (*), Andrew—Jan. 26, 1828. Wm. Long, J. P.—2-198.

BAILEY, John—Anderson, Lucinda—Aug. 14, 1855. T. N. Stewart, M. G.—6-227.

BAILEY, L. C.—Hayden, Helen J.—Oct. 27, 1857. John Frazer, M. G. —7-26.

BAILEY, Margaret—Anthony, George—Sept. 26, 1816 (Recorded) James Hoge, M. G.—2-30.

BAILEY, Margaret—Wallace, Benjamin—Mch. 20, 1842. Z. P. Thompson, M. G.—4-292.

BAILEY, Martha E. (Matilda E.)*—Geotchius, Edmund—Oct. 30, 1859 Jacob Hathaway, M. G.—7-342.
(O. S. J.) (Miss Matilda E. Bailey, all of county, rest same)

BAILEY, Matthew—Harrison, Anna—Sept. 5, 1816. William Brown, J. P.—2-30.

BAILEY, Orrange—Waggoner, Lydia—Aug. 9, 1832. John Eberly, J. P. —3-48.

BAILEY, Phebe Ann—Gohring, Franz—Sept. 25, 1834. Wilhelm Schmidt, M. G.—3-92.

BAILEY, Rachel—O'Harra, Garrett—Oct. 8, 1859—(Oct. 4)* W. T. Grantham, M. G.—77-331.

BAILEY, Rose Manly—Hyde, Cyrus S.—May 30, 1833. Jacob S. Rogers, J. P.—3-55.

BAILEY, Rose Manty—Crego, Isaac—Mch. 14, 1864. No return—8-321.

BAILEY, S. C.—Marple, Jennie—May 2, 1854. H. L. Hitchcock, M. G. —6-117.
O. S. J.—Dr. S. C. Bailey of Gallipolis and Miss Jennie Marple of this city, rest same)

BAILEY, Sarah—Search, Ira—Mch. 4, 1841. Thomas Woods, J. P.—4-238.

BAILEY, Sarah Ann—Hoff, John—Aug. 12, 1849. George H. Earhart, J. P.—5-175

BAILEY, Stewart—Overdear, Martha—Apr. 1, 1816 (Recorded). James Hoge, M. G.—2-20.

BAILEY, William—Free, Margaret—May 21, 1840. William Preston, M. G.—4-21.

BAILEY, William D.—Smith, Eliza—July 6, 1843. H. L. Hitchcock, M. G.—4-29.

BAILEY, William H.—O'Harra, Priscilla—June 26, 1857 (May 26)* Smith Postle, J. P.—6-368.

BAILEY, Cilas & Cylas, (*)—Thompson, Susan—May 4, 1837. Washington Lakin, J. P. Clinton Tp—3-168.

BAILY, Eunice—Bowen (Rec) & (I) (Brown)*, Newton—May 19, 1855. J. B. Mitchell, J. P.—6-216.

BAILY, Hester—Vanscoyke, David—Mch. 5, 1835.
Jesse F. Wixom. 3-112.

BAILY, Jane—Waggoner, Levi—Dec. 14, 1837.
T. R. Creey, M. G.—3-185.

BAILY, Jesse—Wagoner, Lucinda—Mch. 22, 1849.
Shuah Mann, J. P.—5-156.

BAILY, Joel—Wolf, Mary—July 14, 1834. Thomas Wood, J. P.—3-102.

BAILY, Joseph—Wilson, Matilda Ellen—Sept. 6, 1849.
John Rathbun, M. G.—5-179.

MARRIAGE RECORDS, FRANKLIN COUNTY, OHIO
Blanche Tipton Rings

BAILY, Mary—Clover, Zebulon—Oct. 9, 1841 (Oct.)* John Rathbun
M. G.—4-23. *(Consent of her father, Knowlton Bailey, she being
of age, Wit—Samuel Bailey, Oct. 4, 1841*
BAILY, Mary—Davis, Edmond—Oct. 25, 1853.
N. M. Gaylord, M. G.—6-88.
BAILY, Margaret—Anthony, George—Mch. 27, 1817 (Recorded)
James Hoge, M. G.—2-34.
BAILY, Matthew—McHenry, Sarah—Oct. 12, 1835 (Sept. 13)*
John Tipton, J. P.—3-126.
BAILY, Permelia—Giberson, Williams—June 7, 1849.
George H. Earhart, J. P.—5-168.
BAILY, Rhoda—Harrison, Charles—Feb. 27, 1823.
Jacob Grubb, J. P.—2-111.
BAILY, Samuel—Ambrose, Margaret J.—Mch. 17, 1842.
M. Ambrose, J. P.—4-24.
BAILY, & Bayley*, Unice—Loy, James—Mch. 6, 1836.
Henry Innis, M. G.—3-140.
*(James Loy & Mason Mayley say that Eunice Bayley is
over 18 years of age, Mch. 5, 1836).
BAINBRIDGE, William—Harper, Hannah A—Feb. 23, 1860.
Richard Doughty, V. D. M.—7-391.
BAINS & Bain, Elizabeth—Hopcraft, Henry—May 28, 1842.
H. L. Hitchcock, M. G.—4-133.
BAINES, Elizabeth—Rowlands, Thomas—Dec. 23, 1847.
Benjamin Dyorig Evans, M. G.—55-86.
BAIN, Smith—Oglesby, Mary E—Aug. 14, 1864.
J. L. Grover, M. G.—8-394.
BAIR & Barr*, William—Shannon, Amanda M—Mch. 28, 1836.
James Hoge, M. G.—4-21.
*William W. Shannon requests that the bearer, Mr. S have
license to marry my daughter Amanda, Mch. 28, 1836.
BAIRD, Hanna—Pasco, Harvey—Apr. 12, 1832.
Benjamin Britton, J. P.—3-41.
BAIRD, Hannah—Rann, Jacob—Sept. 8, 1842.
Joseph M. Trimble, M. G.—4-230.
BAIRD, Hannah—Buion, Jacob (B-index) Ruion*, Jacob—Sept. 16,
1842.
Joseph M. Trimble, M. G.—4-26.
BAIRD, Thomas N—Vining, Mary W—Apr. 13, 1834. (Apr. 15)
George Jefferies, M. G.—3-85.
BAIRD, William—Blosser, Rachel C—Dec. 20, 1863.
Henry McCracken, M. G.—Dec. 20, 1863.
BAKER, Alexander—McCracken—July 23, 1846.
Rebecca
No return—5-16.
Gabriel Postle says Alexander Baker is his ward and is not
of age but he gives consent).

*—Ohio State Journal.
*—Asterisk denotes verification in newspaper items †—Original record.

BAKER, Alvira Jane—Grate, Joseph—Feb. 8, 1857.
(Almira Jane)*
John A. Kellar, J. P. Franklinton.—6-338.
BAKER, Amory Johanna (Rec) & Jane (I)—Miller, John—Sept. 28, 1864.
No return—8-419.
BAKER, Ann—Still, Oliver—Feb. 17, 1828.
William Dalzell, J. P.—2-195.
BAKER, Ann—Hubburd, Simeon—Dec. 17, 1833 (Dec. 19)*
W. T. Martin, J. P.—3-75.
BAKER, & Barker—, Ann—Watson, Samuel—Feb. 15, 1850.
David Warnock, M. G.—5-217.
BAKER, Anthony—Ditzell, Helene—May 9, 1839.
Wilhelm Schmidt, M. G.—3-220.
*(George Frankenberg says he believes Anthony H. Baker
and Helena Deltzell are of age, May 7, 1839).
BAKER, Catherine—Ballard, Thomas, age 18, consent of his father
Fountain L. Ballard—Apr. 18, 1861.
A. C. Bauer, J. P.—7-574.
BAKER, Cyrus—Washington, Rachel—June 20, 1823.
William Gilmer, J. P. of Madison Tp—2-127.
BAKER, David—Searley, Catherine—Dec. 26, 1831—
George Jefferies, M. G.—3-35.
BAKER, David—Searly; Catherine—Jan. 27, 1832.
George Jefferies, M. G.—3-40.
BAKER, David—Race, Maria Elizabeth—Feb. 11, 1846.
J. P. Bruck, J. P.—4-38.
BAKER, Delila—Hodgskins, Goerge S.—Apr. 10, 1850.
David Warnock, M. G.—5-228.
BAKER, Eliza—Gardiner, Cyrus—Dec. 24, 1840.
David Maltby, M. E. M. G. at Worthington—4-109.
BAKER, Eliza—Hunter, Wm —Apr. 11, 1827 (Apr. 19)*
C. Henkel, M. G.—2-183.
BAKER, Elizabeth—Edwards, Daniel—Sept. 14, 1854.
Wm. Field, J. P.—6-147.
BAKER, Elizabeth—Wilson, George M. Nov. 16, 1864.
Elder G. N. Tusing—8-445.
BAKER, Elizabeth—Sweeny, John—Dec. 12, 1864.
A. G. Byers, M. G.—8-466.
BAKER, Emanuel—Smith, Mary C—Aug. 30, 1842.
Henry Coffman, J. P.—4-26.
BAKER, Ester (I & Rec)—Baker, George W—Dec. 2, 1832.
W. T. Martin, J. P.—3-49.
*Consent of Henry and Nancy Becker or Baker that our
daughter shall marry George W Baker, Nov. 30, 1832).
BAKER, George E—Whistner, Catherine—May 24, 1864.
Vouched by Middleton Poole.
Daniel McCarter—8-360.
BAKER, George H. M—Strickler, Lucy Ann—Nov. 2, 1854.
H. L. Hitchcock, M. G.—6-160.
BAKER, George W—Baker (I & Rec), Ester—Dec. 2, 1832.
W. T. Martin, J. P.—3-49—See Ester Baker.
BAKER, Hannah H—Ashlin, Charles A—Nov. 30, 1852.
J. A. Bruner, M. G.—5-424.

*Charles A Ashlin, D. M.—& Miss Hannah A Baker.
BAKER, Hannah—Fookes, Andrew—Aug. 1, 1863,—8-205.
  J. Kronenbitter, J. P.—8-205.
BAKER, Harriet Ann—Reynolds, William—Apr. 16, 1849.
  W. T. Martin, J. P.—5-161.
BAKER, Henderson—Gilbesh, Mary E—Feb. 27, 1862.
  Joseph M Trimble, M. G.—7-716.
BAKER, (I) & Becker, (Rec & *), Henrietta—Frankinberg & Franken-
  berg   Philip—Apr. 4, 1855.
  Wm. F. Lehman, M. G.—6-198.
BAKER, Rev. Henry (Of Fairfield Co)—March, Lanpton (Miss
  Serepta)*   of Franklin Co.—June 2, 1841.
  James C Bontecon, M. G.—4-22.
BAKER, Isaac—Schoonover, Rebecca—Dec. 24, 1822.
  C. Waddell, Lutheran M. G.—2-110.
BAKER, Isaac D—O'Hale, Rebecca—Dec. 4, 1854.
  Wm. Field, J. P.—6-168.
BAKER, Jacob, L—Bower, Rosina C—Dec. 22, 1853.
  F. Greenwald, M. G.—6-87.
  O. S. J. (Miss Rosina C Bauer, all of city, rest same)
BAKER, James—Freeman, Charlotte—June 30, 1851.
  No return—5-319.
BAKER, James—Riley, Lydia—Nov. 17, 1856.
  No return—6-318.
BAKER, James-Ryan, Elizabeth—May 25, 1857—
  No return—6-364.
BAKER, James—Harter, Charity—July 20, 1861.
  Vouched by A. Collins.
  George Taylor, J. P.—7-607.
BAKER, John—Long, Martha (Miss)*—July 29, 1832.
  Robert O Spencer, M. G.—3-47.
BAKER, John (George)*—Patrick, Jane Feb. 12, 1834.
  Charles Rarey, M. G.—3-80.
BAKER, John H—Bell, Mary—June 27, 1861.
  James T Finch, M. G.—7-600.
BAKER, John W—Greenwood, Elizabeth—Dec. 5, 1843.
  H. L. Hitchcock, M. G.—4-30.
  O. S. J. (J. W. Baker, dentist & Miss Elizabeth, daughter of
  John Greenwood of this city, Dec. 5, 1843).
BAKER, John W—Aged 20 years, personal consent of father.
  Long, Mary A—Nov. 17, 1862.
  B. Tresenrider, J. P.—8-87.
BAKER, Joseph—Bilchner & Bilekim, Josephine—Aug. 8, 1837.
  Thomas Wood, J. P.—3-172.
BAKER, Joseph—Stemens, & Stemen, Barbara—Oct. 26, 1854.
  Jeremiah White, J. P.—6-158.
BAKER, Miss Julia C—aged 17—Edward, Henry—Oct. 6, 1861.
  Thomas Lovegrove, M. G.—7-643.
  *(Elizabeth Baker gives consent for my daughter Julia C.
  Baker, a minor to marry Henry Edwards, the father of said
  Julia is dead. Sept. 28, 1861—Wit, Abraham Sowers 7 Mar-
  tin Baker.

BAKER, Lewis—Mitchell, Mary S.—Sept. 25, 1851. Z. G. Waddle, J. P. —5-333. *(Consent of her father, H. S. Mitchell, she being a minor).

BAKER, Lide—Wallace, John—May 26, 1862. A. B. See, M. G.—8-13.

BAKER, Lorenzom—Nye, Samantha F.—Mch. 6, 1858. No return—7-7..

BAKER, Luana & Livona*—Wissenger & Wissniger* John—July 14, 1841. Z. P. Thompson, J. P.—4-289. See John Wissenger.
Z. P. Thompson, J. P.—4-289. See John Wissenger.

BAKER, Lucinda—Butterbaugh, Nicholas—Nov. 24, 1861.
David Beers, J. P.—7-671.

BAKER, Mahala—Briggs, John A—Dec. 24, 1863.
Thomas Lovegrove, M. G.—8-280.
*(Elizabeth Baker, mother and only surviving parent of Mahala a Baker consents for her to marry John A Briggs. Wit-Ed. Livingston & Richard Briggs. Dec. 24, 1863.

BAKER, Marcellus-Bobo, Sarah E—Mch. 8, 1864. J. Kronenbitter, J. P.—8-316.

BAHER, Margaret—Schonover, Abraham—May 21, 1822. Richard Courtright, J. P.—2-102.

BAKER, Margaret S—Green, William—May 17, 1849. W. T. Martin, J. P.—5-164.

BAKER, Margaret—Shick, Preston—Aug. 26, 1852. Patterson Harrison, J. P.—5-396.

BAKER, Martha J. G. aged 19 yrs. personal consent of her father— Beach, Alva—Apr. 26, 1863. B. Tresenrider, J. P.—8-168.

BAKER, Mary—Gray, George—Dec. 26, 1840. James Gilruth, M. G.— 4-109.

BAKER, Mary—Kelsey, John—May 15, 1849. George C. Krumm, M. G. (Crum*—5-165.

BAKER, Mary Ann—Sterner, Anthong M—Feb. 16, 1854. J. White J. P.—6-99.

BAKER, Mary Ann—Perry, George—Oct. 13, 1863. Henry Innis, M. G.— 8-240.

BAKER, Mary E (Mrs)*—Flagg, Edmund W—Apr. 17, 1856. H. H. Ferris, M. G.—6-276.

BAKER, Mary Jane—Ermme (I & Rec) Willism F.—May 5, 1836. David Beers, J. P.—3-143.

BAKER, Oscar S—Clark, Jennie—Jan. 7, 1864. George W Meeker, J. P. 8-287.

BAKER, Priscilla—Frederick; Jacob—May 1, 1855. Thomas H Hall, M. G.—6-206.

BAKER, Rebecca—Lamberson (I & Rec) & Lambert*, John S.—Dec. 26, 1832. W. T. Martin, J. P.—3-51.

BAKER, Rebecka—Brake, James—Apr. 4, 1839, David Beers, J. P.— 3-217.

BAKER, Rebecca—Baril; Joel—Sept. 20, 1864. E. D. Morris, M. G.— 8-416.

BAKER, Robert—Furguson, Isabella—Mch. 27, 1856. Not signed—6-272.

*—Ohio State Journal.
*—Asterisk denotes verification in newspaper items. †—Original record.

BAKER, Samuel—Bridges, Rebecca—June 8, 1828. Aristarchus Walker, J. P.—2-205.

BAKER, Sarah—Spurling, James—Sept. 9, 1839. James C Retnolds, J. P.—3-223.
*(C. A. Platt says that James Sperling & Sarah Barker are of age.)

BAKER, Sarah E. aged 17 years, personal consent of James Baker. Menoh, Wesley R—Mch. 10, 1864. Samuel Tippett, M. G.—8-315.

BAKER, Sophiah—Riley, Bibedick—May 31, 1852. No return—5-382.

BAKER, Sophia Louiza Ernestine—Frankenberg, Alexander F—1857. (Not dated in anyway but follows license dated Sept. 14, 1857. In presence of subscribing witnesses. Wit—Elizabeth R. Hicks & Wilhelmenia Hosback. Marcus Hicks, V. D. M.—6-383.

BAKER, Stacy—Spade, Frederick—Oct. 22, 1826. C. Henkle, M. G.—2-183.

*BAKER, Susan—Wright, Horton—Nov. 11, 1856. E. D. Morris, M. G.—6-315.

*BAKER, Wila—Higgy, Mary—Jan. 13, 1851. Josiah D. Smith, M. G.—5-281.

*BAKER, (I) & Barker (*) William—Wilson, Barbara A—Oct. 16, 1864. Samuel Kinnear, J. P.—8-428.

*BALDEN, Thomas H—Mills; Matilda Jane—Jan. 11, 1834. both of Jefferson Tp. Lewis Madden, M. G.—3-78.

BALDRIDGE, A. J. (Aymor)—Parsons, Adaline—July 20, 1836. Simeon Woodruff, V. D. M.—3-146.

*BALDWIN, Abel—Grean, Delila Ann—Jan. 20, 1846. James Fancher, J. P. of Truro Tp—4-38.

BALDWIN, Caroline R 7 Candace—Quinn, John—Sept. 26, 1844. Nathan Emery, M. G.—4-221. (John Quinn & Miss Candace P. Baldwin).

BALDWIN, Celia M.—Bragg & Bagg, Ben amin Rush—Nov. 14. 1851. H. L. Hitchcock, M. G.—5-344. *(Charles Baker vouches for Benjamin Rush Bagg & Celia M. Baldwin).

BALDWIN, Deborah—Bishop, Gavriel—May 10, 1827. Nathan Emery, M. G.—2-185.

*BALDWIN, Elias—Dixon, Hannah—Nov. 25, 1852. George W. Williard, M. G.—5-421. (Both of city).

*BALDWIN, Elias—Powers, Jane—May 13, 1823. Nathan Emery, J. P.—2-113.

*BALDWIN, Eliza—Blanett (I & Rec), Abraham B. Sept. 30, 1841. Daniel Hamaker, J. P.—4-23.
*Affidavit is Abraham B. Blauvelt).

BALDWIN, Eliza Jane—Neiswender, Solomon—July 21, 1853. Elder H. Hendren—6-47.

*BALDWIN, Fletcher M.—Clark,, Alice C.—Oct. 4, 1863. James Mitchell, M. G.—8-236.

*BALDWIN, Hannah—Meacham, Riley—Feb. 17, 1821. Reuben Carpenter, J. P.—2-88.
*(Levi Baldwin says the parents of Hannah Baldwin have given their consent).

BALDWIN, Henry S.—Tuller, Elvira—Jan. 30, 1861. J. D. Hathaway, M. G.—7-543.

---

†BALDWIN, Heyman—Booth Ann—Apr. 9, 1839. William Preston M. G.—3-242. O. S. J. (H Baldwin of this city & Miss Ann Booth, formerly of Bridgeport, Conn., Apr. 10, 1839).

BALDWIN, Israel C.—Myers, Martha—Apr. 17, 1831. Zachariah Cornell J. P.—3-32.

†BALDWIN, Joseph F.—Stewart, Sarah B.—Jan. 3, 1843. James Hoge, M. G.—4-33. O. S. J.—Joseph E. Baldwin of Springfield & Miss Sarah E. daughter of Francis Stewart of this city, rest same).

†BALDWIN, Joshua—Northorp & Northrup*, Jane E—Aug. 30, 1836. James Hoge, M. G.—4-21.

†BALDWIN, J. William—Hoge, Margaret—Aug. 13, 1846. James Hoge, M. G.—5-19. O. S. J. (James William Baldwin & Miss Margaret Hoge, daughter of Rev. James Hoge.

†BALDWIN, Levi—Bigalo, Salenda—Nov. 28, 1824. Nathan Emery. in M. E. Ch.—2-131. *(Consent of her mother Salenda White. Levi Baldwin says Salenda Bigalo is daughter of Adi Bigalo, deceased Nov. 24, 1824).

†BALDWIN, Lucy—Westervelt, William—(Both of Blendon)—Oct. 3. 1833. G. W. Hart, J. P.—3-67.

BALDWIN, Mariah—Stagg, Jonah—Nov. 27, 1828. William Long. J. P.—2-208.

†BALDWIN, Marietta—Lee, James—Sept. 23, 1850. Lorenzo English Mayor of Columbus—5-259.

BALDWIN, Mary—Arnold, Randall R.—both of Blendon Tp. Sept. 15. 1827. Gideon W. Hart, J. P.—2-189.

†BALDWIN, Oliver K.—Childs & Childs*, Iva—Dec. 2, 1830. Jacob Gander, J. P.—3-4.

†BALDWIN, Robert—Rudolph, Aurelia—Sept. 7, 1849. W. W. Kile. J. P.—5-186.

†BALDWIN, Roxanna—Thompson, William—Jan. 2, 1817. Joseph S. Hughes—2-34.

†BALDWIN, Ruth Elizabeth*—Ferguson, James—Jan. 2, 1855. James Hoge, M. G.—6-175.

†BALDWIN, Samantha S.—Swigart, George—Aug. 4, 1851—(Sept. 4). Daniel Hamaker, J. P.—5-325.
  *(George Swygert, by him—rest same).

†BALDWIN, Sarah—House, Lymon B.—June 3, 1821. Nathaniel Little. J. P.—2-89.
  *(Consent of James Baldwin, father of Sarah Baldwin for her to marry Lymon B. House—Wit.—Nathaniel Little. Worthington—June 1, 1821).

†BALDWIN, Sarah—Alberry, John—Albenny in Index—Dec. 30, 1832. George Beals, J. P. (*3-71.)

†BALDWIN, Sarah F.—Hook, John C.—Nov. 9, 1862. Elder G. N. Tusing—8-79.

†BALDWIN, Sophia S.—Miller Elia—Oct. 29, 1834 or 1835. Abner Leonard, Presbyterian M. G.—3-128.

BALDWIN, Thadus—Enlows, Elizabeth—Feb. 3, 1842. J. Gilruth, M. G.—4-24.

*—Ohio State Journal.
*—Asterisk denotes verification in newspaper items. †—Original record.

†Baldwin, Thomas R. or K.—Alberry, (Rec) & Albenny*, Mati.da Ann Aug. 15, 1844—Shuah Mann, J. P.—4-33.

†Baldwin, William T.—Quinn, Sarah—Oct. 22, 1840. William W. Davis, M. G.—4-19.

†Bales, Jacob—Wahl, Mary—March 17, 1864. Thomas Heard, M. G.—8-324.

†Baley, Elenor—Macky, Samuel—Filed Apr. 8, 1820. John Trois—2-71.

†Baley, Mary—Bigelow, Daniel—June 24, 1824. C. Waddle, L. M. G.—2-120.

†Eall, Albert—Shakelford, Josephine—Sept. 4, 1849. D. B. Cheney, M. G.—5-181.

†Ball, Andrew & Barr*—Ball, Nancy—Feb. 7, 1811. James Hoge, M. G.—1-89.

†Ball, Caroline—Hamilton & Hamelton, Madison—March 19, 1864. G. H. Graham, Min.—8-326—colored.

†Ball, Charles—Price Elizabeth—Sept. 14, 1854. J. Q. Lakin, M. G.—6-147. O. S. J. (All of this county by Rev. J. Q. Lakin, rest same.)

†Eall, Dr. Charles—Conner, Mary—July 12, 1833. William Lusk, J. P.—3-71.

†Ball, Daniel—McCawley—Lucinda—Feb. 14, 1831. Thomas Wood, J. P.—3-8.

†Ball, Daniel E.—McCormick, Jane—Oct. 7, 1833. Nathan Emery, M. G.—3-125. O. S. J. (Daniel F. Ball and Miss Jane McCormick, daughter of George McCormick of this city, Oct 7, 1835).

Ball, Drussella—Higgins, Charles—Dec. 23, 1828. William Stiarwalt, J. P.—2-227.

†Ball, George—Clark, Betsy—May 22, 1843. Thomas Wood, J. P.—4-29.

†Ball, George D.—and George T.—Lon, Caroline E.—July 10, 1845. Josiah D. Smith, M. G.—4-36.
O. S. J. *George T. Bull & Miss Carolin Elizabeth Long, both of Truro Tp. *July 10, 1845.

†Ball, (I & Rec) & Bell*, John—Heaston, Rebecca—Apr. 21, 1834. James Graham—3-84.

†Ball, John D.—Williams, America—Nov. 15, 1830. James Hoge, M. G.—3-64.

†Ball, Lenuel—Seibert, Catherine—17 years, consent of her guardian, not named—Dec. 29, 1864. Jacob Romick, Elder in U. B. Ch.—8-476.

†Ball, Lucius—Hickman, Susan—Jan. 12, 1834. J. L. Graham, J. P.—3-76.

†Ball, Margaret—Greenwood, William B.—Aug. 1, 1862. J. G. Miller, J. P.—8-36.

†Ball, Mary—Risley, Lewis—Dec. 9, 1823. Charles Waddle, M. G.—2-115.

Ball, Mary Ann—Risley, Orval—March 22, 1832. Robert Spencer, M. G.—3-38.

†Ball, Mary Ann—McDonald, John—Oct. 15, 1835. John C. Harey?, M. G.—3-126.
O. S. J. (John McDonald & Miss Mary Ann Ball, both of Franklinton, Oct. 15, 1835)

ABSTRACT OF WILLS, FRANKLIN COUNTY, OHIO

Compiled by BLANCHE TIPTON RINGS

MOREHEAD, JANE, Harrison Twp. (Vol. A-1), Ex. Son, Fergus Morehead. Signed August 24, 1805, Wit., John Dill, Michael Fisher, Elizabeth Hamilton. Prov. December 6, 1805. Mention— Son, Thomas Morehead; eldest dau. Sally Clemens; dau. Jenny, 'her clothes to her sister, Elizabeth Flennekin;' son, Fergus Morehead.

MULLEN, MICHAEL, yeoman, Franklinton (Vol. A-2), Ex. Benjamin White. Signed April 10, 1804. Wit., James Marshall, Alexander Nance. Prob. (missing). Mention—Benjamin White, Liberty Twp. 'all my clothes that are at Alexander Nance's, that is, a coat, jacket, overhalls, hat and a silk handkerchief and $30 in money;' Robert Young, Liberty Twp., 'all the rest of my clothes . . . found in the county of Franklin.'

YOUNG, ROBERT, Franklinton (Vol. A-4), Ex. Wife, Jane Young, Thomas Morehead, Lucas Sullivant. Signed August 24, 1804. Wit., George Skidmore, Samuel Steele, Stephen Warren. Mention— Wife, Jane Young, 'the use of all my estate for the purpose of raising my younger children, to wit: dau. Nancy Young, aged 6 mo.; son, William Young, aged 2 years—' and if my wife should have a son or daughter within nine months from the date thereof . . . children to be schooled one or two years, that is, if a daughter one year and if a son two years, in each several cases the schooling to be given to each child at a time when they are of proper age and size to receive learning. As each child arrives at full age to wit: my daughters to the age of 18 years and my sons to the age of 21 years, for my said wife to pay over to them one equal dividend of their just proportion of my estate at the appraisement to be made.' Son, Andrew Young, 1 shilling; dau. Fanny white, 1 shilling; dau. Matta Benjamin, 1 shilling—'only sufficient in the eyes of the law to support and keep this my last will and testament, they being better able to provide for themselves without a portion of my small estate.'

Abbreviations:
Executor—Ex.; Administrator—Adm.; Witnesses—Wit.; Township—Twp.; Volume—vol.; Acres— a.; born (nee)—b.; died—d.; codicil—cod.; Probate record—prob.; proven—prov.; daughter—dau.

HESS, BALSER (also Bolser), Clinton Twp. (Vol. A-8), Ex. Wife, Mary Eve Hess; Son, Daniel Hess. Dated December 3, 1806. Wit., John Williams, Joseph Swan. Prov. December 27, 1806. Mention—Wife, Mary Eve Hess; Son, Moses Hess; Son, Daniel Hess; Son, Balser Hess; Dau. Mary Eve Hess; Dau. Catherine Hess; Dau. Elizabeth Hess; Dau. Susannah Hess.

BOGART, EZEKIEL, (Vol. A-10), Ex. Joshua Bogart, Michael Fisher. Signed April 18, 1807. Wit., William Bennett, Solomon Smith, Ellis John. Prov. May 6, 1807. Mention—Son, (elder), Joshua Bogart; Son, Joseph Bogart; Son, James Bogart; Son, George Bogart; Dau. Elizabeth (Betsey) Bogart—minor; Dau. Keziah Bogart—minor, 'Joshua Bogart to have guardianship of minor daughters;' Dau. Jemina Bogart 'now wife of Jobe Welton has had an equal division on her leaving and she to have nothing now' . . . 'the executors to make a deed to William Bennett and Phillip Cherry for land bought of Barnabas Lambert, amounting to 400a.' Cod.— April 20, 1807, Dau. Keziah Bogart 'to be sent to her cousin Jemina Cunningham to be educated.'

SCRIBNER, SAMUEL (also Scrivner), Liberty Twp. (Vol. A-14), Ex., Wife, Hannah Scribner. Signed July 13, 1807. Wit., Avery Powers, Oliver Strong. Prov. October term, 1807. Mention—Wife, Hannah Scribner, 'to have north half where I now live and one-half of residue;' Youngest son, Elias Scribner, 'to have residue.'

MORRISON, ALEXANDER, SR. (also Morison), Worthington, (Vol. A-15), Ex., Son, William Morison, James Kilbourn—'my trust friend.' Dated February 10, 1810. Wit., James Kilbourn, Lincoln Goodale, Cynthia Kilbourn. Prob. November 28, 1812. Mention— Wife, Mahitable Morison; Son, Alexander Morrison, Jr.; Dau. Sally Willson (w. of George); Son, William Morrison; Dau., Polly Pinney (w. of Abner P.); Dau., Orrenda Morison; Dau., Orrellia Morison; Son, Henry Morison. Case 071—Israel Case, guardian of Henry Morison, aged 18 years, October 27, 1812.

LISLE, JOHN, Clinton Twp. (Vol. A-20), Ex., Wife, Rachel Lisle; Oldest son, Robert Lisle. Signed December 24, 1808. Wit., Elijah Fulton, Joseph Cowgill, Daniel Hess. Prob. February term, 1809. Mention—Wife, Rachel Lisle, 'to have a bed and bedding, two cows, one mare, and she to be supported from the proceeds of the place I now live on so long as she lives;' Youngest son, John Lisle, 'the land I now live on when he reaches the age of 21 years;' Oldest son, Robert Lisle, 'a quarter section of land adjoining William Caldwell and Robert Wilson;' Second son, James Lisle, 'land adjoining Robert Wilson near Walnut Creek;' Oldest dau., Market Lisle, '100a which lies on the waters of the Whetstone and adjoining the lands of Jeremiah Armstrong;' each of his other daughters . . . not mentioned . . . shall receive $400 in money or property.'

HORNBAKER, JOHN, Hamilton Twp. (Vol. A-23), Ex. Wife, Elizabeth Hornbaker, Isaac Weatherington. Dated April 26, 1810. Wit., John Barr, Joshua Cole. Prob. March 19, 1811. Mention— Wife, Elizabeth Hornbaker; Dau., Mary Hornbaker; Dau., Catherine

Hornbaker; Dau., Elizabeth Hornbaker; Dau., **Ann** (name not given); Son, John Hornbaker; Dau., Peggy Hornbaker.

GRACE, BENJAMIN, (Vol. A-25). Signed October 4, 1811. Wit., Daniel Brunk, Benjamin Fulton. Prov. November 30, 1811. Adm., Jacob Grubb. The last will is a request 'that the home place he now live on for her and the children to stay on as long as she stays his widow and for the loose property to be sold and all money to be equally divided among the children, also one-half of all the movables to stay on the place and household goods excepted and also the children to have schooling from the profits of the place and the boys to be put to a trade at the age of 15 years in case they do well.'

LAMBERT, DAVID, (Vol. A-26), Ex. Wife, Mary Lambert; Thomas Morris. Signed February 21, 1812. Wit., John Ball, Robert Gordon. Prov., March term, 1812. Mention—Wife, Mary Lambert, 'to have one-third of all real and personal property during her life-time and at her death to be divided between Isaac and Rebecca when they become of age. . . . an unborn child that my wife is pregnant with when it is born into the world and lives it is to have equal share with Isaac and Rebecca;' Son, Isaac Lambert, minor; Dau., Rebecca Lambert, minor.

DYER, JOHN (also Dyre), Pleasant Twp. (Vol. A-28). Dated January 7, 1812. Wit., Alexander Blair, John Turner. Prob. March 22, 1812. Mention—Wife, Jain Dyer; Son, William Dyer; Dau., Mary Reed; Son, Samuel Dyer; Son, Robert Dyer; Son, John Dyer; Son, Morrel Dyer; Son, Joseph Dyer. (*Mention of his grist and saw mills on the Big Walnut Creek.*)

POWER, AVERY, Perry Twp. (Vol. A-29). Ex., Wife, Prudence Power. Dated April 29, 1812. Wit., David Scott, D. Gwynne, Joseph Vance, Gustavus Swan. Prob. October 29, 1812. Mention—Wife, Prudence Power; Son, Benjamin Power; Dau., Mary Power, minor; Son, Hiram Power, minor.

HUGHES, WILLIAM, Franklinton (Vol. A-33), Ex., Wife, Elizabeth Hughes. Dated February 19, 1814. Wit., Orris Parish, John Foley, Thomas Webb. Mention—Wife, Elizabeth Hughes, 'all children born of the body of said Elizabeth Hughes' (*not named*); Grandchild, Richard Thomas, 'who lives with me and goes by the names of Richard Hughes.'

HENDERSON, SAMUEL, Clinton and Franklin Twps., (Vol. A-31), Ex., Son, Alexander Henderson, Elijah Fulton. Dated April 11, 1809. Wit., Hugh Fulton, John Wilson. Prob. June 14, 1813. Mention—Son, Samuel Henderson; Son, Adam Henderson; Son, Alexander Henderson; Dau., Rebeckah; Dau., Marget*; Dau., Jean*; Dau., Elizabeth*; Dau., Mary.* (**last names not given*.)

MONROE, JOHN, Hamilton Twp. (Vol. A-35). Ex., Percival Adams, Esq. Dated April 3, 1814. Wit., J. Lusk, Robert W. Williams, George W. Williams, Percival Adams. Prob. June 20, 1814. Mention—Wife, Rhoda Monroe; Dau. Mary Rumsey; Dau., Elizabeth Jones; Dau., Lucinda Monroe; Son, Sheperd Monroe.

PALMER, LUTHER, Worthington, Sharon Twp. (Vol. A-36), Ex., Eathan Palmer, brother. Dated May 11, 1813. Wit., Henry Mathews, Alexander Morrison, Munson Gregory. Prob. June, 1814. Mention—Brother, Benjamin Palmer, of the state of Connecticut, 'all property I now possess.'

ABSTRACTS OF WILLS, FRANKLIN COUNTY, OHIO
Compiled by BLANCHE TIPTON RINGS

DUKES, JOHN, Hamilton Twp. (Vol. A-37), Ex. Eshmael Davis. Signed March 11, 1814. Wit., John B. Johnston, Asa Dunn, John Thompson, Joseph Gifford. Proven June term, 1814. Mention—Wife, Mary Dukes; Daughters—Lydia Davis, Nancy Dukes, Susanah Dukes; the two youngest daughters to have a good bed and furniture when they become of age.

LANE, PETER, Franklinton, (Vol. A-38), Ex., David S. Broderick. Dated July 8, 1814. Wit., Orris Parish, David Deardorff, Joseph Carter. Mention—Oldest son, Henry Lane. "To my seven children, the property to be equally divided." (*Names not given.*)

LEE, JONATHAN, (Vol. A-39), Ex., Wife, Sarah Lee, John Craun (*Crone*). Wit., Thomas Wilson, Richard Courtright, Reachel Dyer. Prob. October, 1814. Mention—Wife, Sarah Lee; Children (*names not given*), "property to my wife, to raise my family, and at her death or leaving my name, the land to fall equally to my children." (*Case 0360, Apr., 1822, John Crone, Gdn.*)

CORNET, THOMAS, Madison Twp. (Vol. A-40), Ex. (*not given*). Dated February 2, 1814. Wit., William King. Joseph Berkey, Joanna King. Prob. October, 1814. Mention—Wife, Rebecca Cornet, "all to my wife to the maintenance of her and her children and to be disposed of as she thinks fit."

WATT, HUGH, Harrison Twp., (Vol. A-42), Ex., William Read. Dated October 10, 1814. Wit., Isaac Griswold, Francis C. Olmstead. Prob. October 14, 1814. Mention—Wife; youngest daughter, Mary Watt. (*Case 0157, Oct. 19, 1815, Mary Watt, Gdn. Jane, John, Sarah, Elizabeth M., Jane Adam, Mary Watt*, orphans.)

BEACH, SAMUEL, Yeoman, Worthington, (Vol. A-43), Ex., Son, Samuel Beach, Levi Pinney. Signed Dec. 27, 1814. Wit., Amos Hawley, Ezekiel Tuller, Peter Barker, Recompense Stansberry. Proven June 14, 1815. Mention—Wife, Desiah Beach; Son, Samuel Beach; Daughter, Charlotte Pinney.

DEARDORFF, PAUL, (Vol. A-45), (*Perry Twp.*), Ex., Wife, Catherine Deardorff, Son Anthony Deardorff, Alexander Bassett. Signed May 25, 1815. Wit., Griffith Thomas, James Kent. Proven Aug. 16, 1815. Mention—Wife, Catherine, "one-third of land I now live on during her life and the exclusive right to occupy it until my youngest son Isaac arrive at the age of 21 years." Eldest Son, Anthony Deardorff, "land I now live on, on the east bank of the Scioto River"; Son, Peter Deardorff, "land adjoining Anthony"; Youngest Son, Isaac Deardorff; Daughters, Ann Deardorff, a minor, Naomi Deardorff, a minor, Susanna Deardorff, a minor, Elizabeth Gulliford.

HEWS, JAMES, Madison Twp., (Vol. A-48), Ex., Wife, Mary Hews, Joseph Wright. Dated September 1, 1815. Wit., Joseph Wright, Moses Starr, Elam Hews. Prob. Oct. 9, 1815. Mention—Wife, Mary Hews; Son, John Donaldson Hews.

DILL, JOHN, of Ross County in the territory of the United States, North West of the Ohio River, (Vol. A-50-52), Ex., Wife, Mary Dill, Robert Dill. Signed June 5, 1802. Wit., David Jameson, Thomas Morehead, Lucas Sullivant. Proven Feb. 29, 1816. Codicil, same date, Sister, Jane Abbit. Mention—Wife, Mary Dill; Brothers, Robert, Thomas Dill; Sisters, Mary Killbreath (*Galbreath*), Rebecca Johnston; Niece, Mary Dill, "daughter of my deceased brother, Armstrong Dill." Note.—"Moneys and obligations left in the hands of Col. Thomas Campbell in Pennsylvania."

RIDENOUR, MATHIAS, Mifflin Twp. (Vol. A-54), Ex., Son, John Rideonur, Stephen R. Price. Dated Dec. 22, 1815. Wit., Stephen R. Price, George Baughman, James Price. Prob. Feb., 1816. Mention—Catherine Ridenour; Sons, John, David, George, Daniel, a minor; Daughters, Susana Turney, Polly Turney, Catherine Ridenour.

DECKER, JOHN, (Vol. A-58), Ex., Sons, Luke, Jacob Decker. Signed April 5, 1815. Wit., Robert Russell, Esratus Webb, Joseph M. Hays. Proven Dec. 8, 1817. Mention—Wife, Hannah Decker, "to possess and enjoy after my decease the servants that are bound unto me shall serve their full time with my wife for which they were indentured to me." Daughters, Catherine Kuykendale, Sarah Pursell, Hannah Miller, Susannah Miller, Elizabeth and Rebecca Decker; Sons, Luke, Isaac and Jacob Decker.

CASE, DAN, Clinton Twp., (Vol. A-68, 70), Ex., Wife, Alice Case, Sons, Luther, Calvin Case. Dated Sept. 24, 1817. Wit., Ebenezer Washburn, Samuel Maynard, Jane Maynard. Prob. Nov., 1817. Mention—Wife, Alice Case; Sons, William, Rodney, Dan, Luther, Calvin H. Case; Daughter, Rachel.

PALMER, ETHAN, Harrison Twp., (Vol. A-71), Ex., Mr. Cadwell Olmstead. Dated July 26, 1817. Wit., Ebenezer Washburn, William Cooper, Phebe Cooper. Prob. Aug. 21, 1817. Mentions—Wife, Cloe Saville Palmer, "at her death, her one-third of estate to go to the Township of Harrison for the purpose of supporting the Gospel in the Presbyterian Order"; Daughter, Miriam Palmer, a minor. (*Case 0253, guardianship.*)

BENNETT, CHARLES, Muskingum Co., (Vol. A-73), Ex., Wife, Mary Bennett, Son, Nathan Bennett. Signed Sept. 16, 1816. Wit., Ruth Frisby, John Springer. Proven Aug. 10, 1818. Mention— Wife, Mary Bennett; Son, Stephen Bennett, "one dollar"; "rest of the children to share equally."

RORAR, MICHAEL, Madison Twp., (Vol. A-74), Ex., John Rorar, George Rorar. Dated Nov. 11, 1818; Wit., Emmor Cox, Thomas Swan, John Hornbaker, Jacob Hammler, (*signed in German*). Prob. Dec. 12, 1818. Mention—Wife, Mary Rorar; Sons, John, George and Michael Rorar; Son-in-law, John Smith.

PARK, JOSEPH, Franklinton, (Vol. A-76), Ex., Wife, Jane Park, Father-in-law, Robert Culbertson, James Hoge. Dated Feb. 5, 1811. Wit., Jacob Keller, Daniel O'Harra, William Stuart. Prob. Oct., 1818. Mention—Wife, Jane Park, "land received from father-in-law, Col. Robert Culbertson."

CASE, ISRAEL, Sharon Twp., (Vol. A-76), Ex., Sons, Putnam, Abial Case. Dated Jan. 11, 1815. Wit., William Thompson, Samuel Humphrey. Prob. Aug., 1818. Mention—Wife, Joanna Case; Sons, Putnam and Abial Case; Granddaughter, Asenath Case, a minor; Daughters, Joanna, "wife of Butler Andrews, living in N. Eng.," Violet Clemina, "wife of Samuel Beach, Eulia, Ursula, "wife of Alpheas Bigelow."

SPRINGER, ELIZABETH, Franklinton, (Vol. A-79), Ex., David Deardorff, Jacob Grubb. Signed Feb. 22, 1819. Wit., Edmund Pinnex, Abraham Stotts. Proven March 27, 1819. Mention—Son, Charles L. Springer, entire estate.

TURNER, ELIAS, Yeoman, Columbus, (Vol. A-79), Ex., Mary Turner. Signed Nov. 5, 1818. Wit., Nathaniel Haswell, Stephen Smith, Ibbey O'Neil. Proven, March 27, 1819. Mention—Wife, Mary Turner; Daughter, Laviney L. Cane; Sons, Wesley, James, "when he become of age," Elias Turner, "when he becomes of age."

RITTER, FREDERICK, (Vol. A-80), Ex., Wife, Polly Ritter. Dated Sept., 1818. Wit., John R. Parish, John N. Strain, William McElvain. Prob. Aug., 1819. Mention—Wife, Polly Ritter, "children to have the property in equal parts at the death of the said Polly Ritter."

READ, WILLIAM, Clinton Twp., (Vol. A-82), Ex., Sons, Adam, Alexander Read. Dated July 11, 1819. Wit., James Hoge, J. Miller, William Dalzell. Prob. Aug. 9, 1819. Mention—Wife, Peggy Read; Sons, Adam, Alexander, William, George, a minor, Samuel, a minor. Daughters, Jane, Polly and Ann.

ANDRUS RICHARD, Clinton Twp., (Vol. A-86), Ex., Wife, Catherine Andrus, Son, Hiram Andrus. Signed Sept. 2, 1819. Wit., Stephen Maynard, David Lockwood, Thankful E. Maynard. Proven Nov. 1, 1819. Mention—Wife, Catherine Andrus; Sons, Hiram Andrus, Samuel Andrus; Daughters, Julia, wife of Jonathon Hill, Betsey, "after she reaches the age of 18 yrs.," Amanda, "after she reaches the age of 18 yrs.," Mary Ann, youngest, "after she reaches the age of 18 years."

SMITH, WILLIAM, Mifflin Twp., (Vol. A-87), Ex., Stephen R. Price, Sons, John Smith, James Smith. Signed Sept. 30, 1819. Wit., Stephen R. Price, J. Miller, John Stuart. Proven Nov. 1, 1819. Mention—Wife, Sarah Smith; Sons, John James, Robert, Josiah Smith; Daughters, Nancy, Elizabeth Latta and her children, Mary Cunningham, Martha Woodroe, Sarah Bowers, Hannah Hunter, Rebecca Allen (does not give relationship).

BRISTOL, DAVID, Worthington, (Vol. A-91), Ex., Son, Adna Bristol. Signed Feb. 19, 1819. Wit., Ezra Griswold, C. Howard, E. Griswold. Proven March term, 1820. Mention—Wife, Amelia Bristol; Sons, Eri, Adna and David Bristol; Daughters, Polly Ingham, Ssally Ingham, Lois Wilcox.

DELENO, OLIVER (Delano), Clinton Twp., (Vol. A-92). Signed Jan. 2, 1820. Wit., John Soul, Polly Soul, Sylvia Bull. Proven Nov. 4, 1823. Mention—"his wife, his parents and his boys' (names not given).

CASE, RACHEL, Clinton Twp., (Vol. A-93), Ex., John Smith. Dated March 27, 1820. Wit., John Smith, Olive Smith. Prob. June 10, 1810. Mention—Mother, Allice Case "all to her."

OGDON, MOSES (Ogden), Jefferson Twp., (Vol. A-94), Ex., Wife, Lydia Ogdon. Dated Feb. 8, 1821. Wit., William F. Sisco, Peter F. Sisco. Prob. March 16, 1825. Mention—Wife, Lydia; Daughters, Elizabeth Smith, Abigail Edgar, Jane and Sarah Ogdon; Sons, Lewis, Elias, Charles and George Ogdon. "It is my desire and will that should any dispute arise that it may be settled in the same manner as General George Washington, former President of the United States, directed disputes, if any should arise between his heirs and legatees should be settled."

ABSTRACTS OF WILLS, FRANKLIN COUNTY, OHIO

Compiled by BLANCHE TIPTON RINGS

CULBERTSON, ROBERT, Franklinton, (Vol. A-96), Ex., Rev. James Hoge, of Columbus, Ralph Osborn of Columbus, Samuel Culbertson, of Madison County. Signed Feb. 12, 1820. Wit., James Kockin (Kooken), R. W. McCoy, Samuel Persons. Proven March 14, 1820. Mention—Wife, Elizabeth Culbertson; Daughters, Jane Park, Rebecca Moore, Agnes Park, Sarah Jameson; Sons, Andrew and James Culbertson; Grandchildren, "children of my daughter Keziah Brotherton," Elizabeth and Margaret Brotherton, "when they arrive at the age of 18 yrs."; "children of my daughter, Martha Brotherton," Robert Brotherton and Peggy (Brotherton) Breckenridge "children of my daughter, Peggy Keller," Robert and James Keller "at the age of 21," Eliza Keller "at the age of 18 yrs., Rev. James Hoge "for benefit of missionaries $100," "for education of young men for ministry $100."

YENTIS, JOHN, Fairfield Co., late of Franklin Co., Ohio, (Vol. A-99), Ex., Son, William Yentis. Dated December 12, 1816. Wit., Samuel Spangler, Daniel Defenbaugh. Prob., June 12, 1821, Fairfield Co., Mention—Sons, William, Henry, George, John Yentis; Daughters, Sibella. Grandsons, Jacob and Valentine, "sons of my daughter, Ann Mary Smith," Katherine Hedge.

TULLER, BELA, Perry Twp., (Vol. A-100), Ex., Son, Flavel Tuller, Ezra Griswold, Esq.· Signed March 22, 1821. Wit., Ezra Griswold, James Wait. Mention—Wife, Lydia Tuller; Sons, Homer, Holcomb, Achilles Tuller; Daughters, Flora, Lydia and Alvira "under 18 yrs."

SMITH, STEPHEN, Franklin Twp., (Vol. A-102), Ex., Wife, Mary Smith. Signed Sept. 17, 1821. Wit., Stephen Smith, George Clickense. Proven July 3, 1822. Mention—Wife, Mary Smith; Sons, Harden, Stephen, Jonathon Smith; Daughter, Mary Williams; Grandson, Henry Williams. Note.—"Jonathon Smith and Mary Williams each to get one-half of coopers tools."

BADGER, WILLIAM, Jackson Twp., (Vol. A-103), Ex., Sons, William, Jr., Archibald J. Badger. Signed Aug. 7, 1822. Wit., Samuel Clark, William C. Duff. Rec. Aug. 15, 1822. Mention—Wife, Martha Badger; Sons, James, Joseph, Archibald J., Sterrat Badger, a minor; Daughters, Martha "I leave and bequeath to my daughter Martha to be paid yearly and every year out of my estate so long as she remains a widow, delivered out of the produce of the place," Ann, "wife of Joseph Badger Taylor, Franklinton.

SMITH, JONAH, Franklinton, (Vol. A-106), Ex., Son, Silas Smith, Nicholas Demorest, Daniel Demorest. Signed March 18, 1823. Wit., Stewart White, Richard House. Proven Apr. 12, 1823. Mention—Wife, Nancy Smith; Son, Silas C. Smith; Daughters, Lucinda, Phebe and Sally; Grandson, Josiah Smith. (*Case 0400, Apr. 12, 1823, Adms. Silas C. Smith, Nicholas, Daniel P., and Geliam Demorest; and John Lore.*)

DECKER, JACOB, Madison Twp., (Vol. A-108), Ex., Isaac Miller, brother-in-law of Pickaway Co. Dated Apr. 17, 1823. Wit., James K. Corey, William Igle, Christian Plank. Prob. June 9, 1823. Mention—Thomas Vause, brother-in-law, "in trust for children and wife," Nephews, John and William Vause; Niece, Rachel Vause, children of Thomas Vause; Sisters, Elizabeth Vause, Susannah Miller, "wife of Isaac"; Mother, Hannah Decker; Brothers, Luke Decker and Isaac Decker "of Illinois"; Brother-in-law, Isaac Miller, "of Pickaway County"; Nephews, Jacob, s. of Isaac Decker; Jacob, s. of Isaac Miller. Note.—"To Thomas Vause all my right, title and interest in the land situated in the county of Clark, State of Ohio, being the south one-half Sec. 14, Twp. 5, Range 10, between the Miami Rivers and S. Quar. Sec. 8, Twp. 5, Range 10, for the sole use."

MITCHELL, CHARLES, Dublin, Washington Twp., (Vol. A-111), Ex., Wife, Jean Mitchell; Son, John Mitchell; Son-in-law, James Howey. Signed Dec. 18, 1820. Wit., Peter Sells, David Smith. Proven June term, 1823. Mention—Wife, Jean Mitchell; Sons, Charles, William, John, Thomas, David, Hughey Mitchell; Sons-in-law, James Howey, David Norton, John Robinson.

SCHOONOVER, JOHN, (Vol. A-114), Ex., John Schoonover, Joseph Schoonover. Signed June 5, 1820. Wit., Willingslea Bull. Phillip Swamer, Solomon Lee, Rec. June 11, 1823. Mention—Wife, Elizabeth Schoonover; Sons, John, Joseph, Henry, Abraham Schoonover; Daughters, Margaret, Elizabeth, Rebecca Schoonover, Mary Scoby; Grandson, John Fairchild.

CHAPMAN, BENJAMIN, Sharon Twp., (Vol. A-116), Ex., Wife, Sylvia Chapman, Son, Roswell R. Chapman. Signed March 6, 1823, at Sharon Twp. Wit., Isaac E. Fisher, Daniel Upson. Proven June term, 1823. Mention—Wife, Sylvia Chapman; Sons, Albert, Henry and Lucius Chapman; Daughters, Mary, Sally, Lucinda, Sylvia, a minor, Harriet, a minor.

JAMISON, DAVID, Franklin Twp., (Vol. A-118), Ex., Arthur O'Harra, Franklin Twp., "my friend," Adam Brotherlin, Franklin Co. Signed May 22, 1823. Wit., Joseph Grate, William Lusk, Jacob Ebey. Proven Aug. 30, 1823. Mention—Wife, Sarah Jamison; Sons, Andrew, Robert, David, Joseph Jamison. Daughters, Nancy Manning, Eliza, Jane Jamison.

PARKS, JANE, (Vol. A-120), Ex., Arthur O'Harra, "my friend." Signed Sept. 16, 1823. Wit., William Badger, Lewis Risley, Cornelius Marran. Proven Sept. 27, 1823. Mention—Sisters, Rebecky Moore, Sally Jamison, Nancy Park; Brother, James Culbertson. Joseph Breckenridge, Franklin Twp.; Niece, Margaret Brotherton: Nephew, Robert Keller.

McDOWELL, JOHN A. (Vol. A-122), Ex., and Guardian of his children, Lynn Starling, brother-in-law. Signed Sept. 29, 1823. Wit., A. J. McDowell, Richard Howe. Proven, Oct. 7, 1823. (*Will missing March 8, 1934.*)

VANDEMARK, JEREMIAH, (Vol. A-123), Ex., Daniel Vandemark, Nicholas Goetcheus (*Gutches*). Signed Sept. 2, 1823. Wit., Nicholas Goetcheus, Jacob Weaver, W. Clevenger. Proven Oct. 30, 1823.

Mention—Only son, Daniel Vandemark; Grandson, Jeremiah Vande-mark, s. of Daniel; Daughters, Ruth Low, Leah Kite, Elizabeth Wade, Jane Bennett, Catherine Rimer, Mary Blair; Grandson, Gideon Vandemark.

TAYLOR, JOHN D., (Vol. A-125), Ex., Joseph Wright. Dated Sept. 1, 1821. Wit. Billingslea Bull, Mary Ann Derrick, Nicholas Hopkins. Prob. Nov. 1, 1823. Mention—Joseph Wright and Mary, his wife, "All my land in Morgan County, also all money due me from Abraham Bowers," "to convey to John Todd or his legal rep-resentatives, 60 A. of land, it being the south end of the before directed."

BULL, THOMAS, Clinton Twp., (Vol. A-127). Signed Sept. 25, 1823. Wit., John Webster, Daniel Royal, Alvin Fuller. Before Aristachus Walker, J. P. Proven Nov. 3, 1823. Mention—Sons, Hiram, Alonson, Jason and Delia his wife, Thompson and Phidelia his wife; Daughters, Edith, Cloe Comstock. "I hereby reserve one-half acre . . out of my son Jason and Delia's . . . on the Evart line of the new road leading from Columbus to Worthington to contain one-half acre square I give and devise . . . to the Meth-odist Episcopal Church for the purpose of building a comfortable meeting house."

CRAUN, JOHN, (Vol. A-132), Ex., Sons, John, Jacob. Abraham and Isaac Craun. Dated Aug. 8, 1820. Wit., Nicholas Goetcheus, Isaac Rainier, James Waits. Prob. Nov. 3, 1823. Mention—Wife, Abigail Craun; James Bensevter, wife's father; Sons, John Jacob, Abraham and Isaac Craun; Daughters, Elizabeth Greene, Catherine D. Long, deceased, and Sally Craun.

FISHER, MICHAEL, (Vol. A-136), Ex., Son, Michael Fisher. Wit., Samuel Persons, Thomas Johnston. Proven Feb. 16, 1824. Cod., "If the Court does not approve of M. Fisher as executor, I appoint Rev. Jas. Hoge as his aid." Mention—Wife, Sarah Fisher; Sons, Joseph Michael, George, Jacob, Milton Fisher, a minor; Daughters, Cristena——,Elizabeth——,Sally,Maximilla,M.Fisherowned a tanner and saw mill. "If my son Michael should succeed in the practice of phisic I wish him to take my son Milton and teach him that branch . . . the interest of the bank stock to pay for his schooling till he is prepared to go to his study, then to pay for the schooling of George, Jacob, and Milton when they have their education . . . bequeath the bank stock to my five sons to be equally divided."

COLEMAN, ABRAHAM, Hamilton Twp. Non-cupative. (Vol. A-138), Ex., *None.* Dated Feb. 12, 1824. Wit., Andrew Dill, James Badger. Prob. March 4, 1824. Mention—Wife, Abigail Coleman, "I give to my wife Abigail the residue of my property, after my just debts are paid during her natural lifetime."

PETERSON, FREDERICK, (Vol. A-139), (*formerly Cumberland Co., N. J.*), Ex., Sons, Frederick, Aaron Peterson. Signed Dec. 12, 1823. Wit., Billingslea Bull, John Henry. Proven Apr. 17, 1824. Mention—Wife, Eleanor Peterson; Sons, Frederick and Aaron Peterson; Daugh-ters, Pamela, Mary, Mahala, Rhoda, Eleanor and Lydia.

FULTON, JOHN, (Vol. A-140), Adm., Wife, Christian, Richard Suddick, "friend." Signed Dec. 25, 1819. Wit., Richard Suddick, James Suddick, Jane Suddick. Proven Apr. 20, 1824. Mention—Wife, Christiana Fulton, "all."

STARR, JAMES, Sharon Twp., (Vol. A-141), Ex., Henry Crosby, "loving friend." Signed Aug. 24, 1823. Wit., Isaac Fisher, Eliza Hollbrook. Proven Nov. 23, 1824. Mention—Wife, Persis Starr; Children (names not given).

CROSBY, HENRY, Sharon Twp., (Vol. A-142), Ex., Augustin W. Swetland. Dated Sept. 6, 1824. Wit., Persis Starr, George Andrews. Prob. Nov. 23, 1824. Mention—Wife, Hannah F. Crosby; Mother, Mary Crosby, of Hartford, Conn.

JEWETT, ELAM, Clinton Twp., (Vol. A-143), Ex., Benjamin F. Jewett, Alexander Shattuck. Signed Sept. 9, 1824. Wit., Billias H. Skeels, Alvin Fuller, John Saul. Proven Dec. 17, 1824. Mention—Wife, ——; Sons, Benjamin F., Othneil, Caleb R. Jewett; Daughters, Laura Elliot, Lydia Welling, Lucinda, Electa, Harriet, Marinda, Eunice, Catherine Jewett, minors.

FROTHINGHAM, DEBORAH, Worthington, (Vol. A-145), Ex., Son, Stephen Frothingham. Dated Dec. 10, 1818. Wit., Recompense Stansberry, Jacob Fairfield, Henry Ogden. Prob. March 22, 1825. Mention—Son, Stephen Frothingham, "all."

SAUL, GEORGE, Mifflin Twp., (Vol. A-145), Signed Jan. 17, 1825. Wit., James Smith, Jesse Baughman. Proven March 21, 1825. Mention—Sons, George, Leonard, Michael, Jacob, Joseph Saul; Daughters, Rebecca, Catherine and Mariah.

SHOFE, ELIZABETH (Shoaf), Hamilton Twp., (Vol. A-148), Ex., Daniel Stimmel, "my friend." Signed April 20, 1825. Wit., Stephen Berryhill, Jacob Plum. Proven June 23, 1825. Mention—Daughters, Nancy, Rachel, Katherine, Elizabeth, and Mary Shofe; Son, to Abraham, "all my right in my father's, John Plum, estate on condition he support my daughter Nancy during her natural life;" other Sons, Jacob, John, Henry and Joseph Shofe. (Case 0546, June 23, 1825, Michael Stimmel, Gdn., John, Polly, Henry, Joseph and Betsey Shofe.)

DEARDORFF, ISAAC, Perry Twp., Ex., Daniel Beard, "to hold real estate till George is 21 years old." Signed Dec. 29, 1825. Wit., David Smith, Peter Bower. Proven Jan. 16, 1826. Mention—Son, George Deardorff, "all real est."

KAMMEL, JOHN, (Vol. A-150), Ex., James Gardner. Dated Aug. 18, 1824. Wit., Jacob Gundy, Abraham Romine, William Gundy. Prob. June, 1825. Mention—Daughters, Polly ——, Jane Young and Sarah Ann Spoon.

SEEDS, JAMES, Sr., (Vol. A-151), Ex., William Miller, Woolry Coonrad. Signed July 18, 1825. Wit., John Smith, John Fisher, Jr., Cod., Wit., John Fisher, Sr., John Fisher, Jr. Proven Aug. 4, 1825. Mention—Wife, Sarah Seeds; Sons, William, "the amount due me from Solomon Borror, William Seeds and Samuel Gourley, to be paid to my wife Sarah for her use," Robert and John Seeds; Grandson, William Seeds, s. of my son Andrew Seeds.

CLARK, SAMUEL, (Vol. A-152), Ex., William Miller, Franklin Twp., Woolry Coonrod. Dated Sept. 24, 1825. Wit., Smith Dulin, R. W. McMaine. Prob. Dec. 17, 1825. Mention—Wife, Sarah Clark; Sons, Samuel Thomas, John, and Sarafield Clark.

GALBREATH, MARY, Borough of Bellfonte, County of Centre and Commonwealth of Pennsylvania, (Vol. A-154), Ex., Son, John Galbreath. Dated March 20, 1821. Wit., William Petrikin, Thomas Petrikin. Prob. Dec. 17, 1825. Mention—Sons, James Galbreath, "he to pay off suit of Elizabeth Hunt brought against me in the State of Ohio," John and Robert Galbreath; Granddaughters, Maria and Jane Williams, also, "all property in Pennsylvania or Ohio, particularly the property in Franklin County descended to me as one of the heirs of my brother, John Dill.

RAREY, CHARLES, SR., (Vol. A-156), Ex., Sons, Samuel Rarey, Charles Rarey. Signed May 29, 1822. Wit., Benj. Howell, Conrod and Christian Heyl. Mention—Wife, Margaret Rarey; Sons, Parker, William, John, Adam, Charles, Benjamin, George Rarey; Daughters, Catherine Pontius, wife of Phillip, Christin Solomon, wife of John, Elizabeth Harmon.

BACKUS, THOMAS, (formerly Norwich, Conn.), (Vol. A-161), Ex., Wife. Signed Feb. 3, 1817. Wit., Eliza S. Lord, Abner Lord, Betsey Frazer, Gustavus Swan, Hannah George. Proven June 24, 1826. Mention—Wife, "to be guardian of all the children."

McCLOUD, THOMAS, Worthington, (Vol. A-162), Ex., Sons, Wallace, William McCloud. Dated June 20, 1818. Wit., Recompense Stansberry, Isaac Hor, Noah Andrews. Prob. April 14, 1824. Mention—Wife; Sons, Charles, Thomas, John, David, dec'd, William and Wallace McCloud; Daughters, Margaret Rich, Pollsy Washman, Sally Allen "to be paid out of claims I have in Vermont"; Grandchildren, Betsey and Sally McCloud, daughters of my son David; "Julia, Laura, Sophia, and Thomas Comstock, "children of my daughter Esther."

GARNETT, ANN, Queen's County, Md., (Vol. A-164), Ex., Henry D. Sellers, Esq. of Queen's County, Md. Copy of original in Registrar's Office, Philadelphia, Pa. (May 16, 1824—Seller's refused to take office or any interest therein.) Dated June 19, 1822. Wit. Ann Wright, Richard Bayard, Hugh L. Hodge. Prob. Sept. 20, 1822, at Philadelphia, Pa. Mention—Relatives, Maria Burns, Williams Burns, Ann G. Burns, Elizabeth Dawson, Sarah Maria Burn, Ann Garnett Burn, Ann Caroline Bayard of the City of Philadelphia.

CASE, ALLICE, Clinton Twp., (Vol. A-167), Ex., Arora Buttles. Dated Oct. 30, 1826. Wit., Hiland Hulbert, Ebenezer Washburn. Prob. Nov. 4, 1826. Mention—sons, Luther, William, and Calvin Case; Daughter, Rachel, deceased, "her legacy to Cherokee Missions"; Grandchildren, Nancy Rachel Case, daughter "of my son Luther, Douglas Case, so of my son Calvin H. Case."

WORTHINGTON, THOMAS, Ross County, (Vol. A-169), Ex., Sons, James T., Albert G., Thomas Worthington. Date March 15, 1827. Wit., John Renshaw, James G. George S. Milligan. Prob. (Copy

Oct. 15, 1827.) Mention—Wife, Eleanor Worthington; Daughters, Mary McComb, Sarah King, Eleanor, Margaret, Elizabeth Worthington; Sons, James T., Albert G., William, Francis, Thomas Worthington; Grandsons, Thomas, s. of my dau. Sarah King, Thomas McComb.

TAYLOR, MATTHEWS, JR., 3d, Madison Twp., (Vol. A-179), Ex., Wife, Ann Taylor, Abithar V. Taylor, William Taylor; my brother, Wm. Shields, stone cutter. Dated April 10, 1826. Wit., John Melsek, Phillip Melsel, Samuel Hamilton. Prob. Dec. 19, 1826. Mention—Wife, Ann Taylor; Sons, John McKnight Taylor, Harvey Taylor, Mathew Anderson Taylor; Daughters, Rebecca Archabele Taylor and Elizabeth Taylor. Cod., (Elizabeth Taylor, widow of John A., "the use of one cabin house so long as she remains a widow.")

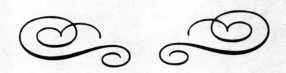

ABSTRACTS OF WILLS, FRANKLIN COUNTY, OHIO

Compiled by BLANCHE TIPTON RINGS

GILLETT, ASA, Worthington, (Vol. A-181), Ex., R. W. Cowles, Arora Buttles, and John W. Ladd. Dated January 10, 1827. Wit., R. W. Coles and William Dunton. Probated February 14, 1827. Codicil, January 23, 1827. Mentions— Mother, Vilet Gillett; Sister, Vilet Hopkins of Hudson, N. Y.; Lansing Hopkins, Maria Tobey and Harriet, children of Charles and Vilet Hopkins; Asa, s. of Timothy Terry of Simsbury, Conn.; Worthington M. E. Society; Brother, James Gillett, Simsbury, Conn. In codicil requests that a tombstone be erected at his grave.

BAKER, JOHN, Madison Twp., (Vol. A-185), Ex., William Stewart. Dated Aug. 21, 1822. Wit., William E. Denoon, David Landes. Prob. Apr. 9, 1827. Mention—Wife, Ann Baker; Daughters, Dorothy Highlen, Eave Stombach, Elizabeth Stombaugh, her heirs; Sons, Henry Baker, John Baker; Grandson, John Sites.

LAWSON, JOHN P., Sharon Twp., (Vol. A-187), Ex., Samuel Cope, Peter P. Lawson. Dated Apr. 19, 1827. Wit., Lyman Andrews, Ebenezer Goodrich. Prob. Sept. 10, 1827. Mention—Wife, Mariah Lawson; Son, Samuel, (eldest), and other five children (not named).

SMITH, JOSEPH, Perry Twp., (Vol. A-188), Ex., Wife, Caty Smith, Son, Abraham Smith. Dated Dec. 5, 1825. Wit., David Smith, Elijah Smith. Prob. Sept. 11, 1827. Mention—Wife, Caty Smith; Sons, Abraham, Isaac, John, Richard; Daughters, Eliza, Caty and Sally.

JOHNSON, ISAAC, Jefferson Twp., (Vol. A-190), Ex., Wife, Sarah Johnson. Dated Feb. 26, 1826. Wit., Hugh Jiams, James Price, Henry Johnson. Prob. Apr. 10, 1826. Mention—Wife, Sarah Johnson; Sons, Lewis, Henry, Isaac, Uriah, and Isaiah Johnson; Dau., Dorcas Johnson.

TAYLOR, ROBERT, Truro Twp., (formerly Nova Scotia), (Vol. A-191), Ex., Sons, David and James Taylor. Dated Mch. 6, 1827. Wit., P. B. Wilcox, J. W. Crosby, R. Brotherton. Prob. Sept. 6, 1828. Mention—Wife, Mehitabel Taylor; Sons, David, Mathew and James W. Taylor; Daughters, Elizabeth and Peggy Long, Susannah and Lydia Taylor.

CUNNING, JOHN, Columbus, (Vol. A-193), Ex., James Hoge, Samuel Persons, Ralph Osborne. Dated Mar. 23, 1828. Wit., John McElvain, Elijah Zinn. Prob. May 31, 1828. Mention—Elizabeth Cunning; Margaret McMaster; Dau., Margaret Cunning, a minor; Son, Samuel Cunning, a minor.

MOOBERRY, WILLIAM, Senior, Madison Twp., (Vol. A-194), Ex., Sons, Wm. and Samuel Mooberry. Dated Jan. 22, 1828. Wit., D. W. Deshler, Samuel Kilgore. Prob. Apr. 7, 1829. Mention—Sons, William and Samuel Mooberry, "all personal property having disposed of and divided among my children my real estate by deeds bearing date Sept. 25, 1827."

CHENOWETH, ELIJAH, Pleasant Twp., (Vol. A-196). Dated July 21, 1828. Wit., Jacob Grubb, Jonathon B. Perrin. Prob. Apr. 7, 1829. Mention— Sons, Thomas, John F., Joseph and Elijah Chenoweth; Daughters, Elizabeth Gheer, Sarah Hains, Cassandra Morgan, Rachel Wood, and Ruth Davison.

FETTERS, PETER (Non-cupative), (Vol. A-197). Dated Jan. 30, 1829. Wit., Mathias Robbins, Jacob Fetters. Prob. Apr., 1829. Mention—Sisters, Susan and (not named), and Jacob.

LEICHTENECHER, GOTTLIEB, Columbus, (Vol. A-197), Ex., Lincoln Goodale, D. W. Deshler. Dated Oct. 8, 1827. Wit., J. R. Swan, Mease Smith. Prob. Jan. 29, 1830. Mention—Wife, Frederica Leichtenecher; Dau., Sebilla Lieber, "now supposed to be in Germany." Cod., Nov. 3, 1827, "at wife's death . . . to go to Gottlieb Rooser and Frederick L. Rooser, minors."

RILEY, WILLIAM, (Vol. A-199), Ex., Wm. Brown. Dated Apr. 27, 1824. Wit., Andrew Armstrong, Wm. C. Duff. Prob. Jan. 14, 1830. Mention— Sons, William, Robert and George Riley; Daughters, Mary Scott, and Eleanor Riley, a minor.

NELSON, DAVID, Marion Twp., (Vol. A-200), Ex., John Barr, Edward Livingston, David Taylor, "husband of my grand daughter Nancy." Dated Nov. 4, 1828. Wit., James Hoge, Wm. McElvain, Adam Read. Prob. Jan. 16, 1830. Mention—Wife, Margaret Nelson; Daughters, Nancy Barr, Mary Livingston, Martha Livingston; Son, David Nelson; Son-in-law, George Gibson; Grandson, Nelson Barr.

SPRINGER, BENJAMIN, Madison Twp., (Vol. A-202), Ex., John More, Abraham Shepherd. Dated Oct. 15, 1823. Wit., Reason Francis, Jacob Francis, Silas Osborn. Prob. Feb. 14, 1825. Mention—Wife, Elizabeth Springer; Sons, Robert, Thomas, and Silas Springer; Son-in-law, Usual Osborn, "husband to my daughter Deborah."

281

DOMIGAN, WILLIAM, Franklinton, (Vol. A-204), Ex., Francis Stewart. Dated June 30, 1830. Wit., Jacob Grubb, Samuel Deardurff, Nathan Cole. Mention—Wife, Mary Domigan; Son, Enoch Domigan; Dau., Marte. "wife of Thomas Biddle;" Grandsons, Lewis Hall, "s. of Richard," William Domigan, "s. of my son Abijah," . . . . "my farm in the fork of the Scioto and Whetstone Rivers—47 acres." Guardian of grandsons, Lincoln Goodale.

SHIELDS, WILLIAM, (Vol. A-206), Ex., Wife, Margaret Shields. Dated Oct. 29, 1830. Wit., Peter Mills, Jr., Joseph Edgar. Mention—Wife. Margaret Shields; Sons, Robert and George Shields, "to be equally divided."

THOMPSON, CHARLES, Worthington, (Vol. A-208), Ex., Moses Wilkinson, Robert Comstock (both of Sharon Twp.). Dated Sept. 11, 1830. Wit., R. W. Cowles, Buckley Comstock. Prob. Nov., 1830. Mention—Wife, Oriel Thompson; Son, Henry Thompson, "all that is left of the estate coming from the estate of my late father, Wm. Thompson, formerly of Sharon township;" Daughters, Pamela, Catherine, Harriet, and Mary Thompson.

MCFEE, JOSEPH, (Vol. A-210), Ex., William McFee. Dated Apr. 1, 1829. Wit., Samuel Dean, Charles Dean. Subscribed Nov., 1830. Mention—Wife, Sarah McFee; Daughters, (not named) "to have a cow and calf each;" Sons, William and (son), a minor, "is to live with son William until he is of age, the oldest to give the youngest (son) 50 acres of land."

STEVENSON, JOHN, Madison Twp., (Vol. A-211), Ex., Wife, Mary Stevenson. Dated Apr. 19, 1831. Wit., Joseph R. Swan, Wm. Scott, Mease Smith. Prob. Nov. 28, 1831. Mention—Wife, Mary Stevenson; Sons, Joshua, Zachariah, Richard and George; Daughters, Hanna and Matilda Stevenson. Rachel Hooper, Sarah Agler, Mary Patterson, and Anna Kalb; Son-in-law, Nathan Stevenson, "husband of my daughter Elizabeth;" Grandchildren, William, Rebecca, and Susan Derick, Mary Ann Taylor, and John Stevenson, "son of my son John."

SWASHGOOD, JOHN, Franklinton, (Vol. A-214), Ex., Stewart White. Dated Sept. 7, 1831. Wit., Jacob Grubb, John Robinson. Prob. Feb. 20, 1832. Mention—Wife, Ann Swashgood, "the home in Franklinton;" Children, Sarah, Elizabeth, Mary Ann, William, and Samuel Swashgood, all minors.

DAVIS, JOHN, Perry Township, (Vol. A-217), Ex., Wife, Ann Davis, Sons, Samuel S. and Joseph Davis. Dated Jan. 22, 1832. Wit., G. Thomas, John Hutchinson. Prob. Feb., 1832. Mention—Wife, Ann Davis; Sons, Samuel S., Joseph, William, Joshua, dec'd, and John Davis; Daughters, Sarah, Nancy, and Eliza.

CRAMER, ANDREW, Madison Twp., (Vol. A-219), Ex., John Swisher. Dated Oct. 6, 1831. Wit., Samuel Hamilton, John Helsel. Prob. Feb. 24, 1832. Mention—Sons, Henry, Jonathon, Michael, Barnabas, and Anthony; Daughters, Charlott, Mary, and Susan; Grandchildren, James and Nancy, "children of my daughter Clara, deceased."

PRICE, STEPHEN R., Mifflin Twp., (Vol. A-221), Ex., John Clark. Dated Mch. 24, 1832. Cod. same date. Wit., Geo. Ridenour, John Starrett. Prob. Aug. 2, 1832. Mention—Wife, Elizabeth Price; Son, James Price; Grandchildren, Martha Price, "who now lives with my wife," Jane, Harriet, and Hugh Price; Stephen Price McCosley; Isabella Smiley.

NOBLE, JONATHON, Blendon Twp., (Vol. A-222-228), Ex., Wife, Hannah Noble, John Billington. Dated Mar. 5, 1832. Wit., Abram Phelps, John Watt. Prob. June 16, 1832. Mention—Wife, Hannah Noble; Sons, Orrin, Lester, Solomon, Lyman, Zenas, Myran, Miles, Elijah, and Horace Noble; Daughters, Lydia, Eliza, and Mary Noble, all minors.

POSTLE, SHADRACH, Prairie Twp., (Vol. A-228), Ex., Son, Stephen Postle. Dated Apr. 24, 1832. Wit., William Stierwalt, Washington Hickman. Prob. June 16, 1832. Mention—Daughter, Elizabeth Brown; Sons, Job, Solomon, John, Stephen; and the heirs of Gabriel, dec'd, ("his daughter, Mary Jane, being a child by his second wife; his sons, Elias, Franklin and Gabriel Postle, sons by his first wife").

GOETCHIUS, HENRY (also Gutches), Franklin Twp., (Vol. A-230). Ex., Wife, Elizabeth Goetchius. Dated Aug. 27, 1814. Wit., Orris Parrish, David

L. Broderick. Prob. May 17, 1832. Mention--Wife, Elizabeth Goetchius, "land in Franklin township which I bought of my brother, Nicholas Goetchius."

HAMILTON, Hon. JAMES, Esq., (Vol. A-232), Ex., Brother, Thomas Hamilton, Esq.; Son, James Hamilton, Esq. Dated Jan. 16, 1819, Gettysburg, Pa. Wit., Jacob Hendle, I. B. Parker. Prob. May 25, 1819. Registered at Carlisle, Pa., Feb. 7, 1832. Mention—Wife, (*not named*), "to have the rent of three house adjoining the said dwelling house, &c;" Son, James; Daughters, Mary, Susan and Emeline, "all property in Pennsylvania, Ohio, and Kentucky to be equally divided between them." Also, "I give $150 to be invested in stock or fund, that the interest be a fund to which I hope more by others will be contributed to be expended in administering to the poor of Carlisle the week of Christmas."

ABBOTT. JANE, Dayton, O., (Vol. A-234), Ex., Elijah Converse, son-in-law. Dated Sept. 18, 1822. Wit., George W. Mytinger, Andrew Crawford. Proven Feb., 1823. Rec. Dayton, Oct. 23, 1828, also Franklin Co., Feb. 20, 1833. Mention—Sons, Richard, Robert, and Thomas Abbott, "land near Abbottstown, Pa., to be sold and divided equally between them;" to son John, "my share of the ground rents in Abbottstown, Pa., and my lands on Big Belly, Ohio, to be sold and my son John to receive for his own use the average price of 55 a." To "the children of my daughter Rebecca Comverse . . . the balance of the money remaining from the sales of lands on Big Belly."

WEATHERINGTON, JOHN, Hamilton Twp., (Vol. A-237), Ex., Sons John and Isaac Weatherington. Dated May 6, 1824. Wit., Andrew Armstrong, John Brigg, Isaac Lorance. Prob. May, 1831. Mention—Wife, Margaret Weatherington; Sons, John, William, and Isaac Weatherington; Daughters, Rebecca (w. of George W. Williams), Comfort (w. of Josiah Williams), Margaret (w. of John Williams), Elizabeth (w. of Archibald Smith); Grandsons, John (s. of Isaac), Thomas Jefferson (s. of John); Son-in-law, John R. Delashmut, "husband of my daughter Sarah."

HEWS. MARY (also Hughes), Madison Twp., (Vol. A-242), Ex., John Courtright. Dated Feb. 28, 1833. Wit., Joshua Glanville, George Glandville. Proven Apr., 1833. Mention—Sisters, Phebe Starr, Elizabeth Hews; Brothers, John D. and Thompson Hews; Nieces. Phebe and Eliza (daus. of Elizabeth Hews), Polly, Courtright, Matilda and Maria (*names not given*); Hiram (s. of Elizabeth Hews), Polly, sister-in-law.

WOLCOTT, WILLIAM (also Walcott), Columbus, (Vol. A-244,), Ex., Son, Robert Wolcott. Dated Apr. 1, 1833. Wit., Samuel C. Andrews, Joshua C. Andrews. Prob. July 1, 1833. Mention—Sons, Robert, Jacob, James, and John M. Wolcott. To Robert, "in consequence of his uncommon care and kindness toward me, all my property and estate, both real and personal."

JONES, LYDIA, (Vol. A-245), Ex., George Jefferies of Columbus. Dated Aug. 14, 1833. Wit., Moses R. Spurgion, Thomas Wood, P. B. Wilcox. Prob. Sept. 19, 1833. Mention—Rachel Jefferies; Magdalene Dandridge, a minor.

LITTLE. HARVEY D., Columbus, (Vol. A-246), Ex., Wife, Mary Little, Joseph Howard, brother-in-law, Samuel Forrer. Dated Mar. 7, 1833. Wit., John Howard, Wm. Hance. Prob. Oct. 14, 1833. Mention—Wife, Mary Little; Dau., Caroline Little; Sons, Horton H., and Richard M. Little. "If my wife re-marries, my highly respected father-in-law, Horton Howard, shall be guardian of my children; or if she die, my esteemed brother-in-law, John Howard."

HOWARD, HORTON, Columbus, (Vol. A-250), Ex., Wife, Hannah Howard; Sons, Joseph and John Howard, Samuel Forrer, son-in-law. Dated Aug. 4, 1833. Wit., Ebenezer Thomas, Amos Menely, W. Hance. Prob. Sept. 20, 1833. Mention—Wife, Hannah Howard; Dau., Mary Little, and her children; Dau. Rachel (*name not given*), dec'd, her children, Henry, Joseph, Horton, Sarah, Mary Ann, and John.

CAMPBELL, JOHN W., (Vol. A-248), Ex., Wife, Eleanor Campbell, and John Patterson. Dated Aug. 12, 1833. No date of probate. Wit., D. Starr, Jacob Haven, Samuel Peymon, George King. Mention—Wife, Eleanor; Brother, James.

"Charles, the heir of my late brother Joseph; Brother Samuel; Sister Betsy Humphrey; Polly Tweed; Phebe Martin; Sister Rebecca Beird; Sister Sarah Rimpton; Sister Fidelia Hopkins; to Elizabeth M. Silley, or Lilley, unmarried; to Elizabeth Ann Rimpon (whom I trust my wife may raise and educate, a minor); to Eleanor Jane Campbell; to each of my nephews bearing my name, and to John Beird." (In proving the will Hiram Paddleford says he is well acquainted with the handwriting of the testator and of D. Starr, deceased.)

LEONARD, ISAAC, Madison Twp., (Vol. A-253), Ex., Wife, Nancy Leonard, and son, Abner Leonard. Dated Sept. 22, 1831. Wit., William Patterson, Esq., and Martha Patterson. Prob. Oct. 17, 1833. Mention—Wife, Nancy; Son, Abner; "to legal heirs of my deceased dau. Eunice; to Harriet Corey; to Jemima Corey; to legal heirs of my dau. (can't read) Tuttle; to legal heirs of my son, Isaac, Jr.; to legal heirs of my dau., Lydia Clause??.

TAILOR and TAYLOR, Samuel, Franklin County, (Vol. A-256), Ex., John Long. Dated Nov. 19, 1833. Wit., Littleton R. Gray and Thomas Gray. Prob. Dec. 5, 1833. To Brother Isaac Fassett; to nephew Isaac (can't read); to sister Lucy's children; to sister Esther's children.

LINDSEY, JAMES, (Vol. A-257), Ex., Brother-in-law John Barr and my eldest son Wilson. Dated Sept. 3, 1833. Wit., Fulton Lindsey and Thomas F. Harbison. Prob. Sept. 23, 1833. He wishes for his children to all live together till they arrive at full age, without charge, or expence for boarding, clothing or schooling as they would enjoy if he were living; to my three daughters, all minors; to niece Eliza Jane Lindsey (who is expected to receive a small legacy from Brown County, Pa., which amount is unknown to me) rest to be divided between my three sons. Requests that John Barr be guardian for all the children during their minority. (In proving the will George Chambers, Esq., of Franklin County, Pa., was to take the deposition of Thomas F. Harbison at Chambersburg, Pa., Oct. 16, 1833.

DYRE, JOHN (also Dyer), Pleasant Twp., (Vol. A-260). Dated Aug. 10, 1833. Wit., John L. Crawford, Ruben P. Mann, Nicholas Hathaway, William Parkinson, John Reed. Prob. Feb. 20, 1834. Mention—Wife. Mary Dyre, "in lieu of her dower, the plantation on which she now resides of about 500 a. . . . so long as she remains my widow or until my death, for the purpose of raising my children, she to sell 50 a. adjoining Henry Clover's purchase to pay my debts."

VORYS, ISIAH (also Voris-Vorhees), Columbus, (Vol. A-262 . Ex., Wife, Charlotte Vorys, John Greenwood. Dated Jan. 14, 1833. Wit., Ralph Osborn, James W. Parker, Jonathon M. Smith. Prob. Apr. 3, 1834. Mention—Wife, Charlotte Vorys; Daughters, Ann Helm, Sarah Helm, Polly Rogers, Hannah Blair; Sons, Abraham, William, and John Vorys.

BAYLEY, THOMAS M., Accomach Co., Va., (Vol. A-265), Ex., Wife, Jane O. Bayley; Son, Thomas Bayley. Dated Mch. 9, 1828. Prob. Jan. 27, 1834. Proven by Thos. R. Jorques, Clk. of Co. Accomah, John G. Jorques, George P. Scarburgh. Mention—Wife, Jane O. Bayley, "not only the slaves but the children of the female slaves, which belonged to her and have been born since her marriage. . . . also, our Plantation called 'The Vale,' in Scarborough's Neck . . . formerly belonged to her father;" Son, Thos. H. Bayley, "10,000 a. of my Ohio land;" Daughters, A. D., Sally, Jane, Elizabeth W., and Margaret P. Bayley.

MAYNARD, MOSES, Worthington, (Vol. A-273), Ex., Son, Moses Maynard. Potter Wright. Dated Dec. 3, 1821. Wit., Recompense Stansberry, Ozeum Gardner, Jonathon Shormon. Prob. Sept. 15, 1834. Mention—Sons, Apollus and Moses Maynard; Daughters, Achsa Johnson, and Lovisa Wright; Grandchildren, Eber P., Lucy, and Harriet Maynard.

WILCOX, ISRAEL S., Lockbourne, Hamilton Twp., (Vol. A-277), Ex., Rennselaer Watson Cowles, Worthington, "my true and trusty friend." Dated Feb. 2, 1834. Wit., James Kilbourn, Joseph Roberts, Thomas Blackburn. Prob. Feb. 2, 1834. Mention—Wife, Sarah D. Wilcox, "if she has no heirs . . . everything to go to the children of Roswell Wilcox (brother) and Moses Messenger (brother-in-law) . . . equal amounts."

PHELPS, ABRAM (Abraham), (Vol. A-279), Ex., Wife, Lucy Phelps. Dated July 15, 1834. Wit., John W. Ladd, Sarah M. Bill, Nancy Landon. Prob. Sept. 15, 1834. Mention—Wife, Lucy Phelps, "the plantation where I now live."

MILLER, WILLIAM, Jackson Twp., (Vol. A-281), Ex., Son, Mathew Miller, Jacob Strader. Dated Sept. 15, 1832. Wit., John Mitchell, David Spangler. Rec. Sept. 15, 1834. Mention—Son, William Miller; Grandson, William Seeds, a minor. "The house and land I now live on, the rest to be equally divided between my five sons."

EDGAR, HARRIET, (Vol. A-283), Ex., Silas Edgar, husband. Dated July 31, 1834. Wit., James E. Edgar, John Compton. Prob. Sept. 15, 1834. Mention—Silas Edgar, husband; Daughter, Catherine Edgar, "my wearing apparel."

YONER, CHARLES W., Sharon Twp., (Vol. A-284). Dated Feb. 27, 1835. Wit., D. L. Terry, Wm. H. Brooks, Thos. Ingersoll. Prob. May, 1835. Mention—G. W. Griswold, Dr. Morrow.

TODD, THOMAS, (Vol. A-291), Ex., Lucy P. Todd. Dated Dec. 22, 1823. Proven Feb., 1826, oaths of John H. Hanna, Luke Munsell, Wm. Washington. Rec. Kentucky, May 8, 1835;* Franklin Co., Ohio, Sept., 1835. Mention—Wife, Lucy P. Todd; Sons, Charles S., John H., Wm. Johnson, and James M. Todd; Child, Madisonia; Edmund S. Starling, "who intermarried with my daughter Ann Maria. (*Signed by Alex. H. Rennick, Clark, and David Waits, J. P.)

MALTBY, WILLIAM, Sharon Twp., (Vol. A-296), Ex., David (of Franklin Co.), Ira, Joseph, and Daniel Maltby (all of Ashtabula Co.). Wit., John W. Ladd, Moses Maynard. Dated May 27, 1835. Prob. Sept. 24, 1835. Mention—Wife,* and children.* Wife "to sell property in Ashtabula county and make payments on property in Sharon twp." (*Not named.)

BLACKE, JAMES, (Vol. A-299), Ex., Sons, John and William Blacke, Thos. Simonton, "friend." Dated Dec. 30, 1808. Wit., Amos Jordan, Francis Jordan. Prob. Jan. 12, 1809 (Prov. 8th). Rec. Aug. 27, 1835, Carlisle, Pa. Rec. Sept., 1835, Franklin Co. Mentions—Sons, John, William, James, Jonathon, and George Blacke; Daughters, Mary, Jane, Rebecca, Abigail, Sarah, Nancy ("intermarried with Robert Elliot"), "to have my real estate on the Scioto River, near Franklinton, 1100 acres . . . those under age shall live with my sons John and William . . . to have them educated so far as is common for their sex."

BURTON, JOSHUA, Madison Twp., (Vol. A-304), Ex., Nathan Perrill. Dated Feb. 25, 1832. Wit., A. L. Perrill, Z. H. Perrill, Nathan Perrill. Prob. Sept. 26, 1835. Mention—Wife, Nancy Burton; Sons, William, Thomas, Basil, John, Joshua, and Walter Burton; also, heirs of Thomas Burton, and Elizabeth Perdue (daughter). To Walter, "my plantation in Franklin county;" To my wife, "if there should be any of my pension due me from the U. S. . . . executor to pay to wife for her use."

PELHAM, PETER, Xenia, O., (Vol. A-306), Ex., Sons, Samuel, Jesse B. Pelham. Dated Feb. 28, 1822. Prob. July 9, 1824, Greene Co., O. Rec. Sept., 1835, Franklin Co. Proven by Phillip Goode and Josiah Grover. Admr. Thomas Davis. Mention—Wife, Parthenia Pelham; Brother, Henry Pelham; Son, Jesse Pelham, "my razor hone, shaving box and razors;" Daughters, Mary and Caroline Pelham, Sarah C. Drougoole (w. of Edward) "land formerly in Champaign county;" Grandson, John B. Pelham, a minor.

WALLACE, JOHN, Montgomery Twp., (Vol. A-310), Ex., Wife, Betsey Wallace, John Wilson, "tanner of Columbus." Dated July 15, 1828. Wit., John Barr, Charles Pettit, James Turner. Prob. Aug. 24, 1835. Mention—Wife, Betsey Wallace; Sons, Samuel Andrews Wallace; John Jos. Wallace; Daughters, Elizabeth and Mary Wallace.

STEPHENSON, RICHARD, Madison Twp., (Vol. A-312), Ex., Wife, Mary Stephenson; Son, Alfred Stephenson. Dated 1835. Wit., Thos. Patterson, John Todd, John Swisher. Prob. Dec. 26, 1835. Mention—Wife, Mary Stephenson; Sons, James,* John,* Richard (youngest)*, Frederick and William; Daughters, Calista Carson, Sarah Needles, Susan Alkire, Ellen Stephens, and

Mary Stephenson. Mention—"lot in Columbus belonging to my second wife to divide between Sylvester W. Piper, Richard Stephenson and the two sons of my second wife." (*"Providing they continue to live with my wife, their stepmother, to help raise the children or till their youngest brother comes of age.")

DECKER, ISAAC D., Madison Twp., (Vol. A-314). Dated Nov. 11, 1833. Wit., Alex. Cameron, Frederick Fruchey. Mention—Wife, Lydia Decker, "the property where we now live;" Daughters, Catherine Tabor, Mary Drake, Sarah Ann Saul, Effy Titler, Eleanor and Eliza Decker.

POWELL, GEORGE, Madison Twp., (Vol. A-315), Ex., Wife, Melinda Powell. Dated Sept. 19, 1835. Wit., Jonathon McComb, George Stevenson. Prob. Dec. 25, 1835. Mention—Wife, Melinda Powell, "all during her life and at her death to go to my children equally."

HUNTER, JOSEPH, Senior, (Columbus), (Vol. A-285), Ex., Sons, Wm. and Joseph Hunter, Jr. Dated Mch., 1828. Wit., J. R. Swan, Freedom Seever, Sam'l Bigger. Cod. Dec. 10, 1829. Wit., J. R. Swan, Mease Smith. Prob. Dec. 8, 1834. Adm., Feb. 16, 1835. Mention—Wife, Mary Hunter; Sons, William and Joseph Hunter; Daughters, Jane (w. of Andrew McElvain), Isabella (w. of Wm. Shaw), Nancy (w. of David Mitchell); Grandchildren, "children of Samuel Robinson and his late wife, Martha."

Ed:—End of Book A.

286

ABSTRACTS OF WILLS, FRANKLIN COUNTY, OHIO

Compiled by BLANCHE TIPTON RINGS

SIMMS, CHARLES, (Also Symmes). Alexandria, D C. (Copy) (Vol. B-1) Ex: Wife, Nancy Simms. Son William Douglas Simms and dau. Catherine Simms and "any other children I may have at my death". First Codicil; Jan. 27, 1799 he says that dau. Catherine has intermarried with Cuthbert Powell since making his will and names as Ex. William Douglas Sims, wife Nancy Simms and son-in-law, Cuthbert Powell. Second codicil, Dec. 16, 1811, adds to the above executors his son, John D. Simms. Third codicil, Feb. 11, 1817 mentions that son William D. Simms has sold land on Montuns Island in Pennsylvania and land on Raccoon Creek in Pennsylvania. Wit: Thomas Swan, Robert J. Taylor, Alexander Henderson. Prob. May 6, 1820.

WALLING, ROBERT, G., (Vol. B-4) Franklin county. Dated Nov. 20, 1835; prob. Mch. 23, 1836, Ross county; wife to be executor and to received all; wit: Eleaxer Cowgill, and James Walling at Ross County.

LEWIS, GEORGE, (Vol. B-6) (Copy) Of Prince George's county, Va.; dated Mch. 19, 1819. Prob. Feb. 6, 1823. Mentions—Wife, Catherine (she to a home any place in Va. she may choose); Son, Dangerfield Lewis and his family to reside with my wife and to have one third of everything, Son, Samuel Lewis is to have one-third of my western lands and one-third of all my negroes and dau., Mary W. Willis is to have same as son, Lewis.; ex.: Sons Samuel and Dangerfield Lewis; wit: William T. Grymes and Dangerfield Lewis. Copy at Franklin County, Nov. 11, 1833.

BLAIR, ARCHIBALD, (Vol. B-7). Dated at Richmond, Va., 1809. Prob. May 17, 1825. Mentions—Wife, (not named) to have the cook. Jenny and her dau. Polly, son John to have negro boy, Jim son of Sally, son Beverly to have negro boy Henry, a son of Sally, son Archibald to have a negro boy Lewis, a son of Sally, dau. Mary to have negro girl, dau. of Sally, and legacy to friend Rev. John Buchanan; ex: Wife (not named), sons John and Beverly Blair with addition of Archibal Blair, his son when he arrives at the proper age; sworn to by Richard Anderson and Nathaniel Sheppard. (He disposed of 1000 acres of land on the Cumberland River in Kentucky and a tract of 718 acres near Chillicothe, Ross Co., Ohio.

TURNER, NATHANIEL, (Vol. B-11). Dated Nov. 8, 1835 at Columbus. Probated May 26, 1836; everything to his wife, Wealthann Turner; wife to be executor; wit: I. G. Jones and Tripheny Smith.

PIKE, JARVIS, (Vol. B-11). Dated Jan. 23, 1836; probated Apr. 3, 1836. Mentions—Wife, Jane Runkle, my wife's nephew Levi Goodwin lishment and everything belonging to the Thompsonian Recorder, being my whole interest in said establishment and wife Rebecca Pike; executor: friends Horatio Woods and Joseph Ridgeway; wit: Jonathan Philips and A. Curtis; signed at Columbus.

GROOM, EZEKIEL, (Vol. B-12). Dated July, 20, 1936; of Madison township. Prob. Sept. 30, 1836. Mentions—Wife, Rhoda Groom, dau. Mary Groom, son Moses, dau. Sarah Stephenson (and Stevenson), dau. Catherine Sawyer, wife of John Sawyer (the land on the county line between Franklin and Pickaway counties where they now live), son Thomas, son William, son John, dau. Tamson Britton; Wit: Isaac Rainier and Alexander Camerson; xecutors; sons Moses and Thomas Groom.

RUNKLE, LEWIS, (Vol. B-14). Dated May, 1830. Prob. Oct. 18, 1836. MentionsWiWfe, Jane Runkle, my wife's nephew Levi Goodwin and son David Goodwin, and my niece Rebecca Runkle, dau. of George Runkle; executor: wife Jane Runkle; wit: William Lusk, John Brooks and Nathaniel W. Brooks. (William Lusk said at time of proving will that Runkle at time of signing was about 40 yrs. or more. Is signed in German).

BROMLOW, JOSEPH, (B-16). Of Washington twp; dated Jan. 19, 1836. Prob. Sept. 29, 1836; wife: Benigna Bromlow (he says "Benigna Geary, otherwise Bruns, otherwise Bromlow, my dear wife now residing with me in the beech woods) trustees: Jesse Stone of Columbus and William Harris of Franklin county; wit: Henry Kaufman (Coffman) and John Sells.

HETH, WILLIAM, (B-17). Signed at Henrico County, Va., proven Apr. 8, 1807 at Richmond, Va. Mention—First and second wives but does not name them, son Henry Heth (by second wife), daus. Elizabeth Agnes, Pleasur, Margaret Thomas Jacqueline and Mary Andrietta Heth, all minors, my acknowledged son, William M. Heth (now commanding the ship, Marshall, of New York, belonging to Archibald Gracie, 2000 acres of military lands to be chosen by himself) (and my Cuckapow mill land in Hampshire county, Virginia), brother John Heth; executors: friend Edward Covington, John Marshall, bro. Henry Heth and son Henry Heth; wit: Thomas Keiser and Joseph Trent.

BOOKER, LEWIS, (B-21). Of Essex County, Va. Dated Dec. 23, 1814. Prob. Feb. 20, 1815 at Tappahannock, Essex Co., Va. Mentions —Wife, Judith Booker (all my property during her life and for the use of my children who are unmarried), son Richard is married and already received share and dau. Dorothy who is married and has received share; executors: James Webb, my friend; James Booker, my son and my son-in-law William Darnell; wit. Lewis Dix, Thomas Dix and Carter Croxton.

SELLS, BENJAMIN, (B-24). Columbus. Dated Feb. 1837. Prob. Mch. 13, 1837. Mentions—Wife, Rebecca Sells (the house on Rich Street, on west side of shop formerly occupied by a pottery), dau. Catherine Skidmore, granddau. Martha Ann Sells (a minor and dau. of the late Ephriam Sells), and grandson John Robinson, Jr. (a minor), grandson younger than John who is an infant not yet named, son Peter. son Ludwick, and dau. Rachel McCoy; executors: Peter Sells and Warren Jenkins; wit: Daniel Whitsel, Mathew Bussard and Warren Jenkins.

WALCUTT, JACOB (also Walcott). (B-26). Dated Apr. 8, 1835. Prob. Mch. 16, 1837. Mentions: wife, Elizabeth Walcott (in lieu of dower, all the plantation occupied now by Nicholas Ollery in Delaware district), mentions his seven children, namely: eldest son Richard, second son Mason, third son Henry, fourth son John, dau. Litty Ann Walcott, fifth son Robert, sixth son William; executor: James Walcutt; wit: James Graham and James O'Hara.

WAGGONER, MARTIN (B-28). Of Jefferson twp. Dated Aug. 27, 1834. Prob. Mch. 13, 1837. Mentions—Step-son, William Havens (unmarried, the 50 acres on which I now live for keeping his mother and me comfortable our life time, if they live till William gets married. he shall find them a comfortable home separate from his own and provide for them), son William, wife Elizabeth, dau. Catherine Datcher, dau. Addy Accorson, dau. Mary Blauvel, dau. Phebe Harris, dau. Susan Davenport. dau. Lydia Peat. dau. Nancy Waggoner, dau. Elizabeth Davice; wit: Andrew Hanna, John R. Smith and Elizabeth Williams.

TOY, CHARLES, (B-30). Of Madison twp. Dated Dec. 20, 1836. Prob. Mch. 13, 1837. Mentions—Three youngest sons: William, Addison and Harrison, and his three daus. (not named); wit: Jacob Weaver, Catherine Weaver and Thomas Gimler.

LENNINGTON, CORNELIUS, (B-31). Of Poughkeepsie, N. Y., now residing in Blendon twp. Dated Sept. 15, 1836. Prob. Mch. 16, 1837. Mentions—Dau. Hannah Westervelt (the use of all my real estate purchased of Royal Carpenter in Blendon twp.*), to the sons of my deceased dau. Mary Westervelt, namely: William, James and Edgar Westervelt), to the heirs of my dau. Hannah Westervelt, namely (Ann Maria, Sarah, Rebecca, Hannah, Matthew, Angeline and Mary Westervelt), to the heirs of my deceased dau. Mary Westervelt, namely: (William, Emline, Edgar, James and Melissa Westervelt), to Cornelius Lennington Westervelt (son of my dau. Hannah Westervelt) (the other undivided half of my land in Poughkeepsie, N. Y.; executor: Samuel Frear and James Fort of Dutchess Co., N. Y.; wit: Gideon W. Hart, Willis Spencer and Horace Loomis. Proven in Franklin county by Gideon W. Hart and Horace Loomis.

Note: Cornelius Lennington died Oct. 1, 1836, aged 64 yrs. and 7 mo. is buried at Westerville, O.

THOMPSON, RUHAMA, (B-33) Dated Oct. 3, 1836. Prob. Mch. 17, 1837; all property to be divided between two daus. equally, namely: Sarah Armstrong and Mary Lacy Shepherd; executor: Robert Armstrong; wit: David W. Deshler and Edward Davis.

Note: This is wife of Col. John Thompson, Revolutionary soldier.

PARRISH, ORRIS, (B-34). Of the town of Columbus; counsellor at law. Dated July 13, 1833. Prob. Sept. 29, 1837; wife Aurelia Parrish to have all property and to be guardian of all their children; wit. N. H. Swayne, William Miner and James Culbertson; re-executed and re-published Mch. 24, 1837; wit: Tripheny Smith and I. G. Jones.

Note: Orish Parish died Apr. 16, 1837, aged 45 yrs. left a widow and 5 children.

BEDINGER, DANIEL, (B-35). Of Jefferson Co., Va. Dated Mch. 10, 1818. Prob. May 26, 1818; copy at Franklin county Oct. 25, 1834. Mentions—Wife Sarah Bedinger (in trust for the benefit of the children who are to be maintained and educated therefrom), dau. Margaret R. Foster (already received her share), dau. Elizabeth C. Washington (the house and lot in Shepherdstown which formerly belonged to my father and which I purchased from his grandson, Henry Swangen, also ½ of the lot purchased from Col. John Monroe), dau. Mary (the Oak Hill Plantation), dau. Susan (Lot 193 in Shepherdstown), dau. Eleanor (40 shares of Capitol stock of the State Bank of Virginia) dau. Virginia, and dau. Henrietta (the two youngest children), son Daniel (land in Livingston Co., Ky.), son Henry (place I now live on), son Edward Gray Bedinger (4 shares of the capitol stock of the Bank of Chillicothe and all lands belonging to me in the State of Ohio); wit: Henry Botcher, Jacob Beadinger and James Brown.

BERGER, PETER, (B-37). Of Hamilton twp. Dated Oct. 4 1837. Prob. Dec. 30, 1837. Mentions—Son Joseph Berger (all real property in Hamilton twp. and all coming from his mother's legacy from her father. Jacob Cershant or Cershaw's estate in New Jersey) and dau. Rachel; executor: son Jasper Berger; wit: John Berger, Cornelius Van Camp and John L. Low.

BOGART, EZRIEK, (B-38).

CHAIN, MATHEW, (B-39). Of Madison twp. Dated Mch. 16. 1838. Prob. May 8, 1838. Mentions—Wife Catherine, son William P., son Joshua W., dau. Hannah M. Chain, dau. Catherine Chain (all under age of 21); friend Alexander Woodbury to be guardian of my sons and wife Catherine to be guardian for my daus.; executors: wife Catherine and friend, John Courtright; wit: James Suddick and Jacob Clickinger.

ABSTRACTS OF WILLS, FRANKLIN COUNTY, OHIO

Compiled by BLANCHE TIPTON RINGS

KILBOURNE, HECTOR, (B-42). Of Huron county, now in Columbus, Ohio. Dated Mch. 18, 1836. Prob. Dec. 30, 1837. Mentions—Father-Col. James Kilbourne of Worthington, step-mother Mrs. Cynthia Kilbourne, Lincoln Kilbourne, Lorita Buttles, Susan Adams, Myra Fay, John Hart, Harriet Githere, Ann Brown, Dorrance Matthews, Fritz James Matthews, Ellin Matthews, Haven Cowls, Cynthia Cowles, bro. Byron, cousin Sally Meeker of Ross county, Douglas Case, bro. James, sister Cynthia Jones, sister Lucy Matthews, sister Laura Cowls, Orril Whiting; executors: Matthew Matthews, Arora Buttles, R. W. Jowels, Esq.: wit: J. Morrison and James A. Frayer or Frazer.

Note: Signing that Lucy Matthews is deceased and left heirs, Dorrance, FitzJames and Ellin Matthews; as her surviving children were the following: Thomas Wood, M. Matthews, Cynthia Cowls, Havens Cowls, A. Buttles, Harriet Buttles, R. W. Cowles, Laura Cowles, J. M. Whiting, Orrel Whiting and Byron Kilbourne.

STARR, JOHN, (B-44). Of Montgomery twp. Dated Oct. 30, 1834. Prob. Mch. 6, 1838. Mentions—Wife Betsy Starr (farm we now reside on in Montgomery twp,) eldest son John Haven Starr, second son Joseph Ruese Starr, third son Simeon Chester Starr (a minor), fourth son William, fifth son Calvin, eldest dau. Betsy Humphrey, second dau. Sophronia Harris, third dau. Lorinda Wildbohr or Wildbohn, fourth dau. Lucinda Starr, fifth dau. Emily Starr (a minor), and sixth dau. Mary Jane Starr (a minor); executors: sons John Havens Starr and John Ruese Starr; wit: G. McCormick, J. C. Broderick, W. T. Martin, E. Backus and R. Neil: wit. to codicil John C. Broderick, Elijah Backus, John Wilson and Robert Neil.

Note: requests that his executors purchase for each of his eleven children, one Bible worth $4.00 to $5.00 apiece and one Confession of Faith of the Presbyterian Church. Also bequests to my six daughters all property or money that may come to my estate from the estate of J. Wood, dec'd.

WAGNER, JACOB, (B-46) (of Madison twp.) Dated Jan. 1, 1838. Prob. May 22, 1838. Mentions—Eldest son James, dau. Catherine Wagner (a minor), son George Wagner (a minor), son David Wagner (a minor), dau. Harriet Wagner (a minor), son John, son-in-law Samuel Horlocker, son Abraham Wagner, to United Brethren in Christ one quarter of an acre of a square lot of land to be taken out of the south west corner of the first above mentioned parcel for the purpose of a meeting house on which said church now stands provided always that if the said James and Abraham be dissatisfied with the above conditions and felt unwilling to comply therewith, then said parcel to be sold by executors and be divided equally between all the heirs and is sold the said Samuel Horlocker to hold peacable possession of his lease until Apr. 1, 1842: executors: Samuel Horlocker and son James Wagner: wit: John Hoover, Samuel Hoover and Daniel Swickard; he appoints Daniel Swickard and Abraham Wagner as guardian of all his children under age.

SMITH, ABRAHAM, (B-48). Of Perry twp. Dated July 26, 1837. Prob. Sept. 18, 1837. Mentions—Wife Sally Smith, adopted child Sally Ann McBurney, and adopted child Guyony McBurney: executors: wife Sally Smith and Peter Mills, Jr.: wit: Moses Wiswell, Peatt F. Sisco, Peter Mills, Jr., and Emial Cook; in codicil "I will that one-half acre of land should be reserved of my above alluded to for a family burying ground being whereon some burials have taken place and I hereby bequeath unto all my brothers and sisters and likewise my father equal right to bury thereon. Witnesses say that at time of of signing Abraham Smith was age of 40 yrs. or upward. Note: This was known as the "Smith Cemetery" but has been destroyed by the late owners.

McCREA, JOHN B. B-50 and again B-99. Of Ballston, County of Saratoga, State of New York, but now of Columbus, Ohio; dated Oct. 10, 1836; prob. Nov. 19, 1839. Mentions: bro. James McCrea, Jr., sister Catherine M. McCrea, bro. Stephen McCrea, father James McCrea, mother Anna McCrea (everything in trust, the income to be used for the support of my father and mother and at their death to go to my two brothers and sister); executor: bro. James McCrea, Jr. and sister Catherine M. McCrea; wit: Anson Brown of Ballston Spa, Saratoga Co., New York and Margaret Williams of Ballston Spa, Saratoga Co., New York, and Mary McCrea Williams of Ballston Spa, Saratoga Co., New York and Sarah Matilda Sargent of Newburgh, Orange Co., New York. Codicil 1: Edward Butcher who resides with mv father. Codicil 2: my cousin Susan McCrea Wilkinson who resides with my father and mother to have $25.00. Wit: Joshua Marshall of Columbus, John Stump of Columbus and Z. Everett of Columbus.

HIGGINS, SAMUEL, SR. B-52. Of Prairie twp.; dated Jan. 14, 1838; prob. June 2, 1838. Mentions: wife Harriet Higgins, dau. Betsy Higgins, dau. Sally Hunter, son Samuel Higgins, sister Susan Reynolds, grandson Samuel Townsend Hickman, grandson Samuel Foster, grandson Charles Hunter, grandson Samuel Clark Higgins, grandson Richard Hickman, son Charles Higgins, dau. Emily Hickman, (the land formerly occupied as a homestead), grandson Tobias Hickman and dau. Eleanor Hickman (the farm called the Manning farm); executors: wife Harriet Higgins and nephew Clark Higgins; wit.: Peter Clover, Solomon Clover and Aron Clover.

BERTSCH, MATTHIAS. B-54. (of Hamilton twp.); dated Oct. 4, 1837; prob. Sept. 18, 1838. Mentions: wife Sarah Bertsch to have the farm where we now reside and all else but if she remarry, it is to come to my heirs, our children (*children not named*); wit: John M. Schrock and Thomas Wood.

LATHAM, WILLIAM. B-54. (Of Columbus); dated July 28, 1838; prob. Sept. 18, 1838: wife Keziah Latham to be sole legatee and executor; wit: P. B. Wilcox and Elizabeth Anderson. (See will of Keziah Latham-C-148) Adm.: Keziah Latham, Jacob Hare and David Smiley.

MONTGOMERY, JOHN. B-54. (Of Clinton twp.); dated Sept. 8, 1838; prob. Sept. 19, 1838; wife Elizabeth to be sole legatee and executor; wit: Joseph Pegg and Matilda Pegg. Note: (Order Bk. 9-75 sys: Joseph Pegg, a citizen of Franklin county swore that John Montgomery, a Revolutionary pensioner, died at his residence in Franklin County on Sept. 12, 1838, leaving Elizabeth Montgomery, his widow and relict.

ROSS, ROBERT. B-56. Of Brown twp; dated Sept. 17, 1838; prob. Sept. 20, 1838; wife Lydia Ross to have all real and personal estate; sole executor: Israel Brown; wit: Lewis A. Burd (Bird) and Joshua Carter of Prairie twp.

FISHER, EPHRIAM. B-57. Of Norwich twp.; dated Nov. 16, 1838; Elias, son William, dau. Elizabeth Stranahan, son Ephriam Henry prob. Dec. 13, 1838. Mentions: wife (*not named*), son George, son Fisher, dau. Catherine Fisher, son Joseph Harvey Fisher, dau. Mary Louisa Fisher, son Andrew Jackson Fisher, and dau. Margaret Fisher; executor: my especial friend Miskell Saunders; wit: Benjamin Scofield and Elvinah Scofield. Note: Ephriam Fisher mar. (1) Catherine Pegg; (2) her sister Margaret Pegg, daus. of Elias Pegg, a Revolutionary soldier.

COONROD, WOOLRY. B-58. (Of Jackson twp.) ; dated Dec. 19, 1838;
prob. Jan. 25, 1839; wife Elizabeth Coonrod, dau. Elizabeth, dau. Mary,
(son Jesse is deceased the estate to go to his three children) ; executors:
sons James Coonrod and Jacob Boror; wit: John Mitchell and Moses
Purcell. Note: Jesse Coonrad died intestate abt. Nov. 16, 1838, left
widow Martha and dau. Nancy aged 2 yrs., son Woolry aged 3 yrs.
and George W. aged 1 yr. James Coonrad left Mary E. aged 7 yrs.,
Catherine aged 6 yrs. and Henry W., aged 3 yrs.

WASHBURN, ALFRED. (In the Index but signed JACOB by him).
B-59. Of Blendon twp; dated May, 1835; prob. Mch. 18, 1839. Mentions: Wife Abigail Williams Washburn (all land in Blendon twp.
and also land in Springfield, Windsor Co., Vermont, until the three
children be of lawful age, dau. Emeline Washburn, dau. Donna Maria
Washburn and son Henry Clinton Washburn; wit: Isaac Griswold,
Joseph P. Eblen and William Schrock. In proving will the witnesses
say that Washburn was of age 40 yrs. or upward.

DEMOREST, GILLIAM. B-59. (Franklin twp.) ; dated Dec. 19, 1838;
prob. Mch. 25, 1839. Mentions: wife Leah Demorest (the farm on
which I now reside during her life time and as long as she is my widow and at her death to go to my children, the sons to have twice as
much as my daughters; wit: Jacob Neff and Edward McMahon.

WIGDON, WILLIAM. B-60. (Of Franklinton) ; dated Mch. 13, 1839.
Mentions: wife Jane Wigdon, sister Hannah, sister Jane; ex: Gus-
tavus Swan; wit: Reuben Golliday, Thomas O'Hail, Nelly O'Hail and
Robert Young. Note: On back of will is a notation that Joseph Wig-
don, Roseville Post Office, Muskingum County, is a brother of
William Wigdon.

GRAHAM, JOHN. B-62-67. Of city of Richmond, Va.; dated July,
1820; codicil Sept. 21, 1820; prob. Oct. 26, 1820. Mentions: Mrs. Dun,
wife of my nephew Walter Dunn of the State of Ohio; to John Brown
son of John Brown; slave Jasper to be emancipated; freedman Reuben
Price; slave Lucy, the cook and her five daughters, Aggy, Jenny, Betsy,
Fanny and Marianni, together with a circle of their children as shall
not exceed four years may be sold to whom they choose; to Robert
Chappel, son of the late Robert Chappel of the county of Lunenberg,
Va.; to Avry Williams, female; to Thomas Mach who is near 3 yrs.
old and who resides with Mrs. Smith, widow of William Smith of
Orange county ($150) per annum for his maintenance and education
till he reaches the age of 14 yrs. and after that he is to get $250 per
annum for same) : to Margaret Glen who is about four months old
and resides with Mrs. Eliza Glen of Orange county in whose care she
was put by me (is to have $120 per annum for maintenance and
education till she reaches age of 14 yrs., then she to get $200 per
annum for the same till age of 21 yrs.) ; to nephew Walter Dunn; to
David (or Daniel) Call; to my nephew John McMuntrie, son of my
sister Christian Graham, widow of Hugh McMuntrie of Port Glasgow,
Scotland; to my sister Elizabeth Graham, widow of James Dun of
Kelsyth, Scotland; to sister Jean Graham, widow of Robert Wilson of
Banton, near Kelsyth, Scotland; to issue of deceased sister Helen Gra-
ham, widow of Pathick Hutcherson of Paisley in Scotland; executors:
Walter Dun and Robert Dun; wit: A. P. Uplher, Joseph May, Jer. and
Manon; in codicil disposes of slave William, son of Aggie; wit. to codicil:
William McKenzie, John Gordon, Robert Bell; recorded at Frankfort,
Ky., Sept 24, 1821.

DUN, WALTER. B-69. Of Fayette county, Kentucky; dated July 24,
1837; prob. Aug. 7, 1838. Mentions: wife, (not named), bro. George
W. Dun, to my five children namely: Mary Anderson Dun mar. to J.
R. Tompkins, eldest son John Graham Dun, second son James Dun,
third son Walter Angus Dun and fourth son Robert George Dun; executors: brothers John and George W. Dun, and sons John Graham and

James Dun; wit: M. S. Scott and James A. Gunstead. He says "If I die at home I wish to be buried on the land where I now reside and a stone to be laid over my grave with my name, age and time of my death engraved upon it." Note: He also owned land in Madison county, Ohio.

JOHNSON, JOHN. B-74. Of Jefferson twp; dated June 11, 1839; prob. July 2, 1839; states he has already disposed of all his real estate. Mentions: friend Job Ayres (to have the household furniture and farming utensils, and animals and money; Isaac Baldwin, nephew (one mare named Kate) and to my other nephews and nieces, $15 to be equally divided among them; executor to be my trusty friend Job Ayres; wit: Susan Ayres, Ezekiel Whitehead and Jesse Squire.

GOULDEN, JOHN. B-75. Of Logan county, Ohio; dated Apr. 1, 1839; prob. Apr. 5, 1839. Mentions: son John, dau. Sarah wife of Alfred L. Williams, and her heirs; son-in-law, John Drake; son Thomas; son-in-law George Witcraft; executor: son Thomas and son-in-law George Witcraft; wit: C. H. Austin and Obediah Johnson.

SCHMIT (Schmidt), WILLIAM. B-76. Of Montgomery twp.; dated Oct. 26, 1839; prob. Nov. 6, 1839. Mentions: wife, Rebecca Schmidt; (the farm in Holmes Co.); nephew, William Georgii, (who is now living with me, son of Frederick William Georgii of Wirtemburgh, payable to the order of his father and at the discretion of my bro. and trustee, Christian Schmidt of Holmes Co.); to Pauline Jaeger, an orphan girl, now living with me and to my children the residue of my estate (children not named); to Rev. John Wagenhals of Lancaster; trustee: bro. Christian Schmidt of Holmes Co.; wit: Lewis Heyl and Charles Jucksch. Note: William Schmidt had a seminary in Columbus, Ohio.

HARRIS, VALENTINE. B.-78; dated June 15, 1839; prob. Sept. 30, 1839; gives to friend, William Williams all real and personal property and he to be executor; wit: Joseph Sullivant and George Davidson.

BECKET, HHMPHREY. B-78 and C-386. Of Pickaway county; dated Aug., 1833; prob. Sept. 24, 1839. Mentions: dau. Martha Becket (all my part of bond held by my attorney in fact, Garland Garth of the County of Albemarle, Virginia on John Jones of aforesaid county to be put into the hands of my son Wiley Becket to buy land); son Wiley, dau. Jemima Churchman, son William, son Winston, son Richard, son Nelson, son James, son Ansel, son Bland; executor: son Wiley H. Becket; wit: Joel Burnley of Darby twp. and J. W. Burnley; codicil in Washington twp., Franklin county, revokes that son Wiley H. Becket be executor and appoints his dau. Patsy Becket in his place; wit. to codicil: Smith Dulin and Anna Dulin.   Note: At time of his death was living with his dau. Jemima Churchman in Washington twp.; is buried near Dublin, Ohio and was a Revolutionary soldier.

ABSTRACTS OF WILLS, FRANKLIN COUNTY, OHIO

Compiled by BLANCHE TIPTON RINGS

DE WOLF, JAMES. B-81-94. Of Vastine, county of Bristol, State of Rhode Island and Providence Plantation, Esq.; prob. July 11, 1839. Mentions: wife Ann De Wolf (the lot I purchased of Lemuel C. Richmond, called "Fox Hill"); son William Bradford De Wolf; bro. William De Wolf, deceased; son James De Wolf, Jr. (land at Louisville, Kentucky); children of my deceased dau., Mary Ann Sumner, late wife of William H. Sumner, Esq. (land in Dighton Cotton Mills and Iron Works establishment in the State of Massachusetts); late bro. Charles De Wolf; son Mark De Wolf (estate on Island of Cuba called Meanaima Plantation, 35 miles west of the City of Havana); son William Henry De Wolf; dau. Harriet Hall, wife of Jonathan Prescott Hall, Esq. (estate in New York City); dau. Nancy B. Homer, wife of Fitzhenry Homer, Esq. (the estate from his wife's father, James De Wolf Neith); infant grandson, James De Wolf, only child of my late son Francis L. B. De Wolf, deceased; dau. Catherine De Wolf, wife of Joshua Dodge, Esq. and dau. Josephine; wit: Levi De Wolf, Byron Dinsan and Martin Bennett.

PHELPS, EDWARD. B-94. Of Blendon twp.; dated Aug. 25, 1834; prob. Sept. 8, 1840. Mentions: wife Azubah Phelps, son Edward, son William, son Homer M., dau. Azubah Phelps, dau. Lucinda Williams, dau. Cloe Gillispie; wit: Rhoda Lee, James Taylor and Timothy Lee. Note: In proving will witness said he was 60 years and upward.

GREGORY, MRS. MARY. B-96. Of City of Columbus; dated Oct. 15, 1840; prob. Nov. 16, 1840. Mentions: eldest dau. Ellen Gregory, dau. Mary, dau. Emily, dau. Virginia, son Charles; my mother, Mrs. Eliza Gregory to be guardian of my children and she to erect a tombstone for my late husband and myself; late husband, Edward N. Gregory; executor: Noah H. Swayne, Esq.; wit: Nehemiah Gregory and C. C. Scheffield. Note: All children are minors under age of 15 years.

RONEY, JAMES. B-98. Of Perry twp.; dated Nov. 6, 1840; prob. Dec. 30, 1840. Mentions: dau. Margaretta Robinson Roney, dau. Eliza Ann Roney, dau. Rachael Marie Roney (*a minor*), son Isaac Henry Jared Roney (*a minor*), son James Hamilton Roney (*a minor*), son John Milton Roney (*a minor*); executor John Kenney of Perry twp. and he is also to be guardian of children; wit: Andrew Lytle and Robert Crooks. He also makes notation that the executor is to purchase a tombstone to be erected for himself and wife and child.

HART, THOMAS. B-104. Late of Berlin; dated July 7, 1831 and Oct. 2, 1832; prob. Aug. 7, 1839. Mentions: Amos Hart, son of my bro. Elihu Hart, deceased; Jonathan Hart, son of my bro., Elihu Hart, deceased; Elizabeth Hart, dau. of I. B. Hart, deceased; Maria Hart, dau. of I. B. Hart, deceased; Jonathan Thomas Hart, son of Eli B. Hart, deceased; Gideon W. Hart, son of my bro. John Hart, deceased; Joseph G. Hart, son of my bro. John Hart, deceased; (Gideon W. and Joseph G. Hart are to have all my share in land granted to my bro. Jonathan Hart in Ohio as military bounty and given him by Congress); Lydia Hart, dau. of my bro. Ebenezer Hart, deceased (all my land in Connecticut); niece Lydia Hart of Berlin and Seth Stanley of Berlin to be executors; wit: Seth Stanley, Sally Stanley, and Deibez Cornwell.

EVANS, CALEB. B-106. Of Norwich twp.; dated Dec. 23, 1839; prob. June 23, 1841. Mentions: wife (*not named*), son Jacob, dau. Elizabeth, dau. Polly, dau. Martha, son Peter, son David, son George, son Abel, son Alexander (the last five sons have had their share); executor: Isaac Davidson; wit: William S. Bowling (also Boaling and Boling) and

Daniel D. Lattimer.   Note: Buried in an old abandoned cemetery in Norwich twp. we find the following inscription on markers:
"Caleb Evans died Apr. 10, 1841, aged 75 yrs."
"Eve C., wife of Caleb Evans, died Nov. 9, 1847, aged 81 yrs."

WALKER, DAVID. B-107-113. Of Juanita, county of Mifflin ' of Pennsylvania; Esq. to my grandchildren, Jane Walker, Eliza Walker and David Walker, and Polly Templeton, wife of Samuel Templeton, the children of my son, James Walker, deceased; to grandchildrn David Stewart, William Stewart, Eliza Stewart and Polly (Mary) Walker Stewart, the children of John and Elizabeth Stewart; to dau. Anny Black, wife of William Black; to dau. Margaret Stinson, wife of Thomas Stinson; to dau. Jane; to great grandson, Wilson Lukens; to Samuel Riddle's son; states he owns land in Franklin county, Ohio; executor: John Stewart, Esq. of Walker twp., County of Mifflin, State of Pa. or John Banks of Mercertown and county of Mercer; signed Aug. 27, 1829; prob. Sept. 6, 1831. He mentions William Black and James Johnston in will; witness: Thomas White and Ephriam Banks; Andrew Banks appears in Formanat county, now Juanita county and says that John Stewart is dead and by his will left all his land to David and William Stewart; recorded in Franklin county, Ohio, Sept. 27, 1831.

BABCOCK, NATHANIEL. B-113. Of Washington twp.; dated Mch. 6, 1835; prob. Sept. 25, 1839; wife Rachel Babcock, son Jacob, dau. Rosemanly, son Ira, son Erastus, son Roswell, dau. Elizabeth, dau. Olive, dau. Wealthy, dau. Cynthia, executor: son-in-law, Noah Smith. Note: Nathaniel Babcock was a Revolutionary soldier and is buried at Dublin, Ohio.

BRAYTON, GEORGE. B-115. Of Wester, county of Oneida, New York; dated Feb. 8, 1837; prob. July 31, 1837 at Rome, New York; certified copy in Franklin county, Ohio, Nov. 21, 1840. Mentions: oldest son Henry, second son Milton, dau. Sarah Boardman wife, of George S. Boardman, grandson George Brayton Boardman, dau. Cynthia Innis, wife of John B. Innis, son George, Jr., son Isaac, dau. Susan Whipple Brayton, son Edward S., dau. Anna S. Brayton, wife Sarah Brayton; executors: three oldest sons, Henry, Milton and George; wit: Harvey Utley or Vitley, Freedom French and Henry W. French.   Note: Henry Utley or Vitley says Brayton died the last of Feb. or first of March at Western, N. Y. and Henry W. French says he died in March.

HART, MOSES. SR. B-119. Of Norwich twp.; dated Aug. 2, 1841; prob. Sept. 29, 1841. Mentions: son Joseph Hart in Norwich twp., son Moses, son John, wife Elizabeth Hart (son John to provide for her), grandsons: John Preston Hart, Moses Washington Hart, and William Madison Hart, sons of my son Valentine Hart; grand dau. Jane Trafsar, dau. of my son Valentine; dau. Elizabeth Cryder and her children Moses and Johnson Cryder, and dau. Mary Jane Cryder; dau. Polly Hart; executor: son John Hart; wit: Miskell Saunders, Abram Sells and George W. Hyde.

DAVIS, EDWARD. B-120. Of Columbus; dated Dec. 14, 1840; prob. Oct. 4, 1841; wife Mary Ann Davis to have all and to be executor; wit: William W. Backus and Alexander Backus.

WINFIELD, RICHARD. B-121. Of Columbus; dated Sept. 15, 1841; prob. Sept. term 1841. Mentions: wife Celia Winfield, son Alfred, son Richard, dau. Maria, son John, son Frank, dau. Eliza Winfield, (a minor); executor; Anthony Baird and Hanson Johnson; wit: William T. Martin, John Witsell and William Sharp.

CLOVER, JOSHUA. B-122 and 126. of Prairie twp.; dated June 14, 1841; prob. Oct. 4, 1841; wife Rachel Clover, eldest son Solomon, second son Orin, third son Zebulon, fourth son George M., fifth son Joshua, dau. Mary, dau. Rachel, dau. Milla Jane Miller; executor: wife Rachel Clover; wit: Warren Frazell, Solomon Clover and Aaron Clover.

295

SEEDS, JOHN. B-123. Late of Jackson twp.; dated Sept. 14, 1841; prob. Sept. term, 1841; wife Elizabeth Seeds (the plantation on which we now reside in Jackson twp. of 200 acres), youngest child, Elizabeth, (a minor), eldest dau. Mary, eldest son James, second dau. Nancy; executor: Adam Gantz; wit: John Gantz and Jacob Dove. Note: The witnesses say testator was about 50 years old.

STRICKLAND, NANCY. B-128. Late of county of Bradford, Pa. but now of Franklin county, Ohio; dated Sept. 18, 1841; prob. Sept. 30, 1841. Mentions: eldest son Stephen Strickland; grandchildren, (all minors), children of my son Amos Strickland and Emily, his wife.(the eldest son is Orlando and the other children all minors and appoints William Casidy of the county of Sanbanen and territory of Iowa to be in charge of the money); dau. Joannah Bayley; dau. Nancy Miles; dau. Rodah Reynolds dau. Polly Reynolds; executor: David Smiley of Franklin county and he is to get Nathan C. Wilcox of Bradford county, Pa. to assist him in anything in Pennsylvania; wit: Nathan Wilcox and Peter Strickland. Note: David Smiley charges $5.00 for burying Nancy Strickland in his own burying ground. Nathan Wilcox refused to serve therefore Edward Overton, Esq. of Pa. was appointed executor.

WHITE, SAMUEL. B-129. Of Franklin twp.; dated Oct. 30, 1841; prob. Dec. 13, 1841. Mentions: dau. Elizabeth White, son George W. White, son Alexander White; executor: Son Samuel M. and son William White; wit: George W. House and Manuel Alkire.

HENDERSON, ALEXANDER. B-130. Of Clinton twp.; dated Sept. 3, 1842; prob. Nov. 16, 1842. Mentions the following heirs: Alexander Fulton, Samuel Fulton, David Fulton, James Fulton, John Curry (his heirs by his first wife Elizabeth Henderson), Elias Hinkle, Margaret Robo or Robb, Anne Thompson, Harriet Hinkle, Robertson J. Hunter (his heirs by Margaret Fulton), James Fulton, (son of Eliza Fulton), James Fulton son of Hughey Fulton, John Anderson (belonging to and of the Reformed Presbytery of North America to dispose of for the use of the church) Samuel Henderson, Robert Wilson, James Smith; wit: Washington Lakin, Aaron Mathes and Jacob Slyh.

WILSON, JOHN. B-131. Of Columbus; dated Mch. 25, 1837; prob. Nov. 20, 1841; wife Margaret Wilson, son Thomas M. Wilson (a minor), dau. Ann Wilson (a minor); wit: Moses H. Kirby, Sr., Matthew Whitworth, John Chestnut and Robert Cutler.

BISHOP, SAMUEL. B-131. Of Madison twp.; dated Apr. 14, 1842; prob. June 14, 1842. Mentions: wife Mary Bishop (to have home farm; son Samuel C.; grandsons Adam and John Bishop, sons of my son, John Bishop, dec'd.; sons of Mathia W. and William W. (to have the land in Alleen county); dau. Patience Young; dau. Rebecca Groom; dau. Sarah Ann Bishop; son Wesley Bishop; executor: friend Thomas Hughs; wit: Alexander Cameron and Riley Gilbert.

HAVELY, ADAM. B-133. Of Madison twp.; dated Apr. 9, 1842; prob. May 6, 1842. Mentions: wife Emily Havely; son Adam, Jr.; (the farm on which we now live); son Samuel D.; dau. Rachel Rarey; dau. Martha Havely; grandchildren: Malachai, Margaret and William Peer, children of my dau. Elizabeth, deceased; (all minors) step-son, John Broshes; executor: friend Alexander Cameron and son Adam Havely; wit: Jesse Wilton and Moses Seymour.

THOMAS, GEORGE. B-135-146. of New York City; dated Sept. 23, 1829. Proven May 7, 1840; Ex: John Jenks Thomas of New York City; mentions: Isaac Fitz as special guardian for George Thomas, (minor), residing in New York City; Hannah Huntington, wife of George Huntington; James S. Thomas; Sarah A. Thomas, widow of Daniel Thomas, residing in the village of Rome in the State of New York; Henry Thomas, George Thomas and Joseph Thomas residing in Norwich in State of Connecticut; William Thomas residing in the town of Urbana, Ohio; James Thomas, George Henry Thomas, Elizabeth Thomas and Mary Ann Thomas residing in the City of Columbus, Ohio; William Thomas and

Frances Thomas whose residence is unknown; (These are the next of kin of George Thomas deceased by proving of will).

CUSHMAN and CASHMAN, MARY. B-147. (Of Hamilton twp.); dated Nov. 5, 1842; prob. Feb. 21, 1843; dau. Popann Smith and her husband William Smith; son Samuel Cashman; wit: Samuel Shannon and John Shoaf; executor: William Smith.

BUTCHER, WILLIAM. B-147. Of Columbus; dated June 16, 1842; prob. July 9, 1842. Mentions: youngest son George Nicholas Butcher and requests that Dr. Wheaton take him and raise him till he is 21 yrs. old; dau. Harriet Butcher and requests that Ormel Sherwood raise her till she is 18 yrs. old; dau. Mary Butcher and equests Dr. Wheaton to raise her till 18 yrs. old; son Robert Butcher; executor: nephew William Butcher; wit: Lyne Starling, Jr. and Lucretia Chavers.

LINE, PETER. B-149. Of Madison twp.; dated Mch. 11, 1840; prob. Feb. 21, 1843; dau. Polly and heirs by her first husband, George Sparr, and no other heirs whatever; dau. Catherine, wife of Amanuel Harmon, her heirs by him and no other heirs whatever (Amanuel Harmon to have none of my estate in his hands in his life time, to dispose of in any way whatever); wit: Henry Dillinger and Martin Fairchild; all real estate and personal property to be divided equally between my children.

EVANS, JOHN W. B-150. Of Columbus; dated Mch. 31, 1843; prob. May 11, 1843. Mentions: John W. Evans (my nephew), son of James Evans, he being a minor; wife's niece Sarah Hanover, dau. of Joseph Hanover, late of Delaware county, deceased; executor: wife Sarah Evans (she to have all during her life); wit: W. T. Martin and Jacob Rickets. Note: Sarah Evans mar. Asa Walling Sept 12, 1844 and she reports on estate Oct. 20, 1848 as "Sarah Walling, late Sarah Evans".

End of Book B.

VAN HORN, WALTER, (C-1). Of Columbus. Dated July 16, 1847. Proven Oct. 20, 1847. Mentions: sister, Elizabeth Moore, wife of James Moore of Indiana; niece, Eliza Kelly, wife of James F. Kelly and her children. Executors: W. T. Martin of Columbus. Witnessed by Charles Knoderer and J. D. Pounds.

HOUSEMAN, DANIEL, (C-2). Of Franklin County. Dated Sept. 16, 1847. Proven Oct. 28, 1847. Mentions: wife, Mary Jane Houseman and five children, as follows: George W, Ann Maria, Charles F, Jane Elizabeth and Mary Emma Houseman. Witnessed by Samuel Black and Nathan Cole.

WAGNER, LOUISA, (C-3). Of Plain Twp. Dated Oct. 28, 1846. Proven Oct. 25, 1847. Mentions: husband, George Wagner (the land in Plain Twp. wherein Francis Clymer was complanent and William S. Clymer, et al, were defendants. No executor named. Witnessed by W. T. Martin and Daniel Barnhart.

SMITH, JOHN J. (C-4). Of Franklin County. Dated May 5, 1844. Proven Oct. 28, 1847. Gives all to his daughter Sarah and she to be executor. Witnessed by Nathan Spencer and Jacob Smith, Jr.

GRISWOLD, RUTH, (C-5). Of Worthington. Dated June 13, 1834. Proven July 22, 1847. Mentions: eldest daughter, Ruth Andrews; youngest daughter, Harriet Burr; grandson George Henry Warren ("the lot in Worthington where I now reside and the brick house erected by my late husband, Ezra Griswold"): eldest son, Ezra Griswold; second son, George Harlow Griswold; daughter, Melissa Howard. No executor named. Witnessed by Victor M. Griswold of Delaware County, George C. Rosett of Delaware County and John Millikan.

WINDERS, ARAMINTA, (C-7). Of Baltimore County, Maryland. Dated Oct. 1, 1844. Proven Feb. 15, 1845. Mentions: four daughters, namely: Mary Stoughton Winders; Sally Rogers Winders; Araminta Sidney Winders and Lydia Hollingsworth Winders; John W. Ward and Thomas A. Emory. Witnessed by Michael Alder, William T. Smith and H. C. Trumbull. Codicil dated Jan. 7, 1845, says that if all daughters die without leaving children, then the principal and residue are to go in trust for Elizabeth Taylor Winders, widow of Edward Winders, the brother of "my" deceased husband, William Sidney Winder. Witnessed by T. Hanson Belt, Henry McElderry and Isaac G. Roberts. Copy in Franklin County, Mch. 4, 1845.

SLAUGHTER, SMITH, (C-14). Of Jefferson County, Virginia. Dated Dec. 22, 1823. Proven Aug. 23, 1834. Frees the following negroes: Jack; Coll; John or Jack; Austin; William Tyler; Mandeville Tyler; Lucy; Agnes and all her increase; James W; Ester's young one whose name is unknown to me; Jenny (sometimes called Bett) with her two children; Presley S. Henry; Nancy and Matilda, the daughters of negro Lucy, who died this fall; $100 is to be paid to them immediately so as to remove them to Scioto, Ohio State and his wagon and horses and 200 acres of land in that country, to them and their heirs forever; the land in Jefferson County is to be sold to John Yates; also Hambleton Jefferson is to have $100 to buy a mourning rug, or otherwise; to his brother, Benjamin Jefferson, $100 to buy a mourning rug or otherwise and his watch; to his sister, Catherine Slaughter Whiting, $50 for the same purpose; to John Robinson Whiting, $100 for the same purpose; Mrs. Jefferson is to have bed, bed stead and all furniture belonging with the draws in his room with all that is in them; the deed of trust from John Taylor to him and Mr. Thomas Griggs, Jr. Esq. as trustees for a tract of land lying near Kable Town for &1700, one half due to Hambleton Jefferson, deceased' heirs; "therefore it is my desire that they should be sold and be equally divided among the heirs of Thomas Slaughter" "these are to receive one fourth part, namely: Polly Slaughter, Jean Slaughter, Faney Slaughter and Milly Akleberger's heirs, if any, and if none, then to Mary Nooe's heirs, namely: Mary Nooe, Nancy Smith Nooe, Charles Nooe and Alexander Nooe; to Gabriel Slaughter's heirs, namely Mary Slaughter and Frances Slaughter; "I give or lend to Thomas Whiting, and after his death, to his son, Smith Slaughter Whiting, to him and his heirs, 100 acres of land lying in Scioto County, the balance of that tract I give to said negroes as before mentioned". Executors: friend, Thomas Griggs and Hambleton Jefferson. Proven by the oaths of Daniel Morgan and James L. Ransom. Copy at Franklin County, Oct. 22, 1847.

HOPKINS, SARAH ANN, (C-16). Of Madison Twp. Dated Jan. 24, 1848. Proven Mch. 2, 1848. Mentions: mother, Ann B. Stevenson; Joshua Stevenson and he to be executor. Witnessed by Joseph Wright and Johannes Alspach.

BYNNER, EDWARD, (C-17). (Of Brown ·Twp.) Dated July 1, 1847. Proven Feb. 19, 1848. Mentions: son Thomas ("the farm where I now live"); son Robert; son John; daughter Susan; daughter Maria; daughter Sinah; grandson Edward Williams; grand daughter Margaret Williams; daughter Jane; daughter Eliza. Executor: sons Thomas and Robert. Witnessed by Thomas Wood and Samuel T. Barnes.

SPANGLER, MARGARET, (C-18). Widow of David Spangler, deceased. Dated Feb. 5, 1848. Proven Feb. 6, 1848. Gives all to her son, Philip. No executor named. Witnessed by J. F. Hildreth and Nicholas Katzel.

OGDEN, SAMUEL, (C-19). Of Franklin Co. Dated Nov. 18, 1847. Proven Feb. 11, 1848. Gives all to his wife, Rachel Ogden. No executor named. Witnessed by John Kitsmiller and Thomas Young.

SMITH, WILLIAM, (C-20). Of Madison Twp. Dated May 24, 1847. Proven Feb. 28, 1848. Mentions: wife, Jane Smith; grand daughter, Christena Thompkins, formerly Christena Scothorn; the five following children of my daughter, Mary Scothorn, deceased, namely: Anna, Sarah, Eliza, William and Abraham Scothorn; son Abraham; son Isaac; daughter Eve Smith; son William; daughter Sarah; son John; dau Christiana; son Adam; son Jackson. Executor: friend, Jacob Bishop. Witnessed by G. T. Wheeler and Peter Bott.

DODGE, LYDIA, (C-22). Of Dublin, Washington Twp. Dated Nov. 9, 1842. Proven May 15, 1848. Gives all to her son, Holcomb Tuller and he to be executor. Witnessed by Mary E. Graham and Daniel Wright.

ELLIOTT, ELIZABETH, (C-23). Of Jackson Twp. Dated Mch. 5, 1848. Proven May 15, 1848. Gives all to her brother, Chapman Elliott. Witnessed by Joseph M. Paxton and John McDaniel.

HAUGHN, PETER, (C-24). Of Franklin County. Dated Sept. 26, 1846. Proven May 13, 1848. Mentions: wife, Mary Haughn; daughter Elizabeth Chambers, wife of William Chambers; and the heirs of his deceased son, Samuel Haughn. Executor: son-in-law, William Chambers. Witnessed by W. T. Martin and B. F. Martin.

LATHAM, BELA, (C-25). Of Columbus. Dated Apr. 8, 1848. Proven May 18, 1848. Mentions: wife, Rosanna Latham; son William A; daughter, Mary C. McKee; son Milton S; son James H, a minor; son Allen, a minor; son Edward H, a minor; son Frank B, a minor; nephew Arthur Latham. Executor: brother Allen Latham and friend, David V. Deshler. Witnessed by Robert H. Thompson and William H. Latham. Requests that brother Allen Latham be guardian of his minor children.

RAREY, WILLIAM, (C-27). Of Madison Twp. Dated May 6, 1848. Proven May 10, 1848. Mentions': wife, Rachel Rarey (the land bequeathed to me by my deceased father, Charles Rarey, Sr); son George Washington Rarey, a minor; daughter, Cynthia Limpert, wife of Casper Limpert; daughter Mary Ann Rarey; daughter Amanda Rarey, a minor. Eyecutors: B. F. Gard and Charles Pontius. Witnessed by B. F. Gard, Parker Rarey and William H. Rarey.

SCHWARZ and SCHWARTZ, HENRY, (C-31). Of Franklin Twp. Dated Jan. 8, 1848. Proven May 22, 1848. Mentions: wife, Katherine Schwartz and she to be guardian of all the children. No executor named. Witnessed by Jacob Adams, John Schwartz and Nicholas Hanover.

BURT, CHRISTOPHER, (C-32). Of Hamilton Twp. No date of signing. Proven May 13, 1848. Mentions: daughter Elizabeth Burt; Sarah Throgmorton; Maria Johnson; Hannah Bennett; Brewer Burt; John Burt; Thomas Burt. Executor: daughter Elizabeth Burt. Witnessed by John Mitchell and Alice Ann Triplett. At time of proving Alice Ann Triplett is Alice Ann Shacklett.

JOHNSTON, JOSEPH C., (C-33). Of Union County. Dated Feb. 28, 1848. Proven May 10, 1848. Mentions: wife (not named); son John; son George; son Clark; daughter Electa Johnston; had recently bought a farm in Franklin County. Executor: Peter Johnston. Witnessed by Peter Johnston and John Johnston to codicil. Witnessed by Christian Myers and Isaac Anderson to will.

SHANNON, SAMUEL, (C-35). Of Franklin County. Dated Feb. 28, 1848. Proven Mch. 18, 1848. Mentions: nephew, James N. P. Shannon; sister, Sally Shannon; nepher, Samuel P. Shannon; neice, Odessa Shannon; brother William; Robert B. Shannon. Executors: brother, William W. Shannon. Witnessed by W. T. Martin and John Kerr.

BIGGERT, JOHN, (C-37). (Of Pleasant Twp) ; Dated June 11, 1836. Proven June 21, 1848. First codicil, Mch. 29, 1842. Second codicil, Nov. 16, 1843. Mentions: wife Margaret Biggert; son John; daughter Charlotte; daughter Rachel; daughter Matilda; daughter Margaret; grandson, John Forgason and grand daughter, Mary Forgason (are to have all the land in Franklin and Madison Counties that he had bought of Allen Latham); son William son Samuel; son Joshua. Witness to will: Robert Armstrong and Lewis Mille; to first codicil: S. Brush and Columbus B. Guthrie; to second codicil: S. Brush and William Baldwin. In proving of will, it is stated that C. B. Guthrie was then of New York City.

PIERCY, JAMES, (C-40). Of Franklin County. Dated Sept. 15, 1839. Proven Oct. 23, 1848. Mentions: wife, Sally Piercy; "the remainder of the estate to be divided equally between the lawfully begotten heirs of Sally Piercy and James Piercy, while living together in marriage, and all heirs before "our marriage" or after my death is not and should not inherit any of my estate except one should be born after my death that was begotten while we was living in marriage"; son John; daughter Nancy Piercy (the last two children are by his first wife, Eleanor Piercy). Executor: wife Sally Piercy and "some one else whom we may select." Witnessed by John Tusing, Henry Kistler and James Tusing. At time of proving will, Sept. 28, 1848, Henry Kistler was of Cass County, Indiana.

FREY, JOSEPH, (C-42). Of Franklin County. Dated Sept. 14, 1839. Proven Nov. 4, 1839. Mentions: first son (not named); second son Phillip; third son, Ludwig; fourth son, Johannes; fifth son, Ludwiner; sixth son, Heinrich. No executor named. Witnessed by Heinrich Lotz, Benedict Shlitt, Gotlieb Hinderer and August Machold.

PENTZ, WEIRICHF, (C-44). Of Franklin County. Dated Aug. 9, 1848. Proven Aug. 19, 1848. Gives all to his mother (not named). Witnessed by W. Whiting, Jr. and W. M. Smith.

Note: (Newspaper obituary: "First Lieut. W. F. Pentz, late of the Second Regiment O. V. died Aug. 13, 1848, aged 28 years") B. T. R.

BUNN, HENRY, (C-45). Of Madison Twp. Dated Mch. 16, 1844. Proven July 15, 1848. Mentions: wife, Elizabeth Bunn; daughters, Sarah and Elizabeth Bunn; son Frederick; daughter, Nancy Landes; daughter, Mary Sharp; daughter, Sarah Bunn; son Henry; daughter Elizabeth Bunn. States that he owns land in Marion County, Ohio. No executor named. Witnessed by Alexander Cameron and Jeremiah White. At time of proving will, Charles Pontius states that Alexander Cameron is now deceased.

WOLFE, ABRAHAM, (C-49 and 217). Of Blendon Twp. Signed at Columbus, Feb. 16, 1846. Proven Sept. 10, 1852. Mentions wife and heirs, altho he names none of them. No executor named. Witnessed by George Cullman and Windsor Atcheson.

SARBER, CHRISTIAN, (C-51). Of Madison Twp. Dated Jan. 25, 1847. Proven Oct. 5, 1848. Mentions: daughter, Mary Courtright, wife of John Courtright; son Leonard; son Jacob; son David; son William; son John. Executors: Leonard and David Sarber. Witnessed by Joshua Glanville and William T. Decker.

HEINRICH, JACOB, (C-52). Of Franklin County. Dated Sept. 26, 1844. Proven Oct. 27, 1848. Mentions: wife, Catherine Heinrich, formerly Kres, is to have every thing and she is to be executor. Witnessed by J. P. Bruck and John Kuenel.

ABSTRACTS OF WILLS, FRANKLIN COUNTY, OHIO
Compiled by BLANCHE TIPTON RINGS

STARLING, LYNE, (C-53). Of Columbus. Dated Mch. 31, 1837. Proven Nov. 24, 1848. Mentions: children of late niece, Susan Ramey; Edmund Starling, the son of brother Thomas; children of sister, Ann Hollaway, namely: John William, Rebecca Stites, Sarah Taylor and Lucy Ann Atkinson; owns land in Territory of Iowa, Missouri and Illinois; nephew, William Hollaway; children of neice, Sarah Taylor by William Taylor (not named); neice, Susan Ramey's eldest son (not named); brother William's children; Maria Campbell and Lucy Davison; nephew, William S. Sullivant, is to have the land in Marion and Crawford Counties for his four youngest sons (not named) and his eldest daughter, Jane Neil; nephew, Michael Sullivant is to have all the lands in Pickaway and Madison Counties; nephew, Joseph Sullivant's eldest and second daughter, who are unmarried (not named); nephew, Joseph Sullivant's three sons (the land in Franklin County called the Carlisle Tract); Joseph Sullivant's eldest son, Lucas Sullivant and his other two sons; children of sister Jane Davison, namely: William and Edmund Davison (to have the land in Indiana); James Smith, eldest son of John A. Smith of Highland County (land in Hardin County, called Wild Cat Lodge); Starling Price, eldest son of John M. Price of Highland County; William Starling, eldest son of Lyne Starling, Jr, of the City of New York and to Sullivant Starling, youngest son of said Lyne Starling, Jr; Edmund Starling, grandson of brother Edmund; eldest son of late neice, Susan Ramey; William Marshall, son of his neice, Sarah Taylor. Executors: John W. Andrews of Franklin County, Lyne Starling, Jr., of New York City and Wray Thomas of Franklin County. Neice Jane Smth, wife of John A. Smith of Highland County; daughter of said neice, Jane Smith, now living (not named); neice, Ann Price, wife of John W. Price of Hghland County; each of other daughters of Ann Price (not named); daughters of Lyne Starling, Jr. of New York City (not named); sons of late brother, William Starling, namely: William, John Madison and Edmund Starling (lands in the counties of Henry, Paulding, Van Wert, Wood, Ottawa, Lucas, Defiance in Ohio and in the State of Michigan and all purchased by him at land sales at Perrysburg or Defiance and entered at Land Office at Lima or Wapaughkonetta; sons of late brother, Edmund Starling, namely: William and Charles (the Conger farm in Franklin County); Madison Starling, as trustee for support of his brother, Samuel Starling; sister, Lucy Bell; children of neice, Susannah Loving, namely: Starling and William Loving; Mary Carter, eldest daughter of Dr. Frank Carter of Franklin County; Judge Bell, his brother-in-law, for the support of nephew, William McDowell; brother, Thomas Starling; Sally and Susan Starling, daughters of brother, Edmund Starling (all bank stock owned by him in the State of Kentucky); Lyne Starling, son of his brother, Edmund Starling; Edmund Starling, grandson of his brother, Edmund Starling; William Starling, son of Lyne Starling, Jr. of New York; Starling Sullivant, son of Joseph Sullivant; Sullivant Starling, son of Lyne Starling, Jr. of New York; nephew, John Madison Starling of Franklin County; nephew, James Smith, son of John A. Smith of Highland County; nephew Starling Price, son of John W. Price of Highland County. Executors: John W. Andrews of Franklin County or Joseph R. Swan. Witnessed by E. W. Gwynne, F. Stewart and Wray Thomas.

First codicil: William Sullivant's three daughters by his present wife (not named); cancels legacy to Jane Neil. Witnessed by E. W. Gwynne and F. Stewart.

Second codicil. Dated Dec. 27, 1847. Revokes bequest to the children of Susan Ramey; gives to Ladies Benevolent Society of New York. Witnessed by E. W. Gwynne, Wray Thomas and F. Stewart.

Third codicil: authorizes executors to assist in repairing substantially the family burial place of his late brother-in-law, Lucas Sullivant, in Franklinton, and to erect therein any suitable monument that they may think proper. Dated June 3, 1848. Witnessed by Wray Thomas and Francis Carter.

Fourth codicil: Dated Sept. 4, 1848. Son of Dr. Hughes who is a grandchild of sister, Jane Davison, and named after his grandfother, Elias Davison. itnessed by Francis Carter and J. R. Swan.

Fifth codicil: Oct. 20, 1848. Witnessed by Wray Thomas and F. Stewart. (A few minor changes made in will).

ARMISTEAD, ROBERT, (C-81). (Of Norwich Twp.). Dated Oct. 7, 1848. Proven Oct. 23, 1848. Divides his property between "all my father's children", namely: Mary Ann Moler; Joseph Armistead; Henry Armistead; William McKendree Armistead; Marie Armistead and the children of deceased sister, Sarah Brackenridge, who are William Robert Brackenridge, Joseph Henry Brackenridge and Mary Elizabeth Brackenridge. No executor named. Witnessed by Nancy Sells, Catherine Davis, Sarah Tuttle and E. M. Pinney.

WHEELER, HENRY F. (C-82). Of Columbus. Dated Apr. 4, 1848. Codicil Oct. 30, 1848. Proven Nov. 15, 1848. Mentions: wife, Jane Wheeler (if she dies or marries within three years of his death, the property is to go to his brothers and sisters). Executors: wife, Jane Wheeler and Dr. I. G. Jones of Columbus.

BRIGGS, JOHN, (C-84). Of Franklin County. Dated Oct. 11, 1847. Proven Oct. 24, 1848. Mentions: wife, Rachel Briggs; son Henry and daughter, Mary Lydia Briggs. Executors: wife, Rachel and son Henry Briggs. Witnessed by Stacy Taylor and Elisha Chambers.

SISSON, PELEG, (C-85). Of Columbus. Dated May 6, 1848. Proven Oct. 24, 1848. Mentions: wife, Eliza Sisson; son Francis; son George P; daughter Eliza; Thomas Sparrow is to sell certain lots and pay the money to daughter, Mary Sisson; son Charles; daughter, Martha Sparrow. Wife is to be guardian to George, Cornelia and Eliza Sisson. Thomas Sparrow is to be guardian to Francis and Mary Sisson. Executor: Thomas Sparrow. Witnessed by Joseph F. Smith and Joseph R. Swan.

BARR, JOHN, (C-88). (Of Franklin County. Dated Oct. 28, 1847.

302

Proven Mch. 23, 1849. Mentions: wife, Nancy Barr; son Samuel; daughter, Susan Vandemann; son Andrew who is now at Princetown Seminary to receive suitable Theological Education to prepare him for the ministry; daughter, Mary McIntire; son, Robert W., now at college in Tennessee studying for the ministry; son Thomas Gibson Barr. Executor: son, Thomas Gibson Barr. Witnessed by W. T. Martin and Samuel Crosby.

GRUBB. JACOB, (C-90). Of Franklinton. Dated Feb. 26, 1849. Proven Mch. 19, 1849. Mentions: wife, Martha Grubb; grand daughter, Mary Starling; grandson, Jacob Starling. Executors: wife, Martha Grubb and grand daughter, Mary Starling. Witnessed by Dr. Samuel M. Smith, Joseph Robinson and Harvey D. Broderick.

HOUSE, SARAH, (C-92). Of Franklin County. Dated Jan. 31, 1845. Proven Mch. 30, 1849. Mentions: son George (to have the family Bible); son William; grand daughters: Sarah Jane and Nancy W. Vanderburgh. No executor named. Witnessed by George Geiger, Jacob White and Benedict House.

GURNEE, JONAH, (C-93). Of the town of Haverstraw, Richland County, State of New York. Dated Feb. 1, 1847. Proven Mch. 16, 1849. Mentions: brother, Richard Gurnee; Ambrose Spencer Gurnee; mother, Sarah Gurnee; widowed sister, Melissa Barlow; brother William. No executor named. Witnessed by A. B. Wambaugh and Richard Page.

SIMMONS, MAGDALENA. (C-95). Of Columbus. Dated Mch. 25, 1848. Proven Mch. 29, 1849. Was formerly Magdalena Scharf. Gives all to her little daughter, Mary Simmons. at present about 15 months old that which she is expecting yet from Germany, namely, her heridatory portion of the inheritance of her deceased mother, Maria Eva Scharf, formerly Scherer, of Hagenbach, Landoommefzariah, Germersheim, Pfabzbaum: her father, Valentine Scharf at present living in Columbus and who has so kindly supported her during her last sickness; her husband, Peter Simmons, who did not pity her in her last sickness, who had left her and he is to be excluded from all participation of her heritage. Executor: father, Valentine Scharf. Witnessed by Michael Zehnacker and F. Gottlieb Hinderer.

WATKINS, ALDRIDGE, (C-98). Of Hamilton Twp. Dated Mch. 9, 1849. Proven Mch. 19, 1849. Mentions: wife, Clarissa Watkins; son Philo B; son Quincy A; son Aldridge; daughter Emmaline Watkins and daughter Madaline Merian Watkins. Executor: son Philo B. Watkins. Witnessed by William H Shannon and Philip Schwartz.

HALL, LURENY, (C-99). Of Franklin County. Wife of Solmon Hall, deceased. Dated Sept. 2, 1848. Proven Apr. 2, 1849. Mentions: son Francis to have all and he is to be executor. Witnessed by S. D. Preston and P. M. Wetmore.

JAMESON, ROBERT, (C-100). Of Blendon Twp. Dated Mch. 20, 1849. Proven Apr. 7, 1849. Mentions: wife, Betsy Jameson; son James W; son Wilson, a minor: had other children but does not name them. Executor: James W. J. Jameson or William Phelps. Witnessed by Timothy Lee and William Cooper.

ALLEN, SAMUEL, (C-102). Of Nicetown in the County of Philadelphia, Pennsylvania. "Gentleman". Died Oct. 24, 1848. No date of signing. Proven Nov. 4, 1848. Copy received here Feb. 26, 1849. Mentions: neice, Eliza A. Evans, now wife of Samuel R. Evans and formerly Eliza A. Climer; sister-in-law, Margaret Hall and her son, Thomas A. Hall, a minor. Executors: Samuel R. Evans and friend, George W. Thorn. Witnessed by Theodore Ashmead, M. D. and Jacob Slingluff.

SMITH, SYDNEY, (C-106). Of New York City. Dated Oct. 15, 1842. Proven June 9, 1849. Place money in trust for his sister, Nancy Harris, wife of Levi Harris, of New Berlin, Chenango County, New York and her daughter, Lucy Harris; nephew, Josiah Cleveland Cady of Providence, Rhode Island; the son of my deceased sister, Lydia (not named). If any of the above die, the money is to be divided between his friends Ralph Clark and Eneas Clark of New York City; gives to James Bogart Clark, Elizabeth B. Clark and Virginia Clark, the minor children of his friend Ralph Clark of New York City. Executors: Ralph Clark, Eneas F. Clark and William H. Bradford. Owned land in Brooklyn, New York. Witnessed by John H. Magher, Attorney, 208 Wooster Street; William H. Maxwell, attorney, 15 Whitehall Street and Henry Smith, 36 Hudson Street, all of New York City.

CLAPP, ABNER, (C-112). Of Sharon Twp. Dated Feb. 21, 1846. Proven June 5, 1849. Mentions: wife, Elizabeth Clapp and at her death is to go to following: son Ralph; son Arnold; and to James Armstrong and John Bodge as trustees for Evaline Clapp, wife of my son, Ela H. Clapp and at her death to go to her children: daughter Emily Rodgers; daughter Jennett Moore; daughter Lucretia A. Rodgers. Executor: son Arnold Clapp. Codicil dated Sept. 28, 1847. Witnessed will: John H. Andrews and J. R. Swan. Witnessed codicil; Joseph R. Swan and B. T. Cushing.

SISCO, MARY F., (C-116). Of Jefferson Twp. Dated Sept. 1, 1843. Proven June 5, 1849. Mentions: son Peter F. Sisco (to have the family Bible); daughter, Emeline F. Sisco (to have all returns from property of her late husband, deceased, now in the hands of Daniel Swickard, administrator of Peter F. Sisco, deceased); grand daughter, Delia Alberry. Executor: Peatt F. Sisco. Witnessed by Shuah Mann and Nathan Spencer.

O'FERRELL, JAMES, (C-117). Of Clinton Twp. Dated Apr. 20, 1849. Proven June 10, 1849. Mentions: wife, Catherine O'Ferrell, and if wife dies, is to go to the Roman Catholic Church of Columbus; Eli H. O'Ferrell. Executor: Andrew Wilson. Witnessed by Archibald Young and James Ferguson.

WAITS, WILLIAM, (C-118) Of Montgomery Twp. Dated July, 1848. Proven June 6, 1849. Wishes to be buried on his own grave lot north of Columbus by the side of his mother; brother James; daughter Mary; son James; daughter Eveline; son William. Executor: William T. Martin of Columbus. Witnessed by John Otstott and Frederick Benevoun.

HOUCHARD, JOHN CHRISTOPHER, (C-119). Of Franklin County. Dated Mch. 29, 1847. Proven June 15, 1849. Mentions: wife, Anaclet Houchard; daughter Agatha Mason; daughter Mary Bey; son Francis. Executors: wife, Anaclet Houchard and John Geary. Witnessed by John Geary and Richard H. Geary.

KOENIG, DANIEL, (C-120). Of Columbus. Dated July 25, 1849. Proven Aug. 8, 1849; proven by Dr. M. Shubert and P. Johnson. German and not translated.

GARD, B. F., (C-121). (BENJAMIN FRANKLIN GARD). Of Columbus. Dated July 11, 1849. Gives to adopted daughter of Mrs. Rebecca Wonderly, named Leona Taylor (all my right to a certain tract of land now in possession of said Rebecca Wonderly). Executor: Charles Pontius. Witnessed by William Miner and Robert Larimore.

BUERCK, BERNHARD, (C-122). Of Columbus. Dated Aug. 20, 1849. Proven Sept. 6, 1849. Mentons: wife, Maria Buerck; children, only two named are John and George, who are minors. Executor: wife, Maria Buerck. Appraisers are to be neighbors, George Hammell, Adam Luckhaupt and Louis Hoster. Witnessed by James H. Stauring, Clement Bahr and Andrew Lang.

WOLPERT, JOHN, (C-123). Of Columbus. Dated Aug. 24, 1849. Proven Sept. 6. 1849. Is written in German and not translated. Witnessed by Konrad Mees, Frederick Schmidt and George D. Fuchs.

CRAIG, DAVID, (C-124). Of Franklin County. Dated Oct. 4, 1849. Proven Nov. 17, 1849. Mentions: Amanda Rarey; Robert Fort; Rachel Rarey. No executor named. Witnessed by William H. McCarty, Parker Rarey and Thomas Hiles.

BUTTERFIELD, JOHN, (C-125). Of Columbus. Dated July 17, 1849. at Lowell, Massachusetts. Probated at Columbus, Ohio, Dec. 10, 1849 and proven at Lowell, Massachusetts, Dec. 18, 1849. Mentions: wife, Sarah Knapp Butterfield and she is to be executor. Witnessed by Elisha Huntington, George H. Carleton and A. H. Brown. Proven by Dr. Elisha Huntington, being 53 years old and of the city of Lowell, Middlesex County and by George H. Carleton of Lowell and by A. H. Brown, being 33 years old and of Lowell, Massachusetts.

GALE, EDGAR, (C-127). Of Columbus. Dated Jan. 20, 1849. Proven Sept. 18, 1849. Mentions: wife, Jane Gale; daughter Henrietta Elizabeth Gale, under 18 years sister Henrietta Elizabth Gale; adopted son, William Henry Harrison Calvert; adopted son, Jarvis Pinckney Calvert. Appoints his wife as guardian of his daughter. Executors: John Walton and Daniel Woodbury. Witnessed by James Aston and John Agler.

GREEN, ANDREW, (C-128). Of Columbus. Dated July 27, 1849. Proven Sept. 24, 1849. Mentions: wife, Sophia Green and at her death is to go to his children (not named). Executors: wife, Sophia Green and brother John Green. Witnessed by J. P. Bruck, Michael L. Zehnacker and N. Anthony.

Note: In settlement of estate gives widow and one child. By Jan. 27, 1854, the widow was married to Nicholas Herrman. (B. T. R.).

ABSTRACTS OF WILLS, FRANKLIN COUNTY, OHIO
Compiled by BLANCHE TIPTON RINGS

PUGH, EVAN (C-129). No date of signing; proven Sept. 22, 1849; mentions: daughter Sarah Pugh and daughter Mary Pugh (all to be equally divided between them; executor; William B. Jarvis, Jr.; witnessed by William Cain and David Davis.

WILSON, JOHN (C-130). Of Clinton Twp.; dated Sept. 28, 1829; proven Oct. 6, 1849; mentions: eldest son John; eldest daughter Martha Thompson; youngest son Andrew; wife Rachel Wilson; youngest daughter Mary Wilson; executor: son Andrew Wilson; witnessed by Elijah Collins and John Smith.

BAKER SILAS (C-131). Of Norwich Twp; dated June 6, 1849; proven Sept. 25, 1849; mentions: wife Rachel Baker is to educate Margaret Baker, daughter of Silas Baker, my son by Malinda Baker and if she dies the money is to go to the Trustees of the Colored Baptist and Methodist Churches of Columbus; he desires to be buried in the old graveyard in Springfield, Ohio "next my children buried there" and requests that Lorenzo D. Taylor and Hanson Johnson attend to this; witnessed by Henry C. Noble, Henry Barrett and Lewis Washington; executor: Wray Thomas.

ROSE, AARON (C-132). Of Jefferson Twp; dated Aug. 28, 1847; proven Mch. 11, 1850; mentions: Stephen G. Rose is to have half of Military lands in Jefferson Twp., and also the money due me from Elijah Mott, living in Deerfield Twp., Portage County; Matilda Spencer; Philip Rose; no executor named; witnessed by Shuah Mann and Benedict Brown of Union County at Richwood. Administrators appointed were Stephen G. Rose, Phillip Rose and Joseph Huffman.

McCORMICK, GEORGE (C-134). Dated Nov. 24, 1846; codicil May 25, 1847; proven Apr. 13, 1850; mentions eight children, namely son Francis Asbury; son Martin Hamilton; son George; son William; daughter Mary High, wife of Hosea High; daughter Eliza Crum, wife of Francis A. Crum; daughter Fanny Kelley; daughter Nancy Grant; executor: friend and relative, William Armstrong; witnessed by W. T. Martin and Goodale Armstrong; codicil witnessed by W. T. Martin and James Crum.

RATHBONE, JOHN (C-138). Of City, County and State of New York; dated Aug. 16, 1842; codicil Oct. 7, 1842; second codicil Jan. 17, 1843; proven Oct. 14, 1845; copy here Nov. 20, 1845; mentions: great grandson John Rathbone; daughter Content Cheesebrough; daughter Eunice Goddard and her four youngest children, namely: James E. Goddard, Inlieke Rathbone Goddard, George W. Goddard and Sarah Wills Goddard;; daughter Mary Rosalie Ruggles and such of her children as are living at her death; daughter Eliza Wetmore is to have the land on which Dr. Charles H. Wetmore now lives; son-in-law Robert Cheesebrough; son Hezekiah; son-in-law Samuel B. Ruggles; children of his deceased grandson, Edward Beverly Rathbone, namely: John, Caroline Lee Rathbone, Julia and Anthony Constant Rathbone, all minors; daughter Juliett Downer; daughter Emma Maria Rhodes; daughter Sophia Smith; deceased daughter, Sarah Downer's children, namely: Joshua, Sarah, and Emily Downer; daughter Clarissa Smith and at her death to go to such of her children as are living, except to Mary Stansbury; grandchildren: namely; Sarah Pettibone, Emily Andrews, Joshua Rathbone Downer, John Rathbone, Caroline Lee Rathbone, Julia Rathbone, Anthony Constant Rathbone; true and faithful servant, Diana Miller; executors: Robert Cheesebrough, Samuel B. Ruggles, William Kent, Esq., Edward R. Weston and Philip R. Kearney; witnessed by Joseph Brandegee, John B. Beck, Maltby Gelston and George Gibson, all of New York City.

HUNDT, JOHN (C-139). Of Columbus; dated Jan. 30, 1850; proven Apr. 2, 1850; mentions: wife, Ann Eliza Hundt; son John; son William; daughter Ann Elizabeth; son Frederick; son Henry; daughter Catherine Hundt; son Thomas, deceased; executor: son John Hundt; witnessed by J. P. Bruck and John Moehl.

SELLS, ELIUD (C-140). Of Dublin, Washington Twp., dated Aug. 14, 1849; proven Mch. 14, 1850; mentions: daughter Harriet; daughter Susan; daughter Lucy; son Franklin; son Eliud; daughter Betsy, a minor; executor: wife Polly Sells; witnessed by Charles E. Davis, Daniel Wright and Woodruff.

(Note: By marriage records Eliud Sells married his cousin Polly Sells.)

TAGERT, JOSEPH (C-141). Of Philadelphia, Pennsylvania; dated Sept. 28, 1846; codicil Aug. 19, 1848; proven Aug. 11, 1849; mentions: daughter Ann Monges?; daughter Maria McCauley; daughter Sarah Tagert; son Joseph; faithful servant Charles Francis; executors: Hugh Campbell of Philadelphia, Francis G. McCauley of Philadelphia and daughter Sarah Tagert; witnessed by W. Patton Jr., Joseph H. Smith and F. A. Vandyke, Jr.; in codicil says daughter Sophia has married James R. Campbell; son Joseph has retired from the firm of McAlpin and Tagert of New Orleans; daughter Ann is widow of late Aristides Monges?; Maria is wife of Francis G. McCauley; Sarah is unmarried; executor: son-in-law James R. Campbell; witnessed by Charles McKeone, Daniel J. Cochran and Benjamin Karrick.

FANCHER, JAMES (C-144). Of Columbus, but late of Illinois; dated Aug. 23, 1827; proven Feb. 8, 1848; mentions: adopted sister, Martha F. Cook (land in Missouri) and if she has no heirs, it is to go to the heirs of David S. Fancher of Franklin County; cousin Eliza Cook; no executor named; witnessed by O. P. Langworthy and Albert Langworthy; was late of Bureau County, Princeton, Illinois.

WINTERSTEIN, JOHN (C-147). Of Madison Twp., dated Dec. 12, 1835; proven Mch. 15, 1850; mentions: wife (not named); daughter Sarah Ann Kile; executor: wife and Thomas Patterson; witnessed by John Swisher and William D. Needles.

LATHAM, KEZIAH (C-148). Of Columbus; dated Dec. 28, 1848; proven Mch. 11, 1850; mentions: daughter Mary, wife of John O'Harra, deceased; son William; daughter Susan, wife of Uriah Stotts (the family Bible); granddaughters, Mary F. O'Harra and Susan O'Harra; grandsons William O'Harra and Henry O'Harra; executor: Arthur O'Harra; witnessed by G. Vandemark and George Krauss.

BROWN, JOSEPH M. (C-150). Of Columbus; dated Apr. 11, 1850; proven Apr. 29, 1850; mentions: wife Lucy R. Brown; children, Albert J. and James George Brown; executors; Robert George and wife Lucy R. Brown and she is to be guardian of their two children; witnessed by F. J. Matthews and C. A. Montrop.

FARIS, JAMES (C-151). Of Clinton Twp; dated Mch. 28, 1850;

proven June 6, 1850; gives all to wife (not named) and at her death is to go to the Missionary Cause of the Methodist Episcopal Church; executor: David Dill; witnessed by Henry Innis and Isabelle P. Innis.

Note. This is also spelled Ferris in many places.

DETRICH, ABRAHAM (C-152). Of Franklin County; dated May 26, 1850; proven June 24, 1850; gives all to wife Lydia Frances Detrich and she is to be executor; witnessed by Lorenzo English, A. S. Weaver, George R. Snow and Orrill Case.

KITTSMILLER, MARY (C-153). Widow; of Franklin County; dated Apr. 5, 1850; proven June 22, 1850; mentions: three daughters: Elizabeth, Mary and Christena; son Jonathan; executor: son John; witnessed by John Clark and Samuel Ogden.

STEVENS, JOHN (C-154). Of Washington Twp.; dated Oct. 16, 1849; proven June 4, 1850; mentions: wife Eliza Stevens; step-daughter Dorothy Gitchell; children by his present wife, namely: Emeline, Salisberry, Levi and Lucinda, all minors; children by his former wife, namely: Bentil, John, Willis, Sally Harrison, Rebecca Duncan, Mary Dennis, Ann Westenhaver, Clement Stevens, Horatio Stevens and Dorcas Ritchie; executor: wife Eliza; witnessed by Jacob Martin and Annie Pool.

TAYLOR, ISAAC (C-155). Of Columbus; dated July 19, 1850; proven Aug. 13, 1850; mentions: wife Mary; daughter Elizabeth Taylor; daughter Mary Wilson; sons John and William, deceased; son Obed; son Daniel; executor: George M. Parsons; witnessed by Daniel Evans and Harvey Coit.

MITCHELL, ANN (C-157). Of Columbus; is as follows "John K. Heyl and Maria Heyl were present during the last sickness of Ann Mitchell of Columbus on the night of July 30, 1850 and she said her sister Betsy was to have all the money due said Ann from her uncle, Christian Heyl, and the money in her chest was to go to the English Lutheran Church." Proven Journal Entry, Vol. 16, page 126; proven Aug. 7, 1850. (Note. Obituary reads: "Mrs. Ann Mitchell died July 30, 1850 of cholera, aged 50 years.")

BUTTLES, JOEL (C-158). Of Columbus; dated Apr. 18, 1849; proven Sept. 20, 1850; mentions: wife (not named) ; son Albert Barnes Buttles; daughters Sarah Phelps Buttles and Emma Buttles, minors; requests that Thomas Moodie, Demas Adams, Jr. and I. G. Jones be guardians for his two daughters; and to hold property as stated, in trust for benefit of son Albert; daughter Eveline, wife of Thomas M. Gwynne land in Williams Cuonty, Ohio and in State of Missouri; son Lucian; 'friend and cousin', Cephas Buttles, who now lives on the land in county of Milwaukee, Wisconsin; executor: Lucian Buttles; witnessed by Charles T. Flowers and Frank K. Hulbard.

WILSON, JAMES C (C-162). Of Clinton Twp; dated June 19, 1850; proven Sept. 30, 1850; mentions: wife Catherine Wilson who was a Gridley before her marriage; two sons, James C. and Cloys B. Wilson; grandchildren: James, Antennet and Wilson Beach, minors; executors: Selah A. Bacon of Clinton Twp. and son David Wilson, now living in Illinois; witnessed by Burton Gardner and Polly Gardner.

ABSTRACTS OF WILLS, FRANKLIN COUNTY, OHIO
Compiled by BLANCHE TIPTON RINGS

CRUM, CORNELIUS (C-164) Of Norwich Twp. dated Aug. 15, 1850; proven Sept. 17, 1850; mentions: wife Margaret Crum; son David S.; son William A.; daughter Rebecca T.; daughter Sarah S.; owns land in forks of Scioto and Whetstone River and also land in Huntingdon County, Pennsylvania; executors: son David S. and daughter Margaret; witnessed by James Gray and Arnold Clapp.

SHOTTS, CHARLES (C-165). Of Columbus:; dated Aug. 2, 1850; proven Sept. 30, 1850; gives one half of all to Charlotte Boos and one half to the Methodist Episcopal Church; watch and chain to Rev. Conrad Gahn; executor: friend and brother, Michael Decker; witnessed by Henry Snider and Mary Capella.

WERT, JACOB. (C-166) Of Groveport. Signed Jan. 9, 1849. Proven Nov. 6, 1850. Mentions: sister Lydia Houck; sister Mary Ameltzer: sister Catherine Welmer; sister Rebecca Brown; only brother Michael Wert who lives at Moulton, Alabama. Mother, Mary Wert; mother-in-law Eliza A. W. Ferguson; wife Julia Wert. Executors: William W. Kile and D. R. Ferguson. Witnesses by M. D. F. Bywaters and M. E. A. Ferguson.

BROOKER, THOMAS (C-167). Of Blendon Twp. dated Oct. 15, 1850; proven Nov. 6, 1850; gives all to his wife, Elizabeth Brooker and at her death is to be equally divided between his natural heirs (not named); executor: Elias Tippy; witnessed by Allen Hickok and Y. W. Durant.

NEFF, ISAAC (C-168). Of Prairie Twp. dated July 7, 1841; proven Nov. 18, 1850; mentions: wife Phebe Neff; three youngest children, namely: Prudence,: Hyram and (can't read) Neff; son Leonard; daughter Dorothy Bivans; son (can't read) daughter Eveline Neff; daughter Elizabeth Neff; daughter Phebe Ransbottom; executor: wife Phebe Neff; witnessed by William M. Scott and Martha Scott.

SAENGER, ANDREASS (C-170). Is in German and not translated. Proven Nov. 6, 1850 by Michael Pickel, Catherine Pickel and Sebastian Bauer.

DAGUE, DANIEL (C-172). Of Plain Twp; dated July 16, 1850; proven Nov. 23, 1850; mentions: wife Susanna; sons Daniel and Benjamin; eldest son Peter; second son Levi; third son George; eldest daughter Elizabeth Dague; second daughter Katherine Dague; fourth son Edward; executors: sons George and Levi; witnessed by Michael Katterman and John Starrett, J. P.

TUSSING, NICHOLAS (C-173). Of Madison Twp; dated July 16, 1849; proven Dec. 4, 1850; mentions: wife Margaret; son John; son J. J.; son George N; daughter Christena Harris; son Adam, a minor (land in Ft. Wayne District, Huntington County, Indiana); son Philip; son S. C.; executors: W. W. Kile and Frederick Swisher; witnessed by William Rower and James Rower; at time of proving will William Rower lives in Putnam County, Ohio.

GRAY, THOMAS, SR. (C-176). Of Madison Twp. dated Feb. 27, 1850; mentions: wife Harriet Gray, from whom he is separated, who is to have $50 per annum as decreed by the Supreme Court of the county; her children, namely: John, Mitchell, Eliza Ann and Wilson Gray; son Alfred Gray to have the farm where I now live; daughter

Rebecca Powell; daughter Harriet Milburn; son Jedediah (these last four are the eldest children); executor: son Alfred; witnessed by W. Kile and Edward Courtright.

FIELDS, HENRY (C-178). Of Columbus; dated Oct. 20, 1850; proven Oct. 25, 1850; all is to be divided equally between his wife, Sarah E. Field and son, Edwin R. Field; executors: brother Arthur Field of Roscoe, Coshocton County, Ohio and F. C. Kelton of Columbus.

GENKINS, ELIZABETH (C-179). Of Franklin County; dated Jan. 13, 1851; proven Mch. 20, 1851; gives all to husband, George G. Genkins, which is arising from her father or grandfather's estate; no executor named; witnessed by James S. Beatty and Zelotes G Waddle.

THOMPSON, SAMUEL. (C-180) Columbus. Dated Nov. 2, 1850. Proven Mch. 27, 1851. Mentions: wife Sarah Ann Thompson; nephew Samuel Augustus Decker. Executor: wife, Sarah Ann Thompson. Witnessed by Samuel M. Mills and Joseph F. Smith. Codicil of Jan. 24, 1851 makes William T. Martin to be co-executor. Witnessed by B. F. Martin and Augustus Platt.

NEEDLES, PHILEMON. (C-182) Of Madison Twp. Dated May 23, 1849. Proven Apr. 15, 1851. Mentions: wife Nancy Needles; daughter Rachel Needles; daughter Anna Gray; daughter Anny or Amy Swisher; son James; son John A; daughter Rebecca Daly; daughter Lucinda Keys; grandson Enoch A Needles, the son of Enoch Asbury Needles; the children of my daughter Anna Gray (who are minors); children of my daughter Lucinda Keys (who are minors); children of my daughter Anny or Amy Swisher who are minors; children of my daughter Rebecca Daly; to Thomas Moodie, Esq. money for the use of the Methodist Church in Delaware, Delaware County, Ohio; son Jedediah; four oldest children: namely: Alfred, Rebecca Powell, Harriet Milburn and Jedediah. Executor: son Alfred Needles. Witnessed by W. W. Kile and Edward Courtright.

DINGES, CATHERINE (C-184) Of Columbus. Signed July 16, 1850. Proven Mch. 25, 1851. Gives all to her husband, Hartman Dinges "All in the United States and out". Executor: Warner Heydt or George Krell or Edward Lilley. Witnessed by Konrad Mees and Konrad Hartman.

WELTON, JOHN (C-184). Of Madison Twp. Signed Dec. 16, 1850. Proven Jan. 8, 1851. Mentions: son Moses; heirs of son Jesse; dau. Annie Gebia; dau. Elizabeth Fruchey; daughter Jemima Welton, for whom John Seymour is to be guardian; daughter Selinda Reber; heirs of daughter Mary, formerly the wife of Jesse Seymour. No executor named. Witnessed by Moses Seymour and C. P. Dildine.

SAVELY, HENRY (C-185). Of Franklin County. Signed Mch. 12, 1851. Proven Apr. 26, 1851. Mentions: son Jacob is to have all of his clothes and those of his brother James, deceased; grand daughter, Mary Catherine Cales; grandson William Henry Cales, a minor; daughter Elizabeth Cales. Executor: Jacob Stanberry and he is to be guardian of the grandchildren. Witnessed by John Rathmell and Patterson Harrison.

MERRILL, LUCINDA M. (C-186) Of Columbus. Signed Mch. 21, 1844. Proven June 12, 1851. Mentions: daughter Pamela Trotter; daughter Mary Eliza Sullivant and her children. Executor: Son-in-law, Joseph Sullivant. Witnessed by Lyne Starling, Jr. and Francis Carter.

PETERS, SAMUEL (C-188). Of Franklin Twp. Signed Jan. 18, 1850. Proven June 7, 1851. Mentions: son Harvey; son Jonathan; daughter

Pamely Joseph; Wife (not named). Executor: son Harvey. Witnessed by George M. Peters, Hiram S. White and Henry N. White.

TIPTON, THOMAS (C-189). Of Columbus. Signed June 10, 1851. Proven June 16, 1851. Owns slaughter house and grocery store. Mentions: wife Elizabeth Tipton; son John; Elizabeth and Alfred K., the children of son John; Clara Celia Tipton and Jasper Jonathon Tipton, the children of son William; son Samuel; daughter Catherine, wife of Stephen Ewing; son John E. Owns lot in Green Lawn Cemetery and wishes for his first wife to be buried there, too. Executor: Han on W. Pollard. Witnessed by B. F. Martin and Augustus Platt.

BRUNK, DANIEL, SR. (C-191). Of Norwich Twp. Signed Mch. 24, 1851. Proven June 2, 1851. Mentions: son Samuel; son Daniel; daughter Susan Nelson, formerly wife of Robert Elliott, but now wife of James Nelson; Sarah, wife of Charles Fields; Margaret Aldrich and Eliza Elliott; Samuel Elliott; Jackson Elliott; Daniel Elliott and David Elliott, the children of Robert Elliott; the eight heirs of son Elijah Brunk (not named); Nathan E. Jacobs and Peggy, his wife; eldest daughter of Mary A. Aldrich, wife of Abraham Aldrich; two youngest sons of son Samuel (the land in the State of Missouri). Executor: Asa Davis of Norwich Twp. Witnessed by Thomas W. Dobbyns, John T. Britton and N. F. Britton.

MAHR, LUDWIG (C-192). Of Jefferson Twp. Signed May 15, 1851. Proven Aug. 11, 1851. Mentions: Elizabeth Mahr; wife Margaret Mahr born Schnur; son Philip (who lives in Jefferson County and is to take care of Elizabeth as long as she lives); son Christopher Ludwig Mahr; son Andreas who is married and lives in Fulton County, Illinois; daughter Anna Catherine, wife of Johann W. Miller in Lancaster, Ohio; daughter Margaretta, wife of Johann Zubrod in Columbus; daughter Maria, wife of Wendel Shrod in Fulton County, Illinois. No executor named. Witnessed by Adam Heintz, Johannas Osban and Ludwig Christopher Mahr.

ROWLAND, JOHN E. (C-195). Of Brown Twp. Signed July 23, 1851. Proven Aug. 11, 1851. Mentions: wife Elizabeth Rowland and son John Rowland. Trustees and executors: Francis Jones and David Edward who were also witnesses to the will.

SMITH, DANIEL (C-196). Of Blendon Twp. Signed Dec. 6, 1849. Proven June 21, 1851. Mentions: daughter Polly, wife of John Sherborn (the land he purchased of Joseph Getznetanner, upon which daughter Polly and husband now reside); Betsy and Lydia Sherborn, daughters of Polly Sherborn; grandchildren (not named, the children of daughter Betsy, deceased; daughter Catherine, widow of John Brown, deceased; daughter Peggy's heirs; and daughter Harriet, wife of Frederick Leaman. Executor: J. B. Connelly. Witnessed by Allen Hickok and Lewis Lake.

DAVENPORT, OBEDIAH, (C-197). Of Plain Twp. Signed Sept. 16, 1850. Proven Sept. term, 1850. Gives all to son William Davenport. Witnessed by Daniel Ealy and Daniel Neiswender. Charles Davenport appointed administrator.

ROBERTS, STEPHEN, (C-198). Of Franklin County. Signed Aug. 16, 1851. Proven Sept. 13, 1851. Mentions wife but does not give her name. Executor: Thoams Roberts is to be guardian of his heirs. Witnessed by Alexander D. Tucker and Maurice Evans.

311

ABSTRACTS OF WILLS, FRANKLIN COUNTY, OHIO
Compiled by BLANCHE TIPTON RINGS

BOWMAN, JACOB L. (C-199). Of the town of Lockbourne. Signed July 17, 1849. Proven Sept. 13, 1851. Gives wife, Sarah D. Bowman all and she is to be executor. Witnessed by A. N. Boalse and C. M. Porter. Proven by C. M. Porter at Lithopolis, Fairfield County, Sept. 13, 1851.

WHITE, CUMMINS, (C-201). Of Franklin County. Signed Oct. 1, 1851. Proven Nov. 28, 1851. Mentions: wife Julia C White and she to be executor; son Albert Sylvanus White; a minor. Witnessed by James Bloomfield, James Smith and Samuel Mills. Proven at Meigs County, Oct. 9, 1851, before Major Reed, J. P. of Migs County, appeared George White, father of within named Cummins J. White, now deceased and Samuel Mills as witnesses.

COROM, KEZIA, (C-203). A colored woman of Columbus. Signed Sept. 24, 1850. Proven Sept. 24, 1850. Mentions five children: Nancy, Margaret, Sarah, Mary Jane aand John Corom. Another daughter mentioned is Eliza Brown. Executor: friend Frederick Roney. Witnessed by William Preston and P. B. Wilcox.

GOLDSMITH, JOHN, (C-204). Of Columbus. Signed Sept. 1, 1851. Proven Feb. 3, 1852. Mentions: Thomas Harris; George Harris; Julia Edmonds Goldsmith; John Goldsmith, Jr.; William H. Goldsmith; Thomas Goldsmith, Jr.; Leah Goldsmith; Mary Jane Goldsmith; Eliza Emily Goldsmith. Executors: Adam Gantz and Abram Detwiler. Witnessed by William White and John D. Miner.

DANIELS, BRINKLEY, (C-209). Of Jackson Twp. Signed Aug. 25, 1851. Proven Feb. 10, 1852. Mentions: wife Jane and she to be executor; son John and his heirs. Witnessed by John Dunn and Abiathar Freeman.

HIGGINS, CLARK, (C-210). Of Columbus. Signed, no date. Proven Mch. 6, 1852. A verbal will by Clark Higgins who died at his home in Columbus states that he owes money to Harriet Higgins; that the estate shall be under the general direction of Francis A McCormick and John Greenwood to be administrators and to keep his market house estate; owns land in Illinois; owns land with Samuel Galloway and to let Galloway sell it; gives his watch to his son John as it was put "in my hands for that purpose by his grandfather." Witnessed by Samuel McClelland and Ezra Martin.

SPENCER, ANN MARIA, (C-211). Of Jefferson Twp. Signed Oct. 29, 1851. Proven Apr. 7, 1852. Gives her husband, Asa Spencer, all her interest and inheritance in her father's estate; to wit: Daniel Houseman, Lot 220 in city. Executor: husband Asa Spencer. Witnessed by Shuah Mann and Nathan Spencer.

BROWN, PETER, (C-212). Of Fairfield County. Signed Aug. 15, 1849. Proven Apr. 12, 1852. Mentions: wife Catherine Brown; sons John, Charles and Peter (who own land in Van Wert County, Ohio); son Levi; daughter Julian Guildner; granddaughter Mary C. Ingham and grandson Simon Young, a minor. No executor named. Witnessed by Henry Harmon and J. B. Evans.

EVANS, JAMES, (C-213). Of Plain Twp. Signed Dec. 22, 1851. Proven June 15, 1852. Mentions: wife (not named); daughter Mary

Evans; son Mark; son John Wesley and daughter Caroline Evans. Executor: Samuel Evans. Witnessed by Daniel Hamaker and James Wagner.

SNOW, JOHN, (C-214). Of Worthington. Signed July 11, 1846. Proven June 16, 1852. Mentions: wife Mary Snow; two sons, William T and and George R. Snow and grandchildren (not named). Executors: wife and two sons. Witnessed by Isaac Thompson, Charles Willey and Elias Lewis.

McMILLEN, GEORGE, (C-215). Of Columbus. Signed July 16, 1852. Proven July 30, 1852. Mentions: wife Nancy McMillen; Daughter Margaret M McMillen, for whom Otis Patten is to be guardian; says he has six children; namely: Susan, wife of Otis Patten; son William L; daughter Elizabeth, wife of Charles M. Stone; daughter Margaret; a minor; and daughter Nancy, a minor. Wishes his land in Cass County, Indiana to be sold. States that he wishes the remains of his first wife and of deceased daughter, Belinda, be removed and reburied on the same lot as himself in Green Lawn Cemetery and that his second wife be buried on the same lot. Executors: Samuel Galloway of Columbus and Samuel W Hibben of Highland County, Ohio. Witnessed by Thomas F. Jones and W. T. Martin.

(Note: Obituary from newspaper: "George McMillen died in this city July 25, 1852. He was born April 5, 1801 in Perry County, Pennsylvania; removed to Ohio in 1807 with his parents who settled in Highland County; resided there till 1846 when he came to Franklin County. He was Superintendent of the Blind Asylum.")

ARNELL, DAVID R. (C-216) Late of Columbia, Tennessee, but now of Columbus, Ohio. Signed Aug. 5, 1852. Proven Aug. 27, 1852. Gives all to his brother William H Arnell and he is to be executor. Witnessed by Thomas Sparrow and John Morrison.

GOODSON, GEORGE, SR. (C-218). Of Harrisburg, Pleasant Twp. Signed Sept. 27, 1851. Prven Oct. 16, 1851. Mentions: Wife (not named but is Rebecca Goodson) son George; grandchild Lucius Moorhead Morow and his heirs; grandchild Rachel Blare and her heirs; grandchild N. W. Goodson and his heirs; Elijah Stone, a minor who lives with me. No executor named. Witnessed by William Walker and Joseph B Mitchell.

ZUPP, JACOB, (C-220). Of Franklin County. Signed Feb. 17, 1851. Proven Sept. 3, 1852. Mentions: wife Margaret Zupp (all real and personal estate) youngest daughter Julia Zupp; daughter Catherine Miller. Executor: Nicholas Katzel or Frederick Schmidt, Jr. or J. P. Bruck. Witnessed by J. Feshoy, John Zettler, Peter Boehm, Charles C. Traunaker and Edward J. Lilley.

BUTCHER, MARY F. (C-221). Of Columbus. Signed July 24, 1852. Proven Sept. 14, 1852. Gives to her beloved friend, Mrs. Lucretia Shackleford, all her right in the undivided half of the east half of Lot 496 in Columbus and she is to erect a suitable monument at my grave. Witnessed by A. B. Wombaugh and Joanna Leach.

KITTSMILLER, EMANUEL, (C-222). Of Franklin County. Signed Aug. 5, 1852. Proven Oct. 2, 1852. Mentions wife Catherine Kittsmiller and son William. No executor named. Witnessed by G. W. Butler, M. Street and Phebe Morris.

ADRIANCE, CHARLES, (C-222). Late of Bridgeport, New York, but at time of signing was a merchant in New York. Signed Sept. 2, 1847. Proven at Bridgeport Jan. 25, 1849. Recorded in Franklin County Oct. 5, 1843. Mentions Wife Phebe; daughters Margaret Smith Adri-

313

ance, Louise and Helen Adriance; son Charles Edward Adriance, a minor; mother (not named); nephew Charles the son of Theodore Adriance. Executors: Theodore Adriance, Samuel L. Mitchell, James D. Adriance and Cornelius Smith. Witnessed by Charles H. Wildenning and Isaac Adriance, both of New York.

ARMSTRONG, JOHN O. (C-226). Of Newark, Licking County. Signed Feb. 23, 1852. Proven Mch. 8, 1852. Mentions: wife Katherine Armstrong; daughter Isabell Moore and her children (to have the farm where I now reside). These grandchildren are John Armstrong Moore, Charles Lee Moore, Martha Jane Moore and Sarah Katherine Moore. Gives to John Armstrong Moore, a minor. Executor: son-in-law A. J. Moore. Witnessed by George D. Graham and William Goldrick.

STARLING, SUSAN L. (C-227). Of Henderson, Kentucky. Signed Sept. 6, 1852. Proven Sept. 28, 1852. Gives all to her father, E. L. Starling and he to be executor. Mother is Ann Maria Starling. Witnessed by T. J. Hopkins and William B Holloway.

FLINTHAM, WILLIAM, (02448). Of Columbus, but on a visit to Philadelphia County, Pennsylvania. He states that he has something coming to him from the estate of his grandfather, Thomas Bradford, deceased, who owned land in Beaver County, Pennsylvania, of which his uncle, Thomas Bradford is executor. Appoints his friend Abraham Rutter of Philadelphia as his executor. Mentions wife and children but does not give their names. Signed July 18, 1850. Proven Nov. 27, 1850. Witnessed by Margaretta F. How and John Mackey. Copy at Franklin County Feb. 19, 1851.

Note: Administrator appointed was Ann Flintham, widow of deceased.

ROBERTS, JOSEPH (C-228). Of Columbus. Signed July 22, 1852. Proven Oct. 26, 1852. Gives the lot of ground opposite the Catholic School House at corner of Fifth Street to his sister, Anne Roberts. now living in New York at 135-12th Street. Executors: brother Marcus Roberts and Rev. James Meagher. Witnessed by Michael Coffay and William Bergin.

FERGUSON, ROBERT. (C-230). Of Franklin County. Signed Sept. 3. 1852. Proven Nov. 3, 1852. Mentions Wife, Elizabeth Ferguson and that the children are to be schooled. Wife to be executor. Witnessed by Jacob Slyh and John Kenny.

LEGG, ELIJAH. (C-231). Of Perry Twp. Signed July 1, 1847. Proven Nov. 3, 1852. Mentions: heirs of son Fielding; daughter Mary Walcutt; son Thomas, Daughter Elizabeth Wiley; Daughter Susannah Walcutt; daughter Lucinda O'Harra; son John; son James. Executor: son James. Witnessed by John Kenny and James Kenny.

GROOM, MOSES (C-332). Of Madison Twp. Signed Nov. 1, 1852. Proven Nov. 8, 1852. Mentions wife and four children (not named) and that his brother Thomas is to maintain their mother. Administrators: wife and C. P. Dildine. Executor: C. P. Dildine. Brother Thomas to be guardian of the children, or his nephew John F. Groom. Witnessed by Henry Long and Daniel E. Russell.

FRIED, GEORGE. (C-233) Of Columbus. Signed Feb. 7, 1852. Proven Nov. 12, 1852. Mentions: wife Anna Maria Fried: children, namely: Lena Kolbenstaetter, Catherine Fried, son Jacob, daughter Anna Maria Fried, and son Christian. Executor: wife Anna Maria Fried or Phillip Schoedinger or Herman Steiner. Witnessed by Wilhelm Keiser, J. Jacob Schulz, B. Distelzweig and Ed. Lilley.

PHIPPS, MARY ANN (C-236) Of Truro Twp. Signed Aug. 28, 1852. Proven Nov. 23, 1852. Gives her husband the house and lot where they now reside in Truro Twp. No executor named. Witnessed by Barnabas Harris and Robert Edwards.

(Note: In the record book this is given as "Nancy Ann Phipps" but the original has "Mary Ann Phipps".)

WELLES, JOSEPH. (C-237) Of Montgomery Twp. Signed Nov. 19, 1845. Codicil Apr. 1, 1846. Proven Dec. 3, 1852. Mentions: wife is deceased; son Joseph N.; daughter Maria; daughter Abigail; daughter Jane E.; daughter Clarissa; son Samuel; daughter Delia, wife of Dr. Weaver; daughter Lucy Welles; daughter Susannah; daughter-in-law, Susannah Welles, widow of his son Edwin, deceased. Executor: Susannah Welles. Witnessed by Robert Thompson and W. T. Martin. Witnesses to codicil: W. T.: Martin and Frederick Ottstott. At time of proving of will, Daniel Otstott says he is well acquainted with the signature of Frederick Otstett and that he is now on the Pacific Coast of America and that he may never return and probably not for some years.

(Note: Obituary from newspaper "Joseph Welles died at his residence near Columbus, Nov. 13, 1853, aged 68 years and was formerly of Glastonbury, Connecticut" and "Mrs. Lucy Welles, consort of Joseph Welles died in Columbus, Aug. 13, 1841, aged 64 years.")

ABSTRACTS OF WILLS, FRANKLIN COUNTY, OHIO

Compiled by BLANCHE TIPTON RINGS

HUMPHREYS, CHAUNCEY (C-241). Of Columbus. Signed July 30, 1851. Proven Jan. 3, 1853. Mention: Wife, Amanda Humphreys. Sons, Lewis, Leonard, Lucrius (*last two are minors*). To son Lewis the pew in the Universalist Church of Columbus. Executors: Son Lewis, and P. B. Wilcox. Witnessed by P. B. Wilcox and D. H. Taft.

TAYLOR, JAMES, (C-243). Signed Dec. 18, 1844. Probated July 14, 1852 at Georgetown, Ky., was presented. The executor James Taylor appeared. Appointed as appraisers were John D. White and William P. Allen. Calls him 'General James Taylor, deceased'; the widow, Keturah L. Taylor. Proven by Samuel Winston, John H. Thornton, and R. T. Thornton. First Codicil, Dec. 6, 1847. Second Codicil July 1, 1848. Witnessed by Samuel Winston and John B. Rose. Owned real estate in Covington and Newport, Ky., in Ohio and in Indiana. Mention: son James; Daughters: Keturah, Ann W., and Jane. Also 'land which his father had patented'. At the time of proving these appear as heirs: James Taylor, Horatio T. Harris and Keturah L., his wife; John W. Tibbetts and Ann W., his wife.

WESTWATER, JOHN, (C-275). Of Columbus. Signed Nov. 3, 1852. Proven Jan. 11, 1853. Mention: Son William and his heirs. All arrangements are to continue the same in the firm of J. Westwater and Son Company, which governed the stock in 1844. Son James M., to be executor. Witnessed by Thos. S. Aston and James D. Aston.

KENT, MARGARET, (C-277). Of Columbus. Signed Mch. 22, 1847. Proven Jan. 24, 1853. Mention: Daughter-in-law Mary F. Kent; Son Columbus W. Kent to be executor. Owns land in city of Baltimore, Md. Witnessed by Lorenzo English and Jacob Zellers.

FIELD, ARTHUR, (C-279). Of Franklin County. Signed Jan. 10, 1853. Proven Feb. 12, 1853. Mention: Wife Mary Louisa Field and mother or her heirs (*not named*). Executor: F. C. Kelton. Witnessed by John Field and H. H. Kimball.

SAMUELS, JOHN, (C-279). Of Brown township. Signed May 25, 1850. Proven May 7, 1852. Mention: Wife; Sons, John, William R., Samuel, James C.; Daughter Maria Ferris; deceased daughter's Ann S. Rowland's two daughters. No executor named. Witnessed by John Harris, Sr., and John Harris, Jr.

BRINKERHOOF, BOLIVER, (C-282). Of Blendon township. Signed Jan. 24, 1852. Proven Mch. 25, 1852. Mention: Stephen, George, Uriah Brinkerhoof, the sons of Catherine Brinkerhoof. Executor Peter Westervelt of Blendon twp. Witnessed by N. E. Samis, C. L. Westervelt and Peter Westervelt.

CARTER, JOSEPH, (C-283). Senior, of Norwich twp. Signed Aug. 23, 1851. Proven May 14, 1852. Mention: wife, Mary Carter; son Benjamin; daughter, Maria Hyser, wife of John Hyser; son, William. States—"I have made application for my bounty land which I am entitled to under a late law granting land to officers and soldiers who have served during the war and if I get it, it is to go to my son Benjamin." Executor, John Geary of Washington twp. Witnessed by William Carter, Jr., and Henry Crawford.

GRAY, LITTLETON R., (C-284). Of Madison township. Signed April 6, 1852. Proven May 22, 1852. Mention: Wife Anna Gray; son Philemon; daughter, Epolda Marshall, wife of James H. Marshall; daughter Sarah Ann Gray; daughter Elizabeth Jane Gray; son Leroy S.; son James T.; daughter Clara Rebecca T. Gray. Executor son Philemon. Witnessed by W. T. Martin and William H. Chain.

RICHARDS, DAN, (C-285). Of Rome, Prairie township. Signed Jan. 22, 1853. Proven Mch. 1, 1853. Mention: Wife Lydia Ann Richards; daughter Mary Jane (minor), son William Samuel, (minor); son John (minor); guardian of the children, William W. Richards, grandfather. Witnessed by Smith Postle and William W. Richards.

(Note): Inscriptions in Clover Cem, "William S. Richards, son of D. & L. A. Richards, died Oct. 14, 1865, aged 15 years, 1 month, and 25 days", also "Dan Richards died Feb. 18, 1853, aged 39 years, 3 months, and 5 days. Born in Wales."

CASE, HARVEY, (C-286). Of Columbus. Signed Feb. 2, 1853. Proven March 23, 1863. Mention: Wife Amelia Case; Harvey C. Allen, son of Rev. Orasmus Allen; George Whitman, son of my sister, Emily Whitman; Elisha and Henry Case, sons of my brother, John Case; Henry Whitman, son of my sister, Emily Whitman; Edwin C. Barber, son of my sister, Delight Griswold Barber; Brother Erastus; Brother John; Sister Electa Hill. "Money is due me in Chicago, Ill., now in the hands of Dr. S. Willard of Auburn, N. Y." No executor named. Witnessed by T. H. Drake and Orasmus Allen.

SHEPHERD, ABRAHAM, (C-288). Of Shepherdstown, Jefferson county, Virginia. Signed Jan. 4, 1817. Proven Oct. 28, 1822. Mention: Wife, Eleanor Shepherd; Son Rezin D. Shepherd; Son James H.; Son Henry ('the farm where I now live, formerly owned by Col. Van Swearingen'); Daughters: Ann and Eliza; Brother John; Sons: Abraham and Moses; Nephew Moses Shepherd of Ohio county, Virginia ('his lands in Ohio'). No executor named. Witnessed by John B. Briscoe and Thomas G. Harris.

SHEPHERD, C. M., (C-291). Of the parish of St. James, State of Louisiana, planter, "this is my olographic will". Signed Apr. 14, 1850. Proven July 2, 1852. Mention: Wife Margaret Ann Shepherd; Children (not named). Executors: Wife Margaret Ann, Brother R. D. Shepherd and Son Charles Moses Shepherd; No witnesses.

NEWHOUSE, ELEANOR, (C-292). Of Columbus. Signed Mch. 21, 1850. Proven Mch. 29, 1853. Widow of John Newhouse and formerly wife of Capt. Van Swearingen, deceased. 'Have received from the war department of the U. S. A., three certificates constituting me a pensioner of the United States of the said Van Swearingen; one certificate dated Feb. 6, 1849, entitled me to a pension of $480 per annum from the 4th day of Mch. 1836; one certificate dated Feb. 6, 1849 entitles me to a pension of $480 per annum for five years from Mch. 4, 1848; also—that she had 'to prosecute the claim and the costs have been met by' her daughter Eliza J. Fracker, wife of William A. Fracker, and that she had been supported by this daughter for many many years'—these certificates all to go to Eliza J. Fracker, daughter. No executor named. Witnessed by S. C. West and Daniel Evans.

GINGRICH, DAVID, (C-293). Of Mifflin township. Signed Apr. 15, 1853. Mention: Wife Mary Gingrich 'is to have all', and the executor George Gingrich is to sell the land in North Lebanon, Penna. Witnessed by John Clark, David Riednour, and William Bieber. Witnesses to Codicil of same date—George J. C. Smith and T. F. Woodruff.

TRABUE, JOHN, (C-294). Of Chesterfield, State of Virginia. Signed Apr. 7, 1826. Proven May 21, 1828. Mention: Son Macon, 'all his lands south of the James River in Virginia and money already loaned to him'; son Alexander P; daughter Ann E. Hatcher; grandson John T. Hatcher 'to have Beverly son of Milly'; granddaughter Frances Ann Trabue 'to have Kitty child of Cynthia'; son Macon 'to have the large family Bible to be kept as a family register and not to be accounted with the estate. Executor, son Macon. Witnessed by Edward Johnson, Henry Ketton, and Benjamin T. Wells.

MILLER, MARGARET, (C-296). Of Truro township. Signed Aug. 11, 1852. Proven June 20, 1853. Mention: son Harvey E., 'house in Reynoldsburg'; grandchildren: Lucy Ann Fell and John E. Fell, minors; son Henry Walter Miller. Executor: son Harvey E. Miller. Witnessed by John E. Rohrer and D. E. Wood.

ABSTRACTS OF WILLS, FRANKLIN COUNTY, OHIO

Compiled by BLANCHE TIPTON RINGS

RATHBUN, JOHN, (C-298-317) (also RATHBONE) and (C-138). Of the City, County and State of New York. Signed Aug. 16, 1842. Codicil: Oct. 7, 1842. Codicil: Oct. 14, 1845. Copy here Nov. 20, 1845. Mention: great grandson, John Rathbone; daughter Content Cheesebrough; daughter Eunice Goddard and her four youngest children, James E. Goddard, Inlieke Rathbone Goddard, George W. Goddard and Sarah Willis Goddard; daughter Mary Rosalie Ruggles and such of her children as are living at her death; daughter Eliza Wetmore; the land on which Dr. Charles H. Wetmore now lives'; son-in-law Robert Cheesebrough; son Hezekiah; son-in-law Samuel B. Ruggles; children of his deceased grandson Edward Beverly Rathbone, all minors; daughter Juliett Downer; daughter Emma Maria Rhodes; daughter Sophia Smith deceased daughter; Sarah Downer's children: Joshua, Sarah, Emily Downer; daughter Clarissa Smith, 'at her death to go to such of her children as are living, except to Mary Stanbury'; grandchildren: Sarah Pettibone, Emily Andrews, Joshua Rathobone Downer, John Rathbone, Caroline Lee Rathbone, Julia Rathbone, Anthony Constant Rathbone; true and faithful servant, Diana Miller. Executors Robert Cheesebrough, Samuel B. Ruggles, William Kent, Esq., Edward R. Weston and Phillip R. Kearney. Witnessed by Joseph Brandegee— 3 Leroy Place; John B. Beck–14 Leor Place; Maltby Gelston–7 Leroy Place; and George Gibson–9 Leroy Place, all of New York City.

CAMPBELL, GEORGE, (C-318). (Of Lockbourne). Signed May 24, 1852. Proven July 13, 1853. Mention: wife Cellia Campbell; brother Charles Campbell to be executor; 'owns land in Fairfield, Iowa, and canal boat "Missouri." Witnessed by A. Clark and H. L. Chany.

MORRIS, THOMAS, (C-319). Of Hamilton township. Signed Mch. 22, 1851. Proven July 18, 1853; also, 'his grave is to be dug my two poor men of the township to be selected by his executors and that each are to have one half of his clothes and $10 in money'; also, 'to be buried in a plain white shirt and winding sheet, and in a plain coffin, no monument or mark or peculiar distinction to be placed on his grave; Mention:The children of his daughter, Sarah Gordon, deceased, (not named); the M. E. Church in the aid of Missionary Cause; the sum of $1000 for the especial use of securing Sabbath preaching perpetually at Walnut Hill Chapel adjoining his farm in Hamilton township; to the American Bible Society that was organized in 1816, to have $100; 'two acres of ground occupied by the Walnut Hill Chapel for a burying ground always to Jeremiah Clark, husband of his deceased daughter Jane, . . . Executor: Friend Jeremiah Clark and Amor Rees. Witnessed by George H. Earhart and George W. Williams.

BRYDEN, MARGARET, (C-323) (Of Columbus). Signed Apr. 13, 1853. Proven Aug. 11, 1853. Mention: Her four children, Son Harrison; Daughter Mary; Son Joshua; Daughter Fanny, the youngest. Executors: John Otstott and John P. Bruck, (latter to be guardian of the two youngest children). Witnessed by M. A. Snowden and Anna Maria Boswell. At time of proving Anna Maria Boswell, now Anna Maria Cornell.

POSTLE, JOHN, (C-324). Of Prairie township. Signed Aug. 27, 1853. Proven Sept. 23, 1853. Mention: Wife (*unnamed*); Children: Kezia, John Stephen, Perrin, Gabriel, Ezra, Anna, Eliza, Jennet **and** Harriet. Executor: George David Kinnaird, and B. F. Jewett. (Note: In settlement of estate, widow is Rebecca Postle).

PERRIN, WILLIAM, (C-326). Of Franklin county. Signed Nov. 21, 1851. Proven June 30, 1853. To Amelia Perrin, wife of Jonathan Perrin. . .; 'Owns land in Perrysburgh, Wood county'. No executor named. Witnessed by William Kramer and M. R. Ewing, (*at that time*) of Licking County.

PLOCK, JACOB, (C-328). Of Columbus. Signed Nov. 1, 1853. Proven Nov. 4, 1853. To wife Christiana Plock 'one-half' and 'the other half to his children' (*not named*). Executor to be my wife, Christiana. Witnessed by Dr. C. E. Benig, Christian Dagenhardt and Wiegand Strack.

ANDREWS, JEANETTE, (C-329). Of Columbus. Signed Dec. 22, 1853. Proven Dec. 28, 1853. Names her husband Sylvester W. Andrews, 'to have all my lots in Lazell Addition, and to be guardian to my only daughter, Jeanette Lazell Andrews; Mother, father, brothers, and sisters (*not named*). Witnessed by Adelia P. Andrews **and** Rebecca Shumway.

STOTTS, URIAH, (C-331). Of Franklin county. Signed Sept. 24, 1853. Proven Jan. 5, 1854. Mention: Wife, Susan Stotts; Brother Abraham; Nephew Hiram Stotts, son of Brother Hiram: Brother Arthur; Sister Polly Hendricks; Sister Rebecca Anderson; Children of deceased sister, Margaret Alden. Executor: Friend Benjamin F. Martin and Lorenzo English. Witnessed by Ezekiel O'harra and Peter Yeiser.

WILLIAM WHITE, (C-333). Of Franklin county. Signed Nov. 29, 1853. Proven Jan. 28, 1854. Mention: Wife Eloner White; Five sons: Hiram S., Henry M., John M., Samuel H. (or M); and Milton H.; Daughter Rebecca Jane. Executor: Wife, Eloner White, and Hiram S. White, oldest son. Witnessed by Clark White and Hiram Watts.

FUNSTON, JOHN, (C-334). Of Columbus. Signed Feb. 1853. Proven Feb. 30, 1854. Mention: Wife (*not named*); Son J. J. Funston, 'the soap and candle factory'; Grandsons: E. B. and John Funston; To Anthony T. (*no other name given*) of Philadelphia, warden of the City Prison—$300; To niece Fanny Mc (*no other name given*) of Pittsburgh; To afflicted brother Christopher, of Philadelphia; Sister Eliza Maxwell of Philadelphia; "my books to my physician", Dr. I. G. Jones, and my son J. J. Funston, equally; clothes to John Riley, "a man who has worked faithfully for me for eight years"; desires "to be buried by the side of his daughter, Rebecca P. Funston, who is already burial in Green Lawn Cemetery. Executor: Thomas Roberts of Columbus. Witnessed by John Van York and Jeffrey Powell.

PAULL, ROBERT, (C-337). Of Mifflin township. Signed Jan. 4, 1854. Proven Mch. 4, 1854. Mention: Son Robert; Daughter Phebe, and her children; Sister Polly 'who lives with him'. Executor: John Latta. Witnessed by John Starrett and T. Harward.

KIDNEY, JACOB, (C-338). Of Columbus. Signed Sept. 18, 1843. Proven Mch. 9, 1854. Mention: Wife Catherine 'to have all and at her death to (same) go to son John; Daughter Ann Maria's heirs; Daughter Rachel, wife of Joseph Styler; Daughter Sarah, wife of Asher Jacobs; Daughter Ester, wife of Andrew Little; Son Henry. Executor:

Wife, Catherine Kidney. Witnessed by John O. Jones and Jacob Leaf. At the time of proving will John O. Jones was at Murphysboro, Jackson co., Illinois. John T. Leaf and Leroy Leaf on Mch. 9, 1854 stated that 'Jacob Leaf was deceased', which was also sworn to by Ebenezer McDonald and John Huffman.

MAHR, ANNA MARGARET, (C-341). Of Columbus. Signed Dec. 1, 1852. Proven Mch. 25, 1854. Mention: 'that she is widow of Phillip Lewis Mahr; Son Peter Andrew of Illinois; Daughter Catherine Miller of Fairfield county; Catherine Margaret Zubrod who now lives in Columbus; Daughter Maria Catherine Schroett (?) of Illinois. No executor named. Witnessed by F. W. Wirth, F. H. Broesghke and J. P. Bruck.

MOORE, BENJAMIN, (C-343). Of Blendon township. Signed Mch. 14, 1854. Proven Mch. 28, 1854. Mention: Son George Alvin; Son Preston; Daughter Amanda M., a minor; Daughter Hannah W. Moore; Elbridge J. Moore. Executors: Virgil D. Moore and Thomas Bell. Witnessed by William H. Grinnell and Angeline Elsten.

DICKEY, OBEDIAH, (C-344). Of Columbus. Signed Feb. 13, 1852. Proven Apr. 13, 1854. Mention: wife, (not named); Children, minors (not named). Executor: Wife. Witnessed by R. B. Booker and James M. Cunningham.

MAECK, HENRY CHRISTIAN, (C-345). Of Columbus. Signed May 12, 1854. Proven May 15, 1854. Mention: Wife Christiana Maech, to have 'all in the United States or out'—owns land in Mercer county, Ohio. Children—three: Henry William 'who left his home'; Henry and Edward, minors; requests that 'his friend Christopher Winkler,' be made guardian. Executors: Friend Phillip Kaemerrer and John Ihrig. Witnessed by Ed. Lilley and K. Mees.

JOHNSON, WILLIAM S., (C-347). Of Blendon township. Signed July 31, 1853. Proven May 17, 1854. To wife Susan 'all', and she to be executor. Witnessed by Caroline A. Wilson and Horace Wilson. At the time of proof, Caroline A. Johnson was of Athens county.

JOHNSTON, ELIZA S., (C-349) (also JOHNSON). Of Franklin county. Signed May 11, 1854. Proven May 19, 1854. To son William Stewart Johnson–the use of her share in the farm, belonging to the heirs of the late William Stewart, deceasd, 'so long as he keeps my family together.' No executor named. Witnessed by N. Merion and E. Stewart.

ROSTON, ISAAC H., (C-350). Of Columbus. Signed Mch. 23, 1854. Proven June 5, 1854. Gives 'all to his wife' Ellen Roston, and at her death 'to be divided equally' between his brother James P. Roston and his wife's nephew, Andrew Jackson Free, a minor, 'who lives with us'. Executor: Brother James P. Roston. Witnessed by W. T. Martin and J. H. Reel.

(Note: Obit.—"Isaac H. Roston died in this city May 18, 1854 in his 38th year". In the settlement of estate–he died about April, 1854–Iowa, and was brought to Columbus with burial in Green Lawn Cemetery).

BROCKWAY, HEIL, (C-352). Of Monroe county, New York, Village of Brockport, in the town of Sweden, county of Monroe. Signed Feb. 28, 1834. Proven Sept. 22, 1852 at Rochester, N. Y. To wife, Phebe Brockway, 'all' and she to be executor. Witnessed by Elias B. Holmes and Augustus F. Brockway, both of Brockport, N. Y. (Copy here June 14, 1854).

321

OERDEL & OEARTEAL, GEORGE, (C-354). Of Madison township. Signed Aug. 24, 1849. Proven June 24, 1854. Mention: Wife (*not named*) 'to have land in Hancock county, Ohio. Heirs: Mary Cathererine, Louisa, Rosania, Abraham and John Oerdell. No executor named. Witnessed by Moses Seymour and Nancy Seymour.

ARMSTRONG, ROBERT, (C-358). Of Columbus. Signed May 1854. Proven July 17, 1854. Names: Daughter Ruhama C. Heffner and her heirs; Grandchildren: Robert Armstrong Heffner, Albert Heffner, and Georgianna Thompson Wasson; Daughter Mary Wasson 'to have the land in Fulton county, Ohio. Executor: Thomas Sparrow, Columbus. Witnessed by W. T. Martin and A. C. Wiswell.

O'HARRA, JAMES, (C-361). Of Franklin township. Signed Sept. 23, 1853. Proven Aug. 24, 1854. Mention: Son Reed; Daughter Rebecca Legg; Wife Sarah O'Harra; Sons Joseph, Arthur and Thomas; Two grandsons: George and James O'Harra; Daughter Susan Rannell. Executor: Son Arthur O'Harra. Witnessed by Lorenzo English and A. Stotts.

JUNIUS, MARY CATHERINE, (C-363). Of Columbus. Signed May 22, 1854. Proven Aug. 28, 1854. Mention: Brothers, George and Joseph Massie, unmarried; Mother Rosina Newman 'shall pay expenses of schooling of said George and Joseph at the colored seminary on Darby Creek in this county; Cousin Margaret Massie; Cousin Rebecca Massie; Aunt Catherine Massie. Executor: Uncle Joseph Massie; Cousin George Massie, 'a minor'. Witnessed by F. J. Matthews and S. S. Mason.

MATTIX, THOMAS, (C-367). Of Perry township. Signed June 7, 1852. Proven Aug. 30, 1854. Mention: Wife, Nancy Mattix; Heirs—four: Nancy, Hety (and Heaty), Sally, Diana—and daughter Abigail. Executors Jacob Poppaw. Witnessed Jacob Poppaw and Jacob Billingslea.

HOFFMAN, PETER, (C-368). Of the City of Baltimore, Md., Gentleman. Signed Dec. 5, 1836. Proven May 16, 1837. Mention: Wife, Deborah Hoffman 'to have the house (they) live in on Lexington Street'; Daughter Elizabeth, wife of Dr. Lenox Birckhead and her children; Brother George's (deceased) sons, Samuel Owing Hoffman and William Alfred Hoffman; Daughter Sally; Daughter, Henriette—unmarried; Grandchildren (*not named*); Daughter Mary; 'Owns land in Loudon county, Virginia'. Brother Jacob, deceased, and his widow Elizabeth; Father-in-law, Samuel Owing of Baltimore county; Son Edward Hoffman; Son George P. Hoffman (*under age of 23 years*). Executors: Hugh Birckhead, L. S. Eichelberger and Grafton D. Spurrier. Copy in Franklin county, Nov. 4, 1852; filed Sept. 7, 1854.

HOFFMAN. WILLIAM ALFRED, (C-374). Of Baltimore, Md. Signed Dec. 13, 1841. Proven Feb. 11, 1842. 'Gives All' to Brother Samuel Owings Hoffman. No executor named. Witnessed by J. Latimer Hoffman, Sally Hoffman and Henrietta Hoffman. Copy here Sept. 7, 1854.

GOLLIDAY, ROBERT, (C-376). Of Alton. Signed Sept. 8, 1854 Proven Sept. 14, 1854. Mention: wife, Maria L. Golliday. Children: Emily Jane, Robert C., Charles B., Franklin P., all minors; Son Washington Golliday. Wife 'to be guardian of the children or Lewis Potter'. Executor: Franklin Postle. Witnessed by S. H. Putnam and L. Woodruff.

ABSTRACTS OF WILLS, FRANKLIN COUNTY, OHIO

Compiled by BLANCHE TIPTON RINGS

NEVILLE, WILLIAM B., (C-379). Of Columbus; signed May 13, 1854; proven Oct. 5, 1854; gives all which is coming from his maternal grand uncle, Jesse Barker, deceased, late of New York, to his brother, Morgan Lafayette Neville, and he to be executor; witnessed by E. Doolittle, Henry R. Rogers and John Warnock.

HELSEL, NICHOLAS, (C-380). Of Franklin County; signed Aug. 14, 1848; proven Oct. 26, 1854; mentions: wife Elizabeth (the land bounded by George and Adam Helzel); nephew Philip Weatherington; Nicholas, son of Philip Helsel; brother Jacob; brother Daniel's son, Titus Helsel; executors: wife Elizabeth and brother Philip Helzel; witnessed by William Weatherington and George Stotts.

MAURER, NICHOLAS, (C-383).

BROOKS, NATHAN, (C-384). Of Columbus; signed Oct. 29, 1854; proven Nov. 11, 1854; mentions: wife (not named); son Frank; daughter Philena Gilchrist; daughter Ann M. Brooks; daughter Mary Brooks; executors: wife and R. S. Gilchrist; witnessed by Franklin F. Lewis and A. D. Adams.

BECKER, HENRY, (C-386). Of Montgomery Twp; (no date of signing); proven Nov. 16, 1854; mentions: wife Helena Becker; daughters Henrietta and Amalie Becker; appoints his friend Otto Zirckel to be guardian of his daughters; executors: George Frankenberg and Otto Zirckel; witnessed by Frederick Busch and Otto Zirckel.

TAYLOR, WILLIAM, (C-388). Of Franklin County; signed Aug. 2, 1852; proven Nov. 18, 1854; mentions: wife Mary Taylor; son George W.; heirs of daughter Nancy; daughters Elizabeth and Sarah; heirs of daughter Dorcas; sons William and James; no executor named; witnessed by H. S. Mitchell and Mahala Mitchell. Administrator appointed was George W. Taylor.

ROBINSON, ELIZA A., (C-389). Of Franklin County; signed Mch. 27, 1854; proven Nov. 28, 1854; husband Jabez Robinson; says that in case she die childless, at her husband's death, all is to go to her brothers and sisters; owns an undivided one-eighth in land in Delaware County, Ohio, once in the hands of H. G. Andrews and James E. Palmer as a trust fund of John Rathbone, under his appointment, for the use of Eliza Wetmore and others; trustee: Prosper M. Wetmore, named in the marriage settlement, where all my individual property remains subject to my disposal; executor: Charles J. Wetmore; witnessed by Henry B. Carrington and W. C. French.

(Note: Obituary "Mrs. Eliza A. Robinson, wife of Dr. J. Robinson, and daughter of Dr. Charles H. Wetmore, died in Oregon, Missouri, May, 1854. Had been married three months.")

WATTERS, GILBERT, (C-391). Of Plain Twp; signed Nov. 12, 1854; proven Dec. 7, 1854; mentions: wife Sally Watters; son O. W. Watters and his heirs; daughter J. A. Mariah Frable; son R. C. Watters, a minor; daughter Harriet Landon; daughter Ann Waters; son Philip Watters; executor: son O. W. Watters; witnessed by T. S. Johnson and George Wagner.

BISHOP, JOHN, (C-393). Of Blendon Twp; signed May 3, 1851; proven Jan. 4, 1855; mentions: son John, a cripple; son William; son Gabriel and his heirs; son Walter; daughter Angaline C. Cornell;

daughter Hillin Philips; daughter Sarah Hart; daughter Elizabeth Ingalls; daughter Hester Ann Bishop; executors: sons William and Walter Bishop and son-in-law John M. Hart; witnessed by George Taylor, G. G. Wilcox and Alvin Fuller.

McDonald Sarah M., (C-395). Formerly Sarah M. White; of Franklin County; signed Sept. 28, 1854; Proven Jan. 6. 1855; mentions: son John M. White; daughter Sarah Neff; daughter Sarah Jane White; son William M. White; wishes a lot to be purchased in Green Lawn Cemetery; no executor named; witnessed by S. W. Andrews and Henry Woolf.

Ringhausen, Henry Jacob, (C-396). Of Columbus; signed Nov. 25, 1854; proven Jan. 22. 1855; mentions: wife Wilhelmenia; six children. namely: George, Conrad, Henry, Elise, Lewis and Frederick. latter two are minors; executor: wife Wilhelmenia; witnessed by Christian Gramlich, Konrad Westor and Robert Clemen.

Marvin, Richard L., (C-397). Of Washington Twp; signed Dec. 2, 1854;proven Jan. 23, 1855; mentions: wife Jane Marvin to have the land he bought of Jacob Babcock; children, all minors, namely: Maria, Amelia, Adelaid, Sarah, John, and Susan; executors: wife Jane and William Graham; codicil of same date was witnessed by John Golden and William Graham; witnesses to will were James Stedman and William Graham. At time of proving will it was stated that John Golden, a transient young man whose address is unknown, but who is said to be in service of the United States.

Frey, Lewis, (C-400). Of Columbus; signed Jan. 16. 1855; proven Jan. 25, 1855; mentions: wife Mary and six 'ars'; no executor named; witnessed by Sebastian Gramlick and Henry Keefer.

Reams, Jonathan W., (C-401). Of Columbus; signed Dec. 3. 1853;; proven Sept. 25, 1854; gives all to wife, Sarah F. Reams and at her death to go equally to all his children and she is to be executor; witnessed by J. B. Smith and D. T. Jones. At time of proving, J. B. Cofforth proves the handwriting of D. T. Jones, formerly of Columbus. (It does not say where he now is).

Mustard, Samuel, (C-402) and also (D-19). Of the County of Pike; signed Mch. 16, 1839; proven Feb. 8, 1855; copy here Aug. 11. 1840 at Pike town; mentions: daughter Lydia Bennett, wife of William Bennett: grandson Samuel Mustard Sargent, son of Thornton W. and Elizabeth Sargent; executor: son-in-law Thornton W. Sargent; witnessed by Hallam Hempstead, Thomas Barnes and William Leach.

Wilson Samuel, (C-404). Of Richland County; signed June 29, 1849; proven Jan. 29, 1855; gives wife Caroline Wilson, all; no executor named; witnessed by Barnabas Burns and Samuel J. Kirkwood.

Harris, Isabel Clark, (C-407). Of Indian River Hundred in Sussex county, State of Delaware; signed Apr. 3, 1839; proven May 7. 1839; mentions: daughter Hester Ann Harris to have the lots in Columbus; or if she die they are to go to Stephen H. Waples, son of Robert Waples; three daughters of Robert Waples; namely: Margaret Ann, Rachel Jane and Mary Elizabeth Waples; executor: Robert Waples; witnessed by John Thoroughgood, Zadock B. Lacy and Mary Harris; copy here Feb. 12, 1855.

Higgins, Charles, (C-409). Of Prairie Twp; signed Apr. 18, 1850; proven Mch. 8, 1855; mentions: wife Drusilla; daughters Jane, Loretta, Charlotte and. Elizabeth; sons: Julian, Samuel Clark and Charles (last two minors); daughter Jane; executor: wife Drusilla;

ABSTRACTS OF WILLS, FRANKLIN COUNTY, OHIO
Compiled by BLANCHE TIPTON RINGS

witnessed by John Gantz and Frederick Postle. At time of proving John Gantz has removed from the state and his writing is proven by M. D. Lathrop and Charles T. Bynner.

CASHNER, JEREMIAH, (C-411). Of Plain Twp; signed Mch. 6, 1855; proven Mch. 30, 1855; mentions: wife Christena and the property at her death to go equally between the following: Joseph, Samuel and William Cashner; Lydia Swickard; Lucy Ann Cashner and Caroline Ulry and her son William Ulry, a minor; executors: wife Christena and son Joseph; witnessed by Isaac Williams and Jonathan Staufer.

LINDNER, PAULUS, (C-412). Of Norwich Twp; signed July 26, 1849 at Columbus; translated into English from German Apr. 7, 1855 by Charles Jucksch; mentions: intended wife, Susanna Denim; six children by his first wife, Anna Barbara Beck (are not named). Hiram and Abraham Kellar are to be guardians of his children; witnessed by William Bolander, Conrad Hartman and Edward Lilley.

(Note: In March, 1860 the following are given as heirs in settling up the estate: Susannah Ebert, wife of Johanna Ebert and formerly widow of Paulus Lindner; daughter Barbara Schoedinger; son John; son Casper, a minor; daughter Kunegunda Miller, formerly Lindner.)

ROSE, PHILIP, (C-415). Of Jefferson Twp; signed Aug. 7, 1850; proven Apr. 10, 1855; mentions: wife Ruth; grandson Philip Rose, the son of Abraham Rose; son Stephen G. Rose. 'and the rest of the children not herein named'; executor: son Stephen G; witnessed by Shuah Mann and Nathan Spencer.

Note: Obituary in paper "Philip Rose died at his residence in Jefferson Township on Feb. 16, 1855, aged 78 years; came to Ohio in 1807, first settled where New Albany now stands and was one of the first settlers in that part where he has resided ever since."

SCOTT, ANDREW M., (C-416). Of Madison Twp; signed Dec. 6, 1851; proven Apr. 27, 1855; mentions: wife Elizabeth; granddaughter Harriet Arabella Scott; Josiah White, a boy now residing and living with us; nephew Mitchell Allen, son of his sister Jane Allen; Andrew John Scott Hutson, the son of Nathaniel Hutson of Truro Twp; daughter Harriet Selbey, wife of Anelcey Selby; son Andrew Scott. Jr; Bennett Gares, son of Samuel Gares of Franklin County; executor George D. Graham; witnessed by James Langworthy and Samuel Gares.

KELL, JANE, (C-418). Of Prairie Twp; signed Nov. 11, 1847; proven May 11, 1855; mentions Lson Samuel; grandson Edmund W. F. Flagg, a minor; Charlotte Huikill, a grand daughter by daughter Jennett; grandson Achilles, son of Samuel Kell; Zebulon Huikill, son-in-law and husband of daughter Charlotte; executors: son Samuel and John Hunter of Madison County; witnessed by Knowlton Bailey. James Haines and Lewis Huddleson.

BENFIELD, AMANDA S., (C-419). Of the city of Columbus; signed May 31, 1854; proven May 23, 1855; directs that the farm in Hamilton township now occupied by Henry Shoaf be sold; that which her mother, Rebecca Stewart, afterward Benfield, daughter of John Stewart, deceased, and to Lydia Stewart, afterwards Jamison and which was sold and deeded to my father, A. Benfield, shall go to the heirs of my grandfather, John Stewart; to my cousin, Samuel Johnston of Columbus; to Aunt Maria E. Benfield; to Aunt Sarah Stewart; to Uncle Francis. Stewart; to the descendants of my Aunt Eliza O. Swindell, namely: Sarah B. Gray, the widow of James H. Swindell and to John M. Swindell, my cousins; directs that the bodies of her parents be removed to Green Lawn Cemetery; executor: Samuel Johnston of Columbus; witnessed by James D. Osborn and W. T. Martin. In a codicil directs that a monument be erected over their graves.

PEARSON, SIMEON, (C-424). Of Franklin County; signed Mch. 28, 1845; proven May 28, 1855; mentions: wife Elizabeth; sons Richard. John and George; executor: George Ridenour; witnessed by Hugh Price, William Price and James Price.

WISER, FREDERICK, (C-426). Of Perry Twp; signed Apr. 25, 1855; proven July 2, 1855; mentions: wife Rachel; John Barnet, his heir at law, now living in Perry County, Pennsylvania; rest of his heirs: namely: Jacob Weiser, John Wiser, Frederick Barnet. Maria Barnet, Hette Fowler, William Barnet, Jane Putnam, Lewis Byram of Darke County; Sarah Barnet; Union Church of Clinton Twp; executors: John Becket and John Grim; witnessed by Samuel Kinnear and Jacob S. Fogle.

SKIDMORE, GEORGE. (C-427). Of Franklin Twp; signed July 6, 1855; proven July 23, 1855; mentions: wife (not named) five sons and one daughter, namely: William, James M; Joshua, Andrew, George W. and Matilda Galliger; Mary L. Say; William M. Skidmore, one of the heirs of John Skidmore, deceased; James M. Skidmore is to pay Mary C. Anderson what he owes; no executor named; witnessed by A. O'Harra and Samuel Brooks.

SUMMERVILLE, GEORGE, (C-428). Of Columbus; signed May 23, 1855; proven July 23, 1855; mentions: Robert Scott, colored, son of Charles Scott, is to have a lot in Delaware; lot he got from Richard Butcher, deceased; two colored Baptist churches; a friend, David Sulivoo; children of Nancy Johnson, wife of his friend, William Johnson; the house is to be rented for ten years and the money to go to the two colored Baptist Anti-Slavery Associations of Columbus; Agnes Scott, daughter of Charles Scott; Matilda, wife of Charles Scott; Robert, son of William Johnson; executor: friend, David Sullivoo of Columbus; witnessed by B. F. Martin and John Statton.

PETERS, TUNIS, (C-430). Of Columbus; signed May 19, 1855; proven Aug. 23, 1855; mentions: wife (not named); son Jonathan, as soon as he may return from California; nephew Tunis Peters, son of his brother Samuel Peters; grand daughter Mary Davis; no executor named; witnessed by Harvey Peters and James M. Ferguson.

Note: By settlement of estate, widow was Mary E. Peters (See her will).

CLOUSE, JOHN, (C-431). Of New Albany; signed June 21, 1855; proven Aug. 28, 1855; mentions: wife (not named); son George; daughter Christine Ealy; son David; daughter Sophia Ealy; son John; son Jeremiah; daughter Mary Headley; son Jacob; grandchildren: Nancy Phelps and John Clouse, the heirs of Daniel Clouse, deceased; four youngest sons: Oliver, Thomas, Benjamin and Napoleon; no executor named; witnessed by Daniel Hamaker and John Neiswender.

ROWLAND, JOHN G., (C-432). Of Franklin County; signed Aug. 29, 1855; proven Sept. 8, 1855; mentions: wife Elizabeth; daughter Sophia and her heirs; no executor named; witnessed by Joseph O'Harra and John F. Borland.

WAGNER, HARRIET ANN, (C-433). (See Jacob Wagner will—B. 46). Signed Aug. 20, 1855; proven Sept. 8, 1855; mentions: brothers George and John; money held in trust for the purchase of seven sets of tombstones for her father, mother, sister Ann, sister Elizabeth. brother Jacob and an infant sister; sister Elizabeth's heirs; brothers James and Abraham; sister Catherine's heirs, who are minors; brother John; brother David's heirs, who are minors; witnessed by Daniel Hamaker and John Robbins; no executor named.

BRIEN, ELIZABETH, (Alias DEVLIN), (C-434). Of Columbus; signed Aug. 23, 1855; proven (no date); asks that Rev. James Meagher of St. Patrick's Church be guardian of her three children, namely: James Devlin, Charles Devlin and William Devlin; witnessed by James Foley and James Collins. She signs her name as "Elizabeth Devlin, alias "Brien" and the Index gives under the name of 'Brien'.

DAGUE, ANDREW, (C-435). Of Plain Twp; signed Aug. 9, 1854; proven Sept. 25, 1855; mentions: eldest daughter Mary Plymier; second daughter Sally Lenard; eldest son Jonathan; sons Frederick and Israel; daughter Nancy Dague; daughter Elizabeth Plymier; daughter Susanna Whoolf; daughter Lydia Swickard; and daughter Catherine Smith; executor: Daniel Swickard; witnessed by George Dague and Daniel Swickard.

McWILLIAMS, WILLIAM, (C-436). Of Franklin County; signed Aug. 22, 1855; proven Oct. 3, 1855; mentions: wife (not named); sons Robert and John; daughter Eliza Stewart; daughter Sarah Ricther; daughter Miriam McWilliams; executors: Samuel Billingsley and William Graham; witnessed by Barzilla Billingsley and Levi Davidson.

TUSSING, MARGARET, (C-438). Of Franklin County; signed July 23, 1855; proven Oct. 6, 1855; mentions: sons John, J. J., George and Samuel; daughter Christena Harris; that whoever is in final attendance at her last sickness to have all her wearing apparel which she has at time of her decease; two youngest sons, Adam L. and Philip C.; executor:friend John Rager or Frederick Swickard; witnessed by Moses Seymour, Adam Rager and Robert L. Seymour.

METZ, JOHN VALENTINE, (C-439). Of Columbus; signed Feb. 25, 1845; proven Oct. 13, 1855; gives all to his brother George Metz and at his death to his heir, Maria Anna Metz; executor: John Ender; witnessed by M. Fisher, Jacob Lohrer and J. P. Bruck.

COE, RANSOM, (C-440). Of Clinton Twp; signed May 20, 1854; proven Oct. 13, 1855; mentions: wife Elizabeth; daughter Salinda, wife of Robert Stewart of Iowa; son Almon; daughter Rachel Stone; daughter Lovila Ackerman; son Alvin and he is to be executor; witnessed by B. F. Martin and W. T. Martin.

HOFFMAN, JACOB, (C-441). Of Columbus; signed Dec. 28, 1854; proven Nov. 9, 1855; gives all to wife Elizabeth Ann Hoffman and she to be executor; witnessed by J. P. Bruck and John Hoffman.

DORBERTH, GEORGE, (C-442). Of Columbus; signed Oct. 25, 1855; proven Nov. 8, 1855; gives to John Dorberth, by a former marriage; and to Margaretha Dorberth; witnessed by Nicholas Dorberth (Is written in German and was translated by Edward Siefert, Deputy Clerk).

BACKUS, ELIJAH, (C-443). Of Columbus; signed Nov. 5, 1855; proven Nov. 10, 1855; mentions no family names; executors: brother Abner L. Baskus and John Greenleaf; witnessed by John W. Andrews and John A. Little.

PINNEY, INTREPID C., (C-444). Of Franklin County; signed Oct. 21, 1855; proven Nov. 14, 1855; mentions: father Chester Pinney; brothers Horace, Samuel Seabury and Cyrus A. Barker Pinney;

mother Cynthia; executors: George Taylor, Esq. of Worthington; witnessed by F. J. Mathews and F. C. Kelton.

BALDWIN, ISRAEL, (C-445). Of Blendon Twp; no date of signing; proven Nov. 6, 1855; mentions the three children of his son, William, deceased, namely: Morris Fletcher Baldwin, Hannah Baldwin and William Oregon Baldwin; executor: Israel C. Baldwin and he is to be guardian of above children; witnessed by F. J. Matthews and Matthew Long.

RATHMELL, THOMAS, (C-445). Of Franklin County; signed Apr. 27, 1855; proven Nov. 17, 1855; mentions:wife Mary Rathmell; son Joseph; daughter Elizabeth Rees; son John; no executor named; witnessed by John Cox and A. Willi.

SLACK, ELIAS, (C-448). Of Truro Twp; signed Nov. 24, 1855; proven Jan. 5, 1856; mentions: wife Jane; witnessed by Emmor Reynolds and John F. Cookes; no executor named; at time of proving will, Emmor Reynolds says that John F. Cookes has since gone to parts unknown.

SCHWARTZ, PETER, (C-449). (Is in German and not translated).

END OF BOOK C

328

ABSTRACTS OF WILLS, FRANKLIN COUNTY, OHIO

Compiled by BLANCHE TIPTON RINGS

BOOK D.

McCoy, ROBERT (D-1) Florist; of Columbus; signed Nov. 21, 1852; proven Jan. 21, 1856; mentions wife Isabella; nephews William A. and James W. McCoy, the sons of his brother William McCoy; nephews William, John and Samuel McCoy, the sons of his brother John McCoy; nephews James C. and Abram S. McCoy, the sons of his brother Alexander McCoy; the children of nephew Alexander McCoy who is the son of his brother William McCoy; nephew John A. McCoy, the son of his sister Sarah; Elizabeth and Jane Sarah, the daughters of his brother John McCoy; children of Sarah Porter and of Margaret Wise, wife of William Wise and who are the daughters of his brother Alexander McCoy; is owner of The American Hotel in Columbus; executors, William A. McCoy and James A. McCoy; witnessed by Lucien Buttles and P. B. Wilcox.

MERION, SALLY (D-6) of Marion Twp.; signed Aug. 10,, 1848; proven Jan. 26, 1856; widow of Nathaniel Merion, deceased; son William; son Nathaniel; dau. Eveline Baylor; dau. Sally Ann Peters; dau. Emily Stewart; son George; Elizabeth Luts, a young woman she has living with her; executor, son George (or if he is not of age at her death) then Rev. Mr. Hitchcock; witnessed by W. T. Martin and A. Schneider.

Note: Obit—"Mrs. Sarah Merion, consort of the late William Merion, died in Montgomery township, Jan. 21, 1856, aged 67 years".

DUVALL, THOMAS (D-7) of Pleasant Twp; signed Sept. 26, 1855; proven Jan. 26, 1856; mentions that wife Mary Duvall is sole heir and she is to be administrator and guardian of his estate; witnessed by H. T. Henderson and William S. Beatty.

GROOM, NOAH (D-8) Of Madison Twp; signed Sept. 19, 1853; proven Apr. 8, 1856; mentions: the children of his son Thomas Groom, late deceased, namely; Irvin M. Martin V, Isaac N., John W. Hosea, Mary A. and Rebecca A. Groom; Davannus Groom, the dau. of my son David Groom, late deceased; dau. Malvina Bennett; son Moses; son Ezekiel; dau. Rebecca L. Bennett; executor, Augustus L. Perrill of Pickaway County; witnessed by R. G. McLan and Joseph Bratner.

LAMSON, NATHAN S. (D-9) Of Columbus; signed May 8, 1856; proven May 12, 1856; mentions: John W. Andrews to act as trustee for my' sister Caroline E. Holmes; in case that Andrews die before the estate is closed up, then Henry C. Noble shall attend to it; nephew William Preston; niece Sarah M. Preston; nephew Edwin Stanton; niece Mary Stewart; John Stump; Justin Pinney; William Pinney; Mrs. Polly Pinney, the wife of A. P. Pinney; Caroline Holmes; Mrs. Anne C. Pinney; Nathan Pinney, the son of Abner P. Pinney; wishes to be buried in Green Lawn Cemetery and to have the bodies of his wife, child, father and mother and all his family removed thereto and a monument erected; executor: John W. Andrews and Henry C. Noble; witnessed by John Morrison and Charles Reynolds.

Note: Obit—"Died at the residence of his brother-in-law, A. H. Pinney, Nathan S. Lamson on May 8, 1856".

329

STEELY, JOHN (D-11) Of Franklin County; signed May 26, 1856; proven June 14, 1856; mentions: wife Hannah, son Joseph, dau. Betsey, dau. Ann, dau. Rebecca; witnessed by David Goodwin, Allen F. Coe and Simeon Moore; proven by William Jamison and Allen F. Coe.

ALKIRE, MARY (D-12) Of Columbus, Montgomery Twp; signed May 21, 1856; proven June 18, 1856; mentions: two sisters, Nancy W. Peate (is to have my house in Columbus and a note on William Alkire) aand Eliza White; brothers, namely—John, William, Joseph, Alexander W., George and James; no executor named; witnessed by John Anderson and John W. Alkire.

ZIMMER, PHILIP (D-13) Of Franklin County; signed Apr. 23, 1853; proven June 25, 1856; mentions; son Eli and his heirs, dau. Sarah Decker, dau. Elizabeth Eply, son George, wife Lydia Zimmer; executor, son Eli Zimmer; witnessed by Henry Nocodemus and C. B. Cannon.

SPRAGUE, ANSON (D-14) Of Franklin County; signed Apr. 17, 1854; proven July 26, 1856; mentions: William R. Sprague; Mary S. Skates; Marinda R. Lemert; Washington A. Sprague; Malissa M. Linn; Willington P. Sprague; Anson Sprague, Jr.; Romolus C. Sprague; Lewis L. Sprague; Anson C. Skates; Adaline D. Sprague; wife Susannah Sprague; executor—William R. Sprague or Willington P. Sprague; witnessed by D. K. Wood and Maria Wood.

WATTS, ADAM (D-15) of Blendon Twp; signed July 6, 1856; proven Aug. 4, 1856; mentions—friends George Watt and Charles Watt; executor—George Watt; witnessed by William H. Grinnell and D. C. Grinnell.

RAYNOLDS, JOHN (D-15) Of Franklin County; signed Aug. 12, 1856; proven Aug. 15, 1856; wife Mary Raynolds and mother Peney Raynolds; no executor named; witnessed by Powell L. Barnett and James Hayden.

SCOTT, ANDREW (D-17) Of Madison Twp; signed June 26, 1856; proven Aug. 30, 1856; mentions: wife Elizabeth Scott, son William, dau. Rebecca Scott, dau. Minerva Scott, friend Rosalthe Porter, the dau. of Joseph W. Porter; Aaron D. Bendum to be guardian of his son William Scott; executor—Joseph W. Porter; witnessed by John L. Parselland, Harvey Keiser.

REES, NANCY (D-16) Of Montgomery Twp; signed Mch. 26, 1856; proven Aug. 21, 1856; mentions: only dau. Mrs. Sarah Ashbrook; son Jacob Rees; no executor named; witnessed by Powell L. Barnett and James Hayden.

SNYDER, OLIVE (D-21) Of Columbus; signed Sept. 12, 1855; proven Sept. 15, 1856; mentions: Frank Work Deshler and Lizzie Green Deshler, the children of Charles G. Deshler; executor—Charles G. Deshler; witnessed by William F. Wheeler, C. E. Boyle and J. Elmer.

UNGER, GEORGE MICHAEL (D-23) Of Columbus; signed June 19, 1851; proven Oct. 9, 1856; mentions: wife (not named); gives to the four children, including a step-child of his brother, John Peter Unger (at present being in Rothenberg on the Tauber River, Kingdom of Bavaria), and among the six children of the sister of his wife, Margaret Barbara Groeninger (late Muchlender) now living with her husband John George Groeninger in Bavaria, Judicial Circuit of Fenchwang, Kingdom of Bavaria; no executor named; witnessed by John Zachman and Frederick Schille.

BETZ, GEORGE CHARLES (D-24) Of Columbus; signed July 29, 1856; proven Oct. 25, 1856; mentions—wife Eva Catherine Betz, four children, namely: George Charles Betz, Dorothy Betz, Christian Betz and

ABSTRACTS OF WILLS, FRANKLIN COUNTY, OHIO
Compiled by BLANCHE TIPTON RINGS

Eva Sophia Betz; wife is to guardian of any of the children under 18 year of age, and if she die, then my brother Christian Betz is to be guardian; states that if any money is coming to him in Germany it should go to his wife Eva; brother Frederick Betz in Schelbach, Kingdom of Wertemberg, Germany; executor—brother Christian Betz; witnessed by Otto Dresel and William White.

SWISHER, ABRAHAM (D-26) Of Madison Twp; signed Sept. 27, 1850; proven Oct. 21, 1856; mentions: wife Margaret Swisher (the land given to Jesse Patterson by his father, William Patterson; son John; oldest dau. Catherine Vesey (land in Truro Twp. formerly owned by the old gentleman, Frederick Sprague) since deeded to him by David Sprague; youngest dau. Margaret Forsman; grandchild Margaret Forsman; grandchildren Mary and John Forsman; executor—son John Swisher; proven by John Swisher and Daniel Caslow.

BAILEY, KNOWLTON (D-28) Of Brown Twp; signed Feb. 23, 1856; proven Oct. 29, 1856; mentions: wife Elizabeth Bailey; the heir of my son Joseph who is Mary E. Bailey; dau. Margaret; son Knowlton (a minor); dau. Mary; son Samuel; dau. Asenath; dau. Elizabeth and dau. Rachel; executors; Daniel Scofield and James O'Harra; witnessed by Daniel Scofield, Jesse W. Scofield and David E. Scofield.

HADDOCK, SAMUEL (D-30) Of Columbus; signed May 6, 1843; proven Nov. 1, 1856; gives wife Abiah Haddock, all and she to be executor; witnessed by W. T. Martin and L. Heyl.

HODGKINS, JANE (D-31) Of Columbus; signed June 20, 1853; proven Nov. 18, 1856; mentions: sons John, Charles B., George S. and Samuel P. Hodgkins; dau. Sarah Frisbee, who is a widow; son Thomas; executor—son Richard O. Hodgkins; witnessed by W. T. Martin and L. Hilbert.

BONDLE, NICHOLAS (D-51) Of Columbus; signed Oct. 12, 1842; proven Mch. 16, 1857; states that his wife Margaret Bondle should continue to live with her dau. Mary Shoemaker and at her death, his dau. Mary Shoemaker is to have all; executor: wife Margaret; witnessed by W. T. Martin and M. Bush. At time of proving will M. Bush is deceased and his signature is proven by J. P. Bruck.

GOODWIN, DAVID (D-32) (Also as GOODIN) Of Mifflin Twp; signed Sept. 7, 1856; proven Dec. 13, 1856; mentions—wife Elizabeth Goodwin, and at her death to be divided between his five children, namely: Orin, Lovina Maze, Laney Agler, Elizabeth Agler and Mary Jane Goodwin; executors: wife Elizabeth and Andrew Agler; witnessed by John M. Pinney and Napoleon Pinney.

STARLING LYNE (D-34) Of Henderson County, Kentucky; signed Feb. 20, 1850; proven Dec. 22, 1851; mentions: son Edmund L. (who is well provided for by his uncle, Lyne Starling, deceased, of Ohio) and who is a minor; wife Mary H. Starling; he is entitled to something from his grandmother Carneal's estate, on the death of his mother; dau. Ann Marie Starling or any children he may have by his wife; executors: Father, Edmund L. Starling and father-in-law, William D. Allison, Clerk of Courts in Henderson County, Kentucky; witnessed by John P. Wilson, John B. Hart and Frederick A. Jones.

ARMSTRONG, THOMAS (D-38) Of Franklin County; signed Apr. 18, 1855; proven Jan. 2, 1857; names: wife Elizabeth Armstrong; children, namely; William F., Thomas, John L., Ann C. Smith, Mariah Trimble; Foreign Missionary Society for the enlightment of the heathen; executors: John Hanson and James O. Kane; witnessed by Michael W. Rogers and N. C. Mason.

KNAPP, HENRY ARNOLD (D-39) Of Columbus; signed June 30, 1856; proven Jan. 14, 1857; mentions: wife Sarah L. Knapp; executor: brother-in-law, James H. Beebe; witnessed by Robert Cutler and Matthew Gooding.

STAGG, ABRAHAM (D-40) Of Franklin County; signed May 10, 1846; proven Jan. 24, 1857; mentions: wife Rebecca; son Levey; scn George W.; son David S.; (all minors); dau. Sally Ann Stagg; dau. Lucinda Stagg; dau. Harriet Jane Stagg; dau. Hannah Speer; son Thomas; son Josiah; in codicil of May 10, 1846, mentions his step son, John Sager; executors: three sons, Levey, George W. and David S. Stagg; no witnesses given.

METTER, RICHARD (D-41) Of Columbus; signed Jan. 10, 1857; mentions: wife Mary Ann Metters to have all and at her death to go to nephews and nieces of himself and wife; executor: friend Charles Shenry; witnessed by J. P. Bruck and Julis F. Albery.

Note: He was a member of the firm of Joseph Hartman and Company composed of Joseph Hartman, Cyrus Bailey and Richard Metters (B. T. R.)

DAVIS, CHRISTOPHER (D-42) Of Prairie Twp; (being advanced in years); signed Feb. 22, 1850; proven Jan. 15, 1857; mentions: wife America Davis; sons John, Obediah, James, William and George W. M. (who is a minor); dau. Elizabeth A., son Christopher, son Joseph, son Jeremiah, dau. Ruhama; dau. Rachel J.; son Smith W., son Clinton H. (last six are minors); 'or any children born of my present wife'; executor: wife America Davis; witnessed by Thomas J. Moorman and Robert E. Ross. At time of proving will, Thomas J. Moorman is of Washington County, Iowa and a desposition taken there by John S. Beaty, Esq., says that he wrote the will at his office in Columbus, Ohio. Also that Robert E. Ross is now of Johnson County, Iowa.

MANNING, WILLIAM (D-44) Of Prairie Twp; signed Mch. 4, 1853; proven Jan. 12, 1857; mentions: two daughters, Minerva Flack, the wife of John Flack, with whom she lives; and Harriet Hand; executor: John Flack; witnessed by Absalom Peters and Samuel Kell.

MOORE, EMORETTA (D-46) Of Pike County, Missouri; signed Jan. 1, 1857; proven Feb. 13, 1857; mentions: brother Simeon Moore of Pike County, Missouri; sister Harriet E. Moore, sister Laura A. Moore; holds a note against Virgil Moore of Blendon Twp; executors: Simeon Moore and Virgil Moore of Blendon Twp; witnessed by George A. Lee, Pike County, Missouri, and Harriet Mitchell of same place.

PHELAN, WILLIAM (D-48) Of Lancaster, Fairfield County; signed Dec. 6, 1852; proven Apr. 18, 1856; mentions: wife Mary M. Phelan; executors—Henry Miers and P. B. Ewing; witnessed by C. F. Garaghty and A. C. Worthington.

JONES, I. G. (D-52) Of Columbus; signed Mch. 19, 1857; proven Mch. 20, 1857; mentions: wife Cynthia K. Jones; son James Kilborne Jones; dau. Louisa C. Jones; dau. Emma Jones; dau. Lizzie; executors: wife Cynthia K. Jones and Lincoln Kilbourne; witnessed by P. B. Wilcox and James A. Wilcox.

ABSTRACTS OF WILLS, FRANKLIN COUNTY, OHIO
Compiled by BLANCHE TIPTON RINGS

LITTLE, ROBERT PARKER (D-54) Of Mercersburg, Franklin County. Pa.; signed Feb. 23, 1852, proven July 1, 1856; mentions: wife Cynthia D. Little, is to have all for her use of the whole family and she to be executor; no witnesses; proven by William H. McDowell and James O. Carson.

TURNEY, DANIEL (D-55) Of Mifflin Twp.; signed Oct. 16, 1856; proven Apr. 15, 1857; gives widow Susannah Turney all; executor: George R. Turney; witnessed by John Dill and T. D. Grover.

MATTOON, WILLIS (D-57) Of Blendon Twp; signed Apr. 2, 1857; proven May 2, 1852; mentions—wife Caroline; an agreement between his brother Calvin and himself to keep their mother, Thankful Mattoon, and this amount is to be set aside for this purpose; wife is to be guardian of the children and she, with Selah R. Sammis, are to be executors; witnessed by George McWhirk and S. R. Sammis.

Note: Obit—'Died at his residence in Blendon Twp. Willis Mattoon on Apr. 7, 1857, aged 51 years'.

GARRETTSON, ANTHEA (D-58) Of Clinton Twp; signed Dec. 4, 1856; proven May 9, 1857; mentions: brother Ezra Wilcox, and at his death his share is to go to the heir of my deceased brother, Ira Wilcox; Thomas Wilcox; Lucius Wilcox; sister Delia Manley; sister Cornelia Phinney; no executor named; witnessed by Maria E. Skeels and Samuel Kinnear.

JONES, RICHARD B. (D-88) Of Brown Twp; signed Apr. 13, 1857; proven May 5, 1857; gives wife Rachel, all and she to be executor; witnessed by Thomas Sparrow and Robert Brooks.

KENNY, PETER (D-59) Of Columbus; signed May 29, 1857; proven May 30, 1857; mentions three children—Jane Margaret Kenny; Catherine Ann Kenny and Deliah Kenny; appoints Rev. James Meagher as their guardian; witnessed by John P. Hale, Michael Fallon, John Early and Thomas F. Harding. On June 10, 1857 Rev. Meagher refused to act as guardian and the Court appointed J. P. Bruck as guardian.

McCLOUD, WILLIAM (D-60) Of Sharon Twp; signed Apr. 15, 1857; proven June 3, 1857; mentions: dau. Eliza Phinney; dau. Maria Pool; dau. Nancy A. Stephens; son William; son James; executors—son William McCloud and Charles E. Burr; witnessed by C. E. Burr and W. H. Lewis.

JENNER, JOHN (D-62) Of Columbus; signed Mch. 17, 1857; proven June 6, 1857; mentions: wife Ann Maria Jenner (to have the right to hold interest in common with Conrad Born and Henry Bohlender and George Lotich, the share in the store); also the land in Nebraska Territory entered by John Bickley in my name; wife to be executor; witnessed by J. P. Bruck, H. N. Bolender and J. Kafer.

KIRKPATRICK, MARTIN (D-64) Of Blendon Twp; signed Feb. 1857; proven July 9, 1857; mentions—wife Eliza Kirkpatrick and Charles W. Benedict; executor—wife Eliza; witnessed by John Newhard and Frederick Miller.

PARNELL, WILLIAM (D-65) Of Franklinton; signed Dec. 13, 1854; proven July 9, 1857; mentions: son William; Mary Jane; Thomas Parnell; Eliza Ann Raymond; the late Urania Saunders' five children; Walter Parnell; Frances Alexander; Martha Shapter; Hariott Short, a minor; executors: Philip Shapter and James Gill; witnessed by R. H. Olive and S. K. Bell of Iowa, Jackson County, Ohio.

MOELLER, JOST (D-67) Of Truro Twp; signed June 5, 1856; proven Sept. 8, 1857; mentions: wife Catherine Moeller to have all 'in North America or out'; dau. Elizabeth Beckel, wife of Peter Beckel; dau. Ann Katherine Klein, wife of Peter Klein; dau. Christina Weiland, wife of George Weiland; dau. Margaret Reiselt, wife of Frederick Reiselt; dau. Catherine Graesle, wife of Ernest Graesle; dau. Julianna Moeller; executor—son-in-law Peter Klein or Ernest Graesle; witnessed by E. G. Frankenberg, Edward Lilley and F. Zelsman.

HOFFMAN, GEORGE (D-69) Of Franklin County; signed July 2, 1857; proven Sept. 19, 1857; mentions—oldest dau. Magdalena Ferguson and her husband Samuel Ferguson; dau. Elizabeth Martin and her husband, David Martin; dau. Anna Hoffman; dau. Leah Hoffman; executor—Samuel L. Detwiler; witnessed by M. C. Whitehurst and Jacob Carty.

WINTER, ABRAHAM (D-71) Of Westerville; signed Aug. 10, 1857; proven Sept. 21, 1857; mentions: wife Leah Winter; three daughters,

Rachel H., Lydia M. and Sarah J. (the farm in Harrison Twp.; Licking County on York Street); executors: William Slaughter and John Wagner; witnessed by Thomas McFadden and William King.

MARK, CHRISTIAN (D-72) Of Franklin County; signed Apr. 20, 1855; proven Sept. 26, 1857; mentions—Daniel Reese and his wife, who is to take care of him and his wife); Peter Harman and his wife and heirs; son Lewis Marks; no executor named; witnessed by Solomon Rush and James Bannister.

BARRETT, WINIFRED (D-73) Of Columbus; signed May 26, 1857; proven Oct. 6, 1857; mentions: brother Anthony Barrett: Sarah Heron, dau. of William Herron; Sarah Maria Clark; Maria Fossett; sister Abigail Bland; sister-in-law, Mrs. Dyer, wife of Stephen Dyer in Canada (my featherbed estimated to be worth $40); Susan Hills of Indiana; Jane Lucas; Sarah Diggins; Mrs. Davis, wife of Rev. Davis; Rev. Davis; executor—brother Anthony and he is to have my large family Bible; witnessed by W. T. Martin and G. B. Harvey.

KELLER, ABRAHAM (D-74) Of Prairie Twp.; signed Oct. 8, 1857; proven Oct. 21, 1857; mentions: wife Margaret Keller and child (she being pregnant at this time); if the child die, at the end of widowhood of my wife, all is to go to my brothers and sisters; his mother is to have the old house to live in; brother Hiram; sister Chloe; Margaret and Jacob Hopper and my sister Rebecca's child (to have the land in Illinois which was bought at the land sale at Palestine, Illinois; no executor named; witnessed by Thomas O'Harra and James Daugherty.

Note: Buried in Clover Cemetery, Prairie Twp; inscription—'Abraham Keller died Oct. 18, 1857, aged 48-5-6'.

ROWLAND, ABRAHAM (D-76) Of Delaware County; signed Nov. 11, 1856; proven Oct. 28, 1857; mentions: dau. Jane Nicely; dau. Catherine Edwards; grand-daus. (not named), the children of son John; dau. Elizabeth and her children; two grand-daus. (not named) the children of his dau. Mary; dau. Ann Griffith; executors—daus. Catherine Edwards and Jane Nicely; witnessed by G. H. Black and Abraham Lloyd.

PINNEY, ABNER H. (D-77) Of Columbus; signed Feb. 21, 1857; proven Oct. 31, 1857; mentions: wife Anne C. Pinney; son Henry C.; son Justin, son William; son Nathan (the youngest); his father and mother are to have a comfortable living upon and from his farm near Worthington; trustee—John W. Andrews and he to be executor; together with Edward J. Connable of Jackson, Michigan; codicil of same date witnessed by Thomas Sparrow and Henry P. Smythe. Will witnessed by Henry C. Noble and Kendall Thomas.

Note: Obit reads 'Died, A. H. Pinney of Columbus, at Jackson, Michigan, Oct. 21, 1857, aged about 55 years'.

TALLMAN, JOHN (D-84) Of Madison Twp; signed Aug. 23, 1856; proven Dec. 2, 1857; mentions: dau. Dinah; son Benjamin; dau. Mary; son Nathaniel; dau. Nancy; dau. Phebe; son David; son John; dau. Grace; dau. Eliza Anna; dau. Elizabeth; grand dau. Sarah Ann Tallman; executors—sons Nathaniel and John Tallman; witnessed by G. T. Wheeler and J. P. Shearer.

HOWARD, NICHOLAS (D-85) Of Pleasant Twp; signed Apr. 29, 1857; proven Sept. 29, 1857; mentions: son James and dau. Sarah Howard, who live with my son in Pleasant Twp; witnessed by J. Helmick and Jacob Werhl.

STAMBAUGH, ANN (D-87) Of Tazell County, Groveland, Illinois; signed July 11, 1857; proven Sept. 30, 1857; mentions: nephew David Martin; nephews John Andrew and George Schneider; neice Mary Ann Schneider; executor: Nathaniel Merion of Montgomery, Ohio; witnessed by John Shannon and George F. Cleveland.

PARSON, SAMUEL (D-89) Also same as Samuel Persons; of Columbus; signed Sept. 11, 1856; proven Jan. 4, 1858; mentions: two children, George M. Parsons and Elizabeth Jane Scott; executors: George M. and son-in-law, William Scott; owns land in Jackson County, Ohio; nephews James Banks, M. D. of Chicago, Illinois to have his medical books; witnessed by G. Swan and Robert Clemen.

Note: Obit 'Died, Samuel Parsons, Dec. 30, 1857 in his 72nd year. Was born at Reading, Conn., July 30, 1786'. (Much more given in Obit but not genealogical).

PHILIP, JOHN, SR. (D-92) Of Franklin County; signed Apr. 30, 1857; proven Jan. 9, 1858; mentions: son John, to have all land in United States and out; sister Elizabeth Evens; son Benjamin; dau. Mary Martin, wife of John Martin; the land in Wales, Kingdom of Great Britain to go to son John but he is to leave the revenue of said lease to his relatives in Wales if they should be in need of it; executors: William Powell and John Smith of Columbus; witnessed by Otto Zirckel and Julius Zirckel.

KAAG, CHRISTIAN GODFREY (D-93) Of Franklin County; signed Dec. 7, 1857; proven Jan. 21, 1858; mentions: wife (not named) dau. Katherine, married; son William, married; dau. Mary, married; son Gottfried; son Charles; son John; dau. Caroline; dau. Louisa; dau. Elizabeth; no executor named; witnessed by John S. Young, Jacob Rush and Jacob Rossi.

WINCHESTER, DANIEL (D-95) Of Columbus; signed Nov. 5, 1856; proven Feb. 2, 1858; mentions: wife Charlotte H. Winchester and at her death is to be equally divided among his heirs; executor: brother Erastus H. Winchester; witnessed by S. E. Samuel and J. William Baldwin.

COVERT, SAMUEL H. (D-96) Of Harrisburg; signed Jan. 23, 1858; proven Feb. 19, 1858; mentions that his wife is to have all; executor —John S. Young; witnessed by John S. Young and A. Poulson.

By deeds wife is proven to be Elizabeth Covert.

CLOUD, ENOCH (D-97) Of Columbus; signed Mch. 9, 1858; proven Mch. 25, 1858; mentions: wife Mary Ann Cloud; daus. Margaret, Julia and Amanda; son Enoch; dau. Rachel; son Joseph C; children of deceased dau., Mary Cantwell (not named); executors: wife and son Enoch; witnessed by R. J. Patterson and S. M. Smith.

BULL, ALONSON (D-99) Of Columbus; signed Aug. 12, 1857; poven Apr. 13, 1858; mentions: wife Hannah Bull; seven children; William B (the land in Livingston County, Illinois;) dau. Mary A. dau. Abiah L. Jones; sons Jason H and James G; dau. Chloe F. Bull; dau. Jane E. J. Bull; executors: Henry Westervelt of Columbus and son William B. Bull; witnessed by Joshua H Wells and Mary E. Wells.

HOFFMAN, JOHN JACOB (D-101) Of Columbus; signed June 13, 1857; proven Apr. 17, 1858; gives all to his dau. Elizabeth Aug. M. Zipp, wife of Henry Jacob Zipp (with whom I live) and at her death to her children; no executor named; witnessed by Otto Dresel and George Distelhorst.

BRINK, JACOB (D-102) Of Pleasant Twp; signed Mch 12, 1858; poven Apr. 12, 1858; gives all his possessions to his wife Elizabeth Brink; witnessed by J. P. Bruck and L. Walton; no executor named.

SPERRY, ABRAHAM (D-103) Of Columbus; signed Feb. 4, 1858; proven May 31, 1858; mentions: wife (not named); grand-dau. Nancy A. Sperry, wife of Isaac N. Thompson of Maion Co, Missouri; two sons Hiram and John C. Sperry and they to be executors; witnessed by George F. O'Harra and John G. Thompson.

KIRKPATRICK, ELIZA (D-104) Of Blendon; wife of Martin Kirkpatrick; signed Feb. 11, 1858; proven June 24, 1858; mentions: adopted son, Charles H. Benedict (and money left to him by the will of Martin Kirkpatrick), a minor; gives all real estate in Blendon to Dayton Rugg and wife (and he is to set up monuments); no executor named; witnessed by Virgil D. Moore and Frederick Annamiller (or Aumiller).

BRUNER, JOHN (D-106) Of Blnedon Twp; signed June 14, 1858; proven July 10, 1858; mentions: wife Mary Bruner (has no children); and the 'bound boy' William Wittar, a minor; the Evangelical Lutheran Church; executor: wife Mary; witnessed by George Pflieger.

HART, JOHN (D-107) Of Norwich Twp; signed May 18, 1858; proven July 13, 1858; mentions: nieces Margaret and Rebecca, the daus. of Moses Hart; Laura Hart, dau. of John P. Hart; Mary, Margaret, Sarah Rebecca and Amanda, the daus. of Moses Hart; John, son of Moses Hart; Moses Van Lair Hart, Jacob and Joseph Hart, the sons of Moses and John P. Hart; executor: John Hart, son of Moses Hart and Samuel D. Crum; witnessed by George Fisher and William Fisher.

PETERS, MARY E (D-108) Of Columbus; widow of Tunis Peters; signed June 22, 1858; proven July 19, 1858; mentions; son Jonathon L (the lot where her husband had built a room for public worship for Predestinarian Baptists); grandchildren, namely: Benjamin S. Davis, George M. Peters, Oscar Peters, Charles Peters, Lucy Ann Peters, Martin H. Peters, Mary E. Peters, Samuel Peters and Alice Peters; executor; son Jonathan; witnessed by P. B. Wilcox and John Mahl.

LUCAS, MARY (D-109) Of Franklinton; signed June 7, 1858; proven July 30, 1858; gives her share of land in Madison Co, Ohio, to her three bros.: namely- William Stirling Lucas, James Alexander Lucas and David Rittenhouse Lucas; all her rights in land in Johnson Co. Iowa, to her sister Anna Kanaga; executor: bro. William Stirling Lucas; witnessed by Thomas Moodie, Martha Grubb and J. W. Swayne.

BROWNING, JAMES (D-110) Of Jefferson Twp; signed Mch. 16, 1857; proven Aug. 3, 1858; gives all to wife (not named); and at her death, to go to Margaret Hartrum; executor: Abram P. Smith; witnessed by Daniel Hamaker and Henry Hamaker.

MORRILL, MILLE (D-119) Of Montgomery Twp; signed Jan. 13, 1857; proven Aug. 5, 1858; codicil Jan. 13, 1857; second codicil Feb. 10, 1857; mentions: son Elijah Glover; gives to Gustavus S. Innis (in trust for use of grand-son, Corrydon Morrill); Vicenia Morrill, widow of son, Moses Morrill (now Mrs. Vicenia M. Green); dau. Lydia Cookman; dau. Sarah C. Innis; children of her dau. Mary Wareham; grand-dau. Nancy Ann Decker; wants Vicenia Morrill to have nothing; Nathaniel Goodman is deceased (was son of Mariah Goodman, deceased, late Morrill and a dau. of the late Moses Morrill, Sr, deceased; executors: Nathaniel Merion, Rollin Moler and Elijah Merion; first codicil mentions grand-dau. Margaret Wareham and grand-dau. Sarah M. Glover; executor: Elijah Glover; witnessed by Franklin Gale and E. L. Glover; second codicil witnessed by George Merion and N. Merion. Will witnessed by William H. Innis and Clemson Guest.

LEISLER, JOHN G. (D-119) Of Columbus; signed Jan. 23, 1855; proven Aug. 10, 1858; mentions: wife. Elizabeth and she to be executor; wife to have all right to his undivided one-fourth in lot 727 in Columbus; witnessed by James Cherry, George Seilman and Conrad Heinmiller.

RODER, JOHN (D-120) (Also Roeder) Of Prairie Twp; signed May 2, 1858; proven Aug. 12, 1858; mentions: wife Dorothea Roeder, formerly Endres (to have all); children are not named; no executor named; witnessed by Simeon Feder, John Geyer and John Grunbaum.

KIDD, JOHN (D-121) Of Franklin Co; signed Dec. 6, 1851; proven Aug 12. 1858; mentions: wife (not named); son Samuel, unmar.; dau. Kate; son William; son John; dau. Alice; dau. Hannah is mar. and has a dau. Alice; son Anthony and his son William; executor; son Anthony and also to be guardian; witnessed by Hiram Smith and Elisha Smith. Codicil: Nov. 18, 1856; witnessed by Jane Russell and Eliza Russell.

SCHLITT, MARGARETA (D-123) (Katherine Margaretta Schlitt) Of Montgomery Twp; signed Nov. 26, 1855; proven Aug. 17, 1858; mentions: son Henry; dau. Katherine Rudolph; grand-dau. Pauline Richer, a minor; executor; bro. Henry Lutz; witnessed by Otto Zirckel and Henry Lutz.

SOUDER, JONAH (D-126) Of Jefferson Twp; signed Sept. 23, 1857; proven Aug. 27, 1858; mentions: wife (not named); son Abraham; son Isaac; son Jacob; son John; son Solomon; dau. Rebecca; dau. Catherine; dau. Sarah; dau. Christena; dau. Roseanne; dau. Mary Ann; his five sons are to take care of their mother, one each year in rotation   beginning with the eldest son; executors: sons Abraham and Isaac; witnessed by Stephen   Stimson and   Jasper Cheney.

HENRY, FREDERICK (D-127) Of Plain Twp; signed Aug. 18, 1858; proven Aug. 31, 1858; mentions: wife, Christena Henry; son Jacob and his heirs; dau. Susan Alspach; dau. Rachel Wagner; dau. Elizabeth Alspach; son Samuel; son George; dau. Mary Ann Henry; son Lewis; executor: son Jacob; wife to be guardian of all minor children; witnessed by George Wagner and Z. F. Guerin.

ARMISTEAD, WILLIAM (D-128) Of Norwich Twp; signed June 4, 1853; proven Sept. 2, 1858; mentions: wife Rachel; daus. Mary Ann, wife of John Moler and Maria Walton, wife of Michael Walton; youngest son, William McKendree Armistead; son Joseph; grandchildren: William Robert Breckenridge, Joseph Henry Breckenridge and Mary Elizabeth, the heirs of Joseph and Sarah Breckenridge, deceased; children of son Robert, deceased (it is my wish that should there ever be a division in court which shall make any difference, the amount that the children by my last wife shall receive of the estate of my son Robert (deceased) estate, than the children by the first wife, so as to equalize both sets of children; executors: John Moler and Michael Walton; witnessed by W. Armstrong, James D. Osborn and W. T. Martin.

CLOUD, ROBERT (D-131) Of Columbus; signed Aug. 16, 1853; proven Oct. 7, 1858; gives wife Anna Cloud, all, and she to be executor; witnessed by Samuel C. Andrews and Robert Brown.

WAMBAUGH, PAUL (D-132) Of Delaware County; signed July 16, 1858; codicil Oct. 9, 1858; proven Oct. 18, 1858; mentions: wife Sibael; Elizabeth H, Mary and Uriah L. Wambaugh, minors under age of 10 years; executor: John Knox of Blendon Twp; witnessed by Peter Guitner and D. Guitner; in the codicil appoints Solomon Wam-

338

baugh to act as guardian for dau. Mary Wambaugh; codicil witnessed by P. Arnold and S. H. Newcomb.

COCHRAN, EMILY (D-134)) Of Columbus; signed Oct. 22, 1857; proven Nov. 1, 1858; mentions: husband Reuben; daus. Sarah (the youngest) and Elizabeth Fairfield; sons William and Albert; dau. Mary Jane Lane; executor: son-in-law William Fairfield; witnessed by W. T. Martin and C. S. Wills.

FERRY, JANE (D-135) Of Brooklyn, N. Y.; signed Feb. 7, 1857; proven Oct. 26. 1858; mentions that her son Theodore Perry is to have all in trust for his children, namely: Angelina J, Israel J. and Charles J. Perry, all minors; copy in Franklin Co. Nov. 19, 1858; witnessed by Samuel G. Magee of 134 Bergen St. and R. C. Magee of 134 Bergen St, Brooklyn, N. Y.

SCHUCHART, FREDERICK (D-138) Of Columbus; signed Aug. 9, 1858; proven Nov. 30, mentions: wife Elizabeth, dau. Barbara Schuchart; son Henry; no executor named; witnessed by Ed. Lilley, Joseph Fitzwater and Josiah S. Holt.

COOK, WILLIAM (D-139) Of Jefferson Twp.; signed Sept. 18, 1858; proven Dec. 17, 1858; mentions: wife Hannah Cook (the farm in Jefferson Twp.) where George Compton now lives); two daus. Mabel Compton and Anna Cook; witnessed by Gideon W. Steel and A. J. Martin.

SHELDON, RICHARD A. (D-140) Of Columbus; signed Nov. 5, 1855; proven Dec. 13, 1858; mentions: wife Mary L. (at her death she to transfer the residue to his nearest or most deserving relative as in her judgment she may point out as most right and proper; executor: wife Mary; witnessed by Lynde L. Huntington, George D. Spencer and William R. Gay at Lebanon, Conn.

FARNHAM, LORINDA (D-142) Of Columbus; signed Jan. 4, 1858; proven Jan. 11, 1859; only son Eugene Soggs (or Loggs?), who now resides at Nevada City, California; wishes to be buried at Green Lawn Cemetery; executor: N. B. Marple; witnessed by H. B. Carrington and Maria Hillery.

SCHURMAN, CATHERINE (D-143) Of Indianapolis, Marion Co.; signed Nov. 26, 1852; proven Oct. 8, 1858; husband Gustavus to have charge of any children I may have, and he to be executor; witnessed by Conrad Lehmann, Josiah Lynn and Thomas Foster at Indainapolis, Indiana and proven there; signature of Josiah Lynn was proven by Fred Knepler and John C. New, as then Lynn was deceased; recorded in Cuyahoga Co., Ohio Jan. 5, 1859 and in Franklin Co. Jan. 17, 1859.

GLAZIER, JOSEPH N. (D-146) Of Columbus; signed Sept. 11, 1858; proven Feb. 9, 1859; mentions: wife Adeline; daus. Jennis Adda and Sallie Domigan Glazier, both minors; son John Newton Glazier; executor: wife Adeline; witnessed by William Armstrong and B. F. Martin.

GOODHUE, JACOB (D-148) Of Columbus; signed Feb. 26, 1849; proven Feb. 21, 1859; mentions: Eliza Lawson, wife of David Lawson of Columbus; Jacob G. Lawson son of David Lawson; Charlotte Farmer, wife of (no name given) Farmer of Columbus; Hannah Shepherd, wife of Thomas Shepherd of Columbus; executor: Hannah Shepherd; witnessed by W. T. Martin and John Funston. At time of proving, Funston is deceased and will is proven by John Van Yorx of Columbus who has known Jacob Goodhue for fourteen years.

ABSTRACTS OF WILLS, FRANKLIN COUNTY, OHIO
Compiled by BLANCHE TIPTON RINGS

BLUE, ELIZABETH (D-150) Of Columbus; signed Aug. 15, 1855; proven Feb. 21, 1859; mentions: dau. Emily S, wife of John Butler; George W. Butler; grand dau. Eliza Butler, a minor; six grandsons, the sons of John Butler, namely: John H. Henry, Charles, Samuel, Nathan and Albert Butler; witnessed by W. T. Martin and J. H. Graves.

REITZ, JOHN (D-151) Of Columbus; no date of signing; proven July 19, 1858; mentions: wife Mary and only child Mary, and if they both should die without issue, then all is to be equally divided between his and his wife's relatives; executor: John P. Bruck; witnessed by Frederick Walter (also spelled Walther); Louis Schimper and Christopher Kammerer.

HOLT, BENJAMIN (D-153) Of Prairie Twp; signed Feb. 25, 1859; proven Mch 24, 1859; mentions: wife Lydia; sons Josiah, Charles and Elias; daus. Sarah and Tracy Ann Roberts; son Thomas, dau. Mary Holt; son Thomas; dau. Mary Holt; son Williamia Ray; grandson James R. Holt; executors: wife Lydia and Josiah Holt; witnessed by Arthur O'Harra and Bartley O'Harra.

WOEHRLE, GEORGE (D-154) Of Prairie Twp; signed Nov. 28, 1857; proven Mch. 25, 1859; mentions: son Jacob; son George and his children; brother-in-law, David Hildebrandt; Matthias Fladt, to be trustee for son George Woehrle; no executor named; witnessed by John P. Bruck, Frederick Weber and Frederick Walter.

STIMMEL, MICHAEL (D-155) Of Hamilton Twp; signed Apr. 13, 1858; proven Apr. 9, 1859; mentions: wife Catherine; Rebecca Parsel, deceased, late of William Parsel (her heirs); Mary Ann Lisle, wife of Eli Lisle; Elizabeth Rohr, wife of John Rohr; dau. Christena, late Christena More; Abraham; Michael, Jr.; John Yost, deceased; dau. Rachel Shoaf, wife of Henry Shoaf; Mary Stimmel; executor: son Abraham; witnessed by Samuel McCleland and George M. Parsons.

HAMMEL, JONATHAN (D-157) Of Jefferson Twp.; signed May 6, 1853; proven Feb. 23, 1859; mentions: wife (not named); sons John and Samuel; dau. Martha Ann Hammell; dau. Mary Caroline Hammell; or any other children I may have to share equally; dau. Nancy, wife of Scott Kimbol; no executor named; witnessed by Nathan Spencer and Shuah Mann. Mch. 15, 1859, deposition was taken of Nathan Spencer of Crawford Co. Illinois, by John Shaw, Esq. and returned to Franklin Co., Ohio, Apr. 11, 1859.

BRADSHAW, SAMUEL (D-160) Of Washington Twp.; signed Feb. 23, 1858; proven Mch. 21, 1859; all is to go to dau. Tempa Johnson; executor: Holcomb Tuller; witnessed by E. W. Tuller and Roda Lee.

MURRAY, MARY (D-162) Of Cincinnati, Hamilton Co.; signed Aug. 16, 1855; proven Apr. 25 and May 15, 1859; was late of Franklin Co.; mentions: dau. Eliza A. Lawson; dau. Mary M. Thorp; dau. Hannah Coffin; son William Israel Murray; son Samuel H.; dau. Eliza A. Lawson is to be guardian of son William Israel Murray during his natural life; executors: William C. Coffin and Richard Power; codicil of Apr. 9, 1859, states that dau. Eliza is to be executor instead of Richard Power; witnesses to codicil; Mrs. E. D. Samson and Dr. S. M. Smith; witnesses to will: J. P. Walker and John Scott.

BANCROFT, SARAH E. (D-167) Of Montpelier, District of Washington, State of Vermont; signed Mch. 12, 1857; proven May 23, 1859; mentions: father Horace M. White and her son, Edwin H. Field, a minor; executor to be Fernando C. Kelton of Columbus, Ohio, or in case of his death, Harvey Bancroft of Columbus, Ohio; Fernando C. Kelton to be guardian of her son, Edwin by a codicil of Mch. 15, 18557; witnessed by F. F. Merrill, Charles Clark and T. R. Merrill; codicil witnessed by F. F. Merrill, Charles Clark and S. E. Wing.

SCHUCHARDT, ELIZABETH (D-170) Of Prairie Twp; signed Nov. 23, 1858; proven May 24, 1859; mentions: son Henry; dau. Barbara Louisa Hoffer; executors: son Henry and Samuel Kell; witnessed by Eli Peters and Jacob Kaiterly.

COLE, CATHERINE (D-171) Of Franklin Co.; signed Apr. 6, 1859; proven May 30, 1859; mentions: mother Sarah Woodruff, all and she to be executor; witnessed by N. Harrington and L. Woodruff.

DENIG, EDWIN T. (D-172) Of Red River Settlement, Red River of the North British Possessions, but formerly of Ft. Union of the Upper Missouri; signed Sept. 12, 1856; proven Mch. 18, 1859; mentions: bro. Augustus M. Denig; son Robert (who evidently of a first marriage); 'my lawfully wedded wife' Hai Kees Kah We Yah Denig; my dau. Sarah Denig known among the Indians as 'Mock pe e dai' or 'The Firey Cloud'; my son Alexander Denig, known as 'Ean och She or 'Boy of Aone'; states that Sarah is to go to an English school until she is fifteen years old or until four years from date of will; son Alexander is to be sent to an English school at the age of twelve years; says 'in as much as my wife is unacquainted with Federal money, it is to be paid to the Hudson Bay Co. for her use'; executors Augustus M. Denig; Robert Morgan and Rev. Priest Bellecour at Paalenan; witnessed by Joseph Forbescue of Red River, Clerk of Hudson Bay Co.; James McKenzie of Red River and Robert Morgan. Codicil states that the children are not to be taken to the United States to be educated nor to be taken from their mother but better a private teacher, perhaps Priest Bellecour will educate them at his house; same witnesses to codicil; proven Dec. 12, 1858 before W. Mactavish, Governor of Assinibia. A note enclosed gives the following statement: Sarah Denig, born Aug. 10, 1844; Alexander Denig born May 17, 1852; Ida Denig born Aug. 22, 1854, all baptized in the Catholic faith.

TURNER, JOSEPH (D-178) Of Franklin Co.; signed Apr. 11, 1855; proven June 22, 1859; mentions: wife Mariah C. Turner and she is to be executor; witnessed by J. W. Young and Barnabas Harris.

MATTHEWS, WILLIAM (D-178) Of Perry Twp.; signed May 14, 1859; proven June 25, 1859; mentions: bros. John and George and they are to occupy the home place; the children of bro. John; Mary Ann Grey; Altha Matthews; Margaret Jane Matthews and Cordelia Matthews; no executor named; witnessed by Amos Brelsford and David Brelsford.

KEIM, PHILLIP (D-179) Of Mifflin Twp.; signed July 11, 1859; codicil same date; proven July 16, 1859; gives wife Susan all; and she to be executor; witnessed by D. R. Kinsell, John Keim and Elam Drake; witness to codicil, John Starrett and John Clark.

NOTE: Newspaper says "Philip Keim died July 12, 1859, at his residence near Mifflin Cemetery, in his 55th year." Is buried at Green Lawn cemetery.

FREED, SHADRACH (D-181) Of Blendon Twp.; signed Mch. 22, 1859; proven Aug. 17, 1859; gives all to wife Elizabeth; no executor named; witnessed by H. Dyxson and Elizabeth Langham.

OLDING, JOHN JOSEPH (D-181) Of Franklinton; signed Aug. 5, 1859; proven Aug. 20, 1859; mentions: wife Mary is to have all in the United States or out and at her death it is to go to his brothers and sisters: namely: John Herman Olding, Margaret Maria Wellen; John Henry Olding and Anna Maria Wellen; executor: friend Herman, Steinke; witnessed by J. P. Bruck and Lorentz Beck.

TRIPLETT, DANIEL (D-183) Of Plain Twp.; signed May 11, 1855; proven Aug. 20, 1859; mentions: wife (not named) son George W; 'other children not named; executors: George W. Triplett and Nelson Wilkin; witnessed by Daniel Hamaker and Alexander Doran. (By papers in estate, wife is Sarah Triplett).

SAMMISS, MARTHA (D-184) Wife of Selah R. Sammis; signed May 29, 1859; gives her husband undivided interest in estate of Robert McCandish late of Fairfield Co., deceased; the other heirs to this beside herself are bro. Smith McCandish; heirs of her deceased sister, Mary Ann Lamb; heirs of her deceased sister, Mary Ann Lamo; heirs of her deceased sister, Elizabeth Emerick; sister Jane McCandish; sister Nancy McCandish; sister Sarah Pyle; executor: husband, Selah R. Sammis; witnessed by R. R. Arnold and Hawes Barbee, Jr.

LUCAS, MARGARET (D-186) Of Franklinton; signed Dec. 22, 1858; proven Sept. 15, 1859; says that she owns land in Madison Co. with her sisters, Martha Grubb and Eliza Y. Lucas and gives her share to them; and at their death to go to nephews; James A. Lucas, David R. Lucas and niece Anna C. Kanaga, and nephew William Stirling Lucas; the land in Iowa to her two sisters and they are to be executors; nephew David R. Lucas, the son of her late bro. John Lucas; witnessed by A. A. Kerr and William W. Hess.

THOMAS, MICHAEL (D-188) late of New Albany; signed Sept. 24, 1859; proven Sept. 30, 1859; mentions: dau. Hannah Hoover; dau. Melisa Dague; other children (not named); no executor named; witnessed by Jacob Ulry and George Dague.

HUNTER, JOHN (D-189) Of Franklin Co.; signed Apr. 11, 1855; proven Sept. 3, 1859; mentions: son James B. who lives in Iowa; son Charles W; son Moses N. (the land in Madison Co.) dau. Ann Eliza; son John W, land in Iowa and $300 more than the others for his support and schooling; executor: William Walker; witnessed by Henry Clover and Byers Adair.

CLOUD, MORDECAI (D-193) Of Front Royal, Warren Co., Virginia; signed July 11, 1855; proven June 20, 1859; copy at Columbus, Sept. 23, 1859; mentions: wife Rebecca B, the land in Ohio and servants Ann and Louisa; eight heirs, namely: Anna Marie, Sarah Bliss, Kitty Reynolds, Daniel, Mary Elizabeth, R. Virginia, Robert Lopscomb and Lucy Ellen Coud; executors: son Daniel and son-in-law, John M. Hopewell; witnessed by Giles Cook, Newman M. Jacobs and Gideon W. Jones.

HEYL, CONRAD (D-196) Of Mifflin Twp.; signed Jan. 7, 1845; codicil Apr. 10, 1858; proven July 27, 1859; mentions: nieces Anna Mitchell and Elizabeth Pilgrim; bro. Christian Heyl; nephew and godson, John Konrod Heyl; children of my deceased niece, Maria more, late of Illinois and Elizabeth Hymrod, wife of John Hymrod; nephews: Lawrence, Lewis, William E., George W. and Charles Heyl; niece Mary A. Henkel; nephew Christian Myer; nieces Catherine Lambert and Mary Kaemerer; nephew John Lambert; executor: nephew Lawrence Heyl; witnesses to will: Fernando C. Kelton and E. N. Stelzer, a clerk in merchant establishment of Kelton, Bancroft and Co. and who was deceased at time of proving will; witnesses to codicil: Henry Bicher and George Katzmyer. At time of proving, Henry Bicher was of Bloom Twp., Fairfield Co., Apr. 10, 1859.

JONES, EDWARD (D-201) Of Columbus; signed May 13, 1858; poven Oct. 25, 1859; mentions: wife Elizabeth Jones; dau. Elizabeth, wife of Thomas Stevens of Origon; dau. Mary, wife of Richard Jones of Columbus; son John of Columbus, and his dau. Mary; no executor named; witnessed by W. T. Martin and R. J. Patterson.

WESTERVELT, CORNELIUS L. (D-203) Of Blendon Twp.; signed Sept. 28, 1859; (died Oct. 22, 1859); proven Oct. 28, 1859; mentions: father Peter Westervelt; sister Sarah Sammis; sister Rebecca Goodspeed; sister Hannah West; sisteer Angeline Westervelt; sister Mary Andrus; sister Anette Blair; sister Maria Ingalls, (deceased,) her children, namely: Rosalie and Geraldine Ingalls; owns property in Ohio and Iowa; executor: Lewis R. Goodspeed; witnessed by James L. Westervelt and J. B. Connelly.

RUSH, GEORGE, (D-204) Of Reynoldsburg; signed Oct. 7, 1859; proven Nov. 23, 1859; mentions: wife Abigail; son Theodore, a minor; wife to be executor; also to be guardian; witnessed by D. K. Wood and David Hissong.

KELLEY, ALFRED (D-206) Of Columbus; signed July 14, 1858; (died Dec. 3, 1859) proven Dec. 6, 1859; mentoins: wife (not named); son Alfred; dau. Maria K. Bates; dau. Helen K. Collins; dau. Anna Kelley; dau. Kate Kelley; dau. Jane K. Collins of Cleveland; executor: James L. Bates of Columbus; witnessed by Samuel Croswell and Benjamin Philips.

STARLING, WILLIAM (D-211) Of Henderson, Kentucky; signed Nov. 19, 1849; proven Nov. 1850; gives all that is coming to him from the estate of Lyne Starling, deceased, late of Columbus, to his father, E. L. Starling and his mother A. M. Starling of Henderson Co., Kentucky; witnessed by M. Kean, Charles T. Starling and Lyne Starling; Dec. 13, 1859.

MEHRING, GEORGE (D-213) Of Franklin Co.; signed July 26, 1859; proven Dec. 22, 1859; mentions; wife Catherine Moehring to have all in the United States or out; daus. Ann Margaret and Mary Elizabeth; son John Conrad Moehring guardian, Paulus Doler or friend, Leonhard Maegerlein; executor: friend John Hundt or Paulus Hartman; witnessed by Ed. Lilley, J. S. Holt, John Otstot and George Welker.

LANGHAM, ROBERT (D-215) Of Westerville; signed June 29, 1859; proven Feb. 1, 1860; mentions: dau. Sarah Ann; son William; no executor named; witnessed by Milton H. Munn and Henry Swickard.

SWAN, GUSTAVUS (D-216) Of Columbus; signed Feb. 20, 1858; proven Feb. 9, 1860; mentions: wife Amelia Swan; two daus. Sarah and Jane; owned land in Newport, Rhode Island; executors: son-in-law, Augustus Whiting and George N. Parsons; witnessed by Samuel C. Andrews and William Burdell.

TRENT, PRINCE (D-218) Of Columbus; signed Mch. 4, 1857;

proven Feb. 16, 1860; mentions: dau. Mary Trent; dau. Martha Buckner; grand-dau. Elizabeth Bugh; son George Henry Trent's children; son Daniel Trent; witnessed by David Sullavon and John T. Ward.

WIND, CHARLES (D-218) Of Franklin Co.; signed Feb. 3, 1860; proven Feb. 17, 1860; gives all to wife Maria and she to be executor; witnessed by Jonathan Miller, Henry M. Cryder and Alexander Mooberry.

SATTLER, JOSEPH (D-221) Of Columbus; signed Feb. 11, 1860; proven Feb. 18, 1860; mentions: Joseph A. Schuler, unmar., his brother-in-law; Maria Sattler; Theresia Sattler; Brigita Sattler; John Sattler; Phitellus Sattler; widow; wishes a tomb-stone be erected; gives money for Mass at Holy Cross Church and the church at Ampiller, Firol witnessed tby Michael Voll; M. D.; John Pirrung and Joseph A. Schuler.

KELLER, JACOB (D-223) Of Norwich Twp.! signed Jan. 24, 1860; (died Feb. 3, 1860; proven Feb. 4, 1860; mentions: wife Sarah; five daus. Mary A., Nancy, Chloe Margaret and Rebecca; son Joseph, the eldest; sons Daniel, Ezekiel and Jacob who are minors; executors: John H. Groff and James Daugherty; witnessed by Solomon Clover and Samuel N. King.

CEMETERY RECORDS

Frank A. Livingston

Inscriptions from Gravestones
Seceder Cemetery

The Seceder Cemetery is located south of Reynoldsburg, Franklin County, Ohio, on the west side of State Route 256, at the Fairfield County line.

The title to the cemetery is in the name of the United Presbyterian Church of Reynoldsburg, Ohio, the successor of the Truro Associate Presbyterian Church organized in 1817. A large part of the original members of this church came to Franklin County from Washington County, New York, in the years between 1805 and 1817.

Ashton, Cheniworth, died Aug. 24, 1872, aged 55 yrs. 9 mos. 23 ds.
    Jesse, son of J. and H., died Oct. 10, 1877, aged 5 mos.
    Laura, wife of T., died Apr. 12, 1876, aged 83 yrs. 6 mos. 14 ds.
    Louisa, dau. of Thomas and Nancy, died Aug. 22, 1835, aged 19 yrs. 6 mos.
    Nancy, wife of Thomas, died Aug. 31, 1828, aged 34 yrs.
    Thomas, died Mar. 18, 1845, aged 54 yrs. 6 mos.
    William, died Feb. 10, 1871, aged 92 yrs. 8 mos. 28 ds.
Bailey, Infant son of O. K. and A. M., born Feb. 13, 1880.
Beals, George, died May 23, 1835, aged 45 yrs. 3 ds.
    Hannah, dau. of George and Mable, born Dec. 22, 1825, died July 4, 1827, aged 2 yrs. 7 mos. 15 ds.
    Mabel, wife of George, died Aug. 16, 1873, aged 82 yrs. 4 mos. 18 ds.
    Beard, Mary J., wife of John, died Jan. 14, 1866, aged 32 yrs. 6 mos. 9 ds.
Bodine, Abigail C., dau. of J. and Lovina, died Apr. 5, 1852, aged 2 yrs. 10 mos. 11 ds.
    James A., son of J. and L., died July 27, 1845, aged 16 ds.
Boyd, Agnes, wife of Robert, native of Scotland, died Mar. 24, 1878, aged 75 yrs. 2 mos.
    Elizabeth, died Jan. 1, 1843, in 81st yr. of her age.
    Ida I., dau. of W. B. and L. A., died Nov. 13, 1859, aged 3 mos. 7 ds.
    Robert Sr., native of Scotland, died Sept. 19, 1874, aged 75 yrs.
Bull, Balinder, dau. of Walter and Betsey, died Feb. 23, 1839, aged 2 yrs. 9 mos. 23 ds.
    Edward, son of W. and B. A., died Mar. 29, 1850, aged 18 yrs. 2 mos. 9 ds.
    Sarah, dau. of Walter and Betsey, died July 26, 1824, aged 10 mos. 11 ds.
Burton, Charles S., son of W. and M., died Nov. 21, 1853, aged 3 yrs. 5 mos. 16 ds.

James W., son of J. and M., died May 17, 1831, aged 3 mos. 11 ds.

Campbell, Jane, wife of James, died Oct. 6, 1853, in 92nd year of age.

Case, Anne, wife of Jacob, died Dec. 28, 1853, aged 44 yrs. 10 mos.

Catherine, dau. of Jacob and Anne Eliza, died Mar. 21, 1841, aged 3 yrs. 1 da.

Jacob, born Feb. 20, 1804, died Feb. 6, 1865.

Lewis, son of Jacob and Anne Eliza, died Dec. 19, 1848, aged 19 yrs.

Clark, Anna Eleanor, died Oct. 26, 1845, aged 56 yrs. 7 mos. 5 ds. (Inscription on Lee monument.)

Clendenning, Royal, son of J. and C. C., died June 21, 1833, aged 21 mos. 11 ds.

Cochran, Amos E., son of E. T. and G., died Sept. 18, 1861, aged 24 yrs. 6 mos. 19 ds.

Emily, dau. of John and Esther, died Feb. 6, 1820, aged 12 yrs. 9 mos. 23 ds.

Francis, E., son of E. T. and G., died Mch. 20, 1865, aged 10 yrs. 11 mos. 17 ds.

John, died Aug. 29, 1825, aged 58 yrs. 10 mos. 23 ds.

J. R., son of S. and E. T., died July 11, 1834, aged 10 mos. 6 ds.

John T., died Oct. 24, 1826, aged 29 yrs. 10 mos. 23 ds.

Mary, died Nov. 10, 1819, aged 18 yrs. 8 mos. 9 ds.

Coit, Hyram Josephus, son of Huldah and E. W., died Aug. 4, 1834, aged 11 mos. 1 da.

Julia Hortentia, dau. of Huldah and E. W., died Apr. 30, 1834, aged 2 yrs. 8 mos. 5 ds.

Collier, James, born May 2, 1810, died Feb. 1, 1844, aged 33 yrs. 8 mos. 29 ds. ("Erected by William Collier in memory of his brother, May 23, 1844.")

Connal, Flora Bell, dau. of James and Rachel, died June 3, 1863, aged 3 yrs. 11 mos. 27 ds.

Helen, wife of James, died Oct. 17, 1854, aged 62 yrs. 8 mos. 10 ds.

James, died June 27, 1855, aged 63 yrs. 6 mos.

Connel, Andrew, son of J. and H., died July 16, 1851, aged 19 yrs. 7 mos.

Connell, Janet Strang, wife of William, died Nov. 5, 1871, aged 73 yrs.

Cowden, Margaret Jane, wife of Dr. A. S. and dau. of James and Ann Morrow, died Nov. 3, 1840, aged 24 yrs. 6 mos. 21 ds.

Crawford, Mathew, died Feb. 8, 1832, in 50th year of age.

James, born Apr. 10, 1751, died June 14, 1838, aged 87 yrs. (Revolutionary War sailor, grave marked with D. A. R. marker.)

Martha, consort of James, died July 10, 1840, aged 88 yrs. 11 mos. 10 ds.

Darby, Elizabeth, wife of J., died Oct. 15, 1854, aged 66 yrs. 1 mo. 12 ds.

Forrester, Esther, wife of W., died Mch. 28, 1887, aged 75 yrs.

Grace B., wife of Robert, died Dec. 17, 1869, in the 60th year of her age.

Margaret, died Oct. 7, 1855, aged 62 yrs. 4 mos. 27 ds.

Rev. Robert, died Nov. 1, 1861, in 56th year of his age, 24th year of his ministry.

William, died Nov. 15, 1870, aged 69 yrs. 6 mos.

Frazier, Elizabeth, wife of George, died July 2, 1852, aged 36 yrs. 3 mos. 7 ds.

French, David H., son of John B. and Rabena, died Oct. 20, 1823, in 14th year of age.

Euphemia B., wife of James M., died Jan. 17, 1859, aged 32 yrs. 5 mos. 7 ds.

James M., died Nov. 25, 1867, aged 47 yrs. 1 mo. 11 ds.

Jane Ann, dau. of Thomas B. and Jane, died Oct. 10, 1834, aged 11 yrs. 8 mos. 26 ds.

"Janet, wife of Jonathan French, Sr., one of the officers of the Revolution of '76, she died July 4th, 1831, in the 75th year of her age."

Jonathan, died May 17, 1838, in the 85th year of his age. (Grave marked with D. A. R. marker.)

John B., died Sept. 16, 1834, in 55th year of his age.

Margaret, dau. of Jonathan and Jannet, died May 9, 1832, aged 7 yrs. 5 mos. 15 ds.

Rabena, wife of John B., died Sept. 29, 1834, in 50th year of age.

(No Christian name.) Son of J. B. and M. R., died Jan. 18, 1854, aged 24 ds.

Fisk, Caroline, dau. of Ira and Polly, died Oct. 10, 1833, aged 4 yrs.

Polly, widow of Ira, and second wife of Daniel Lines, died Dec. 25, 1843, aged 59 yrs. 11 mos.

Freling, John N., son of J. and E., died May 17, 1851, aged 3 yrs. 5 mos.

Mary Elizabeth, died Apr. 22, 1845, aged 15 mos. 9 ds.

Graham, Agness, wife of William, died July 27, 1858, aged 58 yrs.

Amelia, consort of George D., died May 18, 1846, aged 34 yrs. 11 mos. 7 ds.

Anna, wife of George, died Aug. 18, 1864, aged 85 yrs. 1 mo. 18 ds.

Caroline, wife of William G., died Sept. 8, 1853, aged 38 yrs. 11 mos. 26 ds.

*David, died Oct. 7, 1886, aged 85 yrs. 7 mos. 20 ds.

Elizabeth, dau. of William and Agness, died Feb. 19, 1839, 28th year of her age.

Fidelio, died July 18, 1870, aged 3 weeks.

George, died Nov. 24, 1855, aged 78 yrs. 5 mos. 22 ds.

George D., died June 6, 1852, aged 40 yrs. 4 mos. 29 ds.

George W., died Dec. 5, 1842, aged 35 yrs. 5 mos.

James, died Aug. 7, 1843, aged 66 yrs. 6 ds.

James D., died Apr. 13, 1857, aged 38 yrs. 11 mos. 10 ds.

Jennette, wife of Amos, died Aug. 30, 1864, aged 41 yrs.

John J., died Aug. 19, 1849, aged 39 yrs. 9 mos. 21 ds.

John W., died May 29, 1848, aged 72 yrs. 10 mos.

CEMETERY RECORDS

Frank A. Livingston

Inscriptions from Gravestones
Seceder Cemetery, Reynoldsburg, Ohio

Graham—
> Louie, dau. of Amos and Jennette, died Aug. 17, 1864, aged 4 yrs. 1 mo. 2 ds.
> Lydia Murch, wife of James D., died Dec. 13, 1893, aged 75 yrs. 11 mos. 1 da.
> Margaret, wife of G. D., died Sept. 20, 1854, aged 23 yrs. 1 mo. 25 ds.
> Margaret, consort of James, died Aug. 16, 1864, in 80th year of age.
> Margaret, wife of James, died Sept. 17, 1835, aged 55 yrs. 2 mos. 16 ds.
> Margaret, consort of William G., died Nov. 5, 1842, aged 31 yrs. 2 mos. 14 ds.
> Maria, dau. of David and Nancy, died Dec. 13, 1843, in 19th year of age.
> Mary, wife of James M., died June 13, 1850, aged 24 yrs. 9 mos. 23 ds.
> Mary, wife of John, Jan. 4, 1856, aged 50 yrs. 5 mos. 25 ds.
> Mary McBurney, wife of William (Revolutionary War Soldier) died 1819.
> Mary, wife of William G., died Aug. 1, 1836, aged 31 yrs. 5 mos. 25 ds.
> Maud Willard, dau. of D. L. and E. J., died Mch. 8, 1888, aged 3 mos. 20 ds.
> *Nancy, died June 18, 1889, aged 85 yrs. 7 mos. 20 ds.
> Sarah, consort of George J., born Jan. 15, 1809, died Aug. 31, 1841, aged 32 yrs. 1 mo. 16 ds.
> Wallace, Co. F, 1st Ohio Cav.
> William, born Mch. 17, 1750, died Nov. 15, 1822. (Revolutionary War soldier, D. A. R. marker.)
> William G., died Jan. 18, 1854, aged 50 yrs. 28 ds.
> Willie, son of Amos and Jennette, died Aug. 13, 1864, aged 8 yrs. 9 mos. 2 ds.
> Willie G., died July 28, 1867, aged 21 mos.

Hanes, Hannah, died Sept. 2, 1835, aged 75 yrs.
Harmon, Eleanor Lee, wife of A., died July 1, 1842, aged 24 yrs. 7 mos. 18 ds.
> Jacob, died May 22, 1861, aged 37 yrs. 3 mos. 26 ds.
> Jacob, died Feb. 7, 1857, aged 65 yrs. 8 mos. 4 ds.

---

*Inscription on same stone, marked "Our Parents."

Harper, George, died Feb. 30, 1835, aged 73 yrs. ("Erected by Thomas Ashton in memory of George Harper.")
    Jane, died Oct. 27, 1843, aged 71 yrs. 7 mos. 10 ds.
Huber, Charles M., son of D. and J., died June 28, 1852, aged 28 ds.
    Infant, son of D. and J., died Aug. 18, 1853, aged 28 ds.
Hutson, David P., son of William and Jane, died June 30, 1850, aged 19 yrs. 3 mos. 18 ds.
    Ebenezer, son of John and Elizabeth, died Oct. 16, 1835, aged 16 yrs. 8 mos. 28 ds.
    Elizabeth, wife of J., died May 5, 1857, aged 70 yrs. 7 mos. 29 ds.
    Elizabeth, dau. of N. and E., died Oct. 6, 1839, aged 2 yrs. 8 mos.
    J., died June 22, 1826, aged 44 yrs. 8 mos. 1 da.
    Jane, wife of William, died Feb. 19, 1891, aged 79 yrs. 1 mo. 6 ds.
    Nancy M., dau. of J. and E., died Mch. 11, 1855, age 1 yr. 5 mos. 3 ds.
    Nathaniel, son of J. and E., died Mch. 24, 1855, aged 1 yr. 4 mos. 20 ds.
    Nathaniel, died Oct. 3, 1857, aged 47 yrs. 3 mos. 11 ds.
    William, died Aug. 16, 1869, aged 64 yrs. 10 mos. 26 ds.
Hughes, Anna May, dau. of W. L. and M. J., died July 2, 1873, aged 1 yr. 5 mos. 2 ds.
    Emily G., wife of Joseph, died June 20, 1867, aged 45 yrs. 5 mos. 13 ds.
    Jane, wife of Joseph, died Feb. 7, 1862, in the 57th year of her age.
    Joseph, who emigrated from Ireland in 1801, died Sept. 9, 1842, in 64th year of age.
    Joseph, died May 31, 1873, aged 65 yrs. 11 mos. 22 ds.
    Lulu Myrtle, dau. of W. L. and M. J., died Dec. 21, 1871, aged 2 yrs. 8 mos. 21 ds.
    Margaret, wife of J., died Feb. 11, 1843, aged 71 yrs.
    Margaret S., dau. of Joseph and Jane, died Jan. 5, 185–, aged 1 yr. 7 mos.
    William L., died Aug. 19, 1886, aged 48 yrs. 28 ds.
Jamison, James W., son of Thomas and Anne, died Oct. 17, 1843, aged 1 yr. 2 mos.
Johnson, Infant son of Abm. and Sarah, departed 1831.
    Isaac, son of Henry and Mary, died Dec. 4, 1828, in 18th year of his age. ("Made by Abm. Johnson and brother.")
    William, son of Henry and Mary, died Dec. 11, 1828, in 15th year of his age. ("Made by Abm. Johnson.")
Jones, Elizabeth C., wife of J. C., died Feb. 6, 1875, aged 36 yrs. 4 mos.
    Minta, dan. of R. and M., died Feb. 26, 1877, aged 11 mos. 23 ds.
    John C., died Jan. 16, 1869, aged 31 yrs. 9 mos. 9 ds.
    John W., died Mch. 24, 1886, aged 18 yrs. 5 mos. 13 ds.
    Richard, son of B. and J., died June 1, 1849, aged 9 mos.
    Ronella, dau. of J. C. and E. C., died Mch. 11, 1877, aged 14 yrs. 10 mos. 16 ds.

Kurts, Almira, wife of Henrey, died Mch. 27, 1863, aged 69 yrs.
6 mos. 16 ds.

Learn, Betsy J., dau. of Jefferson and Maria, died May 2, 1837, aged
3 yrs. 8 mos.
    Velina, dau. of Jefferson and Maria, died Nov. 10, 1849, aged
    10 mos. 29 ds.

Lee, John, died June 8, 1877, aged 65 yrs. 6 mos. 25 ds.
    Rosannah, died Feb. 1, 1835, aged 13 yrs. 3 mos. 9 ds.
    Rosannah, dau. of Thomas and Sarah, died Feb. 2, 1836, aged
    11 yrs. 3 mos. 11 ds.
    Sarah, wife of Thomas Sr., died Oct. 11, 1848, aged 60 yrs. 9 mos.
    26 ds.
    Susannah, died Jan. 9, 1842, aged 21 yrs. 11 mos. 24 ds.
    Thomas, died Feb. 7, 1818, aged 4 yrs. 3 mos. 28 ds.
    Thomas Sr., died July 31, 1846, aged 57 yrs. 2 mos.

Livingston, Agness, wife of Alexander, born 1761, died 1826, aged
65 yrs.
    Ebenezer, son of John and Mary, died July 3, 1839, aged 2 yrs.
    2 mos. 6 ds.
    F. C., son of W. J. and M. A., died Oct. 26, 1864, aged 5 yrs.
    2 mos. 4 ds.
    Georgie, dau. of John E. and Isabella Strang, died Feb. 26, 1867,
    aged 1 yr. 4 ds.
    Isabella Strang, wife of John E., died May 8, 1868, aged 30 yrs.
    7 mos. 23 ds.
    John, died Feb. 6, 1863, aged 66 yrs. 8 mos. 19 ds.
    John J., son of Alexander W. and Matilda, died Dec. 23, 1848,
    aged 2 yrs. 2 mos. 24 ds.
    Joseph, died June 26, 1851, aged 67 years.
    Mary, wife of John, died Aug. 1, 1841, aged 41 yrs. 8 mos. 4 ds.
    Mary J., dau. of W. J. and M. A., died Mch. 16, 1863, aged 2 yrs.
    1 mo. 17 ds.

Logan, Nancy, wife of John, died June 24, 1858, aged 51 yrs. 5 mos.
9 ds.

Looker, John B., son of John and Elsey, born Jan. 28, 1817, died
Aug. 11, 1827.

McCafferty, Thomas, born Sept. 24, 1781, died Oct. 8, 1823, aged
42 yrs. 15 ds.

McCray, David, new grave 1933.
    Edwin J., died June 14, 1863, aged 1 yr. 8 mos. 8 ds.
    Eunice L., dau. of J. and M. W., died Mch. 29, 1859, aged 4 yrs.
    4 mos. 17 ds.
    Infant, dau. of W. W. and M., died Jan. 15, 1863.
    Infant, son of A. and M. J., died Aug. 15, 1861, aged 1 mo.
    James, died June 5, 1853, aged 69 yrs. 2 mos.
    Jane, new grave 1933.
    John, died Oct. 1, 1834, aged 47 yrs. 10 mos. 12 ds.
    John, died Sept. 1, 1844, age not legible.

Margaret, wife of John, died June 1, 1872, aged 74 yrs. 10 mos. 11 ds.

Margaret P., wife of James, died Oct. 1, 1845, aged 52 yrs. 10 mos. 23 ds.

Nancy A., dau. of William and Sarah, died Apr. 27, 1873, aged 17 yrs. 6 mos. 8 ds.

Nancy Ann, wife of Robert, died Apr. 24, 1881, aged 90 yrs. 2 mos. 21 ds. (On same stone with Robert, marked "Father and Mother.")

Robert, died July 18, 1872, aged 83 yrs. 5 mos.

Sarah Ann, died Oct. 2, 1836, aged 17 yrs. 1 mo. 29 ds.

Zenith J., dau. of J. and M. W., died Dec. 29, 1853, aged 11 mos. 18 ds.

McCullough, R. M., died in his country's service, Oct. 21, 1862, aged 21 yrs. 6 mos. 3 ds.

McIntire, Jane, died Nov. 17, 1865, aged 86 yrs. 7 mos. 7 ds.

Joseph, died May 14, 1843, aged 63 yrs. 2 mos. 12 ds.

Mary, wife of William. (No dates.)

Shepherd Painter, son of J. and J., died Mch. 9, 1822, age not legible.

McVickar, Elizabeth, died Aug. 13, 1883, aged 82 yrs. 20 ds.

William, died Feb. 9, 1872, aged 72 yrs. 3 mos. 8 ds.

Magruder, Mary L., wife of M., born Apr. 19, 1846, died Feb. 26, 1874.

Maxfield, Ann M., dau. of J. and C., died Nov. 19, 1844, aged 19 yrs. 3 mos. 7 ds.

James, died May 2, ——.

Maxwell, John, son of W. and A., died Sept. 21, 1834, aged 12 yrs. 5 mos.

Margaret A., died Sept. 19, 1865, aged 21 yrs. 6 mos.

William, died Sept. 25, 1854, aged 52 yrs.

Mead, Louesa A., dau. of J. and J. C., died Apr. 25, 1855, aged 3 yrs. 4 mos. 15 ds.

Margaret, dau. of A. J. and J., died Oct. 28, 1854, aged 14 yrs. 8 mos. 28 ds.

William, son of A. J. and J., died June 15, 1853, aged 6 yrs. 10 mos. 15 ds.

Miller, James, died Dec. 8, 1839, aged 38 yrs. 5 mos. 10 ds.

Morse, Joseph N., 1812—1889. Susan, 1825—1888.

(Both of above on same stone "Father and Mother.")

Murch, Agnes, dau. of C. and E., born Sept. 10, 1833, died Sept. 22, 1835, aged 2 yrs. 3 mos. 12 ds.

Chauncey, born July 19, 1795, died Feb. 7, 1839, aged 43 yrs. 29 ds.

Elizabeth, wife of C., died Sept. 4, 1869, aged 74 yrs. 7 mos. 24 ds.

Thomas Law, son of Chauncey and Elizabeth, died Dec. 22, 1846, aged 8 yrs. 3 mos. 4 ds.

Nay, Hannah Louisa, dau. of Jeremiah and Mary, died Feb. 20, 1825, aged 6 yrs. 10 mos. 8 ds.

Jeremiah, died June 11, 1844, aged 58 yrs. 9 mos. 26 ds.

Mary, wife of Jeremiah, died Sept. 2, 1827, aged 42 yrs. 1 mo. 27 ds.

Paulina, dau. of Jeremiah and Mary, died Feb. 12, 1835, aged 14 yrs. 5 mos. 10 ds.

Outcalt, Jane M., wife of T. J., died June 7, 1871, aged 35 yrs. 1 mo. 21 ds.

Painter, Jane, dau. of Nathaniel and Martha, died Nov. —, 1834, aged 5 mos.

Joseph, son of Nathaniel W. and Martha, died 1834, (remainder not legible.)

Lizy, (dates not legible.)

Patterson, Agnes N., 1833—1913.

David E., died Apr. 10, 1864, aged 37 yrs. 11 ds.

Emri F., died Oct. 31, 1871, aged 25 yrs. 10 mos. 21 ds.

James, son of R. and S., died June 11, 1862, aged 24 yrs.

John, 1830—1895.

Phillip, died Jan. 2, 1857, aged 38 yrs. 4 mos. 11 ds.

Susannah, wife of R., died Sept. 7, 1881, aged 75 yrs.

William, 1839—1916.

Peacock, William, died Sept. 11, 1861, aged 26 yrs.

Rees, Samuel, died June 15, 1852, aged 51 yrs. 6 mos. 3 ds.

(On same stone "Also his wife Elizabeth.")

Robertson, James, son of Robert and Mary A., died June 13, 1840, aged 2 mos. 8 ds.

Lovett, son of Robert and Mary A., died July 11, 1846, aged 8 mos. 3 ds.

Thaddie, son of W. W. and C. A., died Sept. 29, 1867, aged 3 yrs. 3 mos. 9 ds.

Rose, Elisha, died Mch. 27, 1856, aged 86 yrs. 7 mos. 15 ds.

Margaret A., wife of S. A., died July 4, 1858, aged 22 yrs. 1 mo. 21 ds.

Sarah, died Mch. 4, 1839, aged 70 yrs. 9 mos. 20 ds.

Shaffer, Anna, consort of Jacob, died Oct. —, 1828, aged 31 yrs. 5 mos.

Anna S., dau. of Dr. J. and —— Shaffer, died Dec. 2, 1853, aged 19 yrs. 9 mos. 11 ds.

Isaac, son of Jacob and Anna, died Aug. —, 1835, aged 17 yrs. 4 mos.

Dr. Jacob, born Sept. 2, 1794, died Oct. 20, 1877.

Jennie, wife of John, died Dec. 31, 1870, aged 31 yrs. 4 mos. 8 ds.

Sarah A., wife of Dr. J., born Oct. 5, 1807, died Nov. 30, 1891.

Smith, Elena, died June 23, 1874, aged 51 yrs. 8 mos. 13 ds.

Elizabeth, died Mch. 31, 1898, aged 74 yrs. 1 mo. 19 ds.

Jacob, died July 10, 1867, aged 75 yrs. 1 mo. 19 ds.

Jacob, Jr., died Apr. 29, 1890, aged 64 yrs. 8 mos. 26 ds.

Maggie, dau. of J. and M., died in Germany, (dates not legible.)
Margaret, wife of Jacob, Sr., died in Franklin Co., Pa., Mch. 1, 1835, aged 37 yrs.

Spitler, Daniel, died June 4, 1866, aged 39 yrs. 1 mo. 21 ds.

Sprague, Agnes M., wife of A. E., died Feb. 1, 1869, aged 20 yrs. 5 mos. 19 ds.

Stebout, George J., Co. F, 5th U. S. Colored Infantry.

Stevenson, Isaac M., son of J. and M., died Oct. 26, 1868, aged 2 yrs. 11 mos. 18 ds.
James, died Mch. 9, 1893, aged 73 yrs. 11 mos.
Mary, wife of J., born Dec. 3, 1825, died Apr. 5, 1866, aged 40 yrs. 4 mos. 2 ds.

Strang, Isabel, born Nov. 28, 1795, died Jan. 7, 1851.
Isabella, dau. of M. and I. S., died Dec. 13, 1854, aged 16 yrs. 8 mos. 13 ds.
Isabella S., wife of M. Strang, died May 16, 1861, aged 56 yrs.
Margaret Anne, died July 14, 1868, no age.
Martha, dau. of M. and I. S., died Dec. 20, 1854, aged 15 yrs. 12 ds.
Moses, died Oct. 8, 1871, aged 64 yrs.

Swann, Aaron, died Aug. 27, 1827, aged 34 yrs. 1 mo.
Pollina, died Aug. —, 1826, aged 2 yrs. 11 mos.

Taylor, Elizabeth, wife of George, died Jan. 3, 1864, aged 41 yrs. 10 mos. 23 ds.
Elizabeth, wife of M., died J—— 12, 1858, aged 66 yrs. 6 mos. 12 ds.
Herbert W., son of Jas. and R. A., died Mch. 7, 1856, aged 2 yrs. 7 mos. 28 ds.
James, died Nov. 20, 1886, aged 71 yrs. 7 mos. 10 ds.
Jemima, wife of Eleazar, died Sept. 1, 1859, aged 73 yrs.
John, son of G. and E., died July 13, 1855, aged 8 mos. 9 ds.
John W., son of J. and R. A., died July 6, 1863, at Vicksburg, Miss., aged 20 yrs. 1 mo. 3 ds. Sargent in Co. I, 95th Regiment O. V. I.
Margaret Serena, dau. of Mathew and Martha, died May 23, 1838, aged 16 yrs. 7 mos. 23 ds.
Mathew, died June 2, 1855, aged 69 yrs. 11 mos. 14 ds.
Rebecca A., wife of James, died Aug. 2, 1881, aged 69 yrs. 9 mos. 20 ds.

Torrence, Ezra M., died Feb. 17, 1837, aged 27 yrs.
Mary A., dau. of J. H. and M., died Feb. 25, 1852, aged 2 yrs. 10 mos.
Thomas, died Mch. 26, 1828, aged 86 yrs.
Thomas, died Sept. 3, 1847, aged 71 yrs.
Volney P., died July 11, 1837, aged 23 yrs. 10 mos. 18 ds.

Tucker, Frances, wife of P., died Mch. 13, 1886, aged 67 yrs. 6 mos. 9 ds.
Phinehas, died Oct. 27, 1894, aged 74 yrs. 10 mos. 27 ds.

Woodruff, Almira, dau. of Rice and Elizabeth, died Apr. 10, 1832, aged 1 yr. 3 mos. 29 ds.

Elizabeth, wife of Rice, died Feb. 11, 1833, aged 21 yrs. 7 mos. 9 ds.

George, son of B. and E. W., died Feb. 12, 1860, aged 20 yrs. 4 mos. 18 ds.

Margaret, dau. of B. and E. W., died May 22, 1832, aged 2 yrs. 4 mos. 12 ds.

Margaret, dau. of Rice and Elizabeth, Jan. 27, 1833, aged 11 ds.

Rice, died Apr. 25, 1876, aged 67 yrs. 29 ds.

Ruth, wife of Wiard, died Aug. 22, 1827, aged 63 yrs.

Ruth E., dau. of B. and E. W., died July 30, 1829, aged 10 mos. 8 ds.

Sarah Ann, wife of Rice, died Aug. 16, 1847, aged 27 yrs. 8 mos. 26 ds.

Wiard, died Dec. 12, 1828, aged 67 yrs.

(THE END)

CEMETERY RECORDS

FRANK A. LIVINGSTON

DAVIS BURIAL GROUND

LOCATION: On Riverside Drive about one mile below Dublin Bridge on east side of Scioto River, in Franklin County, Ohio. On land of Amaziah Sells. His wife was Polly, daughter of Joseph Davis.

Brelsford, Abner, died Dec. 29, 1867, aged 75 yrs. 4 mos. 21ds.

Caroline, dau. of A. and S., died Aug. 24, 1831, aged 4 yrs. 1 mo. 21 ds.

Francis M., son of W. H. and R., died May 27, 1845, aged 1 yr. 6 mos. 22 ds.

Jacob M., son of A. and C., died Apr. 21, 1851, aged 17 mos. 24 ds.

Johnnie F., son of P. A. and M. S., died Feb., 1837, aged 1 yr. 8 mos.

Joseph, son of J. and C., died Apr. 25, 1863, aged 21 yrs. 5 mos. 3 ds. Member of Co. H. 46 O. V. I.

Mary, dau. of A. and S., died Sept. 1, 1831, aged 7 mos. 27 ds.

Nancy, wife of Abner, died Sept. 6, 1825, aged 40 yrs. 5 mos. 24 ds.

Brobeck, Catherine, wife of Jacob. died Nov. 30, 1857, aged 67 yrs. 8 mos.

Brown, Sarah, dau of J. and S., died Feb. 5, 1847, aged 17 ds.

Brunk, Daniel, died Aug. 24, 1863, aged 61 yrs. 8 mos. 28 ds.

*Coalman, James, died May 3, 1838, aged 58 yrs. 3 mos. 28 ds.

*Curlman, Mary, dau. of James and Eliza, died Sept. 13, 1834, aged 1 yr. 10 mos. 25 ds.

Davis, Ann, dau. of Samuel and Matilda, died Jan. 25, 1831, aged 1 yr. 3 mos. 4 ds.

Ann Simpson, died June 5, 1851, aged 86 yrs. 5 mos. 8 ds. (This is Ann Simpson Davis, Revolutionary Heroine.)

Byron, son of Samuel and Matilda, died Apr. 10, 1840, aged 4 yrs. 2 mos. 14 ds.

Edith, dau. of J. E. and C. E., born July 22, 1871, died Apr. 4, 1883, aged 11 yrs. 9 mos. 12 ds.

---

*The two stones are together, probably both should be Coalman.

Edith A., wife of Joseph, Sr., died Aug. 14, 1874, aged 77 yrs. 5 ds.

Elizabeth, dau. of Samuel S. and Matilda, died Jan. 24, 1831, aged 4 yrs. 3 mos.

Fred R., son of Joseph W. and Mary, died Oct. 10, 1887, aged 8 yrs. 8 mos. 9 ds.

Horace W., Co. K. 40th Inf., Spanish American War.

Jacob E., died Mar. 21, 1886, aged 50 yrs. 8 mos. 25 ds.

John, died Jan. 25, 1832, aged 71 yrs. 4 mos. 19 ds.

Joseph, born Jan. 27, 1802, died June 29, 1892.

Joseph Watts, born Oct. 19, 1838, died Jan. 25, 1892. Captain in Recruiting Service, U. S. Army. Civil War.

Joshua, died July 24, 1823, aged 27 yrs. 23 ds.

Lucinda, wife of E. A. Swain and dau of E. A. Davis, died Jan. 8, 1855, aged 21 yrs. 7 mos. 25 ds.

Mary Ann, dau. of J. and S., died Apr. 9, 1847, aged 9 yrs. 4 mos.

Mary Ann, wife of Beriah, died Oct. 31, 1847, aged 69 yrs. 8 mos.

Mary Butt, born July 10, 1842, died Oct. 14, 1891.

William W., son of Joshua and Edith, died June 25, 1841, aged 19 yrs. 7 mos. 21 ds.

Everet, Aaron, died Apr. 21, 1847, aged 47 yrs. 3 mos.

Martin, Caroline, died Oct. 15, 1851, aged 5 yrs. 9 mos. 10 ds.

David, died Sept. 29, 1849, aged 47 yrs. 8 mos. 15 ds.

Matilda, died Mar. 8, 1837, aged 19 or 49 yrs. 1 mo. 3 ds.

Mathews, Rachel, dau. of J. and M. J., died July 13, 1846, aged 4 yrs 4 mos. 7 ds.

Mickey, Zephaniah, died Apr. 30, 1847, aged 20 yrs. 5 mos. 4 ds.

Roney, Isaac H. L., died Mar. 12, 1842, aged 17 yrs. 10 mos. 14 ds.

James, died Nov. 26, 1840, aged 43 yrs. 1 mo. 29 ds.

Rachel, wife of James, died Dec. 11, 1832, aged 41 yrs. 7 mos. 13 ds.

Shipman, Androme, dau. of O. and A., died Aug. 15, 1840, aged 1 mo. 9 ds.

Charles, son of O. and A., died Oct.'1, 1841, aged 1 mo. 29 ds.

Oliver, died Apr. 7, 1847, aged 33 yrs. 8 mos. 6 ds.

Wooley, Benjamin, died Apr. 17, 1858, aged 58 yrs. 2 mos. 24 ds.

Sarah, wife of Banjamin, died Aug. 25, 1847, aged 44 yrs. 8 mos. 15 ds.

Wright, Francis M., son of Jacob and Mary, died July 13, 1831, aged 3 yrs. 8 mos. 18 ds.

Jacob, died Sept. 6, 1877, aged 79 yrs. 9 mos.

Mary, wife of Jacob, died — 20, 1886, aged 82 yrs. 4 mos. 15 ds.

(THE END.)

CEMETERY RECORDS

F. A. LIVINGSTON

THE BEARD-GREEN CEMETERY, LICKING COUNTY, OHIO*

The Beard-Green family burying ground, where most of the persons interred were related, either blood kin or by marriage. The cemetery is located in Licking County, Ohio, on the west side of the pike between Newark and Jacksontown, Ohio. It adjoins the south line of the D. B. Dawes estate and arboretum. Among the weeds and brush are numerous beautiful monuments.

Anderson, John, died Aug. 24, 1830, aged 25 years.
Beard, John, died Feb. 15, 1814, aged 61 years. (A Revolutionary War Soldier.)
    Margaret (Kirk), wife of John, born April 12, 1758, died July 7, 1850.
    Thomas, born May 4, 1800, died Aug. 19, 1844.
    Rachel (Pitzer), wife of Thomas, born Aug. 30, 1807, died Nov. 22, 1899.
Clark, G. O., born 1835, died 1904.
    Sarah H., born 1846, died 1920.
    Armina B., born 1864, died 1865.
Dicken, Jesse G., son of John, died Apr. 5, 1885, aged 89 yrs.
    Amos, died May 25, 1884, aged 27 yrs. 3 mos. 7 ds.
    George Dillon, born Apr. 23, 1853, in Hocking County, Ohio. died St. Petersburg, Fla., Feb. 21, 1916.
    Rowena, born 1841, died 19—.
Green, Benjamin, died Sept. 28, 1833, aged 78 yrs. 5 mos. 2 ds.
    Catherine, wife of Benjamin, died Aug. 20, 1821, aged 76 yrs. 10 mos. 16 ds.
    Benjamin Jr., died Nov. 29, 1838, aged 40 yrs. 5 ds.
    Sophia, died June 26, 1844, aged 40 yrs. 2 mos. 3 ds.
    Benjamin, born 1814, died 1895.
    Mary S., born 1810, died 1911.
    Daniel, died Oct. 3, 1875, aged 84 yrs. 4 mos. 17 ds.
    Elizabeth, wife of Daniel, died July 28, 1860, aged 64 yrs. 5 mos.
    Samantha, dau. of Daniel and Elizabeth, died Oct. 24, 1886, aged 56 yrs. 7 mos. 7 ds.
    Sarah, wife of William, died July 31, 1828, aged 24 yrs. 5 mos. 17 ds.
    Rachel, died Apr. 2, 1874, aged 84 yrs.
    Richard, died at Louisville, Ky., May 11, 1865, aged 19 yrs.
Harris, Thomas, died June 26, 1836, aged 51 yrs.
    Rachel, wife of Thomas, died Feb. 9, 1832, aged 40 yrs.
Hillman, Thomas B., born Nov. 30, 1836, died Nov. 10, 1887.
    Phebe Ann, born Dec. 22, 1837, died Feb. 9, 1917.
    (Father and Mother on stone.)
Holden, Alexander, died Sept. 25, 1832, aged 68 yrs. 19 ds.
    Sally, wife of Alexander, died June 18, 1833, aged 70 yrs. 6 mos. 25 ds.
Lane, Charlotte, wife of Joseph, died Apr. 30, 1852, aged 49 yrs. 2 mos. 21 ds.
    Barbara, died July 20, 1849, aged 62 yrs.
    Gelland (?) H., died June 13, 1833, aged 51 yrs.
Langhrey, Edward, died Nov. 26, 1850, aged 59 yrs.
    Elizabeth, wife of Edward, died Sept. 15, 1862, aged 50 yrs.
    John, died Nov. 30, 1816.
Pitzer, Richard, died Dec. 4, 1819, aged 45 yrs.
    John, died Jan. 28, 1864, aged 62 yrs. 4 mos. 10 ds.
    Mary (Green), died Nov. 10, 1885, aged 80 yrs. 8 mos. 20 ds.
Swisher, Jacob, died June 25, 1843, aged 64 yrs. 6 mos. 16 ds.
    Phebe, wife of Jacob, died Dec. 1838, aged 57 yrs. 7 mos. 5 ds. (Phebe Swisher was a daughter of Benjamin Green.)

---

*Contributed by Mrs. L. Bancroft Fant, Newark, Ohio.

Genealogical Notes, concerning some of those buried in the Beard-Green Cemetery:

John Beard, who died Feb. 15, 1814, at 61 years of age, was a private in Captain Benjamin Lemont's Co., and Colonel McCobb's Regiment in Massachusetts. He enlisted July 9, 1779, and was discharged Sept. 24, 1779. (Ref., "Mass. Soldiers and Sailors," Vol. I, also pension files.)

Benjamin Green, who died September 28, 1833, aged 78 years, 5 months and 2 days, served three enlistments in the Revolutionary War from Loudoun County, Virginia. He was present at the surrender of Cornwallis at Yorktown, and was pensioned for six months' service in the Virginia lines. Following his service in the army he removed to Allegheny County, Maryland, and in 1802 he removed to Licking County, Ohio, where he was prominent in religious, civic and financial affairs. His wife's maiden name was Katherine Beem. (See Hills Licking County History and D. A. R. National Numbers 31343, 46433, and 52212.)

Alexander Holden, who died September 25, 1832, aged 68 years and 19 days, is said to have been a Revolutionary War Soldier. He was a Justice of the Peace and County Commissioner for Licking County, Ohio. In 1808 he was elected to the General Assembly of the state of Ohio.

INSCRIPTIONS—OLD BUCKLEY CEMETERY, JACKSON COUNTY, OHIO

Contributed by MAYBURT STEPHENSON RIEGEL

Location: Franklin Twp., Jackson County, Ohio, three-fourths mile east of Oak Hill Pike, eight miles south of Jackson, Ohio.

Thomas Alexander, d. 5–9–1845, age 71 yr. 2 m. 22 ds. (Soldier).
Wife, Sarah, of Thomas Alexander, d. 11–5–1850, aged 67 yrs.
Thomas J., son of Caleb and Mary Alexander, d. 7–31–1852, aged 72 yrs.
Samuel Stephenson, d. 1–1–1851, aged 77 yrs. (Soldier).
Jane, wife of Samuel Stephenson, d. 9–8–1846, aged 63 yrs.
Eli Henson, d. 4–13–1832, aged 36 yrs. 1 m. 8 ds.
Mary, wife of Eli Henson, d. 1855, aged 51 yrs.
Francina M., dau. of A. A. and L. M. McCray, d. 6–27–1830, aged 1 yr.
Angeline, dau. of A. A. Lethe McCray, d. 8–19–1833, aged 1 yr. 1 m.
Barbara, dau. of A. A. and L. M. McCray, d. 9–13–1837, aged 9 m. 10 ds.
Samuel A., son of M. and M. Nelson, b. 4–4–1848, d. 8–9–1849.
(Footstone on grave adjoining above—E. G. N.).
William Buckley, d. 11–14–1855, age 76 yr. 7 m. 2 ds. (Soldier.)
Elizabeth, wife of William Buckley, d. 3–14–1831, age 42 yrs. 4 m. 14 ds.
Mary Buckley, d. 4–18–1870, age 59 yr. 8 m. 12 ds.
Elizabeth E., dau. of Job and R. Buckley, d. 12–13–1852, age 17 yr. 7 m. 26 ds.
Job, son of Job and Rebecca Buckley, d. 7–16–1852, age 2 yr. 7 ds.

CEMETERY RECORDS
CEMETERY AT SANDY CORNERS

Located at corner of Avery and Amlin Roads, Franklin Co., Ohio.

Andress, Randall, died July 16, 1851, aged 40 yrs.

Babcock, Ann E., dau. of R. and J., died Jan. 4, 1850, aged 9 yrs. 9 mos. 25 ds.
> James, son of ———, died Oct. 2, 1852, aged 9 yrs. 2 mos. 1 da.

Bachel, Zachariah, son of Henry and ———, aged 10 mos. 18 ds.

Condren, William, son of John and ———, died July 21, 1854, aged 1 yr. 13 ds.

Davis, H., died Sept, 22, 1878, aged 48 yrs. 6 mos. 16 ds.
> Lona, dau. of H. and S., died Apr. 6, 1877, aged 2 yrs. 6 mos.
> Sarah, wife of H., died Apr. 12, 1877, aged 47 yrs. 8 mos. 4 ds.

Foark, Infant Mary, dau. of J. and K., died Oct. 2, 1876.

Gouldin, Catherine, wife of Thomas, died May 17, 1854, aged 40 yrs.

Hammer, Elizabeth H., dau. of Joseph and Elizabeth, born Dec. 17, 1848, died Aug. 11, 1850.
> Joseph, son of J. and E., died Aug. 19, 1850, aged 12 yrs.
> Josephine, died Aug. 18, 1850, ager 44 yrs. 5 mos.

Horch, Anna M. Ned——— (Abraham Horch), born Feb. 12, 1826, died Oct., 1846.

Huffman, Josephine, wife of Lumbert, died Feb. 9, 1866/68, aged 25 yrs. 10 mos. 7ds.
> Lawrence, son of L. and J., died Oct. 19, 1864, aged 1 yr. 6 mos. 3 ds.

Hunter, Cynthia, wife ofJohn, died Jan. 19, 1850, aged 31 yrs.
> Harriet E., dau. of John and Cynthia.
> James, died June 25, 1861, aged 86 yrs. 20 ds.
> John P., died Sept. 18, 1852, aged 33 yrs.

Kaiser, Barbary, died Sept. 4, 1852, aged 24 yrs. 3 mos. 3 ds.
> Jacob, son of N. and M., died Sept. 24, 1876, aged 8 yrs. 9 mos. 11 ds.
> Margaret, died July 22, 1849, aged 14 ds.

Latham, Ann, wife of David, died Apr. 20, 1855, aged 25 yrs. 2 mos. 1 da.

Miller, Margaret, died Nov. 16, 1860, aged 21 yrs.

Mock, Alice, dau. of S. and M., died Jan. 11, 1856, aged 9 mos. 1 da.

Paulk, Sarah A., wife of M., died May 3, 1851, aged 21 yrs. 6 mos, 11 ds.

Peasley, J. A., Co. K. 97th O. V. I.

Pendleton, Catherine, dau. of J. and J., died Aug. 19, 1851, aged 11 mos. 2 ds.
> Harriet, dau. of James and Jane, died Aug. 10, 1856, aged 8 yrs. 3 mos. 3 ds.
> James, born in Maine, June 23, 1807, died June 26, 1879, aged 72 yrs. 3 ds.
> Mary J., dau. of J. G. and E., died Oct. 11, 1871, aged 9 mos. 28 ds.

Pugsley, Elizabeth, wife of Francis, died 1862, aged 61 yrs. 2 mos. 21 ds.
> Emily L., dau. of F. and E., died Sept. 16, 1848, aged 4 yrs. 6 mos. 13 ds.

Siebert, Ezekiel, died Dec. 5, 1850, aged 25 yrs. 10 mos. 2 ds.
> Mary Ann, wife of Ezekiel, died Nov. 10, 1851, aged 21 yrs. 3 mos. 12 ds.

Strawbridge, Martha A., dau. of C. and P., died Dec. 15, 1847, aged 17 mos. 15 ds.

Temple, Jane, wife of Thomas, died Jan. 17, 1862, aged 64 yrs.

Watts, William, died Aug. 4, 1846, aged 78 yrs.

Wilcox, Harriet E., dau. of Wm. and Susan, died Apr. 8, 1869, aged 2 mos. 7ds.

Rebecca A., dau. of Wm. and Susan, died Oct. 18, 1862, aged 2 mos. 18 ds.

Windle, Abraham, died Feb. 26, 1876, aged 71 yrs. 9 mos.
Abraham, son of E. M. and Mary, died Apr. 14, 1865, aged 10 yrs. 26 ds.
Amy, dau. of E. M. and Mary, died Dec. 12, 1865, aged 15 yrs. 8 mos. 4 ds.
Jacob, son of E. M. and E., died May 1, 1862, aged 2 yrs.
Mary, wife of E. M., died June 11, 1858.

Yeager, Volentine E., died Oct. 11, 1861, aged 81 yrs.

Young, John Sr., born Aub. 6, 1766, died June 15, 1859.
John, died June 26, 1874, aged 74 yrs. 8 mos. 5 ds. "Father"
Rebecca, died Dec. 3, 1861, aged 59 yrs. 11 mos. 18 ds. "Mother"

* * * *

Incomplete Records
————, James, son of Daniel and E.
————, Nannie J.
————, Persey, dau. of
————, Susan, dau. of.
Wolpert, ————.
————, ————, Aug. 11, 1850, aged 8 yrs.

MITCHELL CEMETERY

Located about half a mile north of Dublin on Mitchell Farm, Franklin Co., Ohio

Bishop, Finley, died Feb. 2, 1860, in the 62nd year of his age.
Infant son of Finley and Nancy, died April 24, 1839, aged 22 ds.
Melicia S., dau. of L. and J., died Sept. 25, 1855, aged 7 yrs. 5 mos. 17 ds.
Nancy, wife of Finley, died Apr. 24, 1839, aged 35 yrs.

Ferris, Mary Ann, dau. of L. and M. J., died Mch. 26, ————, aged 4 mos. 15 ds.

Howey, James, died Mch. 29, 1856, aged 37 yrs. 9 mos. 21 ds.
James, died Aug. 19, 1825, aged 38 yrs.
Sara, died Dec. 23, 1877, aged 84 yrs. 6 mos.

Huston, James, died Aug. 9, 1849, aged 28 yrs.

Johnston, Infant son of H. F. and A. E., died Nov. 26, 1861.

Mitchell, Charles, a pioneer of Washington Township, died Mch. 9, 1823, aged 77 yrs.
Charles, died Aug. 2, 1882, aged 35 yrs. 5 mos. 7 ds.
Eliza Reed, born 1812, died 1899.
George R., son of Hugh and Jane, died June 10, 1839, aged 2 yrs.
Hugh, died Sept. 15, 1862, aged 66 yrs. 5 mos.
Iscah, (In Memory of), died Apr. 26, 1832, aged 3 mos.
Jane, wife of Charles, died Aug. 11, 1853, aged 84 yrs.
Jane, wife of Hugh, died Mch. 17, 1879, aged 74 yrs.
Rachel, wife of Thomas, died Sept. 13, 1851, aged 39 yrs. 6 mos. 16 ds.
Thomas R., son of Thomas and Rachel, died May 15, 1842, aged 5 yrs. 1 mo. 5 ds.
William O., son of Thomas and Sarah, died Feb. 7, 1853, aged 2 mos. 1 da.

CEMETERY RECORDS

FRANK A. LIVINGSTON

SWISHER CEMETERY INSCRIPTIONS

Located on Swisher Farm, Licking County, Ohio, now owned by Mr. Fatig.
Compiled by Luella Bancroft Fant, August, 1934.

Axline, Joseph, 1854-1928.
    Mary A., 1849-——.
    H. G. d. Jan 23, 1871, aged 47 yrs. 7 ms. 25 ds.
    Susannah, w. Henry, d. Apr. 13, 1854, aged 22 yrs. 3 ms. 6ds.
    Joseph, d. Feb. 7, 1901, aged 69 yrs.
    Daniel D., 1837-1887.
    Almeda, 1847-1905.
    Daniel, d. Oct. 24, 1855, aged 60 yrs.
    Catherine, d. Feb. 23, 1874, aged 75 yrs. 1 m. 1d.
    Margaret, w. C. W., d. Aug. 27, 1855, aged 21 yrs.
Barnes, ————, d. July 27, 1887, aged 49 yrs. 8 ms. 10 ds.
Beals. Andrew, 1842-1916.
    Melissa McIntosh, w. of Andrew, 1842-1904.
    Ross, 1875-1903.
    Mary L., 1881-——.
Beem, Andrew, d. Nov. 27, 1863, aged 82 yrs.
    Elizabeth, w. Andrew, d. Dec. 12, 1864, aged 73 yrs.
    Frederick, d. May 8, 1853, aged 29 yrs.
Brown, Henry, d. Nov. 22, 1882, aged 41 yrs.
Clark, Rosa, w. A. A., 1867-1908.
Giles, George W., 1840-1908, G. A. R.
    Sarah, w. Geo. ——- ——.
Gorey, James, b. May 11, 1822, d. Apr. 29, 1905.
Headlee, David S., 1827-1890.
    Susan, 1826-1903.
    Martha, 1860-1929.
    Eliza Ann, 1862-1928.
    John. d. May 16, 1856, aged 26 yrs. 8 ms. 4 ds.
    Elizabeth, d. Oct. 11, 1855, aged 4 yrs. 8 ms. 11 ds.
Holcome, George W.. 1836-1907.
    Nancy, w. G. W., d. Dec. 4, 1883, aged 55 yrs. 5 ms. 14 ds.
Hook, Jonathan, d. June 6, 1852, aged 44 yrs.
                    (see Myers)

Ingram, William, 1883-1917.
Johnson, B., 1828-1906.
  Sarah, 1833-1924.
Looker, Thomas, d. Nov. 20, 1893, aged 53 yrs. 9 ms. 5 ds. Mar. Eliza-
  beth Miller. He was son (3) of Michael Beem. Rev. War soldier
  bur. in Licking Co., O. See Roster D. A. R. for Ohio.
McBride, A. L., 1822-1909.
  Lea (?), w. A. L., 1825-1865.
  Susan, w. A. L., 1825-1889.
  John Henry, 1848-1925.
McIntosh, Nancy, June 6, 1871, aged 37 yrs. 8 ms. 27 ds.
       "Go home dear friends, and do not weep
        I am not dead, but hear at sleep
        Though cold and silent is my bed
        My rest is sweet, my sole had fled."
  Caroline, dau. W. & J. M., d. May 25, 1868, aged 28 yrs. 11 ms. 23
    ds. "She lived a life to be admired."
  Jane, w. William, d. Feb. 1, 1858, aged 50 yrs. 8 ms. 9 ds.
McMillan, Victoria, b. July 18, 1850, d. Aug. 30, 1892.
  John, d. Jan. 26, 1885, aged 74 yrs.
  Belle, dau. J. & R. D., d. Sept. 29, 1883, aged 30 yrs.
Martin, Elizabeth, w. Seriaph, d. Sept. 23, 1855, aged 19 yrs. 4 ms. 15 ds.
Merrill, Rebecca, w. Nicholas, d. May 29, 1867, aged 64 yrs. 11 ms.
Mills, Eva Ellen, d. Apr. 4, 1890, aged 28 yrs. 3 ms. 24 ds. "This simple
  tablet marks a sister's bier and those she loved in life, in death
  are near."
  Sarah Lucinda, d. Mar. 23, 1890, aged 23 yrs. 1 m. 1 d.
           "Alas! she has left us
            Her spirit has fled
            Her body now slumbers
            Along with the dead."
Myers, Elizabeth Hook, d. Nov. 13, 1892, aged 75 yrs.
Neel, Bathsheba, 1812-1898. "Farewell dear mother sweet thy rest, God
  called thee home, he thought it best."
  Thomas, 1816- ——.
Palmer. H., d. Oct. 5, 1897, aged 77 yrs. 1 m. 21 ds.
  Rebecca, w. H., d. Sept. 24, 1860, aged 34 yrs. 4 ds.
  Mary, dau. H. & R., d. Dec. 18, 1874, aged 24 yrs. 7 ms.
  Charles, son H. & R., d. Mar. 21, 1878, aged 18 yrs. 3 ms.
  Laura, d. Oct. 31, 1880, aged 22 yrs. 11 ms. 11 ds.
Ritchie, Emily, d. Apr. 5, 1869, aged 27 yrs.
Rose, Elizabeth, w. Elisha Rose, d. Jan. 24, 1882, aged 50 yrs. 8 ms.
Sensabaugh, Dorothy Isaac, d. Oct. 28, 1885, aged 31 yrs.
  Isaac, 1847-1926.
  Susan, 1857- ——.
  Simon, d. Sept. 5, 1853, aged 74 yrs. 8 ms. 10 ds.
  Hester, w. S. Sr., d. Jan. 27, 1854, aged 69 yrs.
  Jacob, b. Jan. 31, 1826, d. Dec. 1, 1883.
  Mary, b. Jan. 17, 1828, d. Jan. 5, 1872.—Co. 1, 95 Ohio Inf.
  Isaac—, 1824-1901.
  Jane, w. I., 1824-1878.
  John, 1849-1875.
  Henry, 1860-1920.
Shannon, Oscar, d. July 2, 1884, aged 38 yrs.
  John, d. Aug. 24, 1852, aged 62 yrs.
  Martin, d. Nov. 28, 1916, aged 75 yrs. 1 m. 18 ds.
  Thomas, 1821-1863.
  Mary, w. T., 1822-1913.
Sherman, Hester, d. Oct. 26, 1854, aged 55 yrs.
Shultz, Anna B., 1866-1904.

Slane, William, Sr., d. Jan. 27, 1879, aged 83 yrs.
   Charles, d. Sept. 1, 1900, aged 73 yrs. 2 ms. 23 ds.
   Dorothy, w. Wm. Sr., d. Jan. 7, 1881, aged 85 yrs.
Swisher, Phillip, d. Apr. 21, 1851, aged 34 yrs.
   Phillip, d. Nov. 4, 1859, aged 83 yrs. 7 ms. 26 ds.
   Catherine, d. Apr. 1, 18.?, aged 74 yrs. 8 ms. 8 ds. wife of Phillip S.
   (A son J. post office Summit. born in Hardy Co., Va. in 1808, is
      son of Phillip & Catherine Swisher who came to Licking Co. 1827.
      J. mar. Dorothy, dau. of John & Dorothy Howser in 1833.
   Hill's Co. History, page 764.)
Swygart, Isaac, b. May 6, 1836, d. Dec. 27, 1890.
   Nancy, b. Aug. 17, 1842, d. May 14, 1895.
   Amriel, d. May 3, 1859, aged 67 yrs. 5 ms.
   Susannah, w Sam. S., d. Mar. 8, 1870, aged 76 yrs.
   David, 1830-1888.
   Ellen, w. 1846-1919.
Tharp, W. P., 1858-1913.
   Kate, w. W. P., 1858-19—.
   Phillis, d. July 19, 1903, aged 79 yrs. 3 ms. 10 ds.
   Mary, w. Phillis, d. Jan. 19, 1911, aged 79 yrs. 8 ms. 7 ds.
   William, 1856-1928.
Tharp, John, d. Dec. 4, 1876, aged 51 yrs. 10 ms. 23 ds.
   Emily, d. w. John, d. Oct. 28, 1908, aged 82 yrs. 8 ms. 22 ds.
   Isaac, d. July 9, 1871, aged 78 yrs. 7 ms. 4 ds. He was a member
      Licking Co. Pioneer Society & Soldier of the War of 1812.
   Magdalena, w. Isaac, d. Oct. 20, 1867, aged 66 yrs. They settled in
      Licking Co. 1814, from Hampshire Co., Va.
   Anna, d. Sept. 1, 1864, aged 25 yrs.
   Isaac R., 1859-1931.
   Martha J., w. I. R., 1859-1906.
   Joseph, d. June 22, 1884, aged 51 yrs. 11 ms. 16 ds.
   Mary, w. Joseph, d. Dec. 4, 1882, aged 45 yrs. 11 ms. 24 ds.
   J. (b. Apr. 9, 1827, Mar. 1848 Susan Swygart.
   (*Hill's Co. Hist., pg. 779*).
Wagy, Jacob, d. Apr. 1, 1892, aged 90 yrs. 4 ms. 13 ds.
   Catherine, w. Jacob, d. June 20, 1893, aged 88 yrs. 10 ms. 20 ds.
   John, d. May 10, 1886, aged 42 yrs. 2 ms. 20 ds.
   Lucinda, w. John, d. Mar. 19, 1889, aged 50 yrs. 2 ms. 5 ds.
   Margaret, w. Philip, d. Aug. 27, 1849, aged 72 yrs.
Whitehead, George, d. Mar. 3, 1863, aged 28 yrs.
Whitney, William, a soldier of the War of 1812, d. Oct. 19, 1882, aged
      92 yrs, 4 ms. 15 ds.
Wolcott, Benjamin, d. Aug. 27, 1834, aged 69 yrs. 6 ms. 15 ds.
   Horace, d. Sept. 28, 1884, aged 31 yrs.
   Henry Allen, d. May 7, 1861, aged 23 yrs.
   Henry, son B. & E., —— 1871, aged 13 yrs.
   Ella May, dau. R. & E., d. Aug. 5, 1899, aged 33 yrs.
   Sarah, w. J. A., b. Sept. 21, 1835. d. Aug. 9, 1861.
   Richard, d. Sept. 30, 1904, aged 70 yrs.
   Peter, d. June 1, 1864, aged 73 yrs.
   Laura, w. Peter, d. Aug. 6, 1882, aged 87 yrs.
   Jacob Wagy and Catherine Swisher were married Jan. 1, 1829, by
Rev. George Callahan, recorded Jan. 25, 1829 in "old book" Newark, O.

CEMETERY RECORDS

FRANK A. LIVINGSTON

DAGUE CEMETERY

Location: On the Johnstown Road, State Route 62, south side of road, near Rocky Fork Creek.

Baughman, Anthony, died Aug. 2, 1914, aged 84 yrs. 5 mos. 1 da.
    Mary, wife of Anthony, died Feb. 20, 1879, aged 44 yrs. 7 mos. 10 ds.

Becktol, Infant dau. of A. E. Becktol, died May 24, 1851.

Crown, Sadie, born 1891, died 1930.

Dague, Benjamin, son of D. and S., died May 17, 1868, aged 25 yrs. 2 mos. 4 ds. (Civil War Veteran). On same stone with Daniel and Susanna Dague, "Mother and Father."
    Susanna, wife of Daniel, died Oct. 8, 1879, aged 75 yrs. 1 mo. 21 ds. On same stone "Father and Mother."
    Daniel, died Nov. 13, 1850, aged 50 yrs. 4 mos. 9 ds. On same stone "Father and Mother."
    Edmund, died Dec. 1, 1893, aged 63 yrs. 3 mos. 25 ds. (Civil War Veteran). On same stone "Father and Mother."
    Sallie, died May 11, 1916, aged 83 yrs. 8 mos. 21 ds.
    Infant, son of Edmund and Sarah, died Oct. 9, 1851.
    Franklin, son of George and H., died Nov. 17, 1854, aged 2 yrs.
    Elmer E., son of George and H., born Jan. 20, 1861, died Nov. 6, 1868.
    Cyrus, son of George and H., born Dec. 10, 1850, died Feb. 12, 1868.
    Susanna, wife of John, died May 20, 1855, aged 22 yrs. 4 mos. 21 ds.
    Elizabeth, wife of Matthias, died Sept. 7, 1821, in 64th year of age.
    Matthias, died Feb. 16, 1847, aged 86 yrs. (Revolutionary War Veteran, S. A. R. marker).

Lyva, John H., son of P. and S., died Dec. 22, 1868, aged 25 yrs. 7 mos. 12 ds.

Rodgers, Elizabeth, wife of William, died June 27, 1855, aged 40 yrs. 1 mo. 27 ds.
    John, son of Wm. S. and E., died Oct. 28, 1838, aged 1 yr. 6 mos.
    Levi, son of Wm. S. and E., died Sept. 15, 1855, aged 21 yrs. 6 mos. 8 ds.
    Mary E., dau. of Wm. S. and E., died Aug. 10, 1855, aged 1 mo. 15 ds.
    Virginnia, dau. of Wm S. and E., died Nov. 12, 1838, aged 2 yrs. 11 mos.

AYERS GRAVEYARD

Location: On Ayers Lane, Jefferson Township, Franklin County, Ohio. This Ayers Lane is one quarter of a mile west of Blacklick Road, about three miles north of Blacklick Station.

Ayers, Austin, son of Samuel and Elizabth, born Aug. 18, 1829, died Aug. 26, 1830, aged 1 yr. 8 ds.
    Ezekiel W., died Jan. 10, 1891, aged 60 yrs. 1 mo. 17 ds.
    Mary B., wife of E. W., died Apr. 29, 1905, aged 74 yrs. 8 mos. 14 ds.
    Job, died Mar. 21, 1877, aged 77 yrs. 7 mos. 23 ds.
    Eliza, wife of Job Ayers, died Apr. 29, 1861, aged 57 yrs. 2 mos. 20 ds.
    John Johnson, son of Job and Eliza, died Sept. 25, 1841, aged 5 yrs. 9 mos. 22 ds.
    Thomas, died Dec. 26, 1847, aged 79 yrs. 11 mos. 12 ds.
    Mary, wife of Thomas, died Apr. 12, 1861, aged 88 yrs. 1 mo. 24 ds.

George W., son of Thomas and Mary, died Jan. 1840, aged 22 yrs.

Browning, Elizabeth Ann, dau. of Isaac and Sarah, died Apr. 8, 1843, aged 8 mos. 14 ds.

Huldah, dau. of Isaac and Sarah, died Aug. 20, 1840, aged 2 yrs. 7 mos. 5 ds.

Carloch, Shadrich B., died Feb. 28, 1848, aged 39 yrs. 2 mos. 10 ds.

Dodd, William S., son of Abijah and Nancy, died Oct. 24, 1838, aged 1 yr. 6 mos. 24 ds.

Farber, William, died Sept. 21, 1821, aged 32 yrs. 4 mos. 17 ds.

Fisher, Infant Dau. of A. V. and R. S., died Mar. 4, 1853, aged 1 da.

Job Albertis, son of Thomas B. and Matilda, died Jan. 5, 1842, aged 9 mos. 1 da.

Forehand, Thomas Charleton, son of———and Hannah, died Mar. 1838, aged 8 yrs. 11 mos. 25 ds.

Freele, Daniel, died Feb. 18, 1859, aged 75 yrs. 5 mos.

Freeman, Elijah, son of Elijah and Mary, died Sept. 30, 1846, aged 21 yrs. 7 mos.

Joana, died Aug. 1846 in her 95th year.

Hanna, Andrew, died Apr. 19, 1840, aged 75 yrs. 6 mos. 15 ds.

Hardin, Hector, died Aug. 7, 1850, aged 4 yrs. 11 mos. 17 ds.

Mary C. C., died Aug. 5, 1850, aged 12 yrs. 6 mos. 8 ds.

William, died Aug. 5, 1850, aged 18 yrs. 11 mos. 21 ds.

Hartrum, James B., son of Benjamin and Margaret, died Apr. 25, 1849, aged 9 mos. 1 da.

Hickol, Mary, died Jan. 10, 1843, aged 29 yrs.

Johnson, John, A native of New Jersey. Born·Sept. 13, 1764, died June 21, 1839, aged 74 yrs. 9 mos. 8 ds. He was a ruling Elder in the Presbyterian Church and its liberal patron.

Rebecca, wife of John Johnson, formerly of Sparty, Sussex County, New Jersey. These lines were inscribed by her affectionate husband. She was the daughter of William and Mary Brasted. Born in Morris Co., New Jersey, Dec. 19, 1766. Married Nov. 4, 1788. Removed with her husband to this place in 1816 and died Jan. 16, 1833. Much lamented by her friends but this loss we trust was to her great gain and could she through this marble address thee O reader she would exclaim "Prepare to meet thy God" "Improve thy golden hours of time for eternity is near with all its dread realities tomorrow may finish up the boon of life and bring thee to thy last account or at most a few more hasty years."

Kelso, Susan E., dau. of D. C., died Feb. 13, 1849, aged 1 yr. 3 mos. 19 ds.

Lalley, Esther Ann, dau. of William and Mary L., died Mar. 25, 1836, aged 3 yrs. 5 mos. 19 ds.

Mann, Amba, died Aug. 4, 1854, aged 75 yrs. 5 mos. 20 ds.

John, son of Amba and Mary, died Oct. 1834, aged 18 yrs.

Sidney, son of Shuah and Nancy, died Feb. 13, 1846, aged 18 yrs. 4 mos. 24 ds.

Pierce, William T., son of Brinkley and Phebey, died Aug. 28, 1840, aged 11 mos. 19 ds.

Squier, Jesse, died Apr. 30, 1846, aged 69 yrs. 6 mos. 5 ds.

Susan, wife of Jesse, died Aug. 9, 1839, aged 65 yrs. 22 ds.

John Oscar, son of John and Sophia, died Dec. 18, 1849, aged 1 yr. 2 mos. 5 ds.

Turney, Infant Daughter of John and Rebecca Turney.

Webb, Elizabeth, wife of Elijah, died Apr. , 1847, aged 31 yrs .5 mos. 6 ds.

Whitehead, Amanda, consort of Jonathan, died Feb. 3, 1830, aged 37 yrs. 4 mos. 7 ds.

Wigfeld, Sarah, wife of Wm., died Mar. 5, 1848, aged 57 yrs. 1 mo. 15 ds.

CEMETERY RECORDS
FRANK A. LIVINGSTON

SHOCKEY CEMETERY

Located in Mad River Township, Champaign County, Ohio, in Section 3. Record made by T. B. Lang, October 3, 1937.

NOTE: Mr. John Shockey, who lives just north of the cemetery on the west side of the road, supplied the names of those interred there but not marked, such names are marked with an asterisk.

Infant, died 1914 (Mother was a Shockey).
*Harper,—(Not related to Shockeys).
*King,—(Husband, wife and two children from Inditna, not related to Shockeys.)
*Ritter, Elijah, died 1892, (A cousin of John Shockey).
Shockey, Abraham, aged 7 yrs.
    Abraham 1816-1892.
    Abraham, 1841-1915.
    Catherine, aged 4 mos.
    Cinderella, 1840-1926.
    Elizabeth, 1813-1865.
    Leona, dau. of A. and N., died Mch. 27, 1834, aged 3 yrs. 10 mos. 23 ds.
    Nancy, wife of Abraham, died Mch. 9, 1842, aged 59 yrs. 11 mos. 9 ds.
Winn, Eliza, 1833-1897 (Not related to Shockey.)

SODOM CEMETERY

Located in Rush Township, Champaign County, Ohio, on U. S. Route 36. Record made by T. B. Lang, September 26, 1937.

Chandler, Hannah, died 1839, aged 9 mos.
Clark,—ra, dau. of J. W. and L., died Aug. 23, 1863, aged 1 yr. 8 mos. 2 ds.
    H. Chancey, son of Wm. and Clarrissa, died Dec. 28, 1842, aged 10 mos. 6 ds.
    James, died July 5, 1862, aged 87 yrs. 20 ds.
    John, son of W. and Clarrissa, died July 26, 1844, aged 5 yrs. 3 mos.
    Martha, wife of James, died Mch. 20, 1868, aged 85 yrs. 10 mos. 13 ds.
    Phebe, dau. of Wm. and Clarrissa, died Sept. 19, 1845, aged 8 yrs. 3 mos.
Edwards, Catherine, wife of E., died Sept. 7, 1863, aged 68 yrs.
    Edward, died Oct. 21, 1844, aged 44 yrs.
    Mary, died Feb. 6, 1888, aged 57 yrs. 5 mos.
Haise, Eliza, dau. of James and Rebecca, died Feb. 15, 1839, aged 1 yr. 5 mos. 5 ds.
    Rebecca, wife of James, died Dec. 29, 1856, aged 54 yrs. 3 mos. 5 ds.
Hawkins, Benjamin, son of Moses and Betsy, died June 1, 1850, aged 23 yrs. 4 mos. 16 ds.
    Martha, dau. of Moses and Betsy, died Nov. 26, 1852, aged 28 yrs. 9 mos. 9 ds.

Sherwood, Eliza, dau. of O. and M., died Sept. 22, 1852, aged 10 mos. 1 da.

James L., died Sept. 25, 1840, aged 37 yrs. 4 mos.

Mary E., dau. of O. and M., died July 15, 1849, aged 2 mos. 18 ds.

Taylor, Martha J., dau. of H. M. and S. J., died Aug. 28, 1851, aged 11 mos. 28 ds.

Willoughby, Clark, son of F. M. and C., died Oct. 4, 1861, aged 1 yr. 11 mos. 4 ds.

Eleanor, died Feb. 22, 1837, aged 26 yrs. 1 mo. 15 ds.

WINN CEMETERY

Located in Urban Township, Champaign County, Ohio. Record made by T. B. Lang, September 6, 1937.

Bishop, John, son of A. and S., died July 1824, aged 7 yrs.

Susanna I., wife of Aquilla, died Sept. 28, 1823, aged 31 yrs.

McRoberts, D. J., son of Wm. and M. I., died Sept. 4, 1818, aged 11 mos.

Martha I., wife of William, died Dec. 19, 1848, aged 58 yrs. 5 mos.

Mary Eliza, dau. of William and M. I., died Sept. 25, 1837, aged 2 yrs. 7 mos.

William, son of William and M. I., died July 31, 1822 aged 10 mos.

William, died Oct. 17, 1860, aged 71 yrs. 4 mos. 8 ds.

Winn, Myrtilla, dau. of J. and M., died Sept. 29, 1849, aged 40 yrs.

Myrtilla, wife of John Sr., died Aug. 1, 1822, aged 58 yrs.

SHARON CEMETERY

Located in Union Township, Champaign County, Ohio, Section 4181, intersection of routes 167-B and 166-A. Record made by T. B. Lang, October 17, 1937.

NOTE: There were originally between 30 to 40 graves in this cemetery but many have been removed.

Bayles, Hezekiah, died Jan. 1, 1868, aged 84 yrs. 7 mos. 24 ds.

Sarah, wife of Hezekiah, died July 25, 1863, aged 72 yrs. 1 mo. 2 ds.

Blair, Flora, dau. of A. and N., died June —, 1861, aged 7 mos. 11 ds.

Coe, Mary, dau. of J. and M., died March 3, 1847, aged 15 yrs. 5 mos. 9 ds.

-r-nez, dau of J. and M., died Aug. 6, 1846, aged 16 yrs. 19 ds.

Daniel, Sarah, wife of J. T. and dau. of Hezekiah and Sarah Bayles, died Dec. 10, 1848, aged 38 yrs. 3 mos.

Johnson, Elizabeth, dau. of J. and E., died Aug. 6, 1851, aged 3 yrs. 6 mos. 12 ds.

Infant, of J. and E., died Nov. 27, 1845.

Samuel, son of J. and E., died July 30, 1847, aged 5 yrs. 6 mos. 15 ds.

Madden, Benjamin

Ropp, Nancy M., dau. of J. and E., died Aug. 24, 1851, aged 1 yr. 9 mos. 8 ds.

366

SHARON CEMETERY

Madden, Benjamin, born 1-23-1776; Died 9-10-1855.
Madden, Mary, wife of Benjamin. Born 4-4-1805; Died 10-4-1848.

CEMETERY RECORDS
FRANK A. LIVINGSTON

HAVEN'S CORNERS

Location: Near Haven's Corners. On the east side of the Reynoldsburg and New Albany Road, 2½ miles north of East Broad Street.
Recorded by: Thelma Blair Lang.

Atwood, James, died Sept. 25, 1888, aged 45 years, 10 mos. 25 days.

Atwood, Harry R. Born 1886, died 1887.

Antabush, James A., son of A. and M. Antabush, died March 15, 1854, aged 7 mos. 17 days.

Ball, Daniel, died Jan. 3, 1863, aged 64 years.

Butler, Mary R., daughter of F. and M. Butler, died Oct. 2, 1881, aged 9 mos. 23 days.

Cheney, Joseph, died Nov. 16, 1875, aged 70 yrs. 19 days.

Cheney, Rebecca, wife of Joseph Cheney, died Nov. 26, 1875, aged 61 yrs., 6 mos, 4 days.

Cheney, Washington J., died March 2, 1886, aged 37 yrs.

Cook, Shaffer, son of N. and N. E. Cook, born Nov. 15, 1842, died near Atlanta, Ga., Aug. 16, 1864, member 46th Reg't. O. V. I. Buried Marietta, Ga.

Nancy E., wife of W. N. Cook, born June 16, 1817, died Dec. 22, 1878.

Marilla, daughter of N. and N. E. Cook, born March 1, 1841, died Feb. 17, 1861.

Marilla Jane, daughter of Nathaniel and Elizabeth Cook, died Feb. 14, 1861, aged 19 yrs. 11 mos. 13 days.

Compton, Mary, born Sept. 20, 1822, died Nov. 6, 1897.

Compton, William, born Sept. 16, 1820, died Jan. 24, 1894.

Chamberlin, Jesse, born Jan. 11, 1800, died Nov. 7, 1887.

Chamberlin, Elizabeth, wife of J. Chamberlin, died March 30, 1868, aged 80 years.

Cheney, Lutecia, wife of Cheney, died Nov. 12, 1866, aged 25 yrs., 8 mos., 4 days.

Doherty, Edwin D., son of Absalom and Emeline D., died Dec. 14, 1872, aged 22 yrs., 7 mos. 8 days.

Doherty, Absolom, died July 20, 1877, aged 62 yrs, 7 mos. 2 days.

Davenport, Lewis, died July 13, 1884, aged 93 years, 3 mos.

Davenport, Susann, wife of Lewis Davenport, died March 13, 1876, aged 75 years.

Davenport, Peter, died July 14, 1874, aged 82 yrs., 5 mos. and 5 days.

Davenport, Samuel, died October 11, 1874, aged 99 years, 11 mos., and 7 days.

Davenport, Margaret S., wife of S. Davenport. Died March 11, 1865, aged 59 years, 11 months and 25 days.

Doran, Rhoda W., wife of J. Doran. Died October 8, 1855, aged 53 years, 11 months and 16 days.

Edwards, Lucinda, wife of A. D. Edwards, died May 31, 1891, aged 64 years, 6 months and 7 days.

Elliott, Anna, died April 2, 1891, aged 9 years.

Elliot, George, died December 13, 1891, age 19 years.

Ealy, Mary, daughter of D. and Rosey Ealy, died August 29, 1821, age 10 months, 24 days.   e

Ealy, Peter, died September 9, 1821, age 33 years, 1 month and 27 days.

Edgar, Joseph, born at Westmoreland County, Pa., died April 3, 1882, aged 86 years, 5 months and 29 days.

Edgar, Riley, son of J. and A. Edgar, died September 29, 1837, age 4 months, 10 days.

Edgar, Charles, son of J. and A. Edgar, died July 28, 1847.

Edgar, Calvin, son of Joseph and Abagail Edgar, died March 17, 1853, aged 28 years, 1 month and 1 day.

Edgar, Joseph, son of J. and A. Edgar, died August 14, 1853. Age 20 years, 4 months, and 24 days.

Edgar, Lewis, son of Joseph and A. Edgar died

Edgar, G. W., born 1829, died 1881.

Edgar, Lucinda, wife of G. W. Edgar, born 1836, died 1906.

Edgar, Daisy, daughter of G. W. and Lucinda Edgar. Died August 2, 1881, aged 6 years, 6 months and 28 days.

Favis, Emma G., daughter of   Died   5, 1860.

Finney, Infant daughter of B. and N. P. Finney. Died September 17, 1859.

Flesher, Ulalia, daughter of W. H. and M. A. Flesher, died October 6, 1863. Age 11 years, 11 months, and 7 days.

Fishpaw, John W., son of W. L. and M. J. Fishpaw, died June 10, 1875, age 2 years, 6 months and 20 days.

Francis, Elizabeth G., wife of T. E. Francis, died February 17, 1876. Age 37 years, 10 months, and 4 days.

Geiger, Thomas J., Son of Joseph and Mary Geiger. Died December 16, 1902, age 61 years, 1 month and 21 days.

Geiger, Harvey, Son of Joseph and Maryy Geiger. Died October 19, 1818, age 4 years, 4 months and, 16 days.

Geiger, George. Son of Joseph and Mary Geiger. Died August 26, 1864. Aged 24 years, 10 months and 3 days.

Geiger, Joseph Sr. Born February 16, 1789, died October 5, 1869, aged 71 years, 7 months and 26 days.

Geiger, Mary, wife of Joseph Geiger, born October 23, 1807, died August 19, 1882, aged 74 years, 7 months, and 26 days.

Geiger, Mary Jane, wife of Joseph Geiger, died December 25, 1871, age 31 years 10 months and 16 days.

Geiger, Joseph, died March 6, 1890, aged 58 years. 5 months, and 6 days.

Geiger, Dora, daughter of J. and M. J. Geiger, died February 8, 1884, aged 13 years, 4 months, and 13 days.

Geiger, Elma, daughter of J. and Mary Geiger, died September 3, 1861, age 11 years, 11 months and 3 days.

Grubs, Laurance, died August 10, 1865, age 57 years, 6 months and 20 days.

Grubs, Sarah, wife of Laurance Grubs, died February 3, 1865, age 65 years, 5 months and 14 days.

Havens, John, died July 29, 1866, age 62 years.

Havens, Rebecca, born November 15, 1809, died May 26, 1894, age 84 years, 6 months, and 11 days.

Havens, Mary Ingersoll, born 1830 and died 1910.

Havens, William Fancher, born 1830 and died 1872.

Haven, John, born Morris Co. N. J., 1800, died July 22, 1842, age 42 years, 3 months, and 7 days.

Harrison, Jesse, died December 15, 1860, aged 69 years, 9 months and 4 days.

Havens, Maud daughter of H. E. and M. J Havens, died November 26, 1877, aged 9 months and 26 days.

Hook, Naomi E., wife of William H. Hook, died December 24, 1870, age 39 years, 8 months, and 26 days.

Kline, Olive E. daughter of C. and C. Kline, died October 22, 1865, age 2 years, 3 months and 16 days.

Landford, Zelotes, died Aurora, Kane Co. Ill., September 1, 1855, age 89 years, 3 months and 16 days.

Link, Bertha, daughter of F. F. and E. J. Link, died February 3, 1880.

Lyons, Alfred, born January 1. 1822. died December 30, 1890.

Lyons, Martha A., born April 25. 1825. died July 12, 1890.

Milburn, Harriett O., born 1820, died 1874.

Milburn, John, Born 1825, died 1874.

Miller, Cadis, son of I. and E. Miller, died August 18, 1867, age 16 years, 10 months, and 4 days.

Martin, Elizabeth Eldora, daughter of A. J. and S. A. Martin, died October 7, 1860, age 1 year, 2 months and 7 days.

Mann Kesiah, wife of Amba Mann, died April 28, 1863, aged

Miller, Oliver, son of A. S. and L. Miller, died March 7, 1854, age 6 years.

Mills, John M., son of W. and Rebecca Mills, died April 23, 1855, aged 71 years, 6 months, and 17 days.

McCauley, Annie, wife of Sam McCaulay, a native of Ireland, in memory of his wife, died August 2, 1876, aged 43 years.

Mann, Infant son of Marcus and Katherine Mann, born June 3, 1877, died June 8, 1877.

Mann, Nancy, wife of Shuah Mann Sr., died August 8, 1871, aged 82 years, 1 month and 7 days.

Mann, Shuah, died July 24, 1865, aged 78 years, 5 months and 9 days.

Moore, Lois, wife of George Moore. Died July 6, 1861, age 90 years, 4 months, 23 days.

Needles, Infant son of J. H. and Hannah, died January 28, 1852.

Painter, Frank, son of L. and A. Painter, died November 3, 1889, age 24 years, 8 months, 6 days.

Peters, Frank O., died June 18, 1891.

Peters, Samuel L., died March 11 1864, aged 54 years, 3 months, 8 days.

Painter, Almira, wife of J. Painter, died November 12, 1891, aged 78 years, 2 months, 16 days.

Painter, Isaac, died June 19, 1872, aged 28 years, 8 months, 26 days.

Painter, Noah, son of Andrew and Rachel Painter, died September 2, 1860, aged 9 years, 18 days.

Painter, Andrew, died August 28, 1886, aged 69 years, 4 months, 24 days.

Rochelle, John Sr., died October 26, 1877, aged 72 years, 9 months.

Rochelle, John, son of J. and L. Rochelle, born March 4, 1833, died at
    Andersonville, Ga., October 11, 1864, aged 31 years, 7
    months, 7 days.
Rochelle, Lucinda, wife of J. Rochelle, born July 9, 1809, died November 16, 1908, aged 99 years, 4 months, 7 days.
Rochelle, Zelotes, died August 15, 1851, aged 24 years, 11 months, 18
    days.
Rochelle, infant son of John and Lucinda Rochelle, died February 16,
    1840.
Rochelle, Victoria, daughter of J. and L. Rochelle, died July 31, 1867,
    aged 2 years, 1 month, 3 days.
Roberts, Emma, daughter of James and Abana Roberts, died April 15,
    1867, aged 18 years, 11 months, 23 days.
Roberts, Hata, daughter of I. and A. Roberts, died June 29, 1861.
Ricketts, Oral S., daughter of W. and W. Ricketts, died September 23,
    1866, aged 18 years, 8 months.
Roberts, Jame, daughter of James and Arrena Roberts, died December 26, 1860, aged 13 years, 5 months, 15 days.*

INSCRIPTIONS IN PENTZ CEMETERY
Knox Township, Columbiana County

This cemetery is located on the s. line of S. E. Quarter of Sec. 5,
Twp. 17, Range 5. Data compiled by Mary P. Borton and Daniel Wilson, Alliance, Ohio, Oct. 2, 1938.

John Hilton, b. April 25, 1803; d. Oct. 23, 1870. Mary, wife of John
    Hilton, family of Jacob Motz, d. August 1855, ag. 58 yrs.,
    6 mos., 23 d.
Susannah, wife of John Steel, d. May 8, 1847, ag. 42 yrs.
In memory of Katherine, wife of Christopher Pentz, d. Aug. 22, 1838,
    ag. 62 yrs., 3 mos., 12 ds.
John Pentz, died Sept. 7, 1883, aged 88 yrs., 6 mos., 12 ds.
Elizabeth, wife of John Pentz, d. Oct. 10, 1877, aged 79 yrs.,
    5 mo., 21 ds.
Christianna Pentz, (d.) May 22, 1894, aged 96 yrs., 10 m., 22 ds.

> Mother thou hast from us flown,
> To the regions far above
> We to thee erect this stone
> Consecrated by our love.

Peter Pentz, died Oct. 8, 1873, aged 80 yrs., 6 ms., 7 ds.

> Rest dear Father in quiet sleep,
> While friends in sorrow o'er thee weep,
> And here their heartfelt offerings bring
> And near thy grave thy requiem sing.

In memory of Phebe, wife of John C. Luke, who died April the 5 A. D.
    1842, aged 20 years, 7 mos., & 8 ds.
    Sarah Jane, daughter of John C. & Phebe Luke, died April 4,
    A. D. 1842, aged 1 yr. 1 mo., 4 ds.
Where this cold memorial weeps a wife   a child and Mother Sleep.
Daniel Borton, died Oct. 28, 1887, aged 84 yrs, 1 mo., 19 ds.
Mary, wife of Daniel Borton, died April 26, 1873, age 70 y.,
    8 m., 27 day.

*Continued on p. 372

Mary M. daughter of D. B. Pierson, died May 7, 1858, aged 2 m. 23 ds.
In memory of Henry the son of Elwood & Rebecca Harlan, d. Dec. 8,
  1845, 2 mo.
Henry Huffer, died Apr. 28, 1869, aged 47 yrs., 3 mos., 22 ds.
Abraham Huffer, died Jan. 27, 1865, aged 85 yrs., 6 mo., 8 d.
Esther, his wife, died May 21, 1869, aged 78 yrs., 5 m., 24 ds.
Sarah E. Huffer, died April 6, 1855.
Luiza M., daughter of A. & C.Cameron, died Dec. 12, 1858, aged 7 yrs.,
  11 mo.
Mary J., daughter of A. & C. Cameron, died May 25, 1862, aged
  26 yrs., 2 mo.
Alexander Cameron, died May 2, 1868, aged 67 yr., 2 m., 2 d.
Joseph B. Cameron, died Oct. 8, 1882, 22 yr., 8 m., 18 d.
Catherine Cameron, born July 22, 1812; died Apr. 24, 1891.
William Cameron, born June 10, 1846; died Mar. 16, 1885.
Charlotte, wife of Amos M. Wilson, died May 20, 1916,
  aged 89 yr., 10 mo.
Amos M. Wilson, died May 27, 1888, aged 55 y., 7 m., 26 d. O. V. I.
  Co. K. Reg. 80.
William A. son of Abraham & Catherine Scott, died April 18, 1861,
  aged 2 mo.
Eliza, dau of Jonas D & Sarah J. Heffner, died Oct. 15, 1858, aged 1 yr.
Mary E., dau. of H. P. & P. S. Borton, died Sept. 10, 1866,
  ag. 1 yr., 11 mo.
Mary E., dau. of A & C Wilson, died Oct. 18, 1863, aged 3 yr., 1 mo.
Cyrus B., son of A & C Wilson, died Sept. 24, 1857, aged 3 yr, 7 mo.
Amos, son of A & C Wilson, died May 22, 1852, aged 1 yr.,
  3 mo., 7 days.
Daniel B., son of A & C Wilson, died Jan. 27, 1850, aged 1 yr., 13 days.
Allisanna, wife of J. Conn, died Feb. 23, 1819, aged 36 yrs, 6 mo.
  20 days.
Mary, dau of D & M. Borton, died Apr. 21, 1842, aged 2 yr., 4 m.,
  6 day.
Others buried here without markers:
Horace Potter Borton, b. Jan. 19, 1832; d. Nov. 3, 1900.
Pauline S. Borton, b. Oct. 17, 1841; d. June 1, 1904
Michael Fou(gh)ty (the grandfather of H. P. Borton) said to have
  been aged 102 years.

371

CEMETERY RECORDS
FRANK A. LIVINGSTON

Sagar, William Henry, son of A. & A. Sagar, died June 11, 1871, aged 21 years, 3 months, 23 days.

Sagar, Catherine, died December 31, 1905, aged 88 years, 6 months, 10 days.

Sagar, Abraham, died May 5, 1881, aged 66 years.

Sagar, George Washington, son of A. & G. Sagar, born August 9, 1837, died January 4, 1874, aged 36 years, 4 months, 25 days.

Sagar, Georgie, son of G. W. & E. E. Sagar, born September 20, 1873, died December 21, 1873, aged 6 months, 3 days.

Sagar, Myrtha E., daughter of G. W. & E. Sagar, died April 6, 1871, aged 2 years, 7 months, 2 days.

Sagar, Laura M. Daughter of E. M. & M. A., died October 24, 1893, aged 4 years, 10 months, 16 days.

Sagar, Walter E., son of D. & K. Sagar, died November 1, 1889, aged 7 months, 26 days.

Sagar, Desiah J. wife of D. Sagar, died August 29, 1893, aged 43 years, 10 months, 23 days.

Simguy, Mirch L., Co. K. 2nd. Ohio Inf. Mex. War

Strau, George Washington, son of George W. & Hattie A. Strau, died April 17, 1883, aged 1 year, 11 months, 9 days.

Strait, Hattie A., wife of George W. Strait, died April 8, 1890, aged 39 years, 11 months, 7 days.

Stoel, Silas, died September 22, 1862, aged 76 years, 4 months, 16 days.

Stoel, Betsy, wife of S. Stoel, died August 30, 1868, aged 72 years, 4 months, 11 days.

Smith, Huldah, daughter, died March 15, 1854, aged 7 months, 17 days.

Shadwick, John, died September 27, 1860, aged 49 years, 5 months, 2 days.

Seadwick, Reynolds, born November 20, 1839. Enlisted March 27, 1864 in 18 O. V. Calv., died and interment at Germantown, Pa. August 2, 1864.

Stagg, Warren, son of L. & M. J. Stagg, died July 27, 1892, aged 28 years, 7 months, 19 days.

Stagg, Sarah R., wife of G. W. Stagg, died November 19, 1869, aged 24 years, 9 months, 18 days.

Shadwick, infant son of Shadwick, born February 27, 1885, died February 28, 1885.

Shadwick, Infant son and daughter of L. & S. B. Shadwick. Born February 22, 1889.

Smith, Elisha, son of J. & S. Smith, born March 19, 1836, died November 16, 1861, aged 25 years, 7 months, 29 days.

Smith, Stephen, son of J. & S. Smith, born August 5, 1837, died September 3, 1859, age 22 years, 28 days.

Smith, Jacob, died July 13, 1886, aged 61 years, 7 months, 10 days.

Smith, Susan, died April 4, 1870 aged 69 years, 10 months, 6 days.

Smith, Egles, died February 4, 1873, aged 41 years, 4 months.

Smith, Henry, son of John & Rebecca Smith, died August 2, 1861, aged 20 years, 10 months, 8 days.

Stoel, Infant daughter of F. B. & H. E. Stoel, died February 2, 1852, aged 2 days.

Stoel, Thomas J., son of S. & S. Stoel, died April 1, 1854, aged 24 years, 3 months, 26 days.

Smith, Josiah, died August 4, 1828, aged 32 years, 10 months, 9 days.

Smith, John, died February 10, 1846, aged 78 years, 4 months, 15 days.

Smith, Elizabeth, wife of John Smith, died August 12, 1826, aged 56 years, 25 days.

Smith, Aaron, died December 12, 1822, aged 2 years, 2 months.

Stagg, Mary Ann, consort of Thomas Stagg, died June 18, 1834, aged 24 years, 10 months, 12 days.

Stagg, Coswell, son of Thos. & Mary A. Stagg, died July 1, 1834, aged 4 months.

Smith, Thomas, son of John & Rebecca Smith, died February 6, 1841, aged 11 months, 25 days.

Smith, John W., son of Ecles & Mary Smith, died October 16, 1853, aged 11 years, 4 months, 19 days.

Smith, Frank, son of Ecles & Mary Smith, died December 16, 1854, aged 17 days.

Smith, Molly R., daughter of E. & M. Smith, died, August 18, 1870, aged 1 year, 6 days.

Smith, Henry, son of John & Rebecca Smith, died August 2, 1861, aged 20 years, 10 months, 8 days.

Smith, Josua, son of Geo. & Sarah Smith, died September 15, 1832 aged 1 year, 2 months, 13 days.

Smith, Gabriel, son of Geo. & Sarah Smith, died August 2, 1820, aged 6 months.

Smith, infant son of Geo. & Sarah Smith, died January 29, 1836, aged 4 days.

Smith, Ina, son of Geo. & Sarah Smith, died February 25, 1847, aged 10 years, 1 day.

Shull, Delilah, wife of Henry Shull, died January 23, 1849, aged 23 years, 8 months, 20 days.

Smith, Infant son of Benjamin & Holly Smith, died October 19, 1852.

Smith, Abraham, died July 27, 1837, aged 46 years, 6 months, 4 days.

Smith, Daniel, son of Jacob & Elizabeth Smith, died, June 26, 1847, aged 28 years.

Smith, Infant son of Benjamin & Hetty Smith, died June 14, 1836.

Smith, William, died, March 23, 1852, aged 50 years, 6 months, 11 days.

Smith, Garden son of Abram & Milly Smith, died November 1847, aged 13 yrs.

Smith, Millissa, daughter of Abram & Milly Smith.

Smith, Jetter, son of Abram & Milly Smith, died December 9, 1840, aged 2 years, 4 months.

Smith, Jacob E., son of Abraham & Milly Smith, died December 24, 1843, aged 16 years.

Smith, Hesterann, daughter of A. & M. Smith, died November 1, 1850.

Stagg, Kes, wife of Abram Stagg, died August 10, 1827, aged 57 years.

Stagg, Eliza, daughter of Abram & Rebecca Stagg, died June 24, 1841, aged 2 yrs.

Stagg, Abraham, died January 19, 1851, aged 80 years 6 months, 2 days.

Stagg, Rebecca A., died February 7, 1895, aged 85 years, 9 months, 6 days.

Stagg, John Rufus, son of Levi & Mary Stagg, died March 13, 1869, aged 9 years, 1 month, 2 days.

Stagg Mary L., wife of Levi Stagg, died April 13, 1899, aged 68 years, 1 month, 24 days.

Stagg, Levi, died August 15, 1875, aged 43 years, 26 days.

Smith, Sally, wife of George Smith, died May 23, 1882, aged 80 years, 7 months, 25 days.

Smith, George, died April 2, 1866, aged 68 years, 1 month, 27 days.

Shull, Hezekiah, son of Henry & Delilah Shull, died April 3, 1866, Aged 17 years, 2 months, 20 days.

Sager, Dallas, Died January 14, 1914, aged 68 years, 11 months, 6 days.

Sager, Nellie daughter of D. & K. Sager, died November 1, 1889, aged 7 months, 20 days.

Todd, Sarah, wife of G. W. Todd, died January 18, 1872, aged 28 years, 5 days.

Townsend, Flora E., daughter of L. & A. Painter and wife of John Townsend died, August 14, 1884, aged 20 years, 10 months 5 days.

Thompson, Abigail, wife of J. Thompson, died, May 31, 1880, aged 73 yrs., 2 months, 3 days.

Thompson, Joseph, died, May 29, 1854, aged 53 years, 5 months, 19 days.

Welch, Amby M., died June 25, 1874, aged 36 years.

Welch, Jane, wife of Welch, died May 11, 1880, aged 72 years, 11 mos., 25 days.

Welch, Martin G., died, January 24, 1888, aged, 81 years.

Williams, William S., died March 23, 1851, aged 61 years, 1 month, 18 days.

Wiswill, George W., son of Wm. & L. Wiswill, died, November 5, 1854, aged 18 years, 8 months, 23 days.

Williams, Keziah, wife of Joseph Williams, died April 17, 1818 or 1848, aged 87 years.

Wiswell, Keziah, wife of Moses Wiswell, died April 2, 1841, aged 54 years, 10 months, 8 days.

Wiswell, Moses, died, May 20, 1849, aged, 20 years, 4 months, 28 days.

Woodruff, Eldora, daughter of N. & E. Woodruff, died, September 24, 1862, aged 7 months.

Wengert, Chester, son of J. & J. Wengert, died, January 31, 1892, aged 7 years, 4 months, 25 days.

Wilson, Grace Edgar, born 1856, died 1884, aged 28 years.

CEMETERY RECORDS
FRANK A. LIVINGSTON

Graveyard on Sunbury Pike, in Delaware County, Ohio, about one-half
 mile north of the Franklin County line on the
  East side of the road.

Bardslee, Tolman D., died September 12, 1846, aged 49 years.

Carr, Evaline M., wife of Bennet, born January 8, 1808, died
  September 16, 1840, aged 32 yrs. 8 mos. 8 ds.

Dixon, Letty Ann*, wife of Alva, born April 9, 1817, died July 31,
  1883.

  Alva,* born June 15, 1810, died March 20, 1884.

  (*On same stone marked "Father and Mother")

  Willie P., son of A. and L. A. died Nov. 4, 1863, aged 7 yrs.
  5 mos. 4 ds.

  Russell, died September 30, 1880, aged 35 yrs. 9 mos. 12 ds.

  Charles, born January 15, 1907, died March 25, 1907.

  Daisy V., born 1882, died 1902, aged 20 yrs.

  Amanda A., born 1843, died 1909.

  Walter L., born 1840, died 19— (Civil War Veteran and on
  same stone as Amanda A. Dixon).

Nutt, Edward, died August 29, 1873, aged 83 yrs. 4 mos.

  Allie, died April 4, 1890, aged 88 yrs. 10 mos. 11 ds.

  (On same stone as Edward Nutt)

  George, Co. G, 47th Ohio Infantry.

  Emily, died April 26, 1847, aged 1 yr. 2 mos. 7 ds.

  Eliza, dau. of Edward and Allie, died February 26, 1851,
  aged 1 yr. 27 ds.

  Dorcas, dau. of Edward and Allie, died December 2, 1864,
  aged 22 yrs.

  Jacob W., born February 19, 1837, died June 23, 1882.

  David H., son of John C. and Elizabeth, died March 12, 1851,
  aged 1 yr. 2 mos. 12 ds.

  Henry, died October 30, 1851, aged 66 yrs. 7 mos. 6 ds.

  David H., born December 30, 1853, died March 12, 1854.

  John, died March 5, 1866, aged 86 yrs. 8 mos. 5 ds.

  Mary, wife of John, died April 30, 1852, aged 67 yrs.
  10 mos. 28 ds.

Nutt, Eliza A. Off,* wife of J. C., born December 18, 1810, died
  November 11, 1845.

  John C.,* born January 24, 1810, died January 4, 1889.

  Eliza J.,* born December 2, 1833, died February 2, 1834.

  William H.,* born June 18, 1839, died July 22, 1860.

  Sarah J.,* born December 29, 1841, died January 24, 1849.

  Eliza A.,* born November 11, 1845, died November 25, 1845.

  (*All on same stone).

  James W., died April 5, 1849, aged 29 yrs. 4 mos. 3 ds.

  Francis M., son of W. L. and M. A., died May 16, 1852, aged
  5 mos. 21 ds.

  Phebe Ann, dau. of Walter L. and Mary A., died December
  22, 1848, aged 11 ds.

Roberts, Amos, born 1857, died 1895, aged 38 yrs.

Rodgers, Grover E., born October 13, 1885, died December 28, 1913.

HOOKER CEMETERY
Contributed by
Virgil B. Tallman
Canal Winchester, Ohio

Located at Hooker, Fairfield Co., O., a little over one-half mile due west of Hooker on the Hooker-Greencastle road on the farm known (1939) as the Laura B. Peter's Farm, west one-half of section 28, township No. 15, range No. 19.

George, son of Susan and B. Imbody, died Mar. 21, 181(9), aged (2) yr., 10 mo., 17 da.

Wilson S. Roller, died July 22, 185(6), aged 3 mo., 19 da.

Loyd Murrey, died July 3, 18(2 or 7)4, aged 73 years, 3 mo., — days.

Martha E. Snider, died Apr. 12, 1857, age about 3 mo.

Nancy Stanbery, wife of R. McFarland, died Nov. 3, 1888, aged 73 years, 27 da.

Robert McFarland, died June 5, 1882, aged 52 yr., 4 mo., 15 da.

Wesley C. McFarland, died July 7, 1853, aged 2 yr. 6 mo. 23 da.

Our grandmother, Mary, wife of John McFarland, died Jan. 22, 1864, aged 84 yrs.

Walter McFarland, Jr., died June 26, 1860, aged 17 (or 47) years, 6 m. and 10 da.

Effie G., dau. of Walter and Margaret McFarland, died Dec. 30, 1825, aged 8 yr. 1 mo., 25 da.

Abraham C., son of Walter and Margaret McFarland, died Nov. 7, 1832, aged 10 yr. 10 m. 12 d.

William McFarland, died Aug. 3, 1839, aged 81 years, 6 months, and 18 days. (A Revolutionary soldier.)

Rebecca, wife of William McFarland, died Aug. 12, 1836, aged 82 years, 4 months, and 2 days.

Henry F., son of Walter and Juliann McFarland, died Oct. 22, 1839, aged 2 years, 7 months and 3 days.

Samantha, dau. of Thos. and Maria Littlefield, died Jan. 23, 1853, aged 15 yrs., 6 mo. 18 da.

Luella Alberta, dau. of J. and O. McFarland, died Aug. 21, 1884, aged 17 yr. 9 mo. 8 da.

Orvilla Lusk, wife of John McFarland, died Apr. 25, 1882, aged 40 yrs. 11 mo. 25 da.

Sarah, wife of E. M. Winter, died July 29, 1873, aged 45 yr. 8 mo. 19 da.

George W. Winter, died Sept. 10, 1881, aged 21 yr. 9 mo. 23 d.

Mary Young, wife of Henry Brusman, died Sept. 18, 1883, aged 49 yr. 2 mo. 18 da.

James Reed, Born in Pennsylvania, May 28, 1782, emigrated to Ohio in 1805. Died Feb. 4, 1858, aged 75 years, 8 mo, 7 da.

Nancy Reed, born in Virginia, May 6, 1792, emigrated to Ohio, 1805. Died June 2, 1866, aged 74 yrs. and 27 ds.

Nancy Reed died Mar. 25, 1890, aged 66 yr. 1 mo. and 13 d.

William J. Reed, (brother of Nancy Reed) died Jan. 11, 1885, aged 70 yr. 1 mo. and 13 d.

Sarah Reed died Oct. 4, 1874, aged 45 yr. 8 m. and 29 da.

Eliza, wife of J. Armbruster, daughter of J. and N. Reed, born May 17, 1836, died Feb. 26, 1862.

General James Wells, died Jan. 29 A. D., 181(4), aged 65 years.

Mrs. Rachel Wells, wife of Gen'l James Wells, died Nov. 1, 1815, aged 55 years.

(The Tallman monument bears the inscription of 'Father and Mother' and appears to be of a more modern type than the markers of the 1820 period. It probably replaced the original markers. The Tallman Bible gives 1825 as the date of Samuel's death and a record in the Bible made by Samuel himself states he married Sarah Wells).

Father and Mother

Samuel Tallman, died Aug. 7, 1823, aged 50 y. 10 mo.

Sally Wells, wife of Samuel Tallman, died Nov. 13, 1837, aged 52 y. 8 m.

(The Brooke monument bears the inscription 'Erected by descendants, 1924.' The original slab lying nearby gives James' birth date Mar. 5.)

James Brooke March 11, 1771; Feb. 8, 1841.

Cornelia Rice Brooke, (birth date left blank), Nov. 7, 1834.

Samuel, son of Michael and Rachel Rice, died Aug. 11, 1812, aged 10 years, 6 months.

Margaret, daughter of Peter and Margaret Marshall, died May 4, 1850, aged 26 years and 8 months.

Janet, daughter of Peter and Margaret Marshall, died June 7, 1848, aged 21 years, 2 mo. and 14 days.

George Hood, died August 14th, 1815, aged 50 years and 5 months.

Elle---r Hoo-, died Aug--t 16, (date obliterated but seems to be 1812), aged (obliterated but may be 45) years and —months.

Two stones, inscriptions illegible.

George, son of Susan and B. Imbody, died Mar. 21, 18(12?), aged 2 yr. 10 mo. 17 da.

James M. Summers, died Mar. 15, 1865, aged 2 (9 ?) yrs.

Samuel Hooker, died June 9, 1880, aged 83 yr. 3 mo. 22 da.

Sarah, wife of Sam. Hooker, died Jan. 7, 1862, aged 53 yr. 10 m. 13 da.

Samuel Hooker, Sen., son of Richard and Martha Hooker, died Oct. 3, 1842, aged 89 yrs. 10 mo. 17 da.

Rachel, wife of Samuel Hooker, died Feb. 7, (rem. tombstone missing).

Mary Jane, dau. of R. and M. E. Hooker, died Dec. 2, 1864, aged 4 yr. 4 mo. 24 da.

Children of R. H. and M. E. Hooker. (individual stones missing)

William Stansberry, Born Nov. 16, 178(3). Died Oct. 6, 1855.

Milcha, wife of William Stansberry died 1838, aged 45 yrs. 4 mo. 3 da.

Margaret, dau. of William and Milcha Stansberry, died 1833, aged 19 yr.

Louisa Stansberry, died 1833, aged 15 yr.

Mary A., wife of John Stansberry, died Aug. 29, 1890, aged 81 yr. 6 mo. 28 da.

Maurice J., son of Jones (so spelled on tombstone) and Rachael W. Gibbony, died Sept. 11, 1851, aged 9 yr. 9 mo. 27 da.

Mary J., dau of Johnes (so spelled) and Rachel W. Gibbony, died Aug. 31, 1854, age 7 yrs. (remainder of inscription underground).

Rufus W., son of J. and R. Gibbony died Sept. 23, 1849, aged 4 ms. 26 days.

Infant son of William and Nancy McCleery, died Aug. 31, 1846.

Priscilla, wife of William McCleery, died May 30, 1844, aged 88 (or 38) years, 4 mo. 21 days.

Father and Mother.
Thomas McCall died June 11, 1853, aged 84 yr. 7 mo. 11 da.

Mary B., wife of Thomas McCall, died July 26, 1828, aged 51 yr. 10 mo. 25 da.

Elizabeth, daut. of T. and M. B. McCall, died Oct. 3, 1888 (?) (date 1888 obscure; cannot tell whether the numbers are 8s or 3s), aged 87 yrs. 7 mo. 15 da. (The date 1888 is probably 1838.)

Philemons B., son of Thomas and Mary McCall, died Mar. 22, 1849, aged 31 yr. 6 mo. 6 d.

John Stansberry, died Jan. 5, 1867, aged 88 years.

Mary Hooker, wife of J. Stansberry, died Oct. 11, 1828, aged 41 yrs.

Abraham Young, March 26, 1807, Feb. 18, 1853. (no other wording on tombstone).

Rachel Stansberry, wife of A. Young, Mar. 7, 1808, Mar. 7, 1886.

Margaret McFarland, died July 6, 1852, aged 68 yrs. 9 mo. and 5 d.

Our Parents

Walter	Julia
McFarland	McFarland
D. Apr. 29,	D. Mar. 31,
1876, aged	1881, aged
83 yr. 1 mo.	81 yr. 7 mo.
14 da.	10 da.
Father	Mother

McFarland

Margareta, wife of William McFarland, died April 17, 185(9?), aged 33 yrs. 2 mo. 9 da.

Twins, born Nov. 25, 1848; Lapale L., son of S. and R. Clippinger, died Dec. 14, 1848. Landon L., son of S. and R. Clippinger, died June 11, 1849.

Rachael, wife of Solomon Clippinger, Died Dec. 3, 1848, aged 30 years, 11 ms. 23 days.

Isaac J. Meason, son of J. and A. Meason, Died Oct. 30, 1844, aged 19 yrs. 1 mo.

Anna, 1st wife of John Meason, born May, 1797, died Jan. 11, 1830, in her 33rd year.

John Meason, born in Fayette Co., Pa., Mar. 26, 1795, died in Fairfield Co., O., Jan. 15, 1876, aged 80 yr. 9 mo. 19 da.

Elizabeth, wife of John Meason, died Aug. 10, 1888, aged 91 y. 2 m. 18 d.

Elijah E. Meason, died Jan. 19, 1876, aged 52 ys. 11 ms. 23 ds.

Anna M. dau. of John and Anna Meason, wife of S. A. Baxter, died Jan. 30, 1879, aged 49 years, 27 days.

Henry F., son of Walter and Juliann McFarland, died Oct. 22, 1839, aged 2 years, 7 months, and 3 days.

John W., son of Jacob and Juliann Switzer died Feb. 19th, 1845, aged 22 years, 8 months and 12 days.

George W. Meason, died Jan. 10, 1847, aged 32 yrs. 9 mos.

Rachel, wife of Isaac Meason who migrated from Fayette Co., Pa., to Ohio in 1799 and died April 25, 1836, aged 61 years, 10 mo. and 8 days.

Isaac Meason, died Feb. 26, 1845, aged (7?)1 yrs., 2 mo. 28 days.

In memory of Isaac W. Meason, 7, son of Isaac and Rachel Meason.

Jeremiah C. Meason, died May 18, 1825, aged 23 years, 9 m. and 18 days.

In memory of Isaac and Rachel Meason and their descendants that lie here. Isaac and Rachel Meason settled within one-half mile of this place in the year 1799.

John M., son of J. and E. Cherry, died Dec. 19, 1827, in the 27th year of his age.

Elsey J., dau. of (believed to be Ralph and Rutha Cherry). Remainder of inscription illegible.

Mary, dau. of Ralph and Rutha Cherry, died Sept. 24, 1823, aged 6 mo. 21 da.

——————— son of Ralph and Rutha Cherry, died Feb. 24, 1826.

Rutha, wife of Ralph Cherry, died Aprile 21, 1826, aged 22 yrs. 3 mo. and 6 days.

Jeremiah Cherry, died Aug. 6, 1801, in the 30 year of his life.

Elizabeth, daughter of George and Sarah Bear, died Sept. 13, 1824, aged 7 yrs. and 10 months.

Ann C. M., daughter of George and Sarah Bear, died Oct. 17, 1825, aged 6 years, 7 mo. 11 da.

Elijah, son of Isaac and Rachel Meason, died Jan. 31, 1825, aged 18 yrs. 10 mo. 5 da.

Hiram C. son of Isaac and Rachel Meason, died June 3, 1802, aged 51 years, 24 days.

A grave marked by G. A. R.; Civil War Vet. Believed to be Cherry.

Abigail, wife of John Abrams, died Oct. 26, 1839, aged 44 yr. and 8 mo.

Francis McCollom, died July 29, 1852, aged 91 years.

Amanda M., dau. of Thomas and Sarah Davis, died Aug. 30, 1845, aged 8 years, 2 mo. 21 d.

TAYLOR GRAVEYARD INSCRIPTIONS
FRANK A. LIVINGSTON

Location: About 200 yards south of the end of Taylor Road, which runs south one-half mile from the Columbus and Lancaster Pike—State Route 31. Franklin Co., Ohio.

In memory of
Rebeckah Taylor consort of Mathew Taylor. She was born in Londonderry, N. H. December 21, A. D. 1761, and departed this life February 20, 1814, in the 53rd year of her age.
Same Stone
In memory of
Mathew Taylor, who was born June 28, A. D. 1755, in Londonderry, N. H., died (stone sunk in ground, could not read death date.)
In memory of
Mathew Taylor, Jr., son of Mathew and Rebeckah Taylor, who was born January 16, 1787, died September 7, 1826, in the 40th year of his age.

In memory of
Milton Taylor 3rd son of Mathew Taylor who was born November 11th, A. D. 1821, and departed this life October 16, 1823.

In memory of
James Taylor, only son of James and Margaret Taylor, who was born June 10th, A. D. 1823, and departed this life December 5th, 1823, aged 5 mos. 25 ds.

James (A?) Taylor, 2nd son of Samuel and Elenor Taylor, born April 13, 1791, died August 17, 1814, aged 24 years.

In memory of Jenny Crossit, consort of Samuel Crossit, youngest daughter of Mathew and Rebeckah Taylor, born Ross County, Ohio, June 27, 1801, departed this life January 31, 1824, aged 23 yrs. 7 mos. 4 ds.

In memory of Samuel Crossit son of John and Ann Crossit, who was born South Granville, Washington County, N. Y. April 11th, 1792, and departed this life September 26, 1823, aged 31 yrs. 5 mos. 15 ds.

Joseph H. Fashinger, died August 27, 1843, aged 27 yrs. 4 mos. 13 ds.

Ebenezer Smith died October 22, 1843, aged 65 yrs. 11 mos. 20 ds.

Anna, first wife of Ebenezer Smith, died August 12, 1823, aged 59 yrs. 1 mo. 3 ds.

In memory of Jane Ross consort of Daniell Ross, died October 11, 1823, aged 49 yrs. 7 ds.

Christiana Ross youngest daughter of Daniell and Jane Ross, died October 8, 1823, aged 12 yrs. 5 mos. 8 ds.

Christiana Fulton, died January 16, 1835, aged 12 yrs. 1 mo.

John Fulton, died August 28, 1823, aged 74 yrs.

Samuel Brown, died January 15, 1816, aged 36 years.

Clarissa, daughter of James Kilgore, died February 2, 1835, aged 15 yrs. 18 ds.

Anna M. Knight consort of John H. Knight, born in Lancaster Co. ———Oct. 12, 1826.

George Edwards departed this life 1817 (?) aged 16 (?) yrs.

In memory of Mary Hamilton, daughter of Samuel and Sally Hamilton born March 22, 1817, died September 22, 1826.

In memory of William, son of Samuel and Sally Hamilton, died August 21, 1832, aged 13 yrs. 10 mos. 3 ds.

Albert B. and Andrew J., sons of Silace and Margaret Ogden, died December 25 —— aged 2 mos. 16 ds.

Mary J., dau. of Silace and Margaret Ogden, died May 23, 1843, aged 2 yrs. 11 mos. 24 ds.

Juliann, dau. of Silace and Margaret Ogden, died March 9, 1846, aged 9 mos. 30 ds.

EAST SPRINGFIELD PIONEER CEMETERY

Reported By
Dr. William S. and Katherine H. Van Fossen, October 13, 1935.

Armantha wife of Wm. McComes died Mar. (May?) 25, 1838 in the 85 yr. of her age.

William McComes died May 27, 1828 in the 89th year of his age.
——————1808   M. Lyon.

Maria Patten Sacred to the memory Maria wife of James Patten and dau. of Daniel & Jane Dunlevy who departed this life March 17th A. D. 1841 in the 39th yr. of her life.

In memory of Jane consort of James Patten who departed this life Dec. 7 A. D. 1838 aged 72 years 1 month 12 days.

In memory of James Patten who departed this life Apr. 8th 1828 aged 56 years.

In memory of Sarah   Patten dau. of James and Jane Patten who departed this life December 25, 1828 aged 20 yrs. 10 mos. 15 days.

Philip Crabs died Feb. 23, 1852, aged 55 yrs. 5 mos. 23 days.

Marian wife of Jas. W. Parr died Dec. 28, 1846 aged 20 yrs.

Calhoon Thomas Calhoon Dec. 19, 1809 Dec. 31, 1897.

His wife Eliza Jan. 24, 1819 May 18 1843.

His wife Harriet Dec. 4, 1821 Mar. 5, 1899.

Moses E. son of T. and H. Calhoon died Sept. 10 1886 aged 23 yrs. 11 mos. 18 days.

John Calhoon died May 2 1871 age 6 yrs. 9 mos. 13 days.

Marion E wife of John Calhoon died May 30 1873 age 59 yrs. 7 mos. 26 days.

In memory of Eliza consort of Thomas Calhoon who departed this life May 18 A. D. 1843 age 24 yrs. 3 mos. 24 days.

In memory of Anne consort of Adley Calhoon who departed this life Dec. 25 A. D. 1843 in the 68 yr. of her age.

Jacob Allensworth died Mar 31 1851 in the 39th yr. of his age.

In memory of Robert Wilson who departed this life April 1835 aged 55 yrs.

Samuel Wilson died Oct. 21, 1869 in his 90th year.

Jane wife of Samuel Wilson died Sept. 13 1872 in the 75th yr. of her age.

In memory of Sarah consort of Samuel Lindsey Sr. who departed this life Sept 26 A. D. 1836 in the 52nd yr. of her age.

In memory of Samuel Lindsey who departed this life July 17 1849 in the 70th year of his age.

CEMETERY RECORDS

F. A. Livingston

METHODIST HILL CEMETERY, REYNOLDSBURG, OHIO
TRURO TOWNSHIP, FRANKLIN COUNTY, LOCATED ON GRAHAM ROAD, NORTHEAST CORNER OF REYNOLDSBURG CORPORATION
Walter E. Osborne

Alwood, Sarah, dau. of A. A. & S. Alwood, Died May 14th, 1867, aged 22 yrs. 10 mos. 22 ds.

> A. A. Died March 13th, 1863, aged 76 yrs. 11 mos.

> Rosa Belle, dau. of G. W. & C. Alwood. Died April 5th, 1863, aged 5 ds.

Atwood, Thomas. Died Jan. 19th, 1866, aged 54 yrs.

> Sarah, wife of Thomas, Died Feb. 15th, 1867, aged 52 yrs.

Ayers, Wm. R. Co. E, 178th Ohio Infantry

Allebaugh, Rachel, wife of Andrew. Died April 1, 1849, aged 54 yrs. 4 mos. 23 ds.

Bethel, David, Died August 12th, 1850, aged 9 yrs.

Bayes, Elizabeth, Died Jan. 18th, 1885, aged 67 yrs. 11 mos. 10 ds.

Brunn, George, Died July 9th, 1856, aged 34 yrs. 4 mos. 4 ds.

> John E., son of Geo. Brunn. Died Jan. 26th, 1845, aged 1 yr. 3 mo. 2 ds.

Baldwin, Delia A., wife of Abel Baldwin. Died Jan. 5th, 1873, aged 48 yr. 3 mo. 13 ds.

> A, son of A. Baldwin, Died July 27th, 1852, aged 3 mos. 1 ds.

> Charles, son of A. Baldwin, Died July 17th, 1852, aged 1 yr. 11 mo. 1 ds.

> Charles, son of A. & D. Baldwin, Died Sept. 8th, 1859, aged 1 yr. 1 mo. 1 da.

Bingaman, Elizabeth, wife of John. Died Mar. 20th, 1854, aged 55 yrs. 5 mo. 19 ds.

> John, Died Feb. 13th, 1880, aged 81 yrs. 7 mo. 20 ds.

Bowsher, Flora G., dau. of Wm. & J. Bowsher. Died Dec. 9th, 1868, aged 6 yrs. 6 mo. 2 ds.

Barr, Eliza Payton, Died Aug. 26th, 1879, aged 44 yrs. 10 mo. 28 ds.

Compton, Martha R., dau. E. & L. F. Compton. Died Dec. 26th, 1816, aged 1 mo. 23 ds.

Chamberlain, Jane M., wife of S. Chamberlain. Died July 10th, 1866, aged 42 yrs. 11 mo.

Clabaugh, Arza. Died Apr. 22nd, 1848, aged 23 yrs. 4 mo. 9 ds.

Cook, Cornelius, son of Louis D. Cook, Died Oct. 27th, 1858, aged 19 yrs. 10 mo. 15 ds.

Conkle, Henry. Co. F 1st Ohio Calvery.   -   —   —

> Adam, Co. A 88th Ohio Infantry   —   —

> Rebecca T. dau. M. A. Conkle. Died Mar. 25th, 1864, aged 5 yrs. 3 mo. 14 ds.

Cabard, Frances A., dau. of J. A. Cabard. Died Feb. 25th, 1851.

Clark, Anjaline, dau. of S. B. Clark. Died July 18th, 1850, aged 2 mos.

> Susan R., dau. of Jack Clark. Died June 6th, 1850, aged 19 yr. 11 mo. 12 ds.

Cook, W. M. Co. B 159 th Ohio Vol. Inf. 1832-1908.

> Mary E., wife of W. M. Cook. Died Jan. 23rd, 1876, aged 39 yrs. 9 mos. 22 ds.

> Sheldon, son of W. M. & Mary E. Died Apr. 6th, 1869, aged 1

yr. 3 mo.

Chamberlain, N. Died Jan. 29th, 1883, aged 66 yrs. 1 mo. 14 da. Born Dec. 12, 1816.

Eliza, Died Jan. 17th, 1895, aged 78 yrs. 4 mos. 18 ds. Born Aug. 28, 1816.

Benjamin, Died. Dec. 31, 1876, aged 25 yr. 9 mos. 11 ds.

Crist, Cornelia Ann, wife Adam B., dau. Stephan P. & Nancy Stiles of New Jersey. Died Sept. 17th, 1845 aged 24 yrs. 5 mo. 14 ds.

Davis, Evan, Died Oct. 20th, 1843, aged 27 yrs.

Marvia, Died July 19th, 1840 aged 17 yr. 11 mos. 27 ds.

Devore, John Died Mar. 25th, 1873, aged 72 yrs. 6 mos. 9 ds.

Phebe, Died Oct. 18th, 1869, aged 65 yrs. 2 mo. 5 ds.

Derlburger, Alba Belle, dau. J. & M. Died Aug. 9th, 1865 aged 12 yrs. 7 mos. 2 ds.

Jacob, son of J. & M. Died July 26th, 1867, aged 4 yrs. 11 mo. 26 ds.

Dennis, Rebecca, wife of John, Died May 27th, 1852, aged 28 yrs. 23 ds.

Infant dau. of J. & R., Died Apr. 29th, 1852, aged 1 mo. 5 da.

Dellinger, Mary, wife of F., Died Dec. 12th, 1875, aged 62 yrs.

Fredric, Died Dec. 8th, 1871, aged 77 yrs.

Fred Payton, son of G. R. & S. E., Died Sept. 17th, 1870, aged 10 mo. 4 ds.

Evans, William 1814-1878

Cynthia, wife of William, Died May 14th, 1871, aged 51 yr. 6 mo. 14 ds.

Mark C., son of Wm. & C., Died May 10th, 1850, aged 2 yr. 2 mo.

Maude, dau. of E. A. Evens, Died Nov. 6th, 1875, aged 1 yr.

Susan, Wife of Maurice, Died Oct. 26th, 1864, aged 72 yrs.

David G., son of D. & A., Died Mar. 23rd, 1867, aged 2 yr. 5 mo. 15 ds.

William H., Died June 16th, 1865, aged 19 yr. 5 mo. 7 ds.

M. A., Died Mar. 2nd, 1904, aged 75 yr. 3 mo. 17 ds.

Evan, Died Oct. 9th, 1867, aged 40 yrs. 1 mo. 12 ds.

Edgar, Eleanor, wife of William, Died May 1st, 1858.

Felch, Alpheus W., son of A. S. & P. B., Died June 22nd, 1871, aged 19 yr. 5 mo. 5 ds.

Flora A., dau. of A. S. & P. B. Died July 12th, 1854 aged 4 mo.

Earnest A. son of A. S. & P. B., Died Dec. 31st, 1860, aged 3 yr. 17 ds.

Harriet E., dau. of A. S. & P. B., Died Oct. 17th, 1854, aged 3 yr. 10 mo.

Fearn, Edward, Died Aug. 16th, 1900, aged 76 yrs.

Grubs, Jesse, Died Dec. 1st, 1851, aged 76 yrs. 1 mo. 20 ds.

Clary, wife of Jese, Died Sept. 13th, 1851, aged 62 yrs.

Goldrick, Josephine E., Died Aug. 9th, 1850 aged 2 yr. 4 ds.

Matilday H., wife of Doct. Goldrich, Died Aug. 13th, 1850, aged 30 yr. 4 mo. 13 ds.

Gains, Charity, wife of Alan Gains, Died Oct. 9th, 1851, aged 56 yrs. 6 mo. 3 ds.

Green, Eliza, wife of Ira Green, Died Apr. 10th, 1889, aged 69 yr. 11 mo. 28 ds.

Graham, Jane, wife of John Green, Died Aug. 20th, 1878, aged 52 yr. 11 mo. 17 ds.

Gordon, James, son of J. P. & M. S., Died Apr. 25th, 1855, aged 1 yr. 11 mo. 11 ds.

Mary S., wife of J. P., Died Feb. 26th. 1857, aged 30 yr. 10 mo. 30 ds.

Hissong, Elizabeth, wife of Hissong, Died Oct. 16th, 1868, aged 48 yr. 4 mo. 22 ds.

Harriete, dau. of G. & E., Died July 31st, 1851, aged 8 mo. 7 ds.

Henderlick, Elizabeth, wife of John, Died Dec. 3rd, 1870, aged 52 yr. 10 mo. 15 ds.

Hanson, John, Died June 22nd, aged 81 yr. 10 mo.

Howard, Silas, Died Dec. 16th, 1854, aged 60 yrs.

Anna S, Wife of Silas, Died May 7th, 1853, aged 58 yr. 2 mo. 28 ds.

Infant dau. Wm. & M. J., Died Oct. 18th, 1856.

Glendora, dau. Wm. & M. J., Died Oct. 24th, 1854, aged 1 yr. 2 mo. 16 ds.

Ellsworth, son of Wm. & M. J., Died Nov. 9th, 1863, aged 1 yr. 3 mo. 24 ds.

Infant dau. Henry & Mary, Died Aug. 16th, 1853, aged 11 mo. 22 ds.

Grant, son of C. & S., Died Apr. 21st, 1856, Aged 2 yr. 10 mo. 13 ds.

Hunt, Rosa Bell, dau. of W. & M. Hunt, Died Oct. 5th, 1862, 1 yr. 3 mo. 7 ds.

Holmes, W. D. Died Oct. 3rd, 1851, aged 40 yr. 2 mo.

Hutchinson, John G., Died July 6th, 1880, aged 62 yr. 10 mo. 19 ds.

Innis, Carrie, wife of J. W., Died Dec. 8th 1870, aged 32 yr. 10 mo. 20 ds.

James, H. son of J. W. & C. C., Died June 23rd, 1877, aged 9 yrs. 10 mo. 27 ds.

Little Willie, son of J. W. & C. C.

Little Charley, son of J. W. & C. C., Died May 10th, 1875, aged 16 ds.

Johnson, Henry Died March 28th, 1867 aged 83 yrs.

Henry, son of F. & S. Died Sept. 21st, 1860, aged 2 yrs. 17 ds.

Andrew, son of F. & S. Died June 7th, 1868, aged 11 yrs. 4 mo.

Jennings, Cordelia, dau. J. & M. Died Aug. 8th, 1853-Aged - 4 mo.

Rebekah, wife of Joseph Died May 16th, 1849, aged 64 yr. 2 mo. 16 ds.

Joseph, Died Feb. 26th, 1862, aged 84 yrs. 2 mo. 1 da.

Jamison, Chas. W., son of T. A. & J. A. Died Aug. 12th, 1875, aged 2 yr. 3 ds.

Kindred, Elizabeth, wife of J. Died Mar. 20th, 1866, aged 64 yrs.

Kraft, Chas. M. son of C. & B., Died Mar. 29th, 1876, aged 4 yrs. 2 mo. 4 ds.

Krall, Priscilla, dau. of Jacob & Mary Died Apr. 6th, 1873 aged 15 yrs. 2 mo. 15 ds.

Geo. W., son of J. & M. Died Sept. 25th, 1865, aged - 4 mo.

Jane, dau. of J. & M., Died Nov. 12th, 1874 aged 1 yr. 1 mo.

Lotland, infant dau. of John W. & Elizabeth A., Died Aug. 20th, 1817.

Adelia, wife of John W. Died Jan. 26th, 1815 aged 28 yrs. 5 mo. 3 ds.

Thomas, son of John W. & Adelia, Died Nov. 18th, 1811 aged 8 yrs.

Lynch, Jonathan, Died Apr. 27th, 1851, aged 29 yrs. 6 mo.

Leasure, Rachel, wife of E. B., Died Jan. 22nd, 1875, aged 61 yrs. 3 mo. 5 ds.

Agnes, dau. of E. B. & R. Died Sept. 2nd, 1874 aged 27 yrs. 11

mo. 24 ds.

Leachman, Chapman, Died Sept. 1st, 1870, aged 66 yrs. 11 mo. 21 ds.
    Isaac G., son of C. & R. Died Jan. 28th, 1867 aged 23 yrs. 2 mo.
    3 ds.

Gordon, Sarah E., dau. of C. & R. Died Dec. 2nd, 1858 aged 1 yr. 1 mo.
    Rachel A. wife of C. Died July 12th, 1890, aged 77 yrs. 4 mo.
    28 ds.

Loeffler, Maryetta dau. of W. C. & L., Died Aug. 21, 1858 aged 3 yr. 7
    mo. 11 ds.

Lanford, Naoma Died June 13th, 1863 aged 76 yrs.
    Luther, Died Jan. 18th, 1857 aged 63 yrs.
    W. H. Co. K. 2nd. U. S. Cavalry
    Clara M. Died Sept. 4th, 1888 aged 15 yrs. 6 mo.

Learn, Jefferson, hus. of Maria, Died Jan. 6th, 1884 aged 70 yr. 5 mo.
    10 ds.
    Maria, wife of Jefferson, Died Feb. 21st, 1889, aged 75 yr. 10
    mo. 28 ds.
    Velina, dau. of J. & M. Died Nov. 10th, 1849 aged—11 mo.
    Betsy, dau. of —. & M. Died May 2nd, 1887, aged 8 yr. 3 mo.
    Matilda dau. of J. & M. Died Nov. 11th, 1877 aged 21 yr. 1 mo.
    3 ds.

Longshore, Thomas, Died Feb. 10th, 1874 aged 79 yr. 5 mo. 19 ds.
    Jane, wife of Thomas Died May 21st, 1852 aged 65 yrs. 2 mo.
    3 ds.

Leckrone, Wm. D. L., son of J. & E. Died Feb. 17th, 1865 aged 11 yr.
    11 mo. 4 ds.

Langheinrich, John F., son of J. & K., Died Nov. 29th, 1872 aged 10
    mo.

Mcrton, Madison M., son of A. M. & C. Died July 16th, 1861 aged 25
    yrs. 8 mo. 19 ds.
    Albert L. son of A. M. & C. Died May 9th, 1869 aged 21 yrs.

Meyers, Nancy, wife of John Died Feb. 14th, 1875 aged 75 yrs. 15 ds.
    Caroline, dau. of John & Nancy, Died Sept. 3 rd, 1860 aged 21
    yr. 13 ds.

Morehead, Louisa, wife of John Died Aug. 15th, 1845 aged 39 yr. 3 mo.
    Francis. M., son of John & Louisa, Died Aug. 11th, 1845 aged
    3 yr. 6 mo. 16 ds.

Mingis, Francis H. dau. of J. & R., Died May 6th, 1861 aged 3 yr. 9
    mo. 14 ds.
    John, Died Aug. 18th, 1865 aged 31 yrs. 10 mo.
    Oscar W., Died May 25th, 1878 aged 41 yrs. 9 mo. 10 ds.
    Lauria G., Died May 12th, 1863 aged 6 yrs. 11 mo.

Martin, John, Died Apr. 17th, 1862 aged 64 yr. 7 mo. 6 ds.
    Jane, Died Mar. 19th, 1856 aged 19 yr. 11 mo. 18 ds.

Mead, Samuel, Jr., Died June 5th, 1844 aged 50 yr. 5 mo. 1 da.

Miller, Margaret, wife of P. Miller, Died Feb. 13th, 1877 aged 36 yr.
    2 mo. 8 ds.
    John H., Died Feb. 20th, 1890 aged 89 yrs.
    Sidney, Died Jan. 2nd, 1890 aged 79 yrs.
    Alice, Died May 15th, 1856 aged 3 yrs. 9 mo.

Mills, Lucina, wife of Peter, Died Apr. 19th, 1845 aged 47 yrs.

Metzner, Eliza, kin. of Geo. Died Apr. 4th, 1834 aged 30 yrs. 1 mo. 20
    ds.

Moyer, Henry, Died Nov. 26th, 1847 aged 68 yrs. 11 mo. 23 ds.

Morris, Willmer ., son of T & R. Died July 18th, 1851 aged 15 yr. 10
    mo. 18 ds.

Chas. son of T & R Died May 15th, 1850 aged 29 yrs.

Mason, John W. Died Nov. 20th, 1872 aged 35 yrs. 11 mo. 1 ds.

Michael, Died Nov. 28th, 1878 aged 70 yrs.

McLean, Henrietta dau. of G. S. & S. J. Died Sept. 11th, 1857 aged 15 yrs.

McCofferty, David W. Died Dec. 26th, 1872 aged 41 yrs. 11 mo. 4 ds.

Eliza C., wife of D. W. Died June 14th, 1874 aged 36 yrs. 27 ds.

McCafferty, Julia, wife of T. Died Apr. 27th, 1863 aged 26 yrs.

T. F. Died Nov. 18th, 1869 aged 34 yr. 3 mo. 6 ds.

McEwen Lucy, dau. of R. & M. Died Sept. 21st, 1872 aged 1 yr. 5 mo. 5 ds.

Francis L. dau. of R. &. M., Died Aug. 12th, 1866 aged 11 mo.

McIntyre, Marietta, dau. of J. & M. Died Sept. 1st, 1855 aged 16 yr. 2 mo.

Wm. Died Feb. 28th, 1886 aged 62 yr. 11 mo. 28 ds.

Sarah, wife of Wm. Died Jan. 29th, 1855 aged 36 yr. 11 mo. 21 ds.

Joseph, died Dec. 23rd, 1851 aged 31 yrs. 21 ds.

Rosetta M., 1848-1902

Susan Ann 1844-1917

Mary Jane, dau. Wm. & S. Died May 31st, 1867 aged 24 yr. 11 mo. 3 ds.

Sarah, wife of Wm., dau. F. T. & J. Longshore Died Jan. 29th, 1855 aged 36 yrs. 11 mo. 21 ds.

Nueomer Uriah, Died Sept 20th, 1847 aged 40 yrs.

Osborn Samuel, Died Jan. 20th, 1857 aged 57 yrs.

William, son of Samuel

Overbore, Maryan, wife of Charles, Died Dec. 29th, 1860 aged 36 yrs. 2 mo. 25 ds.

Odell, Elias in memory of

Phebe in memory of

Mary in memory of

Delia in memory of

Moses, in memory of

Edeng in memory of

Edward in memory of

Martin V. B. in memory of

Powers, Thomas J. Died Sept. 24th, 1889 aged 53 yrs. 1 mo. 10 ds.

Painter Nathaniel Died Nov. 11, 1876 aged 76 yrs. 1 mo. 24 ds.

Parkinson, Edward Died Jan. 31st, 1899 aged 86 yrs. 1 mo.

Margaret, wife of George, Died Aug. 20th, 1871 aged 87 yrs. 2 mo. 26 ds.

Daniel, Died Apr. 14th, 1876 aged 65 yrs. 5 mo.

Reynolds, Minnie A. dau. J. T. & A. Died Aug. 20th, 1879 aged 18 mo.

Lettie dau. E. & A. Died Jan. 19th, 1868 aged 26 yrs.

Read, James, son of O. S. & M. Died Dec. 17th, 1863 aged 2 yrs. 8 mo. 25 ds.

Rush, George D. Died May 17th, 1853 aged 33 yrs.

Flora A. dau. G. & A. Died Apr. 1st, 1854 aged 7 mo.

Rodebaugh, infant son of S. B. & C. Died Aug. 12th, 1875 aged 9 ds.

Austin M., son of S. B. & C. Died Sept. 26th, 1877 aged 3 yr.

Roberts, Thomas, Died Dec. 2nd, 1892 aged 73 yrs. 2 mo. 5 ds.

Mahala

Stephen, Died Aug. 8th, 1851 aged 33 yrs. 8 mo. 15 days.

John, 1850-1869

Rush, Henry, Died Jan. 25th, 1879 aged 28 yrs. 4 mo. 3 ds.

Reynolds, James M. Died Jan. 21st, 1867 aged 27 yrs. 6 mo. 23 ds.
    Christian, wife of E. Died June 27th, 1885, aged 73 yrs. 11 mo.
    21 ds.
Sharp, Temperance A, wife of J. Died May 12th, 1867 aged 60 yrs.
    John, Died Sept. 22nd. 1851 aged 58 yrs.
Scofield, Alanson, Died June 28th, 1882, aged 82 yrs. 7 mo. 28 ds.
    Maria, wife of A. Died Apr. 10th, 1875, aged 74 yrs. 8 mo. 8 ds.
    Ruben, Died Dec. 21st, 1853. Aged 75 yrs. 10 mo. 28 ds.
    Mary, wife of R. Died June 11th, 1857, aged 77 yrs. 9 mo.
    Lousisa, dau. of Alanson & Mary Died May 23; 1848, aged 13
    yr. 11 mo. 2 ds.
Smith, Lydia, Died Apr. 24th, 1883.
Squires Nettie, dau. of E. S. & C. T. Died April 14th, 1884, aged 2 mo.
    5 ds.
Thomas, Edward, Died Dec. 16th, 1877, aged 61 yrs. 6 mo. 14 ds.
    Elizabeth, Died Apr. 9th, 1878. aged 63 yrs. 1 mo. 24 ds.
Tucker, Mary, wife of Phinehas Died Apr. 12th, 1861, aged 44 yrs. 9
    mo. 17 ds.
    M. T. Phinehas, son of P. M. Died Feb. 6th, 1869 aged 19 yr.
    6 mo. 22 ds.
    Sarah, dau. of D. & M. Died Mar. 20th, 1855 aged 3 yr. 9 mo.
    2 ds.
Talmadge, Daniel Died Sept. 8th, 1882. aged 66 yrs. 1 mo.
    David, son of M. Died June 11th, 171 aged 19 yr. 11 mo.
    Mary, dau. of David   Died Oct. 30th, 1860, aged 11 yrs. 3 mo.
    2 days.
    Mary, wife of D.   Died May 2nd, 1852, aged 31 yrs.
    Joseph, Died Oct. 12th, 1862, aged 43 yrs. 9 mo. 2 ds.
Tucker, A. D.   Died Aug. 21st 1865, aged 94 yrs. 2 mo. 10 ds.
    Hanna, wife of A. D.   Died Apr. 9th, 1874, aged 91 yrs. 6
    mo.
Vrooman, William, son of A. & L. A. Died May 25th, 1852 aged 1 yr.
    6 mo.
    Nicklos   Died July 5th, 1850, aged 28 yrs. 5 mo.
Walling, Asa, Died Jan. 9th, 1861, aged 72 yrs. 9 mo. 9 ds.
Winters, Zopher, son of A. & L. Born Sept. 13th, 1839. Died Sept. 17th,
    1885.
    Louis, Died Jan. 1st, 1872, aged 75 yrs. 10 mo.
    Ady, wife of Louis, Died Nov. 9th, 1864 aged 63 yrs. 27 ds.
    Laura M, dau. of J. G. & S. A. Died Sept. 18th, 1877, aged
    19 yrs.
    Sarah,, wife of J. G. Died Oct. 17th, 1895, aged 63 yrs. 25 ds.
Wolf, Jacob L., son of L. & H. Died Nov. 27th, 1868, aged 1 yr. 4 mo.
    19 ds.
Isaac, Died Mar. 14th, 1863, aged 39 yr. 3 mo. 5 ds.
    Margaret, dau. of I. & S. Died Aug. 16th, 1863, aged 4 yr. 3
    mo. 5 ds.
    Mary R. dau. of I. & S. Died July 28th, 1861, aged 8 mo. 5 ds.
    Margaret, wife of Jacob, Died Sept. 2nd, 1872, Born Nov. 6th,
    1792.
    Jacob, Died July 30th, 1869 Born Jan. 28th, 1788.
Whitney, Augusta L. dau. of S. Died Feb. 14th, 1856 aged 3 mo.
    Edward H., son of C. & S. Died Nov. 12th, 1853 aged 2 yr. 6
    mo. 11 ds.
Woodruff, Aota R., dau. of H. & A. Y., Died Aug. 24th, 1870, aged 3 yr.
    10 mo. 12 ds.

CEMETERY RECORDS

FRANK A. LIVINGSTON

JENKINS CHAPEL CEMETERY

Located in Wayne Township, Champaign County, Ohio, On Route 216 on north side of road. Record made by T. B. Lang, August 15, 1937.

BEST, Clarence, son of J. W. and I. M., died Aug. 22, 1888, aged 5 mos. 23 ds.
> Ida M., wife of J. W., died July 16, 1888, aged 23 yrs. 8 mos. 9 ds.
> John, born 1863, died 1924.
> John, born Oct. 3, 1823, died Sept. 29, 1903.
> Mary J., born Oct. 22, 1830, died Aug. 17, 1894.
> Otho, H., born July 21, 1896, died Nov. 13, 1911.
> Sarah J., born 1869, died 19—.

BLACK, Ava M., born Nov. 28, 1887, died Mch. 5, 1897.
> C. B., born Mch. 10, 1868.
> Catherine, born July 27, 1832, died Feb. 11, 1907.
> Cora, (No record).
> Eldise, born 1916, died 1917.
> Emma Irene, dau. of C. B. and M. J., died May 25, 1885, aged 2 mos. 20 ds.
> Henry Edgar, born 1856, died 1907.
> Infant son of C. B. and M. J., died Oct. 17, 1889.
> Jennie, born 1857, died 19—.
> Mable, G., born Nov. 19, 1883, died Dec. 2, 1904.
> Minnie, wife of W. B., born Oct. 11, 1867, died May 10, 1895.
> Nettie, born 1864, died 1915.
> Perry, son of S. C. and Joanna, died July 10, 1878.
> Peter, born May 14, 1828, died Dec. 26, 1899.
> Ruth B., born 1885, died 1922.
> Thurman P., born Nov. 4, 1890, died Dec. 16, 1896.
> Verna, born 1882, died 1906, m. W. L. Turner.

BUCKWALTER, Arthur, born 1879, died 19—.
> Susie Y., born 1884, died 1934.

CHATFIELD, Florence, born Feb. 22, 1892, died Sept. 4, 1892.

CLARK, Isaac, died Feb. 25, 1882, aged 83 yrs. 24 ds.
> Lillian, born Sept. 20, 1879, died Aug. 29, 1897.
> Lucy E., born 1849, died 1914.
> Mary A., died Apr. 6, 1888, aged 77 yrs. 10 mos. 2 ds.
> Minnie, dau. of Peter and Lucy, died July 22, 1879, aged 5 mos. 22 ds.
> Peter, born 1842, died 1924.

CORBET, David L., born Apr. 30, 1827, died May 18, 1892.
> George W., born July 10, 1851, died Feb. 23, 1902.
> Joseph Lee, born Oct. 16, 1936, died Oct. 23, 1936.
> Lorinda, wife of D. L., born Feb. 20, 1826, died Feb. 13, 1901.
> Sarah A., born June 2, 1845, died Sept. 27, 1895.
> William, born June 3, 1840, died Dec. 20, 1890.

CORBETT, Benjamin, born Oct. 19, 1837, died Mch. 3, 1899.
> George, born 1867, died 1885.
> Perry, born 1885, died 1905.
> Susan, (No record).

DODSON, Charles, born 1850, died 1919.
> J. Edwin, adopted son of Charles and M. E., born Feb. 24, 1889, died July 9, 1889.
> Mary Elizabeth, born 1858, died 19—.

DOTY, Amy L. born 1861, died 1891.
DURNELL, Chester, son of F. A. and F. A., born Jan. 11, 1895, died
    Aug. 26, 1896.
    Hiram, born Jan. 22, 1805, died May 18, 1898.
    James, born Aug. 17, 1835.
    Lucindia, wife of James, born Jan. 22, 1842, died May 8, 1908.
    Sarah, wife of Hiram, born June 29, 1815, died Dec. 5, 1902.
EVANS, William E., Co. H. 66, O. V. I.
GALLOWAY, John A., born 1841, died 1912.
GANSON, Chauncey C., died Feb. 3, 1887, aged 1 yr. 5 mos. 24 ds.
    Children J. D. and Lizzie.
    Infant son, died Apr. 13, 1881, aged 1 da.
GLENDENNING, Earl L., born 1877, died 19—.
    Grace, D., born 1883, died 1918.
GRAHAM, Anna, born 1845.
    John, born 1844, died 1895.
    Nettie, born 1873, died 1895.
HAGERDON, Charles S., born 1870, died 1927.
    John, born 1858.
    Martha, born Oct. 7, 1836, died Sept. 7, 1893.
    Mary, born 1859, died 1919.
    Peter, born Aug. 27, 1829, died Nov. 11, 1907.
HATFIELD, Burleigh, born 1872, died 1896.
    Cora E., wife of John M., born 1847, died 19—.
    Francis L., born 1876, died 1900.
    Hamet, born 1844, died 1922.
    John M., born 1841, died 1921, Co. H. 86, O. V. I.
HAWKINS, Betsey, born May 10, 1800, died Aug. 19, 1876.
    Ida G. wife of F. M., died Apr. 10, 1886, aged 21 yrs. 7 mos. 24 ds.
    L. P., son of Betsey, Co. D. 134, O. V. I., born Apr. 1, 1830, died
        Mch. 27, 1900.
HESS, Elizabeth, born May 6, 1798, died Aug. 14, 1889.
    John M., born Oct. 26, 1825, died Oct. 30, 1902.
    Narcissa, born May 26, 1831, died Apr. 29, 1898.
HINTON, Infant of Z. T. and L., died Nov. 6, 1874.
    John, died May 7, 1882, aged 77 yrs. 3 mos. 25 ds.
    Lavinia, wife of Taylor, born Oct. 30, 1849, died Aug. 22, 1933.
    Sarah, wife of John, died Sept. 11, 1888, aged 75 yrs. 11 mos. 2 ds.
    Taylor, Co. D. 134, O. V. I., died June 2, 1903.
JENKINS, Ada K., born 1876, died 1892.
    Flossie B., born 1891, died 1891.
    Kittie, wife of R. P., born 1848, died 1886.
    Martha B., born 1859, died 1909.
    Mattie A., born 1863, died 1913.
    Richard P., born 1847, died 1917.
    Venis C., dau. of C. and S. M., born July 24, 1893, died June 22,
        1894.
    Wretha, born 1873, died 1892.
JOHNSON, George, died Apr. 21, 1873, aged 67 yrs. 9 mos. 25 ds.
    Infant dau. of Geo. and Mary, died Apr. 15, 1878.
    Infant son of O. P. and A. M., died Dec. 2, 1879.
    Irvin, born Feb. 8, 1839, died June 11, 1895.
    John W., born 1854, died 1913.
    Mary E., born 1858, died 1916.
    Mary J., died Jan. 1, 1855, aged 37 yrs. 1 mo. 3 ds.
    Sarah E., born 1856, died 1935.

Sarah J., died Oct. 22, 1895, aged 88 yrs. 5 mos. 13 ds.

JORDON, Edith B., born 1869, died 1912.
Edith, wife of Philip G., born Feb. 8, 1869, died May 1, 1912.
Philip G., born July 10, 1864.

KERNS, Clarenda A., wife of I. E., born Nov. 22, 1846, died Oct. 17, 1886, aged 40 yrs. 20 ds.
Infant son of I. E. and C. A., died Aug. 26, 1890, aged 3 yrs.
Pearlie, son of L. H., died Jan. 14, 1881, aged 1 yr. 8 mos. 11 ds.

KRIDER, Walter, died Aug. 5, 1897, aged 24 yrs. 2 mos. 19 ds.

LARUE, Andrew Jr., born 1853, died 1913.
Mary J., born 1866.

LARY, Julian, died Jan. 31, 1874 aged 69 yrs. 11 mos. 17 ds.

LEOPARD, Elizabeth, born 1860.
Wilmer H., born 1885, died 1918.

MABRY, Edith, born 1895, died 1918.
Millie, born 1911.
Polany, born Jan. 18, 1849, died Aug. 28, 1902.
W. P., born Feb. 18, 1849.

McADAMS, Byron, born 1896, died 1896.
Frank, born Jan. 27, 1866/67, died 1914.
Lou, born 1864, died Mch. 8, 1916.
Robert, born 1894, died 1916.
Samuel, born 1869.
Samuel Sr., born June 16, 1834, died 1919.
Winnie T., born 1837, died 1896.

McAFEE, Archibald, (No record).
Elnora M., born Mch. 6, 1881.
Hannah, wife of Archibald, died Jan. 16, 1887, aged 73 yrs. 5 mos. 22 ds.
Joseph S., born 1840, died 1914.
Scott A., born Jan. 2, 1877, died Nov. 27, 1899.
Tephanes, wife of Joseph, born 1840, died 1877.

McCOLLY, Amazia J., died Mch. 3, 1891, aged 43 yrs. 11 mos. 25 ds.
Charley A., son of C. and R., died Mch. 12, 1877, aged 5 mos. 20 ds.
Edna May, dau. of J. and C., died Mch. 26 1894, aged 10 yrs. 10 mos. 13 ds.
John M., died May 7, 1876, aged 60 yrs.
Margaret, died Feb. 17, 1886, aged 70 yrs. 8 mos. 11 ds.

MIDDLETON, Arthur, born 1856, died 1906.
Charles O. born 1866, died 1934.
Edward, born Jan. 18, 1827, died Jan. 20, 1901.
Elizabeth, wife of John, born July 13, 1783, in Fairfax Co., Va., died Dec. 13, 1873, aged 90 yrs. 5 mos.
Elizabeth, wife of Edward, born Mch. 24, 1830, died Oct. 24, 1894, aged 64 yrs. 7 mos.
Enola J., born 1855, died 19—.
Estaville, wife of Wm.
Harry P., born 1891, died 1906.
Infant children of A. H. and A.
Infant dau. of C. O. and Maggie, born Feb. 26 - 28, 1895.
John, born July 13, 1778, in Fairfax Co., Va., died Aug. 12, 1873, aged 95 yrs. 30 ds.
John Jr., born Apr. 18, 1821, died Mch. 13, 1881.
Maggie, born 1863, died 1924.
Mary Jane, born 1866, died 1910.
Milton G., born 1855, died 1910.

Minnie, dau. of W. W. and S. R., died Nov. 12, 1884, aged 16 yrs. 5 mos. 28 ds.

Sarah R., born 1844, died 1911.

Staten, born 1851, died 19—.

William, died Jan. 1, 1890, aged 87 yrs. 8 mos. 15 ds.

William, born 1841, died 1895, Co. E. 95, O. V. I.

MIDDLLETON, Lorena E., died at age of 17 yrs.

MOODY, Cora, born 1871, died 1921.

Florence W., born 1894, died 1915.

Ogg, (No record).

MORRISON, Mary J., wife of F. W., died Mch. 8, 1877, aged 30 yrs. 4 mos. 24 ds.

MYERS, Robert C., died Feb. 28, 1885, aged 26 yrs. 5 mos. 10 ds.

NINCEHELSER, Henry, born Apr. 8, 1827, died Aug. 7, 1914.

NOLAN, John, born Dec. 25, 1854 died Sept. 23, 1887.

OUTRAM, James, born 1846, died 1896.

Mary E., born 1852, died 1931.

PEES, Nicholas, born Aug. 22, 1798, died July 29, 1869.

PERRY, Charles, son of Evan and Elizabeth, died Mch. 8, 1880, aged 18 yrs. 2 mos. 14 ds.

Elizabeth, died Apr. 21, 1905, aged 85 yrs. 11 mos. 21 ds.

Evan, died Oct. 5, 1872, aged 52 yrs. 11 mos. 9 ds.

Evan Jr., born 1872, died 19—.

George M., born 1848, died 1923.

Jethinea, wife of Evan Jr., born Dec. 6, 1870, died Feb. 9, 1895.

Mary L., born 1872, died 19—.

Melissa J., born 1846, died 1923.

Sterling C., born 1907, died 1932.

REAM, Lizzie, dau. of T. N. and M. J., died Jan. 5, 1874.

Mary Jane, born 1850, died 1924.

Thomas N., born 1842, died 1913.

REED, Ida, born 1866, died 19—.

Oscar, born 1865, died 1924.

RUDISILL, Mable G., wife of Guy Black, born 1883, died 1904.

Sarah J., born 1860, died 1929.

William, born 1853, died 1929.

William M., born Jan. 15, 1824, died Apr. 27, 1886.

SHAUL, Elizabeth, wife of John, died Feb. 8, 1879, aged 77 yrs. 12 ds.

John, died Dec. 21, 1885, aged 76 yrs. 1 mo. 1 da.

Joseph M. born Sept. 30, 1869, aged 30 yrs. 1 mo. 10 ds.

SHIELDS, Beattrice, born 1863, died 1877.

Jno., Co. F. 134, Ohio Inf.

SMITH, Ira, born Dec. 10, 1817, died May 8, 1875.

Joanna M., born 1852, died 1914.

Josiah C., born 1855, died 1926.

Mary, born Mch. 1, 1822, died Dec. 30, 1900.

STEWARD, James, died Dec. 9, 1884, aged 66 yrs. 7 mos. 9 ds.

Lydia, dau. of J. and R., died Mch. 16, 1872, aged 17 yrs. 1 mo. 10 ds.

STROHL, Elizabeth, wife of Reuben, born Oct. 1, 1831, died Aug. 15, 1905.

Hannah, wife of John, died July 22, 1886, aged 59 yrs. 9 mos. 27 ds.

Hester, wife of Jacob, born in Berks Co. Pa. Mch. 14, 1804, died Oct. 8, 1863, aged 59 yrs. 6 mos. 24 ds.

Jacob, born in Berks Co., Pa., Nov. 4, 1801, died Oct. 4, 1878, aged 76 yrs. 11 mos.

Jacob A., born 1866, died 1917.

John, died Dec. 28, 1896, aged 74 yrs. 2 mos. 12 ds.

Mary A., born Nov. 7, 1826, died Aug. 29, 1913.

Reuben, born Mch. 25, 1825, died May 27, 1894.

SWISHER, Infant dau. of Perry and Martha, died Feb. 15, 1879.

TEMPLE, Josie, dau of G. V., died Sept. 23, 1875, aged 2 mos. 2 ds.

THOMPSON, Bertha S., wife of Edward, born 1854.

Edward M., born 1844, died 1918, 134 Reg. O. V. I.

Ella, wife of A. B., born Mch. 3, 1853, died Sept. 21, 1895.

Emma F., dau. of J. and S. M., died Jan. 6, 1874, aged 14 yrs. 6 mos. 11 ds.

George M., son of J. and S., died Dec. 11, 1876.

Infant son of A. B. and E. W.

James, born 1834, died 1903.

Sarah C., born 1844, died 1927 or 1911.

Sarah M., born 1843, died 1919.

Susan, died Dec. 18, 1888, aged 76 ysr. 10 mos. 23 ds.

W. F., born 1865, died 1898.

William, born 1841, died 1932 or 1895.

TURNER, Verna (Black) wife of W. L., born 1882, died 1906.

WALTER, Griffith, born Dec. 27, 1820, died Mch. 5, 1886.

Jane, born Dec. 17, 1833, died Aug. 18, 1921.

WHITE, Henry M., Co. 1 - 66, O. V. I.

WILLIAMS, Infant dau. of Wm. and S., born June 16, 1881, died June 22, 1881.

Warren Edward, born 189-, died 1914.

WILSON, Isaac T., born Sept. 17, 1841, died Jan. 18, 1896.

CEMETERY RECORDS

By F. A. Livingston

BAPTIST CHURCH, REYNOLDSBURG, OHIO

ARMSTRONG, Elvira, wife of William; born May 20, 1803; died Feb. 13, 1897

William; died July 25, 1853; age 78 years

ASHBROOK, Sarah, wife of J. P.; died Aug. 1, 1861; age 59 yrs. 8

mo. 2 da.

W. H. H., 55 Reg. Co. E O. V. I.; born June 7, 1835; died June 6, 1862

BEACH, Horace E., son H. E. & I.; died Oct. 6, 1865; age 13 yrs. 8 da.

BELL, Elijah; born Frederick Co., Md. Oct. 27, 1794; died Sept. 29, 1876

BINGHAM, Ira Elbert, son W. & E. J.; died Oct. 30, 1878; Age 3 yrs. 3 mo. 20 da.

Alva Eldon, son W. & E. J.; died Nov. 6, 1878; Age 12 yrs. 2 mo. 29 da.

Allen E., son W. & E. J.; died March 16, 1864; age 2 yr. 10 mo. 2 da.

John H., son W. & E. J.; died Mar. 17, 1864; age 11 yr. 22 da.

BOEN, Alva, son S. A.; died Oct. 16, 1878; age 1 yr. 8 mo. 5 da.

COONS, Josiah, son Madison & Rachel; died Sept. 17, 1851; age 11 yr. 28 da.

Kittie L., wife O. F.; dau. J. B. & M. E. West; died Aug. 17, 1877; age 25 yrs. 10 mo. 17 da.

Mayor John; died Nov. 4, 1865; age 78 yrs. 7 mo.

Anna G., wife John; died Mar. 29, 1871; age 82 yrs. 9 mo. 21 da.

CLABAUGH, Rebecca, wife Nicholas; died May 20, 1836; age 76 yrs.

COHAGEN, John; died Dec. 26, 1871; age 59 yrs. 7 mo. 3 da .

May J., wife John; died Feb. 25, 1872; age 51 yrs. 23 da.

George W., died Jan. 23, 1872; age 24 yrs. 5 mo. 18 da.

Matilda; died July 29, 1879; age 28 yrs. 9 mo. 23 da.

CORNELL, William; died March 10, 1835; age 62 yrs. 6 mo. 7 da.

Permelia, wife William; died June 27, 1882; age 84 yrs. 3 mo. 19 da.

Infant son of J. W. & M. U.; died Jan. 21, 1881; age 1 mo.

CREIGHTON, Isaac; died Oct. 17, 1867; age 68 yrs. 5 mo. 22 da.

Wilson, son Isaac; died Mar. 26, 1870; age 28 yrs. 3 mo. 28 da.

COLLUM, James W., son J. & E. M.; died Feb. 25, 1872; age 1 yr. 9 mo. 1 da.

DUNNON, Aaron; died Mar. 8, 1843; age 20 yr. 11 mo. 8 da.

DAVIS, Sarah F.; died Sept. 20, 1884; age 60 yrs.

Sarah Orlean; died Sept. 19, 1887; age 25 yrs.

Lot; died May 13, 1862; age 85 yrs.

Harriet, wife Lot; died Dec. 12, 1869; age 87 yrs.

DIXON, James H., son Wm. & Ma.; died Mar. 25, 1848; age 1 yr. 3 mo.

Rosetta, dau. Wm. & M.; died Sept. 22, 1845; age 4 yrs. 10 mo. 11 da.

Manerva J., dau. Wm. & M.; Dec. 18, 1839; age 2 mo. 4 da.

Nancy A., dau. Wm. & M.; died Aug. 14, 1839; age 1 yr. 10 mo. 5 da.

William, father of above; died Aug. 28, 1872; age 63 yrs.

Margaret, wife Wm.; dau. John and Ann Helphrey; died Nov. 18, 1857; age 42 yrs.

DICKSON, John Wesley, son Harriet; died May 19, 1840; age 2 mo. 13 da.

EVANS, Mary E., wife A. N.; died Feb. 26, 1865; age 41 yrs.

EDGAR, Mary, former wife of Thomas Palmer; died Sept. 22, 1865; age 83 yrs. 5 mo. 8 da.

ESSEX, Isaac, W. H., son H. & N. M.; died Sept. 11, 1857; **age 3 yrs.**
3 mo. 3 da.

FELL, Lousanna, wife John; died Jan. 10, 1851

FOLK, Mattie, dau. G. P. & S. T.; died Sept. 11, 1871; **age 7 yrs. 6**
mo. 6 da.

FURRY, James; died Dec. 5, 1874; age 37 yrs. 8 mo. 24 da.

FURRY, Mary A., wife James; died Apr. 19, 1886; age 44 yrs. 7 mo.
28 da.

    Ida, J., dau. J. & M. A.; died June 11, 1882; age 15 yrs.
9 mo. 27 da.

GILBERT, Hiram, son G. W. & N.; died Aug. 2, 1878; age 1 yr. 5 mo.
5 da.

GREEN, Stephen; died Nov. 6, 1864; age 71 yrs. 7 mo. 19 da.

    Margaret, wife S.; died Dec. 8, 1863; age 65 yrs. 11 mo.
24 da.

    David; died Aug. 19, 1864; age 27 yrs. 10 mo. 21 da.

    Elijah G.; died Aug. 19, 1864; age 49 yrs. 4 mo. 1 da.

GRUES, Ardelpha Jane, dau. James & Sarah; died July 28, 1843; age
4 yrs. 10 mo.

    Infant son of W. H. & E. C.; died Apr. 10, 1867

    J. H.; born Jan. 4, 1849; died Nov. 13, 1898

    Celia; born Nov. 5, 1812; died June 21, 1888

    Mary L.; born Feb. 24, 1844; died Dec. 21, 1864

    Celia M., dau. Eli H. & Celia; died Aug. 19, 1840; age 1
yr. 1 mo. 2 da.

    Isaac, son Elijah & Margaret Shaw; died March 28, 1818

    Eli. O., son Eli, H. & C.; died Mar. 2, 1854; age 12 yrs.
1 mo. 24 da.

HEDDON, Prudence A.; died Sept. 30, 1838; age 1 yr. 3 mo. 19 da.

    Edward; died July 10, 1846; age 33 yrs. 10 mo.

HOWARD, Mary E., wife A. S., dau. M. & E. Powers; died Oct. 18,
1862; age 23 yrs. 10 mo. 23 da.

    Sergt. A. S. Co. F. O. V. Cal. no dates shown

    Fatinae, dau. A. S. & M. E.; died July 24, 1858; age 2 yrs.
1 mo. 1 da.

    Clarence O., A. S. & M. E.; died Dec. 5, 1860; age 6 mo.
5 da.

HUTSON, Luella, dau. G. J. & M.; died July 14, 1867; age 8 mo. 19
da.

HICKMAN, infant son of D. & M. A.; died Aug. 8, 1873

IRVING, Thomas, died Jan. 9, 1878, age 34 years.

    Josie, dau. Thom. & E., died Oct. 15, 1877; age 6 yrs. 11
mo. 2 da.

JOHNSON, Martha A., wife of A. D.; died Dec. 11, 1863; age 31 yrs.
4 mo. 9 da.

    Margaret; born Dec. 28, 1802; died Apr. 7, 1889

    Bolin Frank; son of R. R. & E. A.; died June 10, 1857;
age 18 yrs.

    Charles S.; son of R. R. & E. A.; died Feb. 28, 1863; Age
3 yrs. 5 mo. 15 da.

    Hattie V., dau. R. R. & E. A.; died Oct. 25, 1865; age 3
yrs. 11 mo. 15 da.

KISAR, Frank B., son of M.; died Aug. 10, 1858; age 11 mo.

LONGSHORE; Amanda J., dau. J. G. & S.; died Aug. 18, 1850; **age 3**
mo. 20 da.

Damaris **Ann,** dau. J. G. & S.; died Dec. 11, 1849; age 4 yrs. 3 mo.

Ann, wife John G.; died Aug. 17, 1842; age 19 yrs. 6 mo. 21 da.

LONNIS, John; died Mar. 7, 1883; age 81 yrs. 8 mo. 12 da.

King Jacob, son of J. & R.; died July 31, 1869; age 17 yrs. 11 mo. 10 da.

Elbridge G., son of J. & R.; died Nov. 21, 1867; age 9 yrs.

LUNN, B. F., Co. I O. V. I.; died Oct. 1, 1862; age 26 yrs. 1 mo. 22 da.

Jesse; died Feb. 16, 1856; age 69 yrs. 11 mo.

Margaret, wife of Jesse; died Nov. 12, 1855; age 55 yrs.

Benjamin U.; died Jan. 15, 1834; age 31 yrs.

Lewis; died Aug. 22, 1837; age 30 yrs.

Mary; died May 20, 1838; age 75 yrs.

Alice; died Jan. 14, 1879; age 81 yrs. 11 mo. 25 da.

Catherine; died Sept. 13, 1875; age 79 yrs. 7 mo. 14 da.

LYNCH, infant dau. of C. & E.; died May, 1840;

J. R.; son of C. & E.; died Sept. 20, 1834; age 2 yrs. 1 mo. 20 da.

E. H., son of C. & E.; died Sept. 28, 1834; age six weeks.

MCDONALD, wife of S. M., dau. Claris A. Lonnis; died Aug. 5, 1868; age 24 yrs. 17 da.

McFEE, Melissa, wife William; died Mar. 24, 1867; age 32 yrs. 7 mo. 7 da.

MASON, N. C.; died Apr. 27, 1875; age 25 yrs. 3 mo. 20 da.

Mary H., wife N. C. Sr.; died Dec. 16, 1867; age 55 yrs. 3 mo. 18 da.

MATHEW, J. W.; Born 1853; Died 1907

M. E., wife of J. W.; Died 1849

Nathaniel M.; born June 10, 1817; died May 3, 1871

Susana, wife of N. M.; born Mar. 8, 1820; died May 2, 1895

Clara E., dau. J. W. & M. E.; died Mar. 13, 1878; age 11 mo. 21 da.

Bessie L., dau. J. W. & M. E.; died Dec. 2, 1887; age 1 yr. 4 mo. 28 da.

Daisy D., dau. J. W. & M. E.; died Feb. 2, 1888; age 5 yrs. 1 mo. 5 da.

Nellie, dau. J. W. & M. E.; died Aug. 27, 1889; age 1 yr. 3 mo.

MILLER, Mary M., dau. H. E. & Harriet P.; died Aug. 27, 1840; age 2 mo. 5 da.

Granville, son H. E. & Harriet P.; died Feb. 12, 1847; age 6 mo. 24 da.

Leah Jane, dau. H. E. & Harriet P.; died Feb. 7, 1852; age 3 mo. 8 da.

Mary L., dau. H. E. & Harriet P.; died Oct. 13, 1853; age 10 mo. 7 da.

Mary L., dau. H. E. & Harriet P.; died Oct. 13, 1853; age 10 mo. 7 da.

Margaret, mother of H. E. & H. W.; died Apr. 7, 1853; age 65 yrs.

MILLS, Johanna Christiana, wife M. L.; died Sept. 14, 1846; age 62 yrs. 3 mo. 28 da.

NESSLEY, Jonas; died Mar. 5, 1894; age 81 yrs. 5 mo. 25 da.
>Elizabeth, wife Jonas; died Sept. 27, 1887; age 76 yrs. 11 mo. 4 da.
>Harriet E.; died Aug. 18, 1880; age 25 yrs. 10 mo. 3 da.
>Sarah G.; died Apr. 13, 1877; age 22 yrs. 5 mo. 28 da.

NIGHWANDER, Ephraim; died Oct. 14, 1892; age 79 yrs. 11 mo.
>Catherine, wife of E.; died Feb. 7, 1876; age 64 yrs. 9 mo. 20 da.

NISLEY, Abraham; died May 30, 1849; age 72 yrs.   ; mo. 19 da.
>Anna, dau. Abraham & Elizabeth; died Jan. 29, 1845; age 44 yrs. 4 mo. 20 da.

NOE, Isabel A., wife of William; died June 11, 1850; age 30 yrs. 1 mo. 17 da.
>William; died May 21, 1869; age 51 yrs. 8 mo. 11 da.
>George W., son W. & I.; died Feb. 15, 1847; age 10 da.
>Daniel M., son W. & I.; died Apr. 24, 1862; age 17 yrs. 5 mo. 20 da.
>Vol. 46 Reg. O. V. I. wounded at Shiloh, Mem. of Reynoldsburg G. A. R. Post.

PALMER, Thomas, imigrated from Maine 1805; died Apr. 10, 1825; age 54 yrs. 4 mo. 17 da.

PUGH, Thomas; died July 9, 1865; age 44 yrs. 9 mo. 22 da.
>Margaret, wife of T.; died Dec. 11, 1849; age 25 yrs. 6 mo. 3 da.
>Angeline, dau. T. & M.; died Nov. 21, 1848; age 3 mo.
>Edmond, son T. & M.; died Dec. 15, 1845; age 3 yrs. 7 mo. 14 da.
>Amos, son T. & M.; died Nov. 24, 1841; age 3 da.
>David; died Nov. 17, 1877; age 63 yrs. 18 da.
>Hannah, wife David; died Jan. 13, 1883; age 62 yrs.
>Florence H., dau. D. &. H.; died Mar. 9, 1863; age 1 yr. 10 da.
>Thomas, son D. & H.; died Jan. 27, 1863; age 2 yrs. 7 mo.
>David; born Feb. 8, 1769; died Oct. 24, 1857
>Jane, wife David; born Dec. 29, 1790; died Mar. 8, 1857
>Margaret M. dau. D. & J.; died Nov. 9, 1852; age 32 yrs. 4 mo. 15 da.

POWERS, Isaac; died Apr. 15, 1867; age 62 yrs. 6 mo. 11 da.
>Noah; died May 18, 1862; age 50 yrs. 6 mo. 5 da.
>Elizabeth, wife Noah; born Nov. 20, 1808; died Feb. 10, 1882

REESE, Juliann, dau. John & Hannah; died Mar. 5, 1843; age 2 yrs. 6 mo. 17 da.
>Edmond, son John & Hannah; died Nov. 21, 1841; age 3 yrs. 3 mo. 18 da.
>Bonham; died Nov. 20, 1854; age 41 yrs.
>Nancy, wife Thomas; died Aug. 7, 1856; age 81 yrs.

REESE, Jacob; died Jan. 9, 1856; age 48 yrs. 2 mo. 7 da.
>Francis Marion, son of Jacob & Huldah; born June 17, 1844; died Aug. 6, 1846

REYNOLDS, William H. H.; born Mar. 12, 1820; died Dec. 14, 1838

RHODES, Chas. J., son of B. V. & J.; died Oct. 6, 1860; age 11 mo. 11 da.
>Eliza, dau. J. C. & R. R.; died June 4, 1865; age 18 yrs. 3 mo. 26 da.

Ruth J., wife J. C.; died July 5, 1866; age 53 yrs. 7 mo. 17 da.

Margaret J., dau. J. C. & R. R.; died June 26, 1867; age 24 yrs. 3 mo.

John C.; Born 1814; Died 1872

Margaret Jane, wife Richard; died Apr. 7, 1845; age 18 yrs. 8 mo. 13 da.

Charles M., son R. & J. A.; died July 6, 1851; age 1 yr. 6 mo. 21 da.

James A., son R. & J. A.; died Apr. 7, 1853; age 1 mo. 2 da.

RICKETTS, Mary F., dau. E. & S.; died Oct. 30, 1862; age 1 yr. 4 mo. 15 da.

ROBB, Samuel; died Jan. 18, 1844; age 39 yrs. 10 da.

ROACHELL, infant dau. M. S. & M. J.; died Aug. 6, 1861

ROHRER, Anna, dau. J. E. & W. M.; died May 26, 1856; Age 24 da.
Infant dau., J. E. & W. M.; died Sept. 27, 1861

RUSH, Solomon; died Feb. 4, 1879; age 49 yrs.
Cyrus N., son S. & M.; died July 18, 1887; age 29 yrs. 7 mo.

SEILER, Orlando, son R. E. & E.; died June 11, 1863; age 4 yrs.

SIBLE, Hiram, son H. & L.; died Aug. 26, 1845; age 9 months

SINSABAUGH, Hiram; born June 14, 1804; died Aug. 19, 1839
David, son Hiram and Matilda; died Apr. 11, 1840

SKATS, Sarah, wife Jonathan; died Jan. 31, 1838; age 24 yrs. 3 mo. 19 da.

SMITH, James T.; died Aug. 29, 1896; age 83 yrs. 1 mo. 26 da.
26 da.
Eliza, wife J. T.; died June 14, 1880; age 66 yrs. 4 mo.
George, son Timothy and Eliza; died Sept. 14, 1848; age 3 yrs. 7 mo. 27 da.

SMITH, Jones, son Timothy & Eliza; died Dec. 10, 1851; age 5 mo.

STEPHENS, Mary E., wife C. A.; died Mar. 19, 1858; age 22 yrs. 11 mo. 27 da.

SYLER, John; died Mar. 19, 1858; age 70 yrs.

TAFT, Robert H.; died Aug. 6, 1836; age 27 yrs. 7 mo. 6 da.
Elizabeth Aadeline, daughter R. H. & Matilda; born June 6, 1835; died Sept. 20, 1846
Daniell; died Oct. 11, 1851; age 69 yrs.
Mary, wife Daniell; died Aug. 19, 1850; age 67 yrs.

VENNER, John; died Mar. 5, 1864; age 46 yrs. 5 mo. 14 da.

WELCH, William, Co. "A" 88th Ohio Infantry no date
Infant dau. J. & M. E.; died July 15, 1871
George; died June 5, 1862; age 85 yrs. 10 mo. 1 da.
Sarah, wife George; died Nov. 14, 1836; age 48 yrs. 6 mo. 4 da.

WEST, J. B.; born Aug. 15, 1804; died Mar. 14, 1882
Melissa, wife J. B.; died Jan. 24, 1798; died May 11, 1877

MAPLEWOOD CEMETERY
SOUTH OF NEW ALBANY, PLAIN TOWNSHIP, OHIO

Data By C. R. SWICKARD

NOVEMBER 30, 1936

ALBERRY, Charlie; Born June 28, 1872; Died Feb. 7, 1890
George Fay; Born 7, 1870; Died Apr. 10, 1926
Elizabeth; Born June 6, 1868
E. M.; Born April 30, 1837; Died March 13, 1924
Rachel; Born Dec. 25, 1840; Died March 14, 1902
ALBEE, Russell E.; Born 1897; Died 1930
ADAIR, Frankie T.; son of J. A. and M. A.; age 2 yrs., 1 mo., 24 days
Addie G.; daughter of J. A. & M. A.; age 2 yrs., 2 mo., 6 days.
ALTHAUSER, Elizabeth; Born 1846; Died 1919
Michael; Born 1839; Died 1920
ALLEN, Stephen; Born May 17, 1824; Died April 16, 1907
Mary Allen, wife; Born Oct. 22, 1831; Died Sept. 3, 1906
BABBITT, Lydia; Born 1815; Died 1880
LO ll; Born 1817; Died 1887
Charles A.; Born 1854; Died 1922
Roselle; Born 1855; Died 1928
Elizabeth A.; Born 180 ; Died 1876
Sarah J.; Born 1842; Died 1882
Samuel B.; Born 1844; Died 1931
Partha M.; Born 1852; Died 1927
Elnora; Born 1850; Died 1922
Edward C.; Born 1858; Died 1934
BAUGHMAN, Sevilla, wife Adam; Died Sept. 6, 1865; Age 81 yrs. 9 mo. 28 days
Julia A.; wife Reuben; Died May 14, 1870; Age 48-9-24
Albert, son R. & J. A.; Died May 6, 1884; Age 28-11-21
Frank L.; Died March 15, 1899; Age 40 yrs., 1 mo., 15 days
Edward T.; Born 1863; Died 1895
Adam; Died March 26, 1853; In the 75th year of his age

John   (Nothing else)
Simon; Born Oct. 9, 1827; Died Aug. 3, 1902
Ella; Born 1863; Died 1926
Amos; Born 1857; Died 1908
Libby, wife A. R.; Born 8-1-1876; Died Feb. 3, 1902
John; Died March 5, 1873; Age 54 yrs., 10 mo., 24 days
Mary A.; Died Dec. 2, 1898; Age 77 yrs., 7 mo., 5 days
Stella, daughter R. L. & E.; Died Sept. 27, 1886; age 6 mo., 29 days
29 days
Russell, son R. S. & A.; Died May 6, 1851
Eben G., son T. M.; Died May 7, 1872; Age 13 yrs., 1 mo., 16 days
Eden, son F. M.; Died May 28, 1872
Adam R.; Born 1852; Died 1896
P. H.; Died July 31, 1893; Age 77 yrs., 5 mo., 14 days
Myrtle M.; Born 1879; Died 1897
BEAR, Jacob, Co. B.; Born 1861; Died 1865
　　　Edmund, Co. F 4th. Ohio Inf.
　　　Temuel, 133 Ohio Inf.; Born 1861; Died 1865
BURRELL, Charles; Born 1832; Died 1920
BENEDICT, J. W.; Born July 8, 1871; Died June 16, 1897
BASSITT, Elizabeth A.; Born 180 ; Died 1876
BROWN, Almeda; Born 1868; Died 1929
BEAN, Louis Sidney; Born 1908; Died 1932
BOBO, Jonathan; Born Feb. 1, 1803; Died Jan. 27, 1879; Age 75-0-26
　　　Henry, son Jonathan & Catherine; Died 9-1861; Age 20-3-17
BOBO, Phineas J., son J. & C.; Died Dec. 16, 1854; Age 6-5-21
BARNHARD, Peter; Died March 20, 1879; Age 65 yrs., 2 mo., 25 days
　　　Dorris, daughter C. M. & A. D.; Died Aug. 11, 1893; Age 1 year, 10 mo., 18 days
　　　David; Born 1849; Died 1913
　　　Harriett; Born 1850; Died 1900
　　　John W.; Born 1846; Died 1920
　　　Sarah H.; Born 1848; Died 1918
BUTTS, Mary E.; Born July 4, 1854; Died July 14, 1917
　　　Samuel D.; Born Dec. 8, 1844; Died May 23, 1907
BROOKS, Anna; Born 1858; Died 1929
　　　Lewis; Born 1855; Died 1930
　　　Mildred; Born 1924; Died 1928
BROWNING, A. B.; Died May 21, 1868; Age 23 yrs., 5 mo., 27 days
　　　Isaac; Died June 15, 1885; Age 74 yrs., 9 mo., 28 days
　　　Mary E.; daughter I. & Sarah; Died 1-9-1863; Age 18-6-26
BAILEY, Betty Gene; Born 1925; Died 1926
BENNETT, Charles Jr.; Born 1929; Died 1931
　　　Mayme W.; Born 1886; Died 19
　　　Charles E.; Born 1888; Died 19
CREINER, Carrie; Born 1899; Died 1933
CLOUSE, Henry; Born 1864; Died 1928
　　　Eldon; Born 1868; Died 19
　　　Baby Mae; Born March 8, 1908; Died May 4, 1908
　　　Nancy; Born April 15, 1835; Died Aug. 16, 1906
CLAPHAM, Blanche M.; Born 1890; Died 1913
　　　William; Born 1827; Died 1886
CAMPBELL, Dorothy A.; Born 1835; Died 1874

Eliza; Died Nov. 6, 1870; Age 61-2-21

CARPENTER, James; Born 1801; Died 1892
Clyde E.; son T. & E.; Died Aug. 21, 1881; Age 11-11-23
Frances Emma, wife T. and daughter of J. & L. McCurdy;
Died May 8, 1870; Age 57
Thomas; Born 1835; Died 1911
Elizabeth; Born 1849; Died 1931
Freddie A., son T. & E.; Died March 3, 1892; Age 8-1-13
Ethel Estella; Born July 13, 1886; Died Aug. 28, 1886
Sophronia; Born 1849; Died 1925
Alexander; Co. B 113 Ohio Inf.

CHERRY, Mathew; Born 1843; Died 1927
Jerusha; Born 1841; Died 1931
Lou; Born 1870; Died 1932

COONS, Rebecca; Born May 25, 1856; Died Jan. 31, 1904
Elizabeth; Born 1834; Died 1921
John; Born 1854; Died 1914

CAVENDISH, John; Born on the Isle of Mann May 15, 1815; Died May 24, 1870
John E.; Born 1876; Died 1928
William M.; Born Jan. 1, 1851; Died Nov. 28, 1913
F. C.; Born 1882; Died 1925

CAIN, Clara E.; Born 1879; Died 1922

CUMMINS, Mahala L.; Born 1836; Died 1920
William; Born 1826; Died 1916

CLAYPOOL, Mary A.; Born June 24, 1808; Died March 4, 1885; Age 81-8-10

CHIPPY, Lena M.; daughter of W. E. & L.; Died Dec. 23, 1882; Age 2 yrs., 9 mo., 17 days
Lucinda; Born 1837; Died 1912
W. E.; Born 1840; Died 1919; Co. F. 3 rd. Reg. of Md. Inf.

COLE, Kathrine; Died Aug. 15, 1842; Age 87 yrs., 10 mo., 11 days
Frederick; Died July 10, 1885; Age 80 yrs., 1 mo., 14 days

COLE, Edward; Born 1824; Died 1901
Martha Smith; Born 1827; Died 1924
Frederick; Died July 10, 1885; Age 80 yrs., 1 mo., 14 days

CONRAD, Christian; Co. F 160 Ohio Inf.; Born 1861; Died 1865

COMER, Elizabeth Baldwin, wife John Comer; Died Jan. 16, 1876; Age 85 yrs., 1 mo., 4 days
John Jr.; Died April 4, 1876; Age 59 yrs., 4 mo., 27 days

DAGUE, George; Died Jan. 4, 1861; Age 74 yrs., 11 mo., 21 days
Mary, wife of George; Died Sept. 9, 1877; Age 85 yrs., 7 mo., 15 days

DORAN, Ross E.; Born 1894; Died 1909
Fernie L.; Born 1917; Died 1917
Ella S. Swickard; Born 1874; Died 1927
Charles E.; Born 1866; Died 1930

DAILY, Russell; Born May 25, 1907; Died May 7, 1910
Arthur L.; Born Sept. 3, 1884; Died May 17, 1919
George; Born Nov. 2, 1844; Died Feb. 2, 1920

DORAN, Ella A.; Born May 8, 1860; Died March 3, 1877
Rhoda; Born Jan. 21, 1806; Died June 7, 1886
James; Born Jan. 9, 1802; Died March 7, 1885
Alexander; Born 1831; Died 1898
Cynthia A.; Born 1834; Died 1926

Ella M. Swickard; Born 1860; Died 1877
Sadie L.; Born 1874; Died 1924
Emma O.; Born 1874; Died 1920
DAUGUE, Infant son of John; Died May 28, 1928
Ida; Died Nov. 5, 1889; Age 18 yrs., 10 mo., 22 days
Harriett; Born Dec. 10, 1828; Died April 1, 1902
Clark; Born 1895; Died 1930
Phoebe S.; Died April 6, 1900; Age 46 yrs., 5 mo., 16 days
Jonathan; Born Oct. 14, 1814; Died Sept. 6, 1890
Elanliza Thomas, wife John Dague; Born Aug. 25, 1821; Died June 5, 1877
Bessie, daughter of J. D.; Born Nov. 9, 1907; Died age 20 yrs., 9 mo., 22 days
Louisa; Born 1859; Died 1931
Cadus; Born 1859; Died 1930
Mary E., daughter of L. & E.; Died Aug. 26, 1882; Age 32 yrs., 7 mo., 1 day
Eliza; Born 1828; Died 1914
Levi; Died July 22, 1892; Age 73 yrs., 5 mo., 26 days
George; Born Sept. 23, 1821; Died Aug. 16, 1900
DENT, G. W.; Died May 11, 1890
EWING, Bernice; Died June 29, 1890; Age 10 mo.
Nira J.; Born 1847; Died 1928
Abiah P.; Born 1844; Died 1893
EALY, Jeremah; Died Feb. 25, 1873; Age 27 yrs., 11 mo., 18 days
M. O.; Born Dec. 10, 1844; Died Dec. 19, 1908
Lilly D. daughter of M. & M.; Died Oct. 15, 1872; Age 2 yrs. 10 mo.
Bertha L., daughter of M. & M.; Died Dec. 11, 1878; Age 1 yr., 6 mo., 29 days
Angus L.; Died Jan. 28, 1892; Age 2 yrs., 2 mo., 26 days
Mary; Born 1846; Died 1935
Bessie M., daughter E. P. & N. C.; Born Sept. 4, 1905; Died Sept. 19, 1906
Susan Hoppes; Born July 4, 1807; Died Oct. 17, 1901
EVANS, Russell Jay; Died May 3, 1925
Matilda; Died July 23, 1817; Age 6 mo., 21 days
Anna; Died July 18, 1891; Age 30 yrs., 3 mo., 28 days
Rowland; Died Feb. 26, 1882; Age 76 yrs., 8 mo., 10 days
William Keys; Born March 31, 1887; Died July 21, 1901
Martha (Carpenter); Born Oct. 3, 1842; Died April 11, 1908
EASTON, Walter, son of C. O. & Susan; Died July 13, 1888; Age 5 mos., 7 days
Charles Orville; Born 1852; Died 1912
Gulia Elnor; Born 1849; Died 1934
EARL, Wilbur; Porn 1915; Died 1916
ELBON, Clarence William; Born 1883; Died 1933
Laurie B.; Born 1882; Died 1928
FARBER, Clair Eugene; Born 1920; Died 1925
James H.; Born March 25, 1846; Died Aug. 27, 1919
Alvira; Born April 25, 1843; Died Aug. 9, 1915
Clyde, son of J. H. & M. M.; Sept. 16, 1903; Jan. 12, 1904
Sarah; Died March 12, 1865; Age 29 yrs., 11 days
Caleb; Born Aug. 18, 1797; Died Aug. 4, 1881
Eliza; April 7, 1805; Oct. 28, 1864

401

Caleb; Died Feb. 3, 1856; Age 16 yrs., 11 mo., 29 days
Edward; Died Dec. 18, 1864; Age 23 yrs., 3 mo.
James; Sept. 27, 1863; Age 3 yrs., 29 days
Samuel; Died Jan. 3, 1877; Age 68 yrs., 29 days
Evline; Aug. 8, 1832; July 14, 1921
James, son S. E.; Died Sept. 27, 1886; Age 3 yrs. 28 days
FISHER, Roy, son of J. C. & H. N.; Died Dec. 25, 1900; Age 4 yrs. 26
days
FOULK, C. C.; Born Dec. 24, 1881; Died Dec. 15, 1913
John W.; Born 1915; Died 1915
Harriett; Born 1858; Died 1923
George W.; Born 1853; Died 1921
FRAVEL, David; Born Hardy Co., Va. Died Feb. 3, 1829; Age 54 yrs.
10 mo., 28 days
FLATTERY, Elizabeth; Born June 10, 1834; Died Nov. 4, 1922
FRIZZELL, Stella; Born 1872; Died 1911
GOODRICH, Charles W.; Died Jan. 6, 1873; Age 1 yr., 4 mo., 6 days
Margarette; Born March 5, 1919; Died Sept. 14, 1919
Walter Nelson; Born Nov. 5, 1893; Died Nov. 8, 1893
Mary; Born Nov. 5, 1893; Died Nov. 10, 1893—Children of
W. & O. Goodrich
Justus; Born Nov. 30, 1832; Died March 3, 1900
Mary Evans; Born Aug. 5, 1833; Died Oct. 3, 1875
Viola Dell; Born July 9, 1866; Died Feb. 24, 1888
Rose M.; Born Oct. 24, 1888; Died March 14, 1919
John W.; Born 1830; Died 1909
Aridna A.; Born 1846; Died 1916
Fannie; Died Jan. 17, 1871; Age. 67 yrs., 2 mo,. 25 days
John; Born 1790; Died 1878
Linnie Elnora; Died Nov. 1881; Age 4 yrs., 7 mo., 8 days
Malissa May; Died Feb. 8, 1881; Age 1 yr., 2 mo., 15 days
GROVENBERRY, William; Sarg't Co. A 50 O. V. I.; Born 1840; Died
1872
Henry, son William; Born June 2, 1840
Eliza; Died July 10, 1840; Age 29 yrs., 22 days
GROVES, George L.; Born 1907; Died 1925
Charles; Born Feb. 20, 1904; Died June 25, 1905
Levi; Born 1856; Died 1925
Layfayette; Born 1855; Died 1920
GROVES, David; Born 1849; Died 1855
Perry; Born 1857; Died 1918
Jacob; Born 1819; Died 1886
Mary, wife Jacob; Born 1829; Died 1905
GRANGER, Mary; Born 1852; Died 1921
Martha; Born 1823; Died 1902
Jas.; Serg't Co. B 133 Ohio Inf.
GREENWOOD, Ella; Born 1858; Died 1917
Electa; Born 1845; Died 1901
Levi; Born 1840; Died 1929   18th. U. S. I.
Elsie M.; Born 1866; Died 1888
GEORGE, O. C.; Born 1888; Died 1919
GREINER, Carrie; Born 1899; Died 1933
HOLT, George; Born 1911; Died 1926
Susan B.; Born 1829; Died 1907
Bennie, son Charles and Susan; Died Oct. 29, 1887; Age

19 yrs., 1 mo., 20 days
HEISCHMAN, George; Born 1870; Died 1932
    Harold; Born 1904; Died 1907
    Jessie E.; Died Sept. 25, 1895; Age 23 yrs., 2 mo., 5 days
    Dr. Theo.; Died Jan. 30, 1892; Age 42 yrs., 4 mo., 27 days
    Charlie; son of Henry; Died April 9, 1865; Age 7-11-28
    Mary A.; Born April 28, 1841; Died July 28, 1904
    Henry G., Born Feb. 22, 1841; Died June 26, 1919
HAND, Clais V.; Born Feb. 4, 1842; Died Feb. 6, 1865
    J. W.; Born Dec. 12, 1832; Died March 7, 1845
    L. M.; Born Nov. 1, 1853; Died Sept. 22, 1865
    David S.; Born 1834; Died 1901
    C.; Born May 23, 1831; Died June 17, 1932
HORLOCKER, Christian; Died Jan. 14, 1907; Age 75 yrs., 6 mo., 2 days
    Leona; Died Dec. 17, 1876; Age 15 yrs., 1 mo., 19 days
HEDRICK, Minor H.; Born 1858; Died 1927
HORST, Albert H.; Born 1853; Died 1909
HIGGINS, Thelma A.; Born Aug. 31, 1905; Died March 13, 1934
HARRIS, Wilson J.; Born 1857; Died 1930
HARLAN, Elizabeth A.; Born 1828; Died 1920
    Dale; Born 1905; Died 1922
HEADLEY, George H.; Born 1856; Died 1929
    Lucinda J.; Born June 6, 1843; Died April 2, 1905
    Daniel; Born April 20, 1838; Died Dec. 30, 1903
HAMMOND, Harry; Born 1901; Died 1920
HURSEY, John; Born 1903; Died 1935
JOHNSON, John F.; Born 1862; Died 1882
    William H.; Born Jan. 15, 1838; Died Jan. 14, 1862
    Abbie M.; Born 1839; Died 1912
KEYES, Hattie, wife of Otto Benedict; Born 1885; Died 1913
KASHNER, Mary E. Swickard, wife John W.; Born Jan. 18, 1861; Died
    Aug. 13, 1895
KIRTS, George W.; Born 1876; Died 1936
    Julia A.; Born 1887; Died 19
KNODE, Russell; Born 1895; Died 1933
KISSON, Alice; Born 1865; Died 1934
KLICK, Ephriam; Born Nov. 20, 1833
    Eveline; Born Aug. 15   Died June 27, 1902
KIMMEL, Cora E.; Born 1888; Died 1935
KITZMILLER, Blanche, dau. Wm. & F. K.; Died Sept. 11, 1873; Age
    5 mo. 4 days
    William; Died Sept. 27, 1879; Age 37 yrs., 8 mo., 19 days
    R. Vance, son Wm. & E.; Died March 14, 1878; Died 3-9-26
LONGH, A. M.; Born 1833; Died 1906
LOY, Katherine; Died Nov. 10, 1927
LINK, Emma J.; Born 1859; Died 1932
    F. E.; Born 1855; Died 1905
    William, son of F. E. & M. J.; Died Nov. 3, 1898 Age 16
    yrs., 1 mo., 15 days
LANDON, Edward; Died Feb. 23, 1843
    John D.; Died Aug. 17, 1864; Age 22 yrs., 10 mo.
    Charlotte S., wife of Mark; Died March 20, 1867; Age 48
    yrs., 4 mo., 5 days
LAYMAN, N. J.; Born 186—; Died 1921
    N. J. Born 1862; Died 1921

MORRISON, Charles W.; Died Dec. 14, 1871; Age 22 yrs., 11 mo. 30 days
McMILLAN, Hepsah Trumbo; Born 1845; Died 1926
McGUIRE, Nora Noe, wife H.; Died May 18, 1895; Age 17 yrs., 10 mo., 11 days.
    Betty Jean; Born July 5, 1929; Died Feb. 13, 1930
MILLER, John N.; Born 1842; Died 1934
    Francis J.; Born 1845; Died 1920
    Harrison G.; Born 1840; Died 1922
    Ollie B.; Born Jan. 22, 1871; Died July 17, 1883
    Ophella J.; Born 1847; Died 1935
    Anthony; Died Feb. 6, 1862; Aged 53 yrs., 3 mo., 28 days
    Amanda; Died Aug. 28, 1904 Aged 87 yrs., 3 mo., 11 days
    Thomas; Died June 15, 1856; Age 68 yrs., 5 mo., 15 days
    Emma G.; Died Feb. 1862; Age 15 yrs., 1 mo., 25 days
    R. F.; Born Hardy Co., Va. Feb. 6, 1821; Died Jan. 17, 1902
    Mary Miller Taylor; Born 1848; Died 1919
    Margaret Wilkin, wife R. F. Miller; Born Hardy Co. Va. July 12, 1812; Died Nov. 19, 1878
McCURDY, John Lee, son of J. & L.; Died Sept. 4, 1871; Age 17-5-27
    Rhodelle, daughter of J. & L.; Died July 3, 1872; Age 20 yrs., 11 mo., 22 days
    John; Died May 4, 1876; Age 75 yrs., 4 mo.
    Henry H.; Born 1836; Died 1913
    Sarah J.; Born 1842; Died 1905
    Minnie Maude; Died Oct. 2, 1871; Age 7 yrs., 6 mo., 20 days
    Charles D.; Born 1862; Died 1909
McCLAIN, Sarah; Died Jan. 17, 1892; Age 55 yrs., 9 mo., 23 days
MEYERS, Lewis W.; Sept. 21, 1888; Feb. 10, 1910
    Electa J., March 16, 1867; March 3, 1932
    Marvin D.; Oct. 10, 1858; April 25, 1912
MYER, Jacob M.; Born 1862, Died 1928
    Rilla, his wife; Born 1865; Died 19
MEYERS, John Urvin; Born June 2, 1880; Died May 3, 1912
    Electta; Born Dec. 26, 1892; Died April 18, 1929
    Harmon; Born Feb. 17, 1829; Died Sept. 10, 1916
McCORMICK, Joe; Born 1889; Died 1917
MANN, Laura; Born 1854; Died 1925
MIESSE, Julia A., Born Aug. 3, 1852; Died Jan. 1930
    George J.; Born April 13, 1854; Died March 10, 1928
    Harriett E.; Born 1898; Died 1928
MARGARUM, J. Edward; Born Feb. 4, 1856; Died April 7, 1886
NEEDLES, Samuel I.; Born 1853; Died 1919
    Infant of S. L. & E. J.; Sept. 15, 1885
NOE, Arza; Died July 15, 1885; Age 49 yrs., 2 mo., 20 days
NOBLE, Melvin; Born 1873; Died 1935
    Mary O.; Born 1879; Died 19
NOE, Mary M.; Born 1848; Died 1923
    Wilson S.; Born 1840; Died 1917
    Ephbaim: Born March 15, 1887; Age 76 yrs., 6 mo., 22 days should this be Died March 15, 1887
    Orvilla; Died Jan. 1, 1897; Age 88 yrs., 2 mo., 23 days
    Forest, son of J. J. & L.; Born July 6, 1895; Died Aug. 19, 1895
    Gary F., son of M. & M.; Died Oct. 21, 1886; Age 18 yrs., 11 mo., 10 days

OSBORN, S. W.; Born March 29, 1857; Died Dec. 19, 1924
PARK, Lewis; Born 1857; Died 1918
        J. E.; Born 1831; Died 1910
        Sarah J.; Jan. 1, 1884
        Infant; 1888
        David P.; Born 1844; Died 1915
        Mary E.; July 9, 1843; July 29, 1900
        Samuel W.; Jan. 1, 1835; May 13, 1906
        E. Park; Aug. 16, 1808; May 21, 1891
        Elizabeth; Nov. 22, 1811; April 3, 1863
PHELPS, Rollin; Born May 6, 1833; Died Jan. 1, 1913
        Adaline; Born May 8, 1863; Died Sept. 17, 1864
        Clara E.; Born Feb. 6, 1856; Died Sept. 13, 1906.
PRICE, John; Born 1849; Died 1927
        Ellen J.; Born 1854; Died 1936
PRIEST, Sarah, wife of Silas; Died March 7, 1891; Age 65-2-28
        William H.; Born 1853; Died 1932
        Emma; Born 1857; Died 19
PERRY, Rosa Bell; Born 1850; Died 1935
        John; Born 1871; Died 1905
        Susan B.; Born Jan. 31, 1826; Died Jan. 5, 1902
ROSS, Effie M.; Born 1881; Died 1917
        Amanda J.; Born 1839; Died 1925
        Henry; Born 1823; Died 1922
        John Sutton; Born in Philadelphia, Pa., Oct. 10, 1828; Died April 24, 1918
        Emma; Born in London, England March 22, 1825; Died Sept. 10, 1888
REEB, Wilsena C.; Born 1884; Died 1917
RHODES, Irene B.; Born 1894; Died 1925
RANNEY, Joel Jr., Born Sept. 10, 1802; Died Sept. 21, 1877
        Anna May, daughter of B. P. & Cordelia; Born May 14, 1880; Died July 18, 1880
        Cordelia; Born Jan. 14, 1856; Died Oct. 4, 1925
        Mary E.; Born Aug. 30, 1832; Died Dec. 18, 1887
        S. W.; Was an M. D.; Born 3-7-1830; Died 4-13-1897
        Elizabeth M.; Born May 1, 1805; Died Apr. 16, 1869
        Edwin; Born Dec. 19, 1837; Died April 11, 1842
        Eliza; Born June 13, 1843; Died June 3, 1852
        Abiah E.; Born Feb. 12, 1839; Died Jan. 8, 1879
        Joel Sr.; Born Sept. 10, 1774; Died Oct. 19, 1819
        Mary B.; Born Oct. 4, 1777; Died March 24, 1858
SIDNEY, Louise Sidney Bean; Born 1908; Died 1932
SELBERT, John; Born 1844; Died 1932
SINES, William; Born 1867; Died 1933
SHULL, Jerusha; Born 1852; Died 1923
        Lewis; Born May 24, 1843; Died Nov. 3, 1914
        Clyde; Born April 24, 1871; Died July 25, 1917
SUMPTION, John; Born Aug. 28, 1845; Died Dec. 9, 1910
        Amanda; Born Dec. 7, 1845; Died Dec. 7, 1906
SHIRK, Lousetta; Died Apr. 16, 1879; Age 58-2-11
        Laura Ann; Born June 19, 1852; Died Feb. 25, 1882
SIMMONS, Betsey; Died Dec. 11, 1898; Age 74-5-12
        Thomas; Died March 10, 1896; Age 88-11-6
SONDER, Susan; Died Dec. 9, 1871

Mary M.; Died Feb. 24, 1872; Age 92-0-20
Martin; Died Sept. 30, 1864; Age 86-7-0
Johnatahan; Died Aug. 24, 1825; Age 88-2-12
Rachel; Died Nov. 10, 1861

SISCO, Joseph; Born July 28, 1818; Died 1900
Sarah; Born Oct. 23, 1821; Died 1913
Lewis; Died Aug. 21, 1878; Age 26-3-21
Willis W.; Born 1871; Died 1892
Arloia M.; Born 1869; Died 1892
George B.; Born 1844; Died 1908
Catharine; Born 1843; Died 1924

SCHLEPPI, Sonis; Born 1856; Died 1921
Elizabeth; Born 1862; Died 1931

STINSON, Dr. Stephen; Born 1795; Died 1862
Abigail; Born 1798; Died 1880
Dr. Henry; Born 1837; Died 1885

SMITH, W. W.; Born 1854; Died 1924
Hezekiah; Born Oct. 1823; Died Jan. 13, 1911
Harriett; Born Jan. 1, 1830; Died Dec. 11, 1905
Everette?; Born 1833; Died 1856
Augustine; Born Sept. 11, 1836; Died July 20, 1880
Orabell; Born Oct. 26, 1837; Died Feb. 4, 1875
Salinda; Born 1844; Died 1870
Alma Hughes; Born 1814; Died 1895
Richard; Born 1807; Died 1887
Rev. S. Burton; Died March 18, 1907; Age 29-6-14
Baby G. Worthy, son Rev. S. & B.; age 1 mo. 25 days
Bowland; Died March 29, 1883; Age 5-2-2

STRAIT, Carl D.; Born 1890; Died 1919
George L.; Born 1864; Died 1917
Edward L.; son of D. B. & A.; Born March 4, 1864; Died Oct. 4, 1864
Dulcenia, daughter D. B. & A.; Born Jan. 28, 1861; Died Sept. 16, 1876
Ann; Born Nov. 22, 1822; Died April 6, 1901
Dennis; Born May 20, 1824; Died April 2, 1891
Infant daughter Whitney & Ella; Born & Died July 6, 1891
Whitney; Born 1853; Died 1935
Minnie R.; Born Sept. 13, 1888; Died Aug. 19, 1895
Abraham; Died Aug. 10, 1861; Age 70-5-5
Dulcena, wife Abraham; Died March 23, 1845; Age 39-8-13
William Dunn; Born Dec. 6, 1834; Died Feb. 17, 1922
Mary Doran; Born Feb. 1, 1836; Died Sept. 11, 1892
Sophia; Born May 27, 1836; Died April 10, 1915
Nelson; Died Feb. 18, 1872; Age 35-5-2

SWICKARD, Robert A.; Born 1863; Died 1934
Delphus Minnie; Born Oct. 13, 1877; Died Nov. 15, 1899
Frederick; Born Feb. 24, 1831; Died March 21, 1921
Robert A.; Born June 12, 1863; Died Dec. 5, 1934
Mary P.; Born 1851; Died 1926
Gustavus; Born 1840; Died 1912
Burean? Born June 22, 1859; Died Dec. 12, 1928
Donald, Infant son of Frederick; Born June 29, 1917;

Died July 11, 1917
Sarah M.; Born April 25, 1837; Died June 12, 1891
Charles O.; Born 1867
Ida May Dague, wife Chas. O.; Born 1873; Died 1911
Emma B., daughter F. & S. A.; Died March 25, 1873; age 14-9-26
Lucy A.; Born Aug. 16, 1841; Died Nov. 16, 1912
Noah; Born Dec. 12, 1835; Died Oct. 6, 1901
Rosetta; (she is a sister of Robert Swickard)
Effie; (Robert's sister)
James Allen, son J. & S. E.; Died May 13, 1893; Age 17-1-8
Mary A. Swickard Baughman; Born 1856; Died 1915
Stephen Willis, son of J. B. & R. E.; Died Feb. 12, 1888; Age 5 mos. 18 days
Jimmie, Infant of J. B. & B. E.; Age 6 mos. 18 days
Lydia; Died July 20, 1881; Age 60-8-11
Jonathan; Died 1863
Mary M., wife D. S.; Died Jan. 17, 1829; Age 38-10-2
Lydia May, daughter of Alonzo & Sarah; Died Dec. 15, 1880; Age 10 mos., 7 days
Daniel; Died July 7, 1874; Age 84-10-15
Christina, wife Daniel, Died April 10, 1880; Age 82-10-28
Sarah E.; Born 1853; Died 1921
Alonzo; Born 1845; Died 1926
L. Fern; Born 1882; Died 1915
John W.; Born 1842; Died 1916
Frances E., wife J. W., Born 1844; Died 1887
SWICKARD, Martin; Died Jan 12, 1881; Age 72-0-17
Howard; Born 1870; Died 1933
THARP, Francis; Born 1856; Died 1932
Samuel H.; Born 1860; Died 1895
TAYLOR, Mary Miller; Born 1848; Died 1919
Dr. A. P.; Born 1849; Died 1923
Hester; Born Feb. 29, 1848; Died Jan. 17, 1921
J. Buren; Born Jan. 14, 1839; Died March 16, 1926
Stephen W.; Born March 1, 1862; Died April 8, 1922
William T.; Born March 22, 1836; Died Nov. 6, 1900
Lyana T.; Born Sept. 22, 1834; Died Sept. 14, 1903
Herman W.; Born March 31, 1864; Died Oct. 26, 1925
Lorenzo; Born July 28, 1828; Died Jan. 10, 1910
Martha E.; Born Dec. 5, 1827; Died Feb. 23, 1912
Irving, John; Born 1924; Died 1927
William T.; Born 1894; Died 1926
Margaret; Born 1898; Died 1915
TRIPPLETT, Harry; Born Aug. 16, 1888; Died March 5, 1907
Ella; Born Aug. 10, 1868; Died June 27, 1889
Pearl; Born May 13, 1868; Died June 6, 1904
George W.; Born Nov. 22, 1818; Died March 10, 1889
Alice; Died Sept. 20, 1854; Age 1-4-9
Sarah Archer; Died Jan. 27, 1866; Age 79 yrs.
Daniel; Died July 1, 1859; Age 84 yrs.
Daisy D.; Born July 29, 1868; Died Feb. 7, 1902
TRUMBO, Millie Hursey; Born 1870; Died 1921
Infant son of J. H.; Born June 14, 1901; Died June 22,

1901
>Harriett; Died March 9, 1882; Age 40-2-14
>Davis; Died Jan. 30, 1881; Age 77-0-14
>Susan; Born March 22, 1815; Died Oct. 4, 1882

UNKLE, Lottie May, daughter J. J. & A. J.; Born Aug. 5, 1891; Died April 2, 1910

ULRY, Jocie; Died March 26, 1890; Age 12-5-28
>Isaac; Dec. 28, 1845
>Elizabeth; Born July 12, 1854; Died Dec. 19, 1920
>John; Born Oct. 2, 1844
>Esther Marie, R. L. & M. A. Born 1927; Died 1931
>Anna A. B.; Born 4-1845-1905; Died March 25, 1909 (something wrong with above)
>Priscilla; Born 1847; Died 1827 (should this be 1927)
>Albert; Born March 21, 1913; Died Nov. 22, 1913
>Ralsa J.; Born 1848; Died 1853
>Eliza J.; Born 1815; Died 1885
>Jacob; Born 1813; Died 1865
>Christina; Born 1849; Died 1909
>Myrtel V.; Born 1875; Died 1888
>George D.; Born 1844; Died 1925
>Elizabeth Zaff; Born 1864; Died 1922
>Thomas; Died July 22, 1887; Age 84-10-21

VOLKNER, Harriett N.; Born Dec. 16, 1863; Died Oct. 12, 1897

VANDRUFF, Irminta, wife A. B.; Died Feb. 12, 1824; Age 24-4-2
>Albert B., son J. S. & M.; Died March 16, 1876; Age 32-7-26

WOODS, Daniel D.; Born Oct. 6, 1837; Died Feb. 7, 1919

WILLIAMSON, John; Died April 10, 1891; Age 15-4-7

WHITE, Nellie C.; Born 1876; Died 1932
>Wilford S.; Born 1876; Died 1919

WHITHEAD, Died July 5, 1882; Age 62-2-8

WATTS, Betty; Born 1913; Died 1930

WILLIS, Harry; Born 1891; Died 1931

WILLISON, Elsie M.; Born Nov. 5, 1891; Died Oct. 15, 1909
>Nellie

WALLITS, Marie; Born Oct. 9, 1903; Died Jan. 28, 1919

WHEATON, Horton L.; Born March 29, 1877; Died July 27, 1908

WOLCOTT, Clara I.; Born 1847; Died 1917

WAGNER, Raymond; Born 1878; Died 1920
>Lindora; Born 1858; Died 1922
>Ida J.; Born 1858; Died 1922
>John; Born 1855; Died 1928
>Elizabeth, Died June 9, 1836; Age 21
>James; Died April 8, 1876; Age 88-10-7
>Charlie; Died Sept. 1, 1884; Age 19-10-9
>Mattie, dau. J. & E.; Died July 12, 1881; Age 23-3-14
>Lydia, dau. J. & E.; Died Oct. 6, 1864; Age 8-7-18
>Electa, wife James; Died Feb. 17, 1884; Age 60-3-6

WILSON, Robert.; Co. F. 19 U. S. INF.
>Eliza; Born 1864; Died 1866
>John C.; Born 1854; Died 1855
>Augusta; Born 1824; Died 1896
>Job.; Born 1819; Died 1900

WILKIN, Russell; Born 1857; Died 1933

Alica; Born 1857; Died 1935
William H.; Born 1862; Died 1924
Richard Clair; Born 1918; Died 1919
Frederick A.; Born 1895; Died 1912
Nelson; Co. B. 133 Ohio Inf.
Clarinda; Died March 20, 1898; Age 75-2-28
Mary; Died July 21, 1859; Age 80-4-25
Harvey; Died Jan. 12, 1868; Age 60 yrs.
Luona; Born 1868; Died 1926
Armstead; Died July 22, 1874; Age 79-4-7
Emeline; Died June 29, 1915; Age 84-2-28
YOUNG, Osabelle
YANTIS, Elizabeth; Born 1834; Died 1886
Jennie B.; Born 1874; Died 1894
The following may be listed twice
PESTEL, Richard E.; Born Jan. 12, 1936; Died March 16, 1936
WILKIN, Margaret, wife of R. F. Miller, Born Hardy Co., Va. July
12, 1812; Died Nov. 19, 1878

YATES GRAVE YARD

Located on land owned in 1910 by W. A. Bazone on Clarksburg Pike, 2½ miles south of Williamsport, in Pickaway County, Ohio. Supposed to have been about 15 burials here. Only three stones left and they are not standing.

YATES, David, Officer in War 1812, died March 13, 1840, aged 65-5-21
 Rezin, died Jan. 17, 1851, aged 44 years, 1 mo. 7 days
 Marquis L., son D. & M., died Sept. 26, 1852, aged 1-8-2

HANSON GRAVEYARD

On land owned in 1910 by John P. Bennett on Chillicothe Pike, 2½ miles south of Williamsport, in Pickaway County, Ohio.

CHAMP, Joseph, died Feb. 10, 1838, aged 40-1-5

GILMORE, Lidia, died March 24, 1875, aged 70 years
 Ruhe Ann, daughter of H. & M., died Jan. 12, 1870, aged 27-8-5

HANSON, Daniel, died June 2, 1836, aged 50-5-28

HASTINGS, Sciota E., daughter E. P. & M., died July 10, 1852, aged 1-11-4

SMITH GRAVEYARD

Also on land of John P. Bennett, 2½ miles south of Williamsport, Pickaway County, Ohio.

CANNON, Mary Ann, daughter Sylvester & Ketury, died Oct. 9, 1825, aged 2 years

LANDON, Mary, died Feb. 15, 1871, aged 86-9-9

SMITH, Jonas H. W., died March 1, 1821, aged 45 years

WILEY GRAVEYARD

On land owned in 1910 by C. L. Bishop, one fourth mile south of Williamsport, Pickaway County, Ohio. Supposed to have been about 25 buried here, but only one stone left.
REED, George, died Aug. 22, 1812, aged 74 years.

ALEX SMITH GRAVEYARD

On land owned in 1910 by Charles O. Smith, 4 miles south of Williamsport, Pickaway County, Ohio, and on the Chillicothe Pike.

SMITH, Alexander, born July 4, 1817, died Nov. 5, 1886, aged 69-4-1
 James, no death date, aged 45 years.
 Phebe, wife of James, died April 26, 1872, aged 85-4-14

SMITH, Margaret, daughter of J. & P., died Oct. 23, 1840, aged 15-2-9

ANDERSON, Marie, wife of William, died Jan. 23, 1843, aged 22-7-23
 Margaret, dau. Wm. & Marie, died Aug. 18, 1844, aged 2-9-27

ATER, Elizabeth, wife of J., died Jan. 21, 1838, aged 23-8-8

Located in Section 17, Bath Township., Allen County, Ohio. Copied in July 1941, by J. H. Miller of Lima, Ohio.

MILLER, Sollomon, died May 11, 1864, aged 66-4-26
    Daniel, died May 19, 1879, aged 62-3-1
    Mary A., wife Daniel, died Dec. 23, 1872, aged 54-8-5
    Elizabeth, wife J. B., died Jan. 6, 1863, aged 32-11-28
    Samuel, son M. & M. M., died March 8, 1858

ZETTY, Susanna, died Apr. 14, 1862, aged 64 years

WEAVER, Elizabeth, wife of Peter and daughter of P. Zetty of Virginia, died Dec. 21, 1850, aged 56-11-27

NEHER, Abraham, born 1867, died 1938

BOON, Daniel, died May 20, 1877, aged 33-11-27

NEHR, Daniel, son of D. & C., died 1861, aged 27-0-21

WEAVER, Margaret, wife of J. F., died Jan. 25, 1865, aged 19-7-2
    David W., son J. & B. A., died July 22, 1865, aged 18 yrs.
    David William, son Jacob F. & Barbara A., died July 27, 1865, aged 18-9-3

MILLER, Elizabeth, wife of Abraham, died Dec. 22, 1861, aged 24-0-8
    Catharine, wife of Abraham, died June 8, 1877, aged 75-1-5
    Abraham, died Aug. 5, 1862, aged 66-5-2

MARTIN, Father, born 1825, died 1877
    Mother, Mary, born 1828, died 1908

TONY'S NOSE CEMETERY

Located in Bath Township, Allen County, Ohio. Copied in April, 1940 by Bert Hefner, Lima, Ohio.

HOMEN, Elizabeth, wife of A. M., died April 12, 1856, aged 72-0-12

CHENOWETH, John, born July 16, 1812, died Nov. 17, 1844, aged 32-3-29
    Elizabeth, wife of John, born Nov. 24, 1814, died Apr. 12, 1856
    Sgt. William, Rev. War soldier
    Martha A., born 1834, died 1842
    Rebecca, born 1841, died 1842

TUNGET, Peter, died May 28, 1844, aged 77-0-0
    Sarah, wife of Peter, died March 14, 1884, aged 76-10-12
    John, son Peter & Sarah, died Aug. 18, 1852, aged 22-4-8
    ————, son Peter & Sarah, died Aug. 25, 1855, aged 20-8-0

OSMON, Aaron, died Nov. 28, 1876, aged 78-8-4
    Eleanor, wife Aaron, died Sept. 15, 1889, aged 84-6-23

HEFNER, Rachel, wife of William, died Oct. 17, 1884, aged 45-1-14

BEDFORD, Roy, son of W. A. & E. A., died Aug. 18, 1892, aged 2-5-12

DANER, William H., son of John & Mary, died Dec. 5, 1847, aged 2 mos. 20 days.

HOMAN, Eleanor Chenoweth, daughter of Sgt. William Chenoweth, the Revolutionary Soldier

HANSON, Ann, died March 18, 1840, aged 60-9-14

MURÆY, James, son of T. & M., died Nov. 2, 1892, aged 1-0-28

SPYKER, Eliza J., daughter L. & M. E., died Jan. 31, 1863, aged 10-10-2
  Charity H., died Oct. 6, 1872, aged 15 years.

OSBORNE, ———, died 1872, aged 1 year

OSMON, Brazillia, born Oct. 17, 1831, no death date
  Sara L., 2nd. wife of Brazillia, died Mar. 6, 1900, aged 64-6-16
  Sarah L., 1st. wife of Brazillia, died Apr. 26, 1865, aged 26-2-24

CORNS, Henry M., died Sept. 28, 1870, aged 67-3-10
  Cynthia A., died Apr. 29, 1895, aged 87-9-2
  Infant son of J. H. & M. A., died Aug. 13, 1856

WHISTLER, Infant daughter of ?. & L. E., no date

DIXON, Henry, son of J. & S., died March 16, 1862, aged 1-7-19

CORNS, Henry G., son H. M. & C., stone has been reset, dates covered
  David, son H. M. & C., stone has been reset, dates covered
  Little son of H. M. & C., stone has been reset, dates covered

MADDEN, Sarah, wife of James, died Apr. 1, 1858, aged 92-8-22
  Infant son of James & Sarah, no date

SAXTON, Samuel H., Co. A. 20th. Ohio Inf. G A R no date

OSMON, Elizabeth, born 1779, died 1849, aged 70
  Abraham, died Dec. 15, 1858, aged 45-4-2
  Charlotta, wife Abraham, died June 28, 1877, aged 67-2-6
  John H., son Abraham & Charlotta, died July 8, 1839, aged 7-10-0
  Elizabeth A., daughter Abraham & Charlotta, died 1848, aged 9 years
  Harrison H., son Abraham & Charlotta, died Aug. 1858, aged 1 year, 1 month
  William C., Co. C 81st. O.V.I. GAR, died Dec. 31, 1932, aged 68
  Irene J., wife of William C., died July 29, 1890, aged 54-4-22
  Infant son of Irene J. & Wm. C., died Feb. 1, 1860

ATMORE, Infant son of J. H. & H., died Apr. 29, 1860

OSMON, John, died Jan. 4, 1865, aged 20-9-20
  John, died Sept. 9, 1836, aged 44-4-14
  Matilda, died Aug. 9, 1838, aged 1-4-18
  Mary J., dau. N. & S. J., died July 24, 1865, aged 3 mos. 8 days

MUMAUGH, Mary R., dau. C. & B., died May 6, 1893, aged 4 days

MAXWELL, James, died Jan. 12, 1860, aged 62-9-21
  Robert, son James & Margaret, stone reset, date covered
HOLMES, Pricilla, wife Isaac Sr., died Dec .17 ,1855, aged 77-0-27
  Warren, son H. & A., died March 14, 1865, aged 3 mos.—18 days

Wierman, son H. & A., died Mar. 21, 1860, aged 1-7-9
Infant son H. & A., died, no date

DOUGLAS, John, died Feb. 28, 1860, aged 69-11-11
Ann, wife John, died July 6, 1881, aged 78-8-14

SCOTT, Maud, dau. T. F. & V. J., died Dec. 28, 1870, aged 11 days

MUMAUGH, William Sr., died Sept. 28, 1875, aged 80-6-24
Sarah, wife of William Sr., died May 16, 1876, aged 80 years

DOUGLAS, William, died Aug. 23, 1888, aged 49-4-4
Catharine, wife William, died Oct. 3, 1915, aged 72-11-5
Julius, son Wm. & Catharine, born 1866, died 1929
John D., son Wm. & Catharine, born 1864, died 1907

YOAKUM, Lobena, wife N. L., died Mar. 6, 1876, aged 25-2-5
Walter L., son of Norton & Alice, died Aug. 18, 1881, aged 9 mos. 18 days
Stanley W., son Norton & Alice, died Aug. 23, 1884, aged 2-0-18

TUNGET, Hattie Adora, Dau. Geo. & H. A., died Dec. 31, 1870, aged 2-10-9
Hosannah, wife Geo. E., died Dec. 14, 1871, aged 27-8-4
Eliza J., wife Geo. E., died, no date

BEDFORD, William A., born 1852, died 1929
Ella A., wife of William A. (not deceased)
Lloyd R., son William A. & Ella A., born 1892, died 1916
Pauline, born 1896, died 1918

FAMILY HISTORY IN FAMILY BIBLES

Mabel Innis Frey

Family Bible records are primary and authentic sources of information in the compilation of family histories. Often they are important links in the chain of genealogical data. Many people possess old family Bibles in which records of marriages, births, and deaths were recorded by their pioneer ancestors. For this reason the Columbus Genealogical Society has been collecting and preserving family Bible records. The following list contains the names of Bible records now in the possession of the society:

Augustus, John, (b. 1775) formerly lived in Pickaway Co., O., wife Hannah (b. 1778).

Barnes, John, (b. 1811) wife Mary (b. 1813). Bean, Thomas, (b. 1793) wife Sarah Hill (b. 1796) formerly lived in Athens Co. O. Belknap, Foris, (b. 1782) wife Sarah Bateman (b. 1793. Bellows, Cornelius Vanderhoof (b. 1821) wife Mary Ann Blake (b. 1822). Berryhill. Samuel G., (b. 1785). Blakiston, Charles, (b. 1824) Philadelphia, Pa., wife Angelina Cecilia Gay (b. (1827) Lancaster, Pa. Blue (Blew-Blaw) Family formerly lived in New Jersey. Brelsford, William Henry, (b. 1819) wife Rebecca (b. 1818) formerly lived in Dublin, O. Butler, John. Merchant in Baltimore, Maryland, wife Emily S. Blue (m. 1825). This family record goes back to 1610 in Ireland.

Culbertson, William Henry, (b. 1840) wife Minnie (b. 1853). Chaney, Edward Kearney, wife Eliza A. Tallman (m. 1856). Chaffee, Ezra, (b. 1785) wife Mary (b. 1787). Cooley, Asahel, (b. 1753) in Mass., wife Esther Warriner. Emigrated to Ohio about 1796, both buried at Coolville, Athens Co., O. (a very complete record of this family). Corbin, George, (b. 1827) wife Margaret (b. 1830).

Davis, John, (b. 1706) in New York, wife Jane (b. 1708) Charleston, So. Carolina. (A complete record of this Davis family). Dawson, Thomas, (b. 1770) wife Lucretia Wolverton (b. 1766). Doty, Jonathan (son of Zuresha) b. 1767, wife Cynthia Merrill (dau. Jedediah) b. 1771. Dungan, John, (b. 1814) wife Susan Blue.

Eader (Ater), Jacob, (b. 1767) wife Saly (b. 1769). Eberly, Charlie, (b. 1857) wife Anna Corbin. Eberly, John, (b. 1799) wife Hannah Shipman (b. 1811). Evans, George W., (b. 1805) wife Nancy Ricketts.

Filler, Joseph, (b. 1801) wife Lydia Crum (b. 1806).

Guild, Mary Blakiston Family Record 1st entry:—Blakiston, John, (b. 1773) in Philadelphia, wife Harriet Richards (b. 1789). Green, John, (b. 17—) wife Ruhama Nichols (b. 1769). Gardiner, Edmund Gibson, (son of John Gardiner, Sr.) b. 1844, wife Susan J. Barnes (b. 1850). Gardiner, Lebbeus William, (b. 1786) wife Eunice Latimer (b. 1792).

414

Gardner, John Martin, (b. 1766) wife Susanah (b. 1778) both of Lancaster, Co., Pa. Gilruth, Thomas, (b. Blairgourie, Pertshire, Scotland) wife Marion Ingles (b. Edenburg, Scotland) moved to the French Grant, O. from Bellville, Va. Apr. 1797, came to America in 1783. Gilruth, James & Mary, (Westlake) Gilruth. James was a circuit rider of the Methodist Church i nthe early days in Ohio. Good, John, (b. 1774) Written in the German handwriting of Magdalena Landis Good (b. 1776). Geer, Rezin, (b. 1737) wife Mary (Vendenburg or Vanderburgh) Geer, (b. 1745).

Hagler, Samuel, (b. 1794) wife Anna Fudge (b. 1801. Hannum, Perez, (b. 1791) wife 1st Abigail Nutt (b. 1793). 2nd Abigail Smith (b. 1801) Harlow, Jonas, (b. 1801) wife Mary (b. 1800). Hetzer, Phillip, (b. 1774) wife Sarah Dernburger (b. 1775). Herron-Tylor-Ferguson, record. Hibben, James, (b. 1795) son of Thomas and Mary. Hoover, Lucretia Gren of Licking Co., O. a very extensive Bible Record of several branches. Hunter, William Forest, (b. 1808) Alexandria, Va., wife Mary (b. 1812) Allegheny Co., Pa.

Innis, Henry, (b. 1792) wife Isabella Clifford Pegg (b. 1793).

Jeffrey, Joseph Andrew, (b. 1836) Clinton Co., O., wife Celia C. Harris (b. 1849. Jones, Henry, (b. 1812) son of Jacob & Sarah (Kirby) Jones, wife Rebecca Ann (b. 1814) dau. of James & Delila (Perdue) Huston.

Keys, John, (b. 1777) wife Mary Smiley (b. 1787).

Lankford, William Haley, (b. 1828) son of James & Elizabeth Morris Lankford, wife Roseann Violette (b. 1837) dau. of John & Mary E. Violette. Lewis, Newell, (b. 1823) Harrisville, O., wife 1st Elmira J. Brown (b. 1822) 2nd Louisa F. Brown (b. 1818) both women born in Erie Co., N. Y. Lindenberg, Charles H., (b. 1841) Gentien, Prussia, wife Sarah Elizabeth Robbins (b. 1849) Columbus, O. Livingston, David (Rev), (b. 1847) Reynoldsburg, O., son of Alexander W. & Matilda Dickey (Graham) Livingston, wife Lotta Jane Hagler (b. 1852) in Xenia, O., dau. Wm. Leonard & Mary Lyon (Scroggs) Hagler. Loyd, Willis H., (b. 1855) wife Anna M. Franks (b. 1865). This record refers back to 1811 on some lines.

McDonald, William, (b. 1784) New Milford, Conn., wife Mary Jane Davis (b. ———). McMaster, Hugh, (b. 1798) Ontario City, N. Y., wife Ann McGown (b. 1797) Nova Scotia. McPherson, Joseph, (b. 1804) wife Elizabeth Hart (b. 1807). Means, Joseph, (b. 1825) wife Margaret Sutton (b. 1827). Menday-Cummings-Miller. This record goes back to 1700. Merion, Nathaniel, (b. 1750) son of Wm. & Thankful Withington Merion; wife Lydia Gay (b. 1755) both from Mass. Merion, William & Catherine Merion, another generation than the above.

Pillsbury, Geo. Harlen, (b. 1843) wife Sophia PPratt (b. ———). Patterson, Luther, (b. 1783) wife Sarah Neal (b. 1783) both from Mass. Pearce. Joseph (The older Pearces lived in Rhode Island). The line of Betty Simmons, wife of Samuel Pearce (1755) goes back to the Mayflower. Pond, Valorous, (b. 1821) wife Emma Bateman Pond (b. 182—). Purdum, John and Christena Ann, their children only.

Quick, Franklin H., of Jackson Co., Ohio, some dates in this Bible go back to 1827.

Reed, M. W., (b. 1818) wife Nancy Chevalier (b. 1819). Ross, Levi, (b. 1792) Rockingham Co., Virginia, wife Mary Ruffner (b. 1802) Shenandoah Co., Va.

Springer-Stedham & Springer—*—Crooks Records. These two Bible records go back to 1766. Springer, Charles Christopher, (1658), connects in many places with the record formerly mentioned. Simpson, Ann (Davis) (b. 1764) with her husband had Revolutionary Service. Some early dates in our possession. Sells, Ludwick (his children) first date 1771. Very complete record. Sherman, Samuel. (1620-1700) Benjamin, (1661-1741) Nathaniel, (1692 ———) David, (1755-1826) David Thompson, (b. 1794) all of Conn. Shoemaker, Christopher, (b. 1777) wife Marie Barbarie Keller (b. 1788). Mr. Christopher Sherman was born in Paris, France, came to America at the age of five. Mrs. Marie Keller Shoemaker was born in Holland. Shoemaker, Christopher. Jr., (b. 1820) wife Sarah Ann Belknap (1825). Swisher, Jacob, (b. 1803) son of John & Mary Swisher, wife Anah Needles (b. 1811) dau. Philemon & Sarah Needles. Swisher, Frederick. (b. 1807) wife Lydia Landes (b. 1811). Swartz. Christian Daniel. (b. 1822) in Wurtenberg, Germany, wife Hannah Bevilhimer (b. 1826) dau. Geo. & Margaret Bevilhimer. Stephenson, Samuel, (b. 1831) wife Sarah Turner (b. 1836)

BIBLE RECORDS

MABEL INNIS FREY

Name: Samuel Hagler, Xenia, Ohio.
Present Owner: F. A. Livingston, 239 Nineteenth Ave., Columbus, Ohio.

BIRTHS

Samuel Hagler	October 31, 1794
Anna Fudge	August 18, 1801
Elizabeth Ann Hagler	November 2, 1823
Mary Amanda Hagler	January 17, 1825
Sarah Jane Hagler	March 4, 1826
William Leonard Hagler	May 9, 1827
Henry Christian Hagler	August 28, 1828
Marthy Eldy Hagler	April 25, 1830
Katherine Charlotte Hagler	May 31, 1831
John Milton Hagler	December 13, 1832
Moses Allen Hagler	April 30, 1834
Clarissa Rebecca Hagler	September 27, 1835
Hanna Minerva Hagler	August 17, 1837
Emmily Loisa Hagler	December 31, 1838
Samuel Harrison Hagler	August 28, 1840
Anna Samantha Hagler	February 1, 1842
Harriet Rosaltha Hagler	July 27, 1847

MARRIAGES

Samuel Hagler and Ann Fudge	January 16, 1823

DEATHS

Samuel Harrison Hagler	November 10, 1843
Harriet Rosaltha Hagler	July 25, 1849
Henry Christian Hagler	October 18, 1865
Moses Allen Hagler	October 22, 1865
Samuel Hagler	August 7, 1880

Name: Harlow Family Bible.
Present Owner: Blanche Tipton Rings, 70 S. Burgess Ave., Columbus, Ohio.

BIRTHS

Jonas Harlow	April 25, 1801
Nancy Harlow	September 15, 1800

CHILDREN

Lafayette Harlow	April 5, 1825
Mary Jain Harlow	July 10, 1827
Ann Eliza Harlow	May 1, 1829
George W. Harlow	March 18, 1831
Marthaette Harlow	August 25, 1833
William Harlow	December 28, 1836

Jonas Harlow (son of Lafayette)...............December 25, 1845
William Harlow (son of Lafayette).................July 28, 1848
Louisa Harlow (dau. of Lafayette)............September 7, 1852
Franklin A. (son of Eliza Harlow & Frank Hudson)...June 14, 1827
Henrietta B. Webster (dau. Joshua & Catherine Webster), July 5, 1827

MARRIAGES

Jonas & Nancy Harlow........................January 22, 1824
Lafayette Harlow & Nancy (?)................November 2, 1845
Mary Jain Harlow & Clark Coffman...........September 3, 1846
Marthaette Harlow & Francis Riley............December 24, 1856
Ann Eliza Harlow & Thomas Eberly.............January 20, 1857
George Harlow & Mary Martin.................January 26, 1860
William A. Harlow & Fanny Persinger..............July 16, 1865
Henrietta B. Webster.......................November 1, 1848

DEATHS
(Compiled by Jonas Harlow)

Mother Hutchinson dide the 8 of June, 1853, aged 78 yrs. 1 mo. 10 da.
Henrietta Webster died Jan. 21, 1868, aged 40 yrs. no children.
My father dide 13th December, 1836, at Vincennes, Indiana.
My mother dide 22nd March at St. Louis, Missouri.
Brother Jeremiah Harlow dide in the City of New York.
Brother Guy Harlow dide in Texas the 7th April, 1841.
Brother Wm. Harlow dide in Louisville, Ky.
Brother Benjamin Harlow dide in St. Louis, Aug. 21, 1848.
Sister Susan Harlow dide.
Brother Samuel's wife dide the 6th July, 1850, at St. Louis.
First son Lafayette dide in Covington, Ky. Feb. 16, 1855.

BERYHILL–CLARK FAMILIES

Present owner: Clark Family, E. Ward St., Urbana, Ohio.
Condition: Yellow with age, front cover gone as well as pages from
front and back.

BIRTHS

Samuel G. Berryhill.........born...............22nd. June, 1785
Miriam Berryhill............born...............12th. Oct., 1794
Mary McCibben.............born.........7th. Feb., 1801
Eliza B. Berryhill...........born...............29th. Aug., 1810
William M. Berryhill........born...............27th. Dec., 1811
Sarah B. Berryhill..........born...............24th. Apr., 1814
Ruth M. Berryhill...........born...............25th. Mar., 1816
Mary Ann Berryhill........born Sat............15th. Mar., 1818
Alexander L. Berryhill......born Sat............11th. June, 1820
Saml. Berryhill.............born...............18th. July, 1822

John Clark.................born...............25th. Mar., 1777
Miriam Clark...............born...............12th. Oct., 1794

```
Saml. B. Clark..............born................20th. Aug., 1828
Diademma Clark...........born................14th. Feb., 1830
Chambers H. Clark.........born................14th. Sept., 1833
Charles M. Clark..........born................24th. Oct., 1835
```

MARRIAGES

```
John Clark and Miriam Berryhill were married....11th. Sept., 1827
C. M. Clark and Mary A. Baillie were married.....11th. Aug., 1855
Saml. G. Berryhill and Miriam McCibben were married
                                              16th. Oct., 1809
```

DEATHS

```
John Clark.................died...........................1861
Chambers H. Clark.........died................Aug. 29th., 1884
Mirriam S. Clark...........died...................Aug., 1856
Hattie E. Clark.............died.........Oct. 13th., 1898 or 1893
```

HANNUM FAMILY

Present owner: William H. Hannum, 1690 Franklin Ave., Columbus, Ohio.

Bible bound in sheep, last leaf of cover missing.

BIRTHS

```
Father: Perez Hannum........was born.....July 24th, A. D. 1791
Mother: Abigail Nutt.........was born.....July 21st, A. D. 1793
        Abigail Smith........was born...October 7th, A. D. 1801
Harriet Hannum..............was born....Decr. 17th., A. D. 1812
Eliza Hannum................was born....May 30th., A. D. 1814
William Nutt Hannum........was born...March 28th., A. D. 1816
A Child born dead....................January 19th., A. D. 1819
Stillman Bullard Hannum......was born....Decr. 29th., A. D. 1819
Mary Ann Hannum...........was born...April 10th., A. D. 1823
Elijah Cushman Hannum.....was born...Septr. 19th., A. D. 1825
Henry Chappell Hannum.....was born....June 23rd., A. D. 1829
A Child born dead.......................June 29th., A. D. 1833
Ezra Smith Hannum..........was born..March 12th., A. D. 1836
Sarah Hannum...............was born....April 30th., A. D. 1838
```

MARRIAGES

Perez Hannum and Abigail Nutt were married Jany. 19th., A.D. 1812.

Perez Hannum and Abigail Richardson formerly Smith were married June 14th, 1834.

Asa Clark and Eliza Hannum were married.

Stillman B. Hannum and Mary Eliza Read were married Octr. 14th., A. D. 1847.

Elijah Cushman Hannum & Mary Elizth McCabe were married July 3rd., A. D. 1851.

Henry Chappell Hannum and Julia H. Gardner were married September 17th., A. D. 1855.

Perez Hannum and Sarah M. Irvin formerly Tracy were married August 4th., A. D. 1856.

DEATHS

Harriet Hannum..........died.............July **30th.**, A. D. 1813
William Nutt Hannum....died............March 29th., A. D. 1818
Mary Ann Hannum.......died............Decr. 18th., A. D. 1824
Abigail Hannum..........died............June 30th., A. D. 1833
Eliza Clark...............died............Decr. **2nd.**, A. D. 1847
Abigail Hannum..........died.........February 9th., A. D. 1856
Sarah Hannum...........died............Sept. 15th., A. D. 1856
Henry C. Hannum........died............April 10th., A. D. 1863
E. C. Hannum............died..........March 11th., A. D. 1867
Perez Hannum...........died............Aug. 10th., A. D. 1871

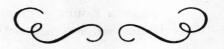

BIBLE RECORDS

MABEL INNIS FREY

Name: McGown McMaster Family.
Present Owner: Bessie Bliss Wiggin Fitz.

BIRTHS

Hugh McMaster........born in Ontario City, N. Y..June 22, 1798
Ann McGown McMaster.born in Nova Scotia......August 18, 1797
Washington McMaster...born in Columbus, Ohio.February 27, 1821
Olive McMaster........born in Columbus, Ohio....March 26, 1823
Matilda A. McMaster...born in Columbus, Ohio.December 11, 1825
David McMaster........born in Columbus, Ohio.....July 19, 1829
Henry Clay McMaster...born in Columbus, Ohio....March 11, 1832
Benjamin McMaster.....born in Columbus, Ohio..February 2, 1834
Robert McMaster.......born in Columbus, Ohio......April 4, 1838

(Children of Isaac and Olive McMaster Wells)

Ann Wells..............born......................July 31, 1842
Lewis Washington Wells.born................November 21, 1843
Matilda Virginia Wells...born................November 29, 1845
Marvel White Wells.....born...................October 6, 1847
Deborah Wells.........born.................November 2, 1849
Mary Wells...........born.................November 27, 1852
Byron Wilbur Wells.....born................September 23, 1856
Simon Winfield Wells....born.....................June 19, 1862

MARRIAGES

Hugh McMaster was married to Ann McGown....February 7, 1820
Isaac Newton Wells was married to Olive McMaster..Dec. 14, 1841
Washington McMaster was married to Mary Carie.....July 2, 1844
Marvel White Bliss was married to Matilda Ann McMaster
August 27, 1844
David McMaster was married to Elizabeth Turner..August 19, 1860

DEATHS

Henry Clay McMaster...died in Columbus, Ohio....August 31, 1833
Ann McMaster.........died in Columbus, Ohio..November 9, 1853
Benjamin McMaster....died in Frankfort, Union Co., O.,
October 11, 1856
Hugh McMaster.......died in Columbus, Ohio..February 20, 1868
Washington McMaster..died in Chillicothe, Ohio.
Olive McMaster Wells...died in Worthington, O....January 13, 1882
(at 6 o'clock and 40 M. of paralysis, aged **59**, nine months
and 13 days)
David McMasters......died at Bloomington, Ill....August 4, 1887
(left a wife and 1 daughter Olive)
Matilda Ann McMaster Bliss, died in Cincinnati, O..March 8, 1892
(at a sanitarium with a disease of the nerves, was buried from
her home in Columbus, O.)

Matilda Virginia Wells...died................December 5, 1926

In one of the marriage columns the following statement is made: "John Megown, a native of Nova Scotia, was given a deed of a tract of land in Columbus, Ohio, called Refugee land, under the administration of Thomas Jefferson." He had two sons, Robert and John, and eight daughters, viz.: Mary, Hannah, Ann, Deborah, Martha, Olive, Jane, Sarah.

Martha....married John Hunter in Columbus.....January 28, 1813
Sarah......married Benjamin Chandler in Columbus...April 1, 1816
Mary......married Jerry Shed in Columbus.....December 21, 1818
Deborah...married Robert Hunter in Columbus..January 22, 1807
Hannah....married Adolf Tolle in Columbus......February 7, 1820
Ann.......married Hugh McMaster in Columbus..February 7, 1820
Jane.......married Hassalton McMaster in Columbus Dec. 21, 1818

On the inside of cover is the following:

"This was Hugh McMaster's and Ann McMaster's Family Bible, he left it with his daughter Olive Wells to keep for his son Robert and give it to him when he called for it. After Olive died, Matilda Bliss took it and kept it until she died. After her death her daughter Anna gave it to me to keep. I prize it very highly and hope I will be guided by its teaching in the way of all truth as well as its former owners, I hope this blessed book will be ever kept in the family.— Miss TILLIE V. WELLS, May 15, 1895. Worthington, Ohio."

Name: Patterson Family Bible.
Present Owner: Ora Patterson Moeller, 2740 Westerville Rd., Columbus, Ohio.

BIRTHS
Luther Patterson..........born................February 11, 1783
Sarah Neal Patterson......born.....................May 1, 1783

CHILDREN
Philander Patterson.......born.....................April 17, 1804
John Patterson...........born............September 30, 1805
Louisa Patterson.........born....................August 9, 1807
Laura Patterson.........born................February 4, 1810
Luther Patterson.........born...............December 15, 1813
Charles Patterson.........born....................April 29, 1815
Angeline Patterson........born................December 16, 1818
Mariah Patterson.........born................December 14, 1820
Sophronia Drake (dau. Elizur & Mary Drake) born January 28, 1818

GRANDCHILDREN
(Children of John and Sophronia Drake Patterson)
Alonzo H. Patterson.......born.....................July 3, 1834
Ellis P. Patterson........born................February 20, 1836
Mary S. Patterson........born................October 24, 1838
Charles Patterson.........born................February 13, 1840

Margaret A. Patterson..... born.....................June 6, 1842
Laura L. Patterson........born....................June 24, 1844
John R. Patterson........born..................March —, 1852

MARRIAGES

Luther Patterson married Sarah Neal

John Patterson and Sophronia Drake were married....May 29, 1834
John Patterson and Amanda Jane Kohn were married Jan. 24, 1875
Ora Patterson and Wm. Moeller were married........June 13, 1898
Cora B. Patterson and Alonzo Brush were married....June 23, 1903
Sherman Patterson and Mary Gordon were married
Mont. Byron Patterson and Inez Wilson were married.July 20, 1918

DEATHS

Luther Patterson..........died...............September 20, 1824
Sarah Neal Patterson......died..................March 29, 1876
John Randolph Patterson..died...........................1928
Amanda Kohn Patterson...died. ....
Charles B. Patterson......died....................June 11, 1869

BIBLE RECORDS

Name: Innis Family Bible.

Present Owner: Mabel Innis Frey, 1329 Lincoln Rd., Columbus, Ohio.

BIRTHS

Henry Innis..............was born.......May 1st, A. D. 1792
Isabella Pegg..............was born.......July 30th, A. D. 1793
Gustavus Swan Innis (son of Henry) was born Feb. 4th, A. D. 1819
Moses Morrill.............was born......April 19th, A. D. 1780
Mille Merion..............was born.....October 21st, A. D. 1777
Sarah G. Morrill (dau. of Moses) was born September 2, A. D. 1821
(Children of G. S. & Sarah G. Innis)
Henry Morrill Innis........was born........May 7th, A. D. 1846
George Swan Innis..........was born.....August 9th, A. D. 1850
Isabella Clifford Innis.......was born...November 6th, A. D. 1852
Mille Merion Innis..........was born....January 26th, A. D. 1858
Frank William Innis........was born..December 24th, A. D. 1854
Charles Frances Innis.......was born....October 25th, A. D. 1862
(Grandchildren of G. S. & Sarah G. Innis)
Mabel Drake Innis (dau. Henry, was born November 26, A. D. 1875
Homer Clarence Innis (son of Geo.) was born December 14, A. D. 1878
Ethelwynne Innis (dau. of Geo. was born...July 22nd, A. D. 1882
Mildred Alice Innis (dau. of Henry) was born Dec. 31st, A. D. 1886
*Clifford Lyman Bohannan (son Mille) was born Sept. 14, A. D. 1884
*Charles Dudley Bohannan (son Mille) was born Oct. 19, A. D. 1887
Raymond Innis Matthews (son of Isabella) born in Williamstown, Ky.

MARRIAGES

Henry Innis and Isabella Clifford Pegg.......June 10th, A. D. 1813
Gustavus Swan Innis and Sarah G. Morrill..March 25th, A. D. 1845
Moses Morrill and Mille Merion.....................April, 1805
Henry Morrill Innis and Alice Arabella Drake.May 23rd, A. D. 1871
George Swan Innis and Alice Van Fossen at
    Appleton, Licking Co., Ohio...........October 23rd, A. D. 1877
Dr. Charles L. Bohannan and Mille Merion Innis
                            November 29th, A. D. 1881
Dr. Newton S. Matthews and Isabella Clifford Innis
                            November 5th, A. D. 1885
Albert L. Frey and Mabel Drake Innis.......May 23rd, A. D. 1904
Dr. Edward A. Rich and Ethelwynn Innis..January 1st, A. D. 1906
Homer C. Innis and Eunice Shofner.........April 7th, A. D. 1909
Clinton Barton Schenck and Mildred Alice Innis,
                            August 30th, A. D. 1910

---

*Born in Tracy, Minn.

Moses Morrill..............died.................July 17th, 1837
Mille Morrill...............died.................July 22nd, 1858
Henry Innis................died.................May 20th, 1865
Isabella C. Innis (wife of Rev. Henry) died........March 31st, 1880
Frank William Innis........died............February 17th, 1855
Isabella Innis Matthews.....died...............August 9th, 1902
   (at Williamstown, Ky.)
Gustavus Swan Innis........died..............January 2nd, 1899
Sarah G. Innis.............died...............June 25th, 1912
Henry Morrill Innis........died...............June 16th, 1927
Charles Frances Innis.......died............February 25th, 1931

BIBLE RECORDS

MABEL INNIS FREY

Name: Miller-Cummings-Menday Family Bible.

Present Owner: Mabel Innis Frey, 1329 Lincoln Rd., Columbus, Ohio.

George Miller, age 18, emigrated from Germany (probably in 1700's). Four children b. in Germany: George and Jacob, twins; John and Daniel. Seven children b. in America: David, Henry, Phillip, Polly, Catherine, Susan, Elizabeth. George m. Elenador Plouegh (Plue) b. at Cynthiana, Ky., of German parents. Moses Miller (son of George and Elenador) b. June 6, 1817, Hamilton Co., Ohio, Big Belt, five miles east of General Harrison's residence; died Oct. 8, 1900, Placerville, Cal., age 83. Moses Miller was married to Matilda Brunner, (b. 17 April, 1817) on January 12, 1839, by Squire Frakers, Storrs Twp., Cincinnati, Ohio.

Emma B. Miller (b. May 15, 1847) m. April 18, 1868, Jesse K. Cummings (d. Sept. 18, 1870, Atlanta, Ga.). Emma B. Miller Cummings m. George Menday (b. Feb. 17, 1838), Winsor, England, June 5, 1872, by Rev. S. K. Hall. (Recorded by Joseph Pearce, July 25, 1835, Bucyrus, Crawford Co., Ohio:

Pearce, James, son of George Pearce, b. Sept. 4, 1691, d. Sept. 24, 1755, aged 64. Martha, his wife, b. —— 22, 1696, died Sept. 22, 1760, aged 64 years. *Wm.* Pearce, son of James and Martha, b. Jan. 19, 1713. *Susannah* Pearce, b. May 19, 1715. *Martha* Pearce, b. Aug. 4, 1717. *James* Pearce, b. Sept. 14, 1719, d. Sept. 17, 1761. *Gyles* Pearce, b. March 25, 1722. *Mary* Pearce, b. Oct. 17, 1724. *George* Pearce, b. Sept. 11, 1727. *Alise* Pearce, b. Jan. 7, 1729. *Phebee* Pearce, b. Sept. 21, 1731. *Samuel* Pearce, b. Jan. 29, 1734, d. Dec. 2, 1793. *Samuel* Pearce m. Betty Simmons, Nov. 9, 1755. *Phebee* Pearce, b. Sept. 8, 1756, d. Jan. 24, 1793. *Pricilla* Pearce, b. Feb. 1, 1758, d. Nov. 14, 1793. *Jeremiah* Pearce, b. March 7, 1760, d. Feb. 22, 1835. *Joseph* Pearce, b. Jan. 14, 1761, d. Sept. 14, 1763.

Joseph Pearce m. Mary Ann Woods Jan. 22, 1821. Narcissa Pearce, b. March 29, 1822, d. April 24, 1909. Mary Ann Pearce, b. July 26, 1823. Mary Ann, wife of Joseph Pearce, d. July 26, 1823, aged 29 yrs. 10 mo. Joseph Pearce m. Mary Cary, July 9, 1825. Sarah Pearce, b. Feb. 16, 1826. Lurainah Pearce, b. Feb. 29, 1829. Joseph Pearce d. Nov. 20, 1840.

Name: The Joseph Pearce Family Bible.

Present owner of Joseph Pearce Bible, Mrs. Georgiana Elliott Rife.

Cary Record—Abel Cary, b. June 13, 1781. Sarah McKeever, b. May 20, 1789. Elizabeth Cary, b. Jan. 4, 1806. Mary Cary, b. Oct. 4, 1807. John S. Cary, b. Sept. 20, 1809. Emily Cary, b. Sept. 20, 1811. William M. Cary, b. Jan. 3, 1814. Mathew Cary, b. Mch. 2, 1816. Isabel Cary, b. Apr. 18, 1818. Entries made by John C. Gale, West Unity, O., April 10, 1905, son of John Gale. Mary Ann Pearce, m. John Gale, May 5, 1842. John Gale d. Nov. —— Mary Ann Pearce Gale, m. James Jackson, Mch. 4, 1850, d. Sept. 25, 1878, at Angola, Ind. Narcissa Pearce, m. Thom. G. Elliott, Mar. 13, 1842. Sarah Pearce, m. Lewis Slusser, Nov. 22, 1849, d. Nashville, Tenn., Feb. 26, 1863, buried Canton, O., Mch. 3, aged 37 yrs. 10 days. Luranah Pearce m. John Green, Dec. 20, 1863. William Eyles, d. Wadsworth, Ohio, Feb. 11, 1870. Mary Pearce Eyles, d. Sept. 26, 1876, Carson City, Nevada. Thomas G. Elliott, b. Sept. 1, 1813, York Co., Pa., d. West Unity, Ohio, Oct. 27, 1897, aged 84 yrs. 1 mo. 26 days. George Pearce Elliott, b. Feb. 29, 1849 (?). Anna Elizabeth Wartz Elliott, b. Jan. 8, 1865, m. George Elliott, Aug., 1894. Georgiana G. Elliott, b. West Unity, Oct. 3, 1899. Geo. P. Elliott and Anna Elizabeth Elliott. William G. Elliott, son of Thomas G. Elliott, b. Feb. 10, 1854, Cleveland, Ohio, d. West Unity, Ohio, Sept. 7, 1905, age 51 years, 6 mo., 21 days. Narcissa Pearce Elliott, dau. Joseph Pearce and Mary Ann Woods Pearce, b. Mch. 29, 1822, d. West Unity, O., Apr. 24, 1909, aged 87 yrs., 25 da.

BIBLE RECORDS

MABEL INNIS FREY

Name: Lakin, Daniel, Family Bible.

Present Owner: Mrs. James S. Lakin, 1575 Virginia St., Charleston, W. Va.

Daniel Lakin, b. Jan. 20, 1757, d. Jan. 4, 1829, m. Ann Sheckell, b. Jan. 18, 1766, d. Jan. 4, 1822. Daniel Lakin and Ann Sheckell were m. in Frederick, Maryland, Feb. 8, 1787. Their children: Benj. Lakin, b. Dec. 23, 1787. d. ???? Elizabeth Lakin, b. Oct. 2, 1789. Jemima Lakin, b. Dec. 6, 1791. Sarah Lakin, b. Feb. 1st, 1794. Lucretia Lakin, b. Apr. 28, 1797. Rebecca Lakin, b. Apr. 18, 1798. Ruth Lakin, b. Jan. 8, 1800. Emiline Lakin, b. Apr. 27, 1801. Daniel Lakin, b. Nov. 17, 1803. Serena & Washington Lakin, b. July 6, 1805. Ann M. Lakin, b. Oct. 5, 1808. John Scheckel Lakin, b. Sept. 5, 1811.

Daniel Lakin, b. Nov. 17, 1803, d. Dec. 29, 1872. m. Dorcas Flenniken (b. July 16, 1808. d. Apr. 30, 1886) on June 27, 1833. Their Children: Samuel Wilson Lakin, b. May 22, 1834. d. ? m. Anna Clagett, Oct. 24, 1858. George Washington Lakin, b. Jan. 1, 1836. d. ? m. Mary E. Johnston on Nov. 3, 1864. Daniel Clinton Lakin, b. Sept. 8, 1838. d. ? m. Eliza C. Lane on Oct. 13, 1859 Ann Elizabeth Lakin, b. Feb. 3, 1845. d. Aug. 12, 1847. Margaret Elizabeth Lakin Shrum b. May 9, 1846. Milton Dwight Lakin. b. Feb. 1, 1850. d. ?? m. Ida Davis in May 1876.

Additional data: David Trowbridge m. Maggie E. Lakin, Nov. 12, 1868. Margaret M. C. Shrum, d. May 9, 1846. Samuel G. Flenniken d. Dec. 25, 1846. Elizabeth Flenniken d. Sept. 7, 1852.

Name: Hetzer, George Marcus; Family Bible.

Present Owner: Francis Henry Hetzer, 1423 Sunbury Rd., Columbus, Ohio.

George M. Hetzer, b. Jan. 31, 1853, d. Apr. 30, 1912, m. Ida Frances Reed of Reedsville, Ohio, Dec. 9, 1847, Wm. Hawley, officiating. Ida F. Reed b. Dec. 27, 1853, d. Dec. 31, 1914. Mentor M. Hetzer, b. Aug. 19, 1875, d. ?? m. Bertha Wells on July 19, 1902. Francis Henry Hetzer, b. Dec. 1, 1878, d. ? m. Flora Skeels on Oct. 17, 1900. Addie S. Hetzer, b. June 28, 1881, d. Oct. 15, 1916, m. Homer Barnett on Sept. 7, 1901. John Milton Hetzer, b. Feb. 1, 1891, d. Nov. 15, 1891.

Name: Waddell, Alexander; Family Bible.

James Wadell (son of Alxeander) b. ?? 7th, 1774, m. Sarah Grimes b. Jan. ? 15, 1780, dau. Felix & Catherine Grimes. "And they were married third day of June (may be July or Jan.) 1798." This data confirmed in "annals of Bath County, Va. 1917, Morton, p. 129 except that calls her Sally Graham instead of Sarah Grimes." Their children are: John Waddell, b. Oct. 13, 1799. Caty, b. May 30, 1801. Elizabeth b. Apr. 23, 1803. Polly, b. Apr. 7, 1808 or 1806. Nancy b. Nov. 8, 1809. Peggy b. June 19, 1811. Sarah b. Nov. 16, 1816. Lydia, b. Aug. 4, 1820. (Note: Sarah and Lydia children of second marriage. Another son by second marriage, James P. R. Waddell, born after Lydia.) Note:—Jack E. Nida has a very complete record of the descendants of Alexander Waddell (1732-1834) Address 1859 W. 1st Ave., Columbus, Ohio.

BIBLE RECORDS

Mabel Innis Frey

Haessley Family.

Present Cwner: Mrs. William Hasley, Elyria, Ohio.

Haessley, Phillip, b. Oct. 25, 1795 at Baden-Baden, Germany; d. Feb. 21, 1890 at Dungannon, Ohio; m. Dec. 30, 1821, Northumberland county, Pa., Anna Maria Spone (Spohn) b. Oct. 20, 1800—Berks county, Pa.; d. Dec. 14, 1889—Ohio.

Children of Phillip and Anna Maria (Spone) Haessley:
Joseph, b. 10-17-1822, Berks county, Pa; d. Mar. 6, 1907—Ohio.
Jacob, b. 3-2-1824, Berks county, Pa; d. May 10, 1922—Ohio.
Jonathan, b. 12-10-1825, Berks county, Pa.
Anna, b. 1-5-1827, Berks county, Pa; d. 1834.
Catharine, b. 2-15-1828, Berks county, Pa; d. Sept. 11, 1911—Ohio.
Phillip, junior, b. 10-12-1829, Berks county, Pa; d. Dec. 8, 1914.
Nathan, b. 2-10-1831, Berks county, Pa; d. Jan. 23, 1865.
Sarah, b. 1-10-1833, Northumberland county, Pa; d. Jan. 8, 1928.
Lucy, b. 12-6-1835, Northumberland county, Pa; d. 1886—Ohio.
George, b. 5-22-1838, Northumberland county, Pa; d. May 1898.
Charles, b. 12-10-1838, Northumberland county, Pa; d Oct. 18, 1911.
Abraham, b. 1-6-1841, Columbiana county, Ohio; d. Jan. 31, 1921.
*William, b. 11-21-1844, Columbiana county, Ohio; living 1938.

Hasley, William, m. November 16, 1875, Columbiana county, Ohio. Annette McMullen* (b. Mar. 3, 1856) dau. of Enos and Mary (Stewart) McMullen, Columbiana county, Ohio. (*Both living in 1938)

Children of William and Annette (McMullen) Hasley:
Wilfred, b. Aug. 22, 1878; m. Aug. 9, 1904, Hattie Vogley.
Pauline, (b. 1881); Eleanor, d. aged 16 years.
Clare, m. Aug. 26, 1911, John Cullin (Lorain county, Ohio).
William, junior, (A. E. F. No. 2242084-26/Engrs.) m. July 11, 1920, Belle Milburn, Columbiana county, Ohio.
Raymond Enos, (A. E. F. No. 2397391, Co. B, 5-Reg-'17) m. Helen Gill, November 16, 1925. (Lorain county, Ohio)

Phillip Haessley (b. 1795) came to Pennsylvania about 1812. He engaged in teaching in the Lehigh district, and for a period of time resided at Milton. (?) About 1839 he immigrated to Ohio, (Columbiana county) bringing with him his entire family.

Ross Bible.

Present Owner: Roy H. Ross, Urbana, Ohio.

Inscription:
On the inside of the front page.

"John Ross his book and pen in hand it being in the year 1766."

Following this the name of James Mahanes.

On the inside of back cover are two names, John Jordan and William Dedilston.

BIBLE RECORDS
MABEL INNIS FREY

THE SPRINGER FAMILY TREE.
Owner, Family of Dr. Chas. S. Hamilton, Columbus, Ohio
A beautiful scroll, maker unknown.

Charles Christopher Springer I, b. 1658. *Christopher Springer II*, b. 1696. His children:—Catharine, b. 1742.—Peter, b. 1729.—Brita, b. 1726. —John, b. 1724.—Joseph, b. 1738.—Susannah, b. 1731.—Solomon, b. 1734.—Abraham, b. 1736.—Charles, b. 1722. Peter (1729) children: Rachel, b. 1755.—Rebecca, b. 1757.—Hannah, b. 1760.—Jesse, b. 1761. Lydia, b. 1763.—Peter, b. 1768.—Catharine, b. 1771.—Sarah, b. 1776.—Mary, b. 1779. Brita (1726) m. J. Hendrickson, 1755. John (1724) had:—John & Catharine, who married a Corbett. Susannah, (1731) was 2nd wife of John, son of Charles Sonn, C. C. had Sarah, b. 1762.—David, b. 1765. Solomon (1734) had Anna, b. 1758.—John, b. 1760.—Solomon, b. 1773. Abraham (1736) m. Christina Anderson, Nov. 1759. Charles (1722) had: Jeremiah, b. 1755.—Catharine, b. 1753.—Rachel, b. 1758.—James, b. 1765.— Reese, b. 1770.—Benjamin. Joseph (1738) had Catharine, b. 1771. —Andrus, b.1776.—Joseph, b. 1778.—Lydia, b. 1781.—Peter, b. 1784 & John. John, son of Joseph, had: Cornelius, born. 1790.—Jacob & Peter (twins) b. 1792. & Lydia. Jeremiah, son of Charles, had: Catharine, b. 1789.—Lavinah, b. 1793.—Sarah, b. 1795.—Sahilla, b. 1803.—Susan & Lewis. James, had Mary, b. 1792. Reese, had Elizabeth. Lydia, dau. of John, m. William Hamilton, had:—Cornelius, S. b. 1821.—John W. b. 1823.—Joseph H. b. 1826.—Isaac N. b. 1828.—Horatio C. b. 1830.— George B. b. 1833.—Thomas B. b. 1836.—Susan R. b. 1838. Catharine, dau. of Jeremiah (1755) m a Justice and had:—Mary, Hannah, Gustavus, Robert, Lewis C. & Sarah C. John W. Hamilton (1823) had:—Catharine, John, William D., Charles S., Thomas E. & Eloise. Cornelius S. Hamilton had:—Laura, b. 1848.—Thomas C. b 1849.—William, b. 1851.—John S. b. 1854.—William, b. 1855.—Cornelius, b. 1861.—Louisa, b. 1862. —Carrie, b. 1864.

SPRINGER–STEDHAM FAMILY RECORD
Bible owned by Paul Andrew Springer, Cleveland, Ohio

John Springer III. descendant of Charles Christopher Springer, b. Sept. 15, 1766, d. June 1, 1837, aged 71; m. Rebecca Stidham (Stedham) b. Nov. 18, 1769, d. June 29, 1861, aged 92. Cornelius Springer, son of John & Rebecca, b. at Wilmington, Del., Dec. 29, 1790. Jacob, b. Sept. 23, 1792. Lydia, b. July 7, 1794. Joseph, b. Dec. 23, 1795. Isaac, b. May 7, 1798, d. Mch. 17, 1853, m. Charlotte d. July 26, 1870. Andrew, b. Dec. 6, 1799. Elenora, b. Feb. 17, 1802. John, b. May 7, 1804. d. Oct. 1804. Jeremiah, b. Apr. 25, 1808. Susan Ann, b. Oct. 19, 1808, d. 1811. Eliza, b. Jan. 8, 1812, d. June 17, 1861, m. a Wiley. Rebecca, b. Oct. 21, 1813, d. May 18, 1848. m. a Cochran.

Andrew Springer, b. Dec. 23, 1800. d. Aug. 20, 1836. m. Elizabeth Crooks, b. Aug. 23, 1804 on Jan. 1, 1824. Elizabeth married, 2nd husband, a Mr. Axline. Elizabeth Springer Axline, d. Apr. 4, 1875. Children: —Rebekahann, b. Oct. 30, 1824.—John C. b. June 20, 1826. d. June 1, 1837.—Maryellen, b. July 22, 1828.—Almedea, b. Apr. 13, 1830. Increas Andrew. b. Apr. 28, 1832.—Lucresia, b. Sept. 29, 1834.

John C. Springer, b. June 26, 1826, d. Mch.. 15, 1900. m. Catherine Martin, b. Nov. 30, 1832, d. June 12, 1899, on May 15, 1808. Elizabeth, b. Aug. 21, 1852, d. Nov. 23, 1893, m. John White, of Roseville, Ohio, on Aug. 1, 1870. William Andrew, b. May 31, 1857, d. May 25, 1866. One death given as follows:—Martha Ellan Evans, dau. of Isaac & Charlotte Springer, d. Jan. 27, 1866.

BIBLE RECORDS
MABEL INNIS FREY

Family Bible of Charles H. Lindenberg.
Original Owner: CHARLES H. LINDENBERG, Columbus, Ohio

FAMILY RECORD
BIRTHS

Charles H. Lindenberg was born at Gentien, Prussia,
January 14, 1841.

Sarah Elizabeth Robbins was born at Columbus, Ohio
February 23, 1849.

Carl Robbins Lindenberg was born at Columbus, Ohio
January 13, 1875.

Francis Hicks was born Madison County, Ohio
June 1, 1875.

Frank Herman Lindenberg was born July 31, 1877.

Desha Darling Hubbard was born at Columbus, Ohio,
December 9, 1880.

Paul Lindenberg was born December 30, 1879.

Robert Lindenberg was born June 7, 1882.

Harry C. Lindenberg was born Feb. 21, 1872.

Charles Robbins was born January 13, 1875.

Frank Herman Lindenberg was born July 31, 1877.

Leo Lindenberg was born July 31, 1884. died.

Harry C. Lindenberg was born July 27, 1875.

MARRIAGES

Charles H. Lindenberg and Sarah Elizabeth Robbins were married
May 16, 1871 at the residence of Charles Robbins, 77 N. Washington Ave., Columbus, Ohio by Rev. D. A. Randall.

Carl Robbins Lindenberg and Frances Hicks were married February
18, 1902 at the residence of Johannes W. Hicks, 1375 East Broad
St., Columbus, Ohio by Rev. F. S. Palmer, or at Broad St. Presbyterian Church.

Frank Herman Lindenberg and Desha Darling Lindenberg were married Sept. 29, 1904 by Rev. Atwood at Trinity Episcopal Church.

Paul Lindenberg was married May 1, 1905 by Rev. John Hewitt at
644 Franklin Ave. at the residence of Darius Talmadge, her father.
She was born Dec. 29, 1885. Does not give her name. B. R.

Robert Lindenberg married October 30, 1906 by Rev. J. Hewitt at St.
Paul's Church. (Does not give her name. B. R.)

NO DEATHS GIVEN

Memorandum.

"Boarding at Mrs. Sentor's High St. From June 1, 1871 until about
Nov. 15, 1871. Then to Ma Robbins until about November 1, 1872.,
went to housekeeping on Friend St., south side second door east of
Seventh st. Moved April 24, to 479 East Friend St. Boarding with
Ma Robbins in spring of 1876. Moved into the house we built North
East corner of Fifth and Oak, on Nov. 1876. Remained there until
April 15, 1884 when we moved to 333 E. Town St. which we bought
March, 1884. Sold the Town St. house conditionally to Dr. J. F.
Baldwin, 1899. Moved to the Southern Hotel Sept. 1899. Moved to
the house known as the Inn at Arlington May 3, 1902. Lived here
two summers, living at the Southern Hotel in the winter. Remained
at the Southern Hotel until March 1, 1905. Began building house on

North E. corner of Broad and Champion, August, 1903 and moved when house was practically completed March 1, 1905".

JONAS D. HEFFNER, Family Bible Record.
    Knox Twp., Columbiana Co., Ohio
Owner: IRA J. HEFFNER, North Canton, Ohio

Heffner, Jonas D. b. Nov. 17, 1828, Chester Co., Pa., d. Sept. 20, 1910, m. Sarah-Jane Wentworth (Kennedy), b. Sept. 8, 1837, Berks Co. Pa. d. Aug. 31, 1921 on Mch. 13, 1856 at Berks Co. Pa. Came to Ohio, 1853, located Knox Twp. Columbiana Co. Eliza J. Heffner (d of Jonas) b. Feb. 11, 1857. d. Dec. 15, 1858. Albert O. Heffner (s. of Jonas) b. Apr. 15, 1859. d. Dec. 16, 1925, 11:45 P. M. m. 1st wife Jennie B. Jolly on Oct. 13, 1887. 2nd wife Martha Albright on Apr. 3, 1890. Walter Ira Heffner (s. of Jonas) b. Apr. 15, 1861. d. Aug. 25, 1923. m. Lauretta Thomas, on Feb. 23, 1882 at Columbiana Co. Ohio. d. Oct. 27, 1886. Omer L. Heffner (s. of Jonas) b. Mch. 10, 1864. d. July 4, 1927 m. Anna L. Furbay on Mch. 3, 1887. Harrie Hamilton Heffner (s. of Jonas) b. Apr. 30, 1870, Knox Twp. d. Dec. 6, 1936, unmarried. Joseph S. Heffner (s. of Walter) b. Sept. 20, 1883. Pearl E. Heffner(d. of Walter) b. Oct. 14, 1886. Ira J. Heffner (s. of Omer L.) b. Jan. 3, 1888. Helen Heffner (dau. of Omer L.) b. Oct. 9, 1889. Thomes R. Heffner (s. of Omer L.) b. Dec. 3, 1892. Katherine Heffner (sister of Jonas D. Heffner) married John Wagner, Amanda, Ohio Eliza Heffner (sister of Jonas D. Heffner) married Michael Springer, Amanda, O. Infant Heffner, (child of Jonas D. and Sarah-Jane) d. Mch. 11, 1858. John Wagner (s. of Katherine and John Wagner) d. buried Old Evang. Cemetery, Amanda, Ohio.

ADDITIONAL BIBLE RECORDS

THE CHRISTOPHER SHOEMAKER, SR. Family Bible Record
Owner: MRS. MAY GLICK, Jackson Center, Ohio
Shoemaker, Christopher. b. Aug. 26, 1777, Paris, France, came to
America with his parents at the age of five. Married Marie Bar-
barie Keller, b. Apr. 30, 1788, in Holland. Their children:—John
David, b. Apr. 16, 1811, died young, Licking Co. Ohio. Katherine
Shoemaker, b. May 17, 1812, m. John Buchanan, lived in Clinton
Twnp. Ohio. Henry Shoemaker, b. May 21, 1815, m. Jane ? ?,
buried "Old North Graveyard" removed to Green Lawn. Mary
Ann Shoemaker, b, Mch. 21, 1817, m. Earl Buxton, lived Licking
Co. Ohio. Christopher Shoemaker, b. July 30, 1820, m. Sarah
Belknap, lived Columbus, O. Marie Antonette Shoemaker, b. Feb.
20, 1823, died young. Seth Shoemaker, b. Oct. 19, 1824, m. Emma
and Eliza Philbuck (sisters) lived Licking Co. Ohio. Joel Shoemaker, b. July 12, 1829, unmarried. Pauline Antonette Shoemaker, b. July 12, 1829, unmarried.

No Deaths Recorded

THE CHRISTOPHER SHOEMAKER, JR. Family Bible Record.
Owner: MR. CLENDID SHOEMAKER, 303 East 5th St., Dallas, Texas
Shoemaker, Christopher Jr. b. July 30, 1820, d. Mch. 17, 1891, m. on
Apr. 7, 1844 Sarah Ann Belknap, b. Apr. 13, 1825, d. Apr. 27,
1901, Columbus, Ohio. Their children: Elias Fassett, b. Jan. 5,
1845., m. Mary Dumbald. Elmira Ann, b. Apr. 10, 1846, d. July
27, 1911, m. Dr. S. M. Sherman, b. Dec. 23, 1842, d. Dec. 26, 1930.
Mary Rozelle, b. Dec. 9, 1847, d. 1872, unmarried. Dubois Devereaux, b. Feb. 20, 1850, d. Nov. 18, 1923, m. Elizabeth Green.
Seth, b. Oct. 5, 1851, m. Amy Peasley. Franklin Pierce, b. Sept.
15, 1854, m. Ida Nash. Eva Leona, b. Sept. 14, 1856, m. Geo. W.
Williams. William Dalton, b. Sept. 19, 1858, m. Anna Buck.
Charles, b. June 24, 1861, m. Ella Claproth. Stella Marie, b. Dec.
20, 1864, d. Feb. 23, 1884, unmarried. Ruth Ambretta, b. July
29, 1866, d. Apr. 25, 1886, married; no issue.

BIBLE RECORDS
MABEL INNIS FREY

Jacob Swisher—Family Bible Record.
Present owner: Mrs. Jennie Preston, Groveport, Ohio.
Swisher, Jacob, b. July 5, 1803, Knowlton Twp., Sussex County, New
     Jersey, d. Jan. 3, 1894, Groveport, Madison Twp.,
     Franklin Co., Ohio, m. (1) Elizabeth Scothorn, Mch. 4,
     1826; m. (2) Anah Needles, b. April 21, 1811, Franklin
     Co., Ohio, dau. of Philemon and Sarah (Collins)
     Needles.
     Children of Jacob and Anah Swisher
Henry Clay, b. Feb. 8, 1837, d.   m. Dec. 18, 1866.
Jane Nau, dau. of Jacob and Margaret Bradley Nau,
     b. Oct. 10, 1844, d. June 10, 1936.
Philemon, b. Sept. 24, 1838, d. Gallatin, Tenn. Dec. 27, 1862.
John Winterstein, b. March 1, 1840, d. Dec. 19, 1915,
     m. S. Pauline Brobst, (b.—, d. Feb. 25, 1888), Dec. 29, 1869.
Sarah Viana, b. Sept. 27, 1841, d. Nov. 9, 1843.
Irvin Trimble, b. Dec. 13, 1843, d. Mar. 18, 1908.
Jacob Edwin, b. Nov. 7, 1845, d. June, 1932. M. Feb. 11, 1869.
     Ella Whetzel, b.—, d. 1929.
Wilhelmina Rebecca, b. July 23, 1847, d. May 2, 1886,
     m. Dec. 27, 1866, Robert Kile, b. Jan. 20, 1844,
     d. Jan. 14, 1921.
Phebe Maria, b. Jan. 5, 1849, d. April 30, 1876.
Elvina Jane, b. Aug. 18, 1852, m. Jan. 3, 1878, George Preston.

Fredrick Swisher Family Record.
Present Owner: Thomas Dickey, Columbus, Ohio.
     Frederick Swisher was a nephew of Jacob Swisher, the son
          of Jacob's brother, Isaac.
     Fredrick Swisher, b. May 1, 1807, d.—. M. March 8, 1832,
          Lydia Landes, b. Jan. 29, 1811.
     Children of Fredrick and Lydia Swisher
Samuel Landes (Landis) Swisher, b. Dec. 16, 1833, d.—.
     m. Phebe Comb.
Mary, b. May 6, 1838, d. Oct. 5, 1836.
John Lincoln, b. Sept. 12, 1838, d. July 8, 1856.
Phebe Catherine, b. Oct. 22, 1840, d. Dec. 29, 1842.
Adoniram Judson, b. Dec. 17, 1842, d.—. M. Dec. 22,
     1875, Rachel McCullock.
Laura A., b. May 14, 1845, d.—, m. Oct. 14, 1869,
     James McCurdy.
Lewis Aten, b. Aug. 11, 1847.
Arza William, b. Oct. 18, 1849.
Meda E. b. Sept. 16, 1851, d. Dec. 28, 1832, m. Thomas
     Dickey, Sept. 11, 1894.

BIBLE RECORDS
Mabel Innis Frey

Latimer-Sensel Family Record
  Bible owned by John Sensel, Dublin, Ohio.
Stephen Latimer, b. Oct. 22. 1775. d. Feb. 26. 1854. m. Dimmis Burns, b. Sept. 26. 1797, d. Sept. 19. 1871, on Oct. 22. 1817, at Bradford County, Penna.   Nathan Latimer, b. Aug. 17. 1819, d ? ? ? ? m 2nd wife, Amanda Urton, on April 7. 1848 m Emerline Perry, June 25, 1840. Nancy Latimer, b. June 28, 1821. d. ? ? ? ? ? ? m. Thomas Wesley Long, Dec. 21, 1846, Union Co. Ohio. Sally Latimer b. Sept. 21, 1823 d. ? ? ? ? ? m. Julius Richards, Feb. 26, 1846. L. S. Latimer, b. Nov. 10, 1825. d. ? ? ? Thomas S. Latimer, b. Dec. 1, 1827, d. Apr. 4th, 1858. m. Elizabeth Dodge, May 3rd 1855, Union County, Ohio. Matilda J. Latimer, b. Feb. 1, 1830, d. ? ? ? ? David B. Latimer, b. Sept. 12, 1832. d. ? ? ? ? ?. George W. Latimer b. Feb. 22, 1835, d. ? ? ? m. Nancy ——, b. Sept. 15, 1863. Lydia B. Latimer, b. Aug. 9, 1837 d. Dec. 29, 1927, aged 90 years, m. John Sensel, b. June 12, 1843, m. Nov. 13, 1864, Union Co., Ohio. L. W. Brown, b. Aug. 18, 1846 (Wiley Brown). Harris Latimer, b. June 18, 1841, Stephen Latimer, b. Feb. 24, 1843. William P. Latimer, b. May 7, 1849. Daniel Long, b. June 26, 1849. Allas Latimer, b. Jan. 23, 1833, d. Nov. 9, 1863. Sarah T. G. Latimer (dau. of Thomas) b. Aug. 31, 1858.
Elizabeth Sensel, b. Aug. 24, 1795. d. June 2. 1874, aged 79.   John Sensel, b. Aug. 25. 1796. August 15. 1876, aged 79.   John Sensel, b. June 12. 1843, Fayette Co. Pa.   Lydia Conn, b. Nov. 27. 1864. (niece of Mrs. Sensel and reared by her) d. Sept. 13 1887, aged 23. Stephen F. Latimer married L. I. James, Jan. 1. 1850.   Mary, daughter of John & Lydia Sensel, d. Jan. 23. 1905.

The Jonas Harlow Family Record
  Bible owned by Jonas Harlow, Dublin, Ohio. Present owner, Blanche Rings.
Jonas Harlow, b. Apr. 25. 1801, m. Nancy Harlow, b. Sept. 15. 1800, on Jan. 22. 1824.   Children:—Lafayette Harlow, b. Apr. 5. 1825, m. Nancy, on Nov. 2. 1845.   Mary Jain Harlow b. July 10. 1827. m Clark Coffman, Sept. 3. 1846.   Ann Eliza, b. May 1. 1829, m. Thomas Eberly Jan. 20. 1857.   George W. Harlow, b. Mch. 18. 1831, m. Mary Martin, Jan. 26. 1860.   Marthaett Harlow, Aug. 25. 1833, m. Francis Riley, Dec. 24. 1856.   William Harlow, b. Dec. 28. 1836, m Fany Persinger, July 16. 1865. Grandchildren: Lafayett's 1st child, named Jonas, b. Dec. 25, 1845. William, b. July 28, 1848. Louisa, b. Sept. 7, 1852. Frank-

lin A., son of Eliza & Frank Hudson, b. June 14, 1827. Henrietta B. Webster, dau of Joshua & Catherine Webster, b. July 5. 1827, m. Nov. 1. 1848.

The following deaths copied as written in this Bible:—
Mother Hutchinson, d. June 8. 1853, aged 78 yrs, 1. mo. 10. da. Henrietta Webster, d. Jan. 21, 1868, aged 40 yrs, no children. My father d. Dec. 13. 1836, at Vincennes, Ind. My Mother d. Mch. 22. St. Louis, Mo. Brother Jeremiah Harlow, d. in the city of New York. Brother Guy Harlow, d. in Texas, Apr. 7. 1841. Brother Wm. Harlow, d. in Louisville Kentucky, Benjamin Harlow, d. in St. Louis, Aug. 21. 1848. Sister Susan Harlow d ? ? ?. Brother Samuel's wife d. July 6. 1850, at St. Louis, Mo. First son of Lafayette d. in Covington, Ky. Feb. 16, 1855.

WILLIS & ANNA M. LOYD

Bible presented by the parents, I. C. & L. C. Franks.
Present owner, unknown.
Willis H Loyd, b. Oct. 14. 1858, Dresden, Ohio. m. Anna M. Franks, b. Feb. 9. 1865, m, at Zanesville, O. Dec. 24. 1885, in presence of Clara B. Franks & Alpheus Loyd, with parents by C. W. Bostwick. The following Birth Records are registered:
Isaac C. Franks, b. May 11. 1840. Lucy C. Franks, b. Feb. 13. 1843. Alice M. Franks, b. July 18, 1863. Anna M. Franks, b. Feb. 9. 1865. Eddie Z. Franks, b. Aug. 26. 1867. Clara B. Franks, b. May 9. 1871. Myrta A. Franks, b. July 12. 1874. Foster C. Franks, b. Apr. 18, 1880. Thos. Franks, b. Mch. 18, 1811. Elizabeth Franks, b. Apr. 13. 1815. Hannah, Loyd. b. May 17, 1850. Elinor T. Loyd. b. Nov. 16. 1851. Martha Loyd, b. June 29. 1853. James E. Loyd, b. Feb. 17. 1855. Wilson S. Loyd, b. Oct. 14. 1858. Willis H. Loyd, b Oct. 14, 1858. Alpha Loyd, b. Jan. 4. 1860. Pheby Loyd, b. June 24. 1862. Lemert B. Loyd, b Mch. 14. 1867. Benjamin Z. Norris, b. Apr. 17. 1867. Martha J. Norris, b. Jan. 31. 1818. Benson Loyd, b. Jan. 11, 1818. Jemima Loyd, b. Mch. 29. 1830.
This data, was followed by these death records:
Isaac C. Franks, d. 1898, aged 58. Lucy Franks, d ? ? ? ? aged 55. Anna M. Franks, d. 1898 aged 33. Eddie Z. Franks, d. 1898, aged 31. Clara B. Franks, d. 1898, aged 27. Myrta Franks, d. 1898, aged 24. Foster Franks, d. 1898, aged 18. The above records were copied from a Bible, in the Columbus Book Exchange, 1932.

THE JOHN EBERLY FAMILY RECORD

Bible owned today by Mr. Chas. Eberly, Dublin, Ohio.
John Eberly, b. Nov. 19. 1799, d. Aug. 6. 1864. m. Hannah Shipman, b. Oct. 1. 1811, d. Nov. 17. 1888, on June 2. 1833. Henry Thomas Eberly, b. Mch. 16, 1834. m. Ann E. Harlow Jan. 20, 1851. Mary C. Eberly, b. Oct. 1835. d. Feb. 24. 1866. m. 1st Benjamin H. Swearingen, d May 23, 1863, on Dec. 28. 1858. 2nd. Howard D. John, Dec. 4. 1864. David S. Eberly, b. Aug. 16. 1837 d. Mch. 31. 1874. m. Eliza J. Atcheson, on Dec. 2. 1860. Jacob M. Eberly, b. June 19, 1840, d. Oct. 6, 1841. John T. Eberly, b. Nov. 30 ,1842, d. Dec. 26, 1914. m. Caroline Brelsford on May 11, 1869. Myra Swearinger, b. June 23. 1862. Mary A. Eberly, b. May 29. 1864. Earl B. Eberly, b. Jan. 5. 1870. Clay E. Eberly, b. July 25. 1871.

The Chas. Eberly Family Record.

Bible owned by Mr. Chas. Eberly, Dublin, Ohio

Henry Thomas Eberly, b. Mch. 16. 1834. d. May 19. 1908. m. Anna E Harlow, b. May 1. 1829 d. Apr. 12. 1899, on Jan. 20. 1857. Chas. Eberly, b. July 8 1857, m Anna Corbin, on Nov. 16. 1880. Myra C. Eberly, b. July 28, 1859, d. Dec. 25, 1860. Mary C. Eberly, b. Oct. 31. 1861, d. Sept. 23. 1863. Grant E. Eberly, b. July 24, 1863, d. Nov. 27, 1902, m. Jennie Smith, on Oct. 18, 1890. Fayette H. Eberly, b. June 11. 1866. Milo F. Eberly, b. June 1. 1881, Ely T. Eberly, b. Sept. 21. 1883. Beulah Eberly, b. July 10. 1891. The following deaths are recorded. Nancy Harlow, d. Jan. 12. 1884, aged 84. Jonas Harlow, d. Aug. 23. 1892, aged 91. John Eberly, d. Aug. 6. 1864, aged 66. Hannah Eberly, d. Nov. 17. 1888, aged 77.

The Geo. W. Corbin Family Record

Present owner of the Bible, Chas. Eberly, Dublin, Ohio.

Geo. W. Corbin, b. Feb. 12, 1827, d. Mch. 23, 1878. m. Margaret Bishop, b. Sept. 20, 1830. d. Sept. 25, 1877 on Sept. 3, 1849. Nathan Corbin, b. Aug. 1, 1850, d. June 9, 1882, m. Josie Evans, on Aug. 10. 1878. John Iden Corbin, b. Nov. 14. 1854. d. Aug. 29. 1913. m. Dillie M. Thomas, on March 26. 1879. Chas. Wm. Corbin, b. Nov. 5. 1859. d. Aug. 24. 1881. Matilda Dilla Corbin, b. Nov. 26. 1865. Elizabeth Matilda Corbin, b. Nov. 26. 1865, d. Mch. 8, 1881. Josie Corbin, b. Nov. 19, 1858. John Leasure and Sarah Bishop m. Sept. 26, 1854. William T. Corbin, son of John P. Corbin, d. Feb. 18, 1869, aged 48 yrs., 10 mo., 2 das.

BIBLE RECORDS
MABEL INNIS FREY

NAME: DOBBINS, WILLIAM N., Family Bible.

PRESENT OWNER: Guy L. Dobbins, Portsmouth, O.

William N. Dobbins, b. Nov. 25, 1815, Bedford Co. Va., d. Nov. 9, 1896, Jackson Co., O. m. July 15, 1841 Lawrence Co., O. Irena Willis (b. Jan. 31, 1826, Ohio Furnace, Lawrence Co., O. d. June 11, 1900). Their children were: Rebecca, b. Oct. 8, 1842, Sophia, b. Oct. 7, 1844, John H., b. Mar. 23, 1847 Andrew b. Aug. 16, 1849, Elizabeth F. b. Jan. 29, 1852, William L., b. Jan. 17, 1854, Matilda, b. Nov. 28, 1856, Thomas G., b. July 18, 1859, Nancy Susan, b. Feb. 10, 1860, James Forsythe, b. May 3, 1861.

MARRIAGES: Elizabeth and William Curby, Oct. 8, 1867, Rebecca and Henry Simmers, Mar. 10, 1870, Andrew and Nancy Bridgeman, July 3, 1870, Sophia and Andrew Kyer, Sept. 3, 1870, John and Louisa Hale, May 16, 1871, William L. and Elizabeth Ward, June 12, 1875, Thomas G. and Cassy Cutter, Dec. 25, 1878, Matilda and Hamilton Booth, Aug. 11, 1879, James and Lida (Eliza Amanda) Jackson, Feb. 21, 1885. William Kyer, only ch. of Sophia, m. Mar. 29, 1898, Matilda Lewis.

BIRTHS: Calla Simmers, b. Dec. 25, 1866, Felia Curby, b. Aug. 15, 1870, Thomas W. Curby, b. Dec. 19, 1871, Luella Curby, b. Feb. 27, 1873, William A. Kyer, b. Aug. 25, 1872, Charlotte D. Boothe, b. Nov. 20, 1877, Charles Boothe, b. Mar. 21, 1879, Calla Boothe, b. Mar. 29, 1881, Thomas Boothe, b. Nov. 16, 1883.   DOBBINS: Flora, b. Apr. 8, 1871, (d. of Andrew), William Melvin, b. Feb. 16, 1872, (s. of John), John William, b. Aug. 31, 1872 (s. of Andrew), Ida, b. Sept. 24, 1874 (d. of Andrew), Luella B., b. Oct. 2, 1875, (d. of William L.), Irena, b. Mar. 25, 1877 (d. of Andrew), William T., b. June 6, 1879 (s. of Thomas G.), Ora Benson, b. Oct. 16, 1885, (s. of James), Ernest, b. Oct. 14, 1880 (s. of William L.), Grace C., b. Feb. 12, 1887 (s. of William L.).

NAME: BENJAMIN, BENONIA, Family Bible.

PRESENT OWNERS: Benjamin family, 1825 Harrisburg Pike, Briggsdale, O.

Printed 1790, original owner of Fairfield Co., O.

Washington Mingomery Benjamin, b. May 24, 1809, Margaret, wife of Washington M., b. Jan. 9, 1809. Martin Mingomery, their son, b. Oct. 20, 1833. (His book, Dec. 29, 1899)
Washington Mingomery Benjamin, son of Benonia Benjamin (b. Apr. 11, 1772) and Anna Benjamin (b. Apr. 3, 1774).

NAME: BENJAMIN, MARTIN MINGOMERY, Family Bible.

PRESENT OWNERS: BENJAMIN family (above).

Margaret E., b. Sept. 17, 1856, Sarah J., b. Nov. 28, 1857, J. J., b. Feb. 3,1860, Hiram W., b. Apr. 5, 1862, William J., b. Mar. 17, 1864, Ida Jenny, b. June 7, 1866, Harry and Hattie, b. May 27, 1869, Charles L., b. Feb. 27, 1872, Martha Clarissa, b. Dec. 5, 1875. Children of M. M. (b. Oct. 20, 1833, d. Dec. 20, 1921) and Nancy H. Benjamin (b. July 15, 1834, d. June 21, 1889).

Bro. John B., d. Sept. 27, 1918, age 83 y. 1 mo. 12 d. Father, Washington Mingomery Benjamin, d. June 15, 1885. Mother, Margaret Benjamin, d. June 21, 1899. Hattie, d. June 15, 1886, Sarah Jane, d. June 8, 1933, Margaret Elizabeth, d. Mar. 19, 1933, Jennie, d. Feb. 27, 1937, James W., d. July 28, 1937.

Wilbur Watkins, b. July 26, 1887, Harry Martin Watkins, b. Apr. 4, 1889, Audrey Watkins, b. Feb. 17, 1896, Ethel Watkins, b. Apr. 20, 1898, Elsie Bell, b. Nov. 21, 1882, Charlie Bell, b. Oct. 23, 1885, Gerald Eugene Bell, b. Oct. 8, 1907, Marene Bell, b. May 28, 1910 Francis C. Bell, b. June 16, 1914, Don Watkins, b. July 26, 1914, Shade Watkins, b. Mar. 12, 1918, Melva E. Benjamin, b. Sept. 5, 1909, Claude C. Benjamin, b. May 10, 1913, Helen Florence Benjamin, b. Mar. 3, 1921, Mattie A. Benjamin, (wife of Chas.—State of Md.), b. Dec. 22, 1885, Layton Bell, b. June 16, 1914, Vera Bell, b. Aug. 24, 1916, Cathalene Watkins, b. June 14, 1916. Melva Benjamin m. Howard Reber, Karon Irene Reber, b. June 2, 1937. Martha C. Benjamin m. Dec. 6, 1894, Thomas J. Woodrow, (he d. Dec. 7, 1929). Harry M. Watkins m. May 23, 1916, Jessie E. Cannon.

NAME: PARKS, JAMES H., Family Bible.

PRESENT OWNERS: Myrtle Parks, Route 1, South Webster, O.

James H., b. July 21, 1841, Mary A. Neary, b. Nov. 28, 1846, Susan, b. Oct. 25, 1869, Frances L., b. Mar. 4, 1871, Edward, b. Mar. 18, 1873, Robert, b. Sept. 20, 1874, Louisa, b. Mar. 16, 1876, Sarah, b. Jan. 31, 1878, Mertie Bell, b. Mar. 8, 1880, Mathew, b. Nov. 17, 1882, Floyd Earl, b. Aug. 20, 1886.

James H. m. Jan. 21, 1869, Mary A. Neary. Susan m. July 21, 1895, James W. Parks. Frances L., m. Sept. 7, 1898, Jonathan Boyer. Sarah P., m. Dec. 24, 1898, Alva A. Lair. Edward, m. Sept. 10, 1902, Nora Humphrey. Louisa, m. Aug. 24, 1906, Walter C. Rice. Robert. m. Mar. 18, 1909, Matilda Altman. Floyd E., m. Dec. 19, 1912, Mertle Finney.

Robert Parks, father, d. May 19, 1882, age 76 y. 10 mo. 17 da. Susann, mother, d. Apr. 15, 1873, age 67 y. 9 mo. 22 da. Mathew, d. Nov. 27, 1882. James H., d. June 28, 1917. Mary Ann, d. June 28, 1922.

BIBLE RECORDS

WALTER E. OSBORNE

WILLIAM STEWART, Original owner.
PROPERTY OF Jay Trowbridge & Co., Columbus, Ohio.
PRINTED BY John Edwin Potter, Philadelphia, Pa.

FAMILY RECORD

Stewart, Sybilla Jane, b. April 27, 1867, at St. Louis, Mo; d. there
July 27, 1867. William James, b. August 31, 1868 at St. Louis,
Mo. Oliver, b. July 15, 1872 at Little Rock, Ark. Robert M. b.
June 19, 1883, at Bellville, Ill. William James, Sr., b. June 19,
1840, Belfest, County Down, Ireland; d. July 14, 1808—at 10 P. M.
aged 68 years, 25 days, at Chicago, Ill. Caroline Miller, b. September 27, 1845, at St. Louis, Mo., d. June 5, 1915, at 12 P. M.
aged 69 years, at Chicago, Ill.

MARRIAGE CERTIFICATE

William Stewart married Carrie Miller, September 16, 1863.

DEATHS

Nancy Campbell, August 30.
Edward King, d. Aug. 30, 1866, of cholera, at St. Louis, Mo.

JAMES HIBBEN, Uniontown, Pa., and Jamestown, Ohio.
PROPERTY OF Mrs. G. A. Robinson, Washington Court House, Ohio.
EDITION BY Rutter, Gaylord & Company.

FAMILY RECORD

James Hibben, son of Thomas and Mary E. Hibben, b. March 23, 1795;
d. August 23, 1836. Ann Watson Allison, dau. of James and Elizabeth Hibben, b. Dec. 27, 1800. Mary Jane Hibben, * dau. of James
and Ann Hibben, b. Oct. 4, 1821; d. Feb. 8, 1903. James Allen
Hibben, b. June 15, 1823. William Wallis Hibben, son of James
and Ann Hibben, b. April 17, 1825. Ann Elizabeth Hibben, dau. of
James and Ann Hibben, b. July 24, 1827; d. April 20, 1846.
Thomas Samuel Hibben, son of James and Ann Hibben, b. August
22, 1832; d. May 28, 1836. Alexander Selkirk Ballard I, husband
of M. J. H. Ballard*, d. Sept. 8, 1864.

HENRY JONES, Harrison, Meigs, and Pike Counties, Ohio.
PROPERTY OF Arden Roberts, Waverly, Ohio.

FAMILY RECORD

Henry Jones, son of Jacob and Sarah (Kirby) Jones, b. 4/8/1812—
Maryland; d. 5/23/1888; m. Nov. 16, 1834, Rebecca Ann Huston.
Rebecca Ann (Huston) Jones, dau. of James and Delila (Purdue)
Huston, b. 7/21/1814; d. 2/18/1897.

CHILDREN:

Lydia Ann, b. 1/21/1836; d. 4/10/1842.
Absolom, b. 11/27/1837; d. 9/6/1861.
Delila, b. 10/8/1839; d. 2/3/1882.
William Henry, b. 9/22/1841; d. 7/17/1880.
Sarah Jane, b. 9/19/1847; d. 9/23/17.
Rebecca Ann, b. 3/19/1849; d. 12/14/1878.
Amanda Melvina, b. 5/2/1850; d. 12/25/1933;
m. * (below)
Emmeline, b. 5/27/1852; d. 7/31/1852.
Tabitha Ophelia, b. 5/8/1854; d. 1/14/1880.
Catherine, b. 10/18/1855; d. 3/14/1920.

James Huston, b. 1788; m. 1813, Delila Purdue; d. 8/25/1875, ag. 87 y. Delila Purdue Huston, b. 1796; d. 8/4/1845, ag. 49 y. William Stanford Roberts, b. 8/27/1849; d. 7/6/1921; married Amanda Melvina Jones *

CHILDREN:

Katie Amanda, b. 8/15/1875; Leroy Van Roberts, b. 2/28/1878; Maud Henry Roberts, b. 11/2/1881; Claudia Gertrude Roberts, b. 1/18/1884; Vivian Winifred Roberts, b. 8/4/1890; d. 4/17/1892.

DEATHS

Jacob Jones, d. 7/30/1859; Sarah Jones, d. 9/8/1859.
Perry Jones, d. 10/8/1837; Susannah Jones, d. 1/1/1839.
Absolom Jones, d. 5/8/1840; Nancy Smith Jones, d. 9/26/1872.
Israel Jones, d. 12/20/1883; Sarah Ann Devault, d. 6/ /1888.
Alexander Huston, d. 8/7/1845.

BIBLE RECORDS

WALTER E. OSBORNE

JAMES HUTSON, Original Owner.
John A. Forgrave, Helena, Ohio, present owner.
Lucile L. Hutson, Sandusky, Ohio. Has a certified copy of these records under date of Aug. 31st, 1936.
Hutson, James, b. Feb. 13th, 1807. Elizabeth Hutson, Wife, b. Feb. 4th, 1807.
Jemima Ann Hutson, b. Dec. 5th, 1829. John Hutson, b. Jan. 22nd, 1832.
Peter Hutson, b. Aug. 26th, 1834. Vincent Hutson, b. June 8th, 1837.
William Marcus Hutson, b. Feb. 20th, 1840. Nathaniel Washington Hutson, b. Dec. 28th, 1842. James Scott Hutson, b. Sept. 23rd, 1843.

MARRIAGES

James Hutson, married Elizabeth Stults, Aug. 28th, 1828.

DEATHS

William Marcus Hutson, d. Oct. 10th. 1854. Vincent Hutson, d. Mar. 10th, 1858. Elizabeth Hutson, d. July 23rd, 1877. Washington Hutson, d. March 20th, 1879. James Hutson, d. June 18th, 1883.

JOHN KEYS SR. Fall Creek, Highland Co. Ohio. Original Owner.
Mrs. James E. Roades, 1141 Highland St., Columbus, Ohio. Present Owner.
Printed by Jesper Harding, Philadelphia, Pa. 1845.
KEYS, John b. Sept. 19th, 1777. Mary Smiley Keys, Wf. b. Sept. 19th. 1787. Samuel Keys, b. Dec. 1st. 1810. James Keys, b. Dec. 3rd. 1812. Alexander Keys, b. Mar. 8th, 1814. Susan S. Keys, b. Mar. 18th. 1816. John Keys Jr. b. Sept. 21st. 1818. William Keys, b. Oct. 7th. 1820. Calvin L. Keys and Andrew Reid Keys. (Twins) b. Aug. 10th. 1823. Hugh L. Keys, b. Nov. 8th. 1826. Joseph Keys, b. Aug. 18th. 1830.

MARRIAGES

John Keys, Mary Smiley, 1810.
Samuel Keys, Susan S. Keys, 1843.
William, Calvin Luther, Andrew Reid. Hugh, not married.

DEATHS

Calvin L., d. Jan. 17th. 1850. John Keys Sr. Feb. 7th. 1855. Hugh L., d. Mar. 8th. 1864. (Killed Civil War). Mary Keys, d. Jan. 13th. 1869. Susan Keys, d. Nov. 5th. 1871. James and Alexander both died young.

* * * * *

FILLER, JOSEPH, Dublin, Ohio. Original Owner.
Howard Wilson, Worthington, Ohio. Present Owner.
Joseph Filler, b. Aug. 13th. 1801. Lydia Crum, Wf. b. Sept. 30th. 1806. Hanna Reed, b. Oct. 1814. William Henry Filler, b. June 21st, 1830. Margaret Ann Filler, b. May 6th, 1833. Frederick Elijah Filler, Dec. 19th. 1834. Hanna Filler, b. Oct. 19th. 1819.

MARRIAGES

Joseph Filler and Lydia Crum Aug. 27th. 1829.
Joseph Filler and Hanna Reed, May 14th. 1843.
Joseph Wilson and Margaret A. Filler, 1857.
Frederick E. Filler and Susan McKitrick, Aug. 6th. 1857.

DEATHS

Margaret Ann Wilson, d. Oct. 4th. 1866. Lydia Crum Filler, Aug. 15th. 1836. Elizabeth Reed, wf. of Samuel Reed, d. Dec. 4th. 1833. Samuel Reed, d. Jan. 11th. 1835. William Henry Filler, d. Feb. 11th. 1832. Joseph Filler, d. Sept. 12th. 1882. Hanna Filler, d. Sept. 2nd. 1899.

SEELEY FAMILY, Westwood Ave., Grandview, Original Owners.
Mrs. Mark Hodson, Present Owner.
Printed and copywrited by M. Carey, Philadelphia, Pa., 1813.
John Seeley, b. July 10th. 1743. Mary Seeley, Wf. b. Feb. 23rd. 1740. James Seeley, b. Oct. 2nd. 1761. John Seeley, b. Apr. 5th. 1764. Mary Seeley, b. Oct. 2nd, 1766. Eliphalet Seeley, b. Apr. 19th. 1769. Thadeus Seeley, b. Nov. 4th. 1772. Ebenezer Seeley, b. June 21st. 1777. Elizabeth Seeley, b. Dec. 8th. 1779. Abigail Seeley, b. Mar. 20th. 1783.

MARRIAGES

Eleophus Seeley and Mary, Oct. 3rd. 1852.
Spencer P. Seeley and Lizzie Gilham, 1860.
Elizann Seeley, Sept. 25th. 1812.
F. B. Seeley, Apr. 29th. 1826.
Laura Seeley, Apr. 24th. 1827.
John Seeley, 1828.
Eugene Seeley, 1830.
Theddus Seeley, 1833.
Theana Seeley, 1830.

DEATHS

Eliphlet Seeley, May 15th. 1793.
"Mother," Oct. 27th. 1795.
"Father," Nov. 24th. 1795.
Thadeus, Dec. 8th. 1825.

BIBLE RECORDS

WALTER E. OSBORNE

DAWSON BIBLE RECORD

Thomas Dawson, b. July 11th. 1770. Lucretia Dawson, b. Mar. 26th. 1766.

Lovicy Gary, b. Dec 31st. 17—. Lucretia, b. June 1st. 1804. John, b. June 12th. 1793. Hannah, b. June 19th. 1795. Daniel, b. Feb. 8th. 1797. Ralph b. July 10th. 1798. Levi, b. July 21st. 1801. Mary. b. Nov. 20th. 1802. Rebeccah, b. Oct. 26th. 1807. Martha, b. Oct. 2nd. 1809. Janet, b. Apr. 4th. 1735. Hannah, b. Sept. 13th. 1818. James, b. Oct. 8th. 1821. Joseph, b. March 27th. 1824. Thomas, b. Dec 5th. 1831. Rachel, b. May 21st. 1826. Margaret, b. Sept. 25th. 1833. Lucretia, b. Mar. 20th. 1837.

MARRIAGES

Thomas Dawson and Lucretia Wolverton, m. Oct. 7th. 1792.
Thomas Dawson and Lovicy Gary, m. Sept. 19th. 1839.
Thomas Dawson and Lucretia Hatfield, m. Apr. 13th. 1843.
John Dawson and Janet ——— m. Oct. 8th. 1818.
Mary Dawson and William Pyrs, m. Dec. 9th. 1823.
Rebecca Dawson and John Miligan, m. Mar. 9th. 1825.
Hanna Dawson and Charles Dockaty, m. May 30th. 1833.
Rachel Dawson and William Donley, m. July 9th. 1829.

DEATHS

Levi Dawson, d. Dec. 4th. 1818. Lucretia Dawson, d. Dec. 22nd. 1839. Lovicy Dawson, d. Mar. 27th. 1841. Thomas Dawson, d. July 10th. 1845. Rachel Dawson, d. Dec. 24th. 1822. Joseph Dawson, d. Jan. 24th. 1849. Jenett, wf. of John, d. Mar. 14th. 1869. John Dawson, d. Oct. 5th. 1874. Lucretia Poling, d. Dec. 11th. 1889. James Dawson, d. Dec. 20th. 1891.

DAVIS BIBLE RECORD

JOSEPH DAVIS, Dublin, Ohio. Original Owner.
Mr. A. H. Sells, Dublin, Ohio. Present Owner.
Sarah Davis, b. Oct. 1784. William Davis, b. 1786. John Davis Jr., b. 1788. Nancy Davis, b. 1790. Samuel Davis, b. 1798. Joshua Davis, b. 1796. Elizabeth Davis, no date. Joseph Davis, b. 1802.
Ann Simpson Davis, Mother, b. 1764.
John Davis, Father, b. 1760.

MARRIAGES

John Davis and Ann Simpson m. 1783. Bucks Co., Pa.
Sarah Davis and Philip Warfield, m. Apr. 29th. 1807.
William Davis and Mary Sullivan, m. Feb. 11th. 1809.
John Davis and Amy Hart, m. Mar. 23rd. 1818.
Nancy Davis and Bazil Brown, m. Mar. 19th. 1807.
Samuel Davis and Matilda Sells, m. June 16th. 1825.
Joshua Davis and Edith DeFord, m. March, 1817.
Joseph Davis and Edith DeFord, m. 1827.
Elizabeth Davis, m. 1st. James Coleman, 2nd. Penwell, 3rd. Downs.

DEATHS

John Davis, d. 1832. John and Ann Simpson Davis had Revolutionary War record.

Note:—Some one (a man) brought this Bible to the State Library for Miss Boardman to see and being there, I copied these records but as it was prior to the time the Ohio Genealogical Quarterly started publishing these records, I did not get the rest of the information to fill in the blank. The Bible belonged to the Dawson Family of Marysville, O.—Blanche T. Rings.

BIBLE RECORDS

GREENE FAMILY BIBLE RECORD.

John Lynde Greene Sr. Original owner.

Lucile L. Hutson, Sandusky, Ohio. Present owner.

BIRTHS

Daniel C. Greene, Sept. 14th, 1829. Charles H. Greene, July 21st, 1831. Frances H. Greene, June 10th, 1834. Louise S. Greene, Jan. 15th, 1836. John Lynde Greene Jr., July 7th, 1837. Geo. S. Greene, Jan. 29th, 1839. James D. Greene, May 29th, 1846. Josephine D. Mead, June 30th, 1842. Ducomb Greene, Nov. 8th, 1848. Franklin L. Greene, Aug. 9th, 1850. Marshall K. Greene, May 17th, 1853. Maggie Rose Greene, Apr. 30, 1856. Julie E. Hutson, Sept. 12th, 1853. Fannie J. Hutson, Aug. 25th, 1855. Charles V. Hutson, May 10th, 1857. William W. Hutson, Feb. 17th, 1870.

MARRIAGES

Louise Stone Greene and John Hutson, Dec. 23rd, 1852.

John L. Greene Sr. and Julia Laura Castle July 16th, 1828.

DEATHS

Julia E. Hutson, Sept. 1853. William W. Hutson, Sept. 26th, 1896. John Hutson, July 8th, 1901. Louise G. Hutson, May 25th, 1903. Chas. V. Hutson, July 15th, 1918. Mary McVey Hutson, Dec. 6th, 1929.

Fannie Hutson McVey, Apr. 24th, 1932.

EVANS FAMILY BIBLE RECORD

George W. Evans, original owner.

Mrs. Samuel H. Davis, present owner.

BIRTHS

George W. Evans, Apr. 8th, 1805. Nancy R. Evans, Sept. 26th, 1806. Geo. Evans, Sept. 26th, 1829. Jessie L. Evans, Nov. 17th, 1831. Henry E. Evans, Feb. 8th, 1834. John E. Evans, Nov. 9th, 1835. Mary Andrews Evans, Nov. 17th, 1837. Charles Evans, Apr. 25th, 1841. Eli Pinney Evans, June 10th, 1842. Lydia Ann Evans, Mar. 29th, 1845. Bell Evans, June 24th, 1841. Mary Andrews, Sept. 26th, 1770.

MARRIAGES

Geo. W. Evans and Nancy Ricketts, Oct. 23rd. 1828.

DEATHS

Chas. Evans, May 1st, 1831. Henry E. Evans, March 24th, 1849. Jessie L. Evans, Jan. 6th, 1858. Geo. W. Evans, Nov. 29th, 1862. Mary C. Evans, July 8th, 1872.

WARD FAMILY BIBLE RECORD

Elias Ward, original owner.

Mrs. Catharine Sharp, Bexley, Ohio, present owner.

BIRTHS

Daniel Ward, July 4th, 1763. Abner Ward, May 4th, 1765. Jemima Ward, Oct. 31st, 1767.

MARRIAGES

Elias Ward and Mary Pierson, Dec. 23rd, 1758.

DEATHS

Jemima Ward, Aug. 11th, 1768. Elias Ward, Nov. 19th, 1790. Daniel Ward, Jan. 29th, 1792. Abner Ward, Dec. 23rd, 1795. Mary Ward, Jan. 5th, 1809.

BEAN FAMILY BIBLE RECORD

Thomas Bean, original owner.

Mrs. Frank L. Bellows, Athens, Ohio, present owner.

BIRTHS

Thomas Bean, Nov. 15th, 1793. Sarah Hill, Sept. 23rd, 1796. Elisha M., Apr. 28th, 1820. William M. Nov. 9th, 1821. Harriett, June 13th, 1823. Ester A. Oct. 11th, 1825. Elizabeth, Mar. 24th, 1828. Diana, Jan. 1831. Joseph M., Nov. 20th, 1832. Mary E., Jan. 3rd, 1835. Samuel, Dec. 13th, 1837.

CHILDREN OF ADAM CLARK MCPHERSON AND MARY E. BEAN

Eva Edell, Dec. 22nd, 1858. William F., June 24th, 1862. Elizabeth A. Aug. 4th, 1864. Charles L., Aug. 3rd, 1866. Joseph A., Sept. 26th, 1869. Addeline M., Nov. 3rd, 1872. George E., July 29th, 1874. Cora A. Feb. 26th, 1877.

CHILDREN OF ADAM CLARK MCPHERSON AND CAROLINE SIDMAN

Odessa M., Aug. 19th, 1884. Arthur E., May 1st, 1887.

MARRIAGES

Adam Clark McPherson and Mrs. C. C. Dill (Caroline Sidman) July 3rd, 1883.

DEATHS

William M. Bean, July 12th, 1822. Mary E. Bean McPherson, July 3rd, 1879. Adeline May McPherson, Jan. 14th, 1873. Eva Edell McPherson Knowlton, May 10th, 1915. Elizabeth Ann Beckley, Oct. 14th, 1887. Adam Clark McPherson, Apr. 9th, 1909.

YOUNG FAMILY BIBLE RECORD

William C. Young, Newark, Ohio, original owner.

Mrs. E. Galloway, Newark, Ohio, present owner.

BIRTHS

William C. Young, June 26th, 1791. Rachel Kauffman Young, Jan. 16th, 1791. Arbelia Young, Jan. 6th, 1819. Rebecca Ann Fulton, Dec. 5th, 1819. David Bell, Jan. 20th, 1822. Sarah Narcisis, July 31st, 1824. Louisa Dorthy, Jan. 30th, 1827. Mary Jane, June 6th, 1824. John Willis, Nov. 8th, 1830. William Benjamine, Nov. 8th, 1830. Rachel Elizabeth Elenor, Mar. 23rd, 1834.

MARRIAGES

William C. Young and Rachel Kauffman, Mar. 18th, 1817.
Arbelia Young, and Abraham Brubaker, Apr. 7th, 1836.
Rebecca Ann Young and John Fulton, Jan. 9th, 1840.
David Bell Young and Angeline Coffman, Jan. 20th, 1846.
Sarah Narcisis Young and John Kinney, Sept. 18th, 1845.
Mary Jane Young and Bruce Moody, Nov. 3rd, 1848.
Rachel E. E. Young and Daniell Kinney, Jan. 1st, 1852.
William B. Young and Louise Morgan, Mar. 22nd, 1855.
Willis J. Young and Mary E. McClelland, Jan. 4th, 1859.

DEATHS

William C. Young, Apr. 12th, 1838. Rachel C. Young, Sept. 19th, 1877. Louisa Dortha, Aug. 23rd, 1827. Dorthea Kauffman, Feb. 28th, 1833. Mary Jane Moody, Apr. 16th, 1851. William B. Young, Apr. 4th, 1866. David B. Young, Oct. 18th, 1871. Sarah Narcisis Young, Apr. 28th, 1911.

BIBLE RECORDS

WALTER E. OSBORNE

TAYLOR FAMILY BIBLE RECORD
Jane Irwin Taylor, Bainbridge, Ohio, original owner.
Van der Veer Taylor, Xenia, Ohio, present owner.

BIRTHS

Joseph Taylor, Sept. 27th, 1770. Jane Irwin, Apr. 25th, 1779. William Taylor, June 11th, 1798. Nancy Taylor, April 3rd, 1800. Jared Taylor, May 22nd, 1802. Price Taylor, July 9th, 1804. Joseph Taylor, Sept. 23rd, 1806. James Taylor, March 25th, 1809. Edward Taylor, Feb. 17th, 1811. Irwin Taylor, July 15th, 1813. Jane Emily Taylor, Dec. 27th, 1815.

MARRIAGES

Joseph Taylor and Jane Irwin, Aug. 8th, 1797.
Price Taylor and Polly Swan, Mar. 11th, 1824.
William I. Taylor and Elizabeth Finch, June 3rd, 1824.
Jared Taylor and Nancy Peppel, May 20th, 1827.
Nancy Taylor and Abraham Peppel, May 21st, 1827.
Edward Taylor and Penelope Virginia Gordon, Nov. 26th, 1833.
Joseph Taylor and Priscilla Bell, Aug. 8th, 1837.
James Taylor and Mariah Ruth Applegate, July 17th, 1838.
Price Taylor and Catharine Smith, Mar. 16th, 1834.
Edward Taylor and Malvina Taylor, Oct. 1st, 1839.
Emily Jane Taylor and Chirstian Platter, Apr. 29th, 1845.

DEATHS

Joseph Taylor, Aug. 25th, 1830. Jane Taylor, Oct. 19th, 1847.
Emily J. Houston, June 14th, 1900. Polly Taylor, Bainbridge, O. No date.
Penelope Taylor, Feb. 28th, 1836. Irwin Taylor, Apr. 4th, 1843.
William I. Taylor, Jan. 28th, 1847. Christian Platter, July 23rd, 1847.

HUNTER FAMILY BIBLE RECORD
William Forrest Hunter Sr., original owner.
Mary E. Hunter, Columbus, Ohio, present owner.

BIRTHS

William F. Hunter, Dec. 10th, 1808. Mary Kincaid Hunter, May 15th, 1812. Mary Ellen Hunter, Dec. 5th, 1831. Richard A. Hunter, Nov. 18th, 1833. Annie Eliz. Hunter, Jan. 18th, 1837. William F. Hunter, May 26th, 1839.

MARRIAGES

William F. Hunter and Mary Kincaid, July 20th, 1830.
Mary Ellen Hunter and Pardon Cooke, Nov. 10th, 1852.
Annie Elizabeth Hunter and William R. Ford, Apr. 26th, 1866.
William F. Hunter and Elizabeth Fitz Randolph, Jan. 1st, 1867.

DEATHS

Richard A. Hunter, Nov. 13th, 1838. Pardon Cooke, died in the military service of the United States, as Surgeon of the 77th O. V. I. Regt. at Durvalls Bluff, Ark. Aug. 30th, 1863.

BIBLE RECORDS

WALTER E. OSBORNE

SCHELL FAMILY RECORD.
Original Owner—Joseph Schnell, North Georgetown, Ohio
Present Owner—Mrs. Ella Clement (D. M.) Alliance, Ohio.
Printed and Copyrighted (no dates available)

Joseph Shell, son of John and Sarah Shell, born in the Year of Our Lord, 1821, April 15, in the State of Pennsylvania; died June 15, 1860, Age 45 yrs. 2 mo.

Annie Mary Shell, dau. of David and Abigail Frifogle, born in the Year of Our Lord, 1820, October 28, in Baltimore County, Maryland, d. Mar. 5, 1894, Age 74 yrs.

Stephen Shell, son of Joseph and Anna Mary Shell, born in the Year of Our Lord, 1846, April 3; d. November 22, 1934, Age 88 yrs.

Malen Shell, son of Joseph and Anna Mary Shell, born in the Year of Our Lord, 1848, June 4; departed this life December, Age 88 yrs.

Elizabeth Anne Shell, dau. of Joseph and Anna Mary Shell, born in the Year of Our Lord, 1849, July 24; d. May 7, 1922, Age 73 yrs. (See Shaffer)

Celesta Shell, dau. of Joseph and Anna Mary Shell, born in the Year of Our Lord, 1851, February 23; d. 1854, Age 2 yrs. 10 mo, 12 das.

Abigail Shell, dau. of Joseph and Anna Mary Shell, born in the Year of Our Lord, October 17, 1852 in Stark County, Ohio.

Rachel Shell, dau. of Joseph and Anna Mary Shell, born in the Year of Our Lord, June 23, 1855; d. November 24, 1861, Age 6 yrs. 5 mos. 1 day.

Perry Shell, son of Joseph and Anna Mary Shell, born in the Year of Our Lord, February 5, 1857; d. May 31, 1934, Age 77 yrs.

Sarah Shell, dau. of Joseph and Anna Mary Shell, born in the Year of Our Lord, January 19, 1859; d. January 8, 1895, Age 36 yrs. (See Liebing).

Ellanora Shell, dau. of Joseph and Anna Mary Shell, born in the Year of Our Lord, May 29, 1863; living 1942.

MARRIAGES

Joseph Shell and Anna Mary Frifogle were married August 22, 1845 in New Lisbon, Ohio, by George G. Gice, Esq.

Stephen Shell and Sarah Knoll were married in June (1854) by the Rev. Cox, at Mount Union, Ohio.

Lizzie Shell and Henry Shaffer were married October 22, 1854 Homeworth, Ohio, by Rev. Feight.

Abbie Shell and Caleb Oyster were married January 12, 1882 at Mount Union, Ohio.

Perry Shell and Ella Ruhl were married September 14, 1887, Rev. J. J. Carmony, at Homeworth, Ohio.

Sarah Shell and William Liebing were married September 14, 1881, Rev. J. J. Carmony, at Homeworth, Ohio.

Ellanora Schell and Daniel M. Clemont were married December 22, 1885, by the Rev. Hoffer at Louisville, Ohio.

DEATHS

Malen, son of Joseph and Anna Mary departed this life December 26th, 1853. Aged 5 yrs., 6 mo., 22 days.
Celesta, 1854, 2 yrs., 10 mo., 12 da.
Rachel, November 24, 1861, 6 yrs. 5 mo., 1 da.
Joseph, June 15, 1860, Age 45 yrs. 2 mo.
Anna Mary (nee Fryfogle) March 5, 1894, 74 yrs.
Sarah Schell Liebing, January 8, 1895, 36 yrs.
Elizabeth Schell Shaffer, May 7, 1922, 73 yrs.
Perry Schell, May 21, 1934, 77 yrs.
Stephen Schell, November 22, 1934, 88 yrs.

BIBLE RECORDS

Walter E. Osborne

LANE FAMILY RECORD.

PRESENT OWNER: Mrs. Irma C. Earle, West Hartford, Conn.

BIRTHS

Children of T. B. Lane and Polly Lane
George, Sept. 27, 1819
Francis and Fraulin, Sept. 24, 1820
Edwin, June 22, 1822
Sarah, June 8, 1824
Nathaniel Batchelder, Aug. 27, 1825

DEATHS

Franklin, Aug. 1, 1821
Edwin, Jany 27, 1876
Polly Coolidge wife of T. B. Lane died Dec 14, 1874
Helen wife of George W. Lane died Oct. 24, 1879

MARRIAGES

Thomas B. Lane, b. Mch. 11, 1788
Sarah Willson, b. May 5, 1786
Thomas B. Lane and Sarah Willson were married March 1, 1808
FAMILY RECORD

BIRTHS

Children of J. B. Lane and Sarah Lane
Agnes, Dec. 15, 1808
Thomas Willson, Oct. 19, 1810
Milton, July 20, 1813
Harriet Newell, September 6, 1814
George, November 4, 1816
Sarah, April 18, 1818

DEATHS

Sarah, wife of T. B. Lane, died Nov. 22, 1818
Agnes, Jany 16, 1815
Milton, Aug. 13, 1813
George, Dec. 5, 1816
Sarah, Nov. 23, 1818
Thomas B. Lane, March 27, 1825

MARRIAGE

Polly Worthen, b. Sept. 6, 1797
Thomas B. Lane and Polly Worthen married May 5, 1819
Copied by Lorena B. Adamson, Columbus, Ohio

447

BLACKWOOD FAMILY BIBLE RECORD

ORIGINAL OWNER: *James Monroe Blackwood*
PRESENT OWNER: James Monroe Blackwood, 2nd, 59 W. Royal Forest
Blvd., Columbus, Ohio.

FAMILY RECORD

BIRTHS

John Chester Blackwood, b. June 29th, 1863
Hattie May Blackwood, b. January 31, 1868
Baptized March 29th, 1868 by Rev. G. Harter
Erdin Eveline Blackwood, b. Nov. 4, 1870
Baptized April 30, 1871 by Rev. Geo. Harter
Frank Walter Blackwood, b. Feb. 27, 1874
Harvey Monroe Blackwood, b. May 18, 1877
Baptized Sept. 2, 1877 by J. Beck
Mable Anna Blackwood, b. January 6, 1885
Baptized Sept. 6, 1885 by Rev. J. Beck
Guy Roland Blackwood, b. 19th March, 1889
Baptized 8th Sept. 1889 by Rev. J. H. Kuhlmann

MARRIAGES

James M. Blackwood, Barbara Whaley joined in wedlock Sept. 2, 1862.
James M. Blackwood, Anna M. E. Zangmeister joined in wedlock,
May 26, 1867.

DEATHS

Barbara Elin Blackwood d. Nov. 2, 1864
Frank Walter Blackwood, d. May 18, 1875
John Chester Blackwood, d. May 2, 1886
James Monroe Blackwood, d. Sept. 6, 1919, 78 yrs. 7 mo. born Feb.
6, 1841.
Anna Elizabeth Blackwood, died Dec. 11, 1921, born June 16, 1850.
Hattie May Barratt, May 23, 1929
Mabel Anna Blackwood, Good Friday, March 25, 1932.
Harvey Monroe Blackwood, d. May 27, 1936.

BIBLE RECORDS

By Walter E. Osborne

WARRICK BIBLE RECORD

Mrs. Edith Warrick Williams, 1449 W. 6th Ave., Columbus, Ohio. Present owner.
John Warrick, Somerton, Belmont Co., Ohio, Original owner.
June 28, 1881
Griffith & Simon, 114 N. 3rd. St., (City missing) Publishers
Stereotype Edition (Large) Calf skin binding. Publish date missing.

BIRTHS

John Warrick, born July 25, 1822
Ann Hooie, born August 15, 1835
Asa Thomas Warrick, son of John and Ann, his wife, born July 30, 1853
Cam T. Warrick, born January 12, 1855
John W. Warrick, born December 7, 1857
Ruth Warrick, born December 19, 1860
Frances Warrick, * born Feb. 15, 1864
Enfield Warrick, born June 4, 1866
Minnie Warrick, born Oct. 11, 1869
* (Note by Mrs. Reigel. This Frances lives in the old home place in Somerton, Ohio)

DEATHS

Minnie Warrick Morehead, died Dec. 5, 1901
Mrs. Annie Warrick, died Feb. 13, 1920
John Warrick, died August 12, 1907

MARRIAGES

John Warrick and Ann Hooie, married August 19, 1852

WARRICK BIBLE RECORD

Mrs. Edith Warrick Williams, 1449 W. 6th Ave., Columbus, Ohio. Present owner.
Cam T. Warrick, Somerton, Belmont Co., Ohio. Original owner.
American Bible Society of New York, Publisher.
Stiff back Morocco binding, Sml., 1887.

MARRIAGES

C. T. Warrick and Sarah Ann Lutes, married September 2, 1886.

BIRTHS

C. T. Warrick, born January 13, 1855.
Annie Warrick, born April 12, 1858.
Clyde Earl Warrick, born November 25, 1887.
Lester B. Warrick, born March 10, 1895.
Howard C. Warrick, born September 7, 1896.
Howard C. Warrick, Jr., born April 10, 1915 at Barnesville, Ohio.

DEATHS

Howard C. Warrick, died November 7, 1914.
C. T. Warrick, died July 1, 1932.
Record copied by Mrs. Mayburt Stephenson Reigel.

BIBLE RECORDS

By Walter E. Osborne

SAMSON FAMILY RECORDS

Bible Records of the Samson Family—In the possession of Miss Mollie Slaughter—Loveland, Colorado.

David Samson, born 1771; died 1832; aged 61 years. Buried at Stockdale, Pike County, Ohio

Sarah (Brouse) Samson, his wife, died 1847—buried at Stockdale, Pike County, Ohio. She came from the town of Bath—Berkeley County, Virginia which is now called Berkeley Springs—Morgan County—West Virginia. The emigration (1802) of ths couple is recorded in "The History of Lower Scioto Valley."

CHILDREN

James born January 28, 1797. Married Margaret Bradford.

Abigail born August 11, 1798. Married Lyttleton Bradford.

Ralph born September 6, 1800. Married Hulda Brown.

David Jr., born October 13, 1802 Pickaway Plains. Married Nancy Bennett.

Samuel born Seputember 5, 1805. Married Jane McDowell.

Lucinda born May 24, 1808. Married Stephen Slaughter.

Sarah born October 30, 1810. Married John Slaughter.

Rev. William Samson born April 21, 1813. Married Eliza Beanchamp.

Elizabeth born June 11, 1815. Married Rev. William Slaughter.

The three Slaughter men were sons of Ezekiel Slaughter, born 1773 in Virginia, and his wife Laetitia (Thompson) Slaughter who emigrated to Ohio in 1813 (land deed recorded at Waver, Pike County, Ohio) from Martinsburg, Berkeley County, Virginia (West).

Lyttleton Bradford, son of Ezra Bradford and Sarah (Curtis) Bradford a record of this family can be found in "History of Scioto County". More information concerning the Brouse family can be found in "History of Scioto County" by Nelson Evans.

Sarah (Brouse) Samson was the daughter of John Andrew Brouse and his wife Elizabeth C. who bought land in 1778—Warm Springs Ridge—Berkeley Co., Virginia where is now the town of Berkeley Springs, Morgan County, West Virginia.

Records found at county seat—Martinsburg—Berkeley County—West Virginia.

This Bible is he property of Ezekiel Slaughter born about 1773 in Virginia. Died before Oct. 21, 1878.

Letitia Thompson Slaughter consort of Ezekiel Slaughter departed this life January 2, 1840 age 63 years.

Their children were born in Martinsburg, West Virginia up to 1812 when they moved to Pike County, Ohio.

BIRTHS

Mary (called Polly) Slaughter was born August 28, 1805; died May 1, 1836.

Turner Slaughter was born December 28, 1807.

John Slaughter was born June 28, 1809; died 1903 at Cheyenne, Wyoming.

Stephen Slaughter was born March 12, 1811.

Anna Slaughter was born March 29, 1814.

William Slaughter was born July 13, 1816.

Elizabeth (called Betsy) Slaughter was born November 13, 1818.

Children of William Slaughter and Elizabeth Samson Slaughter (born June 11, 1815).

James Allen Slaughter was born June 25, 1837.

Ezekiel Birney Slaughter was born May 23, 1839.

Clarinda Slaughter was born March 4, 1841.

Lewis Davis Slaughter was born March 4, 1843.

Sarah Ellen Slaughter was born August 1, 1845.

Rebecca Davis Slaughter was born May 5, 1848.

Sylvia Josephine Slaughter was born April 3, 1851.

Mary Alice Slaughter was born May 17, 1857.

Elizabeth Samson Slaughter the daughter of David Samson and Sarah Brouse. Davis Samson of Mass. died 1832 age 61 years. Buried at Stockdale, Ohio. Sarah Brouse of Warm Springs Virginia died 1847. Buried at Stockdale, Ohio.

MARRIAGES

Turner Slaughter was married to Nancy Miller April 3, 1828.

Judge John Slaughter was married to Sarah Samson August 19, 1829.

Stephen Slaughter was married to Lucinda Samson May 23, 1830.

Anna Slaughter was married to John Martin April 29, 1832.

Eliabeth Slaughter was married to George Martin January 27, 1835.

Mary (Polly) Slaughter was married to John Cochran 1830.

Rev. William Slaughter was married to Elizabeth Samson Sept. 4, 1836.

DEATHS

Ezekiel Birney Slaughter, son of William and Elizabeth Samson Slaughter, died January 1, 1895.

Lewis Davis Slaughter died March 20, 1896.

Clarinda Slaughter Landon died July 6, 1921.

Slyvia Josephine Slaugher, infant daughter of Eliabeth and William Slaughter, died June 28, 1852 age 9 months, 3 weeks and 4 days.

James Allen Slaughter, eldest son of Elizabeth and William Slaughter, died June 5, 1862 age 24 years, 11 months, and 10 days. His decease was at or near Corinth, Mississippi. He died in the hospital of fever. Sweet be his rest in a strange land.

Rev. William Slaughter, husband of Elizabeh Samson Slaughter, died Sept. 13, 1875 age 59 years and 2 months.

Elizabeth Samson Slaughter, widow of Rev. William Slaughter, died December 2, 1894.

Mary Alice Slaughter, daughter of Rev. William and Elizabeth Samson Slaughter, died April 5, 1891.

MARRIAGES

Children of William and Elizabeth Samson Slaughter.
Ezekiel Birney Slaughter and Selina Stenner of Bristol England were married June 7, 1866.

Lewis Davis Slaughter and Laura Smith married.

Clarinda Slaughter and Dr. Chauncey P. Landon married.

Rebecca Davis Slaughter and Dr. Frank H. Houghton married.

Miss Molly Slaughter reports that the records are incomplete as to dates. She has no documentary proof but her own faher, Ezekiel Slaughter, born 1839, lived in the same house with his grandfather, Ezekiel Slaughter born about 1773 and had from his lips many stories of his father, killed in the Revolution. Miss Slaughter believes that the boy mentioned in the will of Ezekiel Slaughter (born 1729) as "my grandson Ezekiel Slaughter" is the very one for whom her father was named. There are many who would be interested in this record so she will continue to make the effort to prove the stories her father told. Ezekiel Slaughter (born 1773) served in the war of 1812.

There are three Slaughters who married three Samson girls. Three sons of Ezekiel Slaughter born 1773 and his wife Latitia Thompson. And three daughters of David Samson of Mass. and his wife Sarah Brouse of Warm Springs, Virginia. The story of this couple who emigrated from Berkeley County, Virginia to Ohio in a covered wagon in 1802 is recorded in "The History of Lower Scioto Valley".

The will of Ezekiel Slaugher born in 1729 can be found in "Tyler's Quarterly Historical and Genealogical Magazine", an article by Mrs. Wirt Johnson Carrington—Vol. 9 (July 1927) Pages 122—133. Also Lineage 76 and 67—Family records.

JAQUITH

The following record was copied from the original by Mrs. Mayburt Riegel. The original is on a sheet of very old yellowed and worn paper, and is the possession of Major Louis W. Jaquith, 926 Geers Ave., Columbus, Ohio.

The parents of Mj. Jaquith were traveling by train sometime past 1850. When nearing Columbus, Ohio the father died, and the mother left the train at Columbus, Ohio and settled in Columbus.

JAQUITH RECORD

Ebenezer Jaquith, son of Ebenezer and Esther Jaquith was born Nov. 20th., 1758.

Sarah Hawthorn, daughter of Collins and Sarah Hawthorn, was born Aug. the 9th., 1767.

Ebenezer Jaquith and Sarah Hawthorn, both of East Jaffrey, New Hampshire were married June 22nd., 1786.

Their Children & Births

Sally Jaquith was born Saturday Nov. 18, 1786
Esther Jaquith was born Saturday, Dec. 22, 1787
Ebenezer Jaquith was born Thursday, June 25, 1789
Collins Jaquith was born Friday March 4, 1791
Joseph Jaquith was born Monday, Oct. 8, 1792
Luke Jaquith was born Thursday, Jan. 30, 1794
Asor Jaquith was born Monday, Aug. 28, 1797
John Jaquith was born Saturday Aug. 3, 1799
Ira Jaquith was born Monday Apr. 19, 1800
Seth Jaquith was born Friday, July 13, 1804
Elijah Jaquith was born Monday June 27, 1808
Abigail Jaquith was born Wednesday Apr. 24, 1811

DEATHS

Esther Jaquith, died Nov. 21, 1789, aged 1 year, 11 months, 29 days
One daughter, born Saturday June 18, 1795 and died June 19th.
John Jaquith, died Aug. 5th., 1802, aged 3 years and 2 days
One son born Monday, Aug 26, 1805
One son born Wednesday Feb. 4, 1807 and died the same day.
Ebenezer Jaquith, son of Ahraham and Hannah Jaquith was born December 29, 1732
Esther French, daughter of Ebenezer and Esther French, was born Feb. 22, 1736
Ebenezer Jaquith and Esther French, both of Billerica, Mass., were married Jan. 19, 1758

Ebenezer Jaquith was born Nov. 20, 1758
Samuel Jaquith was born Oct. 6, 1760
Esther Jaquith was born Sept. 2, 1762
Jesse Jaquith was born Nov. 27, 1764
Hannah Jaquith was born Nov. 12, 1766
Olive Jaquith was born Oct. 19, 1769
Ab;gail Jaquith was born July 21, 1773
Betsy Jaquith was born July 15, 1777
Risport Jaquith was born Nov. 16 1779
Levi Jaquith was born Dec. 11, 1781

BIBLE RECORDS

Walter Osborne

FLEMING BIBLE RECORD

Daniel Fleming Sr., Dublin, Ohio——Original owner
Mrs. Edward Dolby, Columbus, Ohio——Present owner
Printed and copyrighted 1854

BIRTHS

Daniel Fleming, Sr. was born August 27, 1801.
Matilda Fleming was born May 9, 1815.
Priscilla Robinson was born August 1, 1837.
Miss Julia Fleming was born July 10, 1835.
Mr. Williams S. Fleming was born August 23, 1837.
Mr. Alonzo C. Fleming was born December 4, 1839.
Mr. Daniel Fleming, Jr. was born September 9, 1841.
Miss Mary J. Fleming was born May 23, 1844.
Miss Olive S. Fleming was born August 13, 1846.
Mr. Charles H. Fleming was born November 11, 1850.
Mr. George W. Fleming was born November 20, 1853.
Miss Matilda G. Fleming was born June 15, 1851.
Mr. Daniel Craig was born November 13, 1857.
Miss Ella Craig was born November 24, 1867.
Miss Julia Fleming was born June 7, 1858.
Mr. Frank Fleming was born December 25, 1859.
Alonzo F. Fleming was born November 2, 1862.
Miss Lizzie Houston was born July 5, 1866.
Miss Elmira Houston was born January 10, 1868.
Miss Corra Houstin was born January 1, 1871.
Miss Ora May Fleming was born August 18, 1872.

MARRIAGES

Mr. Daniel Fleming and Miss Matilda Bennett were married July 18, 1834.
Mr. Daniel Craig and Miss Tillie Fleming were married July 16, 1882.
Mr. George Fleming and Miss Ella N. Creg were married November 21, 1887.

JACOB ALEXANDER
And some of his Descendants
By WILLIAM H. HANNUM

Jacob Alexander was one of the Scottish immigrants who came to the American colonies by scores of thousands through the 18th century. As most of them were of families that had lived a generation or more in Ulster, they have been called Scotch Irish, though most of them seem to have had no Irish blood. The main movement was from about 1720 to 1750. In the early period Virginia and Maryland were the main destinations, but later it was Pennsylvania. As they were deeply religious people, they and their fathers in the British Isles having suffered bitter persecution for freedom of conscience, they brought with them Presbyterian principles and usages, and their influence in the religious and political development of the American people has been immense.

This statement is a revision of that issued in 1929, 'The Alexanders of Central Ohio.' Further facts and corrections will be welcomed. The following abbreviations, besides those generally recognized, are used here.

Ab.—about
B.—born
Cem.—cemetery
Ch.—church
Chil.—children
Col.—college
D.—died (or death)

Dau.—daughter (or daughters)
Grad.—graduated (or graduate)
M.—married (or marriage)
Prob.—probably
Rem.—removed or (removal)
Res.—resided (or residence)
Univ.—university

1. Jacob[1] Alexander; b. prob. ab. 1710 in County Down, Ireland; rem. to Pa., and prob. ab. 1750 settled in Great Cove, Ayr Tp., Bedford (now Fulton) Co. He d. 1792 prob. in Great Cove[a]. The number and order of his chil. are uncertain. The first 4 named here were b. prob. in Co. Down.

a   Record of Deeds in Court-house, Bedford, Pa.; Vol. E, p. 146; shows a deed of 25 Nov. 1796, naming Jacob Alexander deceased and reciting that he 'did in his lifetime obtain from the proprietaries of Pennsylvania two warrants for land in the Ayr Township aforesaid, the first bearing date the 5th and the second the 6th day of July A. D. 1752. And whereas the aforesaid Jacob Alexander also held by claim other land adjoining the aforesaid land, for which he obtained the Warrants—and did by his last Will and Testament bearing date the 19th day of July A. D. 1778 bequeathe . . . . .'

i   William[2] Alexander; b. prob. ab. 1734; m. (1) prob. ab. 1754[a]; res. Great Cove.

   1   Hugh[3] Alexander; b. prob. ab. 1767; rem. 1804 or before to Lane's Run, Scott Co., Ky.[b]

2   2   Mary; b. Sep. 1769.

William[2] Alexander; m. (2) 11 Nov. 1770 Isabel Alexander[c]; res. Great Cove; served in Revolutionary War and in fights with Indians[d]; prob. 9 chil., order uncertain.

455

a History of Bedford, Somerset and Fulton Counties; 641; mentions Mrs. William Alexander among captives taken in Great Cove by Indians in the year following Braddock's defeat, (1755).

b A letter signed 'your loving Sister Isabel Alexander', from . . . Cove Bedford 12th April 1804' to Mary A., but addressed outside 'Mr. Hugh Alexa . . . Scott C . .. ty favoured by Mr. Shannon', seems intended for Mary to forward to Hugh. (Mary's res. is not shown but the letter was written ab. 5 years before her rem. to Ohio.)

Record of Deeds, Bedford; G 205, 14 Feb. 1805; mentions Hugh as of Scott Co., Ky; & 2 deeds, (H 328, 16 Sep. 1811; & I J 34, 24 Sep. 1813), name him as 'of the State of Csintucky'.

Record of Deeds, Georgetown, Scott Co., Ky., has an entry of 3 Apr. 1835; K 192; signed by the administrator of Hugh's estate, for sale of a tract on 'the waters of Lane's Run'. Several entries refer to the preemption of a tract in Scott Co. by William Alexander, one in the year '179-'. This suggests Hugh's occupancy of land there once owned by his father.

c Dr. John King's record of marriages for Mercersburg Ch., ab. 5 mi. e. of Great Cove. William & Isabel may have been cousins.

d Reported in several posts, in Pa. Archives, 5th Series:

II 53; 1st Lt. in Col. Wm. Thompson's Bat. of Riflemen, Oct. 1775.

II 634; commission in Continental Line, 17 Apr. 1780.

IV 231; private in Bedford Co. Militia.

IV 599; private, paid as of Bedford Co.

V 50, 55; corporal in Capt. Thomas Paxton's Co. of Rangers, 16 Sep. to 13 Nov. 1776.

V 70; elected 10 Dec. 1777, 2nd lt., 5th co., 2nd bat.

V 96; private in 'Undersignated Militia', (prob. 1782, for protection against Indians).

V 98; private in Capt. Charles Taggart's co., 1st bat., Bedford Co. Militia, 6 July to 27 Sep. 1782.

V 103; paid in Militia, 2. 9. 0, & 0. 14. 0.

V 115; enrolled in Capt. Taggart's co., 6th class.

    3 Polly[3] Alexander; b. prob. ab. 1775; m. 13 Mar. 1804 to Thomas McCamish[a].
3   4 Cairns; b. prob. ab. 1778.
4   5 Jacob; b. Oct. 1779.
    6 Isabel; b. prob. ab. 1780; res. 1804 Great Cove[b].
5   7 William Knox; b. prob. 1782.
6   8 Susannah; b. 1783.
    9 Sarah Ann; b. 1784; m. 1825 to William B. Wilson; rem. to Perry Tp., Hocking Co., O., ab. ½ mi. w. of James McClelland's Stone House; d. 23 Jan. 1867 near Middlefork, Perry Tp.
       William B. W.; b. 1787[c]; d. 6 Oct. 1855, both buried in McClelland Cem., Middlefork; no chil. surviving.
    10 Andrew; b. prob. after 1786; m. 25 June 1818 Polly Starling[d].
7   11 John Allen; b. prob. ab. 1788.
       William[2] Alexander; m. (3) prob. ab. 1795 Susannah ————[e]; he d.

a Marriage-record of Presb. Ch. of Mercersburg.

Letter of Isabel A., of 12 Apr. 1804, says; ' . . . sister Polly was in such a . . . Rumatick pains.' (The use of the names Mary and Polly for sisters is not explained. Polly, which is usually a pet-name for Mary, may here stand for some other name.)

b Isabel's letter is dated at ' . . . Cove Bedford', which is taken to mean Great Cove. The letter was found in the papers of Isabel's niece, Jane (Hamilton) Lowe.

c Subscriber, June 1830, for erection of a meeting house for the Presbyterian Society, Tarlton, Pickaway Co., O.

d Andrew is an uncertain figure. Marriage-record at Lancaster, O., shows certificate of this marriage. Polly may have been the dau. of William Starling, whose name appears on the fly-leaf of a book belonging to Hugh Alexander. William S. was prob. related to Lyne Starling of Columbus, O., and to Rev. Joseph S. of Lancaster. Record of Deeds, Bedford; P 339; 2 Apr. 1827; names Clark Alexander with Andrew A. as a witness. (The latter might be a son of William A.)

e Record of Deeds, Bedford; J 23; shows a deed of 24 Mar. 1807 for a tract that 'William Alexander of Air Township & Susanna his wife hath sold'; also P 342; a quit-claim deed of 2 Apr 1827, given by Susannah, widow of William Alexander, ab. Jan. 1819a.

ii Martha Alexander; b. prob. ab. 1737; m. to John Kendall; res. Great Cove; blind for 40 yearsb; d. in old age.

John, son of Robertc and Margaret (Fleming?) K.; b. prob. ab. 1720, Co. Down; d. 1805 Great Cove, buried in Big Spring, McConnellsburgd.

1 Francis3 Kendall; b. 1767 Great Cove; m. 1794 Jane Gibson; d. 3 June 1817 Great Cove.

a Record of Wills, Bedford; I 535; shows the will of William A., of 6 (or 18) Nov. 1818, with provision for his 'dearly beloved Wife' but without naming her. It mentions some of his chil.; ' . . . my son William Knox . . . Next Jacob and Knox, Hugh, Mary and Andrew they have got some part already and the rest of the children I allow to have as mutch' (Knox is taken to mean William Knox.) The will was proved 10 Feb. 1819.

b The family tradition, heard at McConnellsburg, is that Martha, having bad eyes, went to Hagerstown, Md., (some 20 mi. s.e.), for treatment, but by mistake in using the wrong medicine she lost her sight.

c The tradition is that Margaret Kendall came, a widow, to Great Cove, with 2 sons, John & Robert. She had the Alexanders for neighbors, one family on the w. side & one on the e. She d. in 1750. History of Fulton Co., by Miss E. S. Greathead; 2; tells of a visit made in 1750 by Richard Peters, Secretary of the Province of Pa., with an official party, to several settlements illegally made on lands of the Indians. In Great Cove the party expelled 22 families and burned their houses. One of those dispossessed settlers was Robert Kendall.

'The Life-story of Rev. Francis Makemie', by I. M. Page; 214; shows a deed given by John Laws of Somerset Co., Md., 2 Mar. 1702/3, to Francis Makemie, for 200 acres purchased by Laws from John Stratton, 29 Jan. 1689, & by Stratton from William Kendall of Northampton Co., Va.; with no date stated. (Query: was William the father of Robert?)

d Pa. Archives, Series 3, XXV, names James Kendall as warrantee of land in Bedford Co.; 553, 20 July 1784; & 554, 27 Dec. 1794. Record of Deeds, Bedford Co.; E 259: in entry of 1 May 1799, names John K. as having lands in Great Cove. His Will is dated 10 Apr. 1805, with William Alexander Sr., & James & Francis Kendall as executors.

History of Bedford, Somerset & Fulton Counties; 644; names John among 40 men identified certainly as being in Ayr Tp. in 1773 and 1785.

        Jane, dau. of Capt. James G[a].; b. 1773; d. 1847; among their chil. were James ⁴ K[b]; (b. 1798; m. 1830 Margaret, dau. of Thomas Logan; d. 1879); & Sarah, (m. to Clark Alexander; prob. son of Andrew; they rem. to Ia. & and had no chil.)

iii Polly[2] Alexander; b. prob. ab. 1740; d. 1792 or after[c].

iv Margaret; b. prob. ab. 1742; d. 1792 or after[d].

v Hugh; b. prob. ab. 1747; served in Revolutionary War[e].

    Capt. James G., (prob. son of Henry, who was killed in a great massacre by Indians in Great Cove, 1 Nov. 1755); b. 1745; m. ab. 1769 Margaret ———; d. 31 Mar. 1810 Fulton Co.; 3 sons, 7 dau., Jane being the 2nd child.

    b James K. had 12 chil., the eldest of whom was William Andrew[5] K.; b. 6 Dec. 1835; m (1) Sarah Walker, & (2) Sarah (McCain) Linton; d. 1896. Of his 4 chil. the youngest was Helen McCain[6] K.; b. 5 Aug. 1887, Air Tp., Fulton Co.; nurse in hospital at Miraj, Bombay Presidency, India, under Board of Foreign Missions of Presb. Ch. in U. S. A. She was m. 21 Jan. 1926 at Miraj, to Capt. James Keith MacLeod, M. B. E., the present writer solemnizing the marriage. Capt. M. was b. in Aberdeenshire, Scotland; served in World War, was secretary of Soldiers' Christian Association at Agra & c; d. 2 Aug. 1938, Miraj. Helen had no chil. She served in hospital at Ferozepur, Punjab; rem. to Bangalore, Mysore, and in 1939 to Coolville, Athens Co., Ohio.

    c Will of Jacob Alexander, made 19 July 1778 and proved 14 Nov. 1792, names 'Polley' first of his 'Daughteres' & 'Peggey' next.

    d Record of Mercersburg Ch., under admissions to communion, 'Oct[r]. 2[d] Sab 1785 . . . . Margrt Alexander'.

    e Hugh A. is named in Pa. Archives, 5th Series:

        IV   231; private in Bedford Co. Militia.

        IV   599; private, paid as of Bedford Co.

        V   96; private in 'Undesignated Militia; (prob. 1782 for protection against Indians.)

        V   103; paid in Militia L 10. 0. 0 & L 10. 17. 6.

        V   114; enrolled in Capt. Taggart's co. of Militia, 1st class.

(These entries are taken to refer to Hugh, son of Jacob.)

    Record of Deeds, Bedford Co.; E 146; shows a deed of 25 Nov. 1796, naming 'William Alexander of Air Township . . . . eldest son and heir of Jacob Alexander and Hugh Alexander of the aforesaid Township . . . the youngest son and heir of Jacob Alexander.'

    The same record; O 610, 1 June 1827; shows a grant by William K. Alexander & Francis Kendel, executors of William Alexander, to Hugh Alexander, of a trace in Wells Valley, surveyed to Hugh Alexander on a warrant from the land-office of Philadelphia, dated 5 Jan. 1788.

    Pa. Archives, 3rd Series; XXV 450; name Hugh Alexander warrantee of land in Bedford Co.; 6 Feb. 1786, 200 acres; 5 Jan. 1788, 50 acres; & XXV 453; 4 Aug. 1795, 400 acres.

        Oct. 1778 Margaret, dau. of Robert Elder[a]; m (2) 17 Feb. 1789 Mary[b], dau. of Joseph Bell; d. 1825.

vi Isabel; b. prob. ab. 1750; m. 14 Nov. 1770 to William Alexander[c].

vii Susannah; b. prob. 1752; m. 8 July 1772 to John Shannon[d]; d. 1804.

John, son of Samuel S.; rem. prob. to Scott Co., Ky.

2 Mary³ Alexander; b. Sep. 1769; m. (1) 29 Mar. 1807 to David Hamilton[a]; rem. 1809 near Buena Vista (now Middlefork), Perry Tp., Fairfield (now Hocking) Co., Ohio.

David, son of Robert H.[e]; b. ab. 1781 prob. Leacock Tp., Lancaster Co., Pa.; rem. to Great Cove, & near Buena Vista, O.; d. 21 (or 27)

a Dr. John King's record for Mercersburg Ch. states both marriages.

Record of Deeds, Georgetown, Ky., mentions Robert E.; D 27; and B 75, 22 Mar. 1822; suggesting that some of Margaret's family migrated to Scott Co.

b Record of Deeds, Bedford; N 239; shows a power-of-attorney granted by Hugh Alexander & recorded 6 Aug. 1823, 'respecting the estate real or personal of me from my father-in-law Joseph Bell of Bedford Co. . . .'

Record of Deeds, Georgetown; F 438; shows an indenture of 9 Mar. 1829 naming James F. & Joseph N. Bell of Scott Co. as purchasing 'a certain parcel of land . . . in the County of Scott . . . on the waters of Elkhorn.' (Mary's brothers may have been among the immigrants from Pa.)

Deeds recorded at Bedford,; E 37, 25 Nov. 1796; & F 447, 4 Apr. 1803; named Mary, wife of Hugh, but if in both these cases Hugh, son of Jacob, is meant, the name of the wife of Hugh Jr. is still to be ascertained.

c These marriages are recorded by Dr. John King. William and Isabel were prob. cousins. There were several related Alexander families in the County.

d Dr. John King's record: 'David Hamilton—Mary Alexander. Mch. 29, 1807'.

e Robert, prob. son of William & Jean (McMaster) H.; b. prob. Leacock Tp., Lancaster Co., Pa.; rem. to Bedford Co.; d. 1827 or after, prob. Leacock Tp.

Record of Deeds, Bedford; E 144: 'I, Robert Hamilton of Bedford County . . . . yeoman . . . . have granted . . . . all that Tract

June 1813[a]; killed by the fall of a timber in raising a barn on James McClelland's farm; buried Tarlton, Pickaway Co., O.; 3 chil.

i William⁴ Hamilton; b. 16 Mar. 1808 Great Cove; farmer & teacher; commissioned 1834 Colonel of 2nd Regt., 1st Brig., 7th Div., O. Militia[b]; studied surveying in Mr. Roscoe's school, Lancaster, O., & prob. in Rev. Ebenezer Washburne's school, Blendon, Franklin Co., O.; m. 8 Aug. 1839 Rebecca Augustus; res. Oakland, Clearcreek Tp., Fairfield Co., O.; elder in Presb. Ch., Tarlton[c]; county-surveyor; rem. 1856 to Lancaster; d. there 12 Dec. 1856; buried Tarlton.

lying and being in Bedford County on the waters of Redstone Creek . . . . known by the name of Adventure . . . . same Tract . . . granted to Robert Hamilton by a location No. 806 from the Land Office in Philadelphia on the 3rd d. of April 1769 . . . . 24 April 1772.'

Pa. Archives, 5th Series; II 915; 'Continental Line, 3rd Pa., Jan. 1, 1777—Nov. 3, 1783, *Ensigns*, Hamilton, Robert.' (This was prob. the father of David. Ensign Robert H. was brother of Major James H., who was Gen. Washington's aide was noted in the campaign about Yorktown.) Robert's letters show his business in Lancaster, including shipments from Philadelphia to Dublin.

Robert was a son of William of Leacock Tp., (b. ab. 1720, d. 1781), & prob. grandson of James, whose book of sermon-notes indicates that he was, in 1710-11, a student in the Divinity College, Edinburgh. He rem. to Lancaster Co., Pa., & at Conewago, near the Susquehanna River, kept a post for trading with Indians. He d. in 1732.

a The tombstone gives the date 21 June, but the record in the Bible reads 27 June. (The one date may refer to the accident & the other to the fatal termination.) David's school-exercise book, with names & sentiments scribbled later by various persons, also bits of business-letters, has been handed down in the family. The book, with similar ones written by his 3 chil., is in the Archaeological Museum, Columbus, Ohio.

b The record-book of the 2nd Regt., kept by Col. Hamilton, is in the Archaeological Museum, Columbus.

c In his papers was found the list of subscriptions, made in June 1830, for a meeting house for the 'Presbyterian Society' at Tarlton. His name is next to last among 53. The list is in the Archaeological Museum, Columbus.

Rebecca, dau. of John & Hannah (Hendrickson) Augustus[a]; b. 28 June 1809 Oakland; d. 9 Oct. 1889 Lancaster, buried in Forest-rose Cem.; 6 chil., b. Oakland.

1 Jane[5] Hamilton; b. 15 July 1841; m. 19 Dec. 1860 to Ezra Smith Hannum; res. Lancaster, O.; d. 13 Jan. 1877; buried in Forest-rose Cem.

Ezra S., son of Perez & Abigail (Smith, Richardson) H.; (Caleb[5], Aaron[4], William[3], John[2], William[1])[b]; b. 12 Mar. 1836 Baltimore, Fairfield Co., O.; county-surveyor; d. 29 Oct. 1883, Lancaster; 1 dau., 1 son[c], b. there.

2 Mary; b. 28 Sep. 1843; teacher from 1863 in schools of Lancaster,ab. 60 years; m. 30 Mar. 1897 to Samuel Joseph Wolfe; guardian to her sister's 2 chil.; d. 19 Apr. 1927.

a John, son of John & Elizabeth (Springer) Augustus, of Christina Hundred, New Castle Co., Del.; b. prob. there. Elizabeth was a dau. of John & Mary Springer & granddau. of Charles Christopherson S., who was b. 1658 at Stockholm, Sweden. His father, Charles was Swedish minister, London. The son, Charles C., was taken to London for education, but in 1676 he was kidnapped on the street, placed on a ship on the Thames & transported to Va. to labor on a plantation. This was one method of recruiting for the colonies. When released in 1683, he walked to Fort Christina (now Wilmington) & joined his countrymen. He soon became a leader in the Swedish colony & on 26 May 1738, d. & was buried in the 'Old Swedes' Ch. Hannah also was of an old family of that colony. John & Hannah rem. to Va., & ab. 1805, with 3 chil., to Clearcreek Tp., Fairfield Co., O. On his farm ab. 1 mi. s. of Oakland is the old Augustus Cem. John was an associate justice of the Common-pleas Court of Fairfield Co. from 1825 to 1830. He was a member of the Presb. Ch. of Tarlton & he made the largest subscription, ($35.00), for the meeting house there. Hannah was descended from Charles C. Springer, & was prob. a cousin to John.

b See 'William Hannum of New England and some of his Descendants', in the *Register* of the N. E. Historic Genealogical Society, of Boston, April 1936 to April 1937.

c The present writer.

Samuel. J, son of Samuel & Eliza (Kraft) Wolfe; b. 18 Oct. 1845 near Circleville, Pickaway Co., O.; teacher from 1871 nearly 60 years in Lancaster, (with intervals in business), elder in

Presb. Ch.; d. 29 May 1933, both buried in Forest-rose Cem.; no chil.

3   John Allen; b. 5 July 1845; d. 28 Sep. 1856, buried Tarlton.

4   William; b. 31 Mar. 1847; d. 13 Sep. 1856, buried Tarlton.

5   Clark Alexander; b. 11 Oct. 1851; d. 26 Sep. 1856, buried Tarlton.

6   Franklin Augustus; b.22 Jan. 1854; locomotive engineer on C. & M. V. Ry.; m. 21 Aug. 1884 Minnie Comer; res. Lancaster; rem. to Zanesville, O.; served on B. & O. R. R.; d. 20 Mar. 1933, buried Putnam, Zanesville; 2 dau., 1 son.

ii   Jane[4] Hamilton; b. 23 Oct. 1810; m. ab. 1847 to William Henry Lowe; res. on Little Pine Creek, Perry Tp., Hocking Co., O.; rem. ab. 1851 to farm in Clearcreek Tp., Fairfield Co., O., 2 mi. e. of Tarlton; d. 2 Feb. 1879, buried Tarlton.

William H., son of Joseph & Nancy (Wiggins) Lowe; b. 29 May 1812, Frederick, Md.; m. (1) prob. ab. 1832 Louisa Eliza Thompson; res. on Little Pine Creek.

Louisa E. T.; d. 1840; buried in Salt-creek Tp., Pickaway Co., near Adelphi.

Mary[5] Lowe; b. ab. 1832; d. 1840.

William H. L.; d. 26 Feb. 1885, buried Tarlton; 5 chil., 1st 3 b. on Little Pine.

1   Lucinda Ann[5] Lowe; b. 25 July 1848; not m.; d. 15 May 1929 Circleville, O., buried Tarlton.

2   Joseph Mahlon; b. 24 Jan. 1850; grad. O. Wesleyan Univ., Delaware; attorney in Columbus; m. ab. 1888 Anna Taylor Fairchild; d. 8 Mar. 1924 Daytona Beach, Fla.; buried in Greenlawn Cem., Columbus.

Anna T., dau. of William F.; b. 1862 Urbana, O.; grad. O. Wesleyan Univ.; m. (2) 1930 to Charles S. Barnes of Washington Court-house, O.; d. 3 May 1931 Columbus; buried Greenlawn; no chil.

3   David Alexander; b. 6 May 1851; m. ab. 1876 Sara M. Kiefaber; res. on his father's farm, Clearcreek Tp.; d. there 18 Apr. 1888, buried Tarlton.

Sara M., dau. of Bernard & Eliza Jane (Brown) K.; b. 24 Aug. 1858 prob. Oakland, Clearcreek Tp.; 2 dau.

Sara M. K.; m. (2) to Milton C. Lutz; res. Columbus; d. 27 Mar. 1927 Lancaster, buried in Mausoleum, Stoutsville, Fairfield Co., O.

4   John Franklin; b. 9 Dec. 1853; m. 10 Nov. 1881 Clara Ellen Dunkel; res. on his father's farm; rem. 1892 to farm near Butlerville, Warren Co., O., & prob. 1919 to Oakley, Cincinnati, O.; d. there 22 Dec. 1933.

Clara Ellen D.; b. 12 Aug. 1860 Ross Co., O.; d. 22 June 1902 Butlerville; both buried Blanchester, Clinton Co., O.; 2 sons[a]; 5 dau.; 1st 5 chil. b. prob. Clearcreek Tp., Fairfield Co.

5   William Allen; b. 6 Nov. 1855; m. ab. Dec. 1892 Ellen Fredona Lutz; res. on his father's farm; rem. to Circleville; d. there 22 July 1939.

Ellen F. L.; b. Pickaway Co.; d. 18 Oct. 1932, Circleville; both buried Amanda, Fairfield Co.; 1 dau., Dorothy B.; b. ab. 1893; grad. O. State Univ., instructor in home-economics; m. to Wilbert Cathmore Ronan, prof. of architecture, O. State Univ.

a   Eldest of the 7 is Clifton Dunkel Lowe; b. 9 Dec. 1883; grad. 1910 D. V. M., O. State Univ.; m. 22 Dec. 1912, Dalton, Ga., Nora MayAnderson; in Bureau of Animal Industry, Dept. of Agriculture.

Washington, D. C.; 1 son, 1 dau.

iii David Allen[4] Hamilton; b. 6 Jan. 1812; kept tannery in Tarlton[a]; m. prob. ab. 1857 Ann Bailer Banks Slaughter; res. Columbus; kept tannery on e. bank of Scioto River, Rich St.; d. 16 Jan. 1870, Columbus.

Ann B. B., dau. of Robert F. & Sarah (Bond) S[b].; b. 1821 prob. Lancaster, O.; teacher there & in Rev. Samuel S. Rickly's[c] Academy, Tarlton; rem. ab. 1886 to Pasadena, Cal.; d. there 9 Mar. 1892, both buried Greenlawn Cem., Columbus; 2 sons; b. prob. Tarlton.

1 Alexander Slaughter[5] Hamilton; b. prob. 1858; d. 28 Apr. 1860 Columbus.

2 David Allen; b. prob. 1860; d. 28 Jan 1862 Columbus.

Mary[3] (Alexander) Hamilton; m. (2) 1 Feb. 1814 to James Chambers; rem. to Clearcreek Tp., 2 mi. e. of Tarlton; d. 1 Mar. 1843, buried Tarlton.

James, eldest child of Alexander —& Isabelle C.; b. 25 Apr. 1770.

a The tradition is that Allen when working in the tannery at Tarlton became engaged to marry a cousin who was living in a prosperous farming community some distance west, but when after elaborate preparation the appointed day arrived, the expectant bride saw from a window the groom coming on a sulky, with no fine array, and she angrily refused, against the remonstrance of her relatives, to proceed with the ceremony. She later became a farmer's wife, and Allen a comparatively rich manufacturer in Columbus.

b Robert F. S.; b. 1770 Va.; rem. to Ky., & ab. 1796 to Chillicothe, & ab. 1800 to Lancaster, O.; m. 6 Apr. 1807 Sarah Bond; appointed 1805 president judge of common-pleas court; prosecuting attorney 4 years; elected to Ohio Senate 1810-11, & 1827-31, & to House of Representatives 1817, '19, '21, '23, '24; d. Oct. 1846 Lancaster; both buried in Kuntz (or Carpenter) Cem., 1 mi. s. of Lancaster.

c Mr. Rickly afterwards organized an academy at Tiffin, O., now Heidelberg Col.; & later for many years president of Capital City Bank, Columbus, where he was Mrs. Hamilton's adviser on investments. Being made blind by an attack of an angry applicant for a loan, he would have friends read to him, as the present writer used sometimes to do.

prob. Londonderry, Ireland[a]; rem. prob. 1796 to Pa.; employed by Robert Hamilton, Lancaster, Pa., in grain-business[b]; rem. ab. 1804 to Bedford Co., Pa., prob. accompanying his former employer's son David, & following him in 1809 to Buena Vista, O.[c]; subscriber 1830 for Presb. meeting house Tarlton[d]; rem. to farm afterwards owned by William H. Lowe, 2 mi. e. of Tarlton; rem. ab. 1850 to Sidney, O. to live in the family of his dau.; d. there 1 Apr. 1858; 2 dau., b. near Buena Vista.

1 Elizabeth[5] Chambers; b. ab. 1816; not m.; d. 2 Sep. 1839 prob. Clearcreek Tp.

2 Mary Ann; b. 23 Mar. 1818: m. 23 Oct. 1849 to Mahlon Ashbrook; res. Tarlton & Ashville, Pickaway Co., & at Sidney; rem. 1859 to St. Joseph, Mo.; d. there 7 Apr. 1896.

a A letter of John McFarland of 28 Mar. 1842, from Mullaughban near Ballygawly, Co. Tyrone, Ireland, addressed to his son-in-law, John Chambers of Tarlton, O., (brother of James), suggests that Alexander, with James may have come from that County, but the family tradition favors Londonderry. The tradition of James' partial course in divinity at Edinburgh, Scotland, may be correct, though no

JACOB ALEXANDER
And some of his Descendants

By WILLIAM H. HANNUM

definite evidence for it is found. He is said to have crossed the Atlantic three times, & to have served in the war of 1812 & in the Black Hawk war.

 b A certificate given to James by Robert Hamilton was found in the family papers: 'That James Chambers a young man worked for me in July 1797 and has remained in the neighborhood ever since and lives with Capt. William Crawford at present, hath been as far as came to my knowledge an industrious civil man pr. me Robert Hamilton. August 7th 1802'.

 c A land-patent issued 1 Sep. 1820 with signature of President J. Q. Adams, states the grant to James Chambers, Assignee of John Stump, of 160 acres, s. e. quarter of section 18, of township 12, of range 19; i. e. Perry Tp., Hocking Co. That is w. of South Perry, near boundary of Pickaway Co., & may have been the farm occupied by David Hamilton. The record in the Court-house, Lancaster, shows the purchase in 1812,, by James Chambers, of a tract in Clearcreek Tp. That was prob. the farm 2 mi. e. of Tarlton, to which he rem. at his marriage.

 d James was prob. the writer of the elaborate preamble, which is in a neat bold hand.

  Mahlon, son of William Ashbrook; b. 27 Jan. 1813 Ross Co., O.; kept store in Tarlton & hotel in St. Joseph; d. 12 Aug. 1901; both buried in Mt. Mora Cem.; 2 sons, 2 dau., b. Ashville.

3 Cairns[3] Alexander, b. prob. 1778[a]; m. 26 Mar. 1816 Mary Alexander[b]; rem. prob. ab. 1822 near Auglaize River in w. part of O.; d. 1838 or before; 2 sons, b. prob. Great Cove.

 a Record of Deeds, Bedford; G 206; shows *Carns* Alexander as witness to the transfer by Hugh of certain undivided parts of tracts called Alexandria & Bentwood: & the same Record; H 328-330; shows *Carns* as witness to a deed for part of a tract called Stirling. *Carns* &

Carnes are prob. modifications of the Scottish *Cairns*. *Stirling* suggests an ancestral reminiscence of Stirling Castle, seat of Sir William Alexander, (1567 to 1640), reputed progenitor of many Alexander families in Ulster & in the American colonies.

b Record of marriages by Dr. Elliott, Presb. minister of Mercersburg: '1816. Mar. 26 Cairns Alexander and Mary Alexander Bedford Co.' (She may have been the dau. of Andrew Clark Alexander.)

 i William Clark[4] Alexander; b. 1818; d. 20 Oct. 1838 Bloomingburg, Fayette Co., O.[a]

 ii James; b. ab. Dec. 1819[b].

4 Jacob[3] Alexander; b. Oct. 1779; m. 1809 Susannah Morrison[c]; rem. ab. 1817 to Clearcreek Tp., later to Pine Creek, Perry Tp., Hocking Co., O.; d. 15 Dec. 1851, buried in Karshner Cem., Haynes, Salt-creek Tp., Hocking Co.

 Susannah M.; b. 1791; d. 19 Aug. 1861; 6 chil., 1st 3 b. prob. Great Cove.

 i Isabelle[4] Alexander; b. 29 Oct. 1809; m. 1843 to William McClelland; res. near Buena Vista, O.; d. there 19 July 1895; 2 sons, 3 dau.[d]

 ii William; b. prob. ab. 1812; m. (1) — .

 1 Susanna[5] Alexander; m. to John Updike; res. South Perry, Perry Tp.; 1 dau.

 2 Melville; m. — ; res. Pickaway Tp., Pickaway Co.; son Thomas. William A.; m (2) — ; drowned 1875 in Big Walnut Creek.

 iii Esther[4] Alexander; b. 1812; not m.; d. 2 Dec. 1869, buried in McClelland Cem., Middlefork, Perry Tp.

 a A letter of John Allen Alexander of 7 Nov. 1838, states the d. of his nephew, William C. A., from a sudden attack of bilious colic. He was on a tour, making collections, prob. for his father's estate. The letter commends him highly.

 b A letter of John A. A., of 1 Jan. 1841, says: 'James Alexander, my brother Crans's youngest son, had been with a month or more, he is attending school . . . he is just 21 years old . . . a member. I think, of the Methodist Church.'

 c Marriage-record of Path Valley Presb. Ch.: 'J. Alexander — Miss Morrison 1809'

 d See Record of William McClelland below.

 iv Ann; b. prob. ab. 1814; m. 19 Nov. 1834 to Abraham Wheeler; res. prob. near Buena Vista; 4 chil.

 1 Susanna[5] Wheeler; m. to Christopher Seesholtz; res. South Perry; 3 dau., 2 sons.

 2 Charles; m. Amanda (Steel) Crouch; res. South Perry; 4 dau., 2 sons; 1st 5 res. Chicago, Ill.

 3 Jane; m. (1) to — Stump; res. prob. South Perry; m. (2) to — Extine; 3 or 4 chil.

 4 Isabell; m. to Jasper Morris; res. South Perry; many chil.

 v David[4] Alexander; b. ab. 1816 Clearcreek Tp.; m. (1) 24 Dec. 1840, Clearport, Fairfield Co., Kima Julian; res. South Perry; builder & cabinet-maker; rem. prob. ab. 1854 to Lancaster, O.

 Kima J.; d. prob. ab. 1855; 2 sons, 1 dau., b. South Perry.

8 1 Allen W.[5] Alexander; b. 14 Nov. 1842.

 2 Austin; b. 2 Nov. 1846; trained in military academy; printer; M. E. minister; d. 28 Oct. 1874 Chicago, Ill., buried Adelphi, Ross Co., O.

 3 Emma; b. 8 Aug. 1850; res. from ab. 1856 to 1860 at her Grandfather Alexander's, where her 'Aunt Easter' cared for her;

had Uncle William McClelland as guardian from her father's
d. till 1868; from 1863 res. at William H. Lowe's, Clear-creek
Tp.; rem. 1868 to Delaware. O., to live with her brothers;
rem. prob. ab. 1880 to Columbus; dressmaker; m. 22 Oct. 1890
to Benjamin Franklin Menear; res. Columbus; d. 5 Feb. 1940.
Benjamin F. M.; served in civil war; watchman in state-insti-
tutions; d. 24 Sep. 1924 Columbus; both buried Greenlawn
Cem.; no chil.

David A.; m. (2) 1860 or after — ; served in civil war, 75th O.
Vol. Inf., in Va., from Jan. 1862, in many battles & skirmishes;
member of M. E. Ch.; earnest Christian; wounded 2 July 1863
Gettysburg; d. soon after, buried there in National Cem.

vi George Washington[4] Alexander; b. 1 Sep. 1819 on Pine Creek,
Salt-creek Tp., Hocking Co.; m. 26 Aug. 1841 Mary Hemphill;
res. prob. near South Perry; farmer & teacher; in later years
res. in house of son Lewis C., Huntington, W. Va.; d. June 1901
Toledo, O., buried there in Woodlawn Cem.

Mary, dau. of Benjamin H.; b. 4 Oct. 1815; d. 18 Nov. 1864; 5
sons, 2 dau., on Pine Creek.

1 (Son)[5]; b. Oct. 1842; d. 24 Oct. 1842.

9 2 Isaac Newton Alexander; b. 17 Sep. 1843.

10 3 Clark Noble; b. 19 Sep. 1846.

4 Samuel; b. 23 Jan. 1849; m. Lydia Culp; res. Toledo, O.;
employed in factory; killed 20 Sep. 1898 Toledo, in fire in
elevator; no chil.

11 5 Lewis Cass; b. 14 June 1852.

6 Mary; b. 5 Sep. 1854; m. to William Reed; res. Chicago, Ill.,
with her dau., Erma, (m. to — Porritt).

7 Susanna; b. 30 July 1858; m. 8 June 1887 to Reese D. Chesher;
res. Toledo, O.

Reese D. C.; d. 23 Oct. 1929 Toledo; 2 sons, 1 dau., b. prob. there.

5 William Knox[3] Alexander; b. prob. 1782; m. 1815 Susan Reed, of
Spring Valley; res. Air Tp., Bedford Co., Pa.; d. 1829; 5 chil.,
b. prob. there[a].

a Bible-record names William K. A., with b., m., d. & 5 chil. Pa.
Archives, Series 3; XXV 454; name him as warrantee of land in
Bedford Co., 4 Mar. 1828.

Record of Wills, Bedford, II 180; shows will of William Alexander,
dated 8 (or 18?) Nov. 1818, naming his son William Knox & James
Kendall as executors.

i William Clark[4] Alexander; b. prob. ab. 1817; d. at age of 77,
Fonda, Pocahontas Co., Ia.

ii Robert Sloan; m. Esther Irvine.

iii David Knox; m. Harriet McCune.

iv Esther Reed; m. to John McCune.

v John Brown; m. Mary Jane Kerr.

6 Susanna[3] Alexander; b. 1783; m. 30 Sep. 1806 to James McClelland[a]; res. near Buena Vista, O.; subscriber 1830, for meeting
house, Tarlton; d. Aug. 1831.

James, son of Robert M.[b]; b. 2 June 1781 prob. Buena Vista, Pa.;
rem. prob. 1806 near Buena Vista, O.; in 1825 built the Stone
House[c]; d. 27 July 1825; both buried Tarlton; 8 chil., b. (except
Mary Jane) on farm where Stone House stands.

i Alexander[4] McClelland; b. 3 June 1807; m. 4 Oct. 1832 Minerva
Spangler[d]; res. Buena Vista, O.; farmer; justice of peace;

d. 3 Nov. 1890, buried in Stump Cem.; 8 chil., b. prob. on his father's farm.

1 John Allen[5] McClelland; b. 14 Nov. 1833; m. (1) Rachel Cox; res. Perry Tp.; 2 dau., 2 sons; m. (2) ab. 1868 Evaline Record of Deeds, Bedford, names William K. A. as a party in transactions; L 608, 8 May 1819; O 610, 1 June 1827; P 590, 5 Feb. 1829; P 591, 23 Sep. 1829: & as otherwise connected with transactions; W 239, (recorded 6 Aug. 1823); P. 339, 2 Apr. 1827; P 526, 1 Apr. 1828; P 555, 28 Sep. 1829.

    a   Marriage-record of Presb. Ch. of Mercersburg.

    b   Robert McClelland; b. 1754; prob. related to John M. of Westmoreland Co., Pa., who was an officer in revolutionary war & member of Convention of Pa. 1776, & of General Assembly 1778. This Robert may have been the famous scout of that name who served with Gen. Wayne against Indians, (as stated in 'Pioneer People of Fairfield Co., O., by C. M. L. Wiseman, p. 182.) Robert M. d. 25 Oct. 1834, buried Tarlton.

    c   Inscription on gable: 'J McC June 14, 1825' The house is remembered as occupied ab. 1874 by Alexander M., & in 1936 used as store for grain & tools.

    d   Record in Probate Court, Lancaster, O.; 227; '4th Oct. 1832 Cave; res. Laurelville, Hocking Co., O.; d. 1917.

Evaline C.; b. 1840; d. 1934, both buried in M. E. Cem., South Perry; 4 dau., 2 sons.

2 James Harvey; b. 13 Dec. 1834; m. Zelda Hedges; res. near Charleston, Coles Co., Ill.; served in civil war; 2 sons, 3 dau., b. near Charleston.

3 Samuel; b. 17 Feb. 1836; m. 13 Dec. 1860 Marianne Armstrong; res. near Laurelville; served in civil war, in many battles; d. 1883 or after.

Marianne, dau. of William & Sarah (Fetherolf) A.; d. Aug. 1924 Laurelville; 4 sons, 1 dau., b. prob. near Laurelville.

4 Salem Spangler; b. 10 Apr. 1838; m. Margaret Elizabeth Deffenbaugh; res. near Laurelville; d. there prob. ab. 1923; 1 dau., 1 son, b. there.

5 Clark Alexander; b. 1840; d. 1842.

6 Susannah; b. 10 Apr. 1842; m. to James W. McDowell; res. near South Perry; rem. to Columbus, O.; d. about. 1926 Columbus.

James W. M.; b. 1842; served in civil war, Co. I, 58th Regt., O. Vol. Inf.; d. 7 Feb. 1931 Columbus; 4 dau., 1 son.

7 William Enos; b. 2 Dec. 1845; m. Elmira Hedges; res. near South Perry; 4 dau., 1 son, b. there.

8 Charles Morris; b. 8 Mar. 1855; m. Lanora Hedges; d. 2 Dec. 1923.

Lanora H.; d. ab. 1908; 2 sons, 4 dau.

Alexander McClelland was married legally to Minerva Spangler by me. Wm. Jones.'

ii Margaret[4] McClelland; b. 10 Jan. 1809; m. 25 Oct. 1832 to Gustin Wilson; res. 2 mi. s. w. of Lancaster; d. 11 Oct. 1895 Mackinaw, Mich.

Gustin, son of Nathaniel Jr. & Alice (Peters) W.; b. 28 Oct. 1806 s. w. of Lancaster; completed erection of wall of. Wilson cem. on his farm; elder in Presb. Ch., Lancaster; d. 25 Aug. 1882; both buried in Forest-rose Cem., Lancaster; 3 chil. b. on farm.

12 1 Harvey[5] Wilson; b. 13 Oct. 1834.

    2 Noble[a]; b. 18 Sep. 1836; d. 18 Dec. 1836.

    3 Mary A.; b. 2 Sep. 1838; d. in infancy.

iii William[4] McClelland; b. 10 Nov. 1810; m. 1843 Isabella Alexander (his first cousin); res. near Buena Vista; d. there Feb. 1868.

Isabella, dau. of Jacob Alexander, (see above); b. 29 Oct. 1809 prob. Great Cove; rem. ab. 1816 to Pine Creek; d. 19 July 1895 near Buena Vista; both buried there in McClelland Cem.; 2 sons, 3 dau.

1 Martin Van Buren[5] McClelland; b. 8 Apr. 1844; teacher from 1867, for over 50 years, in Hocking & Fairfield Counties; not m.; rem. to Lancaster; d. there 17 Mar. 1925, buried in McClelland Cem.

2 Susannah; b. 25 Aug. 1845; not m.; d. 2 Jan. 1919 in Ill., buried in McClelland Cem.

3 Mary Jane; b. 22 Jan. 1847 Lancaster; m. 25 Dec. 1867 to Isaiah Deffenbaugh; res. near Buena Vista; rem. ab. 1908 to a Named prob. for Col. John Noble, son of Samuel, (who was a farmer of Tarlton.) The family had come from Va. John was a tailor in Lancaster, O., but opened a hotel & became a prominent citizen there, as he did later in Columbus & Cincinnati.

Lancaster; d. there 17 Mar. 1922.

Isaiah, son of James & Lydia (Stump[a]) D.; b. 19 Feb. 1845 near Buena Vista; rem. ab. 1933 to Logan, O.; d. there 1936; 1 dau., 3 sons, b. near Buena Vista.

4 William A.; b. 7 Sep. 1848; d. 28 July 1853 near Buena Vista, buried in McClelland Cem.

5 Ann Elizabeth; b. 14 July 1850; m. to — Kane; rem. to Lancaster; d. there 13 Oct. 1929; 2 sons, 2 dau.

iv John Allen[4] McClelland; b. 15 Nov. 1812; rem. 1837 or before to Lancaster m. Lucinda Trimble; res. Lancaster; tinner; rem. ab. 1871 to a farm in Neb. & later to Lincoln; charter-member of 1st Presb. Ch. there; member of Masonic Lodge; d. 18 Feb. 1882 Lincoln.

Lucinda T.; b. 1821 Fairfield Co., O.; d. 24 Mar. 1895 Lincoln; 1 dau., 2 sons, b. Lancaster.

1 Elizabeth Trimble[5] McClelland; b. 10 Mar. 1854; dressmaker in Lincoln; rem. ab. 1905 to Pasadena, Cal.; member of Highland Park Presb. Ch.; friend of the poor; not m.; d. 9 Dec. 1934 Pasadena; her ashes were buried in the family lot, Lincoln.

2 John Henry; b. 5 July 1857; d. 29 Jan. 1874 Lincoln.

3 George Starrett; b. 18 Feb. 1860; trained as civil engineer; ranchman in Neb. & west; rem. to Pasadena & to Yuma, Ariz.; teamster; friend of Indians; exhibitor of Australian boomerang; not m.; d. 11 Oct. 1925, Yuma, buried Somerton, Yuma Co.

v Isabella[4] McClelland; b. 20 Jan. 1815; teacher 1836, Newport, a Two letters of Lydia Stump, written in 1838 to Col. William Hamilton, who had prob. been her teacher in Perry Tp., are found among his papers.

Vermillion Co., Ind., & from 1838 to 1842 near Yellow Springs, Greene Co.; m. 15 Feb. 1842 to Charles Dickeson Miller; res. near Enon, Clark Co., O.; rem. to Springfield, O.; d. 1 Jan. 1904.

Charles D. M.; b. 1819; farmer; d. 27 Dec. 1868 from accident with threshing machine; 5 cihl., b. near Enon.

1 Mary Eliza[5] Miller; b. 27 May 1844; m. 31 May 1870 to Albert Edward Wooden; res. Centerville, Appanoose Co., Ia.; d. there 4 June 1920.

A. Edward W.; wealthy merchant; d. 1 Mar. 1920 Centerville; 1 son, 1 dau.[a], b. there.

2 Henrietta Augusta; b. 6 Sep. 1846; m. Feb. 1873 to Harrison
Jacobs; res. near Enon; rem. s. of Springfield; d. 30 July 1923.
Harrison J.; b. 1841; farmer; d. 9 Jan. 1913; 1 dau.
3 Laura Adelia; b. 31 Oct. 1848; d. 12 Nov. 1850 near Enon; clothing
caught fire from stove.
4 Charles Robert; b. 9 May 1851; m. Feb. 1885 Matilda Hammaker;
res. near Springfield; rem. near Enon to brick house erected
1825 by Grandfather Miller; d. there 12 May 1931; 1 dau.
5 Franklin Bishop; b. 28 Dec. 1853; m. 1 Sep. 1897 Emma Thomas;
res. Springfield, where he kept music-store in Arcade Building;
rem. 1912 to Romney, Hampshire Co., W. Va.; kept nursery for
trees &c; member of Presb. Ch.; d. 13 May 1939 Romney.
Emma T.; b. 1865 prob. Pendleton, Madison Co., Ind.; member of
Society of Friends; 1 son, 1 dau., b. Springfield.
a Belle Wooden; b. Oct. 1874; m. ab. 1896 to Nathan E. Kendall;
after world-war they went abroad for her health; she d. 18 Mar. 1926
at sea near Naples; buried at Centerville. She left over half-a- million
dollars to her husband, to go eventually to an orphanage at Burlington,
Ia. Nathan E. K. served 1914-18 in Congress & 1920-24 as governor
of Ia.
vi Susanna[4] McClelland; b. 19 Apr. 1817 (or 1816?); d. 14 Aug.
1831, buried Tarlton.
vii Mary Jane; b. 11 Apr. 1820 Lancaster. O.; m. prob. 23 Apr. 1845
to Noah Bishop; res. Enon; rem. to Yellow Springs & to Monroe, Butler Co., O.; to Marysville, Madison Co., Ill., & to Ironton,
Iron Co., Mo.; d. there 6 June 1873.
Noah Bishop; b. Litchfield, Conn.; grad. 1833 Yale Col., & later
Princeton Seminary; teacher there & in theological Seminary,
Xenia, O.; Presb. minister; d. 22 Sep. 1869 Ironton.
1 Anna Louisa[5] Bishop; b. 1 Mar. 1847 near Yellow Springs; m. to
Charles A. Smith; res. St. Louis, Mo.; d. there 10 Jan. 1932,
buried in Bellefontain Cem.
Charles A. S.; b. 1827 Pa.; moulder & revenue-assessor of Iron
Co., Mo.; d. 1902 St. Louis; 5 chil., b. prob. there.
2 Mary Isabel; b. 6 June 1848 Yellow Springs; m. 28 Feb. 1870 to
J. Lewis Moser; res. Ironton, Mo.; d. 22 Jan. 1914 Freemont,
Dodge Co., Neb.; 1 dau. 1 son.
7 John Allen[3] Alexander; b. prob. 1788; m. 30 Oct. 1831 Mrs. Mary
C. (Morrison) Howe; res. near Enon, Clark Co., O.; member of
O. Legislature; d. 1870.
Mary C., prob. dau. of Samuel Morrison; m. (1) to — Howe; 2
sons by 1st m.
i William Hamilton[4] Alexander; b. 24 July 1833 near Enon; student in Antioch Col., Yellow Springs; teacher in boys' school in
Miss.; served in civil war; not m.; d. 3 June 1865 near Enon, of
tuberculosis; buried Yellow Springs.
8 Allen W.[5] Alexander; b. 14 Nov. 1842; trained in military acad-
demy; m. 11 Oct. 1863 Martha A. Crouch; res. South Perry;
rem. to Delaware, O., & to Columbus; 25 years foreman in
printing office; postal clerk on Hocking Valley Ry. till d.; d. 24
May 1897 Columbus.
Martha A. C.; d. Columbus; 5 chil.
i Jennie May[6] Alexander; b. 20 Jan. 1864 prob. S. Perry; not m.;
d. 5 July 1889 Columbus.
ii Clarence; b. 21 Jan. 1868 Delaware; in wholesale grocery, Columbus; sergeant-major in 14th Regt., O. National Guard; m.;

d. 10 Aug. 1894 Columbus; no chil.

iii Nellie; b. 8 May 1870 Delaware; m. 22 Sep. 1887 to William David Ranney; res. Columbus.

William D. R.; machinist & stationary engineer; d. 20 Apr. Columbus; 4 chil., b. there.

1 Adeline[7] Ranney; b. 29 Aug. 1888; m. ab. 24 Aug. 1910 to John Laurance Tidball; res. Columbus; rem. to Mt. Vernon, O., & to Tulsa, Okla.; 1 son, Laurance J. T.

2 William David; b. 5 July 1890; m. 4 Oct. 1911 Myrtle McDonald; res. Columbus; machinist; rem. to Akron, O.; in rubber factory; 2 dau., b. Columbus.

3 Martha; b. 22 July 1892; d. 24 Oct. 1892 Columbus.

4 Myrtle; b. 9 Feb. 1903; m. 11 Apr. 1925 to Dean P. Evans; res. Columbus; 1 dau.

iv Franklin Austin[6] Alexander; b. 20 Aug. 1874 Delaware; m. (1) ab. 1893 Emma Stickle; res. Columbus.

Emma S.; d. 7 Apr. 1894 Columbus.

1 Jennie[7] Alexander; b. 7 Apr. 1894 Columbus; m. 22 Apr. 1913 to Hollis A. Logue; res. Columbus.

Hollis A. L.; meat-salesman; 3 sons, 1 dau., b. Columbus.

Franklin A.[6] A.; m. (2) ab. 1895 Elizabeth Williams; res. Columbus; served in Spanish war; house-decorator; d. 2 Jan. 1931 Columbus; 4 chil., b. there.

2 Helen[7] Alexander; b. 1899.

3 Ruth; b. 1902.

4 William; b. 1905.

5 Harriet; b. 1909.

v Raymond S.[6] Alexander; b. 26 June 1884 Columbus; not m.; d. 21 May 1906 Columbus.

9 Isaac Newton[5] Alexander; b. 17 Sep. 1843 Pine Creek, Hocking Co., O.; m. Oct. 1864 Sophia Shifler; res. Toledo, O.; rem. to Crestline, Crawford Co., O.; in railway service; d. 10 Apr. 1889 Crestline; 2 sons.

i William Lewis[6] Alexander; b. 14 Oct. 1865; m.; res. Toledo; with Terminal Ry.; 9 chil., b. Toledo.

1 Egie M.[7] Alexander; b. 31 May 1892; m. ab. 1917 to — Mosshart; res. Middletown, Warren Co., O.

2 Guy S.; b. 1 Mar. 1894; m.; res. Pasadena, Cal.

3 Harriet; b. 28 June 1896; m. to Floyd Redmond; res. Findlay, O.

4 Dodge V.; b. 1 Nov. 1900.

5 William Lewis; b. 12 June 1904.

6 Frank; b. d.

7 Carroll K.; b. 28 Mar. 1912.

8 Mary; b. d.

9 Robert Newton; b. 20 Jan. 1918.

ii Frank Oscar[6] Alexander; b. 29 May 1868; m. Mary Richter; res. Toledo; d. there 29 May 1923.

1 Helen May[7] Alexander; b. 19 Oct. 1894; m. to — Schriner; res. Toledo.

10 Clark Noble[5] Alexander; b. Sep. 1846 Pine Creek; m. 21 Mar. 1872 Eliza Johnston; res. Toledo; teacher; employed by American Bridge Co.; d. 21 Jan. 1929 Toledo.

Eliza J.; b. prob. South Perry; members, with chil., of M. E. Ch.; both buried in Woodlawn Cem.; 7 chil., b. Toledo.

i Bertie May[6] Alexander; b. 15 Apr. 1873; m. to Carlin Houser; res. Calumet City, Cook Co., Ill.

1 Doris Vashti[7] Houser.
ii Nellie Maude[6] Alexander; b. 9 Apr. 1876; not m.; cashier of hardware firm, Bostwick Braun Co., Toledo.
iii Charles Johnston; b. 1 Nov. 1881; m. Aug. 1909 Mabel Quinn; res. Gallup, McKinley Co., N. M.; rem. to Longmont, Boulder Co., Col.
1 Dorothy[7] Alexander; b. Gallup.
2 Elinor Ruth.
iv Ethel Olive[6] Alexander; b. 17 May 1883; m. 26 June 1918 to William G. Greiner; res. Toledo.
William G. G.; b. of German parents, prob. Toledo; hardware-merchant, automobile salesman; 2 chil., b. Toledo.
1 Margaret June[7] Greiner; student in art, O. State Univ.
2 James Alexander.
v Paul Edwin[6] Alexander; b. 20 Oct. 1886; grad. 1910 O. State Univ.; civil engineer, on municipal building &c; m. 25 May 1911 Belle Reynolds; res. Toledo.
Belle R.; b. Ontario, Canada; 5 chil., b. Toledo.
1 Mary Frances[7] Alexander; b. 23 Aug. 1912; senior in Waite High School; d. 14 Mar. 1930.
2 Carol Belle; b. 26 Dec. 1914; student in art, Univ. of Toledo.
3 Robert Clark; b. 30 Nov. 1918.
4 Jean Elizabeth; b. 24 Nov. 1920.
5 Richard Paul; b. 12 Nov. 1925.
vi Margaret Hemphill[6] Alexander; b. 16 June 1888; kindergartner; m. 11 June 1935 to Charles F. Yeager; res. Toledo.
Charles F. Y.; m. (1) —, (2) —, (3) at Celina, O., Margaret H. A.; machinist in railway shop; members of Disciple Christian Ch.; no chil.
vii Ralph Holding; b. 26 Nov. 1890; m. 16 Aug. 1925 Rhea Wagoner; res. Toledo; automobile salesman; no chil.
11 Lewis Cass[5] Alexander; b. 14 June 1852; m. (1) ab. 20 Aug. 1878 Isabel Shaeffer; res. Mechanicsburg (now Drinkle), Fairfield Co., O., & Barlow, Washington Co., O.; M. E. minister.
Isabel S.; b. near Mechanicsburg; d. ab. 1880.
i Rosanna Blanche[6] Alexander; b. 17 Nov. 1879 Mechanicsburg; grad. of O. Univ., Athens; attended Columbia Univ., N. Y.; teacher, Akron, O.; not m.
Lewis C.[5] A.; m. (2) 5 Nov. 1884 Hannah Shuck; minister, Coolville, Athens Co., O. &c; retired to Huntington, W. Va.; d. there 23 Dec. 1928.
Hannah S.; b. 23 Apr. 1854.
ii Walter Bayliss[6] Alexander; b. 21 Apr. 1887 Barlow; m. 18 Aug. 1919 Blanche Richardson; res. Chesterhill, Morgan Co., O.; rem. to Vincent, Washington Co., O.; to Neb. — to Oakland & Long Beach, Cal.; manager of gasoline stations.
1 Katherine[7] Alexander; b. 16 June 1910 Chesterhill.
2 Helen; b. 8 Oct. 1911 Vincent.
iii Grace Marian[6] Alexander; b. 8 July 1889; m. 5 Sep. 1911 to M. Clifford Blake; res. Huntington, W. Va.; grad. 1933 of Marshall Col., Huntington, & later of Ohio Univ., Athens.
M. Clifford B.; b. 23 Dec. 1891; insurance-agent; municipal clerk; members of M. E. Ch.
1 Rosanna Alexander[7] Blake; b. 16 July 1912 Proctorville, Lawrence Co., O.; A. A. & M. A., Ohio Univ.; student in law-school, Huntington, & in Duke Univ., Durham, N. C.; instructor in Lees

McRae Col., Banners Elk, Avery Co., N. C.

12 Harvey[5] Wilson; b. 13 Oct. 1834; teacher; m. (1) Mary Ann Miller; grad., Heidelberg Col.; Tiffin, O.; minister of Reformed Ch. in U. S., & later of Presb. Ch. in U. S. A.; president of Shelby Col., Shelbyville, Ill., & for 12 years, of Ladies' Seminary, Oakdale, Antelope Co., Neb.; pastor, Shelbyville; Wykoff, Fillmore Co., Minnesota; Indianapolis, Ind.; Dakota City, Neb.; Middlepoint, Van Wert Co., O.; & Mackinaw & Petoskey, Mich.

Mary A., dau. of Martin Philip Miller; b. prob. near Clearport, Fairfield Co., O.; d. prob. Shelbyville; 1 dau., 1 son.; b. on Gustin Wilson's farm.

i Catherine Margaret[6] Wilson; b. 16 May 1863; m. to T. W. Stratton; res. Oakdale, Neb.; rem. near Petersburg, Va.

T. W. S.; d. 1914 near Petersburg.

1 Oliver Wilson[7] Stratton; b. 28 Oct. 1899 Oakdale; m. Celeste —; res. near Petersburg; farmer; 2 dau., 1 son.

ii Mark Harvey[6] Wilson; b. 3 Dec. 1868; m. 14 June 1894 Nettie Priestley; res. Oakdale; rem. 1900 or after to Pomona, Los Angeles Co., Cal.; druggist.

Nettie P.; d. 1912 prob. Pomona; 4 chil., b. prob. Oakdale.

1 Charles Harvey[7] Wilson; b. 11 July 1895; m. Phillipa Speck; res. Los Angeles; no. chil.

2 Virgilia Marie; b. 26 Jan 1897; office-secretary, New York City; m. 10 Aug. 1929 to George Edward Johnson; res. Pomona; rem. to Claremont, Los Angeles Co.

George E. J.; farmer; dealer in automobile accessories; no chil.

3 Imogene Pauline; b. 19 June 1902; m. to Roger Boggess; res. Santa Ana, Cal.; rem. to Pomona; no chil.

4 William Henry; b. 21 Dec. 1906; res. Pomona.

Harvey[5] W.; m. (2) Pauline Blackstone; res. Shelbyville, Petoskey &c; d. 25 Mar. 1918 Petoskey, buried Shelbyville.

Pauline B.; m. (2) to David Ewing; res. Lancaster, O.; rem. after her husband's d., near Petersburg, Va.; d. there ab. 1934. no chil.

David E.; d. 1932 Lancaster.

BOONE-STEVENSON FAMILY

Contributed by JUSTIN J. STEVENSON

WILL OF ROBERT BOONE, ANN ARUNDAL COUNTY, MD. (a copy)

In the name of God Amen, I Robert Boone of Ann Arundal County in the province of Maryland. Gentleman being sick in body but of sound and perfect disposing mind and memory do make and appoint this to be my last will and testament in manner following—First of all I commit my body to earth to be buried in such a manner as my executor hereafter named shall think proper. And as for my worldly goods I give and dispose of them in the manner following—This is to say I give, devise and bequeath unto my dear and beloved wife Elizabeth Boone my bed and furniture that we now lye on Also the following negroes in part of her third of my estate (That is to say) one negro man named Paul, one negro woman named Judith, one negro woman named Phylis and one negro woman named Hannah. Also I give, devise and bequeath unto my son Humphrey Boone a tract of land lying in Ann Arundel County called Burke's Town land containing 100 acres likewise 50 acres of land originally called Swan Cove. Also 150 acres of land being part of a tract of land originally called Broad Crook but now by the resurvey called Swan Cove joined containing by patent of Resurvey 183 acres of land.

I likewise give to my said son Humphrey Boone my great new gun and my scrutoire. Also I give, devise and bequeath unto my son Thomas Boone and his heirs 256 acres of land called Edward and Wills Valleys and Hills and a part of a tract of land called the Enlargement which said lands I purchased of one George Brown and lyes in Baltimore County. But finding the right not good I purchased of Edward Stevenson being the rightful heir. I likewise give to my said son Thomas Boone one negro girl named Rachel, one negro girl named Munsar in full of his part of my estate. Also I give, devise and bequeath unto my son Richard Boone his heirs all that tract or parcel of land called Young Richard containing 225 acres of land lying in Baltimore County also one gun called Harrison. Also I give devise and bequeth unto my grandson John Boone his heirs all that tract or parcel of land called Brown's adventure lying in Ann Arundel County, containing 160 acres of land and likewise 50 acres of land being part of a tract of land called Rattle Snake Neck adjoining to Browns' Adventure. Also I give devise and bequeath unto my grandson Robert Boone son of John Boone and his heirs all that tract or parcel of land called Rockholos Range lying in Ann Arundel County containing 200 acres of land and likewise 100 acres of land being part of a tract called Rattle Snake Neck adjoining to Rockholos Range. I also give and bequeath unto my grandson Nicholas Boone, son of Humphrey Boone one negro boy named Charles and my small Dutch gun. Also I give devise and bequeath all the residue and remaining part of my personal estate after my just debts and legacies are paid and the remaining part of my wife's third deducted unto my two sons Humphrey

472

Boone and Richard Boone to be equally divided between them. And lastly I do hereby constitute ordain and appoint my son Humphrey Boone Executor of this my last will and testament hereby revoking and being nul and void all other wills and testament by me theretofore made and declaring this to be only my last will and testament.

In witness hereof I have hereunto set my hand and affixed my seal this 3rd day of January in the year of our Lord 1758. Robert Boone Witnesses—John Meniken, Joshua Meniken, George Page, Samuel Moss, Nicholas Lewis. Proven—March 24th 1759.

WILL OF THOMAS BOONE, BALTIMORE COUNTY, MD. (copy)

PAGE 2 (first page lost)

two negro boys, Adam and Charles and an unbroke bay colt called Griel-Item I give and bequeath unto my son William Govane Boone and his heirs forever all the remaining part or parcels of that tract of land called the Enlargements that is not heretofore bequeathed to my son John Cockey Robert Burley Boone and to my son Richard Boone and also a negro boy named Solomon and my riding mare named Tipsy—Item I give and bequeath unto my daughter Rebecca and her heirs forever a negro girl named Eve also a feather bed and bolster—Item I give and bequeath unto my daughter Ann Boone and her heirs forever a negro girl named Thenea and a sorrell horse named Dobbin. Item I give and bequeath unto my daughter Elizabeth Boone and her heirs forever a negro girl named Judah—Item I give and bequeath unto my daughter Sarah Boone and her heirs forever a negro girl named Comfort. Item I give and bequeath unto my daughter Susannah Cockey Boone and her heirs forever a negro girl named Casandra.

Lastly all the residue of my estate after my just debts are fully paid and satisfied I give and bequeath unto my Dear and beloved wife Sarah Boone as also my dwelling plantation for and during her natural life that is in case she does not marry but if she should marry I then will that an equal distribution of my effects not already bequeathed should be made and equally divided between my 3 sons and 6 daughters.

And I do hereby make and ordain and appoint my said wife Sarah Boone together with my son John Boone, Executrix and Executor of this my last will and testament—In witness thereof I have hereunto set my hand and affixed my seal this sixth day of December Anno Domini 1774.

THOMAS BOONE

Signed, sealed, published and declared by the testator to be his last will and testament in the presence of us.

signed—John Hopkins, Daniel Evans, Thomas Rutter
A true copy from the original by Edward Cockey.

OTHER ITEMS

In the possession of Mr. Justin J. Stevenson, Columbus, O.—
Lease signed Feb. 17, 1786 being between Daniel Evans, William Stevenson, and John Merryman for the "Merryman Orchard at Popular Hill", for farming.

A letter from Sarah Boone, written March 8th, 1780, Baltimore County, Md. to her son Richard Boone, 7th Maryland Regiment of Captain Richard Anderson's Company.

(Private, 2-8-1777—dis. 11-1-1780, re-inlisted—killed 3-15-1781)

Letter written Feb. 19, 1798 by Caleb Merryman to William Stevenson (c/o John) (mentions Wm. Davis and Joseph Taylor) (another Dec. 31, 1809.)

William Stevenson was administrator of the estate of Richard Boone, who was killed March 15, 1781, while serving in Captain Richard Anderson's Company, 7th Maryland Regiment.

John C. R. B. Boone wrote 2 letters to William Stevenson, Baltimore Co., Md. 6-15-1785 and 8-1-1785.

An old paper possibly used in planning the will of John Stevenson (but not signed).

A tract of land called RIDGLEYS, by the boundary of land called Robert's Park.

13½ acres to George Stevenson.

13 ½ acres to John Stevenson.

13½ acres to William Stevenson.

(Just a part of the whole agreement).

Also an agreement between George R. Stevenson and his wife Catherine of Fairfield Co., O and Joshua Stevenson, 9-2-1843.

William Stevenson, administrator of estate of Sarah Boone Stevenson 3-25-1807. Entire cost of burial $11. Baltimore Co., Md.

Also has—Numerous receipts of Thomas Boone, merchant of Baltimore Co., Md. beginning with July 7, 1749 and including dates in 1756, 1761, and 1762. These are from London, England firms of William Perkins, Henry Carroll, Wm. Barry and George Brash.

ANCESTRY AND DESCENDANTS
OF
MOSES DEMING
1777 — 1868

One of the first group of settlers in 1812 to old Liverpool (now Valley City) Medina County, Ohio in the "Connecticut Western Reserve". (Compiled by Doris Wolcott Strong).

DEMING

BIBLIOGRAPHY:

Private family records kept by Moses Deming (1777-1863), one of first group of settlers from Waterbury, Conn. to Liverpool, Medina Co., Ohio in 1812
Autobiography (manuscript) of Moses Deming Howell's Early History of Southampton, L. I.
Savage's Genealogical Dictionary of New England
Memorial History of Hartford County, Conn.
History of Medina County, Ohio.
Diamond Genealogy

The name of the family appears in early records under various spellings, such as Deming, Demmon, Demond, Dimon, Diamond, Diamont and Dymont, the latter being the first form used in this country.

John and Thomas Dymont (Diamont or Deming) first appear in the Wethersfield records in 1636-45. Savage says they were, perhaps, brothers. This agrees with a tradition of the family. John Deming remained in Wethersfield and vicinity, married Honor Treat. (For his family, see "Deming" in Stiles History of Ancient Wethersfield, Connecticut, also Deming Genealogy.)

Thomas Deming's Yard in Wethersfield in 1648 is mentioned as the place where one of the first ships of the colony (the Tryall) was built. (See Memorial History of Hartford County, Conn.. P. 481). Thomas married Mary Sheaffe in Wethersfield in 1645. They soon removed to Farmington, where their son James was born in 1646. From Farmington, Conn. Thomas removed with his family to Southampton, Long Island, New York, and later to Easthampton, where he died in 1682. His wife, Mary, died August 21, 1706. In his will in 1682 he used the earlier spelling of the name, Dymont, and mentions his wife, Mary, and his children as follows:

James b. 1646
Thomas
Sarah, wife of ————Headley of New Jersey
Abigail
Hannah, wife of ————Bird or Budd
Elizabeth, wife of ————Miller
Ruth, wife of ————Dayton
John, who died before 1682
> (Howell's Early History of Southampton, L. I., 2nd edition, also Diamond Genealogy)

JAMES DYMONT (DEMING) 2, (Thomas 1), b. 1646 in Farmington, Connecticut, died December 13, 1721, in Easthampton, L. I., m. Hannah James (daughter of Rev. Thomas James, minister in Easthampton. (Moses Deming in his autobiography manuscript, mentions the ancestor preacher, who failed to receive the amount agreed upon for his services, and who, in his farewell sermon, stated that "for any person or people to promise what they had not the means to perform, was a trick of the Devil and a devilish trick!") (Howell's Early History of Southampton states Hannah, wife of James, died September 30, 1706, and that he married, second, September 18, 1707, Elizabeth Davis, but this is not given in Diamond Genealogy.)

Issue:

Mary m. Matthias Hopping
Thomas m. Hannah Finney of Bristol, R. I. Jan. 4, 1706-7
John b. c. 1696 (See below)
Hannah m. Joseph Moore or More of Bridgehampton, Jan. 17, 1705
Abigail, m. ————Lupton
Nathaniel

JOHN DYMONT, DIMON, DEMING 3, (James 2, Thomas 1), b. c. 1696 in Easthampton, L. I., d. May 31, 1765, m. (1) December 17, 1718, Deborah Hedges, b. 1696, who died February 18, 1722; (2) Elizabeth Davis, December 25, 1722, who died September 12, 1729; and (3) Rachel Dayton April 23, 1730, who died August 7, 1762. In his will dated March 8, 1764, John Dymont used the spelling Dimon, the first record of a change from Dymont.

Issue:

Deborah bpt. 1724, m. ————Miller
Elizabeth bpt. 1726
John bpt. d. Feb. 7, 1809, m. Anna Knowles (See below)
Elizabeth (2), daughter to third wife, bpt. 1731, m. ———— Hand
Rachel bpt. 1734
(Abraham & Isaac) twins bpt. 1735 (m. Hannah Foster & Eunice Foster) sisters
Mary bpt. 1742

> (Diamond Genealogy)

JOHN DEMING 4, (John 3, James 2, Thomas 1) bpt. 1727, d. February 7, 1809, aged 82, removed to Southbury, Connecticut, married September 14, 1758 Anna Knowles, daughter of Samuel and Elizabeth Knowles of Woodbury. She died August 28, 1809, aged 77. John Deming (Demon) served in the Revolutionary War.

Issue:

Anna b. Aug. 12, 1759, d. 1843, m. Elijah Booth, as his second wife

476

Davis, b. 1762, removed to Albany County, then Onandaga County, N. Y., m. Elizabeth Curtis (See below)

Isaac bpt. Mar. 18, 1764

Betty bpt. Feb. 23, 1766, d. Oct. 12, 1826

Lucretia bpt. Oct. 25, 1767, d. June 19, 1858

John, who settled at Freehold, Chenango County, N. Y. (from manuscript of his brother, Moses Deming)

Mercy, b. 1775, d. Dec. 30, 1858

Moses, b. Dec. 4, 1777, in Southbury, Conn. Dec. 9, 1868, aged 91, in Liverpool, Medina County, Ohio (See below)

(History of Woodbury, Conn)

(Private records of Moses Deming)

DAVIS DEMING 5 (John 4, John 3, James 2, Thomas 1) b. 1762, d. 1839, m. Dec. 19, 1798, Elizabeth Curtis of Stratford, Conn., moved first to Albany County, then to Onandaga County, New York. Served in War of the American Revolution, and received a pension for his service.

Issue:

Delia Ann, b. Sept. 26, 1790, m. 1814 (1) Luke Hitch, (2) 1834, Asa Coleman

Rufus Romeo, (Rev.) b. Feb. 4, 1792, d. 1868, m. Feb. 21, 1825 Julia Ann Porter, dau. Dr. Norton Porter

Electa b. Nov. 28 1793, d. Sept. 14, 1848, m. James Y. Hodges

Cythera b. Apr. 14, 1797, d. Sept. 4, 1848

Sophia b. Nov. 20, 1798, d. Oct. 13, 1850

Lucy b. Nov. 5, 1800, m. Daniel Patten

Stephen Platt, b. Apr. 15, 1803, m. Sarah Carpenter Nov. 28, 1841

Alexander Hamilton b. Feb. 6, 1805

Eliza b. Oct. 20, 1806, m. James Hodges as his second wife

Rutha, b. Oct. 31, 1808, d. Feb. 28, 1812

Charlotte b. Oct. 29, 1810, m. George Poulton

MOSES DEMING 5, (John 4, John 3, James 2, Thomas 1) born December 4, 1777, in Southbury, Connecticut, died December 9, 1868, aged 91, in Liverpool (now Valley City), Medina County, Ohio. He was one of the first group of settlers in Liverpool in 1812. He married (1) June 1, 1802, Ruth Warner, daughter of Justus and Urania (Warner) Warner. She died in Liverpool, Ohio, July 26, 1812———the first death in Liverpool. He married (2) March 11, 1813, Clarissa Cranny, born August 3, 1788, in Brattleborough, Vermont, died June 26, 1814———the second death in Liverpool. He married (3) Nov. 24, 1814, Jerusha Russell, a school teacher from Newburgh, near Cleveland, born Feb. 24, 1785, in Windsor, Conn., died Sept. 10, 1849, in Columbia, Lorain County, Ohio, while on a visit there with her husband, following a runaway accident. Moses Deming was a prominent man in the early days of the settlement, and served as magistrate.

Issue:

(None by first wife).

By second wife:

Clarissa Cranny, b. June 16, 1814, m. Jan. 22, 1833, George Lewis, b. Aug. 16, 1811, d. Aug. 20, 1861

By third wife:

Ralph R. b. Jan. 7, 1816, m. Eliza Phelps

Lucian M. b. Apr. 10, 1818, m. Sallie L. Hastings

Mary Ann b. Dec. 9, 1819, m. Warren Metcalf

Wealthy A. b. July 30, 1824, m. Joseph D. Fuller

CLARISSA CRANNY DEMING 6 (Moses 5, John 4, John 3, James 2, Thomas 1) b. June 16, 1814, in Liverpool, Medina County, Ohio, m. Jan 22, 1833, George Lewis, b. August 16, 1811, d. August 20, 1861.

Issue:

Helen Lewis, b. Mar. 12, 1836
George Henry Lewis, b. June 23, 1838, d. June 2, 1894
Delia A. Lewis, b. Sept. 28, 1839
Charles B. Lewis, b. Feb. 15, 1842
Francis M. Lewis, b. May 16, 1844
William L. Lewis, b. Dec. 12, 1845, d. Oct. 4, 1867
E. Isabelle Lewis, b. May 21, 1847
James Lewis, b. August 3, 1850
Arthur Lewis, b. May 10, 1854
Archie Lewis, b. May 6, 1858

RALPH R. DEMING 6, (Moses 5, John 4, John 3, James 2, Thomas 1) b. Jan. 7, 1816, in Liverpool, Medina County, Ohio, d. Feb. 25, 1852, m. March 10, 1839, M. Eliza Phelps, born Dec. 2, 1818 in Vermont.

Issue:

Mary J. b. Feb. 16, 1840 m. James Elijah Parker
Milton R. b. Jan. 18, 1842, d. August 26, 1862
Albert R. b. Mar. 2, 1847, m. Angie A. Atkinson
Martha E. b. June 12, 1849, m. John J. Warner
Clara C. b. Nov. 18, 1854, m. Otho A. Robinson

LUCIAN M. DEMING 6, (Moses 5, John 4-3, James 2, Thomas 1) born April 10, 1818, in Liverpool, Ohio, died September 29. 1873, married November 8, 1840, Sallie L. Hastings.

Issue:

Juliaette b. August 26, 1841
William D. b. Mar. 3, 1843
Lafayette
Rufus b. May 14, 1849
Francis b. Mar. 18, 1852, d. Apr. 20, 1855
John b. Mar. 20, 1855

MARY ANN DEMING 6, (Moses 5, John 4-3, James 2, Thomas 1) born December 9, 1819, Liverpool, Ohio, d. Feb. 19, 1892, m. March 13, 1836, Warren Metcalf, born in Pike County, New York, Dec. 18, 1810, died July 14, 1889.

Issue:

Milo R. Metcalf b. Sept. 11, 1838, d. Mar. 19, 1864
William Henry Metcalf, b. June 1, 1840, m. Dec. 27, 1867 Sarah Clark
Emily M. Metcalf, b. Feb. 9, 1842, m. Zadock Tillotson
George P. Metcalf, b. Jan. 2, 1844, d. Oct. 4, 1887, m. August 1871 Sarah Stroup
Eliza A. Metcalf, b. Mar. 4, 1846, Edward Clark
Mary J. Metcalf, b. Jan. 22, 1849, m. Sept. 30, 1874 Clay Terrell, son of Jay Terrell (No issue)
Frank D. Metcalf, b. May 29, 1851, m. Alzina Dikeman 1873
Charles A. Metcalf, b. Jan. 17, 1854, m. Carrie R. Boyden

WEALTHY A. DEMING 6, (Moses 5, John 4-3, James 2, Thomas 1) b. Liverpool, Ohio, July 30, 1824, d. July 23, 1887, married Nov. 8, 1840, Joseph D. Fuller, b. Sept. 20, 1819, d. Nov. 16, 1895.

Issue:

Newell J. Fuller, b. Jan. 20, 1844, m. 1871 Carrie A. Fuller, daughter of Ebenezer Fuller

Cordelia A. Fuller, b. April 18, 1853, d. Jan. 6, 1867

William Arthur Fuller, b. Sept. 3, 1869, d. Sept. 24, 1869

MARY J. DEMING 7, (Ralph R. 6, Moses 5, John 4-3, James 2, Thomas 1) b. Feb. 16, 1840, m. July 21, 1860, James Elijah Parker, b. Naples, New York, Jan. 24, 1838, d. Mar. 28, 1894.

Issue:

Maybelle Parker, b. Mar. 16, 1862, m. 1884, James Pillar, born Carlisle, Lorain County, Ohio

Willard Barker Parker, b. August 26, 1868, m. 1891, Nettie Clark

Milton Harlan Parker, b. Sept. 26, 1872, d. Nov. 15, 1874

ALBERT R. DEMING 7 (Ralph E. 6, Moses 5, John 4-3, James 2 Thomas 1) b. Mar. 2, 1847, m. June 14, 1868, Angie A. Atkinson, born June 21, 1846.

Issue:

May Rebecca b. Mar. 23, 1859

Frank Milton b. Apr. 6, 1873

MARTA E. DEMING 7, (Ralph 6, Moses 5, John 4-3, James 2, Thomas 1) b. June 14, 1849, m. August 22, 1866, John J. Warner, b. Sept. 18, 1842

Issue:

Will A. Warner b. Jan. 16, 1869

Clara B. Warner b. June 21, 1872, d. June 26, 1892

CLARA C. DEMING 7 (Ralph 6, Moses 5, John 4-3, James 2, Thomas 1) b. Nov. 18, 1854, m. Dec. 20, 1875, Otho A. Robinson, b. Sept. 28, 1847

Issue:

Grace M. Robinson, b. Nov. 9, 1877

Ellen M. Robinson b. Jan. 26, 1880

Albert O. Robinson b. June 14, 1887, d. Sept. 21, 1887

Otho (or Olo A.) Robinson b. Oct. 5, 1889

WILLIAM HENRY METCALF (son of Warren Metcalf and Mary Ann (Deming) Metcalf, b. June 1, 1840, m. Dec. 27, 1867, Sarah A. Clark.

Issue:

Mary E. Metcalf, b. Feb. 27, 1867, m. Dec. 1896, Frank Yosiger

Orrin G. Metcalf, b. April 2, 1870

Clarence A. Metcalf, b. Jan. 5, 1875

Clark Metcalf, b. May 14, 1880

EMILY M. METCALF (daughter of Warren and Mary Ann (Deming) Metcalf, b. February 9, 1842, m. June 12, 1860, Zadock Tillotson.

Issue:

Albert Z. Tillotson, b. August 2, 1867, m. Sept. 23, 1888, Emily Feakins. They had Roy Tillotson, b. April 1, 1891

Jessie Tillotson b. Dec. 25, 1892

Mary Tillotson b. Nov. 22, 1894

GEORGE METCALF (son of Warren and Mary Ann (Deming) (Metcalf) b. Jan. 2, 1844, died Oct. 4, 1887.

ELIZA A. METCALF (daughter of Warren and Mary Ann (Deming) Metcalf, b. Mar. 4, 1846, m. Dec. 31, 1867, Edward Clark, b. ———died July 1878; m. 2nd., Jan. 10, 1882, D. Ross Brown.

Issue: (by first marriage)
Frank Clark b. Mar. 31, 1869, d. July 31, 1878
Florence Clark, b. Dec. 14, 1874, d. June 28, 1878
(by second marriage)
Ernest Brown b. Feb. 8, 1883
George Brown b. Oct. 22, 1885

MARY J. METCALF (daughter of Warren and Mary Ann (Deming) Metcalf), b. Jan. 22, 1849, m. Sept. 29, 1874 Clay Terrell, son of Jay Terrell of Ridgeville, Lorain County, Ohio. No issue.

FRANK D. METCALF (son of Warren and Mary Ann (Deming) Metcalf), b. May 29, 1851, died April 6, 1877, m. Alzina Dikeman Dec. 16, 1873.

Issue:

Alvira Metcalf, b. Oct. 20, 1874

CHARLES A. METCALF (son of Warren and Mary Ann (Deming) Metcalf), b. Jan. 17, 1854 m. Mary 23, 1882, Carrie R. Boyden. Lived in Elyria, Lorain County, Ohio.

Issue:

Helen B. Metcalf, b. July 11, 1883
George P. Metcalf, b. Mar. 11, 1887
Ruth Metcalf, b. May 6, 1889
Charles A. Metcalf, Jr. b. Feb. 18, 1892

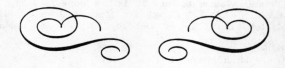

HISTORICAL NOTES ON THE HAWK FAMILY

These Notes Were Compiled by W. J. Hawk

(Contributed by Mrs. John M. Titus)

Our great-grandfather Hawk was a solider in the English army and in a war with Germany, was captured and imprisoned, but made his escape to an island, was taken off by a passing vessel and brought to America where he finally settled on what was then known as Big Capon Cr. The place of his settlement was within 40 miles of Washington. He sent for his family soon after he arrived in this country.

When the Revolutionary broke out, he and his eldest son enlisted in the Continental Army, the son as a drummer boy, being 16 years old at that time. They served under Washington until the close of the war, and were at Valley Forge and Yorktown.

Isaac Hawk went to Greenbrier Co., Va. after he was mustered out and married a widow named Rebecca Collins. His father, Isaac Hawk died at the age of 117 years. When 88 years old Isaac was thrown from a horse and sustained injuries from which he died. He was the father of five sons, viz: Timothy, Isaac, Benjamin, Abraham and Samuel. Timothy located at Circleville, Ohio; Isaac our grandfather, came from Greenbrier Co., Va. and settled on Chickamauga Creek in Gallia Co., O. In 1810 he removed to where Wilkesville, Vinton Co. now stands. He cleared the public square and on the breaking out of the War of 1812, he enlisted in the calvary seervice and with his regiment marched to Sandusky. He was hurt by his horse falling on him, sustaining injuries from which he never fully recovered. He was discharged after three months service and finally settled on a farm two miles north of Wilkesville. The first Divine service ever held in Wilkesville was held in his home by a Rev. Mr. Dixon, a Methodist minister. Grandfather Isaac Hawk married Margaret Lotz, a native of Winchester, Jefferson Co., Va., whose mother's maiden name was Wolf, a niece of Gen. Wolf, hero of Quebec. She died aged 88 years old. Grandfather lived to vote for Abraham Lincoln at his first election, and died in 1862 at the advanced age of 87 years. He and his wife are buried on the top of the hill in the old cemetery at Wilkesville.

They had eleven children, six girls and five boys. Named in the order of their birth, they were Clara, Polly, Benjamin, Henry, Josiah, Michael, Sarah, Susan, Lydia Ann, Jonah and Rachel. The Hawk family is noted for its longevity. All of their children lived to be more than 60 years old with the exception of Clara and Polly. Aunt Lydia Ann Zinn died in Iowa about 1915 at the advanced age of 93. Aunt Rachael Ewing Smith, the last of the family, died at Ewington, Ohio, Aug. 15, 1921, in her 93rd year; Jonah died aged 82; Michael at the age of 84 years.

At the Campbell-Hawk Reunion held at Bethel church near Dundas, O., Aug. 15, 1917, the following grandsons of Isaac and Margaret Hawk were present. Charles E. aged 79 yrs., Layfayette Hawk and Lafayette Gaston each 74 yrs., Cass Hawk aged 80 yrs. and J. J. Hawk aged 69 yrs. The Hawk family did its full share in the war for tho preservation of the union; in all 33 descendants of great-grandfather Hawk served in the Union Army. Of grandfather's immediate family, one son Jonah and six grandsons, viz: Lafayette Gaston, Isaac Eustler, C. O. Hawk, O. F. Hawk, C. E., and Lafayette Hawk served in the Civil War. All lived to return at the close of the war. C. O.

Hawk was with Sherman on his march from Atlanta to the sea. Gaston got a bullet in his shoulder down in Tennesee. Layfayette was made a prisoner at the battle of Kearnstown, Va., July 24, 1865; was confined as a prisoner at Danville, Va., after some two months, he with a number of others escaped and finally reached the Union lines on the Kanaroha river. From there he was not long in making his way home. After a month he returned to his regiment and served until the end of the war.

Michael Hawk, our father, the sixth child of Isaac and Margaret Lotz Hawk was born on the farm two miles north of Wilkesville, Mch. 24, 1816 and died at the same place on Aug. 3, 1900. Margaret Hawk, his wife, was the daughter of Samuel and Margaret Eustler Z'nn, of Jackson Co., O. He was of Irish and she of Dutch descent. Margaret Zinn, their daughter, and our mother, was born July 20, 1821, and died Sept. 18, 1897. She and her husband, Michael, had four sons, named in the order of their birth, Charles E., Lafayette, William, Jasper and Benjamin Lowell. Charles Ephraim was born Oct. 20, 1839 and was married to Christena Barger, a native of Harrison Co., O. on Sept. 13, 1860. He enlisted on Feb. 13, 1864 in Co. C., 36th Ohio Infantry, and was mustered out at Gallipolis, O., June 13, 1865. He was an undertaker and also had a planing mill at Wilkesville with Benton Strong. He died in Wood Co. Nov. 23, 1920, while visiting his daughter Jennie E. Erwin, his home at the time being at Hamden, O. His wife died at Wilkesville.

The old family Bible is in the Ewing family at Ewington.

THE ANCESTRY OF FREDRICK PETERSON
OF SUSSEX COUNTY, NEW JERSEY
AND FRANKLIN COUNTY, OHIO

By Helen Swisher Fuller

Fredrick Peterson with John Swisher, Phillip Swisher, John Winterstein, and others from New Jersey migrated with their families from Sussex County, New Jersey and settled in Madison township, Franklin County, Ohio, in 1807.

Fredrick Feterson married Ellenor P. Lore in Cumberland County, N. J. on November 3, 1775. (Reference: New Jersey Archives). His wife, their grown children, and their younger children, accompanied him to Ohio. His older children had married in New Jersey and brought their families with them. His younger children were reared in Ohio.

Although Fredrick Peterson was old enough to be married in 1775, and hence of age for military service, no reecord of military service in the American Revolution has been found thus far in New Jersey records.

Fredrick Peterson's ancestry may be traced through abstracts of wills in the New Jersey Calendar of Wills, to one Lucas Peterson, (Peterson) (Peters), "planter", who died in 1687. Four generations had preceded Fredrick Peterson in New Jersey.

I. Lucas Peterson, planter.

New Jersey Calendar of Wills, years 1630-1730, page 358. "Lucas Peterson (Peeters) (Feeterson), planter, died Salem Tenth, New Jersey. Will Proven June 20, 1687. Children: Peeter (named executor), Lucas, Haunce, Gabrill, Christian, Elizabeth, Margaret La Croy, wife of John La Croy." Witnesses: Ard Johnson, John La Croy, William Shute.

II. Gabriel Peterson, husbandman fourth
child of Lucas Peterson

New Jersey Calendar of Wills, 1630-1730 page 360. Died at Piles Grove, Salem County, N. J. Will proven Feb. 5, 1728-9. Wife: Cristena. Children: Lucas, Gabriel, Hans, Marget, Mary,

Peter, Lorence, Anna, Abraham, Jonas, Cristena. Executors: Wife, son Lucas ,and Garrett Vanneman. Personal estate 224 pounds, 9 shillings, 4 pence; also included some Swedish books.

III. Peter Peterson Sr. of Morris River,
Salem County, N. J. Yoeman.

New Jersey Calendar of Wills, 1730-1750. Will proven October 18, 1735. Wife: Ann. Children: Peter Peterson, Jr., Henry, Aaron, Gabriel, John, Mathias, Modlena (eldest daughter), Rebecca, Scull, Christian, Elener; Susannah Steelman, daughter of John Steelman also mentioned. Will provides a deed for Andrew Erickson. Witnesses: Henry Hickin, Charles Belitha, Moses Poolson. Executors: Gabriel and Mathias Peterson.

IV. Aaron Peterson of Maurice River (Morris River)

New Jersey Calendar of Wills, 1751-1760. Liber 9, page 334. Will dated July 14, 1759. Will proven August 25, 1759. Wife: Christianna, daughter of Peter Moslander. Children: Aaron, Fredrick, William, Permealy. Legacies to Abraham and Isaac, sons of Hance Peterson of Carolina, deceased. Witnsses: Joseph Savage, Margaret Erexson, Ealse Shaw.

Abstracts of Wills and Settlements of Estates, recorded Franklin County Court House, Columbus, Ohio.

Abstracts of Will—Fredrick Peterson.

(Vol. A. P. 139) "formerly of Cumberland, N. J. Signed Dec. 12, 1823, witnessed by Billingslea Bulls, John Henry. Proven April 17, 1824. Mentions: wife, Eleanor Peterson, sons, Fredrick and Aaron Peterson; daughters, Pamela, Mary, Mahala, Rhoda, Eleanor, and Lydia. Executors: sons Fredrick and Aaron Peterson.

Settlement of Estate (Record No. 0480)

Estate of Fredrick Peterson, April 17, 1824. Fredrick Peterson, Jr. appointed executor with Billingslea Bull and Joseph Wright as sureties.

June 24, 1825, John Swisher was appointed administrator after the death of the executor, with William Godman and Jacob Gander as sureties.

Abstract of Will—John Winterstein of Madison
Township, (Book C, Page 147)

Will mentions wife, daughter, Sarah Ann Kile. Executors: Wife and Thomas Patterson. Witnesses: John Swisher and William D. Needles. Dated Dec. 12, 1835. Proven Mar. 15, 1850.

Abstract of Will—Nicholas Tussing of
Madison Twp., dated July 16, 1849.

Proven Dec. 4, 1850. Wife Margaret, sons, John, J. J.; Margaret, son, George N., daughter, Christena Harris, son,

Adam, a minor. Executors: W. W. Kile and Fredrick Swisher. Settlement of Estate. No. 038. Foos

Guardianship of Nicholas, Margaret, and Polly Foos, infants of John Foos, deceased, October 11, 1809. Guardians named: Jacob De Long, John F. Craun, Fredrick Peterson.

Settlment of Estate No. 0152. Wright

Estate of John Wright. October 9, 1815. Sales to Phileman eedles, John Chaney, Nicholas Winterstein, Phillip Swisher, and others.

***   ***   ***   ***

Sussex County, New Jersey, Marriage Records on file at Court House, Salem, N. J.

Mary Peterson m. John Swisher, Sept. 12, 1802.
Mahala Peterson m. Phillip Swisher, Nov. 27, 1803.
Abraham Swisher Jr. m. Margaret Snyder, Feb. 5, 1805.
Abigail Swisher m. John Winterstein, 1805.

***   ***   ***   ***

Franklin County, Ohio, Marriage Records, Court House, Columbus, Ohio.

Peterson, Lidia m. Samuel Codner, 3-7,1823. Richard Courtright, J. P. Peterson, Rhoda m. Richard Stevenson, June 23, 1807 by Massey Clymer, J. P. Fredrick Peterson gives consent. Witnesses: Phillip Swisher, John Swisher, William Peterson.

***   ***   ***   ***

The Ohio State Journal reported "married Miss Lydia Peterson and Samuel Codner, in Madison Twp. Feb. 7, 1823". The March date of the court record may be the date the return was made to the court by the justice of peace.

***   ***   ***   ***

Graves of the New Jersey pioneer settlers in Ohio have been located as follows:

1. John and Mary (Peterson) Swisher, Hendrew graveyard, Madison Twp., Franklin County, Ohio.
2. Abraham and Margaret Swisher, Truro Cemetery, Truro Twp., Franklin County, Ohio.
3. Mahala, wife of Phillip Swisher, Harrison Twp. Cemetery, Pickaway County, Ohio.
4. James A. Kile, and his wife, Sally Ann Kile, Kile graveyard, Section 6, Madison Twp. John Winterstein and Abigail, his wife, parents of Sally (Sarah) Ann Kile, also are buried here.

Abraham, John, Phillip, and Abigail Swisher were children of Captain Abraham Swisher.* Capt. Swisher and his wife, Hannah Christine, sold land they owned in Knowlton Twp.

* Ohio Genealogical Quarterly Vol. 6, No. 1, p. 500

(p. 519, this volume)

Sussex Co. N. J. in 1811, came to Ohio and purchased land in Harrison Twp., Pickaway Co., Ohio, later owned by their son, Phillip Swisher.

Williams Bros. History of Franklin and Pickaway County, Ohio (1880) page 442, records that "Fredrick Peterson came to Madison township in 1807 from Sussex Co., N. J. and located a mile and a half northeast of Groveport."

Fredrick Peterson's will names sons, Fredrick Jr. and Aaron as executors. It is presumed that Aaron was deceased or had left the community between the time of the writing of Fredrick's will Dec. 12, 1823, and the proving of the will April 17, 1824 as Fredrick Jr. only is named as executor. Less than a year later Fredrick Jr. had died and on June 24, 1825 John Swisher, husband of Fredrick's daughter, Mary, was appointed administrator.

The organization of a Baptist Church in Groveport, Ohio, in 1807 is described in Bareis' History of Madison Twp. Among its first members were Eleanor Peterson (wife of Fredrick) and John and Mary Swisher. Later Fredrick Swisher, son of John and Mary was an active leader in this church for many years.

There are no descendants of Fredrick Peterson by name of Peterson known to be living in Franklin County, Ohio, to-day. There are, however, many descendants of his daughters, Mary Swisher, Lydia Codner, and Rhoda Stephenson (Stevenson).

***   ***   ***   ***

Children of John Swisher and Mary Peterson, his wife.

1. Jacob Swisher b. 7-5-1803, Knowlton Twp. Sussex Co. N. J. d. Groveport, Madison Twp. Franklin Co. Ohio, 12-1-1890.

    m. 1st. Eliza Scothorn (no children); 2nd. Anah Needles,, 3-10-1836. She was born 4-21-1811 in Franklin Co., Ohio d. 9-29-1862, Madison Twp., Ohio.

2. Fredrick Swisher b. May 1, 1807 Franklin Co., Ohio. Lydia Landes b. Jan. 29, 1811, Franklin Co., Ohio. They were married March 8, 1832.

3. Thomas, said to have lived in Marion Co., Ohio.

4. William, said to have "gone west" as did his brother, John, Jr.

5. John Jr. b. 4-3,1815, died 9-25,1872, Montgomery Co. Illinois. m. 1-7-1836, Rebecca Sinker, died 3-31-41, Franklin Co., Ohio m. 2nd. Mary Brown 2-17-1842.

6. Famah b. 5-13, 1809, d. 8-17, 1898. m. 9-14, 1826, Absolom Peters, d. 1-24, 1885. They lived in Pickaway County, O.

7. Marie, m. Michael Plum on 3-5-1829.

8. Phebe, m. William Hoover, on 10-13-1838. They lived on a farm in Crawford Co., Ohio.

THE SPRINGERS OF CHRISTINA
AND RELATED FAMILIES

By William Hamilton Hannum

In the middle of the sixteenth century, in a village identified as Lamstedt in the Province of Hannover, Germany, lived a man called Christopher (probably in German, Christlieb) Springer, that surname probably indicating a residence of the family at Sprin.ge, some nine miles from the town of Hannover. He had a son namd Christopher, born in 1593 probably in Lamstedt, who in 1645, at a town stated as Wisner, perhaps the same as Winsen, which is about 170 miles north of Hannover, married Alma Dorothys Jacobia. In the next year a son was born and was named Lorentze, probably in English to be spelled Lawrence. As he is recorded to have died at Tiverton, R. I., he may be supposed to have been the ancestor of the Springers of New England.

In 1647 Christopher married Henrietta Stuckenrauch and they removed to Stockholm. In 1650 a daughter was born, who was named Christina, apparently for the Queen who was reigning there. A third marriage occurred in 1654, the bride's name being Beata Jacobine Hendrickson (or Hindricsson as then usually spelled). She was known as Lady Beata and was apparently of noble family. She served as lady-companion to Hedwig Eleonora, Queen of Charles X of Sweden, and it may be inferred that Christopher was serving in some royal connection. In Sweden five more children came, the second of whom was Carl, born in 1658. He is often mentioned by historical writers as Charles Christopherson Springer, the patronymic being used as a middle name after the Swedish manner. Christopher was sent as Swedish consul-general to London and the boy, Carl, was taken there for education. When walking on the street one evening, he was seized and forced on board of a ship lying in the river, bound for Virginia. This seems to have been a recognized method of recruiting laborers for the colonial planations. The agents employed by the chartered companies to bring in men may be supposed to have chosen Carl as an able-bodied foreigner, without concern for his family identity.

In Virginia, with other laborers and indentured servants, he was sold, probably at auction, and the purchaser held the legal right to recover his expenditure by a claim on the service of the laborer. Carl thus served for five years, and then, having heard of the Swedish colony at Fort Christina on Christina Creek, later called Willing Town and Wilmington, walked to the place and joined his countrymen in 1683. He married about 1686, his wife's name being Maria (or Marie).

In a few years he attained great infuence, especially in the Lutheran Church, which was under the charge of a Swedish clergyman sent out for the purpose. Records show that in 1691 he was one of two lecturers who presided in certain services and in 1697 he was appointed a scribe of the congregation. He became a church-warden and was the leader in the erection of the edifice which is still standing, called since its transfer to the Anglican body Holy Trinity Church, but commonly called the Old Swedish Church. He is said also to have served as a civil magistrate. He died on the 26th of May 1738, honored for his fine character and for his manifold services. He was buried in the Church, but when some years later it became necessary to alter the position of a wall close beside his grave and the members of the family were asked to have the body moved, they refused and thus the present wall covers the grave. When I saw the place a few years ago, no mark could be found to show the location.

Carl left five sons and two daughters. The second son, John, took a wife named Mary and died in 1772, leaving five sons and three daughters. The seventh of those children, Elizabeth, was born in 1739 and was married at about 20 years of age to John Augustus. The record of Holy Trinity Church has an entry of 1772 of assent given by the vestry to John's request for release from payment of burial fees for his father-in-law, John Springer, at the rate required of strangers, because he had been prevented by blindness from frequenting the Church. John and Elizabeth had eleven children the seventh of whom was another John Augustus who was born in 1775. About 1796 he married Hannah Hendrickson, thus forming a second connection with the old family of that name. They seem to have been third cousins. Hannah's ancestral line has not been definitely traced but it may have been from Cornelis Hendrickson, who is mentioned in local histories as having in 1616 sailed up the Delaware River and landed in what is now the state of Delaware. One authority however states that a Dutchman of the name in 1615 sailed up the Zuydt (i. e. Delaware) River and saw the site of Philadelphia.

In Delaware Co., Pa., at Eddystone, on the north bank of Plum Creek near its confluence with the Delaware, stands an old stone house, on the corner of which is faintly carved the number 1620 (or 1629). It is known as the Hendrickson house and it may have been Hannah's birthplace.

Carl Christopherson Springer's third son, Joseph, had a wife named Annika and he died about 1780. They had nine children, of whom the sixth was another Joseph, born 17th Oct. 1739, and he died in 1832.

488

He had a son John, whose dates seem divergent, but he is said to have had four children, the youngest of whom, Lydia, was married in 1820 to Rev. William Hamilton, of Muskingum and Union Counties, Ohio. Of their eight children the second was John Waterman Hamilton, who was born in 1823 and died on the 1st of January 1898 after a long and distinguished medical practice in Columbus, O. He left six children, two of whom worthily followed in their father's profession in Columbus.

Long ago I was told by my Aunt, the widow of my mother's Uncle, David Allen Hamilton of Columbus, of a conversation that she had had with Dr. J. W. Hamilton, with the conclusion that there was no traceable relation between the two Hamilton families. The link now found through the Springer family is gratifying.

John and Hannah (Hendrickson) Augustus lived in Christiana Hundred, New Castle Co., Del., a few miles from Wilmington, but within a few years, according to family tradition, they removed to Virginia whence about 1805 they went on to Ohio. The location in Virginia and the westward route taken are unknown, but the intended destination was the vicinity of Chillicothe, where John's brother David with his wife, Ann Hart, had settled. As the travellers came along Zane's Trace, in what is now Clearcreek Township, Fairfield County, they were stopped by the death of one of their horses, and making camp they observed the good rolling land with splendid forest and they found a spring with ample flow of cold water, and ascertaining that land was available they settled there. There the family was reared and on that farm is the Augustus cemetery with many graves of the Augustus and Hedges families. The latter family seems to have come from near Wilmington and that may have been one reason for the other's settlement. Close by their farm stood the Augustus School til a generation ago. Though John was a farmer he served about five years as a justice of the court at Lancaster, no legal eduction being then required. A small silver teaspoon, marked 'H. H.', is in my possession, received from Hannah's daughter, my Grandmother, Rebecca (Augustus) Hamilton, and from her also were received other personal articles of her mother's, as a large tortoise-shell comb and a portion of a gay bonnet. A list of subscriptions,* dated 3rd of June 1830, for the erection of a Presbyterian meeting-house at the neighboring village of Tarlton, shows the names of John Augustus, the largest of the fifty-three subscribers, and his sons, David and John. The list is preserved in the Archaeological Museum in Columbus. John and Hannah had two sons and five daughters. Of them Rebecca was married to William Hamilton, who in infancy had been brought by his parents from Ayr Township, Bedford Co., Pa., to Perry Township, Hocking Co., O., but he was reared on a farm in Clearcreek Tp., adjoining that of the Augustus family. He became a teacher in a district-school and served several years as county-surveyor. He was for many years an officer, first a major and then a colonel, in the Ohio Militia, and his regimental record is in the Archaeological Museum in Columbus.

* Ohio Genealogical Quarterly, Page 98. (p. 522, this volume)

STEVENSON-BOONE FAMILY RECORDS

STEVENSON FAMILY BIBLE

In good condition with brown calf-skin binding. Fly leaf gone. Supposedly published in 1696. Pages of family record complete, but torn. Printed by Charles Bill, London, England.

Original owner—William and Mary Boone Stevenson, Baltimore County, Md. *Present owner*—Justin J. Stevenson, Columbus, Ohio. Copied by Mrs. Mayburt Stephenson Riegel, Columbus, Ohio.

FAMILY RECORD, PAGE 1

Jeremiah Mckelvey died Feb. 19, A. D. 1834.

Mary Stevenson died Jan. 13th, 1835.

William Stevenson died Mar. 11th, A. D. 1835.

Joshua B. Stevenson died Mar. 17th A. D. 1848.

Mary B. Taylor died Dec. 31st, 1863.

Susannah L. Bowen died June 15th A. D. 1863.

(Written at later date in other handwriting)—George R. Stevenson died Jan. 7th, 1884.

PAGE 2

William Stevenson, son of John and Susannah Stevenson his wife, was born in the year of our Lord, October the 6th, 1763.

Mary Boone, daughter of Thomas and Sarah Boone was born in the year of our Lord, March the 23rd, 1763.

William Stevenson of John and Susannah his wife and Mary Boone daughter of Thomas and Sarah Boone was married the 15th day of February in the year of our Lord 1784.

William and Mary Stevenson lived together in wedlock 51 years, 10 months, and 29 days.

PAGE 3

Sarah Stevenson, daughter of William and Mary Stevenson, born July 29, 1786. George King Stevenson, son of William and Mary Stevenson, born August 7, 1788. Susannah Stevenson, daughter of William and Mary Stevenson, born May 20, 1790. Jemima Stevenson, daughter of William and Mary Stevenson, born July 21, 1793.

PAGE 4

Mary B. Stevenson, daughter of William and Mary Stevenson, born June 16, 1796. Ann B. Stevenson, daughter of William and Mary Stevenson, born Jan. 9, 1800. Joshua Richard Boone Stevenson, son of William and Mary Stevenson, born April 2, 1803.

PAGE 5

Mary Glanvill, daughter of Stephen and Sarah Glanvill was born in the year of our Lord Dec. 10th, 1811.

Joshua R. Boone Stevenson and Mary Glanvill were married—— (torn).

PAGE 6

Crumwell W. Stevenson, son of Joshua and Mary Stevenson, born Dec. 9, 1827, (d. at birth). Milton G. Stevenson, son of Joshua and Mary Stevenson, born June 11, 1829, Alphaes B. Stevenson, son of Joshua and Mary Stevenson, born June 5, 1831. Irvin E. Stevenson, son of Joshua and Mary Stevenson, born March 17, 1839. Minerva Jane Stevenson, dau. of Joshua and Mary Stevenson, born Dec. 20, 1840 and died Dec. 25, 1885.

Mary, wife of Joshua R. B. Stevenson died Jan. 20 A. D. 1894.

Milton Glanville, son of Joshua R. B. and Mary Stevenson died June 12, 1905.

Irvin E. Stevenson died Jan. 1923.

Milton Lafayette Stevenson, son of Alphaes Boone and Elizabeth Jane Woods Stevenson, born October 1856, died Jan. 15, 1932.

Alice Carey Stevenson, daughter of Alphaes Boone and Elizabeth Jane Woods Stevenson, born October 1858, died May 23, 1933.

Justin Jason Stevenson, son of Alphaes Boone and Elizabeth Jane Woods Stevenson, born Dec. 9, 1871.

Additional dates, on paper written by Alphaes B. Stevenson.

William Stevenson, son of John and Susannah Stevenson, died March 11, 1835.

Mary Stevenson, daughter of Thomas and Sarah Boone, died Jan. 13, 1835.

George K. Stevenson died Jan. 7, 1884. Married Katie Hopkins.

Susan, married Robert Bowen; died June 15, 1863.

Jemima, married ————— McKelvey, died Feb. 9, 1834.

Mary B., Married ————— Taylor, died Dec. 31, 1863.

Ann B., married ————— Hopkins, died Spring 1873.

Joshua R. B. Stevenson died March 17, 1848.

Joshua R. B. Stevenson and Mary Glanville were married Jan. 9, 1827.

Minerva J. Stevenson, born Dec. 20, 1840, and died Dec. 25, 1885, leaving one son John J. Pickering, her son James Pickering having died. Remained a widow.

Susan Stevenson, daughter of William and Mary Stevenson was married to Robert W. Bowen, May 22, 1817. There was born to this union eight children as follows—Thomas G. Bowen was born March 1, 1818, married Lucinda Crouse March 20, 1850. (Children, Minerva Bowen born August 10, 1851 died unmarried; Sept. 10, 1884 —Irvin Bowen born June 24, 1851—Olive L. Bowen, born June 5, 1854—Oliver T. Bowen born Feb. 16, 1854, married ————— Grove.) Lucinda Bowen died Dec. 15, 1855. Thomas G. then married June 20, 1858 Hannah Glanville, daughter of Nathan and Rebecca Glanville. Had one heir by this union, George Lucian Bowen born Nov. 12, 1860. Thomas G. Bowen died April 22, 1882.

Ruth W. Bowen, daughter of Robert W. and Susan Bowen born June 20, 1819, died Sept. 7, 1887.

Mary S. Bowen, born Dec. 12, 1820, married————— Cimer.

Sarah W. Bowen, born Feb. 19, 1823, married ————— Boyd. (widowed).

Susan G. Bowen, born Sept. 8, 1825, married Bolenbaugh. (widowed).

Julia Bowen, born Nov. 17, 1827, married ————— Lyons. (widowed).

Charles Bowen, born May 21, 1830.

Nathan Bowen.

CHARLES ROBERT SWICKARD

April 14, 1864—May 12, 1940

IN MEMORIUM

This issue of the Ohio Genealogical Quarterly is dedicated to the memory of Charles Robert Swickard, trustee of the Columbus Genealogical Society and a member of the committee on Publication, Ohio Genealogical Quarterly.

CHARLES ROBERT SWICKARD

Born April 14, 1864—Died May 12, 1940

Charles R. Swickard, aged 76, a leading real estate broker in Columbus died suddenly at his home 30 South Monroe avenue Sunday, May 12. The funeral was held at Egan-Ryan Chapel with interment in St. Joseph's cemetery. Mr. Swickard had spent Saturday as usual at his office. A native of Westerville, Mr. Swickard had been engaged in the real estate business in Columbus 44 years.

Surviving him are his wife, the former Helena G. Cohan, a daughter, Marion, and a sister, Mrs. Edgar B. Smith, Detroit.

Mr. Swickard was a trustee of the Columbus Genealogical Society, and served on the committee of Publication for the Ohio Genealogical Quarterly. He was interested in genealogy, not for himself, but as a matter of public interest and civic concern. He was a member of the class of 1893, Ohio State University, the Columbus Gallery of Fine Arts, The Virginia Historical Society, The Historical Society of Pennsylvania, The German Society of Pennsylvania, a life member of the Ohio State Archeological and Historical Society, a member of the Sons of the American Revolution and of the Society of Colonial Wars.

A SHORT SKETCH OF THE SWICKARD FAMILY

As given by Charles R. Swickard, at a Reunion at Steubenville, Ohio, July 26, 1935.

As far as known the first Swickard who came to this country was Daniel. He eventually settled in Somerset Township, Washington County, Penna. At the time this part of Pennsylvania was claimed by Virginia and Daniel on Feb. 18, 1780 entered a claim for 400 acres of land but after a survey there was issued to him a Pennsylvania patent April 8, 1788 for 312 acres strict measure. Pennsylvania honored Virginia titles. The farm was patented under he name, THE GERMAN FARM.

This land was originally surveyed under a Virginia certificate in 1780 by Colonel William Crawford, friend and land agent of Colonel George Washington, the same Colonel Crawford who lead the ill fated Expedition against Sandusky.

The latest information as to when Daniel came to this country is derived from a recent publication known as Pennsylvania German Pioneers in which appears the name Dannial Zwigart. This was in 1765. There is a tradition in our branch of the family made known to me December 5, 1894 by a cousin Jonathan Swickard, a grandson of Daniel, brother of Martin and who was thirty-one years of age when this Daniel died. This cousin was reared in the vicinity of where this Daniel resided, after Daniel came to Franklin County, Ohio.

The tradition is that the Swickard family came with two sons Martin and Daniel. They came from Germany about 1764 and were six months "Crossing" (really coming). Martin was about eighteen years of age and Daniel eight years younger.

493

In 1764 Martin actually was eighteen years of age but Daniel was only born that year. As a mistake of one year in the date of coming so far back could easily be made, being handed down by word of mouth for 100 years and more, it seems reasonable to assume that the family who arrived in Philadelphia in 1765 was our family.

No doubt Elizabeth and Eva, known members of the family, and David, probably a member, as well as others, came along. There was a difference of 18 years between the ages of Martin and Daniel. If there were only five children the three in between these two would have been born about five years apart which would have been unusual and the probability is that there were some others who became victims of the long voyage which will be referred to later.

In a history of Washington County, Penna, it is stated that Martin Swickard was born in Penna., but this seems to be an error as all evidence points to his having been born in Germany.

In the Martin Swickard line it is said that the Swickards came from Alsace, France. Alsace was long a part of the German government but at the time the Swickards are thought to have come over here Alsace was a part of France just as it is now. But it had been German so long prior to becoming a part of France and was a part of France such a comparatively short time prior to the coming of the Swickards, that I, myself, am convinced that the Swickards when they came over here were German. The name Zwickart and variants of this as used in Washington County, Penna., and also their writing at that time is plainly German.

Whether from Alsace or just what part of Germany they came from, it seems that they must have come from far up the Rhine. The story of the cousin who told me of their being on the way six months indicates this because upon good authority it required about six months to come from far up the Rhine. Gottleib Mittelberger in his "Journey to Pennsylvania in 1750", tells about this. The Rhine boats from Heilbronn* to Holland had to pass by twenty-six custom houses, at all of which the ships were examined and this was done when it suited the convenience of the custom house officials. In the meantime the ships with the people were detained long so that the passengers had to spend much money. When the ships came to Holland they were detained three to six weeks and because things were expensive the poor people had to spend nearly all they had during that time, From Rotterdam in Holland it was necessary to go to some English port in order to get clearance papers to enter a Province of England. In England there was another delay of one or two weeks when the ships were either waiting to be passed through the custom house or waiting for favorable winds. The voyage proper was marked by much suffering and hardship. The passengers were packed in densely, like herring, without proper food and water and were subject to all

*Heilbronn is on the Neppar river which empties into the Rhine at Mannheim, south of Heidelberg a short distance. But the Rhine extends far up beyond the Neppar into Germany.

sorts of diseases. The children were the first to be attacked by diseases. and died in large numbers. The terrors of disease were much aggravated by frequent storms.

Quote:

"A gale rages for two or three nights and days so that everyone thinks that the ship will sink. When the sea rages and surges the ship is constantly tossed from side to side so that no one can walk or sit or lie and the closely packed people in the berths are thereby tumbled over each other, both sick and well—it can readily be seen that many of these people, none of whom were prepared for hardships, suffered so terribly that they did not survive."

So many passengers were ill on arrival that an island was set apart and a hospital erected there. Many of the sick passengers died. In the year 1754 there were 253 deaths of immigrants on this island.

Just when the Swickards first came to Washington County, Penna., is not positively known, but the Penns who had bought this part of Pennsylvania from the Indians in 1768 for 10,000 pounds in gold coin, were in control and in the spring of 1769 opened the land for settlement and offered it for 5 pounds or about $25.00 per 100 acres. There was an additional charge of one pence per acre Quit Rent. In 1774 the Virginians usurped the land claiming it as part of Virginia. They opened sales giving 100 acres for 10 shillings plus 2 shillings 6 pence for the certificate, making the land purchased from Virginia cost about 1/10 of that bought from Pennsylvania. Disregarding the 2 shillings 6 pence, this Virginia land in our money cost about 2½ cents and acre. Lord Dunmore on behalf of Virginia broke up the court established by the Penns and established his own. The next year, 1775, when the Revolutionary War began, Lord Dunmore was driven out as a Tory but the Virginians divided the southwestern Pennsylvania land into three Virginia counties. The section in which the Swickards settled was presided over by the Yohogania court.

The minutes of this court are preserved and the first records of the Swickard family found in these minutes appear to show them on a farm which was the identical piece of ground in Somerset Township on which they lived for a number of years.

These old courts were jammed with suits about land. The first Swickard record was on the docket of Dunmore's court May 20, 1775, Swigart v. Mills. The title of this case was preceded by "B" and followed by "Adj" both being notations by clerks. Just what "B" means is not surmised. It is possible Adj means adjusted or adjourned.

Again on Yohogania docket are four cases in which two were brought by Francis Morrison, one against Danial Swigart and the other against David Swigart. In one of the other cases Danial Swigart was plaintiff v. James Murphy and in another some Swigart, first name not given on Nov. 25, 1778 was plaintiff v. Clemens, et al.

There appears one in March 23, 1779, Swigart v. Murphy,

Judg. W. I. which is interpreted to mean, judgment with interest in favor of the plaintiff.

These records indicate that there was a David in the family and as the next to the last case mentioned (brought Nov. 25, 1778) was abated by the death of the plaintiff, the presumption is that this was David who may have been a Revolutionary War Casualty.

I have made a careful search of the United States census of 1790 for the name of Swigart in Washington County, but such a name was not found. However, the name Swickard as will appear later was found. From this it is concluded that these court records with Swigart referred to ancestors in our family. If so, and there can scarcely be any doubt about this, these records prove that the Swickards were on their Washington County land as early as 1775 and from the fact that these lands were open to settlement as early as 1769 it is possible they were there at that time. If there is any question in your minds as to the Swickards being over there early, then how is this?

In a Will dated April 27, 1779 made by John Book and proved June 19, 1786, among the witnesses are, Martin Swickert and Danniel Zwigart.

Daniel signed and Martin made his mark. The signature of Daniel is identical with that of Danniel in the Ship Betsey list 1765, which to me is positive evidence that the Swickard family early in Washington County, Pa., was one and the same as the family that landed at Philadelphia in 1765. My opinion is corroborated by that of Dr. Wm. J. Hinke, Editor of Pennsylvania German Pioneers, which work required him to decipher and translate over 30,000 signatures, mostly in German. See copy of his letter. Daniel Jr. only lacked 3 months of being 15, and it is not probable he would have been eligible to witness. Martin is known to have signed his name to deeds by making his mark. Apparently Martin could not write, but when he went on his own bond as Administrator of his father's estate, he did sign and likewise signed his final account filed 31 July 1813, in Washington County, Pa. He also signed a receipt. It is quite evident that Martin himself as well as Daniel the father was there,—only 2 years and 4 months after the Battle of Trenton which to me is significant.

In 1781 or 7 years before Daniel received his Patent for 312 acres, he was assessed for taxes on 200 acres, 3 horses, 2 cattle, 5 sheep.

In Deed Book 1 N, page 620 is a deed Agreement dated January 17, 1798 by which Daniel Swickhart in effect made his last Will and Testament well worthy of study and of being followed in its provisions as to protecting the maker by any parent who executes a similar instrument. A copy of this follows:
"is to have 100 pounds good and lawful money out of the estate and the daughter Eva Lash is to have 100 acres of land of Daniel's son Martin. Then after the demise of both parents it is provided that the son Daniel received the tract of land purchased by the father from David Crawford, and the son Martin received the land originally patented less the 100 acres that went to Eva."

496

This Deed Agreement was accepted in writing by Daniel but there is nothing on the record that shows Martin as having accepteed. There is no doubt but that he actually did accept and received this land.

From the foregoing it is evident that in the family of Daniel and his wife Maria there were at least five children. The United States census of 1790 shows Daniel as having under his roof two males under sixteen. The presumption is that these were the children of David who had apparently died as in the Yohogania court record.

Creigh's History of Washington County gives an account of the Whisky Insurrection of 1794. This grew out of the levying of an excise tax of 10c to 25c upon every gallon of domestic distilled liquor and placed a tax on stills according to their capacity. The population of western Pennsylvania as the time was about 87,000, very small compared with the population in the remainder of the country. This western part of Pennsylvania produced more whiskey than any equivalent section in the colonies. The Continental Congress, a revolutionary body which derived its authority from the success of the Revolution, had put itself on record as opposed to any excise tax and the people of western Pennsylvania felt that this tax was an encroachment on their rights and privileges and all agreed upon the principle enunciated by the Congress of 1774 that an excise law "was the horror of all free states". They were aroused as were the New Englanders who held the Boston Tea Party when England put a tax on tea.

There was little market for the products of western Pennsylvania this side of the mountains and by distilling grain into whisky the people could transport to the east across the mountains in the form of distilled whisky what was the equivalent of 24 bushels of rye or six times as much as could be tranported of the grain itself. Every sixth man became a distiller, and he distilled not only for himself but also for his neighbors so that practically everyone in this section was called upon to pay this tax. Monongahela was the center of this Insurrection.

So serious was this Insurrection that President Washington himself left the seat of government at Philadelphia and appeared in person at Bedford, Penna., before an Army which he had called out for the purpose of ending this Insurrection. This Army did so at a cost to the government in money of over $600,000.00.

Residents of Washington County and perhaps of other counties were required to subscribe to an oath of allegiance. Creighs History gives the list and in it is found Daniel and Martin Swickard and some of their neighbors among them being Isaac Lash. The name of Swickard is there of record in the form of Zuzidant which shows how names become changed when written by another.

Whether the Swickards and Isaac Lash actually took part in the Insurrection is not known and need not be inferred from the fact that they signed the oath of allegiance to the government. None of these names are among those whose stills were seized nor who were earrested or wanted for arrest.

It appears that Daniel the pioneer died late in 1803 or in Jan. 1804 as Martin his son signed a bond as administrator in Washington County, Penna., on January 27, 1804. Martin moved to Jefferson County, Ohio, in 1805 and did not file his Final Account until 1813. In this account is a claim for expenses incurred during five trips made from Jefferson County to Washington County. The Mother is thought to have died before Daniel her husband.

Tradition in the Martin branch of the family is that Daniel resided in Lancaster County and also that Martin resided for some time in the Everglades of Maryland. There is no such place as the Everglades of Maryland, although there is a place known as the Glades which are located in what was then Maryland but are now in what is known as Somerset County, Penna., which adjoins the north line of the western part of Maryland. Tradition in the Daniel Swickard branch of the family is that the Swickards were at one time in Bucks County which is not far from Philadelphia and were in Lancaster County, Penna. before going to Washington County.

By March 1789, Daniel, the pioneer, had acquired 466 acres. Of this 312 acres were patented and 154 acres and 115 perches, bought from David Crawford in 1789 for 154 pounds, 14 shillings and 4½ pence or practically one pound an acre. The total cost of this last parcel being in our money $751.89. Although this deed was executed in 1789 it may be stated as a matter of interest that it was not put on record until March 6. 1811 or twenty-two years after the purchase.

Daniel and his wife Maria were no doubt buried in some one of the small burying grounds near his land.

Apparently Daniel, the brother of Martin, remained in Washington County until 1822. That is the date he moved to Franklin County, Ohio, and the records of Washington County show that he made sales the same year, apparently selling everything he had before he came to Ohio.

On February 26, 1822 he sold to his brother Martin an undivided one half interest in Section No. 26, Township No. 28. Jefferson County, Ohio, of which the two were seized in fee simple.

This Daniel and wife Mary, born Dague, brought up a family of twelve, all of whom in turn brought up families some of which were quite large. The descendants are widely distributed in the northern states between Ohio and California. This Mary Dague who married Daniel a brother of Martin, was a daughter of Frederick Dague, Sr., a Revolutionary Soldier, and some of his descendants are now living over near Scenery Hill, Washington County, Penna. Incidentally I might say that two of his sons were also Revolutionary Soldiers. One of them, Mathias, moved to Franklin County, Ohio, about 1810 and he and his wife and many descendants are buried in the Dague Cemetery near

New Albany. Mary, the daughter of Frederick, is said to have lived to be over 100 years of age.

As Martin Swickard is credited with having been in the Revolutionary War, so also is Philip Saltzman, his brother-in-law, who married Elizabeth the daughter of Daniel, the pioneer, he being of record in Penna. Archives, Series o, vol. 2, page 133 as in Washington County Militia from a return made September 19, 1781.

The records were searched as to Isaac Lash in the Revolutionary War but his name was not found. But little more is known by me of either the Saltzmans or the Lashs, except that Isaac Lash and his family seeemed to have remained in Washington County, Penna., while Philip Saltzman and famliy moved to Jefferson County, Ohio.

Daniel, a son of Daniel, son of Daniel, the pioneer, was in the War of 1812 and enlisted from Jefferson County, Ohio. He moved to Franklin County early and there with his wife who was Mary Magdalene Kintner, daughter of George Kintner of Washington County, Penna., a Revolutionary Soldier, reared a large family. He was a Justice of the Peace for many years and was known as Squire Swickard, married many people and with the help of the others in his family accumulated a number of farms aggregating about 1000 acres, leaving upon his death a farm to each one of his children, there having been ten or so. Three Daniels are of record in the same War from Jefferson County. One was put down as "Big" Daniel and in another record as Daniel, Sr., another as Daniel, Jr. and the other as Daniel. The Daniel and Daniel, Sr. were probably in the Martin line. Saltzmans are also listed in the War of 1812. In the Civil War there were some Swickards in the Daniel line and no doubt some in the Martin line but this I have not investigated. This may also be said of the World War.

Rev. Nathan A. Swickard, a cousin of mine, has it that the first Swickard who came over fought on the side of the colonists, presumably in the Revolutionary War. The assistant to the Librarian at Harrisburg, wrote that she is of the opinion that Daniel the pioneer, served in the Revolutionary War but she could not give any reference. However, the records at Harrisburg and also in Washington as to Soldiers of the Revolution are quite incomplete. Another cousin of mine who resided in the vicinity of Daniel, son of the pioneer, told me that Daniel served in the Revolutionary War but I have been unable to get any official record of this. Daniel the son was only eleven years old when the War began and seventeen when it virtually ended which was Otcober 19, 1781 when Cornwallis surrendered to Washington. The War was not actually over until the Peace Treaty was signed in 1783 when Daniel was nineteen. It is possible he did actually serve and it is hard to think that either he or his Father or both did not serve as so many during those six years of active conflict did get into the War. The very fact that Daniel the pioneer was able to patent land is evidence that he was a patriot. Referring to the Revolutionary War records, I find that about the first question asked by nearly every young person with whom I talk about the family is, "are we entitled to join the D. A. R. or the S. A. R.?" The records show that any descendant of either of the Martin or Daniel line is entitled to join one of these societies.

As a matter of interest it seems fitting to repeat the story related to me a few years ago by Rev. Nathan A. Swickard who is now about 74 years of age. When he was a boy some elderly man at New Albany, Franklin County, Ohio, told him that some years before two courtiers in livery or uniform, each wearing a sword dangling at his side came to New Albany in search of an heir to the title and estates of a nobleman who had died in Germany and who was the last of his family in Germany to have the right to the title and estate. They were looking for an heir in this country and satisfied themselves that one of the Swickards in New Albany, presumably Daniel the brother of Martin, was the right heir. They so informed the Swickard found but he refused to go with them and qualify saying that he was settled in this land of the free, had a large family and was content to remain where he was

The same story so Nathan Swickard informed me was told his Father. Whether it is a fairy tale or was part of an attempted racket such as the racketeering that goes on now I cannot say but its repetition seemed worth while for entertainment if nothing else.

The Swickard family is known to have been and still is represented by those who have devoted their lives to the ministry, to medicine, to the law and to teaching. Some have engaged in business and some in the trades but for the most part, they have been tillers of the soil and hewers of wood, doing in a quiet way their share of the work of the world, a hard working, industrious and law abiding people, representatives of that great middle class, which is the salt of the earth and without which civilization could not carry on. They were here in colonial times before our nation had separated from her unworthy mother country. They and those into whose families they married played an honorable part in making possible this separation. After the separation our forebearers and their descendants, have taken an active part in clearing the forests, making homes, establishing communities, building roads and in all other things necessary in the making of a great country. They have not made for themselves names known far and near but certainly their combined efforts in the making and upbuilding of the nation, I dare say, is equal and in some cases, far superior to the work, judged by its results, of some who have risen to distinguished positions in the affairs of the nation. Yet. while none have become, nationally prominent, however, as time goes on and the younger and coming generations with the new blood from marriages into other families, reap the advantages afforded, there is no telling who and from whence in the

The Swickard Family Chart

Charles Robert
Swickard
b. April 14, 1864
Westerville, O.
d. May 12, 1940
Columbus, O.
m. June 11, 1902
Helena G. Cohan

Florence Belle
Swickard
Amelia Gertrude
Swickard
William Ells-
worth Swickard
Daisy Josephine
Swickard

Henry Swickard
b. Mar. 13, 1835
d. Nov. 30, 1894
m. Jan. 1, 1857

Sarah Langham
b. Jan. 19, 1827
d. Nov. 3, 1902

Jacob Swickard
b. Apr. 27, 1812
d. Dec. 31, 1871
m. Sept. 14, 1832

Mary Baughman
b. Aug. 1, 1813
d. Nov. 25, 1883

Robert Langham
b. Apr. 12, 1796
d. Oct. 11, 1859

Sarah Kinney
b. Jan. 2, 1796
d. Feb. 11, 1848

Daniel Swickard
(Zwigart)
b. 1764; d. Mar.
8, 1849

Mary M. Dague
m.

Adam Baughman
b. 1778; d. Mar.
26, 1853
m.

Priscilla
Huffman
(Stella)
b. Nov. 9, 1783
d. Sept. 6, 1865

Wm. Langham
b. 1756 or 57
d. Aug. 10, 1830
fr. Birmingham,
Eng.

m.
Jennie Fulton
Bailey
an orphan, whose
grandparents
lived and are
buried in Bed-
ford County,
Penna.

Daniel Zwigart b. ab. 1723, Germany; d. 1803,
Wash. Co., Penna.
m. Maria ——, d. before 1808.

Fredrick Dug. b. 1786; d. Oct. 12, 1796
m. Maria ——, b. 1735 (Apr. 15); d. Oct. 28, 1813

Abraham
Baughman
b. 1755

Mary Kat-
arine Deeds
(Dietz)

John Huffman
b. ab. 1750 near
Hagerstown, Md.
d. 1825 or 26
near Columbus,
Ohio
"Capt. John Huff-
man of the In-
dian Wars."
In 1802 he bought
4000 ac. in Plain
twp. in Franklin
Co., Ohio.

m.
Catharine Book
(Buch)

Abraham
Bachman
fr. Wortemberg,
Ger.

Rudolph
Huffman
d. 1794

m. (1) ——
(by whom John
and Henry)

m. (2) Dorothy
(by whom 8 sons,
3 daughters)

Johannes Buch
d. 1786

Jacob Platter
b. 1689;
d. 1734

Nicholas Platter
b. 1722, July 8,
at Neuweiler,
Ger.

m.
Margaret
Platter

Michael Platter
b. ab. 1625
at Erlenbach,
near Berne,
Suisse

m.
Maria ——
b. 1665
d. June 14, 1729

Michael Platter
b. Nov. 3, 1656
d. Dec. 18, 1719

m.
Magdalena ——

m.
Magdalena
Muller

501

family will come those who will attain high places in the nation.

But whether this is ever realized or not, let us bear in mind that work honorably and intelligently performed is what counts in the world and it is not to be thought but that the members of the Swickard family and their descendants, will do their part with credit in the future as they have done in the past. The Swickards, although industrious, ambitious and accumulative, as is shown by their large and widely distributed land holdings, yet, when it comes to forging to the front in public life, they seem not inclined to act in that direction, being of a more retiring disposition, preferring to live their lives in the quiet of their callings and their homes.

We sometimes think life is hard and that we are called upon to do more than our share but let us recall and ever bear in mind the perilous ocean voyage necessary, the sacrifices of our forebearers and other pioneers, the hardships they endured and perils encountered, as they made a place for themselves in this new world, clearing the land, building cabins, encountering ferocious wild animals, required to be alert against the attacks of savages and compelled to huddle in stockades for protection of themselves and their large families, to say nothing of the superhuman efforts required to provide for their families. Comparing those experiences and conditions with the present, the most modestly provided for among us live in comparative luxury and ease.

Our nation is a composite of its family units. Water can rise no higher than its source nor can our nation, the land of our adoption, rise higher than its source, the families of the nation.

As many others, though far too few, show themselves by their works to be worthy of their forebearers, so, I am sure, will the members of the Swickard family show themselves to be worthy of our rich heritage and to be ever eager to carry on the work so well begun but far from completed by our forebearers, and thereby do our part to make this nation a democracy in fact as well as in name, a democracy founded upon the principle of special privileges to none and equal rights to all, with Liberty really enlightening the world.

It seems fitting to close by quoting from Pennsylvania German Pioneers, Volume I, P. X.

"These ancestors of ours were more than mere immigrants, in the everyday sense of the word. They were even more than refugees from a beloved and despoiled homeland. They were pioneers in that they came not to a ready-made republic of opportunity but to a virgin land inhabited by savages. They blazed the trail that helped to transform that land into the America of today, built our institutions and moulded American character. Many were men of eminence in the fatherland; others came up from the penury and virtual slavery of the redemptioner system. Together they worked and won, together they fought America's battles and led in public service, industry, science, invention and in that art of agriculture which is the very foundation of our national wealth and of human progress.

502

ANCESTRY, ALSO DESCENDENTS OF JUSTUS WARNER
WATERBURY, CONNECTICUT
DORIS WOLCOTT STRONG

Records kept by Maria Warner Pierce and Rhoda Warner Hinckley, granddaughters of Justus Warner. Later additions in records made by Percy Everett Pierce, Cleveland, Ohio, a grandson of Maria Warner Pierce. Prepared for publication by Doris Wolcott Strong. All rights reserved by the author.

WARNER

JOHN WARNER, M. 1649 Ann Norton
Issue:
    John d. bef. 1706-7
    Daniel
    Thomas
    Sarah
JOHN WARNER, Jr. (2), (John) d. bef. 1706-7
Issue:
    Dr. Ephraim b. 1670, d. Aug. 1, 1753
    John (Dr)
    Robert
    Ebenezer
    Lydia
DANIEL WARNER 2, (John 1) b. Farmington, Conn.
    Samuel
    Thomas
THOMAS WARNER 2, (John 1)
Issue:
    Daniel
    John
    Abigail
Issue:
    Benjamin
    John
    Mary
    Martha
    Thomas
    Samuel
    Margaret
Dr. EPHRAIM WARNER, b. 1670, d. 1753, m. Esther Richards, daughter of Obadiah Richards and Hannah (Andrews) Richards. Hannah Andrews was daughter of John and Mary Andrews.
Issue:
    Margarett
    Ephraim
    Dr. Benjamin
    John
    Obadiah
    Esther
    Ephraim
    Ebenezer

503

DR. JOHN WARNER 3, (John 2-1)
Issue:
    3 daughters who died young
    Rebecca
    Ebenezer
    Lydia
    John
    Daniel

DANIEL WARNER 3, (Daniel 2, John 1)
Issue:
    2 sons who died young
    Samuel b. Sept. 16, 1698, Farmington, Conn. m. Dec. 21, 1719
        Elizabeth Scott. (Their daughter Huldah was mother of Rhoda
        Williams).
    Sarah
Issue:
    Josiah
    Dinah
    Ruben
    Margaret
    Ruben

    David m. 1753 Abigail Harrison (parents of Urania Warner, wife
        of Justus—see below)
    Benjamin
    Anna
    Ephraim
    Eunice
    Art

JOHN WARNER, Deacon, 4, (Dr. Ephraim 3, John 2-1)
Issue:
    Esther
    Phebe
    Annie
    James
    Mary 7
    Elijah
    John
    Ebenezer
    Abraham
    Abigail
    Mary

SAMUEL WARNER 3, (Thomas 2, John 1)
Issue:
    Twins
    Mary
    Sarah
    Thomas
    Benjamin
    Thankful) twins
    Patience)
    Hannah
    Phebe
    Martha

DR. BENJAMIN WARNER 4, (Dr. Ephraim 3, John 2-1) d. 1772, m.
Mar. 17, 1720 Johanna Strong

504

OBADIAH WARNER 4, (Dr. Ephraim 3, John 2-1)
Issue:
Jerusha
Lydia
Obadiah
Esther
Joseph
Lois
Enos
Sarah
Agnes
Irena
Mary

EBENEZER WARNER 4 (Dr. Ephraim 3, John 2-1)
Issue:
Noah
Ebenezer   d.   y.
Margaret
Ebenezer
Jemima
Annis
Elizabeth
Justus
Mark

JUSTUS WARNER 5, (Ebenezer 4, Dr. Ephraim 3, John 2-1) m. Urania
Warner, daughter of David and Abigail (Harrison) Warner.
Issue:
Chloe m. Seth Worden
Ruth m. Moses Demming. She died leaving no issue.
Alpheus m. Minerva Seymour
Roxy m. Seth Worden as his second wife.
Aaron m. Lucinda Terrell
Adna m. Anna ———
Urania
Justus m. Sally
Leverett
Joanna m. ———Mallett.

ALPHEUS WARNER 6, (Justus 5, Ebenezer 4, Dr. Ephraim 3, John
2-1) m. Minerva Seymour.
Issue:
Sally m. Joah Marsh
Eri
Heli
Ruth
Virgil
Charles
Alpheus m. Catherine ——— (Irish)
Francis

AARON WARNER 6 (Justus, 5, Ebenezer 4, Dr. Ephraim 3, John 2-1)
m. May 30, 1813, at Ridgeville, Ohio, (Lorain County), Lucinda
Terrell, daughter of Oliver Terrell. She was born in Connecticut November 6, 1795, and died Sept. 20, 1871 in Sullivan County, Missouri, at
the home of her daughter Rhoda.
Issue:

Leverett d. aged 16
Maria b. Jan. 16, 1819 m. Henry Pierce
Rhoda b. Oct. 20, 1829, m. (1) Christopher Olin, (2) Dexter
Hinckley

ADNA WARNER 6, (Justus 5, Ebenezer 4, Dr. Ephraim 3, John 2-1)
m. Anna ——— resided in Berea, Ohio.
Issue:
Levi
Rebecca
Elmer
Sarah

JUSTUS WARNER 6, (Justus 5, Ebenezer 4, Dr. Ephraim 3, John 2-10
married Sally ———
Issue:
Urania, died in girlhood

ERI WARNER 7, (ALPHEUS 6, Justus 5, Ebenezer 4, Ephraim 3.
John 2-1)
Issue:
Alpheus
Francelia
Henry
Adelbert

HELI WARNER 7, Alpheus 6, Justus 5, Ebenezer 4, Ephraim 3,
John 2-1)
Issue:
John
Charles
William

SALLY WARNER 7, (ALPHEUS 6, Justus 5, Ebenezer 4, Ephraim 3,
John 2-1) m. (1st) Jaob Marsh, (2nd) Demot.
Issue: (first marriage)
Ransom Marsh
Cemantha "
Harriet "
Minerva "
Homer "
Issue: (second marriage)
Arta

VIRGIL WARNER 7, (Alpheus 6, Justus 5, Ebenezer 4, Ephraim 3,
John 2-1) married Ann ——— "With sons and goods moved to the
West".

CHARLES WARNER, 7 (Alpheus 6, Justus 5, Ebenezer 4, Ephraim 3,
John 2-1) married Jane ———. Had three sons and moved west.

HARRY WARNER 7, (Aaron 6, Justus 5, Ebenezer 4, Ephraim 3,
John 2-1) m. (1) Lucy Ann, (2) Lizzie "the Pennymite"
Issue: (first marriage)
George
Lucinda
Lavina
Aaron
Justus
Issue by second marriage:
Susan

HARRIS WARNER 7, (Aaron 6, Justus 5, Ebenezer 4, Ephraim 3, John
2-1) married Mary Ann Pierce (sister of Henry Pierce, who married
his sister Maria). They resided in Pierceton, Indiana.

Issue:
    Charlotte
    James
    Delilah
    Willie
    Effie d. inf.

MARIA WARNER 7, (Aaron 6, Justus 5, Ebenezer 4, Ephraim 3, John 2-1) born Jan. 16, 1819, died Oct. 29, 1889, married February 26, 1837 Henry Pierce, born September 1, 1811, in Pennsylvania, died February 11, 1882, in Grafton, Lorain County, Ohio.
Issue:
    Francis H. Pierce, b. Feb. 28, 1833, d. Oct. 19, 1906, m. Caroline Biddle. r. Cleveland, Ohio. Had two children, Virginia (Jenny) b. 1866, d. 1907; and Frank Lamont, b. 1875.
    Everett Pierce, b. May 26, 1843, d. July 16, 1860, ae. 16.
    Jay Augustus Pierce, b. Feb. 14, 1848, d. Apr. 18, 1897, m. 1872 in Liverpool, Medina County, Ohio, Louisa Dell, b. —— d. Sept. 1895. Had two sons, Percy Everett Pierce, b. Nov. 26, 1873, Liverpool, Ohio, m. Dec. 11, 1894, Cora May Wolcott, b. Feb. 3, 1875. (See Wolcott Genealogy). Had six children, r. Cleveland, Ohio; and Charles Dell Pierce, b. Sept. 26, 1875, Liverpool, Ohio, d. unmarried April 8, 1924, in Cleveland, Ohio.

RHODA WARNER 7, (Aaron 6, Justus 5, Ebenezer 4, Ephraim 3, John 2-1) born October 20, 1829, in Liverpool, Ohio, d. April, 1893, i nMilan. Missouri. Married 1st, Christopher Olin, and, Dexter Hinckley, Feb. 8, 1851.
Issue: (first marriage)
    Daughter, died infancy.
    Jerome Olin, called Jerome Hinckley
Issue: (second marriage)
    Eva
    Jamie

CHLOE WARNER 6, (Justus 5, Ebenezer 4, Ephraim 3, John 2-1) m. Seth Worden
Issue:
    Rebecca Worden, d. y.
    Justus Worden
    Virgil Worden m. Caroline —,m. 2nd, Lois Ann (——) Gregory
    Aaron Worden
    Justus Worden, m. Eunice——, had Milton and Homer. Eunice married 2nd, Rev. ——Sevell, by whom she had two sons.

ROXY WARNER 6, (Justus 5, Ebenezer 4, Ephraim 3, John 2-1) m. Seth Worden as his second wife, after the death of her sister Chloe.
Issue:
    Chloe Worden, m. Alonzo, had George and Jenny
    Seth Worden

507

EARLY SETTLERS—CHAMPAIGN COUNTY, OHIO

Contributed by THELMA BLAIR LANG

Champaign County was created from the counties of Green and Franklin by an act of the Ohio Legislature, February 20, 1805.

The land that comprised the original Champaign County now includes the following townships and counties:

Champaign County: Mad River, Urbana, Union, Wayne, Salem and Concord Twps.; *Clark County:* Bethel, Boston, Springfield, Harmony, Pleasant, Moorfield and German Twps.; *Logan County:* Lake, Jefferson, Harrison, Miami, Zane and Adams Twps.

Springfield was the first county seat. The first court was held at the home of George Fithian. The commissioners, appointed by the legislature, met at Springfield. In this meeting, William Ward, founder of Urbana, influenced them in the selection of a site for the county seat. He with John Humphrey and James Vance are responsible for Urbana being chosen.

Possibly the only white men in 1800 in the territory later to become Champaign County were Pierre Dugan and William Owen and their families. Pierre Dugan, a French Canadian, had married a squaw wife.

With the organization of the County in 1805, settlers started coming from various states; many came from Virginia through Kentucky. The majority of settlers from the New England States came from Vermont. Woodstock is named for Woodstock, Vt.

The census of 1810 for Champaign County (including lands now part of Logan and Clark Counties) gives a population of 6,303 persons. Champaign County received its present boundaries in 1817 when the legislature set off Logan and Clark Counties. Census reports for Champaign County with its present boundaries are: 1820, 8,479; 1830, 12,131; 1840, 16,721; and 1930, 31,000.

MAD RIVER TOWNSHIP was organized by the associate judges April 20, 1805. In 1797 William Owen, a Virginian, became the first settler of the now Mad River Township. A poor married man, owner of four horses and a wagon, he squatted near Westerville and later bought 240 acres from William Ward for $1.00 per acre. He is credited with bringing the first hogs into this part of the state and was called by the Indians, Hogman; died 1818 leaving 8 children.

Many of the first settlers were Virginians. Settlers with dates of entrance included: *1802,* Christopher, Philip, William and Elijah

Weaver, natives of Bucks Co., Pa., who had settled in Kentucky in 1792; *1804*, Harry Storms, Thomas Redmond; *1804*, from Shenandoah Co., Va., David Loudenback and the families of Pence, Wiant, Kite and Runkle; *1805*, Charles Rector, Basil West, Taylor family; *1805*, from Virginia, Jessie Goddard, Elijah Standerford, Henry Ritter; *1805*, from North Carolina, Jacob Arney and ———— Dibert; *1806*, the following families had settled in Mad River Township by this time: Ambrose, father or grandfather of Newton, probably Frederick; Anderson, James W. or his father, John; Arrowsmith; Bacome; Boone; Boswell; Brown; Broyles; Burns; Curoker; Cain; Campbell; Carter; Chapman; Clark, Colbert; Darnell; Davis; Flemin; Frank; Gard; Glaspie; Haller; Harbor; Harshbarger; Henkle; Hill; Johnson; Kelly; Kenton; Landsdale; Largent; Logan; Mahin; McGrew; McKinley; McMillen; Miller; Mitchell; Montgomery; Mouser; Pence; Pierce; Reynolds; Rhoades; Ritter; Rock; Ross; Rouse; Runkle; Shockey, Abraham; Sims; Smith; Snyder; Stevens; Talbott; Taylor; Trier; Whitmore; Williams.

SALEM TOWNSHIP was organized by the associate judges April 20, 1805. The township lay entirely within military lands. The first settler was ———— Deshicket, 1794. Pierre Dugan, French Canadian, with his squaw wife, settled here prior to 1800. Other early settlers were: *1802*, William Powell, William Wood; *1804*, Arthur Thomas, Matthew Stewart, of Pennsylvania; before *1805*, David Parkinson, George and Jacob Leonard, of Virginia; Abner Barrett, John Guthridge, William Johnson, Jones Turner, John Taylor; John McAdams, of Pennsylvania; *1805*, Joseph Petty; James Vance, from Washington Co., Pa. (became Governor of Ohio; d. 1852); *1857*, Morgan family from Virginia. Several of the families settling in Salem Township were Mennonites from Pennsylvania.

CONCORD TOWNSHIP was set off from Mad River Township in *1811*. Joseph Hill, *1802*, was the first settler; also coming in *1802* were Isaac Anderson and Sampson Talbott (land entered by him is now owned by his great-great-grandson); *1805*, Adam Wise, Alexander Dunlap, James Mitchell. Joseph Longfellow and his wife, both over sixty, from Delaware, through Kentucky walked the entire distance, hauling their goods in a one-horse home-made cart. (They had 22 children.) *1807*, John Duckworth, an Englishman; Felix Rock; Jesse Harbair family from the Carolinas (32 children).

WAYNE TOWNSHIP originally part of Salem Township, was set off by the commissioners in 1811 in a military survey. The first settler, Abner Barnett (1800) was not there in 1811; *1804*, Jacob Johnson, from Maryland, with his wife, Martha Boggs, from Pennsylvania; *1805*, James Devore, from Washington Co., Pa.; Thomas Goode; *1805*, from Dinwiddie Co., Va., Jordan Reams, Spain families, Crowder families; *1810*, Gray Gary, Isaac Everett; *1811*, Alexander St. Clair Hunter, of Virginia; *1812*, Hester Moorecraft, a widow, from New York; *1813*, Isaac Gray, from Virginia; *1815*, Thomas Middleton, of Virginia; *1817*, Thomas Cowgill and families of Igou, Tharp, Paxton, Pickerall, Hughes, Wheaton, Baldwin, Mason, William and Johnson.

UNION TOWNSHIP was established from Military Lands and Congress Lands. The first settlers, Stephen Runyon and James McClain, from the same neighborhood in Virginia, married and came to Ohio in *1801*. Other settlers were: *1803*, Barton Minturn, Donald, Abram and Jesse Jones, from New Jersey; Donald Baker, John Clar; *1805*, Joseph Diltz, of New Jersey, via Kentucky; *1810*, John Lafferty and the families of Bidwell, Carnmell and Wolf; *1813*, Jesse C. Phillips, of Virginia; Jacob Van Meter, Virginia; Samuel Humes, Justice Jones, Thomas Sayres, Peter Sewell, Solomon Vance, John Reynolds, David Marsh, William Hall, James Reed, William Dunlap, Nathan Reese, James Hayes, Neil Gun, Solomon Viss and the Pollock and McAdams (came over from Salem Township) families.

URBANA TOWNSHIP was established in 1811-12 by the county commissioners. Early settlers were: *1803*, Thomas Pearce; *1807*, William Patrick, Col. Douglas Luce, and the families of Powell, Wiley, Fitzpatrick, Knox, Largent, Thomas, Pence, Rhoades, Johnson, Barr, McBeth, Shockey, Moore, Pendeton, Tobar, Dallas, Stuart, Kenaga, Arney.

GOSHEN TOWNSHIP lies within the Military Lands. Early settlers were: *1805*, Jacob Hazle, from Pennsylvania; *1806*, Thomas Lawson, John Cummings, of Massachusetts; Hugh Bay, Joseph Porter; *1808*, Richard Corbis, William Frankbarger, John Cowan, John Pepper and William Burnside.

HARRISON TOWNSHIP was created from Mad River Township in 1817. The first settler, ——— Fuson, of Virginia, came in 1804. Other early arrivals were: *1808*, Jacob Sarver, of Virginia; *1809*, Ralph Robinson; *1811*, William Wilson, b. Ireland, came from Virginia, Jeptha Terrell, Thomas Daniels, from Virginia; *1813*, John McIntire, of Virginia; *1814*, Peter Speece, Virginia; *1815*, Elijah Davis, Kentucky; *1816*, Joseph Wilson, Washington Co., Pa.; *1817*, John Taylor.

JACKSON TOWNSHIP was taken from Mad River Township in 1817. The first settler, Charles Dorsey, of Virginia, served in the American Resolution, came to Ohio, *1802*, and died, 1811. Before *1805*, came John Kain, William Lemon; in *1805*, George Wilson; *1806*, Thomas Grafton, from Rockingham Co., Va.; Sampson Kelley, from Ireland, through Virginia; Thomas Cowie, from Virginia; before *1810*, Joshua Darnell; *1808*, Joshua Howell, from Virginia; David Field, from Kentucky; *1810*, John Fitzpatrich, from Virginia; John Johnson, from Kentucky; before *1815*, William McCrea, from Scotland.

JOHNSON TOWNSHIP was taken from Concord Township. The earliest settler, Silas Johnson, came from Virginia, via Kentucky, in *1802; 1805*, Christian Marsh, from Virginia; the Carter, Cox and Fleming families had left by *1807*. John and Phillip Long came from Rockingham Co., Va., *1807*. From Shenandoah Co., Va., came the following: *1807*, Acory Berry, Lewis Haniback; *1808*, Philip Comer; before *1810*, Adam Hite, Peter Smith, Jacob Maggart, Jacob Judy; *1811*, Joseph Kizer, Louis Lyons, Isaac Good; *1813*,

David and Jeremiah Huffman; *1815*, Samuel Brubaker, also from Virginia were David and Henry Long, Frederick Pence and Campbell.

RUSH TOWNSHIP was set off from Wayne Township in *1828*. Squatters about *1800* were: John Rodgers, William Martin, James Merryfield, Emanuel Merryfield, William Pickerill, Robert Bay, James Stover, Francis Owen. Settlers after *1805* are among those listed under Wayne Township.

ADAMS TOWNSHIP was set off from Mad River Township in *1828*. This township was not settled for several years after other townships because of its inaccessibility. The first settler, Asahel Wilkinson came from Harrison Co., Va., in *1811*. Other early settlers were: 1813, Henry Ritter, from Kentucky, Daniel Neal, of Maryland, Joel Harbour; *1816*, William McCroskey, of Kentucky, Samuel Curry; *1817*, George Halterman, of Virginia; *1819*, Richard Southgate, Archibald Irwin, and before *1820*, Silas and Walker Johnson, of Kentucky. After *1828*, Isaac Curl, Levi Valentine, William Terrell, William Calland (b. Scotland, from Virginia, 1828), Erastus Kinnon, James Lockbridge, Samuel Anderson, John Cunningham, and John Clark.

Champaign County, Ohio, was created by act of the Ohio Legislature February 20, 1805. The names of early officers of the county have been compiled from county histories, family genealogies, and early court records.

The first three associate judges were commissioned February 21, 1805. The presiding judge and the associate judges were elected by the state legislature. The president judge was a man with knowledge of law, but the associate judges usually were resident laymen. The first president judge was Francis Dunleavy, not a resident of Champaign County. The first associate judges were: John Runyon, John Reynolds, and Samuel McCullough. The first representative to the general assembly was John Sterritt, not a resident of Champaign County. The first state senators were Duncan McArthur and George Todd, not residents of Champaign County. The offices of Clerk, Auditor and Recorder were combined under one person; the first one to hold these offices was Joseph C. Vance, who died in office in 1809. The first Surveyor was Solomon McCullough. Arthur St. Clair was the first prosecuting attorney.

It is doubtful if all the records of the first election in 1805 are complete, since there are no records for some offices which should have been in existence at that time. The following are lists of those who early held offices in Champaign County:

COUNTY CLERK:

1805–1809. Joseph C. Vance, who died in office May 16, 1809.	1816–1822. Samuel Gibbs.
	1822–1843. J. C. Pearson.
1809–1816. William Ward.	1843–1850. Samuel H. Robinson.

SHERIFF:

1806–1806. John Daugherty,	1829–1833. John Owen.
1806–1810. Daniel McKinnon.	1833–1837. Frederick Ambrose.
1810–1813. Samuel McCord.	1837–1841. Henry Vanmeter.
1813–1817. David Vance.	1841–1843. John Owen.
1817–1821. John Wallace.	1843–1847. John C. Nigh.
1821–1825. Frederick Ambrose.	1847–1851. John West.
1825–1829. John Wallace.	

RECORDER:

1805–1808. Joseph C. Vance.	1839– R. R. McNemar.
1808–1830. William Ward.	1839–1842. Mathew Magrew.
1830–1836. Mathew Magrew.	1842–1854. Decatur Talbott.
1836–1839. David Vance.	

AUDITOR:

1809–1830. David Vance.	1839–1841. Mathew Magrew.
1830–1836. Mathew Magrew.	1841–1845. E. P. Fyffe.
1836–1838. David Vance.	1845–1855. Francis Wright.

The county surveyors must be determined by the names affixed to the surveys, which makes it hard to give a proven list of the surveyors.

512

SURVEYOR:
1805-1824. Solomon McCullough.
1824-1842. John Arrowsmith. The name of Thomas Cowgill appears on a greater part of the surveys during this period; however, he was not surveyor. It is not certain whether Arrowsmith served continuously during this time.
1842-1843. William Hamilton.
1843-1846. Thomas Cowgill, Jr.
1846-1854. James B. Armstrong.

PRESIDENT JUDGES:
1805-? Francis Dunleavy.
?-1848. John R. Swann, of Columbus, Ohio.
1848-1852. George B. Way, of Champaign Co., Ohio.
1852 was the last year for president judges.

ASSOCIATE JUDGES:
2-21-1805. John Runyon, John Reynolds and Samuel McCullough.
2-17-1809. John Guthridge.
2-25-1816. John Reynolds.
12- 5-1816. Alexander McBeth.
1-27-1818. Samuel Hill.
2- 6-1819. John Runyon.
Legislature 1820. James Smith.
Legislature 1821. George Fithian.
Legislature 1824. A. R. Colwell.
Legislature 1825. Samuel Hill.
1-22-1827. William Runkle.
1-22-1827. William Fithian.

1-22-1827. James Smith.
January, 1831. Obed Horr.
January, 1834. Elisha C. Berry.
January, 1834. David Markley.
January, 1837. Charles Flago.
January, 1837. James Dallas.
January, 1837. John Taylor.
January, 1841. Elisha C. Berry.
January, 1844. James Dallas.
January, 1844. John Owens.
January, 1848. William Patrick.
January, 1851. Edward L. Morgan.
January, 1851. John West.

PROSECUTORS: (Filled by appointment until 1852.)
1805. Arthur St. Clair.
1806. Joshua Collett.
1807. Arthur St. Clair.
1808-1811. Edward W. Pearce.

1811. Henry Bacon.
Moses B. Corwin.
John H. James.
James Cooley.
Samuel V. Baldwin.

ELECTORS, CHAMPAIGN COUNTY, OCTOBER 8, 1811

Alexander Allen, James Askin, Jacob Arney, Frederick Ambrose. Joseph Ayers, Jr.

Henry Bacon, William Bridge, Daniel Baker, Jonathan Brown. Abner Barritt, Gabriel Briant, John Black, John Ballinger, John Barrett. John Bowlman, Sr., John Bowlman, Jr., Robert Blaney, James Brown, David Brown, Jeremiah Bowen, Henry Boswell, Ezekiel Boswell, John Boggs, William Boggs, Peter Bruner, John Beaty, John Brown, James Boggs, David Bayles, John Bayles, David Beaty, John S. Berry, Alexander Brown.

Jacob Conklin, Hiram Cotteral, Bernard Coon, Isaac Custor. William Custor, Philip Comer, Abraham Custor, Benjamin Cheney, William Cheney, Richard Carbus, Ebenezer Cheney, Hiram M. Curry, John Clark. Joseph Cummons, Nicholas Carpenter, Job Clemons, Samuel Clifton.

James Davidson, James Dallas, James Doolittle, John Devore. Elijah T. Davis, John Davis, Henry Davis, Joseph Duncan, Anderson Davis, Jr., Andrew Davis, Sr., Nathan Darnall, Boswell Darnall, Daniel Davis. Joseph Diltz.

Owen Ellis, John Elefrits, Sanford Edmonds.

John Frazel, John Ford, James Fithian, Nathan Fitch, William H. Fyffe, George Fithian, Joseph Ford, Tolson Ford, John Fitcher, William Fagen, George Faulkner, Joel Fuson.

Thomas Grafton, James Grafton, Gershom Gard, George Glass, Miller Gillespy, Allen Galent, John Galent, Samuel Gibbs, Gray Gary, Andrew Grubbs, Jesse Guthridge, John Guthridge Sr., Moses Guthridge, Timothy Giffert, John Glenn, John Gilmore, Hugh Gibbs, William Glenn, Joseph Gordon, Job Gard.

George Hunter, Daniel Hermick, Joseph Hedges, John Huston, Samuel Hoge, Daniel Harr, Wesley Hathaway, Paul Huston, Charles Harrison, Abraham Hughes, Isaac Hughes, Wesley Hughes, Joseph Hill, Joseph Hurings, Phillip Huffman.

Michael Instine.

David Jones, Josse Johnson, Walker Johnson, Silas Johnson, James Johnson, Otho Johnson, Joshua Jones, Daniel Jones, Justus Jones, Daniel Jackson.

Simon Kenton, John Kelly, William Kelly, Philip C. Kenton, William Kenton, Jr., Jark Kenton, Thomas Kenton, John Kain, Sampson Kelly.

Isaac Lansdale, John Logan, Jr., Jonathan Long, Jacob Leonard, Randle Largent, George Leonard, Benjamin Line, Benjamin Lee, John Lafferty, James Lowry, Britton Lovett, Zepaniah Luce, William Largent, John Largent, Daniel Largent, Nelson Largent.

Thomas Moore, Samuel McCord, Nathaniel Morrow, James McGill, John McCord, David Moody, Alexander McCumpsey, James Maryfield, Emanuel Maryfield, Allen Minturn, Israel Marsh, James Mitchell, David Marsh, Jacob Minturn, Alexander McCorkle, Joseph McLain, Barton Minturn, James McLain, Philip Miller, Adam Miller, Archibald McGrew, Sr., James McLaughlin, Samuel Mitchell, Sr., Mathew McGrew, James Mitchell, John McAdams, Job Martin, Robert McFarland, Archibald McKinley, Isaac Myers, James Montgomery, Reuben McSherry.

William Nicholson, Shadrach Northcutt, Nathan Norton, Basil Noel, John Noel, Daniel Noel, Robert Noe, Benjamin Nocholas.

Allen Oliver, James Owen, Francis Owen, David Osburn, John Owen.

Henry Pence, Samuel Pence, John Pence, Abraham Powell, William Powell, Joseph Petty, David Parkison, James Porter, Ezekiel Petty, Reuben Paxton, John Paxton, Jacob Paxton, William Pickrill, John Price, Thomas Pearce, Jr., Thomas Pearce, Sr., Nathaniel Pinkard, Anthony Patrick, William Parkison, Edward W. Pierce, Jacob Pence, Joseph Pence.

James Robinson, John Rigdon, Isaac Robison, John Reynolds, William Rhodes, Andrew Richards, John Rhodes, John Runyon, Jacob Rees, John Ross, Alexander Ross, Stephen Runyon, Richard Runyon, William Ray, Adam Rhodes, John Richardson, Daniel Reed, Felix Rock, William Riddle, John Reed, Joseph Reynolds, Levi Rouze, Elijah Ross, William S. Ross, John Rouze.

Abraham Shockey, Elijah Standiford, Henry Steinberger, John Steinberger, Peter Smith, Mathew Stewart, John Symmes, Archibald Stewart, Christian Stevens, Ezekiel A. Smith, Thomas Stretch, William Stretch, Jacob Sarver, Samuel Smith, John Sutton, Solomon Scott, John Sayre, Enoch Sargeant, Thomas Sayre, George Sargeant, William Stevens, Jacob Slagel, John Schryock, Isaac Shockey, Francis Stevenson, John Stewart.

John Thompson, John Thomas, Enos Thomas, John Trewett, Curtis M. Thompson, Robert Taber, Thomas Trewett, Jeremiah Tucker, Isaac Tucker, Isaac Titsworth, William Tharp, Abner Tharp, John Thomas, Nathan Tharp, Solomon Tharp, Sampson Talbot, Daniel Thomas, John Taylor, James Turner, Francis Thomas, Arthur Thomas.

John Vance, Joseph Vance, William Valentine, Henry Valentine, David Vance.

Lawrence White, John Williams, James Wilkinson, John A. Ward, Thomas West, John White, James Walker, Obed Ward, Abijah Ward, Henry Williams, William Williams, Adam Wise, William Weaver, Sr., William West, William Weaver, Jr., George Wickum, George Wilson, Michael Whisman, William Waukob, Christopher Wood, James Williams, John Williams, Joseph Wilkinson, Thomas Wilkinson.

CHAMPAIGN COUNTY INSCRIPTIONS

Thelma Blair Lang

PISGAH CEMETERY
LOCATION: Section 32. Union township, Champaign county, Ohio; route 236 at the junction of routes 99 and 222A, on the east side of the road. The cemetery altho fenced is in poor repair, and is not used now. Until about 1895 a church stood there which has since been torn down. According to a statement by Mr. and Mrs. Charles Blair, Urbana, members of this church, many of the bodies were removed about 1895. Many of the stones have been carried away in the past twenty years.

AEYERS: James, died————, 26-1874

CLARKE: Ellen Amanda, daughter J. H. & E., died 9-12-1867, age 6 mos. and 2 days
    Job, son Stephen, and Hannah, died 1   (rest not readable)
    Hannah, wife Stephen, died 10-28-1855

CONKLYN: Susan, consort David, died 9-27-1840, age 24-8-27
    David, died 1-20-1852, age 38-10-3
    Emily, daughter J. & E., died 12-24-1847, age 18 months
    Robert, son Jacob & Emily, died 1-18-1849, age 7 days
    Mary Y., daughter of J. & E., died 8-21-1851, age 7-7-9

EARNHART: Margaret F. mother, born 1825, died 1896
    Morton G., father, born 1825, died 1905

GRIM: Mary, wife Henry and daughter of George & Rebecca Kinsinger of Cumberland Co., Pa., died Jan. 1846, age 26-7-0

HUFF: Andrew, son John and Leannah, died 1-10-1838, age 9 weeks

HELLER: Amos, died 4-10-1869, age 32-0-24

JONES: Mary, died 9-20-1840, age 62-11-14
    William Raper, son Mary Jones, died 9-1-1833, age 10 mos. 28 days
    Infant son of T. O. & N. E., died 5-7-1870

KNADLER: Peter, died 7-14-1844, age 96-4-0

LYON: W. G. L. died 12-27-1877, age 21

MINTURN: Nancy, wife B., died 8-23-1847, age 67-6-14
    Allen, died 4-1-1855, age 72-2-4
    Esther, wife Barton, died 7-30-1849, age 76

MILLER: Ruham Jane, daughter John & Blanchey, died 3-7-1836, age 7 mos. and 11 days

McCollum: James, died 4-24-1838, age 50
    V. Co. B., 32 Ohio Inf.

QUINN: John, died 3-13-1876, age 51-2-3
    Elizabeth, wife of John, died 3-11-1857, age 31-1-30
    John D., on J. & E., died 5-28-1856, age 10 mos.
    Eliza, daughter J. & M. J., died 2-6-1877, age 9-10-25
    William, son J. & M. J., died 8-10-1864, age 3 days

MORRISON: William P M. A., son F. & J., died 5-20-1846, age 12 years Mary E. died 1857

REED: James, died 1857, age 71 years
    John R. son J. R., died 1848, age 3 years
    Catherine, daughter J. R., died 1848, age 5 years

RIED: Martha A., wife James, died 3-1-1854, age 54-4-28
    Charles W., son John and M. A., died 7-1-1846, age 20 mos. and 10 days
    Theodore F., son J. R. & M. J., died 6-27-1848, age 2-9-11

RAPER: Wm., son Mary Jones, died 9-1-1833, age 10 mos. 28 days
REIGART: John B., died 10-1852, age 48-1-26
REYNOLDS: , son———— and E. P., died 11-3-1851, age 2-3-0
STONE: or
SLONE: Elenor, died 11-3-1845, age 3-11-0
STRAYER: Infant son of G. W. & S. A., died 3-15-1853
TURNER: John R., son of E. & M., died 12-25-1851, age 12 years
     James, son E. & M., died 12-21-1851, age 15 years
     Margaret G., wife Alexander, died 3-5-1866, age 54-10-3
WILSON: James, wife Rezin, died 8-19-1879, age 84-7-3
     Rozetta, daughter Jane & Rezin, died 12-1-1849, age 25
WILSON: Andrew, son Peter & Sarah, died 1850, age 1-4-0
WHITEHEAD: Adena, daughter E. B. & R. A., died 9-15-1849, age
     1 mo. and 15 days
WREN:: Samuel, died 7-31-1870, age 33-6-20
WHARTON: Samuel, died August 1853, age 8 mos.
WHITE: Children of R. & S.
     Emma, died 8-23-1863, age 1-2-11
     Jacob A., died 9-21-1863, age 1-4-2
——————————, Rolleigh, died 2-2-1843, age 39-5-0
——————————, ——————, died 8-30-1867, age 4-11-18
     (the two above were not readable)

CHAMPAIGN COUNTY INSCRIPTIONS

THELMA BLAIR LANG

————

HOPEWELL CEMETERY

LOCATION: Survey 5820, Union township, Champaign county, Ohio.
Route: Take route 29 from the town of Urbana to route 56; take route 56 to
route 173. The cemetery is on the north side of the road back in a field. Altho
it is not used today, it is fenced, but many of the stones have toppled over.
There are numerous open graves where bodies have been disinterred and the
graves left uncovered.

ALLISON: Susan, wife of W., died 8-5-1855; Age 51-1-28
     Wilford, died 11-5-1867, age 68-7-4
     Mary, wife of John, born 5-13-1811, died 9-24-1880
     John, died 8-26-1865, age 51-10-8
ALEXANDER: Lydie, wife of Joseph O., died 6-5-1853, age 24-0-29
CUMMINGE: Mary, wife of L., died 10-2-1853, age 57-0-16
DOWNS: John N., died ———— 17-1849, age 33-7-14
GROVES: Hannah, wife of John, died 3-12-1844, age 44-1-6
     Henry, died 3-23-1847, age 19-.........-11
GORDON: Pearl, son of G. W. & M., died 1-10-1865, age 6 mo. 3 days
HARBERT: Hosilla, wife J., died 11-18-1848, age 41 yrs.
LAFERTY: Mary, wife of Samuel, died 8-2-1849, age 63 yrs.
LONGBREAK: ——————————, son of A.L.&D., died 3-19-1832, age 1-8-7
OTT: John, son Abraham and Nancy, died 10-22-1849, age 9-3-0
     John J., born 5-5-1830, died 11-19-1869
     Sallie May, daughter J. J. & L. D.,   (rest nor readable)
POLAND: Jane, wife Absalom, died 6-13-1852, age 24-8-0
STEVENSON: Peter, died 9-27-1856, age 57 yrs.

516

THOMAS: Richard, died 12-9-1861, age 21-5-0

WASHINGTON: Arsing, daughter W. & E., died 1-10-1859, age ?-7-0
    Nancy, daughter W. & E., died 12-18-1858, age 15 days
    Harriet, daughter W. & E., born 5-10-1849, died 5-23-1866

ZOLL: Catherine, wife Jacob, died 10-15-1860, age 35-7-0
    Mary, wife James,   (rest not readable)

PRINCE CEMETERY

LOCATION: Section 28, Mad River township, Champaign county, Ohio;
on route 240B just west of route 86, on the north side of the road. The cemetery is in good condition, well fenced and with all stones in order.

BUROKER: Elizabeth, wife of A., died 2-29-1868, age 74-4-24
    Adam, died 9-18-1851, age 65-9-5
    Martin, died 1-1-1855, age 70 years
    Molly, wife M., died 9-25-1848, age 68 years

CRABILL: John, died 6-1866, age 76 years

HOWER: Sarah, wife John, died 11-12-1854, age 62-11-14
    Henry, died 1-21-1854, age 26-3-26

LOUDENBACH: Benjamin, died 4-12-1854, age 12-10-18
    Norah, died 4-17-1854, age 32-9-9
    Adam, died 9-14-1876, age 75-2-28
    Joseph, died 12-11-1858, age 62-5-12
    Salina, daughter Jacob & Sarah, died 12-22-1861, age 8-2-12
    Washington, died 10-31-1863, age 30-0-16

VANCE: William, son D. & A., died 12-13-1850, age 4-11-22
    Sarah, daughter D. & N., died 6-1-1834, age 1-0-2

VENICE: Henry, died 1-21-1859, age 60-5-20
    Mary, died 5-5-1886, age 85-7-27

GEORGE'S CHAPEL CEMETERY

LOCATION: On a line between Sections 4 and 5, Urbana township,
Champaign county, Ohio; on route 29 east of the town of Urbana, on the
north side of the road near the intersection of routes 29 and 130B. The un-
fenced plot is within a farm field, and most of the stones are broken. At one
time this cemetery surrounded George's Chapel, one of the first churches in
Urbana township.

CAMPBELL: Margaret, wife of I., died 12-3-1848, age 34

HUTCHINS: Ida, daughter Mary, died 12-28-1866

KING: George, son John & Jane, died 9-15-1843, age 6 mos.
    John E., died 1849, age 32-2-9

LEECH: Joseph, died 2-22-1843, age 45 years

MILLER: John   (rest not readable)

NEAL: Susannah, daughter S. & Susannah, died 2-22-1837, age 4 mos.
    Galhanna, daughter S. & S., died 10-2-1838, age 6 mos.
    Nelson W., son C. H. & R., died 1-28-1849, age 4-9-11
    Elizabeth, wife Curtis, died 2-14-1850, age 28-0-8

OSBORN: Ira B., son James & Rachel, died 7-15-1845, age 2 mos.
    24 days

WATT: Samuel, son Robert & Margaret, died 2-6-1845, age 24 days

517

OWNERS OF VIRGINIA MILITARY LANDS, PICKAWAY COUNTY, 1822

MAYBURT STEPHENSON RIEGEL

Francis Ayers*, William Bell*, Na. Randolph, Lawrence Butler, John Blackwell, Evans & Owens, Corneilus Baldwin*, Charles Scott, Hance Baker*, Samuel Beavers*, George Carrington*, Joseph Conway*, George Clark*, T. James, John Campbell*, Warren Cash, B. Holmes, A. Shepard, Willis Wilson, J. H. Fitzgerald, James Denny*, Daniel Duvall*, John Parkman, John Dark*, Francis Dade*, P. Hackley, Joseph Evans*, Patrick Finney*, Benjamin Forsythe*, H. Fox;

John Gibson, Alexander Gibson*, John Wallace, J. Goldsbley, J. Holmes, George Greenway, Strother Jones, George Handy, Benjamin Harrison*, Whitehead Coleman, George Hoffman, John Hoffman, Benjamin Hough*, Scott, Medley and Green, Jeremiah Joslin*, W. West, J. Holmes, John Finch, Peter Kelley, Elias Langhorn, Joseph Ladd, William McMahan, John Evans, B. Sublefield, R. White, Elias, E. T., A. L. Langham, Jesse M'Kay*, Francis Mure*, Wallace Codwallader;

F. Seagles, Joseph Mishemore, Samuel M'Ferron*, A. Parkins, Stephen T. Mason*, Ralph Morgan*, William McMeechan*, Good Lavely, John Overton*, Daniel Brown, J. A. Fulton, William Carter, Robert Porterfield*, Alexander Parker, Samuel Peebles*, J. Hoffman, David Ross*, John Tench, Strother Jones, Elias Rector*, John R. Stokes*, Uriah Springer*, Anthony Sheriff*, John Swan*, Samuel Spencer*, David Morgan, John Smith*, John Jacobs, Smith Snead*;

Charles Simmons, William White, Sheldon Clough, A. B. West, John Shearer*, Fred'k Seagles, Thomas Smith, John Steed, Charles Scott, David Walker, Tarlton Woodson, Tillman Walton*, H. Bedinger, Moses Dumnett, John Foggy, Thomas Hill, J. and M. Hobson, John Holmes, Daniel Kuth, James Mishner, William Phillips;

William Robinson, John Rose, Samuel Smith, H. Whiting*, Thomas James, Robert Means. David Kinnear, auditor of Pickaway County, O.

Published—June 7, 1822—**Olive Branch,** Circleville, Ohio. * Owners in 1822.

REVOLUTIONARY SOLDIERS BURIED IN PICKAWAY CO. OHIO..

JOASH MILLER

Joash Miller, early settler of Pickaway Co. Ohio was born in Cocalico Twp. Lancaster Co. Pennsylvania. He enlisted in 1776 as private 4th class under Capt. Andrew Ream, Lancaster Co. Penn. militia, and was promoted to sergeant in 1780. He married Nov. 2, 1777, in Lancaster Co. Anna Stubsh (Nancy on tomb stone) b. 1758, died Aug. 21, 1839, Pickaway Co. Ohio.

Will of Joash Miller, Will Book 1, page 27. Pickaway County Court Records. Oral will given in the presence of John Fisher, William Wilson, and John Brintlinger mentions wife, Nancy, daughters Nancy, Betsy, at home, their four married sisters, Catherine Paulgrove, Rebecca Westenhaver, Mary Hedges, Susannah Hedges, and their two brothers Peter Miller, and Joseph Miller. Joash Miller declared he wished his two sons Peter Miller and Joseph Miller, and his son-in-law John Hedges to administer his estate. Affirmed to have been declared on the sixteenth of February A. D. 1819.

Witnesses: William Wilson, John Fisher, John Brintlinger.

The estate of Joash Miller was inventoried and appraised by Joseph Kelley, Shadrick Cole and Jahez Hedges, April 10, 1819. The inventory was affirmed and notarized Oct. 12, 1819 before Andrew Dildine, J. P.

BIBLE RECORDS (in German)

"Michael Muller, died Sept. 11, 1785 aged 83 yrs. 9 mo. 11 days. wife—Maria Catharine Mulluvim died Dec. 1786, on the second, aged 73 yrs. 11 months, 27 days."

Will probated in Lancaster Co. Pa. Oct. 10, 1785. mentions fact that Michael Muller resided in Cocalico twp. and names eldest son Elan, youngest son, Joas.

CAPTAIN ABRAHAM SWISHER

MILITARY RECORD

Captain Abraham Swisher served as private and sergeant First Regiment Militia, Sussex Co. New Jersey. Nov. 5, 1780 he received certificate No. 780 for 14 S 2 D depreciation of his Continental pay as captain in the Sussex Co. New Jersey Militia during the Revolutionary War. Vol. II P. 337 "Official Roster Soldiers of the American Revolution who lived in Ohio." Also page 413 Official Register, Officers and men of New Jersey in the revolutionary War. Stryker—1872.

NEWSPAPER ITEM from The Herald, Saturday, Nov. 22, 1828. On file the Public Library, Circleville, Pickaway Co., Ohio. "Died in Harrison Twp. Nov. 12, 1828, Abraham Swisher Sr. aged 87 years". Captain Swisher probably was buried in Harrison Twp. Cemetery, altho' his grave has not been located.

INVENTORY RECORD, Pickaway County, Ohio, Court Records. Volume 7, 1826—1829 P. 285.

Phillip Cherry, Emanuel Clover, and Nathaniel Wilkins, appraisers, presented to George Bogart, Justice of the Peace, an inventory of the estate of Abraham Swisher, late of Harrison Twp. Dec. 23, 1828. And also the following:

"A true and correct inventory of the goods and chattels of the estate of Abraham Swisher late of Harrison twp. deceased, presented to us the undersigned appraisers of said estate by Philip Swisher and Abraham Swisher administrators thereof the 23rd Dec. 1828. Nathaniel Wilkins, Emanuel Clover, Philip Cherry.

DEED RECORDED SUSSEX COUNTY, NEW JERSEY, Court House, 1811, reads in part "Captain Abraham Swisher and Hannah Christine, his wife, late of Knowlton Twp. Sussex Co N. J. and now of Pickaway Co. Ohio."

BENJAMIN TALLMAN

MILITARY RECORD—

Benjamin Tallman took the oath of Allegiance in Pennsylvania 7, Aug. 1777, and served an enlistment in the Pennsylvania militia. (Penn. Archives 3rd Series, Vol. 6. P. 314.) In 1779 he removed to Virginia, and settled in Harrisonburg, Augusta Co. (later Rockingham Co.). There Benjamin Tallman joined De Best's Troop of the First Partisan Legion under Col. Armand. (Penn. Archives Second Series. Vol. XI P. 140, 145, 146), and took part in the siege of Yorktown.

BENJAMIN TALLMAN, b. 9, Jan. 1745 Berks Co. Penn. son of William and Anne (Lincoln) Tallman, d. June 4, 1820, near Canal Winchester, Ohio, married 9, Nov. 1764 in Berks Co. Penn. Dinah Boone. Dinah Boone Tallman was born 3 or 10, May, 1749, Berks Co. Penn. died July 25, 1824 near Canal Winchester, Ohio. She was baptized 6, Aug. 1753 St. Gabriel's Episcopal Church at Morlstton (now Douglasville) Penn. Family record states she was born May 3. Baptismal record reads May 10.

CHILDREN: First nine b. in Berks Co. Pa., last five b. near Harrisonburg, Va.

William Tallman b. 27, Jan. 1766.
Patience Tallman b. 2, Oct. 1767.
Sarah Tallman b. 12, April 1769.
James Tallman b. 8, April 1771.
Samuel Tallman b. 18, Oct. 1772.
Thomas Tallman b. 6, July 1774 d. 5, May, 1794.
Benjamin Tallman b. 26, May 1776 d. 29, May 1776.
Annah Tallman b. 6, May 1777 d. Sept. 5. 1778.
Annah Tallman b. 15, Dec. 1778.
Ann (Nancy) Tallman b. 20, May 1781.
Susannah Tallman b. 6, Feb. 1783.
Mary Tallman b. 2, Dec. 1784.
Benjamin Tallman b. 19, Nov. 1786.
John Tallman b. 1788.

Benjamin Tallman and Dinah Boone Tallman his wife are buried on the Peter's Farm, Walnut Twp. Pickaway Co. Ohio. Their graves have been marked appropriately by bronze tablets placed there by the Daughters of the American Revolution.

References: The Tallman Family.

1. The Boone Family, Hazel Atterbury Spraker.
2. The Ancestry of Abraham Lincoln, Lee and Hutchinson.
3. Settlers by the Long Gray Trail, Harrison.
4. The Descendants of Thomas Durfee of Portsmouth, Rhode Island Reed.
5. Austin's Genealogical Dictionary of Rhode Island.

SUBSCRIPTIONS FOR THE MEETING-HOUSE

At Tarlton, Ohio, in 1830

By William Hamilton Hannum

The following subscription-list containing the names of fifty-four early settlers of Pickaway Co., Ohio has been found among the effects of William Hamilton.

Know all men by these presents that we the Undersigned Subscribers here Constitute & Appoint David Agustus Israel Todd & John Agustus Jnr A Board of trustees with full power to Appoint their own treasurer and Collector and fill all Vacancies in their own body for the purpose of building a Meeting House or Church in or Near the Town of Tarlton Pickaway County & State of Ohio which building Shall be begun and Finished As soon as expedient after Sufficient Subscribers Shall have been Obtained in Size Not less than 36 feet in length & 30 in breadth one Story High building when Completed Shall be the property of the Presbyterian Society whch now are or May Hereafter be established in the Said town of Tarlton Who May Preach in the English Language with the privilege of the house Extended to all Other Christian Societies When Not Occupied by the Afforesaid proprietors the said building to be built of Brick In order to Carry the said Object into Effect we hereby bind Ourselves unto David King Treasurer & Collector of the Said trustees to pay him or his order Severally the Amount of our Subscriptions As follows (to wit) the one fourth thereof on the first day of Sept. 1830 and the Remaining three fourths Quarter Annually thereafter excepting Articles of Trade which if Grain or Whiskey Shall be delivered to the Said Treasurer on or before the first of Jan 1831 At Market price in Cash in the Said Town of Tarlton if Materials for building or labor when Called for any person or persons Subscribing Halling or Labor Must board themselves of the Said building to the Trustees of Presbyterian Society as soon as it Shall be so far Completed as to be occupied beneficially by them & Submit there accounts of the Expenses thereof to there Examination holding themselves Responsible to them for the faithful Application of the funds Committed to there Charge arising Either from Subscriptions or donations June 3, 1830.

Subscribers Names	Wheat Rye Corn Oats Whiskey	Labor or Material
(1) Samuel Nobel	$30.00	& all timber for Splitting or Hewing
(2) Robert P. Noble	30.00	
(3) James Chambers	25.00	
(4) David King	30.00 Paid in full	Merchandise
(5) Israel Todd The woodwork of a wagon including bed at $28 or 2,500 feet of inch Popular Boards at 1.12½ per 100 feet—		
(6) John Augustus Sr.	35.00	
(7) David Augustus	10.00	$10.00 in sawing
(8) John Wiley	5.00 $5.00	
(9) Robert Carnes	20.00 $5.00 in hauling	
(10) Saml. Lybrand	20.00 In Brick	
(11) Chs. C. Lybrand	10.00 In leather	
(12) Paid George Dresbach	5.00 Rec'd payment Aug 21 1831	
(13) David Wiley	10.00	
(14) Bartletts	5.00	
(15) Susanna McClelland	20.00	
(16) William Willson	5.00	
(17) Geo. S. Binkley	20.00	
(18) Joseph A. Starling	6.00	
(19) Z. H. Binkley	5.00	
(20) Henry Zehrung	5.00	
(21) Lewis Mays	5 00	
(22) Paid Joseph Foust	5.00	
(23) Settled Elijah Hedges	5.00	
(24) Chd David M. Baldwin	5.00	
(25) Settled J. Larrick	10.00	
(26) Settled J. Marks	10.00	
(22) Settled N. Couldron	10.00	
(28) John Chambers	5.00	
(29) Settled Geo Pontius	5.00	In Work not settled
(30) Abram Dresback	5.00	
(31) John Lyons Jnr	5.00 Recd. 33 ft. Boards 33 Spt. 6, 1832	
(32) Paid	5.00	
(33) Paid Saml Spangler	5.00 Recd. August 14, 1832 five dollors in	Painting
(34) Nim Davison	3.00	
(35) Jacob Ritsel	2.00	
(36) Paid Henry Holler	3.00	
(37) Paid Henry S. Crail	2.00	
(38) Paid Jacob Bingley	2.00	
(39) Paid Geo. Will	1.00	
(40) Paid Fred Julien	1.00 Settled by Joseph A. Starling July 26, 1832	
(41) Chd. Danel Sidle Chd. July 25, 1833	1.00	
(42) Paid William Cregor	1.00	
(443) Paid Jacob Reams	Paid Sept. 24th 1832	1 days Hauling
(44) Paid Simeon Hoffman	.50	
(45) George S. Nigh	4.00	
(46) Ezra Julien	5.00	
(47) Paid Chas. Shoemaker	5.00	
(48) Paid Jno Shoemaker	1.00	
(49) Peter Prough	3.00	
(50) John Shaver Chd. July 25 '33	1.00	
(51) Peter Nigh Chgd	5.00	

(52) Daniel Henry		4.00
(53) Wm. Hamilton	Chgd	2.00 .
July 25 '33		
(54) Eli Julien Chg		1.00
July 25, 33		

The meeting-house was eventually erected on the northern edge of the village of Tarlton, on the Zanesville and Maysville Turnpike. It may have been north of the line in Fairfield County. The 'Presbyterian Society' was under the Presbyterian Church in the U. S. A. The present building of the Presbyterian Church, two blocks south of the turnpike, was for many years used by the Cumberland Presbyterian congregation.

The subscription-list shows 54 names, counting one cancelled because of duplication, that of George Dresbach. Opposite the name of John Lyons Jnr. the entry of settlement was cancelled, having been erroneously entered for him instead of Fred Julien.

William Hamilton's name is next to the last(53rd). He was the eldest child of David and Mary (Alexander) Hamilton and was born in 1808 at Great Cove, in Bedford (now Fulton) County, Pa. He came in infancy to a farm near Beuna Vista (now called Middlefork) in Perry Township, Hocking County, Ohio. The patent, granting that tract to David Hamilton is signed by James Madison in 1812 and counter-signed by Edward Tiffin. William was 22 years old when he placed his signature on this list, and was a farmer, and teacher. Nine years later he married Rebecca, daughter of John Augustus Sr.: they lived just south of Oakland, Clearcreek Township, Fairfield County. William was an elder in the Church at Tarlton. In 1833 he became major of the 2nd Regiment, 1st Brigade, 7th Division, Ohio Militia, and in 1839 Colonel. After serving about 3 years as county-surveyor at Lancaster, Ohio he died there in 1856, and was buried beside the graves of his 3 little sons in the cemetery at Tarlton.

James Chambers, (No. 3 on list), was William Hamilton's step-father, and lived in Clearcreek Township. The patent for Jame's farm there, bears the signature of J. Q. Adams, dated in 1827. James the eldest of 4 sons of Alexander and Isabelle Chambers, was born in 1770, probably in County Tyrone, Ireland, and is thought to have studied theology in Edinburg, Scotland. The preamble of this list appears to be in his neat handwriting, as are also probably 40 or more of the Subscribers' names. Till 1802 he was in the employ of Robert Hamilton, Pa., grandfather of William. James's business-experience seems to have made him the custodian of this list. His wife Mary (Alexander, Hamilton), died in 1843, and was buried at Tarlton. When their daughter, Mary Ann Chambers, had been married to Mahlon Ashbrook in 1849, James sold his farm and removed to Sidney, Ohio., where he died in 1858. The Ashbrooks lived at

Ashville, Pickaway O., till 1859, when they removed to St. Joseph, Mo. where some of their descendants still live.

John Chambers (28) was a younger brother of James. His first wife, living at the time of this subscription, was Elizabeth, daughter of John McFarland, who lived at Mullaughban, near Ballygawley, County Tyrone. John Chambers resided about 4 miles east of Tarlton in Perry Township, Hocking County, near where James had lived. John had 4 sons and 1 daughter and their descendants are living in Pickaway, Allen and other counties in Ohio.

John Augustus Sr. (6) was the eighth of 11 children of John and Elizabeth (Springer) Augustus of Wilmington, Del., and was born in 1775. He married Hannah Hendrickson, both being of the old Swedish and Dutch community. After a stay in Virginia they came about 1805 to Ohio, settling in Clearcreek Township, Fairfield County, about 2 miles northeast of Tarlton. He was a farmer, and in 1817 was elected as associate judge and so served about 5 years in Lancaster. He died in 1847, and was buried, with his wife and several children, in the Augustus cemetery on his farm.

David Augustus(7), who is named as a trustee of the building fund, was the eldest of the 7 children of the foregoing John, and was born in 1799, probably in Wilmington, At the age of 21 he married Catherine Rice of Lancaster, where they lived for a time, removing to Clearcreek Township, where he took up experiments in agriculture. He later went west, probably first to Illinois, but his death occurred in 1858 at Carthage, Mo., where his son William was living.

John Augustus Jr., who is named as a trustee, was the second child of Judge John Augustus, and was born in 1802 in Delaware or Virginia. His first wife Anna, a daughter of Samuel and Mary Kirkwood, died about 2 years after the time of this subscription, and her grave is in the Augustus cemetery. They had 3 children, of whom the eldest, Clark, removed to Bloomington, Ill., and had a large family. John married twice afterward. He removed to Cincinnati and probably about 1849 to Newport, Ind., and later to Bloomington, Ill., where he died in 1883.

Jacob Larrick (25) owned a farm on the north edge of the village, and is said to have been the proprietor of a tannery in Tarlton, and to have removed later to Adelphi about 6 miles south. The grave-record at Tarlton shows his birth about 1779 in Virginia and death 23 July 1862. He seems to have been connected with the Augustus family, for Maria, daughter of David Augustus, is thought to have been married to a Larrick, perhaps a son of Jacob. Maria and her family lived near Bloomington. Wesley Larrick, who lived in Platt Co., Ill., many years, removed to Decatur, and later lived in the Soldier's Home at Danville, may have been Jacob's son. A family named Larrick was keeping a hotel in Tarlton about the time of the civil war or before, and the proprietor may have been Wesley.

Jacob Reams (43) was of a family whose name was also spelled Ream and Rheem, and this Jacob was probably the person known in the family records as Daniel Rheem. The record in the Probate Court at Lancaster states the marriage of Jacob Ream and Sarah Augustus on the 17th April 1834, solemnized by Rev. Henry King, and Daniel Rheem was there clearly meant. Daniel was a son of Samuel and Susan (Wunderlick) Rheem, and had come from Carlisle, Pa. His Wife, Sarah, was a daughter of Judge John Augustus. Daniel lived in Madison Township, Fairfield Co., about 4 mile northeast of Tarlton, and later kept a mill about a mile southwest of Lancaster. He removed with his family, about 1867, to a farm near Lonejack, Jackson Co., Mo., and his descendants live in Missouri, Kansas, California, etc. Daniel (alias Jacob) was probably connected with the large family of Abraham Reams, who operated a mill in Bern Township, Fairfield Co. Both families had come about two generations before from Germany.

William Willson (16) had married Ann, sister of Mary (Alexander-Hamilton) Chambers. The Willsons had come from Bedford Co., Pa., and they lived near Buena Vista, on a farm adjoining that of David Hamilton, and there they died, leaving no children.

Susanna McClelland (15) was the widow of James McClelland and younger sister of Mary and Ann Alexander. James was a son of Robert, who was born in 1754, probably in Lancaster Co., Pa.; migrated to Hocking Co., O., probably about 1805; died there in 1834, and was buried at Tarlton. Robert was probably related to Captain John McClelland, who was born in 1734 in Lancaster Co., removed to Westmoreland Co., was active in the Revolution and died on his farm, probably near Buena Vista, Pa., in 1819. James was born there in 1781 and came to Ohio about 1805. He erected on his farm near Buena Vista, O., the stone house which still stands, marked with his name and the year of its completion, 1825, which was the year of his death. The barn had been built in 1813, and it was then that David Hamilton was killed by a falling log. David was buried at Tarlton, where his wife was laid beside him nearly 30 years later. James McClelland also was buried there, and Susanna too, who died within a year after signing this subscription. They had 3 sons and 5 daughters, and their descendants are numerous in Ohio and other States.

Samuel Noble(1) lived on a farm a mile south of Tarlton. He had come probably in 1816, from Virginia. Hiss will, made 20 Sep. 1832 and recorded at Circleville, names his wife Mary, with 2 sons and 4 daughters. The elder son was Colonel John Noble, who had come to Lancaster, O., about 1815 as a tailor, but he owned and managed the Union Hotel on Main Street, on the site of the later Tallmadge House and Kirn House. In 1832 he opened the National Hotel on High Street in Columbus, on the spot where the erection of the Neil House was begun in 1839. He was a member of the City-Council in Columbus, and in 1846 he was elected to represent Franklin County in the General Assembly. He then became proprietor of the Pearl House in Cincinnati, where in 1848 or 1849 he entertained President-elect Zachary Taylor. John Noble had 2 sons and 3 daughters. One was John W. Noble, who lived in St. Louis, Mo., and was Secretary of the Interior in President W. H. Harrison's brief administration. The other son was Henry C. Noble, a prominent attorney of Columbus. The daughters were the wives of leading men of that city, One of Samuel Noble's daughters was Mary, who in 1816 was married to Samuel Effinger, a coppersmith in Lancaster. Her gravestone in Elmwood Cemetery, Lancaster, gives the record: 'Born Emmetsburg, Md., May 24, 1796; Died March 25, 1859' Samuel died in 1833 soon after the completion of his brick house on the public square. The house, after about 100 years, was demolished, and its front door with some interior parts is preserved in the Columbus Gallery of Fine Arts.

Another of Samuel Noble's daughters, Anne, was married in 1836 to Hugh Wilson, whose farm was close to the Nobles'. She died in 1839, leaving 2 children. Hugh was a son of John Wilson, and was born in 1813 in Ireland. The Wilsons came about 1825 to Washington Co., Pa., and about 1835 to Ohio. Hugh in 1842 married Margaret Kinnear, by whom he had 3 children. In 1851 he married Mary, daughter of Judge John Augustus (Mentioned above) and widow of James Earhart. She had no children, and died in 1855 and was buried in the Augustus cemetery. Hugh in 1856, in Philadelphia, Pa., married Susan, daughter of Samuel Lybrand of Tarlton (mentioned below) Hugh died in 1875, and his son by the second wife, David K. Wilson, occupied the home-place till his death in 1930.

Robert P. Noble (2) was the son of Samuel Noble. Robert's will, made 30 Oct. 1847, names his 2 children, Samuel and Isabella.

Robert Carnes of Scotch Irish descent, had come from Virginia, having been born in 1785. In 1806 he married Nancy Stewart, whose borth occurred in 1785 and death in 1851. They removed from the vicinity of Tarlton to a farm about 3 miles southwest of Lancaster, on the pike, where he bought a section of land and built a tavern. obert died in 1853; he and Nancy were buried in the cemetery at Amanda. His granddaughter, Miss Ellen M. Carnes of Lancaster, has a copy of the coat-of-arms and crest of the family and some of the heirlooms.

Samuel and Charles C. Lybrand (10, 11) lived in Tarlton and worked in the tannery later operated by David Allen Hamilton, brother of William. Samuel had been, from 1818 to 1824, a member of the House of Representatives for the Hocking Pickaway District.

George S. Binkley (17) kept a store. James Chamber's ledger has an inscription on the fly-leaf in James's hand: 'Bot. of Geo. S. Binkley Tarlton Ohio Jan. 14th 1830 Price .87½ Cts.

Joseph A. Starling was the minister, probably leader of the movement for the church-building, and thought to be related to Lyne Starling, the pioneer settler of Columbus. Joseph afterward lived in Lancaster. This grave is in Elmwood Cemetery there. The stone bears the record: 'Rev. Joseph A. Starling, Died June 25, 1855. Aged 56 years. Eleanor Starling Died July 9, 1881. Aged 82 years.'

Henry Sehrung (20) lived about 4 miles west of Tarlton. The name commonly has been spelled Zehring, as in the marriage-record in the Probate Court at Circleville, (III. 19): '1832 Mar. 15 License to Henry Zehring and Susanna Wallace' He was an uncle of John, who is remembered as a tinner in the village.

Elijah Hedges (23) was one of several families of the name, Hedges, in Saltcreek and Clearcreek Townships. Some of that name were buried in the Augustus cemetery.

N. Couldron (22), commonly spelled Coldren, lived about 2 miles northeast of Tarlton. His son Andrew long continued on the same farm.

Nimrod Davison (34) was a druggist in Tarlton. He had 2 daughters, one of whom was the wife of James Cregor, who was probably a son of William (43).

George S. Nigh (45) is thought to have been the keeper of the tavern in the western part of the village. George was probably the father of Frederick W. Nye, a prominent citizen.

John Shaver (50), otherwise spelled Shaeffer, probably lived about 5 miles northeast of Tarlton, in Madison Township, near Mechanicsburg, a place now known as Drinkle.

(The end)

INDEX OF WILLS, PICKAWAY COUNTY, 1810-1837
BOOKS A AND B

Mayburt Stephenson Riegel

Elizabeth Allen, William Allison, Philding Atchison, Samuel Atchison, Heronimous Augusten, Elizabeth Anderson, William Bloxem, William B. Becket, Peter Brown, Jacob Bobbs, Andrew Buzzard, Catharine Brancher, William Boley, John Black, Noah Bishop, Sara Backet, James Bell, Sr., Mary Boggs, Thomas Borr, Peter Borner, Margaret Botkin, Coonrad Butt, Draper Brown, Anthony Bowsher, James Bomer, Aimrod Bright, Henry Burgy, Thomas Bowdle, Cornelius Baldwin;

John Blackwell, Catharine Caldwell, Jane Caldwell, William Caldwell, Woolery Coonrad, Joseph Campbell, Thomas Crow, James C. Chaney, William Close, Burton Creal, Samuel Denny, John Dresbach, William Dungan, Edward Davison;

Samuel Davenport, Anthony Davenport, John Dungan, Christopher East (Ger), Robert Ellis, Thomas Emerson, Washington C. Evans, Caleb Evans, Sr., Sarah Ely, Phillip Foresman, Robert Foresman, George Foresman, Alex. Foresman, Alex. Fleming, Jacob Famulener, George Faybach, John Gay, Sr., George Glaze, John Griffith, Mary Griffith, Jared Graham, John Groce, Dr. Thomas H. Gibson;

Ferdinand Gublick, Mary Hammons, Elizabeth Hogan, George Hitler, Simon Hadley, John Hughes, Peter Hollenbach, Susannah Hollenbach, Anthony Hall, Levi Hays, Joseph Hoffnes, Samuel Hibbs, Sr., John Holstead, Margaret Hane, Francis Horsey, Stephen Horsey, Jacob Hubbard, George Horn, George Harmon, Charles Hays;

Henry Hall, John Hittle, Henry Haller, Robert Johnston, John Justice, Mary Van Kirk, James Kinney, John W. Loofburrow, Andrew Leist, Sr., John Lilley, Valentine Leach, Daniel Ludwig, James Lawrence, Elizabeth Lawrence, Abraham Long, William Love, Zadoc Lewis, Joshua Leazenbey, Nicholas Miller, Joush Miller;

Mary Morris, Ezekiel Morris, Henry Mathias, Melcher Mayer, Leviner Mitten, George Moore, John Magath, Robert Martin, John Martin, Sr., Thomas McFadin, John McAllister, Samule McKinney, William McGraw, George Murray, William Marquis, Daniel Markel, Mary Miller, John Miller, John Manatte, Henry Massie, Peter Muhlenburg, James Morris, Peter Mowry, Rodens Mitchel, George Murray, Samuel Noblem, Daniel Noble, Thomas Noland.

Ed. Ostrander, George Pennywell, John Parcels, George Pontius, John Renick, Henry Rush, John Rector, Henry Reeder, Andrew Ramb, William Reed, William Rout, Ann Rout, Talmage Ross, Jonathon Runnels, Jacob H. Smith, Samuel Smith, James Short, Stephen Short, John Swagert, Conrad Stumpf, Jacob Swingley, Phillip Shuck, John Sharpe, John Stump, Gabriel Stuly, Rachel Snodgrass, James Sisk, Charles Simms, James Smith, Hannah Tanner, Caleb Taylor, Mary Thomas, Archibald Thompson, Thomas Thompson, Aaron Teegardin, Isaac Van Meter, Abraham Vanhise, Mary Van Kirk, Winn Winship, James Wooddell, George West, Tubman Wright, Nancy Wright, Leonhart Weimer, William Wilker, Henry Wisler, John Watts, Nathan Ward, Robert White, John Young, Joseph Yates, Jacob Zeager.

From April 26, 1810=Nov. 1, 1837.—MSS/Riegel

MARRIAGE RECORDS, GREENE COUNTY, OHIO
1803-1805
Contributed by MRS. W. E. KLOPP

JONATHAN Donnel m. Sally Newland—at Xenia—Sept. 6, 1803 by David Huston.

PHILLIP Rock m. Mary Kelly—Aug. 4, 1803—by Jonathan Milhollen.

AARON Goodman m. Polly Chapman—Aug. 23—by Jonathan Milhollen.

MATTHEW Cumpton m. Rachel Campbell—Sept. 1, 1803 by John McKnight.

ARTHUR Layton m. Susannah McHenry—Oct. 16, 1803 by Joseph Layton, J. P.

JOSEPH McCord m. Mary Hall—Nov. 10, 1803 by Andrew Read, J. P.

MARTIN Judy m. Sally Petro—Dec. 8, 1803 by Andrew Read, J. P.

FREDERICK Shegley m. Talmer Bailey—Dec. 29, 1803 by David Huston.

GEORGE Taylor m. Polly Smith—Dec. 29, 1803 by David Huston.

SAMUEL Bone m. Abetha Beason—Nov. 8, 1803 by William I. Stewart.

THOMAS M Penattoe m. Mary Lewis—Nov. 25, 1803 by Jonathan Milhollen.

ABRAHAM Buckles m. Jenny Carman—Nov. 8, 1803 by (not given).

JOHN Marshall m. Ann Shaw—Sept. 1, (presumably 1803).

TIMOTHY Greene m. Haldy Well—Jan. 15, 1804 by Joshua Carman.

JOHN Forger m. Margarte Denny—Apr. 20, 1804 by Joseph Layton.

JACOB Kugler m. Kelly Horner—Mch. 6, 1804 by David Huston.

JESSE Dellin m. Mary Jay—Feb. 8, 1804 by William I. Stewart.

REUBEN Strong m. Anna Wilson—Apr. 19, 1804 by William I. Stewart.

SAMUEL Ruth m. Jane Wilson—May 10, 1804 by William I. Stewart.

JACOB Server m. Nancy Robertson—July 9, 1804 by Jonathan Milhollen, Esq.

JACOB Robertson m. Easter McKinney—July 9, 1804 by Jonathan Milhollen.

JACOB Ryan m. Hannah Bush by Joshua Carman.—Also Samuel Darlington m. Nancy McDonnald—Mch. 18, 1804.

JOSEPH Jones m. Rebeckah Mooney—Aug. 16, 1804 by David Huston, Esq.

JOHN Sail m. Nancy Bonner—July 7, 1804 by Bennet Maxey.

JOHN Martin m. Elizabeth Price— Sept. 6, 1804 by Bennet Maxey.

MOSES Trader m. Elizabeth McDonnel—Sept. 2, 1804 by Bennet Maxey.

JOHN Price m. Hannah Davis—July 12, 1804.

JOHN Coy m. Mary Jones—Sept. 18, 1804 by Joshua Carman.

ELIJAH Forguson m. Mary Rue—Dec. 13, 1804 by William McFarland.

JAMES McDaniel m. Betsey Read—Dec. 7, 1804 by Jonathan Milhollen.

JAMES Bull m. Ann Gowdy—Nov. 8, 1804 by Robert Armstrong.

EPHRIAM Morrison m. Letty Gibson—Nov. 29, 1804 by Willliam Robertson.

DANIEL Rector m. Esiah Reece—Mch. 2, 1805 by Andrew Read.

JOHN Williams m. Elizabeth Owens—Jan. 14, 1805 by William McFarland.

WILLIAM Morgan m. Sarah Vance—Jan. 29, 1805 by Joshua Carman.

MICHAEL Kengrey m. Betsey Webb—Feb. 7, 1805 by Joshua Carman.

ARMSTRONG McCabe m. Eleanor Barrett—Apr. 12, 1805 by Joshua Carman.

RICHARD Warfield m. Elizabeth Ennis—Apr. 11, 1805 by Joshua Carman.

JERMIAH York m. Ann Westfall—Apr. 7, 1805 by Joshua Carman.

JACOB Hall m. Ann McGuin—

JAMES Stevenson m. Anna Galloway—Apr. 3, 1805.

JOSEPH Beason m. Susanna Boane—Apr. 13, 1805 by John McKnight.

ROBERT Frakes m. Margaret Orr—May 2, 1805 by Andrew Read, Esq.

WILLIAM Agin m. Catherine Shoves—May 3, 1805 by Andrew Read, Esq.

MARTIN Myre m. Hannah Adby—June 27, 1805 by John McKnight.

HENRY Rogers m. Susannah Hurley—Aug. 15, 1805 by John McKnight.

THOMAS Robertson m. Lydia Horney—Aug. 15, 1805 by John McKnight.

AARON Lambert m. Mary Turner—Oct. 16, 1805 by John Wilson, Esq.

WILLIAM Ames m. Polley McDonnel—Feb. 9, 1805 by Jonathan Milhollen.

CHRISTIAN Curst m. Easter Staley—Nov. 12, 1805 by David Huston, Esq.

MOSES Hatfield m. Catherine John—Nov. 12, 1805 by David Huston.

SAMUEL Kirkpatrick m. Blancy Derough—Oct. 6, 1805 by David Huston, Esq.

ENOS Cleminger m. Susannah Martin—Sept. 11, 1805 by David Huston, Esq.

JAMES Owens m. Deborah Marshall—Aug. 15, 1805 by William McFarland, Esq.

JAMES Collier m. Rachel Smith—June 5, 1805 by Joshua Carman.

JAMES Pelvey m. Mary Jackson—Apr. 24, 1805 by William McFarland.

ABRAHAM Standley m. Mary Horne—Oct. 3, 1805 by John McKnight.

CHARLES Man m. Lydia Jenkins—Oct. 4, 1805 by John McKnight.

ABRAHAM Pittinger m. Jane Wingate—June 20, 1826 by Daniel Kershner. Consent of her father.

ABRAHAM Reed m. Nancy Cox—Jan. 21, 1821—of lawful age.

ALEXANDER McBeth m. Sarah Demit—Mch. 3, 1831 by John A. Swearing—lawful age.

WILLIAM Cozad m. Mary Demint—Mch. 1, 1832 by William Cozad, J. P.

GEORGE Taylor m. Mary Elizabeth Demetts—Apr. 27, 1832 by Thomas Beacham.

HENRY Zimmerman m. Elizabeth Denmint—July 30, 1833 by J. C. Johnson, J. P.

JAMES Demint m. Mary Hillyard—by personal consent of her father—Aug. 13, 1842.

Greene county was formed May 1, 1803, at the home of Owen Davis, Beaver Creek, it being taken from the counties of Hamilton and Montgomery. It was named for General Nathaniel Greene of Revolutionary War fame.

References: "History of Greene County, Ohio", 1902, George F. Robinson.

DATA TAKEN FROM OBITUARIES

of Early Ministers of the Methodist Episcopal Church,

Members of Ohio Conference. (published in 1880)

Agard, Rev. Horace, born Jan. 1776 and died 1850, aged 64 years.

Ayars, Rev. Charles W., Born Feb. 22, 1836 in Philadelphia, died Nov. 18, 1869.

Alverson, Rev. John B., Born Oct. 1793 in Seneca, Ontario Co., N. Y. died Sept. 21, 1850.

Akins, Rev. James, a native of Ireland, born 1778, came to America 1792, settling in Penna.

Amedon, Rev. Moses, born Oct. 10, 1794, in Reedsborough, Vt. and died March 21, 1830.

Anderson, Rev. William R. born in Ross Co., Ohio, in 1810 and died in Franklin, Ohio in 1845.

Austin, Rev. James B. born in Surry Co., N. Carolina, August 16, 1806; removed to Ohio in 1811.

Bangs, Rev. Nathan, born in Stratford Conn., May 2, 1778 and died in New York City.

Bristow, Rev. James H., born in Clark Co., Ky. July 26, 1813.

Boehm, Rev. Henry born in Penna. June 8, 1775 and died December 28, 1875, aged 100 years, 6 months and 21 days.

Baer, Rev. John, born in Virginia October 9, 1794 and died in Baltimore, Md. March 11, 1879.

Brasse, Rev. Gortlich was born in Prussia, Nov. 8, 1833 and died June 3, 1876.

531

DATA FROM OBITUARIES

EARLY CLERGYMEN

By Rosalie Haddox

BROWN, Rev. William, born near Amsterdam, New York, March 7, 1828; died June 8, 1871.

Rev. James Willis, born in Indiana, May 24, 1850; died March 2, 1874.

Rev. Azra, born in Hampton, Mass., Aug. 13, 1792, came to Ohio 1824; died at Evanston, Ill., Aug. 1869.

BLAIN, Rev. John D., born in Kingston, N. J., Feb. 24, 1819; died July 12, 1872.

BERRY, Rev. T. S., died at Corning, Iowa, April 10, 1880.

BANGS, Rev. Herman, born in Fairfield, Conn., April 1790; died Nov. 2, 1869.

BARTINE, Rev. David, born in Winchester County, N. Y. Jan. 26, 1776; died Apr. 26, 1850.

BECKLEY, Rev. William, born Alexandria, Va. Oct. 5, 1817; died Feb. 10, 1880.

BOWDISH, Rev. Leonard, born in New Lisbon, N. Y. in 1812; died at Bainbridge, Ohio May 23, 1870.

BLOOD, Rev. H. P., born in Buckport, Maine, Feb. 1825; died in Sacremento, Calif. Feb. 21, 1874.

BARR, Rev. George S., born in Quarryville, Lancaster Co., Pa., Dec. 4, 1832; died July 1, 1867. Daughter Adelie mentioned.

BIGELOW, Rev. Russel, born 1792; died in Columbus, Ohio July 1, 1835.

BUTLER, Rev. Frederick B., born July 22, 1803, in Prince George Co., Va.

BALDWIN, Rev. Charles R., born in Stockbridge, Mass., March 19, 1803; died in Parkersburg, W. Va.

BROWN, Rev. Stephen D., born 1816; died in New York, Feb. 19, 1875.

BIBBINS, Rev. Samuel, born 1812; died in Burtus, N. Y. Jan. 6, 1880.

BEALL, Rev. Isaac, born in Ohio, Sept. 18, 1823; died in Fairfield, Green County, Ohio, Oct. 27, 1860.

BUNTING, Rev. Jabez, D. D., born at Manchester, May 13, 1799; died June 16, 1858.

BROWN, Rev. David, born Feb. 1760 in County Down, Ireland, died Sept. 15, 1803.

BAKER, Rev. Thomas, born in Monongalia C., Va., Dec. 6, 1808; died April 4, 1845.

BROCKUNIER, Rev. S. J., born in Pa., June 12, 1795; died in Bloomingdale, Ohio, July 12, 1867.

BRUCE, Rev. Phillip, born in North Carolina, a descendant of the Huguenots, and a soldier of the Revolution; died in Giles Co., Tenn. May 10, 1826.

BUDD, Rev. Thomas, born Feb. 19, 1783 in Burlington Co., N. J.; died June 17, 1810.

CAPERS, Rev. William, D. D., bishop of the M. E. Church South. Born in South Carolina, Jan. 26, 1790; died in Anderson, South Carolina, Jan. 29, 1855.

CLARK, Rev. Davis W., born on the island of Mt. Desert off the coast of Maine, Feb. 25, 1812; died in Cincinnati, May 23, 1871.

CRUME, Rev. Moses, born in Virginia, 1766; died in Oxford, O., April

1, 1839.

CRANE, Rev. James Lyons, D. D., born in Ohio, Aug. 30, 1823; died in Ill., 1879.

CALLUHAN, Rev. George, born in Maryland, Dec. 27, 1765; came to Ohio from Penna., an early settler in Licking Co., died Feb. 19, 1839.

COOPER, Rev. Benjamin, born in Perry Co., O., June 3, 1802; died in Hancock Co., Ind., May 13, 1846.

COLLINS, Rev. John, born in New Jersey, 1769; died Aug. 21, 1845.

CONNER, Rev. Aaron, born in Ind., May 22, 1822; died Sept. 28, 1878.

COREY, Rev. David, born 1797; died Aug. 23, 1844.

COLES, Rev. George, born in Stewkley, England, June 2, 1792; died in New York, May 1, 1858.

COOKMAN, Rev. Alfred, born in Columbus, on the Susquehanna river, Jan. 4, 1828; died in Newark, N. J., Sept. 13, 1871, a brother, John and a sister-in-law, Mrs. Rebecca Bruner, a son George, mentioned.

CURRY, Rev. H. M., born in Adams Co., O., April 7, 1818; died in Fletcher, Miami Co., O., March 3, 1874. Son, Morris, aged 10, mentioned.

CULVER, Rev. Aaron L., born at Dobb's Ferry, N. Y., Feb. 19, 1841; died Nov. 11, 1877; married 1865.

CLARK, Rev. Alexander, born in Jefferson Co., O., March 10, 1834; died at Atlanta, Ga., July 6, 1879.

CAMPBELL, Rev. George A., born in Baltimore, Hundred, Delaware, Sept. 3, 1846; died in Frankford, Del. Sept. 7, 1876.

CHRISTIE, Rev. William Burr, born in Wilmington, O., Sept. 2, 1802; died in Cincinnati, O., March 26, 1842. Wife and two small sons mentioned.

CLARK, Rev. Abner, born in Salem, New Hampshire, May 1, 1788; died Feb. 20, 1814.

CHAPLIN, Rev. Jonathan E., born in Chaplin, Windham Co., Conn., in 1789.

CARSON, Rev. Joseph, born in Winchester, Va., Feb. 19, 1785; died in Culpepper Co., Va., April 15, 1875.

CHANDLER, Rev., William, born June 22, 1764; died in 1822.

CUNNINGHAM, Rev. Nathaniel Pendleton, born in Pendleton Co., Va., Aug. 1807; wife and daughter Virginia, mentioned.

DATA FROM OBITUARIES

Early Clergymen
By Rosalie Haddox

DANFORTH, Rev. Calvin, born in Covington, Franklin County, New York, died at St. Augustine, Florida, May 15, 1839.

DAUGHADAY, Rev. Thomas, born in Baltimore County, Maryland in 1777; died in Uniontown Fayette County, Pa. Oct. 12, 1810.

DAVISSON, Rev. Daniel D., born in Clarksburg, Va. 1786; died in Dayton, Ohio.

DELAY, Rev. Jacob, born in Penn., December 17, 1781, died in Jackson County, Ohio Oct. 18, 1845.

DILLON, Rev. John, born near Zanesville, Ohio, Oct. 27, 1815, died at McArthur, Ohio Aug. 26, 1876.

DIXON, Rev. William, son of Rev. William Dixon, and was born in England, Dec. 27, 1816. In 1834 he emigrated to the United States and settled at Windsor, Connecticut.

DOBBINS, Rev. Robert, born in 1768, died in 1860, a daughter, Eliza, is mentioned.

DONKERSLEY, Rev. Richard, born in Yorkshire, England, landed in America in 1842, died at Elizabeth, Ill. Nov. 3, 1875.

DUKE, Rev. H. S. died in Lexington, Ky., May 3, 1836.

DURBIN, Rev. John Price, D. D., born in Bourbon County, Ky., in 1800. Came to Ohio 1820, died in Philadelphia Oct. 1876.

EBBERT, Rev. Isaac, D. D., born at Ellicott Mills, Maryland, March 2, 1817, died in 1871 at Paducah, Ky.

EDDY, Rev. Augustus, born in Massachusetts, Oct. 5, 1798, died Feb. 9, 1870 in Ind. A wife and son, Thomas, mentioned.

EDDY, Rev. Thomas Mears, son or Rev. Augustus, born near Cincinnati, Ohio Sept. 23, 1823, died in New York, Oct. 7, 1874. Granddaughter, Nancy and grandson, Spencer, mentioned.

EDGERTON, Rev. Daniel, born July 2, 1850, died June 1878.

EDMONDS, William, born in Lancaster County, Virginia, Feb. 16, 1804.

ELLIOTT, Rev. Arthur, born in Baltimore County, Maryland, Feb. 22, 1784, died in Paris, Ill. Jan. 18, 1858.

Rev. James, nephew of Dr. Charles Elliott, born June 13, 1813 in Ireland, died May 2, 1870.

Rev. Simon, born Oct. 25, 1809 in Ireland, came to America in 1814.

ELLIS, Rev. Thomas, born in Mastyn, Flintshire, North Wales, Jan. 1, 1806; died at Pine Plains, New York, May 30, 1873.

ELLSWORTH, Rev. William Innis, born in Clinton County, Ohio, Aug. 9, 1807, died in Springfield, Ohio in 1875.

EMERY, Richard, youngest son of John & Abiah Emery, born in Haverhill, West Parish, Mass., Nov. 23, 1794.

EMORY, Robert, born in Philadelphia, July 29, 1814, died May 18, 1848.

FARNANDIS, Rev. Henry S., born Dec. 1, 1793 in Loudoun Co., Va. came to Ohio 1819 and died May 17, 1845.

FAY, Rev. Arial, born 1808, died in Royalton, Vermont, Dec. 29, 1836.

FERREE, Rev. John, born in Lancaster County, Pa. in Nov. 22, 1792, came to Ohio 1825.

FIELD, Rev. Andrew Craig, born in Hobart, New York, Feb. 6, 1815, died in Tarrytown, New York, Jan. 13, 1872.

Rev. Hezekiah, born in Mansfield, Conn., in 1768, lived at Woodstock, Vt., in 1801, died Jan. 2, 1843.

FINLEY, Rev. James W., eldest son of the late John P. & Sarah; born in Highland County, Ohio Dec. 24, 1806.

FISK, Rev. Wilbur, D. D., born in 1791, died Feb. 21, 1838.

FLETCHER, Rev. John, born 1729, died Aug. 14, 1785, wife mentioned.

FOOT. Hon. Senator Solomon, born in Cornwall, Vt., Nov. 19, 1802, died in Washington City, March 26, 1866.

FOSS, Rev. Cyrus, born in Barrington, New Hampshire, 1799, died at Carmel, New York Feb. 29, 1849.

FOULKS, William W., born in Monmouth, New Jersey, Sept. 25, 1788.

FOWBLE, Rev. John Wesley, born in Baltimore, Md., Nov. 5, 1814. Came to Ohio in 1838 married Miss Susan L. Quinn, daughter of the late Rev. James Quinn.

FOX, Rev. Robert, born in Va. Oct. 29, 1826, died in Guyandotte W. Va. July 1, 1873.

FULLER, Daniel, born in Paris, Maine in 1804, died July 27, 1847.

FURLONG, Rev. Henry, born in Baltimore, Maryland, March 21, 1796 died Aug. 29, 1876.

GALE, Elijah, died Sept. 9, 1847, born in Windham, Vermont in 1816.

GARRETTSON, Freeborn, born in Maryland in 1752, died at the home of a friend, George Suckley, Esq., in New York, September 26, 1827.

GATCH, Rev. Philip, born near Baltimore, Md. March 2, 1751, died at his home in Milford, Clermont County, Ohio.

GEORGE, Bishop, born in Lancaster, Va. 1768.

GIBBINS, Rev. Thomas H., born in Springfield, Washington County, Ky., July 19, 1807, died Georgetown, Ky. June 24, 1838. On July 1, 1834 he was married in Cincinnati, Ohio to Miss Eliza Weath, a daughter Mary, and infant son Thomas Emory mentioned.

GIBSON, Rev. Tobias, born in Liberty County, S. Carolina, Nov. 10, 1771.

GILBERT, Rev. Samuel, born in Connecticut, 1818, died Aug. 1, 1866.

GIVENS, Rev. Thomas, died in Potosi, Missouri, Sept. 1, 1835.

GOODE, Rev. William H., D. D., born in Warren County, Ohio, June 19, 1807, died in Richmond, Ind. Dec. 16, 1879.

GORSUCH, Rev. Thomas, born in Hartford County, Md., Jan. 1, 1816; died in the village of Monroe in the Miami Valley, Ohio May 12, 1855.

GREENE, Rev. Elihu, born in Madison County, Ky. July 28, 1814; died Sept. 10, 1845.

GREEN, Rev. Henry Forest, born in Somerset, Ohio, Feb. 18, 1830; died at the home of his father, Bainbridge, Ross Co., Ohio May 6, 1856.

GRIFFIN, Rev. John, born 1784, died Dec. 22, 1844.

GRIFFIS, Rev. Daniel, born near Princeton, Butler Co., Ohio, March 29, 1827; died there Aug. 28, 1861.

GRIFFITH, Rev. Alfred, born 1798, near Greencastle, Pa.; died April 14, 1871. A daughter survived.

GRUBER, Rev. Jacob, born of German parentage in Pennsylvania Feb. 3, 1778.

GUETHING, Rev. George Adam, born Oct. 20, 1741; died in Md., June 28, 1812.

GURLEY, Rev. Leonard B., born in Norwich, Conn., March 10, 1804; died in Delaware, Ohio March 26, 1889. He was married twice—in 1835 to Miss Mary Walcott of Columbus, Ohio. In 1848 he was married to Miss Christina Banks, who survived him. Rev. William, father of Rev. Leonard, born in Wexford, Ireland, March 12, 1757, he died 1848.

GUYER, Rev. James, born in Huntington County, Pa. Jan. 3, 1817; died Aug. 12, 1846 at the home of his father-in-law, Hon. G. Crawford in Clinton County, Pa.
Rev. John, born in Pa. Feb. 13, 1808; died in 1867.

HALL, Rev. Emanuel, born in Ritchie County, Va., Jan. 1824; died in Anderson, Iowa, March 29, 1880. His wife Rosa and son William mentioned.

HAMILTON, Rev. Jefferson, D. D., born in Worchester County, Mass. Aug. 22, 1805; died at Opelika, Alabama, Dec. 16, 1874. Wife, children and grandchildren mentioned.

HAMLINE, Rev. (Bishop) Leonidas L., born in Burling, Conn., May 10, 1797; died 1865.

HANCE, Rev. Alfred, born in New Jersey, Jan. 8, 1810, came to Ohio in 1810, died Jan. 29.

HARMER, Rev. James, born in Philadelphia County, Pa., April 29, 1808; died Sept. 8, 1850.

HARRIS, Rev. G. W., born in Frederick County, Va. Nov. 14, 1823; died near Springfield, Ohio Nov. 5, 1862. In 1852 he married Miss Lizzie Kenaga.

HAVEN, Bishop Gilbert, born in Malden, Mass. Sept. 19, 1821; died Jan. 3, 1880. In 1851 he married Miss Mary Ingraham, who died in 1860. They had a son and a daughter.

HAW, Rev. Uriel, born May 13, 1799, the son of Rev. James Haw.

HEDDING, Bishop Elijah, born in Duchess County, New York in 1780; died April 9, 1852.

HIBBARD, Rev. William, born in Norwich, Conn. Feb. 24, 1771; died April 24, 1823.

HILL, Rev. Jeremiah, born in Providence, Rhode Island, Oct. 2, 1816; died in Ohio in 1836.

HOPKINS, Rev. James H., born Dec. 6, 1804 in Huntingdon, Luzerne County, Pa., came to Ohio to Morgan County in 1808. He married Jane Alderman in 1822; died Dec. 16, 1872.

HOUSEWEART, Rev. James J., born in New Jersey, Aug. 15, 1806; died in 1839.

HOWARD, Rev. Solomon, son of Cyrus and Lucy Howard, born in Cincinnati, Ohio Nov. 14, 1811. He married Margaretta Garroutte of Highland County, Ohio in 1836. He married a second time to Mrs. Eliza Varian of Piqua, Ohio in 1841. He died in Calif. Aug. 11, 1880. They had two children, a daughter, the wife of Rev. D. J. Starr and a son, drowned at Athens, Ohio in 1860.

HUDSON, Rev. Wesley C., born in 1813; died in New Brunswick, Apr. 2, 1844.

HUMELBAUGH, Rev. H. Y., born in Adams County, Pa. July 10, 1835; died at Chambersburg on Oct. 13, 1868. Wife and son mentioned.

HUSTED, Rev. Harvey, born in Alford, Mass. Feb. 2, 1803, died Oct. 4, 1871.

EARLY DEATHS IN COLUMBUS

From Vital Statistics, Original records on file in the Department of Health, Columbus City Hall, Columbus, Ohio.

Compiled by MABEL INNIS FREY AND LORENA B. ADAMSON

Abbreviations: w—white; mar—married; b—born; par—parents; res—residence; bur.—buried; mcht—merchant; cptr—carpenter; drsmkr—dressmaker.

1874

| January 1 | No. 1 | Cynthia Blake, w, mar, b. 1815 Franklin county; par. unknown; res. Noble & Front Sts; d. 6/1—bur 6/8. |

2   2   George H. Cowley, w, butcher, mar, b. 2/24/1846 England; par. Robert & Caroline Cowley; res. Friend St; d. 1/2—bur 1/3.

?   3   Paddie Washington, c, single, b. 8/7/1861 Virginia, par. Archable and Anice; res. No. d & Long Sts; d. 1/2—bur 1/4.

3   4   John Joseph Trott, w, laborer, single, b. 11/21/1861 Columbus, par. Alban & Theresia; res. Columbus; d. 1/3—bur 1/5.

3   5   Frances Stewart, w, mcht, mar, b. 3/2/1788 York Pine, par. J & Anna; res. Columbus; d. 1/3—bur. 1/6.

3   6   Addy Brown, w, drsmkr, single, b. 7/8/1861 Columbus, par. Moses & E; res Columbus; d. 1/3—bur 1/5.

4   7   Julie Stevens, w, cptr, mar, b. 6/1/1823 Columbus, par. Germany; res. Loganport, Ind; d. 1/4—bur 1/7.

5   8   James H. Wing, w, rr, single, b. 3/14/1839 Baltimore, par. Wm. & Electa; res. Columbus; d. 1/6—bur. 1/7.

6   9   Caroline Reichbach, w, single, b. 1/5/1874 Baltimore, par. John & Frances; res. Columbus; d. 1/6—bur 1/7.

6   10   Sarah Davenport, w, mar, b. Virginia; par. Sarah & Fred; res. Columbus; d. 1/6—bur. 1/8.

6   11   Evan Javis, w, laborer, single, b. Virginia; d. 1/6—bur 1/8.

7   12   Sophia Stoertzbach, w, single, b 7/22/1871 Ohio;

par. Charles & Elizabeth; res. Columbus; d. 1/7
—bur 1/8.

10 13 George Harper, w, single, par. J & M; res Columbus; d 1/7—bur 1/8.

10 14 Infant, w, b. 1/10/1874 Columbus; par. J. S. Palmer & Clara; res. Columbus; d. 1/10—bur 1/11.

11 15 Mary Hawkins, w, mar, b. 1847 Ireland, par. Patrick & Jane Hagerty; res. Columbus; d. 1/11 —bur 1/13.

11 16 C. H. Davis, w, single, b. 10/15/1867 Columbus; par. Robert & Mary Davis; res. Columbus; d. 1/11 —bur. 1/17.

11 17 Mary Ann Sutherly, w, mar, b. 2/1824 England, par. Salomon & Eliz. Sprage; res. Columbus; d. 1/11—bur 1/17.

12 18 Wilhelmina Wahl, w, mar. b. 1843 Germany, par Christ & Christina Rebel; res. Columbus; d. 1/12 —bur 1/14.

12 19 Frank Lang, w, single, b. Columbus, par. W. & C. Lang; res. Columbus; d. 1/12—bur 1/14.

20 Mary C. Puffs, w, single, b. 3/10/1873 Columbus; par. Henry & Mary Puffs; res. Columbus; d. 1/12 —bur. 1/14.

13 21 Fred Collins, w, mar. b. England, par. F. & S. Collins; res. Columbus; d. 1/13—bur 1/14.

22 Keller, w, b. 1/13/1874 Columbus, par. Christ & Mary Keller; res. Columbus; d. 1/13—bur 1/14.

15 23 Ernst Wobring, w, single, b. 8/25/1873 Columbus, par. Phillip & Heneryeta; res. Columbus; d. 1/13 —bur /14.

24 Georgetta Nichlone, w, single, b. 8/4/1864 Ohio, par. Fred & Mary; res. Columbus; d. 1/15 —bur 1/16.

25 N. E. Lang, w, single, b. 12/14/1873 Columbus, par. J. & K. Lang; res. Columbus; d. 1/15 —bur 1/17.

16 26 Benj. F. Romaine, w, clergy, single, b. 12/14/1873 New York, res. Columbus; d. 1/16—bur 1/19.

27 Charles Neistling, w, single, b. 9/20/1872 Columbus, par. Lewis & Christina; res. Columbus; d. 1/16—bur 1/18.

17 28 Katharina Stalder, w, single, b. 9/20/1867 Columbus, par. Lewis & Christina; res. Columbus; d. 1/17 —bur 1/18.

18 29 Ewing Jones, w, single, b. 1861 Columbus, par William & Mary; res. Columbus; d. 1/18—bur. 1/20.

30 James Clanehan, w, single, b. 9/12/1861 Columbus, par. William & Mary; res. Columbus; d. 1/18 —bur 1/20.

31 Mrs. Mary Druny, w, mar. b. 3/10/1810 Columbus, par. Adam Druny; res. Columbus; d. 1/18 —bur 1/20.

32 Josephine Mutter, w, mar. b. 6/11/1812 Germany, par. Lucas Gerber; res. Columbus; d. 1/18 —bur 1/20.

19 33 Rachel Probenn, w, mar. b. 5/3/1846 Wales, par

W & Ely Williams; res. Columbus; d. 1/19

34 James Doyle, w, mar. b. 10/18/1839 Ireland, par. Mary Doyle; res. Columbus; d. 1/19—bur 1/21.

20 35 George Coleman, w, mar. b. 7/16/1870 Ohio, par. Mary, res. Columbus; d. 1/20—bur 1/22.

36 Harriett Warren, w, single, b. 1/13/1874 Columbus, par. Henry & Mary; res. Columbus; d. 1/20 —bur 1/22.

37 Jacob Schwemberger, w, single, b. 1/30/1874 Columbus, par. Jeremia & Elizabeth; res. Columbus; d. 1/20—bur 1/22.

38 George Schmidt, w, mar, b. 3/1827 Germany, par. George Henry; res. Columbus; d. 1/20—bur 1/22.

39 Polly Churchwell, w, single, b. 1801 Virginia, par. ——; res. Columbus; d. 1/20—bur 1/23.

40 Jeromia Mara, w, blacksmith, mar, b. 9/4/1824 Ireland, par. Sally; res. Columbus; d. 1/20 —bur 1/22.

21 41 William Korell, w, Laborer, mar, b. 1813 Germany, par. William & Margareta; res. Columbus; d. 1/21 —bur 1/24.

42 James Graham, w, mar, b. 1/21/1818 Pennsylvania; res. Columbus; d. 1/21—bur 1/23.

22 43 Alfred Hollenbach, w, laborer, mar, b. 1/7/1822 Germany, par. Amos & Tabitha; res. Columbus; d. 1/22—bur 1/25.

44 Amanda Miller, w, mcht, mar, b. 10/5/1848 Lancaster, par. Henry & Amanda; res. Columbus; d. 1/22—bur 1/24.

45 Siling Rawson, w, tailor, mar, b. 1818; res. Columbus; d. 1/22—bur 1/23.

24 46 Ann M. Phillips, w, mar. b. 1819 Wales; par. Thomas & Ann Davis; res. Columbus; d. 1/22 —bur 1/23.

47 Minerva Sheridan, w, b. 5/24/1866 Columbus, par. Michel & Mary; res. Columbus; d. 1/24—bur 1/25.

48 Lucy Masey, w, mar, b. 3/12/1812 Columbus, par. Ed. Masey; res. Columbus; d. —bur 1/26 Aged 62 yrs.

26 49 Mary Scoot, w, single, b. 2/22/1866 Columbus, par. Richard & Mary; res. Columbus; —bur 1/27 Aged 8 yrs.

27 50 Daniel Simmons, w, mar, b. 1/2/1829 Columbus; res. Columbus; —bur 1/29 Age 51 yrs.

51 Charles Zapp, w, butcher, mar, b. 10/28/1823 Germany; par. Charles & Elizabeth; res. Columbus; bur 1/29 Aged 51 yrs.

52 William Arthur, w, grocer, mar, b. 12/9/1833 Columbus, par. Richard & Margaret; res. Columbus; bur. 2/1, Age 41 yrs.

28 53 Cetty Ruegg, w, single, b. 3/19/1864 Columbus, par. Chasper Reugg; res. Columbus; bur. 1/29, Aged 10 yrs.

539

EARLY DEATHS IN COLUMBUS

From VITAL STATISTICS—Original Records on file,
Dept. of Health, City Hall, Columbus, Ohio

1 8 7 4

January 30 No. **54** George Schween, w, single, b. 12/22/1871 in Columbus; par. George & Mary; res. Columbus; d. age 3; bur. 2/2/1874.

31 **55** Emma L. Dickie, w, married, b. 10/17/1843 in Indiana; par. Grove & Hannah Lampman; res. Columbus; d. age 41; bur. 2/1/1874.

February 1 No. **56** David M. Robert, w, single, b. 1/13/1873 in Ohio; par. Benjamin & Rachel; res. Columbus; d. age 1 yr.; bur. 2/2/1874.

1 **57** George Kirk, w. married, b. 3/28/1839 in England; par. George & Ellen; res. Columbus; occupation Liveryman; d. age 45; bur. 2/3/1874.

2 **58** Jacob Schaffhauser, w, married, b. 10/13/1815 in Germany; par. Andreas & Marie; res: Columbus; occupation Cooper; d. age 59; bur. 2/3/1874.

4 **59** Bridget Lene, w, single, b. 9/14/1840 in Ireland; par. unknown; res. Columbus; died age 34; bur. 2/6/1874.

6 **60** Thomas Y. Miles, w, married, b. 10/19/1799 in Pa.; par. Giddion & Anna; res. Columbus; died age 75; bur. 2/8-1874; occupation Plasterer.

6 **61** Franck Hays, w, married, b. 10/18/1845 in Germany; par. unknown; res. Columbus; died age 29; bur. 2/8/1874; occupation Laborer.

7 **62** Rebecca Anderson, w. married, b. 1793 in Virginia; par. unknown; res. Columbus; died age 81; bur. 2/10/1874.

February 7 No. **63** Francis Hay, w, married, b. 12/8/1771 in Germany; par. John & Margaretta; res. Columbus; Occupation Physician; died age 102; bur. 2/11/1874.

9 **64** Katy Wilkon, w, single, b. 7/10/1873 in Columbus; Par. William & Katy, res. Columbus, died age 1 yr.; bur. 2/10/1874.

10 **65** Sarah E. Watkins, w, married, b. 12/3/1835 in Ohio; par. Levy and Abigail Baley; res. Columbus, died age 39; bur. 2/15/1874.

10 **66** Josephine Ball, c, married, b. 1833 in Ohio; par. Schacleford; d. age 41; bur. 2/12/1874.

10 **67** Mary Bucannan, w, married, b. 8/15/1789 in Germany; par. unknown; d. age 85 in Columbus; bur. 2/15/1874.

12 **68** Mary Evans, w. single, b. 9/11/1858 in Ohio; Par. Elizabeth & Richard; d. age 16 in Columbus; bur. 2/13/ 1874.

12	69	Katy Brown, w, single, b. 11/18/1862 in Columbus; par. unknown; d. age 12 in Columbus; bur. 2/14/1874.
13	70	Allen Jackson, w, married, b. 2/6/1842 in Ohio; par. Abraham & Hana; d. age 32 in Columbus; bur. 2/13/1874.
14	71	George Krum, w, single, b. 12/14/1863 in Columbus; par. George & Ellen; d. age 11; bur. 2/16/1874.
16	72	S. Schwaigert, w, married, b. 1812 in Germany; par. unknown; occupation Teamster; d. age 62 in Columbus; bur. 2/17/1874.
17	73	Katharina Reichert, w, single, b. 11/19/1857 in Columbus; par. Jacob & Katherine; d. age 17 in Columbus; Bur. 2/20/1874.
February 17 No.	74	Henry Sanforth Kach, w, single, b. 3/21/1869 in Pa.; par. N. B. & Meny; d. age 5 in Columbus; bur. 2/18/1874.
19	75	Fredricka Bittlemayer, w, married, b. 5/14/1840 in Germany; par. Fredrich & Fredericka Schute; d. age 34 in Columbus; bur. 2/22/1874.
20	76	Thomas Conway, w, single, b. 10/18/1832 in Ireland; par. unknown; d. age 42 in Columbus, bur. 2/22/1874.
21	78	John Mood, w, single, b. 1/18/1814 in Columbus; par. John & Mary; d. age 60; bur. 2/22/1874.
21	79	Ellen Moody, w, single, b. 1871 in Columbus; par. John & Mary; d. age 3; bur. 2/26/1874.
23	80	———— Phillips, w, single, b. Sept.. 1873 in Columbus; par. not given; d. age 1 year; bur. 2/25/1874.
24	81	Marie A. Mubury, w, married, b. 3/23/1791 in Maryland; par. Simon & Mary Reynolds; d. age 85; bur. 2/26/1874.
26	82	Emma Enricht, w, single, b. 8/14/1856 in Columbus; par. Mike & Ellen; d. age 18; bur. 2/28/1874.
26	83	Mary Enricht, w, single, b. 9/18/1852 in Columbus; par. Mike & Ellen; d. age 22; bur. 2/28/1874.
26	84	Thedora Lindenberg, w, married, b. 11/13/1807 in Germany; par. Henry & Augusta; died age 67; bur. 3/1/1874; Occupation Clerk.
26	85	John Fairvis, w, single, b. 1874 in Md.; par. William; died age 0; bur. 3/1/1874; Occupation of Father, Huckster.
27	86	Anna Korn, w, married, b. 8/6/1817 in Pa.; par. Robert & Anna Nelson; died age 53; bur. 3/1/1874.
February 28 No.	87	Ferdinand Eichensee, w, single, b. 2/5/1850 in Germany; par. John & Dorothea; died age 24; bur. 3/4/1874; Occupation Composition.
28	88	Franz Mehling, white, single, b. 4/1/1822 in Germany; par. John & Katherina; died age 52; bur. 3/4/1874; Occupation Plasterer.

EARLY DEATHS IN COLUMBUS

March 1 No. 89 John Benboe, w, single, b. 12-2-1873 in Columbus; par. John & Mary; d. age 1 yr.; bur. 3/3/1874.

1 90 John G. Hinbeer, w, married, b. 1-20-1805 in Germany; par. John & Christine; d. age 69; bur. 3/3/1874.

4 91 Rosa Lang, w, single, b. 4-24-1856 in Columbus; par. George & Rosa; d. age 18; bur. 3 5 1874.

4 92 William Wylie, w, single, b. 11-26-1873 in Columbus; par. James & Catherine; d. age 1; bur. 3-6-1874.

4 93 Melina Daniel, w, married, b. 11-11-1837 in Ohio; par. John & Margaret Patterson, d. age 41; bur. 3-6-1874.

5 94 James Wylie, w, single, b. 1-24-1874 in Columbus; par. James & Catherine; d. 8 mos.; bur. 3-6-1874.

6 95 Daniel Brunner, w, single, b. 4-3-1870 in Columbus; par. Zirol & Emmelia; d. age 3 yrs; bur. 3-8-1874.

6 96 Emmilia Brunner, w, s, b. 7/17/1867 in Columbus; par. Zirol & Emmelia; d. age 6; bur. 3/8/1874.

7 97 Sarah Dennison, w, married, b. 10/25/1842 in Columbus; par. George Dennison; d. age 32; bur. 3/9/1874.

8 98 Carolina Wedan, w, married, b. 4/9/1833 in Germany; par. Heiden; d. age 41; bur. 3/10/1874.

8 99 Mary Hoff, w, single, b. May, 1834 in Virginia; par. unknown; d. age 40; bur. 3/9/1874.

8 100 Rosalia Wolf, w, single, b. 1/13/1869 in Columbus; par. Michael & Rosalia; d. age 5; bur. 3/9/1874.

8 101 Henry M. Failing, w, single, b. 9/21/1825 in N. Y.; par. Joseph & Mary; d. age 49; bur. 3/11/1874; occupation, bookkeeper.

March	10 No.	102	Oliver A. Banks, w, single, b. 3/11/1874 in Columbus; Par. O. A.; d. age 5 days; bur. 3/17/1874.
	12	103	S. L. Brown, w, single, b. 5/20/1863 in Ohio; par. William; d. age 6; bur. 3/15/1874.
	12	104	Anton Roling, w, married, b. 4/4/1799 in Germany; d. age 75; bur. 3/14/1874; occupation, Laborer.
	15	105	Mary Buttler, w, single, b. 10/18/1862 in Columbus; par. James & Mary; d. age 12; bur. 3/17/1874.
	16	106	James Patterson, w, single, b. 1/19/1871 in Ohio; par. Jasper & Mary; d. age 3; bur. March, 1874.
	16	107	Nancy A. Snyder, w, married, b. 5/31/1854 in Ohio; par. Jonathan & Mahaly Ream; d. age 20; bur. 3/18/1874.
	17	108	Barbara Bierbrener, w, married, b. 9/12/1830 in Germany; par. Schneider; d. age 44; bur. 3/18/1874.
	14	109	Emma Dell, w, married, b. 8/12/1833 in Switzerland; par. John & Mary Reimeyer; d. age 40; bur. 3/15/1874.
	18	110	Bridget Moore, w, married, b. 9/18/1845 in Columbus; par. James Moore; died age 29; bur. 3/18/1874.
	18	111	Mary F. Cox, w, single, b. 3/17/1872 in Columbus; par. William and M. Cox; d. age 1 yr.; bur. 3/19/1874.
	18	112	Sarah E. Spicer, w, married, b. 10/27/1833 in Ohio; par. unknown; d. age 41; bur. 3/19/1874.
	18	113	Ratie Bulland, w, single, b. 12-7-1873 in Columbus; d. age 1 yr; bur. 3/19/1874.
	18	114	Adam Silbernagel, w, single, b. 4/23/1847 in Germany; d. age 27 in Columbus; bur. 3/20/1874.
	20	115	Bridget Carney, w, married, b. 8/18/1846 in Ireland; par. Karney; d. age 28; bur. 3/21/1874.
March	20 No.	116	A. Trott, w, single, b. 3/20/1874 in Columbus; par. A. Trott; d. at birth; bur. 3/21/1874.
	21	117	Olca Harris, w, single, b. Aug. 1873 in Columbus; par. unnamed; d. age 6 mos.; bur. 3/23/1874.
	23	118	Michael Elurham, w, married, b. 9/24/1843 in Ireland; par. unknown; d. age 31 in Columbus; bur. 3/25/1874.
	23	119	Wm. H. Perjus, w, single, b. 10/4/1865 in Ohio; d. age 9; bur. 3/24/1874.
	23	120	John Schaart, w, single, b. 4/23/1811 in Germany; d. age 62 in Columbus; bur. 3/24/1874.
	23	121	Catherine Rancy, w, single, b. 1/11/1819 in Ohio; d. age 52 in Columbus; bur. 3/25/1874.
	23	122	Molly Booker, w, single, b. unknown; in Virginia; age at death unknown; bur. 3/25/1874.

No Entry

24	124	William Woolard, w, single, b. 1/4/1873 in Columbus; bur. 3/25/1874.
24	125	Anna Dieble, w, single, b. 3/27/1869 in Columbus; par. Casper & Crecentia; d. age 4; bur. 3/26/1874.
24	126	Catherine Scott, w. married, b. 1808 in Virginia; par. Mosley; d. age 66; bur. 3/26/1874.
25	127	Harry Carr, w, married, b. 10/14/1838 in Me.; par. Harry & Ellen; d. age 36; bur. 3/28/1874.
25	128	Henry Cherry, w, single, b. 9/19/1872 in Columbus; par. Bruce & Catherine; d. age 2; bur. 3/26/1874.
27	129	John Obrien, w, single, b. 5/12/1864 in Columbus; par. Michael & Mary; d. age 10; bur. 3/26/1874.
27	130	Eliza C. Swagert, w, married, b. 10/1857 in Pa.; par. Binklinger; d. age 17; bur. 3/28/1874.
March 27 No.	131	The Lindel child, w, single, b. died at birth; par. George & Catherine, bur. 3/28/1874.
27	132	The Gressle child; w, single, b. 3/20/1874 in Columbus; par. Jacob & Anna; died age 3 days; bur. 3/28/1874.
28	133	Mary Collins, w, married, b. 8/18/1836 in Ireland; par. John & Mary; d. age 38; bur. 3/29/1874.
29	134	Elizabeth Rolether, w, married, b. 11/1/1807 in Germany; par. Anton & Eva Stebig; d. age 61; bur. 3/31/1874.
30	135	Male infant Atkins, w, single, b. 3/11/1874; par. David & Christina; d. age 19 days; bur. 4/2/1874.
31	136	James Ritson, w, married, b. 3/8/1811 in England; par. James and Mary; died age 63; bur. 4/2/1874.
31	137	John Maeler, w, single, b. 2/5/1874 in Columbus; par. Henry & Elizabeth; d. age 2 mos; bur. 4/2/1874.
31	138	Margaretha Hoy, w, married, b. 6/17/1777 in Germany; par. Jos. & Mary Haring; d. age 97; bur. 4/2/1874.

MISCELLANY

Thelma Blair Lang

Residents of Columbus a Century Ago

Professional men who were residing in Columbus, Franklin Co., Ohio, March 1, 1834, included the following groups of persons*:

United States Officers—William Miner, Clerk of the United States Courts; John Patterson, Marshal for the District of Ohio; Noah H. Swayne, District Attorney; Bela Latham, Postmaster; Henry Brewerton, Superintendent of the National Road; David Scott, Engineer and Inspector of the National Road; John McElvain, Indian Agent.

Ohio State Officers—Benjamin Hinkson, Secretary of State; Henry Brown, Treasurer of State; John A. Bryan, Auditor of State; Timothy Griffith, Chief Clerk, Auditor's Office; William W. Gault, Keeper of the Penitentiary; Nathaniel Medbury, Superintendent of New Penitentiary; Zachariah Mills, State Librarian; Christopher Neiswanger, Quarter-Master General; Samuel C. Andrews, Adjutant General.

Practicing Lawyers—Gustavus Swan, P. B. Wilcox, Nease Smith, Orris Parrish, Lyne Starling, Jr., John G. Miller, John D. Munford, Noah H. Swayne, M. J. Gilbert, Samuel C. Andrews.

Practising Physicians—John M. Edmiston, Peter Jackson, William M. Awl, J. S. Lander, N. M. Miller, Samuel Parsons, P. Sisson, P. H. Eberle, M. B. Wright, Robert Thompson, S. Z. Seltzer.

Officiating Preachers—James Hoge, D. D., Presbyterian; L. B. Gurley, Methodist (stationed); Thomas Asbury, local preacher, Methodist Episcopal; J. F. Wixom, Methodist Episcopal; William Preston, Episcopalian; Russell Bigelow, Methodist Episcopal (agent for Temperance Society); George Jeffries, Baptist; Edward Davis, Baptist.

Columbus' Officials—The first election under a charter was held by the City of Columbus in the spring of 1834. The results were: MAYOR: John Brooks. COUNCILMEN: FIRST WARD, Joseph Ridgeway, Sr.; Robert W. McCoy, Otis Crosley, Henry Brown; SECOND WARD, Jonathan Neereamer, Francis Stewart, Noah H. Swayne, William Long; THIRD WARD, John Patterson, Christian Heyl, William Miner, and William T. Martin. OFFICERS OF COUNCIL: Robert W. McCoy, President; William T. Martin, Recorder; and William Long, Treasurer.

*From Franklin County Register, William T. Martin, Scott and Wright, publishers, Columbus, Ohio. 1834.

ACCOUNT OF WORK AT THE TOLL BRIDGE
LEADING FROM LANCASTER TO MARIETTA

by C. KING

Micheal Hensel 19 days of work at 50 cents per day. Boarding 25 cents, whiskey 12½ cents, tools 2¼, cents per day.

Henry Ansel, Jacob Heeler, John Pennybaker, Henry Hansel, George Wagoner, Jacob Ream, Jacob Ream, Jr., Phillip Ream, Benjamin Wolham, Nicholas Tipple, William Carpenter, John Dodd, Peter Zarley, Jacob Erick, Sr., Jacob Erick, Jr., Henry O. Zebaugh, John Carpenter, Jacob L. Eckert, John Hansel, George Carpenter.

John Harrh, John Roland, Henry Heizer, William Traverse, Samuel Stookey, John Rods, Sr., John Rods, Jr., Peter Saunders, John Stallings, Benjamin Bradle, Michael Blank, Benjamin Bougher, Abraham Mayer, John Stookey, Henry Smith, David Carringer, Patrick Sharran, Daniel Phillips, Christian Blank, John Lisho.

John Brooks, Abraham Ritcher, Christian Beery, Chriolian Meser, George Hansel, John Isles, Abraham Lisho, Robert Watts, George S. Watts, Danial Hock, Jacob Ream, Peter Myers, John Beery, Henry Rudolph, John Bonsey, Solomon Dodd, Henry Rudolph, Samuel Carpenter, John Schvare, Abraham Ream, Absolum Ream, George Bixler, Peter Sturgeon, John Dodd, Isaac Coons, Henry Stoushp, Luke Stegevt, William Carpenter, George Dodd, James Parrigin.

Daniel Fenk, Henry Gunder, George Carpenter, Mule Torole, William Jackson, Jonathian Lynch, William Dulton, Christian Wistnhaver, William Ream, Sampson Ream, Peter Gunder, Thomas Reynolds, Benjamin Reynolds, John Sellers, Jacob Garuk, Huffman Ream, Baker Dulton, David Carpenter, Elijah Bonam, John Addison, Frederuk Huffman, Timothy Green, Old Lukehart, James Baley, Jacob Beary, James Brooks, John Roland, William Long, Bear at Vaumetres, Jipe Stugeon.

Henry Shellenbarger, Jipe Hedges, Joseph Wonk, Michael Stoker, John Hoffman, Ezra Torrence, Sebastin Carpenter, John Crooks, James Crooks, John Vanmetre, Abraham Sellenbarger, John Winters, Mathias Wadman, Elijah Williams, Abraham Hestead, Ephran Reynolds, William Crooks, James Purl, Lewis Sites, William Traverse, Thomas Coloson, John Euks, John Purl, Hezekiah Purl, Even Perkins, John Carpenter, Sam Fosler, E. B. Memen, John Carpenter, Isaac Schaeffer.

Henry Sloushpring, Philip Huffman, Peter Menlong, Robert Harper, Jacob Gassell, Jacob Huffman, Philip Bratz, Peter Stookey, Fred Arney, John Freaker, Peter Rudolph, Robert Young, Job Fowler, John Huffman, Daniel Arnold, Samuel Watt, Henry Abrams, Andrew Crockett, Rudolph Pilcher, Michael Shoag, William W. Irwin, Emuel Carpenter, Sr., Emuel Carpenter, Jr., John Adams Soladay, Alexander McEntire, Matin Landes, Michael Shellenbarger, John Trumph, Samuel Crats, James Buchert (negro).

Jacob Burg, Peter Ebersole, Elijah Lamb, Joseph Lienbien, Robert Pettgren, Richard Richardson, John Cook, James H. Collins, M. Phillips, Jacob Sellers, William Gassell, Elias Bixler, Jacob Meeks, John Pennybaker, Frederick Downey, John Laleher, Warren Spitter, William Chambers, John Hover, Conrad Pratz, Jacob Forman, Daniel Mayers, Henry Pralz, Larkinson Reynolds, Burton Reynolds, John Bibler, Jacob Bibler, Jonathan Amsbaugh, John Shesler, Henry Shellenbarger.

Abraham Reynolds, William Brennan, Samuel Shellenbarger, Marshal Pero (to hauling 1 day), John Kreasey, Jacob Boos, John Baldwin, Casper Huffard, Samuel Graybill, Joseph Stewart, Peter Rivers, Abraham Eversole, Jacob Myers, Peter Sturgeon, Valentine Bratz.

Amount of work expended on Turnpike from Lancaster to Marietta ————$360.10.

Total amount expended by C. King ———— $1613.50.

August 22, 1811, Book No. 1 County Recorder's office, Fairfield County, Ohio

---

EARLY SETTLERS OF JACKSON COUNTY, OHIO
MARCH 1818-SEPTEMBER 1846
MAYBURT STEPHENSON RIEGEL

Charles O'Neil, John James, Edmund Richmond, Jr., Nathaniel W. Andrews, Jared Strong, J. W. Ross, Hugh Poor, David Paine, Wm. Givens, Absolom M. Faulkner, Andrew Donnally, Hooper Hurst, David Mitchell, Vincent Southard, Elias Long, John N. Moore, Alex. Miller, John N. Rathburn, Patrick Shearer, Christopher Hanna, Ezekiel Boggs, John Stinson, N. R. Clough, Geo. W. Hale, James Hale, Robert Mims, Hugh G. Hale, Wm. Stephenson, Andrew Cremeens, Gabriel McNeel, N. W. Andrews, Gabriel McNeel, Lewis Adkins, Timothy Darling,

Seth Richmond, Beverly Keenan, Anthony Fought, D. Hoffman, Oliver N. Tyson, Banister Brown, James McQuality, Jacob Westfall, Daniel Perry, Joseph Armstrong, Levi Dungan, Henry Poffenberger, Levi M. Mercer, Samuel McDowell, C. W. Long, Wm. Branson, Sam'l Carrick, John Martin, S. L. Craig, Moses Hale, James Miller, James Stephenson, Lewis Leach, Robert Ward, Abraham Cassill, James Dempsey, Thompson Leach, Abraham French, Thos. W. Leach, Reuben Rickabaugh, Henry Cassill, George Burris, C. M. Martin, Peter Pickrel, Nelson Cavett, Asa Dudley, Thomas Vaughn, Wm. Ransom, Wm. White, Wm. Givens, John Gillispie, Thomas Dougerty, John Duncan, Robert Dawthitt,

Wm. Gillispie, Wm. Stockham, Jas. Chapman, John Ream, Elisha Vernon, Solomon Brown, W. McCarlesy, Jesse Savage, Isaac Exline, David W. Cartmel, Jas. Brady, Abraham Dehaven, John Burnsides, Solomon Mackley, Geo. Poore, Wm. Bowen, John Stropes, Jas. Kelly, Courtney Martin, Samuel Wooden, Alex. Daniel, Elzey Landrum, John Farney, Sam'l M. Burt, John Stropes, Sam'l Gray, Elihu Johnson, Asa W. Isham, David C. Bolles, James Hughes, A. Walterhouse, Stephen Radcliff, Wm. Trago, Sam'l Gilliland, Andrew Stephenson,

Nottingham Mercer, Leander Weeks, Sabin Griffis, John Millikin, Jas. Farrer, Wm. McKinnis, Thos. W. Leach, Anson Hanna, Robt. Johnston, John D. Hoffman, Martin Owens, Henry Hawk, Hickman Powers, John Griffiths, John Griffis, J. C. Chriswiser, W. Cunningham, John V. Hank, Jas. Hanlin, John S. Hanlin, Wm. C. Roberts.

(Compiled from Record Book, Recorders Office, Jackson.)

Walter Armstrong, B. Joseph Banker, C. John Copeland, Baziel Clark, Joseph Case, Sen., D. Wm. Douglass, Joseph Davis, E. John S. Edwards, Esq., G. John Gregg, H. James Hunter, Peter Hall, K. John Krepp, L. Hetty Lowe, David Lewis, Wm. Lary, John Lauderbach, M. Wm. Martaindall, Rev. Wm. M'Daniel, N. Wm. Nicholson, P. Simon Perkins, Wm. Polk, Allen Powell, R. John Roberts, Nathan Richardson, S. Christopher Snnesman, Nathan Siver, Jun., William Shane, Thomas Sherwood, T. Nathan Taylor, Mr. Taylor, P. M. Lebanon, —W. Thomas Wilson, Michael Wise, Joseph Wright, John Whittusey, John Wallace, Robert Watkins.

—Mattias Ross, P. M. Lebanon, Ohio. 30, September, 1810.

LETTERS IN THE POST OFFICE

List of letters remaining in the Post Office at Columbus, Ohio, November 5, 1814:

Ebenezer Butler	Christiana Fahon	Edward Livingston
Dr. Budge	John Garcer	Alexander McLaughlin
Patrick Bresland	John Huff	Andrew Shaw
James Cockson	Jacob Hare	Henry Streight
John Coughran	Robert Hulekson	John Taylor
James Fame	George Inglish	

(From the *Ohio Monitor*, pub. Columbus.)

LETTERS IN THE POST OFFICE

New Salem, Ohio, July 1, 1817

Arnold, Daniel; Burnhouse, John; Bunier, George; Cessna, Wm.; Crow, John; Conte, Widow; Coefeed, Mr.; Dorrence, Samuel; Duel, John; Ebersole, John; Eccles, Allen; Endsley, Andrew; Fort-Esq, Jo; Folley, Robert W.; Ford, Nichodemus; Ford, Stephen; Haft, Jacob; Holmes, Isaac; Hafman, David; Leslie, Alex; Leas, John or Jacob; Mills, James; McMaster, James; M'Queen, Wm.; Mugg, Wm.; Moreland, Caleb; Morrison, Alex; Mastin, Luman; Nossinger, Abraham; Peart, Thomas; Rhodes, Frederick; Robinson, Abel; Rhodes, Moses; Reed, Jos.

Stinger, George; Sweaney, Wm.; Shiel, Frederick; Shreve, Stacy; Stales, John (Stoles); Stewart, Edward; Smith, John; Shick, John; Shock, Jacob; Tittore, Rareel (Rafeel Ditore); Viers, Brill; Wolf, John; Wilson, Amos; Woolman, jun., Samuel; Wilkinson, John; Woods, Wm.-Robert Baird, P. M.—Western Herald-Gazette (Steubenville)

LETTERS IN THE POST OFFICE

Steubenville, Ohio, October, 1817.

Sterling Adams, George Atkinson, James Andrews, Wm. Abraham, Rob't. Anderson, Martha Adams, Jonathan Arnold, Abram Skeely, James Ball, Wm. Boden, George Butler, Rob't Boid, George Birty, Gardner Baird, Thomas Burton, Elisha Brooks, Samuel Bigestaff (Bickerstaff), Joseph Baley, Mr. Butchers, Wm. Bell, Ruth Brown, David Bryson, Gilbert Brewston, Stephen Brown, Joseph S. Batchelor, James Brown, Sr.

John Crawford, Rebecca Clark, Thomas Clear, John Craig, Frances Crawford, Stephen Cooper, Thomas Chandler, Elisha Fox, Hugh

Cosgrove, James L. Crain, Adam Curfman, Robert Cassidy, James Clark, Isabella Carey, Adley Caldron, John Cunningham, Alex. Campbell, Garrot Creson, Zach Dowdon, Samuel Dorsey, Mary Draper, James Daly, Baz. Donley, Joseph Dolbey, Martin Easterday, Andrew Elliot, Esq., Jacob Eberhart, Wm. Elliot, Jun., John Eskin, Simon Elliott.

Rev. James B. Finley, Wm. Fetherson, Jacob Fickes, John Fulton, Wm. J. Fithem, David Frederick, George Fauble, Sam'l B. Fleming, Susanna'h Freet, Alex. Fergeson, James Finley, Hannah Graham, Thomas Gray, John Gasset, Mary Grubb, Josiah Gamble, Thomas George, Mrs. Jere Gray, Jeremiah Gray, Geo. Hull, Frances Heans, David Hull, Noble Hunter, Uriah Harries, M. Hildebrant, Clark Herrington, Susana Holmes, Andrew Huff, Margaret Hurt, Jas. Heeston, J. Hathaway, John Heairien, Thos. Jones, Hugh Johnson, Richard Jackson, Jas. Jelly, John Jones, Margaret Johnson, Ts. R. Kirkpatrick, Geo. Kinzer, Balzer Kolp, James Karr, Margratta Kissinger, Margaret Lion, Mr. Latour, Michael E. Lukes, Olive Little, Wm. Longhead, Wm. Lee.

Peter McCleary, Alex. Montgomery, James Murdock, Wm. Murray, Robert Marshall, Martha Mahan, John Miller, David Maginnis, Any Millen, William Mitchell, Thos. Mellen, Thos. McMillen, David Mum, Lydia M'Manniman, James W. M'Grew, Wm. Mardes, John McGuire, Charles McCutcheon, Luke Malbird, Ann M'Fadden, James Monroe, Benj. Morris, Wm. M'Gowen, Rev. Wm. M'Kendree, H. Montgomery, Charles Maxwell, Joseph M'Connel. Thos. Morton, John Niven. Thos. Orr, John Orr, Charles Osborn. Matthew Porter, John Patterson, Thomas Plummer, Benj. Powel, John Porter, Thos. G. Plummer, Elizabeth Price, Charles Porter, Silas Paul, John Pollock, Jacob Piles.

Wm. Rippie, Joseph Robeson, Andrew Ralston, John Reynolds, John Rizer, Sam'l Ramsey, John Robey, John Reilly, Eliphelett Richards, Mary Ann Read, May Randle, Elenor Reynolds, John Riddel, Mathew Rielly. Sam'l Stokely, Wm. Snyder, Ambrose Shaw, Frederick Salmon, Robert Strain, Henry Swearingen, Thomas Smith, Jones Sams, Robert A. Sherrard, John Sheets, Samuel Sample, Jas. Sutton, Thomas Shepherd, Robings Stowill, Elizabeth Swegars, Charles Shaw, Alex. Shaw, Charles Stewart, John Smith, Benj., or Wm. Speaker, Sam'l Sharrard, John Shoup. Abel Thompson, Hugh Taggart, Mathew Tennant, Wm. Todd, Lewis Timer, Edw. W. Thirston, Margaret Vankirk, Mr. Wilson. Jas. Whittingham, Mahlon H. West, John Warner, Wm. Walker, James Wetherow, Louis Whitman, Benj. Weldon, Wm. Wright, Hez. Whitney, Wm. Westbrook, John Ward, John Woods, Joshua Wright, Joseph Waters. George Wilcox, George Whitefield, John Wilson, James Withrow, Isaac Wilson. Thos. Young, Robert Young. Peter Zebold. David Larimore—P. M. (Western Herald & Steubenville Gazette)

LETTERS IN THE POST OFFICE AT IRVILLE, JANUARY 1818

Bell, David; Barecroft, John; Henry, Wm. F.; Johnston, John; Shaffer, Lucy; Morgan, Morgan; Fisher,   ; Gass, Jonathan—2; Pentecost, James.—Jared Brush, P. M.

From the Muskingum Messenger, Feb., 1818

LETTERS IN THE POST OFFICE
Knoxville, Jefferson County, Ohio

January 1, 1818:
Thomas George, Peter Householder, George James, Wm. Jones, Wm. Mills, Moses Marshall, Joseph Redd, Rodgers at Pgh, Wm. Robb, Streibly & Fox, Isaac White.—Samuel Hawley, P. M.

April 25, 1818:

New Salem, Jefferson County

January 16, 1818
John Adams, Sally Arbuckle, Charles Clinton, Robert Carnes, Baltzer Culp, Zadoc Elliot, Wm. Jameson, Robert Jackson, James Hair, Sara Mills, Gasper Markle, Michael Myers, Sam'l Miller, Geo. Punches, Thos. Rodgers, Elimelick Swearingen, John Workman.—Sam'l Hawley, P. M. (Western Herald)

Thomas Beatty, John Collins, George Chambers, Wm. Chambers, John Crown, Capt. P. Collens, Joseph Elliot, John Ebersole, Jacob Fryman, Jacob Gans, John Crowall, Daniel Gaskill, Harmon Girt, Adam Hoobler, Wm. Hibbs, Jacob Henry, James Hammen, Jonathan Hough, Geo. Kelly, Thomas Kezarte, Dr. T. Kimmings, Thomas Luckshon, C. Leslie, Joshua Lemmon, Dan'l Leezer, James Meholm, Oliphant Marten, James M'Mastin, George Morrow, Jasent M'Donnel, Benj. Marshall, Thomas Mory, Sam'l Patterson, Wm. Risinger, John Rareigh, Dan'l Simmons, Peter Salsbury, Andrew Stranger, James Tolerton, Elizabeth Tope, Dorsey Viers, Sam'l Viers, Robert Woods, Isaac Woods, Joseph Walker.—Robert Baird, P. M. *(Western Herald)*

Richmond, Jefferson County.

July 1, 1818—A. Farquhar, P. M.
John S. Adams, John Adams-schoolmaster, John Adams, Elizabeth Adams, John Crawford, Frederick Nicholas, Allen Hanlon, John Marvan, Cheney Porter, Wm. Stone, Joseph Wood. It is probable that these letters were intended for Richmond, Ross co. (Western Herald)

LIST OF LETTERS IN POST OFFICE
New Lisbon, September, 1855

Adams, Esther G.; Ashton, Thos.; Arter, Dr. Daniel; Atterholt, George; Bricker, David; Baker, Worthington; Benner & McGeehan; Barber, Mary L.; Bell, Thos.; Brown, John; Bilzer, John R.; Bonsell & Sharp-Davis; Bridensine, Martin; Beeabout, Jaybez; Boyer, J. B.; Calhoon, J.; Crothers, G.; Crawford, Robert; Crawford, Thomas; Donley, Charles; Fawcett, Elizabeth; Fox, Joseph; Grine, Franklin; George, Thos.; Gtrayer (Stroyer), Jeremian; Gamit, Wm.; Gemmet, Wm.; Howard, George; Hinkman, Jesu J.; Heller, Peter; Haler, M.; Hetrick, Moses; Hoffman, The; Koontz, John; Knowles, John W.; Miller, Marthal; Miller, Jane; Mills, L. E.; Moffit, Mrs. Phere-2; Martin, J. H.; Mons, Mary B. E.; Petit, Wm. V.; Rooney, Francis; Rudisill, Jones; Rymer, Wm.; Sitler, Velind; Scattergood, Alfred; Seechrist, Mich; Stockberger. Frederick; Steward, John-2; Sword, Hugh C.; Travis, Wm.; Totten, F. Samuel; Ward, Juliana; Welsh, Edward (care); Withers, James; Worman, Samuel; Way, Joseph; Whan, Elizabeth; Wilson, John T.; Wilken, Valinlen; McCullough, Michael; McLain, Margaret; McLaughlin, Lizzie A.; McConnell, Samuel. A. G. McCaskey, P. M. Ohio Patriot.

LICENSED TAVERN KEEPERS OF CENTRAL OHIO

The Ohio country was the gateway to the Northwest Territory. Travelers on their way westward passed through Franklin County. Taverns and inns dotted the old National Road, passing through Reynoldsburg, Columbus, and Franklinton. Taverns existed in many other places in the county as well. Columbus, the state capital, attracted a large transient population.

The traveler was assured of a warm personal welcome at any of the many taverns. The inn-keeper was a public citizen esteemed by the community. Frequently licenses stipulated that "spirituous liquors" could not be sold. Unique advertisements of taverns and inns appeared in the early newspapers of central Ohio. Many of these are verified by the tavern licenses recorded in the Franklin County Court House.

TAVERNS IN FRANKLIN COUNTY—FROM 1806 TO 1847.

Licenses were issued to the following persons:

COLUMBUS—Armstrong, Jeremiah, 1817–1834; Alsten, C. H., 1845; Armstrong, John, 1846; Barr, Samuel, 1823–1824; Beard, John, 1813–1814; Blankner, John, South Columbus, 1846; Brodrick, David, 1816; Brooks, David, 1832–1834; Brown, Henry, 1825; Browning, Edmund, 1828; Bush & Granger, "The Buckeye House," 1846; Coles, Major, 1846; Collett, John, 1814; Courtney, Richard, 1817; Cuser (Cooser), Daniel, 1813; Davis, Isaac, "The Broadway House," 1846–1847; Gale, Edgar, 1845–1847; Gardiner, James B., 1816–1821; Heyl, Christian, 1814–1834; Hurd, Hinman, 1842–1843; Kelsey, William, "American Hotel," 1842–1846; Kent, Columbus W., 1846; Kincaid, Thomas, 1815–1817; Knoderer, Charles, 1845–1846; Kooser, Daniel, 1813–1814; Krause, George, 1843–1846; Lampson, William, 1828; Lewis & Brown, "Franklin House," 1846; Lindsey, James, 1821; Lolliker (Lolligher), Rudolph, 1821–1823; Manelly, Amos, 1829–1846; Martin, John, 1817–1818; Michael, Gotlieb, 1845; McCollum, Thomas, 1814 (started in 1812, by newspaper advertisement); Neil, William, 1823; Nichols, William, 1815; Noble, John, 1832–1836; O'Hale, Thomas, 1832–1836; O'Harra, Charles, 1815–1816; Olmstead, R. H., 1846; Oyler, Jacob, 1843; Paine, Only (Olney), 1813; Patterson, Nathaniel, 1844; Rockwell, Elkanah, 1839–1846; Russell, Robert, 1819–1843; Sibel, Hiram, 1847; Stotts, Uriah, 1843–1846; Vorhes, Isaiah, ——; Waas, Henry, 1842–1844; Whiting & Upson, 1816; Zollinger, Jacob, 1842–1847.

MONTGOMERY TOWNSHIP—Bennignus, Frederick, 1843–1845; Cadwallader, Thomas, 1832–1847; Coles, Major, 1844; Culbertson, James, 1811–1823; Gale, Edgar Montgomery, 1843–1845; Kaemerly (Kimmerly), George, 1844–1846; Miller, Daniel, 1810–1814; Morrell, Moses, 1832–1833; Seibert, Henry, 1838; Warner, Levi, 1814; Watson, John, 1830–1831 (Proven by taxes); Williams, George W., 1813–1814; Wynkoop, Strickland, 1825; Cowles, R. B., 1843–1846 (By tax records).

FRANKLINTON—Armstrong, John, 1816–1818; Badger, Archibald J., 1830; Beamon, George, 1814; Broderick, David S., 1813–1814 (Then to Columbus, 1816); Deardorff, Samuel, 1825–1844 (By taxes);

Domigan, William, 1808-1831; Foos, Joseph, 1806-1819; Goetchius, Nicholas, 1815-1816; Headington, William, 1846; Innis, Henry, 1817-1818; Jamison, Andrew, 1828; Jamison, David. 1816 (By advertising); Jenkins, John, 1844; Kintz, George, 1842: Marshall, Wm., 1818 (At the west end of Sullivants Bridge where he lives); O'Harra, John, 1810-1811; Overdear, John, 1809-1810; Pratt, Cary, 1814-1816; Read, Jonathon, 1819; Ritter, Frederick, 1810; Robinson, John, 1832; Sellman, Beal, 1839; Sells, Benjamin, 1806; Simpson, William, 1843; Stephenson, Wm. H., 1832-1842; Stephenson, John, 1843-1845; Stewalt, John, 1808-1816; Stutler or Stettler, Benjamin, 1840-1846; Wiatt & Wyatt, H. L., 1841-1843.

Licensed Tavern Keepers of Central Ohio

Persons wishing to open a tavern in the earlier times were required to file an application with county officials, and when the license was granted, were assessed a license fee of one dollar.

Licenses were issued as follows:

FRANKLIN TOWNSHIP—Samuel Higgins, 1816, 1819; Richard Higgins, March 2, 1819.

JACKSON TOWNSHIP—Kious, John H., June 1841; Kissinger, John, September 2, 1829.

MADISON TOWNSHIP—From 1811 to 1847

Oyler, Jacob (George), June 30, 1841; Bishop, George, Aug. 13, 1811. Aug. 13, 1813; Blair, Jesse,, Apr. 12, 1824, June 25, 1825, Aug. 20, 1826; Blair, John, (Jesse) Dec. 13, 1827; Borgholthames, Fredrick W., May, 1835; Bott, Peter, Mar. 1838; Champ, John, May 24, 1839; Crouse, Daniel, Oct. 27, 1846, Oct. 20, 1847; Decker, Isaac D. Feb. 22, 1813, Sept. 19, 1833, Feb. 15, 1835; Dildine, Elisha D. May 14, 1832; Dudgeon, George, May 20, 1844; Durel, Thomas G. Apr. 1, 1847; Flack, John, May 21, 1844; Fleming, James, March 1837, July 6, 1841; Logan, S. W. June 2. 1824; Moore, Isaac M. Sept. 25, 1843; Rarey, Adam, March 5. 1816, June, 1821, June 24, 1830, May 13, 1836, May 1838; Rarey, Charles W. March 17, 1840, March 19, 1841; Strode, Harvey, May 1836, May 23, 1840; Strong, J. P. Sept. 18, 1838; Vaudemark, Daniel, (Peter) Sept. 2, 1829; Vaudermark, Jeremiah, March 2, 1819, March 4, 1823; Watt, Samuel, June 2, 1834.

TRURO TOWNSHIP—From 1816 to 1847

Armstrong, Thomas, Sept. 29, 1832, Oct. 27, 1846, Feb. 14, 1848; Butler, Amon, Apr. 15, 1833, March, 1838; Demorest, Nicholas, April 15, 1833, June 2, 1834; Fell, John, Nov. 13, 1844; Fredrick, Morford, Feb. 20, 1834; Gares, Samuel H. Sept. 24, 1835, April 1, 1845, July 14, 1846; Grafton and Buzard, May 21, 1837; Hammond, Francis S. March 1840; Hunter, William, May 1838, May 22, 1839; Kelly, John, May 25, 1837; Peters and Rickley, Sept. 27, 1837; Pew, ———, Nov. 29, 1830; Puch. David, Aug. 2, 1816, Nov. 28, 1817; Rennick, John (Rhenick), April 15, 1833; Sells, Seurs, March 17, 1840, July 25, 1860, July 15, 1847; Sensebaugh, Matilda, June 10, 1840, June, 1841; Smith, John D. Sept. 8, Sept. 9, 1840; Vauderberg, Peter, Sept. 24, 1835, Sept. 1836; Walcutt, John, M. Sept. 26, 1835; Wilson, Levi, E. Sept. 1838, Sept, 24, 1839; Zahringer, Christian, May 15, 1846.

MISCELLANY

Thelma Blair Lang

SHARON TOWNSHIP—Adams, Demas, 1819-21; Aumack, Christopher, 1839; Beers, Uriah, 1838-46; Brundage, James, 1844-46; Burr, Izias, 1821; Buttles, Aurora (or Amon Butler), 1835; Cole, Marcus, 1837-45; Geer, Isaac W., 1821; Goodrich, John, 1820-23; Griswold, Ezra, 1807; Griswold, George H., 1819-22; Grace, Benjamin, 1819; Johnston, John, 1832-35; Kilbourne, James, 1828-37; Russ, Lyman, 1846; Salisbury, G. L., 1834; Starr, John, 1818; Topping, Dayton, 1835; Vinning, Elam, 1806; Wilcox, Morris, 1840; Wilson, James C., 1828-29; Wilson, James, 1831.

BLENDON TOWNSHIP—Clark, Sylvester, 1838-42; Clark, Jonathan P., 1844; Grinnell, Wm. H., 1838-44; Griswold, Isaac, 1826, 1832; Hays, Brice, 1846; Ninnon, John, 1838; Olmstead, A. J., 1834; Olmstead, Francis C., 1824-30; Shafter, John, 1835.

PLAIN TOWNSHIP—Arnold, George, 1829-34; Foos, Franklin, 1844-45; Landon, Noble, 1835; Read, George B., 1841; Ulry, Jacob, (New Albany) 1844, (County) 1845-47; Whitcomb, D. G., 1832-33.

CLINTON TOWNSHIP—Buck, John, 1842; Haraff, Peter, 1813; Kinnear, Sam'l 1832-37; Wilcox, Roswell, 1819-24; Wilcox, Israel S., 1821-31.

HAMILTON TOWNSHIP—Coleman, Abram, 1819-23; Dukes, John, 1813; Dukes, Mary, 1814; Durell, Thomas G., 1847; Fleming, James, 1837-41; Gatton, Edw. H., (also Galton) 1834; Ketchum, Philander, 1830-32; Kimberly, John Geo. (also Kaemerly), 1839-42; Kissinger, John, 1829; Logan, S. W., 1824; Manning, John, 1839; Middleton, John, 1826-27; Miller, Elizabeth, 1840-43; Miller, John, 1829; Obetz, Charles, 1838-47; Powell, Wm., 1816 (formerly by M. Dukes); Stillwell, Alanson, 1840; Strong, J. P., 1835 (Lockbourne); Williams, Geo. W., 1816-29 (formerly in Montgy twp.); Wynkoop, Strickland, 1824-25.

PRAIRIE TOWNSHIP—Cryder, Jefferson, 1834-39; Fleming, Daniel, 1843; (Alton) Foley, Moses, 1839; Graham, Thomas, 1825-39; Harris, Daniel, 1841; Higgins, Charles, 1829-37; Higgins, Richard, 1820; Kinnaird, David, 1846; (Georgesville) Littlejohn, Joseph, 1818-19; (Georgesville) Mantle, Batzer, 1826-33; Michael, Gotlieb, 1846; (Georgesville) Reynolds, Thomas, 1828-33; Postle, David, 1844-46; Sharp, James, 1839-40.

WASHINGTON TOWNSHIP—Tuller, Bela M., 1808-14; (Dublin) Coffman, Henry, 1840-45; (Dublin) Hutchinson, Zenas, 1836-46; (Dublin) Sells, Iliad, (Eliud) 1832-47; (Dublin) Sells, John, 1816.

HARRISON TOWNSHIP—Bogart, Joseph, 1808; Creighton, Hugh, 1807; Osborn, George, 1824-39; Holmes, Jonathon, 1806-08; Robinson, John, 1807, 1825.

JEFFERSON TOWNSHIP—Painter, Isaac, 1820; Stagg, Michael, 1832-33.

MIFFLIN TOWNSHIP—Read, George P., 1841.

PLEASANT TOWNSHIP—(Harrisburg) Ketchum, Obediah, 1846; Goodrich, George W., 1846-47; Stark, Samuel, 1817.

NORWICH TOWNSHIP—Brunk Samuel (Daniel), 1833-35; Saunders, Miskell, 1836.

BERKSHIRE TOWNSHIP—(Later Delaware county) Patterson, John, 1807.

LIBERTY TOWNSHIP—Shaw, John, 1807.

ON THE NATIONAL ROAD—(Big Darby) McCray, Joseph, 1840; (Rome) Comly, John, 1837-38.

MARRIAGES

SOME EARLY MARRIAGES TAKEN FROM THE ORIGINAL PERMITS, WHICH WERE ISSUED AUTHORIZING THE MINISTER OR JUSTICE OF THE PEACE TO PERFORM THE CEREMONY. THE ORIGINALS ARE IN THE POSSESSION OF THE COLUMBUS GENEALOGICAL SOCIETY.   By Thelma Lang.

KNOX COUNTY, OHIO

George Ely and Lucinda Forescythe, March 5, 1832 by Alex. Elliott, Clerk

Samuel McCarty and Elizabeth Veatch, Sept. 5, 1831 by Alex. Elliott, Clerk

Stepehen Rumsey and Susan Stricker, Jan. 23, 1834 by Alex. Elliott, Clerk

Alfred W. Tilton and Mrs. Mary Ellen Taylor, July 30, 1833 by Alex. Elliott, Clerk

Samuel (not Legible) and Hetty Wolfe, Aug. 30, 1832 by Elex. Elliott

W. Henry Deal and Elizabeth Baughman, Feb. 26, 1829 by James Smith

W. John Ely and Elizabeth Storm, Oct. 2, 1826 by James Smith

William Schooler and Delilah Horn, Jan. 2, 1832 by Alex. Elliott, Clerk

Daniel Chadwick and Emly Loveland, Feb. 16, 1850 by Samuel Forquhar, Clerk

Hardman Horn & Rachel Porter, Sept. 20, 1834 by Alex. Elliott, Clerk

John Saucerman and Susan Wolf, Oct. 18, 1830 by Alex. Elliott, Clerk

Samuel Thompson and Sarah Forbes, March 22, 1830 by James Smith, Clerk

Peter Snediker and Sarah Anderson, April 26, 1848 by Samuel Farquhar

Joseph Blystone and Delila Wolf, Dec. 22, 1828 by James Smith, Clerk

James Cox and Priscilla Ann Gould, Feb. 10, 1834 by A. Elliott, Clerk

Wm. John Batch and Malinda Hall, Sept. 30, 1833 by Alex, Elliott, Clerk

Wm. Tuttle and Nancy Mattox, Aug. 6, 1833, by Alex. Elliott, Clerk

Nathaniel Johnston and Betsey Beach, March 18, 1833 by Alex. Elliott, Clerk

Nathaniel Johnston and Sarah Mattocks, May 15, 1833 by Alex. Elliott, Clerk

Thomas Mattocks and Nancy Taylor, Sept. 10, 1833 by Alex. Elliott Clerk

554

Nelson B. Robinson and Sarah Ann Johnston, April 26, 1833 by Alex. Elliott, Clerk

Jefs Mattox and Mrs. Elizabeth Dickison, Aug. 6, 1833 by Alex. Elliott

DELAWARE COUNTY, OHIO

Henry Green and Amanda Spaulding, Sept. 10, 1844 by W. D. Heim, Clerk

MUSKINGUM COUNTY. OHIO

James Atwood and Hannah Haines, Sept. 26, 1825, Ezekiel Cox, Clerk

COSHOCTON COUNTY. OHIO

Daniel Berry and Ann Dillon, July 21, 1833 by John Frew, Clerk

MEMORIAL TO CAPT. ABRAHAM WESTFALL
MT. ZION CEMETERY, CARROLL COUNTY, OHIO

On the day following Memorial Day, 1939, a small group of descendants of Abraham Westfall, an early resident of Carroll County and a Captain in the Revolutionary War, were present at the erection of a monument to his memory in Mt. Zion Cemetery in Augusta Township.

Abraham Westfall came from a long line of German and Hollandish ancestors, the earliest of whom was Juryan Westvael, who settled near Kingston, Ulster County, N. Y., in 1654.

Captain Westfall was in Dunmore's Campaign before the Revolutionary War, at the battle of Fort Montgomery, Grand Creek, below Wheeling, Stony Point, Bloody Run and Brandywine. He was wounded at the Battle of Stony Point.

There were twelve children in the Westfall family, seven born in Orange County, N. Y., and five in Washington County, Pa., before the family removed to Carroll County, Ohio. Names and dates of birth of the children are as follows:

Joseph, born June 14, 1782; Hannah, born February 25, 1784, married John Morledge, descendants in Sparta, Wisconsin; Anna, born February 9, 1786, married Levi Marshall, residence near Cleveland; Eunice, born March 12, 1788, married ————— Gamble in Washington County, Pa; Levi, born December 7, 1790, married Sallie Cameron, second wife, Elizabeth Hales Myers; Naomi, born Feb. 2, 1793, married ————— Sargent, Tuscarawas County, O; Simeon, born March 4, 1795, married Cassandra Shaw, Carrollton, Ohio; Catherine, born January 30, 1798, married James Patrick, Tuscarawas County, Ohio; John, born June 22, 1800, married Amy Beatty, Carrollton County, Ohio; Thomas, born Sept. 28, 1802, married ————— —————; Abraham, born April 13, 1809, married Nancy Sutton English; James, born January 31, 1811.

Abraham Westfall died September 5, 1829, and was buried in a private cemetery on what is known as the Potter farm.

Broken pieces of his head stone and the complete foot stone were found by two of his descendants, Mr. Tipton Westfall of Carrollton, Ohio, and Miss Nova Westfall of Alliance, Ohio, and this fact was brought to the attention of Mr. Ralph Eckley Westfall of Columbus, Ohio, a great grandson of Capt. Westfall.

He had the grave stones and a bronze tablet placed in a cement slab, forming a memorial marker to perpetuate the record of the life of a patriotic ancestor of a large branch of the Westfall family. This monument was placed beside the grave of Abraham Westfall's wife, Blandina (Dinah) Van Etten Westfall, who was buried in Mt. Zion cemetery twenty years after the death of her husband.

The wording of the tablet is as follows:—
Born Nov. 18, 1755   Died Sept. 5, 1829.
In memory of Abraham Westfall, Captain in the War of the Revolution. The only child of Petrus Westfael and his wife Arientje Rosenkrans. He and his wife Blandina (Dinah) Van Etten were born in Orange County, N. Y. With their seven children they moved in May, 1797, to Washington County, Pa., where five more children were born. In April 1817, they moved to Carroll County, Ohio, where they both died. The fragments of his grave stones preserved below by his descendants, were found on the Potter farm.

Those present when the memorial was erected were Mr. and Mrs. John H. Westfall of Carrollton, Mrs. Helen Westfall Bodurtha of Delaware, Ohio, and Mr. and Mrs. Ralph E. Westfall, of Columbus, Ohio.

A PETITION FROM REFUGEES TO THE
CONTINENTAL CONGRESS

While the American Revolution was in progress, refugees sympathetic to the cause of the American colonies, were forced to flee from their homes in Nova Scotia and to seek shelter in Massachusetts. They addressed a memorial from Boston to the Continental Congress on March 3 1778. This memorial* "humbly sheweth, that your Memoralists by reason of their zealous attachment to the glorious cause of American Liberty, and their firm and unshaken resolution to stand or fall with it, have been driven by the enemy from their Families, Estates, and Connections, and compelled to take shelter in the state of Massachusetts Bay and other of these United States. . "

The memorial recounts that the Province of Nova Scotia at the beginning of the War was invited to join the rebelling colonies and states that the answer returned did not represent the opinion of the majority of the inhabitants of Nova Scotia, especially of the counties of Cumberland and Sunbury, and the townships of Onslow, Truro, and Londonderry in the county of Halifax.

Regretting that the Articles of Confederation made it difficult for Nova Scotia to be admitted to the "Alliance of the United States," the petitioners "humbly Pray, that your Honors would be pleased to take our case into your wise consideration, and admit the Province of Nova Scotia into the Alliance and Confederation of the United States of America, and grant us such other Relief in the Premises, as to your Honors shall seem meet, and your Memoralists as in Duty bound shall ever pray Etc.."

Boston, March 3rd, 1778.

Seth Noble	Anthony Burke	Josiah Lodge
Jona Eddy	Wm. Howe	William Eddy
Phil Nevers	William Maxwell	Jas. (or) Jos. Avery
Sam Rogers	Edward Hampton	Nath-il Reynolds
Daniel Earl	Christopher Payne	Zebulen Coe
Elijah Ayer	John McGowen	John Ackley
Jonathan Nevers	John Ackley	
Parker Clarke	John (Tom) Ship	
Robert Foster	Edward C-helon (?)	

---

*The papers of the Continental Congress, Memorials. No. 41, Vol. VII, page 21. Library of Congress.

Resolutions passed by Congress, April 23, 1783, and April 13, 1785, assured the refugees that on account of their attachment to the interest of the United States, they were recommended to the humanity and particular attention of the several states in which they reside and that "whenever Congress can consistently reward them by grants of land they will do so, by making such reasonable and adequate provision for them on our public domain as will amply remunerate them."

April 17, 1798, Congress provided that all refugees who were claimants of land should make their claims to the War Department within two years.

Feb. 18, 1801, Congress provided for these and other refugees by establishing the Refugee Tract of about 100,000 acres in Ohio. This was a tract four and a half miles wide, extending eastward from the Scioto River toward the Muskingum River about 48 miles and terminating in Muskingum County not far east of Gratiot. Two and one half miles of this four and a half mile strip belonged to the United States Military tract, the other two miles were Congress lands. The refugee tract was located chiefly in Franklin, Licking, Fairfield, and Perry Counties; few if any locations were made in Muskingum County by refugees. Settlers came to Truro Township, Franklin County, Ohio, from Truro Township, Nova Scotia. Land in Licking County adjoining Truro Township also was settled by refugees from Nova Scotia.

Helen E. Swisher

Revolutionary Soldiers, Franklin County, Ohio

A list of Revolutionary soldiers who applied for pensions from Franklin County, Ohio is found in the early records of our Court House. Those found are as follows:

James Armstrong, Mathaniel Babcock, Michael Baker, George Baughman, Henry Baumgardner, Christopher Beard, Adam Blont, Jacob Carey or Casey, John Champ, Roswell Cook, Matthias Dague, John Davison, Samuel Davis, Isaac Davis, George Emery, Jacob Fisher, Isaac Fisher, Jacob Foster, Henry Hill, John Hoover, Lemuel Hungerford, Joseph Ingals, Robert Justice, George Kohr or Kuhn, Joseph Lewis, Joseph Mapes, William Manning, Jesse Mannelly, (sometimes spelled Menely) Hugh McMillen, Henry Miller, Josiah Miller, John Montgomery, Simeon Moore, Joseph Price, Moses Rugg, Thomas Sibbless, Abijah Staus, Edward Whaley, John White, Samuel White, George Wightman (sometimes spelled Weightman) Jenks Wait, Samuel McKee, Francis Olmstead, John Denoon, John Walcott, John Starrett and Archibald McNinch.

MISCELLANY

REVOLUTIONARY PENSIONERS

Revolutionary soldiers who applied for pensions from Franklin County, Ohio, as found in the early records of Franklin County Court House at Columbus are as follows:

James Armstrong, Nathaniel Babcock, Michael Baker, George Baughman, Henry Baumgardiner, Christopher Beard, Adam Blont or Blair, Jacob Carey or Casey, John Champ, Roswell Cook, Matthias Dague, Samuel Davis, George Emery, Jacob Fisher, Isaac Fisher, Jacob Foster, Henry Fix, Henry Hill, John Hoover, Lemanuel Hungerford, Joseph Ingals, Robert Justice, George Kohn or Kuhn, Joseph Lewis, Joseph Mapes, William Manning, Jesse Mannelly (sometimes spelled Menely), Hugh McMillen, Henry Miller, Josiah Miller, John Montgomery, Simeon Moore, Elias Pegg, Joseph Price, Moses Rugg, Thomas Sibbless or Sibbles, Abijah Straus or Stow or Staur, Edward Whaley, John White, Samuel White, Col. John Thompson, George Wightman (sometimes spelled Weightman), Jenks Wait, Samuel McKee, Francis Olmstead, John Denoon, John Walcott, John Starrett, Archibald McNinch, W. L. Moore, James Crawford and John Trusler.

The following additional names were taken from the Pension Book at the State Library:

John Anderson, William Ballard, Benjamin Chapman, James Durry, Samuel Franklin, Richard Gale, John Halton, Patrick Logan, James McBurney, Samuel McElvain, Moses Lickens, Wm. Patterson, Roger Smith, Thos. Smith, John Stewart or Staurt, Isiah Vory, John Wheatherholt, John Stowell.

The following names were taken from obituaries in old newspapers of Franklin County, Ohio, which stated that the deceased had been a soldier of the Revolution:

John McGown, James Butterfield (this pension was rejected), Neil Mahon, Ephriam Evans and Ebenezer Butler.

WILL OF WILHELM WILDERMUTH

Copied by Charles Wagner

April 11, 1814   In the Name of the Lord, Amen.

I, Wilhelm Wildermuth of Greenfield Township, Fairfield County, State of Ohio, have considered to make a will and testament. I am in my right mind, thanks to God.

I wish to divide my little savings and land the following way:

First, I wish to give my soul in to the hands of the "Almighty God". And my body shall be buried in an orderly Christian way. After I am dead, please see to it that all my bills are being paid, and whatsoever I owe be paid in full.

As far as my children are concerned, every one shall have his.

First: My son David has his in full, he has no more to ask for.

Second: My son Johann has his part given to him in money, and no more to ask for.

Third: My daughter Marie has also her share of money, and no more to ask for.

Fourth: My son Heinrich has his share given him in land, in this township, and has no more to ask for.

Fifth: And now my son Abraham has also received his share in full in land and no more to ask for.

Sixth: My son Daniel shall have the land, house, barns, outhouses, etc. house furniture, wagon and horses and all farm implements, including live stock, after my death.

Now though if Daniel should die before I do I reserve the right to keep everything as long as I live.

No one may sell it without my consent. After my death everything mentioned above shall go to Daniel.

For now I shall keep the house where I live in. It shall be kept in good condition. We shall have a little garden, keep one cow, the cow shall graze with Daniel's cows. I shall keep a few chickens. For all this I will help as much as possibe on the farm for my rent and upkeep. Daniel shall give us whatever we need, on bread, milk, butter, grain, corn, wood to burn, and two pigs from 125 lbs. to 150 lbs. each. As long as I live I reserve the right to keep Church or Christian Meetings in my home.

After I am dead shall be divided as stated.

I hope everyone is satisfied with my Will and Testament.

In the Name of the Lord Amen.

This was written the 11th. day of April 1814 at Greenfield Township, Fairfield County, State of Ohio.
I herewith sign this   Wilhelm Wildermuth, father

                                        Daniel Wildermuth, son

Witnesses: Jacob Alspach
           Heinrich Fisher
Fairfield County, Ohio.

At a court of Common Pleas entered and held at Lancaster in the aforesaid County, on the 2nd day of February 1816 the foregoing will is proven by the subscribing Witnesses thereto on which it is ordered to be recorded.

                              Attested. Hugh Boyl, Clerk

The above Wilhelm Wildermuth was born in Germany, came to America with parents in 1752, lived in Berks County, Pa., until April of 1805 when he removed to Greenfield Township, Fairfield County, Ohio. He was the great great grand father of Charles W. Wagner, of Columbus, Ohio.

(Does not include the 1810
tax lists on pp. 101-159)

Adam (cont.)
Helena 230
Adams, (?) 81
A. D. 323
A. H. 229
Abraham 21
Addison 229
Amanda 229
Andrew 229
B. 49
B. (Rev.) 47
Bailey 229
Barbara 229
Charles B. 229
Chloe 230
Delia 230
Demas 187, 188, 197,
204, 207, 216, 230,
553
Demas (Jr.) 308
Edmond C. 233
Edward 230
Eli 182
Elijah (Jr.) 42
Elisa 230
Elizabeth 230, 550
Elizabeth B. 230
Eri 230
Esther G. 550
Fredona 230
George W. 230
H. (Jr.) 81
H. L. 230
Harriet G. 230
Harriet J. 230
Henry 77, 230
Isaac J. 230
J. Q. 523
J. Q. (Pres.) 463
Jacob 300
James 230
James W. 230
Jane 230
John 77, 230, 550
John N. 231
John Q. 33
John Quincy 87, 231
John S. 550
Joseph 231
Julia Ann 38
Lucinda 231
Margaret 231, 255
Margaret A. 231
Martha 231, 548
Marvin 47
Mary 231
Mary Ann 231
Mary E. 231
Milka (Mrs.) 77
Minerva Ann 231
Nancy 231
Nancy (Mrs.) 96
Nelson 232
Percival 167, 168,
169, 171, 184, 191,
194, 195, 196, 205,
209, 231, 232, 233,
270
Percivlal 209
Samuel N. (Col.) 45
Sarah 233
Sarah B. 233
Sterling 548
Susan 233, 290
Susan C. 233
Therusha 47
Thomas 233
William 233

Adams (cont.)
William A. 233
William J. 233
William L. 233
Adamson, Lorena B. 92,
96, 447, 537
Adby, Hannah 530
Addams, Delia 230
Addis, A. 60
Addison, John 546
Ade, Josephine 233
Adey, Anne 233
Adkins, Lewis 547
Adkinson, Levi 186
Adler, Eliza 233
Samuel 233
Adriance, Charles 313,
314
Charles Edward 314
Helen 314
Isaac 314
James D. 314
Louise 314
Margaret Smith 313
Phebe (Mrs.) 313
Theodore 314
Aeyers, James 515
Agard, (?) (Mrs.) 41
Horace (Rev.) 531
Salmon 41
Agatha, Anna 233
Agile, Messlus 233
Agilo, Messlus 233
Agin, David 233
James 53
Martha (Mrs.) 53
Martha Frances 53
Peter 233
William 530
Agler, (?) 192
Andrew 331
Andrew J. 233
Clinton W. 233
Elizabeth 192, 233
Elizabeth (Mrs.) 331
Emma 233
Flora 233
Franklin 233
Frederic 182
Frederick 18, 187,
192, 233
George 233
George W. 233
John 182, 187, 233,
305
John A. 233
Laney (Mrs.) 331
Lewis 192, 224, 233
Lovina 233
Lucinda 233
Luther 233
Margaret 187, 192, 234
Mary A. 234
Mary Adaline 234
Mary Ann 234
Matilda Ida 234
Peter 224, 234
Sally 234
Sarah 234, 282
Sophia D. 234
Susan Ann 234
William 192, 234
Agnew, Thomas 233
Agustus, David 521
John (Jr.) 521
Ahlefeld, Nathan 234
Ahler, Wilhelmenia 234
Aigin, Stephen B. 52

Ainsworth, Juliett M.
234
Akenbreck, Elizabeth 234
Aker, Mary 228
Akin, Charles B. 234
Akins, (?) 208
Charles B. 208
Elizabeth A. 208
James 208, 234
James (Rev.) 531
Margaret M. 208
Martha 208
Richard 208
Samuel 208
Akleberger, Milly 299
Albany, Rhoda 234
Albee, Russell E. 398
Alben, Elijah 234
Albenny, John 266
Matilda Ann 235, 267
Alberm, Susan Ann 235
Alberry, (?) (Dr.) 13
Amanda A. 255
Anna M. (Mrs.) 234
Charlie 398
Delia 304
Delila 234
E. M. 398
Eliza Jane 234
Elizabeth 398
Emily 234
George Fay 398
Hannah 234
Henry M. 234
Herman B. 234
James M. 234
John 234, 266
Mary 235
Mary Ellen 235
Matilda Ann 235, 267
Pater 235
Rachel 398
Rhoda 234
Thomas J. 235
William 235
Albers, John H. 235
Albert, Ann 235
Anthony 235
Anton 235
Barbara 235
Elizabeth 235
George 235
Heman 235
John 235
Levi 235
Regina 235
Susan 235
Albertson, Dorothy 235
Albery, Francis 238
Harvey 234
Jerusha 234
Jonathan 235
Julis F. 332
Philip 235
Philip G. 235
Albin, Susan Ann 235
Albrecht, Aandrew 235
Andrew 235, 256
Catherine 235, 255
Albright, Andrew 235,
256
Barbra (Mrs.) 34
Elijah 208
Gotlieb 34
Martha 431
Thomas 235
Alcheins, Elizabeth 234
Alcorn, Hiram 235

564

Allen (cont.)
Jesse 238
John R. 238
Katherine 256
Livinia 238
Lucinda 238
Lucinda Jane 238
Lucy Frances 239
Margaretha J. 238
Mary 93, 239
Mary Allen (Mrs.) 398
Minnie A. 239, 255
Minus 239
Mitchell 239, 325
O. 238, 239, 255
O. (Rev.) 238
Orasmus 317
Orasmus (Rev.) 317
Oril 239
Owen W. 239
Rebecca 274
Rosella 239, 245
Sally (Mrs.) 35, 279
Samuel 303
Sarah 239
Stephen 239, 398
Stephen B. 41
Titus 58
Warren H. 46
William 239
William P. 316
Wilson D. 239
Allensworth, Jacob 381
William 239
Aller, Catherine 239
John 239
Phebe 239
William 239
Alley, Eleanor 239
Allger, Sarah 236
Allgier, Adaline 239
Allgire, Adaline 239
Eliza 239
Henry 239
Joshua 239
Ruth 236
Alliger, Angeline 239
Allis, Edwin J. 239
Phebe Ann 239
Allison, A. 202, 238
Andrew 190, 194
John 516
Mary (Mrs.) 516
Mary H. 331
Nancy 239
Susan (Mrs.) 516
W. 516
Wilford 516
William 30, 528
William D. 331
Allman, Elizabeth 241
Eve 239
William 199
Allspatch, Charles 239
Allspaugh, Jacob 239
Alltman, Eve 239
Allwood, A. A. 241
Cynthia 240
Eliza Jane 240
Maria 240
Samuel 240
Susan 241
Almy, A. O. 242
Alpaw, Susan 240
Alslpach, Levi 254
Alspach, Catherine 240
Christena 240
Daniel 72

Alspach (cont.)
Elizabeth 240
Elizabeth (Mrs.) 338
Esther 90
Henry 73
Jacob 240, 561
Johannes 299
John 20
Jonas (Jr.) 240
Judy 240
Levi 240
Rebecca 240
Sarah 240
Susan 240
Susan (Mrs.) 338
Susannah 240
William 240
Alspau, Jonathan 240
Alspaugh, David 210
Hannah 240
Jacob 240
John 206
Jonathan 240
Susan 240
Alsten, C. H. 551
Alston, Anthony 240
Peter 240
Alt, Adam 240
Altes, Charles 240
Althaln, Elizabeth 240
Althan, Elizabeth 240
Althauser, Elizabeth 398
Michael 398
Althen, Ann Maria 240
Henry L. 240
John 240
Althes, Charles 240
Althohn, George 240
Katherine 241
Altholhn, George 240
Althouse, Christian 241
Isaac 241
Altin, Katherine 241
Altman, Caroline M. 241
David 241
Elizabeth 241
Frederick 241
John G. 241
Lavina A. 241
Margaret 241
Maria 241
Mary M. 241
Matilda 438
Salome 241
Seloma 241
Silome 241
Sophia 241
William H. 241
Altmeyer, Martin 241
Altmon, Catherine 241
Altun, David 241
Altwood, Eliza Jane 240
Alverson, John B. (Rev.)
531
Alvord, Elijah S. 241
George 241
Alward, Elizabeth 241
Alwood, A. A. 382
C. (Mrs.) 382
Eliza J. 39
G. W. 382
Mary Jane 241
Rosa Belle 382
S. (Mrs.) 382
Sarah 382
Sarah (Mrs.) 382
Susan 241
Thomas 382

Amann, Johanna 241
Amas, George 242
Ambos, Caroline 242
Peter 242
Ambrose, D. 242
Frederick 509, 512,
513
M. 242, 261
Margaret J. 242, 26?
Margaret Jane 242
Newton 509
Silas J. 242
Ambrosher, John 242
Ambroshier, John 242
Amburge, Theresa 242
Amedon, Moses (Rev.) ?
Ameltzer, Mary (Mrs.)
309
Ames, Catherine 242
Cyrus (Cpt.) 25
Lois 44
Slome 51
William 530
Amlin, Eliza J. 242
Zeloria 242
Amold, George J. 242
Lavina 242
Sarah L. 242
Amos, George 242
John 242
Mary 242
Walter 242
Amrstrong, Robert 177
Amsbaugh, Jonathan 54?
Amspher, Amos 242
Amy, Frances A. C. 242
Anchor, Hope V. 95
Ander, Mary 242
Andereg, Conrad 244
Anderick, John W. 242
Anders, Abram Y. 242
Elmira 243
Lucinda 242
Timothy 242
Anderson, (?) 243
Andreas 242
Andrew 59, 60
Andrianas M. 242
Christina 429
Daniel 243
Edmund 243
Eliza J. 243
Elizabeth 53, 291, 5
Elizabeth J. 243
Elmira 243
Esther 167, 169
Ezekiel 167, 169
Fanna 243
Fanny 38, 63, 243
George H. 243
Georgianna 243
H. 244
Hannah 243
Isaac 300, 509
James 63, 243
James W. 509
Jane 167, 169, 243
John 167, 169, 194,
243, 244, 296, 330
356, 509, 559
John M. 243
John T. 243
Joseph (Rev.) 61
Joseph R. 243
Levi 243
Louisa 243
Lucinda 243, 260
Margaret 167, 169, 4?

Anderson (cont.)
  Margaret (Mrs.) 167
  Marie 410
  Marie (Mrs.) 410
  Mary 167, 169, 243
  Mary C. 326
  Mary E. 243
  Nancy 244
  Nora May 461
  Polly 244
  Rebecca 540
  Rebecca (Mrs.) 320
  Rebecca A. 244
  Rebecca Jane 244
  Richard 287
  Richard (Cpt.) 474
  Rob't 548
  Robert D. 244
  Rose A. 244
  Rose M. 244
  Samuel 511
  Sarah 244, 554
  Sarah D. 244
  Thomas 170, 194
  W. J. 244
  William 410
  William F. 244
  William H. 244
  William R. (Rev.) 531
  William T. 244
  Wilson 244
  Wm. 410
Andlitz, Anna 244
Andover, Maria 244
Andre, (?) (Maj.) 84
Andrea, Joanna Maria
  Sophia 244
Andregg, Conrad 244
Andres, Charles 244
  George H. 243
  John 244
  Mahala 244
Andress, Mahala 244
  Randall 358
Andrew, John 335
Andrews, Abner 244
  Abner L. 245
  Adam 245
  Adelia P. 320
  Amanda 245
  Amelia 177
  Anne 245
  Annjennett 245
  Betsy 177, 245
  Bradford L. 245
  Butler 273
  Clara Ann 245
  Clarinda 245
  Clarissa 245
  Cynthia 245
  Edward 245
  Edwin 245
  Eliza 245
  Elizabeth 245
  Emily 307, 319
  George 278
  George B. 245
  George C. 239, 245
  George H. 211, 217
  George H. (Cpt.) 246
  George T. 239
  H. A. 36
  H. G. 40, 323
  Hannah 503
  Hiram 177, 211, 214,
    224
  Hiram (Maj.) 247
  James 245, 548

Andrews (cont.)
  James L. 245
  Jeanette (Mrs.) 320
  Jeanette Lazell 320
  Jesse 169, 246
  John 245, 503
  John C. 245
  John H. 304
  John W. 245, 301, 302,
    327, 329, 335
  Joshua C. 283
  Juliet 245
  Laura 246
  Lavina 242
  Lydia 246
  Lyman 198, 246, 281
  Mahala 246
  Maila R. 246
  Margaret 246
  Maria 244
  Martha 246
  Mary 246, 443
  Mary (Mrs.) 503
  Mary Ann 177, 246
  Mary L. 246
  Mary Lucinda 246
  Moses 22
  Myra 246
  N. W. 547
  Nathaniel W. 547
  Noah 185, 187, 246,
    279
  Peggy 246
  Polly 247
  Qualzy 246
  Ray W. 246
  Richard 169, 176, 177,
    245
  Ruth (Mrs.) 298
  S. W. 324
  S. W. (Gen.) 246
  Samuel 172, 177, 195,
    246
  Samuel C. 190, 195,
    219, 246, 283, 338,
    343, 545
  Simon P. 246
  Sylvester W. 246, 320
  Thomas 246
  Timothy 242
  Titus A. 246
  Titus D. 217
  William 246
  William C. 246, 247
  Zelda 246, 247
Andrick, Christian 246
  Elizabeth 247
  John 246, 247
  John W. 242
  Lydia 247
  Mary M. 247
  Rufus Edward 247
Andricks, Ann 246
  Daniel 247
Andrix, Mary A. 247
Andros, Jesse 170
  Warren 170
  William C. 247
Andrus, Abner 244
  Amanda 274
  Betsey 274
  Bradford L. 245
  Catherine 247
  Catherine (Mrs.) 274
  Harriet 41
  Harvey 247
  Hiram 274
  Julia 274

Andrus (cont.)
  Mary (Mrs.) 343
  Mary Ann 246, 274
  Polly 247
  Richard 176, 246, 247,
    274
  Samuel 247, 274
  Sarah L. 247
Andus, Lorinda 242
Angel, Michael 247
Angle, A. R. 247
  Jacob B. 247
Anline, Jacob 247
Anlon, Jacob 247
Annamiller, Frederick
  337
Annmeiller, Frederick
  247
Annold, Cathron 247
  George W. 247
  Martha 247
Annon, Margaret 247
Ansel, Henry 546
Anson, Ann 226
Ant Dess, Thomas 244
Antabush, A. 367
  James A. 367
  M. (Mrs.) 367
Anthony, Anna (Mrs.) 248
  Anna Eva 247
  Annie J. 247
  Caroline S. 248
  Frederick 248
  George 177, 182, 190,
    248, 260, 261
  Jacob 248
  Lewis 248
  N. 305
  Nicholas 248
  Rosina 248
  Susannah 248
Antoni, Sophia 248
Antony, Nicholas 248
Apols, Dorothea 248
Apple, Jane 248
  Peter 29
  Thomas 248
Applegait, Anna 248
Applegate, Anna 248
  Mariah Ruth 445
Appleguts, William 248
Appleman, Lucinda 248
  Peter 239
Appling, (?) (Col.) 80
Apt, Elizabeth 70
Arbuckle, John 164
  Sally 550
Archer, G. L. (Rev.) 242
  George J. 229
  Robert H. 248
  Sarah 248
  William 248
Ardle, John D. 248
Armand, (?) (Col.) 520
Armbruster, J. 377
  Mathias 250, 259
  Matthias 250
Armentrought, Martha 248
Armentrout, Elias 249
  Gideon 228, 249
  Ishmael 249
  Jacob 249
  Jemima 248
  Lydia 249
  Marion 249
  Martha 248
  Merion 249
  Ruhama 249

Bristol (cont.)
Eri 274
Lois 274
Polly 274
Ssally 274
Bristow, James H. (Rev.)
531
Britton, Alexander 97
B. 255
Benj. 165, 173, 180
Benjamin 217, 224,
243, 247, 254, 261
Edward 251
Hosea 180
J. T. 249, 252
John 184
John T. 254, 311
N. F. 311
Tamson (Mrs.) 287
Brobeck, Catherine
(Mrs.) 354
Jacob 354
Brobst, S. Pauline 433
Brock, (?) (Dr.) 13
Brockover, Noe 54
Brockunier, S. J. (Rev.)
532
Brockway, Augustus F.
321
Heil 321
Mary (Mrs.) 36
Phebe (Mrs.) 321
Broderick, David 168,
171, 184
David L. 283
David S. 271, 551
George 184
Harvey D. 303
J. C. 202, 290
John B. 197
John C. 173, 187, 205,
207, 210, 211, 216,
290
John G. 206
Brodrick, David 551
W. H. 244
William H. 244
Broesghke, F. H. 321
Bromlow, Benigna (Mrs.)
288
Joseph 288
Bronson, (?) 13
Benjamin 225
Brooke, (?) 377
Cornelia Rice 377
James 377
Brooker, Elizabeth
(Mrs.) 309
Thomas 309
Brookhover, Nelson 42
Brooks, Ann M. 323
Anna 399
Cyrus 249
David 188, 551
DeLorma 64
Elisha 548
Frank 323
James 546
John 288, 545, 546
Joseph S. 208
Lewis 399
Mary 323
Mildred 399
Nathan 241, 246, 257,
323
Nathaniel W. 288
Philena 323
Robert 334

Brooks (cont.)
Samuel 326
W. C. 233
Wm. H. 285
Broome, (?) (Gov.) 76
Broonhall, James 87
Broshes, John 296
Brotherlin, Adam 189,
207, 212, 276
Brothers, Hays 13
Brotherton, A. 207
Adam 176, 178, 179,
180, 183, 186, 191,
195, 211
David 88
Elizabeth 275
Keziah (Mrs.) 88, 275
Margaret 275, 276
Martha 275
Peggy 275
R. 207, 224, 225, 281
Robert 164, 166, 169,
171, 174, 175, 176,
183, 186, 187, 188,
190, 192, 193, 195,
196, 198, 199, 200,
202, 205, 207, 208,
209, 210, 211, 212,
213, 214, 215, 216,
219, 221, 222, 275
Robt. 225
Brouse, (?) 451
Elizabeth C. (Mrs.)
451
John Andrew 451
Sarah 450, 451, 452
Browder, Isham 31
Brown, (?) 82, 210, 509,
551
(?) (Rev.) 26
A. H. 305
Ady 537
Adelia 238
Albert J. 307
Alexander 172, 513
Allen 253
Almeda 399
Ann 290
Anson 291
Banister 547
Bazil 442
Benedict 306
Catherine (Mrs.) 312
Charity 52
Charles 46, 67, 312
D. Ross 479
Daniel 180, 518
Daniel M. 165
David 513
David (Rev.) 532
Draper 528
E. (Mrs.) 537
Eliza (Mrs.) 312
Eliza Jane 461
Elizabeth 75, 172,
232, 256
Elizabeth (Mrs.) 282
Elmira J. 415
Ernest 480
Ezekiel 91, 214
George 29, 33, 472,
480
H. 174
Henry 166, 168, 170,
171, 174, 179, 181,
182, 184, 185, 186,
193, 200, 201, 221,
225, 360, 545, 551

Brown (cont.)
Hiram 82
Hiram J. L. 53
Hulda 450
Israel 291
Israel P. 178, 193
J. 354
James 41, 168, 289,
513
James (Sr.) 548
James George 307
Jane 48
John 210, 240, 292,
311, 312, 513, 550
John S. 48, 227
John W. 51
Jonathan 513
Joseph 30
Joseph M. 307
Joseph S. 234
Josiah 193
Julian 312
Katy 541
L. W. 434
Levi 312
Louisa F. 415
Lucy R. (Mrs.) 307
Margaret 171, 172
Margaret (Mrs.) 28
Martha 172
Mary 486
Mary A. (Mrs.) 46
Matthew 213
Minerva 35
Moses 537
Newton 260
Patsy 210
Peter 312, 528
Peter J. 53
Polly 40
Putman 214
Rebecca (Mrs.) 309
Richard (Col.) 59
Robert 338
Robert George 307
Ruth 548
S. (Mrs.) 354
S. L. 543
Samuel 171, 172, 210,
380
Sarah 354
Solomon 547
Sophia M. 235
Stephen 548
Stephen D. (Rev.) 532
Susanna 70
Thomas J. (Col.) 35
Walter (Rev.) 33
Wiley 434
William 167, 169, 180,
191, 198, 205, 207,
210, 228, 258, 260,
543
William (Rev.) 532
William Mary Ann 210
Wm. 162, 164, 167,
168, 281
Wm. (Jr.) 161, 168
Browne, John W. (Rev.)
88
Brownell, Joshua 32
Brownfield, W. (Rev.) 67
Browning, A. B. 399
Edmund 551
Elizabeth Ann 364
Huldah 364
I. 399
Isaac 364, 399

Browning (cont.)
James 337
Josiah 198
Mary E. 399
Sarah (Mrs.) 364, 399
William 25
Broyles, (?) 509
Brubaker, Abraham 444
Samuel 511
Bruce, J. G. (Rev.) 47
Phillip (Rev.) 532
Bruck, J. P. 233, 236,
240, 259, 262, 301,
305, 307, 313, 321,
327, 331, 332, 334,
336, 342
John P. 319, 340
Bruckman, Sam'l 31
Brundage, James 553
Brundige, Sarah 35
Bruner, J. A. 239, 244,
251, 262
John 337
Louis A. 247
Mary (Mrs.) 337
Peter 513
Rebecca (Mrs.) 533
Brunk, Daniel 165, 173,
180, 204, 231, 270,
311, 354, 553
Daniel (Sr.) 311
Elijah 311
Mary A. 231, 311
Samuel 180, 311, 553
Sarah 311
Susan 311
Brunn, Eliza 255
Geo. 382
George 382
John E. 382
Brunner, Daniel 542
Emmelia (Mrs.) 542
Emmilia 542
Matilda 426
Zirol 542
Bruns, Benigna 288
Brunt, Henry 240
Bruny, Mary B. 227
Brush, Alonzo 423
George W. 242
Henry 31
Jared 549
S. 300
Brusman, Henry 376
Bryan, John A. 545
Bryant, Charles 70
John 13
Mary A. 231
Bryden, Fanny 319
Harrison 319
James 188, 214, 218
Joshua 319
Margaret (Mrs.) 319
Mary 319
Bryson, David 548
Mary 86
Bucannan, Mary 540
Buch, Johannes 501
Buchanan, George (Rev.)
64
John 432
John (Rev.) 287
Buchert, James 546
Buck, Anna 432
Collins 58
E. 54
Edmund 50, 51
Elizabeth 162

Buck (cont.)
John 38, 199, 211,
243, 553
Joseph 161, 162
Lucy H. 50
Mathilda 50
Nancy 55
Buckingham, Bradley 97
Eb. (Jr.) 99
Stephen 93
Buckles, Abraham 529
Buckley, Elizabeth
(Mrs.) 357
Elizabeth E. 357
Job 357
Mary 357
R. (Mrs.) 357
William 357
Buckner, Martha (Mrs.)
344
Buckwalter, Arthur 388
Susie Y. (Mrs.) 388
Budd, (?) 475
(?) (Dr.) 45
Remembrance 45
Thomas (Rev.) 532
Budge, (?) (Dr.) 548
Buerck, Bernhard 304
George 304
John 304
Maria (Mrs.) 304
Bugh, Catharine 66
Peter (Sr.) 65
Buion, Jacob 261
Bull, Abiah L. 336
Alanson 177, 184
Alonson 277, 336
B. A. (Mrs.) 345
Balinder 345
Betsey (Mrs.) 345
Billingslea 166, 277,
484
Billingsley 181, 182,
184, 187
Billingsly 183, 186
Caty 187
Chloe F. 336
Cloe 277
Delia (Mrs.) 277
Edith 277
Edward 345
George T. 267
Hannah (Mrs.) 336
Hiram 177, 277
Horace J. 246
James 529
James G. 336
Jane E. J. 336
Jason 169, 184, 187,
202, 211, 257, 258,
277
Jason (Rev.) 258
Jason H. 336
Lucy 258
Lucy C. 257
Mary A. 336
Phildelia 277
Sarah 345
Sylvia 274
Thomas 177, 184
Thompson 198, 203, 277
W. 345
Walter 345
William B. 336
Willingslea 276
Bulland, Ratie 543
Bulls, Billingslea 484
Bumgardener, Henry 206

Bumgardener (cont.)
Nancy (Mrs.) 206
Bumgardner, Henry 206
Jacob 95
Nancy (Mrs.) 206
Bunier, George 548
Bunker, Isaac 52
Isaac (Jr.) 52
Joseph 52
Lydia 50
Pegleg 51
Reuben 45
Bunn, Elizabeth 300
Elizabeth (Mrs.) 300
Frederick 300
Henry 175, 203, 300
Mary 300
Nancy 300
Sarah 300
Bunting, Jabez (Rev.)
532
Burd, Lewis A. 291
Burdell, William 343
Burg, Jacob 547
Burge, Christian (Rev.)
39
George 59
John 45
Burgess, John 59
John (Rev.) 59
O. (Rev.) 59
Burgett, George 225
Burgy, Henry 528
Burke, Andrew L. 186
Anthony 557
Burn, Ann Garnett 279
Sarah Maria 279
Burnell, Anthony 173
Burnet, Hiram 212
Margaret 212
Tobias 75
Burnett, Anthony 174
Belinda 174
Henry 173
Hiram 174
Burnham, William 95
Burnhouse, John 548
Burnley, J. W. 293
Joel 293
Burns, (?) 509
Ann G. 279
Barnabas 324
Dimmis 434
Jeremiah 75
Maria 279
Williams 279
Burnside, William 510
Burnsides, John 547
Buroker, A. 517
Adam 517
Elizabeth (Mrs.) 517
M. 517
Martin 517
Molly (Mrs.) 517
Burr, Agnes C. 238
C. E. 334
Catherine 179
Charles E. 334
Eleanor N. (Mrs.) 38
Erastus 245
Harriet (Mrs.) 298
Izias 553
Ozias 38, 178, 179,
184, 207
Philo 227
Burrell, Charles 399
Burris, George 547
Burroughs, Mathilda A.

Cloud (cont.)
  R. Virginia 342
  Rachel 336
  Rebecca B. (Mrs.) 342
  Robert 338
Clough, N. R. 547
  Sheldon 518
Clouse, Baby Mae 399
  Benjamin 326
  Christine Ealy 326
  Daniel 326
  David 240, 326
  Eldon 399
  George 326
  Henry 399
  Jacob 172, 326
  Jeremiah 326
  John 326
  Mary 326
  Nancy 399
  Napoleon 326
  Oliver 326
  Sophia Ealy 326
  Thomas 326
Clover, Aaron 295
  Aron 291
  Emanuel 519, 520
  George M. 295
  Henry 178, 284, 342
  Joshua 175, 295
  Mary 295
  Milla Jane 295
  Orin 295
  Peter 208, 291
  Rachel 295
  Rachel (Mrs.) 295
  Solomon 208, 291, 295,
    344
  William A. 249
  Zebulon 261, 295
Clymer, (?) 223
  Francis 218, 298
  John 20, 218, 223
  Louisa 219, 223
  Mary 218
  Massey 485
  William S. 298
Coalman, James 354
Coartney, Margaret 236
Coates, Thomas M. 61
Cobb, David 97
Cochran, (?) 191, 219,
    224, 429
  Albert 339
  Amos E. 346
  Daniel J. 307
  E. T. 346
  Eliza 47
  Elizabeth 190, 339
  Emily 346
  Emily (Mrs.) 339
  Esther (Mrs.) 346
  Francis E. 346
  G. (Mrs.) 346
  Glass 22, 169
  J. R. 346
  John 30, 179, 187,
    190, 191, 219, 346,
    451
  John T. 346
  Mary 346
  Mary Jane 339
  Michael 224
  Peter 97
  Reuben 339
  Robert 47
  S. 346
  Sarah 339

Cochran (cont.)
  Simeon 194
  Thomas 170
  Westley 194
  William 47, 339
Cochrane, John 185
Cockey, Edward 473
Cockrell, Elijah 27
  Jesse 27
  John 27
Cockson, James 548
Code, Phinehas 31
Codner, Lydia (Mrs.) 486
  Samuel 485
Codwallader, Wallace 518
Coe, -r-nez 366
  Allen F. 330
  Almon 327
  Alvin 327
  Eliza Ann 233
  Elizabeth (Mrs.) 327
  J. 366
  Katy Ann 52
  Lovella 228
  Lovila 327
  M. (Mrs.) 366
  Mary 366
  Mina 238
  Rachel 327
  Ransom 327
  Salinda 327
  Zebulen 557
Coefeed, (?) 548
Coffay, Michael 314
Coffeen, Clarissa 75
Coffin, Hannah (Mrs.)
    340
  William C. 340
Coffman, Angeline 444
  Clark 417, 434
  H. 207
  Henry 262, 288, 553
  Samuel 66
Cogley, James 79
  John 79
  Joseph 79
  Joseph M. 79
  Robert 79
Cohagen, George W. 393
  John 393
  Matilda 393
  May J. (Mrs.) 393
Cohan, Helena G. 493
Coil, Fanny 64
Coit, E. W. (Mrs.) 346
  Edwin W. 66
  Harvey 308
  Huldah 346
  Hyram Josephus 346
  Julia Hortentia 346
Colbert, (?) 509
  John W. 78
Coldrain, Isaac 34
Coldren, Andrew 527
  N. 527
Coldshine, John 186
Cole, Abraham 42
  Barbara A. 257
  Bateman 176
  Catherine 341
  Chester P. 176
  D. P. 234, 249, 253,
    254, 259
  Edward 400
  Frederick 400
  John 172
  Joshua 269
  Julia Ann 39

Cole (cont.)
  Kathrine 400
  Marcus 553
  Martha Smith 400
  Mordeccai 60
  Nathan 180, 282, 298
  Shadrick 519
  Stephen 72
Coleman, Abigail 232
  Abigail (Mrs.) 277
  Abraham 185, 277
  Abram 553
  Asa 477
  George 538
  James 185, 442
  John 194, 243
  John L. 239
  Mary (Mrs.) 538
  Whitehead 518
Coler, Barbary (Mrs.) 64
  Christian Henry 64
Colerick, (?) (Mrs.) 95
Coles, (?) (Maj.) 551
  George (Rev.) 533
Coleshine, (?) 189
  Jackson 189
  John 189
  Margaret 189
Colestock, Elizabeth 33
Colhoun, Narcissa 85
Collens, P. (Cpt.) 550
Colleson, Alex. 61
Collet, Joshua 78
Collett, John 167, 170,
    177, 551
  Joshua 513
Collier, James 346, 530
  Melinda 66
  William 346
Collins, A. 263
  Axy 67
  Blanche 24, 33, 38,
    44, 59, 60, 62, 65,
    68, 74, 78, 80, 84,
    88, 89, 90
  Elijah 306
  F. 538
  Fred 538
  Helen K. (Mrs.) 343
  James 327
  James H. 547
  Jane (Mrs.) 343
  Jas. 67
  John 544, 550
  John (Rev.) 25, 533
  John A. 69
  Mary 544
  Mary (Mrs.) 544
  Mary E. 245
  Rebecca (Widow) 481
  S. (Mrs.) 538
  Sarah 433
  William 216
Collison, Alexander 26
  Moses 26
Collum, E. M. (Mrs.) 393
  J. 393
  James W. 393
  Nelson 49
Coloson, Thomas 546
Colshine, Henry 187
Colver, John 98
  Nathaniel 98
Colvin, David 177
Colwell, A. R. (Jdg.)
    513
  Robert 29
Comb, Phebe 433

Crist (cont.)
Susanna 72
Critz, Daniel 29
Crockett, Andrew 546
Crockwell, James 26
Croker, (?) 509
Cromwell, John S. 243
Joseph S. 253
Crone, Aalexander 177
Alex 181
John 173, 179, 271
Croninshield, George
(Cpt.) 62
Crook, J. 73
Crooks, (?) 415
Elizabeth 429
James 546
John 546
Robert 294
William 546
Crosby, Adam 70
Hannah F. (Mrs.) 278
Harry 187
Henry 278
J. W. 281
James 29
Libbie 259
Mary (Mrs.) 278
Otis 197, 209, 216,
220, 222, 223
P. W. (Mrs.) 48
S. 220
Samuel 201, 216, 220,
223, 303
William 198, 255
Crosley, Otis 545
William 30, 177
Cross, Mary Ann 230
Crosset, William 183
Crossett, Elizabeth 185
Samuel 183, 185
William 183, 185
Crossit, Ann (Mrs.) 380
John 380
Samuel 380
Croswell, Samuel 343
Crothers, G. 550
Crouch, Amanda (Mrs.)
464
Martha A. 468
Crouse, Daniel 183, 186,
552
Lucinda 491
Crow, John 548
Thomas 528
Crowall, John 550
Crowder, (?) 509
Crowl, Hannah 33
John 33
Crown, John 550
Sadie 363
Croxton, Carter 288
Crum, Amos 212
Cornelius 309
David S. 309
Francis A. 306
G. C. 231
George C. 243, 264
James 306
Lydia 414, 441
Margaret 309
Margaret (Mrs.) 309
Rebecca T. 309
Samuel D. 337
Sarah S. 309
William 249
William A. 309
Crumb, Abraham 188

Crumb (cont.)
Anthony 188
Jacob 188
Crume, Moses (Rev.) 532
Crumley, Catherine 241
Cryder, Catharine Ann 35
Elizabeth (Mrs.) 295
Henry M. 344
Jefferson 553
Johnson 295
Mary Jane 295
Moses 295
Culbertson, (?) 200
(?) (Rev.) 84, 85
Agnes 275
Andrew 193, 200, 275
Elizabeth 200
Elizabeth (Mrs.) 275
Emily 187
Esther 193
J. (Rev.) 85
James 168, 169, 176,
187, 200, 275, 276,
289, 551
James (Rev.) 40, 93
Jane 273, 275
Jas. 91
Margaret (Mrs.) 92
Minnie (Mrs.) 414
Rebecca 275
Robert 161, 164, 165,
178, 273, 275
Robert (Col.) 273
S. W. 98
Samuel 178, 200, 275
Sarah 275
William 92
William Henry 414
Cullin, John 428
Cullman, George 301
Culp, Baltzer 61, 550
Lydia 465
Culver, Aaron L. (Rev.)
533
Cumins, James L. 47
Cumminge, L. 516
Mary (Mrs.) 516
Cummings, (?) 205, 415,
426
Alexander 205
Jesse K. 426
John 190, 510
Samuel Parker 205
Cummins, (?) (Mrs.) 34
Alexander 205
Daniel 205
James 34
Mahala L. 400
William 400
Cummons, Joseph 513
Cumpton, Matthew 529
Cunard, S. T. 46
Cunning, (?) 201
Elizabeth 281
John 176, 195, 196,
201, 281
Margaret 201, 281
Mary Ann 199
Sam'l 201
Samuel 199, 201, 281
Cunningham, Barney 42
Daniel 93, 98
Hugh 35
James M. 321
Jemina 269
John 49, 511, 549
Martha (Mrs.) 35
Mary 274

Cunningham (cont.)
Mary (Mrs.) 42
Nathaniel Pendleton
(Rev.) 533
Thomas 30, 168
Virginia 533
W. 547
Cunnins, (?) 205
John 79
Sarah (Mrs.) 79
Curby, Felia 437
Luella 437
Thomas W. 437
William 437
Curfman, Adam 549
Curl, Isaac 511
Curlman, Eliza (Mrs.)
354
James 354
Mary 354
Curry, Elizabeth 184
Elizabeth C. 184
H. M. (Rev.) 533
Hiram M. 513
Hiram M. (Rev.) 25
John 184, 296
Mary 179
Morris 533
Moses 179
Samuel 511
Curst, Christian 530
Curtis, A. 287
Elizabeth 476, 477
Ezekiel 180
Jeremiah 22
Sarah 451
Curty, Wm. 68
Cuser, Daniel 551
Cushen, Eliza 75
Cushing, B. T. 304
Cushman, Mary (Mrs.) 297
Popann 297
Custard, Jacob 33
Custor, Abraham 513
Isaac 513
William 513
Cutler, Betsey 253
Cynthia 41
David 78
Ephriam 31
James 192, 206
John 171, 173, 179,
185, 186, 191, 195,
196
Manasseh 3
Robert 216, 220, 296,
332
Cutter, Cassy 437
John 184
Lewis 54
Robert 218
Dabus, Adam 241
Dade, Francis 31, 518
Dagenhardt, Christian
320
Dague, (?) 363
Andrew 327
Benjamin 309, 363
Catherine 327
Cyrus 363
D. 363
Daniel 20, 309, 363
Edmund 363
Edward 309
Elizabeth 309, 327
Elizabeth (Mrs.) 363
Elmer E. 363
Franklin 363

Dague (cont.)
Frederick 327, 499
Frederick (Sr.) 498
George 20, 309, 327,
342, 363, 400
H. (Mrs.) 363
Israel 327
Jonathan 327
Katherine 309
Levi 309
Lydia 327
Mary 327, 498, 499
Mary (Mrs.) 400
Mary M. 501
Mathias 20, 498
Matthias 363, 558, 559
Melisa (Mrs.) 342
Nancy 327
Peter 309
S. (Mrs.) 363
Sallie 363
Sally 327
Sarah (Mrs.) 363
Susanna 327
Susanna (Mrs.) 309,
363
Daily, Arthur L. 400
George 400
Russell 400
Dale, Daniel 175
Jeremiah 85
John 175
Dales, Elizabeth 310
Mary Catherine 310
William Henry 310
Dallas, (?) 510
James 513
James (Jdg.) 513
Daly, James 549
Rebecca (Mrs.) 310
Dalzell, John 18
William 182, 198, 262,
274
Damond, (?) 475
Dana, William (Cpt.) 25
Dandridge, Magdalene 283
Daner, John 411
Mary (Mrs.) 411
William H. 411
Danforth, Calvin (Rev.)
534
Daniel, Alex. 547
Harris 553
J. T. 366
John 194
John M. (Cpt.) 77
Melina (Mrs.) 542
Sarah (Mrs.) 366
Daniels, Brinkley 312
Jane (Mrs.) 312
John 312
Thomas 510
Danielson, (?) (Gen.) 92
Timothy E. (Lt.) 92
Danner, Catherine S. 72
John 72
Darby, Elizabeth (Mrs.)
346
J. 346
John 220
Ruth 254
Dark, John 31, 518
Darling, Desha 430
Timothy 547
Darlington, D. N. 45
Samuel 529
Darnall, Boswell 513
Nathan 513

Darnell, (?) 509
Joshua 510
William 288
Darragh, (?) (Lt.) 100
Datcher, Catherine
(Mrs.) 288
Daughaday, Thomas (Rev.)
534
Daugherty, Catharine 86
Henry 86
James 335, 344
John 87, 181, 512
Daugue, (?) 401
Bessie 401
Cadus 401
Clark 401
E. (Mrs.) 401
Elanliza Thomas (Mrs.)
401
Eliza 401
George 401
Harriett 401
Ida 401
J. D. 401
John 401
Jonathan 401
L. 401
Levi 401
Louisa 401
Mary E. 401
Phoebe S. 401
Davenpor, John T. 31
Davenport, Anthony 528
Charles 311
David 241
Fred 537
John T. 29
Lewis 367
Margaret S. (Mrs.) 367
Obediah 311
Peter 367
S. 367
Samuel 367, 528
Sarah 537
Sarah (Mrs.) 537
Susan (Mrs.) 288
Susann (Mrs.) 367
William 311
Davice, Elizabeth (Mrs.)
288
Davids, John E. 55
Davidson, (?) 191, 193
Abednigo 193
Adonijah 193
George 293
Isaac 294
James 174, 513
Joseph 191, 202
Levi 327
Mary 191
Ruth (Mrs.) 202
Samuel 190
Thomas 28
Davies, James (Rev.) 40
John 40
Davis, Ann (Mrs.) 539
(?) 183, 197, 442,
509, 550
(?) (Mrs.) 335
(?) (Rev.) 335
Alfred 197
Amanda M. 379
Amasa 236
America (Mrs.) 332
Amoss 236
Anderson (Jr.) 513
Andrew (Sr.) 513
Ann 354, 415

Davis (cont.)
Ann (Mrs.) 282
Ann M. 539
Ann Simpson 354, 442
Asa 311
Ashe A. (Rev.) 41
Benjamin S. 337
Beriah 245, 355
Brice 245
Byron 354
C. E. (Mrs.) 354
C. H. 538
Catherine 302
Charles E. 252, 307
Christopher 200, 219,
222, 332
Clinton H. 332
Daniel (Sr.) 513
David 306
E. A. 355
Ebenezer 30
Edith 354
Edith (Mrs.) 355
Edith A. (Mrs.) 355
Edmond 261
Edward 213, 218, 230,
254, 289, 295
Edward (Rev.) 545
Elijah 510
Elijah T. 513
Eliza 282
Elizabeth 355, 442,
475
Elizabeth A. 332
Ellen Jane 247
Eshmael 271
Evan 383
Francis 206
Fred R. 355
George W. M. 332
H. 358
Hannah 529
Harriet (Mrs.) 393
Henry 513
Henry F. 258
Horace W. 355
Ida 427
Isaac 32, 551, 558
Isaac Newton 197
Ishmael 163, 177, 179,
197
J. 355
J. E. 354
Jacob E. 355
James 31, 197, 332
Jane (Mrs.) 414
Jeremiah 332
John 92, 168, 186,
197, 200, 211, 248,
282, 332, 355, 414,
442, 513
John (Jr.) 442
John (Mrs.) 92
John W. 239
Joseph 30, 207, 211,
282, 332, 354, 355,
442, 548
Joseph (Sr.) 355
Joseph W. 355
Joseph Watts 355
Joshua 186, 282, 355,
442
L. 233
Lewis 183
Lona 358
Lot 393
Lucinda 355
Marvia 383

Demetts, Mary Elizabeth 530
Deming, (?) 475
  Albert R. 478, 479
  Alexander Hamilton 477
  Anna 475
  Betty 476
  Charlotte 477
  Clara C. 478, 479
  Clarissa Cranny 477, 478
  Cythera 477
  Davis 476, 477
  Delia Ann 477
  Electa 477
  Eliza 477
  Francis 478
  Frank Milton 479
  Isaac 476
  James 475, 477, 478, 479
  John 475, 476, 478, 479
  Juliaette 478
  Lafayette 478
  Lucian M. 477, 478
  Lucretia 476
  Lucy 477
  Martha E. 478, 479
  Mary Ann 477, 478, 479, 480
  Mary J. 478, 479
  May Rebecca 479
  Mercy 476
  Milton R. 478
  Moses 475, 476, 477, 478, 479
  Ralph R. 477, 478, 479
  Rufus 478
  Rufus Romeo (Rev.) 477
  Rutha 477
  Sophia 477
  Stephen Platt 477
  Thomas 475, 477, 478, 479
  Wealthy A. 478
  William D. 478
Demint, James 530
  Mary 530
Demit, Sarah 530
Demming, Moses 505
Demmon, (?) 475
Demon, John 475
Demond, (?) 475
Demorest, Dan'l 182
  Daniel 275
  Daniel P. 275
  Geliam 275
  Gilliam 292
  Gillian 182
  Lean (Mrs.) 292
  Nicholas 182, 194, 220, 275, 552
Demorst, Gilliam 192, 193
  Nicholas 192
Demot, (?) 506
  Arta 506
Dempsey, James 547
Dempster, Pere 62
Dener, Elenor 70
Denig, A. L. 257
  Alexander 341
  Augustus M. 341
  Edwin T. 341
  G. (Dr.) 241
  George 257
  George (Dr.) 257

Denig (cont.)
  Hai Kees Kah We Yah 341
  Harriet L. 257
  Ida 341
  Maria 241
  Robert 341
  Sarah 341
Denim, Susanna 325
Denison, Thomas 238
Denmint, Elizabeth 530
Denney, James 177
Dennis, Isaac 236
  J. 383
  John 383
  Mary (Mrs.) 308
  R. (Mrs.) 383
  Rebecca (Mrs.) 383
  Sarah 230
Dennison, George 542
  George H. (Dr.) 52
  Sarah 542
  W. 216
Denny, David 162, 163
  James 31, 518
  Jane 25
  John 163
  Margarte 529
  Samuel 196, 528
Denoon, Barbara 233
  John 558, 559
  William E. 281
Dent, G. W. 401
  L. 94
  William 245
Denune, Alexander 234
  John 214
  Lucinda 233
Derick, Rebecca 282
  Susan 282
  William 282
Dering, Harriet L. 257
Derlurger, Alba Belle 383
  J. 383
  Jacob 383
  M. (Mrs.) 383
Dernburger, Sarah 415
Derough, Blancy 530
Derrick, Mary Ann 277
  Richard 170
Derrikson, William 176
Deshicket, (?) 509
Deshler, Charles G. 330
  D. G. 234
  D. W. 182, 190, 192, 199, 217, 281
  Daniel 182
  David 182, 186, 187
  David W. 180, 183, 192, 193, 197, 198, 203, 205, 208, 220, 222, 289, 299
  Frank Work 330
  Lizzie Green 330
Detrich, Abraham 308
  Lydia Frances (Mrs.) 308
Detwiler, Abram 312
  Samuel L. 334
Deuel, Benjamin 38
Deval, Marion H. 30
Devault, Sarah Ann 440
Deviney, Jacob 255
  Jacob C. 256
Devlin, Charles 327
  Elizabeth (Mrs.) 327
  James 327

Devlin (cont.)
  William 327
Devol, Gilbert (Jr.) 98
Devore, J. 58
  James 509
  John 383, 513
  Phebe 383
Dex, Rachel 242
Deyo, Aaron 242
  David 242
  Elizabeth 242
Diamond, (?) 475
  James 475
  Thomas 475
Diamont, (?) 475
  John 475
Dibert, (?) 509
Dice, Charles 259
Dicken, Amos 356
  George Dillon 356
  Jesse G. 356
  John 356
  Rowena 356
Dickerson, Susannah 231
Dickey, (?) 13
  Matilda 415
  Michael 163, 164
  Obediah 321
  Thomas 433
Dickie, Emma L. (Mrs.) 540
Dickinson, Anna 9
Dickison, Elizabeth (Mrs.) 555
Dickson, Harriet (Mrs.) 393
  John Wesley 393
  Joseph 161, 163
  Moses 255
  Rachel 86
  Wm. 68
Dicus, Aaron 247
Dieble, Anna 544
  Casper 544
  Crecentia (Mrs.) 544
Diemer, Jacob B. 219, 258
Diens, Aaron 247
Dieterick, Jacob D. 66
Dietz, Mary Katharine 501
Diffenbaugh, George 67
Diggins, Sarah 335
Dike, Abigail 55
Dikeman, Alzina 478, 480
Dikes, James 235
Dildine, Andrew 170, 173, 207, 519
  C. P. 310, 314
  Elisha 217
  Elisha D. 552
  Henry 186, 208, 211, 221
Dile, Henry 69
Dill, (?) 198
  Andrew 179, 180, 183, 185, 187, 188, 191, 193, 198, 200, 210, 211, 212, 277
  Andrew C. 198
  Armstrong 272
  C. C. (Mrs.) 444
  David 308
  Esther 198
  Frances 78
  Isabella 198
  James A. 233
  John 18, 160, 161,

Dill (cont.)
164, 165, 167, 168,
170, 172, 268, 272,
279, 333
John A. 198
Lucinda 75
Mary 272
Mary (Mrs.) 272
Rebecca 272
Robert 172, 272
Thomas 198, 272
Dilley, Susan 25
Dillinger, Henry 210,
212, 297
Dillon, Ann 555
Isaac P. 86
John (Rev.) 534
Mary 87
Diltz, Joseph 513
Dimon, (?) 475
Abraham 475
Deborah 475
Elizabeth 475
Isaac 475
John 475
Mary 475
Rachel 475
Dinges, Caherine (Mrs.)
310
Hartman 310
Dinsen, Byron 294
Disney, Julia (Mrs.) 68
Wm. 68
Distelhorst, George 336
Distelzweig, B. 314
Ditore, Rafeel 548
Ditzell, Helene 262
Diver, John 69
Dix, Lewis 288
Peres M. 48
Rachel 242
Stephen 56
Thomas 288
Dixon, (?) (Rev.) 481
A. 375
Alva 375
Amanda A. 375
Blythe 17
Charles 375
Daisy V. 375
Hannah 265
Henry 412
J. 412
James H. 393
Jesse 191
Jesse F. 191
Joseph 167
L. A. (Mrs.) 375
Letty Ann (Mrs.) 375
M. (Mrs.) 393
Ma. (Mrs.) 393
Manerva J. 393
Margaret (Mrs.) 393
Nancy A. 393
Rosetta 393
Russell 375
S. (Mrs.) 412
Walter L. 375
William 30, 393
William (Rev.) 534
Willie P. 375
Wm. 96, 393
Dlowd, Phoebe D. 246
Dobbins, Andrew 437
Eliza 534
Elizabeth F. 437
Ernest 437
Flora 437

Dobbins (cont.)
Grace C. 437
Guy L. 437
Ida 437
Irena 437
James 437
James Forsythe 437
John 437
John H. 437
John William 437
Luella B. 437
Matilda 437
Nancy Susan 437
Ora Benson 437
Rebecca 437
Robert (Rev.) 534
Sophia 437
Thomas G. 437
William L. 437
William Melvin 437
William N. 437
William T. 437
Dobbs, (?) 533
Dobbyns, Thomas W. 311
Dobyns, T. W. 228, 249
Dockaty, Charles 442
Dodd, Abijah 364
Alexander F. 257
George 546
John 546
Nancy (Mrs.) 364
Solomon 546
William S. 364
Doddridge, Baron (Dr.)
27
Eliza Maria 62
J. (Rev.) 62
Julia Ann 27
P. 63
Dodds, John Milton 54
Mary (Mrs.) 54
Mathilda L. 57
William C. 54
Dodge, Elizabeth 434
Joshua 294
Lodemia 45
Luther 245
Lydia 299
Dodson, Charles 388
J. Edwin 388
Louisa 40
M. E. (Mrs.) 388
Mary Elizabeth 388
Doherty, Absalom 367
David 182
Edwin D. 367
Emanuel 182
Emeline E. (Mrs.) 367
John 181, 182
Keziah 181
William 179, 183, 185,
186, 190, 192, 196,
197, 198, 204, 210,
212, 215, 222
William H. 197
Wm. 181, 182, 203
Dolbey, Joseph 549
Dolbier, M. (Rev.) 35
Dolby, Edward (Mrs.) 454
Doldear, Sophia 48
Doler, Paulus 343
Domigan, Abijah 282
Abram 168
Enoch 282
Marte 282
Mary (Mrs.) 282
William 160, 179, 185,
187, 207, 252, 282,

Domigan (cont.)
552
Wm. 163, 164, 166,
168, 173, 174
Domigon, William 252
Donahoo, James T. 236
Donahue, (?) 13
Donald, Cornelius 98
Rachel O. 98
Donaldson, Moses 162
Donally, Andrew 26
Mary 26
Donalon, Valentine 69
Donalson, John (Rev.) 12
Donaworth, George 248
Donkersley, Richard
(Rev.) 534
Donley, Baz. 549
Charles 550
William 442
Donnally, Andrew 547
Donnel, Jonathan 529
Donnon, (?) (Dr.) 13
Donovan, John 167
Doolittle, E. 323
Ephriam 31
James 513
N. 227, 251, 252, 253
Doran, Alexander 342,
400
Charles E. 400
Cynthia A. 400
Ella A. 400
Ella M. Swickard 401
Ella S. Swickard 400
Emma O. 401
Fernie L. 400
J. 368
James 400
Rhoda 400
Rhoda W. (Mrs.) 368
Ross E. 400
Sadie L. 401
Dorberth, George 327
John 327
Margaretha 327
Nicholas 327
Dorigan, Wm. 164
Dorrence, Samuel 548
Dorsam, Catherine 241
Dorsey, Charles 510
Samuel 549
Dort, Titus 166
Doty, Amy L. 389
Jonathan 414
Peter 47, 50
Zuresha 414
Dougerty, Thomas 547
Doughty, Richard 261
Douglas, Ann (Mrs.) 413
Catharine (Mrs.) 413
Hannah 238
James 238
Jane 86
John 413
John D. 413
Joseph 86
Julius 413
William 413
Wm. 413
Douglass, A. J. 246
Almira 36
Archibald 180
Wm. 548
Douty, Dora L. 247
G. 247
Dove, Jacob 296
Dowdon, Zach 549

590

Downer, Emily 40, 306, 319
  Joshua 306, 319
  Joshua Rathbone 307, 319
  Juliett (Mrs.) 306, 319
  Sarah 306, 319
  Sarah (Mrs.) 49, 306, 319
  Sarah Ann 46
Downey, Frederick 547
  Henry 65
  Sallie (Mrs.) 65
Downing, (?) 204
  Dorcas 204
  Elizabeth 204
  Francis 204
  John 163
  Mary 204
  Simeon 204
Downs, (?) 210, 442
  James 187, 210
  John N. 516
  Wilber 210
Doyle, James 538
  Mary (Mrs.) 538
Drake, (?) (Cpt.) 88
  Alice Arabella 424
  Daniel S. 42
  Elam 341
  Elizur 422
  Hannah 233
  Harriet 34
  J. 49
  J. (Rev.) 39, 41, 44, 45, 48, 58
  Jacob (Rev.) 35, 44, 88
  John 293
  Lewis (Col.) 76
  Lucinda 233
  Mary 56
  Mary (Mrs.) 76, 286, 422
  Patience 88
  Sophronia 422, 423
  Sylvester 88
  T. H. 317
  William S. 34
Draper, Mary 549
Draun, John 271
Drenning, (?) 60
Dresbach, Daniel 29
  George 522, 523
  John 528
Dresback, Abram 522
Dresel, Otto 331, 336
Dreshmann, Mary 240
Drougolle, Edward 285
  Sarah C. (Mrs.) 285
Drummond, Benj. 170
Druny, Adam 538
  Mary (Mrs.) 538
Duckworth, John 509
Dudgeon, George 552
Dudles, (?) (Col.) 92
Dudley, Asa 547
Duel, John 548
Duff, William 198
  William C. 183, 191, 205, 245, 275
  Wm. C. 281
Duffy, James 249
  John 192
Dugan, Peter 85
  Pierre 508, 509
Duke, H. S. (Rev.) 534

Duke (cont.)
  William 177
Dukes, Andrew 30
  Dellia 171
  John 168, 171, 200, 271, 553
  Lewis 171
  Lydia 271
  M. 553
  Mary 168, 553
  Mary (Mrs.) 271
  Nancy 171, 271
  Nicholas 171
  Richard 171
  Susanah 271
  Susannah 171
Dulin, Anna 293
  Francis 252
  Smith 279, 293
Dulton, Baker 546
  William 546
Dulty, Michael 191
Dumbald, Mary 432
Dumegan, John 44
Dumnett, Moses 518
Dun, (?) (Mrs.) 292
  George W. 292
  James 292, 293
  John 292
  John Graham 292
  Robert 26, 292
  Robert George 292
  Walter 292
  Walter Angus 292
Duncan, (?) (Rev.) 49
  Adrew 59
  Jennet 86
  John 86, 547
  Joseph 513
  Rebecca (Mrs.) 308
  Robert 86
Dundass, Elizabeth 63
Dungan, John 414, 528
  Levi 547
  William 528
Dunham, Clark 49
  Eleazer 35
  Fanny 235
  Jeremiah 51
  Obadiah 47
  Silas 35
  Spencer 39
Dunkel, Clara Ellen 461
  John 66
Dunlap, Alexander 509
  Joseph (Col.) 34
  William 510
Dunleavy, Francis (Jdg.) 512, 513
Dunlevy, Daniel 381
  Jane (Mrs.) 381
  Maria 381
Dunmore, (?) 555
  (?) (Lord) 495
Dunn, (?) 202
  (?) (Mrs.) 292
  Asa 161, 168, 169, 184, 186, 202, 209, 271
  Caleb 196, 202
  Jabob 239
  John 208, 209, 235, 241, 312
  Mahala 186
  Mary 186, 202
  Matthew 186
  Nancy 202
  Richard 86

Dunn (cont.)
  Susan 202
  Virginia A. (Mrs.) 239
  Walter 292
  William 86
Dunnon, Aaron 393
Dunton, Solomon 243
  William 280
Durant, Y. W. 309
Durbin, John P. (Rev.) 75
  John Price (Rev.) 534
Durel, Thomas G. 552
Durell, Thomas G. 553
Durfee, G. 40
  Thomas 520
Durfey, Celinda (Mrs.) 46
  Philen 42
Durfy, James 37
Durling, Benjamin 39
Durnell, Chester 389
  F. A. 389
  F. A. (Mrs.) 389
  Hiram 389
  James 389
  Lucinda (Mrs.) 389
  Sarah (Mrs.) 389
Durphy, Dexter 35
  Ebenezer 35
Durry, James 559
Dust, David 90
Dustin, Sarah A. 46
Dutcher, William 44
Dutton, Mary (Mrs.) 56
  Wm. 68
Duvall, Daniel 518
  Mary (Mrs.) 329
  Thomas 329
Duwall, Dan'l 31
Dyche, (?) (Mrs.) 76
  Frederick 76
Dyer, (?) (Mrs.) 335
  Herman 36
  Jain (Mrs.) 270
  Jane 165, 214
  John 163, 165, 214, 270, 284
  Joseph 270
  Mary 219, 270
  Mary (Mrs.) 284
  Morrel 270
  Reachel 271
  Robert 163, 270
  Samuel 165, 173, 178, 179, 185, 188, 194, 198, 270
  Stephen 335
  William 270
Dyerd, John 219
Dykes, James 235
Dymont, (?) 475
  Abigail 475
  Elizabeth 475
  Hannah 475
  James 475
  John 475
  Mary 475
  Nathaniel 475
  Ruth 475
  Sarah 475
  Thomas 475
Dyre, John 270, 284
  Mary (Mrs.) 284
Dysart, (?) (Dr.) 13
Dyxson, H. 342
Eader, Jacob 414
  Saly (Mrs.) 414

Ealy, Angus L. 401
  Bertha L. 401
  Bessie M. 401
  D. 368
  Daniel 311
  E. P. 401
  Jeremah 401
  Lilly D. 401
  M. 401
  M. (Mrs.) 401
  M. O. 401
  Mary 368, 401
  N. C. (Mrs.) 401
  Peter 368
  Rosey (Mrs.) 368
  Susan Hoppes 401
Earhart, Adam 180
  George 81
  George H. 260, 261,
    319
  James 526
  M. K. 233, 255
  Martin 80, 81
  Nicholas 81
Earl, Daniel 557
  Wilbur 401
Earle, Irma C. (Mrs.)
    447
Early, John 334
Earnfight, Susan 75
Earnhart, Margaret F.
    (Mrs.) 515
  Morton G. 515
East, Christopher 30,
    528
  George 30, 66
  Henry 30
Easterday, Martin 549
Eastman, W. (Rev.) 52
Easton, C. O. 401
  Charles Orville 401
  Susan (Mrs.) 401
  Walter 401
Eastwood, Jane 233
Eatherton, Margaret 52
Eaton, Barsheba (Mrs.)
    44
  John 44
  Martha W. 49
  W. (Gen.) 92
  William (Jr.) 234
Ebbert, Isaac (Rev.) 534
Ebberton, Lucinda 259
Eberhart, Jacob 549
Eberle, P. H. (Dr.) 545
Eberlee, Jacob 222
  Peter 222
Eberly, Beulah 436
  Charlie 414
  Chas. 435, 436
  Clay E. 435
  David S. 435
  Earl B. 435
  Ely T. 436
  Fayette H. 436
  Grant E. 436
  Hannah 436
  Henry Thomas 435, 436
  Jacob M. 435
  John 252, 260, 414,
    435, 436
  John T. 435
  Mary A. 435
  Mary C. 436
  Milo F. 436
  Myra C. 436
  Thomas 417, 434
Ebersole, John 548, 550

Ebersole (cont.)
  Peter 547
Ebert, Barbara 325
  Casper 325
  Johanna 325
  John 325
  Susannah (Mrs.) 325
Ebey, Jacob 178, 191,
    276
Ebinger, John 79
  Nancy (Mrs.) 79
Eblen, Joseph P. 292
Eby, George 163
  Jacob 180
  Polly 254
Eccles, Allen 548
Eckehene, Jacob 31
Eckert, Jacob L. 66, 546
Eckles, Charles 86
Eddy, Augustus (Rev.)
    534
  Jona 557
  Nancy 534
  Spencer 534
  William 557
Eddye, Joseph 77
Edem, Catherine 229
Edgar, A. (Mrs.) 368
  Abagail (Mrs.) 368
  Abigail (Mrs.) 274
  Calvin 368
  Catherine 285
  Charles 368
  Daisy 368
  Eleanor (Mrs.) 383
  G. W. 368
  Harriet 221
  Harriet (Mrs.) 285
  J. 368
  James 219
  James E. 285
  John 167, 168, 169,
    173
  Joseph 178, 190, 194,
    201, 216, 282, 368
  Lewis 368
  Lucinda (Mrs.) 368
  Mary 393
  Riley 368
  Silas 285
  William 383
Edgerton, Daniel (Rev.)
    534
Edginton, John 63
Edminston, John W. 170
Edmiston, John M. 182
  John M. (Dr.) 173,
    222, 545
Edmonds, Sanford 513
  William 534
Edmundson, Mary 9
Edward, David 311
  Henry 263
Edwards, (?) 202
  A. D. 368
  Alice 85
  Catherine (Mrs.) 335,
    365
  Charles 202
  Daniel 262
  E. 365
  Edward 365
  Edward H. 26
  Elizabeth 42
  Francis 202
  Fred 26
  George 201, 202, 380
  John Gill 202

Edwards (cont.)
  John S. 548
  Joseph 241
  Lucinda (Mrs.) 368
  Lucius H. 202
  Mary 365
  Rebecca 202
  Robert 315
  Samuel 26
  Stephen 202
Effinger, Samuel 526
Egan, Peter 233
Egbert, Daniel (Dr.) 78
  John 79
Egenbrought, (?) (Rev.)
    51
Eggenbrecht, Elizabeth
    234
Eichelberger, L. S. 322
Eichensee, Dorothea
    (Mrs.) 541
  Ferdinand 541
  John 541
Eirick, P. 257
Eisler, Frederick 216
Eister, T. 218
Elbon, Clarence William
    401
  Laurie B. 401
Elder, (?) 213
  (?) (Rev.) 55
  Jesse 213
  Margaret 458, 459
  R. J. 257
  R. S. (Rev.) 54, 58
  Robert 458, 459
  Thomas 211
  William 183, 211, 213
Eldridge, Daniel 243
Elefrits, John 513
Elias, E. T. 518
Eliott, J. W. 50
Ellen, Jerusha 238
  Margaretha J. 238
Elliot, Andrew 549
  Christiana 33
  George 368
  J. W. 45
  James S. 36
  Joseph 550
  Joseph W. 35
  Laura (Mrs.) 278
  Robert 180, 193, 204,
    285
  Thos. 60
  Wm. (Jr.) 549
  Zadoc 550
Elliott, (?) (Dr.) 464
  A. 554
  Alex 554
  Alex. 555
  Anna 368
  Anna Elizabeth 426
  Arthur (Rev.) 534
  Chapmann 299
  Charles (Dr.) 534
  Daniel 311
  David 231, 311
  Elex. 554
  Eliza 311
  Elizabeth 299
  Geo. P. 426
  George 426
  George Peace 426
  Georgiana G. 426
  J. W. 46, 53
  Jackson 311
  James (Rev.) 534

Fisher, (?) 88, 221,
  364, 549
  (?) (Dr.) 13
  A. V. 364
  Andrew Jackson 291
  Catherine 291
  Cristena 277
  Daniel 72
  Elias 291
  Elizabeth 277, 291
  Ephraim 180, 192
  Ephriam 291
  Ephriam Henry 291
  Fisher 291
  George 185, 277, 291,
    337
  George (Dr.) 33
  George Josiah H. 217
  H. N. (Mrs.) 402
  Heinrich 561
  Henry 64, 239
  Isaac 242, 243, 278,
    558, 559
  Isaac E. 276
  J. C. 402
  Jacob 185, 219, 236,
    277, 528, 559
  Jane 221
  Job Albertis 364
  John 32, 190, 519
  John (Jr.) 278
  John (Sr.) 278
  Joseph 200, 203
  Joseph Harvey 291
  Joseph Michael 277
  Josiah 178, 246
  M. 277, 327
  Margaret 291
  Mary 243
  Mary Louisa 291
  Matilda (Mrs.) 364
  Maximilla 277
  Michael 161, 165, 167,
    169, 172, 174, 184,
    185, 186, 194, 214,
    219, 221, 268, 269,
    277
  Michael (Jr.) 184
  Milton 185, 186, 277
  Molly 227
  R. S. (Mrs.) 364
  Roy 402
  Ruth B. 242
  Sally 277
  Sarah 186, 277
  Thomas B. 364
  William 291, 337
Fishpaw, John W. 368
  M. J. (Mrs.) 368
  W. L. 368
Fisk, Caroline 347
  Emma 258
  Ira 347
  Polly (Mrs.) 347
  Wilbur (Rev.) 535
Fist, Jacob 249
Fitch, Nathan 514
  Ruth 25
Fitcher, John 514
Fithem, Wm. J. 549
Fithian, George 508, 514
  George (Jdg.) 513
  James 514
  William (Jdg.) 513
Fitz, Bessie Bliss
    Wiggin 421
  Isaac 296
  John 241

Fitz Randolph, Elizabeth
  445
Fitzgerald, Edward 259
  Edward M. 233
  Edwin 236
  J. H. 518
Fitzpatrich, John 510
Fitzpatrick, (?) 510
Fitzwater, Joseph 339
Fix, Henry 559
Flack, John 332
Fladt, Matthias 340
Flagg, Edmund 221
  Edmund W. 264
  Edmund W. F. 325
  Jane 223
Flago, Charles (Jdg.)
  513
Flanagan, Martha 50
Flanner, Abigail 9
Flannery, Thomas C. 195
Flattery, Elizabeth 402
Fleischhauer, Cecilly
  233
Flemin, (?) 509
Fleming, (?) 454, 510
  Alex. 528
  Alonzo C. 454
  Alonzo F. 454
  Archibald 244, 252
  Charles H. 454
  Daniel 454, 553
  Daniel (Jr.) 454
  Daniel (Sr.) 454
  Eliza 175
  Elizabeth (Mrs.) 160
  Frank 454
  George 454
  George W. 454
  James 217, 552, 553
  Jean 168
  Joseph 160, 168, 175
  Julia 454
  Margaret 168, 175, 457
  Mary Ann 42
  Mary J. 454
  Matilda 454
  Matilda G. 454
  Olive S. 454
  Ora May 454
  Peggy 175
  Robert 160
  Sally 175
  Sam'l B. 549
  Sarah 168, 175
  Tillie 454
  William 160, 168, 175,
    179
  Williams S. 454
  Willy 168
  Wm. 174
Flemming, Daniel 98
  John 57
Flennekin, Elizabeth 268
Flenniken, Ann 236
  Dorcas 427
  Eliza S. 243
  Elizabeth 427
  Isaac W. 180
  Martha 236
  Samuel 174, 183
  Samuel C. 216
  Samuel G. 167, 172,
    173, 427
Flenniker, Eliza S. 243
  Samuel G. 217
Flennikin, Sam'l G. 170
Flesher, M. A. (Mrs.)

Flesher (cont.)
  368
  Ulalia 368
  W. H. 368
Fletcher, Elizabeth 96
  John (Rev.) 535
Flieschmann, F. C. 49
Flintham, Ann (Mrs.) 314
  William 314
Flipp, (?) (Cpt.) 88
Flood, Elizabeth 248
  Thomas 84, 85
Flournay, T. C. 175
Flourney, Thomas G. 176
Flowers, Charles T. 308
  Mary E. 244
Foark, J. 358
  K. (Mrs.) 358
  Mary 358
Foggy, John 518
Fogle, Jacob S. 326
Foley, James 327
  John 164, 270
  Moses 258, 553
  Wm. 164
Folk, G. P. 394
  Mattie 394
  S. T. (Mrs.) 394
Folley, Robert W. 548
Folsom, Joshua 195
Fookes, Andrew 263
Foos, (?) 485
  Franklin 553
  Jane 160
  John 160, 164, 485
  Jos. 176
  Joseph 160, 552
  Margaret 164, 485
  Nicholas 164, 485
  Polly 164, 485
  Valentine 160
Foot, Solomon 535
Forbes, Sarah 554
Forbescue, Joseph 341
Ford, John 514
  Joseph 514
  Nichodemus 548
  Stephen 548
  Tolson 514
  William R. 445
Foreaker, William 94
Forehand, Hannah (Mrs.)
  364
  Thomas Charleton 364
Forescythe, Lucinda 554
Foresman, Alex. 528
  Alexander 29
  George 528
  Jane 30
  Phillip 528
  Robert 528
  Robert K. 30
  William 30
Forester, Robert 11
  Robert (Rev.) 12
  William 15
Forgason, John 300
  Mary 300
Forger, John 529
Forgrave, John A. 440
Forguson, Elijah 529
Forman, Catherine (Mrs.)
  79
  Jacob 547
Forney, Daniel 19
  James F. 200
Forquhar, Samuel 554
Forrer, John 197

Griffis (cont.)
 John 547
 Sabin 547
Griffith, (?) 449
 (?) (Dr.) 13
 Alfred (Rev.) 536
 Ann (Mrs.) 335
 Deleloh 41
 Isaac 189
 John 528
 Lewis 75
 Robert 87
 Timothy 545
Griffiths, John 547
Griggs, Ann (Mrs.) 76
 Matthew 76
 Phebe 76
 Thomas 299
 Thomas (Jr.) 298
Grim, Henry 515
 John 326
 Mary (Mrs.) 515
Grimes, Catherine (Mrs.)
 427
 Felix 427
 Sarah 427
Grine, Franklin 550
Grinnell, D. C. 330
 William H. 321, 330
 Wm. H. 553
Griswold, (?) 170
 Alexander Viets 21
 E. 274
 Ezra 22, 59, 90, 162,
 164, 170, 171, 176,
 178, 180, 245, 246,
 274, 275, 298
 Ezra (Jr.) 174
 G. H. 246
 G. H. (Gen.) 37
 G. W. 285
 Geo. Harlow 180
 George H. 180, 207
 George Harlow 298
 Harriet 298
 Isaac 168, 199, 212,
 272, 292, 553
 Melissa 298
 Ruth 59, 246, 298
 Ruth (Mrs.) 298
 Samuel A. 44
 Sylvanus (Cpt.) 88
 Victor M. 48, 298
Groce, John 528
Groeninger, George 330
 Margaret Barbara
 (Mrs.) 330
Groff, J. H. (Rev.) 243
 John H. 344
Groom, Catherine 287
 Davannus 329
 David 329
 Elizabeth 258
 Ezekiel 171, 287, 329
 Irvin M. Martin (V)
 329
 Isaac N. 329
 John 287
 John F. 314
 John W. Hosea 329
 Malvina 329
 Mary 287
 Mary A. 329
 Moses 287, 314, 329
 Noah 329
 Rebecca (Mrs.) 296
 Rebecca A. 329
 Rebecca L. 329

Groom (cont.)
 Rhoda (Mrs.) 287
 Sarah 287
 Tamson 287
 Thomas 287, 314, 329
 William 287
Groomis, David 224
 Mary 224
Grooms, Thomas 207
Grove, (?) 208, 491
 Catharine 32
 Caty 30
 Elizabeth 208
 Jacob 203, 208
 John 208
 Livina 208
 Martin 97, 208
 Michael 208
 William 208
Grovenberry, Eliza 402
 Henry 402
 William 402
Grovenbery, Salinda 252
Grover, Aaron C. 57
 Ira 36, 216
 Isaac 65
 J. L. 258, 261
 Josiah 285
 Louisa 57
 Mary (Mrs.) 36
 T. D. 333
Groves, (?) 206
 Charles 402
 David 402
 George L. 402
 Hannah (Mrs.) 516
 Henry 516
 Horsey H. 30
 Jacob 206, 402
 John 516
 Jonas 206
 Layfayette 402
 Levi 402
 Mary (Mrs.) 402
 Perry 402
 Peter 206
Growel, Samuel 40
Grub, Jacob 173, 211
Grubb, Jacob 160, 161,
 162, 163, 164, 165,
 166, 167, 168, 173,
 176, 177, 178, 179,
 180, 182, 183, 184,
 189, 191, 195, 206,
 207, 231, 249, 251,
 253, 261, 270, 273,
 281, 282, 303
 Martha 337
 Martha (Mrs.) 303, 342
 Mary 549
Grubbs, Andrew 514
Gruber, Jacob (Rev.) 536
Grubs, (?) 394
 Ardelpha Jane 394
 C. (Mrs.) 394
 Celia 394
 Celia (Mrs.) 394
 Celia M. 394
 E. C. (Mrs.) 394
 Eli H. 394
 Eli O. 394
 Eli. H. 394
 Elijah 394
 Isaac 394
 J. H. 394
 James 394
 Laurance 368
 Mary L. 394

Grubs (cont.)
 Sarah (Mrs.) 368, 394
 W. H. 394
Grunbaum, John 338
Grymes, William T. 287
Gtrayer, Jeremian 550
Gublick, Ferdinand 528
Guerin, Z. F. 338
Guest, Clemson 337
Guething, George Adam
 (Rev.) 536
Guffin, (?) 99
Guild, Mary Blakiston
 414
Guildner, Julian (Mrs.)
 312
Guitner, D. 338
 Peter 338
Guitteau, Abner L. 257
Guldner, John 226
Gulick, Johannah 74
Gulliford, Elizabeth
 (Mrs.) 272
Gun, Neil 510
Gunder, Henry 546
 Peter 546
Gundy, Jacob 178, 189,
 199, 200, 255, 259,
 278
 Joseph 178
 William 278
Gunn, James 31
Gunstead, James A. 293
Gurley, L. B. (Rev.) 37,
 545
 Leonard B. (Rev.) 536
 William (Rev.) 536
Gurnee, Ambrose Spencer
 303
 Jonah 303
 Melissa 303
 Richard 303
 Sarah (Mrs.) 303
 William 303
Gustin, Samuel 76
Gutches, Nicholas 171,
 276
 Paul M. 230
Guthridge, Jesse 514
 John 509
 John (Jdg.) 513
 John (Sr.) 514
 Moses 514
Guthrie, C. B. 300
 Columbus B. 300
Guy, Ann 219
 Hiram 219
Guyer, James (Rev.) 536
 John (Rev.) 536
Gwynn, David 25
 Frances Ann 25
 Thomas 25
 Thomas Peyton 25
Gwynne, D. 270
 E. W. 302
 Eli W. 193, 216, 222
 Evan 199
 Lavinia 245
 Thomas 164
 Thomas M. 222, 308
Gyers, A. G. 262
Gypson, John 40
Hackley, P. 518
Haddock, Abiah (Mrs.)
 331
 Enoch 176
 Hannah 176
 Samuel 331

Hanes, Hannah 348
Haniback, Lewis 510
Hank, John V. 547
Hanlin, Jas. 547
  John S. 547
Hanlon, Allen 550
Hanna, Andrew 288, 364
  Anson 547
  Benjamin 9
  Christopher 547
  James 13
  John H. 285
  Marcus A. 9
Hannah, Ann 248
Hannam, John 60
Hannaman, William 29
Hannum, (?) 419
  Aaron 460
  Abigail 420
  Caleb 460
  E. C. 420
  Elijah Cushman 419
  Eliza 419
  Ezra S. 460
  Ezra Smith 419, 460
  Harriet 419, 420
  Henry C. 420
  Henry Chappell 419
  John 460
  Mary Ann 419, 420
  Perez 415, 419, 420,
    460
  Sarah 419, 420
  Stillman B. 419
  Stillman Bullard 419
  William 460
  William H. 419, 455,
    463
  William Hamilton 487,
    521
  William Nutt 419, 420
Hanover, Joseph 297
  Nicholas 300
  Sarah 297
Hansbarger, G. 82
Hansel, Henry 546
  John 546
Hanson, (?) 410
  Ann 411
  Daniel 31, 410
  John 173, 186, 188,
    214, 216, 225, 332,
    384
Hany, Abraham 81
Haraff, Peter 553
Harbair, Jesse 509
Harbaugh, Sila 64
  Wm. 64
Harbert, Hosilla (Mrs.)
  516
  J. 516
Harbison, Thomas F. 284
Harbor, (?) 509
Harbour, Joel 511
Hard, Elisha 217
Harden, Lavina H. 234
Harder, Jos. 55
  Mary A. (Mrs.) 55
  Mary Emily 55
Hardin, Erastus 58
  Hector 364
  Mary C. C. 364
  Nathan 250
  Sophia 235
  William 364
Harding, Jesper 440
  Thomas F. 334
Hardy, Kinzie 84

Hardy (cont.)
  Leanah (Mrs.) 84
Hare, Benjamin F. 241
  Jacob 186, 222, 291,
    548
  Joseph 86
  Rebecca 86
Harey, John C. 267
Haring, Jos. 544
  Margaretha 544
  Mary (Mrs.) 544
Harkness, Edward 97
Harlan, Dale 403
  Elizabeth A. 403
  Elwood 371
  George 6
  Henry 371
  Rebecca (Mrs.) 371
Harlow, (?) 417
  Ann E. 435
  Ann Eliza 417, 434
  Anna E. 436
  Benjamin 417, 435
  Eliza 417
  Franklin A. 417
  George 417
  George W. 417, 434
  Guy 417, 435
  Jeremiah 417, 435
  Jonas 415, 417, 434,
    436
  Lafayette 417, 434,
    435
  Louisa 417, 434
  Marthaett 434
  Marthaette 417
  Mary (Mrs.) 415
  Mary Jain 417, 434
  Nancy 417, 434, 436
  Nancy (Mrs.) 417, 434
  Samuel 417, 435
  Susan 417, 435
  William 417, 434
  William A. 417
  Wm. 417, 435
Harman, John 30, 65
  Peter 335
Harmer, Daniel 30
  James (Rev.) 536
Harmon, A. 348
  Amanuel 297
  Eleanor Lee (Mrs.) 348
  Elizabeth (Mrs.) 279
  George 528
  Henry 312
  Jacob 348
  Michael 30
Harper, (?) 365
  Clayton 170
  Frances (Mrs.) 253
  George 349, 538
  Hannah A. 261
  James 97
  Jane 349
  Josiah 64
  Martha Jane 253
  Mary 75
  Robert 546
Harr, Daniel 514
Harrh, John 546
Harries, Uriah 549
Harrington, N. 341
  Stephen (Cpt.) 88
Harris, Abraham 66
  Amos 94
  Barnabas 315, 341
  Bethiah (Mrs.) 28
  Celia C. 415

Harris (cont.)
  Christena (Mrs.) 309,
    327, 484
  Enoch 9
  G. W. (Rev.) 536
  George 94, 312
  Harvey D. 247
  Hester Ann 324
  Horatio T. 316
  Isabel Clark (Mrs.)
    324
  J. C. (Rev.) 39
  James 179, 186, 206,
    218, 220, 221
  Jane 95
  Jane (Mrs.) 94
  John 48
  John (Jr.) 316
  John (Sr.) 316
  Levi 304
  Lucy 304
  Lucy (Mrs.) 51
  Mary 324
  Morrison H. 246
  Nancy (Mrs.) 303
  Nathaniel 18
  Norman 51
  Olca 543
  Phebe (Mrs.) 288
  R. 47
  Rachel (Mrs.) 356
  Sophronia (Mrs.) 290
  Thomas 312, 356
  Thomas G. 317
  Timothy (Rev.) 28
  Tmothy 93
  Valentine 293
  William 288
  Wilson J. 403
Harrison, (?) (Gen.) 426
  Abigail 503, 505
  Anna 260
  Benjamin 31, 518
  Charles 194, 206, 261,
    514
  George 66
  Isaac 49, 168, 191
  J. S. (Rev.) 46
  James 237
  Jesse 369
  Patterson 246, 248,
    264, 310
  Sally (Mrs.) 308
  W. H. (Pres.) 526
  William 206
Harruff, (?) 176
  Mary 176
  Peter 175
Harrupp, W. 172
Harshbarger, (?) 509
Hart, Amanda 337
  Amos 294
  Amy 442
  Ann 489
  Anna 173
  Ashael 173
  Ebenezer 294
  Eli B. 294
  Elihu 294
  Elizabeth 294, 295,
    415
  Elizabeth (Mrs.) 295
  G. W. 226, 266
  Gideon W. 191, 199,
    253, 266, 289, 294
  Gracy (Widow) 204
  Harriet 173
  I. B. 294

Henry (cont.)
Jacob 338, 550
John 277, 484
Lewis 338
Mary (Mrs.) 79
Mary Ann 338
Mary Ann (Mrs.) 338
Presley S. 298
Rachel 338
Samuel 338
Sarah 240
Susan 338
William 79, 203
Wm. F. 549
Hensel, George 546
Michael 546
Henson, Eli 357
Mary (Mrs.) 357
Henthorn, Mary (Mrs.) 65
Hephner, Jacob 33
Herbert, Lemuel 41
Herdman, David 186
Elias 186
Herickle, Jacob F. 85
Hermick, Daniel 514
Heron, Sarah 335
William 335
Herr, W. 238
Herrington, Clark 549
Herrman, Nicholas 305
Herron, (?) 415
Sarah 335
William 335
Hersey, Henry 239
Hershey, Elizabeth C.
236
Hersley, Henry 239
Heser, Elizabeth 239
Hesler, Elizabeth 257
Hess, Balser 160, 161,
269
Baltzer 160, 164
Bolser 269
Catherine 172, 239,
269
Daniel 161, 166, 167,
269
Elizabeth 269, 389
Isaac 172
John M. 389
Mary Eva (Mrs.) 161
Mary Eve 269
Mary Eve (Mrs.) 269
Moses 269
Narcissa 389
Polly 172
Susan K. 66
Susannah 269
William W. 342
Hestead, Abraham 546
Heth, Elizabeth Agnes
288
Henry 288
Jacqueline 288
John 288
Margaret 288
Mary Andrietta 288
Pleasur 288
William 288
William M. 288
Hetrick, Moses 550
Hetsel, John 201, 202
Phillip 204
Hetzel, Catharine 69
Hetzer, Addie S. 427
Francis Henry 427
George M. 427
John Milton 427

Hetzer (cont.)
Mentor M. 427
Phillip 415
Hevy, Samuel 240
Hewitt, J. (Rev.) 430
John (Rev.) 430
Moses 98
Hews, Elam 272
Eliza 283
Elizabeth (Mrs.) 283
Hiram 283
James 272
James D. 210
Jeremiah 170
John D. 283
John Donaldson 272
Mary 170, 214, 283
Mary (Mrs.) 272
Phebe 283
Thompson 283
Walter 215
Heydt, Warner 310
Heyl, C. 182, 210, 216,
218
Charles 343
Christian 90, 190,
204, 207, 208, 210,
218, 222, 279, 308,
342, 545, 551
Christopher 169, 201
Conrad 209, 342
Conrod 279
George W. 343
John K. 308
John Konrod 342
L. 331
Lawrence 343
Lewis 293, 343
Mary (Mrs.) 308
William E. 343
William L. 228, 238,
254
Wm. L. 259
Heyle, Christian 188
Heylin, Marcus 28
Hibbard, William (Rev.)
536
Hibben, Ann (Mrs.) 439
Ann Elizabeth 439
Ann Watson Allison 439
Elizabeth (Mrs.) 439
James 415, 439
James Allen 439
Mary (Mrs.) 415
Mary E. (Mrs.) 439
Mary Jane 439
Samuel W. 313
Thomas 415, 439
Thomas Samuel 439
William Wallis 439
Hibbs, Adin G. 219
Samuel (Sr.) 528
Wm. 550
Hickin, Henry 484
Hickman, (?) 394
D. 394
Eleanor (Mrs.) 291
Emily (Mrs.) 291
Jane 172
Joseph 164
M. A. (Mrs.) 394
Richard 291
Samuel Townsend 291
Susan 267
Tobias 291
Townsend 172
Washington 213, 282
Hickok, Allen 309, 311

Hickol, Mary 364
Hicks, Elizabeth R. 265
Francis 430
Johannes W. 430
Marcus 265
Higgins, (?) 205
Ann Maria 183, 184
Betsy 291
Charles 267, 291, 324,
553
Charlotte 324
Clark 179, 184, 205,
219, 224, 291, 312
Drusilla (Mrs.) 324
Eleanor 291
Elizabeth 324
Emily 291
George 205
George W. 179
George Washington 183
Harriet 312
Harriet (Mrs.) 291
Jane 324
John 312
Joshiah 91
Joshua 183, 184
Julian 324
Loretta 324
Maria A. 179
Mary D. 178
Richard 178, 179, 183,
205, 552, 553
Sally 291
Samuel 178, 183, 552
Samuel (Sr.) 291
Samuel C. 183, 205
Samuel Clark 205, 291,
324
Susan 291
Thelma A. 403
Thomas 179
Wealtha 179
Willey Ann 205
Willy Ann 183
Higgy, Mary 265
High, David 44
Hosea 306
Highlen, Dorothy (Mrs.)
281
Hight, Abraham 32
Highwarden, Benego 32
Hilbert, L. 331
Hildebrandt, David 340
Hildebrant, M. 549
Hildreth, Emma A. 230
Emma A. (Mrs.) 230
J. F. 299
Hilendale, Adam 244
Hiles, Thomas 305
Hill, (?) 509
Alanson 78
Caroline M. 45
Electa (Mrs.) 317
Henry 192, 558, 559
Jeremiah (Rev.) 536
Jonathon 274
Joseph 509, 514
Moses 87
Roger 20
Rowlad (Rev.) 37
Samuel (Jdg.) 513
Sarah 414, 444
Thomas 31, 518
Hillery, Luther 216
Maria 339
Hillman, Phebe Ann 356
Thomas B. 356
Hills, Elmira 234

Hills (cont.)
  Emma 234
  James H. 170
  James H. (Dr.) 34
  James Harvey 39
  Lorin 19, 20
  Maria 234
  Rachel 51
  Ralph (Dr.) 38
  Susan 335
Hillyard, Mary 530
Hillyer, P. D. 43, 44,
  47
  Picton D. 58
Hilton, John 370
  Mary (Mrs.) 370
Hinbeer, Christine
  (Mrs.) 542
  John G. 542
Hinckley, Dexter 506,
  507
  Eva 507
  Jamie 507
  Jerome 507
  Rhoda Warner 503
Hinde, Thomas S. 24, 25
Hinderer, F. Gottlieb
  303
  Gotlieb 300
Hindricsson, Beata
  Jacobine 487
Hines, Amy 64
  Sarah 71
  Valentine 73
Hinke, Wm. J. (Dr.) 496
Hinkle, Charles 196
  Elias 296
  Harriet 296
Hinkman, Jesu J. 550
Hinkson, Benjamin 545
Hinshaw, William Wade 6
Hinton, (?) 389
  John 389
  L. (Mrs.) 389
  Lavinia (Mrs.) 389
  Sarah (Mrs.) 389
  Taylor 389
  Z. T. 389
Hipple, G. 58
Hiser, Benjamin 228
Hissong, (?) 384
  David 343
  E. (Mrs.) 384
  Elizabeth (Mrs.) 384
  G. 384
  Harriete 384
Hitch, Luke 477
Hitchcock, (?) (Rev.)
  329
  Alma (Mrs.) 51
  H. L. 230, 241, 243,
    244, 254, 260, 261,
    262, 263, 265
  T. W. 51
  William Harvey 51
Hite, Adam 510
  James 258
Hitler, George 528
Hitt, Daniel (Rev.) 68
  Samuel M. 68
Hittle, John 528
Hoadly, Helen M. 54
  Laura H. (Mrs.) 54
  Thomas L. 54
Hobbs, George 168
Hobson, J. 518
  M. 518
Hock, Danial 546

Hockman, Jacob 205, 220
Hodgden, H. 50, 51
  Henry 42, 47, 48
Hodge, Hugh L. 279
Hodges, James 477
  James Y. 477
Hodgins, Henry 42
Hodgkins, Charles B. 331
  George S. 331
  Jane (Mrs.) 331
  John 331
  Richard O. 331
  Samuel P. 331
  Sarah 331
  Thomas 331
Hodgskins, Goerge S. 262
Hodson, Mark (Mrs.) 441
Hoff, John 260
  Mary 542
Hoffer, (?) (Rev.) 446
  Barbara Louisa (Mrs.)
    341
Hoffet, John 39
Hoffman, Anna 334
  Christian 31
  D. 547
  Daniel 29
  Deborah (Mrs.) 322
  Edward 322
  Elizabeth 322, 334,
    336
  Elizabeth (Mrs.) 322
  Elizabeth Ann (Mrs.)
    327
  George 31, 322, 334,
    518
  George P. 322
  Henrietta 322
  J. 518
  J. Latimer 322
  Jacob 322, 327
  Jno. 31
  John 29, 327, 518, 546
  John D. 547
  John Jacob 336
  Leah 334
  Magdalena 334
  Margaret 238
  Mary 322
  Peter 322
  Sally 322
  Samuel Owing 322
  Samuel Owings 322
  Simeon 522
  The 550
  William Alfred 322
Hoffnes, Joseph 528
Hogan, Elizabeth 528
Hoge, (?) (Rev.) 25, 48
  Asa 86
  J. (Rev.) 36
  James 175, 176, 178,
    190, 198, 199, 200,
    201, 205, 226, 227,
    230, 231, 232, 233,
    234, 238, 239, 241,
    243, 244, 248, 251,
    252, 256, 258, 260,
    261, 266, 267, 273,
    274, 281
  James (Rev.) 253, 266,
    275, 545
  Jas. (Rev.) 277
  Margaret 266
  Samuel 514
Hogg, John 9
Hoglin, Amos 62
Hoit, Jacob 177

Hoit (cont.)
  Joab 177
  Stephen 177
Holbert, Eleanor 239
Holcomb, Homer 275
Holcome, George W. 360
  Nancy (Mrs.) 360
Hold, Eliza N. 235
Holdeman, David 30
Holden, Alexander 356,
  357
  Sally (Mrs.) 356
Holder, Daniel 71
Holdsbury, Sally 94
Hole, Charles 33
Hollaway, Ann (Mrs.) 301
  John William 301
  Lucy Ann 301
  Rebecca 301
  Sarah 301
  William 301
Hollbrook, Eliza 278
Hollenbach, Alfred 539
  Amos 539
  Peter 528
  Susannah 528
  Tabitha (Mrs.) 539
Hollenback, Amos 32
Holler, Henry 522
Hollingsworth, (?) 81
  Joshua 78
Holloway, William B. 314
Holmes, (?) 413
  A. (Mrs.) 412, 413
  Alexander 24
  Altha (Mrs.) 48
  B. 518
  B. W. 53
  Caroline 329
  Caroline E. (Mrs.) 329
  Elias B. 321
  Frances (Mrs.) 53
  H. 412, 413
  Isaac 548
  Isaac (Ssr.) 412
  J. 518
  John 518
  Jonathan 163
  Jonathon 553
  Mary 85
  Nancy 67
  Pricilla (Mrs.) 412
  Susana 549
  W. D. 384
  Warren 412
  Wierman 413
Holsclaw, Nancy C.
  (Mrs.) 36
Holstead, John 528
Holt, Benjamin 340
  Bennie 402
  Charles 340, 402
  Elias 340
  George 402
  J. S. 343
  James R. 340
  Josiah 340
  Josiah S. 339
  Lydia (Mrs.) 340
  Mary 340
  Mary (Mrs.) 340
  Sarah 340
  Susan (Mrs.) 402
  Susan B. 402
  Thomas 340
  Tracy Ann 340
  Williamia Ray 340
Holton, James L. 201

Hunter (cont.)
Moses N. 342
Nancy 286
Noble 549
Orville S. 225
Return I. 225
Richard A. 445
Robert 174, 182, 422
Robertson J. 296
Robinson P. 194
Sally (Mrs.) 291
Samuel 64, 178, 193,
194, 195, 200
Sarah E. (Mrs.) 73
William 195, 203, 208,
221, 223, 286, 552
William F. 445
William Forest 415
William Forrest (Sr.)
445
Wm. 262, 286
Huntington, Elisha 305
Elisha (Dr.) 305
George 296
Hannah (Mrs.) 296
Jedidiah (Gen.) 85
Lynde L. 339
Samuel 84
Hurd, Hinman 551
Hurin, Susan 75
Hurings, Joseph 514
Hurley, Susannah 530
Hursey, John 403
Hurst, Hooper 547
Hurt, Margaret 549
Huse, Walter 170
Husted, Harvey (Rev.)
537
Huston, Alexander 440
Andrew 31
C. 182
Caleb 182
David 529, 530
Hugh 214
James 359, 415, 439,
440
John 192, 514
Paul 514
Rebecca Ann 415, 439
Hutcherson, Pathick 292
Hutchins, Ida 517
Mary (Mrs.) 517
Hutchinson, (?) 219,
435, 520
(?) (Mrs.) 417
Amaziah 180, 184, 192,
193, 209, 221, 224,
255
Amaziah (Jr.) 184, 254
Amazian 174
Emorilla 246
John 219, 282
John G. 384
Lewis 219
N. 63
Samuel 219
Silas 81
Zenas 553
Hutchison, James 86
Hutson, Andrew John
Scott 325
Charles 11
Charles V. 443
Chas. V. 443
David P. 349
E. (Mrs.) 349
Ebenezer 349
Elizabeth 349, 440

Hutson (cont.)
Elizabeth (Mrs.) 349,
440
Fannie J. 443
G. J. 394
J. 349
James 440
James Scott 440
Jane (Mrs.) 349
Jemima Ann 440
John 185, 190, 349,
440, 443
Julie E. 443
Louise G. 443
Lucile L. 440, 443
Luella 394
M. (Mrs.) 394
Mary McVey 443
N. 349
Nancy M. 349
Nathaniel 325, 349
Nathaniel Washington
440
Peter 440
V. 13, 15
Vincent 440
Washington 440
William 349
William Marcus 440
William W. 443
Hutsonpillar, Sarah 26
Hyde, Cyrus S. 260
George W. 295
John 28
Joseph 217
Hymrod, Elizabeth (Mrs.)
343
Jennie Z. 245
John 343
Hyser, John 316
Iams, Hugh 192, 202
John 59, 193
Igel, Peter 228
Igle, William 276
Igou, (?) 509
Ihrig, John 321
Ike, Paul 30
Imbody, B. 376, 377
George 376, 377
Susan (Mrs.) 376, 377
Impson, Benjamin 243
Ingalls, Elizabeth
(Mrs.) 324
Geraldine 343
Maria (Mrs.) 343
Rosalie 343
Ingals, Joseph 558, 559
Thomas 184, 188
Ingersoll, Thos. 285
Ingham, Abraham 180
Mary C. 312
Polly (Mrs.) 274
Ssally (Mrs.) 274
Ingles, Marion 415
Inglis, Elizabeth 238
Inglish, George 548
Ingman, Wm. 67
Ingraham, Mary 536
Ingram, Katherine 163
Lena 253
Rotha 163, 164
William 361
Inks, John 167, 173
Sarah 173
Inman, Esack 230
Esau 230
Innis, (?) 424
C. C. (Mrs.) 384

Innis (cont.)
Carrie (Mrs.) 384
Charles Frances 424,
425
Ethelwynne 424
Frank William 424, 425
G. S. 424
Geo. 424
George Swan 424
Gustavus S. 337
Gustavus Swan 424, 425
Henry 202, 261, 264,
308, 415, 424, 425,
552
Henry (Rev.) 425
Henry Morrill 424, 425
Homer C. 424
Homer Clarence 424
Isabella 425
Isabella C. (Mrs.) 425
Isabella Clifford 424
Isabelle P. 308
J. W. 384
James H. 384
John B. 295
Little Charley 384
Little Willie 384
Mabel Drake 424
Mildred Alice 424
Mille Merion 424
Sarah C. (Mrs.) 337
Sarah G. 425
Sarah G. (Mrs.) 424
William H. 337
Inskeep, Abram (Jr.) 163
Instine, Michael 514
Irhie, Luke 54
Iron, (?) 86
Irvin, Sarah M. (Mrs.)
419
Wm. 66
Irvine, Esther 465
Irving, E. (Mrs.) 394
Josie 394
Thom. 394
Thomas 394
Irwin, Archibald 511
Harriet (Mrs.) 164
Jacob 46
Jane 445
Jno. 31
Sally 92, 175
Sarah 41
William 30, 32
William W. 546
Wm. 164
Wm. (Dr.) 164
Iseler, Frederick 216
Isham, Asa W. 547
Isles, John 546
Itzkin, Philip 98
Jack, Hannah 75
Jackson, (?) 15
(?) (Gen.) 81, 82
Abraham 541
Allen 541
Andrew (Jr.) 70
Benjamin 219
Catherine 186
D. 47
Daniel 514
Elemuel G. 81
Eliza Amanda 437
George (Col.) 96, 97
Hana (Mrs.) 541
James 28, 29, 426
John 229
Lida 437

Jackson (cont.)
Malaban 42
Mary 28, 530
Peter (Dr.) 545
Prudence 97
Richard 549
Robert 550
William 186, 546
Jacobia, Alma Dorothys
487
Jacobs, Asher 320
Benjamin 179
Elijah 179
Harriet (Mrs.) 84
Harrison 468
Jacob (Dr.) 28
John 518
Nathan E. 311
Newman M. 342
Peggy (Mrs.) 311
Thomas 84
Jacobus, Ruliff 53
Jacoby, Jacob 41
Nicholas 36
Jaeger, Dorothy 242
Doroty 242
Pauline 293
Jager, Dorothy 242
Doroty 242
Jalkes, Richard 86
James, Aaron 76
Catherine (Mrs.) 75
David 160
Elizabeth (Mrs.) 66
George 550
Hannah 475
John 547
John H. 513
Joseph 78, 81
L. I. 434
Lester 242
Lucy A. 44
Marion 54
Oliver 439
Polly (Mrs.) 76
Robert M. 439
T. 518
Thomas 518
Thomas (Rev.) 475
William 439
William (Sr.) 439
Wm. 66
Jameson, (?) 209
A. 209
Andrew 187
Betsy (Mrs.) 303
David 161, 174, 183,
209, 272
Eliza 249
J. M. 241
James 209
James W. 303
James W. J. 303
Jane 230
Joseph 209, 212
Mary 209
Moses Bradford 59
Robert 303
Sarah 209
Sarah (Mrs.) 275
Thomas 209
William 217
Wilson 303
Wm. 550
Jamison, Andrew 276, 552
Anne (Mrs.) 349
Chas. W. 384
David 161, 276, 552

Jamison (cont.)
Eliza 276
J. A. (Mrs.) 384
J. M. 238
James M. 40
James W. 349
Jane 276
Joseph 276
Lydia (Mrs.) 325
Nancy 276
Robert 276
Robert (Sr.) 48
Sally (Mrs.) 276
Sarah (Mrs.) 276
T. A. 384
Thomas 349
William 330
Jamiston, Harriet 40
Janes, Charlotte 47
H. B. (Mrs.) 56
Maria 36
Jaquith, (?) 453
Abigail 453, 454
Abraham 453
Asor 453
Betsy 454
Collins 453
Ebenezer 453, 454
Elijah 453
Esther 453, 454
Esther (Mrs.) 453
Hannah 454
Hannah (Mrs.) 453
Ira 453
Jesse 454
John 453
Joseph 453
Levi 454
Louis W. (Maj.) 453
Luke 453
Olive 454
Risport 454
Sally 453
Samuel 454
Seth 453
Jarmor, George (?) 172
Jarvis, William B. (Jr.)
306
Javis, Evan 537
Jay, Mary 529
Jaycocks, Abraham 194
Jeams, Hugh 173
Jefferies, George 235,
244, 248, 261, 262,
283
Rachel 283
Jefferson, (?) (Mrs.)
298
Benjamin 298
Hambleton 298, 299
Thomas 243, 422
Jeffords, (?) 197
Caroline 197
John 176, 179, 197
Mary 197
Sally 179
Jeffrey, Betsey 75
Joseph Andrew 415
Jeffrie, James 93
Jeffries, George 214,
215, 216
George (Rev.) 545
Jelly, Jas. 549
Jenkins, Ada K. 389
Amon 206
Amos 186
Betseyann 40
C. 389

Jenkins (cont.)
Flossie B. 389
George 241
John 552
Kittie (Mrs.) 389
Lydia 530
Martha B. 389
Mattie A. 389
R. P. 389
Richard P. 389
S. M. (Mrs.) 389
Venis C. 389
Walter 81
Warren 288
Wretha 389
Jenkinson, Isaac 64
Jenner, Ann Maria (Mrs.)
334
John 334
Jennings, Cordelia 384
Cyrenus 81
David 87
J. 384
Joseph 384
M. (Mrs.) 384
Obediah (Rev.) 64
Rebekah (Mrs.) 384
Simeon 98
Jerman, Riley 187
Sally 187
William 187
Jessup, Saraj 36
Jester, Eli 30
Jewell, Moses 209, 222
Jewett, B. F. 320
Benjamin F. 187, 216,
278
Caleb R. 278
Catherine 278
Elam 177, 187, 278
Electa 278
Eunice 278
Harriet 278
Henry 216
Laura 278
Lucinda 278
Lydia 278
Marinda 278
Moses 182
Othneil 278
Jiams, Hugh 281
Jinkins, John 35
Martin 40
Jinks, A. (Rev.) 39, 50
Ahab (Rev.) 35, 46,
47, 51
William 50
Jobs, James 30
John, Catherine 530
Ellis 269
Howard D. 435
Mar. Ann 257
Peter 259
Wm. 175
Johnes, F. C. 36
Nancy D. 36
Johns, (?) (Rev.) 36
Levi 33
Johnson, (?) 349, 366,
389, 509, 510
A. D. 394
A. M. (Mrs.) 389
Abbie M. 403
Abm. 349
Abram 13
Achsa (Mrs.) 284
Andrew 384
Ard 483

Kinnaird, David 553
  George David 320
Kinnear, Andrew (Rev.)
    40
  David 518
  Francis 29
  Margaret 526
  Sam'l 553
  Samuel 233, 234, 242,
    265, 326, 334
Kinner, Hanner 238
Kinney, Daniell 444
  Jacob 31
  James 31, 528
  John 444
  Leah 31
  Sarah 501
Kinnon, Erastus 511
Kinsell, D. R. 341
Kinsely, Abraham 98
  Jacob 98
Kinsinger, George 515
  Mary 515
  Rebecca (Mrs.) 515
Kinsley, Abraham 98
  Jacob 98
Kintner, George 499
  Mary Magdalene 499
Kintz, George 552
Kinzer, Geo. 549
Kious, (?) 219, 220
  Daniel 212
  John 190, 214, 219,
    220
  John H. 219, 552
  Maria 220
  Solomon 201, 220
  Zeniah 219
Kirby, Anna 245
  M. H. (Col.) 36
  Moses H. 225
  Moses H. (Sr.) 296
  Sarah 415, 439
Kirk, Ellen (Mrs.) 540
  George 540
  James 171
  Margaret 356
Kirker, (?) 94
  James 92
Kirkland, William 87
Kirkpatrick, Eliza
    (Mrs.) 334, 337
  Joseph (Sr.) 27
  Maria 26
  Martin 334, 337
  Moses 27
  Samuel 530
  Thomas 25
  Ts. R. 549
  William 27
Kirkwood, Anna 524
  Mary (Mrs.) 524
  Samuel 524
  Samuel J. 324
Kirts, George W. 403
  Julia A. 403
Kisar, Frank B. 394
  M. 394
Kisner, Henry 30
Kissel, Martin 240
Kissell, Elizabeth 239
Kissinger, Andrew 233
  John 224, 552, 553
  Margratta 549
Kisson, Alice 403
Kistler, Henry 300
Kite, (?) 509
  Leah (Mrs.) 277

Kitsmiller, John 254,
    299
  Thomas 254
Kittsmiller, Catherine
    (Mrs.) 313
  Christena 308
  Elizabeth 308
  Emanuel 313
  John 308
  Jonathan 308
  Mary 308
  Mary (Mrs.) 308
  William 313
Kitzmiller, Blanche 403
  E. (Mrs.) 403
  F. K. (Mrs.) 403
  R. Vance 403
  William 403
  Wm. 403
Kizer, Joseph 510
Klein, Catherine 258
  Frederick 60
  John S. 60
  Peter 334
  S. S. (Rev.) 41, 44,
    45, 46
  Samuel S. (Rev.) 40
Klick, Ephriam 403
  Eveline 403
Kline, C. 369
  C. (Mrs.) 369
  Joshua 39
  Olive E. 369
Klopp, W. E. (Mrs.) 529
Knadalon, Joseph 228
Knadler, Peter 515
Knap, Elisha 90
Knapp, Henry Arnold 332
  Sarah L. (Mrs.) 332
Knedel, Mary A. 235
Knepler, Fred 339
Knight, Anna M. (Mrs.)
    380
  Benjamin S. (Cpt.) 42
  Jemima 240
  John H. 380
Knobs, William 226
Knode, Elizabeth 164
  Russell 403
Knoderer, Charles 213,
    298, 551
  Charles (Jr.) 213
  Frederick C. 218
  Frederick W. 218
Knodoean, Joseph 228
Knoll, Sarah 446
Knop, David 27
Knouff, John 86
  Mary Ann 86
Knowles, Anna 475
  Elizabeth (Mrs.) 475
  John W. 550
  Samuel 475
Knowls, Ephriam 31
Knox, (?) 510
  Catherine 76
  John 57, 338
  Martha 75
  William 456, 457
Koch, George 254
  Magdalina 228
Kockin, James 275
Koenig, Daniel 304
Kohn, Amanda Jane 423
  George 559
Kohr, George 558
Kolbenstaetter, Lena
    (Mrs.) 314

Kolp, Balzer 549
Konitzer, C. F. 229
Kooken, James 176, 179,
    180, 215, 216, 275
  James (Cpt.) 47
Koons, Frederick W. 46
  Matilda 242
Koontz, John 550
Kooser, (?) 200, 222
  Conrad 222
  Daniel 179, 200, 551
  Elizabeth 179, 200,
    222
  Frederick 222
  Frederick L. 200
  Gottileb 200
  Gottilieb 222
  John 200
  Margaret 200
  Sarah 200
Korell, Margareta (Mrs.)
    539
  William 539
Korn, Anna (Mrs.) 541
Kraft, B. (Mrs.) 384
  C. 384
  Chas. M. 384
  Eliza 460
Krall, Geo. W. 384
  J. 384
  Jacob 384
  Jane 384
  M. (Mrs.) 384
  Mary (Mrs.) 384
  Priscilla 384
Kramer, Anthony 225
  David 20
  Henry 242
  Ludwig 225
  Mary Ann 240
  William 320
  Zachariah 18
Krause, George 551
Krauss, George 307
Krayer, Sophia 256
Kreamer, Joseph 228
Kreasey, John 547
Krell, George 310
Krepp, John 548
Kres, Catherine 301
Krider, Walter 390
Kronenbitter, J. 230,
    233, 235, 236, 238,
    239, 242, 244, 247,
    248, 252, 263, 264
Krouse, Daniel 171, 182
  Hannah 171
  Lydia 171
  Mary 171
  Michael 171
  Nancy 171
Krug, George 234
Krum, Ellen (Mrs.) 541
  George 541
Krumm, George C. 264
Kuehlwein, George L. 228
Kuenel, John 301
Kugler, Jacob 529
Kuhlmann, J. H. (Rev.)
    448
Kuhn, George 558, 559
Kulp, Margaret 257
Kunkle, Jacob 180
Kunkleman, Julia 58
Kuntz, Henry 86
Kurts, Almira (Mrs.) 350
  Henrey 350
Kuth, Daniel 518

Kuth (cont.)
    Price 33
Kuts, George 171
    James 171
    Patience (Mrs.) 171
Kuykendale, Catherine
    (Mrs.) 272
Kyer, Andrew 437
    William 437
    William A. 437
La Croy, John 483
Labaree, (?) (Rev.) 42
    Jos. (Rev.) 53
    Joseph (Rev.) 49, 57,
        58
Lacey, Jno. 31
Lachenmeur, Gottlieb 259
Lacy, John 170
    Zadock B. 324
Ladd, Benjamin W. 64
    Charles H. 59
    John W. 166, 180, 198,
        205, 221, 246, 280,
        285
    Joseph 31, 518
Laferty, Mary (Mrs.) 516
    Samuel 516
Lafferty, John 510, 514
Laghenmur, Gottlieb 259
Lain, William 254
Lair, Alva A. 438
Laird, John 77
Lake, (?) 191
    Lewis 311
    Thomas 191
    William 191
Lakin, Ann Elizabeth 427
    Ann M. 427
    Benj. 427
    Benjamin 249
    Daniel 427
    Daniel Clinton 427
    Elizabeth 427
    Emiline 427
    George Washington 427
    J. Q. 267
    J. Q. (Rev.) 267
    James S. (Mrs.) 427
    Jemima 427
    John 222
    John Scheckel 427
    Lucretia 427
    Maggie E. 427
    Margaret Elizabeth 427
    Milton Dwight 427
    Rebecca 427
    Ruth 427
    Samuel Wilson 427
    Sarah 427
    Serena 427
    Washington 260, 296,
        427
Laleher, John 547
Lalley, Esther Ann 364
    Mary L. (Mrs.) 364
    William 364
Lamar, Elizabeth 34
Lamb, Cynthia 52
    Elijah 547
    Emily 247
    Henry (Maj.) 37
    Mary Ann 342
    Mary Ann (Mrs.) 342
    Reuben 160
    Reuben (Dr.) 52, 160
    Reuben A. 46
Lamber, John H. (Dr.) 91
Lamberson, John S. 264

Lambert, Aaron 530
    Ann (Widow) 179
    Barnabas 162, 269
    Catherine 343
    David 164, 165, 167,
        270
    Isaac 167, 270
    John 343
    John H. 179
    John S. 264
    Mary (Mrs.) 270
    Polly 165, 167
    Rebecca 167, 270
Lamon, Isaac 233
Lamphear, Wesley (Rev.)
    33
Lampman, Emma 540
    Grove 540
    Hannah (Mrs.) 540
Lampson, Harriet 245
    John 34
    Nathan 199
    Sarah (Mrs.) 199
    William 551
    William K. 199
Lamson, (?) 221
    Harriet 245
    James 221
    Nathan 329
    William K. 221
Lander, J. S. (Dr.) 545
    William 85, 93
Landes, (?) 203
    David 281
    Elizabeth 203
    Lydia 416, 433, 486
    Matin 546
    Nancy (Mrs.) 300
    Rudolph 162
    Samuel 162, 164, 165,
        181, 203
Landford, Zelotes 369
Landis, Benjamin 224
    John 224
Landon, Charlotte S.
    (Mrs.) 403
    Chauncey P. (Dr.) 452
    Edward 403
    Elizabeth 42
    Harriet (Mrs.) 323
    John D. 403
    Mark 403
    Mary 410
    Nancy 285
    Noble 50, 553
Landrum, Elzey 547
Landsdale, (?) 509
Lane, (?) 447
    Agnes 447
    Barbara 356
    Charlotte (Mrs.) 356
    Edwin 447
    Eliza C. 427
    Elizabeth 178
    Francis 447
    Franklin 447
    Fraulin 447
    Gelland (?) H. 356
    George 180, 447
    George W. 447
    Harriet Newell 447
    Helen (Mrs.) 447
    Henry 271
    J. 178
    J. B. 447
    James 180
    John 180, 182, 242
    Joseph 356

Lane (cont.)
    Lemuel 178
    Mary Jane (Mrs.) 339
    Milton 447
    Nathaniel Batchelder
        447
    Peter 168, 271
    Polly (Mrs.) 447
    Sarah 447
    Sarah (Mrs.) 447
    T. B. 447
    Thomas B. 447
    Thomas Willson 447
    William 179, 180
Lanfare, Sally 65
Lanford, Clara M. 385
    Luther 385
    Naoma 385
Lang, Andrew 304
    C. (Mrs.) 538
    Frank 538
    George 182, 542
    J. 538
    John 176, 198
    John M. 247
    K. (Mrs.) 538
    N. E. 538
    Rosa 542
    Rosa (Mrs.) 542
    T. B. 365, 366, 388
    Thelma Blair 367, 508,
        512, 515, 516, 545,
        559
    W. 538
Langham, A. L. 518
    Angus L. 24, 31
    Elias 31
    Elizabeth 342
    Robert 343, 501
    Sarah 501
    Sarah Ann 343
    William 343
    Wm. 501
Langhear, Isaac N. 252
Langheinrich, J. 385
    John F. 385
    K. (Mrs.) 385
Langhorn, Elias 518
    John L. 29
Langhrey, Edward 356
    Elizabeth (Mrs.) 356
    John 356
Langmeister, Henry 226
Langworthy, Albert 307
    James 325
    O. P. 307
Lankford, James 415
    William Haley 415
Lanning, (?) 203
    John 203
    Joseph 203
Lanpton, (?) 263
    Serepta 263
Lansdale, Isaac 514
Lape, John 30
Lapping, Wm. 163, 164
Largent, (?) 509, 510
    Daniel 514
    John 514
    Nelson 514
    Randle 514
    William 514
Larick, Jacob 29
Larimore, David 549
    Robert 304
Larkin, David 31
Larrick, (?) 524
    J. 522

Larrick (cont.)
Jacob 524
Wesley 524, 525
Larue, Andrew (Jr.) 390
Mary J. 390
Larvin, John 31
Lary, Julian 390
Wm. 548
Lash, (?) 499
Eva (Mrs.) 496
Isaac 497, 499
Lashmut, Jane D. (Mrs.)
90
Latham, Allen 299, 300
Ann (Mrs.) 358
Arthur 299
Bela 217, 219, 299,
545
David 249, 358
Edward H. 299
Frank B. 299
James H. 299
Keziah 307
Keziah (Mrs.) 291
Mary 307
Mary C. 299
Milton S. 299
Rosanna (Mrs.) 299
Susan 307
William 291, 307
William A. 299
William H. 299
Lathem, Bela 179, 187,
195, 201
Lathrop, M. D. 325
M. D. (Dr.) 77
Latimer, (?) 434
Allas 434
Daniel Long 434
David B. 434
Eunice 414
George W. 434
Harris 434
L. S. 434
Lydia B. 434
Lyndes L. 255
Mary A. 238
Matilda J. 434
Mercy A. 238
Nancy 434
Nancy (Mrs.) 434
Nathan 434
Sally 434
Sarah T. G. 434
Stephen 434
Stephen F. 434
Thomas 434
Thomas S. 434
William P. 434
Latmore, Lynd L. 192
Peter 207
Latour, (?) 549
Latta, Elizabeth (Mrs.)
274
James 18
John 320
Martha 63
Thos. 63
Lattimer, Daniel D. 295
Lucy 255
Lauderbach, John 548
Laug, John 217
Laughlin, (?) 93
A. M. 93
Laughrey, John 168
Laughry, John 179
Launsby, Frederick 213
Lavely, Good 518

Lawrence, Benjamin 236
Elizabeth 528
Isaac 188
James 528
Maragaret 37
Sarah 93
Laws, James 236, 251
John 457
Lawson, David 222, 339
Eliza (Mrs.) 339
Eliza A. (Mrs.) 340
Jacob G. 339
Jeremiah 26
John P. 198, 281
Losana 222
Mariah (Mrs.) 281
Mathilda (Mrs.) 26
Peter 198, 201, 213,
222
Peter P. 281
Samuel 281
Thomas 510
Lawyer, John 214
Layman, Maria (Mrs.) 257
N. J. 403
Layton, Arthur 529
David 222
Joseph 529
Lazell, Jeanette 246
John A. (Jdg.) 246
LePert, George 56
William 57
Leach, Joanna 313
Lewis 547
Thompson 547
Thos. W. 547
Valentine 528
William 324
Leachman, C. 385
Chapman 385
Isaac G. 385
R. (Mrs.) 385
Lead, Valentine 30
Leaf, Jacob 321
John T. 321
Leroy 321
Leak, Charlotte 48
Leaman, Frederick 311
Leamon, Isaac 233
Learn, Betsy 385
Betsy J. 350
J. 385
Jeff 11
Jefferson 350, 385
M. (Mrs.) 385
Maria (Mrs.) 350, 385
Matilda 385
Velina 350, 385
Learned, Clarinda 50
Leas, Jacob 548
John 548
Leasure, Agnes 384
E. B. 384
John 436
Rachel (Mrs.) 384
Leathers, Jacob 71
Mary 66
Samuel 71
Leavell, John 29
John (Maj.) 31
Leavens, John 95
Leazenbey, Joshua 528
Leby, David 26
Mary 26
Leckrone, E. (Mrs.) 385
J. 385
Wm. D. L. 385
Lee, (?) 217, 346, 520

Lee (cont.)
Asa 217
Benjamin 514
Charles B. 217
George A. 217, 332
James 179, 266
Jeremiah 37
John 244, 350
Jonathan 168, 179, 271
Joseph 179
Margaret 231
Margret 257
Nancy 231
Newton D. 217
Oren A. 217
Rhoda 294
Roda 340
Rosannah 350
Sally 217
Sarah (Mrs.) 168, 271,
350
Sarah Jane 252
Solomon 276
Susannah 350
T. 255
Thomas 64, 350
Thomas (Sr.) 350
Timothy 217, 223, 294,
303
Wm. 549
Leech, Joseph 517
Leef, Jacob 66
Leezer, Dan'l 550
Lef, Samuel 86
Lefever, Samuel 66
Legg, Elijah 314
Elizabeth 314
Fielding 314
James 314
John 314
Lucinda 314
Mary 314
Rebecca (Mrs.) 322
Susannah 314
Thomas 215, 314
Lehew, Ann 85
Lehman, John K. 240
William F. 226, 258
Wm. F. 248, 263
Lehmann, (?) 224
Conrad 339
Gabriel 224
Herrman 224
William F. 228, 235,
239, 240, 241, 242,
248, 250, 253, 255,
257, 258, 259
Wm. F. 259
Leiby, Joseph 206, 208
Leichtenecher, Frederica
281
Gottlieb 281
Leidy, Joseph 216
Leighnecker, Gottlieb
200
Leightenecher, Goetleib
188
Leightnecker, G. 199,
201
Gottlieb 199, 205
Gottlieb 192
Leiser, Joseph 40
Leisler, Elizabeth
(Mrs.) 338
John G. 338
Leist, (?) (Rev.) 30
Andrew (Sr.) 528
John W. 29

621

Mathew (cont.)
Daisy D. 395
J. W. 395
M. E. (Mrs.) 395
N. M. 395
Nathaniel M. 395
Nellie 395
Susana (Mrs.) 395
Mathews, (?) (Dr.) 13
F. J. 328
Henry, 239, 271
Increase 99
J. 355
John 99
M. J. (Mrs.) 355
Matthew 195
Rachel 355
Mathias, Henry 528
John 43
Matters, Joanna 238
Matthews, Altha 341
Bathsheba 174
Cordelia 341
Dorrance 290
Ellin 290
Errin 290
F. J. 307, 322, 328
FitzJames 290
Fritz James 290
George 341
H. 239
Henry 246
Henry (Rev.) 68, 70
Isabella Innis (Mrs.) 425
John 341
Lucy (Mrs.) 290
M. 208, 210, 222, 290
Margaret Jane 341
Mary Ann 341
Mathew 173, 174, 187, 210, 211, 213
Matthew 194, 197, 199, 202, 203, 221, 222, 290
Newton S. (Dr.) 424
Raymond Innis 424
William 341
Mattison, (?) 216
Mary 216
William 216
Mattix, Abigail 322
Diana 322
Heaty 322
Hety 322
Nancy 322
Nancy (Mrs.) 322
Sally 322
Thomas 322
Mattocks, Sarah 554
Thomas 554
Mattoon, Calvin 333
Caroline (Mrs.) 333
Thankful 333
Willis 333, 334
Mattox, Jefs 555
Nancy 554
Mauk, Joseph 27
Mauker, George 65
Maurer, Nicholas 323
Maxey, Bennet 529
Maxfield, Ann M. 351
C. (Mrs.) 351
J. 351
James 351
Maxwell, A. (Mrs.) 351
Charles 549
Eliza (Mrs.) 320

Maxwell (cont.)
Emmy 63
James 412
John 351
Margaret (Mrs.) 412
Margaret A. 351
Rob't (Sr.) 63
Robert 412
W. 351
William 351, 557
William H. 304
May, Jeremiah 203
Joseph 292
Katherine 247
Mayer, Abraham 546
Melcher 528
Mayers, Daniel 547
Mayley, Mason 261
Maynard, (?) 224
Achsa 284
Apollus 284
E. (Mrs.) 89
Eber P. 221, 284
Elnathan 224
Harriet 284
Horace 224
J. P. 54
Jane 273
Jane (Mrs.) 163
Jefferson T. 224
Lovisa 284
Lucy 284
Moses 163, 164, 170, 175, 221, 284, 285
Moses (Jr.) 221
Samuel 273
Stephen 162, 163, 165, 169, 175, 176, 177, 178, 180, 214, 224, 245, 252, 274
Stephen (Dr.) 89
Stephen (Jr.) 175, 180
Thankful E. 274
William W. 224
Mays, Lewis 522
Maze, Lovina (Mrs.) 331
Mc, Fanny 320
McAdams, (?) 510
Byron 390
Frank 390
John 509, 514
Lou 390
Robert 390
Samuel 390
Samuel (Sr.) 390
Winnie T. 390
McAfee, Archibald 390
Elnora M. 390
Hannah (Mrs.) 390
Joseph 390
Joseph S. 390
Scott A. 390
Tephanes (Mrs.) 390
McAffee, (?) 217
Dinah 217
Joseph 217
Thomas B. 217
William 217
McAfferty, (?) 193
Almire 193
Hiram 193
James 193
Nancy 193
Thomas 193
McAllister, John 528
McAlpin, (?) 307
McArthur, Columbus 240
Duncan 512

McArthur (cont.)
J. C. (Rev.) 12
Wesley 73
McBeth, (?) 510
Alexander 530
Alexander (Jdg.) 513
McBratney, Robert 217
McBride, A. L. 361
Hugh Calvin 241
John Henry 361
Lea (?) (Mrs.) 361
Susan (Mrs.) 361
McBurney, Guyony 290
James 559
Sally Ann 290
McCabe, (?) (Rev.) 58
Armstrong 529
Mary Elizth 419
McCafferty, John 220
Julia (Mrs.) 386
Rachel 187
T. 386
T. F. 386
Thomas 187, 350
McCain, Sarah 458
McCall, Elizabeth 378
M. B. (Mrs.) 378
Mary B. (Mrs.) 378
Philemons B. 378
T. 378
Thomas 378
McCamish, Thomas 456
McCan, John 219
McCandish, Elizabeth 342
Jane 342
Mary Ann 342
Nancy 342
Robert 342
Sarah 342
Smith 342
McCanley, (?) 68
McCann, Ann 249
McCarlesy, W. 547
McCarroll, Rebecca 86
McCarter, Daniel 262
McCarthy, John 222
McCartney, Mary L. 33
Wm. D. (Rev.) 33
McCarty, Hannah 80
John 215
Samuel 554
William H. 305
McCaskey, A. G. 550
McCaulay, Annie (Mrs.) 369
Sam 369
McCauley, Francis G. 307
Maria (Mrs.) 307
Thomas 189
McCausland, Thomas 59
McCawley, Lucinda 267
McCibben, Mary 417
Miriam 419
McClain, James 510
John 31
Sarah 404
McClane, John 252
McClara, Sarah 236
McClary, Pheby 236
Sarah J. 236
McClean, John 31
McCleary, John 73
Peter 549
McCleery, (?) 378
Alice 73
Carpenter 72
James 73
Nancy (Mrs.) 378

McMaster (cont.)
James 548
Jean 459
Margaret 281
Matilda A. 421
Matilda Ann 421
Olive 421, 422
Robert 421, 422
Robert G. 50
Washington 421
McMasters, Hugh 195, 209
McMeechan, William 518
McMeechen, William 31
McMillan, Belle 361
Hepsah Trumbo 404
John 361
John P. 63
Victoria 361
McMillen, (?) 509
David 178
Elizabeth 313
George 313
Hugh 558, 559
J. F. 252
Margaret M. 313
Nancy (Mrs.) 313
Susan 313
Thos. 549
William L. 313
McMullen, Annette 428
Enos 428
McMullin, John 203, 204
McMuntrie, Hugh 292
John 292
McNary, J. W. (Rev.) 12
Sam'l 59
McNeal, William H. H.
253
McNeel, Gabriel 547
McNemar, R. R. 512
McNinch, Aarchibald 559
Archibald 558
McNutt, James 164
John 164
Robert 164
Samuel 164
McOwen, Rachel 234
McPherson, Adam Clark
444
Addeline M. 444
Adeline May 444
Arthur E. 444
Charles L. 444
Cora A. 444
Elizabeth A. 444
Eva Edell 444
George E. 444
Joseph 415
Joseph A. 444
Odessa M. 444
William F. 444
McQuality, James 547
McRoberts, D. J. 366
M. I. (Mrs.) 366
Martha I. (Mrs.) 366
Mary Eliza 366
William 366
Wm. 366
McSherry, Reuben 514
McSowell, A. J. 215
McVey, Fannie Hutson 443
McVickar, Elizabeth 351
William 351
McWhirk, George 334
McWilliams, Eliza 327
John 327
Miriam 327
Robert 327

McWilliams (cont.)
Sally 50
Sarah 327
William 327
MeLene, Jeremiah 190
Meacham, Milo 50
Riley 265
Mead, A. J. 351
Asenith 86
Elizabeth 175
George 175
Hezekiah 175
J. 351
J. (Mrs.) 351
J. C. (Mrs.) 351
Josephine D. 443
Julia 175
Linus 222
Louesa A. 351
Louisa 222
Margaret 351
Nash 175
Samuel (Jr.) 385
William 351
Meagher, James 233
James (Rev.) 314, 327,
334
Meally, James (Maj.) 60
Means, Elizabeth (Mrs.)
63
James 63
Joseph 415
Robert 518
Thomas 98
Meason, A. (Mrs.) 378
Anna (Mrs.) 378
Anna M. 378
Elijah 68, 379
Elijah E. 378
Elizabeth (Mrs.) 378
George W. 379
Hiram C. 379
Isaac 68, 379
Isaac J. 378
Isaac W. 379
J. 378
Jeremiah C. 379
John 378
Rachel (Mrs.) 379
Medbury, Josiah 12
Nathaniel 219, 545
Medley, (?) 518
Meek, Mary 45
Meeker, Aaron 72, 212
Elisha 72
Forrest 57
Geo. W. 254
George W. 264
Jacob 72
Sally 290
Meeks, Jacob 547
Mees, Conrad 258
K. 226, 228, 229, 230,
234, 235, 236, 240,
241, 242, 244, 246,
247, 248, 254, 255,
256, 257, 258, 259,
321
Konrad 228, 247, 257,
259, 305, 310
Meese, K. 243
Meets, Adam 30
Megown, Ann 422
Deborah 422
Hannah 422
Jane 422
John 422
Martha 422

Megown (cont.)
Mary 422
Olive 422
Robert 422
Sarah 422
Mehling, Franz 541
John 541
Katherina (Mrs.) 541
Meholm, James 550
Mehring, Ann Margaret
343
Catherine (Mrs.) 343
George 343
John Conrad 343
Mary Elizabeth 343
Melhorn, Daniel 248
Mellen, Thos. 549
Melsek, John 280
Melsel, Phillip 280
Memen, E. B. 546
Mench, Wesley R. 265
Menday, (?) 415, 426
George 426
Mendenhall, J. Z. 47
Joel 46
Joel Z. 48, 52
John H. 57
Menear, Benjamin F. 465
Benjamin Franklin 465
Menely, Amos 283
Hannah 188
Jesse 188, 558, 559
Joseph S. B. 188
Meniken, John 473
Joshua 473
Menlong, Peter 546
Mercer, John 86
Levi M. 547
Lydia 86
Nottingham 547
Merchant, Rachel (Mrs.)
67
Thomas 86
Merion, Elijah 179, 337
Emily 329
Eveline 329
George 329, 337
Mille 424
N. 321, 337
Nathaniel 329, 335,
337, 415
Sally (Mrs.) 329
Sally Ann 329
Sarah (Mrs.) 329
William 195, 197, 329
Wm. 415
Merrian, Wm. 164
Merrill, Cynthia 414
F. F. 341
Jedediah 414
Lucinda M. (Mrs.) 310
Mary Eliza 310
Nicholas 361
Pamela 310
Rebecca (Mrs.) 361
T. R. 341
Merrion, William 188
Wm. 167
Merryfield, Emanuel 511
James 511
Merryman, Caleb 474
John 473
Merwin, Elijah B. 84
Maria 85
Meser, Chriolian 546
Messenger, Adonijah 91,
167
Elmyra (Mrs.) 36

Messenger (cont.)
Madison 40
Moses 284
Zephaniah 167
Zepheniah 91
Messer, Jacob 93
Messmore, Robert C. 184
Metcalf, Alvira 480
Charles A. 478, 480
Charles A. (Jr.) 480
Clarence A. 479
Clark 479
Eliza A. 478, 479
Emily M. 478, 479
Frank D. 478, 480
George 479
George P. 478, 480
Helen R. 480
Mary E. 479
Mary J. 478, 480
Milo R. 478
Orrin G. 479
Ruth 480
Warren 477, 478, 479,
480
William Henry 478, 479
Metter, Mary Ann (Mrs.)
332
Richard 332
Metters, Mary Ann (Mrs.)
332
Richard 332
Metz, George 327
John Valentine 327
Maria Anna 327
Mary 42
Metzner, Eliza 385
Geo. 385
Meyers, Caroline 385
Electa J. 404
Electta 404
Harmon 404
John 219, 385
John Urvin 404
Lewis W. 404
Marvin D. 404
Nancy (Mrs.) 385
Michael, Gotlieb 551,
553
Michel, Charles 214
Thomas 214
Michell, Matthew 163
Michey, Daniel 163
Elizabeth 163
Thomas 163
Mickey, Jane 207
Thomas 207
Zephaniah 355
Mickles, Christian 29
Middlesworth, Wm. 66
Middleton, (?) 390
A. (Mrs.) 390
A. H. 390
Arthur 390
C. O. 390
Charles O. 390
Edward 390
Elizabeth (Mrs.) 390
Enola J. 390
Estaville (Mrs.) 390
Harry P. 390
John 242, 390, 553
John (Jr.) 390
Maggie 390
Maggie (Mrs.) 390
Mary Jane 390
Milton G. 390
Minnie 391

Middleton (cont.)
Rachel (Mrs.) 99
S. R. (Mrs.) 391
Sarah R. 391
Somerset 32
Staten 391
Thaddeus Andrews 99
Thomas 509
W. W. 391
William 391
Wm. 390
Middlleton, Lorena E.
391
Miers, Henry 332
Miesse, George J. 404
Harriett E. 404
Julia A. 404
Milburn, Belle 428
Harriet (Mrs.) 310
Harriet O. 369
John 369
Miles, Anna (Mrs.) 540
Giddion 540
Nancy (Mrs.) 296
Polly 25
Solomon S. (Rev.) 30
Thomas Y. 540
Milhollen, Jonathan 529,
530
Milhouse, William 86
Miligan, John 442
Milikan, William 49
Mill, Lewis 216
Millar, (?) (Mrs.) 63
James 63
Mille, Lewis 300
Millege, John 84
Millen, Any 549
Miller, (?) 221, 415,
426, 468, 475, 509
A. S. 369
Abraham 65, 411
Adam 44, 246, 514
Alex. 547
Alice 385
Amanda 404, 539
Amanda (Mrs.) 539
Andrew 183
Anna 47
Anthony 404
Belle Wooden 468
Betsy 519
Blanchey (Mrs.) 515
Cadis 369
Caroline 439
Carrie 439
Catharine (Mrs.) 411
Catherine 426, 519
Catherine (Mrs.) 313,
321
Charles 98
Charles C. 37
Charles Dickeson 467
Charles Robert 468
Daniel 215, 411, 426,
551
Daniel P. 207
David 205, 426
Diana 307, 319
E. (Mrs.) 369
Edward W. 467
Elia 266
Elizabeth 361, 426,
553
Elizabeth (Mrs.) 411
Emma B. 426
Emma G. 404
Francis J. 404

Miller (cont.)
Franklin Bishop 468
Frederick 334
George 48, 78, 426
Granville 395
H. E. 395
Hannah (Mrs.) 272
Harriet P. (Mrs.) 395
Harrison G. 404
Harvey 13
Harvey E. 318
Henrietta Augusta 468
Henry 219, 426, 558,
559
Henry (Mrs.) 539
Henry Walter 318
Hugh 31
I. 369
Isaac 29, 276
J. 274
J. B. 411
J. G. 227, 239, 252,
267
J. H. 411
Jacob 69, 207, 276,
426
James 27, 351, 547
James B. 244
Jane 550
Janette (Mrs.) 35
Jesse 207, 214
Joash 519
Johann W. 311
John 11, 13, 69, 250,
262, 426, 515, 517,
528, 549, 553
John Conrad 69
John G. 35, 48, 221,
241, 247, 251, 259,
545
John H. 385
John N. 404
John S. 211
John W. 253, 254
Jonathan 344
Jos. 175, 176
Joseph 91, 176, 178,
179, 519
Josiah 558, 559
Joush 528
Justice 173
Kitty 93
Kunegunda (Mrs.) 325
L. (Mrs.) 369
Laura Adelia 468
Leah Jane 395
M. 411
M. M. (Mrs.) 411
Margaret 358
Margaret (Mrs.) 318,
385, 395
Mariah S. 227
Martha 230
Marthal 550
Martin Philip 471
Mary 50, 404, 519, 528
Mary A. (Mrs.) 411
Mary Ann 471
Mary Eliza 467
Mary Frances 233
Mary L. 395
Mary M. 395
Mathew 285
Matthew 183, 221
Milla Jane (Mrs.) 295
Moses 426
N. M. (Dr.) 545
Nancy 451, 519

627

Moslander (cont.)
    484
    Peter 484
Mosley, (?) 544
    Catherine 544
Moss, Margaret (Mrs.) 67
    Samuel 473
Mosshart, (?) 469
Mossman, Huldah 228
Motlinger, Elizabeth
    (Mrs.) 33
    George 33
Mott, Elijah 306
Motz, Jacob 370
Moulton, Samuel (Dr.) 30
Mount, (?) (Widow) 83
Mouser, (?) 509
    David 244
Mower, Isabelle 93
Mowry, Peter 528
Moyer, Henry 385
Mubury, Marie A. (Mrs.)
    541
Muchlender, Margaret
    Barbara (Mrs.) 330
Muenscher, Joseph (Rev.)
    49
Mugg, Wm. 548
Muhlenberg, Francis S.
    (Col.) 69
    Peter 24
Muhlenburg, Peter 528
Muir, Francis 31
Mulford, Lewis 47
Mullen, Michael 268
Muller, Elan 519
    Joas 519
    Magdalena 501
    Michael 519
Mulliken, George Fayette
    32
Mulluvim, Maria
    Catharine 519
Mulvany, Catharine A. 86
    P. 86
Mum, David 549
Mumaugh, B. (Mrs.) 412
    C. 412
    Mary R. 412
    Sarah (Mrs.) 413
    William (Sr.) 413
Munford, John D. 545
Munger, Elizabeth 75,
    202
    Timothy 202
Munn, Milton H. 343
Munro, Josiah 93
Munsell, Luke 285
Munson, Jeremiah (Maj.)
    93
    Jesse 92
    Mary 34
Murch, Agnes 351
    C. 351
    Chauncey 351
    E. (Mrs.) 351
    Elizabeth (Mrs.) 351
    Robert L. 251
    Thomas Law 351
Murdick, Daniel (Jr.) 90
    Elizabeth (Mrs.) 90
Murdock, James 94, 549
Mure, Francis 518
Murey, James 412
    M. (Mrs.) 412
    T. 412
Murphy, (?) 495
    Bridget 228

Murphy (cont.)
    James 495
    John 41, 259
    Mary 97
    Nicholas 94, 97
    William 24
Murray, Caroline 243
    Eliza 259
    Eliza A. 340
    George 528
    Hannah 340
    Joseph 215
    Julianna Doddridge 64
    Mary 340
    Mary M. 340
    Nichlas (Cpt.) 64
    Samuel H. 340
    William Israel 340
    Wm. 549
Murrey, Loyd 376
Murrill, (?) (Rev.) 33
Muskemore, James 31
Mustard, Elizabeth 324
    Lydia 324
    Samuel 324
Mustin, Luman 548
Mutchler, Valentine 30
Mutter, Josephine (Mrs.)
    538
Myer, Christian 343
    Jacob M. 404
    Rilla (Mrs.) 404
Myers, (?) 59
    (?) (Mrs.) 28
    Christian 219, 300
    Ebenezer 26
    Elizabeth 69
    Elizabeth Hales 556
    Elizabeth Hook 361
    George 68, 179
    Henry M. 252
    Isaac 514
    Jacob 227, 547
    John 176, 179
    Joseph 28, 163, 177
    Lavinia 255
    Levinia 255
    Lydia 177
    Martha 266
    Michael 550
    Peter 546
    Robert C. 391
    Sally 179
    Thomas 255
    William 32
Mynier, Elizur P. 48
Myre, Martin 530
Mytinger, George W. 283
Myyers, Jacob 227
Nachtrieb, Gotlieb 235
Nafus, Jane 37
Nagle, John Martin 259
Nambath, Friedrich 200
Nance, Alexander 268
Nash, (?) 201
    George W. 201
    Ida 432
    James 201
    R. K. 228, 238, 246
Nashee, (?) 198
    Esther 198
    George 197, 198
    Jane K. (Mrs.) 197
    Sarah 198
Nau, Jacob 433
    Jane 433
Nay, Hannah Louisa 352
    Jeremiah 11, 352

Nay (cont.)
    Mary (Mrs.) 352
    Paulina 352
Naylor, Sarah 75
Neal, C. H. 517
    Curtis 517
    Daniel 511
    Elizabeth (Mrs.) 517
    Galhanna 517
    Nelson W. 517
    R. (Mrs.) 517
    S. 517
    S. (Mrs.) 517
    Sarah 415, 422, 423
    Susannah 517
    Susannah (Mrs.) 517
Neary, Mary A. 438
Nebucker, Lucius 29
Needler, Philemon 210
Needles, (?) 369, 404
    Alfred 310
    Amy 310
    Anah 416, 433, 486
    Andrew 170
    Anna 310
    Anny 310
    Archibald 172
    Cubbage 219
    E. J. (Mrs.) 404
    Elijah 172
    Elizabeth 172
    Enoch A. 310
    Enoch Asbury 310
    Hannah (Mrs.) 369
    Harriet Milburn 310
    J. H. 369
    James 310
    James A. 234
    Jedediah 310
    John 172
    John A. 310
    Lucinda 310
    Nancy 172
    Nancy (Mrs.) 310
    Phileman 485
    Philemon 170, 211,
        310, 416, 433
    Philomen 172
    Polly 172
    Rachel 238, 310
    Rebecca 310
    Rebecca Powell 310
    S. L. 404
    Sally 66
    Samuel 240
    Samuel I. 404
    Sarah 172
    Sarah (Mrs.) 285, 416
    William D. 307, 484
Neel, Bathsheba 361
    Thomas 361
Neeley, Martha 227
Neereamer, Jonathan 545
Neff, Abraham 72
    Catherine 73
    Dorothy 309
    Elizabeth 309
    Eveline 309
    Francis 30
    George 72
    Henry 86
    Hyram 309
    Isaac 309
    Jacob 182, 292
    John 73, 222
    Leonard 309
    Phebe 309
    Phebe (Mrs.) 309

Ransburgh, John 191
Ransom, Calvin N. (Rev.)
  41
  James L. 299
  Wm. 547
Raper, Mary Jones (Mrs.)
  516
  William 515
  Wm. 516
Rareigh, John 550
Rarey, Adam 177, 192,
  279, 552
  Amanda 299, 305
  Benjamin 279
  Catherine 279
  Charles 166, 171, 192,
    215, 217, 226, 263,
    279
  Charles (Sr.) 279, 299
  Charles W. 552
  Christin 279
  Cynthia 299
  Elizabeth 279
  George 279
  George Washington 299
  John 279
  Margaret (Mrs.) 279
  Mary Ann 299
  Parker 203, 279, 299,
    305
  Rachel 305
  Rachel (Mrs.) 296, 299
  Samuel 279
  William 192, 209, 279,
    299
  William H. 299
Rathbone, Amos 186
  Anthony Constant 307,
    319
  Caroline Lee 306, 307,
    319
  Clarissa 306, 319
  Content 306, 319
  Demming L. 197
  Edward Beverly 306,
    319
  Eliza 306, 319
  Emma Maria 306, 319
  Eunice 306, 319
  Hezekiah 306, 319
  John 306, 307, 319,
    323
  Julia 306, 307, 319
  Julia Constant 306
  Julia Putman 197
  Juliett 306, 319
  Mary Rosalie 306, 319
  Sarah 306, 319
  Sophia 306, 319
  Thomas 186
Rathbun, John 260, 261,
  319
Rathburn, John 249
  John N. 547
Rathmell, Elizabeth 328
  John 310, 328
  Joseph 328
  Mary (Mrs.) 328
  Thomas 179, 184, 203,
    206, 210, 328
  Thos. 175
Rawlings, Michael 163
Rawlins, Moses 32
Rawson, Siling 539
Ray, Elizabeth 50
  William 514
  William C. 239
Raymond, Eliza Ann

Raymond (cont.)
  (Mrs.) 334
  Polly 44
  William B. 84
Raynolds, John 330
  Mary (Mrs.) 330
  Peney (Mrs.) 330
Read, Adam 169, 176,
  188, 209, 223, 274,
  281
  Alex 176
  Alexander 169, 274
  Andrew 198, 529, 530
  Ann 274
  Betsey 529
  George 19, 274
  George B. 553
  George P. 553
  James 386
  Jane 274
  Jonathon 552
  M. (Mrs.) 386
  Mary Ann 549
  Mary Eliza 419
  O. S. 386
  Peggy (Mrs.) 274
  Philip 222
  Phillip 209, 211
  Polly 91, 274
  Samuel 274
  William 18, 169, 176,
    272
  Willian 274
Reader, (?) 210
  Elizabeth 210
  John 210
Readinghouse, William
  240
Ream, Abraham 546
  Absolum 546
  Andrew (Cpt.) 519
  Barbara 69
  Eliza 69
  Elizabeth 70
  Huffman 546
  Jacob 66, 525, 546
  Jacob (Jr.) 546
  John 547
  Jonathan 543
  Lizzie 391
  M. J. (Mrs.) 391
  Mahaly (Mrs.) 543
  Mary Jane 391
  Nancy A. 543
  Phillip 546
  Sampson 69, 546
  T. N. 391
  Thomas N. 391
  William 546
Reams, Abraham 525
  Jacob 522, 525
  Jonathan W. 324
  Jordan 509
  Sarah F. (Mrs.) 324
Reamy, Jenny 244
Reardon, George 187, 206
Reason, John 259
Rebel, Christ 538
  Christina (Mrs.) 538
  Wilhelmina 538
Reber, Howard 438
  Karon Irene 438
  Selinda (Mrs.) 310
Recher, Peter 257
Rector, Charles 509
  Daniel 529
  Elias 518
  John 528

Redd, Joseph 550
Redenhauer, Daniel 174
  David 202
  George 202
  Mathew 174
Redmond, Floyd 469
  Thomas 509
Reeb, Wilsena C. 405
Reece, Esiah 529
  Jacob 95
  Nancy 223
  Thomas 223
Reed, (?) (Maj.) 312
  Abraham 530
  Adam 176, 189
  Alex 176
  Alice 97
  Andrew 29
  Catherine 515
  Charles 168
  Danforth B. 258
  Daniel 514
  David 81
  Eliza 377
  Elizabeth (Mrs.) 441
  Emeline 231
  Erma 465
  George 212, 410
  Hanna 441
  Ida 391
  Ida F. 427
  Ida Frances 427
  J. 377
  J. R. 515
  James 376, 510, 515
  John 284, 514
  John R. 515
  Jos. 548
  Joseph 30
  M. W. 415
  Mary (Mrs.) 270
  N. (Mrs.) 377
  Nancy 377
  Oscar 391
  Phillip 215
  S. K. (Rev.) 238
  Samuel 81, 441
  Sarah 377
  Stephen 97
  Susan 465
  William 171, 465, 528
  William J. 377
  Wm. 167, 174
Reeder, David 77
  Henry 528
  John 81
Reel, Henry (Jr.) 259
  J. H. 321
Rees, Amor 319
  Elizabeth (Mrs.) 328,
    352
  Jacob 330, 514
  John 13
  Nancy (Mrs.) 330
  Samuel 352
  Sarah 330
  Susannah 85
Reese, Bonham 396
  Daniel 335
  Edmond 396
  Francis Marion 396
  Hannah (Mrs.) 396
  Huldah (Mrs.) 396
  Jacob 223, 396
  John 396
  Juliann 396
  Nancy (Mrs.) 396
  Nathan 510

Ried (cont.)
John 515
M. A. (Mrs.) 515
M. J. (Mrs.) 515
Martha A. (Mrs.) 515
Theodore F. 515
Riednour, David 318
Riegel, Mayburt (Mrs.) 453
Mayburt Stephenson 357
Mayburt Stephenson (Mrs.) 490
Mayburt Stephenson 86, 518, 528
Rielly, Mathew 549
Rierdan, George 217
Robert 216
Rife, Georgiana Elliott (Mrs.) 426
Rigby, Wm. 66
Rigdon, John 514
Riggle, Samuel 20
Righter, Jacob 78
Riley, Bibedick 265
E. 58
Eleanor 281
Esther 47
Francis 417, 434
George 281
John 320
John S. 50
Lydia 263
Mary 281
Moses 67
Robert 187, 281
Robert W. 187, 235
Samuel 189
William 205, 281
Rimer, Catherine (Mrs.) 277
Daniel 242
Rimpon, Elizabeth Ann 284
Rimpton, Sarah (Mrs.) 284
Rinehart, Samuel 239
Ring, G. 65
Robert 244
Ringhausen, Conrad 324
Elise 324
Frederick 324
George 324
Henry 324
Henry Jacob 324
Lewis 324
Wilhelmenia (Mrs.) 324
Ringle, Lewis 195
Ringrose, John 186
Rings, Blanche 434
Blanche T. 442
Blanche Tipton 229, 232, 237, 241, 244, 250, 259, 261, 264, 266, 268, 271, 275, 280, 287, 290, 294, 301, 306, 309, 312, 316, 319, 323, 325, 329, 333, 340, 417
Riordan, George 212, 225
Robert 216, 233
Rippie, Wm. 549
Riser, Elizabeth 258
Risinger, Wm. 550
Risley, Lewis 178, 191, 207, 267, 276
Orval 267
Orville 215
Washington 215

Risly, Lewis 180
Ritcher, Abraham 546
Ritchey, Samuel 78
Ritchie, Dorcas (Mrs.) 308
Emily 361
James 254
Robert (Jr.) 64
Ritsel, Jacob 522
Ritson, James 544
Mary (Mrs.) 544
Ritter, (?) 509
Elijah 365
Frederick 176, 186, 273, 552
Henry 509, 511
Maria 186
Polly (Mrs.) 273
Ritzmann, Fredericka 240
Rivers, Frank 238
Rizer, Elizabeth 258
John 549
Roachell, (?) 397
M. J. (Mrs.) 397
M. S. 397
Roades, James E. (Mrs.) 440
Roads, Joseph G. 234
Robb, Margaret 296
Samuel 397
Wm. 550
Robbins, (?) 212, 430
Charles 430
David 212
Eliza 212
John 327
Mathias 281
Minerva 212
Samuel 212
Sarah Elizabeth 415, 430
Westley 212
Robe, William 169, 181
Wm. 165, 167
Robert, Benjamin 540
David M. 540
Rachel (Mrs.) 540
Roberts, A. (Mrs.) 370
Abana (Mrs.) 370
Alden 439
Amos 375
Anne 314
Arrena (Mrs.) 370
Claudia Gertrude 440
Emma 370
Hata 370
Henry Floy 251, 254, 258
I. 370
Isaac G. 298
Jacob 174
Jame 370
James 370
John 386, 548
Joseph 221, 284, 314
Katie Amanda 440
Leroy Van 440
Lewis 56
Mahala 386
Marcus 314
Maud Henry 440
Owen 170, 210
Samuel 238
Sarah (Mrs.) 340
Stephen 311, 386
Thomas 49, 81, 165, 168, 173, 199, 311, 320, 386

Roberts (cont.)
Tracy Ann (Mrs.) 340
Vivian Winifred 440
William C. 235
William Stanford 440
Wm. C. 547
Robertson, (?) (Dr.) 13
C. A. (Mrs.) 352
Charles 29
Jacob 529
James 352
Lovett 352
Mary A. (Mrs.) 352
Nancy 529
Robert 352
Thaddie 352
Thomas 29, 530
W. W. 352
William 529
Robeson, Arena 35
Joseph 549
Robey, John 549
Robinson, (?) 222
Abel 548
Albert O. 479
Ann 221, 222
Eliza A. (Mrs.) 323
Ellen M. 479
G. A. (Mrs.) 439
Gain (Dr.) 30
George 33
George F. 530
Godfrey 221
Grace M. 479
Henry 164
J. 178
J. (Dr.) 323
Jabez 323
James 94, 184, 187, 196, 205, 221, 222, 514
John 20, 160, 161, 178, 211, 276, 282, 552, 553
John (Jr.) 288
John P. 191
Joseph 303
Martha (Mrs.) 286
Mary 222
Mary (Widow) 221
Nelson B. 555
Olo A. 479
Otho 479
Otho A. 478, 479
Priscilla 454
Ralph 510
Robert 79
Samuel 286
Samuel H. 512
Thomas 30
William 518
Robison, Isaac 514
Roby, Betsy 27
Rochel, Dency 255
Rochell, John 255
Lucinda (Mrs.) 255
Rochelle, (?) 370
J. 370
John 370
John (Sr.) 369
L. (Mrs.) 370
Lucinda (Mrs.) 370
Victoria 370
Zelotes 370
Rock, (?) 509
Felix 509, 514
Phillip 529
William 30

Rockhill, William 83
Rockwell, Elkanah 551
Rodebaugh, (?) 386
  Austin M. 386
  C. (Mrs.) 386
  S. B. 386
Roder, John 338
Rodes, Peter 196
Rodgers, (?) 550
  Chandler 220
  Chandlers 246
  David 47
  E. (Mrs.) 363
  Elisha (Mrs.) 89
  Elizabeth (Mrs.) 363
  Emily (Mrs.) 304
  Grover E. 375
  John 363, 511
  Levi 363
  Lucretia A. (Mrs.) 304
  Mary E. 363
  Thomas 26
  Thos. 550
  Virginnia 363
  William 363
  Wm. S. 363
  Zephaniah 207
Rodney, Caesar A. 77
Rods, John (Jr.) 546
  John (Sr.) 546
Roe, Morris 240, 253
  Sarah 74
Roeder, Dorothea (Mrs.)
  338
  John 338
Roger, J. S. 235
Rogers, Alexander M. 50
  C. (Rev.) 45
  Chandler 177, 179,
    191, 204, 214, 242
  Chandler (Rev.) 251
  Charles 191
  David 64, 245, 246,
    251, 258
  Henry 530
  Henry R. 323
  J. S. 228, 248, 249,
    251, 256
  Jacob S. 217, 219,
    256, 260
  John 171
  John Chandler 242
  Lizzie 33
  Mary (Mrs.) 41
  Michael W. 332
  Polly (Mrs.) 284
  Rachel 40
  Sam 557
  Thomas B. 245
  William 28
  William K. 246
Rohr, Elizabeth (Mrs.)
  340
  Geo. 175
  George 184
  John 175, 210, 240,
    340
  Margaret 210
  Michael 175, 184
Rohrer, (?) 397
  Anna 397
  J. E. 397
  John E. 318
  W. M. (Mrs.) 397
Roland, John 546
Rolether, Elizabeth
  (Mrs.) 544
Roling, Anton 543

Roller, Wilson S. 376
Roloson, Catharine 49
  John 46
Romaine, Abraham 193
  Benj. F. 538
Romick, Jacob 267
Romine, Abraham 278
  Abram 208, 222
  Miranda 234
Romines, Abraham 168
Ronan, Wilbert Cathmore
  461
Roney, (?) 223
  Eliza Ann 223, 294
  Frederick 312
  Isaac H. L. 355
  Isaac Henry Jared 294
  Isaac L. 223
  James 223, 294, 355
  James Hamilton 294
  John Milton 294
  Margaretta 223
  Margaretta Robinson
    294
  Mary Jane 223
  Rachael Marie 294
  Rachel (Mrs.) 355
Rook, Frederick 82
  Mary R. (Mrs.) 75
Rooney, Francis 550
Roose, Phillip 172
Rooser, Frederick L. 281
  Gottlieb 281
Ropp, E. (Mrs.) 366
  J. 366
  Nancy M. 366
Rorar, George 273
  John 273
  Mary (Mrs.) 273
  Michael 273
Roscoe, (?) 459
Rose, Aaron 306
  Abraham 325
  Elisha 352, 361
  Elizabeth (Mrs.) 361
  Jacob 45
  James 236
  John 518
  John B. 316
  Levi 99
  Margaret A. (Mrs.) 352
  Philip 306, 325
  Ruth 246
  Ruth (Mrs.) 325
  S. A. 352
  Sarah 352
  Stephen G. 306, 325
  Tmothy 92
  William 48
Rosecrans, Charles R. 55
  Jane 51
  Sophronia 52
Rosemiller, P. (Rev.) 52
Rosenberg, L. 242
Rosenkrans, Arientje 556
Rosett, George C. 298
Roshon, Israel 72
Ross, (?) 428, 509
  Alex. 182
  Alexander 85, 514
  Amanda J. 405
  Ann 183
  Christena 190
  Christiana 380
  Daniel 169, 181, 182,
    183
  Daniell 380
  David 518

Ross (cont.)
  Edward M. 183
  Effie M. 405
  Elijah 95, 514
  Emma 405
  Henry 405
  Hugh 182
  Hugh M. 207
  Hugh W. 183
  J. W. 547
  James 63
  Jane 182, 183
  Jane (Mrs.) 380
  John 199, 212, 428,
    514
  John F. 182, 207
  John Sutton 405
  Levi 415
  Lydia (Mrs.) 291
  Mary 183
  Mattias 548
  Moses 64
  Robert 197, 291
  Robert E. 332
  Robert L. 231
  Roy H. 428
  Sarah 75
  Talmage 528
  William S. 514
Rossi, Jacob 336
Roston, Ellen (Mrs.) 321
  Isaac H. 321
  James P. 321
Roth, Peter 196
Rouse, (?) 509
Rout, Ann 528
  Samuel 30
  William 30, 528
Rouze, John 514
  Levi 514
Rowan, (?) (Mrs.) 37
  A. H. 37
  John (Jdg.) 37
  William 37
Rower, James 309
  William 309
Rowland, Abraham 335
  Ann 335
  Ann S. (Mrs.) 316
  Catherine 335
  Edward (Dr.) 51
  Elizabeth 335
  Elizabeth (Mrs.) 311,
    326
  Jane 335
  John 311, 335
  John E. 311
  John G. 326
  Mary 335
  Sophia 326
Rowlands, Thomas 261
Rowley, James M. 259
Royal, Daniel 277
Royce, David 208
Rude, Caleb 87
  Margaret (Mrs.) 87
Rudilson, Jane C. 233
Rudisill, Guy Black 391
  Jane 233
  Jones 550
  Mable G. (Mrs.) 391
  Sarah J. 391
  William 391
  William M. 391
Rudolph, Aurelia 266
  Christian 70
  Henry 546
  Katherine (Mrs.) 338

Rudolph (cont.)
  Peter 546
Rue, Benjamin 81
  Benjamin (Cpt.) 76
  Benjamin S. 76
  Mary 529
Ruegg, Cetty 539
  Chasper 539
Ruff, John 79
  Polly (Mrs.) 79
Ruffner, Mary 415
Rugg, Dayton 337
  Moses 558, 559
Ruggles, Alfred 42
  Benjamin 84
  John 30
  Mary Rosalie (Mrs.)
    319
  Samuel B. 306, 307,
    319
  Tirzah (Mrs.) 84
Ruhl, Ella 446
Ruion, Jacob 261
Rumser, Nicholas 68
Rumsey, Amelia 69
  Daniel 180
  Mary (Mrs.) 270
  Stephen 554
Runion, Absolom 81
Runkle, (?) 509
  George 288
  Jane 287
  Jane (Mrs.) 288
  Lewis 288
  Rebecca 288
  William (Jdg.) 513
Runnels, Jonathon 528
Runyan, Absalom 76
  Mary Ann 76
Runyon, John 514
  John (Jdg.) 512, 513
  Joseph 64
  Rebecca (Mrs.) 64
  Richard 514
  Stephen 510, 514
Ruse, Solomon 68, 240
Rush, A. (Mrs.) 386
  Abigail (Mrs.) 343
  Cyrus N. 397
  Flora A. 386
  G. 386
  George 343
  George D. 386
  Henry 386, 528
  Jacob 336
  John 31
  Josiah 13
  M. (Mrs.) 397
  Rachel (Mrs.) 65
  S. 397
  Saul 13
  Solomon 335, 397
  Theodore 343
  William 13
Rusk, Robert 243
Russ, Lyman 553
Russel, Wm. 66
Russell, Daniel E. 314
  Eliza 338
  Elizabeth 239
  James 166, 198
  Jane 338
  Jerusha 477
  John R. 75
  Jonathan 80
  Robert 25, 29, 178,
    201, 213, 272, 551
  William 75

Ruster, Rebecca 248
Ruth, Price 33
  Samuel 529
Rutter, Abraham 314
  George 81, 82
  Henry 73
  Thomas 473
Ryan, Elizabeth 263
  Jacob 529
  John 84
Rymer, Wm. 550
Rynearson, Nicholas 76
Saber, George 247
Sackett, Rachel (Mrs.)
  163
Sackreiter, Elisabeth 66
Sader, L. L. 230
Saenger, Andreass 309
Safford, Fanny 93
Sager, A. 372
  A. (Mrs.) 372
  Abraham 372
  Catherine 372
  Christiana 220
  D. 372, 374
  Dallas 374
  Desiah J. (Mrs.) 372
  E. (Mrs.) 372
  E. E. (Mrs.) 372
  E. M. 372
  G. W. 372
  George Washington 372
  Georgie 372
  John 220, 332
  K. (Mrs.) 372, 374
  Laura M. 372
  M. A. (Mrs.) 372
  Myrtha E. 372
  Nellie 374
  Walter E. 372
  William Henry 372
Sail, John 529
Saint, James 33
  John 33
  Joseph 33
  Levi 33
  Lucinda 33
  Thomas 33
  William 33
Sale, Robert 77
Salida, Juliann 257
Salidee, Juliann 257
Salisberry, Emeline
  (Mrs.) 308
Salls, Peter 209
Salmon, Frederick 549
  Sarah 59
Salor, Melicia V. 235
Salsberry, George L. 217
Salsbury, Peter 550
Saltzman, (?) 499
  Philip 499
Samis, N. E. 316
Sammis, S. R. 334
  Sarah (Mrs.) 343
  Selah R. 333
Sammiss, Martha (Mrs.)
  342
  Selah R. 342
Sample, Samuel 549
Sams, Jones 549
Samson, (?) 450
  Abigail 450
  David 450, 451, 452
  David (Jr.) 450
  E. D. (Mrs.) 340
  Elizabeh 452
  Elizabeth 450, 451,

Samson (cont.)
  452
  James 450
  Lucinda 450, 451
  Ralph 450
  Samuel 450
  Sarah 450, 451
  William (Rev.) 450
Samuel, S. E. 336
Samuels, Ann S. 316
  James C. 316
  John 316
  Maria 316
  Samuel 316
  William R. 316
Sanders, Dennis 64
  Josiah M. 57
  Robert 244
Sands, Levin L. 46
Sandusky, John 163
Sanford, (?) 213
  William 213
Sarber, Adam 180
  Christian 180, 192,
    301
  David 301
  Jacob 301
  John 301
  Leonard 301
  Mary 301
  William 301
Sarbor, Adam 205
Sargeant, Enoch 514
  George 514
Sargent, (?) 556
  Abel M. (Rev.) 81
  Samuel Mustard 324
  Sarah Matilda 291
  Thomas F. (Dr.) 38
  Thornton W. 324
Sarver, Jacob 514
Sattler, Brigita 344
  John 344
  Joseph 344
  Maria 344
  Phitellus 344
  Theresia 344
Saucer, Isaac 96
Saucerman, John 554
Saul, (?) 199, 213
  Aaron 199
  Catherine 278
  George 188, 199, 213,
    278
  Jacob 278
  John 18, 177, 213,
    220, 278
  Joseph 278
  Leonard 188, 198, 199,
    213, 235, 278
  Mariah 278
  Mary 199
  Michael 278
  Rebecca 278
  Samuel 198
  Sarah Ann (Mrs.) 286
  Susanna 227
Saunders, Miskell 224,
  291, 295, 553
  Peter 546
Savage, (?) 475
  George 45
  Jesse 547
  Joseph 484
Savely, Henry 310
  Jacob 310
  James 310
Saver, Jacob 510

Sawyer, Catherine (Mrs.)
  287
  John 287
Saxton, Joseph 47
  Samuel H. 412
Say, Mary L. (Mrs.) 326
Saylor, Michael 30
Sayre, Benjamin 81
  John 514
  Thomas 514
Sayres, Thomas 510
Scarburgh, George P. 284
Scattergood, Alfred 550
Schaad, Martin (Rev.)
  230
Schaart, John 543
Schacleford, (?) 540
  Josephine 540
Schaeffer, Almira 227
  C. F. 226
  Charles F. 235, 248,
    251, 253, 258
  Isaac 546
  Rachel 73
Schaffhauser, Andreas
  540
  Jacob 540
  Marie (Mrs.) 540
Scharf, Magdalena 303
  Magdalens 303
  Maria Eva (Mrs.) 303
  Valentine 303
Schaub, Frederick 239
Scheffield, C. C. 294
Scheiff, Louisa 235
Schell, (?) 446
  Joseph 446
  Perry 447
  Stephen 447
Schenck, Clinton Barton
  424
Scherer, Maria Eva 303
Schille, Frederick 330
Schimper, Louis 340
Schleich, Isaac 69
Schleppi, Elizabeth 406
  Sonis 406
Schlitt, Henry 338
  Katherine 338
  Katherine Margaretta
    338
  Margareta (Mrs.) 338
Schmidt, Caroline 248
  Christian 293
  Frederick 305
  Frederick (Jr.) 313
  George 539
  George Henry 539
  Hannah 43
  Jacob 43
  Rebecca (Mrs.) 293
  Wilhelm 226, 240, 248,
    260, 262
  William 293
Schmit, William 293
Schmitt, Elizabeth 254
Schneider, (?) 543
  A. 329
  Balentine 257
  Barbara 543
  Catherine 257
  George 335
  Mary Ann 335
  Valentine 257
Schnitzer, Frederick F.
  257
Schnur, Margaret 311
Schoedinger, Barbara

Schoedinger (cont.)
  (Mrs.) 325
  Mary 228
  Phillip 314
Schoffhauser, John 241
Schonatt, William 228,
  257
Schonover, Abraham 264
Schooler, William 554
Schoonover, (?) 216
  Abraham 216, 276
  Angeline 216
  Ava 216
  Charles W. 216
  Elizabeth 276
  Elizabeth (Mrs.) 276
  Henry 170, 276
  John 182, 215, 216,
    276
  Joseph 182, 185, 217,
    276
  Margaret 216, 276
  Mary 276
  Rebecca 263, 276
  William 216
Schorempf, Sellina 259
Schott, Sophia 241
Schriner, (?) 469
Schrock, John M. 291
  T. G. 18
  William 252, 292
Schroett, Maria Caherine
  (Mrs.) 321
Schryock, John 514
Schuchardt, Barbara
  Louisa 341
  Elizabeth (Mrs.) 341
  Henry 341
Schuchart, Barbara 339
  Elizabeth (Mrs.) 339
  Frederick 339
  Henry 339
Schuler, Joseph A. 344
Schultz, Margaret 226
Schulz, J. Jacob 314
Schulze, J. A. 254
Schuman, Catharine 67
Schurman, Catherine
  (Mrs.) 339
  Gustavus 339
Schute, Fredericka 541
  Fredericka (Mrs.) 541
  Fredrich 541
Schutz, Margaret 226
Schvare, John 546
Schwaigert, S. 541
Schwartz, Henry 300
  John 300
  Katherine (Mrs.) 300
  Philip 303
Schwarz, Catherine 235
  Henry 300
Schwatz, Peter 328
Schween, George 540
  Mary (Mrs.) 540
Schwemberger, Elizabeth
  (Mrs.) 539
  Jacob 538
  Jeremia 539
Schwing, Jacob 82
Scoby, Mary (Mrs.) 276
Scofield, A. 387
  Alanson 387
  Benjamin 291
  Daniel 331
  David E. 331
  Elvinah 291
  Jesse W. 331

Scofield (cont.)
  Lousisa 387
  Maria (Mrs.) 387
  Mary (Mrs.) 387
  R. 387
  Ruben 387
Scoot, Mary 539
  Mary (Mrs.) 539
  Richard 539
Scothorn, Abraham 299
  Anna 299
  Christena 299
  Eliza 299, 486
  Elizabeth 433
  Mary (Mrs.) 299
  Sarah 299
  William 299
Scott, (?) 219, 518, 545
  Abraham 371
  Agnes 326
  Andrew 168, 330
  Andrew (Jr.) 325
  Andrew M. 325
  Catherine (Mrs.) 371,
    544
  Charles 217, 222, 239,
    326, 518
  Charles G. 44
  David 166, 171, 173,
    176, 270, 545
  Elizabeth 503
  Elizabeth (Mrs.) 325,
    330
  Elizabeth Jane (Mrs.)
    336
  Flora M. 239
  G. M. 232
  Geo. 170
  George 25, 219
  Hannah (Widow) 54
  Harriet 325
  Harriet Arabella 325
  Hugh 97
  James 167, 177
  Jane 325
  John 18, 212, 340
  Louise (Mrs.) 57
  M. S. 293
  Maria L. 251
  Maria Louisa 251
  Martha 309
  Mary (Mrs.) 281
  Mary M. 51
  Matilda (Mrs.) 326
  Maud 413
  Minerva 330
  Rebecca 330
  Robert 326
  Seymour 57
  Solomon 514
  T. F. 413
  Thos. 63
  V. J. (Mrs.) 413
  William 209, 330, 336
  William A. 371
  William M. 309
  Wm. 63, 282
Scovell, E. 46
  H. 45, 50
  Hurlburt 44, 52
Scovelle, Carlton G. 47
Scribner, Elias 269
  Hannah (Mrs.) 162, 269
  Samuel 162, 269
Scrivener, Hannah (Mrs.)
  162
  Samuel 162
Scroggs, Mary Lyon 415

643

Shannon (cont.)
Thomas 361
William 224, 300
William H. 303
William W. 193, 213,
219, 224, 261, 300
Shaplor, Jacob 60
Shapter, Martha (Mrs.)
334
Philip 334
Sharon, (?) 366
Sharp, (?) 194, 550
Andrew 188, 194
Catharine (Mrs.) 443
Clarissa 194
George 169, 171, 179,
188
J. 387
Jacob 168
James 553
John 175, 176, 188,
203, 387
Mary (Mrs.) 300
Nancy 245
Parthena 194
Sally 194
Temperance A. (Mrs.)
387
William 295
William W. 242
Sharpe, Jeptha 86
John 528
Sharran, Patrick 546
Sharrard, Sam'l 549
Shattuck, Alexander 187,
214, 278
Shaug, (?) (Dr.) 66
Wm. 66
Shaul, Elizabeth (Mrs.)
391
John 391
Joseph M. 391
Shaver, (?) (Prof.) 49
John 522, 527
Shaw, Aaron 40
Alex. 549
Ambrose 62, 549
Andrew 548
Ann 529
Cassandra 556
Charles 549
Daniel D. 45
Ealse 484
John 340, 553
Margaret 394
Margaret (Mrs.) 25
Samuel P. 256
William 192
Wm. 286
Shay, Abraham 86
Isaac 86
John 86
Shead, Jared 209
Sheaders, James 254
James J. 254
Sheaffe, Mary 475
Shearer, J. P. 335
John 26, 518
Patrick 547
Shearman, Rebecca 39
Sheckell, Ann 427
Shed, Jerry 422
Sheehy, William 236
Sheesley, Rovenia 254
Sheets, John 549
Mary A. 43
Shegley, Frederick 529
Sheilds, William 195

Sheldon, Mary L. (Mrs.)
339
Richard A. 339
Shell, Abbie 446
Abigail 446
Anna Mary (Mrs.) 446,
447
Annie Mary 446
Celesta 446, 447
David 446
Elizabeth Ann 446
Ellanora 446
John 446
Joseph 446, 447
Lizzie 446
Malen 446, 447
Perry 446
Rachel 446, 447
Sarah 446
Sarah (Mrs.) 446
Stephen 446
Shellar, Nancy 75
Shellenbarger, Henry
546, 547
Michael 546
Samuel 547
Shellhouse, Laure 53
Shenefelt, Henry 242
Shenry, Charles 332
Shepard, A. 518
Henry C. 251
Luther 26
Shepherd, (?) 201, 222
Abraham 281, 317
Adam 207
Alexander 201
Ann 317
C. M. 317
Charles Moses 317
E. S. (Rev.) 55
Eleanor (Mrs.) 317
Eliza 317
Hannah (Mrs.) 339
Henry 317
James 201
James H. 317
Jane 201
John 193, 201, 317
Margaret Ann (Mrs.)
317
Mary 222
Mary Lacy (Mrs.) 289
Moses 317
R. D. 317
Ruhama 201
Sally 201
Sarah 201
Thomas 339, 549
W. (Dr.) 18
Sheppard, Nathaniel 287
Sherborn, John 311
Lydia 311
Petsy 311
Sheridan, Mary (Mrs.)
539
Michel 539
Minerva 539
Sheriff, Anthony 518
Sherman, (?) 482
Benjamin 415
Charles 54
Christopher 416
David 415
David Thompson 415
Hester 361
J. 180
Jonathan 181, 197
Nathaniel 415

Sherman (cont.)
S. M. (Dr.) 432
Samuel 415
Sherrard, Robert A. 549
Sherwood, Eliza 366
Hannah 66
James L. 366
M. (Mrs.) 366
Mary E. 366
O. 366
Ormel 297
Thomas 548
Shesler, John 547
Shick, John 548
Preston 264
Shide, Lewis (Rev.) 67
Shiderly, Andrew 81
Shiel, Frederick 548
Shields, Beattrice 391
George 282
Jno. 391
John 167, 171, 172,
174, 186
Margaret 208
Margaret (Mrs.) 282
Robert 282
William 201, 208, 282
Wm. 280
Shifler, Sophia 469
Shin, Levi 169
Ship, John 557
Tom 557
Shipman, A. (Mrs.) 355
Androme 355
Charles 355
Hannah 414, 435
O. 355
Oliver 355
Shirey, (?) 215
Michael 215
Shirk, Laura Ann 405
Lousetta 405
Shirley, Lawrence 30
Shlitt, Benedict 300
Henry S. 242
Shlusher, Dannie 182
Tobias 182
Shoaf, Elizabeth 172
Elizabeth (Mrs.) 278
Henry 325, 340
John 297
Shoag, Michael 546
Shock, Jacob 548
Shockey, (?) 365, 510
A. 365
Abraham 365, 509, 514
Catherine 365
Cinderella 365
Elizabeth 365
Isaac 514
John 365
Leona 365
N. (Mrs.) 365
Nancy (Mrs.) 365
Shoemaker, Abraham 180,
210, 211, 213, 220,
222, 233, 236, 239,
240
Abram 247
Charles 432
Chas. 522
Christopher 416, 432
Christopher (Jr.) 416,
432
Christopher (Sr.) 432
Clendid 432
Dubois Devereaux 432
Elias Fassett 432

645

649

Stevens (cont.)
Horatio 308
John 308
Julie 537
Levi 308
Lucinda 308
Mary 308
Rebecca 308
Sally 308
Thomas 343
William 514
Willis 308
Wm (Rev.) 69
Wm. (Rev.) 69
Stevenson, (?) 472, 490
Alfred 235
Alice Carey 491
Alphaes B. 490
Alpheas B. 491
Alpheas Boone 491
Ann B. 490, 491
Ann B. (Mrs.) 299
Catherine (Mrs.) 474
Crumwell W. 490
E. C. 233
Edward 472
Elizabeth (Mrs.) 282
Francis 514
George 282, 286, 474
George H. 210
George K. 491
George King 490
George R. 474, 490
Hanna 282
Irvin E. 490
Isaac M. 353
J. 353
James 60, 353, 530
Jemima 490, 491
John 170, 210, 282,
474, 490, 491
Joshua 210, 282
Joshua B. 299, 490
Joshua R. B. 490, 491
Joshua R. Boone 490
Joshua Richard Boone
490
Justin J. 472, 473,
490
Justin Jason 491
M. (Mrs.) 353
Mary 210, 490, 491
Mary (Mrs.) 282, 353,
490, 491
Mary B. 490, 491
Mary Jane 236
Matilda 282
Milton G. 490
Milton Glanville 490
Milton Lafayette 491
Minerva J. 491
Minerva Jane 490
Nathan 282
Peter 516
Rhoda (Mrs.) 486
Richard 168, 170, 210,
282, 485
Sarah 490
Sarah (Mrs.) 287
Sarah Boone 474
Susan 236, 491
Susannah 490
Susannah (Mrs.) 490,
491
Thomas 491
William 187, 473, 474,
490, 491
Zachariah 169, 170,

Stevenson (cont.)
205, 210, 225, 282
Stevison, Anna (Mrs.) 86
Isaac 86
Stewalt, John 552
Steward, J. 391
James 391
John 550
John N. 234
Lydia 391
R. (Mrs.) 391
Stewart, (?) 203
Adam 165
Anna (Mrs.) 537
Archibald 514
Catharine 66
Charles 549
Charles A. 24
Daniel 33
David 295
E. 321
Edward 548
Eliza 295
Eliza (Mrs.) 327
Elizabeth (Mrs.) 295
Emily (Mrs.) 329
F. 302
Frances 170, 217, 218,
219, 224, 225, 537
Francis 171, 174, 175,
183, 184, 186, 187,
189, 190, 193, 200,
202, 203, 205, 206,
207, 209, 210, 211,
212, 213, 218, 221,
222, 223, 266, 282,
326, 545
Hannah (Mrs.) 65, 94
Hugh 27
J. 537
James 94
Jane (Mrs.) 94
John 165, 295, 325,
326, 514, 559
Joseph 167, 547
Lydia 165
Lydia (Mrs.) 325
Mary 329, 428
Mary Walker 295
Mathew 514
Matthew 509
Minerve Ann 37
Nancy 526
Nathan 22, 161
Polly Walker 295
Rebecca (Mrs.) 325
Reuben 40
Robert 327
Sarah 326
Sarah B. 266
Sarah E. 266
Spencer 203
Sybilla Jane 439
T. N. 239, 243, 260
Venal 253
Vinal 246
William 179, 184, 185,
193, 205, 206, 209,
211, 212, 213, 219,
233, 281, 295, 439
William I. 529
Wm. 175, 179
Wm. C. 33
Stiarwalt, William 267
Stichts, (?) (Rev.) 80
Stickle, Emma 469
Stidham, Rebecca 429
Stienbeck, Charles 48

Stienbeck (cont.)
William 43
Stierwalt, William 178,
179, 213, 282
Wm. 172
Stierwell, John 174
William 174
Stiles, (?) 475
Cornelia Ann 383
Nancy (Mrs.) 383
Stephan P. 383
Still, Jane 49
Oliver 262
Stillwell, Alanson 553
Stimmel, Abraham 340
Catherine (Mrs.) 340
Christena 340
Daniel 278
Frederick 168
Jacob 223
John 53
Mary 340
Michael 169, 205, 208,
214, 278, 340
Michael (Jr.) 340
Peter 223
Rachel 340
Stimmell, Daniel 189
Jacob 218, 219
Michael 189, 195, 218
Peter 181, 203
Stimmuell, Michael 181
Stimson, Stephen 338
Stinekerner, Mary 66
Stiner, Nancy 58
Stinger, George 548
Stinson, Abigail 406
Henry (Dr.) 406
John 547
S. 20
Stephen (Dr.) 406
Stinton, Thomas 295
Stipp, John 169
Stirling, (?) 464
Stirrat, Alex. 69
Stites, Rebecca (Mrs.)
301
Stith, James 245
Stoake, (?) 60
Stockberger, Frederick
550
Stocker, Anna Maria
(Mrs.) 65
Stockham, Wm. 547
Stockton, Ann (Mrs.) 26
Stoel, (?) 373
Betsy (Mrs.) 372
F. B. 373
H. E. (Mrs.) 373
S. 373
S. (Mrs.) 373
Silas 372
Thomas J. 373
Stoertzbach, Charles 538
Elizabeth (Mrs.) 538
Sophia 537
Stokely, Sam'l 549
Stoker, Michael 546
Stokes, John R. 177, 518
Stoles, John 548
Stoll, William 177
Stombach, Eave (Mrs.)
281
Elizabeth (Mrs.) 281
Stombaugh, Frederick 198
John 166, 206
Stone, (?) 516
Charles M. 313

Stone (cont.)
  Elijah 313
  Enos 250
  Jesse 288
  Mary L. (Mrs.) 85
  Noyce (Cpt.) 85
  Rachel (Mrs.) 327
  Willliam C. 41
  Wm. 550
Stonerock, John 31
Stookey, John 546
  Peter 546
  Samuel 546
Storm, Delia 46
  Elizabeth 554
  George 46, 58
  Harriet 39
  May C. (Mrs.) 57
Storms, Harry 509
Stotts, A. 322
  Abraham 273
  Abrahan 320
  Abram 186, 195
  Arthur 320
  George 323
  Hiram 320
  Polly 320
  Rebecca 320
  Susan (Mrs.) 320
  Uriah 195, 307, 320,
    551
Stouffer, Amos 248
Stoushp, Henry 546
Stover, James 511
Stow, Abijah 559
Stowell, John 559
Stowill, Robings 549
Strack, Wiegand 320
Strader, Jacob 176, 221,
  285
Strain, Elizabeth 182
  Jane 259
  John 182
  John M. 177
  John N. 273
  Robert 549
Strait, (?) 406
  A. (Mrs.) 406
  Abraham 406
  Ann 406
  Carl D. 406
  D. B. 406
  Dennis 406
  Dulcena (Mrs.) 406
  Dulcenia 406
  Edward L. 406
  Ella (Mrs.) 406
  George L. 406
  George W. 406
  Hattie A. (Mrs.) 372
  Mary Doran 406
  Minnie R. 406
  Nelson 406
  Sophia 406
  Whitney 406
  William Dunn 406
Stranahan, Elizabeth
  (Mrs.) 291
  John 172, 206
  William 210
Strang, I. S. (Mrs.) 353
  Isabel 353
  Isabella 353
  Isabella S. (Mrs.) 353
  M. 353
  Margaret Anne 353
  Martha 353
  Moses 11, 353

Stranger, Andrew 550
Strate, John 168
Stratton, Celeste (Mrs.)
  471
  John 457
  Oliver Wilson 471
  T. W. 471
Strau, George W. 372
  George Washington 372
  Hattie A. (Mrs.) 372
Straus, Abijah 559
Strawbridge, C. 358
  Martha A. 358
  P. (Mrs.) 358
Strayer, (?) 516
  G. W. 516
  John 68
  S. A. (Mrs.) 516
Streacher, John 198
Street, Ebenezer 22
  M. 313
Streibly, (?) 550
Streight, Henry 548
Stretch, Thomas 514
  William 514
Stricker, Susan 554
Strickland, Amos 296
  Emily (Mrs.) 296
  Joannah 296
  Nancy 296
  Nancy (Mrs.) 296
  Orlando 296
  Peter 296
  Polly 296
  Rodah 296
  Stephen 296
Strickler, Lucy Ann 262
  Martha 75
Strode, Harvey 552
Strohl, Elizabeth (Mrs.)
  391
  Hannah (Mrs.) 391
  Hester (Mrs.) 391
  Jacob 391
  Jacob A. 392
  John 391, 392
  Mary A. 392
  Reuben 391, 392
Strohm, Henry C. 230
Strole, Elizabeth 69
Strong, Benton 482
  David 180
  Doris Wolcott 475, 503
  J. P. 552, 553
  Jared 547
  Johanna 503
  L. C. 244
  Lucius 180, 244
  Lucius C. 246
  Marcus 180
  Mina (Mrs.) 47
  Oliver 269
  Reuben 529
  Truman 241
Stropes, John 547
Stroub, Barbara 40
Stroup, Sarah 478
Stroyer, Jeremian 550
Stuart, (?) 510
  John 62, 274
  Snowden 93
  William 273
Stubbs, Isaac 86
  Joseph 86
Stubsh, Anna 519
  Nancy 519
Stuckenrauch, Henrietta
  487

Stugeon, Jipe 546
Stukey, Mary 72
Stults, Elizabeth 440
Stuly, Gabriel 528
Stumbaugh, John 231
Stump, (?) 464
  John 291, 329, 463,
    528
  Lydia 467
  William 30
Stumpf, Conrad 528
Sturdevant, Chauncey 49
  Lewis C. 45
Sturgeon, Peter 546, 547
  Wm. 66
Stutler, Benjamin 552
Stutz, Charles 233
Stygler, D. 18
Styler, John 320
Styre, Abraham 57
Sublefield, B. 518
Suckley, George 535
Suddick, Edward T. 186
  James 186, 278, 289
  Jane 278
  Richard 169, 186, 278
Sulivant, Joseph 210
  Michael 209
  William 220
Sulivoo, David 326
Sullavon, David 344
Sullivan, (?) (Gen.) 45
  Aaron 29, 30, 31
  Julia 233
  Mary 442
Sullivant, (?) 195
  Jane 301
  Joseph 186, 293, 301,
    302, 310
  Lucas 160, 161, 166,
    173, 174, 175, 176,
    178, 179, 180, 183,
    186, 195, 268, 272,
    301, 302
  Mary Eliza (Mrs.) 310
  Michael 195, 213, 301
  Michael L. 186
  Starling 302
  William 302
  William S. 186, 301
Sullivoo, David 326
Summers, James M. 377
Summerville, George 326
Sumner, William H. 294
Sumption, Amanda 405
  John 405
Sunderland, Mary 69
Sunton, Samuel (Rev.) 50
Sutherland, Alex. 60
Sutherly, Mary Ann
  (Mrs.) 538
Sutton, Jas. 549
  John 514
  Margaret 415
  William 258
Swagert, Eliza C. (Mrs.)
  544
  John 528
Swain, Betsy 187
  E. A. 355
  Mathew 187
  Matthias 179
  Phoebe 187
Swamer, Phillip 276
Swan, Amelia (Mrs.) 343
  G. 336
  Gustaus 212
  Gustavus 166, 167,

653

663